IMMIGRATION LAW

IMMIGRATION LAW

Kevin Browne, LLB, Solicitor

Published by

College of Law Publishing,
Braboeuf Manor, Portsmouth Road, St Catherines, Guildford GU3 1HA

British Library Cataloguing-in-Publication Data
A catalogue record for this book is available from the British Library.

ISBN 978 1 910661 64 2

Typeset by Style Photosetting Ltd, Mayfield, East Sussex
Printed in Great Britain by Polestar Wheatons, Exeter

Preface

This book is intended to provide an introduction to immigration law and practice. I hope that it will be of use to students studying in this area, as well as practitioners who are new to the various topics covered or who wish to update their knowledge.

After a short, practical introduction in **Chapter 1** (which includes a list of useful websites at **1.2.8**), the book deals with British nationality and the right of abode in the United Kingdom in **Chapter 2**. This is followed by a detailed analysis of immigration controls in **Chapter 3**. The unique immigration status of EEA nationals and their family members is considered in **Chapter 4**, along with how a family member of a British citizen who has engaged Treaty rights might use EU rather than domestic law to enter the UK. The next four chapters then address the key immigration categories of entry to the UK. Asylum seekers and refugees are considered in **Chapter 9**. Enforcement of immigration law, the appeals system and judicial review are dealt with in the last three chapters. In each chapter I have tried to present the information in a logical, structured order with practical examples. I would welcome comments from readers which can be sent via CLP (clponline.co.uk).

Immigration law and practice constantly change. At least one major piece of legislation is introduced each year and, as at 1 October 2015, there had already been four statements of changes to the Immigration Rules in 2015. In this edition, I have included developments in nationality law, biometric residence permits, criminal record certificates, deportation, removal and the introduction of the immigration health charge. In addition, **Chapters 5** and **11** have been rewritten in light of the significant changes made to the visitor category and appeals system respectively.

New cases in this edition include: R *(on the application of DA (Iran)) v Secretary of State for the Home Department* (2014) (naturalisation), *Pham v Secretary of State for the Home Department* (2015) (deprivation), R *(on the application of Agyarko) v Secretary of State for the Home Department* (2015) (deportation), *Secretary of State for the Home Department v SS (Congo)* (2015) (ECHR, Art 8) and *MA (Somalia) v Secretary of State for the Home Department* (2015) (removal).

In the interests of brevity, the masculine pronoun has been used throughout to include the feminine.

I would like to thank David Stott, Sue Hall and the team at CLP for all their hard work on this title.

I would also like to thank my wife, children, colleagues and past students for their help and inspiration.

This edition is dedicated to Alistair, Mary, Chris, Tom, Phil, Harry and Rene. All much missed.

Kevin Browne
The University of Law,
London

Contents

Table of Cases

S

T

Table of Statutes

Table of Secondary Legislation

Page numbers in **bold** refer to text of legislation in the Appendices

Table of Abbreviations

AI(TC)A 2004	Asylum and Immigration (Treatment of Claimants, etc) Act 2004
BNA 1981	British Nationality Act 1981
BOCs	British overseas citizens
BOTCs	British overseas territories citizens
CAS	Confirmation of Acceptance for Studies
CPR 1998	Civil Procedure Rules 1998
CUKC	citizen of the UK and colonies
DCB	designated competent body
DfWP	Department for Work and Pensions
ECHR	European Convention on Human Rights
ECtHR	European Court of Human Rights
ECJ	European Court of Justice
ECO	Entry clearance officer
EEA	European Economic Area
EU	European Union
FCA	Financial Conduct Authority
HA 1985	Housing Act 1985
HMRC	HM Revenue and Customs
HND	Higher National Diploma
HRA 1998	Human Rights Act 1998
IA	Immigration Act
IAA 1999	Immigration and Asylum Act 1999
IAC	Immigration and Asylum Chamber
IANA 2006	Immigration, Asylum and Nationality Act 2006
I(EEA) Regs 2006	Immigration (European Economic Area) Regulations 2006
IHC	Immigration health charge
NHS	National Health Service
NIAA 2002	Nationality, Immigration and Asylum Act 2002
NQF	National Qualification Framework
NVQ	National Vocational Qualification
SIAC	Special Immigration Appeals Commission
UNHCR	United Nations High Commissioner for Refugees

CHAPTER 1

INTRODUCTION

1.1 PUBLIC LAW AND PRACTICAL PROBLEMS

This book aims to provide an introduction to immigration and nationality law and practice.

This is a public law subject, dealing with relations between the State and the individual, concerned fundamentally with the exercise of discretion by officials. It is easy to understand the practical problems which arise in this area of the law, as it concerns the individual's ability to live, work and enjoy family life in the country of his or her choice. In practice, it involves a great deal of client contact, argument with officials, advocacy in tribunals and familiarity with a wide range of legal sources. It therefore calls upon the full range of legal skills.

1.2 SOURCES OF IMMIGRATION LAW AND GENERAL PRINCIPLES

1.2.1 Legislation

The main piece of legislation dealing with immigration law is the Immigration Act 1971 (IA 1971). This replaced existing immigration controls and introduced the concept of the right of abode in the United Kingdom (UK). The starting point for any immigration practitioner is the following general principles set out in s 1:

(1) All those who are in this Act expressed to have the right of abode in the United Kingdom shall be free to live in, and to come and go into and from, the United Kingdom without let or hindrance except such as may be required under and in accordance with this Act to enable their right to be established or as may be otherwise lawfully imposed on any person.

(2) Those not having that right may live, work and settle in the United Kingdom by permission and subject to such regulation and control of their entry into, stay in and departure from the United Kingdom as is imposed by this Act ...

As to s 1(1) and the right of abode in the UK, see **1.4.1**.

Section 1(2) establishes what are known as immigration controls: see **1.4.2**.

The IA 1971 has been amended by numerous subsequent Acts, almost on an annual basis.

British nationality law is dealt with mainly in the British Nationality Act 1981 (BNA 1981) (as amended). This Act came into force on 1 January 1983 and Pt 1 sets out the provisions which determine whether or not a person is a British citizen. The date is significant, as different tests apply to determine British citizenship depending on whether or not the individual was born before 1983 (ie up to and including 31 December 1982) or after 1982 (ie from and including 1 January 1983). Note that British citizenship is also affected by whether or not the person was born in the UK. Full details are to be found in **Chapter 2**.

A British citizen has the right of abode in the UK. Therefore a British citizen is not subject to immigration controls. So a preliminary question for an immigration practitioner to answer when seeing a new client is whether or not the client is a British citizen.

1.2.2   The Immigration Rules

Whilst the IA 1971 (as amended) is the framework of immigration law, it does not contain any detail. This is because ss 1(4) and 3(2) permit rules to be laid down and amended by the Secretary of State as to the practice to be followed in the administration of the Act for regulating the entry into and stay in the UK of persons not having the right of abode. These are the Immigration Rules. A copy can be found in **Appendix 1**. Quickly skim through the contents to get some idea of their wide coverage.

The Immigration Rules structure the discretion given by the IA 1971 to grant leave to enter, to vary leave, or to make a deportation order. They bind immigration officers, but not the Home Secretary who, in the exercise of his discretion, may, in appropriate circumstances, depart from the Rules he has laid down, for instance granting leave to remain in the UK when the Rules would require refusal. They are, therefore, not rules of law in the strict sense (R v Secretary of State for the Home Department, ex p Hosenball [1977] 3 All ER 452; Odelolar v Secretary of State for the Home Department [2008] EWCA Civ 308). But as the Rules are laid before and approved by Parliament, published Government policy guidance cannot add requirements that are not in the Rules themselves: see Secretary of State for the Home Department v Pankina [2010] EWCA Civ 719 and R (on the application of Alvi) v Secretary of State for the Home Department [2012] UKSC 33.

Nevertheless, a lawyer can base his advice on the Rules because they are normally followed by the immigration authorities, and because failure to apply them may give grounds for appeal, administrative review or judicial review (see **Chapters 11** and **12**).

The current Rules are cited as the Statement of Changes in Immigration Rules 1994 (HC 395). As the Rules are not delegated legislation, they are cited as a House of Commons Paper and not as a statutory instrument. Later amendments to the Rules are cited similarly.

1.2.3   Home Office practices

Since the Home Office has considerable discretion not governed by the Rules, it is inevitable that informal practices evolve in order to ensure that comparable cases are treated in like ways. These practices are not generally binding, although under the administrative law doctrine of legitimate expectation, a decision which disregards them may be quashed as unreasonable (R v Secretary of State for the Home Department, ex p Asif Mahmood Khan [1984] 1 WLR 1337).

The Home Office has made public some of the internal instructions to staff on the handling of immigration cases. These are available via the Internet (see **1.2.8**).

1.2.4   Case law

Immigration cases have in recent years formed the largest single category of applications to the High Court for judicial review. In addition, cases may reach the higher courts by way of appeal. These cases may be reported in the standard series of law reports, but may also be found in the specialist Immigration and Nationality Law Reports (INLR), published six times a year by Jordans, and the Immigration Appeal Reports (Imm LR), published quarterly by The Stationery Office.

1.2.5   EU law

Nationals of EU and EEA Member States (see the list in **Appendix 2**) have special rights under EU law (eg under Article 45 TFEU (freedom of movement of workers)). These rights are set out in detail in EU Regulations and Directives. The rights often have direct effect and so override conflicting provisions of UK immigration law. The UK Government will try to ensure that legislation and the Immigration Rules give effect to EU law, but be aware that UK provisions may be open to challenge.

In addition, there is a considerable body of case law of the European Court of Justice (ECJ) on the meaning and effect of Treaty provisions and legislation. This is binding on UK courts. Directives, Regulations, EU judgments, etc can be found on the European Union on-line website at www.europa.eu.

Probably the most significant Directive is Directive 2004/38/EC of the European Parliament and Council. A copy appears at **Appendix 3**. This sets out the terms and limits of the right of free movement. It has been implemented into domestic law by the Immigration (European Economic Area) Regulations 2006 (I(EEA) Regs 2006) (see **Chapter 4** and **Appendix 4**).

It is important to note that a family member of a British citizen may sometimes be able to use EU law rather than domestic UK immigration law to enter the UK. The most common example is where a British citizen goes to work in another EEA country, thereby exercising and engaging EU Treaty rights. The British citizen marries or enters into a civil partnership with a non-EEA national. The couple then want to travel to the UK to live together. The British citizen has a right of abode in the UK and so is not subject to immigration controls (see **1.2.1** and **Chapter 2**). His or her spouse or civil partner may be able to seek entry to the UK under EU law rather than domestic law (see **4.4.12** and **8.3** respectively).

1.2.6 The European Convention on Human Rights and the Human Rights Act 1998

The Human Rights Act 1998 (HRA 1998) interprets, rather than incorporates, the European Convention on Human Rights (ECHR). Although the legislation requires UK courts to apply Acts of Parliament even if they are incompatible with the Convention, it contains a number of measures which will enable practitioners to rely on the Convention in immigration cases. In outline these are as follows.

Section 3 requires UK courts to try to interpret an Act of Parliament in a way which is compatible with listed Convention rights, whether or not the Act is ambiguous.

Section 4 enables the courts to make a declaration that an Act is incompatible with Convention rights. The court must still apply the Act in the case before it, but s 10 enables the Government to introduce fast-track delegated legislation to alter the law.

Section 6 is probably the most far-reaching provision. It states that it is unlawful for public authorities (such as the Home Office) to act in a way which infringes Convention rights, unless required to do so by Act of Parliament. So, when exercising a discretion, the Home Secretary must take Convention rights into account and, if statute permits it, must avoid decisions which infringe them. As the Immigration Rules themselves are made in the exercise of a discretion, both the Rules and decisions made under them are open to challenge if they infringe Convention rights. So, in applying the Rules and exercising powers, the Secretary of State must respect Convention rights, whether or not the Rules explicitly refer to them: see R (Syed) v Secretary of State for the Home Department [2011] EWCA Civ 1059.

So immigration lawyers need a good working knowledge of human rights. The main Convention rights that might be relevant are set out in **Appendix 5**. Detailed references to human rights cases and principles can be found in the **Chapters 9, 10** and **11**.

1.2.7 Practitioner texts

The practitioner in immigration law relies heavily on a limited number of secondary sources. These include:

(a) *Macdonald's Immigration Law and Practice* (Butterworths): the leading practitioner text;

(b) *Butterworths Immigration Law Service*: in the form of a loose-leaf encyclopaedia, particularly useful as a source for Home Office practices;

(c)   *Tolley's Immigration and Nationality Law and Practice*: a quarterly journal;

(d)   *Immigration, Nationality and Refugee Law Handbook* (Joint Council for the Welfare of Immigrants): an invaluable practical guide (*JCWI Handbook*);

(e)   Fransman, *British Nationality Law* (Butterworths);

(f)   Webb and Grant, *Immigration and Asylum Emergency Procedures* (Legal Action Group).

1.2.8 Websites

There are many useful websites, most of which have links to other, related sites. You might start with the following:

Home Office: www.gov.uk/government/organisations/uk-visas-and-immigration

European Union on-line: www.europa.eu

Immigration and Asylum (Chamber) Tribunal: www.justice.gov.uk/immigration-asylum-tribunal

European Court of Human Rights: www.echr.coe.int

Ministry of Justice: www.justice.gov.uk

The Supreme Court: www.supremecourt.gov.uk

Joint Council for the Welfare of Immigrants: www.jcwi.org.uk

UNHCR UN Refugee Agency: www.unhcr.org

Electronic Immigration Network: www.ein.org.uk

1.3 INSTITUTIONS

1.3.1 The Home Office

Under the IA 1971, the Home Secretary has overall responsibility for the administration of immigration control. The Act designates the Home Secretary as the person who makes the Immigration Rules, appoints immigration officers, and takes specific decisions such as the decision to deport. The law generally recognises that, in practice, the Home Secretary acts through civil servants (*Carltona Ltd v Commissioner of Works* [1943] 2 All ER 560). However, there is a division of functions under s 4 of the IA 1971. The immigration service is specifically made responsible for granting leave to enter the UK, whilst the Home Office in general deals with the subsequent variation of leave.

1.3.2 The immigration service

The immigration service consists of immigration officers, chief immigration officers and inspectors appointed by the Home Secretary. As explained in **1.3.1**, they are responsible for control on entry to the UK. They operate from the various ports of entry (including airports). Division of functions between the immigration service and the Home Office in general is not always clear-cut, as the Home Secretary may validly delegate some functions (eg the decision to deport overstayers) to the immigration service (*Oladehinde v Secretary of State for the Home Department; Alexander v Secretary of State for the Home Department* [1990] 3 WLR 797).

1.3.3 UK Visas and Immigration

UK Visas and Immigration is a department within the Home Office that is responsible for managing border controls, as well as enforcing immigration and customs regulations. It considers applications for permission to enter or remain in the UK, citizenship and asylum.

1.3.4 The Identity and Passport Service

This is an executive agency of the Home Office. It issues UK passports.

1.3.5 International Group

The International Group is part of the Home Office. It operates visa offices, manned by entry clearance officers, in 250 locations throughout the world. The largest handles 300,000 applications a year; the smallest fewer than 10.

1.3.6 The First-tier Tribunal (Immigration and Asylum Chamber)

Some, but far from all, of the decisions made by an official in an immigration context are appealable to the First-tier Tribunal (Immigration and Asylum Chamber). Any further appeal on a point of law is to the Upper Tribunal and the Court of Appeal. See further **Chapter 11**.

1.4 IMMIGRATION CONTROLS

1.4.1 Right of abode in the UK

As we have seen, a British citizen has a right of abode in the UK. So, if a British citizen leaves the UK, he is free to return at any point in time and enter the UK via an airport or a port. Subject to producing evidence of that right of abode, usually by way of a British passport, he is not subject to immigration controls. This applies equally to a British citizen born abroad who travels to the UK for the first time.

Note that certain Commonwealth citizens also have a right of abode in the UK (see **2.3**). Also, EEA nationals are not subject to domestic UK immigration laws when entering the UK under EU law (see **Chapter 4**).

1.4.2 Entry clearance, leave to enter and leave to remain in the UK

Immigration controls are dealt with in detail in **Chapter 3**. However, it is important to grasp the following points at this stage. As a general rule, immigration controls may exist at three particular points in time, namely:

(a)   before a person travels to the UK. This is known as entry clearance, and most persons, apart from some people who wish to enter for less than six months, must obtain it;

(b)   on arrival in the UK at the port of entry. This is known as leave to enter the UK. All people who are subject to immigration controls must obtain permission to enter the UK when first arriving;

(c)   after arrival, if an extension of the initial limited time granted for the stay is required.

1.4.3 Visa nationals

A 'visa national' is a person who always needs entry clearance in advance of travelling to the UK for whatever purpose. The entry clearance document he needs to obtain from the British High Commission or embassy in his own country before travelling is a visa, and this will state the purpose of the entry to the UK, for example as a visitor or student, etc. Most visas appear as a stamp in the person's passport. A list of countries whose nationals must obtain visas appears in Appendix 1 to the Immigration Rules (see **Appendix 1** to this book).

Upon arriving at a UK port of entry, a visa national usually requires leave to enter the UK, that is, he must convince the immigration officer that entry is pursuant to the terms of his visa. If leave is given, a stamp to that effect is put in his passport.

> **EXAMPLE**
>
> Kim is Chinese. He is a visa national. He wishes to come to the UK for a holiday. If he is to be given leave to enter the UK, he must, as a general rule:
>
> (a)   obtain a visa in China before travelling; and
>
> (b)   on arrival in the UK, convince the immigration officer that he is entering as a genuine visitor.

1.4.4 Non-visa nationals

A non-visa national is a person who is not on the visa list. He does not require entry clearance in advance of travelling to the UK for short-term purposes, ie a stay of up to six months in the UK, such as a visitor (see **Chapter 5**). However, he will require it for long-term purposes (ie a stay of more than six months), for example as an employee or a businessman, or if he wishes to stay permanently in the UK. The entry clearance document he needs to obtain from the British High Commission or embassy in his own country before travelling is an entry certificate. This will state the purpose of the entry to the UK, for example 'settlement as spouse', and usually appears as a stamp in the person's passport.

Upon arriving at a UK port of entry, a non-visa national will require leave to enter the UK, ie he must convince the immigration officer that entry is pursuant to the Immigration Rules.

> **EXAMPLE**
>
> Bob is an American. He is a non-visa national. He wishes to come to the UK for a holiday (ie for up to six months). He does not have to obtain an entry certificate in America before travelling but, on arrival, he must convince the immigration officer that he is entering as a genuine visitor, if he is to be given leave to enter. But if Bob wanted to enter and stay for more than six months, he would need to obtain an entry certificate before travelling to the UK.

1.4.5 Settled status

A person with 'settled status' (also known as unconditional leave, permanent stay, permanent residence, indefinite leave and settlement) does not have the right of abode in the UK and so, in theory, can be deported (see **Chapter 10**). This is a person who is legally in the UK without any conditions or restrictions being placed on his residence. Hence, it is not limited in time. If a person with settled status leaves the UK, he will be subject to immigration control on return, ie he will need leave to enter the UK on the basis that he is returning to reside again (see **3.8.3**).

1.4.6 Summary: who does what?

- Entry clearance officer (ECO) – visas and entry certificates;
- Immigration officer – leave to enter the UK;
- Home Office – extension of stay in UK, including switching of category.

CHAPTER 2

BRITISH NATIONALITY AND RIGHT OF ABODE

2.1 INTRODUCTION

The law relating to nationality or citizenship forms the background to immigration law because a person's right to live in the country of his choice often depends on his nationality. This is true in UK law, in that a British citizen has a right to live in the UK.

There are two categories of people who have a statutory 'right of abode in the UK': all British citizens (see **2.2**) and certain Commonwealth citizens (see **2.3**). A person with the right of abode can freely enter the UK (ie he is not subject to immigration controls (see **1.4** and **Chapter 3**)). Moreover, he cannot be excluded from the UK (ie he cannot be removed or deported (see **Chapter 10**)). Nationals of the EEA do not have the right of abode, although they have a right of entry to and residence in the UK under EU law (see **Chapter 4**).

2.2 BRITISH CITIZENSHIP

British nationality law has changed considerably over the last century. For an historical analysis, see **2.4**. The BNA 1981 was implemented on 1 January 1983, thereby creating the nationality of British citizenship. The starting points for determining whether a person is a British citizen or not is to ask two questions:

(a) was he born before 1983 or after 1982; and

(b) was he born in the UK or elsewhere?

There is a summary of the key requirements at **Appendix 6**.

2.2.1 People born in the UK before 1983

A person is a British citizen if, before 1983 (ie, up to and including 31 December 1982), he was born in the UK.

2.2.2 People born outside the UK before 1983

A person is a British citizen if, before 1983, he was born outside the UK and:

(a) his father was born in the UK; *or*

(b) his father was registered or naturalised (see **2.2.6.1** and **2.2.7**) as a British citizen in the UK before the child's birth (if a father becomes British after the child's birth, this does not retrospectively make the child British); *and*

(c) his parents were married, or subsequently marry in a country where that marriage operates to legitimise the child.

So, before 1983, a father could pass on his British citizenship acquired in the UK only to his legitimate child. An illegitimate child could not 'inherit' British citizenship through his father.

EXAMPLES

1. Joshua was born in 1962 in the UK. He is therefore a British citizen (see **2.2.1**). In 1980 he married Grace (who is not a British citizen). In 1981 their daughter, Sophie, was born outside the UK. Sophie is a British citizen as her father was born in the UK and married to her mother at the time of Sophie's birth.

2. Harry was born in 1961 in the UK. He is therefore a British citizen (see **2.2.1**). In 1979 he started a relationship with Lynda (who is not a British citizen). In 1981 their son, Michael, was born outside the UK. In 1982 Harry and Lynda married in a country where their marriage operated to legitimise Michael who thereby became a British citizen.

3. James was born in 1960 in the UK. He is therefore a British citizen (see **2.2.1**). In 1978 he started a relationship with Lilly (who is not a British citizen). In 1981 their daughter, Katie, was born outside the UK. James and Lilly never marry. Katie is not a British citizen on these facts.

Before 1983, a mother could not pass on her British citizenship acquired by her birth, registration or naturalisation in the UK to any child born outside the UK. However, in those circumstances, the Home Office allowed for the child to be registered as British, and this is now possible pursuant to BNA 1981, s 4C (see **2.2.6**).

EXAMPLE

Ruby was born in 1959 in the UK. She is therefore a British citizen (see **2.2.1**). In 1980 she married Gary (who is not a British citizen). In 1982 their son, Simon, was born outside the UK. Although Ruby is a British citizen at the time of her son's birth, she cannot pass that citizenship on to him. However, she could have applied to register him as a British citizen whilst he was a child, or he may do so as an adult: see **2.2.6**.

2.2.3   People born in the UK after 1982

A person is a British citizen if, after 1982 (ie, from and including 1 January 1983), he was born in the UK and at the time of his birth either of his parents was:

(a)   a British citizen; or

(b)   settled in the UK. (As to settled status, see **1.4.5** and **3.8**. Note that for these purposes a Commonwealth citizen with the right of abode (see **2.3**) is treated as 'settled'.)

Note that until the Nationality, Immigration and Asylum Act 2002 (NIAA 2002) came into force on 1 July 2006, a 'parent' in this context did not include a father of a child who was not married to the child's mother. However, the BNA 1981, as amended by the NIAA 2002, provides at s 50(9A) that from 1 July 2006 a child's father is:

(a)   the husband, at the time of the child's birth, of the woman who gives birth to the child (and remember that if the parents subsequently marry that may operate to legitimise the child); or

(b)   where a person is treated as the father of the child under s 28 of the Human Fertilisation and Embryology Act 1990, that person; or

(c)   where neither paragraph (a) nor (b) applies, any person who is proven to be the natural father by the production of such evidence (eg a birth certificate, DNA test report or court order) as may satisfy the Secretary of State on this point.

This means that subject to satisfying (c) above, an illegitimate person born in the UK on or after 1 July 2006 is a British citizen if his father was either a British citizen or settled at that time. What if an illegitimate person can meet these requirements but he was born in the UK before July 2006? In these circumstances the person may apply to register as a British citizen under s 4G of the BNA 1981 (when he will have to satisfy the Secretary of State that he is of good character).

EXAMPLES

1. Evie was born in 1965 in the UK. She is therefore a British citizen (see **2.2.1**). In 1990 she gave birth to her daughter, Charlotte, in the UK. Charlotte is a British citizen as her mother was a British citizen at the time of Charlotte's birth.

2. Chloe was born outside the UK in 1967 as a visa national. In 1970 she entered the UK with her family for the purposes of settlement. She had indefinite leave to remain in the UK when she gave birth to her son, Lewis, in 1987 in the UK. Lewis is a British citizen as his mother was settled in the UK at the time of his birth.

3. John was born in 1970 in the UK. He is therefore a British citizen (see **2.2.1**). In 1995 he married Helen (who is not a British citizen). In 1997 their daughter, Sally, was born in the UK. Sally is a British citizen as her father was a British citizen and married to her mother at the time of Sally's birth.

4. Oliver was born outside the UK in 1980 as a visa national. In 1992 he entered the UK with his family for the purposes of settlement. He had indefinite leave to remain in the UK when his girlfriend, Jessica, gave birth to his son, Alfie, in 2008 in the UK. Jessica had limited leave to remain in the UK at that point in time. Alfie is a British citizen if Oliver and Jessica subsequently marry in a country where their marriage operates to legitimise him; or if the Secretary of State accepts evidence that Oliver is his father.

5. What if, in Example 4, Alfie had been born before 1 July 2006? In those circumstances Alfie could be registered as a British citizen at the discretion of the Secretary of State. See further **2.2.6**.

Note that if, at any time after his birth but before he reaches 18, either of his parents becomes a British citizen or settled in the UK, he may be able to register as a British citizen (see **2.2.6.1**).

2.2.4 People born outside the UK after 1982

A person is a British citizen if, after 1982, he is born outside the UK, and:

(a) his father or mother was a British citizen otherwise than by descent by birth in the UK (see **2.2.5**); *or*

(b) his father or mother was a British citizen otherwise than by descent (see **2.2.5**), having been registered or naturalised (see **2.2.6.1** and **2.2.7**) as a British citizen in the UK before the child's birth (if either parent becomes British after the child's birth, this does not retrospectively make the child British).

As noted at **2.2.3**, until the NIAA 2002 came into force on 1 July 2006, a 'parent' in this context did not include a father of a child who was not married to the child's mother.

This means that subject to satisfying condition (c) of s 50(9A) of the BNA 1981 (**2.2.3**), an illegitimate person born outside the UK on or after 1 July 2006 is a British citizen if his father was a British citizen otherwise than by descent (see **2.2.5**), or registered or naturalised as a British citizen before the child's birth. What if an illegitimate person can meet these requirements but he was born outside the UK before July 2006? In these circumstances he may apply to register as a British citizen under s 4G of the BNA 1981 (when he will have to satisfy the Secretary of State that he is of good character).

EXAMPLES

1. Amelia was born in 1970 in the UK. She is therefore a British citizen otherwise than by descent (see **2.2.5.1**). In 1990 she gave birth to her son, Charles, outside the UK. Charles is a British citizen (by descent: see **2.2.5.2**) as his mother was a British citizen otherwise than by descent at the time of Charles's birth.

2. Benjamin was born in 1972 in the UK. He is therefore a British citizen otherwise than by descent (see **2.2.5.1**). In 1997 he married Adela, a visa national. In 1999 their daughter, Ramona, was born outside the UK. Ramona is a British citizen (by descent: **2.2.5.2**) as her father was a British citizen otherwise than by descent and married to her mother at the time of Ramona's birth.

3. Ethan was born in the UK in 1980. He is therefore a British citizen otherwise than by descent (see **2.2.5.1**). In 2007 his girlfriend, Alice, gave birth to his son, Zach, outside the UK. Alice is a visa national. Zach is a British citizen by descent (see **2.2.5.2**) if Ethan and Alice subsequently marry in a country where their marriage operates to legitimise him; or if the Secretary of State accepts evidence that Ethan is his father.

2.2.5   British citizenship: what about subsequent generations?

2.2.5.1   British citizen otherwise than by descent

A person who acquires British citizenship by birth in the UK (see **2.2.1** and **2.2.3**), or as a child by registration in the UK (see **2.2.6.1**) or as an adult by naturalisation in the UK (see **2.2.7**), is classified as a *British citizen otherwise than by descent*. This means he can automatically pass on British citizenship to a child born outside the UK in the circumstances described at **2.2.2** and **2.2.4** above.

2.2.5.2   British citizen by descent

Where a person is born outside the UK (see **2.2.2** and **2.2.4**) and acquires British citizenship only because one or both of his parents is a British citizen, he is classified as a *British citizen by descent*. This means that he cannot automatically pass on British citizenship to any child who is also born abroad. However, some second-generation children can be registered abroad at the British consulate as British citizens (by descent) if:

(a)   one of the parents is a British citizen by descent; and

(b)   the British parent has a parent who is or was British otherwise than by descent; and

(c)   the British parent had at some time before the child's birth lived in the UK for a continuous period of three years, not being absent for more than 270 days in that period.

In addition an applicant aged 10 or over will have to satisfy the Secretary of State that he is of good character (see **2.2.7.1(f)**). In these circumstances a child is registered as a British citizen by descent – the registration takes place outside the UK and is based not on any residence in the UK by the child but by his British parent in the past before the child's birth.

What if (a) and (b) are met but not (c)? It will be possible to register the child in the UK as a British citizen if during his childhood his father and mother come and live in the UK with him for a continuous period of three years and are not absent during that time for more than 270 days. Note that the requirement is that both parents live in the UK unless one of them is dead or the couple have divorced. In addition an applicant aged 10 or over will have to satisfy the Secretary of State that he is of good character (see **2.2.7.1(f)**). In these circumstances a child is registered as a British citizen otherwise than by descent because the registration takes place in the UK and is based on the family's residence in the UK.

> **EXAMPLE**
>
> James was born in Germany in 1975. His father, Larry, was born in London, England in 1945. Larry had married James's mother in 1965. In 1990, James married Steffi, a German national. In 2005, their son, Thomas, was born in Germany.
>
> Larry was born before 1983 in the UK and is therefore a British citizen otherwise than by descent. His son, James, was born outside the UK before 1983 and is therefore British by descent. Thomas can be registered as a British citizen by descent if James has lived in the UK at some time for a continuous period of three years before Thomas's birth.
>
> What if James has not lived in the UK for the requisite period before Thomas's birth or, alternatively, the family are just about to move to the UK to live there permanently? If James, Steffi and Thomas all come to live in the UK whilst Thomas is still a child, and do so for a continuous period of three years, Thomas may be registered as a British citizen otherwise than by descent.

Can a British citizen by descent apply for naturalisation as a British citizen (see **2.2.7**) in order that his children born abroad automatically become British citizens? No, held the Court of Appeal in the case of *R v Secretary of State for the Home Department, ex p Azad Ullah* [2001] INLR 74.

2.2.6 Registration as a British citizen

2.2.6.1 Child born in the UK after 1982

A child can apply to register as a British citizen, pursuant to s 1(3) and (4) of the BNA 1981, if he was born in the UK after 1982 and, after his birth:

(a)   one of his parents becomes a British citizen or settled in the UK (see **3.8**) before he is 18; or

(b)   he remains in the UK for the first 10 years of his life and is not absent for more than 90 days each year during that period. By s 1(7), a longer period of absence may be acceptable.

In addition, an applicant aged 10 or over will have to satisfy the Secretary of State that he is of good character (see **2.2.7.1(f)**).

Such a person is a British citizen otherwise than by descent (see **2.2.5**).

2.2.6.2 Child born outside the UK before 1983

As we saw at **2.2.2**, a British mother could not before 1983 transmit her British citizenship acquired in the UK to her child born outside the UK. However, by concession, the Home Office did allow such a child to be registered as British (by descent), provided the application was made before the child reached 18. What if no such registration occurred, given that the concession, by its very nature, expired at the end of 2000? Section 4C of the BNA 1981 now gives a right to such a person born before 1 January 1983 to apply to register as a British citizen. An applicant under s 4C has to satisfy the Secretary of State that he is of good character (see **2.2.7.1(f)**) before being registered.

Such a person is a British citizen by descent (see **2.2.5**).

2.2.7 Naturalisation

If a foreign national adult living in the UK has settled status (see **1.4.5** and **3.8**), he may wish to apply to become a British citizen (otherwise than by descent) by a process known as naturalisation. Under s 6 of the BNA 1981, the Home Secretary has a discretion to grant a certificate of naturalisation to any person aged 18 or over who is not a British citizen. The grant of British citizenship under s 6 is not a fundamental human right: *R v Secretary of State for the Home Department, ex p Al Fayed* [2001] Imm AR 134 and *R (AHK) v Secretary of State for the Home Department* [2009] EWCA Civ 287. As Blake J stated at first instance in *AHK* (in a judgment entitled *MH v Secretary of State for the Home Department* [2008] EWHC 2525, at [41]), 'In general terms ... no claimant [under s 6] has a right to British citizenship, but only a right to have an application fairly considered under the statutory scheme.'

The requirements are slightly different, depending on whether or not the applicant is married to or in a civil partnership with a British citizen at the time the application is made. Broadly, those requirements are as follows.

2.2.7.1 If the applicant is married to, or in a civil partnership with, a British citizen

The applicant:

(a)   must be settled (see **3.8**) at the time of the application;

(b)   must have been living in the UK legally for at least three years continuously before making the application;

(c)   must have been physically present in the UK on the date three years before the application is made. The start of the qualifying period of three years is the day after the corresponding application date. So, for example, if the application is received by the Home Office on 5 January 2014, the three-year qualifying period starts on 6 January 2011;

(d)   must not have been absent for more than 270 days in total during the three-year qualifying period, and not more than 90 days in the year immediately before the application. The Home Office has indicated that it will normally disregard 30 days and 10 days respectively over these limits, provided all the other requirements are met. If the absences are greater than that, see the Home Office guidance, 'Naturalisation Booklet – The Requirements' on the Home Office website (see **1.2.8**). What is the purpose of this residence requirement? Home Office guidance is that it allows an applicant to demonstrate close links with, and commitment to, the UK, and enables the Home Secretary to assess the strength of that commitment as well as the applicant's suitability on the other grounds;

(e)   must have (i) sufficient knowledge of the English language and (ii) sufficient knowledge about life in the UK. How can an applicant demonstrate this? The answer is to be found in the British Nationality (General) Regulations 2003 (SI 2003/548, as amended), reg 5A. Broadly, the requirements are that the applicant:

(i)   demonstrates knowledge of the English language by:

(A)   possessing a Home Office approved qualification or passing a Home Office prescribed test as specified in Sch 2A to the 2003 Regulations; or

(B)   possessing a degree which the Home Office accepts was taught in English (see **7.4.3.3**); or

(C)   having met this requirement when making an earlier, successful application for indefinite leave to remain (see **3.8.7**); or

(D)   satisfying the Secretary of State that he is a national of a Home Office designated majority English speaking country (see the list of relevant nationalities at **7.4.3.2**);

(ii)   demonstrates knowledge about life in the UK by passing the test known as the 'Life in the UK Test' administered by a Home Office approved educational institution.

What is the 'Life in the UK Test'? The test has to be taken on a computer and consists of 24 questions, such as: where is the Prime Minister's official home in London, and is it true or false that UK citizens can vote in an election at the age of 18? It is based on the Government handbook, 'Life in the United Kingdom: A Guide for New Residents'. It can be taken only at an official testing centre. Note that in Wales and Scotland the test can be taken in Welsh or Scottish Gaelic, as appropriate. Full details are on the website, www.lifeintheuktest.ukba.homeoffice.gov.uk.

In what circumstances will the Home Office waive these requirements? If the applicant is suffering from a long-term illness or disability that severely restricts his ability to learn English or prepare for the Life in the UK test, or has a mental condition and is not able to speak or learn the relevant language.

What other physical conditions may prevent an applicant from meeting the requirement? The Home Secretary will consider how the condition would stop the applicant from taking the Life in the UK test or learning English, for example, if the applicant is deaf or without speech or has a speech impediment which limits his ability to communicate in the relevant language.

Life in the UK test centres and many colleges can cater for a variety of disabilities, such as blindness. An applicant may be able to do the test even if he produces evidence of a disability.

If an applicant claims to have a physical or mental condition, he must provide original and current medical evidence from a medical practitioner. This must state the condition, and explain why it is unreasonable to expect the applicant to take the Life in the UK test or learn English; and

(f)   must show good character. This requirement is not defined in the BNA 1981. In *R (Thamby) v Secretary of State for the Home Department* [2011] EWHC 1763 Parker J stated, at [41]:

> It is a term capable of carrying a range of meanings, and requires an exercise in evaluation to apply it. It is established that this means that the proper approach of the courts to considering the standard of good character adopted by the Secretary of State and the application of the concept in a particular case is to ask whether the standard and its application were such as could reasonably be adopted in the circumstances: *ex p Al Fayed* [2001] Imm AR 134, [41] (Nourse LJ), [93] (Kennedy LJ) and [97] (Rix LJ). It is open to the Secretary of State, so long as she acts rationally, to adopt a high standard of good character, and one higher than other reasonable decision-makers might have adopted: *ex p Al Fayed* at [41] (Nourse LJ).

The applicant must disclose on the application form details of all criminal convictions both within and outside the UK. These include road traffic offences.

The onus is on the applicant to establish his good character (*R (on the application of DA (Iran)) v Secretary of State for the Home Department* [2014] EWCA Civ 654).

So what convictions affect an application? **Table 2.1** gives examples of sentences, along with the relevant sentence-based threshold. In calculating the threshold, it is the prison sentence that counts, not the time served. Note that a suspended sentence counts as if it were a non-custodial sentence unless that sentence is subsequently activated.

Table 2.1 Criminality requirement

Sentence	Impact on nationality application
4 years' or more imprisonment	Application should be refused, regardless of when the conviction occurred
Between 12 months' and 4 years' imprisonment	Application should be refused unless 15 years have passed since the end of the sentence
Up to 12 months' imprisonment	Application should be refused unless 10 years have passed since the end of the sentence.
A non-custodial sentence or other out of court disposal	Application should be refused if the conviction occurred in the last 3 years.

2.2.7.2   If the applicant is neither married to, nor in a civil partnership with, a British citizen

The applicant:

(a)   must have been settled (see **3.8**) for at least one year before the application;

(b)   must have been living in the UK legally for five years continuously before making the application;

(c)   must have been physically present in the UK on the date five years before the application is received by the Home Office;

(d)   must not have been absent for more than 450 days in total during the five-year qualifying period, and not more than 90 days in the year immediately before the application is made (see **2.2.7.1(d)** for Home Office policy where this is exceeded);

(e)   must have sufficient knowledge of the English language and sufficient knowledge about life in the UK (see **2.2.7.1(e)**);

(f)   must show good character (see **2.2.7.1(f)**); and

(g)   must show an intention to live in the UK. Home Office guidance is that this requirement is usually met if the applicant's stated intention is to have his home or, if more than one, his principal home in the UK. Factors affecting this will include whether a home here (owned or rented) has already been established and the reason for any past or intended future absences.

2.2.7.3 EEA nationals

Certain EEA nationals are treated as settled for the purposes of naturalisation: **3.8.9**.

2.2.8 Formalities for registration and naturalisation

These are governed by the BNA 1981 and the British Nationality (General) Regulations 2003 (SI 2003/548). In particular, applicants of full age are required to make an oath of allegiance and pledge. The latter states that the person will respect the rights and freedoms of the UK and will uphold its democratic values, observe its laws, and fulfil the duties and obligations of citizenship.

2.2.9 Deprivation of citizenship obtained by registration or naturalisation

This is governed by s 40 of the BNA 1981 and the British Nationality (General) Regulations 2003 (SI 2003/548). The Secretary of State may by order deprive a person of his British citizenship status if satisfied that it would be conducive to the public good. Home Office guidance is that this can be done in cases involving national security, terrorism, serious organised crime, war crimes and unacceptable behaviour such as preaching *jihad*.

The Secretary of State may also by order deprive a person of his British citizenship status where it was obtained by registration or naturalisation, if satisfied that such was obtained by means of fraud, false representation or concealment of a material fact.

The Secretary of State may not normally make either of the above orders if it would make a person stateless, unless he reasonably believes that the person can acquire another nationality or citizenship: see *Al-Jedda v Secretary of State for the Home Department* [2010] EWCA Civ 212. The Court held that the burden is on the appellant to show on the balance of probabilities that he will become stateless. See also *B2 v Secretary of State for the Home Department* [2013] EWCA Civ 616 and *Pham v Secretary of State for the Home Department* [2015] UKSC 19 for discussion of the meaning of statelessness under the BNA 1981. The exception to the normal rule is where the Secretary of State is satisfied that the deprivation is conducive to the public good because the person has conducted himself in a manner seriously prejudicial to the vital interests of the UK.

Before making a deprivation order the Secretary of State must give the person concerned written notice specifying that a decision has been made to make the order and the reasons for it. The notice must also advise the person of his right to appeal (see **Chapter 11**). Does the fact that the person has to conduct his appeal from outside the UK render the exclusion decision procedurally unfair? No, held the Court of Appeal in *GI v Secretary of State for the Home Department* [2012] EWCA Civ 867. On appeal, the Tribunal has to ask itself 'does the evidence in the case establish that citizenship was obtained by fraud?' If it does then it has to answer the question 'do the other circumstances of the case point to discretionary deprival?' See *Arusha and Demushi (deprivation of citizenship – delay)* [2012] UKUT 80 (IAC).

2.3 COMMONWEALTH CITIZENS WITH RIGHT OF ABODE

There are two categories of Commonwealth citizens who have the right of abode in the UK, ie the right to enter the UK without being subject to immigration controls (see **1.4** and **Chapter 3**). There is a list of Commonwealth countries in **Appendix 9**.

2.3.1 Parental link

The first category concerns those Commonwealth citizens with a 'parental link' to the UK. The requirements are that:

(a)   the person was a Commonwealth citizen on 31 December 1982, and continues to be such; and

(b)   either parent was born in the UK. 'Parent' in this context includes the mother, but not the father, of an illegitimate child.

> **EXAMPLE**
>
> Bill was born in New Zealand in 1979. His mother, Ada, was born in London, England. His father was a citizen of New Zealand. Assuming that Bill is a citizen of New Zealand under that country's nationality laws and so remained, Bill was a Commonwealth citizen on 31 December 1982. Bill cannot be a British citizen by descent as his father was not British and, before 1983, mothers could not pass on their citizenship (see **2.2.2**). However, as a Commonwealth citizen, he has the right of abode in the UK by virtue of his mother's birth in the UK. Query if Ada registered him as British in these circumstances before he reached 18 or, if she failed to do so, whether he can now apply (see **2.2.6.2**).

2.3.2 Acquired by marriage

The second category concerns those Commonwealth citizen women who acquired the right of abode by marriage. The requirements are that:

(a)   the woman was a Commonwealth citizen on 31 December 1982 and continues to be such; and

(b)   on or before 31 December 1982, she married a man who at the time of the marriage was either:

   (i)   born, registered or naturalised in the UK, or

   (ii)   was a Commonwealth citizen with a right of abode through a parental link (see **2.3.1**).

Note that any subsequent divorce or the death of the husband does not affect her status.

> **EXAMPLES**
>
> 1.   Anna was a citizen of Barbados on 31 December 1982 and continues to be such. In 1980 she married Frank. He had been born in the UK in 1960. Anna acquired the right of abode in the UK by marrying Frank.
>
> 2.   Barbara was a citizen of Fiji on 31 December 1982 and continues to be such. In 1975 she married Luke. He had been born in Fiji in 1955 and was a Fijian national. His mother had been born in the UK. Provided Barbara can produce evidence that Luke was a Commonwealth citizen with the right of abode by his parental link (see **2.3.1**), she acquired the right of abode by marrying him. There is no requirement that Luke must have obtained his own certificate evidencing his right of abode.

2.3.3 Certificate of entitlement

A Commonwealth citizen with the right of abode will travel under his or her own country's passport. Before travelling to the UK for the first time, he or she should apply to the British High Commission for a certificate showing that right of abode.

To get the certificate in the first category, the applicant will need to produce:

(a) evidence of being a Commonwealth citizen on 31 December 1982 and that he remains a Commonwealth citizen;

(b) his own full birth certificate naming the appropriate parent;

(c) the appropriate parent's full UK birth certificate; and

(d) if claiming through the father, the parent's marriage certificate or evidence of relationship.

A check should always be made to see if the applicant can claim British citizenship (see **2.2.2**).

To get the certificate in the second category, the applicant will need to produce:

(a) evidence of being a Commonwealth citizen on 31 December 1982 and that she remains a Commonwealth citizen;

(b) her marriage certificate; and

(c) evidence that her husband was either British by birth, registration or naturalisation in the UK (eg his UK birth, registration or naturalisation certificate), or a Commonwealth citizen with his own right of abode (as above).

2.3.4 Excluded Commonwealth nationals

It is important to note that as Cameroon, Mozambique, Namibia, Pakistan and South Africa were not members of the Commonwealth on 31 December 1982, nationals of those countries cannot take advantage of the above provisions.

2.3.5 Deprivation of right of abode

Section 2A of the IA 1971 gives the Secretary of State power to remove this right of abode if it is conducive to the public good to remove or exclude the Commonwealth citizen from the UK. There is a similar power for deprivation of British citizenship (see **2.2.9**).

There is a right of appeal to the IAC or, if issues of national security arise, to the Special Immigration Appeals Commission (see **Chapter 11**).

2.3.6 Flow diagram: summary

We have seen that before 1983 some Commonwealth citizens acquired the right of abode in the UK. The requirements are summarised in the flow diagram at **Appendix 10**.

2.4 HISTORICAL BACKGROUND

One of the difficulties in understanding the law in this area is that a person's citizenship may change over time. Someone born in the UK in 1940 would have had the status of 'British subject' at common law. Under the British Nationality Act 1948, he would have become a citizen of the UK and colonies (CUKC). Under the BNA 1981, he would become a British citizen. The problem is that his current citizenship status is defined in the legislation in terms of his earlier status. Thus, it is necessary to know a little of the history of citizenship law – in particular, three major developments, illustrated in the diagram that follows.

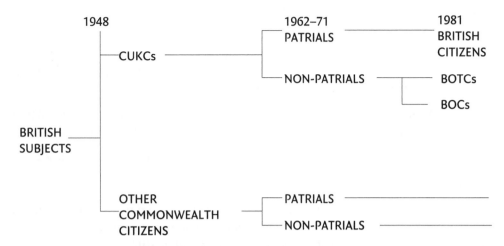

The terms used in the diagram have the broad meanings set out in **2.4.1** to **2.4.7** below.

2.4.1 British subjects

Before 1948, anyone who owed allegiance to the Crown, regardless of the Crown territory in which he was born.

2.4.2 CUKCs

After 1948, anyone connected with the UK or a Crown colony (such as Hong Kong).

2.4.3 Commonwealth citizens

After 1948, anyone having citizenship of an independent Commonwealth country, according to the law of that country. Independent Commonwealth countries included the former Dominions (eg Canada, Australia, New Zealand) and also former colonies (eg Jamaica) when they gained independence. On independence, existing citizens who were CUKCs might lose that status by becoming citizens of the newly independent Commonwealth country. The current list of countries whose citizens are Commonwealth citizens is given in **Appendix 9**. In addition, anyone who has British citizenship, British overseas territories citizenship or British overseas citizenship (see **2.4.5** to **2.4.7** below) is also a Commonwealth citizen.

2.4.4 Patrials

Anyone who under the IA 1971 had the right of abode in the UK. Until 1962, Commonwealth citizens and CUKCs could enter the UK freely. From that year, controls were introduced which were finally enacted in the 1971 Act. The controls extended to both CUKCs and Commonwealth citizens, but CUKCs and Commonwealth citizens who had a close connection with the UK were recognised as 'patrials', having the right of abode.

2.4.5 British citizens

Anyone who at 1 January 1983 was a CUKC with right of abode in the UK, and anyone who acquired British citizenship after that date (eg by birth in the UK, see **2.2.1**). British citizenship and the following categories of citizenship were created by BNA 1981.

2.4.6 British overseas territories citizens (BOTCs)

Anyone who at 1 January 1983 was a non-patrial CUKC, with a close connection with a colony, together with those later becoming BOTCs (eg by birth in the colony). The list of British overseas territories is given in **Appendix 11** to this book. By the Overseas Territories Act 2002, all BOTCs were granted British citizenship.

2.4.7 British overseas citizens (BOCs)

Anyone who at 1 January 1983 was a non-patrial CUKC, but without a close connection with a colony. This category included CUKCs living in a colony which gained independence, who did not acquire citizenship of the newly independent country (eg those of Asian origin in former colonies in East Africa).

This list is not exhaustive. There are other minor categories such as British protected persons, British nationals (overseas) and British subjects under the 1981 Act.

The following other major categories of citizens were unaffected by these changes in UK law.

2.4.8 Irish citizens

Citizens of the Republic of Ireland. They were not Commonwealth citizens under the British Nationality Act 1948. They are not subject to immigration controls (see **3.9**, Common Travel Area), but may be liable to deportation (see **Chapter 10**).

2.4.9 Aliens

Broadly, anyone who does not fall into the above categories. Immigration controls were introduced for aliens in 1905. They do not have the right of abode. However, UK law does permit dual nationality, so that someone who lacks the right of abode as an alien, may nevertheless have it if he can also claim British citizenship.

2.5 SUMMARY OF BRITISH CITIZENSHIP

A summary of British citizenship is set out in **Table 2.2** below.

Table 2.2 Summary of British Citizenship

	British citizen otherwise than by descent	British citizen by descent
Born in the UK before 1983	X	
Born in the UK after 1982 and either parent a British citizen or settled in the UK.	X	
Born in the UK after 1982 and subsequently either parent becomes a British citizen or settled in the UK before applicant is 18.	X	
Born in the UK after 1982 and remains in the UK for the first 10 years of life, and is not absent for more than 90 days each year during that period.	X	
Born outside UK before 1983 and father born, registered or naturalised in the UK and married to mother (or parents subsequently marry in a country where that marriage operates to legitimise the child).		X
Born outside UK before 1983 and mother born, registered or naturalised in the UK and registered child before reached 18 (or registers subsequently).		X
Born outside UK after 1982 and either parent a British citizen otherwise than by descent		X

	British citizen otherwise than by descent	British citizen by descent
Born outside UK after 1982 and one parent a British citizen by descent; and the British parent has a parent who is or was British otherwise than by descent; and the British parent had at some time before the child's birth lived in the UK for a continuous period of three years, not being absent for more than 270 days in that period.		X
Born outside UK after 1982 and one parent a British citizen by descent; and the British parent has a parent who is or was British otherwise than by descent; and the family lives in the UK during applicant's childhood for a continuous period of three years and is not absent during that time for more than 270 days.	X	
Naturalised in UK	X	

CHAPTER 3

IMMIGRATION STATUS

3.1 IMMIGRATION CONTROLS

As we saw at **1.4**, a person with the right of abode in the UK (British citizens – see **2.2** – and certain Commonwealth citizens – see **2.3**) can enter without being subject to any immigration controls. All that person has to do is produce documentary evidence of that right of abode, usually a British passport or a Commonwealth country passport with a certificate of the right of abode.

Nationals of the EEA may enter the UK under EU law (see **Chapter 4**) rather than domestic UK law.

Everyone else is subject to immigration controls. Full details are given at **3.4**.

3.2 IMMIGRATION RULES

3.2.1 An overview

You will find it useful to take a brief look at the contents of the Immigration Rules. You will see that they start with a brief introduction, and importantly there are some useful definitions of key terms in para 6. The Rules are then divided into 13 Parts, each Part dealing with a discrete topic. So, for example, Part 1 sets out the general provisions regarding leave to enter or remain in the UK.

3.2.2 Structure

Parts 2 to 8 of the Rules set out the various different categories of entry to the UK. Why is the structure of the Rules for some categories different from others? This is because some categories require entry clearance, whilst a few do not for non-visa nationals. Also, some categories can lead to settlement, whilst others cannot.

In 2008 the Government introduced a points system for entry to work in the UK (see Part 6A, dealt with in **Chapter 7**). It took that opportunity to restructure the paragraphs dealing with those categories, which now clearly state which requirements are for entry clearance etc. Likewise, when in 2012 the Government made significant changes to most family reunion routes into the UK (see **Chapter 8**), it modernised the structure and content of the new requirements.

3.2.3 Legal status of the requirements

After entering the UK an entrant does not commit a criminal offence by no longer meeting any particular requirement. For example, a student may no longer be following any course of study at all (see *OO v Secretary of State for the Home Department* [2008] EWCA Civ 747). However, if that comes to the attention of the Home Office, it may end the leave by what is known as curtailment (see **3.7**). If an application is made to extend or vary the leave (see **3.6**), it is likely to be refused.

3.3 CONDITIONS OF LIMITED LEAVE

By s 3(1) of the IA 1971, a person granted limited leave to enter or remain in the UK may be subject to all or any of the following conditions:

(a)   a condition restricting his employment or occupation in the UK;

(b)   a condition requiring him to maintain and accommodate himself, and any dependants of his, without recourse to public funds;

(c)   a condition requiring him to register with the police;

(d)   a condition requiring him to report to an immigration officer or the Secretary of State; and

(e)   a condition about residence.

3.3.1 Restricting employment or occupation

The category of entry will determine the nature of this condition, and the answer can be found by looking at the relevant paragraph under which leave is granted. A student may work only within prescribed guidelines (see para 95 and **6.6.4**). An entrepreneur is not permitted to take employment, other than working for the business or businesses which he has established, joined or taken over (see para 245M and **7.4**).

Note that para 6 defines 'employment' as including paid and unpaid employment, paid and unpaid work placements undertaken as part of a course or period of study, self-employment and engaging in business or any professional activity.

3.3.2 Not to have recourse to public funds

3.3.2.1 What are public funds?

All entrants with limited leave are subject to a condition not to have recourse to public funds. This is because all entrants are supposed to be self-sufficient and able to maintain and accommodate themselves and any dependants. So what count as public funds? All that follow:

(a)   housing of homeless persons under Pts VI or VII of the Housing Act 1996 and under Pt II of the Housing Act 1985;

(b)   the non-means tested welfare benefits of attendance allowance, carer's allowance, child benefit, personal independence payment, and disability living allowance;

(c)   the means-tested benefits of universal credit, income support, income-related employment and support allowance, income-based jobseeker's allowance, council tax benefit and a council tax reduction under a council tax reduction scheme, housing benefit, State pension credit, child tax credit and working tax credit; and

(d)   a Social Fund payment.

The following do not count as public funds:

(a)   the National Insurance-based welfare benefits of contribution-based jobseeker's allowance, contributory employment and support allowance, State pension and bereavement benefits;

(b)   National Health Service treatment and education for a child at a local authority maintained school.

3.3.2.2 Additional public funds

Very often entry to the UK is for the purposes of family reunion (see **Chapter 8**), for example a child joining a parent who is already settled in the UK. The person settled in the UK is often known as the 'sponsor'. If a sponsor already receives public funds, will entry clearance be refused? Paragraph 6A makes an important qualification to this condition. It states that

> For the purpose of these Rules, a person (P) is not to be regarded as having (or potentially having) recourse to public funds merely because P is (or will be) reliant in whole or in part on public funds provided to P's sponsor unless, as a result of P's presence in the United Kingdom, the sponsor is (or would be) entitled to increased or additional public funds (save where such entitlement to increased or additional public funds is by virtue of P and the sponsor's joint entitlement to benefits under the regulations referred to in paragraph 6B).

So, for example, if P seeks entry clearance to live permanently with his sponsor (S) in the UK, the application will not necessarily fail if S already receives one or more of the public funds. It will fail, however, if S becomes entitled either to an increase in the amount of his existing public funds, or to another public fund because of P's joining S in the UK.

Paragraph 6B provides as follows:

> Subject to paragraph 6C, a person (P) shall not be regarded as having recourse to public funds if P is entitled to benefits specified under section 115 of the Immigration and Asylum Act 1999 by virtue of regulations made under subsections (3) and (4) of that section or section 42 of the Tax Credits Act 2002.

Normally a person with limited leave to enter or remain in the UK is excluded from claiming mainstream welfare benefits (including those on the public funds list) by s 115 of the IAA 1999. However, a claim might be made by such a person if he meets the exceptions in subsections (3) and (4). Also, if the person has a partner who is entitled to apply for child and/or working tax credits, uniquely the application can be made jointly, and both count when the tax credits are calculated under the 2002 Act.

Paragraph 6C provides as follows:

> A person (P) making an application from outside the United Kingdom will be regarded as having recourse to public funds where P relies upon the future entitlement to any public funds that would be payable to P or to P's sponsor as a result of P's presence in the United Kingdom (including those benefits to which P or the sponsor would be entitled as a result of P's presence in the United Kingdom under the regulations referred to in to paragraph 6B).

What is the effect of paragraph 6C? First, note that it only concerns an application by P for entry clearance. That application will be refused if P shows that he will be adequately maintained in the UK only by relying upon his or his sponsor's future entitlement to any public funds, including tax credits or those payable to him under the IAA 1999, s 115(3) and (4).

This form of sponsorship should not be confused with the more formal and detailed sponsorship of students and workers, etc under Part 6A of the Immigration Rules (see **Chapters 6** and 7). Also see **3.4.4**.

3.3.3 Registration with the police

Adult nationals of certain countries are listed in Appendix 2 to the Immigration Rules (see **Appendix 1** to this book) as they are required to register with the police within seven days of arriving in the UK (see Part 10 of the Rules). To register they need to produce their passports and pay a registration fee. If they are staying in the Metropolitan Police area in London, they should register at the Overseas Visitors Records Office, Brandon House, 180 Borough High Street, London, SE1 1LH. Otherwise they should contact their local police station for the address and opening hours of the nearest police registration office.

3.3.4 Reporting to an immigration officer or Secretary of State

This condition and the next (**3.3.5**) were introduced by s 16 of the UK Borders Act 2007. The Government's view was that without these powers it was difficult for the Home Office to maintain contact with foreign nationals during the currency of their limited leave, and to enforce their removal should that leave be curtailed (see **3.7**). The Government stated that it would apply these conditions to foreign national criminals, who cannot currently be removed due to the ECHR, and to certain children about whom there are particular concerns or who have been placed on discretionary leave (see **9.10**) with a view to their removal when they reach 18.

3.3.5 Residence

See **3.3.4** above.

3.3.6 Consequences of breach of a condition

Although it is an offence under s 24(1)(b) of the IA 1971 for a person with limited leave knowingly to breach a condition of leave, it is unusual for the Home Office to prosecute. Government policy is that if the breach is sufficiently serious, the person should be removed from the UK (see **10.4**).

3.4 ENTRY CLEARANCE

3.4.1 The general rule

The entry clearance procedure is, in effect, a form of pre-entry control, in which a UK official known as a visa or entry clearance officer (ECO) acts as an immigration officer, applying the Immigration Rules, but usually in the country in which the entrant is living before travel to the UK.

The form of clearance depends on the nationality of the entrant. The Immigration Rules specify countries whose nationals (known as 'visa nationals') require entry clearance in the form of a visa (usually stamped on the passport). A list of these countries is given in Appendix 1 to the Immigration Rules (**Appendix 1** to this book). In the case of some 'non-visa nationals', entry clearance is required for a stay of more than six months (see **2.1**). In this case, the entry clearance is shown by a different stamp, known as an entry certificate (see para 25 of the Immigration Rules).

An applicant for entry clearance as a visitor must apply to a particular designated post. However, any other type of application must be made to the appropriate designated post in the country or territory where the applicant is living. Applicants from certain countries can apply on-line at www.visa4uk.fco.gov.uk, although it should be noted that the website currently only supports applications made in English. Once they have submitted their on-line applications they are given an appointment to produce their original passports and supporting documents, and pay the appropriate fees if they have not already done so on-line. At that appointment the applicant's biographic and biometric data are collected (see **3.4.3**). These are then transmitted to the UK for checks.

Nationals listed in Appendix T of the Immigration Rules must undergo compulsory screening for active pulmonary tuberculosis if applying to enter the UK for more than six months.

Forms and guidance notes for making an application in writing can be found at www.ukvisas.gov.uk/en/howtoapply/vafs.

3.4.2 Leave under the Immigration and Asylum Act 1999

The IAA 1999 provides for greater flexibility in the way permission to enter the UK and to remain may be granted. Instead of leave to enter always having to be given in writing at a port of entry, the IAA 1999 allows for additional ways of giving leave to enter to be specified, eg that a visa or other entry clearance is to be treated as leave to enter. This means that holders of visas, for example, will be able to pass through the port control with only a quick check on identity and on the rightful ownership of the travel document and entry clearance, unless there is a need to examine for, among other matters, change of circumstances.

Most entry clearance now takes effect as leave to enter as well. This means that there are two significant dates to look out for on a visa or entry certificate, namely, the *effective date* and the *expiry date*. In most cases, the effective date will be the date on which the entry clearance is issued. However, some people may not intend or be able to travel to the UK immediately following their application, and in these circumstances an ECO will usually exercise his discretion to defer the effective date for up to three months after entry clearance has been authorised. So, in order to avoid the cost of making an unnecessary application for an extension of stay, an applicant should always confirm his date of travel.

For applicants in categories that require a qualifying period to be met before applying for settlement, or who have a limit imposed on their total length of stay in that category, their leave to enter will normally begin on the date they arrive in the UK within the three-month limit. This ensures that the maximum leave to which they are entitled is given.

The expiry date on a visa or entry certificate reflects the date on which the entry clearance and leave to enter are no longer effective. After this date the entry clearance will not be valid for travel to the UK, neither will it confer leave to enter.

3.4.3 Biometric information

All applicants are now routinely required to provide 10-digit fingerscans and a digital photograph when applying for UK entry clearance. The applicant attends a pre-arranged appointment. Fingerprints are taken on a glass screen scan. A digital photograph is taken. The biometric data are stored on a central government database in the UK and checked against UK government records.

Where an applicant is issued with a visa exceeding six months, he will also receive a biometric residence permit. This is a standard credit card size (86mm x 54mm) and looks similar to this type of permit issued by other EU countries.

3.4.4 Financial undertakings

Often entry clearance is sought for the purposes of immediate or ultimate settlement (eg child joining parent in UK, or grandparent joining grandchild in UK or spouse joining partner in UK, etc). The person based in the UK is usually known as 'the sponsor'. See the definition in Immigration Rules, para 6. This does not necessarily mean that that person has signed a written agreement with the DfWP to be financially responsible for the entrant. As para 35 of the Immigration Rules states, '[a] sponsor of a person ... may be asked to give an undertaking in writing to be responsible for that person's maintenance [and] accommodation'. However, it will always be required when the adult dependent relative of a British citizen or a person settled in the UK seeks entry clearance to settle in the UK (see **8.11.6**). As to what constitutes a written undertaking, see *Ahmed v Secretary of State for Work and Pensions* [2005] EWCA Civ 535.

The Home Office uses Sponsorship Undertaking Form SU07. It can be found on the Home Office website (see **1.2.8**).

3.4.5 Refusal of entry clearance

3.4.5.1 Mandatory grounds

The general grounds for refusal of entry clearance (and leave to enter) are set out in para 320 of the Immigration Rules. Some of these are described as mandatory grounds, although in such cases an ECO should always consider any human rights grounds (in particular the right to family life under Article 8 ECHR) which would justify issuing the entry clearance.

Mandatory grounds for refusal are given in para 320(1)–(7D). These include that entry clearance must be refused in the following circumstances:

(a)   Where entry clearance is being sought for a purpose not covered by the Rules.

(b)   Where the applicant is currently the subject of a deportation order (see **10.1**) or has a relevant criminal conviction (see **Appendix 8**).

(c)   Where the applicant has failed to produce a valid national passport or other document satisfactorily establishing his identity.

(d)   Where the Secretary of State has personally directed that the exclusion of a person from the UK is conducive to the public good.

(e)   Where the Medical Inspector has confirmed that, for medical reasons, it is undesirable to admit a person seeking entry clearance to the UK and an ECO is satisfied that there are no strong, compassionate reasons justifying admission.

(f)   Where false representations have been made or false documents have been submitted (whether or not material to the application, and whether or not to the applicant's knowledge), or material facts have not been disclosed, in relation to the application. This includes false representations made in order to obtain supporting documents for an application, for example using false representations to obtain a genuine qualification.

Home Office guidance is that a false representation is made when an applicant or third party lies or makes a false statement in an application, either orally or in writing. To refuse the application, an ECO must be satisfied to a high standard that a false representation has been made. It is irrelevant that the applicant might later in interview correct the false statement. As the Court of Appeal observed in SS (Nepal) v Entry Clearance Officer [2013] All ER (D) 314 (Jul), an applicant has to be honest throughout the process; otherwise, an applicant would be permitted to lie on the application form and when found out could later make a true statement. That is contrary to common sense.

The Home Office gives the following two examples of false representations:

(i)   A visa applicant states that he is a project manager for a company, earning a significant salary. It is discovered that he is in fact the cleaner for the company on a low salary.

(ii)   An applicant applies for entry clearance on the basis of his marriage to a British citizen, and states in his application form that he has never been married before. But a marriage certificate is received from another wife, which is verified, showing that he is already married.

Does a false statement mean one made dishonestly? Yes: see AA (Nigeria) v Secretary of State for the Home Department [2010] EWCA Civ 773. This is because 'a false representation stated in all innocence may be simply a matter of mistake, or an error short of dishonesty' (per Rix LJ at [68]).

What is a false document? Home Office guidance is that this includes a genuine document which has been altered or tampered with; a counterfeit document (one that is completely false); a genuine document that is being used by an impostor; a genuine document which has been fraudulently obtained or issued; and a genuine document which contains a falsified or counterfeit visa or endorsement.

Must the applicant have created the false document or even be aware that it is false? No, as Rix LJ observed in Adedoyin v Secretary of State for the Home Department [2010] EWCA Civ 773:

> 67. First, 'false representation' is aligned in the rule with 'false document'. It is plain that a false document is one that tells a lie about itself. Of course it is possible for a person to make use of a false document (for instance a counterfeit currency note, but that example, used for its clarity, is rather distant from the context of this discussion) in total ignorance of its falsity and in perfect honesty. But the document itself is dishonest. It is highly likely therefore that where an applicant uses in all innocence a false document for the purpose of obtaining entry clearance, or leave to enter or to remain, it is because some other party, it might be a parent, or sponsor, or

agent, has dishonestly promoted the use of that document. The response of a requirement of mandatory refusal is entirely understandable in such a situation. The mere fact that a dishonest document has been used for such an important application is understandably a sufficient reason for a mandatory refusal. That is why the rule expressly emphasises that it applies 'whether or not to the applicant's knowledge'.

See also *JK (India) v Secretary of State for the Home Department* [2013] EWCA Civ 1080.

What about material facts that have not been disclosed? Here the ECO will need to show that the withheld information would have been relevant to his decision. Note that an ECO cannot refuse an applicant on this ground if he has not indicated to the applicant the kind of information that is relevant to the application. The Home Office gives the following example. The wife of a man in the UK who has limited leave to remain as a highly-skilled worker (see **7.3**), applies to join her husband as his dependant, but does not mention that the marriage has broken down. The husband has sent a letter stating that the marriage no longer subsists.

(g)   Where the applicant has previously breached the UK's immigration laws and was over 18 at the time of the most recent relevant breach. That breach must be the result of overstaying by more than 90 days; breaching a condition attached to leave; being an illegal entrant; or using deception in an application for entry clearance, leave to enter or remain (whether successful or not). All of these are dealt with in **Chapter 10**.

Are there any exceptions to this? Yes, but these result in time limits being imposed on the applicant applying again.

Table 3.1 below summarises the position.

Table 3.1 Time limits applicable where there are exceptions to mandatory refusal on ground (g)

Exceptions	Length of ban
Left the UK voluntarily and not at the expense (directly or indirectly) of the Secretary of State	12 months from date left the UK
Left the UK voluntarily; at the expense (directly or indirectly) of the Secretary of State; and the date the person left the UK was no more than 6 months after the date on which the person was given notice of the removal decision, or no more than 6 months after the date on which the person no longer had a pending appeal, whichever is the later	2 years from date left the UK
Left the UK voluntarily and at the expense (directly or indirectly) of the Secretary of State	5 years from date left the UK
Removed or deported from the UK	10 years from date left the UK
Used deception in an application for entry clearance	10 years from date deception used

EXAMPLES

1.   Alan overstays his leave by 50 days before departing the UK voluntarily. He pays his own travel costs (so not at the expense (directly or indirectly) of the Secretary of State). As Alan overstayed for less than 90 days, he will not in these circumstances be subject to any ban.

2.   Brenda overstays her leave by 100 days before departing the UK voluntarily. She pays her own travel costs (so not at the expense (directly or indirectly) of the Secretary of State). As Brenda overstayed for more than 90 days, any application she makes for entry clearance within 12 months of leaving the UK will, in these circumstances, be subject to mandatory refusal.

If an applicant has previously been refused entry clearance because a false document was used or a false representation was made, the applicant may claim that he was unaware that the document or representation was false. Unless the applicant can prove this, he must be automatically refused entry clearance under this ground for 10 years from the date the deception was used.

Note that where more than one breach of the UK's immigration laws has occurred, only the breach which leads to the longest period of absence from the UK is relevant. The Home Office gives the following example. An applicant left the UK voluntarily at her own expense in January 2008 and applied for entry clearance using false documents in February 2008. Any subsequent entry clearance application must be automatically refused for 10 years, until February 2018. This is the longer refusal period where deception has been used in an entry clearance application. The shorter refusal period of one year for leaving the UK voluntarily is not applicable.

(h)   Where the applicant has failed, without providing a reasonable explanation, to comply with a request made on behalf of the ECO to attend an interview.

Note that only ground (c) above applies to an application for entry clearance and leave to enter as a family member under Appendix FM of the Immigration Rules (see **Chapter 8**).

3.4.5.2 Discretionary grounds

The general grounds on which entry clearance (and leave to enter) should normally be refused are set out in para 320(8)–(20) of the Immigration Rules, and these include the following:

(a)   Failure to supply any information, documents, copy documents or medical report that has or have been formally requested.

(b)   Where the applicant has previously contrived in a significant way to frustrate the intentions of the Immigration Rules by:

(i)   overstaying; or

(ii)   breaching a condition attached to his leave; or

(iii)   being an illegal entrant; or

(iv)   using deception in an application for entry clearance, leave to enter or remain, or in order to obtain documents from the Secretary of State or a third party required in support of the application (whether successful or not);

and there are other aggravating circumstances, such as absconding, not meeting temporary admission or reporting restrictions or bail conditions, using an assumed identity or multiple identities, switching nationality, making frivolous applications or not complying with the re-documentation process.

All cases must be considered on their merits, taking into account family life in the UK and the level of responsibility for the breach in the case of children.

There is, of course, an overlap here with the mandatory ground for refusal highlighted at (g) in **3.4.5.1**. Home Office guidance is that where an applicant falls to be refused under the mandatory ground, an ECO must also consider whether it is also appropriate to refuse the applicant on this discretionary ground. If an applicant is exempt from the mandatory ground refusal, an ECO must consider whether a refusal under this discretionary ground is appropriate.

(c)   Refusal by a sponsor to give, if requested to do so, an undertaking in writing (see **3.4.2**) to be responsible for that person's maintenance and accommodation for the period of any leave granted.

(d)   Refusal to undergo a medical examination when required to do so.

(e)   Relevant criminal convictions as detailed in **Appendix 8**.

(f)   Where, from information available, it seems right to refuse the application on the ground that exclusion from the UK is conducive to the public good; if, for example, in the light of the character, conduct or associations of the person seeking leave to enter, it is undesirable to grant the application. The Home Office gives the following examples: where a person's admission could adversely affect the conduct of foreign policy; where there is reliable evidence that a person has been involved in criminal activities, even though he has not been convicted; where the person's admission would be contrary to internationally agreed travel restrictions; where the person's admission might lead to infringement of UK law; where the person's admission might lead to an offence being committed by someone else; and where a person's activities are such that his presence in the UK is likely to cause a public order concern. What is involved is an evaluation of risk to the public. The question the ECO must answer is whether or not there a substantial risk of disorder: see *CB (United States of America) v Entry Clearance Officer (Los Angeles)* [2008] EWCA Civ 1539.

(g)   Where one or more relevant NHS body has notified the Secretary of State that the person seeking entry or leave to enter has failed to pay a charge or charges with a total value of at least £1,000 in accordance with the relevant NHS regulations on charges to overseas visitors.

Note that only ground (b) above applies to an application for entry clearance and leave to enter as a family member under Appendix FM of the Immigration Rules (see **Chapter 8**).

3.5 LEAVE TO ENTER

3.5.1 The general rule

Leave to enter is dealt with in paras 7–11 of the Immigration Rules. Everyone must, on arrival in the UK, produce a passport or other document establishing his nationality and identity. On examination by an immigration officer, the entrant must furnish such information as may be required to enable the officer to decide whether he requires leave to enter, whether leave should be given, and the terms of leave. It is para 2(1) of Sch 2 to the IA 1971 which gives an immigration officer the power to examine any person who arrives in the UK and sets out the purpose for which such an examination is conducted, namely to determine whether:

(a)   he is or is not a British citizen; and, if not,

(b)   if he may or may not enter the UK without leave; and, if not,

(c)   if he has been given leave which is still in force, or should be given leave and for what period or on what conditions (if any), or should be refused leave.

If it is concluded that a person is a British citizen, the immigration officer takes no further action. If he is not a British citizen, however, he will be examined to determine whether or not he requires permission to enter the UK. This permission is called leave to enter. If a person qualifies for leave to enter then the immigration officer will go on to decide the length of the leave and any conditions, such as permission to work, which will apply. Finally, if a person does not qualify for leave to enter then the immigration officer may refuse leave to enter.

These controls do not, however, apply to persons arriving from another part of the Common Travel Area (see **3.9**).

3.5.2 Documentary evidence

Documentary evidence to be produced to an immigration officer may include:

(a)   a UK passport: required to be produced by a British citizen as evidence of his right of abode;

(b)   a certificate of entitlement issued by the UK Government: evidence of right of abode which may be produced as an alternative to (a) above (by a Commonwealth citizen who has the right of abode, see **2.3**);

(c)   entry clearance in the form of a visa or entry certificate;

(d)   a non-UK passport or identity card: identity cards may be used as a substitute for a passport by EEA nationals.

3.5.3 Grant of limited leave

The immigration officer grants leave by written notice, usually in the form of a stamp on the entrant's passport. The stamp gives the date and port of entry, the time limit of the leave, and any conditions imposed, but does not indicate the Rule under which leave has been granted.

However, if a person's entry clearance also takes effect as leave to enter the UK (see **3.4.2**), an immigration officer may still question that person to establish that he is the rightful holder of the document, that the document does take effect as limited leave, that the passport is genuine and that there are no circumstances under which the entry clearance should be cancelled (see **3.5.4**).

3.5.4 Refusal of limited leave

An immigration officer may refuse leave to enter the UK on exactly the same grounds that an ECO may refuse entry clearance (see **3.4.5**).

Paragraph 321 of the Immigration Rules provides three instances where a person seeking leave to enter the UK who holds an entry clearance which was duly issued to him and is still current may be refused leave to enter. These are where an immigration officer is satisfied of any of the following:

(a)   False representations were made or false documents were submitted (whether or not material to the application, and whether or not to the holder's knowledge), or material facts were not disclosed, in relation to the application for entry clearance.

(b)   A change of circumstances since it was issued has removed the basis of the holder's claim to admission, except where the change of circumstances amounts solely to the person becoming over age for entry in one of the categories contained in paras 296 to 316 of the Rules since the issue of the entry clearance.

(c)   Refusal is justified on grounds of restricted return ability; on medical grounds; on grounds of criminal record; because the person seeking leave to enter is the subject of a deportation order; or because exclusion would be conducive to the public good.

Paragraph 321A sets out the grounds on which a person's leave to enter which is in force on his arrival in, or whilst he is outside, the UK may be cancelled by an immigration officer. These include that:

(a)   There has been such a change in the circumstances of that person's case since the leave was given, that it should be cancelled.

(b)   False representations were made or false documents were submitted (whether or not material to the application, and whether or not to the holder's knowledge), or material facts were not disclosed, in relation to the application for leave.

(c)   For medical reasons it is undesirable to admit the person.

(d)   The Secretary of State has personally directed that exclusion is conducive to the public good.

After admission, any extension of the time limit, or variation of conditions, is dealt with by an application to the Home Office (see **3.6**).

3.5.5 Temporary admission

If a decision on whether to grant leave cannot be reached quickly, the immigration officer will usually issue a notice of temporary admission (in Form IS96). This tells the entrant that he is liable to detention, but may physically enter the UK without having leave to enter. He may be directed to reside at a particular place, and is asked to report back to an immigration officer at a specified time. He may not take employment.

As an alternative to temporary admission, the entrant can be detained, but may apply to an Immigration Judge for bail if he remains detained seven days after his arrival in the UK.

3.5.6 Entry without a passport

By s 2(1) of the Asylum and Immigration (Treatment of Claimants, etc) Act 2004 (AI (TC)A 2004), a person commits an offence if, when seeking leave either to enter or remain in the UK or asylum, he does not have with him a passport (or similar immigration document) which is in force and satisfactorily establishes his identity and nationality or citizenship. By s 2(4) various defences may be raised, such as proving a reasonable excuse for not being in possession of the required document. The defendant has the legal burden of proving the defence on the balance of probabilities: see R *v Navabi and Embaye* [2005] EWCA Crim 2865.

However, note that by s 2(7) the fact that a document was deliberately destroyed or disposed of is not such a reasonable excuse unless it is shown that the destruction or disposal was for a reasonable cause, or that it was beyond the control of the person charged with the offence. So what is a 'reasonable cause'? By s 2(7)(b) this does not include the purpose of (i) delaying the handling or resolution of a claim or application or the taking of a decision, (ii) increasing the chances of success of a claim or application, or (iii) complying with instructions or advice given by a person who offers advice about, or facilitates, immigration into the UK, unless in the circumstances of the case it is unreasonable to expect non-compliance with the instructions or advice.

3.6 LEAVE TO REMAIN IN THE UK: EXTENSION OR VARIATION OF EXISTING LEAVE

3.6.1 Application made to Home Office

The general framework is laid down by s 3(3) of the IA 1971, which provides that limited leave may be varied, whether by restricting, enlarging, or removing the time limit, or by adding, varying, or removing conditions. If the time limit is removed, the leave becomes indefinite and any conditions cease to have effect. Indefinite leave cannot be varied.

Application for variation is made to the Home Office. Immigration officers have no powers to deal with variations. Application should be made before expiry of the time limit on leave, because overstaying is a criminal offence, and may result in refusal of the application to extend leave.

If the application is granted, an appropriate entry is made in the applicant's passport and that is returned with a covering letter. Any refusal (see **3.6.5**) is notified to the applicant by letter, stating the reasons for the refusal and setting out any rights of review (see **Chapter 11**).

3.6.2 Effect of application on existing leave

By s 3C of the IA 1971, when a person applies for variation of his leave before that leave expires, but it then expires before a decision is taken, the leave is automatically extended to the point at which the appropriate period for appealing a refusal expires (see **Chapter 11**). This will protect the immigration status of that person and prevent him from becoming an overstayer. All conditions attached to the leave will still apply. So if a person who entered the UK as a fiancé(e) subsequently applies to stay as a spouse following the marriage, until the variation is granted by the Home Office, the applicant cannot lawfully work (see **8.4.10**). A person will not be able to submit further applications during the leave as extended under this section, although he would be able to vary his original application: this is to ensure that all issues raised are covered by one decision (see further **Chapter 11**).

3.6.3 Switching categories

In many cases, an entrant will apply to vary his leave by switching from one category of entry to another. For example, someone who has entered as a student may wish to remain as the spouse of someone living in the UK. In every case, it will be necessary to check the detailed provisions of the Rules relating to the new category.

Is there any danger in applying to switch categories? The danger is that the Home Office may refuse the application and curtail the existing leave (see **3.7**).

3.6.4 Procedure for variation

3.6.4.1 Specified forms

Paragraphs 34 and 34A to 34J of the Immigration Rules lay down the procedure that must be followed for most applications to the Home Office (apart from EEA matters: see **3.6.4.3**). First, certain applications must be made on the form specified by the Home Office. The main forms are:

FLR(M): application for an extension of stay in UK as the partner of a person present and settled here, the partner of a person with limited leave as a refugee or with humanitarian protection, or on the basis of a right to family and/or private life.

FLR(O): application for extension of stay in UK for any purpose not covered by other application forms.

SET(DV): application for indefinite leave to remain in UK as a victim of domestic violence.

SET(M): application for indefinite leave to remain in UK as the spouse, civil partner or unmarried partner of a person who is present and settled here.

SET(O): application for indefinite leave to remain in UK on completion of five years of continuous leave to remain in UK in categories such as Tier 1 entrepreneur or investor migrant and person with UK ancestry. The form is also used to apply for indefinite leave to remain in one of the following categories: long residence in UK, bereaved partner, and any other purpose or reason not covered by other application forms.

SET(F): application for indefinite leave to remain in UK as a family member (other than husband or wife or unmarried partner) of a person present and settled in UK.

BUS: application for an extension of stay (FLR) or for indefinite leave to remain in UK (SET) as a sole representative.

Tier 1 (entrepreneur): application to switch or extend stay as an entrepreneur.

Tier 1 (graduate entrepreneur): application for leave to remain as a graduate entrepreneur.

Tier 1 (investor): application to switch or extend stay as an investor.

Tier 2 Migrant: application to switch or extend stay as a Tier 2 Migrant.

PBS (dependant): application for extension of stay as dependant of person granted leave to remain under points-based system.

Tier 4 (general): application to switch or extend stay as a student.

Tier 5 (temporary worker): application for leave to remain as Tier 5 worker.

3.6.4.2 Following the specified forms procedure

It is absolutely vital that an applicant follows the specified form procedure or his application will be invalid. An invalid application is returned to the applicant and treated as if it was never made. Of course, if a valid application is not made in time, the applicant becomes an overstayer liable to removal from the UK (see **3.6.5** and **Chapter 10**).

What will make an application invalid? Any of the following:

(a)   failing to use the specified form;

(b)   failing to pay the specified fee, or paying it in a manner not specified in the form and/or guidance notes;

(c)   failing to complete in full those parts of the specified form marked as mandatory. Every question in these parts of the form must be answered and all the information required given;

(d)   failing to provide biographical or biometric information as required;

(e)   failing to provide any photographs or documents specified as mandatory (see, for example, *R (Fu) v Secretary of State for the Home Department* [2010] EWHC 2922);

(f)   failing to sign the form as required;

(g)   failing to deliver the form in the manner stated on it.

As the requirements for an application to be valid are part of the Immigration Rules there is an element of discretion, but Home Office guidance is that this is limited to exceptional circumstances, such as where an applicant is unable to sign the form or to provide photographs because of a serious illness or accident.

It is vital that the Home Office receives the specified form before the applicant's current leave expires. If possible, therefore, it should be delivered by hand to the public enquiry office and a receipt obtained. If it is posted, the application is treated as made on the day it was posted by reference to the postmark.

If an application is rejected but then re-submitted, and fully complies with the requirements of para 34A, the date of application is the date that it is re-submitted.

Note that if parts of a specified form which are not designated as mandatory are incomplete, a Home Office caseworker may attempt to obtain the missing information from the applicant, or consider the application on the basis of the information provided, but the application will be valid.

3.6.4.3   EEA forms

Note that the following four forms all relate to EEA nationals (see **Chapter 4**) and are not forms specified under para 34.

EEA1: application for a registration certificate by an EEA national.

EEA2: application for a residence card by a non-EEA family member of an EEA national.

EEA3: application for permanent residence by an EEA national.

EEA4: application for permanent residence by a non-EEA family member of an EEA national.

3.6.5   Refusal by Home Office

In addition to the grounds for refusal of extension of stay for the various immigration categories set out in Parts 2 to 8 of and Appendix FM to the Immigration Rules, para 322 provides a list of grounds similar to those used by entry clearance officers and immigration officers to refuse entry clearance (see **3.4.4** and **3.5.4**).

The provisions concerning the refusal of an application made by an overstayer were amended in July 2012. Now an application for further leave to remain after the applicant's previous period of leave has expired by more than 28 days will be refused. Note, however, the following concessions:

(a)   Where an applicant submits an application before his previous period of leave to enter or remain expires, but the application is rejected as invalid after his leave expires, the 28-day window in which the application may be submitted as an overstayer will start from the date on which the application was rejected, rather than when leave expired.

(b)   The Home Office caseworkers have discretion to consider exceptional cases. Applicants who have overstayed by more than 28 days may provide evidence of exceptional circumstances which prevented them from submitting their application in time. Home Office guidance is that the threshold here is high, but it could include delays resulting from:

(i)   serious illness which meant that the applicant or his representative was unable to submit the application in time (where supported by appropriate medical documentation);

(ii)   travel or postal delays, which meant that the applicant or his representative was unable to submit the application in time; or

(iii) inability to provide necessary documents. This would apply only to exceptional or unavoidable circumstances beyond the applicant's control, such as the Home Office being at fault in the loss of, or delay in returning, travel documents; or delay in the applicant being able to replace documents following loss as a result of theft, fire or flood (where supported by evidence of the date of loss and the date replacement documents were sought).

(c)   A breach of immigration laws by remaining in the UK beyond a period of leave to enter or remain will not be a determinative factor when considering applications in the following circumstances:

(i)   the applicant has a dependent child under the age of 18 years who is a British citizen or who has lived in the UK for at least the preceding seven years, and it would be unreasonable to expect the child to leave the UK (see EX.1 at **8.5.1**); or

(ii)   the applicant has lived in the UK for more than 20 years; or

(iii) the applicant is seeking leave to remain as a bereaved partner (see **8.7**) or as a victim of domestic violence by her partner (see **8.8**).

3.6.6 Overstaying: a summary

Note that by para 6 of the Immigration Rules, 'overstayed' and 'overstaying' mean that an applicant for leave to remain has stayed in the UK beyond the latest of:

(a)   the time limit attached to the last period of leave granted; or

(b)   the period that his leave was extended under ss 3C or 3D of the IA 1971 (see **3.6.2**); or

(c)   the date that an applicant receives the notice of invalidity declaring that an application for leave to remain is not a valid application, provided the application was submitted before the time limit attached to the last period of leave expired (see **3.6.4.2**).

3.7 CURTAILMENT OF EXISTING LEAVE TO ENTER OR REMAIN

If a person enters the UK in one category and before his limited leave expires he applies to switch to another category, there is a danger not only that the application might be refused but also that the existing leave might be curtailed (or the applicant removed from the UK).

> **EXAMPLE**
>
> Bob enters the UK as a student with 12 months' limited leave. After three months he applies to remain in the UK as the spouse of a British citizen. The suspicion may well be that he never intended to leave the UK because he always intended to marry. Not only might his leave be curtailed, but alternatively he may be removed from the UK as an illegal entrant (see **Chapter 10**).

The power to curtail a person's leave is contained in s 3(3)(a) of the IA 1971. It may be used when a person has failed to comply with certain requirements of the Immigration Rules or has lost the justification for his presence here, eg an employee's job ends. It is only available when a person has limited leave. Guidance from the Home Office is that curtailment should not normally be used unless the person has at least six months' leave outstanding.

Paragraph 323 of the Immigration Rules allows curtailment, for example, if:

(a)   false representations have been made or material facts not disclosed in order to obtain leave to enter or a previous variation of leave;

(b)   the person has failed to comply with any conditions attached to his leave;

(c)   the person has failed to maintain and accommodate himself and any dependants without recourse to public funds;

(d)   the person ceases to meet the requirements of the Rules under which that leave was granted;

(e)   the person has, within the first six months of being granted leave to enter, committed an offence for which he is subsequently sentenced to a period of imprisonment.

As curtailment is a matter of Home Office discretion it is not automatic. The burden of proof rests with the Secretary of State. Very often a person will be removed rather than his leave curtailed, eg where a person has failed to disclose relevant facts or has made false representations in order to obtain leave, consideration may be given to curtailing any subsisting leave, but it is more usual to proceed directly to administrative removal (see **Chapter 10**) or, in the case of leave to enter, removal for illegal entry (also **Chapter 10**). Equally, although leave may be curtailed where a person fails to observe the conditions of his leave to enter or remain, normally the Home Office proceeds direct to administrative removal for breach of conditions (see **Chapter 10**). Curtailment therefore is normally considered only where the person's actions are not so serious as to merit enforcement action, but where it would be inappropriate to let him remain for the duration of his leave.

3.8 SETTLEMENT

3.8.1 What is it?

A person is settled according to the definition in s 33(2A) of the IA 1971 if he is ordinarily resident in the UK without being subject under the immigration laws to any restriction on the period for which he may remain. The status will be acquired by a person given unlimited leave who satisfies the 'ordinary residence' test (see **3.8.2**). A person who has been given indefinite leave to remain in the UK would not be 'settled' in the UK under the IA 1971, if he has emigrated to another country and is no longer ordinarily resident in the UK.

A person who is settled in the UK has, subject to the Immigration Rules, the right to continue to live in the UK. Unlike a person with right of abode, he may be deported (see **Chapter 10**).

3.8.2 Ordinarily resident

This is a condition of settled status. It has a quite distinct meaning. Case law from various fields suggests that a person can be 'ordinarily resident' without having the right, or the intention, to reside here permanently. All that is necessary is that a person resides in a place with a 'settled purpose' (eg to undertake a course of education). It is possible to have ordinary residence in more than one place at the same time. A person may be ordinarily resident in the UK even though temporarily absent (eg on holiday). Generally, however, for purposes other than exemption from deportation, a person cannot be so resident at a time when he is in breach of immigration laws (eg overstaying) (see the IA 1971, s 33(2)).

EXAMPLES

(1)   Erasmus has been in the UK for the last eight years, periodically renewing his leave to remain.

       He is 'ordinarily resident' in the UK, but not 'settled' as he is subject to limited leave.

(2)   Farooq was given indefinite leave to remain in the UK 10 years ago, but emigrated six years ago. He is now here for a holiday, having been admitted as a visitor.

> He is not 'ordinarily resident'. Neither is he 'settled', as his indefinite leave to remain was not renewed on his return to the UK.
>
> (3)   As (2), but Farooq has been admitted as a student, with 12 months' leave. He is 'ordinarily resident' but not 'settled'.

3.8.3   Returning resident rule

If a person with settled status leaves the UK and returns within two years, his leave will continue, leave to enter has to be given again and his settled status in effect confirmed. This is usually automatic under para 18 of the Rules, dealing with 'returning residents', provided that the entrant satisfies the immigration officer that he had indefinite leave to enter or remain in the UK when he last left, that he has not been away for longer than two years, and that he now seeks admission for the purpose of settlement. If a person is returning periodically only for a limited period simply to show residence in the UK within two years of each departure, then eventually he or she is likely to be denied the benefit of para 18 of the Immigration Rules.

What if a person with settled status does not return to the UK within two years of last leaving it? See para 19 of the Immigration Rules.

3.8.4   Who is treated as settled under the Immigration Rules?

Note that the Immigration Rules use the term 'settled' to cover British citizens (see **2.2**) and Commonwealth citizens who have the right of abode (see **2.3**), as well as those people who have indefinite leave.

3.8.5   Entry clearance

Only certain family members of a person already settled in the UK may apply for entry clearance for the purposes of settlement in the UK with that relative. These are dealt with in **Chapter 8**.

3.8.6   Switching where permitted

Some categories of entrants with limited leave are by their very nature temporary and so cannot lead to settlement, eg visitors (see **Chapter 5**) and students (see **Chapter 6**). However, most other categories may lead to settlement, and the answer is always found by studying the appropriate Immigration Rules. For example, a Tier 1 (Entrepreneur) Migrant can apply for settlement under para 245DF. See further **Chapters 7 and 8**.

3.8.7   Knowledge of language and life in the UK

Any individual between the ages of 16 and 65, who has entered the UK with limited leave and subsequently applies for settlement, must satisfy the English language and life in the UK requirements detailed in Appendix KoLL of the Immigration Rules.

3.8.8   The long-residence rules

Even where the requirements of the Immigration Rules for a switch to settled status are not met, it may be possible to obtain indefinite leave by virtue of long residence in the UK. Pursuant to the Immigration Rules, paras 276B and 276ADE, it is Home Office practice to consider this in cases where the applicant has been continuously resident in the UK either for 10 years lawfully (see **3.8.8.2**), or for most of his life (see **8.13**).

3.8.8.1   Key requirements

Both provisions share the key requirement of 'continuous residence'. By para 276A(a), this means residence in the UK for an unbroken period. Does that mean that the applicant must not have been absent from the UK at all? No, for these purposes a period is not considered broken where an applicant is absent from the UK for six months or less at any one time, provided that the applicant has existing limited leave to enter or remain on his departure and return. So in what circumstances is a period broken? This occurs if the applicant:

(a)   has been administratively removed or deported (see **Chapter 10**), or has left the UK having been refused leave to enter or remain here; or

(b)   has left the UK and, on doing so, evidenced a clear intention not to return; or

(c)   left the UK in circumstances in which he could have had no reasonable expectation at the time of leaving that he would lawfully be able to return; or

(d)   has been convicted of an offence and was sentenced to a period of imprisonment or was directed to be detained in an institution other than a prison (including, in particular, a hospital or an institution for young offenders), provided that the sentence in question was not a suspended sentence; or

(e)   has spent a total of more than 18 months absent from the UK during the period in question.

For the long residence provision based on 10 years' continuous residence (see **3.8.8.2**) there is an additional key requirement of 'lawful residence'. By para 276A(b), this means residence which is continuous residence pursuant to:

(a)   existing leave to enter or remain; or

(b)   temporary admission within s 11 of the 1971 Act (see **3.5.5**) where leave to enter or remain is subsequently granted; or

(c)   an exemption from immigration control, including where an exemption ceases to apply if it is immediately followed by a grant of leave to enter or remain. People exempt from immigration control include diplomats and members of the armed forces. These are beyond the scope of this book.

Is an applicant no longer lawfully resident if at any point he became an overstayer? Yes, held the Court of Appeal in *MD (Jamaica) v Secretary of State for the Home Department* [2010] EWCA Civ 213, as para 276A(b) has an exhaustive definition of lawful residence. However, Home Office guidance is that any period of overstaying for 28 days or less will be disregarded. If the period is longer but there are extenuating reasons for this, such as a postal strike, hospitalisation or an administrative error by the Home Office, caseworkers may exercise discretion to grant indefinite leave to remain, provided the application meets all the other requirements.

Continuous residence is considered to be broken by the Home Office if the applicant has:

(a)   been absent from the UK for a period of more than six months at any one time, or is absent from the UK for a shorter period but does not have valid leave to enter the UK on his return, or valid leave to remain on his departure from the UK; and/or

(b)   spent a total of 18 months outside the UK throughout the whole 10-year period.

Home Office guidance is that continuous residence is not broken if the applicant is absent from the UK for six months or less at any one time, or had existing leave to enter or remain when he left and when he returned (this can include leave gained at a port when returning to the UK as a non-visa national), or departed the UK after the expiry of his leave to remain but applied for fresh entry clearance within 28 days of that previous leave's expiring.

What about any time spent in prison by an applicant? Continuous residence is broken if he receives a custodial sentence by a court of law and is sent to prison, a young offender's institution or a secure hospital. So any leave accumulated before sentencing will be disregarded and only residence after release from custody counts. Note that continuous residence is not broken if an applicant receives a suspended sentence.

3.8.8.2   Ten years' residence provision

By para 276B, the requirements to be met by an applicant for indefinite leave to remain on the ground of long residence in the UK are that:

(a)   he has had at least 10 years' continuous lawful residence in the UK (see **3.8.8.1**);

(b)   having regard to the public interest, there are no reasons why it would be undesirable for him to be given indefinite leave to remain on the ground of long residence, taking into account his:

    (i)   age, and

    (ii)   strength of connections in the UK, and

    (iii)   personal history, including character, conduct, associations and employment record, and

    (iv)   domestic circumstances, and

    (v)   compassionate circumstances, and

    (vi)   any representations received on the person's behalf; and

(c)   the applicant does not fall for refusal under the general grounds for refusal (see **3.6.5**);

(d)   the applicant has sufficient knowledge of the English language and sufficient knowledge about life in the UK by passing the test known as the 'Life in the UK Test' (see **3.8.7**), unless he is under the age of 18 or aged 65 or over at the time he makes his application.

What is the Home Office guidance on the public interest factors in para 276B(ii) ((b) above)?

(a)   Age may be a relevant factor if the applicant is an unaccompanied child under the age of 18, or if the applicant or his dependants have spent their formative years in the UK and adapted to life here.

(b)   The family life a person has in the UK must be taken into account in assessing the strength of that person's connections to the UK. This may be particularly strong if he is married to or has established a similar relationship with a settled person. The person may have other close relatives settled in the UK. The strength and closeness of the relationship will determine how strong a factor this may be. Similarly, if a person's close relatives are not in the UK, this may call into question the strength of the person's connection to the UK.

Owning property or a business may support the view that an applicant has shown long-term commitment and a connection to the UK. However, on its own, this would not be a significant factor. Factors such as the length of time the individual has owned the business or property, or whether the business is legally operating, must be considered. If someone mentions his business interests as proof of commitment to the UK, he must provide supporting documentary evidence. The applicant will be required to show further proof of strong connections to the UK.

If the applicant has contributed positively to society, for example through significant investment or charitable work, this may be another factor in his favour, although this is unlikely to be decisive on its own.

(c)   Character, conduct and associations go beyond criminal convictions and enable the caseworker to consider whether the applicant's activities in the UK or abroad make it undesirable to grant indefinite leave. This could include concerns about the applicant on the basis of national security, war crimes, crimes against humanity and serious criminality, whether convicted or not. As to applicants with a conviction, see para 276B(iii).

A history of anti-social behaviour or low-level criminality might be a ground to refuse indefinite leave, especially if it has led to the issuing of an anti-social behaviour order (ASBO).

The applicant's employment record will often be a significant consideration. The caseworker must consider what the person has been doing while he has been in the UK, and what economic contribution, if any, he has made. Whilst not having a sound employment record is not in itself a reason to refuse leave, a sound employment record, along with strong ties with the UK, would count in a person's favour, if he has not been a burden on public finances but has, in fact, contributed through income tax and national insurance contributions.

(d) If the applicant has dependent children who have adapted to life in the UK, this could be a factor against refusal. The presence of another settled person who is routinely dependent on the applicant, for example a disabled relative, might also be a factor against refusal.

(e) It is not possible to define all potential compassionate circumstances, but it might, depending on the situation, include significant or serious illness, frailty and particularly difficult family circumstances.

(f) All representations raised on behalf of the applicant must be carefully assessed, even if these have been dismissed in previous applications. The caseworker must weigh those factors against the compassionate circumstances, if any, and all the other circumstances of the case, and then decide whether a grant of indefinite leave would be against the public interest.

Note that if the applicant cannot meet the requirements of paras 276B(iii) and/or (iv), he may under para 276A2 be granted an extension of his stay on the ground of long residence in the UK for a period not exceeding two years.

The application will be refused if the applicant does not meet the requirements for indefinite leave to remain or further leave to remain on the ground of long residence in the UK.

3.8.9 EEA nationals

Nationals of the EEA do not need leave to enter or remain while exercising rights in EU law (see **Chapter 4**). Does this mean that while in the UK they have no restriction on the period for which they can remain and are therefore 'settled' under UK immigration law? The answer is, 'No'. However, by reg 15(1) of the I(EEA) Regs 2006 (see **4.4.9** and **Appendix 4**), EEA nationals acquire the right to reside in the UK permanently where, as a general rule, they have resided in the UK in accordance with the Regulations for a continuous period of five years. In limited circumstances, the right to reside in the UK permanently may be acquired more quickly, eg under reg 15(1) by a worker or self-employed person who has ceased activity as defined in reg 5. People falling within reg 15(1) are treated as settled for the purposes of applying for naturalisation (see **2.2.7**).

3.8.10 Criminality requirement for settlement

In April 2011 the Government introduced a requirement that any person applying for settlement under the Immigration Rules must show that he does not have any relevant convictions as detailed in Part 9. Are criminal convictions imposed outside the UK relevant? Yes, as para 6 of the Immigration Rules provides that 'conviction' means conviction for a criminal offence in the UK or any other country. Home Office guidance is that offences do not need to have an identically named provision or carry similar penalties as in the UK, provided that there is a comparable offence, for example homicide and murder. However, offences which do not constitute a criminal offence in the UK are ignored, such as homosexuality and proselytising (attempting to convert someone to another religion). The details are in **Appendix 8**.

3.9 THE COMMON TRAVEL AREA

The Common Travel Area consists of the UK, Ireland, the Channel Islands and the Isle of Man. The basic principle, set out in s 1(3) of the IA 1971, is that persons arriving on local journeys to the UK from elsewhere in the Common Travel Area are not subject to immigration control, and no leave to enter is required. Control operates only on initial entry to the Area from outside. This is subject to some exceptions, for example under the Immigration (Control on

Entry through the Republic of Ireland) Order 1972 (SI 1972/1610). This subjects some persons to immigration control (such as visa nationals without a visa for entry to the UK). If such persons enter the UK, for example, from Ireland, they are illegal entrants, even though they have never been examined by the immigration service. The 1972 Order also imposes conditions in other cases (eg where a person who is not Irish, and does not have the right of abode in the UK, travels to the UK from outside the Area, via the Republic). Usually such persons will have deemed leave to enter for three months, with a prohibition on employment and business for non-EEA nationals. As the person will not have passed through immigration control, there will be no indication of these conditions on his passport.

3.10 IMMIGRATION HEALTH CHARGE

The immigration health charge (IHC) was introduced by s 38 of the IA 2014. The details can be found in the Immigration (Health Charge) Order 2015 (SI 2015/792). Broadly, it must be paid by most applicants seeking entry clearance, limited leave to enter and limited leave to remain for more than six months. So the largest group of entrants not liable to pay the IHC are standard visitors (see **5.2**) and those entering for settlement or applying in the UK for indefinite leave to remain.

Who is exempt from the IHC? The main groups are:

- non-EEA family members of EEA nationals exercising EU Treaty rights in the UK (see **Chapter 4**)
- Tier 2 intra-company transfer migrants (see **7.8.1.1**)
- nationals of Australia and New Zealand
- Appendix FM domestic violence concession applicants (see **8.8**), and
- asylum seekers and applicants for humanitarian protection (see **Chapter 9**).

The IHC must be paid at the time of making the application. If it is not paid, the application will not be granted. How much is it? It costs £150 per year for a student visa and £200 per year for all other visa and immigration applications. What if the period of leave to enter or remain will be less than a year or include part of a year? If the part year is six months or less, the amount payable for that part is half of the specified annual amount; but if it is more than six months, the amount payable for that part is the full specified annual amount.

Dependants usually pay the same amount as the applicant.

EEA NATIONALS

4.1 WHO ARE EEA NATIONALS?

'EEA nationals' are nationals of the Member States of the European Union together with Iceland, Liechtenstein and Norway (which are parties to the European Economic Area Agreement). See **Appendix 2** to this book for the full list of relevant countries.

Note that by an Agreement on the Free Movement of Persons made between the EC (now EU) and the Swiss Confederation (Cm 4904), Swiss nationals and their family members were from 1 June 2002 given broadly similar rights of entry to and residence in the UK as are enjoyed by EEA nationals. See the Immigration (Swiss Free Movement of Persons) (No 3) Regulations 2002 (SI 2002/1241).

4.2 WHAT IS THEIR IMMIGRATION STATUS?

Nationals of the EEA have a hybrid status. They do not have the right of abode possessed by British citizens but, unlike other aliens, they do not require leave to enter or remain while exercising rights in EU law (s 7(1) of the IA 1988). Paragraph **4.3** outlines their rights in EU law. These have been implemented in UK law by the I(EEA) Regs 2006, considered in detail in the rest of this chapter.

4.3 RIGHTS UNDER EU LAW

Article 20 TFEU states that:

1. Citizenship of the Union is hereby established. Every person holding the nationality of a Member State shall be a citizen of the Union. Citizenship of the Union shall be additional to and not replace national citizenship.

2. Citizens of the Union shall enjoy the rights and be subject to the duties provided for in the Treaties.

Article 21(1) TFEU provides that:

Every citizen of the Union shall have the right to move and reside freely within the territory of the Member States, subject to the limitations and conditions laid down in the Treaties and by the measures adopted to give them effect.

It can be seen that Article 21 TFEU provides for a right of residence and movement of EEA nationals throughout the EU. Directive 2004/38/EC of the European Parliament and Council of 29 April 2004 sets out the terms and limits of this right of movement. It is a consolidation and modernisation of existing EU secondary legislation in this area. It has been implemented into domestic law by the I(EEA) Regs 2006 (see **4.4**). This book will look at the detail of the 2006 Regs. There is a chart at **4.5** which sets out where the 2006 Regs implement the 2004 Directive. A copy of the Directive is set out in **Appendix 3**.

More detailed treatment of this topic is to be found in Part III of **Legal Foundations**. The following is a summary of the main principles.

4.3.1 Free movement of workers

Article 45 TFEU requires free movement for workers within the Union. Article 45(3) TFEU provides that this entails the right to:

(a)   accept offers of employment;

(b)   move freely within the EU for this purpose;

(c)   stay in a Member State for employment;

(d)   remain after employment, subject to conditions.

4.3.2 Self-employed activities and establishment of businesses

Article 49 TFEU requires abolition of restrictions on the freedom of establishment of EU nationals. This freedom includes the right to pursue activities as self-employed persons, and to set up and manage undertakings such as companies or firms.

4.3.3 Provision of services

Article 56 TFEU requires abolition of the restrictions on freedom to provide services within the Union in respect of nationals of Member States who are established in a State of the Union other than that of the person for whom the services are intended.

Article 57 TFEU states that the provider of a service (including industrial, commercial, craft, and professional activities) may temporarily pursue his activity in a State where the service is provided. Permanent provision of the service would involve 'establishment'.

Freedom of movement extends not only to the providers, but also to the recipients of services. In Joined Cases 286/82 and 26/83 *Luisi (Graziana) and Carbone (Giuseppe) v Ministero del Tesoro* [1984] ECR 377, the ECJ held that this covered tourists, and those who travel for medical treatment, education or business.

Does the EEA national have to travel to another EEA country and provide services there? 'No', held the ECJ in *Alpine Investments BV v Minister van Financiën* (Case C-384/93) [1995] ECR I-1141 – an offer to provide services over the telephone to potential recipients established in other Member States is sufficient. On a proper construction, Article 56 applies to services which a provider supplies, without moving from the Member State in which he is established, to recipients established in other Member States.

4.3.4 When the 2004 Directive applies

The 2004 Directive applies only to EEA nationals exercising Treaty rights. So a non-EEA national cannot directly benefit from it. This is because the Directive determines how, and under what conditions, EEA citizens can exercise their right to freedom of movement within the territory of the Member States. Accordingly, the Directive concerns the travel and residence of an EEA citizen in a Member State other than that of which he is a national: see *McCarthy (European citizenship)* [2011] 3 CMLR 10. A non-EEA national may only indirectly benefit from the Directive if he is the family member of an EEA national (see **4.4.6**).

An EEA national will exercise his Treaty rights by, for example, moving to another EEA country and living there. This is the combined effect of Articles 20 and 21 TFEU (see **4.3**). The EEA national might take employment pursuant to Article 45 TFEU (see **4.3.1**), or run a business under Article 49 (see **4.3.2**). His right of entry to and residence in the host EEA country will be governed by the 2004 Directive as implemented into the domestic law of the host EEA country; as we saw at **4.3**, in the UK that means the 2006 Regs.

EXAMPLES

(1) Abdus is a citizen of Pakistan. He is a single man. He travelled from Pakistan and entered Spain, an EEA country, pursuant to domestic Spanish immigration laws. Abdus is not an EEA national. He cannot exercise Treaty rights.

(2) Marie is a French national living in Paris. She is single and an EEA national. She has a right of entry to and residence in the other EEA countries. She travels to Madrid, Spain (an EEA country) and starts working there. She is thereby exercising her Treaty rights.

(3) Boris is a German national living in Berlin. He travels to Jamaica and works there for several years. He marries Alisha, a Jamaican national. The couple decide that they want to live together in Germany. As Jamaica is not an EEA country, Boris has not exercised his Treaty rights. Alisha will have to comply with domestic German law to enter and live with Boris there.

(4) Marie, from example (2) above, meets Abdus from example (1) in Spain. They fall in love and marry. The couple subsequently decide to live together in France. As Marie is an EEA national who has exercised her Treaty rights, Abdus, as her spouse, can benefit indirectly. Rather than applying under domestic French immigration law to enter France with Marie, he can choose to rely on EU law and enter as the spouse of an EEA national. See further **4.4.6** and **4.4.7**.

4.4 THE IMMIGRATION (EUROPEAN ECONOMIC AREA) REGULATIONS 2006

The I(EEA) Regs 2006 enact EU law rights of free movement in UK law. A copy may be found at **Appendix 4** to this book. The immigration adviser can refer directly to the I(EEA) Regs 2006 but should be aware that, in the event that they fail to give effect to EU law, EU law will prevail. In addition, EU case law may affect the interpretation of the Regulations.

All references in the rest of this chapter are to the I(EEA) Regs 2006 unless otherwise stated.

4.4.1 Right of admission for EEA nationals (reg 11(1))

An EEA national must be admitted to the UK if he produces on arrival a valid national identity card or passport issued by an EEA State.

4.4.2 Right of admission for family members of EEA nationals (reg 11(2))

A person who is not an EEA national must be admitted to the UK if he is a family member of an EEA national and he produces on arrival a valid passport or an EEA family permit (see **4.4.7**), a residence card (see **4.4.8**) or a permanent residence card (see **4.4.10**).

The family member may be travelling with the EEA national to the UK, or joining the EEA national who is already in the UK. If the family member is travelling independently of the EEA national and not joining him in the UK then the Immigration Rules apply.

4.4.3 Initial right of residence for three months (reg 13)

An EEA national and his family member(s) are entitled to reside in the UK for a period not exceeding three months. The only condition is that the EEA national and any family member must not become an unreasonable burden on the social assistance system of the UK (see further **4.4.5.4**).

4.4.4 Residence beyond three months (reg 14)

An EEA national is entitled to reside in the UK for a period exceeding three months if he is a qualified person. Indeed, he has the right to reside in the UK for as long as he remains a qualified person. His family member(s) have the same right.

It is important to appreciate that the family member's right to reside is dependent upon the EEA national's having a right to reside. The problem that arises if the EEA national dies or leaves the UK, etc is considered at **4.4.11**.

4.4.5 Who is a qualified person? (reg 6)

A qualified person is an EEA national who is in the UK in any of the following categories:

(a)   a jobseeker;

(b)   a worker;

(c)   a self-employed person;

(d)   a self-sufficient person; or

(e)   a student.

4.4.5.1 Jobseeker

A 'jobseeker', as defined in reg 6(4), is an EEA national who either:

(a)   entered the UK in order to seek employment; or

(b)   is now present in the UK seeking employment immediately after enjoying a right to reside as a qualified person in another category.

In addition, he must provide evidence that he is seeking employment and has a genuine chance of being engaged.

As to (a), an EEA national has an initial right to reside in the UK for three months (see **4.4.3**), and so any right to reside in this category commences after this period.

How long can an EEA national look for work in this category? By reg 6(7), for no longer than 91 days, unless he can provide compelling evidence that he is continuing to seek employment and has a genuine chance of being engaged. The Home Office gives the example of an EEA national who enters the UK to study and shortly afterwards commences employment. After 13 months he is made redundant and registers with Job Centre Plus. Eight months later, he is still seeking work, but provides evidence to show that he has recently undertaken further training which, when he finishes it in two months' time, will guarantee him a position as an apprentice. This is sufficient evidence to show that he has a genuine chance of being engaged in work.

To what extent is it possible for an EEA national to enjoy repeat periods of residence in the UK as a jobseeker? The answer is in reg 6(8), which allows the 91-day period for jobseekers to look for work to be split across multiple occasions but not exceeded. So where a jobseeker has previously enjoyed a right to reside in that capacity for 91 days, it will usually only be possible to enjoy jobseeker status again following a period of absence from the UK. A former jobseeker who has been absent from the UK for less than 12 months may only enjoy a period of jobseeker status if he is able to provide compelling evidence of a genuine prospect of engagement from the outset. A former jobseeker who has been continuously absent from the UK for more than 12 months will be able to enjoy a fresh period of residence as a jobseeker without being subject to that requirement.

4.4.5.2 Worker

Regulation 4(1)(a) defines a worker by a simple cross-reference to Article 45 TFEU (see **4.3.1**), namely an employee.

So what constitutes employment? Does it include part-time employment? Yes, held the ECJ in *Levin v Secretary of State for Justice* [1982] ECR 1035, although it will not include activities on such a small scale as to be regarded as purely marginal and ancillary. Work means to pursue an economic activity.

Note that by reg 6(2), an EEA national who has worked in the UK but is currently not working may in certain limited circumstances still be classified as a worker, eg if he is temporarily unable to work due to illness or accident. So a woman who ceases work because she is pregnant does not retain the status of a worker since pregnancy is not an illness: see *JS v Secretary of State for Work and Pensions* [2011] EWCA Civ 806. An employed woman will, of course, still remain a worker whilst on maternity leave. Note that a woman who gives up work, or seeking work, because of the physical constraints of the late stages of pregnancy and the aftermath of childbirth retains the status of worker provided she returns to work or finds another job within a reasonable period after the birth of her child: see *Saint Prix v Department for Work and Pensions* (Case C-507/12) (2014).

Also note the definition of a worker who has ceased activity in reg 5(2)–(5). This includes, for example, an EEA national who has resided in the UK for more than three years and worked for at least 12 months before ceasing work when reaching retirement age, and also an EEA national who has resided in the UK for at least two years prior to termination of his work or self-employment due to a permanent disability. The definition is important, as such a person may acquire permanent residence in the UK (see **4.4.9**).

What is the difference between a worker who is 'temporarily' unable to work due to illness or accident (reg 6(2)(a)) and a worker with a 'permanent' incapacity to work (reg 5(3))? According to Blake J in *FMB (Uganda) v Secretary of State for the Home Department* [2010] UKUT 447 at para 23 'if a person's inability or incapacity is not permanent, then it should be regarded as temporary'. This was approved by the Court of Appeal in *De Brito v Secretary of State for the Home Department* [2012] EWCA Civ 709.

4.4.5.3   Self-employed person

Regulation 4(1)(b) defines a self-employed person by a simple cross-reference to Article 49 TFEU (see **4.3.2**).

Note that by reg 6(3), an EEA national who is temporarily unable to work due to illness or accident retains the stautus of a self-employed person.

Also note the definition of a self-employed person who has ceased activity in reg 5(2)–(5). This includes, for example, an EEA national who has had to stop work due to a permanent incapacity, and either he resided in the UK for more than two years before that incapacity or the incapacity results in his becoming entitled to a pension payable in whole or part by a UK institution. The definition is important, as such a person may acquire permanent residence in the UK (see **4.4.9**).

4.4.5.4   Self-sufficient person

A 'self-sufficient person', as defined in reg 4(1)(c), is an EEA national who has (i) sufficient resources not to become a burden on the social assistance system of the UK during his period of residence; and (ii) comprehensive sickness insurance cover in the UK. Guidance from the Home Office is that, for example, a retired person would be self-sufficient if he could demonstrate that he was in receipt of a pension and/or had sufficient funds or income from investments not to become a burden on the UK's social assistance system. Can resources supplied by another person be taken into account? Yes: see *Commission v Belgium* [2006] ECR I-2647.

Is a set amount of money required to demonstrate self-sufficiency? Directive 2004/38/EC, Article 8(4) prohibits this. However, reg 4(4) provides that a person's resources are regarded as sufficient if they exceed the maximum level of resources which a UK national and his family members may possess if he is to become eligible for social assistance under the UK benefit system.

If an EEA national claims a UK 'minimum subsistence benefit' like income support or income-based jobseeker's allowance, at what point might he become an unreasonable burden on the UK's welfare benefits system? The UK Government should carry out a proportionality test, and recital 16 of the 2004 Directive suggests that the following questions need to be posed and answered:

(1)   Duration
   •   For how long is the benefit being granted?
   •   Outlook: is it likely that the EEA citizen will get out of the safety net soon?
   •   How long has the residence lasted in the UK?

(2)   Personal situation
   •   What is the level of connection of the EEA citizen and his family members with the society of the UK?
   •   Are there any considerations pertaining to age, state of health, family and economic situation that need to be taken into account?

(3)   Amount
   •   Total amount of aid granted?
   •   Does the EEA citizen have a history of relying heavily on social assistance?
   •   Does the EEA citizen have a history of contributing to the financing of social assistance in the UK?

Only receipt of social assistance benefits can be considered relevant to determining whether the person concerned is a burden on the UK's social assistance system. As long as the beneficiaries of the right of residence do not become an unreasonable burden on the social assistance system of the UK, they cannot be expelled for this reason.

Is the requirement that the EEA national has comprehensive sickness insurance cover in the UK strictly enforced? Yes. It is not a mere formality but an integral part of the concept of self-sufficiency under the Regulations: see *Kamau (Kenya) v Secretary of State for the Home Department* [2010] EWCA Civ 1302.

4.4.5.5   Student

A 'student', according to reg 4(1)(d), is an EEA national who:

(a)   is enrolled, for the principal purpose of following a course of study (including vocational training), at a public or private establishment which is financed from public funds; or otherwise recognised by the Secretary of State as an establishment which has been accredited for the purpose of providing such courses or training within the law or administrative practice of the part of the UK in which the establishment is located;

(b)   has comprehensive sickness insurance cover in the UK; and

(c)   assures the Secretary of State, by means of a declaration, or by such equivalent means as the person may choose, that he has sufficient resources not to become a burden on the social assistance system of the UK during his period of residence.

4.4.6   Who is a family member of an EEA national?

Under reg 7, as a general rule, the following are family members of an EEA national:

(a)   his spouse or his civil partner;

(b)   direct descendants (children, grandchildren, etc) of him, his spouse or his civil partner who are–
   (i)   under 21, or
   (ii)   dependants of him, his spouse or his civil partner;

(c)   dependent direct relatives in his ascending line (parents, grandparents, etc) or that of his spouse or his civil partner.

As to (a), what if an EEA national has more than one lawful spouse or civil partner? Only one counts. Why? Because reg 2 provides that a spouse or civil partner does not include the spouse or civil partner of an EEA national where a spouse or civil partner is already present in the UK.

4.4.6.1 Spouse or civil partner

A spouse or civil partner ((a) in **4.4.6** above) will not cease to be a family member in the event of marital breakdown or separation as long as the EEA national continues to exercise Treaty rights in the same Member State: see *Diatta v Land Berlin* [1985] ECR 567 and *Amos v Secretary of State for the Home Department* [2011] EWCA Civ 552. The right of residence will continue until any divorce is finalised by decree absolute, or until a civil partnership is dissolved. See further **4.4.11**.

4.4.6.2 Marriage or civil partnership of convenience

Note that by reg 2, a 'spouse' does not include a party to a marriage of convenience; and a 'civil partner' does not include a party to a civil partnership of convenience.

The 'convenience' referred to involves the non-EEA national seeking to obtain a right of residence in the UK under EU law by marriage to, or entering into a civil partnership with, an EEA national. That might occur whilst the parties are outside the UK, and so the non-EEA national seeks to enter under an EEA family permit (see **4.4.7**), or whilst they are in the UK. The objective is to avoid UK domestic immigration law. Typically, but not always, it takes place after the non-EEA national has been refused entry clearance or leave to remain in the UK.

Article 35 of the 2004 Directive (see **Appendix 3**) allows the UK Government to refuse, terminate or withdraw any rights conferred on the non-EEA national in these circumstances, provided that is a proportionate response, taking into account Article 8 of the ECHR (see **Appendix 5**), and subject to the safeguards in Articles 30 and 31 of the Directive. Further details may be found in Pt 4 of the I(EEA) Regs 2006 (see **Appendix 4**).

What factors might suggest a marriage or civil partnership of convenience? In *TC (Kenya) v Secretary of State for the Home Department* [2008] EWCA Civ 543, the Court of Appeal indicated that these may include the fact that the marriage occurs after the non-EEA national has been refused leave to remain under domestic law; that the application for a residence certificate or card (see **4.4.8**) is made quickly after the marriage or civil partnership ceremony; a lack of financial support between the parties; a considerable difference in age or background between the parties; no common language; the limited time that the parties to the relationship spend together; lack of cohabitation; the length of time which any party spends abroad without any compensating cohabitation whilst in the UK; the fact that the couple never go away together on holiday; one party being vague about the other's movements; the lack of credibility or reliability of a party as a witness; and limited (or no) supporting evidence from family and friends about the relationship between the parties.

The Home Office has published its policy in this area. Factors taken into account by an ECO when considering an application for a family permit include:

(a)   *Evidence of previous relationship.* In all cases, in order to refuse on the basis of a marriage of convenience, an ECO must be satisfied that there is little or no evidence of a relationship between the applicant and the EEA national. An applicant might provide email exchanges, letters, joint bank accounts, photographs, etc to show evidence of their relationship.

There are a number of other factors which may cause an ECO to suspect that the applicant is party to a marriage of convenience. The following may raise doubts as to the credibility of a relationship:

(b) *The applicant has an adverse immigration history.* The applicant may have had previous entry clearance applications refused or had otherwise attempted to gain entry or leave to remain in the UK, eg a failed asylum application.

(c) *Intention to live together in the UK.* The applicant and the EEA national should generally intend to live together in the UK. This should be evidenced by a clear commitment from both parties that they will do so following the outcome of the application.

(d) *Claims of previous marriage.* The applicant may have previously claimed to be married to someone else. In such cases they should produce documentary evidence of that marriage being dissolved.

(e) *Reason to question the plausibility of the marriage.* For example, factors may include considerable differences in age and background or where the applicant and EEA national have no common language.

(f) *A sum of money has been handed over in order for the marriage to be contracted.* This would not include money given in the form of a dowry in the cases of nationals of countries where the provision of a dowry is common practice.

Guidance on the point may be found at COM (2009) 313 Final. This confirms that the 2004 Directive does not prevent Member States from investigating individual cases where there is a well-founded suspicion of abuse; for instance, where the couple are inconsistent about their respective personal details, about the circumstances of their first meeting or about other important personal information concerning them. The guidance also includes the following example:

> S, a third country national, was ordered to leave in one month as she had overstayed her tourist visa. After two weeks, she married O, an EU national who had just arrived to the host Member State. The authorities suspect that the marriage might have been concluded only to avoid expulsion. They contact the authorities in O's Member State and find out that after the wedding his family shop was finally able to pay a debt of 5000 EUR, which it had been unable to repay for two years.
>
> They invite the newly-weds for an interview, during which they find out that O has meanwhile already left the host Member State to return home to his job, that the couple is not able to communicate in a common language and that they met for the first time one week before the marriage. There are strong indications that the couple may have married with the sole purpose of contravening national immigration laws.

In *Papajorgji (EEA Spouse – Marriage of Convenience) Greece* [2012] UKUT 38, the Tribunal held that when an applicant applies for a family permit, there is an evidential burden on the ECO to justify having a reasonable suspicion that the marriage or civil partnership was entered into for the predominant purpose of securing residence rights. Only then is the burden of proof on the applicant because reasonable suspicions have arisen, and the matter will be resolved against him unless those suspicions are determined in his favour.

4.4.6.3 Direct descendants

The direct descendants ((b) in **4.4.6** above) of the EEA national, his spouse or civil partner also count. So this will include children, grandchildren, great-grandchildren, etc who are either under 21 years of age or dependent on the EEA national, his spouse or civil partner. As to dependency, see **4.4.6.7**.

'Children' include step-children, and adopted children provided that the adoption is recognised by the UK.

4.4.6.4 Dependent direct relatives in ascending line

The parents, grandparents, etc of the EEA national and his spouse or civil partner count. As to dependency, see **4.4.6.7**.

4.4.6.5 Family members of a student after three months

Whilst the list of those who constitute family members in **4.4.6** above is the general rule, there is a major exception. Once a student has been residing in the UK for a period of three months, his family members are limited to (i) his spouse or his civil partner, and (ii) his dependent children or those of his civil partner.

4.4.6.6 Other (extended) family members

What about direct descendants (children, etc) aged 21 or over, or direct relatives in the ascending line (parents, etc) who cannot show dependency? What about other relatives, such as brothers and sisters, uncles and aunts, cousins, etc? These may fall within reg 8, which deals with 'extended family members'. These are any of the following:

(a)   a person who is a relative of an EEA national, his spouse or his civil partner and –

   (i)   who is residing in a country other than the UK and who is either dependent upon the EEA national or a member of his household,

   (ii)   who satisfied the condition in para (i) and is accompanying the EEA national to the UK or wishes to join him here, or

   (iii)   who satisfied the condition in para (i), has joined the EEA national in the UK and continues to be either dependent upon him or a member of his household;

(b)   a person who is a relative of an EEA national, or his spouse or his civil partner and, on serious health grounds, who strictly requires the personal care of the EEA national, his spouse or his civil partner;

(c)   a person who is a relative of an EEA national and who would meet the requirements in the Immigration Rules (other than those relating to entry clearance) for indefinite leave to enter or remain in the UK as a dependent relative of the EEA national were the EEA national a person present and settled in the UK (see **8.11**);

(d)   a person who is the partner of an EEA national (other than a civil partner) and who can prove to the decision maker that he is in a durable relationship akin to marriage or a civil partnership with the EEA national. The Home Office advises that the test it imposes is similar to that in the Immigration Rules, Appendix FM (see **8.3.1**). Note that the fiancé(e) or proposed civil partner of an EEA national is not his or her family member under EU law. Such a person would have to apply under the Immigration Rules, Appendix FM (see **8.3.5.1**).

In category (a), when is someone a member of the EEA national's household? Home Office guidance is that the family member should normally have lived with the EEA national under the same roof for at least six months.

In category (a), evidence is required of recent dependency or recent household membership. Historic but lapsed dependency or membership is irrelevant to the Directive policy of removing obstacles to the Union citizen's freedom of movement and residence rights: see *Bigia v Entry Clearance Officer* [2009] EWCA Civ 79, *SM (India) v Entry Clearance Officer* [2009] EWCA Civ 1426 and *Oboh v Secretary of State for the Home Department* [2013] EWCA Civ 1525.

Are there two or four different ways of meeting (a)? The Upper Tribunal held that there are four ways, in *Storey v Secretary of State for the Home Department* [2012] UKUT 79, each of which requires proving a relevant connection both prior to arrival in the UK and in the UK, namely: prior dependency and present dependency; or prior membership of a household and present membership of a household; or prior dependency and present membership of a household; or prior membership of a household and present dependency.

It does not matter whether it is the EEA national or his extended family member who arrives in the UK first: see *Aladeselu v Secretary of State for the Home Department* [2013] EWCA Civ 144.

Note that in *Secretary of State for the Home Department v Islam & Another* [2012] EUECJ C-83/11 the Court of Justice stated that the dependence must exist in the country from which the family member in question comes, at least at the time when such a family member makes an application for entry.

EXAMPLES

(1)   Marta is a citizen of Latvia. Her cousin, Mikhaila, a non-EEA national, has lived with her in the capital, Riga, for the last two years. Marta may seek to enter the UK as an EEA national. Mikhaila could travel with her to, or soon afterwards seek to join her in, the UK as her extended family member, as someone who was and will remain a member of Marta's household.

(2)   Patrik is a citizen of Slovakia. His aunt, Kata, a non-EEA national, has lived in another part of Slovakia for the last 12 months. She has been financially dependent on Patrik during that time and remains so. Patrik may seek to enter the UK as an EEA national. Kata could travel with him to, or soon afterwards seek to join him in, the UK as his extended family member, as someone who is financially dependent on Patrik.

(3)   Mahbur, a Bangladeshi national, marries Molly, an Irish national who is working in the UK. Following that marriage, Mahbur's brother, Muhammad, in Bangladesh becomes financially dependent on the couple. He may apply for an EEA family permit in order to enter and reside in the UK as Molly and Mahbur's dependant.

Does it count if the applicant is dependent on the spouse or civil partner of the EEA national or a member of his household? This might arise where the EEA national and his spouse or civil partner live separately, perhaps for work reasons, before moving to the UK. The Court of Appeal answered the question in the negative in *Soares v Secretary of State for the Home Department* [2013] EWCA Civ 575. Dependence or household membership can only count when it relates to the EEA national.

What are the requirements in order to meet category (b) above? The Tribunal in *TR (reg 8(3) EEA Regs 2006) Sri Lanka* [2008] UKAIT 00004 held that the 'serious health grounds' need to be significantly beyond ordinary ill-health and require detailed medical evidence in support. Personal care must be provided on a day-to-day basis and relate either or both to the physical and mental tasks and needs required for a person to function. 'Strictly' is a restrictive or limiting requirement and imports a need for complete compliance or exact performance, and reinforces the need for personal care to be provided on a day-to-day basis. Home Office guidance is that this would include an applicant who is totally dependent on his EEA national family member, or his spouse or civil partner, for basic everyday care, like helping with personal hygiene or preparing meals.

For further Home Office guidance on extended family members, see **4.4.6.8** below.

4.4.6.7   Meaning of dependency

Some of the above categories have a test of dependency on the EEA national. Guidance from the Home Office is that the dependency may be one of choice rather than necessity, but the definition of 'dependency' includes only financial dependency and not emotional dependency. Financial dependency might be shown by the family member being unemployed.

According to the case of *Lebon* [1987] ECR 2811, the status of 'dependent' family member is the result of a situation characterised by the fact that material support for that family member is provided by the EEA national, or by his spouse or partner. In order to determine whether a family member is dependent, it must be assessed in the individual case whether, having regard to his financial and social conditions, he needs material support to meet his essential needs in his country of origin or the country from which he came at the time when he applied to join the EEA national (ie not in the host Member State where the EEA national resides).

In the case of *Jia* [2007] ECR I-0001, when addressing the concept of dependency, the Court did not refer to any level of standard of living for determining the need for financial support by the EEA national. The 2004 Directive does not lay down any requirement as to the minimum duration of the dependency, or the amount of material support provided, as long as the dependency is genuine and structural in character.

In *Bigia v Entry Clearance Officer* [2009] EWCA Civ 79, the Court stated that the dependency test was met where the EEA national provided his adult daughter with rent-free accommodation and sent her money on a regular basis for 'bills, daily expenses and clothes'. She had no other source of income. The Court concluded that without that support she would be unable to meet her essential needs.

Can the UK Government require a direct descendant, who is 21 years old or older, to show that he has previously tried unsuccessfully to obtain employment or subsistence support in his country of origin, in order to be regarded as dependent? No – see *Reyes* [2014] EUECJ C-423/12.

4.4.6.8 Home Office guidance on extended family members

Guidance from the Home Office is that Directive 2004/38 refers in Article 3 only to facilitating the entry and residence of extended family members. When deciding whether to issue a residence card, the Home Office must assess whether refusal would deter the EEA national from exercising his EU Treaty rights, or would create an effective obstacle to the exercise of those rights. An example is given that it might be appropriate to issue a residence card where the family member was very elderly or incapacitated. In assessing such a case, the Home Office states that it would be important to consider whether there were relatives to care for the person in the home country.

In considering cases under reg 8, the Home Office normally refuses those who have, for example, their own family unit (unless there are sufficient compassionate circumstances), or who lived as part of the EEA national's household many years ago.

4.4.7 Does a family member need a travel document? (reg 12)

To be admitted to the UK, a family member should apply to an ECO for a travel document known as an EEA family permit before travelling to the UK. It is required only where the family member is not an EEA national. In order to obtain the permit the family member will have to produce documentation demonstrating the relationship with the EEA national (eg marriage certificate, etc).

4.4.8 How can an EEA national or family member confirm his right of residence?

Under regs 16 and 17, an EEA national or a non-EEA family member entitled to residence may apply to the Secretary of State for a residence certificate or residence card respectively. A residence certificate or card is normally valid for five years.

A family member may find it useful to obtain a residence card, particularly when applying for employment, as it confirms his entitlement to take employment in the UK. Also, if he leaves the UK, it will prove his right of re-entry (otherwise he will need to obtain an EEA family permit: see **4.4.7**).

4.4.9 Permanent right of residence in UK (reg 15)

The following persons may acquire the right to reside in the UK permanently:

(a)   an EEA national who has resided in the UK in accordance with the 2006 Regulations for a continuous period of five years;

(b)   a family member of an EEA national (who is not himself an EEA national) who has resided in the UK with the EEA national in accordance with the 2006 Regs for a continuous period of five years;

(c)   a worker or self-employed person who has ceased activity;

(d)   the family member of a worker or self-employed person who has ceased activity;

(e)   a person who was the family member of a worker or self-employed person where –

    (i)   the worker or self-employed person has died,

    (ii)   the family member resided with him immediately before his death, and

    (iii)   the worker or self-employed person had resided continuously in the UK for at least the two years immediately before his death, or the death was the result of an accident at work or an occupational disease;

(f)   a person who –

    (i)   has resided in the UK in accordance with the 2006 Regulations for a continuous period of five years; and

    (ii)   was, at the end of that period, a family member who has retained the right of residence.

So as to (a), this would include an EEA national who works in the UK for two years and then is unable to work for the next three years due to illness – this person would initially be a worker as defined in reg 6(1)(b) and would remain a worker when subsequently temporarily unable to work due to illness under reg 6(2)(a). The Home Office may well require medical evidence that there was a genuine inability to work during those three years. These are the facts of *FMB (Uganda) v Secretary of State for the Home Department* [2010] UKUT 447.

Note that as to (b) above (and subject to reg 10: see **4.4.11**), the family member must have held that status for five years. So an extended family member who was in a durable relationship with an EEA national but whose relationship breaks down before he fulfils the five-year requirement is excluded: see *CS (Brazil) v Secretary of State for the Home Department* [2009] EWCA Civ 480.

In (b) above, does the 'residing with' requirement relate just to presence in the UK or does it require living in a common family home? In *PM v Secretary of State for the Home Department* [2011] UKUT 246, the Tribunal held the former. So, in respect of a spouse, (b) is met where the couple entered a genuine marriage; both parties have resided in the UK for five years since the marriage; the EEA national's spouse has resided as the family member of a qualified person or otherwise in accordance with the Regulations and the marriage has not been dissolved. Obviously, if the parties have separated there may be an issue as to whether the marriage is one of convenience (see **4.4.6.2**). But that did not apply in the case as there was genuine matrimonial cohabitation for some time, a child had been born to the couple and there were continuing social relations by the parties to the marriage in the context of contact with the child.

Note that as to (c) above (a worker or self-employed person who has ceased activity), this category of person is defined by reg 5. So, for example, it includes a worker or self-employed person who has to stop work as a result of a permanent incapacity (see **4.4.5.2**) and who had resided in the UK continuously for more than two years prior to his work ending.

So if an EEA national with the right of permanent residence in the UK under (c) marries or enters into a civil partnership with a non-EEA national, that spouse or civil partner acquires the permanent right of residence in the UK under (d): see *RM (Zimbabwe) v Secretary of State for the Home Department* [2013] EWCA Civ 775.

Some of the above categories are based on a period of continuous residence in the UK. What about any periods of absence? Regulation 3 provides that continuity of residence is not affected by:

(a)   periods of absence from the UK which do not exceed six months in total in any year;

(b)   periods of absence from the UK on military service; or

(c)   any one absence from the UK not exceeding 12 months for an important reason, such as pregnancy and childbirth, serious illness, study or vocational training, or an overseas posting.

Is any period of continuous residence in the UK broken if the person is imprisoned? Yes, see *C v Secretary of State for the Home Department* [2010] EWCA Civ 1406, as 'the worker is not legally resident in the host state as an EEA worker during the period of imprisonment and that any period, which includes that period of imprisonment, cannot be part of the necessary "continuous" period for the purpose of calculating the five years continuous legal residence necessary to acquire the right permanently to reside here' (per Longmore LJ at [47]). Likewise, a period of imprisonment in the UK by a family member of an EEA national cannot be taken into consideration in the context of the acquisition by the family member of the right of permanent residence: *Onuekwere* [2014] EUECJ C-378/12.

Can the right of permanent residence be lost once acquired? Yes, but only through absence from the UK for a period exceeding two consecutive years.

4.4.10   How can an EEA national or family member confirm his permanent residence?

Under reg 18, an EEA national or non-EEA family member entitled to permanent residence can apply to the Secretary of State for a document certifying permanent residence or a permanent residence card respectively.

A document certifying permanent residence does not have an expiry date. A permanent residence card is valid for 10 years and is renewable.

4.4.11   What is the status of a family member who has not acquired permanent residence on the death or departure from the UK of the qualified person, or the termination of marriage or civil partnership?

Until a family member acquires his own right of permanent residence he is in a vulnerable position: what if the qualified person dies or leaves the UK? If his right of residence is dependent on marriage to, or on a civil partnership with, a qualified person, what is his immigration status when that relationship formally ends?

The answer is to be found in reg 10, which allows certain family members to retain the right of residence. This includes, for example, under reg 10(2), a person who:

(a)   is a family member of a qualified person when the qualified person dies;

(b)   resided in the UK in accordance with the 2006 Regs for at least the year immediately before the death of the qualified person; and

(c)   if he had been an EEA national himself, would qualify as a worker, a self-employed person or a self-sufficient person as defined by reg 6, or who is the family member of such a person.

A non-EEA ex-spouse or ex-civil partner may retain the right of residence under reg 10(5) if:

(a)   he ceased to be a family member of the qualified person on the termination of their marriage or civil partnership;

(b)   he was residing in the UK in accordance with the 2006 Regs at the date of the termination;

(c)   had he been an EEA national himself, he would qualify as a worker, a self-employed person or a self-sufficient person as defined by reg 6 (or as the family member of such a person); and

(d)   either –

(i)   the marriage or civil partnership had lasted for at least three years prior to the initiation of the proceedings for its termination, and the parties had resided in the UK for at least one year during its duration;

  (ii) he has custody of a child of the qualified person;

  (iii) he has the right of access to a child of the qualified person, where the child is under the age of 18 and where a court has ordered that such access must take place in the UK; or

  (iv) his continued right of residence in the UK is warranted by particularly difficult circumstances, such as he or another family member having been a victim of domestic violence while the marriage or civil partnership was subsisting.

For (b) above, the applicant will need to demonstrate that at the date of termination his ex-spouse or ex-civil partner was a qualified person. So, if the EEA national was then working, his payslips, bank statements, accounts, letters from employers or customers may help if the applicant can obtain such. On any appeal to the Tribunal (see **Chapter 11**) the applicant may be able to apply for a witness summons requiring his ex-spouse or ex-civil partner to attend and give evidence. Additionally, or alternatively, a direction may be sought requiring the Secretary of State to provide any information necessary for the determination of the appeal: see *Amos v Secretary of State for the Home Department* [2011] EWCA Civ 552. But note that the interpretation of this provision has been referred to the ECJ by the Court of Appeal in *NA (Pakistan) v Secretary of State for the Home Department* [2014] EWCA Civ 995.

Home Office guidance is that it will normally revoke, or refuse to issue or renew, a residence card where a family member's marriage to, or civil partnership with, a qualified person terminates, or there is evidence that the EEA national has left the UK, unless the family member has retained the right of residence under reg 10.

The burden is on the applicant to show that the conditions under which the right of residence is said to be retained are met: *Okafor v Secretary of State for the Home Department* [2011] EWCA Civ 499.

Can a family member who retains the right of residence ever acquire permanent residence? Yes, after five years' continuous residence in the UK, provided that has been in accordance with the 2006 Regs (see **4.4.9**).

4.4.12 British citizens who exercise Treaty rights and then return to the UK (reg 9)

If a British citizen travels to another EEA country to work or otherwise exercise Treaty rights, he is entitled to be accompanied by, or later joined by, his family members. Equally, if a British citizen travels to the UK from an EEA country after exercising Treaty rights there as a worker or self-employed person, his family may accompany him. So, for example, the Indian spouse of a British citizen who has worked in another EEA country may take advantage of Article 44 TFEU, acquiring rights of residence in the UK itself beyond those given by UK immigration law – see *R v Immigration Appeal Tribunal and Surinder Singh, ex p Secretary of State for the Home Department* [1992] 3 CMLR 358. The facts of the case were as follows.

Mr Singh, an Indian national, married a British citizen in the UK in 1982. At no time did the authorities allege that the marriage was a sham. It appears that Mr Singh was lawfully in the UK, but his immigration status is not clear from the case report. In 1983 Mr and Mrs Singh went to Germany, where they were both employed for two years. At the end of 1985 the couple returned to the UK to open a business. The ECJ held that the provisions of the Council Regulations and Directives on freedom of movement within the EU for employed and self-employed persons provide that Member States must grant the spouse and children of such a person rights of residence equivalent to those granted to the person himself. A national of a Member State might be deterred from leaving his country of origin in order to pursue an activity as an employed or self-employed person as envisaged by the Treaty in the territory of another Member State if, on returning to the Member State of which he is a national in order to pursue an activity there as an employed or self-employed person, the conditions of his entry and residence were not at least equivalent to those which he would enjoy under the Treaty or secondary law in the territory of another Member State. He would in particular be deterred from so doing if his spouse and children were not also permitted to enter and reside in the territory of his Member State of origin under conditions at least equivalent to those granted them by EU law in the territory of another Member State.

Regulation 9 is said to give effect to the *Surinder Singh* judgment.

4.4.12.1 Regulation 9(2)(a)

Where a British citizen is residing in an EEA State as a worker or self-employed person, or was so residing before returning to the UK, he is entitled to be accompanied by his family members (spouse, civil partner, partner in a durable relationship, child under 21, etc: see **4.4.6**).

Does reg 9(2)(a) require that the British citizen must be residing in an EEA State as a worker or self-employed person immediately before returning to the UK? No, held the Upper Tribunal in *OB (Morocco) v Secretary of State for the Home Department* [2010] UKUT 420. In the case the UK national married a national of Morocco in August 2006 whilst both were in the Republic of Ireland. The couple stayed there until July 2008. During that time the UK national worked from November 2006 to April 2007. In July 2008 the UK national returned to Northern Ireland, UK (where she had previously lived) to live and work there permanently. Her husband joined her and in September 2008 he applied for a residence card as the spouse of a UK national who had exercised Treaty rights. This application was granted. The Tribunal stated that the link between the UK national's right under EU law to reside and work in the Republic of Ireland and her right to return to the UK accompanied by her family members had not been broken. Further, in general, a period of interruption of employment for maternity and child rearing purposes, temporary illness or involuntary unemployment would also not break such a link.

4.4.12.2 Regulation 9(2)(b)

If the family member of the British citizen is his or her spouse or civil partner, there are additional requirements. Either:

(a)   the couple are living together in the EEA State before the British citizen returns to the UK; or

(b)   the couple entered into the marriage or civil partnership and were living together in the EEA State before the British citizen returned to the UK.

4.4.12.3 Regulation 9(2)(c)

This provides that the centre of the British citizen's life must have transferred to the EEA State where he resided as a worker or self-employed person.

What does this mean? Regulation 9(3) lists the following relevant factors:

(a)   the period of residence in the EEA State as a worker or self-employed person;

(b)   the location of the British citizen's principal residence; and

(c)   the degree of integration of the British citizen in the EEA State.

Home Office guidance is that these factors are indicative and it is not necessary to meet all three.

As to (a), the longer the British citizen has resided in another EEA State as a worker or self-employed person, the more likely it is that he has transferred the centre of his life to that State. The Home Office gives the following example:

> A British citizen who has lived and worked in another member state for a period of two years is more likely to meet the requirement of regulation 9(2)(c) than a British citizen who was employed in another Member State for a period of four months.

As to (b), the Home Office states that the principal residence is the place and country where the British citizen's life is primarily based. It gives the following example:

A British citizen worked in France for three months, staying in a hotel during the week and returning to their main home in the UK at the weekends. In this case they are unlikely to meet the requirements of regulation 9(2)(c) as their principal residence would be considered to be the UK.

In this context, 'primarily' does not mean 'solely'. So refusal should not occur if the British citizen returns to the UK regularly, so long as his principal residence is in another EEA State.

As to (c), Home Office guidance is that the more of the following questions that can be answered in the affirmative, the more likely the British citizen will be considered to have transferred his centre of life:

a.   Does the British citizen have any children born in the host member state? If so, are the children attending schools in the host member state?

b.   Does the British citizen have any other family members resident in the host member state?

c.   Has the British citizen immersed themselves into the life and culture of the host member state? For example, have they bought property there? Do they speak the language? Are they involved with the local community?

The Home Office gives the following examples:

A British citizen is working in France, is fluent in French and has bought a house there. Their children were born in France and are educated in a French school where the British citizen sits on the school council. In this example it is likely that the British citizen has moved the centre of their life to France.

Contrast with the example of a British citizen who will be working in France for three months, who resides in a hotel and returns to the UK every weekend. They don't speak the language and educate their children in a school in the UK. In this second example they are less likely to have moved the centre of their life from the UK to France.

4.4.12.4   Rights of family members

Home Office guidance is that because EEA nationals have an initial three-month right of residence in the UK (see **4.4.3**), there is no requirement for the British citizen to be the equivalent of a qualified person on arrival back in the UK. However, the first two questions on the application form for an EEA family permit are: what is the main purpose of your visit to the UK, and how long do you intend to stay in the UK? Detailed disclosure is then required of the couple's financial situation, as well as details of where they intend to live in the UK, etc. If an ECO takes the view that after three months in the UK the British citizen will not then be the equivalent of a qualified person (see **4.4.4**), it is possible that the application may be refused. However, note that Home Office guidance is that where the ECO has strong grounds to doubt that the EEA (or thereby British) national is, or will be, a qualified person, he should first interview the couple.

Does it make any difference if the British citizen deliberately went to another EEA country and worked there in order that he might use EU rather than domestic law to bring a family member back to the UK? No, held the ECJ in *Secretary of State for the Home Department v Akrich* [2003] 3 CMLR 26, provided the British citizen was properly a worker and, in the case of a spouse or civil partner, the relationship is genuine and not one of convenience. As to the latter, see **4.4.6.2**.

Additionally, a family permit might be refused on public policy, public health or public security grounds (see **4.4.14**) or, where the non-EEA national is the spouse or civil partner of the British national, on the ground that the relationship is one of convenience (see **4.4.6.2**).

On entering the UK the family member will be entitled to a residence card (see **4.4.8**) and, in due course, permanent residence (see **4.4.9**) under the same conditions as any family member of an EEA national.

If the family member of the British citizen is his spouse or civil partner, he has the choice of entry under EU law or domestic law (see **8.3**). If he chooses EU law and is successful, he will be issued with a family permit and a residence card. He may qualify for permanent residence after five years.

4.4.13 Derivative rights (reg 15A)

In 2012 the 2006 Regs were amended (see the Immigration (European Economic Area) (Amendment) Regulations 2012 (SI 2012/1547)) to give effect to the judgments of the ECJ in Case C-200/02 *Chen*, Case C-310/08 *Ibrahim* and Case C-480/08 *Teixeira*. Broadly, these cases established the right of entry and residence for primary carers of self-sufficient EEA national children, children of EEA national workers or former workers where the child is in education in the UK, primary carers of children of EEA national workers or former workers where that child is in education in the UK, and dependent children under the age of 18 of those primary carers.

In 2012 the 2006 Regs were further amended (see the Immigration (European Economic Area) (Amendment) (No 2) Regulations 2012 (SI 2012/2560)) to give effect to the judgment of the ECJ in the case of *Zambrano v Office national de l'emploi (ONEm)* (Case C-34/09) [2011] 2 CMLR 46. This provides that if a child in the UK is a British citizen, his primary carer (usually a parent) is a non-EEA national and there is no other parent, guardian or carer on whom the child is dependent or who could care for the child if the primary carer left the UK, the carer will have a right of residence.

Regulation 15A sets out the conditions which a person must satisfy in order to qualify for a derivative right of residence. Why derivative? Because the right does not stem directly from the 2004 Directive. As a result the person's wider family members have no right of entry to the UK and the person cannot acquire permanent residence here.

4.4.14 Summary of key terms

'Qualified person'	An EEA national who is exercising Treaty rights as a jobseeker; worker; self-employed person; a self-sufficient person or student.
'EEA family permit'	A form of entry clearance issued to a non-EEA national who is the family member of an EEA national.
'Registration certificate'	This is issued to an EEA national who is exercising Treaty rights (reg 16).
'Residence card'	This is issued to a non-EEA national who is the family member of a qualified person (reg 17).
'A document certifying permanent residence'	This is issued to an EEA national who has been residing in the UK for at least five years exercising Treaty rights (reg 18).
'A permanent residence card'	This is issued to a non-EEA national who is the family member of a qualified person, when he has resided for at least five years with a qualified person, who, during those five years has exercised Treaty rights (reg 18).

4.4.15 Excluding and removing an EEA national from the UK

Regulation 19 of the I(EEA) Regs 2006 provides for the exclusion and removal of an EEA national or his family member who has ceased to qualify, or whose removal is justified on the grounds of public policy pursuant to reg 21. Note that protection from removal is enhanced if the person has a permanent right of residence after five years ('serious grounds of public policy or public security' are required under reg 21(3))) and further enhanced after continuous residence of 10 years ('imperative grounds of public security' are required under reg 21(4))). As to the meaning of these terms, see *VP (Italy) v Secretary of State for the Home Department* [2010] EWCA Civ 806 and *FV (Italy) v Secretary of State for the Home Department* [2012] EWCA Civ 1199.

Further, note that in *HR (Portugal) v Secretary of State for the Home Department* [2009] EWCA Civ 371 it was held that both these qualifying periods must consist of lawful residence and so do not include time spent in prison. Can time spent in the UK before a period of imprisonment be included in a qualifying period? The matter has been referred to the ECJ: see *Onuekwere (Nigeria)* [2012] UKUT 269 and *MG (Portugal)* [2012] UKUT 268.

For a person to be excluded or removed on public policy grounds under reg 21, he must present a serious threat to the fundamental interests of society by his personal conduct. Guidance from the Home Office provides that previous criminal convictions are not in themselves sufficient grounds, unless the offence(s) are particularly serious (eg rape, murder, drug smuggling) and it is likely that the person will reoffend. A person charged with minor customs offences is not refused admission on that basis alone, whereas a person who is the leader of an extreme political party might present such a threat. Facilitation of illegal entry may, in itself, be sufficient grounds to refuse admission to EEA nationals. National security may also fall under this heading.

Public security under reg 21 does not necessarily equate with national security. Public security may also be a matter of personal security within society. Certain medical conditions (eg drug addiction or profound mental disturbance) may pose a threat to public policy or public security. These conditions might provide reasons for exclusion on public policy or public security grounds, but not on public health grounds.

As to public health, only a disease that has epidemic potential as defined by the World Health Organisation, or a disease to which s 38 of the Public Health (Control of Disease) Act 1984 applies (detention in hospital of a person with a notifiable disease), will constitute a ground for a decision to exclude or remove. However, if the person concerned is in the UK, any disease occurring after the initial three-month period does not count.

Home Office guidance is that once it is established that the threat posed by a person is sufficient in principle to justify his deportation on grounds of public policy or security under EU law, there will be a presumption that the public interest requires deportation. Regulation 21(5)(a) of the I(EEA) Regs 2006 requires such a decision to deport to comply with the principle of proportionality. Regulation 21(6) lists the type of considerations that must be taken into account, such as age; state of health; family and economic situation; length of residence in the UK; social and cultural integration into the UK and the person's links with his country of origin. The proportionality test under EU law requires that any interference with a person's free movement rights must be both appropriate in the circumstances of the case and go no further than is necessary to achieve the public policy or public security need; and the consideration of proportionality encompasses human rights considerations.

4.5 CHART CROSS-REFERENCING KEY ASPECTS OF 2006 REGULATIONS AND 2004 DIRECTIVE

Coverage	2006 Regulations	2004 Directive
Definitions	reg 2 'EEA national'	Art 2 'Union citizen'
	reg 7 'family member'	Art 2
	reg 8 'extended family member'	Art 3(2)
Right of entry	reg 11	Art 5
Initial right of residence up to 3 months	reg 13	Art 6
Right of residence for more than 3 months	reg 14	Art 7

Coverage	2006 Regulations	2004 Directive
Issue of residence cards	reg 17	Art 10
Retention of right of residence by family members on death or departure of qualified person	reg 10	Art 12
Retention of right of residence by family members on formal ending of marriage or registered civil partnership with qualified person	reg 10	Art 13
Right of permanent residence	reg 15	Arts 16, 17 and 18
A document certifying permanent residence	reg 18	Art 19
A permanent residence card	reg 18	Art 20
Continuity of residence	reg 3	Art 21
Protection against expulsion	reg 21	Art 28
Public health	reg 21	Art 29

VISITORS

5.1 INTRODUCTION – WHO IS A VISITOR?

A person may want to enter the UK temporarily as a visitor for many different reasons – for a holiday, to visit family or friends, to conduct some sort of business, to have private medical treatment, get married or enter into a civil partnership, etc. Appendix V to the Immigration Rules deals with these different routes into the UK for a visitor, and we shall look at the key categories in this chapter.

5.1.1 Entry clearance

Except in the case of visa nationals (see **1.4.3**), no entry clearance is normally required for a visit to the UK of up to six months. So it is possible for non-visa nationals (see **1.4.4**) to arrive at a UK port and seek leave to enter from an immigration officer. It may, however, reduce any potential problems for those who are not simply tourists if entry clearance is obtained in advance. In addition, there are some exceptions to the normal rule, as a non-visa national must apply for entry clearance if visiting the UK to marry or to form a civil partnership, or to give notice of this (see **5.10**), or when seeking to visit the UK for more than six months.

5.1.2 Leave to enter and conditions

Most kinds of visitors under Appendix V will be given leave to enter the UK for a period not exceeding six months, subject to a condition prohibiting employment (see **3.3.1**), but this does not prohibit any work-related permitted activities (see **5.4**). There will also be a condition of no study, although this does not prohibit the incidental study allowed by the permitted activities (see **5.4.15**). Like all limited leave entrants, visitors will be subject to the condition not to have recourse to public funds (also see **3.3.2**).

There is a useful chart at para V 1.5 of Appendix V to the Immigration Rules that summarises the types and lengths of visit visa and leave to enter or remain.

Note that within the period for which a visit visa is valid, a visitor may enter and leave the UK multiple times, unless the visit visa is endorsed as a single or dual entry visa (see **5.2.4**).

5.1.3 Frequency of visits

Is there any restriction on the number of visits a person may make to the UK? Is there any requirement that a specified period of time must elapse between successive visits? The answer to both these questions is 'No'. Home Office guidance is that a person who has made a series of visits to the UK with only brief intervals between them would not, in the absence of any other relevant factors, be refused entry as a visitor. However, an immigration officer will consider the stated purpose of a visit in light of the length of time that has elapsed since previous visits. See further *Sawmynaden (Family visitors – considerations)* [2012] UKUT 00161 (IAC).

Note that the Home Office accepts that, occasionally, a visitor carrying out a permitted activity associated with business (see **5.4**) may be required to stay for a period of weeks or even months in the UK, for example where machinery is being installed or faults are being diagnosed and corrected. An immigration officer should be satisfied, however, that a person's presence in the UK on business for more than six out of any 12 months does not mean that he is basing himself here and holding down a specific post which constitutes employment, and which would therefore require the individual to seek entry under the points-based system (see **Chapter 7**).

Home Office guidance accepts that there is no specified maximum time a visitor can spend in the UK in any period, such as '6 months in 12 months'. However, if it is clear from a visitor's travel history that he is making the UK his home, the application will be refused (see further **5.2.2.2**).

5.2 STANDARD VISITOR

All visitors must meet the general suitability and eligibility requirements set out in Parts V3 and V4 of Appendix V to the Immigration Rules.

5.2.1 Suitability

Whilst visitors are not subject to the general grounds for refusal in Part 9 of the Immigration Rules, the suitability requirements in paras V 3.2 to V 3.16 of Appendix V are broadly the same (see **3.4.5**).

5.2.2 Genuineness and credibility

5.2.2.1 Requirements

Paragraph V 4.2 provides that an applicant must be a 'genuine' visitor. This means that the applicant:

(a)   will leave the UK at the end of his visit; and

(b)   will not live in the UK for extended periods through frequent or successive visits, or make the UK his main home; and

(c)   is genuinely seeking entry for a purpose permitted by Appendix V; and

(d)   will not undertake any prohibited activities (see 5.3).

5.2.2.2 Home Office policy

What should have struck you when reading the above requirements for a standard visitor is that they concern the applicant's intention. So he must *genuinely* be seeking entry as a visitor and *intend* to leave the UK at the end of his visit, and he must *not intend* to make the UK his main home, etc. The burden of proof is on the applicant, but to what standard? It is the balance of probabilities. Home Office guidance to its decision makers is that the following factors may be relevant:

- the applicant's previous immigration history, including visits to the UK and other countries

- the duration of previous visits, and whether this was significantly longer than originally stated on the applicant's visa application or on arrival

- the applicant's financial circumstances, as well as his family, social and economic background

- the applicant's personal and economic ties to his country of residence

- the cumulative period of time the applicant has visited the UK and his pattern of travel over the last 12-month period; and decision makers should assess whether this amounts to 'de facto' residence in the UK

- whether the information and the reasons for the visit provided by the applicant are credible and correspond to his personal, family, social and economic background

- the applicant's country of residence and/or country of nationality, including information on immigration non-compliance by individuals who applied for a visit visa from the same geographical region as the applicant.

Whilst visitors can undertake multiple activities whilst they are in the UK, Home Office guidance is that an applicant should be able to explain at the visa application stage and on entry his main reason for coming to the UK. So when might an ECO and/or an immigration officer doubt an applicant's intentions in visiting the UK? This may include the following circumstances:

- the applicant has few or no family and economic ties to his country of residence and has several family members in the UK

- the political, economic and security situation in the applicant's country of residence, including whether it is politically unstable, a conflict zone or at risk of becoming one, may lead to doubts about the applicant's intention to leave the UK at the end of his visit

- the applicant, his sponsor (if he is visiting a friend or relative) or other immediate family member has, or has attempted to, deceive the Home Office in a previous application for entry clearance, leave to enter or leave to remain

- there are discrepancies between the statements made by the applicant and the statements made by the sponsor, particularly on points where the sponsor could reasonably be expected to know the facts but does not

- it has not been possible to verify information provided by the applicant despite attempts to do so

- the information that has been provided or the reasons stated by the applicant are not credible

- a search of the applicant's baggage and vehicle at the border reveals items that demonstrate an intention to work and/or live in the UK.

5.2.3 Maintenance and accommodation

5.2.3.1 Requirements

Paragraph V 4.2(e) provides that an applicant must have sufficient funds to cover all reasonable costs in relation to his visit without working or accessing public funds (see **3.3.2**). This includes the cost of the return or onward journey, any costs relating to dependants and the cost of any planned activities such as private medical treatment.

An applicant must have access to sufficient resources to maintain and accommodate himself adequately for the whole of his planned visit to the UK. Is there a set level of funds for an applicant to show this? No. So what are the key questions to be answered? These will include:

(a)   where the applicant will be staying;

(b)   the costs likely to be incurred, including any on-going financial commitments the applicant may have in his country of residence, such as rent or mortgage payments and any dependants whom the applicant supports financially, including those who are not travelling with him;

(c)   the sources of revenue that are available to the applicant.

Home Office guidance is that an applicant's income or savings, minus his financial commitments, must be sufficient to meet the likely costs he will incur in the UK and be reasonable expenditure in light of his financial situation.

5.2.3.2   Third party assistance

Paragraph V 4.3 provides that an applicant's travel, maintenance and accommodation may be provided by a third party, as long as that third party:

(a)   has a genuine professional or personal relationship with the visitor; and

(b)   is not, or will not be, in breach of UK immigration laws at the time of decision or the visitor's entry to the UK; and

(c)   can and will provide support to the applicant for the intended duration of his stay.

Typical third parties include family members, friends and business associates.

Home Office guidance is that when assessing whether the relationship is genuine and whether the third party intends to provide support, the decision maker should consider the relationship between the applicant and the third party sponsor (including, if appropriate, where they met, and how often and by what method they communicate), and the third party's previous history of 'sponsoring' visitors (as previous failures to support visitors may call into question the sponsor's intention and ability to do so for this applicant).

If the third party sponsor is an individual, such as a friend or family member providing financial support for the visitor, he must demonstrate that he has enough funds available to adequately support himself, and anyone normally dependent on him, as well as the applicant.

The third party may be asked to give an undertaking in writing to be responsible for the visitor's maintenance and accommodation during the visitor's stay (see **3.3.2**).

> **EXAMPLE**
>
> Ada, aged 22, is a non-visa national. She arrives in the UK without an entry certificate. She informs the immigration officer that she is visiting her sister in the UK for six months. When questioned, she discloses that:
>
> (a)   she recently lost her job;
>
> (b)   she will be looking after her sister's children whilst she is in the UK, because her sister and brother-in-law have just got jobs;
>
> (c)   her sister will not pay her but will provide her with food and accommodation;
>
> (d)   she has only a few pounds in cash on her;
>
> (e)   her sister bought her a one-way ticket to the UK.
>
> The immigration officer may decide that she does not meet the requirements for a standard visitor, as follows:
>
> (a)   Ada is not genuinely seeking entry as a standard visitor for six months; rather, her purpose is to enter the UK to be a child-minder for her sister and brother-in-law indefinitely.
>
> (b)   Ada does not intend to leave the UK after six months, especially as she has no return ticket and no apparent means of saving enough money to buy one whilst in the UK.
>
> (c)   Ada intends to take unpaid employment.

> (d) Ada has no evidence to support her claim that she will be maintained and accommodated adequately by her sister.
>
> (e) Ada has no evidence that she can meet the cost of her return journey after six months.
>
> In particular, the immigration officer will take into account Home Office guidance that states, 'Where a family member is coming to look after a child in the UK, this is permitted provided it is for a short visit and does not amount to the relative being employed as a child-minder. You must be satisfied that the visit is of a short duration and the relative is a genuine visitor.'

5.2.4 Multi-entry visa

Visit visas are normally valid for six months, 12 months, two years, five years and 10 years. A visa is valid for unlimited journeys within its period of validity. However, a person with a visit visa may remain in the UK for a maximum of only six months on any one visit, or until the visa expires if less than six months.

5.3 PROHIBITED ACTIVITIES

5.3.1 Work

An applicant must not intend to work in the UK. This includes:

- taking employment in the UK
- doing work for an organisation or business in the UK
- establishing or running a business as a self-employed person
- doing a work placement or an internship
- direct selling to the public and providing goods and services.

Are there any exceptions? Yes, where expressly allowed by the permitted activities (see **5.4**). However, permitted activities must not amount to the applicant's taking employment, or doing work which amounts to his filling a role or providing short-term cover for a role within a UK-based organisation. In addition, where the applicant is already paid and employed outside of the UK, he must remain so. Payment may only be allowed in the specific circumstances set out below.

5.3.2 Payment

The applicant must not receive payment from a UK source for any activities undertaken in the UK, except for the following:

(a) reasonable expenses to cover the cost of the applicant's travel and subsistence, including fees for directors attending board-level meetings;

(b) prize money;

(c) billing a UK client for the applicant's time in the UK, where the applicant's overseas employer is contracted to provide services to a UK company and the majority of the contract work is carried out overseas. Payment must be lower than the amount of the applicant's salary;

(d) where the applicant is employed by a multi-national company that, for administrative reasons, handles payment of its employees' salaries from the UK;

(e) where the applicant is engaged in Permitted Paid Engagements (see **5.11**), provided the applicant holds a visa or leave to enter in this category; or

(f) paid performances at a permit-free festival (see **5.4.11**).

5.4 PERMITTED ACTIVITIES

5.4.1 Tourism and leisure

Traditionally this route has been used for applicants to visit friends and family and/or come to the UK for a holiday.

5.4.2 Volunteering

A visitor can undertake 'incidental volunteering'. What is that? It means that the applicant may volunteer for no more than 30 days in total of his visit for a charity that is registered with either the Charity Commission for England and Wales, or the Charity Commission for Northern Ireland or the Office of the Scottish Charity Regulator.

As to entering the UK as a charity voluntary worker, see **7.12.2**.

5.4.3 Business: general activities

What sort of general business activities can a visitor in the UK undertake? Appendix 3, para 5 of Appendix V to the Immigration Rules provides that a visitor may:

(a)   attend meetings, conferences, seminars, interviews;

(b)   give a one-off or short series of talks and speeches, provided these are not organised as commercial events and will not make a profit for the organiser;

(c)   negotiate and sign deals and contracts;

(d)   attend trade fairs, for promotional work only, provided the visitor is not directly selling;

(e)   carry out site visits and inspections;

(f)   gather information for the visitor's employment overseas;

(g)   be briefed on the requirements of a UK-based customer, provided that any work for the customer is done outside of the UK.

Home Office guidance is that the decision maker should assess whether the period of leave requested is credible in view of the activities the applicant is seeking to carry out. For example, as to conferences and seminars falling within (a), these will usually be formal, speaker-led events lasting for a couple of days and focused on a specific topic or sector, but they can also include familiarisation programmes for people coming to learn about UK practices on law, finance, etc. However, they must not amount to the person's undertaking work experience or longer study.

5.4.4 Business: corporate activities

What activities can an employee of an overseas-based company undertake whilst in the UK in this category? In relation to a specific internal project with UK employees of the same corporate group, provided no work is carried out directly with clients, the employee may:

(a)   advise and consult;

(b)   trouble-shoot;

(c)   provide training; and

(d)   share skills and knowledge.

Home Office guidance is that these activities should be of a short duration, linked to a specific project and not involve the visitor in working directly with or for clients. The applicant should be mainly based at the company's offices in the UK and not at client sites, unless that it is for meetings.

An internal auditor may also carry out regulatory or financial audits at a UK branch of the same group of companies as the visitor's employer overseas. Are there any restrictions on the nature of the regulatory audits? No, as long as they are internal to the group of companies, including a branch or subsidiary. Home Office guidance gives the example of an auditor inspecting the quality of car productions at a manufacturing plant.

5.4.5 Prospective entrepreneur

This category allows an individual entrepreneur to come to the UK to secure funding to set up a business here. At the time of applying for entry clearance, the applicant must be in discussions with a Home Office-designated funding body to secure funding in order to join, set up or take over, and be actively involved in the running of, a business in the UK. Which funding bodies are designated? These are:

(a)   registered venture capitalist firms regulated by the Financial Conduct Authority (FCA);

(b)   UK entrepreneurial seed funding competitions that are listed as endorsed on the UK Trade & Investment website; and

(c)   one or more UK government departments.

What is a venture capitalist firm? It is a company that draws on private equity funds to invest in new businesses with high growth potential, and in exchange it takes a stake in the business (which it subsequently hopes to sell at a profit). A registered firm is one regulated by the FCA.

What UK entrepreneurial seed funding competitions are listed as endorsed on the UK Trade & Investment website? See **7.4.2.2**.

If, after entering the UK, the applicant secures funding, he may be able to apply to switch to the Tier 1 (Entrepreneur) Migrant category (see **7.4**). Otherwise he must leave the UK at the end of his limited leave.

5.4.6 Manufacturing and supply of goods to the UK

An employee of a foreign manufacturer or supplier may install, dismantle, repair, service or advise on equipment, computer software or hardware where it has a contract of purchase or supply or lease with a UK company or organisation.

Home Office guidance is that this activity should normally take less than one month to carry out, given that the applicant will be in employment overseas.

5.4.7 Clients of UK export companies

A client of a UK export company may be seconded to the UK company in order to oversee the requirements for goods and services that are being provided under contract by the UK company or its subsidiary company, provided that the two companies are not part of the same group. Employees may exceptionally make multiple visits to cover the duration of the contract, but there should be a clear end date for the work.

Home Office guidance is that there should be a contract of service between the two companies for the UK company to provide goods and/or services to the overseas company. An example given is that of a UK company contracting defence services to an overseas company.

5.4.8 Science, research and academia

Scientists and researchers may:

(a)   gather information and facts for a specific project that relates directly to their employment overseas; and

(b)   share knowledge or advise on an international project that is being led from the UK, provided the visitor is not carrying out research in the UK.

Researchers and scientists must remain paid and employed overseas, and may only carry out activities that are incidental to their jobs overseas. The Home Office gives the examples of providing advice on an international project, or sharing knowledge on research being conducted overseas.

Academics may:

(a)   take part in formal exchange arrangements with UK counterparts (including doctors);

(b)   carry out research for their own purposes if they are on sabbatical leave from their home institution; and

(c)   if they are eminent senior doctors or dentists, take part in research, teaching or clinical practice, provided this does not amount to filling a permanent teaching post.

An academic can carry out research for his own purposes, such as for a book or for his employment overseas, but the research should not be for commercial gain.

Eminent senior doctors or dentists must have been working for a number of years in their profession. They may come to the UK to take part in research, teaching or clinical practice, as long as this remains incidental to their employment overseas.

Also see **5.9**.

5.4.9   Legal

An overseas lawyer may enter in this category in order to advise a UK-based client on specific international litigation and/or an international transaction.

An expert witness may visit the UK to give evidence in a UK court.

A non-expert witness may visit the UK to attend a court hearing in the UK, but only if summoned in person by a UK court. The decision maker is likely to require evidence to confirm why the witness's attendance in person is necessary, and whether his evidence could be given by video-link instead.

5.4.10   Religion

A religious worker may visit the UK to preach or do pastoral work. The applicant must not be seeking to take up an office, post or appointment in the UK.

What are pastoral duties? Home Office guidance is that these include one-off engagements, such as conducting wedding ceremonies or funerals, provided the applicant will not receive payment and will continue to be in employment overseas.

5.4.11   Creative

An artist, entertainer, or musician may:

(a)   give performances as an individual or as part of a group;

(b)   take part in competitions or auditions;

(c)   make personal appearances and take part in promotional activities; and

(d)   take part in one or more cultural events or festivals on the list of permit-free festivals in Appendix 5 of Appendix V to the Immigration Rules.

Who is an artist? Home Office guidance is that an artist can include anyone coming to the UK to undertake an activity that is connected to the arts. Amateur and professional artists are included, such as poets, film crew, photographers and designers.

Who is an entertainer according to the Home Office? The category includes dancers, comedians, members of circus acts and members of film crew.

Can personal or technical staff (such as conductors, choreographers, stage managers, make-up artists, personal bodyguards and press officers) accompany the artist, entertainer or musician to the UK? Yes, provided they are attending the same event as the applicant and are employed to work for the applicant outside of the UK.

Film crew (including actors, producers, directors and technicians) employed by an overseas company may visit the UK to take part in a location shoot for a film or programme, provided that it is produced and financed overseas.

5.4.12   Sport

A sports person may:

(a)   take part in a sports tournament or sports event as an individual or part of a team;

(b)   make personal appearances and take part in promotional activities;

(c)   take part in trials, provided they are not in front of a paying audience;

(d)   take part in short periods of training, provided he is not being paid by a UK sporting body; and

(e)   join an amateur team or club to gain experience in a particular sport if he is an amateur in that sport.

Sportspersons are able to take part as visitors in tournaments or events in the UK, but not in a professional domestic championship or league, including where one or more of the fixtures or rounds takes place outside the UK. A professional sportsperson who is to be employed by a team based in the UK should apply under Tier 2 or Tier 5 of the points-based system (see **Chapter 7**).

Personal or technical staff of the sportsperson (such as physiotherapists, coaches, dieticians and press officers), as well as sports officials, including referees, assistant referees and umpires, may also enter for these permitted activities, provided they are attending the same event as the sports person.

5.4.13   Overseas business roles requiring specific activities in the UK

It is possible for the following types of professional workers to visit the UK to carry out their work in relation to their employment overseas:

(a)   a translator and/or an interpreter may support a business person in the UK, provided he will attend the same event(s) as the business person and he is employed by that business person outside of the UK;

(b)   personal assistants and bodyguards may support an overseas business person in carrying out permitted activities, provided they will attend the same event(s) as the business person and are employed by him outside the UK. They must not be providing personal care or domestic work for the business person;

(c)   a driver on a genuine international route delivering goods or passengers from abroad to the UK;

(d)   a tour group courier, contracted to a company with its headquarters outside the UK, who is entering and departing the UK with a tour group organised by that company;

(e)   a journalist, correspondent, producer or cameraman gathering information for an overseas publication, programme or film;

(f)   archaeologists taking part in a one-off archaeological excavation;

(g)   a professor from an overseas academic institution accompanying students to the UK as part of a study abroad programme, who may provide a small amount of teaching to the students at the host organisation. However, this must not amount to filling a permanent teaching role for that institution.

5.4.14   Work-related training

Employees of an overseas company or organisation may receive training from a UK-based company or organisation in work practices and techniques required for their employment overseas and not available in their home country.

An employee of an overseas-based training company may deliver a short series of training to employees of a UK-based company, where the trainer is employed by an overseas business contracted to deliver global training to the international corporate group to which the UK-based company belongs.

What is training? Home Office guidance is that it should typically be class-room based and/or involve familiarisation or observation. Is practical training allowed? Yes, provided it does not amount to training on the job or the person filling a role. It is acceptable for a visitor to learn how to use a piece of equipment in the UK, but it must not amount to working for that company in the UK.

Overseas graduates from medical, dental or nursing schools may:

(a)   undertake clinical attachments or dental observer posts provided these are unpaid, and involve no treatment of patients; and

(b)   take certain Home Office-approved tests and examinations.

5.4.15 Study

As we saw at **5.1.2**, a standard visitor's limited leave is subject to a condition of no study, but this does not prohibit the incidental study allowed by the permitted activities. So what is incidental study? It is studying:

(a)   on educational exchanges or visits with a UK state or independent school; or

(b)   a total of up to 30 days on either –

    (i)   recreational courses (but not English language training), or

    (ii)   a short course (which includes English language training) at an accredited institution as defined in Appendix 1 of Appendix V to the Immigration Rules.

As to (a), the children must be in full-time education in their home country, and any teachers or other adults accompanying the group must be employed overseas. Home Office guidance is that exchanges and educational visits should be mainly about broadening horizons and deepening intercultural understanding.

For (b)(i), the Home Office give examples of a visitor coming to the UK for a holiday and undertaking a diving, horse-riding or dancing course. The Home Office accepts that any bona fide institution in the UK can offer recreational courses. However, courses that lead to formal qualifications are not normally considered recreational.

Must the permitted 30 days be completed in just one period? No, it may consist of multiple periods totalling no more than 30 days, for example study in two blocks of 15 days. However, the visitor must not make repeat visits in order to complete a longer course of study that should be carried out under the short-term student route (see **5.13**) or Tier 4 of the points-based system (see **Chapter 6**).

5.4.16 Medical treatment

As to when a visitor may enter the UK to receive private medical treatment, or act as an organ donor or be assessed as a potential organ donor to an identified recipient in the UK, see **5.6** and **5.7** respectively.

5.5 CHILD VISITOR

A child is a person under the age of 18 at the date of applying for a visitor visa. A child might be travelling to the UK alone or with an adult. Usually the purpose of the visit is to see family, but it may be for some short-term educational reason.

5.5.1 Requirements

In addition to meeting the requirements for a standard visitor (see **5.2**), a child applicant must demonstrate that adequate arrangements have been made for his travel to, reception in and care in the UK (see **5.5.1.1**).

What if the child applicant is not applying or travelling with a parent or guardian based in his home country or country of ordinary residence who is responsible for his care? Then that parent or guardian must confirm that he consents to the arrangements for the child's travel to, and reception and care in the UK. Where requested, this consent must be given in writing. What if the child's parents are divorced? Written consent must be given by the parent who has residence or legal custody, or sole responsibility for the child.

Where a child is travelling in the company of an adult, he must hold a visa that identifies the adult with whom he seeks to enter the UK. The identification is by way of the adult's passport number, initial and surname, which is included on the child's visa document.

5.5.1.1 Adequate travel, reception and care arrangements in UK

Where a child is applying to come to the UK as a visitor, he is not expected to have funds in his own name but instead will usually meet the requirement by showing that he has access to funds from his parents, guardians or a third party. Home Office guidance is that where there are no other factors giving cause for concern, this requirement may simply involve the inclusion of the child in the travel and accommodation arrangements of the parent(s), relative(s) or friend(s) accompanying him, or a letter from a relative or friend at the UK address, inviting the child to visit.

What evidence will an ECO require for entry clearance purposes? He will need the name, address and landline telephone number of the parent or carer in the child's home country, the host in the UK and the person accompanying the child. Where these details are missing or unclear, or other factors raise concerns about the child's welfare, further enquiries will be undertaken to confirm the identity and residence of the host, and that the child is expected in the UK. The application will be refused if the ECO remains concerned about the child's welfare in the UK.

Where an immigration officer considering leave to enter has concerns about the child's welfare, the Home Office's policy is that both the social service departments in the host's area and those local to the port of entry should be contacted, so that enquiries can be made to ascertain the host's suitability.

5.6 PRIVATE MEDICAL TREATMENT VISITOR

This provision allows a person who is genuinely seeking entry for the purpose of receiving private medical treatment in the UK to do so. The ECO and immigration officer must be satisfied that he does not intend to seek free treatment under the National Health Service; that he does not represent a danger to public health; that the treatment is of finite duration; and that he has sufficient funds available to pay for the cost of treatment and all other expenses until the treatment ends.

5.6.1 Requirements

An applicant must meet the requirements for a standard visitor (see **5.2**).

If the applicant is suffering from a communicable disease, he must satisfy a Home Office-appointed medical inspector that he is not a danger to public health (see **5.6.1.1**).

The applicant must arrange his private medical treatment before travelling to the UK, and must provide a letter from his doctor or consultant detailing:

(a)   the medical condition requiring consultation or treatment;

(b)   the estimated costs and likely duration of any treatment, which must be of a finite duration (see **5.6.1.2**); and

(c)   where the consultation or treatment will occur.

If the applicant is applying for an 11-month visit visa for the purposes of private medical treatment, he must:

(a)   provide evidence from his medical practitioner in the UK that the proposed treatment is likely to exceed six months but not more than 11 months; and

(b)   if required under the Immigration Rules (para A39 and Appendix T, Part 1), provide a valid medical certificate issued by a Home Office-approved medical practitioner, confirming that he has undergone screening for active pulmonary tuberculosis and that this tuberculosis is not present in the applicant.

5.6.1.1 No danger to public health

A person suffering from a communicable disease may be given leave to enter if he satisfies the medical inspector that there is no danger to public health. However, an applicant who otherwise meets all the requirements may still be refused entry under para V 3.13 of Appendix V if the port medical inspector confirms that his admission is undesirable for medical reasons.

5.6.1.2 Proposed course of treatment is of finite duration

Home Office guidance is that a long period of treatment, for example 11 months, may be acceptable, provided there is a clear need for the patient to be in the UK to receive treatment and he has enough funds to meet all the costs. It is for the decision maker to assess how long treatment is likely to take, for example fertility treatment can go on for some years. With the applicant's consent, the decision maker may speak to the consultant who is due to treat him. If the treatment is open-ended, the application will be refused.

5.7 ORGAN DONOR VISITOR

This provision allows entry by a person who genuinely intends to donate an organ, or who is to be assessed as a potential organ donor to an identified recipient in the UK with whom he has a genetic or close personal relationship

5.7.1 Requirements

An applicant must meet the requirements for a standard visitor (see **5.2**).

An applicant must satisfy the decision maker that he genuinely intends to donate an organ, or that he is to be assessed as a potential organ donor to an identified recipient in the UK with whom he has a genetic or close personal relationship (see **5.7.1.1**).

The applicant must provide written confirmation of medical tests to show that he is a donor match to the identified recipient, or that he is undergoing further tests to be assessed as a potential donor to the identified recipient.

The applicant must provide a letter, dated no more than three months prior to his intended date of arrival in the UK, from either:

(a)   the lead nurse or co-ordinator of the UK's NHS Trust's Living Donor Kidney Transplant team; or

(b)   a UK registered medical practitioner who holds an NHS consultant post, or who appears in the Specialist Register of the General Medical Council.

The letter must confirm that the applicant meets these requirements, and give details of when and where the planned organ transplant or medical tests will take place.

The applicant must be able to demonstrate, if required to do so, that the identified recipient is legally present in the UK, or will be at the time of the planned organ transplant.

5.7.1.1 Genetic or close personal relationship

Home Office guidance is that a genetic relationship exists where the donor is a blood relative to the identified recipient in the UK.

Close personal relationships typically include the visitor's spouse, partner or close friends. They do not extend to relations established via social media campaigns.

5.7.1.2 Persons accompanying a donor

Where a family member, friend or nurse is to accompany the applicant, he must apply as a standard visitor (see **5.2**).

5.8 APPROVED DESTINATION STATUS AGREEMENT VISITOR

The Approved Destination Status Agreement allows groups of Chinese tourists to enter the UK. A very limited number of designated tour operators have been accredited and trained by the British Embassy in China, and these may submit visa applications to the British Embassy for each member of the proposed tour group. The details are to be found in para V 4.21.

5.9 ACADEMIC VISITOR IN EXCESS OF SIX MONTHS

Academics who wish to apply for a 12-month visit visa, or an extension for up to 12 months, must be highly qualified within their field of expertise and working in that area before entering the UK. This will generally apply to people with at least a PhD in their field.

5.9.1 Requirements

An applicant must meet the requirements for a standard visitor (see **5.2**).

An applicant must satisfy the decision maker that he intends to carry out one or more of the permitted activities set out at **5.4.8**. In addition, he must be highly qualified within his own field of expertise, and currently working in that field at an academic institution or institution of higher education overseas.

If required under the Immigration Rules (para A39 and Appendix T Part 1), the applicant must provide a valid medical certificate issued by a Home Office-approved medical practitioner confirming that he has undergone screening for active pulmonary tuberculosis and that this tuberculosis is not present in the applicant.

5.10 MARRIAGE AND CIVIL PARTNERSHIP VISITOR

If a person wishes to enter the UK to marry or to enter into a civil partnership, this route may be used, provided, of course, that the couple do not intend to stay in the UK after the marriage or civil partnership ceremony.

If the couple wish to remain in the UK permanently, the applicant should apply as a fiancé(e) or proposed civil partner (see **8.7**).

5.10.1 Requirements

An applicant must meet the requirements for a standard visitor (see **5.2**).

An applicant must be aged 18 or over.

An applicant must satisfy the decision maker that he intends, within the validity period covered by his visit visa, to give notice of marriage or civil partnership, or to marry or form a civil partnership. That must not be a sham marriage or sham civil partnership (see **5.10.1.1**).

On arrival in the UK, a visitor coming to marry or form a civil partnership, or give notice of this in the UK, must have a valid visit visa endorsed with this purpose and the name of his or her fiancé(e) or proposed civil partner.

5.10.1.1   Sham marriage or sham civil partnership

What is the sham here? That the marriage or civil partnership is to be entered into for the purpose of avoiding the effect of one or more provisions of UK immigration law or the Immigration Rules (see further **4.4.6.2** and **8.3.5.5**).

5.11   PERMITTED PAID ENGAGEMENT (PPE) VISITOR

What if a UK higher education institution wants to pay a visiting academic to examine its students, chair a selection panel, or give one or more lectures? Or what if a person wants to pay an advocate to act for him at a court or tribunal hearing, arbitration or other form of alternative dispute resolution process in the UK? Or say that a UK-based arts or sports organisation or broadcaster wants to pay a professional artist, entertainer or sports person to carry out activities relating to his main profession. In these circumstances, but strictly limited to those activities listed in Appendix 4 of Appendix V to the Immigration Rules, an applicant may apply as a PPE visitor.

5.11.1   Requirements

An applicant must meet the requirements for a standard visitor (see **5.2**).

An applicant must intend to do one or more of the permitted paid engagements set out in Appendix 4 of Appendix V to the Immigration Rules. The activity must be:

(a)   arranged before the applicant travels to the UK,

(b)   declared as part of the application for a visit visa or leave to enter; and

(c)   evidenced by a formal invitation as required by Appendix 4.

In addition, the activity must relate to the applicant's area of expertise and occupation overseas.

An applicant must not be a child.

This is an alternative route to requiring sponsorship under the points-based system for these activities (see **Chapter 7**).

5.12   TRANSIT VISITOR

Who is a visitor in transit? This refers to any passenger whose sole purpose is to pass through the UK within 48 hours and who either:

(a)   arrives at one port or airport and needs to transfer to another port or airport to continue his journey; or

(b)   wishes to spend the time between his arrival and embarkation outside the transit area (ie pass through immigration controls at the port or airport).

Full details can be found in Part V7 of Appendix V to the Immigration Rules.

5.13   SHORT-TERM STUDY VISA

There are three potential short-term study visa categories:

(a)   a short-term student (six months) for applicants aged 18 and over for a maximum of six months' study;

(b)   a short-term student (11 months) for applicants aged 18 and over for a maximum of 11 months' English language study only;

(c)   a short-term student (child) for applicants aged under 18 for a maximum of six months' study.

Full details can be found in paras A57A to A57H of the Immigration Rules and the relevant Home Office guidance.

STUDENTS

6.1 WHO IS A STUDENT?

6.1.1 Tier 4 of the points-based system

Part 6A of the Immigration Rules deals with the points-based system of entry to the UK. Students come within Tier 4. The other tiers deal with working and conducting business in the UK (see **Chapter 7**).

There are two main types of student categories in Tier 4. First, an adult student, known in the Immigration Rules as a Tier 4 (General) Student. Here an adult is any person coming to the UK for post-16 education. We shall focus on this category in this chapter, as it attracts a large number of applicants. Secondly, a child student or a Tier 4 (Child) Student. This category covers children aged between 4 and 17 who wish to enter the UK for their education. Note that a child aged between 4 and 15 may be educated only at an independent fee-paying school. The details of this second category, which has a limited number of applicants, are beyond the scope of this book.

The following special considerations apply to a student aged 16 or 17:

(a) If he wants to study a course at National Qualification Framework (NQF) level 3 or above, he can apply as an adult or a child student, but if the course is longer than two years, the Home Office recommends that the application is made as an adult student. If he is proposing to study a course below NQF level 3, he must apply as a child student. Note that the NQF sets out the levels against which a qualification may be recognised in England, Wales and Northern Ireland. Broadly, the levels are as follows: 1 (GCSE at grades D–G), 2 (GCSE at grades A★–C), 3 (A Level), 4 (Certificate of Higher Education), 5 (HND, HNC), 6 (Bachelor's degree), 7 (Master's degree) and 8 (Doctorate). Full details can be found at www.qcda.gov.uk.

(b) If he wants to study for an English language qualification at the Common European Framework of Reference for Languages (CEFRL) level A2 or above, he must apply as an adult student. Note that the CEFRL provides a basis for the mutual recognition of language qualifications in the EEA.

For further details of the courses that may be studied, see **6.3.2.4**.

All students can enter to study at a Home Office-approved education provider only (see **6.2**). This is otherwise known as sponsorship.

6.1.2 Entry clearance

All Tier 4 students must apply for entry clearance. As part of the visa or entry certificate application they must produce certain documentation (see **6.3.2**) from the Home Office-approved educational institution at which they will be studying in the UK.

6.2 SPONSORSHIP: APPROVED EDUCATION PROVIDER

6.2.1 Obtaining a licence from the Home Office

All education providers that want to provide courses for international students need a licence from the Home Office. One key step is for the provider to obtain a satisfactory review or inspection by one of the publicly recognised inspection bodies approved for Tier 4 purposes (namely Ofsted and its equivalents in the devolved administrations, the Quality Assurance Agency and the Department for Education-approved inspectorates for independent schools). In addition, a provider must be able to show that it has allocated a number of key roles to its staff using the Home Office online sponsorship management system; it can comply with its sponsorship duties; and it has the appropriate human resource systems in place to be able to monitor its students' attendance.

For ease of reference, throughout the rest of this chapter we shall refer to an approved education provider as the 'sponsor'.

6.2.2 Sponsorship duties

The key duties of a sponsor are to keep copies of all students' passports, to keep up-to-date contact details for students, and to tell the Home Office if a student has any unauthorised absences, fails to enrol on his course or stops his studies.

6.2.3 Tier 4 register

Once a sponsor has a licence, it is added to the Tier 4 register with details of its name and location. The register can be found on the Home Office website (see **1.2.8**).

6.3 TIER 4 (GENERAL) STUDENT

6.3.1 Requirements

Paragraph 245ZV provides that to qualify for entry clearance as a Tier 4 (General) Student, an applicant must meet the following key requirements:

(a) The application must not fall for refusal under the general grounds for refusal (see **3.5.4**).

(b) The applicant must have a minimum of 30 points under paras 113 to 119 of Appendix A ('Sponsorship' – see **6.3.2**).

(c) The applicant must have a minimum of 10 points under paras 10 to 13 of Appendix C ('Maintenance' – see **6.3.3**).

(d) The applicant must, if required to do so on examination or interview, be able to demonstrate, without the assistance of an interpreter, English language proficiency of a standard to be expected from an individual who has reached the standard specified in his CAS (see **6.3.2.1**). Home Office guidance is that the applicant will not be subject to a test at the standard set for his CAS.

(e) The ECO must be satisfied that the applicant is a genuine student. Home Office guidance is that refusal on this ground will normally occur only after the applicant has been interviewed. In 2012 the Government announced that following a successful pilot, a targeted interview system for students was being introduced, concentrating on so-called high-risk applicants. An applicant may be interviewed (in person or on the telephone) and asked a number of questions about his immigration and education history, study and post-study plans, as well as his financial circumstances. One thing the ECO will look for is the standard of English used by the applicant at the interview (see (d) above). Up to 14,000 students are expected to be interviewed each year. See further **6.3.4**.

An applicant therefore needs to score 40 points to qualify. Although the wording of para 245ZV(b) and (c) suggests that a range of points may be available to collect to meet the minimum required, the tests in Appendix A and Appendix C in fact only have 30 and 10 points available each, so either the applicant scores the necessary number of points by meeting the tests or he does not.

6.3.2 Sponsorship points

A Tier 4 (General) Student is awarded 30 points only if he has obtained from a sponsor a confirmation of acceptance for studies.

6.3.2.1 The Confirmation of Acceptance for Studies

Once a sponsor has been granted a licence, the sponsor can access the Home Office's IT sponsorship management system. This may be used to create and assign a Confirmation of Acceptance for Studies (CAS). This is therefore not an actual certificate or paper document. It is a virtual document similar to a database record. Each CAS has a unique reference number and contains information about the course of study for which it has been issued and the student's personal details.

An application for entry clearance or leave to remain must be made no more than three months before the start date of the course of study as stated on the CAS. A CAS expires if it is not used to apply for entry clearance or leave within six months of being issued. In addition, a CAS can be used only once.

Before allocating a CAS, the sponsor must ensure that the student is competent in English language at a set minimum level. This is met if the student is a national of a Home Office-recognised majority English-speaking country (see the list at **7.4.3.2**) or has successfully completed an academic qualification, at least equivalent to a UK Bachelor's degree, which was taught in a Home Office-recognised majority English-speaking country (see the list at **7.4.3.3**). Otherwise, the student must have passed an approved English language test that is still within its validity date. Normally a student must demonstrate knowledge of English equivalent to level B2 of the Council of Europe's Common European Framework for Language Learning, or above. Details are on the Council's website at <www.coe.int/T/DG4/Linguistic/CADRE_EN.asp>. A list of Home Office-approved test providers and their contact details are on the Home Office website.

6.3.2.2 Supporting documents

In order to be awarded points, the applicant must also supply documentary evidence, such as qualification certificates and references, that he used to obtain the offer of the place on the course from the sponsor. The specified documents are listed in para 120-SD of Appendix A to the Immigration Rules.

Note that students who are nationals of the countries listed in Appendix H to the Immigration Rules – currently Argentina, Australia, Barbados, Botswana, Brunei, Canada, Chile, Hong Kong, Japan, Malaysia, New Zealand, Oman, Qatar, Singapore, South Korea, Taiwan, Trinidad and Tobago, United Arab Emirates and the United States of America – who apply for entry clearance in their country of nationality or for leave to remain in the UK, are treated by the Home Office as 'low risk' and so generally do not have to produce any supporting documents (see also **6.3.3.2**) unless required by the Home Office to do so. Evidence of the student's nationality will be his passport. A 'low risk' student has to confirm that he meets the points requirements on his visa or entry clearance application form and that he has the required documentary evidence. Entry clearance officers do spot checks and sometimes require such a student to send the documents.

6.3.2.3 Re-sitting examinations or repeating course module

If an applicant is re-sitting examinations or repeating a module of a course, he must not previously have re-sat the same examination or repeated the same module more than once. If this requirement is not met, no points will be awarded.

If a student's leave will expire before he is able to re-sit an exam, he will not get an extension as a Tier 4 student unless he scores the required points. It is therefore not possible for a student to remain in the UK just to re-sit an exam. Such a student is expected to leave the UK and revise for the re-sit in his own country (or at least outside the UK). The student should then seek entry to take the re-sit exam as a student visitor (see *RS (Pakistan) v Secretary of State for the Home Department* [2011] EWCA Civ 434 and **5.5**).

6.3.2.4 Academic requirements and approved qualifications

Points are awarded only if the course in respect of which the confirmation is issued satisfies each of the following requirements:

(a)   The course must meet the Home Office's minimum academic requirements and must lead to an approved qualification. The minimum academic requirement is that the course must be a full-time course of study, as either:

(i)   a full-time course of study that leads to a UK-recognised bachelor degree, postgraduate degree, postgraduate diploma or postgraduate certificate;

(ii)   an overseas course of degree level study that is recognised as being equivalent to a UK Higher Education course and is being provided by an overseas Higher Education Institution; or

(iii)   a full-time course of study involving a minimum of 15 hours per week organised daytime study and, except in the case of a pre-sessional course, lead to a qualification below bachelor degree level.

The following are approved qualifications:

(i)   level 3 or the same as or above on the NQF (see **6.1.1**);

(ii)   short-term study abroad programmes in the UK as part of a qualification at an overseas higher education institution, as long as the qualification is confirmed as the same as a UK degree level by the National Academic Recognition Information Centre for the United Kingdom (UK NARIC) (see **7.4.3.3**).

(iii)   an English language course at level B2 or above of the CEFRL (see **6.1.1**).

(b)   Other than when the applicant is actually on a work placement (see **6.6.2**), all study that forms part of the course must take place on the premises of the sponsor.

6.3.3 Maintenance points

6.3.3.1 How much maintenance?

To score the required 10 points, the level of maintenance funds that the applicant will have to show that he has available depends on two factors: how long the course is, and where the course is being studied.

If the applicant has already paid to his sponsor some of his course fees (this may include expenditure on study materials, such as books, purchased from the sponsor), that amount may be deducted from the total required provided that it is confirmed in the CAS or the student is able to produce an original paper receipt issued by his sponsor.

What if the Tier 4 (General) Student will be staying in accommodation provided by his sponsor (eg halls of residence) and he has already paid towards it? In these circumstances, up to a maximum of £1,265 may be deducted from the total required (but no more than that, even if the student has paid in excess of £1,265). Again, either the amount paid must be included in the student's CAS, or the student must produce the sponsor's original written receipt.

If the applicant is receiving all or any of his funding from an official financial sponsorship or government sponsor, see **6.3.3.3**.

Table 6.1 below sets out the details regarding maintenance funds.

Table 6.1 Amount of maintenance funds dependent on length of course and location

Length of course	Location	Amount of maintenance funds needed
Nine months or less	In London	Course fees and £1,265 to cover living costs for each calendar month (or any part of a month) of the course
Nine months or less	Outside London or anywhere else in the UK	Course fees and £820 to cover living costs for each calendar month (or any part of a month) of the course
More than nine months	In London	First year's course fees and £11,385 to cover living costs for the first nine months in the UK
More than nine months	Outside London or anywhere else in the UK	First year's course fees and £7,380 to cover living costs for the first nine months in the UK

When is a Tier 4 (General) Student considered to be studying in London? The answer is if more than 50% of his study time is spent studying at the University of London, or institutions wholly or partly within the area comprising the City of London and the Former Metropolitan Police District as defined in para 12AA of Appendix C to the Immigration Rules.

6.3.3.2 Supporting documents

The money to be used for the applicant's maintenance must be in the form of cash. Shares, bonds, pension funds and similar savings accounts are not acceptable.

The applicant will need to produce documentary evidence to show that the minimum level of maintenance funds has been available to him for a consecutive period of at least 28 days ending no more than 31 days before the date of the application. Provided it covers that period, any of the following documents are acceptable (provided it meets all of the detailed requirements of para 1B of Appendix C to the Immigration Rules):

(a) personal bank or building society statements;

(b) a building society pass book;

(c) a letter from the applicant's bank confirming that the funds are available;

(d) a letter from a financial institution regulated either by the FCA or, in the case of overseas accounts, the home regulator (official regulatory body for the country the institution is in and where the money is held) confirming that the funds are available;

(e)   a letter from a financial institution regulated either by the FCA or, in the case of overseas accounts, the home regulator (official regulatory body for the country the institution is in and where the money is held) confirming that the funds are available as a loan.

The applicant's specified financial documents must be from institutions acceptable to the Home Office. A check should always be made in Appendix P to the Immigration Rules, where there are lists of financial institutions approved or not approved for certain countries (currently Sri Lanka, Bangladesh, Cameroon, India, Ghana, Pakistan, Iran and The Philippines).

What if a student is relying on money held by a parent or legal guardian? In addition to providing the above evidence of available funds, the applicant will have to produce:

(a)   evidence of the relationship, eg the student's birth certificate showing the names of his parent(s), or the student's certificate of adoption showing the names of his parent(s) or legal guardian, or a court document naming his legal guardian. The original document or a notarised copy must be produced;

(b)   a letter from his parent(s) or legal guardian confirming the relationship and consenting to the student using their funds to study in the UK.

Remember that if the student is 'low risk' (see **6.3.2.2**), he will have to produce documentation only if required.

6.3.3.3   Official financial sponsorship

An applicant might receive financial help from the UK Government, his home government, the British Council or any international organisation, company or university.

Details must either be set out in the CAS, or a letter is required from any official financial sponsor confirming the length of the sponsorship, that it will cover all of the applicant's fees and living costs, or the amount available. The applicant must produce evidence to meet any shortfall.

6.3.3.4   Family members

If an applicant is bringing any family members (spouse, civil partner, unmarried or same-sex partner and children under 18) with him, he will have to demonstrate that additional maintenance funds are available (see **6.8**).

6.3.4   Genuine student

Home Office guidance is that when assessing whether the applicant is a genuine student, the ECO must consider the application in the round and might take into account factors such as:

(a)   the immigration history of the applicant in the UK and other countries; and

(b)   the applicant's education history, study and post-study plans. So an ECO might ask: How long has elapsed since the applicant last studied? Does the applicant have sound reasons for returning to, or commencing, formal study in this area, particularly after any significant gap? What is the applicant's knowledge of, and level of research undertaken into, the proposed course of study and sponsoring institution, and living arrangements in the UK? What are the applicant's personal circumstances, and would these make it difficult to complete a full-time course of study? What is the relevance of the course to the applicant's post-study plans?

Home Office guidance is that whether the applicant has the academic ability to study the proposed course is not a relevant consideration for the ECO and should not form part of any conclusion reached. The academic ability of the applicant is a judgement for the sponsor to make with the benefit of its educational expertise. Similarly, the fact that the course does not represent academic progression is not a decisive factor.

The relevance of the course to post-study plans, or vagueness about the nature of post-study plans, should not be used as a sole reason to refuse an applicant; rather, it is one of a range of factors to be considered. In this context, whether the course will add to the applicant's employability, or whether the course could be undertaken more cheaply in the applicant's home country, should not be taken into account.

For those considered to be genuine students, intention to leave the UK at the end of the course is not relevant as there are many bases on which an individual might lawfully remain in the UK.

6.4 LEAVE TO ENTER THE UK

If granted entry clearance, how long will a Tier 4 (General) Student get as limited leave in the UK? The answer depends on the nature and length of the course, as set out in **Table 6.2** below.

Table 6.2   Amount of limited leave

Length of course	Amount of limited leave granted
Less than six months	The full length of the course plus one month after the end of the course
At least six months but less than 12 months	The full length of the course plus two months after the end of the course
12 months or more	The full length of the course plus four months after the end of the course
Postgraduate doctor or dentist	The full length of the course (up to a maximum of three years) plus one month after the end of the course

Note that if a Tier 4 (General) Student has an official financial sponsor (see **6.3.3.3**) who pays all his fees and living expenses but limits the time the student may study in the UK, the permission to stay is limited to the same length of time plus the usual post-course period specified in **Table 6.2**.

6.5 EXTENDING LIMITED LEAVE

After finishing one course, a Tier 4 (General) Student may wish to take another course. In these circumstances the student will need to meet the same requirements as he did to secure entry clearance (see **6.3.1** above). The only difference will be as to the level of maintenance required if the student has within the last four months completed a course of at least six months' duration. In such a case, the figures in **Table 6.3** below will apply.

Table 6.3   Amount of maintenance funds required for extending limited leave

Length of course	Location	Amount of maintenance funds needed
Two months or less	In London	Course fees and £1,265 to cover living costs for each calendar month of the course up to a maximum of two months
Two months or less	Outside London or anywhere else in the UK	Course fees and £820 to cover living costs for each calendar month of the course up to a maximum of two months
More than two months	In London	First year's course fees and £2,530 to cover the first two months of living costs in the UK

Length of course	Location	Amount of maintenance funds needed
More than two months	Outside London or anywhere else in the UK	First year's course fees and £1,640 to cover the first two months of living costs in the UK

Note that there are limits as to how long a Tier 4 (General) Student may study in the UK. Generally, it is for a maximum of two years studying at below degree level and five years at degree level or above. In certain circumstances this may be extended to six years when doing a master's degree and eight years for a PhD (see para 245ZX(h)(ha) of the Immigration Rules). Note that the five years or more limits operate in addition to the maximum time permitted for studying at below degree level.

6.6 WHAT CAN A TIER 4 (GENERAL) STUDENT DO IN ADDITION TO STUDYING?

6.6.1 Students' union sabbatical officer

A students' union sabbatical post is a full-time, salaried, elected executive union position. A Tier 4 (General) Student may take up this post for a maximum of two years, either during his course of study or in the academic year immediately after he graduates. The post must be at the institution which is the student's sponsor.

6.6.2 Work placement

A course of study for a Tier 4 (General) Student may include a work placement, but it must not exceed one-third of the length of a non-degree course or half of the length of a degree course in the UK, unless the student is doing a course where there is a statutory requirement for it to contain a specific period of work placement.

For example, if a degree course is two years long, the first year of the course might involve full-time study and the last year might involve a work placement.

In addition, the work placement must form an assessed part of the course.

A sponsor remains responsible for the student throughout the term of his work placement, and must continue to comply with all the sponsor duties throughout this time.

6.6.3 Extra studies

Tier 4 (General) Students are allowed to undertake supplementary courses, for example evening classes. These do not need to relate to the course of study for which the student was granted entry clearance or leave. No permission is needed and the student does not have to inform his sponsor.

6.6.4 Employment

A Tier 4 (General) Student following a course with a sponsor which is a UK higher education institution, or on a short-term study abroad degree programme at an overseas higher education institution, may work whilst in the UK. This is in addition to any work placement (see **6.6.2**) he is doing as part of his course. However, the student must not fill a full-time, permanent vacancy (other than on a recognised Foundation Programme).

Students may work full time during vacations, but only part time for a prescribed maximum number of hours during term time. What are the limits?

(a)   Students following a course at NQF 6 (Bachelor's degree level) or above with a sponsor which is a UK higher education institution, or undertaking a short-term study abroad degree programme at an overseas higher education institution, can work for no more than 20 hours per week in term time.

(b)   Students following a course at NQF 3, 4 or 5 (below degree level) with a sponsor which is a UK higher education institution can work for no more than 10 hours per week in term time.

Students following a course at any level with a sponsor which is a publicly-funded further education college are not entitled to work.

The following categories of employment are not permitted at any time:

(a)   self-employment;

(b)   employment as a doctor in training (other than on a recognised Foundation Programme);

(c)   employment as a professional sports person (including a sports coach); and

(d)   employment as an entertainer.

6.7 CONDITIONS ATTACHED TO LEAVE

A Tier 4 (General) Student's limited leave is subject to the following conditions:

(a)   no recourse to public funds (see **3.3.2**);

(b)   registration with the police, if this is required (see **3.3.3**);

(c)   no employment except:

    (i)   (as detailed at **6.6.4**),

    (ii)   employment as part of a course-related work placement (see **6.6.2**),

    (iii)   employment as a Student Union Sabbatical Officer, for up to two years, provided the post is elective and is at the institution which is the applicant's sponsor (see **6.6.1**);

(d)   no study except:

    (i)   study at the institution that the Home Office records as the migrant's sponsor;

    (ii)   supplementary study (see **6.6.3**).

Note the effect of condition (d)(i) is to tie the student's leave to his sponsor. So a student cannot lawfully change courses and study with a different sponsor without obtaining a CAS from the new sponsor and further leave to remain from the Home Office.

6.8 FAMILY MEMBERS OF A TIER 4 (GENERAL) STUDENT

6.8.1 Entry clearance and leave to remain and permission to work

Can all Tier 4 (General) Students bring their family members to the UK? No. So who can? Only either:

(a)   students sponsored by a higher education institution on a course at NQF level 7 or above that lasts 12 months or more; or

(b)   Government-sponsored students following a course that is longer than six months.

Who are family members? If subject to immigration controls, the spouse, civil partner, unmarried or same-sex partner ('the Partner') and children under 18 will require entry clearance in order to enter the UK as the family member. If relevant, they should subsequently apply for an extension at the same time as the Tier 4 (General) Student.

Note that such a family member is able to work in the UK.

6.8.2 Partner

6.8.2.1 Requirements

The requirements are set out in para 319C, as follows:

(a)   The applicant must not fall for refusal under the general grounds for refusal (see **3.5.4**) and, if applying for leave to remain, must not be an illegal entrant (see **10.4.2**).

(b)   The applicant must be the spouse or civil partner, unmarried or same-sex partner of a person who:

    (i)   has valid leave to enter or remain as a Tier 4 (General) Student; or

    (ii)   is, at the same time, being granted entry clearance or leave to remain as a Tier 4 (General) Student.

(c)   An applicant who is the unmarried or same-sex partner of a Tier 4 (General) Student must also meet the following requirements:

    (i)   any previous marriage or civil partnership or similar relationship by the applicant or the Tier 4 (General) Student with another person must have permanently broken down;

    (ii)   the applicant and the Tier 4 (General) Student must not be so closely related that they would be prohibited from marrying each other in the UK; and

    (iii) the applicant and the Tier 4 (General) Student must have been living together in a relationship similar to marriage or civil partnership for a period of at least two years (see further **Chapter 8**).

(d)   The marriage or civil partnership, or relationship similar to marriage or civil partnership, must be subsisting at the time the application is made.

(e)   The applicant and the Tier 4 (General) Student must intend to live with the other as their spouse or civil partner, unmarried or same-sex partner throughout the applicant's stay in the UK.

(f)   The applicant must not intend to stay in the UK beyond any period of leave granted to the Tier 4 (General) Student.

(g)   There must be a sufficient level of funds available to the applicant, as set out in Appendix E.

6.8.2.2   Maintenance funds

As to (g) in **6.8.2.1** above, the same requirements for available maintenance funds apply to a partner as to an applicant (see **6.3.3**). Appendix E to the Immigration Rules (see **Appendix 1**) sets out the following requirements:

(a)   If the Tier 4 Migrant is studying in London, there must be £845 in funds for each month for which the applicant would, if successful, be granted leave, up to a maximum of nine months.

(b)   If the Tier 4 Migrant is studying outside London, there must be £680 in funds for each month for which the applicant would, if successful, be granted leave, up to a maximum of nine months.

> **EXAMPLE**
>
> Anne applies for entry clearance as a Tier 4 (General) Student. She has a CAS issued by a London-based sponsor. She has a place on a 24-month master's degree course. She does not have an official financial sponsor. She has not yet paid anything towards her course fees or the accommodation arranged by her sponsor. Her civil partner, Brenda, will be travelling with her. In addition to meeting the requirements of para 319C(a)–(f) above, what maintenance funds under (g) do they need to have available? Anne needs the amount of her first year's course fees and £11,385 to cover living costs for the first nine months in the UK (see **6.3.3.1**). As she will get 28 months' leave (see **6.4**), there must be the maximum additional amount available for Brenda of £7,605.

6.8.2.3   Leave and conditions

If the application is successful, the partner is granted entry clearance and leave to remain for a period which expires on the same day as the leave granted to the Tier 4 (General) Student.

That leave will be subject to conditions not to have recourse to public funds and registration with the police, if this is required (see **3.3.2** and **3.3.3** respectively).

6.8.3 Child

6.8.3.1 Requirements

The requirements are set out in para 319H, as follows:

(a) The applicant must not fall for refusal under the general grounds for refusal (see **3.5.4**) and, if applying for leave to remain, must not be an illegal entrant (see **10.2.2**).

(b) The applicant must be the child of a parent who:

   (i)   has valid leave to enter or remain as a Tier 4 (General) Student; or

   (ii) is, at the same time, being granted entry clearance or leave to remain as a Tier 4 (General) Student.

(c) The applicant must be under the age of 18 on the date the application is made, or if over 18 and applying for leave to remain, must have, or have last been granted, leave as the child of a Tier 4 (General) Student.

(d) The applicant must not be married or in a civil partnership, must not have formed an independent family unit, and must not be leading an independent life. See further **Chapter 8.**

(e) The applicant must not intend to stay in the UK beyond any period of leave granted to the Tier 4 (General) Student parent.

(f) Both of the applicant's parents must either be lawfully present in the UK, or being granted entry clearance or leave to remain at the same time as the applicant, unless:

   (i)   the Tier 4 (General) Student is the applicant's sole surviving parent; or

   (ii) the Tier 4 (General) Student parent has and has had sole responsibility for the applicant's upbringing (see **Chapter 8**); or

   (iii) there are serious or compelling family or other considerations which would make it desirable not to refuse the application and suitable arrangements have been made in the UK for the applicant's care (see **Chapter 8**).

(g) There must be a sufficient level of funds available to the applicant, as set out in Appendix E.

It is important to note the effect of (c) above in respect of a child now aged 18 or over. That child will still qualify for an extension of leave in this category, provided he had previously obtained such leave when under 18.

6.8.3.2 Maintenance funds

As to (g) in **6.8.3.1** above, the additional available maintenance funds are exactly the same as for any partner (**6.8.2.2**).

> **EXAMPLE**
>
> Lewis applies for entry clearance as a Tier 4 (General) Student. He has a CAS issued by a sponsor based outside London. He has a place on a 12-month master's degree course. He does not have an official financial sponsor. He has not yet paid his course fees. He is not using accommodation arranged by his sponsor. His wife, Alice, and 6-year-old son, John, will be travelling with him. In addition to meeting the requirements of paras 319C and 319F(a)–(f) respectively, what maintenance funds under (g) do they need to have available? Lewis needs the amount of his course fees and £7,380 to cover living costs for the first nine months in the UK (see **6.3.3.1**). As he will get 16 months' leave (see **6.4**), there must be the maximum additional amount available for his wife, Alice, of £6,120 and also the maximum additional amount available for his son, John, of £6,120.

6.8.3.3   Leave and conditions

If the application is successful, the child is granted entry clearance and leave to remain for a period which expires on the same day as the leave granted to his Tier 4 (General) Student parent. This will be subject to conditions of no recourse to public funds and registration with the police, if this is required (see **3.3.2** and **3.3.3** respectively).

6.9   WHO CAN SWITCH TO BECOME A TIER 4 (GENERAL) STUDENT?

The following migrants already in the UK may switch from their current category and apply for leave to remain as a Tier 4 (General) Student, namely a:

(a)   Tier 2 General Migrant (see **7.9**);

(b)   Tier 2 Intra-Company Transfer Migrant (see **7.9**);

(c)   Tier 2 Minister of Religion (see **7.10**);

(d)   Tier 4 Child Student (see **6.1.1**).

6.10   TIER 4 (GENERAL) STUDENT SWITCHING TO ANOTHER CATEGORY

A Tier 4 (General) Student may be able to switch categories whilst in the UK. The most usual routes would be into the category of a Tier 1 (Entrepreneur) Migrant (see **7.4**), Tier 1 (Investor) Migrant (see **7.5**), Tier 2 Migrant (see **7.7**), the spouse, or civil partner or the same-sex partner of a person settled in the UK (see **Chapter 8**).

Note that if a Tier 4 (General) Student switches to a category that may lead to settlement, the time spent in the student category cannot count towards the time needed to qualify for settlement.

6.11   SUMMARY OF POINTS AND EVIDENCE REQUIRED FOR A TIER 4 (GENERAL) STUDENT

Points	How obtained	Evidence required
30	Sponsorship – studying a course that meets the Home Office's minimum academic requirements and leads to an approved qualification with a licensed education provider (see **6.3.2**).	Confirmation of acceptance for studies from the sponsor with supporting documents (see **6.3.2**).
10	Maintenance – having enough cash available to pay course fees and monthly living costs (see **6.3.3**).	Bank statement or letter confirming level of cash funds (see **6.3.3.2**). It must be shown that the applicant has held the money for at least 28 days ending no more than 31 days before the date of the application.

CHAPTER 7

EMPLOYMENT, BUSINESS AND INVESTMENT

7.1 INTRODUCTION

7.1.1 Who can work, conduct business or invest in the UK?

In this chapter we shall consider entry to the UK for the specific purpose of working, conducting business or investing.

Nationals of the EEA can work, conduct business and invest in the UK exercising their EU Treaty rights (see **Chapter 4**). If a UK business wants to employ an EEA national, it will not have to use any of the domestic law routes of entry dealt with in this chapter.

A general visitor (see **5.1.2**) is prohibited from working. A student (see **6.6.4**) is restricted as to what work he may do. But the following people may freely carry out any of these activities:

(a) anyone admitted for settlement (see **Chapter 8**);

(b) anyone given limited leave with a view to settlement, eg spouses, civil partners and those in a non-marital relationship (see **Chapter 8**);

(c) refugees and those granted humanitarian protection (see **Chapter 9**);

(d) anyone admitted, without prohibition on employment, as the dependant of someone with limited leave in the UK, eg the spouse or civil partner of a Tier 1 or Tier 2 Migrant (see **7.6** and **7.8.9**).

7.1.2 Overview of the categories covered in this chapter

A person seeking to enter the UK may fall into one of the following categories:

(a) A person with officially recognised 'exceptional talent' in the field of science, humanities, engineering or the arts; an entrepreneur (business person); a graduate with officially recognised entrepreneurial skills; and an investor. These are known as *Tier 1 Migrants*. They form part of a points-based system detailed in paras 245AA to 245DF.

In the Immigration Rules, these Tier 1 Migrants (apart from those with exceptional talent and the graduate entrepreneur) are normally given limited leave initially for three years. This may be extended for two years, followed by an application for settlement. Note that in certain circumstances an entrepreneur or investor may be able to apply for settlement earlier. The graduate entrepreneur may be allowed two periods of limited leave to remain of 12 months, but is expected either then to depart the UK or to switch into another category, such as an entrepreneur. Those with exceptional talent are normally given limited leave for five years.

See further **7.2**.

(b)   A skilled (general) worker, minister of religion or sports person. These applicants are known as *Tier 2 Migrants* and form part of the points system detailed in the Immigration Rules, paras 245G to 245HF. Each person must have a UK-based sponsor who is licensed by the Home Office. Limited leave is initially for three years. This may be extended for two years, followed by an application for settlement. See further **7.8**.

(c)   Temporary work in the creative and sporting sector, charity and religious workers, government authorised exchange workers, workers under an international agreement and workers under a youth mobility scheme. These are known as *Tier 5 Migrants* and form part of the points system detailed in the Immigration Rules, paras 245ZI to 245ZS. Each category has its own sponsorship arrangements. As this tier provides for temporary work only, leave is usually limited to one or two years and cannot lead to settlement. See further **7.12**.

(d)   A sole representative of an overseas firm who will establish a wholly-owned subsidiary or branch in the UK. This is a long-standing category and it is not part of the points system. The requirements are set out in para 144 of the Immigration Rules. A person who meets the requirements is given three years' limited leave. That may be extended for two years, followed by an application for settlement. See further **7.13**.

(e)   A Commonwealth citizen with a UK-born grandparent. This is a long-standing category reflecting the UK's historical links with the Commonwealth. It is not part of the points system. The requirements are set out in para 186 of the Immigration Rules. A person who meets the requirements may enter the UK to look for, or take up, work. Five years' limited leave is given, after which an application for settlement can be made. See further **7.14**.

Note that at the time of writing the Government has indicated that it does not intend to implement Tier 3 for low-skilled workers for the foreseeable future.

7.2   OVERVIEW OF TIER 1

7.2.1   A profile of each category

7.2.1.1   Exceptional talent

This category allows a person who is internationally recognised as a world leader or potential world-leading talent in the field of science, humanities, engineering or the arts to work in the UK, provided he has the official endorsement of a Home Office-specified Designated Competent Body (DCB).

7.2.1.2   Entrepreneur

This category might otherwise be called the 'business person' route into the UK. The individual (or team of two entrepreneurs) must be investing in the UK. How? By either setting up a new business, or joining or taking over an existing business. Note that the minimum investment in a business is either £200,000 from any source, or £50,000 from a Home Office-approved source such as a registered and regulated venture capital firm.

7.2.1.3 Investor

This category is for an individual who is able to make substantial financial investment of at least £2 million in the UK.

7.2.1.4 Graduate entrepreneur

This category allows a graduate from a Home Office-approved UK Higher Education Institution, who has been identified as having developed world-class innovative ideas or entrepreneurial skills, to stay in the UK after graduation to establish one or more businesses in the UK. Leave is normally only for 12 months (with the possibility of one 12-month extension) and then the person is expected to depart the UK or switch into another category, such as an entrepreneur.

7.2.2 Common features: entry clearance

7.2.2.1 Points system

An entrepreneur and a graduate entrepreneur are required to score 95 points from three different areas, namely, attributes (a minimum of 75 points), English language (10 points) and maintenance (10 points).

A person with exceptional talent and an investor are required to score 75 points for attributes. These categories are not subject to the English language and maintenance requirements in order to obtain entry clearance. However, a person with exceptional talent will need to meet the English language requirement when applying for an extension of leave (see **7.3.3**).

7.2.2.2 Attributes

Briefly, the specific attributes for each category are as follows:

(a) Person with exceptional talent – the applicant must have the official endorsement of a Home Office-specified DCB.

(b) Entrepreneur – the applicant must have access to at least £200,000 that is in a regulated financial institution, being disposable in the UK to invest in business; or £50,000 in a Home Office-approved source such as a registered and regulated venture capital firm.

(c) Investor – the applicant must have access to £2 million that is in a regulated financial institution and disposable in the UK.

(d) Graduate entrepreneur – the applicant must have the official endorsement of a Home Office-approved UK Higher Education Institution.

Full details are set out below, where each category is considered further.

7.2.2.3 English language test for entrepreneur and graduate entrepreneur

An entrepreneur and a graduate entrepreneur must have a minimum level of English language. This requires scoring 10 points by an entrepreneur either passing a Home Office-prescribed English language test, or being a national of a Home Office-designated majority English-speaking country or having a Home Office-recognised degree that was taught in English. Only the last applies to a graduate entrepreneur. Further details are given at **7.4.3** and **7.7.3**.

7.2.2.4 Available maintenance funds test for entrepreneur and graduate entrepreneur

An entrepreneur and graduate entrepreneur must be able to demonstrate that he can support himself in the UK. This requires scoring 10 points for available maintenance funds of at least £3,310 and £900 respectively. Further details are set out at **7.4.4** and **7.7.4**.

7.2.2.5 Self-assessment

A Tier 1 applicant may assess the likely number of points he will score by using the Home Office online points-based calculator. This is at <www.ukba.homeoffice.gov.uk/pointscalculator>.

7.2.2.6 Forms and guidance notes

Applicants can find application forms and guidance notes on the Home Office website.

7.2.2.7 Not liable to refusal on general grounds

An applicant will fail if his application is liable to be refused under the general grounds in Part 9 of the Immigration Rules (see **3.4.5**).

7.2.2.8 Criminal record certificates

A Tier 1 (Investor) and Tier 1 (Entrepreneur) applicant must produce a criminal record certificate from every country in which he has lived continuously for 12 months or more during the previous 10 years. Information for applicants on the practices of different countries in issuing such certificates appears on the UKVI website.

7.2.3 Common features: extension of leave

Just before the initial limited leave of a Tier 1 entrepreneur and investor expires, an application should be made to extend it. Basically the applicant will have to demonstrate that the original requirements have been met, eg an entrepreneur must show that the full amount of cash has been invested in business in the UK; and an investor must show that he has invested at least £2 million within three months.

Before the leave of a graduate entrepreneur expires, an application should be made to switch categories (assuming the person wishes to remain in the UK). Note that a graduate entrepreneur may be granted only one extension of 12 months' limited leave to remain in this category.

An applicant will fail if his application for an extension is liable to be refused under the general grounds in Part 9 of the Immigration Rules (see **3.4.5**) or he is an illegal entrant (see **10.2.2**), or if he is in the UK in breach of immigration laws, except that any period of overstaying for 28 days or less is ignored.

See further **7.3.3, 7.4.5, 7.5.3** and **7.7.2**.

7.2.4 Common features: limited leave conditions

In each category it will be a condition of a person's limited leave that he does not have recourse to public funds (see **3.3.2**).

A person must also register with the police if this is necessary under the Immigration Rules, para 326 (see **3.3.3**).

Additionally, it is a condition of an entrepreneur's limited leave that he does not take employment other than working for the business or businesses that he has established, joined or taken over, nor as a professional sportsperson (including as a sports coach).

Also, it is a condition of the limited leave of a person with exceptional talent that he does not take employment as a doctor or dentist in training, or as a professional sportsperson (including as a sports coach).

Additionally, it is a condition of a graduate entrepreneur's limited leave that he works for the business or businesses that he has established, and that any other employment must not exceed 20 hours per week. Also, he must not take employment as a doctor or dentist in training, nor as a professional sportsperson (including as a sports coach).

7.2.5 Common features: settlement

As a general rule, once a person with exceptional talent, entrepreneur and investor has spent a continuous period of five years in the UK in that category, an application may be made for settlement.

Note that an entrepreneur can apply to settle more quickly if he creates 10 jobs or turns over £5 million in a three-year period. See further **7.4.6**.

Note also that an investor is able to settle here faster if he invests larger sums of money. Those who invest at least £5 million can apply to settle after three years, whilst those investing £10 million or more can apply to settle after two years. See further **7.5.4**.

Obviously, a graduate entrepreneur cannot apply for settlement. He may, of course, be able to switch into another category, such as an entrepreneur, which may ultimately lead to settlement.

7.2.6 Common features: family members

Who are the family members of a Tier 1 applicant? The answer is his spouse, civil partner, unmarried or same-sex partner, and children under 18.

Does a family member have to obtain entry clearance? Yes. The requirements are in the Immigration Rules, paras 319A–319K. See further **7.6**.

7.2.7 Common features: verification of documentation

Each application form and the relevant Immigration Rules (Appendix A for attributes, Appendix B for English language and Appendix C for maintenance) list the various specified documents (see **3.6.4.1**) that are needed. Where a Home Office officer has a reasonable doubt that a specified document is genuine, it is normal practice to verify the document with an independent person or government agency.

There are three possible outcomes of a document verification check:

(a)   If the document is confirmed as genuine, the application will proceed unaffected.

(b)   If the document is confirmed as false, the application will be refused, whether or not the document is essential to the application.

(c)   If the verification check is inconclusive then that document will be ignored as evidence for scoring points.

7.3 TIER 1: (EXCEPTIONAL TALENT) MIGRANT

7.3.1 Overview

An applicant must be internationally recognised in his field as a world-leading talent and be endorsed by a Home Office-specified DCB.

7.3.2 The attributes

An applicant must score 75 points for the specific attribute of having been issued with the endorsement of a Home Office-specified DCB. Each DCB's criteria for the endorsement of an applicant are set out in Appendix L to the Immigration Rules.

What DCBs have been specified by the Home Office? These include: the Arts Council for arts and culture applications; The British Academy for humanities and social science applications; The Royal Society for natural sciences and medical science research applications; The Royal Academy of Engineering for engineering applications; and Tech City UK for digital technology applications.

So what steps must an applicant take? An application must be submitted to the Home Office and not to the DCB. The Home Office sends the relevant documentation to the applicant's chosen DCB, which will advise the Home Office whether the applicant meets its endorsement criteria. If so, the Home Office will then consider the application, taking into account whether the DCB has endorsed the applicant, make its decision and notify the applicant of the result.

7.3.3 Post-entry: extension

Where historically under previous schemes the person with exceptional talent was granted less than five years limited leave (typically only three years limited leave), an application should be made to extend it under the Immigration Rules, para 245BD.

An applicant will fail if his application is liable to be refused under the general grounds in Part 9 of the Immigration Rules (see **3.4.5**) or he is an illegal entrant (see **10.2.2**), or if he is in the UK in breach of immigration laws, except that any period of overstaying for 28 days or less is ignored.

The applicant must have earned money in the UK as a result of employment or self-employment in his expert field as endorsed by his DCB; and the DCB must not have withdrawn its endorsement. See para 6 of Appendix A to the Immigration Rules as to the specified documents the applicant must produce to prove his earning.

7.3.4 Post-entry: settlement

Once a person with exceptional talent has spent a continuous period of five years in the UK in that category (or any other Tier 1 or Tier 2 category), an application may be made for settlement under the Immigration Rules, para 245BF. The applicant will have to show that he:

(a)   does not fall for refusal under the general grounds for refusal (see **3.4.5**) and is not an illegal entrant (see **10.4.2**);

(b)   has spent a continuous period of five years lawfully in the UK as a Tier 1 (Exceptional Talent) Migrant;

(c)   has earned money in the UK as a result of employment or self-employment in his expert field as endorsed by his DCB (see para 6 of Appendix A to the Immigration Rules as to the specified documents the applicant must produce to prove this), and the DCB has not withdrawn its endorsement; and

(d)   has sufficient knowledge of the English language (see **7.4.3**) and sufficient knowledge about life in the UK (see **3.8.7**).

If an applicant has any family members (spouse, civil partner, unmarried or same-sex partner and children under 18) living with him, they may be able to apply for settlement at the same time (see **7.6**).

7.3.5 Tier 1 (Exceptional Talent) Migrant annual limit

At the time of writing, the Government has stated that the maximum annual number of endorsements in this category will be 1,000.

7.4 TIER 1: ENTREPRENEUR

7.4.1 Overview

This category might otherwise be called the 'business person' route into the UK.

The applicant (or a team of two entrepreneurs) must either be setting up a new business, joining or taking over an existing business by investing in it.

How much is required? A minimum of £200,000 from any source or £50,000 from a Home Office-approved source such as a registered and regulated venture capital firm.

In addition, the applicant must be able to speak English and have enough money to support himself and any dependants.

See the flow diagram summary at **Appendix 12**.

The investment must be in one or more UK businesses. A business is considered to be in the UK only if:

(a)   it is trading within the UK economy;

(b)   it has a registered office in the UK, except where the applicant is registered with HM Revenue and Customs (HMRC) as self-employed and does not have a business office;

(c)   it has a UK bank account; and

(d)   it is subject to UK taxation.

Multinational companies that are registered as UK companies with either a registered office or head office in the UK are acceptable.

Where two entrepreneurs apply as a team, each must separately pass the English language and maintenance tests.

7.4.2   The entrepreneur attributes

An applicant must score 75 points for specific attributes regarding the level of his investment, where the money is held and the fact that it is disposable in the UK.

The details are set out in Table 4 of Appendix A to the Immigration Rules (see **Appendix 1** to this book).

7.4.2.1   Points

The points required for specific attributes are shown in **Table 7.1** below.

Table 7.1   Entrepreneur – specific attributes points

Investment	Points
The applicant has access to not less than £200,000; or	25
The applicant has access to not less than £50,000 from:	
(a) one or more registered venture capitalist firms regulated by the Financial Conduct Authority; and/or	
(b) one or more UK entrepreneurial seed funding competitions listed as endorsed on the UK Trade & Investment website; and/or	
(c) one or more UK government departments, and made available by the department(s) for the specific purpose of establishing or expanding a UK business.	
The money is held in one or more regulated financial institutions	25
The money is disposable in the UK	25

It can be seen that to score the required 75 points the applicant must meet all three requirements. We shall now look at each in more detail.

7.4.2.2   The applicant has access to the prescribed investment

First, let us consider the £200,000 route.

An applicant must demonstrate that he has at least £200,000 of his own money available to make a fresh investment into business in the UK. In this context, 'available' means that the funds must be in the applicant's own possession, or in the financial accounts of a UK incorporated business of which he is the director, or (if applicable) available from the third party or parties named in his application.

Note that making a fresh investment excludes spending on the following:

(a)   the applicant's own remuneration;

(b)   buying the business from a previous owner where the money ultimately goes to that previous owner (irrespective of whether it is received or held directly or indirectly by that previous owner) rather than into the business being purchased (this applies regardless of whether the money is channelled through the business en route to the previous owner, for example by means of the applicant or business purchasing 'goodwill' or other assets that were previously part of the business);

(c)   investing in businesses other than those the applicant is running as a self-employed person or a director; and

(d)   any spending not directly for the purpose of establishing or running the applicant's own business or businesses.

Home Office guidance is that the applicant may include money made available by one or more other people ('a third party or parties'). This includes another investor or corporate body, as well as an applicant's spouse, civil partner, unmarried or same-sex partner. In those circumstances the applicant must also provide a declaration from each third party that the money is available to the applicant, together with confirmation from a legal representative that the declaration document is valid (see **7.4.2.5**).

Secondly, what about the £50,000 alternative route?

An applicant must demonstrate that he has access to at least £50,000 to invest in business. Those funds can be made up of any combination of the three prescribed sources. But an applicant cannot use any of his own funds to meet this requirement.

What is a venture capitalist firm? It is a company that draws on private equity funds to invest in new businesses with high growth potential, and in exchange it takes a stake in the business (which it subsequently hopes to sell at a profit). A registered firm is one regulated by the FCA.

Where a UK government department is providing all or some of the funds specifically for the purpose of setting up or expanding a business in the UK, the funding package may be considered for the award of points here.

Note that a prospective entrepreneur visitor (see **5.12**) may seek to switch into this category on the basis of having secured funding of at least £50,000 from one or more of the three prescribed sources.

Also note that a Tier 1 (Graduate Entrepreneur) Migrant (see **7.7**) may seek to switch into this category on the basis of having at least £50,000 of his own money to invest and/or already invested in UK business. This may include money made available by third parties.

7.4.2.3   The money is held in one or more regulated financial institutions

The financial institution or institutions that provide confirmation that the money is available to the applicant must be regulated by the home regulator, ie an official financial regulatory body in the country where the financial institution operates and the funds are located. This body must be appropriate to the type of financial transaction. For example, where a financial institution does business in the UK, the appropriate regulator is the FCA.

7.4.2.4   The money is disposable in the UK

If the money is held in the UK then it must be with an institution that is regulated by the FCA. Where the money is held outside the UK, all of the amount required to qualify must be freely transferable to the UK and able to be converted to pounds sterling.

If the money is held overseas but in an institution that has a presence in the UK and is regulated by the FCA, the Home Office requires no further evidence that the money can be transferred into the UK. In all other cases that evidence is needed by way of a document from the bank or financial institution.

Funds in a foreign currency are converted into pounds sterling using an official exchange rate currency converter recognised by the Home Office at <www.oanda.com>. This is done on the date on which the application is made.

7.4.2.5 Specified documents

To satisfy each of the three requirements and thereby score 25 points for each, the applicant must produce the documents specified in para 41-SD of Appendix A to the Immigration Rules. These include, for example, an original letter, on official headed paper, from each financial institution holding the applicant's funds, confirming that the stated amount of money is available and disposable in the UK.

Each letter must have been produced within the three months immediately before the date of the application. Each letter must also confirm that the institution is regulated by the appropriate body. Details of the amount of money being provided by any third party must also be given.

If the applicant is relying on third-party funding, he must supply a declaration from every third party that they have made the money available for the applicant to invest in a business in the UK, and a letter from a legal representative confirming the validity of signatures on each third-party declaration provided.

7.4.2.6 Team of two entrepreneurs

The required investment funds can be shared by an entrepreneurial team of two people. Each member of the team may apply to come to the UK in this category using the same investment funds.

Where two applicants apply using funds from a third party, each provider of funds must confirm that both applicants have equal access to, and are able to dispose of, the money in the UK.

7.4.2.7 Genuine application

The ECO must be satisfied that:

(a) the applicant genuinely intends and is able to establish, take over or become a director of one or more businesses in the UK within the following six months;

(b) the applicant genuinely intends to invest the funds; and

(c) that those funds are genuinely available to the applicant, and will remain available to him until such time as it is spent by his business or businesses.

'Available to him' in this context means that the funds are in his own possession, or in the financial accounts of a UK-incorporated business of which he is the director, or available from any declared third party or parties.

The ECO must also be satisfied that the applicant does not intend to take any other employment in the UK.

In making this assessment, the ECO will assess the balance of probabilities and may take into account the following factors:

(a) the evidence the applicant has submitted;

(b) the viability and credibility of the source of the funds;

(c) the viability and credibility of the applicant's business plans and market research into his chosen business sector;

(d) the applicant's previous educational and business experience (or lack thereof);

(e) the applicant's immigration history and previous activity in the UK.

The applicant must provide a written business plan. This must set out his proposed business activities in the UK and how he expects to make his business succeed.

If the ECO is not satisfied with the genuineness of the application, no points will be scored for specific attributes.

7.4.3 English language

An applicant must score 10 points for English language. There are three different ways in which an applicant might achieve this, as set out in Appendix B to the Immigration Rules (see **Appendix 1** to this book). In summary these are that the applicant:

(a)   has passed a Home Office-approved English language test;

(b)   is a national of a Home Office-designated majority English-speaking country; or

(c)   holds a degree accepted by the Home Office as taught in English that is equivalent to a UK Bachelor's degree or above.

7.4.3.1 English language Home Office-approved test

An applicant must demonstrate knowledge of English equivalent to level B1 (intermediate) of the Council of Europe's Common European Framework for Language Learning, or above. Details are on the Council's website at <www.coe.int/T/DG4/Linguistic/CADRE_EN.asp>. A list of Home Office-approved tests may be found in Appendix O to the Immigration Rules.

Ten points are be awarded for passing an English language test only if the applicant has the relevant level of English language required and provides with his application the original English language test document which is within its validity date and clearly shows:

(a)   the applicant's name;

(b)   the qualification obtained, which must meet or exceed the relevant level in all four components (reading, writing, speaking and listening), unless the applicant was exempted from sitting a component on the basis of a disability; and

(c)   the date of the award.

7.4.3.2 National of a Home Office-designated majority English-speaking country

Nationals of Home Office-designated majority English-speaking countries automatically meet the English language requirement. To prove their nationality they must produce a current valid original passport or travel document.

Nationals of the following countries are designated for these purposes by the Home Office:

Antigua and Barbuda
Australia
The Bahamas
Barbados
Belize
Canada
Dominica
Grenada
Guyana
Jamaica
New Zealand
St Kitts and Nevis
St Lucia
St Vincent and the Grenadines
Trinidad and Tobago
United States of America

7.4.3.3 Degree accepted by the Home Office as taught in English

An applicant meets the English language requirement if he can produce an academic qualification (not a professional or vocational qualification) from an educational establishment in a Home Office-prescribed country listed below. These are deemed by the

National Academic Recognition Information Centre for the United Kingdom (UK NARIC) to meet or exceed the recognised standard of at least a Bachelor's degree in the UK.

Academic qualifications from the following countries count:

Antigua and Barbuda
Australia
The Bahamas
Barbados
Belize
Dominica
Grenada
Guyana
Ireland
Jamaica
New Zealand
St Kitts and Nevis
St Lucia
St Vincent and the Grenadines
Trinidad and Tobago
United Kingdom
United States of America

The applicant should produce with his application the original certificate of the award. If he cannot do so, see para 7(ii)(2) of Appendix B to the Immigration Rules. What if an applicant's relevant qualification was taught in English but not in one of the above countries? Points will be awarded if the qualification is equivalent to at least a UK bachelor's degree and the degree was taught to a competent standard of English equivalent to level B1 on the Council of Europe's Common European Framework of Reference for Languages. In these circumstances an applicant should use the Home Office's points-based calculator on its website (see **7.2.2.5**).

7.4.4 Available maintenance funds

Applicants must be able to support themselves for the entire duration of their stay in the UK without needing public funds (see **3.3.2**). An applicant must score 10 points for having available sufficient maintenance funds. As to what constitute 'sufficient' funds, the requirement is set out in Appendix C to the Immigration Rules (see **Appendix 1** to this book).

An applicant must have at least £3,310 of personal savings. The applicant must demonstrate that he has held at least that amount for a consecutive 90-day period of time, ending no earlier than 31 days before the date of his application. So access to a bank overdraft facility in excess of that amount will not satisfy this requirement: see R *(Adeyemi-Doro) v Secretary of State for the Home Department* [2011] EWCA Civ 849.

Points will be awarded only if the Home Office receives the specified documentary evidence of the applicant's personal savings as set out in para 1B of Appendix C to the Immigration Rules. So, for example, where an applicant produces personal bank or building society statements, or building society passbooks, these must clearly show the applicant's name; the account number; the date; the financial institution's name and logo; transactions covering the 90-day period; and a balance that does not fall below £3,310.

If an applicant is bringing any family members (spouse, civil partner, unmarried or same-sex partner and children under 18) with him, he will have to demonstrate that additional maintenance funds are available. See **7.6**.

The applicant's specified documents must be from institutions acceptable to the Home Office. A check should always be made in Appendix P to the Immigration Rules, where there are lists of financial institutions approved or not approved for certain countries (currently Sri Lanka, Bangladesh, Cameroon, India, Ghana, Pakistan, Iran and The Philippines).

An applicant may not use any moneys included in his investment as evidence of maintenance funds.

7.4.5   Post-entry: extension

Just before the initial three years' limited leave of an entrepreneur expires, an application should be made to extend it under para 245DD of the Immigration Rules.

An applicant will fail if his application is liable to be refused under the general grounds in Part 9 of the Immigration Rules (see **3.5.4**) or he is an illegal entrant (see **10.4.2**), or if he is in the UK in breach of immigration laws, except that any period of overstaying for 28 days or less is ignored.

Basically, the applicant has to demonstrate that the original requirements have been met, ie the entrepreneur must show that the full amount of £200,000 or £50,000 (as appropriate) in cash has been invested in a genuine business in the UK and the applicant must again score at least 75 points. See **7.4.5.1**.

As the applicant will have satisfied the English language test when applying for entry clearance, that requirement does not apply again.

The applicant will have to demonstrate that he has maintained and will continue to maintain himself (and any dependants): see **7.4.5.6**.

7.4.5.1   Attributes for an extension

An applicant must score 75 points for specific attributes in relation to the investment steps he has taken since entering the UK.

The details are set out in Table 5 of Appendix A to the Immigration Rules (see **Appendix 1** to this book), as shown in **Table 7.2** below.

Table 7.2   Entrepreneur – attributes points for an extension

Investment and business activity	Points
The applicant has invested, or had invested on his behalf, not less than £200,000 or £50,000 (as appropriate) in cash directly into one or more businesses in the UK.	20
The applicant has: (a) registered with HMRC as self-employed; (b) registered a new business in which he is a director; or (c) registered as a director of an existing business. Where the applicant's last grant of entry clearance, leave to enter or leave to remain was as a Tier 1 (Entrepreneur) Migrant, this condition must have been met within six months of his entry to the UK (if he was granted entry clearance in this category and there is evidence to establish his date of arrival to the UK), or, in any other case, the date of the grant of leave to remain.	20
On a date no earlier than three months prior to the date of application, the applicant was: (a) registered with HMRC as self-employed; (b) registered a new business in which he is a director; or (c) registered as a director of an existing business.	15

Investment and business activity	Points
The applicant has: (a) established a new business or businesses that has or have created the equivalent of at least two new full-time jobs for persons settled in the UK; or (b) taken over or joined an existing business or businesses, and his services or investment have resulted in a net increase in the employment provided by the business or businesses for persons settled in the UK by creating the equivalent of at least two new full-time jobs.	20
Where the applicant's last grant of entry clearance or leave to enter or remain was as a Tier 1 (Entrepreneur) Migrant, the jobs must have existed for at least 12 months of the period for which the previous leave was granted.	

It can be seen that to score the required 75 points the applicant must meet all four requirements. We shall now look at each in more detail.

7.4.5.2 Invested at least £200,000 or £50,000 (as appropriate) cash in UK business

The applicant must show that the full amount of £200,000 or £50,000 (as appropriate) in cash has already been invested in business in the UK. If the entrepreneur is no longer involved in a business, evidence of the investment must still be produced.

What property, if any, purchased by the applicant counts as an investment? Home Office guidance is that only commercial premises count, and it does not include the value of any residential accommodation, nor property development or property management. If the applicant has bought property which includes residential accommodation for himself and his family, the value of that part is excluded.

If the applicant has made the investment in the form of a director's loan, does that count? Yes, but only if it is unsecured and ranks after any third-party creditors of the company. The original legal agreement between the applicant and the company must be provided.

What other documentary evidence is required? If the business is a registered company that is required to produce audited accounts, these must be provided. Businesses that are not required to produce audited accounts must provide their unaudited management accounts, together with a certificate of confirmation from an UK regulated accountant. Audited accounts, or management accounts accompanied by an accountant's certificate, must show how much the applicant has invested in the business.

For each business that an applicant relies on to claim points, the documents specified by para 46-SD of Appendix A to the Immigration Rules must be provided.

7.4.5.3 Registration requirement

Self-employed applicants must provide either their original welcome letter from HMRC, or any Small Earnings Exemption Certificate from HMRC.

A director of a new or existing company must provide his Current Appointment Report from Companies House.

Each document must be dated no more than six months after the date the applicant entered the UK (or, where there is no evidence of that, the date his entry clearance was granted).

7.4.5.4 Engaged in a business activity

Although an applicant does not have to be engaged in the same business in which he was working when he first entered the UK, he must still be either a self-employed business person or a director of a company at the time the extension application is made. A self-employed person might prove this by producing evidence of payment of Class 2 National Insurance Contributions. A director should produce his Current Appointment Report from Companies House. The report must show that the applicant is a director of the business, and that it is actively trading and not struck off, dissolved or in liquidation. As proof that the applicant is still engaged in business the specified evidence must be dated no earlier than three months prior to the date of application.

7.4.5.5 Created at least the equivalent of two new full-time jobs

What is the purpose of this requirement? The Home Office states that the creation of employment for settled workers shows the applicant's contribution to the UK economy. However, the jobs do not have to exist at the time of the application. The requirement is that during the entrepreneur's three years' limited leave he must have created jobs that existed for at least 12 months of that period.

A self-employed applicant must employ the settled workers directly. If the applicant is a director of a business, he must show that his business has created the new posts for settled workers.

What is a full-time job? The Home Office considers a 30-hour working week to be full-time. The employment must be for at least two separate jobs that exist for at least 12 full months each. The Home Office gives the following examples:

(a)   the working hours of two part-time workers can be combined to add up to 30 hours a week or more, and form the equivalent of one full-time post;

(b)   another worker can replace a worker who is employed for part of a year and then leaves the job, so that the employment as a whole adds up to 12 months. However, if there is a gap between one worker's leaving a post and another worker's starting employment, the period when the post is not filled is ignored. Only periods during which a worker is employed in a post count.

What documents need to be produced? These include copies of the documents kept by the employer as evidence that the employee is a settled worker; documents registering the employee with HMRC; Form P11 (a report to HMRC recording the earnings of each separate employee); and payslips.

How does an applicant who has taken over or joined an existing UK business show that he has created new posts that result in a net increase? The applicant must produce a duplicate Form P35 (this is an annual return made to HMRC listing the names of employees of the business) and an original accountant's letter verifying that the new posts have been created.

7.4.5.6 Available maintenance funds

The level of funds required on an extension application is £945. The same documentation (see **7.4.4**) is required, evidencing that the applicant has held at least that amount for a consecutive 90-day period of time, ending no earlier than 31 days before the date of his application.

If an applicant has any family members (spouse, civil partner, unmarried or same-sex partner and children under 18) living with him, he will have to demonstrate that additional maintenance funds are available. See **7.6**.

7.4.6 Post-entry: settlement

Once an entrepreneur has spent a continuous period of five years in the UK in that category (or three years in the circumstances set out in **Table 7.3** below), an application may be made for settlement under the Immigration Rules, para 245DF. The applicant will have to show that he:

(a)   does not fall for refusal under the general grounds for refusal (see **3.5.4**) and is not an illegal entrant (see **10.2.2**);

(b)   scores 75 points for specific attributes (see **7.4.6.1**);

(c)   has sufficient knowledge of the English language and sufficient knowledge about life in the UK (see **3.8.7**); and

(d)   has established, taken over or become a director of one or more genuine businesses in the UK, and has genuinely operated that business or businesses while he had leave as a Tier 1 (Entrepreneur) Migrant. In addition, he must demonstrate that he has genuinely invested the money referred to in **Table 7.3** at **7.4.6.1** below into one or more businesses in the UK to be spent for the purpose of that business or businesses, and genuinely intends to continue operating one or more businesses in the UK.

If an applicant has any family members (spouse, civil partner, unmarried or same-sex partner and children under 18) living with him, they may be able to apply for settlement at the same time, provided they have lived together in the UK for at least five years (see **7.6**).

An entrepreneur's child may apply for settlement at the same time as the entrepreneur, as long as the child meets the requirements of the Immigration Rules.

7.4.6.1   Specific attributes for settlement

An applicant must score 75 points for specific attributes in relation to the investment steps he has taken since entering the UK. The details are set out in Table 6 of Appendix A to the Immigration Rules (see **Appendix 1** to this book), as shown in **Table 7.3** below.

Table 7.3   Entrepreneur – attributes points for indefinite leave to remain

Investment and business activity	Points
The applicant has invested, or had invested on his behalf, not less than £200,000 (or £50,000 if, in his last grant of leave, he was awarded points for funds of £50,000) in cash directly into one or more businesses in the UK. The applicant will not need to provide evidence of this investment if he was awarded points for it in his previous grant of entry clearance or leave to remain as a Tier 1 (Entrepreneur) Migrant.	20
On a date no earlier than three months prior to the date of application, the applicant was: (a) registered with HM Revenue and Customs as self-employed, or (b) registered with Companies House as a director of a new or an existing business. Directors who are on the list of disqualified directors provided by Companies House will not be awarded points.	20
The applicant has: (a) established a new business or businesses that has or have created the equivalent of at least two new full-time jobs for persons settled in the UK; or (b) taken over or joined an existing business or businesses, and his services or investment have resulted in a net increase in the employment provided by the business or businesses for persons settled in the UK by creating the equivalent of at least two new full-time jobs. Where the applicant's last grant of entry clearance or leave to enter or remain was as a Tier 1 (Entrepreneur) Migrant, the jobs must have existed for at least 12 months during the last grant of leave.	20

Investment and business activity	Points
The applicant has spent the specified continuous period lawfully in the UK in this category, with absences from the UK of no more than 180 days in any 12 calendar months during that period.	15

The specified continuous period is:

(a)   three years if the number of new full-time jobs referred to above is at least 10;

(b)   three years if the applicant has:

    (i)   established a new UK business that has had an income from business activity of at least £5 million during a three-year period in which the applicant has had leave as a Tier 1 (Entrepreneur) Migrant;

    (ii)   taken over or invested in an existing UK business and his services or investment have resulted in a net increase in income from business activity to that business of £5 million during a three-year period in which the applicant has had leave as a Tier 1 (Entrepreneur) Migrant, when compared to the immediately preceding three-year period; or

(c)   five years in all other cases.

It can be seen that to score the required 75 points the applicant must meet all four requirements. The first 60 points are the same as for an extension (see **7.4.5.3** and **7.4.5.4**). Securing the remaining 15 points will determine when the application can be made. The specified documents in para 46-SD of Appendix A to the Immigration Rules must be provided.

7.5   TIER 1: INVESTOR

7.5.1   Overview

This category is for an individual aged 18 or over who is able to make a substantial financial investment of at least £2 million in the UK.

An applicant does not have to meet on entry any English language requirement because he is investing in the UK and may choose whether or not he wants to work. In addition, given the level of investment, he does not have to demonstrate that he has enough money to maintain himself (and any dependants).

7.5.2   The investor attributes

An applicant must score 75 points for having access to £2 million that is in a regulated financial institution and disposable in the UK, set out in Table 7 of Appendix A to the Immigration Rules (see **Appendix 1** to this book).

The applicant must show that he can make an investment of at least £2 million in the UK. The money may already be in the UK or held overseas at the time of application. If it is not in pounds sterling, the applicant must convert its value into that using the Oanda website (see **7.4.2.4**) on the date on which the application is made.

The applicant must open an account with a UK regulated bank for the purposes of investing not less than £2 million in the UK. The applicant must provide with his application an original letter issued by that bank on its official letter-headed paper, which is dated within the three months immediately before the date of the application. The letter must state the applicant's name as the account holder and include the account number. It must also confirm that the applicant opened the account for the purposes of investing not less than £2 million in the UK, and that the bank is regulated by the FCA for the purposes of accepting deposits.

Can an applicant rely on money that he owns jointly with his spouse, civil partner, unmarried or same-sex partner? Yes – see paras 61 and 61-SD of Appendix A to the Immigration Rules.

An applicant must produce the documents specified in para 64A-SD of Appendix A to the Immigration Rules to earn 75 points by this route. In summary, these include:

(a)   A portfolio report or breakdown of investments in a letter produced by a UK regulated financial institution covering the three consecutive months in the period immediately before the application.

If the money has already been invested in the UK in the last 12 months or is held abroad, but in either case the applicant has such a report, he may use it as evidence that the money is available. Alternatively, the applicant may supply a breakdown of his investments in a letter from an authorised financial institution.

Only investments made in the UK within the 12 months immediately before the date of the application are eligible for the award of points. What investments count? Those in government bonds, share capital or loan capital in active and trading companies registered in the UK.

(b)   Where the applicant manages his own investments or has a portfolio manager who does not operate in the UK, he must produce documentary evidence of his holdings. This may include certified copies of bonds, share certificates and audited accounts. All documents must cover the three consecutive months in the period immediately before the application.

(c)   If the funds are in a bank account, the applicant must provide personal bank statements from a bank that is regulated by the official regulatory body for the country in which the institution operates and the funds are located. These must show the amount of money available in the name of the applicant and/or his spouse, civil partner, unmarried or same-sex partner. Consecutive bank statements covering the three months immediately before the date of application are required. Alternatively a letter from that bank may be acceptable.

What if the money has not been held in a portfolio or bank account for at least three months prior to the application? Then the applicant will have to provide evidence of the source of the money as outlined in **Table 7.4** below.

Table 7.4   **Investor – sources of funds**

Source of funds	Supporting evidence key points
Gift	The original irrevocable memorandum of gift and a letter from a legal adviser confirming that it is valid and binding according to the laws of the country in which it was made.
Deeds of sale	The original deeds of sale of assets (such as property or business) and a letter from a legal adviser confirming that the sale was genuine and that the money is available to the applicant.
Evidence from a business	Business accounts and a letter from a legal adviser confirming that the applicant can lawfully extract the money from the business.
Will	A notarised copy of the will and a letter from a legal adviser confirming the validity of the will.
Divorce settlement	A notarised copy of the terms of the divorce settlement and a letter from a legal adviser confirming that the document is valid.
Award of winnings	A letter from the organisation issuing the financial award or winnings and a letter from a legal adviser confirming the money has been transferred.

In all other cases the applicant will need to produce original documentation as evidence of the source of the money, together with independent supporting evidence. For example, if the money was received as a result of court action, the Home Office requires original documents in the form of a letter of confirmation of the court proceedings and a suitable letter from the applicant's solicitor.

(d)   Applicants who have funds that are not held in the UK, or who have a portfolio of investments that are not in the UK, must provide a letter from their bank or financial institution confirming that the money can be transferred into the UK.

An ECO may refuse the application if there are reasonable grounds to believe that the applicant is not in control of the investment funds; the funds were obtained unlawfully (or by means which would be unlawful if they happened in the UK); or the character, conduct or associations of a party providing the funds mean that approving the application is not conducive to the public good.

7.5.3   Post-entry: extension

Just before the initial three years' limited leave of an investor expires, an application should be made to extend it under para 245ED of the Immigration Rules.

An applicant will fail if his application is liable to be refused under the general grounds in Part 9 of the Immigration Rules (see **3.5.4**) or he is an illegal entrant (see **10.2.2**), or if he is in the UK in breach of immigration laws, except that any period of overstaying for 28 days or less is ignored.

Basically, the applicant has to demonstrate that the original requirements have been met, ie the investor has made the required investment, and the applicant must again score at least 75 points. The attributes are set out in Table 8A of Appendix A to the Immigration Rules (see **Appendix 1** to this book), as shown in **Table 7.5** below.

Table 7.5   Investor – attributes for extension

Money and investment	Points
The applicant has invested not less than £2 million in the UK by way of UK Government bonds, share capital or loan capital in active and trading UK registered companies, subject to the restrictions set out in paragraph 65. The investment referred to above was made: (1) within 3 months of the applicant's entry to the UK, if he was granted entry clearance as a Tier 1 (Investor) Migrant and there is evidence to establish his date of entry to the UK, unless there are exceptionally compelling reasons for the delay in investing, or (2) where there is no evidence to establish his date of entry in the UK or where the applicant was granted entry clearance in a category other than Tier 1 (Investor) Migrant, within 3 months of the date of the grant of entry clearance or leave to remain as a Tier 1 (Investor) Migrant, unless there are exceptionally compelling reasons for the delay in investing, or (3) where the investment was made prior to the application which led to the first grant of leave as a Tier 1 (Investor) Migrant, no earlier than 12 months before the date of such application, and in each case the level of investment has been at least maintained for the whole of the remaining period of that leave. 'Compelling reasons for the delay in investing' must be unforeseeable and outside of the applicant's control. Delays caused by the applicant failing to take timely action will not be accepted. Where possible, the applicant must have taken reasonable steps to mitigate such delay.	75

7.5.3.1   Investment

By para 65 of the Immigration Rules, certain investments do not count. These include an offshore company or trust, open ended investment companies, investment trust companies or pooled investment vehicles, companies mainly engaged in property investment, property management or property development, deposits with a bank, building society or other enterprise whose normal course of business includes the acceptance of deposits, ISAs, premium bonds and saving certificates issued by the National Savings and Investment Agency.

7.5.3.2 Maintaining the level of investment

By para 65C of the Immigration Rules, points for maintaining the level of investment for the specified continuous period of leave are only to be awarded:

(a) if the applicant has maintained a portfolio of qualifying investments for which he paid a total purchase price of at least £2 million throughout such period; and

(b) if the applicant sells any part of the portfolio of qualifying investments during the specified continuous period of leave such that the price he paid for the remaining portfolio falls below £2 million, the shortfall is fully corrected within the same reporting period by the purchase of further qualifying investments.

7.5.4 Post-entry: settlement

Once an investor has spent a continuous period of five years in the UK in that category (or a shorter period of two or three years in the circumstances set out in **Table 7.6** below), an application can be made for settlement under para 245EF of the Immigration Rules.

The applicant will have to show that he:

(a) does not fall for refusal under the general grounds for refusal (see **3.5.4**) and is not an illegal entrant (see **10.4.2**);

(b) scores 75 points for specific attributes; and

(c) has sufficient knowledge of the English language and sufficient knowledge about life in the UK (see **3.8.7**).

If an applicant has any family members (spouse, civil partner, unmarried or same-sex partner and children under 18) living with him, they may be able to apply for settlement at the same time (see **7.6**).

Home Office guidance is that the partner of an investor may apply for settlement at the same time as the investor, provided they have lived together in the UK for at least five years before applying for settlement.

An investor's child may apply for settlement at the same time as the investor, as long as the child meets the requirements of the Immigration Rules.

7.5.4.1 Specific attributes for settlement

An applicant must score 75 points for specific attributes in relation to the investment steps he has taken since entering the UK. The details are set out in Table 9A of Appendix A to the Immigration Rules (see **Appendix 1** to this book), as shown in **Table 7.6** below.

Table 7.6   Investor – attributes points for indefinite leave to remain

Row	Money and investment	Points
1	The applicant has invested money of his own under his control amounting to at least: (a) £10 million; or (b) £5 million; or (c) £2 million in the UK by way of UK Government bonds, share capital or loan capital in active and trading UK registered companies, subject to the restrictions set out in paragraph 65.	40

2	The applicant has spent the specified continuous period lawfully in the UK, with absences from the UK of no more than 180 days in any 12 calendar months during that period. The specified continuous period must have been spent with leave as a Tier 1 (Investor) Migrant. The specified continuous period is: (a) 2 years if the applicant scores points from row 1(a) above; (b) 3 years if the applicant scores points from row 1(b) above; or (c) 5 years if the applicant scores points from row 1(c) above. Time spent with valid leave in the Bailiwick of Guernsey, the Bailiwick of Jersey or the Isle of Man in a category equivalent to the categories set out above may be included in the continuous period of lawful residence, provided the most recent period of leave was as a Tier 1 (Investor) Migrant in the UK. In any such case, the applicant must have absences from the Bailiwick of Guernsey, the Bailiwick of Jersey or the Isle of Man (as the case may be) of no more than 180 days in any 12 calendar months during the specified continuous period.	20
3	The investment referred to above was made no earlier than 12 months before the date of the application which led to the first grant of leave as a Tier 1 (Investor) Migrant. The level of investment has been at least maintained throughout the relevant specified continuous period referred to in row 2, other than in the first 3 months of that period, and the applicant has provided the specified documents to show that this requirement has been met. When calculating the specified continuous period, the first day of that period will be taken to be the later of: (a) the date the applicant first entered the UK as a Tier 1 (Investor) Migrant, (or the date entry clearance was granted as a Tier 1 (Investor) Migrant) or the date the applicant first entered the Bailiwick of Guernsey, the Bailiwick of Jersey or the Isle of Man with leave in a category equivalent to Tier 1 (Investor) if this is earlier; or (b) the date 3 months before the full specified amount was invested in the UK, or before the full required amount in an equivalent category was invested in the Bailiwick of Guernsey, the Bailiwick of Jersey or the Isle of Man.	15

7.6 FAMILY MEMBERS OF A TIER 1 MIGRANT

7.6.1 Entry clearance and leave to remain

If subject to immigration controls, the spouse, civil partner, unmarried or same-sex partner ('the Partner') and children under 18 of a Tier 1 Migrant will require entry clearance in order to enter the UK, and should usually subsequently apply for an extension at the same time as the Tier 1 Migrant. The requirements are set out in the Immigration Rules, paras 319A–319K.

7.6.1.1 Partner

The requirements are set out in para 319C as follows:

(a)   The applicant must not fall for refusal under the general grounds for refusal (see **3.5.4**), and if applying for leave to remain must not be an illegal entrant (see **10.4.2**) nor in the UK in breach of immigration laws, except that any period of overstaying for 28 days or less is ignored.

(b)   The applicant must be the spouse or civil partner, unmarried or same-sex partner of a person who:

    (i)   has valid leave to enter or remain as a Tier 1 Migrant; or

    (ii)   is, at the same time, being granted entry clearance or leave to remain as a Tier 1 Migrant.

(c)   An applicant who is the unmarried or same-sex partner of a Tier 1 Migrant must also meet the following requirements:

    (i)   any previous marriage or civil partnership, or similar relationship by the applicant or the Tier 1 Migrant with another person must have permanently broken down;

    (ii)   the applicant and the Tier 1 Migrant must not be so closely related that they would be prohibited from marrying each other in the UK (see **8.3.5.3**); and

    (iii)   the applicant and the Tier 1 Migrant must have been living together in a relationship similar to marriage or civil partnership for a period of at least two years (see further **8.3**).

(d)   The marriage or civil partnership, or relationship similar to marriage or civil partnership, must be subsisting at the time the application is made (see **8.3.5.5**).

(e)   The applicant and the Tier 1 Migrant must intend to live with the other as his spouse or civil partner, unmarried or same-sex partner throughout the applicant's stay in the UK (see **8.3.5.9**).

(f)   The applicant must not intend to stay in the UK beyond any period of leave granted to the Tier 1 Migrant.

(g)   If the applicant's partner is a Tier 1 Entrepreneur Migrant, there must be a sufficient level of funds available to the applicant, as set out in Appendix E.

As to (g) above, the same requirements for available maintenance funds for an applicant (see **7.4.4**) apply to a partner. Appendix E to the Immigration Rules (see **Appendix 1** to this book) sets out the following requirements:

(a)   Where the Tier 1 Entrepreneur Migrant to whom the application is connected is outside the UK, or has been in the UK for a period of less than 12 months, there must be £1,890 in funds.

(b)   Where the Tier 1 Entrepreneur Migrant to whom the application is connected has been in the UK for a period of 12 months or more, there must be £630 in funds.

(c)   Where the applicant is applying as the partner of a Tier 1 Entrepreneur Migrant, the relevant amount of funds must be available to either the applicant or the Tier 1 Entrepreneur Migrant.

(d)   Where the Tier 1 Entrepreneur Migrant is applying for entry clearance or leave to remain at the same time as the applicant, the amount of funds available to the applicant must be in addition to the level of funds required separately of the Tier 1 Entrepreneur Migrant.

EXAMPLES

Adam applies for entry clearance as a Tier 1 Entrepreneur Migrant. His civil partner, Brian, will be travelling with him. In addition to meeting the requirements of para 319C(a)–(f) above, what maintenance funds do they need to have available? Adam needs £3,310 for himself (see **7.4.4**). As he is applying from outside the UK there must be an additional £1,890 available for Brian.

Janet has been in the UK for the last two years as a Tier 1 Entrepreneur. She recently married David, a foreign national. He is outside the UK and is applying for entry clearance to join Janet in the UK. In addition to meeting the requirements of para 319C(a)–(f) above, there must be £630 in maintenance funds available for David.

If the application is successful, the partner is granted entry clearance and leave to remain for a period which expires on the same day as the leave granted to the Tier 1 Migrant (but if the Tier 1 Migrant already has indefinite leave to remain, the partner will be granted limited leave for a period of three years). That leave will be subject to conditions not to have recourse to public funds and registration with the police, if this is required (see **3.3.2** and **3.3.3** respectively). The partner will be free to work in the UK, but not normally as a doctor or dentist in training (see para 319D(iii) of the Immigration Rules).

7.6.1.2 Child

The requirements are set out in para 319H as follows:

(a)   The applicant must not fall for refusal under the general grounds for refusal (see **3.5.4**), and if applying for leave to remain must not be an illegal entrant (see **10.4.2**) nor in the UK in breach of immigration laws, except that any period of overstaying for 28 days or less is ignored.

(b)   The applicant must be the child of either:

(i)   one parent who has valid leave to enter or remain as a Tier 1 Migrant, or is, at the same time, being granted entry clearance or leave to remain as a Tier 1 Migrant where –

(1)   that parent is the applicant's sole surviving parent, or

(2)   that parent has and has had sole responsibility for the applicant's upbringing (see **8.9.4.3**), or

(3)   there are serious and compelling family or other considerations which would make it desirable not to refuse the application and suitable arrangements have been made for the applicant's care (see **8.9.4.4**); or

(ii)   parents –

(1)   one of whom has valid leave to enter or remain as a Tier 1 Migrant and one of whom has leave as the partner of a Tier 1 Migrant, or

(2)   who are at the same being granted entry clearance or leave to remain as a Tier 1 Migrant and as the partner of a Tier 1 Migrant, or

(3)   where one parent has valid leave to enter or remain as the partner of a person who has either limited leave to enter or remain as a Tier 1 Migrant, indefinite leave to remain as a Tier 1 Migrant, or who has subsequently become a British Citizen.

(c)   The applicant must be under the age of 18 on the date the application is made, or if over 18 and applying for leave to remain, must have, or have last been granted, leave as the child of a Tier 1 Migrant.

(d)   The applicant must not be married or in a civil partnership, must not have formed an independent family unit, and must not be leading an independent life. See further **8.9.4.6**.

(e)   The applicant must not intend to stay in the UK beyond any period of leave granted to the Tier 1 Migrant parent.

(f)   If the applicant's parent is a Tier 1 Entrepreneur Migrant, there must be a sufficient level of funds available to the applicant, as set out in Appendix E.

(g)   An applicant who is applying for leave to remain must have, or have last been granted leave as the child of a parent who had leave under any category of the Immigration Rules.

(h)   All arrangements for the child's care and accommodation in the UK must comply with relevant UK legislation and regulations.

It is important to note the effect of (c) above in respect of a child now aged 18 or over. That child will still qualify for an extension of leave in this category, provided he had previously obtained such leave when under 18.

As to (f) above, the same requirements for available maintenance funds for an applicant (see **7.4.4**) apply to a child. For details of (f) and Appendix E, see **7.6.1.1**. In addition, note that the required funds must be available either to the child, or to the parent who is the Tier 1 Entrepreneur Migrant or to the child's other parent. In the case of the other parent, he or she must either be lawfully present in the UK, or being granted entry clearance or leave to enter or remain, at the same time.

EXAMPLES

Mona applies for entry clearance as a Tier 1 Entrepreneur Migrant. Her daughter, Janice, will be travelling with her. Janice's father is dead. In addition to meeting the requirements of para 319H(a)–(e) above, what maintenance funds need to be available? Mona needs £3,310 for herself (see **7.4.4**). As she is applying from outside the UK there must be an additional £1,890 available for Janice.

Clive has been in the UK for the last three years. He applies to switch to a Tier 1 Entrepreneur worker. Clive's wife and 6-month-old baby live with him. What maintenance funds do they need to have available? Clive needs £945 for himself (see **7.4.5.6**). As Clive has been in the UK for longer than 12 months, he needs £630 for his wife and £630 for his child.

If the application is successful, the child is granted entry clearance and leave to remain for a period which expires on the same day as the leave granted to his Tier 1 Migrant parent or partner, as appropriate. This will be subject to conditions of no recourse to public funds and registration with the police, if this is required (see **3.3.2** and **3.3.3** respectively).

7.6.2 Settlement by a partner

Once a Tier 1 Migrant is in a position to apply for settlement, the applicant's partner may apply for settlement at the same time, provided the couple have lived together for at least five years (or later when that requirement is met).

All the requirements are set out in the Immigration Rules, para 319E, as follows:

(a) The applicant must not fall for refusal under the general grounds for refusal (see **3.5.4**) and must not be an illegal entrant (see **10.4.2**).

(b) The applicant must be the spouse or civil partner, unmarried or same-sex partner of a person who is being, or has been, granted indefinite leave to remain as a Tier 1 Migrant (or who has subsequently become a British citizen).

(c) The applicant must have, or have last been granted, leave as the partner of the Tier 1 Migrant who is being or has been granted indefinite leave to remain (or who has subsequently become a British citizen).

(d) The applicant and the Tier 1 Migrant must have been living together in the UK in marriage or civil partnership, or in a relationship similar to marriage or civil partnership, for a period of at least five years. During that time the applicant must have had continuous leave as the partner of the Tier 1 Migrant and met all of the requirements of para 319C(a)–(e) (see **7.6.1.1**).

(e) The marriage or civil partnership, or relationship similar to marriage or civil partnership, must be subsisting at the time the application is made (see **8.3.5.5**).

(f) The applicant and the Tier 1 Migrant must intend to live permanently with the other as spouse or civil partner, unmarried or same-sex partner. See further **8.3.5.9**.

(g) The applicant must have sufficient knowledge of the English language and sufficient knowledge about life in the UK (see **3.8.7**) (unless the applicant is aged 65 or over at the time the application is made).

7.6.3 Settlement by a child

Once a Tier 1 Migrant is in a position to apply for settlement, the applicant's children may apply for settlement at the same time, provided the following requirements in the Immigration Rules, para 319J are met:

(a)   The applicant must not fall for refusal under the general grounds for refusal (see **3.5.4**) and must not be an illegal entrant (see **10.4.2**).

(b)   The applicant must be the child of:

    (i)   a parent who has been granted or is at the same time being granted indefinite leave to remain as a Tier 1 Migrant where –

        (1)   that parent is the applicant's sole surviving parent, or

        (2)   that parent has and has had sole responsibility for the applicant's upbringing (see **8.9.4.3**), or

        (3)   there are serious and compelling family or other considerations which would make it desirable not to refuse the application and suitable arrangements have been made for the applicant's care (see **8.9.4.4**); or

    (ii)   a parent who is at the same time being granted indefinite leave to remain as the partner of a person who has indefinite leave to remain as a Tier 1 Migrant, or who has subsequently become a British citizen.

(c)   The applicant must have, or have last been granted, leave as the child of the Tier 1 Migrant who is being granted indefinite leave to remain.

(d)   The applicant must not be married or in a civil partnership, must not have formed an independent family unit, and must not be leading an independent life (see **8.9.4.6**).

(e)   Both of an applicant's parents must either be lawfully present in the UK, or being granted entry clearance, limited leave to remain, or indefinite leave to remain at the same time as the applicant, unless:

    (i)   the Tier 1 Migrant is the applicant's sole surviving parent;

    (ii)   the Tier 1 Migrant parent has and has had sole responsibility (see **8.9.4.3**) for the applicant's upbringing; or

    (iii)   there are serious and compelling family or other considerations which would make it desirable not to refuse the application, and suitable arrangements have been made for the applicant's care (see **8.9.4.4**).

(f)   The applicant must have sufficient knowledge of the English language and sufficient knowledge about life in the UK (see **3.8.7**), unless the applicant is under the age of 18 at the time the application is made.

(h)   All arrangements for the child's care and accommodation in the UK must comply with relevant UK legislation and regulations.

7.7 TIER 1: (GRADUATE ENTREPRENEUR) MIGRANT

7.7.1 Overview

This category allows a graduate from a Home Office-approved UK Higher Education Institution who has been identified as having developed world-class innovative ideas or entrepreneurial skills to stay in the UK after graduation to establish one or more businesses in the UK.

Leave is normally only for 12 months (with the possibility of one 12-month extension) and then the person is expected to depart the UK or switch into another category, such as an entrepreneur.

7.7.2   The attributes

An applicant must score 75 points for specific attributes regarding his endorsement. The details are set out in Table 10 of Appendix A to the Immigration Rules. Note that these cover the requirements for initial leave and an extension in this category.

7.7.2.1   Points

The points required for specific attributes are shown in **Table 7.7** below.

Table 7.7   Graduate entrepreneur – specific attributes points

Criterion	Points
The applicant has been endorsed by UK Trade and Investment OR The applicant has been endorsed by a UK Higher Education Institution which: (a) has Highly Trusted Sponsor status under Tier 4 of the Points-Based System, (b) is an A-rated Sponsor under Tier 2 of the Points-Based System if a Tier 2 licence is held, (c) is an A-rated Sponsor under Tier 5 of the Points-Based System if a Tier 5 licence is held, and (d) has established processes and competence for identifying, nurturing and developing entrepreneurs among its undergraduate and postgraduate population.	25
The applicant has been awarded a degree qualification (not a qualification of equivalent level which is not a degree) which meets or exceeds the recognised standard of a Bachelor's degree in the UK. For overseas qualifications, the standard must be confirmed by UK NARIC.	25
The endorsement must confirm that the institution has assessed the applicant and considers that: (a) the applicant has a genuine, credible and innovative business idea, and (b) the applicant will spend the majority of his working time on developing business ventures, and (c) if the applicant's previous grant of leave was as a Tier 1 (Graduate Entrepreneur), he has made satisfactory progress in developing his business since that leave was granted and will, on the balance of probabilities, qualify for leave to remain as a Tier 1 (Entrepreneur) Migrant within the next 12 months.	25

It can be seen that to score the required 75 points the applicant must meet all three requirements. We shall now look at each in more detail.

7.7.2.2   Endorsement

Table 7.7 shows which UK Higher Education Institutions may be eligible to provide endorsements. In order to be approved, the institution must confirm to the Home Office that it wishes to take part in the scheme and that it has established processes and competence for identifying, nurturing and developing entrepreneurs among its undergraduate and postgraduate population.

It should be noted that the Government has capped the number of possible endorsements at 2,000 annually.

7.7.2.3 Qualification

See further **6.3.2.4**.

7.7.2.4 Business idea

To be awarded the points for this requirement, the endorsement from the UK Higher Education Institution must confirm that the institution has assessed the applicant and considers that he has a genuine, credible and innovative business idea, and that he will spend the majority of his working time on developing business ventures.

Note that on an application for an extension of leave in this category, the endorsement must confirm that the applicant has made satisfactory progress in developing his business and will, on the balance of probabilities, qualify for leave to remain as a Tier 1 (Entrepreneur) Migrant within the next 12 months.

7.7.2.5 Content of endorsement

The above points will be awarded only if:

(a)   the endorsement is issued to the applicant no more than three months before the date of application;

(b)   the endorsement has not been withdrawn by the relevant Higher Education Institution at the time the application is considered by the Home Office; and

(c)   the applicant provides the original endorsement which sets out the information prescribed by para 70(c) of Appendix A to the Immigration Rules.

7.7.3 English language

If an applicant successfully achieves 75 points for attributes, he will automatically satisfy the English language requirement. This is because he will have shown that he was awarded a degree level qualification taught in English (see **7.7.2.3**).

7.7.4 Available maintenance funds

As the applicant is already in the UK, normally as a Tier 4 (Student), his application is for leave to remain in this category and so he must have at least £945 of personal savings. The applicant must show that he has held at least that amount for a consecutive 90-day period of time, ending no earlier than 31 days before the date of his application. He must produce documents demonstrating this as specified in para 1B of Appendix C to the Immigration Rules.

If the applicant has, or wishes to be joined by, any family members, additional maintenance funds will be required (see **7.6.1**).

7.8 OVERVIEW OF TIER 2

7.8.1 A profile of each category

7.8.1.1 Tier 2 (General) Migrant and Tier 2 (Intra-company Transfer) Migrant

A Tier 2 (General) Migrant must have a job offer from a UK-based employer which holds an appropriate licence from the Home Office. However, note that migration here is only for the purpose of filling gaps in the UK labour force that cannot be filled by the resident workforce. So there are tests that have to be met to demonstrate that. In particular, the Tier 2 (General) Migrant must be skilled. How skilled? The job skill level must be at graduate level or above (apart from some shortage occupations: see **7.9.3.1**).

The Tier 2 Intra-company Transfer category is for existing employees of multi-national companies who are being transferred from outside the EEA by their overseas employer to a training position or skilled job in a related UK entity. The transfer must be for training purposes, or to fill a specific vacancy at graduate level or above that cannot be filled by a British or EEA worker.

The applicant must be paid at or above the appropriate rate for the job in accordance with codes of practice in Appendix J to the Immigration Rules (see **7.9.1**).

7.8.1.2 Minister of religion

This category is for a religious worker within a recognised religion and anyone who ministers, whether regularly or occasionally, and/or performs pastoral duties.

Note that Tier 5 (see **7.12**) will cover ministers of religion entering the UK on a temporary basis as religious workers in a non-pastoral role, whose duties include performing religious rites.

7.8.1.3 Sports person

This category is for an elite sports person or a coach who wishes to be based in the UK. The person must be internationally established at the highest level, and his employment should make a significant contribution to the development of the particular sport at the highest level in the UK.

7.8.2 Common features: entry clearance

7.8.2.1 Sponsorship

A Tier 2 Migrant cannot apply for entry clearance without a certificate of sponsorship issued by a UK-based sponsor which has been licensed by the Home Office (see **7.8.3**). Note that a certificate of sponsorship does not guarantee that entry clearance will be given.

7.8.2.2 The points system

Each Tier 2 Migrant is required to score 70 points from three different areas, namely, attributes (50 points), English language (10 points) and maintenance (10 points).

Note, however, that an intra-company transfer migrant who does not wish to remain in the UK beyond three years only has to score 60 points from two different areas, namely, attributes (50 points) and maintenance (10 points).

7.8.2.3 Attributes

For each category an applicant must score 50 points for specific attributes. Briefly, these are as follows:

(a)   General migrant – attributes are based on sponsorship and annual salary.

(b)   Minister of religion and sports person – the only attribute concerns sponsorship.

Full details are set out below, where each category is considered in detail.

7.8.2.4 English language

A Tier 2 Migrant (apart from an intra-company transfer migrant) must have a minimum level of competence in the English language. This requires scoring 10 points for either:

(a)   passing a prescribed English language test at the required minimum level (as set out in **Table 7.8** below); or

Table 7.8   English language test requirements

Entry Clearance Applicant	Council of Europe's Common European Framework for Language Learning Level
Tier 2 (General)	B1
Tier 2 (Minister)	B2

Entry Clearance Applicant	Council of Europe's Common European Framework for Language Learning Level
Tier 2 (Intra-company Transfer)	A1
Tier 2 (Sports Person)	A1

(b)   being a national of a Home Office-designated majority English-speaking country (see the list at **7.4.3.2**); or

(c)   having obtained a Home Office-recognised academic qualification (not a professional or vocational qualification) which is deemed by UK NARIC to meet or exceed the recognised standard of a Bachelor's degree in the UK (see **7.4.3.3**).

Note that an intra-company transfer migrant needs to demonstrate the required English

7.8.2.5   Available maintenance funds

A Tier 2 Migrant must be able to demonstrate that he can support himself in the UK. This requires scoring 10 points for available maintenance funds of at least £945 of personal savings. These must have been held for a consecutive 90-day period of time, ending no earlier than 31 days before the date of the application. Alternatively, if the Tier 2 Migrant has an A-rated sponsor (see **7.8.3**), that sponsor may provide a written undertaking that, should it become necessary, it will maintain and accommodate the migrant until the end of the first month of the migrant's leave. The undertaking may be limited, provided the limit is at least £945.

If any family members (see **7.8.9**) of the Tier 2 Migrant are travelling with him, each must have available savings of at least £630, which must have been held for a consecutive 90-day period of time, ending no earlier than 31 days before the date of the application. Alternatively, if the Tier 2 Migrant has an A-rated sponsor (see **7.8.3**), that sponsor may provide a written undertaking that, should it become necessary, it will maintain and accommodate the dependant until the end of the first month of the migrant's leave. The undertaking may be limited, provided the limit is at least £630 per dependant.

The details are otherwise the same as for Tier 1 (see **7.4.4**).

7.8.2.6   Forms and guidance notes

Applicants can find detailed guidance and application forms on the Home Office website (see **1.2.8**).

7.8.2.7   Not liable to refusal on general grounds

An applicant will fail if his application is liable to be refused under the general grounds in Part 9 of the Immigration Rules (see **3.5.4**).

7.8.2.8   Length of initial limited leave

Normally a Tier 2 General Migrant may be granted leave up to 3 years and 1 month. That may be followed by an application for an extension and subsequently for settlement. However, it was announced in March 2014 that on payment of a higher fee, a Tier 2 General Migrant may be granted leave up to 5 years and 1 month.

A Tier 2 Minister of Religion or Sportsperson Migrant may be granted leave up to 3 years and 1 month. That may be followed by an application for an extension and subsequently for settlement.

As to Tier 2 Intra-company Transfer Migrants, the length of initial leave is as follows: 6 months for the Skills Transfer sub-category; 12 months for the Graduate Trainee or Short Term Staff sub-categories; and 5 years and 1 month for the Long Term Staff sub-category.

7.8.3 Common features: sponsorship

7.8.3.1 An appropriate sponsor

Each Tier 2 Migrant must be sponsored as shown in **Table 7.9** below.

Note that if the sponsor is a limited company, the applicant must not own more than 10% of the sponsor's shares (unless he is applying as an intra-company transfer migrant or as a general migrant with an annual salary of at least £155,300).

Table 7.9   **Tier 2 Migrant – appropriate sponsors**

Tier 2 category	UK-based sponsor
General migrant	A genuine organisation or sole trader operating legally in the UK.
Intra-company transfer migrant	An UK entity with a direct link by common ownership or control with the overseas entity where the migrant is currently working. For definitions of common ownership or control see **Appendix 13**.
Minister of religion	A genuine religious institution, which is a registered, excepted or exempt UK charity according to the relevant charity legislation in force in its part of the UK, or is an ecclesiastical corporation (either corporation sole or body corporate) established for charitable purposes.
Sports person	A genuine club, or equivalent, which has a recognised governing body. A list of approved bodies is expected to be published by the Home Office in due course.

7.8.3.2 How to become a sponsor

Sponsorship applies to Tiers 2, 4 (see **Chapter 6**) and 5 (see **7.12**). Full details are beyond the scope of this book and the Home Office-published guidance on its website (see **1.2.8**) should be consulted.

In outline, a prospective sponsor must apply for a licence for each Tier that it requires and indicate the number of certificates of sponsorship it intends to issue. The application must be made online, and the applicant must pay a prescribed fee and submit certain specified documents. Once licensed, a sponsor can issue certificates of sponsorship up to a set number. A licence lasts for four years, unless it is withdrawn or surrendered before then.

A licensed sponsor is rated A or B according to the Home Office's assessment of any risk posed. A sponsor that is B-rated must comply with a time-limited action plan, which will set out the steps it needs to take in order to gain or regain an A-rating. If the sponsor does not comply with this action plan, it is likely to lose its licence altogether.

7.8.3.3 Duties of a sponsor

A licensed sponsor must comply with certain duties, including reporting the following situations to the Home Office:

(a) the migrant does not turn up for his first day at work;

(b) the migrant is absent from work for more than 10 working days without permission;

(c) the migrant's contract of employment ends, including if he resigns or is dismissed;

(d) the name and address of any known new employer;

(e) any significant changes in the migrant's circumstances, for example change of job or salary;

(f) any suspicions that the migrant is breaching the conditions of his leave;

(g)   any significant changes in the sponsor's circumstances, for example if it stops trading or becomes insolvent, or substantially changes the nature of its business, or is involved in a merger or is taken over.

A sponsor must also keep proper records of the migrants it sponsors, including contact details and the migrant's identity card details.

7.8.3.4   Certificates of sponsorship

A licensed sponsor will provide its proposed Tier 2 Migrant with a certificate of sponsorship. But this is not an actual certificate or a paper document. It is a unique reference number that the sponsor issues to the migrant, along with details of the sponsorship. This information needs to be produced to the ECO with the entry clearance application. The certificate acts as confirmation from the sponsor that it wishes to bring the migrant to the UK and that to the best of its knowledge the applicant meets the requirements for the issue of the certificate of sponsorship. The certificate does not guarantee that entry clearance will be given. The ECO will check the application against the requirements of the Immigration Rules, including whether the applicant has enough points.

7.8.3.5   Job or sponsorship ends

What happens if a migrant's employment ends before his limited leave has expired? Or if, during his limited leave, his sponsor does not renew its licence or has it withdrawn? In these circumstances the Home Office will curtail (see **3.7**) the person's leave to 60 days, unless only six months or less is remaining. During that time the person could apply for leave to remain in another category or as a Tier 2 Migrant with another sponsor if he finds one.

7.8.4   Common features: extension

Just before the initial three years' limited leave of a Tier 2 Migrant expires, an application should be made to extend it under para 245GD of the Immigration Rules. Basically, the applicant will have to demonstrate that the original requirements have been met. Note that the migrant must be issued with a further certificate of sponsorship (see **7.8.3.3**) for his continued employment before making the application.

An applicant will fail if his application for an extension is liable to be refused under the general grounds in Part 9 of the Immigration Rules (see **3.5.4**) or he is an illegal entrant (see **10.4.2**), or if he is in the UK in breach of immigration laws, except that any period of overstaying for 28 days or less is ignored.

7.8.5   Common features: change of employment

What if a Tier 2 Migrant changes his employment, either within the same organisation or with a new organisation? He will need to apply for an extension of leave, and this will involve passing the relevant attributes test.

In these circumstances the migrant will automatically receive points for English language ability because he will have shown this for the initial application, although this may not apply to an intra-company transfer migrant (see **7.8.2.4**).

The migrant will also not have to give fresh evidence of maintenance.

7.8.6   Common features: supplementary employment

Can a Tier 2 Migrant work in addition to that for which he was granted leave? Yes, but any supplementary work must be:

(a)   a job on the shortage occupations list (see **7.9.3.1**) or a job in the same profession and at the same professional level as the main employment;

(b)   no more than 20 hours a week; and

(c)　　outside of the applicant's normal working hours for which his certificate of sponsorship was issued.

In addition, a migrant may do voluntary work in any sector, provided he is not paid and does not receive any other payment for his work except reasonable expenses.

7.8.7　Common features: limited leave conditions

In each category it will be a condition of a person's limited leave that he does not have recourse to public funds (see **3.3.2**).

A person must also register with the police if this is required by the Immigration Rules, para 326 (see **3.3.3**).

Additionally, it is a condition that the Tier 2 Migrant cannot take up employment except for his sponsor in the employment stated in his certificate, supplementary employment (see **7.8.6**) and voluntary work (see **7.8.6**).

7.8.8　Common features: settlement

Once a Tier 2 Migrant has spent a continuous period of five years in the UK in that category (but including any time as a Tier 1 Entrepreneur or Investor), an application can be made for settlement under para 245GF of the Immigration Rules.

7.8.9　Common features: family members

Who are the family members of a Tier 2 applicant? The answer is the spouse, civil partner, unmarried or same-sex partner, and children under 18.

A family member will have to obtain entry clearance and a subsequent extension. He or she may be able to apply for settlement at the same time as the Tier 2 Migrant. The provisions are exactly the same as for a Tier 1 Migrant family member: see **7.6**.

7.8.10　Switching

Switching to a Tier 2 Migrant category (apart from intra-company transfer) is by way of an application to the Home Office. The applicant must be lawfully in the UK already as a Tier 1 Migrant (see **7.2**), another Tier 2 Migrant, a Tier 4 Migrant (see **Chapter 6**) or a Tier 5 (Temporary Worker) Migrant (see **7.12**).

7.9　TIER 2: GENERAL MIGRANT AND INTRA-COMPANY TRANSFER WORKER

7.9.1　Overview

A general migrant must already have a job offer from a UK-based licensed employer that fills a recognised gap in the UK labour force.

An intra-company transfer worker is an employee of multi-national company who is being transferred by an overseas employer to a skilled job in a related UK entity. There are four sub-categories of intra-company transfer workers:

(a)　　Long Term Staff – the applicant has been working for the organisation for at least 12 months and is being transferred to a skilled job in the UK to fill a post which cannot be filled by a settled worker for a period of more than 12 calendar months (up to a maximum stay of five years or nine years for any staff earning £155,300 a year or more).

(b)　　Short Term Staff – the applicant has been working for the organisation for at least 12 months and is being transferred to a skilled job in the UK to fill a post which cannot be filled by a settled worker for a maximum period of 12 months.

(c)　　Graduate Trainee – the applicant is a recent graduate of a multi-national company who is being transferred to the UK branch of the same organisation as part of a structured graduate training programme, which clearly defines progression towards a managerial or specialist role.

(d)   Skills Transfer – the applicant is an overseas employee of a multi-national company who is being transferred to the UK branch of the same organisation in a graduate occupation to learn the skills and knowledge he will need to perform his job overseas, or to impart his specialist skills to the UK workforce.

The certificate of sponsorship (see **7.8.3.4**) must confirm that the job is at NQF level 6 (degree or above) or in a creative sector occupation skilled to NQF level 4 (Certificate of Higher Education), or the job is at NQF level 4 and appears on the list of shortage occupations (see **7.9.3.1**). This does not mean that the applicant must be educated to this level but that the job is at that level.

What is a job at NQF level 4 or 6 or above? If a sponsor has any doubts, the Home Office website reproduces the standard occupational classification codes produced by the Office for National Statistics. This contains nine major groups consisting of managers and senior officials, professional occupations, associate professional and technical occupations, administrative and secretarial occupations, skilled trades occupations, personal service occupations, sales and customer service occupations, process, plant and machine operatives, and elementary occupations. Having identified the appropriate group, the sponsor should check the relevant occupational code of practice in Appendix J to the Immigration Rules. There, occupations skilled to NQF level 6 or above are set out in Table 2 and occupations skilled to NQF level 4 or above are set out in Table 3.

7.9.2   The attributes

Table 7.10   General migrant – attributes points

Certificate of sponsorship	Points
Shortage occupation	30
Job offer passes Resident Labour Market Test	30
Job offer with annual salary of £155,300 or more	30

Appropriate salary	Points
Appropriate annual salary of £20,800 or more	20

To score the required 50 points, the general migrant applicant has to be entitled to a certificate of sponsorship for one of the three possible reasons and also have an appropriate salary.

We shall look at each of these in more detail at **7.9.3.1–7.9.3.4.**

Table 7.11   Intra-company transfer worker – attributes points

	Points
Certificate of sponsorship	30
Appropriate annual salary	20

It can be seen that to score the required 50 points the intra-company applicant will have to be entitled to a certificate of sponsorship and also have an appropriate salary.

We shall look at each of these in more detail at **7.9.3.5–7.9.3.6.**

7.9.3 Attributes: what the requirements mean

7.9.3.1 General migrant: shortage occupations list

For many years the UK has had a shortage of workers in certain occupations – that is to say, there are not enough resident workers to fill available jobs in particular sectors of the UK's economy. Historically this has included various healthcare and teaching jobs.

The Home Office has published a list of shortage occupations in Appendix K to the Immigration Rules.

If an applicant is to be awarded 30 points here, the job must, at the time the certificate of sponsorship was assigned to him, have appeared on the list in Appendix K, and his contracted working hours must be for at least 30 hours a week.

7.9.3.2 General migrant: resident labour market test

The Home Office recognises that it may be necessary for a sponsor to recruit a migrant from outside the UK to fill a particular vacancy that cannot be filled by a settled worker and that is not on the list of shortage occupations list (see **7.9.3.1**). However, this will be possible only if the sponsor can show that no suitably qualified settled worker is available to fill that vacancy.

How does a sponsor satisfy this test? The vacancy must usually be advertised as follows:

(a) If required by para 2 of Appendix J to the Immigration Rules the job must be advertised in Jobcentre Plus. Details can be found on its website at <www.jobcentreplus.gov.uk>.

(b) The sponsor must also advertise the vacancy in accordance with a code of practice specific to the type of sector or job. The codes of practice can be found in Appendix J to the Immigration Rules.

(c) The vacancy must be advertised to settled workers for a minimum of 28 days during the six-month period immediately before the date the sponsor assigns the certificate of sponsorship to the applicant. See para 78B(c) of the Immigration Rules.

(d) The sponsor must use the medium of advertising required by para 2 of Appendix J to the Immigration Rules and set out in the relevant code of practice, often a professional journal or the employment section of a national UK newspaper. The advertisement must include the job title; the main duties and responsibilities of the job; the location of the job; an indication of the salary package or salary range or terms on offer; the skills, qualifications and experience required; and the closing date for applications.

Can a sponsor use other recruitment methods? Yes, if allowed by the appropriate code of practice. These may include Internet advertising, as well as the use of a recruitment agency or head-hunters.

If the recruitment process produces no suitable resident workers, the sponsor can recruit from abroad, but any certificate of sponsorship must be issued within six months of the advertisement being placed. Why? Because that will ensure that the results of the advertising reflect the current availability of the skills the sponsor requires.

7.9.3.3 General migrant: job offer with annual salary of £155,300 or more

In order for the applicant to be awarded 30 points here, the applicant's certificate of sponsorship must show that his gross annual salary, including such allowances as are acceptable for this purpose (see **7.9.3.4**), to be paid by his sponsor is £155,300 or more.

7.9.3.4 General migrant: appropriate annual salary of £20,800 or more

In order for the applicant to be awarded 20 points here, the applicant's certificate of sponsorship must show that his gross annual salary, including such allowances as are acceptable, to be paid by his sponsor is £20,800 or more.

So what counts? Paragraph 81E of Appendix A to the Immigration Rules states that Home Office considers the basic gross pay (before tax) plus any allowances, such as London weighting, which would also be paid to a local settled worker in similar circumstances, provided these allowances are part of the applicant's guaranteed salary package.

What is not taken into account? The Home Office will not consider overtime or benefits such as bonus or incentive pay, travel and subsistence (including travel to and from the applicant's home country).

Points are only awarded for up to a maximum of 48 hours a week, even if the applicant will be working more than this. For example, if the applicant will earn £10 per hour, working 60 hours per week, the salary taken into account is £24,960 (£10 x 48 x 52).

No points are awarded for appropriate salary if the salary is less than the appropriate rate for the job as stated in the codes of practice in Appendix J to the Immigration Rules.

7.9.3.5   Intra-company transfer: certificate of sponsorship

Table 7.12   **Intra-company transfer worker – 30 points for certificate of sponsorship**

Certificate of sponsorship for long term or short term staff
The applicant has been employed by his sponsoring organisation for at least 12 months immediately before the date of the application either outside the UK; and/or in the UK if the applicant has or was last granted leave to work for his sponsoring organisation in the category of Tier 2 (Intra-Company Transfer: Short Term Staff) or Tier 2 (Intra-Company Transfer: Established Staff).
Certificate of sponsorship for graduate trainee
The applicant has been employed outside the UK by his sponsoring organisation as part of a graduate training programme for at least three months immediately before the date of the application.
Certificate of sponsorship for skills transfer
The applicant has been employed outside the UK by his sponsoring organisation immediately before the date of his application. The sole purpose of the transfer to the UK branch of the multi-national company must be for the applicant to learn the skills and knowledge needed to
perform his role overseas or to transfer skills and knowledge to the sponsor's UK workforce. The applicant's appointment must be additional to his sponsor's UK staffing requirements; if it were not for the need for skills transfer, the role in the UK would not exist.

7.9.3.6   Intra-company transfer: appropriate salary

Table 7.13   **Intra-company transfer worker – 20 points for appropriate annual salary**

Long Term Staff	at least £41,500
Short Term Staff, Graduate Trainee or Skills Transfer	at least £24,800

These annual salary figures are the minimum. It is the gross salary that is taken into account and calculated as for a general migrant (**7.9.3.4**). The actual rate of pay must meet the rate set out in the appropriate code of practice.

7.9.3.7   Genuine vacancy

By para 81H of Appendix A to the Immigration Rules, no points will be awarded for a Certificate of Sponsorship if the Secretary of State has reasonable grounds to believe that:

(a)   the job described in the application is not a genuine vacancy; or

(b)   the stated requirements of the job described in the application and in any advertisements for the job are inappropriate for the job on offer and/or have been tailored to exclude resident workers from being recruited.

7.9.4   Tier 2 (General) Migrant monthly limit

From April 2011, the Government introduced a monthly limit on the number of certificates of sponsorship that can be issued for Tier 2 (General) Migrants. Currently, the monthly limit is 1,650 certificates. Note that this does not apply to an applicant filling a vacancy with an annual salary of £155,300 or more, nor to an application to switch into this category.

How does the Home Office apply the limits? For the full and rather complex details, see para 83 of Appendix A to the Immigration Rules.

7.9.5   Tier 4 (General) Student switching to Tier 2 (General) Migrant

What if a Tier 4 (General) Student graduate (see **Chapter 6**) obtains a job offer from a UK-based employer? After graduating, can the student apply to remain in the UK as a Tier 2 (General) Migrant? Yes, provided:

(a)   the Tier 4 (General) Student's leave has not expired;

(b)   the student has lawfully completed and passed a UK Bachelor or postgraduate degree, Postgraduate Certificate in Education or Professional Graduate Diploma of Education, or has completed a minimum of 12 months' study in the UK towards a UK PhD; and

(c)   the course was studied at a UK institution that is a UK recognised or listed body, or which holds a sponsor licence under Tier 4 of the points-based system (see **6.1.1**).

The applicant should apply from within the UK to switch into Tier 2 (General) following graduation. His sponsoring employer does not have to satisfy the resident labour market test (as the applicant is awarded 30 points for sponsorship), but all the other Tier 2 (General) criteria apply.

7.9.6   Minimum salary required for settlement

From 6 April 2016, a Tier 2 (General) Migrant who applies for settlement must be paid at least £35,000 gross per annum (or, if higher, the rate set by the relevant Code of Practice in Appendix J to the Immigration Rules).

Note that this amount will increase in future years as follows:

£35,500 if applying on or after 6 April 2018;
£35,800 if applying on or after 6 April 2019; and
£36,200 if applying on or after 6 April 2020.

This minimum salary requirement does not apply to an applicant on the shortage occupation list (see **7.9.3.1**), or to the occupations skilled to PhD-level listed in the Codes of Practice in Appendix J to the Immigration Rules.

7.10   TIER 2: MINISTER OF RELIGION

7.10.1   Overview

This category is for a religious worker within a recognised religion and anyone who ministers, whether regularly or occasionally, and/or performs pastoral duties. Pastoral duties include leading worship regularly and on special occasions; providing religious education for children and adults by preaching or teaching; officiating at marriages, funerals and other special services; offering counselling and welfare support to members of the congregation; recruiting, training and co-ordinating the work of any local volunteers and lay preachers.

This category is also for a migrant coming to work in the UK as a missionary, a member of a religious order such as a monastic community of monks or nuns, or a similar religious community which involves permanent commitment.

As to English language, see **7.8.2.4**.

7.10.2   Attributes: sponsorship

The minister must score 50 points by way of sponsorship. This requires the following:

(a)   The minister must be qualified to do the job in question. For example, he must be an ordained minister of religion where ordination is prescribed by a religious faith as the sole means of entering the ministry.

(b)   The minister must intend to be based in the UK for the duration of his limited leave.

(c)   The minister must intend to depart from the UK when his leave expires.

7.10.3   Resident labour market test

What about the resident labour market test (see **7.9.3.2**)? Unless the role is exempt from the test, the sponsor must confirm that the minister will not be displacing or denying an employment opportunity to a suitably qualified member of the resident UK labour force. Either the sponsor must have undertaken an appropriate resident labour market test for the role, or, if that is inappropriate, the migrant must be additional to the sponsor's normal staffing requirements. The minister must not be taking a position that would otherwise need to be filled by a resident UK worker.

7.10.4   Maintenance

As to maintenance, note that the sponsor must provide an undertaking to support the minister through funds and/or accommodation that are sufficient for the minister to maintain himself throughout the duration of the certificate of sponsorship.

7.11   TIER 2: SPORTS PERSON

7.11.1   Overview

This category is for elite sports people and coaches who are internationally established at the highest level, whose employment will make a significant contribution to the development of their sport at the highest level in the UK, and who intend to base themselves in the UK.

7.11.2   Attributes: sponsorship

The sports person must score 50 points by way of sponsorship. This requires the following:

(a)   The sports person must be qualified to do the job in question.

(b)   The sports person must intend to be based in the UK for the duration of his limited leave.

(c)   The sports person must intend to depart from the UK when his leave expires.

All migrants in this category must have the approval of the appropriate governing body for their sport as listed in Appendix M to the Immigration Rules. This is officially known as an endorsement. This endorsement will confirm that the sports person meets the code of practice as agreed between the Home Office and the sporting body, and also confirms that:

(a)   the migrant is internationally established at the highest level;

(b)   the migrant will make a significant contribution to the development of his sport at the highest level in the UK; and

(c)   it is appropriate to fill the post with a migrant who is not settled in the UK. The endorsement therefore replaces the resident labour market test for this category.

As to English language and maintenance, see **7.8.2.4** and **7.8.2.5** respectively.

7.12 TIER 5: TEMPORARY MIGRANTS

This tier covers temporary sponsored workers (and their family members) who can remain in the UK for no longer than 12 months (creative and sporting workers and charity workers) or 24 months (religious workers, Government authorised exchange workers, international agreement workers and workers under a youth mobility scheme), or up to a maximum of 72 months (Government authorised exchange workers). We shall consider each type of worker briefly in turn. Details of sponsorship are given at **7.8.3**.

Note that a Tier 5 Migrant cannot switch into any other immigration category. However, during his limited leave he can do additional work, provided that it is for no longer than 20 hours per week, it is outside his normal working hours, and it is in the same sector and at the same level as the work for which his certificate of sponsorship was issued.

Applicants can find detailed guidance and application forms on the Home Office website (see **1.2.8**).

7.12.1 Creative and sporting worker

7.12.1.1 A profile

This category is for creative artists (performers and entertainers) and sports people who wish to work in the UK for up to 12 months. Entertainers may be individuals, or part of a large touring entourage working in areas such as dance and theatre. Sports people should be internationally established at the highest level in their sport, and/or their employment in the UK should make a significant contribution to the development and operation of that particular sport in this country. A sports coach must be suitably qualified.

7.12.1.2 Sponsorship

In order to gain a licence as a sponsor of creative workers and their entourage, the prospective sponsor must be operating, or intend to operate, in the creative sector. Examples include a national body, event organiser, producer, venue, agent or other similar organisation.

In order to gain a licence as a sponsor of sports people, the prospective sponsor must be a sporting body, sports club, events organiser or other organiser operating, or intending to operate, in the sporting sector. Appendix M to the Immigration Rules contains a list of sports and their respective governing bodies.

7.12.1.3 Resident labour market test

A sponsor of creative artists operating in dance, theatre, film and television must follow the codes of practice for taking into account the needs of the resident labour market in these areas. Otherwise the sponsor must conduct a resident labour market test, unless the migrant falls into one of the following categories that are deemed to be making an additional contribution to the UK creative sector and therefore are not a threat to the resident labour force:

(a) The migrant is required for continuity in the creative sector. Here the migrant must have worked for a period of one month or more on the same production outside the EEA prior to coming to the UK.

(b) The migrant is internationally famous in his field.

(c) The migrant is established at the highest level in his profession within the creative sector, ie he has performed at the highest level and has established a reputation in his profession. This category also includes groups of people.

(d) The migrant is engaged by a unit company within the creative sector. A unit company is a large group of entertainers who have regularly performed together in their own country and overseas as part of an established production before entering the UK. Home Office guidance is that pop and music groups are not classed as unit companies.

If a Tier 5 sports person does not have the endorsement of his governing body (see **7.11.2**), the resident labour market test must be carried out.

7.12.1.4   The points system

The migrant must score 40 points, as shown in **Table 7.14** below.

Table 7.14   Tier 5 creative and sporting worker – the points system

Criteria	Requirements	Points
Sponsorship	The migrant is seeking entry to the UK to work or perform in the UK in the relevant sector,	30
	The migrant is not intending to establish himself in business in the UK, His employment must not threaten the resident labour force, *and* The migrant must comply with the conditions of leave and will depart when his limited leave ends.	
Maintenance	£945 and £630 for each dependant or the certificate of sponsorship is issued by an A-rated sponsor and the sponsor certifies that the migrant will not claim benefits while in the UK. However, the sponsor cannot certify maintenance for any dependants.	10

7.12.2   Charity worker

7.12.2.1   A profile

This category is for a charity worker undertaking voluntary activity and not paid employment. The migrant should intend to carry out fieldwork directly related to the purpose of the sponsoring organisation.

As the migrant is not taking paid employment, the resident labour market test does not apply.

7.12.2.2   Sponsorship

In order to gain a licence as a sponsor of voluntary workers, the employer must be a registered, excepted or exempt UK charity according to the relevant legislation in force in its part of the UK.

7.12.2.3   The points system

The migrant must score 40 points, as shown in **Table 7.15** below.

Table 7.15   Tier 5 charity worker – the points system

Criteria	Requirements	Points
Sponsorship	The migrant must intend to do voluntary work directly relating to the sponsor's purpose. The migrant must not be paid or otherwise remunerated for his work. The migrant must not take up a permanent position. The migrant must comply with the conditions of leave and depart when his limited leave ends.	30

Criteria	Requirements	Points
Maintenance	£945 and £630 for each dependant or the certificate of sponsorship is issued by an A-rated sponsor and the sponsor certifies that the migrant will not claim benefits while in the UK. However, the sponsor cannot certify maintenance for any dependants.	10

7.12.3 Religious worker

7.12.3.1 A profile

This category is for either:

(a) a religious worker; or

(b) a visiting religious worker who is employed overseas in the same capacity as that for which he is seeking to come to the UK, although the exact detail of his duties in the UK may differ. This employment should be ongoing, and the time spent in the UK should be consistent with a break from the worker's employment.

In either case the worker may perform religious rites, such as tending to deities or reading scripture aloud to the congregation, but cannot carry out any of the pastoral duties of a Tier 2 minister (see **7.10**).

7.12.3.2 Sponsorship

In order to gain a licence as a sponsor, the employer must be a genuine religious institution, which is a registered, excepted or exempt UK charity according to the relevant charity legislation in force in its part of the UK, or an ecclesiastical corporation (either corporation sole or body corporate) established for charitable purposes.

7.12.3.3 Resident labour market test

When issuing a certificate of sponsorship, the sponsor thereby certifies that the migrant will not be displacing or denying an employment opportunity to a suitably qualified member of the resident labour force.

7.12.3.4 The points system

The migrant must score 40 points, as shown in **Table 7.16**.

Table 7.16   Tier 5 religious worker – the points system

Criteria	Requirements	Points
Sponsorship	The migrant must be qualified to do the job in question. The migrant must not intend to take employment for the sponsor except as a visiting religious worker or a religious worker. The migrant must not claim benefits while in the UK. The migrant must be filling a genuine vacancy that cannot be filled with a suitable qualified member of the resident labour force. *and* The migrant must comply with the conditions of leave and depart when his limited leave ends.	30

Criteria	Requirements	Points
Maintenance	£945 and £630 for each dependant or the certificate of sponsorship is issued by an A-rated sponsor and the sponsor certifies that the migrant will not claim benefits while in the UK. However, the sponsor cannot certify maintenance for any dependants.	10

7.12.4   Government authorised exchange worker

7.12.4.1   A profile

This category is for migrants coming to the UK through approved schemes that aim to share knowledge, experience and best practice. It is for work experience. It cannot be used to fill a job vacancy.

7.12.4.2   Sponsorship

Sponsorship for this category is rather novel. Government policy is that in order to prevent potential abuse of this category and the formation of small individual schemes, employers and organisations cannot sponsor migrants. Instead, there will be an overarching body to administer the exchange scheme. This overarching body will be the sponsor and will need to apply for a licence. The scheme and the body must have the support of a UK government department. The body will issue certificates of sponsorship to migrants who meet the requirements of the scheme. A list of approved schemes can be found in Appendix N to the Immigration Rules.

> **EXAMPLE**
>
> The Law Society is an overarching body that can authorise eligible firms to issue certificates of sponsorship to prospective short-term migrants under internship and secondment programmes.

7.12.4.3   The points system

The migrant must score 40 points, as shown in **Table 7.17**.

Table 7.17   Tier 5 government authorised exchange worker – the points system

Criteria	Requirements	Points
Sponsorship	The migrant must be taking part in a work experience scheme, The migrant must not be filling a genuine vacancy, The migrant's work must be in addition to the normal staffing needs, The migrant must be undertaking skilled work at S/NVQ level 3 or above, *and* The migrant's work must conform with relevant UK and European legislation.	30
Maintenance	£945 and £630 for each dependant or the certificate of sponsorship is issued by an A-rated sponsor and the sponsor certifies that the migrant will not claim benefits while in the UK. However, the sponsor cannot certify maintenance for any dependants.	10

7.12.5 International agreement worker

This category is for migrants who are coming to the UK under contract to provide a service that is covered under international law, including the General Agreement on Trade in Services; similar agreements between the UK and another country; employees of overseas governments and international organisations; and private servants in diplomatic households.

This is a specialised category the details of which are beyond the scope of this book.

7.12.6 Worker under a youth mobility scheme

7.12.6.1 A profile

This is a novel category, as the sponsors under the youth mobility scheme are the national governments of the Home Office-approved participating countries listed in Appendix G to the Immigration Rules – currently Australia, Canada, Japan, Monaco, Taiwan, South Korea, Hong Kong and New Zealand. Places on the scheme for each of those countries are capped each year by the UK Government. Once the limit is reached, no further applications will be considered that year.

So how young does a national of an approved participating country have to be? The answer is between the ages of 18 and 30 inclusive when his entry clearance is granted.

Anything else? Yes, two matters.

First, an applicant must not previously have been in the UK in this category (or its predecessor, which was known as the 'working holidaymaker scheme').

Secondly, an applicant must not have dependent children, ie children under 18 who either are living with the applicant or for whom he is financially responsible.

What about a spouse or partner? The Home Office guidance is that there is nothing to prevent an applicant who is married or has a partner from participating in the scheme, whether his spouse or partner accompanies him or not. However, spouses and partners of participants under the scheme cannot enter as dependants. They may accompany a participant, or join him in the UK, provided that they qualify and obtain an entry clearance in their own right either under the scheme or in another category.

A young foreign national who has entered the UK in this category may, during his two years' limited leave, do whatever work he likes, except for setting up his own business, professional sport, or working as a doctor in training. An employer is therefore free to employ a youth mobility participant on that basis.

A person can be granted leave in this category only once.

7.12.6.2 The points system

The migrant must score 50 points in three areas, as shown in **Table 7.18**.

Table 7.18   Tier 5 worker under a youth mobility scheme – the points system

Criteria	Requirements	Points
Sponsorship	Citizen of an approved participating country (currently Australia, Canada, Japan, Monaco and New Zealand) and that country's quota of places has not been exhausted, or a British Overseas Citizen, British Overseas Territories Citizen or British National (Overseas) Citizen (see **2.4**).	30
Age	The applicant must be between 18 and 30 years of age inclusive at the date that his entry clearance becomes valid for use, and under the age of 31 on the date his application was made.	10

Criteria	Requirements	Points
Maintenance	The applicant must be able to support himself from the point at which he enters the UK until he begins earning. An applicant will need to demonstrate sufficient funds for the first two months following arrival in the UK in the amount of £1,890 which is held in his personal bank account on the date his application was made.	10

7.13 SOLE REPRESENTATIVE OF AN OVERSEAS FIRM

7.13.1 A profile

If an overseas firm has no branch, subsidiary or representative in the UK, it may wish to send one of its senior employees to the UK to establish a wholly-owned subsidiary or branch in the UK. This is a long-standing category and it is not part of the points system. The requirements are set out in the Immigration Rules, para 144, as follows.

7.13.2 Paragraph 144(i) requirement

The first requirement to be met by a person seeking leave to enter the UK as a sole representative is that the applicant has been recruited and taken on as an employee outside the UK as a representative of a firm which has its headquarters and principal place of business outside the UK and which has no branch, subsidiary or other representative in the UK.

The overseas firm must be a genuine commercial enterprise. This is judged in the round, taking into account the length of time that the company has been established, its turnover, profitability, the number of employees, etc. It must be the intention that the business remains centred abroad. This does not mean, however, that an otherwise sound application is refused because of evidence of an intention to make the branch in the UK flourish so vigorously that it might, at some time in the longer term, overshadow the overseas parent company. Companies which have been trading for less than 12 months are required to justify the need to establish an overseas branch here.

The overseas parent company must be sending the sole representative to the UK in order that he establishes a commercial presence for the company here in the form either of a registered branch or of a wholly-owned subsidiary. A 'branch' is a part of a company which is organised so as to conduct business on behalf of the company. This means that a person is able to deal directly with the branch in the UK, instead of the company overseas. The company setting up a branch in the UK must apply to register with Companies House within one month of having opened the branch. A wholly-owned subsidiary is a separate corporate body and is not subject to these registration requirements, being treated in the same way as any other company incorporated in the UK.

Lastly, note that the branch of the overseas business which is to be established in the UK must be concerned with the same type of business activity as the overseas firm.

7.13.3 Paragraph 144(ii) requirement

The second requirement is that the applicant must seek entry to the UK as a senior employee with full authority to take operational decisions on behalf of the overseas firm for the purpose of representing it in the UK by establishing and operating a registered branch or wholly-owned subsidiary of that overseas firm.

The sole representative must have been recruited outside the UK and joined the parent company abroad. Home Office guidance is that 'he is likely to be someone who has been employed by the parent company for some time and holds a senior position there'. If the sole representative is not an existing employee, or has been employed for a short time only, then he must be able to demonstrate a good track record in the same or in a closely related field, in order to show that the reasons for his appointment are compelling. Sole representatives must, in the first instance, be employed by the overseas firm direct (although they may later be employed by the UK subsidiary). Agents who are hired to market the company's product in the UK are normally self-employed and provide their services for a fee. Such people cannot therefore qualify as sole representatives. Neither can sales representatives or others, such as buyers, who fulfil a single function only. However, senior sales staff who have other responsibilities, such as marketing and distribution, are not debarred from qualifying as sole representatives.

The applicant is required to provide a document detailing the terms and conditions of his employment. The importance of the position should be reflected in the salary and other benefits. The Home Office expects a sole representative to be vested with the authority to take the majority of decisions locally, but accepts that it is unreasonable to expect him to take unilateral decisions on all matters.

7.13.4 Paragraph 144(iii) requirement

The applicant must intend to be employed full time as a representative of that overseas firm.

Sole representatives are expected to base themselves in the UK and to spend a minimum of nine months of the year here. However, applications may be approved from those who intend to spend less time in the UK, provided that the additional absences are essential to the running of the UK business, for example, if the UK office is to be the centre of European operations. Applicants who intend to spend less than four months of the year in the UK are unlikely to satisfy the Home Office that they are making genuine efforts to establish a commercial presence in the UK. Such persons should be advised to apply instead as business visitors (see **5.4**).

7.13.5 Paragraph 144(iv) requirement

The applicant must not be a majority shareholder in the overseas firm.

Majority shareholders in the parent company are not eligible for entry as sole representatives. When the sole representative is a major shareholder in the parent company, Home Office guidance provides that care must be taken to establish that the arrangement is not one devised simply to circumvent the more rigorous requirements of the business rules. As a rule of thumb, shareholdings in excess of 30% should attract detailed scrutiny. If it is evident that the applicant, as well as being a major shareholder, is also the driving force behind the parent company such that his presence in the UK is likely to mean that the centre of operations has shifted to this country, the application should be refused. The factors to be weighed in deciding this include:

(a)   the size of the applicant's shareholding;

(b)   his position within the firm;

(c)   the number of senior employees who will remain abroad; and

(d)   the extent to which the company's success seems linked to the applicant's specific talents and performance.

7.13.6 Paragraph 144(v) requirement

The applicant must not intend to take other employment.

Sole representatives are required to work full time as such, but this is not linked to a set number of hours per week. The main consideration is that the parent firm should be paying a 'full-time' salary sufficient for the sole representative to support and accommodate himself and any dependants without taking other work or resorting to public funds.

7.13.7 Paragraph 144(vi) requirement

The applicant must be able to demonstrate English language skills at a basic user standard. How can he do this?

(a) he is the national of a Home Office-designated English-speaking country (see the list at **7.4.3.2**);

(b) he has a Home Office-recognised qualification from a prescribed country (see the details at **7.4.3.3**);

(c) he has a recognised qualification that was taught or researched in English to a prescribed minimum standard; or

(d) he passes a prescribed English language test.

7.13.8 Paragraph 144(vii) requirement

The applicant must be able to maintain and accommodate himself and any dependants adequately without recourse to public funds.

Sole representatives may be offered a remuneration package consisting of a basic salary and commission. This is acceptable to the Home Office as long as the salary element is sufficient to support the applicant and his family without recourse to public funds. As this category is not part of the points system, no set amount is prescribed for maintenance. Full details may be found at **8.3.6.9**.

7.13.9 Paragraph 144(viii) requirement

The applicant must hold a valid UK entry clearance for entry in this capacity.

Entry clearance is mandatory for a person who wishes to enter the UK in this category.

It is not possible to switch into this category.

7.13.10 Supporting documentation for entry clearance

The Home Office requires the following documents to support the application:

(a) a full description of the company's activities with details of the company's assets and accounts, including full details of the company share distribution for the previous year;

(b) confirmation that the overseas company will establish a wholly-owned subsidiary or register a branch in the UK;

(c) the applicant's job description, salary and contract of employment;

(d) confirmation that the applicant is fully familiar with the company's activities and that he has full powers to negotiate and take operational decisions without reference to the parent company;

(e) a notarised statement from the company that the applicant will be its sole representative and that it has no other branch, subsidiary, or representative in the UK;

(f) a notarised statement confirming that the company's operations will remain centred overseas;

(g) a notarised statement that the applicant will not engage in business of his own, neither will he represent any other company's interest.

7.13.11 Extension

Leave is initially given for three years. Towards the end of that time an application may be made to the Home Office for a two-year extension of stay under the Immigration Rules, para 147.

This requires that the sole representative:

(a) entered the UK with a valid UK entry clearance as a sole representative of an overseas firm;

(b) can show that the overseas firm still has its headquarters and principal place of business outside the UK;

(c) is employed full time as a representative of that overseas firm and has established and is in charge of its registered branch or wholly-owned subsidiary;

(d) is still required for the employment in question, as certified by his employer;

(e) meets the requirements of para 144(v)–(vii) (see **7.13.6–7.13.8**); and

(f) must not be in the UK in breach of immigration laws except that any period of overstaying for a period of 28 days or less will be disregarded.

The application should be supported by the following evidence:

(a) a letter from the parent company stating that it wishes to continue to employ the applicant as previously;

(b) evidence in the form of accounts of the business generated (this form can be flexible according to the nature of the company's business);

(c) evidence of the salary paid to the applicant in the first two years of operation and the terms on which the salary will be paid in future;

(d) evidence that he has established and is in charge of a registered branch or wholly-owned subsidiary of the overseas parent company.

7.13.12 Settlement

When a sole representative has remained in the UK for five years in this capacity, he may be eligible to apply for settlement under the Immigration Rules, para 150.

This requires that the sole representative:

(a) has spent a continuous period of five years in the UK in this capacity;

(b) has met the requirements of para 147 (see **7.13.11**) throughout the five-year period;

(c) is still required for the employment in question, as certified by his employer;

(d) has sufficient knowledge of the English language and sufficient knowledge about life in the UK (see **3.8.7**);

(e) does not fall for refusal under the general grounds for refusal (see **3.5.4**); and

(f) is not in the UK in breach of immigration laws except that any period of overstaying for a period of 28 days or less will be disregarded.

7.13.13 Family members of a sole representative

The spouse, civil partner, same-sex or unmarried partner and children under 18 of an applicant will need to apply for entry clearance (see paras 194 and 197 respectively). They may also subsequently apply for settlement (see paras 196D and 198 respectively). See further **Chapter 8**.

7.14 COMMONWEALTH CITIZEN WITH UK ANCESTRY

7.14.1 A profile

A Commonwealth citizen (see the list at **Appendix 9**), aged 17 or over, who can show that one of his grandparents was born in the UK (and Islands) and who intends to take or seek employment in the UK and support himself without needing public funds, may be granted entry clearance in this category. Entry clearance is compulsory and limited leave is given of five years. Thereafter an application can be made for settlement.

In this category an applicant does not need to meet the requirements of the points system under any of the tiers. The requirements to be met are set out in the Immigration Rules, para 186, as follows.

7.14.2 A Commonwealth citizen

The applicant must satisfy the ECO that he is a citizen of a Commonwealth country.

7.14.3 Aged 17 or over

The applicant must satisfy the ECO that he is or will be at least 17 years of age when entering the UK.

7.14.4 Proof of ancestry

The applicant must be able to provide proof that one of his grandparents was born in the UK and Islands, and that any such grandparent is the applicant's blood grandparent or grandparent by reason of an adoption recognised by the laws of the UK relating to adoption.

As regards proof of birth in the UK and Islands, the applicant must be able to demonstrate that the grandparent on whom the claim is based was born in:

(a)   the UK;

(b)   Channel Islands;

(c)   the Isle of Man; or

(d)   if the grandparent was born before 31 March 1922, what is now the Republic of Ireland.

Home Office guidance is that birth on a British registered ship or aircraft also counts.

The applicant may be related to that grandparent in one of two ways. First, by blood. So a qualifying connection can be made through a legitimate or an illegitimate line. Secondly, by adoption. An applicant who has been adopted, or whose parents were, can qualify if:

(a)   he has been adopted by someone who has a UK-born parent; or

(b)   one of his parents was adopted by a person born in the UK; or

(c)   his natural grandparents were born in the UK.

No claim can be made through step-parents.

What sort of proof of the relationship is required by an ECO? The applicant should produce his own full birth certificate; where appropriate the marriage certificates of his parents and appropriate grandparents (or, if unmarried, evidence of the relationship if the claim is made through the paternal line); if applicable the legal adoption papers of the applicant or his parents; and the full birth certificates of the parent and grandparent through whose ancestry he is making the application.

> **EXAMPLE**
>
> Charles is a Commonwealth citizen, aged 20. His mother, Florence, was not born in the UK. His grandmother, Rose, on his maternal siECOde (ie Florence's mother) was born in the UK. What documents should Charles produce to prove this ancestral link? A minimum of three documents are required to confirm the following details:
>
> (a)   his birth certificate naming Florence as his mother;
>
> (b)   Florence's birth certificate naming Rose as her mother; and
>
> (c)   Rose's UK birth certificate showing she was born in the UK.

7.14.5 Able to work and intends to take or seek employment in the UK

Entry clearance is for the purpose of work in the UK, not to study or visit. The applicant must satisfy the ECO that he has arranged employment in the UK already, or that he genuinely intends to seek employment and has a realistic prospect of securing it. Home Office guidance is that the ECO will consider such factors as the applicant's age and health, eg any medical problems that may prevent the applicant from taking employment.

7.14.6   No recourse to public funds

The applicant must be able to maintain and accommodate himself and any dependants adequately without recourse to public funds (see **3.3.2**).

As this category is not part of the points system, no set amount is prescribed for maintenance. Full details can be found at **8.3.6.9**.

7.14.7   Holds a valid UK entry clearance for entry in this capacity

Entry clearance is mandatory for a person who wishes to enter the UK in this category.

It is not possible to switch into this category.

7.14.8   Settlement

Near to the end of the person's five years' limited leave he should apply for settlement. The requirements are set out in para 192, as follows:

(a)   the applicant meets the requirements of para 186(i)–(v) (see **7.14.2–7.14.7**);

(b)   the applicant has spent a continuous period of five years in the UK in this capacity;

(c)   the applicant has sufficient knowledge of the English language and sufficient knowledge about life in the UK (see **3.8.7**);

(d)   does not fall for refusal under the general grounds for refusal (see **3.5.4**); and

(e)   must not be in the UK in breach of immigration laws except that any period of overstaying for a period of 28 days or less will be disregarded.

Although (b) above requires the applicant to have resided continuously in the UK in this category for five years, there is no requirement that any employment taken must be continuous. Home Office guidance is that if the applicant is in employment at the time of the application then all that is required is a letter from his current employers confirming the employment will continue. If, however, the applicant is not employed then he will need to produce evidence of his employment record throughout the five years and evidence of the attempts made to find employment. If it is clear that the applicant has not been in employment for any length of time over the five years, he will be asked to provide reasons as to why he has failed to obtain employment. Unless there is a very good reason for this, the application will be refused. The Home Office will also make enquiries as to how the applicant has been supporting himself without a regular income.

7.14.9   Family members

The spouse, civil partner, same-sex or unmarried partner and children under 18 of an applicant will need to apply for entry clearance (see paras 194 and 197). They may also subsequently apply for settlement (see paras 196D and 198). See further **Chapter 8**.

7.15   ILLEGAL WORKING IN THE UK

7.15.1   Employer's duties

The law on preventing illegal migrant working in the UK has evolved over time. An employer's legal responsibilities may therefore vary according to when he recruited his existing staff. There is a very useful summary of the previous legal requirements on the Home Office website (see **1.2.8**). The current law may be found in ss 15 to 26 of the IANA 2006. This makes an employer liable to payment of a civil financial penalty of up to £10,000 if he employs a person aged 16 or over who is subject to immigration control and who has no permission to work in the UK, or who works in breach of his conditions of stay in the UK (see **3.3.1**).

Note that it is essential that any appeal against a civil penalty is made promptly as the court has no discretion to extend the time limits laid down in the IANA 2006: see *Massan v Secretary of State for the Home Department* [2011] EWCA Civ 686.

7.15.2 Civil penalty

How can an employer avoid civil liability? This is answered by the Immigration (Restrictions on Employment) Order 2007 (SI 2007/3290, as amended). The employer must obtain from the prospective employee certain original documents that need to be checked in accordance with art 6, for example, if the document contains a date of birth, the employer must be satisfied that this is consistent with the appearance of the prospective employee. The employer must keep a copy of any document for a period of not less than two years after the employment comes to an end. So what documents count? The employer can choose from documents in the Schedule. This consists of two lists: list A, which includes a British or EEA national's passport; and list B, which includes a biometric immigration document issued by the Home Office to the holder which indicates that the person named in it can stay in the UK and is allowed to do the work in question. List A documents only have to be checked once by the employer. However, list B documents must be checked at least once every 12 months.

7.15.3 Criminal offence

An employer commits a criminal offence if he knowingly employs a person aged 16 or over who is subject to immigration control and who has no permission to work in the UK, or who works in breach of his conditions of stay in the UK. What sentence might the employer face? An unlimited fine and/or a maximum two-year prison sentence can be imposed.

FAMILY REUNION

8.1 OVERVIEW

8.1.1 Background

Until July 2012, Part 8 of the Immigration Rules had dealt with most family reunion situations. Now the only significant group left in Part 8 are children seeking to join either a parent, both parents or a relative in the UK for the purposes of settlement (see para 297, detailed at **8.9** below). It is Appendix FM to the Immigration Rules that currently sets out the requirements for a person to enter or remain in the UK on the basis of his family life with a person who is a British citizen (see **2.2**), or settled in the UK (see **3.8**), or in the UK with limited leave as a refugee (see **9.8**) or a person granted humanitarian protection (see **9.10.1**).

Broadly, Appendix FM covers entry clearance, extensions and switching, as well as settlement by partners (see **8.3**), parents (see **8.10**) and adult dependent relatives (see **8.11**). It also provides for entry by a child of a parent already in the UK with limited leave as a partner or parent (see **8.12**).

In this chapter we shall also consider one other category, namely, a person allowed to remain in the UK and ultimately settle on the basis that he has established a private life here under Article 8 ECHR (see **8.13**).

8.1.2 Partners

8.1.2.1 Terminology

The member of the couple who is not a British citizen, nor settled in the UK nor in the UK with limited leave as a refugee or humanitarian protection, is known as the applicant. The applicant's spouse, civil partner, fiancé(e), proposed civil partner or the person with whom he is in a long-term heterosexual or same-sex relationship is known as the applicant's partner (or sometimes as his 'sponsor').

8.1.2.2 Immigration controls for a fiancé(e) or proposed civil partner

There is no provision for a person already in the UK to switch into the category of fiancé(e) or proposed civil partner. So the applicant must be outside the UK and will have to apply for entry clearance. If successful, he will be granted entry clearance for a period not exceeding six months. This will be subject to a condition of no recourse to public funds (see **3.3.2**), a prohibition on employment (see **3.3.1**) and, if appropriate, registration with the police (see **3.3.3**).

The applicant will therefore have six months in the UK for the marriage or civil partnership to take place. He should then apply to the Home Office for leave to remain in the UK as a spouse or civil partner (see **8.1.2.3**).

8.1.2.3 Immigration controls for all other partners

Where the applicant is outside the UK he will have to apply for entry clearance.

If successful, he will be granted entry clearance for an initial period not exceeding 33 months, subject to a condition of no recourse to public funds (see **3.3.2**) and, if appropriate, registration with the police (see **3.3.3**). The applicant will be free to work in the UK. Just before an applicant has completed 30 months with limited leave as a partner, he should make an application for further leave to remain for 30 months. After 60 months' leave in total he will be eligible to apply for indefinite leave to remain. This is known as the 'five-year family route'.

Note that if an applicant cannot meet the usual requirements for an extension of limited leave as a partner, it may be possible to remain by establishing a claim under Article 8 ECHR. In those circumstances the applicant will have a longer route to settlement, namely, 10 years (granted in four periods of limited leave of 30 months, with a fifth application for indefinite leave to remain). This is known as the '10-year family route'.

These five- and 10-year limited leave periods are often called 'probationary periods'.

If a person is already in the UK, it may be possible for him to apply for leave to remain as a partner and so start on a five- or 10-year family route to settlement.

What if the applicant's partner dies before the relevant probationary period is completed? See **8.7**.

What if the couple separate due to domestic violence by the applicant's partner before the relevant probationary period is completed? See **8.8**.

8.1.3 Children

8.1.3.1 Entering for immediate settlement

A child may seek entry clearance and be granted indefinite leave to enter the UK to join one or both parents who are already settled in the UK. Exceptionally he might be joining a relative who is here and settled. See **8.9**.

8.1.3.2 Entering with or to join a parent who has limited leave

Note that if a child's parent has only limited leave to enter or remain in the UK, the child can apply under an associated Immigration Rule to travel with or join that parent during the parent's leave (see, eg, **7.6.1.2** and **8.12**).

8.1.3.3 Entering with limited leave

A child might enter the UK with limited leave in his own right under the Immigration Rules, eg as a student (see **Chapter 6**).

8.1.4 Parents

A parent with sole parental responsibility for, or access rights to, a British citizen child or settled child who is living in the UK, may apply for entry clearance and subsequently leave to remain under Appendix FM to the Immigration Rules.

A parent already in the UK may switch into this category. This most commonly occurs when a person has entered the UK with limited leave as the partner of a British citizen or settled person (see **8.3**) but can no longer remain in the UK in that category as the relationship has broken down. If that person has sole parental responsibility for, or is exercising access rights to, his British or settled child, an application may be made for leave to remain.

Ultimately it may be possible to apply for settlement in this category.

See **8.10**.

8.1.5 Adult dependent relatives entering for immediate settlement

This route allows a non-EEA adult dependent relative of a British citizen in the UK or a person settled in the UK to enter and settle because, as a result of age, illness or disability, he requires a level of long-term personal care that can only be provided in the UK by his relative here. See **8.11**.

8.2 EXEMPT GROUPS

Part 8 of and Appendix FM to the Immigration Rules do not apply to those people who do not need leave, or who are seeking entry under other provisions of the Immigration Rules. For example:

(a)   persons who already have the right of abode in the UK (see **2.2** and **2.3**);

(b)   EEA citizens and family members entering by virtue of EU law (see **4.4.6**);

(c)   family members of a British citizen who has exercised EU Treaty rights (see **4.4.12**);

(d)   persons with settled status re-entering as returning residents (see **3.8.3**);

(e)   persons who are entering in another category under the Rules (eg visitors, etc).

EXAMPLE 1

Ben is a citizen of Canada. He was born in Canada in 1972. Ben's father is Canadian but his mother was born in the UK and she is a British citizen. Ben has recently married Sue, a British citizen. The couple now wish to travel to the UK to set up home together in Manchester, England.

As a British citizen, Sue can freely enter the UK as she is not subject to immigration controls.

Ben is a Commonwealth citizen with right of abode in the UK. So Ben can enter the UK freely as he is not subject to immigration controls and therefore does not need to comply with the provisions in Appendix FM to the Immigration Rules. (Ben will need a 'certificate of entitlement' in his Canadian passport: see **2.3**. A check could also be made to see if he is registered as a British citizen and holds, or is entitled to, a British passport: see **2.2.6.2**.)

EXAMPLE 2

Vlad is a citizen of Russia who is married to Maria, a citizen of Austria. The couple wish to come and live together in the UK.

As an EEA national, Maria can enter the UK. Vlad may enter as her family member (spouse) under EU law with an EEA Family Permit (see **Chapter 4**).

Vlad could not apply to enter the UK under Appendix FM to the Immigration Rules as his partner, Maria, is not a British citizen or settled in the UK, nor in the UK with limited leave as a refugee or humanitarian protection leave.

> **EXAMPLE 3**
>
> Liz is a British citizen. For the last 18 months she has been working in Paris, France (an EEA country). She is thereby exercising her EU Treaty rights. Three months ago she married Bill, an American citizen. The couple now wish to come and live together in the UK.
>
> As a British citizen, Liz can freely enter the UK as she is not subject to immigration controls.
>
> Bill has a choice. He could seek entry clearance to the UK under Appendix FM to the Immigration Rules as Liz's partner (see **8.3**), or he could enter as her family member (spouse) with an EEA Family Permit (see **4.4.12**).

> **EXAMPLE 4**
>
> Carla is a citizen of The Philippines. She married Denis, a British citizen, whilst he was on holiday in The Philippines last month. Denis has just returned to the UK without Carla. She has not yet agreed to join him in the UK. She intends to apply for a visa to enter the UK as a general visitor in order to decide whether she would wish to live in the UK with Denis.
>
> In principle, Carla could obtain a general visitor visa, but she would need to satisfy the ECO that she did intend to leave the UK at the end of her visit (see **5.2.1** at **(b)**).

8.3 ENTRY CLEARANCE AS A PARTNER

8.3.1 Who is a partner?

A partner, for the purposes of Appendix FM (see para GEN 1.2), is:

(a)   the applicant's spouse;

(b)   the applicant's civil partner;

(c)   the applicant's fiancé(e) or proposed civil partner; or

(d)   a person who has been living together with the applicant in a relationship akin to a marriage or civil partnership for at least two years prior to the date of application.

For (a) and (b) the parties must have entered into a valid marriage or valid civil partnership (see **8.3.5.6**).

For (c) the parties must intend to marry or enter into a civil partnership within six months of entering the UK (see **8.3.5.7**).

As to (d), Home Office guidance is that 'living together with' should be applied fairly tightly, in that the couple should show evidence of cohabitation for the preceding two-year period. Short breaks apart may be acceptable for good reasons, such as work commitments or looking after a relative, which take one partner away for a period of up to six months, where it was not possible for the other partner to accompany the first partner and it can be seen that the relationship continued throughout that period by visits, letters, etc. The phrase 'akin to a marriage or civil partnership' is said to refer to a relationship that is similar in its nature to a marriage or a civil partnership, which therefore includes both heterosexual and same-sex relationships. In order to demonstrate a two-year relationship, evidence of cohabitation is needed. In order to show a relationship akin to a marriage or a civil partnership, the Home Office looks for evidence of a committed relationship. The following type of supporting evidence might therefore be useful in this respect:

- joint commitments (such as joint bank accounts, joint investments, joint tenancy agreement, joint mortgage account, etc);
- if there are children of the relationship, a full birth or adoption certificate naming the parties as parents;

- correspondence which links them to the same address (eg household bills in joint names, etc); and
- any official records of their address (eg doctors and dentist records, government records, etc).

EXAMPLE 1

Zach and Yvonne are engaged to be married. Zach is a visa national. Yvonne is a British citizen. The couple are living in Zach's home country, but they now wish to travel to the UK to get married and set up home together.

Zach can apply to enter the UK under Appendix FM to the Immigration Rules as Yvonne's partner (fiancé), provided they intend to marry within six months of entering the UK.

EXAMPLE 2

David is a British citizen. He has worked abroad for several years and for the last 18 months has been living in the USA with John, an American citizen. David now wishes to return to the UK and John wishes to travel with him. If John is admitted to the UK he intends to live with David permanently, but the couple do not wish to enter into a civil partnership.

David and John are not civil partners, neither do they intend to enter into a civil partnership. They have not been living in a relationship akin to a civil partnership for at least two years prior to the date of John's wishing to make an application. So the couple's relationship will need to continue for another six months before John can apply under Appendix FM to the Immigration Rules as David's partner.

EXAMPLE 3

Alice and Brian are both citizens of New Zealand. They were both born there and have never been to the UK before. They have recently married and now wish to travel to the UK to set up home together. Whilst they are both Commonwealth citizens, neither has the right of abode in the UK.

Appendix FM to the Immigration Rules does not apply. Whilst the couple are partners (spouses), neither Alice nor Brian is a British citizen or settled in the UK, or in the UK with limited leave as a refugee or person granted humanitarian protection.

8.3.2 An overview of the requirements

The requirements in Appendix FM to be met for entry clearance as a partner (see para EC-P.1.1) are that:

(a) the applicant must be outside the UK;

(b) the applicant must have made a valid application for entry clearance as a partner;

(c) the applicant must not fall for refusal under any of the grounds in Section S-EC: Suitability–entry clearance (see **8.3.3**); and

(d) the applicant must meet all of the requirements of Section E-ECP: Eligibility for entry clearance as a partner (see **8.3.4**).

8.3.3 Suitability requirements in detail

Section S-EC, paras S-EC.1.2 to S-EC.1.7 set out the following mandatory grounds on which an ECO will refuse an application:

S-EC.1.2   The Secretary of State has personally directed that the exclusion of the applicant from the UK is conducive to the public good.

S-EC.1.3   The applicant is at the date of application the subject of a deportation order.

S-EC.1.4   The exclusion of the applicant from the UK is conducive to the public good because they have been convicted of an offence for which they have been sentenced to a period of imprisonment of (a) at least 4 years; or (b) at least 12 months but less than 4 years, unless a period of 10 years has passed since the end of the sentence; or (c) of less than 12 months, unless a period of 5 years has passed since the end of the sentence. Where this paragraph applies, unless refusal would be contrary to the Human Rights Convention or the Convention and Protocol Relating to the Status of Refugees, it will only be in exceptional circumstances that the public interest in maintaining refusal will be outweighed by compelling factors.

S-EC.1.5   The exclusion of the applicant from the UK is conducive to the public good or because, for example, the applicant's conduct (including convictions which do not fall within S-EC.1.4.), character, associations, or other reasons, make it undesirable to grant them entry clearance.

(For each of the above, see further **Chapter 10.**)

S-EC.1.6   The applicant has failed without reasonable excuse to comply with a requirement to –
   (a)   attend an interview;
   (b)   provide information;
   (c)   provide physical data; or
   (d)   undergo a medical examination or provide a medical report.

S-EC.1.7   It is undesirable to grant entry clearance to the applicant for medical reasons.

Paragraphs S-EC.2.2 to S-EC.2.5 set out the following discretionary grounds on which an ECO will normally refuse an application:

S-EC.2.2   Whether or not to the applicant's knowledge –
   (a)   false information, representations or documents have been submitted in relation to the application (including false information submitted to any person to obtain a document used in support of the application); or
   (b)   there has been a failure to disclose material facts in relation to the application.

S-EC.2.3   One or more relevant NHS body has notified the Secretary of State that the applicant has failed to pay charges in accordance with the relevant NHS regulations on charges to overseas visitors and the outstanding charges have a total value of at least £1,000.

S-EC.2.4   A maintenance and accommodation undertaking has been requested or required under paragraph 35 of these Rules or otherwise and has not been provided.

S-EC.2.5   The exclusion of the applicant from the UK is conducive to the public good because (a) within the 12 months preceding the date of the application, the person has been convicted of or admitted an offence for which they received a non-custodial sentence or other out of court disposal that is recorded on their criminal record; or (b) in the view of the Secretary of State (i) the person's offending has caused serious harm; or (ii) the person is a persistent offender who shows a particular disregard for the law.

Note that despite the wording of para S-EC.2.2, Home Office guidance on (b) is that refusal for failure to disclose material facts in relation to the application can be imposed only where the applicant acts with knowledge. An applicant must not therefore be refused on the grounds that he unknowingly failed to disclose material facts in relation to his application.

8.3.4   Eligibility requirements in outline

An applicant must meet all of the eligibility requirements in paras E-ECP.2.1 to E-ECP.4.2. Broadly these are as follows:

(a)   relationship requirements (see **8.3.5**);

(b)   financial requirements (see **8.3.6**)

(c)   accommodation requirements (see **8.3.7**); and

(d)   English language requirement (see **8.3.8**).

8.3.5 Relationship requirements (paras E-ECP.2.1 to E-ECP.2.10)

8.3.5.1 Immigration status of applicant's partner

By para E-ECP.2.1, the applicant's partner must be:

(a) a British citizen in the UK; or

(b) present and settled in the UK; or

(c) in the UK with refugee leave or with humanitarian protection.

For (a) and (b), does this mean that the application will be refused if the British citizen or person settled in the UK is currently living abroad with his partner and will be travelling with the partner to the UK? No, because para GEN.1.3(b) provides that 'references to a person being present and settled in the UK also include a person who is being admitted for settlement on the same occasion as the applicant'. Paragraph 6 of the Immigration Rules also defines 'present and settled' as meaning that the person concerned is settled in the UK and, at the time that an application under the Rules is made, is physically present here or is coming here with or to join the applicant, and intends to make the UK his home with the applicant if the application is successful. In addition, note that para GEN.1.3(c) states that 'references to a British Citizen in the UK also include a British Citizen who is coming to the UK with the applicant as their partner'.

The relationships of fiancé(e) and proposed civil partner are not recognised by EU law (see **4.4.6.6**). So in what circumstances can an EEA national satisfy (b) above? Paragraph 6 of the Immigration Rules provides the answer: it is when an EEA national holds a registration certificate or a document certifying permanent residence issued under the 2006 Regulations (see **4.4.14**).

8.3.5.2 Minimum age

By paras E-ECP.2.2 and E-ECP.2.3, both the applicant and his partner must be aged 18 or over at the date of application.

8.3.5.3 Relationship not within prohibited degree

By para E-ECP.2.4, the applicant and his partner must not be within any prohibited degree of relationship. Three statutory provisions apply, as follows:

(a) The Marriage Act 1949 prohibits a marriage by a man to any of the persons mentioned in **Table 8.1** below, and prohibits a marriage between a woman and any of the persons mentioned in **Table 8.2** below.

Table 8.1 Prohibited degrees for a man

Mother
Daughter
Father's mother
Mother's mother
Son's daughter
Daughter's daughter
Sister
Father's sister
Mother's sister
Brother's daughter
Sister's daughter

Table 8.2 Prohibited degrees for a woman

Father
Son
Father's father
Mother's father
Son's son
Daughter's son
Brother
Father's brother
Mother's brother
Brother's son
Sister's son

(b)   The Marriage (Prohibited Degrees of Relationship) Act 1986 prohibits a marriage between those listed in **Table 8.3** below until both parties are aged 21 or over, and provided that the younger party has not at any time before attaining the age of 18 been a child of the family in relation to the other party.

Table 8.3 Prohibited degrees

Daughter of former wife
Son of former husband
Former wife of father
Former husband of mother
Former wife of father's father
Former husband of father's mother
Former wife of mother's father
Former husband of mother's mother
Daughter of son of former wife
Son of son of former husband
Daughter of daughter of former wife
Son of daughter of former husband

(c)   The Marriage (Prohibited Degrees of Relationship) Act 1986 also prohibits a marriage between those listed in **Table 8.4** below.

Table 8.4 Prohibited degrees

Mother of former wife, until the death of both the former wife and the father of the former wife
Father of former husband, until after the death of both the former husband and the mother of the former husband
Former wife of son, until after the death of both his son and the mother of his son
Former husband of daughter, until after the death of both her daughter and the father of her daughter

8.3.5.4   The parties have met in person

Paragraph E-ECP.2.5 requires the applicant and his partner to have met in person. What does this mean?

The Home Office guidance, following *Meharban v ECO, Islamabad* [1989] Imm AR 57, is that 'met' requires the parties to have 'made the acquaintance of one another'. This need not have been in the context of marriage or a civil partnership. So if, for example, the parties had originally been childhood friends, perhaps going to the same school for several years, they may be said to have met in person and become acquainted.

'Met' implies a face-to-face meeting which results in the making of mutual acquaintance. There is a requirement of 'at least an appreciation by each party of the other in the sense of, for example, appearance and personality'. Therefore a relationship developed over the Internet by Facebook messages, Skype calls or the like would potentially satisfy this requirement, but only if it includes a personal face-to-face meeting between the couple which itself results in the making of their mutual acquaintance. Evidence of a face-to-face meeting might include travel documents, photographs, statements from witnesses, or relevant email or text message exchanges detailing meetings.

8.3.5.5   The relationship is genuine and subsisting

Paragraph E-ECP.2.6 requires the relationship between the applicant and his partner to be genuine and subsisting. Neither term is defined in the Immigration Rules or the Home Office guidance. However, in *GA ('Subsisting' marriage) Ghana* [2006] UKAIT 00046, the Tribunal held that the requirement that a relationship is subsisting requires more than just double-checking the legal status of that relationship. The nature and quality of the substance of the relationship – therefore including whether or not it is genuine – is under scrutiny. As the Tribunal indicated at para 14, this means that when assessing the subsistence of a relationship, the decision-maker:

> will plainly have to bear in mind the cultural context and the wide differences that exist between individual lifestyles, whether by choice, or by circumstances, or by economic necessity. He will also be able to put the claim into the context of the history of the relationship and to assess whether and to what extent this illuminates the nature of the parties' present relationship and future intentions.

Home Office guidance to its caseworkers is that they must be alert and sensitive to the extent to which religious and cultural practices may shape the factors present or absent in a particular case, particularly at the entry clearance and leave to remain stages. For example, a couple in an arranged marriage may have spent little, if any, time together prior to the marriage. For many faiths and cultures marriage marks the start of a commitment to a lifelong partnership and not the affirmation of a pre-existing partnership. Home Office guidance is that its caseworkers must also take into account normal practices for marriages and family living according to particular religious and cultural traditions. In particular, evidence of pre-marital cohabitation and joint living arrangements can be a factor associated with a genuine relationship; equally, their absence can be too. In some cultures it is traditional for the household accounts, bills, etc to be in the name of the male head of the household (who could be the male partner, or his father or grandfather).

Home Office guidance makes it clear that its caseworkers have discretion to grant or refuse an application based on their overall assessment, regardless of whether one or more of the factors contained in the guidance is, or is not, present in the case. As the guidance stresses, consideration of whether a relationship is genuine and subsisting is not a checklist or tick-box exercise.

It is for the applicant to show the requirement is met on the balance of probabilities: see *Naz (subsisting marriage – standard of proof) Pakistan* [2012] UKUT 00040.

In assessing whether a relationship is genuine and subsisting, Home Office guidance to its caseworkers as to what factors might be taken into account is as follows:

Factors which may be associated with a genuine and subsisting relationship

(i)   The couple are in a current, long-term relationship and are able to provide satisfactory evidence of this.

(ii)   The couple have been or are co-habiting and are able to provide satisfactory evidence of this.

(iii) The couple have children together (biological, adopted or step-children) and shared responsibility for them.

(iv)   The couple share financial responsibilities, eg a joint mortgage/tenancy agreement, a joint bank account and/or joint savings, utility bills in both their names.

(v)   The partner and/or applicant have visited the other's home country and family and are able to provide evidence of this. (The fact that an applicant has never visited the UK must not be regarded as a negative factor, but it is a requirement of the Immigration Rules that the couple have met in person).

(vi)   The couple, or their families acting on their behalf, have made definite plans concerning the practicalities of the couple living together in the UK. In the case of an arranged marriage, the couple both consent to the marriage and agree with the plans made by their families.

Factors which may be associated with a relationship which is not genuine and subsisting

If a case contains one or more of the factors listed below, this may prompt additional scrutiny of the application but will not necessarily result in a negative decision. Caseworkers must continue to look at the circumstances of the case as a whole.

Even where additional scrutiny has been prompted by any of the following factors, it does not necessarily mean that the relationship is not genuine and subsisting.

The factors which may prompt additional scrutiny of an application include those listed below. Some factors may also, where specifically stated, lead to a refusal of an application without additional scrutiny but again, before deciding, caseworkers must continue to look at the circumstances as a whole:

(i)   If the marriage or civil partnership took place in the UK, a report – of a suspected sham marriage or civil partnership – was made by the registration service under section 24 of the Immigration and Asylum Act 1999.

(ii)   The applicant or partner makes a public statement that their marriage is a sham. An application can be refused on the basis of such a public statement alone.

(iii)   The applicant or partner makes a public statement (not in confidence) that they have been forced into marriage. An application can be refused on the basis of such a public statement alone.

(iv)   A sibling of the partner or applicant has been forced into marriage.

(v)   The applicant, partner or an immediate family member of either is or has been the subject or respondent of a forced marriage protection order under the Forced Marriage (Civil Protection) Act 1997 or the Forced Marriage etc (Protection and Jurisdiction) (Scotland) Act 1999.

An application can be refused on the basis alone of a current order involving the applicant or partner.

(vi)   There is evidence from a reliable third party (eg the Forced Marriage Unit, police, social services, registration service or a minister of religion) which indicates that the marriage is or may be a sham marriage or a forced marriage. (It may not be possible for this information to be used in any refusal notice). The fact that a third party indicates that in their opinion a marriage, partnership or relationship is genuine must not be afforded any weight.

(vii)   The applicant or partner does not appear to have the capacity to consent to the marriage, partnership or relationship, eg owing to learning difficulties, and independent evidence, eg from a social services assessment, has not been provided to confirm that such capacity exists.

(viii) There is evidence of unreasonable restrictions being placed on the applicant or partner, eg being kept at home by their family, being subject to unreasonable financial restrictions, attempts to prevent the police or other agencies having reasonable, unrestricted access to the applicant or partner.

(ix)   Failure by the applicant or partner to attend an interview, without reasonable explanation, where required to do so to discuss the application or their welfare, or seeking to undermine the ability of the [Home Office] to arrange an interview, eg by unreasonable delaying tactics by the couple or a third party.

(x)   The couple are unable to provide any information about their intended living arrangements in the UK or about the practicalities of the applicant moving to the UK.

(xi)   The circumstances of the wedding ceremony or reception, eg no or few guests and/or no significant family members present.

(xii)   The couple are unable to provide accurate personal details about each other (eg name, age, nationality, employment, parent's names and place of residence), provide inconsistent evidence, or do not have a shared understanding of the core facts of their relationship, eg how and where they met for the first time.

(xiii) The couple are unable to communicate with each other in a language understood by them both.

(xiv)   There is evidence of money having been exchanged for the marriage to be contracted (unless this is part of a dowry).

(xv)   There is a lack of appropriate contribution to the responsibilities of the marriage, partnership or relationship, eg a lack of shared financial or other domestic responsibilities.

(xvi)   Matrimonial co-habitation is not maintained (except where one party is working or studying away from home) or there is no evidence that they have ever co-habited since the marriage.

(xvii) The applicant is a qualified medical practitioner or professional, or has worked as a nurse or carer, and the partner has a mental or physical impairment which currently requires medical assistance or personal care in their own accommodation.

(xviii) The partner has previously sponsored another partner to come to or remain in the UK.

(xix) The partner has previously been sponsored as a partner to come to or remain in the UK (ie the partner has obtained settlement on this basis) and that marriage, partnership or relationship ended shortly after the partner obtained settlement. This excludes circumstances where the partner is a bereaved partner, or where the partner obtained settlement on the basis of domestic violence perpetrated by their former partner.

(xx)   If the partner was married to or in a partnership with the applicant at an earlier date, married or formed a partnership with another person, and is now sponsoring the original partner to come to or remain in the UK.

(xxi) The past history of the partner and/or the applicant contains evidence of a previous sham marriage or forced marriage, or of unlawful residence in the UK or elsewhere.

(xxii) The applicant has applied for leave to enter or remain in the UK in another category and been refused.

In this guidance 'additional scrutiny' means that where a caseworker has doubts that a relationship is genuine and subsisting, they must consider whether further information needs to be obtained, and the application investigated further, before they are able to make a decision on the case.

Also see **4.4.6.2**.

8.3.5.6   Valid marriage or civil partnership

Paragraph E-ECP.2.7 states that if the applicant and partner are married or in a civil partnership, it must be a valid marriage or civil partnership, as specified.

Home Office guidance is that the type of marriage must be recognised in the country in which it took place, it must satisfy the legal requirements of that country and there must not be anything in the law of either party's country of domicile that restricted their freedom to enter into the marriage.

Home Office guidance includes a list of countries where it recognises a civil partnership as valid.

8.3.5.7   Fiancé(e) or proposed civil partner entering UK for marriage or civil partnership

Paragraph E-ECP.2.8 states that if the applicant is a fiancé(e) or proposed civil partner, he must be seeking entry to the UK to enable his marriage or civil partnership to take place. The couple will usually need to produce adequate documentary evidence of the arrangements already made in the UK for the marriage or civil partnership ceremony.

8.3.5.8   Any previous relationship broken down permanently

Paragraph E-ECP.2.9 provides that if the applicant and/or his partner has previously been married or in a civil partnership, the applicant must provide suitable evidence that that relationship has ended (eg decree absolute of divorce, or dissolution order terminating a civil partnership), unless it is a polygamous marriage or civil partnership which falls within para 278(i) of the Immigration Rules. Home Office guidance includes further details.

8.3.5.9   Intention to live together permanently in the UK

By para E-ECP.2.10, the applicant and his partner must intend to live together permanently in the UK. Paragraph 6 of the Immigration Rules defines this as an intention to live together, evidenced by a clear commitment from both parties that they will live together permanently in the UK immediately following the outcome of the application in question or as soon as circumstances permit thereafter.

There is an obvious overlap here with the requirement in para E-ECP.2.6 that the relationship between the applicant and his partner is genuine and subsisting (see **8.3.5.5**), since a relationship that is found to be a sham is a relationship where the parties have no intention of living together at all.

A caseworker may question whether parties meet this requirement if they have lived apart following their marriage or civil partnership. Usually the couple will respond by producing an explanation for the separation, and details of letters sent and telephone calls made during this period, to illustrate their 'intervening devotion'.

In the case of *Amarjit Kaur* [1999] INLP 110, the Immigration Judge had found that the applicant's 'overriding wish was to marry someone from abroad. The letters and phone calls were evidence, not of intervening devotion, but merely of intervening contact'. No further evidence of letters or phone calls was produced to the Tribunal, and although the sponsor had visited his wife in India, the appeal was dismissed. The Immigration Judge had taken a dim view of the fact that the sponsor was a divorcée, 20 years older than the applicant, and that the applicant had turned down Indian-based suitors in order to marry the sponsor. The Tribunal did not demur from that.

Contrast *Amarjit Kaur* with the case of *Goudey (subsisting marriage – evidence) Sudan* [2012] UKUT 00041 (IAC). There the Tribunal concluded that the applicant and her partner were

> the right age for each other, and the [partner] as a young man would undoubtedly be of an age when he would want to have the company of a wife. She appears to have moved homes when the marriage was being arranged. He travelled to Egypt to meet his wife and there is some evidential support for the proposition given in his oral account that the relationship was conducted by telephone. We see no basis on which the judge could dismiss the consistent evidence that they intended to live together as man and wife as lacking in credibility.

The question whether parties intend to live together permanently in the UK is basically one of fact, and decisions often turn on the credibility of the available evidence.

8.3.6   Financial requirements (paras E-ECP.3.1 to 3.3)

8.3.6.1   Overview

When applying for entry clearance (and usually for leave to remain and settlement: see **8.4** and **8.6** respectively) the applicant will have to provide specified documentary evidence that a prescribed minimum gross annual income is available. Home Office guidance is that this sets a benchmark for financial stability and independence on the part of the couple. However, a different test will apply if the applicant's partner is at the time of the application in receipt of certain UK welfare benefits (see **8.3.6.9**).

To satisfy the financial requirement the applicant will have to meet all of the following:

(a)   the level of financial requirement applicable to the application under Appendix FM (see **8.3.6.2**); and

(b)   the requirements specified in Appendix FM and Appendix FM-SE as to:
    (i)   the permitted sources of income and savings (see **8.3.6.3** to **8.3.6.7**);
    (ii)   the time periods and permitted combinations of sources applicable to each permitted source relied on (see **8.3.6.3** to **8.3.6.7**); and
    (iii)   the documentary evidence required for each permitted source relied upon (see **8.3.6.8**).

8.3.6.2   The prescribed minimum gross annual income

Currently, by para E-ECP.3.1, the applicant must provide specified evidence, from the sources listed in para E-ECP.3.2, of a specified gross annual income of at least £18,600.

What if the applicant's child or children will be living with the couple in the UK? An extra £3,800 is required for the first child and a further £2,400 for each additional child.

> **EXAMPLE**
>
> Ivan, a citizen of Russia, has recently married Judith, a British citizen. Ivan and his 8-year-old twin daughters, Olga and Nina, are applying under Appendix FM to the Immigration Rules to enter the UK where they will live with Judith and her 6-year-old son, Mark. What gross annual income must Ivan demonstrate?
>
> The answer is £24,800 (£18,600 for Ivan; £3,800 for Olga; and £2,400 for Nina).

Note that for these purposes a child is defined by para E-ECP.3.1 as a dependent child of the applicant who is:

(a) under the age of 18 years, or who was under the age of 18 years when first granted entry under this route;

(b) applying for entry clearance or is in the UK as a dependant of the applicant;

(c) not a British citizen or settled in the UK; and

(d) not an EEA national with a right to remain in the UK under the 2006 Regulations.

Note that the set amount of £18,600 was held in *MM (Lebanon) v Secretary of State for the Home Department* [2013] EWHC 1900 (Admin) to disproportionately interfere with the ability of partners to live together contrary to their rights under the Article 8 ECHR. However, the Government successfully overturned that decision in the Court of Appeal; see [2014] EWCA Civ 985.

8.3.6.3 Meeting the prescribed minimum gross annual income

Paragraph E-ECP.3.2 sets out the only financial resources that count, namely:

(a) income of the partner (and/or the applicant if he is in the UK with permission to work and applying for leave to remain or settlement) from specified employment or self-employment);

(b) specified pension income of the applicant and partner;

(c) any specified maternity allowance or bereavement benefit received by the partner in the UK;

(d) other specified income of the applicant and partner; and

(e) specified savings of the applicant and partner.

It is clear from the above that certain financial resources on which a couple might wish to rely are excluded. Importantly, para E-ECP.3.2 has the effect of overruling the Supreme Court decision in *Ahmed Mahad (previously referred to as AM) (Ethiopia) v ECO* [2009] UKSC 16, as financial support from a third party, such as relatives or community groups, cannot be counted. If third parties wish to assist a couple, they might do so by gifting them money which can then count towards the couple's savings, provided it is received at least six months before the date of the application (see **Category D** below).

Home Office guidance is that the allowable financial resources can be used to meet the financial requirements in seven different possible ways, which it categorises A to G as follows.

Category A: salaried employment for the last six months

Where the applicant's partner (and/or the applicant if he is in the UK with permission to work and applying for leave to remain or settlement) is in salaried employment at the date of the application and has been with the same employer for at least the last six months, the applicant can count the gross annual salary (at its lowest level in those six months if there has been any increase) towards the financial requirement.

If necessary to meet the level of the financial requirement applicable to the application, the applicant can add to this, as permitted, from Categories C, D and E (see below).

> **EXAMPLE**
>
> The applicant's partner, Alan, is employed in the UK, earning £20,000 gross a year. He has worked for the same firm for over a year. The applicant has no dependent children. Alan should meet the financial requirement under Category A (subject to checking all his salary counts: see **8.3.6.4**).
>
> Note that if Alan had been promoted into his current role within the last six months from a salary of £18,000, he would not fall within Category A. Alan would either have to wait until he had completed six months at his new salary of £20,000, or, if relevant, use income from Categories C, D and E.

But what if the applicant's partner meets the above requirement in respect of salaried employment abroad and is returning with the applicant to the UK to take up employment here? In these circumstances the partner must also have confirmed salaried employment to return to in the UK, starting within three months of their return. This must have an annual starting salary sufficient to meet the financial requirement applicable to the application either alone or in combination with any, or all, of the items in Categories C, D and E as permitted.

For what counts as salaried employment, see **8.3.6.4**.

Category B: salaried employment for less than the last six months

Under Category B, salaried employment at the date of the application with the same employer but for less than the last six months counts in the same way as Category A above, but only if an additional test is met. The couple must also have received in the 12 months prior to the application the level of income required to meet the financial requirement based only on:

(a) the gross salaried employment income of the applicant's partner (and/or the applicant if he is in the UK with permission to work and applying for leave to remain or settlement);

(b) the gross amount of any specified non-employment income received by the applicant's partner, the applicant or both jointly;

(c) the gross amount of any State (UK or foreign) or private pension received by the applicant's partner or the applicant; and/or

(d) the gross amount of any UK maternity allowance, bereavement allowance, bereavement payment and widowed parent's allowance received by the applicant's partner or the applicant.

> **EXAMPLE**
>
> The applicant's partner, Brenda, is employed in the UK. She started her current employment last month. Her gross annual salary is £32,500. Over the last 12 months she has had two other salaried jobs and earned £28,750 from these in total. The applicant has no dependent children.
>
> Brenda will not qualify under Category A above as she has not been with the same employer for at least six months. However, she will qualify under Category B as she has earned more than £18,600 in the last 12 months from salaried employment and is currently in employment at a salary of at least £18,600. This is subject to checking that all her salary payments count: see **8.3.6.4**.

Category B operates differently where the applicant's partner is abroad and returning with the applicant to the UK to take up employment. The partner does not have to be in employment abroad at the date of application. Instead, the following two tests must be met.

First, the couple returning to the UK must have received in the 12 months prior to the application the level of income required to meet the financial requirement, based only on:

(a)   the gross salaried employment income overseas of the applicant's partner;

(b)   the gross amount of any specified non-employment income received by the applicant's partner, the applicant or both jointly;

(c)   the gross amount of any state (UK or foreign) or private pension received by the applicant's partner or the applicant; and/or

(d)   the gross amount of any UK maternity allowance, bereavement allowance, bereavement payment and widowed parent's allowance received by the applicant's partner or the applicant.

Secondly, the applicant's partner must in addition have confirmed salaried employment to return to in the UK (starting within three months of his return). This must have an annual starting salary sufficient to meet the financial requirement applicable to the application either alone or in combination with any, or all, of the items in Categories C, D and E as permitted.

For what counts as salaried employment, see **8.3.6.4**.

Category C: specified non-employment income

The specified non-employment income (see **8.3.6.5**) (excluding pension and allowances under Category E below) the applicant's partner and/or the applicant have/has received in the 12 months prior to the application can count towards the applicable financial requirement, provided they continue to own the relevant asset (eg property, shares, etc) at the date of application.

This income may also be used in combination with other categories as described.

Category D: cash savings

An amount based on any cash savings above £16,000 held by the applicant's partner, the applicant or both jointly for at least six months prior to the application and under their control, can count towards the applicable financial requirement.

At entry clearance and the leave to remain stages, the amount above £16,000 must be divided by 2.5 (to reflect the 2.5 year or 30-month period before the applicant will have to make a further application) to give the amount which can be used.

On an application for indefinite leave to remain, the whole of the amount above £16,000 can be used.

The amount based on cash savings may also be used in combination with other categories as described.

For further details, see **8.3.6.6**.

Category E: pension and allowances

The gross annual income from any State (UK basic State pension and additional or second State pension, or foreign) or private pension received by the applicant's partner or the applicant can count towards the applicable financial requirement. The annual amount may be counted where the pension has become a source of income at least 28 days prior to the application. This income can also be used in combination with other categories as described.

The gross amount of any State (UK or foreign) or private pension received by the applicant's partner or the applicant in the 12 months prior to the application can be used, alone or in combination with other income, for that period as described.

The gross amount of any UK maternity allowance, bereavement allowance, bereavement payment and widowed parent's allowance received by the applicant's partner or the applicant in the 12 months prior to the application can be used in combination with other income for that period as described.

Only the above UK welfare benefits count. So even if the applicant's partner receives other benefits, such as tax credits, child benefit, etc, these cannot count.

Category F: self-employment (last financial year)

The applicant's partner (and/or the applicant if he is in the UK with permission to work and applying for leave to remain or settlement) must be in self-employment at the date of the application and in the last full financial year received self-employment and other income (salaried, specified non-employment and pension) sufficient to meet the applicable financial requirement.

Note that cash savings cannot be used in combination with Category F.

> **EXAMPLE**
>
> The applicant's partner, Noel, is currently self-employed in the UK and in the last full financial year earned £20,575. The applicant has no dependent children.
>
> Noel will qualify under Category F as he is currently self-employed and in the last full financial year earned at least £18,600.

Category G: self-employment (last two financial years)

The applicant's partner (and/or the applicant if he is in the UK with permission to work and applying for leave to remain or settlement) must be in self-employment at the date of the application and as an average of the last two full financial years received self-employment and other income (salaried, specified non-employment and pension) sufficient to meet the applicable financial requirement.

Note that cash savings cannot be used in combination with Category G.

8.3.6.4   Further details about Categories A and B

For the purposes of Categories A and B, what counts as salaried employment?

Employment may be full-time or part-time. It can also be permanent, a fixed-term contract or with an agency.

Salary, basic pay, plus skills-based allowances and UK location-based allowances, eg London weighting, count as income. But any such allowances must form part of the contracted salary package and, if they exceed 30% of the total salary, only the amount which would correspond to 30% of the total salary will be counted towards the financial requirement. Overtime, commission-based pay and bonuses also count.

United Kingdom and overseas travel, subsistence and accommodation allowances, and allowances relating to the additional cost of living overseas cannot be included.

8.3.6.5   Further details about Category C

What income falls within Category C? The specified sources of non-employment income are:

(a)   dividends or other income from investments, stocks, shares, bonds and trust funds;

(b)   property rental income;

(c)   interest from savings; and

(d)   maintenance payments from a former partner in relation to the applicant and former partner's child or children dependent on and cared for by the applicant.

These sources of income must be in the name of the applicant's partner, the applicant or both jointly.

The relevant asset such as shares, bonds, property, etc must be held by the applicant's partner, the applicant or both jointly at the date of application.

In what circumstances can rent received from a property count? The property, whether in the UK or overseas, must be owned by the applicant's partner, the applicant or both jointly, and must not be their main residence (therefore income from a lodger in that residence cannot be counted). If the applicant's partner or applicant shares ownership of the property with a third party, only income received from the applicant's partner's and/or applicant's share of the property can be counted. Income from property which is rented out for only part of the year, eg a holiday let, can be counted. The equity in a property cannot be used to meet the financial requirement.

EXAMPLE

The applicant's partner, William, has been employed in the UK by the same employer for the last 12 months, earning £16,000 gross a year. He also receives £9,000 a year in rent from a house that he lets out. The house was left to him by his grandfather several years ago. It is in his sole name. The applicant has no dependent children.

William should meet the financial requirement of £18,600 under a combination of Category A income of £16,000 (subject to checking all his salary counts: see **8.3.6.4**) and Category C income of £9,000, so totalling £25,000.

8.3.6.6 Further details about Category D

To be counted, the applicant's partner, the applicant or both jointly must have cash savings of more than £16,000, held by the applicant's partner, the applicant or both jointly (but not with a third party) for at least six months at the date of application and under their control.

Only the amount of cash savings *above* £16,000 can be counted against any shortfall in the £18,600 income threshold (see **8.3.6.2**) or the relevant higher figure where at least one child of the applicant is included (see **8.3.6.2**). How is this done? At the entry clearance and limited leave to remain stages, the amount above £16,000 is divided by 2.5 (to reflect the 2.5 year or 30-month period before the applicant will have to make a further application). On an application for settlement, the whole of the amount above £16,000 can be used.

EXAMPLE

Zach and Yvonne are engaged to be married. Zach is a visa national. Yvonne is a British citizen. The couple are living in Zach's home country but they now wish to travel to the UK to get married and set up home together. Zach has no dependent children.

Zach applies for entry clearance under Appendix FM to the Immigration Rules as Yvonne's partner (fiancé). The couple have no income to count towards the financial requirement, but they do have £70,000 in cash savings which they have held in a joint account for at least the last six months. Will they qualify?

Under Category D, Zach and Yvonne's cash savings exceed £16,000 by £54,000. That figure divided by 2.5 is £21,600. As they require £18,600, they meet the financial requirement, provided they can produce the specified documents for these cash savings.

The level of savings required to meet any shortfall income must be based on the level of employment-related and/or other income at the date of application.

Table 8.5 below sets out some examples of the minimum amount of savings required to meet a shortfall where £18,600 (applicant with no dependent children) is the prescribed minimum gross annual income.

Table 8.5 Minimum amount of savings required to meet shortfall

Income	Entry clearance and leave to enter or remain: minimum amount of savings required
No other relevant income	£62,500 (£16,000 + (shortfall of £18,600 x 2.5))
Other relevant income of £15,000	£25,000 (£16,000 + (shortfall of £3,600 x 2.5))
Other relevant income of £18,000	£17,500 (£16,000 + (shortfall of £600 x 2.5))

8.3.6.7   Further details about Categories F and G

What income from self-employment counts for the purposes of Categories F and G? Where the self-employed person is a sole trader, or is in a partnership or franchise agreement, the income taken into account is the gross taxable profits from that person's share of the business. Allowances or deductible expenses which are not taxed are not counted towards income. What if the self-employed person has set up his own registered company and is listed as a director of that company? The income that counts will then be any salary drawn from the post-tax profits of the company.

8.3.6.8   Specified documents

Full details of the documents that must be produced in order to meet the financial requirement are set out in Appendix FM-SE to the Immigration Rules.

8.3.6.9   When applicant is exempt a maintenance test applies

By para E-ECP.3.3(a), the applicant is exempt from the financial requirement if the applicant's partner is receiving one or more of the following UK welfare benefits:

(a)   disability living allowance or personal independence payment;

(b)   severe disablement allowance;

(c)   industrial injury disablement benefit;

(d)   attendance allowance; or

(e)   carer's allowance.

Para 12 of Appendix FM-SE requires the applicant to produce official documentation from the DfWP confirming the entitlement to the relevant benefit or allowance and the amount received, as well as at least one personal bank statement showing payment of the benefit or allowance into the partner's account.

If the applicant is exempt from the financial requirement then, by para E-ECP.3.3(b), the applicant must provide evidence that his partner is able to maintain and accommodate himself, the applicant and any dependants adequately in the UK without recourse to public funds. As to public funds, see **3.3.2**; and as to accommodation, see **8.3.7**. By para 6 of the Immigration Rules, 'adequately' in relation to this maintenance requirement means that, after income tax, National Insurance contributions and housing costs have been deducted, there must be available to the family the level of income that would be available to them if the family was in receipt of income support.

Home Office guidance to its caseworkers is that the following five steps should be taken:

Step 1   Establish the applicant's partner's (and/or the applicant's if he is in the UK with permission to work and applying for leave to remain or settlement) current income. The gross income should be established and if the income varies, an average should be calculated.

Income from disability benefits can be included as income. Job offers or the prospects of employment are not taken into account.

Promises of third party support are not acceptable as Home Office guidance is that the applicant and his partner must have the required resources under their own control, not somebody else's.

Evidence of employment might include wage slips, a letter from the employer (confirming the employment and annual salary) and bank statements showing where the salary has been paid in.

Evidence of income from benefits received by the applicant's partner, such as disability benefits, may include the notice of award, but the best evidence will be the applicant's partner's bank statement showing where it has been paid into the account (see *Ahmed (benefits: proof of receipt; evidence) Bangladesh* [2013] UKUT 84 (IAC)).

Step 2   Establish the applicant's partner's current housing costs from the evidence provided.

Step 3   Deduct the housing costs from the gross income.

Step 4   Calculate how much the family would receive if they were on income support.

Note that the income support level in 2013/14 was £112.55 a week for a couple and £65.62 a week for a child.

Step 5   The gross income after deduction of housing costs must equal or exceed the income support rate.

Note that if on making any future application for leave or settlement the applicant's partner no longer receives an exempting welfare benefit, the financial requirement (**8.3.6.2**) will apply instead, unless para EX.1 then applies (see **8.5**).

8.3.7 Accommodation requirements (para E-ECP.3.4)

8.3.7.1 Adequate accommodation

By para E-ECP.3.4, the applicant must provide evidence that there will be adequate accommodation, without recourse to public funds, for the family, including other family members who are not included in the application but who live in the same household, which the family own or occupy exclusively.

Accommodation is not regarded as adequate if it is, or will be, overcrowded (or it contravenes public health regulations).

8.3.7.2 Owned or occupied exclusively

The couple will have to provide documentary evidence where the property is either owned or rented by them. This may be in the form of a letter from their mortgagee, if the property was bought with the aid of a mortgage, a copy of the property deeds and, in the case of rented accommodation, a rent book and tenancy agreement.

Where the accommodation is rented from a local authority or housing association, correspondence from the landlord is normally regarded as genuine and sufficient by the Home Office.

Can a third party provide accommodation for the couple? Yes, provided it is a firm arrangement. In *AB (Third-party provision of accommodation)* [2008] UKAIT 00018, the sponsor wife was living in premises provided by a relative. She contributed to the household bills but did not pay any rent. The relative was happy for this arrangement to continue if she was joined by her husband. The Tribunal indicated that the mere mention of a relative or friend who was prepared to accommodate the parties was probably not enough, but a real and stable arrangement for accommodation provided by another might be. In this case the offer of accommodation was a real and stable one. It was credible and practical, and satisfied the requirement. In these circumstances it obviously helps if the third party supplies a statement setting out the accommodation arrangements.

If the accommodation is not owned but shared, para 6 of the Immigration Rules provides that 'occupy exclusively' in relation to accommodation means that part of the property must be for the exclusive use of the family. But what does this mean in practice? In *KJ ('Own or occupy exclusively') Jamaica* [2008] UKAIT 00006, the Tribunal observed that

> it is clear that it cannot mean either 'alone' nor 'with a legal right to exclude all others' ... it ought not to be enough for an applicant to say that he will be accommodated by a series of friends allowing him to sleep on sofas, or that he has enough money to put up his dependants in hotels from time to time, or that he or they will find space in hostels. What appears to be required is that there is somewhere that the person or people in question can properly, albeit without any legal accuracy, describe as their own home. They may not own it; and they may share it; but it is adequate for them, it is in a defined place, and it is properly regarded as where they live, with the implications of stability that that phrase implies. (*per* Mr CMG Ockelton, Deputy President, at para 9)

Home Office guidance is that where accommodation is shared with other family members, use of a separate bedroom or bedrooms may suffice.

8.3.7.3 Overcrowding

The Housing Act 1985 (HA 1985), s 324 contains two tests to determine whether or not accommodation is overcrowded. If by coming to live in the property the applicant will cause it to be overcrowded under either test, the application will fail. The relevant law is as follows:

324   Definition of overcrowding

A dwelling is overcrowded for the purposes of this Part when the number of persons sleeping in the dwelling is such as to contravene—

(a)   the standard specified in section 325 (the room standard), or

(b)   the standard specified in section 326 (the space standard).

325   The room standard

(1)   The room standard is contravened when the number of persons sleeping in a dwelling and the number of rooms available as sleeping accommodation is such that two persons of opposite sexes who are not living together as husband and wife must sleep in the same room.

(2)   For this purpose—

(a)   children under the age of ten shall be left out of account, and

(b)   a room is available as sleeping accommodation if it is of a type normally used in the locality either as a bedroom or as a living room.

326   The space standard

(1)   The space standard is contravened when the number of persons sleeping in a dwelling is in excess of the permitted number, having regard to the number and floor area of the rooms of the dwelling available as sleeping accommodation.

(2)   For this purpose—

(a)   no account shall be taken of a child under the age of one and a child aged one or over but under ten shall be reckoned as one-half of a unit, and

(b)   a room is available as sleeping accommodation if it is of a type normally used in the locality either as a living room or as a bedroom.

(3)   The permitted number of persons in relation to a dwelling is the number specified in the following Table but no account shall be taken for the purposes of the Table of a room having a floor area of less than 50 square feet.

Table

Number of rooms	Number of persons
1	2
2	3
3	5
4	7.5
5	10
6 or more	2 persons for each room

As you will have noted, the first test is called 'the room standard'. It means that a property is overcrowded if two people aged 10 or more of the opposite sex, other than the applicant and the applicant's partner, have to sleep in the same room. The second test is 'the space standard'. Basically, this determines whether or not the number of people sleeping in the property exceeds that permitted by the Act. The table sets out the limits. The applicant can meet the accommodation requirement only if both tests are satisfied.

EXAMPLE

Ian, a widower, lives in a house with three rooms that can be used for sleeping. Living with him is his son, Lionel, aged 12, and his daughter, Diane, aged 13. Ian's mother, Mary, also lives with them. Ian recently travelled to Moscow and married Vika, a Russian national. Will the house be overcrowded if she is allowed to join Ian in the UK?

First, apply the room standard and answer the question: who can sleep in each room?

By HA 1985, s 325(1), Ian and Vika, as husband and wife, can share one room.

In light of HA 1985, s 325(1) and (2)(a), Lionel, aged 12, and Diane, aged 13, as two persons of 10 years old or more of the opposite sex, cannot share. So they must be in separate rooms. The house will not be overcrowded, therefore, if Diane shares with Mary (two persons of 10 years old or more but of the same sex) and Lionel has a room of his own.

Secondly, apply the space standard and answer the question: will the permitted number of persons for this property be exceeded?

Here, with three rooms available to sleep in, the limit under HA 1985, s 326(3) is five persons, and that will not be exceeded as there will be only five people in the household if Vika joins them, namely, Ian (an adult counts as one), Vika (an adult counts as one), Lionel (aged 12, so 10 years old or more and counts as one), Diane (aged 12, so 10 years old or more and counts as one) and Mary (an adult counts as one).

A check should be made that each of the three rooms has a floor area of at least 50 square feet for the purposes of HA 1985, s 326(3).

8.3.8 English language requirement (para E-ECP.4.1)

8.3.8.1 Meeting the requirement

By para E-ECP.4.1, the applicant will meet the English language requirement if he provides specified evidence that he:

(a) is a national of a Home Office-designated majority English-speaking country (see **7.4.3.2**);

(b) has an academic qualification recognised by NARIC UK to be equivalent to the standard of a Bachelor's or Master's degree or PhD in the UK, which was taught in English (see **7.4.3.3**);

(c)   has passed an English language test in speaking and listening at a minimum of level A1 of the Common European Framework of Reference for Languages with a provider approved by the Home Office. A list of Home Office-approved tests can be found in Appendix O to the Immigration Rules; or

(d)   is exempt from the English language requirement (see **8.3.8.2**).

The requirement does not breach Article 8 ECHR: see R *(on the application of Bibi) v Secretary of State for the Home Department* [2013] EWCA Civ 322.

8.3.8.2   Exempt from English language requirement

By para E-ECP.4.2, the applicant is exempt from the requirement to provide a suitable English language test certificate if at the date of the application he is is aged 65 or over, or has a disability (physical or mental condition) which prevents him from meeting the requirement, or if there are exceptional compassionate circumstances which prevent him from meeting the requirement prior to entering the UK.

Home Office guidance is that exemption applies only where someone has a physical or mental impairment which prevents him from learning English and/or taking a test. This is not a blanket exemption, as some disabled people are capable of learning English and taking an English test. So the exemption is granted only on production of satisfactory medical evidence from a medical practitioner who is qualified in the appropriate field, which specifies the disability and from which it may be concluded that exemption is justified.

What exceptional compassionate circumstances might lead to exemption? Home Office guidance is that the applicant must demonstrate that as a result of his circumstances he is unable to access facilities for learning English before coming to the UK. Evidence of an inability to attend, prior or previous attendance, or attempts to access learning must be clearly provided. This evidence must be provided by an independent source, eg from an appropriately qualified medical practitioner, or alternatively must be independently verified by a caseworker.

Home Office guidance is that situations which might, subject to receipt of all necessary evidence in support, lead a caseworker to conclude that the applicant can properly claim exceptional compassionate circumstances, include the following:

(a)   if the applicant's partner in the UK is seriously ill and requires immediate support or care from the applicant whilst receiving medical attention in the UK, and there is insufficient time for the applicant to access learning and/or to take a test; and

(b)   where a country or region is affected by conflict or humanitarian disaster, the Home Office will consider whether the situation makes it unreasonable for individuals to learn English and/or to take a test. In such circumstances a caseworker will consider the nature of the situation, including the infrastructure affected, and whether it would be proportionate to expect an applicant to meet the English language requirement.

It will be extremely rare for exceptional circumstances to apply when the applicant is applying in the UK for leave to remain, as applicants already here will have access to a wide variety of facilities for learning English.

Financial reasons, or claims of illiteracy or limited education are not acceptable to the Home Office.

Applicants who are nationals of a country with no test centre and who have made an application for entry clearance from that country are exempt from the requirement.

Note that if an applicant has been granted an exemption due to exceptional compassionate circumstances at entry clearance, he will be required to meet the English language requirement when he applies for further leave to remain after 30 months.

8.3.9 Decision on application

By para D-ECP.1.1, only an applicant who meets the requirements for entry clearance as a partner will be granted entry clearance. This will be for an initial period not exceeding 33 months and subject to a condition of no recourse to public funds. However, if the applicant is a fiancé(e) or proposed civil partner, the applicant will be granted entry clearance for a period not exceeding six months and subject to a condition of no recourse to public funds and a prohibition on employment.

By para D-ECP.1.2, where the applicant does not meet the requirements for entry clearance as a partner the application will be refused.

8.4 LEAVE TO REMAIN IN THE UK AS A PARTNER

8.4.1 Who can apply?

There are six different situations to be considered here, namely:

(a) where a person entered the UK as a partner under Appendix FM and now seeks an extension of his limited leave for a further 30 months;

(b) where a person entered the UK as a fiancé(e) or proposed civil partner under Appendix FM and now, following marriage or civil partnership, applies to switch to the category of a partner under Appendix FM;

(c) where a person is in the UK in a different immigration category has married or entered into a civil partnership and now wishes to switch to the category of a partner under Appendix FM;

(d) where a person switched in the UK to the category of a partner under Appendix FM and now applies for an extension of his limited leave for a further 30 months;

(e) where a person wishes to start on the 10-year family route to settlement under Appendix FM (see **8.1.2.3**) by relying on his Article 8 ECHR rights under para EX.1 (see **8.5**). This application might be made, for example, by an overstayer who has married a British citizen or a person settled in the UK, and who otherwise faces administrative removal from the UK (see **10.4**);

(f) where a person is on the 10-year family route to settlement under Appendix FM and now seeks an extension of his limited leave for a further 30 months.

8.4.2 An overview of the requirements

The requirements in Appendix FM to be met for leave to remain as a partner (see para R-LTRP.1.1) are that:

(a) the applicant and his partner must be in the UK;

(b) the applicant must have made a valid application for limited or indefinite leave to remain as a partner; and either

(c) (i) the applicant must not fall for refusal under Section S-LTR: Suitability – leave to remain, and

    (ii) the applicant meets all of the requirements of Section E-LTRP: Eligibility for limited leave to remain as a partner;

    or

(d) (i) the applicant must not fall for refusal under Section S-LTR: Suitability – leave to remain, and

    (ii) the applicant meets the eligibility requirements of paras E-LTRP.1.2–1.12 and E-LTRP.2.1, and

    (iii) para EX.1 applies.

The suitability requirements are detailed at **8.4.3**, the eligibility requirements at **8.4.4** and para EX.1 at **8.5**.

8.4.3 Suitability requirements

Paragraphs S-LTR.1.2–1.7 and S-LTR.2.2–2.4 set out respectively the mandatory and discretionary grounds on which the Home Office will normally refuse an application. You will see that broadly these are the same as for entry clearance (see **8.3.3**).

S-LTR.1.2 The applicant is at the date of application the subject of a deportation order.

S-LTR.1.3 The presence of the applicant in the UK is not conducive to the public good because he has been convicted of an offence for which he has been sentenced to imprisonment for at least four years.

S-LTR.1.4 The presence of the applicant in the UK is not conducive to the public good because he has been convicted of an offence for which he has been sentenced to imprisonment for less than four years but at least 12 months.

S-LTR.1.5 The presence of the applicant in the UK is not conducive to the public good because, in the view of the Secretary of State, his offending has caused serious harm or he is a persistent offender who shows a particular disregard for the law.

S-LTR.1.6 The presence of the applicant in the UK is not conducive to the public good because his conduct (including convictions which do not fall within paras S-LTR.1.3–1.5), character, associations, or other reasons, make it undesirable to allow him to remain in the UK.

S-LTR.1.7 The applicant has failed without reasonable excuse to comply with a requirement to attend an interview; provide information; provide physical data; or undergo a medical examination or provide a medical report.

S-LTR.2.2 Whether or not to the applicant's knowledge: (a) false information, representations or documents have been submitted in relation to the application (including false information submitted to any person to obtain a document used in support of the application); or (b) there has been a failure to disclose material facts in relation to the application.

S-LTR.2.3 One or more relevant NHS body has notified the Secretary of State that the applicant has failed to pay charges in accordance with the relevant NHS regulations on charges to overseas visitors and the outstanding charges have a total value of at least £1,000.

S-LTR.2.4 A maintenance and accommodation undertaking has been requested under para 35 of the Rules and has not been provided.

Note that when the Secretary of State is considering whether the presence of the applicant in the UK is not conducive to the public good (see S-LTR.1.3–1.6 above), any legal or practical reasons why the applicant cannot presently be removed from the UK must be ignored.

8.4.4 Overview of eligibility requirements

If an applicant meets all of the eligibility requirements in paras E-LTRP.1.2–4.2, he may be granted limited leave to remain and proceed on the five-year family route to settlement. Alternatively, if the applicant can meet the eligibility requirements of paras E-LTRP.1.2–1.12 and E-LTRP.2.1, and also meets para EX.1 (see **8.5** below), he may be granted limited leave to remain and proceed on the 10-year family route to settlement.

The eligibility requirements are as follows:

(a)   relationship requirements (see **8.4.5**);

(b)   immigration requirements (see **8.4.6**);

(c)   financial requirements (see **8.4.7**);

(d)   accommodation requirements (see **8.4.8**); and

(e)   English language requirement (see **8.4.9**).

8.4.5   Relationship requirements

Paras E-LTRP.1.2–1.10 set out the same relationship requirements as for entry clearance (see **8.3.5**). Note that para E-LTRP.1.10 provides, in addition, that the applicant must produce evidence that, since entry clearance as a partner was granted or since the last grant of limited leave to remain as a partner, the applicant and his partner have lived together in the UK, or there is good reason, consistent with a continuing intention to live together permanently in the UK, for any period in which they have not done so.

Note that para E-LTRP.1.11 provides that if the applicant is in the UK with leave as a fiancé(e) or proposed civil partner and the marriage or civil partnership did not take place during that period of leave, there must be good reason why it did not, and evidence must be produced that it will take place within the next six months. In those circumstances any further leave will be for six months only and subject to a condition of no recourse to public finds and a prohibition on employment.

Paragraph E-LTRP.1.12 provides that the applicant's partner cannot be the applicant's fiancé(e) or proposed civil partner, unless the applicant was granted entry clearance as that person's fiancé(e) or proposed civil partner.

8.4.6   Immigration requirements

Paragraph E-LTRP.2.1 excludes certain people already in the UK from switching into this category, namely, a visitor (see **Chapter 5**), or a person with valid leave granted for a period of six months or less, unless that leave is as a fiancé(e) or proposed civil partner, or a person on temporary admission (see **3.5.5**).

By para E-LTRP.2.2, the applicant must not be in the UK in breach of immigration laws (disregarding any period of overstaying for a period of 28 days or less), unless para EX. 1 applies (see **8.5**).

8.4.7   Financial requirements

Generally, by paras E-LTRP.3.1–3.3 the same financial provisions apply as for entry clearance (see **8.3.6**). The key differences to note are as follows:

(a)   Income from specified lawful employment or self-employment (Categories A, B, F and G – see **8.3.6.3**) of the applicant can now be included to meet the financial requirement, provided he is in the UK with permission to work. The only partner prohibited from working is a fiancé(e) or proposed civil partner.

> **EXAMPLE**
>
> Luke is a visa national. Over two years ago he entered the UK as the partner (spouse) of Rachel, a British citizen. He was accompanied by his dependent child, Ambrose. Luke and Ambrose are now applying for leave to remain for a further 30 months under Appendix FM to the Immigration Rules. The financial requirement Luke must meet is a minimum gross annual income of £22,400 (ie £18,600 for himself and £3,800 for Ambrose).
>
> Both Rachel and Luke have had the same jobs for over a year. Luke produces the specified documents evidencing the following financial resources: his annual salary from employment of £11,750, plus Rachel's annual salary from employment of £13,250. Together that totals £25,000 and so the minimum gross annual income is met.

(b)   An applicant does not have to meet the financial requirement, nor the alternative maintenance test (see **8.3.6.9**) if para EX.1 applies (see **8.5**).

8.4.8 Accommodation requirements

By para E-LTRP.3.4, the same accommodation provisions apply as for entry clearance (see **8.3.7**) unless para EX.1 applies (see **8.5**).

8.4.9 English language requirement

If the applicant has not already met this requirement in a previous application for leave as a partner, the applicant must now do so unless para EX.1 applies (see **8.5**). The details are the same as for entry clearance (see **8.3.8**).

8.4.10 Decision on application

If the applicant meets all the requirements he will be granted limited leave to remain for a period not exceeding 30 months and subject to a condition of no recourse to public funds. The applicant will be eligible to apply for settlement after a continuous period of at least 60 months (five years) with such leave (see **8.6**). This includes any period spent in the UK with entry clearance as a partner under para D-ECP1.1, but does not include any period of entry clearance or limited leave as a fiancé(e) or proposed civil partner.

A fiancé(e) or proposed civil partner will be able to work only once he has received notification from the Home Office that his application for leave to remain has been granted.

If the applicant can meet the suitability requirements, the eligibility requirements of paras E-LTRP.1.2–1.12 (the relationship requirements at **8.4.5**) and E-LTRP.2.1 (the first immigration requirement at **8.4.6**), and para EX.1 (see **8.5**) applies, he will be granted leave to remain for a period not exceeding 30 months. This will be subject to a condition of no recourse to public funds (unless there are exceptional circumstances set out in the application which require access to public funds to be granted on grounds of destitution). He will be eligible to apply for settlement after a continuous period of at least 120 months (10 years) with such leave (see **8.6**). This includes any period spent in the UK with entry clearance as a partner under para D-ECP1.1, but does not include any period of entry clearance or limited leave as a fiancé(e) or proposed civil partner.

8.5 PARAGRAPH EX.1

If the applicant can meet the suitability requirements (**8.4.3**) and the eligibility requirements of paras E-LTRP.1.2-1.12 (the relationship requirements at **8.4.5**) and E-LTRP.2.1 (the first immigration requirement at **8.4.6**), the application will be granted if para EX.1 applies. Broadly, this allows an applicant to remain in the UK on the basis of his family life with a child and/or a partner if it would breach Article 8 ECHR to remove the applicant. In these circumstances the applicant will have a longer route to settlement, namely 10 years, granted in four periods of 30 months' limited leave, with a fifth application for indefinite leave to remain.

Note that if the applicant is being deported having committed a criminal offence or criminal offences in the UK, and so does not meet the suitability requirements at **8.4.3**, then different considerations will apply instead of para EX.1: see **10.3.4**.

Further note that if the applicant is liable to being removed from the UK, perhaps as an overstayer, he may still meet the suitability requirements at **8.4.3**, and para EX.1 will then apply: see **10.4.6**.

8.5.1 Family life in UK with a child

Paragraph EX.1 applies if the applicant has a genuine and subsisting parental relationship with a child (under the age of 18 years) who is in the UK, who is a British citizen or who has lived in the UK continuously for at least the seven years immediately preceding the date of application, and it would not be reasonable to expect that child to leave the UK.

8.5.1.1 Genuine and subsisting parental relationship

Home Office guidance to its caseworkers is that when considering whether the relationship is genuine and subsisting, the following questons are likely to be relevant:

(a) Does the applicant have a parental relationship with the child? What is the relationship – biological, adopted, step-child, legal guardian? Is the applicant the child's *de facto* primary carer?

(b) Is it a genuine and subsisting relationship? Does the child live with the person? Where does the applicant live in relation to the child? How regularly do they see one another? Are there any relevant court orders governing access to the child?

(c) Is there any evidence or other relevant information provided within the application, eg the views of the child or other family members, or from social work or other relevant professionals? To what extent is the applicant making an active contribution to the child's life?

Factors which might prompt closer scrutiny include:

(a) that there is little or no contact with the child, or contact is irregular;

(b) any contact is only recent in nature;

(c) support is only financial in nature, there is no contact or emotional or welfare support;

(d) the child is largely independent of the person.

8.5.1.2 Child is a British citizen or been in the UK for a continuous period of seven years

Home Office guidance is that its caseworkers should establish the age and nationality of each child affected by the decision, and where they are foreign nationals their immigration history in the UK, eg how long they have lived in the UK and where they lived before.

In establishing whether a non-British citizen child has been in the UK continuously for more than seven years, the time spent in the UK with and without valid leave can be included. Short periods outside the UK, for example for holidays or family visits, would not count as a break in the seven years required. However, where a child has spent more than six months out of the UK at any one time, this normally should count as a break in continuous residence unless any exceptional factors apply.

8.5.1.3 It would be unreasonable to expect the child to leave the UK

If the child is a British citizen, the applicant is the child's primary carer and there is no other parent, guardian or carer on whom the child is dependent or who could care for the child if the primary carer left the UK, the applicant will have a right of residence under EU law (*Zambrano v Office national de l'emploi (ONEm) (Case C-34/09) [2011] 2 CMLR 46*) (see **4.4.13** and **10.5.2**). In these circumstances the Home Office's European case working team will review the case and, if the claim is established, issue the appropriate documentation.

If the child is a British citizen but *Zambrano* does not apply, the Home Office normally accepts that it would be unreasonable for the child to leave the UK with the applicant where the applicant would be returned to a country outside of the EU. Home Office guidance is that leave to remain may be refused where the conduct of one of the parents gives rise to considerations of such weight as to justify separation, provided the British citizen child could otherwise stay with another parent or primary carer in the UK. The circumstances envisaged by the Home Office include minor criminality falling below the thresholds set out in para 398 of the Immigration Rules (see **10.3.4**) and/or a poor immigration history. In considering whether refusal may be appropriate caseworkers need to consider the impact on the child of any separation.

Where the child is a British citizen, *Zambrano* does not apply and the applicant would be returned to a country in the EU, the Home Office applies the factors at **8.5.1.4** below.

8.5.1.4   Non-British citizen child has been in the UK for more than seven years

The Home Office states that the seven-year threshold recognises that over time children start to put down roots and integrate into life in the UK, to the extent that being required to leave the UK may be unreasonable. It directs its caseworkers to consider whether in the specific circumstances of the case it would be reasonable to expect the child to live in another country. Caseworkers must consider the facts for each child within that family and for the family in the round. They should also engage with any issues explicitly raised by the family, or by or behalf of each child. Relevant considerations are likely to include:

(a)   whether there would be a significant risk to the child's health, for example if there is evidence that the child is undergoing a course of treatment for a life- threatening or serious illness and treatment is not likely to be available in the country of return;

(b)   whether the child would be leaving with its parent(s). It is generally the case that it is in a child's best interests to remain with its parents. Unless specific factors apply, it will generally not be unreasonable to expect a child to leave the country with its parents, particularly if the parents have no right to remain in the UK;

(c)   the extent to which the child is dependent on any wider family members in the UK;

(d)   whether the child is likely to be able to (re)integrate readily into life in the country where the parent would be sent. Relevant factors weighing in favour of successful (re)integration include:

   (i)   whether the parent(s) or child is a citizen of the country and so able to enjoy the full rights of being a citizen in that country,

   (ii)   whether the parents and/or child have lived in or visited the country before for periods of more than a few weeks. The question here is whether, having visited or lived in the country before, the child would be able to adapt and/or the parents would be able to support the child in adapting to life in the country,

   (iii)   whether the child or parents have existing family or social ties with the country. A person who has extended family or networks of friends should be able to rely on them for support to help reintegrate on return,

   (iv)   whether the child or parents have relevant cultural ties to the country Caseworkers should consider any evidence of exposure to and the level of understanding of the cultural norms in the country. For example, a period of time spent living mainly amongst a diaspora from the country may in and of itself give a child an awareness of the culture in the country,

   (v)   whether the child can speak, read and write in a language of that country, or is likely to achieve this within a reasonable time period. Fluency is not required – an ability to communicate competently with sympathetic interlocutors would normally suffice,

   (vi)   whether the child has attended school in that country;

(e)   any country-specific risks (reference should be made to any relevant country guidance – see **9.7**);

(f)   other specific factors raised by, or on behalf of, the child.

Families or children may highlight the differences in quality of education, health and wider public services, and economic or social opportunities between the UK and the country of origin, and argue that these work against the best interests of the child. Home Office guidance is that other than in exceptional circumstances, this would not normally be regarded as a relevant consideration, particularly if the parent(s) or wider family have the means or resources to support the child on return, or the skills, education and training to provide for their family on return.

8.5.1.5 Exceptional factors

If para EX.1 does not apply the application is normally be refused. However, the Home Office accepts that there may be exceptional factors which would make refusal unreasonable. Its caseworkers should consider any other exceptional factors raised in relation to the child's best interests and question whether refusal is still appropriate in light of those factors. In some cases it may be appropriate to grant leave on a short-term temporary basis to enable particular issues relating to the child's welfare to be addressed before return.

Home Office guidance is that whilst all cases are to an extent unique, those unique factors do not generally render them exceptional. Furthermore, a case is not exceptional just because the exceptions to para EX.1 have been missed by a small margin. Rather, the Immigration Rules establish the thresholds as determining when leave would be appropriate bar other factors. However, in assessing exceptionality the matters identified in para EX.1 need to be considered along with all other aspects of the case. The decision maker then needs to determine whether removal would have such severe consequences for the child that exceptionally refusal or return is not appropriate. Finally, the decision maker should be prepared to take into account any order made by the UK Family Court, but that is not determinative of the immigration decision. However, the judgment of the family court, with all the tools at its disposal (including the assistance of the Children and Family Court Advisory and Support Service (CAFCASS) and the opportunity to assess all the adults), could and should inform the decision maker: see *Mohan v Secretary of State for the Home Department* [2012] EWCA Civ 1363.

8.5.2 Family life in UK with a partner

Paragraph EX.1 additionally, or alternatively, applies if the applicant has a genuine and subsisting relationship (see **8.3.5.5**) with a partner who is in the UK and who is a British citizen, settled in the UK, or in the UK with refugee leave or humanitarian protection, and there are insurmountable obstacles to family life with that partner continuing outside the UK.

8.5.2.1 Insurmountable obstacles

In determining whether there are 'insurmountable obstacles', para EX.2 provides that the decision maker should consider if there are very significant difficulties that would be faced by the applicant or his partner in continuing their family life together outside the UK, and which could not be overcome or would entail very serious hardship for the applicant or his partner.

Home Office guidance emphasises that the assessment of whether there are 'insurmountable obstacles' is a different and more stringent assessment than whether it would be 'reasonable to expect' the applicant's partner to join him overseas. For example, a British citizen partner who has lived in the UK all of his or her life, has friends and family here, works here and speaks only English may not wish to uproot and relocate halfway across the world, and it may be very difficult for him or her to do so, but a significant degree of hardship or inconvenience does not amount to an insurmountable obstacle.

Sales LJ held, in *R (on the application of Agyarko) v Secretary of State for the Home Department* [2015] EWCA Civ 440:

> 21. The phrase 'insurmountable obstacles' as used in this paragraph of the Rules clearly imposes a high hurdle to be overcome by an applicant for leave to remain under the Rules. The test is significantly more demanding than a mere test of whether it would be reasonable to expect a couple to continue their family life outside the United Kingdom.
>
> 22. This interpretation is in line with the relevant Strasbourg jurisprudence. The phrase 'insurmountable obstacles' has its origin in the Strasbourg jurisprudence in relation to immigration cases in a family context, where it is mentioned as one factor among others to be taken into account in determining whether any right under Article 8 exists for family members to be granted leave to remain or leave to enter a Contracting State: see eg *Rodrigues da Silva and Hoogkamer v Netherlands* (2007) 44

EHRR 34, para [39] ('... whether there are insurmountable obstacles in the way of the family living together in the country of origin of one or more of them ...'). The phrase as used in the Rules is intended to have the same meaning as in the Strasbourg jurisprudence. It is clear that the ECtHR regards it as a formulation imposing a stringent test in respect of that factor, as is illustrated by *Jeunesse v Netherlands* [(2015) 60 EHRR 17] (see para [117]: there were no insurmountable obstacles to the family settling in Suriname, even though the applicant and her family would experience hardship if forced to do so).

The Home Office states that Article 8 of the ECHR does not oblige the UK to accept the choice of a couple as to which country they would prefer to reside in.

Home Office guidance is that the lack of knowledge of a language spoken in the country in which the couple would be required to live would not usually amount to an insurmountable obstacle. Why? Because it is reasonable to conclude that the couple must have been communicating whilst in the UK. Therefore, it is possible for family life to continue outside the UK, whether or not the partner chooses to also learn a language spoken in the country of proposed return.

Does being separated from extended family members, such as might happen where the partner's parents and/or siblings live here, amount to an insurmountable obstacle? Would a material change in the quality of life for the applicant and his partner in the country of return, such as the type of accommodation they would live in, or a reduction in their income, amount to an insurmountable obstacle? No, answers the Home Office, not unless there were particular exceptional factors in either case.

According to the Home Office, the factors which might be relevant to the consideration of whether an insurmountable obstacle exists include, but are not limited to, the following:

(a) The ability of the family to lawfully enter and stay in another country.

(b) Cultural barriers where the partner would be so disadvantaged that he or she could not be expected to go and live in that country, for example, a same sex couple where the UK partner would face substantial societal discrimination, or where the rights and freedoms of the UK partner would be severely restricted.

(c) Whether or not either party has a mental or physical disability, a move to another country may involve a period of hardship as the person adjusts to his or her new surroundings. But a physical or mental disability could be such that in some circumstances it could lead to very serious hardship, for example due to lack of health care.

(d) In some circumstances, there may be particular risks to foreign nationals which extend to the whole of the country of return.

8.5.2.2 Exceptional circumstances

Where the applicant does not meet the requirements set out above, refusal of the application will be appropriate. However, leave may be granted outside the Rules where exceptional circumstances apply.

The Home Office decision maker needs to determine whether refusal or removal would have such severe consequences for the individual that this would not be proportionate given the nature of his family life, notwithstanding the fact that there are no insurmountable obstacles to family life with the applicant's partner continuing outside the UK. Home Office guidance is that is likely to be the case only very rarely.

In determining whether there are exceptional circumstances, the decision maker must consider all relevant factors, such as the following:

(a) The circumstances around the applicant's entry to the UK and the proportion of the time he has been in the UK legally as opposed to illegally. Did he form his relationship with his partner at a time when he had no immigration status or this was precarious?

Family life which involves the applicant putting down roots in the UK in the full knowledge that his stay here is unlawful or precarious should be given less weight, when balanced against the factors weighing in favour of removal, than family life formed by a person lawfully present in the UK.

(b)   Cumulative factors should be considered. For example, where the applicant has family members in the UK but his family life does not provide a basis for staying and he has a significant private life in the UK. Although under the Rules family life and private life are considered separately, when considering whether there are exceptional circumstances private and family life should be taken into account.

(c)   The public policy considerations in s 117A of the NIAA 2002 (see **10.3.4.2**).

If the application is granted because exceptional circumstances apply, leave outside the Immigration Rules for a period of 30 months is usually given.

8.6 INDEFINITE LEAVE TO REMAIN (SETTLEMENT) AS A PARTNER

8.6.1 Who can apply?

There are two different situations to be considered here, namely:

(a)   where a person has completed the five-year family route to settlement, ie two periods of 30 months' leave in the UK as a partner; and

(b)   where a person has completed the 10-year family route to settlement, ie four periods of 30 months' leave in the UK as a partner.

8.6.2 An overview of the requirements

The requirements in Appendix FM to be met for indefinite leave to remain as a partner (see para R-ILRP.1.1) are that:

(a)   the applicant and his partner must be in the UK;

(b)   the applicant must have made a valid application for indefinite leave to remain as a partner;

(c)   the applicant must not fall for refusal under any of the grounds in Section S-ILR: Suitability – indefinite leave to remain (see **Appendix 16**);

(d)   the applicant must meet all of the requirements of Section E-LTRP: Eligibility for leave to remain as a partner (see **8.4.4**); and

(e)   the applicant must meet all of the requirements of Section E-ILRP: Eligibility for indefinite leave to remain as a partner (see **8.6.3**).

8.6.3 Eligibility requirements for indefinite leave to remain

Note that whilst the applicant must meet all of the requirements of Section E-LTRP: Eligibility for leave to remain as a partner (see **8.4.4**), where the financial requirement applies, any cash savings in Category D that exceed £16,000 are taken into account in full.

Table 8.6 below sets out some examples of the minimum savings required to meet a shortfall where £18,600 (applicant with no dependent children) is the prescribed minimum gross annual income.

Table 8.6 Minimum savings required to meet a shortfall

Income	Indefinite leave to remain: minimum savings required
No other relevant income	£34,600 (£16,000 + shortfall of £18,600)

Income	Indefinite leave to remain: minimum savings required
Other relevant income of £15,000	£19,600 (£16,000 + shortfall of £3,600)
Other relevant income of £18,000	£16,600 (£16,000 + and shortfall of £600)

By para E-ILRP.1.2, the applicant must be in the UK with valid leave to remain as a partner (disregarding any period of overstaying for a period of 28 days or less).

By para E-ILRP.1.3, the applicant must have completed a continuous period of at least 60 months with limited leave as a partner (under para R-LTRP.1.1(a) to (c), or in the UK with entry clearance as a partner under para D-ECP.1.1), or a continuous period of at least 120 months with limited leave as a partner (under para R-LTR.P.1.1(a), (b) and (d), or in the UK with entry clearance as a partner under para D-ECP.1.1) or a continuous period of at least 120 months with limited leave as a partner under a combination of these paragraphs. Note that any period of entry clearance or limited leave as a fiancé(e) or proposed civil partner cannot be included.

By para E-ILRP.1.4, only those periods of limited leave when the applicant's partner is the same person can be taken into account.

8.6.4   Absences from the UK

There is no requirement that the entire five- or 10-year leave periods, as appropriate, must be spent in the UK. Home Office guidance is that where an applicant has spent a limited period outside of the UK in connection with his or his partner's employment, this should not count against him. However, if he has spent the majority of the period overseas, there may be reason to doubt that all the requirements of the Immigration Rules have been met, eg that the couple intend to live together permanently in the UK (see **8.3.5.9**). The Home Office states that each case must be judged on its merits, taking into account reasons for travel, length of absence, and whether the applicant and his partner travelled and lived together during the time spent outside the UK. These factors will need to be considered against the relevant requirements of the Immigration Rules.

8.6.5   Decision on the application

By para D-ILRP.1.1, if the applicant meets all of the requirements at **8.6.2** he will be granted indefinite leave to remain unless para EX.1 applies (see **8.5**). Where paragraph EX.1 applies, the applicant will be granted further limited leave to remain as a partner for a period not exceeding 30 months under para D-ILRP.1.2 (see immediately below).

What if the applicant cannot meet all the requirements? Paragraph D-ILRP.1.2 has a limited concession. It provides that if the applicant does not meet the requirements for indefinite leave to remain as a partner only for one or both of the following reasons:

(a)   para S-ILR.1.5 or 1.6 applies; and/or

(b)   the applicant does not have sufficient knowledge of the English language and sufficient knowledge about life in the UK;

then the applicant will be granted further limited leave to remain as a partner for a period not exceeding 30 months and subject to a condition of no recourse to public funds.

Where an applicant is granted further limited leave under para D-ILRP.1.2 he should be advised that should the reason at (a) and/or (b) be overcome, he can make a further application for settlement at any time within the 30-month period.

The application will be refused if the applicant does not meet all the eligibility requirements for indefinite leave to remain as a partner and does not qualify for further leave to remain as a partner under para D-ILRP.1.2.

8.7 INDEFINITE LEAVE TO REMAIN (SETTLEMENT) AS A BEREAVED PARTNER

What if, before the relevant five- or 10-year probationary period is completed, the applicant's partner dies? In these circumstances, if the bereaved partner wishes to remain in the UK permanently, he should apply for settlement.

By para BPILR.1.1, the applicant will have to meet the following requirements:

(a) the applicant must be in the UK;

(b) the applicant must have made a valid application for indefinite leave to remain as a bereaved partner;

(c) the applicant must not fall for refusal under any of the grounds in Section S-ILR: Suitability – indefinite leave to remain (see **8.6.2(c)**); and

(d) the applicant must meet all of the requirements of Section E-BPILR: Eligibility for indefinite leave to remain as a bereaved partner (see **8.7.1**).

8.7.1 Eligibility requirements

By para E-BPILR.1.2, the applicant's last grant of limited leave must have been as:

(a) a partner (other than a fiancé(e) or proposed civil partner) of a British citizen or a person settled in the UK; or

(b) a bereaved partner.

By para E-BPILR.1.3, the person who has died must have been the applicant's partner at the time the applicant was last granted limited leave under Appendix FM.

By para E-BPILR.1.4, at the time of the partner's death the relationship between the applicant and the partner must have been genuine and subsisting (see **8.3.5.5**), and each of the parties must have intended to live permanently with the other in the UK (see **8.3.5.9**).

Home Office guidance is that normally detailed enquiries as to the subsistence of the marriage, civil partnership or relationship will not be made unless there are already doubts expressed on the file. In most cases, provided the eligibility requirements are met, the application will be granted on sight of the partner's death certificate and without further enquiry.

In cases of doubt, for example where there were doubts expressed at the time of granting the initial period of leave to remain, or where allegations have since been made about the genuine and subsisting nature of the relationship, it may be appropriate to refuse the application. However, as the Home Office guidance recognises, it must be borne in mind that the burden of proof on the Secretary of State will be very high in view of the fact that the applicant will no longer be in a position to prove the subsistence of the relationship.

8.7.2 Timeliness of application

Home Office guidance is that this provision is intended to benefit only those whose sponsor has died during the probationary period and who make their application whilst they still have limited leave to enter or remain in the UK.

The provision is also applied where the sponsor dies after an application for settlement has been submitted but before a decision has been reached.

Is the fact that a sponsor dies during the very early stages of the probationary period considered by the Home Office as an adverse factor in reaching a decision? No: Home Office guidance is that where an applicant can meet the requirements, the application is to be granted regardless of how much of the probationary period has been completed.

What if the application is made after the applicant's existing leave has expired? Home Office guidance is that an applicant does not need to comply with the requirement not to have overstayed by more than 28 days (para E-LTRP 2.2 at **8.4.6**), provided that the circumstances of any period of overstaying relates to a period of bereavement and where compassionate circumstances therefore apply. Applications made out of time where all the other requirements are met should be considered sympathetically. An application should not normally be refused solely on the grounds that the applicant is here without leave. Acceptable reasons for the delay in making an application could be that the partner's death only occurred shortly before the application for settlement was due, or that the stress of the situation led the applicant to overlook the need to regularise his immigration status.

8.7.3 Decision on application

If the applicant meets all of the requirements set out at **8.7** above, he will be granted indefinite leave to remain.

But what if the applicant cannot meet all of the requirements? Paragraph D-BPILR.1.2 has a limited concession. It provides that if the only requirement not met is either para S-ILR.1.5 or 1.6, he will be granted further limited leave to remain for a period not exceeding 30 months (subject to a condition of no recourse to public funds). The applicant should be informed that if he is granted a further period of limited leave under para D-BPILR1.2, he can make a further application for settlement at any time within the 30-month period if the requirement is met.

If the applicant does not meet the requirements for indefinite leave to remain as a bereaved partner, or limited leave to remain as a bereaved partner under para D-BPILR.1.2, the application will be refused.

What if the applicant does not wish to settle in the UK but intends to leave the UK, eg to return to his country of origin? In these circumstances, Home Office guidance is that the applicant may be granted further leave to remain for six months, subject to the same conditions, to give him time to sort out his affairs.

8.8 INDEFINITE LEAVE TO REMAIN (SETTLEMENT) AS A PARTNER WHO IS A VICTIM OF DOMESTIC VIOLENCE

What if the couple separate due to domestic violence before the relevant probationary period is completed? In these circumstances, if the applicant wishes to remain in the UK permanently, he should apply for settlement.

By para DVILR.1.1, the applicant will have to meet the following requirements:

(a)   the applicant must be in the UK;

(b)   the applicant must have made a valid application for indefinite leave to remain as a victim of domestic violence;

(c)   the applicant must not fall for refusal under any of the grounds in Section S-ILR: Suitability – indefinite leave to remain (see **8.6.2(c)**); and

(d)   the applicant must meet all of the requirements of Section E-DVILR: Eligibility for indefinite leave to remain as a victim of domestic violence (see **8.8.1**).

8.8.1 Eligibility requirements

By para E-DVILR.1.2, the applicant's last grant of limited leave must have been:

(a)   as a partner (other than a fiancé(e) or proposed civil partner) of a British citizen or a person settled in the UK;

(b)   granted to enable access to public funds pending an application under this provision; or

(c)   granted under para D-DVILR.1.2 (see **8.8.2**).

Paragraph E-DVILR.1.3 provides that the applicant must provide evidence that during the last period of limited leave as a partner, his relationship broke down permanently as a result of domestic violence. Note first that there needs to be a causal link between the infliction of domestic violence on the applicant and the permanent breakdown of the relationship. Secondly, consideration needs to be given as to what evidence might be available. Has the applicant's partner been convicted of assaulting the applicant or formally cautioned by the police? Many victims of domestic violence do not tell anyone. Whatever the circumstances, the detailed guidance issued by the Home Office on this requirement should be consulted.

8.8.2   Decision on application

If the applicant meets all of the requirements set out at **8.8**, he will be granted indefinite leave to remain.

But what if the applicant cannot meet all of the requirements? Paragraph D-DVILR.1.2 has a limited concession. It provides that if the only requirement not met is para S-ILR.1.5 or 1.6, he will be granted further limited leave to remain for a period not exceeding 30 months. The applicant should be informed that if granted a further period of limited leave under para D-DVILR.1.2, he can make a further application for settlement at any time within the 30-month period if the requirement is met.

If the applicant does not meet the requirements for indefinite leave to remain as a victim of domestic violence, or further limited leave to remain under para D-DVILR.1.2, the application will be refused.

8.9   CHILDREN ENTERING FOR IMMEDIATE SETTLEMENT

8.9.1   Who is a child?

A child is a person under the age of 18 at the date he applies for entry clearance. So it is irrelevant if he turns 18 before the ECO decides his application or before travelling to the UK under his visa or entry certificate (see paras 27 and 321(ii) respectively of the Immigration Rules).

This route is only available to a child outside the UK. A child cannot switch into this route whilst in the UK.

8.9.2   Exempt groups

A child will usually need to apply for entry clearance under Part 8 of the Immigration Rules to join a parent, both parents or a relative who is already settled in the UK. The child will need to apply for entry clearance, and if granted can enter the UK for the purposes of immediate settlement. However, those Rules will not apply to the following:

(a)   children who are British citizens (see **Chapter 2**);

(b)   children who have rights of residence in the UK as the family member of an EEA national (see **Chapter 4**).

> **EXAMPLE**
>
> Eva is a German citizen, aged 17. Her father, also German, is working in the UK. She is entitled to enter the UK in her own right (I(EEA) Regs 2006, reg 11). Whether she has any right of residence beyond three months (reg 14) depends on establishing a qualifying status under reg 6. In the alternative, she can enter and reside as the family member of her father who is an EEA national. The Immigration Rules do not apply.

8.9.3   Who is a parent?

The term 'parent', for the purposes of the Immigration Rules, is defined in para 6 and includes:

(a)   the step-father of a child whose father is dead, and the reference to 'step-father' includes a relationship arising through civil partnership;

(b)   the step-mother of a child whose mother is dead, and the reference to 'step-mother' includes a relationship arising through civil partnership;

(c)   the father, as well as the mother, of an illegitimate child where he is proved to be the father;

(d)   an adoptive parent (provided that the child was legally adopted in a country whose adoption orders are recognised by the UK – see **8.9.6**);

(e)   in the case of a child born in the UK who is not a British citizen, a person to whom there has been a genuine transfer of parental responsibility on the ground of the original parent's/parents' inability to care for the child.

8.9.4   Entry clearance requirements

Normally a child will be seeking entry clearance to join one or both parents who are already settled in the UK. Exceptionally, he might be joining a relative who is here and settled. Note that these people are often called the child's 'sponsor'.

The requirements are set out in para 297.

8.9.4.1   Overview of requirements

The starting point is to identify the parent, parents or relative the child is seeking to join in the UK, as listed in para 297(i)(a)–(f). Unless one of those categories is established, the application will fail at this first hurdle.

Then proceed to consider the remaining requirements in para 297(ii)–(v). The main issues normally concern the child's maintenance and accommodation in the UK.

As you would expect, there is a requirement to obtain entry clearance (see para 297(vi)).

8.9.4.2   Parent, parents or relative

There are four straightforward categories of entry for a child. These are listed in para 297(i), as follows:

(a)   both parents are present and settled in the UK; or

(b)   both parents are being admitted on the same occasion with the child for settlement; or

(c)   one parent is present and settled in the UK and the other parent is being admitted on the same occasion with the child for settlement; or

(d)   one parent is present and settled in the UK or being admitted on the same occasion with the child for settlement, and the other parent is dead.

As can be seen, (a)–(c) involve both parents; in (d) one parent is dead.

The remaining two categories impose additional tests. This is because one parent is alive but will *not* be involved in the family reunion. This is likely where the parents have never lived together, or have separated or divorced. On what basis will the child be allowed to join the one parent who is present and settled in the UK? This is provided for in para 297(i), as follows:

(e)   one parent is present and settled in the UK or being admitted on the same occasion with the child for settlement, and has had sole responsibility for the child's upbringing; or

(f)   one parent or a relative is present and settled in the UK or being admitted on the same occasion with the child for settlement, and there are serious and compelling family or other considerations which make exclusion of the child undesirable and suitable arrangements have been made for the child's care.

The sole responsibility test in (e) is discussed at **8.9.4.3**. The serious and compelling reasons test in (f) is examined at **8.9.4.4**.

You will have noted that the only way a child can join a relative other than a parent in the UK is under category (f).

8.9.4.3 Sole responsibility

According to Home Office guidance, the phrase 'sole responsibility' is intended to reflect a situation where parental responsibility for a child, to all intents and purposes, rests chiefly with one parent. Such a situation is in contrast to the ordinary family unit where responsibility for a child's upbringing is shared between the two parents (although not necessarily equally).

In *Suzara Ramos v Immigration Appeal Tribunal* [1989] Imm AR 148, the Court of Appeal (per Dillon LJ) held that

> the words 'sole responsibility' have to carry some form of qualification in that the rule envisages that a parent who is settled in the United Kingdom will or may have had the sole responsibility for the child's upbringing in another country. Obviously there are matters of day-to-day decision in the upbringing of a child which are bound to be decided on the spot by whoever is looking after the child in the absence of the parent settled here, such as getting the child to school safely and on time, or putting the child to bed, or seeing what it has for breakfast, or that it cleans its teeth, or has enough clothing, and so forth. ... The question must be a broad question.
>
> Direction and control of upbringing are ... factors which are part of the total pattern of facts on which the adjudicator had to make his decision. Another matter was of course the extent of contact that the mother had had with the child since the mother went to the United Kingdom ...

A parent claiming to have had 'sole responsibility' for a child must satisfactorily demonstrate that he has, for a period of time, been the chief person exercising parental responsibility. For such an assertion to be accepted by the Home Office, it must be shown that he has had, and still has, the ultimate responsibility for the major decisions relating to the child's upbringing, and provides the child with the majority of the financial and emotional support he requires. It must also be shown that he has had and continues to have care and control of the child.

In the case of *Nmaju v Entry Clearance Officer* (2000) *The Times*, 6 September, the Court of Appeal held that this requirement could be satisfied even where the parent in question had exercised sole responsibility only for a short period of time (namely, about two and a half months on the facts). The Court said that the question posed by the rules was: Had the parent settled in the UK sole responsibility for the upbringing of the child? In this case the Tribunal had found that the mother had had sole responsibility for the upbringing of the appellants. Having concluded that, the Tribunal was not at liberty under the rules to find that the appellants did not qualify for entry merely because that sole responsibility had not been assumed for a period of in excess of much over two months.

In *Nmaju* the Court of Appeal indicated that:

> While legal responsibility under the appropriate legal system will be a relevant consideration, it will not be a conclusive one. One must also look at what has actually been done in relation to the child's upbringing by whom and whether it has been done under the direction of the parent settled here. (per Schiemann LJ)

In *Cenir v Entry Clearance Officer* [2003] EWCA Civ 572 Buxton LJ stated that the following was a useful rule of thumb:

> [A]ll the important decisions in the child's life, questions concerning health and place of abode, schooling and probably going as far as serious questions of behaviour, mode of dress and the like must

be under the oversight of the parent claiming sole responsibility or delegated to someone obliged to consult and act upon her instructions. To have responsibility means to be answerable.

Home Office guidance lists the following factors which may be relevant when deciding this issue:

(a)   the period for which the parent in the UK has been separated from the child;

(b)   what the arrangements were for the care of the child before that parent migrated to this country;

(c)   who has been entrusted with day-to-day care and control of the child since the sponsoring parent migrated here;

(d)   who provides, and in what proportion, the financial support for the child's care and upbringing;

(e)   who takes the important decisions about the child's upbringing, such as where and with whom the child lives, the choice of school, religious practice, etc;

(f)   the degree of contact that has been maintained between the child and the parent claiming sole responsibility;

(g)   what part in the child's care and upbringing is played by the parent not in the UK and his relatives.

8.9.4.4   Serious and compelling reasons

Guidance from the Home Office on the meaning of 'serious and compelling reasons' in para 297(i)(f) states:

> [T]he objective of this provision is to allow a child to join a parent or relative in this country only where that child could not be adequately cared for by his parents or relatives in his own country. It has never been the intention of the Rules that a child should be admitted here due to the wish of or for the benefit of other relatives in this country. This approach is entirely consistent with the internationally accepted principle that a child should first and foremost be cared for by his natural parent(s) or, if this is not possible, by his natural relatives in the country in which he lives. Only if the parent(s) or relative(s) in his own country cannot care for him should consideration be given to him joining relatives in another country. It is also consistent with the provisions of the European Convention on Human Rights, and the resolution on the harmonization of family reunification agreed by EU Ministers in June 1993.

The degree to which these considerations should be taken into account, and whether they should relate solely to the child or include the circumstances of the sponsor, is determined by two factors, namely:

(a)   whether the sponsor is a parent or other relative of the child; and

(b)   whether or not the sponsor is settled here.

If the sponsor is not a parent but another relative (eg an aunt or grandparent), the factors which are to be considered relate only to the child and the circumstances in which he lives or lived prior to travelling to the UK. These circumstances should be exceptional in comparison with the ordinary circumstances of other children in his home country. It is not, for instance, sufficient to show he would be better off here by being able to attend a State school.

> The focus needs to be on the circumstances of the child in the light of his or her age, social background and developmental history and will involve inquiry as to whether: (i) there is evidence of neglect or abuse; (ii) there are unmet needs that should be catered for; (iii) there are stable arrangements for the child's physical care. The assessment involves consideration as to whether the combination of circumstances [is] sufficiently serious and compelling to require admission. (per Blake J in *Mundeba* (*s.55 and para 297(i)(f)*) [2013] UKUT 88 (IAC) at [37])

The circumstances relating to the sponsors here (eg the fact that they are elderly or infirm and need caring for) are not taken into account.

If the sponsor in the UK is one of the child's parents, consideration needs to be given to whether or not that parent is settled here or being admitted for settlement. If he is not, the relevant circumstances relate solely to the child (as detailed above). But if the child's sponsor is one of his parents and he is settled here (or being admitted for settlement), the considerations to be taken into account may relate either to the child and his circumstances in the country in which he lives or lived prior to travelling here, or to the parent who is settled here or being admitted for settlement.

The circumstances surrounding the child must be exceptional in relation to those of other children living in that country, but in this case, circumstances relating to the parent here, both of an emotional and of a physical nature, may be taken into account. Such circumstances may include illness or infirmity which requires assistance.

EXAMPLE

Marlene is the mother of Dora, aged 14. Both are citizens of Barbados. Marlene is divorced from Dora's father, who never contacts his daughter. He is still living in Barbados. When Dora was 8 years old, Marlene came to the UK and left Dora in Barbados in the care of her grandmother, who alone has supported her granddaughter financially. Marlene now has indefinite leave to remain in the UK. She wishes to know whether Dora can join her in the UK.

Marlene cannot establish her sole responsibility (see **8.9.4.3**) for Dora, as she has not provided any financial support for her from the UK. She must instead show that there are serious and compelling considerations which make Dora's exclusion undesirable (eg if Dora's grandmother becomes seriously ill and incapable of looking after her). If this requirement is not met, Dora cannot currently be admitted for settlement in the UK.

Marlene may be able to establish sole responsibility (see **8.9.4.3**) over the next few months if she provides all or the majority of Dora's financial and emotional support, and takes responsibility for the major decisions in Dora's life.

8.9.4.5   Age

By para 297(ii), the child must be under the age of 18. See further **8.9.1**.

8.9.4.6   Dependent life-style

By para 297(iii), the child must not be leading an independent life, must be unmarried and not a civil partner, and must not have formed an independent family unit.

Paragraph 6 of the Immigration Rules provides that 'must not be leading an independent life' means that the applicant:

(a)   does not have a partner as defined in Appendix FM (see **8.1.2.1**);

(b)   is living with his parents (except where he is at boarding school, college or university as part of his full-time education);

(c)   is not employed full-time (unless aged 18 years or over);

(d)   is wholly or mainly dependent upon his parents for financial support (unless aged 18 years or over); and

(e)   is wholly or mainly dependent upon his parents for emotional support.

Obviously the above general factors may have to be adapted when applied to the different categories of possible entry in para 297(i): see **8.9.4.2**.

8.9.4.7   Accommodation

By para 297(iv), the child must be accommodated adequately by the parent, parents or relative the child is seeking to join, without recourse to public funds, in accommodation which the parent, parents or relative the child is seeking to join own or occupy exclusively.

The equivalent provision for partners under Appendix FM is detailed at **8.3.7**.

> **EXAMPLE**
>
> In the case of *Loresco* [1999] INLP 18, three teenage children (one girl and two boys) sought to join their mother in the UK. Was her two-bedroomed flat, with a living room that was also available as sleeping accommodation, too small for her, her husband, their 1-year-old child and the three teenagers? The Tribunal said 'Yes'. Three rooms were available to sleep in. There was one room for the sponsor and her husband, one room for the girl over 10, and the third room for the two boys over 10. So the room standard was met.
>
> Under the space standard, with only three available rooms, the permitted number of persons was five. But the child aged 1 year counted as half a unit, and as everyone else was aged 10 or over, that meant the total number of people in the flat would be five and a half persons with the three teenage children. Their application was therefore refused as the flat was overcrowded under the space standard (see **8.3.7.3**).

8.9.4.8 Maintenance

By para 297(v), the child must be maintained adequately by the parent, parents or relative the child is seeking to join, without recourse to public funds. As to public funds, see **3.3.2**.

The equivalent provision for partners under Appendix FM is detailed at **8.3.6.9**.

8.9.4.9 General grounds for refusal

The application must not fall for refusal under the general grounds for refusal (see **3.4.5** and the criminality requirements in **Appendix 8**).

8.9.5 Adopted children

Adopted children are dealt with in paras 309A–316F of the Immigration Rules. The details are beyond the scope of this book.

8.10 PARENT OF A CHILD SETTLED IN THE UK

8.10.1 Who can apply?

A parent with sole parental responsibility for, or access rights to, a British citizen child or settled child who is living in the UK, can apply for entry clearance (see **8.10.2**) and leave to remain (see **8.10.3**) under Appendix FM to the Immigration Rules. Ultimately it may be possible to apply for settlement in this category (see **8.10.4**).

A parent already in the UK may switch into this category. This most commonly occurs when a person has entered the UK with limited leave as the partner of a British citizen or settled person (see **8.3**), but can no longer remain in the UK in that category as the relationship has broken down. If that person has sole parental responsibility for, or is exercising access rights to, his British or settled child, an application may be made for limited leave to remain (see **8.10.3**).

Who is a parent for these purposes? See **8.9.3**.

8.10.2 Entry clearance

By para EC-PT.1.1 of Appendix FM to the Immigration Rules, the requirements to be met for entry clearance as a parent are:

(a)   the applicant must be outside the UK;

(b)   the applicant must have made a valid application for entry clearance as a parent;

(c) the applicant must not fall for refusal under any of the grounds in Section S-EC: Suitability – entry clearance; and

(d) the applicant must meet all of the requirements of Section E-ECPT: Eligibility for entry clearance as a parent.

Note that the suitability requirements are the same as for a partner under Appendix FM, and these are detailed at **8.3.3**. As to the eligibility requirements, see **8.10.2.1**.

8.10.2.1 Eligibility requirements in outline

An applicant must meet all of the eligibility requirements in paras E-ECPT.2.1–4.2. Broadly these are as follows:

(a) relationship requirements (see **8.10.2.2**);

(b) financial requirements (see **8.10.2.3**)

(c) accommodation requirements (see **8.10.2.4**); and

(d) English language requirement (see **8.10.2.5**).

8.10.2.2 Relationship requirements (paras E-ECPT.2.1–2.4)

By para E-ECPT.2.1, the applicant must be aged 18 years or over.

Paragraph E-ECPT.2.2 provides that the child of the applicant must be:

(a) under the age of 18 years at the date of application;

(b) living in the UK; and

(c) a British citizen (see **2.2**) or settled in the UK (see **3.8**).

By para E-ECPT.2.3, either:

(a) the applicant must have sole parental responsibility for the child (see **8.9.4.3**); or

(b) the parent or carer with whom the child normally lives must be –

    (i) a British citizen in the UK or settled in the UK;

    (ii) not the partner of the applicant; and

    (iii) the applicant must not be eligible to apply for entry clearance as a partner under Appendix FM (see **8.3**).

By para E-ECPT.2.4, the applicant must provide evidence that he has either:

(a) (i) sole parental responsibility for the child; or

    (ii) access rights to the child; and

(b) the applicant must provide evidence that he is taking, and intends to continue to take, an active role in the child's upbringing.

What evidence is required?

Home Office guidance is that to demonstrate access rights, the applicant will need to produce either a residence or a contact order granted by a court in the UK, or a sworn affidavit from the UK resident parent or carer of the child confirming that the applicant can have access to the child and describing in detail the access arrangements. If the contact with the child is supervised, the supervisor must swear the statement.

How can an applicant show that he is taking, and intends to continue to take, an active role in his child's upbringing? The application form states:

> Please provide details of how you have been involved in the upbringing of your child(ren). You should include information on what role you played in choosing their care arrangements in the UK or which nursery/school they attend. What role have you played in choosing their academic options? How often do you speak to or see your child(ren)? Have you been present for key events in their lives eg religious

events, birthdays etc? How do you keep in touch (telephone, email, letters etc)? Please provide any documentary evidence that you have to support your answer.

8.10.2.3 Financial requirements

By para E-ECPT.3.1, the applicant must provide evidence that he will be able to maintain and accommodate himself and any dependants in the UK adequately without recourse to public funds. As to public funds, see **3.3.2**.

The equivalent provision for partners under Appendix FM is detailed at **8.3.6.9**.

8.10.2.4 Accommodation requirements

By para E-ECPT.3.2, the applicant must provide evidence that there will be adequate accommodation in the UK, without recourse to public funds, for the family, including other family members who are not included in the application but who live in the same household, which the family own or occupy exclusively. Accommodation will not be regarded as adequate if:

(a)   it is, or will be, overcrowded; or

(b)   it contravenes public health regulations.

The equivalent provision for partners under Appendix FM is detailed at **8.3.7**.

8.10.2.5 English language requirement

The requirement in para E-ECPT.4.1 is exactly the same as for a partner seeking entry clearance under Appendix FM, and the details are at **8.3.8**.

8.10.2.6 Decision on application

If the applicant meets the requirements for entry clearance as a parent, he will be granted entry clearance for an initial period not exceeding 33 months and subject to a condition of no recourse to public funds.

8.10.3 Leave to remain

8.10.3.1 Who can apply?

There are five different situations to be considered here, namely:

(a)   where an applicant entered the UK as a parent under Appendix FM and now seeks an extension of his limited leave for a further 30 months;

(b)   where a person entered the UK in a different category, often a partner under Appendix FM, and now applies to switch to this category;

(c)   where a person switched in the UK to this category and now wants an extension of his limited leave for a further 30 months;

(d)   where a person seeks to start on the 10-year family route to settlement under Appendix FM by relying on his Article 8 ECHR rights under para EX.1 (see **8.5**). This application might be made, for example, by an overstayer with no partner in the UK but a child, and who otherwise faces administrative removal from the UK (see **10.4**);

(e)   where a person is on the 10-year family route to settlement under Appendix FM and now seeks an extension of his limited leave for a further 30 months.

8.10.3.2 An overview of the requirements

The requirements to be met for limited leave to remain as a parent (see para R-LTRPT.1.1) are that:

(a)   the applicant and the child must be in the UK;

(b)   the applicant must have made a valid application for limited leave to remain as a parent; and either

(c)   (i)   the applicant must not fall for refusal under Section S-LTR: Suitability – leave to remain (see **8.10.3.3**), and

(ii)   the applicant must meet all of the requirements of Section E-LTRPT: Eligibility for leave to remain as a parent (see **8.10.3.4**), and

(iii)   para EX.1 (see **8.5**) has not been applied; or

(d)   (i)   the applicant must not fall for refusal under Section S-LTR: Suitability – leave to remain, and

(ii)   the applicant meets the eligibility requirements of paras E-LTRPT.2.2–2.4 and E-LTRPT.3.1; and

(iii)   para EX.1 applies.

8.10.3.3   Suitability requirements

Paragraphs S-LTR.1.2–1.7 and S-LTR.2.1–2.4 set out the mandatory and discretionary grounds on which the Home Office will normally refuse an application. These are detailed at **8.4.3**.

8.10.3.4   Overview of eligibility requirements

If an applicant meets all of the eligibility requirements in paras E-LTRPT.1.2–5.2, he may be granted limited leave and proceed on a five-year route to settlement. If he meets the eligibility requirements of paras E-LTRPT.2.2–2.4 and E-LTRPT.3.1, and para EX.1 (see **8.5**) applies, he may be granted limited leave and proceed on a 10-year route to settlement.

The eligibility requirements are as follows:

(a)   relationship requirements (see **8.10.3.5**);

(b)   immigration requirements (see **8.10.3.6**);

(c)   financial requirements (see **8.10.3.7**)

(d)   accommodation requirements (see **8.10.3.8**); and

(e)   English language requirement (see **8.10.3.9**).

8.10.3.5   Relationship requirements

Paragraphs E-LTRPT.2.2–2.4 set out virtually the same relationship requirements as for entry clearance (see **8.10.2.2**). However, note that by para E-LTRPT.2.2 the following additional fourth category of child of the applicant is included, namely, where the child has lived in the UK continuously for at least the seven years immediately preceding the date of application and para EX.1 (see **8.5**) applies.

8.10.3.6   Immigration requirements

Paragraph E-LTRPT.3.1 excludes certain people already in the UK from switching into this category, namely, a visitor (see **Chapter 5**), or a person with valid leave granted for a period of six months or less, or a person on temporary admission (see **3.5.5**).

By para E-LTRPT.3.2, the applicant must not be in the UK in breach of immigration laws (disregarding any period of overstaying for a period of 28 days or less), unless para EX. 1 (see **8.5**) applies.

8.10.3.7   Financial requirements

Paragraph E-LTRPT.4.1 set out the same financial requirements as for entry clearance (see **8.10.2.3**), unless para EX. 1 (see **8.5**) applies.

8.10.3.8 Accommodation requirements

Paragraph E-LTRPT.4.2 set out the same accommodation requirements as for entry clearance (see **8.10.2.4**), unless para EX. 1 (see **8.5**) applies.

8.10.3.9 English language requirement

Paragraph E-LTRPT.5.1 set out the same English language requirements as for entry clearance (see **8.10.2.5**), unless para EX. 1 (see **8.5**) applies.

8.10.3.10 Decision on application

If the applicant meets all the requirements for limited leave to remain as a parent, the applicant will be granted limited leave to remain for a period not exceeding 30 months and subject to a condition of no recourse to public funds. The applicant will be eligible to apply for settlement (see **8.10.4**) after a continuous period of at least 60 months with such leave or in the UK with entry clearance as a parent under para D-ECPT.1.1.

If the applicant can meet the suitability requirements, the eligibility requirements of paras E-LTRPT.2.2–2.4 (the relationship requirements at **8.10.3.5**) and E-LTRPT.3.1 (the first immigration requirement at **8.10.3.6**), and para EX.1 (see **8.5**) applies, he will be granted leave to remain for a period not exceeding 30 months. He will be eligible to apply for settlement (see **8.10.4**) after a continuous period of at least 120 months with such leave, with limited leave as a parent under para D-LTRPT.1.1, or in the UK with entry clearance as a parent under para D-ECPT.1.1.

8.10.4 Indefinite leave to remain (settlement) as a parent

8.10.4.1 Who can apply?

There are two different situations to be considered here, namely:

(a)   where a person has completed the five-year route to settlement, ie two periods of 30 months' leave as a parent; and

(b)   where a person has completed the 10-year route to settlement, ie four periods of 30 months' leave as a parent.

8.10.4.2 An overview of the requirements

The requirements in Appendix FM to be met for indefinite leave to remain as a parent (see para E-ILRPT.1.1) are:

(a)   the applicant must be in the UK;

(b)   the applicant must have made a valid application for indefinite leave to remain as a parent;

(c)   the applicant must not fall for refusal under any of the grounds in Section S-LTR: Suitability – leave to remain (see **8.4.3**);

(d)   the applicant must meet all of the requirements of Section E-LTRPT: Eligibility for leave to remain as a parent **(see 8.10.3.4)**; and

(e)   the applicant must meet all of the requirements of Section E-ILRPT: Eligibility for indefinite leave to remain as a parent (see **8.10.4.3**).

8.10.4.3 Eligibility requirements for indefinite leave to remain

By para E-ILRPT.1.2, the applicant must be in the UK with valid leave to remain as a parent (disregarding any period of overstaying for 28 days or less).

Paragraph E-ILRPT.1.3 provides that the applicant must have completed a continuous period of at least 60 months with limited leave as a parent (under paras R-LTRPT.1.1.(a)–(c) or in the UK with entry clearance as a parent under para D-ECPT.1.1), or a continuous period of at least

120 months with limited leave as a parent (under paras R-LTRPT.1.1(a), (b) and (d) or in the UK with entry clearance as a parent under para D-ECPT.1.1) or a continuous period of at least 120 months with limited leave as a partner under a combination of these paragraphs.

By para E-ILRPT.1.4, the applicant must at the date of application have no unspent convictions (see **Appendix 8** and **8.10.4.4**).

Paragraph E-ILRPT.1.5 requires the applicant to have sufficient knowledge of the English language and sufficient knowledge about life in the UK (see **3.8.7** and **8.10.4.4**).

8.10.4.4   Decision on the application

By para D-ILRPT.1.1, if the applicant meets all of the requirements listed at **8.10.4.2**, he will be granted indefinite leave to remain unless para EX.1 applies. Where para EX.1 applies, the applicant will be granted further limited leave to remain as a parent for a period not exceeding 30 months under para D-ILRPT.1.2 (see immediately below).

But what if the applicant cannot meet all the requirements? Paragraph D-ILRPT.1.2 has a limited concession. It provides that if the applicant does not meet the requirements for indefinite leave to remain as a parent only for one or both of the following reasons:

(a)   the applicant has an unspent conviction; and/or

(b)   the applicant does not have sufficient knowledge of the English language and sufficient knowledge about life in the UK;

then the applicant will be granted further limited leave to remain as a parent for a period not exceeding 30 months and subject to a condition of no recourse to public funds.

Where an applicant is granted further limited leave under para D-ILRPT.1.2, he should be advised that should the reason at (a) and/or (b) be overcome, he can make a further application for settlement at any time within the 30-month period.

The application will be refused if the applicant does not meet the requirements for indefinite leave to remain as a parent, or further leave to remain as a parent under para D-ILRPT.1.2.

8.11   ADULT DEPENDENT RELATIVES ENTERING FOR IMMEDIATE SETTLEMENT

8.11.1   Who can apply?

The purpose of this route is to allow a non-EEA adult dependent relative of a British citizen in the UK, a person settled in the UK, or a person in the UK with refugee leave or humanitarian protection, to enter and settle. On what basis? It must be demonstrated that the applicant, as a result of age, illness or disability, requires a level of long-term personal care that can only be provided in the UK by his relative here and without recourse to public funds.

Note that the applicant's qualifying relative in the UK is known as his 'sponsor'.

Not all relatives can apply. Only the sponsor's parent aged 18 years or over; grandparent; brother or sister aged 18 years or over; and son or daughter aged 18 years or over are able to apply.

Note that this route is available only to an applicant outside the UK. A person cannot switch into this route whilst in the UK.

8.11.2   Entry clearance requirements

By para EC-DR.1.1, the requirements to be met for entry clearance as an adult dependent relative are:

(a)   the applicant must be outside the UK;

(b)   the applicant must have made a valid application for entry clearance as an adult dependent relative;

(c)   the applicant must not fall for refusal under any of the grounds in Section S-EC: Suitability for entry clearance (see **8.3.3**); and

(d)   the applicant must meet all of the requirements of Section E-ECDR: Eligibility for entry clearance as an adult dependent relative (see **8.11.3**).

8.11.3   Eligibility requirements in outline

To meet the eligibility requirements for entry clearance as an adult dependent relative all of the requirements in paras E-ECDR.2.1–3.2 must be met. Broadly these are:

(a)   relationship requirements (see **8.11.4**);

(b)   care needs requirements (see **8.11.5**);

(c)   financial requirements (see **8.11.6**).

8.11.4   Relationship requirements

By para E-ECDR.2.1, the applicant must be related to the sponsor in the UK in one of the following ways:

(a)   a parent aged 18 years or over;

(b)   a grandparent;

(c)   a brother or sister aged 18 years or over; or

(d)   a son or daughter aged 18 years or over.

Note that para E-ECDR.2.2 provides that if the applicant is the sponsor's parent or grandparent, he must not be in a subsisting relationship with a partner unless that partner is also the sponsor's parent or grandparent and is applying for entry clearance at the same time as the applicant.

Evidence of the family relationship should normally take the form of birth or adoption certificates.

By para E-ECDR.2.3, the sponsor must at the date of application be:

(a)   aged 18 years or over; and

(b)   (i)   a British citizen in the UK; or

    (ii)   present and settled in the UK; or

    (iii)   in the UK with refugee leave (see **9.8**) or humanitarian protection (see **9.10.1**).

8.11.5   Care needs requirements

By para E-ECDR.2.4, the applicant (or, if the applicant and his partner are the sponsor's parents or grandparents, the applicant's partner) must, as a result of age, illness or disability, require long-term personal care to perform everyday tasks.

Home Office guidance is that everyday tasks include washing, dressing and cooking. The inability to carry out these tasks may have started recently, eg due to a serious accident resulting in long-term incapacity, or it could be the result of deterioration in the applicant's condition over several years.

By para 34 of Appendix FM-SE, medical evidence that the applicant's physical or mental condition means that he cannot perform everyday tasks must be obtained from a doctor or other health professional. Note that paras 36–39 of the Immigration Rules give the ECO the power to refer the applicant for a medical examination, and to require that this be undertaken by a doctor or other health professional on a list approved by the British Embassy or High Commission.

Paragraph E-ECDR.2.5 provides that the applicant (or, if the applicant and his partner are the sponsor's parents or grandparents, the applicant's partner) must be unable, even with the practical and financial help of the sponsor, to obtain the required level of care in the country where he is living, because:

(a)   it is not available and there is no person in that country who can reasonably provide it; or

(b)   it is not affordable.

As to (a), Home Office guidance is that the ECO should consider whether there is anyone in the country where the applicant is living who can reasonably provide the required level of care. This might be a close family member such as a son, daughter, brother, sister, parent, grandchild or grandparent. But it can include any person who is able to provide care, eg a home-help, housekeeper, nurse, carer, or care or nursing home. If an applicant has more than one close relative in the country where he is living, those relatives may be able to pool resources to provide the required care.

The ECO should bear in mind any relevant cultural factors, such as in countries where women are unlikely to be able to provide support.

Evidence that the required level of care is not, or is no longer, available in the country where the applicant is living could be obtained from a central or local health authority, a local authority, or a doctor or other health professional. If the required care has been provided through a private arrangement, the applicant must provide details of that arrangement and why it is no longer available. See paras 35 and 36 of Appendix FM-SE.

As to (b), if payment was made for arranging care, Home Office guidance is that the ECO should ask to see records and for an explanation of why this payment cannot continue. If financial support has been provided by the sponsor or other close family in the UK, the ECO should ask for an explanation of why this cannot continue or is no longer sufficient to enable the required level of care to be provided (see para 37 of Appendix FM-SE).

8.11.6 Financial requirements

By para E-ECDR.3.1, the applicant must provide evidence that he can be adequately maintained, accommodated and cared for in the UK by the sponsor without recourse to public funds.

The maintenance and accommodation requirements are similar to those for partners under Appendix FM, and are detailed at **8.3.6.9** and **8.3.7** respectively. However, in addition the ECO must be satisfied that the required level of care can and will be met by the sponsor in the UK without recourse to public funds.

Note that by para E-ECDR.3.2, if the applicant's sponsor is a British citizen or settled in the UK, the applicant must provide an undertaking signed by the sponsor confirming that the applicant will have no recourse to public funds, and that the sponsor will be responsible for his maintenance, accommodation and care, for a period of five years from the date the applicant enters the UK if he is granted indefinite leave to enter.

Home Office guidance is that maintenance may be provided by the sponsor, or by any combination of the funds available to the sponsor and the applicant. Promises of third party support will not be accepted, as these are vulnerable to a change in another person's circumstances or in the sponsor's or the applicant's relationship with that party. Cash savings which have originated in a gift (not a loan) from a third party may count towards the required maintenance, but those cash savings must be in an account in the name of the sponsor or the applicant and under that person's control.

What evidence should the sponsor provide? Home Office guidance is:

(a)   original bank statements covering the last six months;

(b)   other evidence of income – such as pay slips, income from savings, shares and bonds – covering the last six months;

(c)   relevant information on outgoings, eg council tax, utilities, etc, and on support for anyone else who is dependent on the sponsor;

(d)   a copy of a mortgage or tenancy agreement showing ownership or occupancy of a property; and

(e)   planned care arrangements for the applicant in the UK (which can involve other family members in the UK) and the cost of these (which must be met by the sponsor, without undertakings of third party support).

8.11.7   Home Office example scenarios taken from guidance

Example 1

A person (aged 25) has a learning disability that means he cannot feed, wash or dress himself. His parents have recently died in an accident and his only surviving close relative is a brother in the UK who has been sending money to the family for some time. The person has been cared for temporarily by family friends since his parents' death, but they are no longer able to do this. The sponsor is unable to meet the costs of full-time residential care, but he and his family have sufficient financial and other means to care for the applicant in their home. **This could meet the criteria if the applicant can demonstrate that he is unable even with the practical and financial help of the sponsor to obtain the required level of care in the country where he is living because it not available and there is no person in that country who can reasonably provide it or it is not affordable and other relevant criteria are met.**

Example 2

A person (aged 30) has lived alone in Sri Lanka for many years. His parents are settled in the UK; other siblings live in the UK and USA. The person has recently been involved in a road accident and as a result has developed a long-term condition which means that he can no longer care for himself. The mother has been visiting Sri Lanka to care for her son, but needs to return to the UK to care for her younger children. **This could meet the criteria if the applicant can demonstrate that he is unable even with the practical and financial help of the sponsor to obtain the required level of care in Sri Lanka where he is living because it not available and there is no person in that country who can reasonably provide it or it is not affordable and other relevant criteria are met.**

Example 3

A husband and wife (both aged 70) live in Pakistan. Their daughter lives in the UK. The wife requires long-term personal care owing to ill health and cannot perform everyday tasks for herself. The husband is in good health, but cannot provide his wife with the level of care she needs. They both want to come and live in the UK. The daughter can care for her mother full time in her home as she does not work whilst her husband provides the family with an income from his employment. Her sister in the UK will also help with care of the mother. The applicant provides the ECO with the planned care arrangements in the UK. **This could meet the criteria if the applicant can demonstrate that she is unable even with the practical and financial help of her sponsor to obtain the required level of care in Pakistan because it not available and there is no person in that country who can reasonably provide it or it is not affordable and other relevant criteria are met.**

8.11.8   Decision on application

By para D-ECDR.1.1, if the applicant meets the requirements for entry clearance as an adult dependent relative of a British citizen or person settled in the UK, he will be granted indefinite leave to enter.

Paragraph D-ECDR.1.2 provides that if the applicant meets the requirements for entry clearance as an adult dependent relative and the sponsor has limited leave as a refugee or with humanitarian protection, the applicant will be granted limited leave of a duration which will expire at the same time as the sponsor's limited leave. This will be subject to a condition of no recourse to public funds. If the sponsor applies for further limited leave, the applicant may apply for further limited leave of the same duration, if the requirements in para EC-DR.1.1(c) and (d) (see **8.11.2**) continue to be met (again subject to no recourse to public funds). In due course an application could be made for settlement – see Section R-ILRDR of Appendix FM.

8.12 CHILD ENTERING WITH OR TO JOIN A PARENT WHO HAS LIMITED LEAVE

8.12.1 Where parent has limited leave as a partner or parent under Appendix FM

8.12.1.1 Entry clearance

By para EC-C.1.1, the requirements to be met for entry clearance as a child are:

(a) the applicant must be outside the UK;

(b) the applicant must have made a valid application for entry clearance as a child;

(c) the applicant must not fall for refusal under any of the grounds in Section S-EC: Suitability for entry clearance; and

(d) the applicant must meet all of the requirements of Section E-ECC: Eligibility for entry clearance as a child.

Note that the suitability requirements are the same as for a partner under Appendix FM, and these are detailed at **8.3.3**. As to the eligibility requirements, see **8.12.1.2**.

8.12.1.2 Eligibility requirements in outline

To meet the eligibility requirements for entry clearance as a child, all of the requirements of para E-ECC.1.2–2.4 must be met. Broadly these are:

(a) relationship requirements (see **8.12.1.3**);

(b) financial requirements (see **8.12.1.4**);

(c) accommodation requirements (see **8.12.1.5**).

8.12.1.3 Relationship requirements

By para E-ECC.1.2, the applicant must be under the age of 18 at the date of application.

Paragraph E-ECC.1.3 provides that the applicant must not be married or in a civil partnership.

By para E-ECC.1.4, the applicant must not have formed an independent family unit.

Paragraph E-ECC.1.5 provides that the applicant must not be leading an independent life. See further **8.9.4.6**.

By para E-ECC.1.6, one of the applicant's parents must be in the UK with limited leave to enter or remain, or be applying, or have applied, for entry clearance as a partner (see **8.3**) or a parent (see **8.10**) under Appendix FM (the 'applicant's parent') and (a) the applicant's parent's partner is also a parent of the applicant or (b) the applicant's parent has had and continues to have sole responsibility for the child's upbringing (see **8.9.4.3**) or (c) there are serious and compelling family or other considerations which make exclusion of the child undesirable and suitable arrangements have been made for the child's care (see **8.9.4.4**).

8.12.1.4 Financial requirement

The equivalent provision for partners under Appendix FM applies, as detailed at **8.3.6**.

8.12.1.5   Accommodation requirements

The equivalent provision for partners under Appendix FM applies, as detailed at **8.3.6**.

8.12.1.6   Decision on application

If the applicant meets the requirements for entry clearance as a child, he will be granted entry clearance of a duration which will expire at the same time as the leave granted to the applicant's parent and subject to a condition of no recourse to public funds.

8.12.1.7   Leave to remain and settlement

When the applicant's parent applies for further leave to remain and settlement, the applicant should do so as well.

As to leave to remain, see generally Section R-LTRC, para 1.1 of Appendix A. As to settlement, see **8.6** and **8.10.4**.

8.12.2   Other provisions applying to children of parents with limited leave

There are separate requirements applying to children of a parent (or parents) in each of the other categories of limited leave already covered in this book. The relevant provisions are set out in **Table 8.7** below.

Table 8.7 Provisions applying to children of parents with limited leave

Child of	See text	Immigration Rules, paras
Tier 4 General Student	Chapter 6	319F–319K
Tier 1 Migrant	7.6.1.2	319F–319K
Tier 2 Migrant	7.8.9	319F–319K
Sole representative	7.13.13	197–199
Person with UK ancestry	7.14.9	197–199

8.13   PRIVATE LIFE IN THE UK

8.13.1   Limited leave to remain

8.13.1.1   Who can apply?

A person who has lived in the UK for at least 20 years continuously, lawfully or unlawfully, can apply to the Home Office for leave to remain in the UK on the basis of the Article 8 ECHR right to respect for private life. Alternative provisions allow an applicant to be granted limited leave to remain in the UK on the basis of private life after seven years' continuous residence if he is under the age of 18; or if he has spent at least half of his life in the UK if he is aged between 18 and 24; or if the applicant has less than 20 years' continuous residence in the UK but there would be very significant obstacles to the applicant's integration into his country of origin.

Most commonly an application will be made as an alternative to an asylum claim (see **Chapter 9**) and when opposing the administrative removal (see **10.4**) of the applicant.

8.13.1.2   Requirements for leave to remain

By para 276ADE(i)–(vi) of the Immigration Rules, the requirements to be met by an applicant for leave to remain on the grounds of private life in the UK are that at the date of application, the applicant:

(a)   does not fall for refusal under any of the grounds in Section S-LTR 1.2 to S- LTR 2.3 and S-LTR.3.1 in Appendix FM (see **8.4.3**); *and*

(b)   has lived continuously in the UK (see **3.8.8.1**) for at least 20 years (discounting any period of imprisonment); *or*

(c) is under the age of 18 years and has lived continuously in the UK for at least seven years (discounting any period of imprisonment) and it would not be reasonable to expect him to leave the UK; *or*

(d) is aged 18 years or above and under 25 years, and has spent at least half of his life living continuously in the UK (discounting any period of imprisonment); *or*

(e) is aged 18 years or above, has lived continuously in the UK for less than 20 years (discounting any period of imprisonment) but there would be very significant obstacles to the applicant's integration into the country to which he would have to go if required to leave the UK (see **8.13.1.3**).

How does a caseworker assess the length of time that the applicant has resided in the UK? Home Office guidance is that an applicant needs to provide credible evidence from an independent source, for example letters from a housing trust, local authority, bank, school or doctor. The caseworker must be satisfied that the evidence provided has not been tampered with or otherwise falsified, and that it relates to the person who is making the application. In order to be satisfied that the applicant's residence in the UK was continuous, the caseworker should normally expect to see evidence to cover every 12-month period of the length of continuous residence and travel documents to cover the entire period, unless the caseworker is satisfied on the basis of a credible explanation provided as to why this has not been submitted.

8.13.1.3 The very significant obstacles to integration ground

As to the ground in para 276ADE(vi)(e) (in **8.13.1.2** above), how should a caseworker assess this? Home Office guidance is that the starting point is to assume that the applicant will be able to integrate into his country of return, unless he can demonstrate why that is not the case. The onus is on the applicant to show that there are very significant obstacles to that integration, not on the decision maker to show that there are not.

The decision maker will expect to see original, independent and verifiable documentary evidence of any claims made in this regard, and will place less weight on assertions which are unsubstantiated. Where it is not reasonable to expect corroborating evidence to be provided, consideration will be given to the credibility of the applicant's claims.

The Home Office states that a very significant obstacle to integration means something which would prevent or seriously inhibit the applicant from integrating into the country of return. The decision maker is looking for more than the existence of obstacles but whether those are 'very significant' obstacles. This is a high threshold. Very significant obstacles will exist where the applicant demonstrates that he would be unable to establish a private life in the country of return, or where establishing a private life in the country of return would entail very serious hardship for the applicant.

The decision maker must consider all the reasons put forward by the applicant as to why there would be obstacles to his integration in the country of return. These reasons must be considered individually and cumulatively to assess whether there are very significant obstacles to integration. In considering whether there are very significant obstacles to integration, the decision maker should consider whether the applicant has the ability to form an adequate private life by the standards of the country of return and not by UK standards. The decision maker will need to consider whether the applicant will be able to establish a private life in respect of all its essential elements, even if, for example, his job, or his ability to find work, or his network of friends and relationships may be differently constituted in the country of return.

The fact that the applicant may find life difficult or challenging in the country of return does not mean that there are very significant obstacles to integration. The decision maker must consider all relevant factors in the person's background and the conditions he is likely to face in the country of return.

The decision maker will need to consider the specific obstacles raised by the applicant. He will also need to set these against other factors in order to make an assessment in the individual case. Relevant considerations set out in Home Office guidance include the following:

(a) *Cultural background.* Is there evidence of the applicant's exposure to and level of understanding of the cultural norms in the country of return? Where the person has spent his time in the UK living mainly amongst a diaspora community from that country, then it may be reasonable to conclude that he has cultural ties with that country even if he has never lived there or has been absent from that country for a lengthy period. If the applicant has cultural ties with the country of return, then it is likely that it would be possible for him to establish a private life there. Even if there are no cultural ties, the cultural norms of that country may be such that there are no barriers to integration.

(b) *Length of time spent in the country of return.* Where the applicant has spent a significant period of time in the country of return, it will be difficult for him to demonstrate that there would be very significant obstacles to integration into that country. The decision maker must consider the proportion of the person's life spent in that country and the stage of life the person was at when in that country.

(c) *Family, friends and social network.* An applicant who has family or friends in the country of return should be able to turn to them for support to help him to integrate into that country. The decision maker must consider whether the applicant or his family have sponsored or hosted visits in the UK by family or friends from the country of return, or the applicant has visited family or friends in the country of return.

The decision maker must consider the quality of any relationships with family or friends in the country of return, but they do not have to be strong familial ties and can include ties that could be strengthened if the person were to return.

The Home Office guidance includes the following examples of common claims made under this provision:

(a) That the applicant has no friends or family members in the country of return. Where there are no family, friends or social networks in the country of return, that is not in itself a very significant obstacle to integration. Why? Because many people successfully migrate to countries where they have no ties.

(b) If there are particular circumstances in the applicant's case which mean that he would need assistance to integrate, it will also be relevant to consider whether there are any organisations in the country of return which may be able to assist with integration.

(c) That the applicant has never lived in the country of return or only spent early years there. If an applicant has never lived in the country of return, or only spent his early years there, this will not necessarily mean that there are very significant obstacles preventing him from integrating, particularly if he can speak a language of that country, eg if the country of return is one where English is spoken or if a language of the country was spoken at home when he was growing up. For these purposes, fluency is not required – conversational level language skills or a basic level of language which could be improved on return would be sufficient. The cultural norms of the country and how easy it is for the person to adapt to them will also be relevant.

(d) That the applicant cannot speak any language spoken in the country of return. Where there is credible evidence that an applicant cannot speak any language which is spoken in the country of return, this will not in itself be a very significant obstacle to integration unless he can also show that he would be unable to learn a language of that country, for example because of a mental or physical disability.

(e) That the applicant would have no employment prospects on return. Lack of employment prospects is very unlikely to be a very significant obstacle to integration. In assessing a claim that an absence of employment prospects would prevent an applicant from integrating in the country of return, his circumstances on return should be compared to the conditions that prevail in that country and to the circumstances of the general population, not to his circumstances in the UK.

Less weight will be given to generalised claims about country conditions that have not been particularised to take account of the applicant's individual circumstances.

(f)   The applicant's private life in the UK. The degree of private life an individual has established in the UK is not relevant to the consideration of whether there are very serious obstacles to integration into the country of return. However, this will be relevant to the consideration of whether, where the applicant falls for refusal under the Immigration Rules, there are exceptional circumstances which would make refusal unjustifiably harsh for the applicant.

8.13.1.4   Decision on application

By para 276BE, limited leave to remain on the grounds of private life in the UK may be granted for a period not exceeding 30 months if the requirements in para 276ADE are met (or, in respect of the requirements in para 276ADE(iv) and (v) ((c) and (d) in **8.13.1.2**), were met in a previous application which led to a grant of limited leave to remain under this para). The applicant may be able to apply for further periods of leave in this category and settlement after 120 months (see **8.13.2**).

What if one or more requirement in para 276ADE is not met? Home Office guidance is that the caseworker should consider whether there are any exceptional circumstances (see **8.13.1.5**) which would make refusal and the removal of the applicant from the UK a breach of Article 8 ECHR.

8.13.1.5   Exceptional circumstances

If the requirements in para 276ADE (see **8.13.1.2**) are not met, what exceptional circumstances would make refusal and the requirement for the applicant to leave the UK a breach of Article 8 ECHR? Home Office guidance is that the caseworker should determine whether removal would have such severe consequences for the individual that refusal of the application and his removal from the UK would not be proportionate given the nature of his private life. The Home Office states that this will rarely be the case.

In determining whether a case is exceptional, the decision maker must consider all relevant factors, such as:

(a)   The best interests of any child in the UK affected by the decision.

(b)   The nature of the family relationships involved, such as the length of the applicant's marriage and how frequently he has contact with his children if they do not live with him. What evidence is there that the couple do or do not have a genuine family life?

(c)   The immigration status of the applicant and his family members. The decision maker should take into account the circumstances around the applicant's entry to the UK and the proportion of the time he has been in the UK legally as opposed to illegally. Did he form his relationship with his partner at a time when he was in the UK unlawfully? Family life formed in the knowledge that his stay here is unlawful should be given less weight (when weighed against the public interest in his removal) than family life formed by a person lawfully present in the UK.

(d)   The nationalities of the applicant and his family members. The nationality of any child of an applicant is a matter of particular importance given the intrinsic importance of citizenship, and the advantages of growing up and being educated in their own country.

(e)   How long the applicant and his family members have lawfully lived in the UK, and how strong their social, cultural and family ties are with the UK.

(f)   The likely circumstances the applicant's partner and/or child would face in the applicant's country of return. It is relevant to consider how long the applicant resided in the country of return and what social, cultural and family ties he has retained with that country, as well as the degree of exposure his partner and/or child has had to that country and to its language and culture.

(g)   Whether there are any factors which might increase the public interest in removal, for example where the applicant has failed to meet the suitability requirements because of deception or issues around his character or conduct in the UK, or the fact that he does not speak English or is not financially independent.

(h)   Cumulative factors should be considered, for example, where the applicant has family members in the UK but his family life does not provide a basis for stay and he has a significant private life in the UK. Although, under the Rules, family life and private life are considered separately, when considering whether there are exceptional circumstances, private and family life should be taken into account.

Cumulative factors weighing in favour of the applicant should be balanced against cumulative factors weighing in the public interest in deciding whether refusal would be unjustifiably harsh for the applicant or his family.

8.13.2   Indefinite leave to remain (settlement)

8.13.2.1   Who can apply?

Once an applicant has been granted four periods of 30 months' limited leave under para 276BE and so spent 10 years in the UK on that basis, he may apply for indefinite leave to remain.

8.13.2.2   Requirements

By para 276DE, the requirements to be met for the grant of indefinite leave to remain on the grounds of private life in the UK are:

(a)   the applicant has been in the UK with continuous leave on the grounds of private life for a period of at least 120 months;

(b)   the applicant meets the requirements of para 276ADE (see **8.13.1.2**);

(c)   the applicant does not fall for refusal under the general grounds for refusal (see **3.5.4**);

(d)   the applicant has sufficient knowledge of the English language and sufficient knowledge about life in the UK by passing the test known as the 'Life in the UK Test' (see **3.8.7 and 8.10.4.4**), unless the applicant is under the age of 18 or aged 65 or over at the time the applicant makes the application; and

(e)   there are no reasons why it would be undesirable to grant the applicant indefinite leave to remain based on the applicant's conduct, character or associations, or because the applicant represents a threat to national security.

8.13.2.3   Decision on the application

By para 276DF, if the applicant meets all of the requirements at **8.13.2.2** he will be granted indefinite leave to remain.

But what if the applicant cannot meet all the requirements? Paragraph 276DG has a limited concession. It provides that if the applicant does not meet the requirements for indefinite leave to remain only for one or both of the following reasons:

(a)   para S-ILR.1.5 or 1.6 applies (see **8.6.2(c)**); and/or

(b)   the applicant does not have sufficient knowledge of the English language and sufficient knowledge about life in the UK;

then the applicant may be granted further limited leave to remain on the grounds of private life in the UK for a period not exceeding 30 months.

Where an applicant is granted further limited leave under para 276DG, he should be advised that should the reason at (a) and/or (b) above be overcome, he can make a further application for settlement at any time within the 30-month period.

The application will be refused if the applicant does not meet the requirements for indefinite leave to remain, or further leave to remain on the grounds of private life in the UK under para 276DG.

8.14 CLAIMS UNDER ARTICLE 8 ECHR

Under the IA 1971, the Secretary of State has a wide residual discretion to grant leave to enter the UK outside the Immigration Rules where an applicant cannot show that he satisfies the conditions in the Rules themselves (see R (Munir) v Secretary of State for the Home Department [2012] UKSC 32). An applicant who does not satisfy the conditions stipulated in the Rules may nonetheless have a good claim to be entitled to enter the UK by reason of his rights under Article 8 ECHR. Such a claim arises by virtue of the obligation of the Secretary of State under s 6(1) of the HRA 1998 to act in a manner compatible with an individual's Convention rights.

The position under Article 8 in relation to an application for leave to enter the UK on the basis of family life with a person already in the UK was summarised by the Court of Appeal in *Secretary of State for the Home Department v SS (Congo)* [2015] EWCA Civ 387 at [39] as follows:

i)   A person outside the United Kingdom may have a good claim under Article 8 to be allowed to enter the United Kingdom to join family members already here so as to continue or develop existing family life: see eg *Gül v Switzerland* (1996) 22 EHRR 93 and *Sen v Netherlands* (2001) 36 EHRR 7. Article 8 does not confer an automatic right of entry, however. Article 8 imposes no general obligation on a state to facilitate the choice made by a married couple to reside in it: R (Quila) v Secretary of State for the Home Department [2011] UKSC 45; [2012] 1 AC 621, para [42]; *Abdulaziz, Cabales and Balkandali v United Kingdom* (1985) 7 EHRR 471, [68]; *Gül v Switzerland*, [38]. The state is entitled to control immigration: *Huang* [[2007] UKHL 11], para [18].

ii)   The approach to identifying positive obligations under Article 8(1) draws on Article 8(2) by analogy, but is not identical with analysis under Article 8(2): see, in the immigration context, *Abdulaziz, Cabales and Balkandali v United Kingdom*, paras [67]–[68]; *Gül v Switzerland*, [38]; and *Sen v Netherlands*, [31]–[32]. See also the general guidance on the applicable principles given by the Grand Chamber of the ECtHR in *Draon v France* (2006) 42 EHRR 40 at paras [105]–[108], summarising the effect of the leading authorities as follows (omitting footnotes):

'105.   While the essential object of Art 8 is to protect the individual against arbitrary interference by the public authorities, it does not merely require the State to abstain from such interference: there may in addition be positive obligations inherent in effective "respect" for family life. The boundaries between the State's positive and negative obligations under this provision do not always lend themselves to precise definition; nonetheless, the applicable principles are similar. In both contexts regard must be had to the fair balance that has to be struck between the competing interests of the individual and the community as a whole, and in both contexts the State is recognised as enjoying a certain margin of appreciation. Furthermore, even in relation to the positive obligations flowing from the first paragraph, "in striking [the required] balance the aims mentioned in the second paragraph may be of a certain relevance".

106.   "Respect" for family life ... implies an obligation for the State to act in a manner calculated to allow ties between close relatives to develop normally. The Court has held that a state is under this type of obligation where it has found a direct and immediate link between the measures requested by an applicant, on the one hand, and his private and/or family life on the other.

107.   However, since the concept of respect is not precisely defined, States enjoy a wide margin of appreciation in determining the steps to be taken to ensure compliance with the

Convention with due regard to the needs and resources of the community and of individuals.

108.   At the same time, the Court reiterates the fundamentally subsidiary role of the Convention. The national authorities have direct democratic legitimation and are, as the Court has held on many occasions, in principle better placed than an international court to evaluate local needs and conditions. In matters of general policy, on which opinions within a democratic society may reasonably differ widely, the role of the domestic policy-maker should be given special weight.'

iii)   In deciding whether to grant [leave to enter] to a family member outside the United Kingdom, the state authorities may have regard to a range of factors, including the pressure which admission of an applicant may place upon public resources, the desirability of promoting social integration and harmony and so forth. Refusal of [leave to enter] in cases where these interests may be undermined may be fair and proportionate to the legitimate interests identified in Article 8(2) of 'the economic well-being of the country' and 'the protection of the rights and freedoms of others' (taxpayers and members of society generally). A court will be slow to find an implied positive obligation which would involve imposing on the state significant additional expenditure, which will necessarily involve a diversion of resources from other activities of the state in the public interest, a matter which usually calls for consideration under democratic procedures.

iv)   On the other hand, the fact that the interests of a child are in issue will be a countervailing factor which tends to reduce to some degree the width of the margin of appreciation which the state authorities would otherwise enjoy. Article 8 has to be interpreted and applied in the light of the UN Convention on the Rights of the Child (1989): see In re E (Children) (Abduction: Custody Appeal) [2011] UKSC 27; [2012] AC 144, at [26]. However, the fact that the interests of a child are in issue does not simply provide a trump card so that a child applicant for positive action to be taken by the state in the field of Article 8(1) must always have their application acceded to; see In re E (Children) at [12] and ZH (Tanzania) v Secretary of State for the Home Department [2011] UKSC 4; [2011] 2 AC 166, at [25] (under Article 3(1) of the UN Convention on the Rights of the Child the interests of the child are a primary consideration – ie an important matter – not the primary consideration). It is a factor relevant to the fair balance between the individual and the general community which goes some way towards tempering the otherwise wide margin of appreciation available to the state authorities in deciding what to do. The age of the child, the closeness of their relationship with the other family member in the United Kingdom and whether the family could live together elsewhere are likely to be important factors which should be borne in mind.

v)   If family life can be carried on elsewhere, it is unlikely that 'a direct and immediate link' will exist between the measures requested by an applicant and his family life (Draon, para. [106]; Botta v Italy (1998) 26 EHRR 241, para [35]), such as to provide the basis for an implied obligation upon the state under Article 8(1) to grant LTE; see also Gül v Switzerland, [42].

CHAPTER 9

ASYLUM-SEEKERS AND REFUGEES

9.1 OVERVIEW

People may flee their own countries for many different reasons – social, economic, political, religious, etc. On arrival in the UK or subsequently, they may state that they do not wish to return to their country of nationality or habitual residence.

An asylum-seeker is a person who flees because of a fear of persecution in his own country and who, as a consequence, is seeking the protection of the UK Government. Such protection is granted if that person is given the immigration status of a refugee. Otherwise, on human rights grounds, he may be granted what is known as humanitarian protection or discretionary leave (see **9.10**).

9.2 LAW AND PROCEDURE

9.2.1 Relevant law

Set out below is a list of the key legal provisions referred to in this chapter:

(a) The United Nations' 1951 Convention and 1967 Protocol Relating to the Status of Refugees (generally known as 'the Refugee Convention').

(b) UNHCR *Handbook on Procedures and Criteria for Determining Refugee Status*.

(c) Parts 11 and 11B of the Immigration Rules.

(d) The Refugee or Person in Need of International Protection (Qualification) Regulations 2006 (SI 2006/2525) ('Qualification Regulations 2006'). A copy is reproduced at **Appendix 14.**

(e) UK and ECHR case law.

(f) Home Office asylum policy instructions and process guidance.

9.2.2 Procedure

Asylum claims are dealt with by the Home Office. Those who wish to have a detailed understanding of the procedures should consult the Home Office guidance, issued to its asylum staff and published on its website (see **1.2.8**).

Anyone in the UK can make an asylum claim, whatever his immigration status. He may be someone who has arrived without a visa or with forged documents, or someone who has obtained limited leave to enter for a different reason (eg as a visitor), an overstayer, or even an illegal entrant. The claim can be made on entry or after entry to the UK.

9.3 WHAT IS AN ASYLUM CLAIM?

9.3.1 The Refugee Convention

The Immigration Rules, para 327 defines an applicant for asylum as a person who makes a request to be recognised as a refugee under the Refugee Convention on the basis that it would be contrary to the UK's obligations under that Convention for him to be removed from or required to leave the UK, or otherwise makes a request for international protection.

To be granted asylum, or the status of a refugee, a claimant must meet the following requirements as set out in Article 1 A. of the Refugee Convention:

> [The claimant,] owing to well-founded fear of being persecuted for reasons of race, religion, nationality, membership of a particular social group or political opinion, is outside the country of his nationality and is unable or, owing to such fear, is unwilling to avail himself of the protection of that country; or who, not having a nationality and being outside the country of his former habitual residence ... is unable, or owing to such fear, is unwilling to return to it.

By para 334 of the Immigration Rules, an asylum applicant will be granted asylum in the UK if the Secretary of State is satisfied that:

(a)   he is in the UK or has arrived at a port of entry in the UK;

(b)   he is a refugee falling within Article 1 A. (see **9.4**) and not excluded (see **9.5.1**);

(c)   there are no reasonable grounds for regarding him as a danger to the security of the UK (see **9.5.2**);

(d)   he does not, having been convicted by a final judgment of a particularly serious crime, constitute danger to the community of the UK (see **9.5.2**); and

(e)   refusing his application would result in his being required to go (whether immediately or after the time limited by any existing leave to enter or remain) in breach of the Refugee Convention, to a country in which his life or freedom would be threatened on account of his race, religion, nationality, political opinion or membership of a particular social group.

9.3.2 Sources of persecution

Before we look in detail at each requirement of Article 1 A., and in particular at what may amount to persecution, we shall consider the possible source of that fear. It might be the government or State itself. Legislation may discriminate against or persecute a certain group, for example, laws may discriminate against women or homosexuals. Or the persecution might come from State bodies, like the police or the army, acting on government orders. Additionally, there may be persecution if the State fails to take steps to protect its citizens from officials who abuse their authority. This might include, for example, a policeman who rapes a woman for his own sexual gratification.

A person may also fear being persecuted by people who have nothing to do with the government. These are known as non-State actors (see further **9.4.1.5**). Common examples concern political or religious intolerance, such as where one section of society does not respect the political or religious beliefs of another. Here we need to remember that part of the

Refugee Convention test is that the claimant is unwilling to avail himself of the protection of his country. The question is whether or not the State has a system of criminal law which makes attacks by non-State actors punishable *and* if the State is prepared to take reasonable steps to enforce that law.

9.4 MEETING THE REQUIREMENTS OF THE REFUGEE CONVENTION

9.4.1 Well-founded fear of persecution

9.4.1.1 Subjective and objective tests

The claimant must be in fear of persecution, but his claim can be rejected if there is no real risk or reasonable likelihood of persecution (*R v Secretary of State for the Home Department, ex p Sivakumaran and conjoined appeals (UN High Commissioner for Refugees Intervening)* [1988] 1 All ER 193). The main issue will be the credibility of the claimant's testimony (see also **9.6.2**) that he has a genuine fear (the subjective test), but the Home Office may rely on evidence of conditions in the country from which he is fleeing to show that there is insufficient basis for the fear (the objective test). The Home Office Country of Origin Information Service has produced assessments of certain countries that produce a significant number of asylum claims. These are used for background purposes by caseworkers (see further **9.7**).

In some cases applicants may be able to provide some documentary evidence to support their claims, such as newspaper or Internet articles, passports or identity cards, political party membership cards, arrest warrants, photographs and medical reports. Organisations such as Amnesty International and the US Department of State (country reports) may be able to provide helpful evidence. As to medical evidence of torture, an applicant may be able to obtain a report from the charity Medical Foundation for the Care of Victims of Torture (see www.torturecare.org.uk). This organisation provides medical and social care, practical assistance and therapy to survivors of torture. If the applicant is already seeing a doctor or consultant, he may be able to provide a report.

When obtaining medical evidence of a claimant's injuries or scarring, it is important that the expert assesses how they were caused: see *SA (Somalia)* [2006] EWCA Civ 1302 and *RT (medical reports, cause of scarring) Sri Lanka* [2008] UKAIT 00009. Where the expert makes findings that there is a degree of consistency between the injuries or scarring and the claimant's allegations as to how they were caused by his persecutors, the expert should also include any other possible causes (whether many, few or unusually few), and gauge how likely they are, bearing in mind what is known about the individual's life history and experiences. Where possible an expert should be instructed to consider the degree of consistency on the following scale:

(1) *Not consistent*: the injury or scarring could not have been caused as alleged.
(2) *Consistent with*: the injury or scarring could have been caused as alleged, but it is non-specific and there are many other possible causes.
(3) *Highly consistent*: the injury or scarring could have been caused as alleged, and there are few other possible causes.
(4) *Typical of*: this is an appearance that is usually found with this type of injury or scarring, but there are other possible causes.
(5) *Diagnostic of*: this appearance could not have been caused in any way other than that alleged.

9.4.1.2 Benefit of the doubt

Obviously, the applicant may find it difficult to provide evidence of events in his home country and many statements may be unsupported. According to the UNHCR *Handbook*, statements should not necessarily be rejected for that reason: 'If the applicant's account appears credible, he should, unless there are good reasons to the contrary, be given the benefit of the doubt' (para 196). Unsupported statements need not, however, be accepted if they are inconsistent with the general account put forward by the applicant (para 197).

9.4.1.3   Acts of persecution

'Persecution' is not defined in the Refugee Convention. The UNHCR *Handbook* suggests that while it will often involve a threat to life or liberty, it could extend to other threats. Discrimination against a particular group does not of itself amount to persecution; but it may do so if serious, for example if it stops someone practising his religion, or earning a livelihood. 'Persecution' does not mean 'punishment'. A person who fears punishment for commission of a common-law crime will not normally be regarded as a refugee, unless, for example, the law under which he is to be punished is seriously discriminatory.

Further examples of persecution are listed in reg 5(2) of the Qualification Regulations 2006. These include an act of physical or mental violence, including an act of sexual violence; a legal, administrative, police, or judicial measure which in itself is discriminatory, or which is implemented in a discriminatory manner; and prosecution or punishment which is disproportionate or discriminatory.

In R *(Sivakumar) v Secretary of State for the Home Department* [2003] 2 All ER 1097, the House of Lords held that it is the severity of the treatment inflicted on the applicant that has a logical bearing on the issues. Excessive or arbitrary punishment can amount to persecution. See further the discussion in the Court of Appeal case of *MI (Pakistan) v Secretary of State for the Home Department* [2014] EWCA Civ 826 at [55]–[58].

Regulation 5(1) of the Qualification Regulations 2006 provides that an act of persecution must be sufficiently serious by its nature or repetition as to constitute a severe violation of a basic human right, in particular a right from which derogation cannot be made under Article 15 ECHR. The basic human rights from which derogation cannot be made under the ECHR include Article 2 (right to life – save that derogation is permitted in respect of deaths resulting from lawful acts of war); Article 3 (prohibition of torture, inhuman or degrading treatment or punishment); Article 4(1) (prohibition of slavery) and Article 7 (no punishment without law). Alternatively, persecution may arise from an accumulation of various measures, including a violation of a human right which is sufficiently severe as to affect an individual in this manner.

A person does not have to be singled out for adverse treatment in order to be said to be persecuted (see R *v Secretary of State for the Home Department, ex p Jeyakumaran (Selladurai)* [1994] Imm AR 45). Discrimination may amount to persecution – this accords with the Tribunal decision of *Padhu* (12318), concerning the inability to work and deprivation of State benefits due to ethnic origin. What if the persecution feared comes from non-State actors? In the case of *Gashi and Nikshiqi v Secretary of State for the Home Department (United Nations High Commissioner for Refugees Intervening)* [1997] INLR 96, the Tribunal held that persecution includes the failure of a State to protect:

(a)   those rights which are non-derogative even in times of compelling national emergency (the right to life; prohibition against torture and cruel, inhumane or degrading treatment);

(b)   those rights which are derogative during an officially recognised life-threatening public emergency (freedom from arbitrary arrest and detention; fair trial);

(c)   some aspects of those rights which require States to take steps to the maximum of their available resources to realise rights progressively in a non-discriminatory manner (the right to earn a livelihood; the right to a basic education; the right to food, housing and medical care).

9.4.1.4   Current fear and past acts of persecution

Whilst there must be a current fear of persecution for a Convention reason upon return (see *Adan v Secretary of State for the Home Department* [1999] 1 AC 293), persecution suffered in the past is relevant to whether a person has a current, well-founded fear of persecution. This is recognised by para 339K of the Immigration Rules. It provides that the fact that a person has already been subject to persecution, or to direct threats of such persecution, will be regarded as a serious indication of the person's well-founded fear of persecution, unless there are good reasons to consider that such persecution will not be repeated. Equally, whilst a past history of no persecution is not determinative of future risks, unless circumstances in an asylum-seeker's return country have deteriorated or some other special factor is present, it is inevitable that an asylum-seeker will have difficulty in showing future risk in the absence of any finding of past persecution: see *Becerikil v Secretary of State for the Home Department* [2006] EWCA Civ 693.

9.4.1.5   Persecution by non-State actors

The applicable law as to persecution by non-State actors is the House of Lords' decision in *Horvath v Secretary of State for the Home Department* [2001] 1 AC 489. This established that persecution implied a failure by the State to make protection available against the ill-treatment or violence which had been suffered at the hands of the persecutors. In such a case, the failure of the State to provide protection was an essential element, and accordingly the person claiming refugee status had to show that the feared persecution consisted of acts of violence against which the State was unable or unwilling to provide protection. Such a conclusion was consistent with the principle of surrogacy which underpinned the Convention, namely that the protection afforded by the Convention was activated only upon the failure of protection by the home State. Moreover, the application of that principle rested upon the assumption that the home State was not expected to achieve complete protection against random and isolated attacks.

Accordingly, in determining whether the protection afforded by the applicant's home country was sufficient for the purposes of the Convention, the court had to apply a practical standard which took proper account of the duty owed by a State to all its nationals, rather than a standard which eliminated all risk. Thus, the sufficiency of State protection was to be measured not by the existence of a real risk of an abuse of human rights but by the availability of a system for the protection of the citizen and a reasonable willingness to operate that system. This is now reflected in reg 4 of the Qualification Regulations 2006.

9.4.1.6   Attacks on applicant's family members

Can an attack upon an applicant's spouse or close family member amount to persecution of the applicant for the purposes of an asylum claim, even though there was no direct threat to the applicant himself? 'Yes', said the Court of Appeal in *Frantisek Katrinak v Secretary of State for the Home Department* [2001] INLR 499. As Schiemann LJ said:

> If I return with my wife to a country where there is a reasonable degree of likelihood that she will be subjected to further grave physical abuse for racial reasons, that puts me in a situation where there is a reasonable degree of risk that I will be persecuted. It is possible to persecute a husband or a member of a family by what you do to other members of his immediate family. The essential task for the decision taker in these sort of circumstances is to consider what is reasonably likely to happen to the wife and whether that is reasonably likely to affect the husband in such a way as to amount to persecution of him.

9.4.1.7   Should the applicant have to change his behaviour to avoid persecution if returned?

Is a claimant required to take reasonable measures if returned home to avoid persecution? For example, where an applicant claims to have been persecuted as a homosexual, is it relevant to take into account whether it would be reasonable to expect him to behave 'discreetly' if returned? No, held the Supreme Court in *HJ (Iran) v Secretary of State or the Home Department* [2010] UKSC 31. In considering such a claim, the Home Office must address the following issues.

(a)   Is it satisfied on the evidence that the applicant is gay, or that he would be treated as gay by potential persecutors in his country of nationality?

(b)   Is it satisfied on the available evidence that gay people who lived openly would be liable to persecution in the applicant's country of nationality?

(c)   What will the applicant do if returned to that country?

(d)   If he would in fact live openly and thereby be exposed to a real risk of persecution, then he has a well-founded fear of persecution – even if he could avoid the risk by living 'discreetly'.

(e)   If, on the other hand, the applicant would in fact live discreetly and so avoid persecution, the question to be answered is why he would do so.

(f)   If the conclusion is that the applicant would choose to live discreetly simply because that was how he himself would wish to live, or because of social pressures, eg not wanting to distress his parents or embarrass his friends, then his application should be rejected.

(g)   If, on the other hand, the material reason for the applicant living discreetly on his return would be a fear of the persecution which would follow if he were to live openly as a gay man, then, other things being equal, his application should be accepted. Such a person has a well-founded fear of persecution. To reject his application on the ground that he could avoid the persecution by living discreetly would be to defeat the very right which the Convention exists to protect – his right to live freely and openly as a gay man without fear of persecution.

So, equally, as 'a general proposition a person found to have genuine political beliefs cannot be refused refugee status merely because they have declined to hide those beliefs, or to act "discreetly", in order to avoid persecution': per Carnwath LJ in *RT (Zimbabwe) v Secretary of State for the Home Department* [2010] EWCA Civ 1285 at [25].

9.4.1.8   Examples

EXAMPLE 1

Bela has fled from his own country which is engaged in civil war. His farm has been destroyed in a battle, and he has no other means of earning his living.

The Home Office may argue that Bela is a displaced person rather than a refugee, unless he can show, for example, that he is likely to suffer persecution because he is identified with one of the sides in the civil war.

EXAMPLE 2

Chaka has left his country because high taxes and an economic crisis have caused his business to fail.

The Home Office may argue that he is an economic migrant rather than a refugee, unless he can show, for example, that the tax measures were directed at a particular ethnic group of which he is a member, designed to destroy their economic position.

9.4.2 'For reasons of race, religion, nationality, membership of a particular social group or political opinion'

9.4.2.1 Race

The concept of race includes, for example, colour, descent, or membership of a particular ethnic group. The fact that a claimant belongs to a certain racial group is not normally enough to prove a claim.

9.4.2.2 Religion

As to the meaning of the word 'religion', see *Omoruyi v Secretary of State for the Home Department* [2001] INLR 33. In the case the applicant was a Nigerian Christian persecuted by a group described variously as 'a secret cult ... associated with idol worshipping to the extent of drinking blood', 'a mafia organisation involving criminal acts', and a 'devil cult' carrying out 'rituals', namely 'the sacrificing of animals to a graven image'. The court held that the persecution was not for a Convention reason (ie it was not related to the applicant's beliefs but to the fact that he had failed to comply with certain demands made by the cult) and therefore his application for asylum failed.

Note that reg 6(1)(b) of the Qualification Regulations 2006 provides that the concept of religion includes, for example, the holding of theistic, non-theistic and atheistic beliefs; the participation in, or abstention from, formal worship in private or in public, either alone or in community with others; other religious acts or expressions of view, or forms of personal or communal conduct based on or mandated by any religious belief.

9.4.2.3 Nationality

The term 'nationality' includes citizenship, or the lack of it, as well as membership of a group determined by such matters as its cultural, ethnic, or linguistic identity. Persecution for reasons of nationality may consist of adverse actions and measures against a national, ethnic or linguistic minority, and in certain circumstances the fact of belonging to such a minority may in itself give rise to a well-founded fear of persecution.

Note that nationals of certain countries may have their asylum claims certified by the Secretary of State as unfounded (see **11.15**).

9.4.2.4 Membership of a particular social group

Over recent years, the courts have given much consideration as to what is meant by the expression 'particular social group'. In the joint cases of *Islam (Shahana) v Secretary of State for the Home Department; R v Immigration Appeal Tribunal and Secretary of State for the Home Department, ex p Syeda Shah* [1999] INLR 144, the House of Lords had to decide if two Pakistani women, who had fled Pakistan after false allegations of adultery and violence by their husbands, were part of such a group. The House held that a 'particular social group' consists of a group of persons who share a common, immutable characteristic that either is beyond the power of an individual to change, or is so fundamental to the individual's identity or conscience that he ought not to be required to change it. Thus, as gender is an immutable characteristic that is beyond the power of the individual to change, and as discrimination against women is prevalent in Pakistan, in violation of fundamental rights and freedoms, women in Pakistan constitute a particular social group.

In the *Islam* and *Shah* appeals, Lord Hoffmann asked:

> What is the reason for the persecution which the appellants fear? Here it is important to notice that it is made up of two elements. First, there is the threat of violence to Mrs Islam by her husband and his political friends and to Mrs Shah by her husband. This is a personal affair, directed against them as individuals. Secondly, there is the inability or unwillingness of the State to do anything to protect them. There is nothing personal about this. The evidence was that the State would not assist them because they were women. It denied them a protection against violence which it would have given to

men. These two elements have to be combined to constitute persecution within the meaning of the Convention.

See also *RG (Ethiopia) v Secretary of State for the Home Department* [2006] EWCA Civ 339, where it was held that women and girls in Ethiopia constitute a particular social group. The Court found institutionalised discrimination, since the penal law in Ethiopia legitimises the marriage of abducted and raped girls to their violators, which marriage then exempts the latter from punishment. This, and the evidence of a lack of protection of women against sexual abuse and serious discrimination, shows a degree of complicity by the State in the treatment of women in Ethiopia, sufficient to conclude that women constitute a particular social group.

Regulation 6(1)(d) of the Qualification Regulations 2006, as interpreted in *K v Secretary of State for the Home Department; Fornah v Secretary of State for the Home Department* [2006] UKHL 45, [2007] 1 All ER 671, provides two useful guidelines defining a particular social group. First, where members of that group share an innate characteristic, or a common background that cannot be changed, or share a characteristic or belief that is so fundamental to identity or conscience that a person should not be forced to renounce it. Secondly, where the group has a distinct identity in the relevant country, because it is perceived as being different by the surrounding society.

9.4.2.5   Political opinion

To show persecution on grounds of political opinion, it is not enough for the claimant to establish that he holds opinions which his government opposes. He must show that that government will not tolerate his opinions, and that it is aware that he holds them. Where the claimant has committed criminal offences in the course of political opposition, he cannot base a claim to refugee status on fear of his country's normal punishment for that offence.

> **EXAMPLE**
>
> Enrico is a member of a minority linguistic group, and of the political party which represents it. The party is campaigning for language rights, for example in regional schools, and its political activities are permitted. His national government will not concede these rights and pursues discriminatory policies. Enrico has fled the country after setting fire to a school which refused to use the minority language.
>
> The Home Office may argue that Enrico does not fear persecution on grounds of his political opinions, but rather punishment for an ordinary criminal offence. However, he may be able to show that his punishment would be excessive or arbitrary, which would amount to persecution. The discriminatory measures in themselves may not be sufficiently serious to amount to persecution on grounds of nationality.

In what circumstances may a person who objects to carrying out compulsory military service be granted asylum? In *Sepet v Secretary of State for the Home Department* [2003] 3 All ER 304, the House of Lords held that refugee status should be accorded to a person who refuses to undertake compulsory military service on the grounds that such service would or might require him to commit atrocities or gross human rights abuses, or participate in a conflict condemned by the international community, or where refusal to serve would earn grossly excessive or disproportionate punishment.

Even if a claimant does not hold political views which his government opposes, it may well be that the government believes that he does. So a person to whom a political opinion is imputed may qualify for refugee status: see *Sivakumar v Secretary of State for the Home Department* [2002] INLR 310. Imputed political opinion may include those who are perceived to be members or supporters of an opposition party, as well as anyone who is unable to demonstrate support for, or loyalty to, the government regime or ruling political party: see *TM (Zimbabwe) v Secretary of State for the Home Department* [2010] EWCA Civ 916.

> **EXAMPLE**
>
> Alexander has fled from his own country because his brother has been imprisoned for political activities.
>
> The Home Office may argue that Alexander's fear is not well founded, unless he can show that persecution is for an imputed political opinion or extends to the social group associated with the political activity.

9.4.3 'Is outside the country of his nationality'

No one can claim to be a refugee until he has left the country of which he is a citizen. This means that a claimant cannot normally obtain a visa from a UK entry clearance officer in his country, clearing him to enter the UK as a refugee. He must (somehow) find his way to the UK and make the claim on arrival. This may be difficult, as airlines are fined for carrying people without correct travel documents (Immigration (Carriers' Liability) Act 1987).

9.4.3.1 The internal flight alternative or internal relocation

The claimant must be outside his country owing to fear of persecution there. What if the persecution is to be feared in only part of the country? Paragraph 339O of the Immigration Rules provides that the Secretary of State will not grant asylum if in part of the country of origin a person would not have a well-founded fear of being persecuted, and the person can reasonably be expected to stay in that part of the country. So if someone would be safe only if he lived in a remote village, separated from his family, his flight from the country can still be said to be based on a fear of persecution there (see *R v Immigration Appeal Tribunal, ex p Jonah* [1985] Imm AR 7).

The House of Lords, in *Januzi v Secretary of State for the Home Department* [2006] UKHL 5, gave further guidance on this issue. Lord Hope of Craighead said (para 47):

> The question where the issue of internal relocation is raised can, then, be defined quite simply. As Linden JA put it in *Thirunavukkarasu v Canada (Minister of Employment and Immigration)* (1993) 109 DLR (4th) 682, 687, it is whether it would be unduly harsh to expect a claimant who is being persecuted for a Convention reason in one part of his country to move to a less hostile part before seeking refugee status abroad. The words 'unduly harsh' set the standard that must be met for this to be regarded as unreasonable. If the claimant can live a relatively normal life there judged by the standards that prevail in his country of nationality generally, and if he can reach the less hostile part without undue hardship or undue difficulty, it will not be unreasonable to expect him to move there.

9.4.3.2 Safe third country exception (AI(TC)A 2004, Sch 3)

There will be no breach of obligation if the UK returns the refugee to a 'safe country' which itself has an obligation to grant him asylum, and which could be expected to fulfil the requirements of the Refugee Convention. The general principle operated by governments is that a refugee should seek asylum in the first 'safe country' he reaches.

Under EU Regulation 604/2013 ('the Regulation') or the Dublin [3] Convention, the UK may return an asylum seeker to the EU Member State which has responsibility for the asylum claim under the terms of the Refugee Convention (eg because that State granted him a visa, or he first entered that State as an illegal entrant). The Home Office will not remove the asylum seeker until the State receiving him has accepted its responsibility under the Regulation or the Dublin Convention. Once that has happened, the Home Office will assume that the receiving State will itself consider the claim and grant refugee status if the claim is well founded.

In these cases, it is possible for someone who meets the Refugee Convention's definition of 'refugee' to claim asylum in the UK, but for his claim, on examination by the Home Office, to fall outside the statutory definition of an asylum claim in the UK. Because return is to a 'safe country', the Home Office may refuse these claims 'without substantive consideration', that is without looking at other aspects of the claimant's case, such as whether he fears persecution in his home country (Immigration Rules, para 345).

Schedule 3 to the AI(TC)A 2004 (which replaced earlier similar provisions) is intended to deal with the fact that many Regulation or Dublin Convention cases were, in the Government's opinion, subject to unnecessary and lengthy delay as a result of judicial review applications which challenged the safety of the transfer. The Schedule sets out in Parts 2 to 5 a graduated approach to the 'safety' of third countries for the purposes of the Refugee Convention and the ECHR. Broadly, these are as follows.

Part 2 of Sch 3 deals with countries that are deemed safe for Refugee Convention purposes and for claims that onward removal from the State would breach the ECHR. All human rights claims against removal will be certified by the Secretary of State as clearly unfounded unless he is satisfied that they are not. The countries listed at para 2 of Part 2 are those which are subject to or have agreed to be bound by the Dublin Convention, currently the members of the EU (see **Appendix 2** to this book) together with Norway, Switzerland and Iceland. In *Nasser v Secretary of State for the Home Department* [2009] UKHL 23, the claimant challenged the legality of the Part 2, para 2 list. The House of Lords held that whilst the statute creates an irrebuttable presumption that the claimant may be removed from the UK to a country listed at para 2 of Part 2, the presumption does not preclude an inquiry into whether the claimant's Article 3 ECHR rights would be infringed for the different purpose of deciding whether the provision is incompatible with his Convention rights. In this case the Secretary of State accepted that that if removal to the country would infringe those rights then the conclusive presumption would be incompatible. See also *R (on the application of EM (Eritrea)) v Secretary of State for the Home Department* [2014] UKSC 12.

Paragraph 4 of Part 2 disapplies s 77 of the NIAA 2002 (which prevents removal while an asylum claim is pending) where the Secretary of State certifies that a person is to be removed to a listed State and he is not a national or citizen of that State. Paragraph 5 of Part 2 prevents a person being removed from bringing an appeal within the UK on the basis that the country is not safe for Refugee Convention purposes or ECHR purposes in terms of onward removal. Paragraph 5 provides that where a human rights claim made on another basis is certified as clearly unfounded, a person being removed is similarly prevented from bringing an appeal within the UK. Lastly, para 5 provides that any human rights claim against removal (other than on the basis of onward removal) will be certified by the Secretary of State as clearly unfounded unless he is satisfied that it is not.

9.4.3.3   Sur place claims

Can a claimant have a well-founded fear of being persecuted or a real risk of suffering serious harm based on events which take place after he leaves his country of origin and/or activities in which he engages since leaving his country of origin? Yes, this provision can be found in the Immigration Rules, para 339P. It will apply, in particular, where it is established that the activities relied upon constitute the expression and continuation of convictions or orientations held in the country of origin by the claimant. The most common example is a claimant who carries on political activities in the UK. However, the provision applies equally to a claimant who was a conformist before leaving his country of origin but who becomes politicised in exile, even if those political activities were designed to create or enhance an asylum claim. As Kay LJ stated in *KS (Burma) v Secretary of State for the Home Department* [2013] EWCA Civ 67 at [32], 'It is unpalatable that someone may become entitled to refugee status as a result of his cynical manipulation but if, objectively, he has a well-founded fear of persecution by reason of imputed political opinion, that may be the reality.'

In assessing a *sur place* claim, the key question is whether the claimant's activities create a real risk of persecution in his home country. The claim fails if the activities are not likely come to the attention of the authorities of that country or the authorities are likely to ignore them: see *TM (Zimbabwe) v Secretary of State for the Home Department* [2010] EWCA Civ 916.

How should a *sur place* claim be assessed? In *BA (Demonstrators in Britain – risk on return) Iran CG* [2011] UKUT 36 the Tribunal identified the following factors:

(i) *Nature of* sur place *activity*

- Theme of demonstrations – what do the demonstrators want (eg reform of the regime through to its violent overthrow); how will they be characterised by the regime?

- Role in demonstrations and political profile – can the person be described as a leader; mobiliser (eg addressing the crowd); organiser (eg leading the chanting); or simply a member of the crowd; if the latter is he active or passive (eg does he carry a banner); what is his motive, and is this relevant to the profile he will have in the eyes of the regime?

- Extent of participation – has the person attended one or two demonstrations, or is he a regular participant?

- Publicity attracted – has a demonstration attracted media coverage in the United Kingdom or the home country; nature of that publicity (quality of images; outlets where stories appear etc)?

(ii) *Identification risk*

- Surveillance of demonstrators – assuming the regime aims to identify demonstrators against it, how does it do so: through filming them, having agents who mingle in the crowd, reviewing images/recordings of demonstrations etc?

- Regime's capacity to identify individuals – does the regime have advanced technology (eg for facial recognition); does it allocate human resources to fit names to faces in the crowd?

(iii) *Factors triggering inquiry/action on return*

- Profile – is the person known as a committed opponent or someone with a significant political profile; does he fall within a category which the regime regards as especially objectionable?

- Immigration history – how did the person leave the country (illegally; type of visa); where has the person been when abroad; is the timing and method of return more likely to lead to inquiry and/or being detained for more than a short period and ill-treated (overstayer; forced return)?

(iv) *Consequences of identification*

- Is there differentiation between demonstrators depending on the level of their political profile adverse to the regime?

(v) *Identification risk on return*

- Matching identification to person – if a person is identified, is that information systematically stored and used; are border posts geared to the task?

9.4.4 'And is unable, or, owing to such fear, is unwilling to avail himself of the protection of that country'

A claimant would be unable to avail himself of his country's protection if, for example, it refused entry to him, or refused to issue him with a passport. A claimant who fears persecution will normally be unwilling to accept his government's protection, and it is inconsistent with his claim to refugee status if, for example, he wishes to retain his national passport.

9.5 EXCLUSION FROM REFUGEE STATUS

Even if an applicant meets the tests under the Refugee Convention, the UK Government will in certain circumstances refuse to grant him refugee status (**9.5.1**) or forcibly remove him (**9.5.2**). However, in either circumstance it must still go on to consider if it is appropriate to award the applicant humanitarian protection or discretionary leave (see **9.10**).

9.5.1 Exclusion under Article 1 F.

Article 1 F. of the Refugee Convention excludes the following claimants from asylum because they are considered not to be deserving of international protection. This is because there are serious reasons for considering that they:

(a)   have committed a crime against peace, a war crime or a crime against humanity; or

(b)   have committed a serious non-political crime outside the country of refuge prior to admission into that country; or

(c)   are guilty of acts contrary to the purposes and principles of the United Nations.

The Home Office has set up a War Crimes Team to focus on modern-day war crimes. The team assists in the identification of people who may have committed or been complicit in war crimes, and supports action taken against them.

There is an evidential burden on the Secretary of State to establish serious reasons for considering that a claimant has committed an act under Article 1 F. (see *JS (Sri Lanka) v Secretary of State for the Home Department* [2010] UKSC 15). However, it does not have to be shown to the criminal standard of proof, ie beyond reasonable doubt (see *Al-Sirri v Secretary of State for the Home Department* [2009] EWCA Civ 222).

So when does Article 1 F. apply?

> I would hold an accused disqualified under Article 1F if there are serious reasons for considering him voluntarily to have contributed in a significant way to the organisation's ability to pursue its purpose of committing war crimes, aware that his assistance will in fact further that purpose. (per Lord Brown in *R (on the application of JS) (Sri Lanka) v Secretary of State for the Home Department* [2010] UKSC 15 at para 38)

What is a 'crime against humanity' for the purposes of Article 1 F.(a)? The starting point is the following definition in Article 7(1) of the Rome Statute of the International Criminal Court 2002:

> 1.   ... any of the following acts when committed as part of a widespread or systematic attack directed against any civilian population, with knowledge of the attack:
>
> (a)   Murder;
>
> (b)   Extermination;
>
> ...
>
> (e)   Imprisonment or other severe deprivation of physical liberty ...;
>
> (f)   Torture;
>
> ...
>
> (h)   Persecution ... on political, racial, national, ethnic, cultural, religious, gender ... grounds ...;
>
> (i)   Enforced disappearance of persons;
>
> ...
>
> (k)   Other inhumane acts of a similar character intentionally causing great suffering, or serious injury to body or to mental or physical health.
>
> (See *SK (Zimbabwe) v Secretary of State for the Home Department* [2012] 1 WLR 2809.)

Article 25 of the Rome Statute 2002 regulates individual criminal responsibility for a crime against humanity falling within Article 7. Article 25(3) provides:

3.   In accordance with this Statute, a person shall be criminally responsible and liable for punishment for a crime within the jurisdiction of the Court if that person:

(a)   Commits such a crime, whether as an individual, jointly with another or through another person, regardless of whether that other person is criminally responsible;

(b)   Orders, solicits or induces the commission of such a crime which in fact occurs or is attempted;

(c)   For the purpose of facilitating the commission of such a crime, aids, abets or otherwise assists in its commission or its attempted commission, including providing the means for its commission;

(d)   In any other way contributes to the commission or attempted commission of such a crime by a group of persons acting with a common purpose. Such contribution shall be intentional and shall either:

(i)   Be made with the aim of furthering the criminal activity or criminal purpose of the group, where such activity or purpose involves the commission of a crime within the jurisdiction of the Court; or

(ii)   Be made in the knowledge of the intention of the group to commit the crime.

...

For a detailed discussion of this exclusionary provision, see *AA-R (Iran) v Secretary of State for the Home Department* [2013] EWCA Civ 835.

Note that reg 7(2) of the Qualification Regulations 2006 interprets the meaning of Article 1 F.(b) as follows:

The reference to 'serious non-political crime' includes a particularly cruel action, even if it is committed with an allegedly political objective. The reference to the crime being committed outside the country of refuge prior to his admission as a refugee shall mean the time up to and including the day on which a residence permit [signifying the grant of refugee status] is issued.

Note that in *AH (Article 1F (b) – 'serious') Algeria* [2013] UKUT 382 it was said: 'The examination of seriousness should be directed at the criminal acts when they were committed, although events in the supervening passage of time may be relevant to whether exclusion is justified: a formal pardon, or subsequent acquittal, or other event illuminating the nature of the activity may be relevant to this assessment.'

Also note that s 54 of the IANA 2006 interprets the meaning of Article 1 F.(c). It provides that acts of committing, preparing or instigating terrorism, or encouraging or inducing others to do so, are included within the meaning of what constitutes 'acts contrary to the purposes and principles of the United Nations'. See further *AH (Algeria) v Secretary of State for the Home Department* [2012] EWCA Civ 395 and *Al-Sirri v Secretary of State for the Home Department* [2013] 1 AC 745.

The application of Article 1 F.(c) will be straightforward in the case of an active member of an organisation that promotes its objects only by acts of terrorism. There will almost certainly be serious reasons for considering that he has been guilty of acts contrary to the purposes and principles of the United Nations. However, what if the organisation pursues its political ends in part by acts of terrorism and in part by military action directed against the armed forces of the government? A person may join such an organisation because he agrees with its political objectives, and may be willing to participate in its military actions, but he may not agree with and may not be willing to participate in its terrorist activities. The higher up in the organisation a person is, the more likely will be the inference that he agrees with and promotes all of its activities, including its terrorism.

> **EXAMPLE**
>
> Danilow fled from his country after being imprisoned for distributing political leaflets. In order to finance his escape he commits an armed robbery.

Whether the armed robbery amounts to a serious non-political crime depends on whether it has been committed for political motives, or for personal reasons or gain, and whether the act was proportionate to the alleged objective. The Home Office may well argue that Danilow's criminal character outweighs his character as a bona fide refugee (see *T v Secretary of State for the Home Department* (1996) *The Times*, 23 May).

9.5.2 Enforced removal under Article 33(2)

Article 33(2) of the Refugee Convention allows the UK Government to remove a person who is otherwise a refugee where there are reasonable grounds for regarding him as a danger to the security of the UK, or who, having been convicted by a final judgment of a particularly serious crime, constitutes a danger to the community of the UK.

Home Office guidance is that for a person to be a danger to the security of the UK, the actions or anticipated actions of that person need not create a direct threat to the UK's system of government or its people. The interests of national security could be threatened indirectly by activities directed against other States. Thus the definition of a threat to national security is very wide: for example, depending on the specific facts of the case, if someone is believed or known to be a terrorist then, due to the nature of international terrorism, and regardless of the immediate threat of his particular terrorist group, it may be reasonable to regard the person as a threat to the UK's national security.

What is a particularly serious crime such that the person constitutes a danger to the community of the UK? By s 72 of the NIAA 2002, there is a general presumption of this where the person was sentenced to a period of imprisonment of at least two years. Note, however, that in *EN (Serbia) v Secretary of State for the Home Department* [2009] EWCA Civ 630, the Court of Appeal held that the presumption is rebuttable and that the Nationality, Immigration and Asylum Act 2002 (Specification of Particularly Serious Crimes) Order 2004 (SI 2004/1910), which specifies a large number of offences as offences to which s 72 applies, irrespective of the sentence imposed, is ultra vires and unlawful.

The Court in *EN (Serbia)* stressed that the second ground for enforced removal under Article 33(2) requires two conditions to be met: first, that the refugee has been convicted by a final judgment of a particularly serious crime; and, secondly, that he constitutes a danger to the community. The presumption that each of these conditions is met is rebuttable. So, for example, if the refugee can demonstrate that he is not a danger to the community, Article 33(2) cannot apply. Note, however, that the Court indicated (at [45] and [46]) that where a person is convicted of a particularly serious crime, and there is a real risk of its repetition or the recurrence of a similar offence, he is likely to constitute a danger to the community. The Court also gave the example of a person convicted of a particularly serious offence of violence whom the Government can establish is a significant drug dealer as being one where removal under Article 33(2) is likely.

On an asylum appeal, the Secretary of State may issue a certificate pursuant to s 72(9)(b) that the presumption applies. Thereafter, the tribunal hearing the appeal must begin its substantive deliberation by considering the certificate. If, after giving the appellant the opportunity for rebuttal, it agrees that the presumption applies, it must dismiss the appeal in so far as it relies on the ground that to remove the appellant would breach the UK's obligation under the Refugee Convention. See further *Secretary of State for the Home Department v JR (Jamaica)* [2014] EWCA Civ 477.

9.6 CONSIDERATION OF CASES

9.6.1 The Home Office checklist

Home Office asylum case owners use the following checklist when assessing a claim:

(a)   What is the applicant's basis of claim?

(b)   Which of the applicant's claims about past events can be accepted?

Are the applicant's claims as to his past experiences consistent with objective country of origin information (see **9.7**) relating to the relevant period, including generally known facts?

Are the applicant's claims consistent with other evidence submitted, eg the evidence of other witnesses, family members or documents specifically referring to the applicant?

Are any of the applicant's claims about his past experiences not able to be corroborated by reference to country of origin information or other evidence? If so, can the benefit of the doubt be given to any of these claims? If not, why not?

After due consideration of the principle of the benefit of the doubt, which of the applicant's material claims can be accepted, and which can be rejected?

(c)   Taking into account the applicant's statements and behaviour, does the applicant have a subjective fear of persecution?

(d)   Objectively, are there reasonable grounds for believing that the harm feared might in fact occur in the applicant's country of origin?

Who are the actors of persecution? Do the authorities of the home country conduct the persecution, or support persecution committed by others?

How far is the State or organisations controlling the State (including international organisations) able to provide protection from persecution caused by others? What laws are in place and are they enforced effectively?

Has the applicant sought the protection of the authorities? If so, what was the outcome? If not, why not?

Considering the objective country of origin information, the past experiences of the applicant and the attitude of the State authorities, is there a reasonable likelihood that the applicant would experience harm if returned?

(e)   Can the applicant return to a part of the country in which he would not be subject to the harm feared (see **9.4.3.1**)?

(f)   Is the harm feared a form of persecution (see **9.4.1.3**)?

Is the harm of sufficient gravity to constitute persecution, or is it something less serious?

Does the cumulative effect of lesser prejudicial actions or threats amount to persecution?

If the applicant has a fear of prosecution or punishment for an offence, is the punishment discriminatory or disproportionate? Does this give rise to a fear of persecution?

If the fear of prosecution is due to draft evasion or desertion, special considerations may apply.

(g)   If the harm feared is serious enough to constitute persecution, would it be inflicted for one or more of the reasons set out in the Refugee Convention, ie race, religion, nationality, membership of a particular social group or political opinion? See further **9.4.2**.

(h)   In the light of (a)–(g) above, does the applicant satisfy all the criteria of the 1951 Convention?

(i)   Should the applicant be excluded from international protection by operation of the exclusion clauses of the Convention? See further **9.5**.

(j)   If an applicant fails to qualify for asylum, decision makers should consider whether to grant humanitarian protection or discretionary leave (see **9.10**).

9.6.2 Adverse inferences

9.6.2.1 Claimant's duties

The Immigration Rules (paras 339I–339N) list some factors which are taken into account. These start by imposing a duty on the claimant to submit to the Secretary of State, as soon as possible, all material factors needed to substantiate the asylum claim. These material factors include the claimant's statement of the reasons for making an asylum claim; all documentation at the claimant's disposal regarding his age, background, identity, nationality(ies), country(ies) and place(s) of previous residence, previous asylum applications, and travel routes; and identity and travel documents.

It is further the duty of the claimant to substantiate the claim. Paragraph 339L of the Immigration Rules provides that where aspects of the claimant's statements are not supported by documentary or other evidence, those aspects will not need confirmation when all of the following conditions are met:

(a)   the claimant has made a genuine effort to substantiate his asylum claim;

(b)   all material factors at the claimant's disposal have been submitted, and a satisfactory explanation regarding any lack of other relevant material has been given;

(c)   the claimant's statements are found to be coherent and plausible, and do not run counter to available specific and general information relevant to his case;

(d)   the claimant has made an asylum claim at the earliest possible time, unless he can demonstrate good reason for not having done so; and

(e)   the general credibility of the claimant has been established.

Paragraph 339M of the Immigration Rules provides that the Secretary of State may consider that a person has not substantiated his asylum claim if he fails, without reasonable explanation, to make a prompt and full disclosure of material facts, either orally or in writing, or otherwise to assist the Secretary of State in establishing the facts of the case. This includes, for example, a failure to attend an interview, failure to report to a designated place to be fingerprinted, failure to complete an asylum questionnaire or failure to comply with a requirement to report to an immigration officer for examination.

9.6.2.2 Statutory adverse inferences

Section 8(1) of the AI(TC)A 2004 includes similar guidelines for assessing the credibility of the claimant. The key provisions are as follows:

(1)   In determining whether to believe a statement made by or on behalf of a person who makes an asylum claim or a human rights claim, a deciding authority shall take account, as damaging the claimant's credibility, of any behaviour to which this section applies.

(2)   This section applies to any behaviour by the claimant that the deciding authority thinks—

(a)   is designed or likely to conceal information,

(b)   is designed or likely to mislead, or

(c)   is designed or likely to obstruct or delay the handling or resolution of the claim or the taking of a decision in relation to the claimant.

(3)   Without prejudice to the generality of subsection (2) the following kinds of behaviour shall be treated as designed or likely to conceal information or to mislead—

(a)   failure without reasonable explanation to produce a passport on request to an immigration officer or to the Secretary of State,

(b)   the production of a document which is not a valid passport as if it were,

(c)   the destruction, alteration or disposal, in each case without reasonable explanation, of a passport,

(d)   the destruction, alteration or disposal, in each case without reasonable explanation, of a ticket or other document connected with travel, and

(e) failure without reasonable explanation to answer a question asked by a deciding authority.

(4) This section also applies to failure by the claimant to take advantage of a reasonable opportunity to make an asylum claim or human rights claim while in a safe country.

(5) This section also applies to failure by the claimant to make an asylum claim or human rights claim before being notified of an immigration decision, unless the claim relies wholly on matters arising after the notification.

(6) This section also applies to failure by the claimant to make an asylum claim or human rights claim before being arrested under an immigration provision, unless—

(a) he had no reasonable opportunity to make the claim before the arrest, or

(b) the claim relies wholly on matters arising after the arrest.

9.6.2.3 How adverse?

What is the effect of s 8(1)? In *JT (Cameroon) v Secretary of State for the Home Department* [2008] EWCA Civ 878, the Court of Appeal held that the section lays down a framework of factors that may potentially damage a claimant's credibility. However, it is for the decision maker to decide the extent to which that person's credibility is damaged, if at all, and what weight should be given to any adverse finding of credibility. In this case the claimant had used false papers to enter the UK and false identities whilst in the UK. The Home Office refused the claimant asylum and the Tribunal determined that under s 8 the claimant's conduct had seriously damaged his credibility.

9.6.2.4 Reasonable explanation

What is a reasonable explanation for the purposes of s 8(3)(a) and (c)–(e)? Home Office guidance is that this may include exceptional situations where the applicant could not easily have disobeyed the instructions of an agent who facilitates immigration into the UK; cases where an adult is severely traumatised, or where cultural norms may make it difficult for a person to answer questions at interview or to disobey instructions, including instructions about documents; situations where a person can show that a document was destroyed or disposed of as a direct result of force, threats or intimidation, eg where an individual was forced at knifepoint to give a document to someone else; or where the document has been lost or stolen and the individual can substantiate such a claim, usually with a police report of the loss or theft.

What is a safe country for the purposes of s 8(4)? It is any country listed in Part 2 of Sch 3 to the AI(TC)A 2004 (see **9.4.3.2**). What is a reasonable opportunity to claim asylum in such a country? Home Office guidance is that the claimant could have approached the authorities at the border or internally, as long as there is no reason to think that the claim would not have been received. For example, it might be thought that someone who spent several weeks in France before coming to the UK must have had a reasonable opportunity to claim asylum there; but this would not be reasonable if the applicant was imprisoned by traffickers throughout that time.

As to what is an immigration decision for the purposes of s 8(5), see **11.2**.

As to s 8(6), Home Office guidance is that an applicant's credibility must be treated as damaged if the claim is made after the applicant's arrest under an immigration provision unless there was no reasonable opportunity to make the claim before the arrest, or the claimant relies wholly on matters arising after the arrest. An applicant has had a reasonable opportunity to claim asylum before being arrested if he could have approached the authorities at any time after his arrival in the UK. Each case should be considered on its merits. So, for example, someone who is apprehended by the police soon after getting out of a back of a lorry is less likely to have been able to make a claim before arrest than someone who passed through immigration control when arriving in the UK.

9.7 COUNTRY OF ORIGIN INFORMATION

The Country of Origin Information Service (COI Service) produces key documents that are used by Home Office asylum staff as part of assessing a claim. These include Country of Origin Information Reports, Country of Origin Bulletins and Country of Origin Key Documents.

The Reports provide a brief summary of the general, political and human rights situations in particular countries, and describe common types of claim. There are over 30 country reports.

The Bulletins are issued on an ad hoc basis and aim to provide clear guidance on how to deal with particular country-specific issues arising in asylum and human rights applications.

The Key Documents provide an indexed list of reports, papers and articles produced by a wide range of recognised external information sources, mainly on human rights issues. They do not contain any Home Office opinion or policy.

Full details and the documents can be found at www.homeoffice.gov.uk/rds/country_reports.html.

9.8 REFUGEE STATUS

9.8.1 Five years' limited leave

A refugee is normally granted five years' leave to remain in the UK. Pursuant to para 339Q(i) of the Immigration Rules, the Secretary of State issues what is known as a UK Residence Permit valid for five years. During this time the refugee is free to work and claim all mainstream welfare benefits.

9.8.2 Settlement

After holding limited leave for five years, a refugee may apply for settlement (when the usual criminality requirements will apply by para 339R of the Immigration Rules).

9.8.3 Review of status

A refugee's status is liable to a review which may lead to that status being withdrawn, cancelled or revoked. Such a step does not in itself affect the person's leave but, in practice, it will normally result in curtailment of any limited leave (see **3.7**) or revocation of any indefinite leave, and in action being taken to remove the person from the UK (see **Chapter 10**).

9.8.3.1 Withdrawal of refugee status

Paragraph 339A of the Immigration Rules gives the Secretary of State power to withdraw refugee status from a person where:

(a) he has voluntarily re-availed himself of the protection of the country of nationality;

(b) having lost his nationality, he has voluntarily re-acquired it; or

(c) he has acquired a new nationality, and enjoys the protection of the country of his new nationality;

(d) he has voluntarily re-established himself in the country which he left or outside which he remained owing to a fear of persecution;

(e) he can no longer, because the circumstances in connection with which he has been recognised as a refugee have ceased to exist, continue to refuse to avail himself of the protection of the country of nationality;

(f) being a stateless person with no nationality, he is able, because the circumstances in connection with which he has been recognised a refugee have ceased to exist, to return to the country of former habitual residence.

Note that (a)–(d) are voluntary steps taken by the refugee. In respect of (e) and (f) the Secretary of State must issue a Ministerial Statement announcing that significant and non-temporary changes have occurred in a particular country such that nationals can be expected to return, or that there are exceptional circumstances for that.

9.8.3.2 Cancellation of refugee status

Paragraph 339A of the Immigration Rules gives the Secretary of State power to cancel a person's refugee status where:

(a) he should have been or is excluded from being a refugee in accordance with reg 7 of the Qualification Regulations 2006 (see **9.5.1**);

(b) his misrepresentation or omission of facts, including the use of false documents, was decisive for the grant of asylum;

(c) there are reasonable grounds for regarding him as a danger to the security of the UK (see **9.5.2**);

(d) having been convicted by a final judgment of a particularly serious crime he constitutes danger to the community of the UK (see **9.5.2**).

9.8.3.3 Revocation of refugee status

Home Office guidance is that revocation of refugee status may be appropriate where a refugee's conduct is so serious that it warrants withdrawal of that status. Where there are serious reasons for considering that a person has committed a crime or act that falls within the scope of Article 1 F.(a) or (c) (see **9.5.1**), subsequent to the grant of asylum, it will be appropriate to revoke a person's refugee status.

9.9 HUMAN RIGHTS ISSUES

A person may claim that he should be allowed to remain in the UK as his removal would be a breach of his human rights and that he cannot reasonably be expected to return voluntarily.

9.9.1 Domestic and foreign cases

The House of Lords in *R (Ullah) v Special Adjudicator; Do v Secretary of State for the Home Department* [2004] UKHL 26 distinguished between what it called domestic and foreign cases. A domestic case is where an applicant alleges that the UK has acted in a way which infringes the applicant's enjoyment of a Convention right within the UK. The most common example is where a person claims that his removal would separate him from his family in the UK and so breach Article 8 ECHR.

A foreign case is where a person claims that requiring him to leave the UK will lead to a violation of his Convention rights in the country of return, ie the alleged violation of the Convention right will occur outside the UK. For example, an applicant may allege that on return he will suffer death contrary to Article 2; inhuman or degrading treatment in breach of Article 3; unlawful detention breaching Article 5; an unfair trial contrary to Article 6; or restrictions on his freedom of religion or expression in breach of Articles 9 and 10. Article 8 claims may arise in respect of a claimant's private life. For example, a person may claim that he would be unable to be openly homosexual in the receiving State because of societal prejudice and/or legislation banning homosexuality, and that his removal from the UK would therefore lead to a breach of his right to respect for private life in the receiving country.

9.9.2 Article 2 ECHR

Home Office guidance is that it will not normally seek to return a person to a country where there are substantial grounds for believing that there is a real risk he would be unlawfully killed either by the State, or through the State being unable or unwilling to protect him. In *R (Ullah) v Special Adjudicator; Do v Secretary of State for the Home Department* (**9.9.1** above), the House of Lords cited the decision of the ECtHR in *Dehwari v Netherlands* (2000) 29 EHRR CD 74, where the Court doubted whether a real risk was enough to resist removal under Article 2 and suggested that the loss of life must be shown to be a 'near-certainty'.

9.9.3 Article 3 ECHR

A person will not be removed from the UK to a country where there are substantial reasons for believing that he faces a real risk of serious harm or other treatment contrary to Article 3. This includes torture, as well as treatment or punishment that is degrading because it arouses in the victim feelings of fear, anguish or inferiority capable of humiliating and debasing him, and possibly breaking his physical and moral resistance. Severe discrimination based on race, sex or other grounds is also capable of constituting degrading treatment. For a review of the case law, see *BB v Secretary of State for the Home Department* [2015] EWCA Civ 9.

Ever since the ECtHR held in *D v United Kingdom* (1997) 24 EHRR 423 that the expulsion of an AIDS sufferer to St Kitts would breach Article 3 ECHR, the Strasbourg Court has sought to distinguish that case. In the case of D, the Court extended the reach of Article 3. The Court noted that Contracting States have the right, as a matter of well-established international law and subject to their treaty obligations including the ECHR, to control the entry, residence and expulsion of aliens. The Court applied Article 3 in what it described as the 'very exceptional circumstances' of that case, namely that the applicant was in the final stage of a terminal illness, AIDS, and had no prospect of medical care or family support on expulsion to St Kitts. In *N(FC) v Secretary of State for the Home Department* [2005] UKHL 31, [2005] 2 WLR 1124, the House of Lords was not persuaded to extend Article 3 any further. The House held that it must be shown that the applicant's medical condition has reached such a critical state that there are compelling humanitarian grounds for not removing him or her to a place which lacks the medical and social services which he or she would need to prevent acute suffering. This approach was confirmed when the case was appealed to the ECtHR: see *N v UK* [2008] LTL 28 May (App No 00026565/05).

It can be seen that the case of *D v United Kingdom* establishes that Article 3 may be engaged where the harm will not result from inhuman and degrading treatment by the receiving authority. For example, in *Bensaid v United Kingdom* [2001] ECHR 82, the applicant suffered from long-term schizophrenia. He claimed that his condition would seriously deteriorate if he were returned to his home country because of difficulties in obtaining suitable medication there. The Court stated, at para 37:

> Deterioration in his already existing mental illness could involve relapse into hallucinations and psychotic delusions involving self-harm and harm to others, as well as restrictions in social functioning (such as withdrawal and lack of motivation). The Court considers that the suffering associated with such a relapse could, in principle, fall within the scope of Article 3.

However, the Court went on to find that Article 3 would not be violated in this case as there were no exceptional circumstances. Ultimately, the question is whether what is likely to befall the claimant crosses the high threshold and the test of exceptionality (*GS (India) v Secretary of State for the Home Department* [2015] EWCA Civ 40). Whether or not the required level of severity is reached in a particular case for an adult or a child depends on all the circumstances of that case (*AE (Algeria) v Secretary of State for the Home Department* [2014] EWCA Civ 653).

9.9.4 Other Convention Articles

When considering a foreign case involving an article other than Articles 2 and 3 ECHR, Home Office guidance is that case owners should assess the likelihood of the alleged treatment or conduct occurring on return and whether that would be a breach of the ECHR; then they should consider whether any breach would be sufficiently serious that it would amount to a flagrant violation of the relevant Convention right.

Where a claim is based on Article 8 ECHR, Home Office guidance is that pursuant to para 326B of the Immigration Rules, it should be considered in line with Appendix FM (family life) (see **8.5**) and paras 276ADE to 276DH (see **8.13**). If the claim for asylum (or humanitarian protection) is refused but the claimant qualifies for leave under either of these provisions, he should be granted leave to remain of 30 months, and he may be eligible to apply for settlement after 120 months of such leave.

9.10 HUMANITARIAN PROTECTION AND DISCRETIONARY LEAVE

9.10.1 Humanitarian protection

9.10.1.1 Overlap with asylum claim

The great majority of claims for humanitarian protection are likely to arise in the context of asylum claims. However, where an individual claims that although he is in need of international protection he is not seeking asylum, and the reasons given clearly do not engage the UK Government's obligations under the Refugee Convention (ie the fear of persecution is clearly not for one of the five Convention reasons: see **9.4.2**), then it is accepted as a stand-alone claim for humanitarian protection.

9.10.1.2 Paragraph 339C requirements

A person will be granted humanitarian protection in the UK if the Secretary of State is satisfied that the following requirements of para 339C of the Immigration Rules are met:

(a)   he is in the UK or has arrived at a port of entry in the UK; and

(b)   he does not qualify as a refugee (see **9.1**); and

(c)   substantial grounds have been shown for believing that the person concerned, if he returned to the country of return, would face a real risk of suffering serious harm and is unable, or, owing to such a risk, unwilling to avail himself of the protection of that country; and

(d)   he is not excluded from a grant of humanitarian protection. Exclusion is on the same grounds as that for asylum: see **9.5**.

For the purposes of (c) above, serious harm is defined as:

(a)   the death penalty or execution;

(b)   unlawful killing;

(c)   torture, or inhuman or degrading treatment or punishment of a person in the country of return; or

(d)   serious and individual threat to a civilian's life or person by reason of indiscriminate violence in situations of international or internal armed conflict.

In considering whether there are substantial grounds for believing that a person would face a real risk of suffering serious harm (para 339C(iii)), the standard of proof applied is that of a reasonable degree of likelihood or a real risk.

9.10.1.3 Grant of humanitarian protection

A person granted humanitarian protection is normally granted five years' leave to remain in the UK. Pursuant to para 339Q(i) of the Immigration Rules, the Secretary of State issues what is known as a UK Residence Permit, valid for five years. After holding limited leave for five years an application can be made for settlement. Life a refugee, this status is liable to a review, which may lead to its being withdrawn, cancelled or revoked (see **9.8.3**).

9.10.2   Discretionary leave

9.10.2.1   Overlap with asylum claim

The great majority of claims for discretionary leave are likely to arise in the context of asylum claims. However, a stand-alone human rights claim may also result in a grant of discretionary leave if the qualifying criteria are met.

9.10.2.2   Qualifying criteria for discretionary leave

In exceptional cases a person's medical condition, or severe humanitarian conditions in the country of return, can make his removal contrary to Article 3 ECHR. Home Office guidance is that the fact that the applicant is suffering from a distressing medical condition involving, say, a limited life expectancy or affecting his mental health, may not, in itself, be sufficient. An applicant will need to show exceptional circumstances that prevent return, namely that there are compelling humanitarian considerations, such as the applicant being in the final stages of a terminal illness without prospect of medical care or family support on return.

There may be some extreme, albeit rare, cases where a person would face such poor conditions if returned, like absence of water, food or basic shelter, that removal could be a breach of the UK's Article 3 obligations.

Home Office guidance is that discretionary leave may be appropriate where the breach would not give rise to a grant of humanitarian protection but where return would result in a flagrant denial of an ECHR right in the person's country of origin. However, it cautions that it will be rare for return to breach another Article of the ECHR in this way without also breaching Article 3.

9.10.2.3   Grant of discretionary leave

Where an applicant would have established that he was a refugee under the Refugee Convention (see **9.1**) or eligible for humanitarian protection (see **9.10.1**) but for the fact that he was excluded from that protection (see **9.8.3** and **9.10.1.3**), he is normally granted discretionary leave for six months which is then reviewed. For an example, see R (C) v Secretary of State for the Home Department [2008] LTL, 25 September.

A grant of discretionary leave is otherwise usually made for three years initially. It may then be extended. All applicants need to complete at least six years in total, or at least 10 years in excluded cases, before being eligible to apply for settlement.

Life a refugee and those granted humanitarian protection, this status is liable to a review, which may lead to its being withdrawn, cancelled or revoked (see **9.10.1.3**).

9.10.3   Asylum claims

All asylum claims are treated by the Home Office as containing an implied claim for humanitarian protection on the ground that the applicant will face a real risk of serious harm in the country of return, and/or a claim for discretionary leave on the basis that requiring the applicant to leave the UK will otherwise breach the UK's obligations under Article 3 because of the ill-treatment the applicant alleges he will suffer on return. In other words, all asylum claims should be treated as an implied Article 3 foreign case (see **9.9.1**); and if the asylum claim is refused, consideration should be given to whether return would breach the UK's obligations under Article 3, first by reference to the requirements for humanitarian protection and then by reference to any residual Article 3 issues that may entitle the applicant to discretionary leave.

9.11 CLAIMS CERTIFIED AS BEING UNFOUNDED

Section 94 of the NIAA 2002 allows the Secretary of State to certify that certain asylum or human rights claims are unfounded. The result is that there is no right of appeal in the UK. Further details are given at **11.11**.

9.12 DANGER OF UNSUCCESSFUL CLAIMS

In many cases, an entrant may feel that he has nothing to lose in making an asylum claim. However, his adviser should consider whether he has any other basis for remaining in the UK which might be prejudiced by an unsuccessful claim. If an applicant already has limited leave, the Home Office may, having refused asylum, proceed to consider whether he still meets the requirements of the Rules under which he was admitted to the UK. If he does not, his existing leave can be curtailed (see **3.7**) and he may then be removed from the UK.

> **EXAMPLE**
>
> Manuel was admitted to the UK as a student with 12 months' leave. Three months later he claims asylum. The Home Office refuses the claim. The Home Office may argue that he no longer meets the requirements of the Immigration Rules (see **6.2**), for example because he does not intend to leave the UK at the end of his studies. His leave can be curtailed (see **3.7**) so that he is required to leave his course before it ends.

9.13 ASYLUM APPEALS

A person refused asylum can appeal under s 82 of the NIAA 2002 (see **11.2**).

9.14 MAKING A 'FRESH' ASYLUM (OR HUMAN RIGHTS) CLAIM

What can a claimant do if his asylum (or human rights) claim has been refused by the Home Office and all his appeal rights (see **Chapter 11**) have been exhausted?

Successive UK Governments have taken the view that many failed asylum seekers attempt to prolong their stay in the UK by making more than one claim. This has led to two key powers being given to the Secretary of State. First, the ability to certify an asylum (or human rights) claim as clearly unfounded, with the result that no appeal can be made in the UK (see s 94 of the NIAA 2002 at **11.11**). Secondly, another possible bar to an appeal lies in s 96 of the NIAA 2002. This enables the Secretary of State (or an immigration officer) to issue a certificate preventing an appeal when a second asylum (or human rights) claim relies on a matter that should have been raised in an appeal against the first claim (see **11.5**).

Now let us answer the question we posed above. Further submissions in support of an asylum claim can be made to the Home Office. If these are accepted, asylum will be granted. But what if they are rejected? Is there any right of appeal in the UK? Only if the further submissions amount to a 'fresh claim' for the purposes of para 353 of the Immigration Rules. When will the submissions amount to a fresh claim? Only if they are 'significantly different from the material that has previously been considered' because:

(a) the content has not already been considered; and

(b) taken together with the previously considered material, the claim has a realistic prospect of success, notwithstanding its rejection.

Note that para 353B of the Immigration Rules provides that where further submissions have been made and the decision maker has established whether or not they amount to a fresh claim under para 353, the decision maker should decide if there are exceptional circumstances which mean that claimant's removal from the UK is no longer appropriate. In doing so the decision maker should take into account the claimant's:

(a)　character, conduct and associations, including any criminal record and the nature of any offence of which the migrant concerned has been convicted;

(b)　compliance with any conditions attached to any previous grant of leave to enter or remain, and compliance with any conditions of temporary admission or immigration bail where applicable; and

(c)　length of time spent in the UK spent for reasons beyond the claimant's control after the human rights or asylum claim has been submitted or refused.

If the Secretary of State concludes that a fresh claim has not been made, this can be challenged by way of judicial review on the traditional *Wednesbury* ground of irrationality: see R (MN (Tanzania)) v Secretary of State for the Home Department [2011] EWCA Civ 193. This will involve the tribunal answering two questions:

> First, has the Secretary of State asked himself the correct question? The question is not whether the Secretary of State himself thinks that the new claim is a good one or should succeed, but whether there is a realistic prospect of an [immigration judge], applying the rule of anxious scrutiny, thinking that the applicant will be exposed to a real risk of persecution on return ... The Secretary of State of course can, and no doubt logically should, treat his own view of the merits as a starting-point for that enquiry; but it is only a starting-point in the consideration of a question that is distinctly different from the exercise of the Secretary of State making up his own mind. Second, in addressing that question, both in respect of the evaluation of the facts and in respect of the legal conclusions to be drawn from those facts, has the Secretary of State satisfied the requirement of anxious scrutiny? If the court cannot be satisfied that the answer to both of those questions is in the affirmative it will have to grant an application for review of the Secretary of State's decision. (per Buxton LJ in WM (DRC) v Secretary of State for the Home Department [2006] EWCA Civ 1495)

See also **Chapter 12**.

9.15　ASYLUM CHECKLIST

Consider the following questions when advising an asylum claimant. If a claim is refused, check any appeal rights (see **9.13**).

(a)　Can the applicant return to a part of the country in which he would not be subject to the harm feared (see **9.4.3.1**)?

(b)　Does the safe third country exception apply (see **9.4.3.2**)?

(c)　Is the harm feared a form of persecution (see **9.4.1.3**)? Identify acts of past persecution.

(d)　What ECHR Articles are engaged (see **9.9**)?

(e)　Is that fear of persecution well founded? Taking into account the applicant's statements and behaviour, does the applicant have a subjective fear of persecution (see **9.4.1**)?

(f)　Is that fear of persecution well founded? Objectively, are there reasonable grounds for believing that the harm feared might in fact occur in the applicant's country of origin (see **9.4.1**)?

(g)　What evidence is available or should be obtained (including medical reports)?

(h)　Are any adverse inferences to be drawn (see **9.6.2**)?

(i)　Check any relevant Country of Origin Information Reports, Country of Origin Bulletins and Country of Origin Key Documents (see **9.7**).

(j)　If the harm feared is serious enough to constitute persecution, would it be inflicted for one or more of the reasons set out in the Refugee Convention, ie race, religion, nationality, membership of a particular social group or political opinion (see **9.4.2**)?

(k)　Is the applicant saying he will act discreetly if returned (see **9.4.1.7**)?

(l)　Are there any relevant sur place activities (see **9.4.3.3**)?

(m)　Should the applicant be excluded from international protection by operation of the exclusion clauses of the Convention (see **9.5**)?

(n)　If an applicant fails to qualify for asylum, should he be granted humanitarian protection or discretionary leave (see **9.10**)?

CHAPTER 10

Deportation and Administrative Removal

10.1 DEPORTATION

10.1.1 Introduction

Under s 5 of the Immigration Act 1971 (IA 1971), the Secretary of State has a discretionary power to make a deportation order. This requires a person to leave the UK and prohibits him from lawfully re-entering while the order is in force. It also invalidates any existing leave to enter or remain.

British citizens and others with the right of abode in the UK (see **2.2** and **2.3**) cannot be deported. Some Commonwealth and Irish citizens are exempt from deportation (see **10.1.2**). Anyone else, including a person who is settled in the UK (see **3.8** and the example of *Samaroo and Sezek v Secretary of State for the Home Department* [2001] UKHRR 1150), is liable to deportation.

10.1.2 Exemption from deportation

The main exemptions from deportation are dealt with in s 7(1)(b) and (c) of the IA 1971. They apply only to Commonwealth or Irish citizens who had that citizenship at 1 January 1973 and were then ordinarily resident in the UK. Such persons are exempt from deportation on any ground if they have been ordinarily resident in the UK and Islands for five years before the date of the Secretary of State's decision to deport.

The term 'ordinarily resident' is considered in **3.8.2**. However, s 7(2) provides that, for the purpose of this exemption, if a person has at any time become ordinarily resident in the UK, he does not lose that status by remaining in breach of immigration laws. This means that a person who has overstayed, or broken conditions of entry, may nevertheless qualify for exemption.

10.1.3 Grounds for deportation

subsection

The Secretary of State may order that a person is to be deported, but only on the alternative grounds specified in s 3(5)(b) and (6) of the IA 1971. These are as follows:

(a) that the Secretary of State considers his deportation to be 'conducive to the public good' (see **10.1.4**);

(b) a person is a member of the family of a deportee (see **10.1.10**);

(c)   a court has recommended deportation, in the case of a person aged 17 or over convicted of an offence punishable with imprisonment (but see the case of R v Kluxen at **10.1.5**).

As to the steps the Secretary of State should take to establish any ground, see DA (Colombia) v Secretary of State for the Home Department [2009] EWCA Civ 682.

10.1.4   When is deportation conductive to the public good?

In OH (Serbia) [2009] INLR 109 (approved by the Court of Appeal in RU (Bangladesh) v Secretary of State for the Home Department [2011] EWCA Civ 651) the court identified three important features of the public interest in deportation, namely:

(a)   the risk of re-offending by the person concerned;

(b)   the need to deter foreign nationals from committing serious crimes by leading them to understand that, whatever the other circumstances, one consequence for them may well be their deportation; and

(c)   the role of deportation as an expression of society's revulsion at serious crimes and in building public confidence in the criminal justice system's treatment of foreign citizens who have committed serious crimes.

As to (a), the risk of re-offending is normally addressed in the report prepared for sentencing and commented on by the trial judge when giving reasons for the sentence imposed.

The Secretary of State has traditionally determined that deportation is beneficial for the public good where a person has been convicted either of one serious crime or of a series of lesser offences. The former category has been largely superseded by the fact that foreign nationals sentenced to a period of imprisonment of at least 12 months are invariably deported 'automatically' (see **10.1.5**). But an offender who repeatedly commits minor offences, or a person who commits a single offence involving, for example, the use of false identity documents for which he receives a custodial sentence of less than 12 months, may be deported at the Secretary of State's discretion.

10.1.5   Automatic deportation of foreign criminals

By s 32 of the UK Borders Act 2007, the Secretary of State must, subject to limited exceptions in s 33, make a deportation order in respect of a foreign adult criminal. This is a person who is not a British citizen (see **2.2**), nor a Commonwealth citizen with the right of abode (see **2.3**) or exempt (see **10.1.2**), and who has been convicted in the UK of an offence for which he was sentenced to a period of imprisonment of at least 12 months.

Moreover, a person may appeal on the ground that his removal from the UK would breach his ECHR rights and/or the UK's obligations under the Refugee Convention (see, eg, RU (Bangladesh) v Secretary of State for the Home Department [2011] EWCA Civ 651; AP (Trinidad & Tobago) v Secretary of State for the Home Department [2011] EWCA Civ 551; **Chapter 9** and **11.3**).

A person liable to automatic deportation might seek to oppose it by claiming asylum in the UK. However, even if the asylum claim is accepted, the person may still be removed if he had been sentenced to a term of imprisonment of at least two years (see **9.5.2**).

What if the foreign criminal is an EEA citizen? He is an exception to the rule on automatic deportation if removal would breach rights he is exercising under the EU Treaties. He may be removed only on grounds of public policy, public security or public health in accordance with reg 19(3)(b) of the I(EEA) Regs 2006 (see **4.4.14**).

What is the effect of s 32 on a criminal court's power to recommend deportation? The Court of Appeal, in R v Kluxen [2010] EWCA Crim 1081, held that:

(a)   in cases to which the 2007 Act applies, it is no longer necessary or appropriate to recommend the deportation of the offender concerned; and

(b)   in cases to which the 2007 Act does not apply (eg the foreign criminal does not receive any single custodial sentence of 12 months or more, or receives a non-custodial sentence), it will rarely be appropriate to recommend the deportation of the offender concerned. Those cases remain within the discretion of the Secretary of State (see **10.1.4**).

10.1.6   Effect

What are the effects of a deportation order? A person may not legally enter the UK whilst an order is in force. By para 320(2) of the Immigration Rules, entry clearance and leave to enter will be refused to such a person.

See **10.1.9** as to revoking an order.

10.1.7   Procedure

The general procedure is described in paras 381, 382 and 384 of the Immigration Rules. Initially, the Home Office takes a decision to deport. Notice of this is then normally given to the deportee. He may then exercise his rights of appeal. If he fails to appeal, or loses his appeal, the Secretary of State may then sign the deportation order. Under Sch 3 to the IA 1971, the deportee may then be removed to the country of which he is a national, or to another country which is likely to receive him.

The deportee may be detained following the decision to deport. The power to detain a person who is subject to deportation action is set out in para 2 of Sch 3 to the IA 1971 and s 36 of the UK Borders Act 2007. This includes those whose deportation has been recommended by a court pending the making of a deportation order, those who have been served with a notice of intention to deport pending the making of a deportation order, those who are being considered for automatic deportation or pending the making of a deportation order as required by the automatic deportation provisions, and those who are the subject of a deportation order pending removal.

Note that a similar power to detain an illegal entrant or a person liable to administrative removal (or someone suspected to be such a person) (see **10.4**) is found in para 16(2) of Sch 2 to the IA 1971.

Rights of appeal against deportation decisions are dealt with in **Chapter 11**.

10.1.8   Voluntary departure

What if a person is subject to enforcement action but a deportation order has not yet been signed? As an order cannot be made against a person who is not in the UK, it is open to the person to leave the UK voluntarily. Enforcement action will cease if it is known that a person has embarked. The advantage is that the person is not subsequently debarred from re-entering the UK, although he must, of course, satisfy the requirements of the Immigration Rules for which he is seeking entry in the normal way.

10.1.9   Revocation of a deportation order

By para 390 of the Immigration Rules, an application may be made for revocation of a deportation order, and this will be considered in the light of all the circumstances, including the following:

(a)   the grounds on which the order was made;

(b)   any representations made in support of revocation;

(c)   the interests of the community, including the maintenance of an effective immigration control; and

(d)   the interests of the applicant, including any compassionate circumstances.

Note that by para 391, if an applicant was deported following conviction for a criminal offence then revocation will not occur:

(a)   in the case of a conviction for an offence for which the person was sentenced to a period of imprisonment of less than four years, unless 10 years have elapsed since the making of the deportation order, or

(b)   in the case of a conviction for an offence for which the person was sentenced to a period of imprisonment of at least four years, at any time.

In other cases, revocation of the order will not normally be authorised unless the situation has materially altered, either by a change of circumstances since the order was made, or by fresh information coming to light which was not before the appellate authorities or the Secretary of State. The passage of time since the person was deported may also in itself amount to a change of circumstances justifying revocation of the order.

Revocation of a deportation order does not entitle the person concerned to re-enter the UK. It merely renders him eligible to apply for admission under the Immigration Rules.

10.1.10   Family members of deportee

By s 5(4) of the IA 1971, the family members liable to be deported with the deportee are his spouse or civil partner and his or her children under 18. For these purposes an adopted child, whether legally adopted or not, may be treated as the child of the adopter and, if legally adopted, must be regarded as the child only of the adopter. Also an illegitimate child (unless adopted) is regarded as the child of the mother.

Note that no family deportation can be made once eight weeks have elapsed since any other family member was deported (see IA 1971, s 5).

This can be a controversial ground for deportation, as someone who is deported as the family member of the deportee may have committed no breach of immigration law or indeed any other laws. Remember, however, that it cannot be used to deport any family member who has the right of abode in the UK (see **2.2** and **2.3**) or is exempt (see **10.1.2**).

By para 365 of the Immigration Rules, the Secretary of State will not normally decide to deport the spouse or civil partner of a deportee where:

(a)   he has qualified for settlement in his own right; or

(b)   he has been living apart from the deportee.

By para 366 of the Immigration Rules, the Secretary of State will not normally decide to deport the child of a deportee where:

(a)   he and his mother or father are living apart from the deportee; or

(b)   he has left home and established himself on an independent basis; or

(c)   he married or formed a civil partnership before deportation came into prospect.

Note that para 389 of the Immigration Rules provides that a family member of a deportee may be able to seek re-admission to the UK under the Immigration Rules where:

(a)   a child reaches 18 (when he ceases to be subject to the deportation order); or

(b)   in the case of a spouse or civil partner, the marriage or civil partnership comes to an end.

As to arguments opposing deportation based on human rights see **10.2** and **10.3**, and on EU law see **10.5**.

Note that Government policies on marriage and cohabitation known as DP 3/96 and DP 2/93 were withdrawn in April 2008.

10.1.11 Presumption that the public interest requires deportation

Paragraph 396 of the Immigration Rules provides that where a person is liable to deportation, the presumption shall be that the public interest requires deportation.

Paragraph 396 of the Immigration Rules also states that it is in the public interest to deport where the Secretary of State must make a deportation order in accordance with s 32 of the UK Borders Act 2007 (see **10.1.5**).

So in what circumstances is the presumption rebutted? Paragraph 397 provides that a deportation order will not be made if the person's removal pursuant to the order would be contrary to the UK's obligations under the Refugee Convention (see **Chapter 9**) or the Human Rights Convention (see **10.2** and **10.3**). However, it is stressed that where deportation would not be contrary to these obligations, it will be only in exceptional circumstances that the public interest in deportation is outweighed.

10.2 HUMAN RIGHTS CHALLENGES TO DEPORTATION OTHER THAN ARTICLE 8 ECHR

10.2.1 Articles 2 and 3 ECHR

A person will not be expelled from the UK to a country where there are substantial reasons for believing that he faces a real risk of:

(a)   being unlawfully killed either by the State, or through the State being unable or unwilling to protect him contrary to Article 2 ECHR; or

(b)   suffering serious harm or other treatment contrary to Article 3 ECHR. This includes torture, as well as treatment or punishment that is degrading because it arouses in the victim feelings of fear, anguish or inferiority capable of humiliating and debasing him, and possibly breaking his physical and moral resistance. Severe discrimination based on race, sex or other grounds is also capable of constituting degrading treatment.

Home Office guidance is that Article 3 ECHR may also be engaged where the person has an illness that has reached such a critical stage (ie he is dying) that it would constitute inhuman treatment to deprive him of the care he is currently receiving and send him home to an early death, unless there is care available there to enable him to meet that fate with dignity.

In *Bensaid v United Kingdom* [2001] ECHR 82, the applicant suffered from long-term schizophrenia. He claimed that his condition would seriously deteriorate if he were returned to his home country because of difficulties in obtaining suitable medication there. The Court stated (at para 37):

> Deterioration in his already existing mental illness could involve relapse into hallucinations and psychotic delusions involving self-harm and harm to others, as well as restrictions in social functioning (such as withdrawal and lack of motivation). The Court considers that the suffering associated with such a relapse could, in principle, fall within the scope of Article 3.

However, it should be noted that the Court in *Bensaid* went on to find that Article 3 ECHR would not be violated in the case as there were no exceptional circumstances. Ultimately, the question is whether what is likely to befall the claimant crosses the high threshold and the test of exceptionality (*GS (India) v Secretary of State for the Home Department* [2015] EWCA Civ 40). Whether or not the required level of severity is reached in a particular case for an adult or a child depends on all the circumstances of that case. See *AE (Algeria) v Secretary of State for the Home Department* [2014] EWCA Civ 653. This was a case where a very severely disabled child was to be returned to her home country. The evidence was that the available healthcare provision there was substantially inferior to that in UK, but no evidence pointed to the likelihood of her early death as a result.

Also see **9.9.2** and **9.9.3**.

10.2.2 Articles 5 and 6 ECHR

In resisting expulsion on the ground that his Article 5 ECHR right will be threatened in the country to which he is sent, a person must establish that there are substantial grounds for believing that, if removed, he will face a real risk of a flagrant breach of that Article. In this context, a flagrant breach is a breach the consequences of which are so severe that they override the right of a State to expel an alien from its territory. In describing such a breach of Article 5 in R *(Ullah) v Special Adjudicator* [2004] UKHL 26, Lord Steyn (at [43]) gave by way of example the case of intended expulsion to a country in which the rule of law is flagrantly flouted, *habeas corpus* is unavailable and there is a real risk that the individual may face arbitrary detention for many years.

Before the expulsion of a person will be capable of violating Article 6 ECHR, there must be substantial grounds for believing that there is a real risk:

(a)   that there will be a fundamental breach of the principles of a fair trial guaranteed by Article 6 ('[w]hat is required is that the deficiency or deficiencies in the trial process should be such as fundamentally to destroy the fairness of the prospective trial', per Lord Phillips in RB *(Algeria) v Secretary of State for the Home Department* [2009] UKHL 10 at [136]); and

(b)   that this failure will lead to a miscarriage of justice that itself constitutes a flagrant violation of the victim's fundamental rights. This was the situation in *RB (Algeria)*, where the appellant had already been tried in his absence and sentenced to life imprisonment. There were substantial grounds for believing that he would not be able to obtain a retrial and would be imprisoned to serve the sentence imposed in his absence.

What is required is a breach of the principles of fair trial guaranteed by Article 6 ECHR which is so fundamental as to amount to a nullification of, or destruction of the very essence of, the right guaranteed by that Article: see *Othman (Abu Qatada) v UK* [2012] ECHR 56. Note that in this case the ECtHR held that the applicant's deportation to Jordan would be in violation of Article 6 on account of the real risk that evidence obtained by torturing third persons would be admitted when the applicant was (re-)tried in Jordan.

Article 6 ECHR might also be engaged where the person has an outstanding civil claim in the UK for private law damages, eg a personal injury claim, or is a prospective party to such a civil claim which he actively is pursuing. Home Office guidance is that it may be relevant if the person:

(a)   does not have access to communication facilities in the country of return;

(b)   needs to undertake a medical examination;

(c)   will not have access to funding to pursue his civil claim;

(d)   will not be able to have access to interpreters;

(e)   wants to represent himself in court;

(f)   is required to give evidence in court; and

(g)   needs direct personal contact in order to instruct his UK legal representatives.

Other factors may include the complexity of the case; access to telephone and conferencing facilities in the country to which the individual is to be returned; the reliability of postal, email and fax facilities in that country; and whether or not liability has been admitted.

10.3 ARTICLE 8 ECHR CHALLENGES TO DEPORTATION

10.3.1 Article 8: private life

For the purposes of Article 8 ECHR, what is a person's private life in the UK? The answer is found by establishing the strength of his ties to the UK, which he has established here in terms of friends, education, work and leisure activities.

Can a person's contribution to society whilst in the UK, such as voluntary work for a charity, be taken into account as a factor in the balancing exercise necessary to decide whether his expulsion from the UK will breach this right? The Court of Appeal answered this question in the affirmative in *UE (Nigeria) v Secretary of State for the Home Department* [2010] EWCA Civ 975. The Court held that a person's contributions to the community in which he lived would reduce the need to maintain effective immigration control for administrative removal (see **10.4**) purposes, but they would be unlikely to make much difference in a deportation case. However, the greater the person's contribution, the more weight the factor might be given, especially if the person is an essential worker in a company engaged in a successful export business, or a social worker upon whom a local community depends or a scientific research worker engaged on research of public importance.

The fact that a foreign criminal's prospects for rehabilitation are better in the UK than in his country of origin is not a factor which should be taken into account in an appeal against deportation based on Article 8 ECHR. An offender cannot rely on his own partially unreformed criminality as a factor relevant to his private (or family) life: *SE (Zimbabwe) v Secretary of State for the Home Department* [2014] EWCA Civ 256.

10.3.2 Article 8: family life

Article 8 ECHR may also be engaged where the person claims that to expel him from the UK will separate him from his family here and would therefore constitute a breach of his right to respect for family life in the UK. Who might form part of a family? Partners in a lawful and genuine marriage or civil partnership, or a relationship akin to such, will normally constitute family life. Home Office guidance is that a relationship between unmarried and same-sex partners of sufficient substance or stability will qualify even if the couple do not meet the usual two years' cohabitation requirement in Appendix FM to the Immigration Rules (see **8.3**). In any event, such relationships would fall within a person's private life. A new or casual relationship will not suffice.

In the case of natural parents and their minor children, there is a general presumption of family life. Further, the relationship between an adoptive parent and an adopted person is in principle the same. The Home Office accepts that family life may exist between a child and his natural parent even if at the time of birth the relationship between the two parents has ended, and even if the child does not live with his parent. However, the fact that a parent has only infrequent contact with his child may be relevant to the question of whether removal would disproportionately interfere with their family life.

Family life may continue between parent and child after the child has attained his majority because it does not suddenly stop when the child reaches 18: see *Secretary of State for the Home Department v HK (Turkey)* [2010] EWCA Civ 583, where Sir Scott Baker said, at [16]:

> [I]t is apparent that the respondent had lived in the same house as his parents since 1994. He reached his majority in September 2005 but continued to live at home. Undoubtedly he had family life while he was growing up and I would not regard it as suddenly cut off when he reached his majority.

Relationships of grandparents and grandchildren, uncles and aunts, nephews and nieces, may fall within the scope of family life, depending upon the strength of the emotional ties. It is rare for relationships between adult siblings or adult children and their parents to count (*Odawey v Entry Clearance Officer* [2011] EWCA Civ 840), unless there are special elements of dependency beyond normal emotional ties (*Kugathas v Secretary of State for the Home Department* [2003] EWCA Civ 31), for example the support of an elder brother for his very sick younger brother in *R (Ahmadi) v Secretary of State for the Home Department* [2005] EWCA Civ 1721.

10.3.3 The traditional five questions

As Article 8 ECHR is a qualified right, traditionally five questions have been posed in determining its role in a person's expulsion:

Question 1: Does the person have a private and/or family life in the UK? See **10.3.1** *and* **10.3.2** *above.*

Question 2: If a private and/or family life exists, will removal interfere with that?

As to family life, the answer depends to some extent on whose family life is being considered – only that of the person being removed, or that of all members of his family unit? The House of Lords, in *Beoku-Betts v Secretary of State for the Home Department* [2008] UKHL 39, held that the effect of expulsion on all members of the person's family unit should be taken into account. Together these members enjoy a single family life, and whether or not the removal would interfere with it has to be looked at by reference to the family unit as a whole and the impact of removal upon each member.

In *Huang v Secretary of State for the Home Department* [2007] UKHL 11, the House of Lords held that the expulsion of the person must prejudice his family life in a manner sufficiently serious to amount to a breach of Article 8 ECHR. However, as Sedley LJ indicated in *AG (Eritrea) v Secretary of State for the Home Department* [2007] EWCA Civ 801, at [28], the threshold of engagement is not a specifically high one. So, for example, in *A (Afghanistan) v Secretary of State for the Home Department* [2009] EWCA Civ 825, the Court held that the interference with family life which would result from not allowing a husband and his heavily pregnant wife in a genuine and subsisting marriage to cohabit, engaged the operation of Article 8 ECHR.

The burden is on an applicant to establish positive answers to questions 1 and 2 (see *PG (USA) v Secretary of State for the Home Department* [2015] EWCA Civ 118).

Question 3: If there is interference with a private and/or family life, is it in accordance with the law?

The answer will be yes, provided the decision is in accordance with the relevant statutory provisions, Immigration Rules and the published policies of the Home Office.

Question 4: Is the interference in pursuit of one or more of the permissible aims set out under Article 8(2)?

This may include the maintenance of effective immigration controls by administrative removal (see **10.4**) and public safety, the prevention of crime and disorder, and national security by deportation (see **10.1.4**).

The answer will be yes, provided the decision is in accordance with the stated Government policy.

Question 5: Is the interference proportionate to the permissible aim or aims?

This is normally the key question, and often a difficult one to answer as the assessment of proportionality is a balancing exercise between the individual's private interests and the Government's permissible aims. It is this question that the Immigration Rules seek to address.

10.3.4   Immigration policy

10.3.4.1   Criminality thresholds

When is it a proportionate step to deport a person for the purposes of Article 8 ECHR? Current government policy, reflected in the Immigration Act 2014 and the Immigration Rules, is that:

(a)   the more serious the offence committed by a foreign criminal, the greater the public interest in deportation;

(b)   the more criminal convictions a foreign criminal has, the greater the public interest in deportation;

(c)   it is in the public interest to deport a foreign criminal even where there is evidence of remorse or rehabilitation or that he presents a low risk of reoffending;

(d)   the need to deter other non-British nationals from committing crimes – by leading them to understand that, whatever the other circumstances, one consequence may well be deportation – is a very important facet of the public interest in deporting a foreign criminal;

(e)   the role of deportation as an expression of society's revulsion at serious crimes, and in building public confidence in the treatment of non-British nationals who have committed serious crimes, is a very important facet of the public interest in deporting a foreign criminal; and

(f)   where a foreign criminal has also been convicted of an offence outside the UK, the overseas conviction will usually add to the public interest in deportation. An example of an exception to this general rule might be where there is evidence that prosecution was pursued solely for political reasons.

Home Office guidance also indicates that the following factors are capable of adding weight to the public interest in deportation, namely, where a foreign criminal:

(a)   is considered to have a high risk of reoffending;

(b)   does not accept responsibility for his offending or express remorse;

(c)   has an adverse immigration history or precarious immigration status;

(d)   has a history of immigration-related non-compliance (eg failing to co-operate fully and in good faith with the travel document process) or frustrating the removal process in other ways;

(e)   has previously obtained or attempted to obtain limited or indefinite leave to enter or remain by means of deception;

(f)   has used deception in any other circumstances (eg to secure employment, benefits or free NHS healthcare to which he was not entitled); and

(g)   has entered the UK in breach of a deportation order.

In particular, s 117C of the Immigration Act 2014 and para 398 of the Immigration Rules address the situation where a person claims that his deportation would be contrary to the UK's obligations under Article 8 ECHR.

By sub-para (b) of para 398, if the person has been convicted of an offence for which he has been sentenced to a period of imprisonment of less than four years but at least 12 months, or under sub-para (c) if, in the view of the Secretary of State, his offending has caused serious harm (see **10.3.5**) or he is a persistent offender who shows a particular disregard for the law (see **10.3.6**), then the Secretary of State may decide not to deport that person but grant him limited leave to remain (see **10.3.10)** should he meet the requirements of paras 399 (see **10.3.7** and **10.3.8**) or 399A (see **10.3.9**); otherwise, the public interest in deportation will only be outweighed by other factors where there are very compelling circumstances over and above those described in paras 399 and 399A (see **10.3.7**, **10.3.8** and **10.3.11**).

By sub-para (a) of para 398, if the person has been convicted of an offence for which he has been sentenced to a period of imprisonment of at least four years, it will be only in very compelling circumstances (see **10.3.11**) that the public interest in deportation will be outweighed by other factors.

What does 'sentenced to a period of imprisonment' mean? Home Office guidance is that the determinative factor is the sentence imposed and not the actual time spent in prison. However, this does not include a suspended sentence, unless that sentence is subsequently activated, nor convictions which are subsequently quashed on appeal. Where sentences are subsequently increased or reduced on appeal but the person nevertheless remains convicted of the offence, the revised sentence length applies.

It is important not to confuse consecutive and concurrent sentences of imprisonment in this context. For a consecutive sentence, the period of imprisonment equals the sum of all the sentences. But for a concurrent sentence, the period of imprisonment equals the length of the longest sentence.

10.3.4.2   Other public policy considerations

Section 117A of the NIAA 2002 (inserted by s 19 of the Immigration Act 2014) provides that whenever a court or tribunal is required to determine whether a decision made under the Immigration Acts breaches a person's right to respect for private and family life under Article 8 ECHR, in considering whether an interference with the person's right to respect for private and family life is justified under Article 8(2) ECHR, the court or tribunal must (in particular) have regard to the following:

(a)   The maintenance of effective immigration controls is in the public interest.

(b)   It is in the public interest, and in particular in the interests of the economic well-being of the UK, that persons who seek to enter or remain in the UK (i) are able to speak English, and (ii) are financially independent, because such persons are less of a burden on taxpayers and better able to integrate into society.

(c)   Little weight should be given to (i) a private life, or (ii) a relationship formed with a qualifying partner (see **10.3.8**), that is established by a person at a time when the person is in the UK unlawfully.

(d)   Little weight should be given to a private life established by a person at a time when the person's immigration status is precarious (see **10.3.8**).

10.3.5   Paragraph 398(c): what is meant by 'serious harm'?

Home Office guidance is that references to an 'offence which has caused serious harm' includes, but is not limited to, causing death or serious injury to an individual or group of individuals. A person does not need to be convicted of specifically causing a death or serious injury. Examples might include, but are not limited to, manslaughter; dangerous driving; driving whilst under the influence of drink and/or drugs; and arson.

10.3.6   Paragraph 398(c): who is a persistent offender?

Home Office guidance is that references to a 'persistent offender who, in the view of the Secretary of State, has shown a disregard for the law' involve a case-specific assessment of the nature, extent, seriousness and impact of the person's offending, taking into account the following non-exhaustive list of factors:

(a)   *The number of offences committed.* The decision maker must look at how many offences have been committed by the individual. There is no numerical value or limit at which deportation begins to outweigh the person's right to family or private life. But this should be borne in mind when looking at the factors at (b), (c), (d) and (e) below in reaching a decision about persistence and whether the public interest is served by that person's deportation.

(b)   *The seriousness of those offences.* The sentence or disposal should be the primary indicator of the seriousness of the offence, but the decision maker should nevertheless consider the nature of any offence(s) of which the person has been convicted and whether there are offences which give rise to the public interest being met.

(c)   *Any escalation in seriousness of the offences.* The decision maker must consider whether the pattern of offending gives particular cause to believe that the public interest would be served by the person's deportation and that it would outweigh that person's right to family or private life. The aim for the decision maker is to identify a pattern of escalating offending and intervene before a very serious offence is committed.

(d)   *The timescale over which the offences were committed.* The decision maker must consider over what timescale the offending has taken place and how recently the last of the offending took place. Less weight might be placed on a series of offences committed over a very short period of time which has long since ceased, particularly if this could be attributed to a particular incident or issue in the person's life which would make deportation now a disproportionate response. But repeated criminality over a lengthy period of time would weigh in favour of deportation. The length of time the person has spent in the UK will be an appropriate consideration. For example, a person who has committed four offences in the 10 years he has spent in the UK might not be viewed as a persistent offender; a person who commits three offences in the course of just six months' residence might be so viewed.

(e) *The frequency within which they were committed.* Again, the length of time the person has spent in the UK will be an appropriate consideration. The less time a person has spent in the UK relative to the number of offences and level of offending, the more deportation begins to outweigh that person's right to family or private life.

(f) *Any action taken to address the cause of the offending.* The decision maker should consider any programs or activities aimed at addressing the cause of the offending. Examples might include courses aimed at reduction of alcohol dependency or drug dependency, and anger management. These must demonstrate that they are having the necessary impact, such that the person's offending can be seen to have significantly reduced to the extent that his right to family or private life outweighs the public interest in deporting him.

10.3.7 Paragraph 399: exception based on relationship with a child

What weight should be given to the best interests of children who are affected by the decision to remove one or both of their parents from the UK? The Supreme Court addressed this question in *H (Tanzania) v Secretary of State for the Home Department* [2011] UKSC 4. The Court held that the best interests of the child must be a primary consideration. A decision maker must identify what the best interests of the child require, and then assess whether the strength of any other consideration, or the cumulative effect of other considerations, outweighs the consideration of the best interests of the child.

Home Office guidance is that where a person asserts that he has a family life with a child or children in the UK, the decision maker must ensure that the person can satisfy all of the following requirements of para 399 (emphasis added):

(a) the person has a genuine and subsisting parental relationship with a child under the age of 18 years who is in the UK [see **8.5.1.1**], *and*

  (i) the child is a British Citizen [see **2.2**]; *or*

  (ii) the child has lived in the UK continuously for at least the 7 years immediately preceding the date of the immigration decision [see **8.5.1.2**]; *and in either case*

    (a) it would be unduly harsh for the child to live in the country to which the person is to be deported, and

    (b) it would be unduly harsh for the child to remain in the UK without the person who is to be deported.

In what circumstances is it proportionate to remove a parent where the effect will be that a child who is a British citizen will also have to leave? The Supreme Court also addressed this question in *H (Tanzania) v Secretary of State for the Home Department*. The Court stated that whilst nationality is not a 'trump card', it is of particular importance in assessing the best interests of any child. The intrinsic importance of British citizenship should not be played down. As a British citizen, a child has rights which he will not be able to exercise if he moves to another country. He will lose the advantages of growing up and being educated in his own country, his own culture and his own language.

10.3.7.1 Would it be unduly harsh for the child to live in the country to which the person is to be deported?

Home Office guidance is that although a child's nationality and length of residence in the UK are both important factors to be considered, it is not inherently unduly harsh to expect a child who is a British citizen and/or has lived in the UK for at least seven years to leave the UK. That is why the rules expressly provide for a child's nationality and length of residence to be considered separately from the unduly harsh question. It will depend on the circumstances of the case. The Home Office takes the view that many people around the world reasonably and legitimately take their children to live in another country either temporarily or permanently, and where this complies with the law, the state does not interfere with those decisions. It is the responsibility of the foreign criminal to consider the impact on his family of the consequences of his criminal activity.

In the same vein, the Home Office asserts that, although children are innocent of any wrongdoing, sometimes they will be affected by the consequences of a foreign criminal's offending. In a deportation context, that can mean the child will go and live in another country, usually because the parents decide that the child should go with the foreign criminal (and perhaps the other parent) to that country, or in a smaller number of cases because the child cannot remain in the UK without the presence of the foreign criminal. Just as there is no automatic bar to sentencing a parent to a period of imprisonment despite the adverse impact on a child (and imprisoning a parent does not mean the child is being punished), there is no automatic bar to deporting a parent and the consequences of deportation are not a punishment for the child. However, Parliament accepts that where a foreign criminal has not been sentenced to a period of imprisonment of four years or more and the effect of deportation on a child would be unduly harsh, the child's best interests outweigh the public interest in deporting the parent.

The following is a non-exhaustive list of relevant factors that the Home Office provides to its decision makers when assessing whether it would be unduly harsh for a child to live in the country to which the foreign criminal will be deported:

(a)   the age and nationality of the child;

(b)   whether the child could obtain citizenship or a visa to reside in the country of return;

(c)   whether the child would be able to adapt to life in the country of return or whether there would be very significant obstacles to his integration there, and, if so, the nature and extent of those obstacles;

(d)   whether the child could be raised by both parents in the country of return (including, if the other parent lives in the UK, whether it is open to him or her to choose to go with the foreign criminal and the child to the country of return);

(e)   the prevailing conditions in the country of return and whether they are such that it would be unduly harsh for the child to live there (this is likely to be rare, and the onus is on the foreign criminal to particularise the impact country conditions will have on the child; decision makers should assess claims on the basis of country conditions with reference to the country guidance used in asylum cases);

(f)   whether the child has formed any family or private life in the UK outside of the home and the strength of those ties;

(g)   the ECJ judgment in *Ruiz Zambrano* (European citizenship) [2011] EUECJ C-34/09 (see **4.4.13**). Note that the Government's position is that criminality which reaches the deportation threshold (conducive to the public good) is capable of outweighing a *Zambrano* right of residence.

The Home Office anticipates that families or children may highlight the differences in quality of education, health and wider public services and economic or social opportunities between the UK and the country of return and argue that these work against the best interests of the child. The Home Office states that, other than in exceptional circumstances, this would not normally mean it is unduly harsh for the child to live in the country of return, particularly if one or both parents or wider family have the means or resources to support the child on return or the skills, education and training to provide for their family on return, or if facilitated return scheme support is available.

The Home Office accepts that consideration must also be given to the extent of a child's private life in the UK, taking into account factors such as the child's age, length of residence, dependence on wider family in the UK and any other ties to the community, to determine whether it would be unduly harsh to expect the child to live in a country other than the UK.

10.3.7.2   Would it be unduly harsh for the child to remain in the UK without the person who is to be deported?

To answer this question, it is first necessary to establish whether the child would be able to remain in the UK when the foreign criminal is deported. The following is a non-exhaustive list of relevant factors the Home Office takes into account:

(a)   whether the child has a legal guardian, a family member who has a legal obligation to care for the child (for example, responsibility or a residence order) or an existing relationship with a family member;

(b)   whether someone other than the foreign criminal is the child's primary or joint-primary carer and whether that person normally has day-to-day care and wider welfare and developmental responsibility for the child;

(c)   whether the person who cared for the child while the foreign criminal was in prison would be able to care for the child when the foreign criminal is deported;

(d)   whether it is reasonable to expect the other person to fulfil the role of primary carer (eg whether he or she has fulfilled that role in the past, whether he or she is able to care for the child, whether he or she cares for any other children or has done so before);

(e)   whether there are any factors which undermine the ability of that person to act as the primary carer of the child or would suggest that he or she is unsuitable (eg criminal convictions, concerns expressed by social services, etc).

Is it relevant, when answering this question, that another person would have to make a choice about working full time or part time or not at all and might need to arrange suitable childcare? The Home Office states that this is not likely to be a determinative factor in his or her ability to care for the child, particularly in the case of someone with a legal responsibility towards the child, and particularly where family life was formed in full knowledge that the foreign criminal may not be able to remain in the UK (because his immigration status was unlawful or precarious, or because he was liable to deportation). The Home Office view is that all parents and guardians have to make difficult choices about how to balance their working lives and their parental responsibilities.

What if the only way a child could remain in the UK if a foreign criminal is deported would be in the care of social services or foster care that is not already in place (excluding care provided by a family member or a private fostering arrangement)? The Home Office accepts that this would usually be unduly harsh, unless there is evidence that the child's best interests would be better served in such care than in the care of the foreign criminal. However, consideration must be given to the age of the child and how long he is likely to remain in care.

Is it appropriate for a decision maker to conclude that a child can remain in the UK in the care of another person who is him- of herself liable to removal or deportation? No. Home Office guidance is that if there is someone who would be able to care for the child in the UK but for having no immigration status then that person's status should be resolved before it can be determined whether it would be unduly harsh for the child to remain in the UK without the foreign criminal. Decision makers must check whether the person has an outstanding application for leave to remain in his or her own right. If he or she does, decision makers should liaise with the other caseworking unit to ensure that the application is decided before the foreign criminal's claim is considered. If the person is granted leave to remain then this will factor into the consideration of the unduly harsh question.

If it is established that the child is able to remain in the UK when the foreign criminal is deported, the following is a non-exhaustive list of relevant factors used by the Home Office when assessing whether it would be unduly harsh for the child to continue living in the UK without the presence of the foreign criminal:

(a)   whether there are any reasons (related to the foreign criminal's offending history, or other reasons) why it would be in the child's best interests to be separated from the foreign criminal;

(b)   the age of the child;

(c)   how in practice the child would be affected by the foreign criminal's absence;

(d)   whether there is credible evidence that the foreign criminal's presence is needed to prevent the child from being ill treated, his health or development being significantly impaired, or his care being other than safe and effective;

(e)   the extent of any practical difficulties the remaining parent or guardian would face in caring for the child alone (if he or she is not already effectively caring for the child alone);

(f)   whether there is credible evidence that the child would lose all contact with the foreign criminal, eg because telephone and internet contact would not be possible and there would be no possibility of visits either to the country of return or a third country. If so, whether this is unduly harsh will depend on the severity of the foreign criminal's conduct, the nature of the relationship the foreign criminal has with the child, and the impact on the child of the loss of contact.

Where a child's parents or guardians have a choice about whether the child leaves or remains in the UK, it will not be appropriate for the decision to deport to prescribe any particular outcome for the child. According to the Home Office, it is the responsibility of the family to decide for themselves whether the child will accompany the foreign criminal overseas or whether to make suitable arrangements for the child to remain in the UK based on where they think the child's best interests lie. The decision to deport requires the child's parents or guardians to make this decision.

10.3.7.3   Seeking the views of children

In deportation cases where the consequence of the decision may be to separate a child from a parent, the decision maker, when assessing the best interests of the child, must be prepared to discover the views of any affected children. These may already be available or known from information and representations supplied. If not available, and there are no reasons for their non-availability, consideration should be given to obtaining them by means of a request in writing to a parent, legal adviser or other suitable adult (eg social worker or other family member). The decision maker should be prepared to consider hearing the views of the child directly, if requested or deemed necessary.

If there are ongoing proceedings in the UK family courts concerning the child, should the decision to deport be delayed? No, stated the Court of Appeal in *Mohan v Secretary of State for the Home Department* [2012] EWCA Civ 1363, if the material in favour of the applicant lacks substance and the public interest in deportation is overwhelming. But, otherwise, the judgment of the family court, with all the tools at its disposal (including the assistance of the Children and Family Court Advisory and Support Service (CAFCASS) and the opportunity to assess all the adults), can and should inform the decision maker on the issue of the proportionality of deportation in relation to the best interests of the child. See further *RS (immigration/family court liaison: outcome) India* [2013] UKUT 82 (IAC) where the family court held that the child's best interests did not lie with her parents but by being placed in long-term foster care in the UK. The family court regarded it as acceptable for the child to have contact with his parents face-to-face annually by visiting them in India and monthly by means of Skype. On that basis, the deportation of the child's father did not interfere with the child's best interests.

10.3.8   Paragraph 399: exception based on relationship with a partner

Home Office guidance is that where a person asserts that he has a family life with a qualifying partner in the UK, the decision maker must ensure that the person can satisfy all of the following requirements of para 399 (emphasis added):

(b)   the person has a genuine and subsisting relationship [see **8.3.5.5**] with a partner who is in the UK and is a British Citizen [see **2.2**] or settled in the UK [see **3.8**], *and*

(i)   the relationship was formed at a time when the person (deportee) was in the UK lawfully and their immigration status was not precarious; and

(ii)   it would be unduly harsh for that partner to live in the country to which the person is to be deported, because of compelling circumstances over and above those described in paragraph EX.2. of Appendix FM [see **8.5.2.1**]; and

(iii) it would be unduly harsh for that partner to remain in the UK without the person who is to be deported.

10.3.8.1   The immigration status of the deportee

The starting point here is s 117B(4) of the NIAA 2002, which provides that little weight should be given to a relationship formed by a deportee at a time when he is in the UK unlawfully, that is when he required leave to enter or remain but did not have it. Likewise, a relationship formed at a time when the foreign criminal had a precarious immigration status will be less capable of outweighing the public interest. For these purposes, a person's immigration status is precarious if he is in the UK with limited leave to enter or remain, or he has settled status which was obtained fraudulently.

The onus is on the foreign criminal to provide evidence that the relationship with his partner was formed when he was in the UK lawfully with indefinite leave to enter or remain and before the criminality which he should have been aware would make him liable to removal or deportation.

10.3.8.2   Unduly harsh for partner to live in the country to which the person is to be deported

Here, unduly harsh means compelling circumstances over and above the very serious hardship described in para EX.2 of Appendix FM, as follows: 'the very significant difficulties which would be faced by the applicant or their partner in continuing their family life together outside the UK and which could not be overcome or would entail very serious hardship for the applicant or their partner.' But note that it is only the impact on a foreign criminal's partner which will be considered by the Home Office, not the impact on the foreign criminal.

In determining whether the unduly harsh threshold is met, decision makers should consider the difficulties which the partner would face and whether they entail something that could not (or could not be expected to) be overcome, other than with a very severe degree of hardship for the partner. According to the Home Office, lack of knowledge of a language spoken in the country in which the foreign criminal and his partner would be required to live would not reach the unduly harsh threshold. Why? Because it is reasonable to conclude that the couple must have been communicating whilst in the UK. Therefore, it is reasonable for that to continue outside the UK, whether or not the partner chooses to learn the (or a) language spoken in the country to which the foreign criminal is to be deported.

According to the Home Office, being separated from extended family members would also be unlikely to reach the unduly harsh threshold, such as might happen where a partner's parents and siblings live in the UK, unless there were particular very compelling factors in the case.

Home Office guidance is that the factors which might be relevant to the consideration of whether it would be unduly harsh for a partner to live in the country to which the foreign criminal is to be deported include, but are not limited to, the following:

(a)   *The ability of the partner lawfully to enter and stay in the country to which the foreign criminal is to be deported.* The onus is on the foreign criminal to show that this is not possible in order for the unduly harsh threshold to be met. A mere wish/desire/preference to live in the UK would not meet the threshold.

(b)   *Cultural barriers.* This might be relevant in situations where the partner would be so disadvantaged that he or she could not be expected to go and live in that country. It must be a barrier which either cannot be overcome or would present very severe hardship such that it would be unduly harsh.

(c)   *The impact of a mental or physical disability.* Whether or not a partner has a mental or physical disability, a move to another country may involve a period of hardship as the person adjusts to new surroundings (just as there may have been when a foreign national first comes to live in the UK). But a mental or physical disability could be such that in some cases it could lead to very severe hardship such that it would be unduly harsh.

10.3.8.3   Unduly harsh for partner to remain in the UK without the deportee

When assessing whether it would be unduly harsh for a partner who could not accompany the foreign criminal to the country of return to be separated from the foreign criminal, consideration must be given to the practical impact of separation on the partner and whether that impact is unduly harsh. The onus is on the foreign criminal to submit evidence demonstrating that the effect would be unduly harsh, not on the Secretary of State to demonstrate that it would not be.

Home Office guidance gives as an example of what might be considered unduly harsh, depending on the facts in an individual case, where there is credible evidence that the foreign criminal's presence is essential to prevent the partner's health from being severely impaired because it would not be possible to receive adequate care from other family members, medical professionals, social services, etc.

10.3.9   Paragraph 399A private life exceptions

Home Office guidance is that where a person asserts that he has a private life in the UK, the decision maker must ensure that the person can satisfy the following set of requirements of para 399A (emphasis added):

(a)   the person has been lawfully resident in the UK for most of his life; *and*

(b)   he is socially and culturally integrated in the UK; *and*

(c)   there would be very significant obstacles to his integration into the country to which it is proposed he is deported.

10.3.9.1   The deportee has been lawfully resident in the UK for most of his life

Lawful residence for the purposes of this requirement means that the deportee had limited or indefinite leave to enter or remain, had a right of residence in accordance with the EEA Regulations 2006, or was in the UK while exempt from immigration control.

In assessing a foreign criminal's residence in the UK, the Home Office states that 'most of his life' means more than half of his life.

10.3.9.2   The deportee is socially and culturally integrated in the UK

Home Office guidance is that positive and negative factors need to be balanced against each other to form an overall assessment of whether a foreign criminal meets this requirement.

The Home Office places reliance here on s 117B(2) of the NIAA 2002, which provides that it is in the public interest that persons who seek to remain in the UK are able to speak English. So if a foreign criminal cannot speak English, the Home Office will take this as an indication that he is not integrated in the UK because he is unable to communicate with the majority of the population. However, if a foreign criminal can speak English, this alone will not be sufficient to demonstrate integration, although it will count in the foreign criminal's favour when balancing all the evidence for and against integration.

There is no prescribed standard of English which must be met for this requirement and no prescribed evidence which must be submitted. However, the Home Office may accept the following:

(a)   evidence of citizenship (eg a passport) of a country where English is the (or a) main or official language;

(b)   evidence of an academic qualification that was taught in English;

(c)   evidence of passing an English language test;

(d)   evidence that he has been interviewed (eg in connection with an asylum claim) or given evidence at an appeal hearing in English.

In this context, the Home Office also places reliance on s 117B(3) of the NIAA 2002, which provides that it is in the public interest that persons who seek to remain in the UK are financially independent. If a foreign criminal cannot demonstrate that he is financially independent, this will indicate to the Home Office that he is not integrated in the UK because he may be reliant on public funds, wider family members or charities, rather than contributing to the economic wellbeing of the country. However, if a foreign criminal can demonstrate that he is financially independent, this alone will not be sufficient to demonstrate to the Home Office his integration, but it will count in the foreign criminal's favour when balancing all the evidence for and against integration.

Home Office guidance is that financial independence means not being a burden on the taxpayer. It includes not having access to income-related benefits or tax credits, on the basis of the foreign criminal's income or savings or those of his partner, but not those of a third party. There is no prescribed financial threshold which must be met and no prescribed evidence which must be submitted. Decision makers should consider all available information, though less weight will be given to claims unsubstantiated by original, independent and verifiable documentary evidence, eg from an employer or regulated financial institution.

The Home Office also treats the foreign criminal's immigration status as important in this context. Why? Because the Home Office takes the view that a person who has been in the UK with limited leave to enter or remain is less likely to be integrated because of the temporary nature of his immigration status. A person who is in the UK unlawfully will have even less of a claim to be integrated. Criminal offending will also often be an indication of lack of integration. The nature of offending, such as anti-social behaviour against a local community or offending that may have caused a serious and/or long-term impact on a victim or victims (eg sexual assault, burglary), may be further evidence of non-integration.

According to the Home Office, it will usually be more difficult for a foreign criminal who has been sentenced more than once to a period of imprisonment of at least 12 months but less than four years to demonstrate that he is socially and culturally integrated. Why? Because he will have spent more time excluded from society, than for a foreign criminal who has been convicted of a single offence.

To outweigh any evidence of a lack of integration, the foreign criminal will need to demonstrate to the Home Office strong evidence of integration. Home Office guidance is that mere presence in the UK is not an indication of integration. Positive contributions to society may be evidence of integration, eg an exceptional contribution to a local community or to wider society, which has not been undertaken at a time that suggests an attempt to avoid deportation. If such a claim is made, decision makers will expect to see credible evidence of significant voluntary work of real practical benefit.

10.3.9.3   There would be very significant obstacles to the deportee's integration into the country to which it is proposed he is deported

Home Office guidance is that the starting point for this requirement is to assume that the applicant will be able to integrate into his country of return, unless he can demonstrate why that is not the case. The onus is on the applicant to show that there are very significant obstacles to that integration.

Decision makers expect to see original, independent and verifiable documentary evidence of any claims made in this regard, and will place less weight on assertions which are unsubstantiated. Where it is not reasonable to expect corroborating evidence to be provided, consideration is given to the credibility of the applicant's claims.

A very significant obstacle to integration means something which would prevent or seriously inhibit the applicant from integrating into the country of return. The decision maker is looking for more than obstacles. They are looking to see whether there are 'very significant' obstacles, which is a high threshold. Very significant obstacles will exist where the applicant demonstrates that he would be unable to establish a private life in the country of return, or where establishing a private life in the country of return would entail very serious hardship for the applicant.

The decision maker must consider all the reasons put forward by the applicant as to why there would be obstacles to his integration in the country of return. These reasons must be considered individually and cumulatively. The question is whether the applicant has the ability to form an adequate private life by the standards of the country of return – not by UK standards. The decision maker will take into account whether the applicant will be able to establish a private life in respect of all its essential elements, even if, for example, his job, or his ability to find work, or his network of friends and relationships may be differently constituted in the country of return.

The decision maker will need to consider the specific obstacles raised by the applicant. They will also need to set these against other factors in order to make an assessment in the individual case. Relevant considerations include:

(a)   *Cultural background by way of the applicant's exposure to and level of understanding of the cultural norms in the country of return.* Where the person has spent his time in the UK living mainly amongst a diaspora community from that country, then it may be reasonable to conclude that he has cultural ties with that country even if he has never lived there or has been absent from that country for a lengthy period. If the applicant has cultural ties with the country of return, then it is likely that it would be possible for him to establish a private life there. Even if there are no cultural ties, the cultural norms of that country may be such that there are no barriers to integration.

(b)   *Length of time spent in the country of return.* Where the applicant has spent a significant period of time in the country of return, it will be difficult for them to demonstrate that there would be very significant obstacles to integration into that country. The decision maker must consider the proportion of the person's life spent in that country and the stage of life the person was at when in that country.

What if the applicant has never lived in the country of return, or only spent his early years there? Home Office guidance is that this will not necessarily mean that there are very significant obstacles preventing him from integrating, particularly if he can speak a language of that country, eg if the country of return is one where English is spoken or if a language of the country was spoken at home when he was growing up. For these purposes, fluency is not required – conversational level language skills or a basic level of language which could be improved on return would be sufficient. The cultural norms of the country and how easy it is for the person to adapt to them will also be relevant.

What if there is credible evidence that an applicant cannot speak any language which is spoken in the country of return? The Home Office states that this will not in itself be a very significant obstacle to integration unless he can also show that he would be unable to learn a language of that country, for example because of a mental or physical disability.

(c) *Family, friends and social network.* An applicant who has family or friends in the country of return should be able to turn to them for support to help them to integrate into that country. The decision maker must consider whether the applicant or his family have sponsored or hosted visits in the UK by family or friends from the country of return, or the applicant has visited family or friends in the country of return. The decision maker must consider the quality of any relationships with family or friends in the country of return, but they do not have to be strong familial ties and can include ties that could be strengthened if the person were to return.

Where there are no family, friends or social networks in the country of return, that is not in itself a very significant obstacle to integration. Why? The Home Office states that many people successfully migrate to countries where they have no ties.

Home Office policy is that the degree of private life an individual has established in the UK is not relevant to the consideration of whether there are very serious obstacles to integration into the country of return. However, it is relevant to the consideration of whether, where the applicant falls for refusal under the Immigration Rules, there are exceptional circumstances which would make refusal unjustifiably harsh for the applicant.

10.3.10 Grant of limited leave under paras 399 or 399A

By para 399B, where para 399 (see **10.3.7** and **10.3.8**) or 399A (see **10.3.9**) applies, the person may be granted limited leave for a period not exceeding 30 months. Can further periods of limited leave be granted? Yes, the requirements for further leave are that the applicant continues to meet the criteria set out in paras 399 or 399A.

10.3.11 Very compelling circumstances

If a person falls within para 398(a) (he has been convicted of an offence and sentenced to a period of imprisonment of at least four years (see **10.3.4**)), or otherwise does not fall within any of the para 399 (see **10.3.7** and **10.3.8**) or para 399A (see **10.3.9**) exceptions, the person's deportation will be the proper course in all but very exceptional cases.

Home Office guidance is that in determining whether there are very compelling circumstances, decision makers must consider all relevant factors that weigh in favour of and against deportation.

Decision makers should be mindful that whilst all cases are to an extent unique, those unique factors do not generally render them exceptional. For these purposes, exceptional cases should be numerically rare. Furthermore, a case is not exceptional just because the exceptions to deportation in paras 399 or 399A have been missed by a small margin. Rather, the Immigration Rules establish those thresholds as determining when deportation would be appropriate bar other factors. However, in assessing if there are very compelling circumstances, the matters identified in paras 399 and 399A need to be considered along with all other aspects of the case. The decision maker then needs to determine whether removal would have such severe consequences for the individual or his family that very exceptionally deportation is not appropriate despite the clear articulation of the public interest in para 398 (see **10.3.4**). Home Office guidance is that that is likely to be the case only very rarely indeed.

10.3.12 Decision maker's approach

The Immigration Rules constitute a complete code for the application of Article 8 ECHR in this context (*MA (Somalia) v Secretary of State for the Home Department* [2015] EWCA Civ 48):

42.   ... [In] approaching the question of whether removal is a proportionate interference with an individual's article 8 rights, the scales are heavily weighted in favour of deportation and something very compelling (which will be 'exceptional') is required to outweigh the public interest in removal. In our view, it is no coincidence that the phrase 'exceptional circumstances' is used in the new rules in the context of weighing the competing factors for and against deportation of foreign criminals.

43.   The word 'exceptional' is often used to denote a departure from a general rule. The general rule in the present context is that, in the case of a foreign [criminal] to whom paragraphs 399 and 399A do not apply, very compelling reasons will be required to outweigh the public interest in deportation. These compelling reasons are the 'exceptional circumstances'.

44.   We would, therefore, hold that the new rules are a complete code and that the exceptional circumstances to be considered in the balancing exercise involve the application of a proportionality test as required by the Strasbourg jurisprudence ... (per Lord Dyson MR in *MF (Nigeria) v Secretary of State for the Home Department* [2013] EWCA Civ 1192).

The reasons why it is important to assess the matter within the Immigration Rules rather than outside them were spelled out by Sales LJ in *Secretary of State for the Home Department v AJ (Angola)* [2014] EWCA Civ 1636:

39.   The fact that the new rules are intended to operate as a comprehensive code is significant, because it means that an official or a tribunal should seek to take account of any Convention rights of an appellant through the lens of the new rules themselves, rather than looking to apply Convention rights for themselves in a free-standing way outside the new rules ...

40.   The requirement that claims by appellants who are foreign criminals for leave to remain, based on the Convention rights of themselves or their partners, relations or children, should be assessed under the new rules and through their lens is important, as the Court of Appeal in *MF (Nigeria)* has emphasised. It seeks to ensure uniformity of approach between different officials, tribunals and courts who have to assess such claims, in the interests of fair and equal treatment of different appellants with similar cases on the facts. In this regard, the new rules also serve as a safeguard in relation to rights of appellants under Article 14 to equal treatment within the scope of Article 8. The requirement of assessment through the lens of the new rules also seeks to ensure that decisions are made in a way that is properly informed by the considerable weight to be given to the public interest in deportation of foreign criminals ...

10.4 ADMINISTRATIVE REMOVAL

10.4.1 Grounds for removal

Removal from the UK is often described as 'administrative removal', as that is what it is in reality, namely, an administrative step. Under s 10 of the Immigration and Asylum Act 1999 (IAA 1999) a person may be removed from the UK under the authority of the Secretary of State or an immigration officer if the person requires leave to enter or remain in the UK but does not have it. This means that the following people may be administratively removed from the UK:

(a)   anyone who has failed to observe the conditions attached to his leave (see **3.3**);

(b)   overstayers (see **3.6.6**);

(c)   anyone who has obtained leave to remain by deception, or who sought to obtain such leave by deception;

(d)   the family members (partner or child) of such people (see the Immigration (Removal of Family Members) Regulations 2014 (SI 2014/2816)).

The most common grounds for administrative removal are that a person has remained beyond the period specified in his limited leave, or has broken a condition attached to it. For example, a person's leave to enter or remain will often either prohibit or restrict his freedom to take employment, and the person is liable to administrative removal procedures if he is found to be working without authority. Home Office guidance is that there must be firm and recent (within six months) evidence of working in breach. The immigration officer will look for at least an admission by the offender under caution of working in breach; or a statement by the employer; or pay slips or the offender's details on the payroll; or visual observation, by the immigration officer, of the applicant working.

As explained in **3.6.2**, a person who wishes to extend his stay should apply for a variation before his leave expires. He commits a criminal offence under s 24(1)(b) of the IA 1971 if he knowingly overstays or fails to observe a condition of the leave. Note that it is not usual practice for a prosecution to occur. Removal does not require a knowing breach, and so normally the person is removed and not prosecuted.

In addition, illegal entrants (see **10.4.2**) may be removed from the UK in the same way.

10.4.2 Definition of illegal entrant

An illegal entrant is a person who unlawfully enters or seeks to enter in breach of a deportation order or of the immigration laws. This includes a person who has so entered.

Typically, a person might enter the UK without leave clandestinely, eg concealed in a vehicle such as a lorry. Or he might present a forged or false British or EEA passport to an immigration officer.

A person who, contrary to the IA 1971, knowingly enters the UK in breach of a deportation order or without leave commits a criminal offence under s 24(1)(a). However, it is possible to be an illegal entrant without having committed any criminal offence, for instance where a person obtains leave by producing false documents, without knowing them to be false (R v Immigration Officer, ex p Chan [1992] 1 WLR 541).

A person will be an illegal entrant if he obtains leave to enter by deception, although mere non-disclosure of material facts will not amount to deception, as the entrant has no positive duty to reveal facts if a relevant question is not asked. It is for the Home Office to prove the deception (R v Secretary of State for the Home Department, ex p Khawaja [1984] AC 74).

10.4.3 Procedure

If the Home Office decides not to remove the person, he is normally granted indefinite to leave to remain.

If, after consideration of all the relevant facts, the Home Office decides that administrative removal is the correct course of action, a notice of liability to administrative removal is served. The immigration officer normally serves the notice in person. It still remains open to the person who is subject to enforcement action to leave the UK voluntarily. Otherwise the immigration officer will set removal directions. The costs of complying with removal directions (so far as reasonably incurred) are met by the Secretary of State.

10.4.4 Effect of administrative removal

Unlike someone who has been deported, a person who is subject to administrative removal does not need to have the decision to remove him rescinded before he may return to the UK, provided that he otherwise qualifies for admission under the Immigration Rules.

10.4.5 Government policy: deportation and administrative removal

It is important to remember that deportation may be automatic (see **10.1.5**), or otherwise there is a presumption of deportation (see **10.1.11**). But administrative removal is never automatic, neither is there a presumption of administrative removal. Why the difference? It is because different government policies are pursued by the use of deportation and administrative removal, as methods to expel a person from the UK.

As we saw at **10.1.4,** there are three important features of the public interest in deportation, namely:

(a)   the risk of re-offending by the person concerned;

(b)   the need to deter foreign nationals from committing serious crimes by leading them to understand that, whatever the other circumstances, one consequence for them may well be their deportation; and

(c)   the role of deportation as an expression of society's revulsion at serious crimes and in building public confidence in the criminal justice system's treatment of foreign citizens who have committed serious crimes.

In UE (Nigeria) v Secretary of State for the Home Department [2010] EWCA Civ 975, the Court identified that the main element of public interest in administrative removal is the need for the Government to maintain a firm policy of immigration control.

The difference in aims is important, because it explains why the factors in favour of expulsion are capable of carrying greater weight in a deportation case than in a case of administrative removal. This led Richards LJ, in JO (Uganda) v Secretary of State for the Home Department [2010] EWCA Civ 10, to observe (at [29]):

> The maintenance of effective immigration control is an important matter, but the protection of society against serious crime is even more important and can properly be given correspondingly greater weight in the balancing exercise. Thus I think it perfectly possible in principle for a given set of considerations of family life and/or private life to be sufficiently weighty to render expulsion disproportionate in an ordinary removal case, yet insufficient to render expulsion disproportionate in a deportation case because of the additional weight to be given to the criminal offending on which the deportation decision was based.

10.4.6   Human rights challenges to removal

See **10.2** as to challenges based on provisions other than Article 8 ECHR.

As to Article 8 ECHR, para 400 of the Immigration Rules provides that where a person claims that his removal would be contrary to the UK's obligations under Article 8, the Secretary of State may require an application under para 276ADE (private life) or Appendix FM (family life) of the Rules. Where an application is not required, in assessing that claim the Secretary of State or an immigration officer will, subject to para 353 (see **9.14**), consider that claim against the requirements to be met under para 276ADE or Appendix FM, and if appropriate the removal decision will be cancelled.

10.4.6.1   Paragraph 276ADE

A person who has lived in the UK for at least 20 years continuously, lawfully or unlawfully, can apply to the Home Office for leave to remain in the UK on the basis of the Article 8 ECHR right to respect for private life. Alternative provisions allow an applicant to be granted limited leave to remain in the UK on the basis of private life after seven years' continuous residence if he is under the age of 18; or if he has spent at least half of his life in the UK if he is aged between 18 and 24; or if the applicant has less than 20 years' continuous residence in the UK but there would be very significant obstacles to the applicant's integration into his country of origin.

Full details are given at **8.13**.

10.4.6.2   Appendix FM (family life)

Under para EX.1 of Appendix FM to the Immigration Rules, an applicant may be allowed to remain in the UK on the basis of his family life with a child and/or a partner if it would breach Article 8 ECHR to remove him.

Paragraph EX.1 applies if the applicant has a genuine and subsisting parental relationship with a child (under the age of 18 years) who is in the UK, who is a British citizen or who has lived in the UK continuously for at least the seven years immediately preceding the date of application, and it would not be reasonable to expect that child to leave the UK. See **8.5.1**.

Paragraph EX.1 additionally, or alternatively, applies if the applicant has a genuine and subsisting relationship with a partner who is in the UK and who is a British citizen, settled in the UK, or in the UK with refugee leave or humanitarian protection, and there are insurmountable obstacles to family life with that partner continuing outside the UK. See **8.5.2**.

10.4.6.3 Future developments

When s 1 of the Immigration Act 2014 comes into force, it will replace s 10 of the IAA 1999 with a new power for the Secretary of State or an immigration officer to authorise the removal of a person who requires leave to enter or remain in the UK but does not have it.

10.5 INTERFERENCE WITH EU TREATY RIGHTS BY DEPORTATION OR ADMINISTRATIVE REMOVAL

10.5.1 Partner

What if a British citizen is exercising EU Treaty rights but his non-EEA partner is threatened with expulsion from the UK? In *Carpenter v Secretary of State for the Home Department* [2003] 2 WLR 267, Mrs C was a national of The Philippines. She was given leave to enter the UK as a visitor in September 1994 for six months. She overstayed that leave and failed to apply for any extension of her stay. In May 1996 she married Mr C, a British citizen. Mr C ran a business selling advertising space in medical and scientific journals, and offering various administrative and publishing services to the editors of those journals. A significant proportion of the business was conducted with advertisers established in other Member States of the EU. Mr C travelled to other Member States for the purpose of his business.

In July 1996 Mrs C applied to the Secretary of State for leave to remain in the UK as the spouse of a British citizen. Her application was refused, and the Secretary of State also decided to make an order removing her to The Philippines. Mrs C argued that since her husband's business required him to travel around in other Member States, providing and receiving services, he could do so more easily as she was looking after his children from his first marriage. Therefore, her removal would restrict her husband's right to provide and receive services. It was accepted that Mrs C's marriage was genuine and that she played an important part in the upbringing of her stepchildren. It was also accepted that her husband was a provider of services for the purposes of EU law.

Mrs C accepted that she had no right of her own to reside in any Member State but claimed that her rights derived from those enjoyed by Mr C to provide services and to travel within the EU. Her removal would either require Mr C to go to live with her in The Philippines, or separate the members of the family unit if he remained in the UK. The ECJ agreed that the separation of Mr and Mrs C would be detrimental to their family life and, therefore, to the conditions under which Mr C exercised his fundamental EU Treaty rights. Those rights could not be fully effective if Mr C were deterred from exercising them by obstacles raised by the UK Government to the residence of his spouse.

The ECJ then went on to link the interference with Mr C's EU rights with the interference with his Article 8 ECHR rights. The decision to remove Mrs C did not strike a fair balance between the competing interests, on the one hand, of Mr C to respect for his family life and, on the other hand, the UK Government's removal policy. Although Mrs C had infringed UK immigration laws, her conduct since her arrival in the UK had not been the subject of any other complaint. The Court held that to remove Mrs C constituted an infringement which was not proportionate to the objective pursued of maintaining immigration control. However, in deportation cases where the criminality threshold is reached (see **10.3.4**), it is most likely that the Home Office's position will be that the public interest in deportation (see **10.1.4**) will ordinarily outweigh any right of the non-EEA partner to remain in the EU in these circumstances and that the couple can continue their family life in a country outside the EU.

10.5.2 Child

What if a child is a British citizen and the parent being expelled is not an EEA national? Can the child's EEA rights assist the parent if the child will otherwise be leaving the UK with that parent? In *Zambrano v Office national de l'emploi (ONEm)* (Case C-34/09) [2011] 2 CMLR 46, the applicant and his wife were both Columbian nationals who had sought and been refused refugee status in Belgium. However, the couple were allowed to stay in Belgium temporarily, and had two children who acquired Belgian nationality under national law.

The Court held that Article 20 TFEU (see **4.3**) confers the status of citizen of the EU on every person holding the nationality of a Member State. Since the children of the applicant possessed Belgian nationality under Belgian law, they undeniably enjoyed that status. Further, Article 20 TFEU precludes national measures which have the effect of depriving citizens of the EU of the genuine enjoyment of the substance of the rights conferred by virtue of their status as citizens of the EU. A refusal to grant a right of residence to a third country national with dependent minor children in the Member State where those children were nationals and resided, had such an effect. Such a refusal would lead to a situation where those children, citizens of the EU, would have to leave the territory of the EU in order to accompany their parents. In these circumstances, the children, as citizens of the EU, would, as a result, be unable to exercise the substance of the rights conferred on them by virtue of their status as citizens of the EU.

So if the child is a British citizen, the applicant is the child's primary carer and there is no other parent, guardian or carer on whom the child is dependent or who could care for the child if the primary carer left the UK, the applicant will have a right of residence under the case (see **8.5.1.3**). However, in deportation cases where the criminality threshold is reached (see **10.3.4**), Home Office guidance is that a decision maker considering Article 8 ECHR can use the argument that family life could continue in a country outside the EU because the British citizen child could accompany his primary carer. This is because in such cases the Home Office's position is that the public interest in deportation (see **10.1.4**) will ordinarily outweigh the right of the British citizen child to remain in the EU, and therefore there will be no contradiction between refusing to recognise a right of residence under the case for the primary carer and arguing that the British citizen child can continue his family life in a country outside the EU.

10.6 REMOVAL TO REQUIRE ENTRY CLEARANCE

In *Chikwamba v Secretary of State for the Home Department* [2008] UKHL 40, the House of Lords had to answer this question: When determining an appeal under s 82 of the NIAA 2002 (see **Chapter 11**) on the ground that to remove the appellant would interfere disproportionately with his Article 8 right to respect for his family life, when, if ever, is it appropriate to dismiss the appeal on the basis that the appellant should be required to leave the country and seek leave to enter from an ECO abroad?

The answer was 'comparatively rarely, certainly in family cases involving children, should an Article 8 appeal be dismissed on the basis that it would be proportionate and more appropriate for the appellant to apply for leave from abroad' (per Lord Brown of Eaton-under-Heywood, at [44]).

For an example of an exceptional case justifying removal for an application to be made, see *R (Kotecha) v Secretary of State for the Home Department* [2011] EWHC 2070.

CHAPTER 11

APPEALS AND REVIEWS

11.1 APPEALS: THE GENERAL RULE

The NIAA 2002 (as amended) sets out a system of appeals, including a system for a 'one stop' comprehensive appeal. It replaces all rights of appeal established in earlier legislation. The Act establishes the principle that there is one right of appeal against a limited number of decisions made by the Secretary of State (see **11.2**). Where multiple decisions would result in multiple rights of appeal, these are subsumed into one appeal. All appealable grounds can and should be raised in an appeal (see **11.5**). Only some appeal rights can be exercised by the appellant in the UK (see **11.4**).

11.2 DECISIONS AGAINST WHICH THERE IS A RIGHT OF APPEAL

By s 82(1) of the NIAA 2002, an appeal can be made against the decision of the Secretary of State to:

(a) refuse a protection claim;

(b) refuse a human rights claim; or

(c) revoke protection status.

As to the grounds of appeal, see **11.3**.

What if there is no right of appeal? It may be possible to apply for administrative review of the refusal of an application, provided it is an eligible decision and on the basis that a case working error has occurred (see **11.16**).

11.2.1 Protection claim and status

A protection claim is a claim for asylum or humanitarian protection.

A person has protection status when granted leave to remain as a refugee, or humanitarian protection.

See **Chapter 9**.

11.2.2 Human rights claim

A human rights claim includes the following applications made under the Immigration Rules:

(a)   long residence under para 276B (see **3.8.8**);

(b)   private life under paras 276ADE(1) or 276DE (see **8.13**);

(c)   asylum under Part 11 (see **Chapter 9**);

(d)   family member under Appendix FM, but not BPILR (bereavement) or DVILR (domestic violence) (see **Chapter 8**).

11.2.3 EEA claims

There are appeal rights against the refusal to issue an EEA family permit and certain other EEA decisions under reg 26 of the I (EEA) Regs 2006 (see **11.10**).

11.2.4 Deprivation of citizenship

Under s 40A of the BNA 1981, there is a right of appeal against a decision to make an order depriving a person of a British citizenship status (see **2.2.9** and **11.9**).

11.2.5 Transitional provisions

Note that refusal of entry clearance and refusal to vary leave to remain may in some situations be appealable where the application was made before the IA 2014 came into force. These transitional provisions are outside the scope of this book.

11.3 GROUNDS OF APPEAL

An appeal under s 82(1)(a) of the NIAA 2002 (refusal of protection claim – see **11.2.1**) must be brought on one or more of the following grounds:

(a)   that removal of the appellant from the UK would breach the UK's obligations under the Refugee Convention;

(b)   that removal of the appellant from the UK would breach the UK's obligations in relation to persons eligible for a grant of humanitarian protection;

(c)   that removal of the appellant from the UK would be unlawful under s 6 of the HRA 1998 (public authority not to act contrary to the ECHR).

An appeal under s 82(1)(b) (refusal of human rights claim – see **11.2.2**) must be brought on the ground that the decision is unlawful under s 6 of the HRA 1998.

An appeal under s 82(1)(c) (revocation of protection status – see **11.2.1**) must be brought on one or more of the following grounds:

(a)   that the decision to revoke the appellant's protection status breaches the UK's obligations under the Refugee Convention;

(b)   that the decision to revoke the appellant's protection status breaches the UK's obligations in relation to persons eligible for a grant of humanitarian protection.

11.4 WHERE APPEAL RIGHTS ARE EXERCISABLE

Section 92 of the NIAA 2002 determines whether an appeal right is exercisable whilst the appellant is in the UK, or if it can be made only from abroad. The general rule is that where the appellant was outside the UK when he made the claim, he must appeal from outside the UK. When the appellant was inside the UK when he made the claim, he may appeal from within the UK unless the claim has been certified under s 94 (see **11.11**) or s 94B (see **11.12**).

11.5 THE 'ONE STOP' PROCESS

11.5.1 Notice of appealable decision

The Immigration (Notices) Regulations 2003 (SI 2003/658) provide that a decision maker (eg ECO, immigration officer, Secretary of State) must give written notice to a person of any appealable decision. The notice must include, or be accompanied by, a statement of the reasons for the decision to which it relates.

The notice must also include, or be accompanied by, a statement advising the person of his right of appeal and the statutory provision on which his right of appeal is based; whether or not such an appeal may be brought while in the UK; the grounds on which such an appeal may be brought; and the facilities available for advice and assistance in connection with such an appeal.

Further, by s 120 of the NIAA 2002, the notice will set a deadline for the appellant to provide, where appropriate:

(a)   his reasons for wishing to enter or remain in the UK;

(b)   any grounds on which he should be permitted to enter or remain in the UK; and

(c)   any grounds on which he should not be removed from or required to leave the UK.

After being served with a s 120 notice, the appellant has an on-going duty, so that a further statement should be made if a new reason or ground for remaining in the UK arises. Any reasons or grounds should be raised as soon as reasonably practicable. There is no requirement to reiterate the same grounds or reasons of which the Secretary of State is already aware, or any that have been considered.

11.5.2 Consequences of failing to disclose all grounds of appeal

What if a s 120 notice is not answered? Any attempt to raise such grounds later on may lead to certification under s 96 of the NIAA 2002, with the effect that there can be no appeal against the decision, or that those grounds cannot be raised in connection with a further appeal.

Before the Secretary of State can lawfully decide to certify, four steps must be taken:

(Step 1)   The Secretary of State must be satisfied that the person was notified of a right of appeal under s 82 of the Act against another immigration decision (s 96(1)), or that the person received a notice under s 120 by virtue of an application other than that to which the new decision relates or by virtue of a decision other than the new decision (s 96(2)).

(Step 2)   The Secretary of State must conclude that the claim or application to which the new decision relates relies on a matter that could have been raised in an appeal against the old decision (s 96(1)(b)), or that the new decision relates to an application or claim that relies on a matter that should have been but has not been raised in a statement made in response to that notice (s 96(2)(b)).

(Step 3)   The Secretary of State must form the opinion that there is no satisfactory reason for that matter's not having been raised in an appeal against the old decision (s 96(1)(c)), or that there is no satisfactory reason for that matter's not having been raised in a statement made in response to that notice (s 96(2)(c)).

(Step 4)   The Secretary of State must consider whether, having regard to all relevant factors, he should exercise his discretion to certify, and must conclude that it is appropriate to exercise the discretion in favour of certification.

As to the interpretation of the word 'matter' in Steps 2 and 3, see *Khan v Secretary of State for the Home Department* [2014] EWCA Civ 88.

11.5.3 Other certificates under s 96

Certificates can be issued under s 96 of the NIAA 2002 otherwise than in relation to s 120 notices (see **11.5.2**).

Note that no appeal can be brought on any ground against an otherwise appealable decision if the Secretary of State or immigration officer certifies that the person was notified of a right of appeal against another decision (whether or not any appeal was lodged or completed) *and* that in his opinion the person made the claim or application in order to delay removal, or the removal of a family member, *and* that in his opinion the person had no other legitimate purpose for making the claim or application. If an appeal has already been brought, the appeal may not be continued if a certificate is issued.

Further, s 96 prevents an appeal being brought if the Secretary of State or immigration officer certifies that a new decision relates to a ground that was raised on an earlier appeal, or which could have been raised at an appeal had the applicant chosen to exercise a right of appeal. If an appeal has already been brought, the appeal may not be continued if a certificate is issued. See, for example, *Khan v Secretary of State for the Home Department* [2014] EWCA Civ 88.

Lastly, where a further appeal right does arise, the Secretary of State or immigration officer may certify that certain grounds of appeal were already considered in an earlier appeal. The appellant is not then allowed to rely on those grounds.

The certificate may be challenged by way of an application for judicial review: see *R (Adebisi) v Secretary of State for the Home Department* [2011] LTL 5 May; *R (J) v Secretary of State for the Home Department* [2009] EWHC 705; and **Chapter 12**.

11.6 THE APPEALS SYSTEM

11.6.1 The First-tier Tribunal (Immigration and Asylum Chamber)

A right of appeal against an appealable decision lies to the Immigration and Asylum Chamber (IAC) under s 82 of the NIAA 2002 (see **11.2**).

The title of the legally-qualified member of the IAC is an Immigration Judge. All IAC appeals are heard in various appeal centres across the UK.

An appeal to the IAC may only be started by giving notice of appeal on a prescribed form in accordance with the Tribunal Procedure (First-tier Tribunal) (Immigration and Asylum Chamber) Rules 2014 (SI 2014/2604). Practitioners should be familiar with the Rules. Normally there is an initial case management review hearing. This will determine the issues in dispute and the evidence necessary to deal with them. Directions are usually given as to the filing of evidence, etc.

At the appeal hearing, the Immigration Judge determines whether or not to uphold the original decision. If it is upheld, appeal lies on a point of law to the Upper Tribunal (Immigration and Asylum Chamber). Permission to appeal is required from the IAC or, failing that, the Upper Tribunal. If both the IAC and the Upper Tribunal refuse permission to appeal, that decision can be judicially reviewed, but limited to the grounds that either:

(a)   the proposed appeal would raise some important point of principle or practice; or

(b)   there is some other compelling reason for the court to hear the appeal: see *R (Cart) v The Upper Tribunal* [2011] UKSC 28.

As to ground (b), note that in *PR (Sri Lanka) v Secretary of State for the Home Department* [2011] EWCA Civ 988, the Court of Appeal (per Carnwath LJ at [35]) stated that 'compelling means *legally* compelling, rather than compelling, perhaps, from a political or emotional point of view, although such considerations may exceptionally add weight to the legal arguments'. See also **Chapter 12**.

Appeal on a point of law from the Upper Tribunal lies to the Court of Appeal (see **11.6.2**). It is necessary to obtain that Court's permission first.

11.6.2   Appeals to the Court of Appeal

The Court of Appeal has the power to give any decision that might have been given by the IAC. It can also remit the matter for rehearing and determination by the IAC, and then may offer the IAC its opinion and make directions with which the IAC must comply.

11.7   PENDING AND ABANDONED APPEALS

Section 104 of the NIAA 2002 sets out when an appeal is pending and when it ends: it clarifies that an appeal ceases to be pending when it is 'abandoned'. An appeal may be treated as abandoned because the appellant leaves the UK, is granted leave to enter or remain, or a deportation order is made against him. However, an appeal continues to be pending so long as a further appeal may be brought, and until such further appeal is finally determined.

As a general rule, while an appeal is pending, the leave to which the appeal relates and any conditions subject to which it was granted continue to have effect. Hence, the person has a right to remain in the UK whilst pursuing the appeal. But what does 'the leave to which the appeal relates' mean? It is referring to the leave the appellant had when he made the application that has been refused. It does not mean the leave for which the appellant applied.

By s 77 of the 2002 Act, while a person's claim for asylum is pending he may not be removed from or required to leave the UK in accordance with a provision of the Immigration Acts. However, this does not prevent the giving of a direction for the claimant's removal from the UK, the making of a deportation order in respect of the claimant, or the taking of any other interim or preparatory action.

By s 78, while a person's appeal under s 82 is pending he may not be removed from or required to leave the UK in accordance with a provision of the Immigration Acts. However, this does not prevent the giving of a direction for the appellant's removal from the UK, the making of a deportation order in respect of the appellant (subject to s 79 – see below), or the taking of any other interim or preparatory action.

Section 78 only applies to an appeal brought while the appellant is in the UK in accordance with s 92 (see **11.4**).

By s 79, a deportation order may not be made in respect of a person while an appeal under s 82 against the decision to make the order could be brought (ignoring any possibility of an appeal out of time with permission) or is pending.

Note that s 99 provides that where a certificate is issued under s 97 (see **11.8**) in respect of a pending appeal, that appeal lapses.

11.8   NATIONAL SECURITY AND SIMILAR MATTERS

Section 97 of the NIAA 2002 provides that an appeal under s 82 cannot be made or continued where the Secretary of State certifies that a decision was taken to exclude or remove a person from the UK:

(a)   in the interests of national security;

(b)   in the interests of the relationship between the UK and another country; or

(c)   otherwise in the public interest.

However, under the Special Immigration Appeals Commission Act 1997, an appeal can be made to the Special Immigration Appeals Commission (SIAC). This body was set up specifically to deal with appeals where national security and other sensitive matters are a consideration. The proceedings of the SIAC are governed by the Special Immigration Appeals Commission (Procedure) Rules 2003 (SI 2003/1034).

11.9   DEPORTATION ORDER MADE ON NATIONAL SECURITY GROUNDS

Section 97 of the NIAA 2002 (see **11.8**) does not apply where the Secretary of State certifies that the decision to make a deportation order (see **10.1**) in respect of a person was taken on the grounds that his removal from the UK would be in the interests of national security. In those circumstances s 97A applies instead, and an appeal can be made only from outside the UK. If the appellant makes a human rights claim the appeal can be brought in country, unless the Secretary of State certifies that removal would not breach the ECHR. Provision is made for an appeal against such a certificate to the SIAC.

11.10   EEA NATIONALS

The I(EEA) Regs 2006 give rights of appeal that have been prescribed under EU law for EEA nationals, members of their family and certain non-EEA nationals who are members of a UK national's family (see **4.4**). There are also additional categories of persons who are entitled to similar rights under agreements to which the UK is a party or by which it is bound. The rights of appeal cover decisions relating to admission, residence and the issue or withdrawal of relevant documentation. Appeals against decisions will be heard by the IAC or, where appropriate, by the SIAC. A copy of the Regulations may be found in **Appendix 4** to this book.

11.11   UNFOUNDED CLAIMS

By s 94(1) of the NIAA 2002, the Secretary of State may certify that a protection claim (see **11.2.1**) or a human rights claim (see **11.2.2**) is clearly unfounded.

Note that if the Secretary of State is satisfied that a claimant is entitled to reside in a State listed in s 94(4), he *must* certify the claim unless he is satisfied that it is not clearly unfounded. The s 94(4) States considered to be generally safe in the context of protection and human rights claims are:

(a)   the Republic of Albania;

(b)   Bosnia-Hertzegovina;

(c)   Jamaica;

(d)   Macedonia;

(e)   the Republic of Moldova;

(f)   India;

(g)   Bolivia;

(h)   Brazil;

(i)   Ecuador;

(j)   South Africa;

(k)   Ukraine;

(l)   Mongolia;

(m)   Ghana (in respect of men);

(n)   Nigeria (in respect of men);

(o)   Gambia (in respect of men);

(p)   Kenya (in respect of men);

(q)   Liberia (in respect of men);

(r)   Malawi (in respect of men);

(s)   Mali (in respect of men);

(t)   Mauritius;

(u)   Montenegro;

(v)   Peru;

(w)   Serbia;

(x)   Sierra Leone (in respect of men);

(y)   Kosovo;

(z)   South Korea

The Home Office gives the following as examples of clearly unfounded claims:

(a)   A claim which raises nothing that could be construed as amounting to an expression of a fear of mistreatment upon return. For example, a person says he is seeking asylum but gives as his reason that he is fleeing poverty or unemployment.

(b)   The claimant expresses a fear of mistreatment, but from the objective evidence it is not arguable that the mistreatment, even if it occurred, would amount to persecution or treatment contrary to Article 3 ECHR.

(c)   The claimant expresses a fear of persecution or Article 3 treatment by non-State actors, but the State provides a sufficiency of protection against such actions.

Further, a person may not bring an appeal if the Secretary of State certifies that it is proposed to remove the person to a country of which he is not a national or citizen, and there is no reason to believe that the person's rights under the ECHR will be breached in that country. In determining whether a person in relation to whom such a certificate has been issued may be removed from the UK, the country specified in the certificate is to be regarded as a place where a person's life and liberty is not threatened by reason of his race, religion, nationality, membership of a particular social group, or political opinion, and a place from which a person will not be sent to another country otherwise than in accordance with the Refugee Convention.

Home Office guidance is that claims should be assessed at their highest and are certified only when they are bound to fail (following *R (Yogathas) v Secretary of State for the Home Department* [2002] UKHL 36).

A certificate may be challenged by way of judicial review:

> It follows that a challenge to the Secretary of State's conclusion that a claim is clearly unfounded is a rationality challenge. There is no way that a court can consider whether her conclusion was rational other than by asking itself the same question that she has considered. If the court concludes that a claim has a realistic prospect of success when the Secretary of State has reached a contrary view, the court will necessarily conclude that the Secretary of State's view was irrational. (per Lord Phillips in *ZT (Kosovo) v Secretary of State for the Home Department* [2009] UKHL 6 at [23])

How should the Secretary of State set about making the decision? His Lordship explained (at [22]) that five steps need to be taken, namely, that the Secretary of State should:

(i)   consider the factual substance and detail of the claim,

(ii)   consider how it stands with the known background data,

(iii)   consider whether in the round it is capable of belief,

(iv)   if not, consider whether some part of it is capable of belief,

(v)   consider whether, if eventually believed in whole or in part, it is capable of coming within the Convention.

If the answers are such that the claim cannot on any legitimate view succeed, then the claim is clearly unfounded; if not, not.

See further **Chapter 12**.

Where a certificate is issued concerning a national of a country listed in s 94(4) of the NIAA 2002, the first challenge may be as to whether the country in question has been properly listed. To succeed, the claimant will have to demonstrate that the evidence clearly establishes that there is a serious risk of persecution in that country that affects a significant number of people: see *R (MD (Gambia)) v Secretary of State for the Home Department* [2011] EWCA Civ 121. It follows that if the listing is lawful, the next question is whether the Secretary of State was obliged to certify the claim on the basis that it was clearly unfounded.

Note that in R (on the application of Brown (Jamaica)) v Secretary of State for the Home Department [2015] UKSC 8, the Supreme Court held that the inclusion of Jamaica on the list was unlawful.

11.12 HUMAN RIGHTS CLAIMS MADE BY PERSONS LIABLE TO DEPORTATION

By s 94B of the NIAA 2002, if a human rights claim is made by a person who is liable to deportation (see **10.1.3**), the Secretary of State may certify that claim if he considers that, despite the appeals process' not having been begun or not having been exhausted, the appellant's removal to the country or territory to which it is proposed to remove him, pending the outcome of an appeal in relation to the claim, would not be unlawful under s 6 of the HRA 1998.

The grounds on which the Secretary of State may certify a claim include in particular that the appellant would not, before the appeals process is exhausted, face a real risk of serious irreversible harm if removed to the country or territory to which it is proposed to remove him.

11.13 PERSONS EXCLUDED FROM ASYLUM

Where the Home Office decides that a claimant is excluded from asylum (see **9.5**), the Secretary of State will issue a certificate to that effect. As a result, any appeal made to the IAC or SIAC must start by considering the statements made in the Secretary of State's certificate. By s 55(4) of the IANA 2006, if the Tribunal or Commission agrees with those statements, it must dismiss such part of the appeal as amounts to an asylum claim before considering any other aspect of the case.

11.14 EUROPEAN COMMON LIST OF SAFE COUNTRIES OF ORIGIN

Section 94A of the NIAA 2002 allows the Secretary of State by order to prescribe a list of States to be known as the European Common List of Safe Countries of Origin. This is pursuant to EC Council Directive 2005/85, which provides that the Council shall adopt a minimum common list of third countries that shall be regarded by Member States as safe third countries of origin. At the time of writing no order had been made.

If a national of a State listed in the European Common List of Safe Countries of Origin, or a stateless person who was formerly habitually resident in such a State, makes an asylum claim or a human rights claim (or both), the Secretary of State will certify such claim as unfounded under s 94, unless he is satisfied that there are serious grounds for considering that the State in question is not safe given the particular circumstances of the claimant.

11.15 DEPRIVATION OF CITIZENSHIP ORDERS

By s 40A of the BNA 1981, a person given notice of a decision to make an order depriving him of his British citizenship (see **2.2.9**) has a right of appeal to the IAC. Where, however, the Secretary of State has certified that the decision to deprive was based wholly or partly in reliance on information which he believes should not be made public, the appeal at first instance will instead be heard by the SIAC.

11.16 ADMINISTRATIVE REVIEW

As we saw at **11.2**, there are very few decisions against which an appeal can be made. In those circumstances it will often be possible to apply for an administrative review of a refusal of an application, provided it is an 'eligible decision' and on the basis that a 'case working error' has occurred. The detail is set out in Appendix AR of the Immigration Rules and summarised below.

11.16.1   What decisions can be reviewed?

Only an 'eligible' decision can be reviewed. This is either the refusal of an application or its approval, but a review is sought of the period and/or conditions of leave granted. The decision must concern:

(a)   in country Tier 4 applications (see **Chapter 6**);

(b)   in country Tiers 1, 2 or 5 Migrant applications (see **Chapter 7**); or

(c)   in country applications for leave to remain, unless the applicant applied as a visitor (see **Chapter 5**) or made a protection claim (see **11.2.1**) or human rights claim (see **11.2.2**).

For applicants at the UK border, eligible decisions are those cancelling leave to enter or remain that were in force with the result that the applicant has no leave to enter or remain, due either to a change of circumstances, or to false representations or failure to disclose material facts. The applicant will be granted temporary admission if he is allowed to enter the UK to make an administrative review application.

A person who receives an eligible decision on an entry clearance application may apply for administrative review. For applicants overseas, an eligible decision is a decision to refuse an application for entry clearance, unless it was made in the category of short-term student or visitor (see **Chapter 5**), or as a human rights claim (see **11.2.2**).

11.16.2   What is a case working error?

If an eligible decision has been made, only the following case working errors can be reviewed:

(a)   That the original decision maker's decision was incorrect in relation to either:

    (i)   refusing an entry clearance application on the basis of paras 320(7A) or 320(7B) of the Immigration Rules (false representations, false documents or information, failure to disclose material facts or previous breach of conditions – see **Chapter 3**), or

    (ii)   refusing an in country application on the basis of para 322(1A) of the Immigration Rules (refusal on the basis of false representations, documents or information or failure to disclose material facts – see **Chapter 3**), or

    (iii)   cancelling leave to enter or remain that is in force as a visitor under paras V9.2 or V9.4 of Appendix V to the Immigration Rules (see **Chapter 5**),

    (iv)   cancelling leave to enter or remain that is in force at the border under para 321A(2) of the Immigration Rules (change of circumstances, false representations or failure to disclose material facts – see **Chapter 3**).

(b)   That the original decision maker's decision to refuse an application on the basis that the date of application was beyond any time limit in the Immigration Rules, was incorrect.

(c)   That the original decision maker otherwise applied the Immigration Rules incorrectly.

(d)   That the original decision maker failed to apply the Secretary of State's relevant published policy and guidance in relation to the application.

(e)   That there has been an error in calculating the correct period or conditions of immigration leave either held or to be granted.

The following examples are taken from Home Office guidance.

Examples

Case working error	Facts
Where the original decision maker's decision to refuse an application under para 322(1A) on the basis that the supporting documents were not genuine, was incorrect.	The migrant has submitted Internet bank statements that appear to have been stamped in a branch to authenticate them. The statements were verified and the issuing bank stated that they were false. The migrant has evidence from the bank stating that the verification was done incorrectly and the statements are genuine.
Where the original decision maker has incorrectly refused an application on the basis that it was made more than 28 days after leave expired.	The original decision maker uses the date on which the application was input as the date of application, rather than the date the application was posted. The 28-day period has therefore been calculated incorrectly.
Where the original decision maker applied the wrong Immigration Rules.	The caseworker applies the rules for Tier 4 (General) students rather than Tier 4 (Child) students.
Where the original decision maker applied the Immigration Rules incorrectly.	The caseworker refuses the application because a resident labour market test has not been carried out, but the applicant's occupation is exempt from this requirement.
Where the original decision maker has considered some or all of the evidence submitted incorrectly, as evidenced in the eligible decision.	Where the migrant has submitted multiple sets of bank statements and the amounts have been added up incorrectly by the original decision maker, resulting in a decision to refuse on the grounds of insufficient funds.
Where the original decision maker failed to apply the Secretary of State's relevant published policy and guidance.	The migrant's original sponsor loses his licence while the application is under consideration. The original decision maker fails to correctly apply the policy to allow the migrant 60 days to find a new sponsor and vary his application.

11.16.3   Applying for an administrative review

The requirements for an administrative review application are set out in paras 34M to 34Y in Part 1 of the Immigration Rules. A valid application can only be made either by completing the relevant online application, or by using the specified application form.

What is the deadline? An in country request must be made within 14 calendar days after the date on which the applicant received the decision, but that will be only seven calendar days if the applicant is in immigration detention. If the request is about a decision made overseas, the deadline is 28 calendar days.

What if the deadline is missed? The Secretary of State may waive the time limit if it is just to do so and the application was made as soon as reasonably practicable. The applicant will normally have to provide evidence to persuade the Secretary of State that it would be unjust not to accept the late application. Home Office guidance gives the example of an applicant who is prevented from making the application before the deadline because he is admitted to hospital as an emergency admission for immediate treatment and a period of recuperation. Here, a letter from the consultant should be produced, confirming the dates of admission and discharge and the nature of the emergency treatment. The applicant must make the application as soon as he is well enough to do so.

As a general rule an applicant is allowed one valid administrative review for each eligible decision. The exception to this is where, following an administrative review, the Home Office maintains its refusal of leave decision but on additional or different grounds. Only in these circumstances is the applicant entitled to a further administrative review, but that is limited to the new grounds.

11.16.4 How an administrative review is conducted

The Home Office case worker, immigration officer or ECO conducting the administrative review is known as the 'reviewer'. Will the reviewer be the same person who made the initial decision? No: Home Office guidance is that an administrative review is carried out by a different person on an independent team.

Home Office instructions to the reviewer are that he must:

(a) normally only consider the specific aspects of the decision the applicant is challenging. However, if it becomes clear during the review that the original decision contained errors that have not been identified, those errors must also be corrected;

(b) carefully consider all the claimed errors raised in the application and address each of them in the review decision;

(c) request additional information if the applicant is allowed to provide it (see **11.18.1**) and it is needed to conduct the review;

(d) not consider any new evidence or information unless it impacts on the decision and the applicant is allowed to provide new evidence (see **11.18.1**);

(e) consider if correcting the case work error would change the outcome of the original decision (whether or not the outcome of the review is that the original decision is overturned).

11.16.5 Evidence

The reviewer will not consider any evidence that was not before the original decision maker, except where such evidence is submitted to demonstrate that a case working error has occurred in the following circumstances:

(a) the original decision maker did not consider all the evidence submitted with the original application;

(b) the original decision maker reached an unreasonable decision as to the credibility of the applicant, where the Immigration Rules allow the original decision maker to consider credibility;

(c) documents provided with the original application were genuine; or

(d) the original decision maker incorrectly refused the application on the basis that it was made more than 28 days after leave expired.

As to (b), what test is applied by the reviewer? Home Office guidance is that the reviewer must determine whether it is more likely than not, based on the evidence and facts available, that the original decision maker made the right decision that the applicant is not credible. The following example is based on Home Office guidance.

> **EXAMPLE**
>
> Angela applies for a student visa (see Chapter 6). Her application is refused on the basis that she is not a genuine student. Angela applies for the decision to be reviewed.

> The reviewer must check whether the original caseworker made an error. He must decide whether any errors were made in respect of the relevant Immigration Rules and Home Office guidance based on the information supplied by Angela with her application, any interview with her and the caseworker's reasoning in the case notes and decision notice. The reviewer must then consider whether, based on those factors and that information, it is more likely than not that the original caseworker made the right decision.

11.16.6 Outcomes of a review

The review may conclude in any of the following ways:

(a)   it is successful and the decision is withdrawn;

(b)   it fails and the decision remains in force, and all of the reasons given for the decision are maintained;

(c)   it fails and the decision remains in force, but one or more of the reasons given for the decision is or are withdrawn; or

(d)   it fails and the decision remains in force, but with reasons different from or additional to those specified in the decision under review.

If the outcome of the administrative review is that the decision on the original application is withdrawn and leave is granted, the Home Office will refund the fee. This includes reviews of granted cases where the outcome of the review is that the original grant of leave was issued for the wrong period or subject to the wrong conditions.

CHAPTER 12

JUDICIAL REVIEW PROCEEDINGS

12.1 WHAT IS JUDICIAL REVIEW?

Judicial review involves a challenge to the legal validity of the decision. It does not allow the court of review to examine the evidence with a view to forming its own view about the substantial merits of the case. It may be that the tribunal whose decision is being challenged has done something which it had no lawful authority to do. It may have abused or misused the authority which it had. It may have departed from the procedures which either by statute or at common law as matter of fairness it ought to have observed. As regards the decision itself it may be found to be perverse, or irrational, or grossly disproportionate to what was required. Or the decision may be found to be erroneous in respect of a legal deficiency, as for example, through the absence of evidence, or of sufficient evidence, to support it, or through account being taken of irrelevant matter, or through a failure for any reason to take account of a relevant matter, or through some misconstruction of the terms of the statutory provision which the decision-maker is required to apply. But while the evidence may have to be explored in order to see if the decision is vitiated by such legal deficiencies it is perfectly clear that in a case of review, as distinct from an ordinary appeal, the court may not set about forming its own preferred view of the evidence. (per Lord Clyde in *Reid v Secretary of State for Scotland* [1998] UKHL 43)

12.1.1 Use of judicial review in immigration cases

As we saw at **11.2**, the NIAA 2002 sets out those immigration decisions against which there is a right of appeal. But what about those decisions where there is no right of appeal? Or where all appeal rights have been exhausted? This is where judicial review proceedings may be an appropriate step for the client to take.

Judicial review will be refused if an alternative remedy is more appropriate, such as where an applicant has failed to use a right of appeal, unless he can show that the circumstances are exceptional: see *R v Secretary of State for the Home Department, ex p Swati* [1986] 1 All ER 717. It is not enough to show that the right of appeal is a less convenient remedy, for instance because it must be conducted from abroad: see *Soon Ok Ryoo v Secretary of State for the Home Department* [1992] Imm AR 59. However, if it would be practically impossible to conduct the appeal from abroad, permission may be given: see *R v Chief Immigration Officer, Gatwick Airport, ex p Kharrazi* [1980] 1 WLR 1396 and *R v Secretary of State for the Home Department and Immigration Officer, Waterloo International Station, ex p Canbolat* [1997] INLR 198.

The vast majority of judicial review proceedings concern aspects of asylum and human rights claims, eg when the Secretary of State does not accept that a fresh claim was made (**9.14**), or certifies a claim as no longer appealable (**11.5.2** and **11.5.3**) or unfounded (**11.11**); deportation and removal cases (particularly human rights-based challenges: **Chapter 10**); as well as cases where the Secretary of State refuses to register or naturalise a person as a British citizen (**Chapter 2**).

12.1.2 Grounds for judicial review

The most common grounds for judicial review are set out in the extract from *Reid* at **12.1**.

The usual starting point is to consider if the decision-maker made an error of law, eg did the Secretary of State ask the right question? Otherwise, in many cases the client will be arguing that the decision made was irrational or unreasonable. The test for this was originally laid down by Lord Greene MR in the landmark Court of Appeal case of *Associated Provincial Picture Houses Ltd v Wednesbury Corporation* [1948] 1 KB 223, namely, having regard to relevant considerations only, did the decision-maker come to a conclusion that was so unreasonable that no reasonable authority could ever have come to it? Note that here consideration needs to be given as to whether the Secretary of State took into account factors that were irrelevant and/or omitted to take relevant matters into account. Equally, it should be asked whether the Secretary of State gave undue weight to one or more factors over other relevant factors.

Subsequently, the test of irrationality has been refined. In *CCSU v Minister for Civil Service* [1984] 3 All ER 935, Lord Diplock stated that, to be irrational, a decision needs to be so outrageous in its defiance of logic, or of accepted moral standards, that no sensible person could have arrived at it. In the later case of *R v Ministry of Defence, ex p Smith* [1996] 1 All ER 257, the Court of Appeal found that, to establish irrationality, the decision or policy should be beyond the range of reasonable responses open to the decision-maker.

When making a decision, the Secretary of State or a court must take all relevant considerations into account. This is often known as the 'anxious scrutiny' requirement. In *WM (DRC) v Secretary of State for the Home Department* [2006] EWCA Civ 1495, Buxton LJ stated, at [7], that in an asylum case, for example, 'the consideration of all the decision-makers, the Secretary of State, the [Immigration Judge] and the court, must be informed by the anxious scrutiny of the material that is axiomatic in decisions that if made incorrectly may lead to the Applicant's exposure to persecution.' As Carnwath LJ later explained in *R (YH) v Secretary of State for the Home Department* [2010] EWCA Civ 116, at [24], the requirement has 'by usage acquired special significance as underlining the very special human context in which such cases are brought, and the need for decisions to show by their reasoning that every factor which might tell in favour of an Applicant has been properly taken into account'.

12.1.3 Remedies

The most common remedy sought in an immigration case is for the decision to be quashed, ie declared void. The court may, in addition, remit the case to the Secretary of State for the Home Department, or relevant tribunal, with a direction to reconsider it according to the findings of the court. See further **12.3.6**.

12.2 MAKING A CLAIM: PRE-ACTION STEPS

Before an application is made to the court, the Pre-Action Protocol for Judicial Review should be consulted (there is a copy at **Appendix 15**). The Protocol sets out a code of best practice and contains the steps which parties should normally follow before starting court proceedings. The Protocol will not be appropriate where judicial review is required of a tribunal decision or in urgent cases, for example when directions have been set, or are in force, for the client's removal from the UK.

When following the Protocol, a claimant must always have in mind the fact that any application for judicial review must be filed promptly, and in any event, not later than three months after the grounds to make the claim first arose.

12.2.1 Letter before claim

Where the Protocol applies, the claimant should send a letter before claim to the defendant. This will be the Secretary of State for the Home Department. The relevant address is the

Judicial Review Unit at St Anne's House, 20–26 Wellesley Road, Croydon CR9 2RL. The letter should clearly, succinctly and accurately identify the issues in dispute and seek to establish whether litigation can be avoided. Normally, the suggested standard format for the letter outlined at Annex A should be used, but in addition you should include, where known and appropriate, the client's Home Office, Port, Tribunal and National Asylum Support Service reference numbers. Otherwise, ensure the client's full name, nationality and date of birth are set out.

There is a specimen letter before claim at **12.5**.

12.2.2 Home Office response

Home Office guidance is that if the caseworker decides the representations in the letter before claim have merit then he should try to rectify the problem without the need for court proceedings. If the representations are without merit, the letter of response should fully explain the reasons for that decision and answer any queries the claimant has made. If the caseworker decides that some of the claim has merit but other points do not, the response should comprehensively set out the reasons for this decision, with a full explanation of what is agreed and what steps will be taken to rectify this, and why the other points are not accepted.

12.3 COURT PROCEEDINGS

Judicial review proceedings must be started in the High Court (see the Senior Courts Act 1981, s 31). Claims are dealt with by the Administrative Court (save a challenge to the Secretary of State's refusal to treat submissions as a fresh asylum or human rights claim (**9.14**) as these reviews are normally transferred to the Upper Tribunal under the Senior Courts Act 1981, s 31A).

The judicial review procedure is governed by Part 54 of the Civil Procedure Rules 1998 (SI 1998/3132) (CPR 1998). By r 54.1(2)(a), a 'claim for judicial review' is defined as 'a claim to review the lawfulness of an enactment; or a decision, action or failure to act in relation to the exercise of a public function'.

12.3.1 The two stages of an application

The judicial review procedure has the unusual feature of two separate stages. First, the claimant must start the proceedings by filing a CPR 1998, Part 8 claim form and obtain the court's permission to proceed with it. If permission is granted then, secondly, after the parties have filed various documents, a full judicial review hearing takes place.

12.3.2 The need for a prompt application

An application for permission to apply for judicial review must be made promptly, and in any event within three months from the date when grounds for the application first arose. The time limit cannot be extended by agreement between the parties. The court may extend the period if there is good reason for the delay, but delay may still result in refusal of a remedy at the final hearing (R (*Lichfield Securities Ltd*) *v Lichfield District Council* (2001) *The Times*, 30 March).

12.3.3 Applying for permission

The claim form and other documents prescribed by CPR 1998, Practice Direction 54A (such as a detailed statement of the grounds for bringing the claim, a statement of the facts relied on, any written evidence relied on and a copy of any order sought to have quashed) must be filed and served on the defendant and any interested party. Where the review is sought of a tribunal decision, the Secretary of State will be an interested party. Rule 6.10 of the CPR 1998 provides that service on a government department must be effected on the solicitor acting for that department, which in the case of the Home Office is the Treasury Solicitor. The address for the Treasury Solicitor can be found in the Annex to Part 66 of the CPR 1998.

The defendant and any interested party have 21 days to acknowledge service of the claim form. Where a party filing an acknowledgment intends to contest the claim, a summary of the grounds on which it will be contested must be included.

12.3.4 Permission hearing

Normally the court determines whether or not to grant permission to proceed without an oral hearing. Permission is granted if the claimant can show on the materials filed a case which is 'arguable' and so requires a full investigation of the substantive merits (see R v Inland Revenue Commissioners, ex p National Federation of Self-Employed and Small Businesses Ltd [1982] AC 617).

If permission to proceed is refused or granted subject to conditions and/or on certain grounds only, the claimant may within seven days request an oral hearing for that decision to be reconsidered.

12.3.5 Next steps if permission granted

If permission to proceed is granted, the court will normally give case management directions as to how the parties are to prepare for the final hearing. This normally includes the the filing and service of a detailed response by the defendant and any interested parties, along with their written evidence. The claimant will prepare the trial bundle and each party should file a skeleton argument.

12.3.6 The hearing

The hearing usually takes place before a single judge nominated to hear cases in the Administrative Court. The parties' advocates make their respective submissions on the evidence filed. Only in exceptional cases will any witnesses be called and cross-examined.

What if the key factual evidence submitted to the court is disputed? The court's approach to this issue was summarised by Silber J in R (McVey) v Secretary of State for Health [2010] EWHC 437 as follows (at [35]):

(i)   The basic rule is that where there is a dispute on evidence in a judicial review application, then in the absence of cross-examination, the facts in the defendants' evidence must be assumed to be correct;

(ii)   An exception to this rule arises where the documents show that the defendants' evidence cannot be correct; and that

(iii) The proper course for a claimant who wishes to challenge the correctness of an important aspect of the defendant's evidence relating to a factual matter on which the judge will have to make a critical factual finding is to apply to cross-examine the maker of the witness statement on which the defendant relies.

What are the court's powers when making a quashing order? The court will usually remit the matter to the decision-maker, direct it to reconsider the case and reach a decision in accordance with the judgment of the court.

When can the court substitute its own decision? Only if that decision was made by a court or tribunal, the decision is quashed on the ground that there was an error of law, and without that error there would have been only one decision which the court or tribunal could have reached.

12.4 APPEALS FROM JUDICIAL REVIEW DECISIONS

What if permission to proceed is refused at an oral hearing or on reconsideration? The claimant can apply within seven days to the Court of Appeal for permission to appeal that decision. Note that the Court of Appeal is not limited to granting permission to appeal but may grant permission for the judicial review. What if the Court of Appeal refuses permission to appeal? That is the end of the matter. Only if permission to appeal is granted but permission to proceed with the judicial review claim is refused can an appeal be made to the Supreme Court.

What if a party does not agree with the outcome of a judicial review? Permission to appeal can be sought from the court or the Court of Appeal. Any further appeal will be to the Supreme Court.

12.5 SPECIMEN LETTER BEFORE CLAIM

To
The Secretary of State for the Home Department,
Judicial Review Unit,
St Anne's House, 20–26 Wellesley Road,
Croydon, CR9 2RL.

The claimant
Christopher Katongo

Reference details
Home Office reference number [   ].

The details of the matter being challenged
The decision made by the Secretary of State under Section 94 of the Nationality Immigration and Asylum Act 2002 (NIAA 2002) to certify as clearly unfounded the claimant's claim that his removal from the UK would be a disproportionate interference with his right to a family and private life under Article 8 of the European Convention on Human Rights (ECHR).

The issue

1. *Date of decision:* [   ]

2. *Relevant law*

A case which is clearly unfounded is one which has no real prospect of success if an appeal was made to the First Tier Tribunal, Immigration and Asylum Chamber.

The Secretary of State was required to give the claim anxious scrutiny. In determining whether the test was met, the Secretary of State had to consider, amongst other matters, the factual substance and detail of the claim; how it stands with the known background data; whether in the round it is capable of belief; if not, whether some part of it is capable of belief; and whether if eventually believed, in whole or in part, it is capable of coming within the ECHR. Only if the answers are such that the claim cannot on any legitimate view succeed is the claim clearly unfounded (*ZT (Kosovo) v Secretary of State for the Home Department* [2009] UKHL 6).

The Secretary of State had to approach the matter by addressing the questions set out by Lord Bingham in paragraph 17 of *R (Razgar) v Secretary of State for the Home Department* [2004] 2 AC 368, as further explained by the subsequent case of *R (Huang) v Secretary of State for the Home Department* [2007] UKHL 11, namely:

(a) Will the proposed removal be an interference by a public authority with the exercise of the applicant's rights to respect for his private or, as the case may be, family life?

(b) If so, will such interference have consequences of such gravity as potentially to engage the operation of Article 8?

(c) If so, is such interference in accordance with law?

(d) If so, is such interference necessary in a democratic society in a number of legitimate interests including, on the established case law, the maintenance of effective immigration control?

(e) If so, is such interference proportionate to the legitimate public ends sought to be achieved?

The relationship of a nephew and his aunt as adults falls within the scope of family life as it started when the nephew was a child and continued after he reached 18 (*Secretary of State for the Home Department v HK (Turkey)* [2010] EWCA Civ 583), and there are special elements of dependency beyond normal emotional ties (*Kugathas v Secretary of State for the Home Department* [2003] EWCA Civ 31 and *Odawey v Entry Clearance Officer* [2011] EWCA Civ 840).

By paragraph 276ADE of the Immigration Rules the Secretary of State had to consider granting the claimant leave to remain on the grounds of his private life in the UK as he is over 18, he has lived continuously in the UK for less than 20 years and has no ties (including social, cultural or family) with the country to which he would have to go if required to leave the UK, namely, Zambia.

As to proportionality, the Supreme Court (then the House of Lords) in *Huang* stated at paragraph 20 that the ultimate question for the appellate authority is whether the refusal of leave to enter or remain, in circumstances where the life of the family cannot reasonably be expected to be enjoyed elsewhere, taking full account of all considerations weighing in favour of the refusal, prejudices the family life of the applicant in a manner that is sufficiently serious to amount to a breach of the fundamental right protected by Article 8.

3. Relevant facts

The claimant is a national of Zambia, aged 22. He was born in Zambia and lived there until he was 15. When he was 5 years old, his mother died. Shortly afterwards his father was diagnosed with a terminal illness. The claimant was an only child. He was cared for, together with his father, by his paternal grandmother. His father died when he was 10. The claimant's grandmother died when he was 15. It was at this point that the claimant was invited by his aunt, Mrs Francis, to visit her and her family in Huddersfield, England. Mrs Francis is a British citizen and the claimant's only living relative.

The claimant entered the UK as a minor. His passport was stamped with a 6-month visitor's visa but he stayed on in the UK when that period expired. His case, supported by Mrs Francis, is that Mrs Francis decided the claimant should stay with her family in the UK permanently but she overlooked applying for the appropriate permissions for the claimant from the immigration authorities.

The claimant had no formal education in Zambia. He can speak little English. He cannot speak Bemba which is spoken nationwide in Zambia. He has no understanding of the cultural norms in Zambia. Mrs Francis describes him as very slow in his learning. She says that he is not capable of looking after himself as an adult. The claimant is dependent on her both financially and emotionally. This is supported by a doctor's report. The report also confirms that the claimant has suffered from time to time with depression and that he has mentioned on occasions that he was thinking of committing suicide because he is very lonely and, in particular, because he misses his father.

4. Why the decision is wrong

The claimant has established a family and private life in the UK. He entered as a child and has been here for approximately 7 years. During that time he has been staying with and has been both financially and emotionally dependent on his aunt, Mrs Francis. The Secretary of State failed to give sufficient weight to the significant relationship that the claimant has with, and his dependency on, Mrs Francis. He is dependent upon her for his day to day health and wellbeing. He has no family, friends or social network to turn to for support in Zambia.

To remove the claimant from the UK is a disproportionate interference with that established family life. The Secretary of State's conclusion that the claimant entered the UK by deception is erroneous. It is the claimant's case that when he arrived in the UK he told the Immigration Officer that he was coming to stay with his aunt in Huddersfield and his visa was stamped. It is Mrs Francis' evidence that she had given the claimant a letter to hand to the immigration authorities confirming this. It was only after the claimant had lived with the family in Huddersfield for several months that it was decided the claimant should remain here permanently with them. This is not a case where the claimant chose to enter or remain in the UK unlawfully. Nor is it a case where the claimant has developed a private and family life in flagrant disregard of orders requiring him to leave the UK.

The claimant is a depressed young man who is suffering from the loss of all of his immediate family members. He was brought up in a family environment and this has continued for the last 7 years in the UK. To separate him from Mrs Francis' family unit, will, as the medical report states, significantly contribute to his state of alienation and depression.

In all these circumstances the Secretary of State's conclusion that the claimant would be able to establish and maintain a private life in his own right on his return to Zambia is irrational.

The claimant has a realistic prospect of persuading an appeal tribunal that to remove him from the UK would be a disproportionate interference with the family life that he has established here.

The details of the action that the defendant is expected to take
The Secretary of State is asked to review the decision and revoke the certificate.

The details of the legal advisers dealing with this claim and the claimant's address for reply and service of court documents
The details of the claimant's legal advisers and his address for service are as follows:

XYZ Lawyers LLP
1 The Avenue
Nowhere
Mythshire
MY11 1AB
Tel: 012345678
Ref: 123/ABC/CK

The details of any interested parties
n/a

Information sought and documents that are considered relevant and necessary
If the Secretary of State intends to rely on additional information and/or documents, please ensure that full details and copies are enclosed with the reply to this letter.

Proposed reply date
Please ensure that a reply is given within 14 days.

APPENDICES

Immigration Rules

The Immigration Rules are updated to 17 September 2015

	Paragraph number
Introduction	
Implementation and transitional provisions	4
Application	5
Interpretation	6
Public funds clarification	6A–6C
Part 1: General provisions regarding leave to enter or remain in the United Kingdom	
Leave to enter the United Kingdom	7–9
Exercise of the power to refuse leave to enter the United Kingdom	10
Suspension of leave to enter or remain in the United Kingdom	10A
Cancellation of leave to enter or remain in the United Kingdom	10B
Requirement for persons arriving in the United Kingdom or seeking entry through the Channel Tunnel to produce evidence of identity and nationality	11
Requirement for a person not requiring leave to enter the United Kingdom to prove that he has the right of abode	12–14
Common Travel Area	15
Admission for certain British passport holders	16–17
Persons outside the United Kingdom	17A–17B
Returning residents	18–20
Non-lapsing leave	20A
Holders of restricted travel documents and passports	21–23
Leave to enter granted on arrival in the United Kingdom	23A–23B
Entry clearance	24–30C
Variation of leave to enter or remain in the United Kingdom	31–33A
Specified forms and procedures for applications or claims in connection with immigration	A34–34D
Variation of applications or claims for leave to remain	34E–34F
Determination of the date of an application or claim (or variation of an application or claim) in connection with immigration	34G–34I
Withdrawn applications or claims for leave to remain in the United Kingdom	34J–34K
Specified forms and procedures in connection with applications for administrative review	34L–34Y
Undertakings	35
Medical	36–39
Students	39A
Specified documents	39B
Indefinite leave to enter or remain	39C
Part 2: Transitional provisions Part 2 and Appendix V: Immigration Rules for Visitors	

	Paragraph number
Part 3: Persons seeking to enter or remain in the United Kingdom for studies	
Requirements for leave to enter the United Kingdom to take the Professional and Linguistic Assessments Board (PLAB Test) or an Objective Structured Clinical Examination (OSCE)	75A – 75F
Requirements for leave to enter to undertake a clinical attachment or dental observer post	75G – 75M
Spouses or civil partners of students or prospective students granted leave under this part of the Rules	76–78
Children of students or prospective students granted leave under this part of the Rules	79–81
Prospective students	A82–87
Part 4: Persons seeking to enter or remain in the United Kingdom in an 'au pair' placement, as a working holidaymaker or for training or work experience	
Spouses of persons with limited leave to enter or remain under paragraphs 110–121	122–124
Children of persons with limited leave to enter or remain under paragraphs 110–121	125–127
Part 5: Persons seeking to enter or remain in the United Kingdom for employment	
Work permit employment	128A–135
Requirements for indefinite leave to remain as a highly skilled migrant	135G–135HA
Representatives of overseas newspapers, news agencies and broadcasting organisations	136–143
Representatives of Overseas Business	144–151
Private servants in diplomatic households	152–159
Domestic workers in private households	159A–159H
Overseas government employees	160–169
Ministers of religion, missionaries and members of religious orders	170–177
Airport based operational ground staff of overseas-owned airlines	178–185
Persons with United Kingdom ancestry	186–193
Partners of persons who have or have had leave to enter or remain under paragraphs 128–193 (but not paragraphs 135I–135K)	193A–196F
Children of persons with limited leave to enter or remain under paragraphs 128–193 (but not paragraphs 135I–135K)	196G–199B
Part 6: Persons seeking to enter or remain in the United Kingdom as a businessman, self-employed person, investor, writer, composer or artist	
Part 6A: Points-Based System	
General requirements for indefinite leave to remain	245AAA
Documents not submitted with applications	245AA
Specified documents for students previously sponsored by an overseas government or international scholarship agency	245A
Tier 1 (Exceptional Talent) Migrants	245B–245BF
Tier 1 (General) Migrants	245C–245CE
Tier 1 (Entrepreneur) Migrants	245D–245DF
Tier 1 (Investor) Migrants	245E–245EF
Tier 1 (Graduate Entrepreneur) Migrants	245F–245FC
Tier 2 (Intra Company Transfer) Migrants	245G–245GF
Tier 2 (General) Migrants, Tier 2 (Minister of Religion) Migrants and Tier 2 (Sportsperson) Migrants	245H–245HF

	Paragraph number
Tier 5 (Youth Mobility Scheme) Temporary Migrants	245ZI–245ZL
Tier 5 (Temporary Worker) Migrants	245ZM–245ZS
Tier 4 (General) Student	245ZT–245ZY
Tier 4 (Child) Student	245ZZ–245ZZE
Part 7: Other Categories	
Persons exercising rights of access to a child resident in the United Kingdom	A246–248F
EEA nationals and their families	255–257B
Retired persons of independent means	266–270
Partners of persons who have or have had limited leave to enter or remain in the United Kingdom as retired persons of independent means	271–273F
Children of persons with limited leave to enter or remain in the United Kingdom as retired persons of independent means	274–276
Long residence	276A–276D
Private life	276ADE–276DH
HM Forces	276DI–276QA
Spouses, civil partners, unmarried or same-sex partners of persons settled or seeking settlement in the United Kingdom in accordance with paragraphs 276E to 276Q (HM Forces rules) or of members of HM Forces who are exempt from immigration control under section 8(4)(a) of the Immigration Act 1971 and have at least 5 years' continuous service	276R–276W
Children of a parent, parents or a relative settled or seeking settlement in the United Kingdom under paragraphs 276E to 276Q (HM Forces rules) or of members of HM Forces who are exempt from immigration control under section 8(4)(a) of the Immigration Act 1971 and have at least 5 years' continuous service	276X–267AC
Spouses, civil partners, unmarried or same-sex partners of armed forces members who are exempt from immigration control under section 8(4) of the Immigration Act 1971	276AD–276AF
Children of armed forces members who are exempt from immigration control under Section 8(4) of the Immigration Act 1971	276AG–276AI
Limited leave to enter for relevant Afghan citizens	276BA1–276BS1
Parent of a Tier 4 (child) student	276BT1–276BV1
Part 8: Family members	
Transitional provisions and interaction between Part 8 and Appendix FM	A277–A281
Spouses and civil partners	277–289
Victims of domestic violence	289A–289C
Fiance(e)s and proposed civil partners	289AA–295
Unmarried and same-sex partners	295AA–295O
Children	296–316F
Parents, grandparents and other dependent relatives	317–319
Family members of relevant points-based system migrants	319A–319K
Other family members of persons with limited leave to enter or remain in the United Kingdom as a refugee or beneficiary of humanitarian protection	319L–319U
Parents, grandparents and other dependent relatives of persons with limited leave to enter or remain in the United Kingdom as a refugee or beneficiary of humanitarian protection	319V–319Y

	Paragraph number
Part 9 – General grounds for the refusal of entry clearance, leave to enter, leave to remain, variation of leave to enter or remain and curtailment of leave in the United Kingdom	
Refusal of entry clearance or leave to enter the United Kingdom	A320–320
Refusal of leave to enter in relation to a person in possession of an entry clearance	321–321A
Refusal of variation of leave to enter or remain or curtailment of leave	322–323C
Crew members	324
Part 10: Registration with the police	325–326
Part 11: Asylum	326A–352H
Part 11A: Temporary Protection	354–356B
Part 11B: Asylum	357–361
Part 12: Procedure and Rights of appeal	353–352B
Part 13: Deportation	A362–400
Part 14: Stateless persons	401–416
Part 15: Condition to hold an Academic Technology Approval Scheme (ATAS) clearance certificate	417
Appendix 1: DELETED	
Appendix 2: Countries or territories whose nationals or citizens are relevant foreign nationals for the purposes of Part 10 of these Rules	
Appendix 3: DELETED	
Appendix 4: DELETED	
Appendix 5: DELETED	
Appendix 6: Disciplines for which an Academic Technology Approval Scheme certificate from the Counter-Proliferation Department of the Foreign and Commonwealth Office is required for the purposes of Tier 4 of the Points Based System	
Appendix 7 – Statement of Written Terms and Conditions of employment required in paragraphs 159A (v), 159D(iv) and 159EA(iii)	
Appendix A: Attributes	
Appendix AR	
Appendix Armed Forces	
Appendix B: English language – English language	
Appendix C: Maintenance (funds)	
Appendix D: Immigration rules for leave to remain as a Highly Skilled Migrant as at 28 February 2008	
Appendix E: Maintenance (funds) for the family of Relevant Points Based Systems Migrants	
Appendix F: Archived Immigration Rules	
Appendix FM: Family members	
Appendix FM-SE: Family members – specified evidence	
Appendix G: Countries and territories participating in the Tier 5 Youth mobility scheme and annual allocations of places for 2014	
Appendix H: Applicants who are subject to different documentary requirements under Tier 4 of the Points Based System	
Appendix I: Pay requirements which the Secretary of State intends to apply to applications for indefinite leave to remain from Tier 2 (General) and Tier 2 (Sportspersons) migrants made on or after 6 April 2016	

	Paragraph number
Appendix J: Codes of practice for Tier 2 sponsors, Tier 5 sponsors and employers of work permit holders	
Appendix K: Shortage occupation list	
Appendix KoLL: Knowledge of language and life	
Appendix L: Designated competent body criteria for Tier 1 (Exceptional talent) applications	
Appendix M: Sports governing bodies for Tier 2 (Sportsperson) and Tier 5 (Temporary worker – creative and sporting) applications	
Appendix N: Approved Tier 5 Government authorised exchange schemes	
Appendix O: List of English Language tests that have been assessed as meeting the UK Border Agency's requirements	
Appendix P: Lists of financial institutions that do not satisfactorily verify financial statements, or whose financial statements are accepted	
Appendix Q: DELETED	
Appendix R: DELETED	
Appendix S: DELETED	
Appendix T: Tuberculosis screening	
Appendix V: Immigration Rules for visitors	

Introduction

The Home Secretary has made changes in the Rules laid down by him as to the practice to be followed in the administration of the Immigration Acts for regulating entry into and the stay of persons in the United Kingdom and contained in the statement laid before Parliament on 23 March 1990 (HC 251) (as amended). This statement contains the Rules as changed and replaces the provisions of HC 251 (as amended).

2.   Immigration Officers, Entry Clearance Officers and all staff of the Home Office will carry out their duties without regard to the race, colour or religion of persons seeking to enter or remain in the United Kingdom

3.   In these Rules words importing the masculine gender include the feminine unless the contrary intention appears.

Implementation and transitional provisions

4.   These Rules come into effect on 1 October 1994 and will apply to all decisions taken on or after that date save that any application made before 1 October 1994 for entry clearance, leave to enter or remain or variation of leave to enter or remain other than an application for leave by a person seeking asylum shall be decided under the provisions of HC 251, as amended, as if these Rules had not been made.

Application

5.   Save where expressly indicated, these Rules do not apply to those persons who are entitled to enter or remain in the United Kingdom by virtue of the provisions of the 2006 EEA Regulations. But any person who is not entitled to rely on the provisions of those Regulations is covered by these Rules.

Interpretation

6.   In these Rules the following interpretations apply:

‘the **Immigration Acts**’ has the same meaning as it has in the Interpretation Act 1978.

‘**the 1993 Act**’ is the Asylum and Immigration Appeals Act 1993.

‘**the 1996 Act**’ is the Asylum and Immigration Act 1996

‘**the 2006 EEA Regulations**’ means the Immigration (European Economic Area) Regulations 2006

‘**adoption**’ unless the contrary intention appears, includes a de facto adoption in accordance with the requirements of paragraph 309A of these Rules, and ‘adopted’ and ‘adoptive parent’ should be construed accordingly.

In Appendix FM references to **'application for leave to remain'** include an application for variation of leave to enter or remain of a person in the UK.

'Approved Destination Status Agreement with China' means the Memorandum of Understanding on visa and related issues concerning tourist groups from the People's Republic of China to the United Kingdom as a approved destination, signed on 21 January 2005.

'a bona fide private education institution' is a private education institution which:

(a)   maintains satisfactory records of enrolment and attendance of students, and supplies these to the Border and Immigration Agency when requested;

(b)   provides courses which involve a minimum of 15 hours organised daytime study per week;

(c)   ensures a suitably qualified tutor is present during the hours of study to offer teaching and instruction to the students;

(d)   offers courses leading to qualifications recognised by the appropriate accreditation bodies;

(e)   mploys suitably qualified staff to provide teaching, guidance and support to the students;

(f)   provides adequate accommodation, facilities, staffing levels and equipment to support the numbers of students enrolled at the institution; and

(g)   if it offers tuition support to external students at degree level, ensures that such students are registered with the UK degree awarding body.

'Business day' means any day other than Saturday or Sunday, a day which is a bank holiday under the Banking and Financial Dealings Act 1971 in the part of the United Kingdom to which the notice is sent, Christmas Day or Good Friday.

'civil partner' means a civil partnership which exists under or by virtue of the Civil Partnership Act 2004 (and any reference to a civil partner is to be read accordingly);

'conviction' means conviction for a criminal offence in the UK or any other country.

'curtailment' in relation to the curtailment of a person's leave to enter or remain in the UK, means curtailing their leave such that they will have a shorter period of, or no, leave remaining.

'degree level study' means a course which leads to a recognised United Kingdom degree at bachelor's level or above, or an equivalent qualification at level 6 or above of the revised National Qualifications Framework, or levels 9 or above of the Scottish Credit and Qualifications Framework.

Under Part 8 of these Rules, **'post-graduate level study'** means a course at level 7 or above of the revised National Qualifications Framework or Qualifications and Credit Framework, or level 11 or above of the Scottish Credit and Qualifications Framework, which leads to a recognised United Kingdom postgraduate degree at Master's level or above, or an equivalent qualification at the same level.

'foundation degree' means a programme of study which leads to a qualification awarded by an English higher education institution with degree awarding powers which is at a minimum of level 5 on the revised National Qualifications Framework, or awarded on a directly equivalent basis in the devolved administrations.

'Pathway Course' means a course which prepares a student for progression to another course at a specific UK recognised body or a body in receipt of public funding as a higher education institution from the Department of Employment and Learning in Northern Ireland, the Higher Education Funding Council for England, the Higher Education Funding Council for Wales or the Scottish Funding Council. It does not include a pre-sessional course.

'primary degree' means a qualification obtained from a course of degree level study, which did not feature as an entry requirement a previous qualification obtained from degree level study. An undergraduate degree is a primary degree. A Masters degree that has a Bachelor degree as an entry requirement is not a primary degree.

A **'UK recognised body'** is an institution that has been granted degree awarding powers by either a Royal Charter, an Act of Parliament or the Privy Council. For the purposes of these Rules we will consider the Foundation Programme Office, Health Education South London and the Health Education Yorkshire and Humber as equivalent to UK recognised bodies.

'Embedded College offering Pathway Courses' means a sponsor recognised by the Home Office as a private provider, usually part of a network and operating within or near to the premises of a higher education institution, delivering pathway courses which prepare students for entry to higher education programmes at that a higher education institution. This does not include pre-sessional courses. The higher education institution must be a UK recognised body, or a body in receipt of public funding as a higher education institution from the Department for Employment and Learning in Northern Ireland, the Higher Education Funding Council for England, the Higher Education Funding Council for Wales, or the Scottish Funding Council.

A '**UK listed body**' is an institution that is not a UK recognised body but which provides full courses that lead to the award of a degree by a UK recognised body.

'**Academy**' means an institution defined by and established under the Academies Act 2010, as amended. This includes academy schools, 16-19 academies and alternative provision academies.

An '**Independent School**' means a school which is:

(a)   a school in England and Wales at which full time education is provided for five or more pupils of compulsory school age (whether or not such education is also provided at it for pupils under or over that age) and which is not a) a school maintained by a local education authority, or b) a special school not so maintained;

(b)   a school in Scotland at which full-time education is provided for pupils of school age (whether or not such education is also provided for pupils under or over that age), not being a public school or a grant-aided school'; or

(c)   a school in Northern Ireland that has been registered with the Department of Education; and

(d)   is not an Academy.

'**EEA national**' has the meaning given in regulation 2(1) of the 2006 EEA Regulations.

'**an external student**' is a student studying for a degree from a UK degree awarding body without any requirement to attend the UK degree awarding body's premises or a UK Listed Body's premises for lectures and tutorials.

A '**Short-term student**' means a person who is granted leave under paragraphs A57A to A57H of these Rules.

'**United Kingdom passport**' bears the meaning it has in the Immigration Act 1971.

'**a UK Bachelors degree**' means

(a)   A programme of study or research which leads to the award, by or on behalf of a university, college or other body which is authorised by Royal Charter or by or under an Act of Parliament to grant degrees, of a qualification designated by the awarding institution to be of Bachelors degree level; or

(b)   A programme of study or research, which leads to a recognised award for the purposes of section 214(2)(c) of the Education Reform Act 1988, of a qualification designated by the awarding institution to be of Bachelors degree level.

'**Immigration Officer**' includes a Customs Officer acting as an Immigration Officer.

'**Multiple Entry work permit employment**' is work permit employment where the person concerned does not intend to spend a continuous period in the United Kingdom in work permit employment.

'**public funds**' means

(a)   housing under Part VI or VII of the Housing Act 1996 and under Part II of the Housing Act 1985, Part I or II of the Housing (Scotland) Act 1987, Part II of the Housing (Northern Ireland) Order 1981 or Part II of the Housing (Northern Ireland) Order 1988;

(b)   attendance allowance, severe disablement allowance, carer's allowance and disability living allowance under Part III of the Social Security Contribution and Benefits Act 1992;, income support, council tax benefit and housing benefit under Part VII of that Act; a social fund payment under Part VIII of that Act; child benefit under Part IX of that Act; income based jobseeker's allowance under the Jobseekers Act 1995, income related allowance under Part 1 of the Welfare Reform Act 2007 (employment and support allowance) state pension credit under the State Pension Credit Act 2002; or child tax credit and working tax credit under Part 1 of the Tax Credits Act 2002;

(c)   attendance allowance, severe disablement allowance, carer's allowance and disability living allowance under Part III of the Social Security Contribution and Benefits (Northern Ireland) Act 1992;, income support, council tax benefit and, housing benefit under Part VII of that Act; a social fund payment under Part VIII of that Act; child benefit under Part IX of that Act; income based jobseeker's allowance under the Jobseekers (Northern Ireland) Order 1995 or income related allowance under Part 1 of the Welfare Reform Act (Northern Ireland) 2007;

(d)   Universal Credit under Part 1 of the Welfare Reform Act 2012 or Personal Independence Payment under Part 4 of that Act;

(e)   Universal Credit, Personal Independence Payment or any domestic rate relief under the Northern Ireland Welfare Reform Act 2013;

(f)   a council tax reduction under a council tax reduction scheme made under section 13A of the Local Government Finance Act 1992 in relation to England or Wales or a council tax reduction pursuant to the Council Tax Reduction (Scotland) Regulations 2012 or the Council Tax Reduction (State Pension Credit) (Scotland) Regulations 2012.

'**settled in the United Kingdom**' means that the person concerned:

(a)   is free from any restriction on the period for which he may remain save that a person entitled to an exemption under Section 8 of the Immigration Act 1971 (otherwise than as a member of the home forces) is not to be regarded as settled in the United Kingdom except in so far as Section 8(5A) so provides; and

(b)   is either:

    (i)   ordinarily resident in the United Kingdom without having entered or remained in breach of the immigration laws; or

    (ii)   despite having entered or remained in breach of the immigration laws, has subsequently entered lawfully or has been granted leave to remain and is ordinarily resident.

'**a parent**' includes

(a)   the stepfather of a child whose father is dead and the reference to stepfather includes a relationship arising through civil partnership;

(b)   the stepmother of a child whose mother is dead and the reference to stepmother includes a relationship arising through civil partnership and;

(c)   the father as well as the mother of an illegitimate child where he is proved to be the father;

(d)   an adoptive parent, where a child was adopted in accordance with a decision taken by the competent administrative authority or court in a country whose adoption orders are recognised by the United Kingdom or where a child is the subject of a de facto adoption in accordance with the requirements of paragraph 309A of these Rules (except that an adopted child or a child who is the subject of a de facto adoption may not make an application for leave to enter or remain in order to accompany, join or remain with an adoptive parent under paragraphs 297–303);

(e)   in the case of a child born in the United Kingdom who is not a British citizen, a person to whom there has been a genuine transfer of parental responsibility on the ground of the original parent(s)' inability to care for the child.

'**date of application**' means the date of application determined in accordance with paragraph 30 or 34G of these rules as appropriate.

'**a valid application**' means an application made in accordance with the requirements of Part 1of these Rules.

'**refugee leave**' means limited leave granted pursuant to paragraph 334 or 335 of these rules and has not been revoked pursuant to paragraph 339A or 339B of these rules.

'**humanitarian protection**' means limited leave granted pursuant to paragraph 339C of these rules and has not been revoked pursuant to paragraph 339G or 339H of these rules.

'**Protection claim**' has the same meaning as in section 82(2)(a) of the Nationality, Immigration and Asylum Act 2002.

'**a period of imprisonment**' referred to in these rules has the same meaning as set out in section 38(2) of the UK Borders Act 2007.

'**Overstayed**' or '**Overstaying**' means the applicant has stayed in the UK beyond the latest of:

(i)   the time limit attached to the last period of leave granted, or

(ii)   beyond the period that his leave was extended under sections 3C or 3D of the Immigration Act 1971.

'**intention to live permanently with the other**' or '**intend to live together permanently**' means an intention to live together, evidenced by a clear commitment from both parties that they will live together permanently in the UK immediately following the outcome of the application in question or as soon as circumstances permit thereafter. However, where an application is made under Appendix Armed Forces the words 'in the UK' in this definition do not apply. Where an application is made under Appendix FM and the sponsor is a permanent member of HM Diplomatic Service, or a comparable UK-based staff member of the British Council, the Department for International Development or the Home Office on a tour of duty outside the UK, the words 'in the UK' in this definition do not apply.

'**present and settled**' or '**present and settled in the UK**' means that the person concerned is settled in the United Kingdom and, at the time that an application under these Rules is made, is physically present here or is coming here with or to join the applicant and intends to make the UK their home with the applicant if the application is successful.

Where the person concerned is a British Citizen or settled in the UK and is:

(i)   a member of HM Forces serving overseas, or

(ii)   a permanent member of HM Diplomatic Service, or a comparable UK-based staff member of the British Council, the Department for International Development or the Home Office on a tour of duty outside the UK, and the applicant has provided the evidence specified in paragraph 26A of Appendix FM-SE,

then for the purposes of Appendix FM the person is to be regarded as present and settled in the UK, and in paragraphs R-LTRP.1.1.(a) and R-ILRP.1.1.(a) of Appendix FM the words 'and their partner must be in the UK' are to be disregarded.

For the purposes of an application as a fiancé(e) or proposed civil partner under paragraphs 289AA to 295 or Appendix FM, an EEA national who holds a document certifying permanent residence issued under the 2006 EEA Regulations is to be regarded as present and settled in the UK.

'**sponsor**' means the person in relation to whom an applicant is seeking leave to enter or remain as their spouse, fiance, civil partner, proposed civil partner, unmarried partner, same-sex partner or dependent relative, as the case may be, under paragraphs 277 to 295O or 317 to 319 or the person in relation to whom an applicant is seeking entry clearance or leave as their partner or dependent relative under Appendix FM.

'**overcrowded**' means overcrowded within the meaning of the Housing Act 1985, the Housing (Scotland) Act 1987 or the Housing (Northern Ireland) Order 1988 (as appropriate).

'**working illegally**' means working in breach of conditions of leave or working when in the UK without valid leave where such leave is required.

'**in breach of immigration laws**' means without valid leave where such leave is required, or in breach of the conditions of leave.

'**adequate**' and '**adequately**' in relation to a maintenance and accommodation requirement shall mean that, after income tax, national insurance contributions and housing costs have been deducted, there must be available to the family the level of income that would be available to them if the family was in receipt of income support.

'**occupy exclusively**' in relation to accommodation shall mean that part of the accommodation must be for the exclusive use of the family.

'**must not be leading an independent life**' or '**is not leading an independent life**' means that the applicant does not have a partner as defined in Appendix FM; is living with their parents (except where they are at boarding school, college or university as part of their full-time education); is not employed full-time (unless aged 18 years or over); is wholly or mainly dependent upon their parents for financial support (unless aged 18 years or over); and is wholly or mainly dependent upon their parents for emotional support. Where a relative other than a parent may act as the sponsor of the applicant, references in this definition to 'parents' shall be read as applying to that other relative.

'**prohibited degree of relationship**' has the same meaning as in the Marriage Act 1949, the Marriage (Prohibited Degrees of Relationship) Act 1986 and the Civil Partnership Act 2004.

'**visa nationals**' are the persons specified in Appendix 2 to Appendix V: Visitors who need a visa for the United Kingdom for a visit or for any other purposes where seeking entry for 6 months or less.

'**non-visa nationals**' are persons who are not specified in Appendix 2 to Appendix V Immigration Rules for Visitors.

'**specified national**' is a person specified in Appendix 3 to these Rules who seeks leave to enter the United Kingdom for a period of more than 6 months.

'**employment**' unless the contrary intention appears, includes paid and unpaid employment, paid and unpaid work placements undertaken as part of a course or period of study, self employment and engaging in business or any professional activity.

'**the Human Rights Convention**' means the Convention for the Protection of Human Rights and Fundamental Freedoms, agreed by the Council of Europe at Rome on 4th November 1950 as it has effect for the time being in relation to the United Kingdom.

'**Biometric immigration document**' means a document recording biometric information issued in accordance with regulations under section 5 of the UK Borders Act 2007.

'**immigration employment document**' means a work permit or any other document which relates to employment and is issued for the purpose of these Rules or in connection with leave to enter or remain in the United Kingdom.

'**Employment as a Doctor in Training**' means employment in a medical post or training programme which has been approved by the Postgraduate Medical Education and Training Board, or employment in a postgraduate training programme in dentistry.

'**these Rules**' means these immigration rules (HC 395) made under section 3(2) of the Immigration Act 1971.

A '**refugee**' is a refugee as defined in regulation 2 of The Refugee or Person in Need of International Protection (Qualification) Regulation 2006.

In part 6A of these Rules, 'relevant grant allocation period' means a specified period of time, which will be published by the Secretary of State on the visas and immigration pages of the gov.uk website, during which applications for entry clearance or leave to enter in respect of a particular route may be granted subject to the grant allocation for that period;

In part 6A of these Rules, 'grant allocation' means a limit, details of which will be published by the Secretary of State on the visas and immigration pages of the gov.uk website, on the number of grants of entry clearance or leave to enter which may be granted in respect of a particular route during the relevant grant allocation period;

Under Part 6A of these Rules, '**Highly Skilled Migrant**' means a migrant granted leave under paragraphs 135A to 135G of the Rules in force before 30th June 2008.

Under Part 6A of these Rules, '**Highly Skilled Migrant Programme Approval Letter**' means a letter issued by the Home Office confirming that the applicant meets the criteria specified by the Secretary of State for entry to or stay in the UK under the Highly Skilled Migrant Programme.

Under Part 6A of these Rules, '**Innovator**' means a migrant granted leave under paragraphs 210A to 210F of the Rules in force before 30th June 2008.

Under Part 6A of these Rules, '**Participant in the Fresh Talent Working in Scotland Scheme**' means a migrant granted leave under paragraphs 143A to 143F of the Rules in force before 30th June 2008.

Under Part 6A of these Rules, '**Participant in the International Graduates Scheme**' means a migrant granted leave under paragraphs 135O to 135T of the Rules in force before 30th June 2008.

Under Part 6A of these Rules, '**Postgraduate Doctor or Dentist**' means a migrant who is granted leave under paragraphs 70 to 75 of these Rules.

Under Part 6A of these Rules, '**Self-Employed**' means an applicant is registered as self-employed with HM Revenue & Customs, or is employed by a company of which the applicant is a controlling shareholder.

Under Part 6A of these Rules, '**Student**' means a migrant who is granted leave under paragraphs 57 to 62 of these Rules.

Under Part 6A of these Rules, '**Student Nurse**' means a migrant who is granted leave under paragraphs 63 to 69 of these Rules.

Under Part 6A of these Rules, '**Student Re-Sitting an Examination**' means a migrant who is granted leave under paragraphs 69A to 69F of these Rules.

Under Part 6A of these Rules, '**Student Writing-Up a Thesis**' means a migrant who is granted leave under paragraphs 69G to 69L of these Rules.

Under Part 6A of these Rules, '**Work Permit Holder**' means a migrant who is granted leave under paragraphs 128 to 133 of these Rules.

Under Appendix A of these Rules, an '**A-rated Sponsor**' is a Sponsor which is recorded as being 'A-rated' on the register of licensed Sponsors maintained by the United Kingdom Border Agency.

Under Part 6A of these Rules, '**Tier 4 Sponsor**' means a sponsor which is recorded as having 'Tier 4 Sponsor status' on the register of licensed sponsors maintained by the Home Office.

Under Part 6A of these Rules, '**Probationary Sponsor**' means a Tier 4 sponsor which is recorded as having 'Probationary Sponsor status' on the register of licensed sponsors maintained by the Home Office.

Under paragraph 34K of these Rules, a 'Premium Sponsor' is a Sponsor which is recorded as holding Premium status on the register of licensed Sponsors maintained by the United Kingdom Border Agency.

Under Part 6A of these Rules, '**Certificate of Sponsorship**' means an authorisation issued by the Secretary of State to a Sponsor in respect of one or more applications, or potential applications, for entry clearance, leave to enter or remain as a Tier 2 migrant or a Tier 5 migrant in accordance with these Rules.

Under Part 6A and Appendix A of these Rules, '**Confirmation of Acceptance for Studies**' means a unique reference number electronically issued by a sponsor via the Sponsor Management System to an applicant for entry clearance, leave to enter or remain as a Tier 4 Migrant in accordance with these Rules.

Under Parts 6A and 9 of these Rules, '**Certificate of Sponsorship Checking Service**' means a computerised interface with the Points Based System computer database which allows a United Kingdom Border Agency caseworker or entry clearance officer assessing a migrant's application for entry clearance, leave to enter or leave to remain to access and review details of the migrant's Certificate of Sponsorship, including details of the migrant's Sponsor, together with details of the job and other details associated with the circumstances in which the Certificate of Sponsorship was issued.

Under Part 6A and Appendix A of these Rules, '**length of the period of engagement**' is the period beginning with the employment start date as recorded on the Certificate of Sponsorship Checking service entry which relates to the Certificate of Sponsorship reference number for which the migrant was awarded points under Appendix A and ending on the employment end date as recorded in the same entry.

Under Part 6A and Appendix A of these Rules, a '**genuine vacancy**' is a vacancy which exists in practice (or would exist in practice were it not filled by the applicant) for a position which:

(a) requires the jobholder to undertake the specific duties and responsibilities, for the weekly hours and length of the period of engagement, described by the Sponsor in the Certificate of Sponsorship relating to the applicant; and

(b) does not include dissimilar and/or unequally skilled duties such that the Standard Occupational Classification (SOC) code used by the Sponsor as stated in the Certificate of Sponsorship relating to the applicant is inappropriate.

Under Part 6A and Appendix A of these Rules, working for '**the same employer**' or '**the same Sponsor**' includes working for a different employer or Sponsor in circumstances which constitute a 'relevant transfer' under Regulation 3(1) of the Transfer of Undertakings (Protection of Employment) Regulations 2006, or similar protection, provided the worker's duties remain unchanged.

Under Part 6A and Appendix A of these Rules, '**Designated Competent Body**' means an organisation which has been approved by the UK Border Agency to endorse applicants as a Tier 1 (Exceptional Talent) Migrant.

Under Part 6A and Appendix A of these Rules, '**Tier 1 (Exceptional Talent) Unique Reference Number**' means a unique reference number issued for the purposes of managing the Tier 1 (Exceptional Talent) Limit and provided by the UK Border Agency to an applicant prior to making his application as a Tier 1 (Exceptional Talent) Migrant.

'Notice of liability for removal' means a notice given that a person is or will be liable for removal under section 10 of the Immigration and Asylum Act 1999 as amended by the Immigration Act 2014. For cases that pre-date the Immigration Act 2014 coming into force, 'notice of liability for removal' refers to a decision to remove in accordance with section 10 of the Immigration and Asylum Act 1999, a decision to remove an illegal entrant by way of directions under paragraphs 8 to 10 of Schedule 2 to the Immigration Act 1971 or a decision to remove in accordance with section 47 of the Immigration, Asylum and Nationality Act 2006.

'Pending appeal' has the same meaning as in section 104 of the Nationality, Immigration and Asylum Act 2002.

Under Part 6A of these Rules, '**Confirmation of Acceptance for Studies Checking Service**' means a computerised interface with the Points Based System computer database which allows a United Kingdom Border Agency caseworker or entry clearance officer assessing a migrant's application for entry clearance, leave to enter or leave to remain as a Tier 4 migrant under these Rules to access and review details of the migrant's Confirmation of Acceptance for Studies, including details of the migrant's Sponsor, together with details of the course of study and other details associated with the circumstances in which the Confirmation of Acceptance for Studies was issued.

Under Part 6A of these Rules, '**Established Entertainer**' means an applicant who is applying for leave to remain as a Tier 2 (General) Migrant or a Tier 2 (Intra-Company Transfer) Migrant in respect of whom the following conditions are satisfied:

(a) the Certificate of Sponsorship Checking Service entry to which the applicant's Certificate of Sponsorship reference number relates, records that the applicant is being sponsored in an occupation which is defined in the United Kingdom Border Agency's Transitional Guidance as being a job in the entertainment sector,

(b) the applicant has, or has previously had, entry clearance, leave to enter or leave to remain in the UK as a Work Permit Holder, and the work permit that led to that grant was issued in the sports and entertainment category to enable him to work in the occupation in which he is, at the date of the application for leave to remain, currently being sponsored,

(c) the applicant's last grant of leave was:

(i)   as a Work Permit Holder in the sports and entertainment category, provided the work permit on the basis of which that leave was granted was issued in the sports and entertainment category to enable him to work either in the occupation in which he is, at the date of the current application for leave to remain, currently being sponsored, or in another occupation which is defined in the UK Border Agency's Transitional Guidance as being a job in the entertainment sector, or

(ii)   leave to remain as a Tier 2 (General) Migrant or a Tier 2 (Intra-Company Transfer) Migrant, provided (in either case):

    (1)   he previously had leave as a Work Permit Holder in the sports and entertainment category to work as described in (i) above,

    (2)   he has not been granted entry clearance in this or any other route since his last grant of leave as a Work Permit Holder, and

    (3)   his last grant of leave was made to enable him to work either in the occupation in which he is, at the date of the current application for leave to remain, currently being sponsored or in another occupation which is defined in the UK Border Agency's Transitional Guidance as being a job in the entertainment sector,

(d)   the Certificate of Sponsorship Checking Service entry to which the applicant's Certificate of Sponsorship reference number relates records:

    (i)   that the applicant will be paid a salary for the job that is at or above the appropriate entertainments industry rate, as listed in the United Kingdom Border Agency's Transitional Guidance; and

    (ii)   that before agreeing to employ the applicant, the Sponsor consulted with such bodies as the United Kingdom Border Agency's Transitional Guidance indicates that it should consult with before employing someone in this capacity, and

(e)   the applicant has not spent a period of 5 years or more in the UK, beginning with the last grant of entry clearance, as a Qualifying Work Permit Holder, Tier 2 (General) Migrant or Tier 2 (Intra-Company Transfer) Migrant, or in any combination of these.

Under Part 6A of these Rules, '**Qualifying Work Permit Holder**' means a Work Permit Holder who was issued a work permit in the business and commercial or sports and entertainment work permit categories.

Under Part 6A of these Rules, '**Senior Care Worker**' means an applicant who is applying for leave to remain as a Tier 2 (General) Migrant or a Tier 2 (Intra-Company Transfer) Migrant in respect of whom the following conditions are satisfied:

(a)   the Certificate of Sponsorship Checking Service entry to which the applicant's Certificate of Sponsorship reference number relates, records that the applicant is being sponsored in an occupation which is defined in the codes of practice for Tier 2 sponsors published by the UK Border Agency as being a Senior Care Worker role,

(b)   the applicant's last grant of leave was:

    (i)   as a Qualifying Work Permit Holder, or

    (ii)   leave to remain as a Tier 2 (General) Migrant or a Tier 2 (Intra-Company Transfer) Migrant, provided (in either case):

    (1)   he previously had leave as a Qualifying Work Permit Holder, and

    (2)   he has not been granted entry clearance in this or any other route since his last grant of leave as a Qualifying Work Permit Holder.

(c)   the work permit or Certificate of Sponsorship that led to the last grant of leave was issued to enable the applicant to work as a senior care worker, and

(d)   the applicant has not spent a period of 5 years or more in the UK, beginning with the last grant of entry clearance, as a Qualifying Work Permit Holder, Tier 2 (General) Migrant or Tier 2 (Intra-Company Transfer) Migrant, or in any combination of these.

Under Part 6A of these Rules, '**Sponsor**' means the person or Government that the Certificate of Sponsorship Checking Service or Confirmation of Acceptance for Studies Checking Service records as being the Sponsor for a migrant.

Under Part 6A of these Rules, a reference to a '**sponsor licence**' means a licence granted by the Secretary of State to a person who, by virtue of such a grant, is licensed as a Sponsor under Tiers 2, 4 or 5 of the Points Based System.

'In Part 6A and Appendices A and J of these Rules, '**settled worker**' means a person who:

(i)   is a national of the UK,

(ii)   is a person with a right of residence in accordance with the Immigration (European Economic Area) Regulations 2006 or, except where that person is subject to worker authorisation, the regulations made under section 2 of the European Union (Accessions) Act 2006 in combination with section 2(2) of the European Communities Act 1972 or the regulations made under section 4 of the European Union (Croatian Accession and Irish Protocol) Act 2013,

(iii)   is a British overseas territories citizen, except those from Sovereign Base Areas in Cyprus,

(iv)   is a Commonwealth citizen with leave to enter or remain granted on the basis of UK Ancestry (paragraphs 186 to 193 of these Rules), or

(v)   has settled status in the UK within the meaning of the Immigration Act 1971, as amended by the Immigration and Asylum Act 1999, and the Nationality, Immigration and Asylum Act 2002.'

Under Part 6A of these Rules, **'supplementary employment'** means other employment in a job which appears on the Shortage Occupation List in Appendix K, or in the same profession and at the same professional level as that which the migrant is being sponsored to do provided that:

(a)   the migrant remains working for the Sponsor in the employment that the Certificate of Sponsorship Checking Service records that the migrant is being sponsored to do,

(b)   the other employment does not exceed 20 hours per week and takes place outside of the hours when the migrant is contracted to work for the Sponsor in the employment the migrant is being sponsored to do.

Under part 6A and Appendix A of these Rules, **'overseas higher education institution'** means an institution which holds overseas accreditation confirmed by UK NARIC as offering degree programmes which are equivalent to UK degree level qualifications, and which teach no more than half of a degree programme in the UK as a study abroad programme.

'Business person' means a migrant granted leave under paragraphs 200 to 208 of the Rules in force before 30th June 2008.

'Investor' means a migrant granted leave under paragraphs 224 to 229 of the Rules in force before 30th June 2008.

'Self-employed Lawyer' means a migrant granted entry clearance, or leave to enter or remain, outside the Rules under the concession for Self-employed lawyers that formerly appeared in Chapter 6, Section 1 Annex D of the Immigration Directorate instructions.

'Points Based System Migrant' means a migrant applying for or granted leave as a Tier 1 Migrant, a Tier 2 Migrant, a Tier 4 Migrant or a Tier 5 Migrant.

'Tier 1 Migrant' means a migrant who is granted leave as a Tier 1 (Exceptional Talent) Migrant, a Tier 1 (General) Migrant, a Tier 1 (Entrepreneur) Migrant, a Tier 1 (Investor) Migrant, a Tier 1 (Graduate Entrepreneur) Migrant or a Tier 1 (Post-Study Work) Migrant.

'Tier 1 (Exceptional Talent) Migrant' means a migrant who is granted leave under paragraphs 245B to 245BF of these Rules.

'Tier 1 (General) Migrant' means a migrant who is granted leave under paragraphs 245C to 245CE of these Rules.

'Tier 1 (Entrepreneur) Migrant' means a migrant who is granted leave under paragraphs 245D to 245DF of these Rules.

'Tier 1 (Investor) Migrant' means a migrant who is granted leave under paragraphs 245E to 245EF of these Rules.

'Tier 1 (Graduate Entrepreneur) Migrant' means a migrant who is granted leave under paragraphs 245F to 245FB of these Rules in place on or after 6 April 2012.

'Tier 1 (Post-Study Work) Migrant' means a migrant who is granted leave under paragraphs 245F to 245FE of the Rules in place before 6 April 2012.

'Tier 2 Migrant' means a migrant who is granted leave as a Tier 2 (Intra-Company Transfer) Migrant, a Tier 2 (General) Migrant, a Tier 2 (Minister of Religion) Migrant or a Tier 2 (Sportsperson) Migrant.

Tier 2 (Intra-Company Transfer) Migrant' means a migrant granted leave under paragraphs 245G to 245GF of these Rules.

'Tier 2 (General) Migrant' means a migrant granted leave under paragraphs 245H to 245HF of these Rules and who obtains points under paragraphs 76 to 84A of Appendix A.

'**Tier 2 (Minister of Religion) Migrant**' means a migrant granted leave under paragraphs 245H to 245HF of these Rules and who obtains points under paragraphs 85 to 92 of Appendix A.

'**Tier 2 (Sportsperson) Migrant**' means a migrant granted leave under paragraphs 245H to 245HF of these Rules and who obtains points under paragraphs 93 to 100 of Appendix A.'

'Tier 4 (General) Student' means a migrant granted leave under paragraphs 245ZT to 245ZY of these Rules.

'Tier 4 (Child) Student' means a migrant granted leave under paragraphs 245ZZ to 245ZZD of these Rules.

'Tier 4 Migrant' means a Tier 4 (General) Student or a Tier 4 (Child) Student.

'expected end date of a course leading to the award of a PhD' means the date the PhD is expected to be formally confirmed, by the sponsor, as completed to the standard required for the award of a PhD and recorded on the confirmation of acceptance for studies accompanying the application for leave to remain as a Tier 4 (General) Student on the doctorate extension scheme.

'Tier 5 (Youth Mobility) Temporary Migrant' means a migrant granted leave under paragraphs 245ZI to 245ZL of these Rules.

'Tier 5 (Temporary Worker) Migrant' means a migrant granted leave under paragraphs 245ZM to 245ZS of these Rules.

'Deemed sponsorship status' means that the country or territory is not required to issue its nationals or passport holders with a Certificate of Sponsorship in order to enable a successful application under the Tier 5 Youth Mobility Scheme and is held by a country or territory listed as such at Appendix G of these Rules.

'Tier 5 Migrant' means a migrant who is either a Tier 5 (Temporary Worker) Migrant or a Tier 5 (Youth Mobility) Temporary Migrant.

Under Part 6A of these Rules '**Government Authorised Exchange Scheme**' means a scheme under the Tier 5 (Temporary Worker) Government Authorised Exchange sub-category which is endorsed by a Government Department in support of Government objectives and provides temporary work in an occupation which appears on the list of occupations skilled to National Qualifications Framework level 3, as stated in the codes of practice for Tier 2 Sponsors published by the UK Border Agency, and where the migrant will be supernumerary.

Under Part 6A of these Rules '**Work Experience Programme**' means work experience including volunteering and job-shadowing, internships and work exchange programmes under a Government Authorised Exchange Scheme.

Under Part 6A of these Rules '**Research Programme**' means research programmes and fellowships under a Government Authorised Exchange Scheme where the migrant is working on a scientific, academic, medical, or government research project/s at either a UK Higher Education Institution or another research institution operating under the authority and/or financial sponsorship of a relevant Government Department.'

Under Part 6A of these Rules '**Training Programme**' means a training programme under a Government Authorised Exchange Scheme where the migrant either receives formal, practical training in the fields of science and / or medicine or will be trained by HM Armed Forces or by UK emergency services, or meets the requirements of paragraph 245ZQ(b)(vi)(2) to (4).

Under Part 6A of these Rules 'Overseas Government Language Programme' means an overseas Government sponsored professional language development programme under the Government Authorised Exchange Scheme where the migrant delivers language training and participates in a cultural exchange programme that is fully or partially paid for by the overseas government or an organisation affiliated to an overseas government.

Under Part 6A of these Rules, '**Temporary Engagement as a Sports Broadcaster**' means providing guest expert commentary on a particular sporting event.'

'**Contractual Service Supplier**' means a migrant who is granted entry clearance, leave to enter or leave to remain under paragraphs 245ZP(e) and 245ZR(b)(ii)(3) of these Rules on the basis that the circumstances in which such leave is sought engage the United Kingdom's commitments in respect of contractual service suppliers under the relevant provisions of one of the agreements specified in paragraph 111(f)(i) of Appendix A of these Rules.

'**Independent Professional**' means a migrant who is granted entry clearance, leave to enter or leave to remain under paragraphs 245ZP(e) and 245ZR(b)(ii)(3) of these Rules on the basis that the circumstances in which such leave is sought engage the United Kingdom's commitments in respect of independent professionals under the relevant provisions of one of the agreements specified in paragraph 111(f)(i) of Appendix A of these Rules.

'Jewish Agency Employee' means a migrant granted leave outside of these Rules under the concession that formerly appeared in Chapter 17 Section 5 Part 2 of the Immigration Directorate Instructions.

'Member of the Operational Ground Staff of an Overseas-owned Airline' means a migrant granted leave under paragraphs 178 to 185 of the Rules in force before 27 November 2008.

'Minister of Religion, Missionary or Member of a Religious Order' means a migrant granted leave under paragraphs 170 to 177A of the Rules in force before 27 November 2008.

'Overseas Qualified Nurse or Midwife' means a migrant granted leave under paragraphs 69M to 69R of the Rules in force before 27 November 2008.

'Participant in the Science and Engineering Graduates Scheme' means a migrant granted leave under paragraphs 135O to 135T of the Rules in force before 1 May 2007.

'Representative of an Overseas Newspaper, News Agency or Broadcasting Organisation' means a migrant granted leave under paragraphs 136 to 143 of the Rules in force before 27 November 2008.

'**Student Union Sabbatical Officer**' means a migrant granted leave under paragraphs 87A to 87F of the Rules in force before 27 November 2008.

'**Working Holidaymaker**' means a migrant granted leave under paragraphs 95 to 97 of the Rules in force before 27 November 2008.

A '**visitor**' is a person granted leave to enter or remain in the UK under paragraphs 40–56Z, 75A–M or 82–87 of these Rules before 24 April 2015 or under Appendix V: Immigration Rules for Visitors on or after 24 April 2015.

An '**Amateur**' is a person who engages in a sport or creative activity solely for personal enjoyment and who is not seeking to derive a living from the activity.

A '**Series of events**' is two or more linked events, such as a tour, or rounds of a competition, which do not add up to a league or a season.

'**Writer, Composer or Artist**' means a migrant granted leave under paragraphs 232 to 237 of the Rules in force before 30th June 2008.

In paragraph 320(7B) and paragraph 320(11) of these Rules:

'**Deception**' means making false representations or submitting false documents (whether or not material to the application), or failing to disclose material facts.

'**Illegal Entrant**' has the same definition as in section 33(1) of the Immigration Act 1971.

In paragraph 320(22) and 322(12) of these Rules, and in paragraphs S-EC.2.3., S-LTR.2.3. and S-ILR.2.3. of Appendix FM to these Rules.

'**relevant NHS body**' means

(a)   in relation to England–

    (i)   a National Health Service Trust established under section 25 of the National Health Service Act 2006,

    (ii)   a NHS foundation trust.

(b)   in relation to Wales–

    (i)   a Local Health Board established under section 11 of the National Health Service (Wales) Act 2006,

    (ii)   a National Health Service Trust established under section 18 of the National Health Service (Wales) Act 2006,

    (iii)   a Special Health Authority established under 22 of the National Health Service (Wales) Act 2006.

(c)   in relation to Scotland–

    (i)   a Health Board or Special Health Board established under section 2 of the National Health Service (Scotland) Act 1978 (c. 29),

    (ii)   the Common Services Agency for the Scottish Health Service established under section 10 of that Act,

    (iii)   Healthcare Improvement Scotland established under section 10A of that Act.

(d)   in relation to Northern Ireland–

    (i)   the Regional Health and Social Care Board established under the Health and Social Care (Reform) Act (Northern Ireland) 2009,

(ii)   a Health and Social Care trust established under the Health and Personal Social Services (Northern Ireland) Order 1991 (S.I. 1991/194 (N.I. 1)) and renamed under the Health and Social Care (Reform) Act (Northern Ireland) 2009.

'**relevant NHS regulations**' means

(i)   The National Health Service (Charges to Overseas Visitors) (Amendment) (Wales) Regulations 2004 (2004 No 1433);

(ii)   The National Health Service (Charges to Overseas Visitors) (Scotland) Regulations 1989 as amended (1989 No 364);

(iii)   The Health and Personal Social Services (Provision of Health Services to Persons not Ordinarily Resident) Regulations (Northern Ireland) 2005 (2005 No 551); or

(iv)   The National Health Service (Charges to Overseas Visitors) Regulations (2011 No 1556).

'**administrative review**' means a review conducted in accordance with Appendix AR of these Rules;

'**eligible decision**' means a decision eligible for administrative review as referred to in paragraphs AR3.2, AR4.2 or AR5.2 of Appendix AR of these Rules;

'**working day**' means a business day in the part of the UK in which the applicant resides or (as the case may be) is detained.

6A.   For the purpose of these Rules, a person (P) is not to be regarded as having (or potentially having) recourse to public funds merely because P is (or will be) reliant in whole or in part on public funds provided to P's sponsor unless, as a result of P's presence in the United Kingdom, the sponsor is (or would be) entitled to increased or additional public funds (save where such entitlement to increased or additional public funds is by virtue of P and the sponsor's joint entitlement to benefits under the regulations referred to in paragraph 6B).

6B.   Subject to paragraph 6C, a person (P) shall not be regarded as having recourse to public funds if P is entitled to benefits specified under section 115 of the Immigration and Asylum Act 1999 by virtue of regulations made under sub-sections (3) and (4) of that section or section 42 of the Tax Credits Act 2002.

6C.   A person (P) making an application from outside the United Kingdom will be regarded as having recourse to public funds where P relies upon the future entitlement to any public funds that would be payable to P or to P's sponsor as a result of P's presence in the United Kingdom, (including those benefits to which P or the sponsor would be entitled as a result of P's presence in the United Kingdom under the regulations referred to in to paragraph 6B)'.

Part 1 – General provisions regarding leave to enter or remain in the United Kingdom

Leave to enter the United Kingdom

7.   A person who is neither a British citizen nor a Commonwealth citizen with the right of abode nor a person who is entitled to enter or remain in the United Kingdom by virtue of the provisions of the 2006 EEA Regulations requires leave to enter the United Kingdom.

8.   Under Sections 3 and 4 of the Immigration Act 1971 an Immigration Officer when admitting to the United Kingdom a person subject to immigration control under that Act may give leave to enter for a limited period and, if he does, may impose all or any of the following conditions:

(i)   a condition restricting employment or occupation in the United Kingdom;

(ii)   a condition requiring the person to maintain and accommodate himself, and any dependants of his, without recourse to public funds;

(iii)   a condition requiring the person to register with the police; and

(iv)   a condition restricting his studies in the United Kingdom.

He may also require him to report to the appropriate Medical Officer of Environmental Health. Under Section 24 of the 1971 Act it is an offence knowingly to remain beyond the time limit or fail to comply with such a condition or requirement.

9.   The time limit and any conditions attached will be made known to the person concerned either:

(i)   by written notice given to him or endorsed by the Immigration Officer in his passport or travel document; or

(ii)   in any other manner permitted by the Immigration (Leave to Enter and Remain) Order 2000.

Exercise of the power to refuse leave to enter the United Kingdom or to cancel leave to enter or remain which is in force

10. The power to refuse leave to enter the United Kingdom or to cancel leave to enter or remain which is already in force is not to be exercised by an Immigration Officer acting on his own. The authority of a Chief Immigration Officer or of an Immigration Inspector must always be obtained.

Suspension of leave to enter or remain in the United Kingdom

10A. Where a person has arrived in the United Kingdom with leave to enter or remain which is in force but which was given to him before his arrival he may be examined by an Immigration Officer under paragraph 2A of Schedule 2 to the Immigration Act 1971. An Immigration Officer examining a person under paragraph 2A may suspend that person's leave to enter or remain in the United Kingdom until the examination is completed.

Cancellation of leave to enter or remain in the United Kingdom

10B. Where a person arrives in the United Kingdom with leave to enter or remain in the United Kingdom which is already in force, an Immigration Officer may cancel that leave.

Requirement for persons arriving in the United Kingdom or seeking entry through the Channel Tunnel to produce evidence of identity and nationality

11. A person must, on arrival in the United Kingdom or when seeking entry through the Channel Tunnel, produce on request by the Immigration Officer:

    (i)   a valid national passport or other document satisfactorily establishing his identity and nationality; and

    (ii) such information as may be required to establish whether he requires leave to enter the United Kingdom and, if so, whether and on what terms leave to enter should be given.

Requirement for a person not requiring leave to enter the United Kingdom to prove that he has the right of abode

12. A person claiming to be a British citizen must prove that he has the right of abode in the United Kingdom by producing either:

    (i)   a United Kingdom passport describing him as a British citizen or as a citizen of the United Kingdom and Colonies having the right of abode in the United Kingdom; or

    (ii) a certificate of entitlement duly issued by or on behalf of the Government of the United Kingdom certifying that he has the right of abode.

13. A person claiming to be a Commonwealth citizen with the right of abode in the United Kingdom must prove that he has the right of abode by producing a certificate of entitlement duly issued to him by or on behalf of the Government of the United Kingdom certifying that he has the right of abode.

14. A Commonwealth citizen who has been given limited leave to enter the United Kingdom may later claim to have the right of abode. The time limit on his stay may be removed if he is able to establish a claim to the right of abode, for example by showing that:

    (i)   immediately before the commencement of the British Nationality Act 1981 he was a Commonwealth citizen born to or legally adopted by a parent who at the time of the birth had citizenship of the United Kingdom and Colonies by his birth in the United Kingdom or any of the Islands; and

    (ii) he has not ceased to be a Commonwealth citizen in the meanwhile.

Common Travel Area

15. The United Kingdom, the Channel Islands, the Isle of Man and the Republic of Ireland collectively form a common travel area. A person who has been examined for the purpose of immigration control at the point at which he entered the area does not normally require leave to enter any other part of it. However certain persons subject to the Immigration (Control of Entry through the Republic of Ireland) Order 1972 (as amended) who enter the United Kingdom through the Republic of Ireland do require leave to enter. This includes:

    (i)   those who merely passed through the Republic of Ireland;

    (ii) persons requiring visas;

    (iii) persons who entered the Republic of Ireland unlawfully;

(iv)   persons who are subject to directions given by the Secretary of State for their exclusion from the United Kingdom on the ground that their exclusion is conducive to the public good;

(v)   persons who entered the Republic from the United Kingdom and Islands after entering there unlawfully or overstaying their leave.

Admission of certain British passport holders

16.   A person in any of the following categories may be admitted freely to the United Kingdom on production of a United Kingdom passport issued in the United Kingdom and Islands or the Republic of Ireland prior to 1 January 1973, unless his passport has been endorsed to show that he was subject to immigration control:

(i)   a British Dependent Territories citizen;

(ii)   a British National (Overseas);

(iii)   a British Overseas citizen;

(iv)   a British protected person;

(v)   a British subject by virtue of Section 30(a) of the British Nationality Act 1981, (who, immediately before the commencement of the 1981 Act would have been a British subject not possessing citizenship of the United Kingdom and Colonies or the citizenship of any other Commonwealth country or territory).

17.   British Overseas citizens who hold United Kingdom passports wherever issued and who satisfy the Immigration Officer that they have, since 1 March 1968, been given indefinite leave to enter or remain in the United Kingdom may be given indefinite leave to enter.

Persons outside the United Kingdom

17A.   Where a person is outside the United Kingdom but wishes to travel to the United Kingdom an Immigration Officer may give or refuse him leave to enter. An Immigration Officer may exercise these powers whether or not he is, himself, in the United Kingdom. However, an Immigration Officer is not obliged to consider an application for leave to enter from a person outside the United Kingdom.

17B.   Where a person having left the common travel area, has leave to enter the United Kingdom which remains in force under article 13 of the Immigration (Leave to Enter and Remain) Order 2000, an Immigration Officer may cancel that leave. An Immigration Officer may exercise these powers whether or not he is, himself, in the United Kingdom. If a person outside the United Kingdom has leave to remain in the United Kingdom which is in force in this way, the Secretary of State may cancel that leave.

Returning Residents

18.   A person seeking leave to enter the United Kingdom as a returning resident may be admitted for settlement provided the Immigration Officer is satisfied that the person concerned:

(i)   had indefinite leave to enter or remain in the United Kingdom when he last left; and

(ii)   has not been away from the United Kingdom for more than 2 years; and

(iii)   did not receive assistance from public funds towards the cost of leaving the United Kingdom; and

(iv)   now seeks admission for the purpose of settlement.

18A.   Those who qualify for admission to the United Kingdom as returning residents in accordance with paragraph 18 do not need a visa to enter the UK.

19.   A person who does not benefit from the preceding paragraph by reason only of having been away from the United Kingdom too long may nevertheless be admitted as a returning resident if, for example, he has lived here for most of his life.

19A.   Sub paragraphs (ii) and (iii) of paragraph 18 shall not apply where a person who has indefinite leave to enter or remain in the United Kingdom accompanies on an overseas posting, a spouse, civil partner, unmarried partner or same-sex partner who is:

(i)   a member of HM Forces serving overseas;

(ii)   a permanent member of HM Diplomatic Service;

(iii)   a comparable United Kingdom based staff member of the British Council;

(iv)   a staff member of the Department for International Development who is a British Citizen or is settled in the United Kingdom; or

(v)   a Home Office employee.

20.   The leave of a person whose stay in the United Kingdom is subject to a time limit lapses on his going to a country or territory outside the common travel area if the leave was given for a period of six months or less or

conferred by a visit visa. In other cases, leave lapses on the holder remaining outside the United Kingdom for a continuous period of more than two years. A person whose leave has lapsed and who returns after a temporary absence abroad within the period of this earlier leave has no claim to admission as a returning resident. His application to re-enter the United Kingdom should be considered in the light of all the relevant circumstances. The same time limit and any conditions attached will normally be reimposed if he meets the requirements of these Rules, unless he is seeking admission in a different capacity from the one in which he was last given leave to enter or remain.

Non-lapsing leave

20A. Leave to enter or remain in the United Kingdom will usually lapse on the holder going to a country or territory outside the common travel area. However, under article 13 of the Immigration (Leave to Enter and Remain) Order 2000 such leave will not lapse where it was given for a period exceeding six months or where it was conferred by means of an entry clearance (other than a visit visa).

20B. Those who seek leave to enter the United Kingdom within the period of their earlier leave and for the same purpose as that for which that leave was granted, unless it

(i) was for a period of six months or less; or

(ii) was extended by statutory instrument or by section 3C of the Immigration Act 1971 (inserted by section 3 of the Immigration and Asylum Act 1999);

do not need a visa to enter the UK.

Holders of restricted travel documents and passports

21. The leave to enter or remain in the United Kingdom of the holder of a passport or travel document whose permission to enter another country has to be exercised before a given date may be restricted so as to terminate at least 2 months before that date.

22. If his passport or travel document is endorsed with a restriction on the period for which he may remain outside his country of normal residence, his leave to enter or remain in the United Kingdom may be limited so as not to extend beyond the period of authorised absence.

23. The holder of a travel document issued by the Home Office should not be given leave to enter or remain for a period extending beyond the validity of that document. This paragraph and paragraphs 21–22 do not apply to a person who is eligible for admission for settlement or to a spouse or civil partner who is eligible for admission under paragraph 282 or to a person who qualifies for the removal of the time limit on his stay.

Leave to enter granted on arrival in the United Kingdom

23A. A person who is not a visa national and who is seeking leave to enter on arrival in the United Kingdom for a period not exceeding 6 months for a purpose for which prior entry clearance is not required under these Rules may be granted such leave, for a period not exceeding 6 months. This paragraph does not apply where the person is a British National (Overseas), a British overseas territories citizen, a British Overseas citizen, a British protected person, or a person who under the British Nationality Act 1981 is a British subject.

23B. A person who is a British National (Overseas), a British overseas territories citizen, a British Overseas citizen, a British protected person, or a person who under the British Nationality Act 1981 is a British subject, and who is seeking leave to enter on arrival in the United Kingdom for a purpose for which prior entry clearance is not required under these Rules may be granted such leave, irrespective of the period of time for which he seeks entry, for a period not exceeding 6 months.

Entry clearance

24. The following must produce to the Immigration Officer a valid passport or other identity document endorsed with a United Kingdom entry clearance issued to him for the purpose for which he seeks entry:

(i) a visa national;

(ii) any other person (other than British Nationals (Overseas), a British overseas territories citizen, a British Overseas citizen, a British protected person or a person who under the British Nationality Act 1981 is a British subject) who is seeking entry for a period exceeding six months or is seeking entry for a purpose for which prior entry clearance is required under these Rules.

Such a person will be refused leave to enter if he has no such current entry clearance. Any other person who wishes to ascertain in advance whether he is eligible for admission to the United Kingdom may apply for the issue of an entry clearance.

25.   Entry clearance takes the form of a visa (for visa nationals) or an entry certificate (for non visa nationals). These documents are to be taken as evidence of the holder's eligibility for entry into the United Kingdom, and accordingly accepted as 'entry clearances' within the meaning of the Immigration Act 1971.

25A.   An entry clearance which satisfies the requirements set out in article 3 of the Immigration (Leave to Enter and Remain) Order 2000 will have effect as leave to enter the United Kingdom. The requirements are that the entry clearance must specify the purpose for which the holder wishes to enter the United Kingdom and should be endorsed with the conditions to which it is subject or wish a statement that it has effect as indefinite leave to enter the United Kingdom. The holder of such an entry clearance will not require leave to enter on arrival in the United Kingdom and, for the purposes of these Rules, will be treated as a person who has arrived in the United Kingdom with leave to enter the United Kingdom which is in force but which was given to him before his arrival.

26.   An application for entry clearance will be considered in accordance with the provisions in these Rules governing the grant or refusal of leave to enter. Where appropriate, the term 'Entry Clearance Officer' should be substituted for 'Immigration Officer'.

27.   An application for entry clearance is to be decided in the light of the circumstances existing at the time of the decision, except that an applicant will not be refused an entry clearance where entry is sought in one of the categories contained in paragraphs 296–316 *or paragraph EC-C of Appendix FM* solely on account of his attaining the age of 18 years between receipt of his application and the date of the decision on it.

28.   An applicant for an entry clearance must be outside the United Kingdom and Islands at the time of the application. An applicant for an entry clearance who is seeking entry as a short-term student must apply to a post designated by the Secretary of State to accept applications for entry clearance for that purpose and from that category of applicant. Subject to paragrapgh 28A, any other application must be made to the post in the country or territory where the applicant is living which has been designated by the Secretary of State to accept applications for entry clearance for that purpose and from that category of applicant. Where there is no such post the applicant must apply to the appropriate designated post outside the country or territory where he is living.

28A.   (a)   An application for entry clearance as a Tier 5 (Temporary Worker) Migrant in the creative and sporting sub-category of Tier 5 may also be made at the post in the country or territory where the applicant is situated at the time of the application, provided that:

   (i)   the post has been designated by the Secretary of State to accept applications for entry clearance for that purpose and from that category of applicant,

   (ii)   the applicant is in that country or territory for a similar purpose to the activity he proposes to undertake in the UK, and

   (iii)   the applicant is able to demonstrate to the Entry Clearance Officer that he has authority to be living in that country or territory in accordance with its immigration laws. Those applicants who are known to the authorities of that country or territory but who have not been given permission to live in that country or territory will not be eligible to make an application.

   (b)   An application for entry clearance as a Tier 1 (Exceptional Talent) Migrant or as a Tier 5 (Youth Mobility Scheme) Temporary Migrant may also be made at the post in the country or territory where the applicant is situated at the time of the application, provided that:

   (i)   the post has been designated by the Secretary of State to accept applications for entry clearance for that purpose and from that category of applicant, and

   (ii)   the applicant is able to demonstrate to the Entry Clearance Officer that he has authority to be living in that country or territory in accordance with its immigration laws and that when he was given authority to live in that country or territory he was given authority to live in that country or territory for a period of more than 6 months. Those applicants who are known to the authorities of that country or territory but who have not been given permission to live in that country or territory will not be eligible to make an application.

29.   For the purposes of paragraph 28 'post' means a British Diplomatic Mission, British Consular post or the office of any person outside the United Kingdom and Islands who has been authorised by the Secretary of State to accept applications for entry clearance. A list of designated posts is published by the Foreign and Commonwealth Office.

30.   An application for an entry clearance is not made until any fee required to be paid under the Consular Fees Act 1980 (including any Regulations or Orders made under that Act) has been paid.

30A.   An entry clearance may be revoked if the Entry Clearance Officer is satisfied that:

(i)   whether or not to the holder's knowledge, false representations were employed or material facts were not disclosed, either in writing or orally, for the purpose of obtaining the entry clearance; or

(ii)   a change of circumstances since the entry clearance was issued has removed the basis of the holder's claim to be admitted to the United Kingdom, except where the change of circumstances amounts solely to his exceeding the age for entry in one of the categories contained in paragraphs 296–316 of these Rules since the issue of the entry clearance; or

(iii)   the holder's exclusion from the United Kingdom would be conducive to the public good.

30B.   An entry clearance shall cease to have effect where the entry clearance has effect as leave to enter and an Immigration Officer cancels that leave in accordance with paragraph 2A(8) of Schedule 2 to the Immigration Act 1971.

30C.   An Immigration Officer may cancel an entry clearance which is capable of having effect as leave to enter if the holder arrives in the United Kingdom before the day on which the entry clearance becomes effective or if the holder seeks to enter the United Kingdom for a purpose other than the purpose specified in the entry clearance.

Variation of leave to enter or remain in the United Kingdom

31.   Under Section 3(3) of the 1971 Act a limited leave to enter or remain in the United Kingdom may be varied by extending or restricting its duration, by adding, varying or revoking conditions or by removing the time limit (where upon any condition attached to the leave ceases to apply). When leave to enter or remain is varied an entry is to be made in the applicant's passport or travel document (and his registration certificate where appropriate) or the decision may be made known in writing in some other appropriate way.

31A.   Where a person has arrived in the United Kingdom with leave to enter or remain in the United Kingdom which is in force but was given to him before his arrival, he may apply, on arrival at the port of entry in the United Kingdom, for variation of that leave. An Immigration Officer acting on behalf of the Secretary of State may vary the leave at the port of entry but is not obliged to consider an application for variation made at the port of entry. If an Immigration Officer acting on behalf of the Secretary of State has declined to consider an application for variation of leave at a port of entry but the leave has not been cancelled under paragraph 2A(8) of Schedule 2 to the Immigration Act 1971, the person seeking variation should apply to the Home office under paragraph 32.

32.   DELETED

33.   DELETED

33A.   Where a person having left the common travel area, has leave to enter or remain in the United Kingdom which remains in force under article 13 of the Immigration (Leave to Enter and Remain) Order 2000., his leave may be varied (including any condition to which it is subject in such form and manner as permitted for the giving of leave to enter. However, the Secretary of State is not obliged to consider an application for variation of leave to enter or remain from a person outside the United Kingdom.

33B.–33G.   DELETED

Specified forms and procedures for applications or claims in connection with immigration

A34.   An application for leave to remain in the United Kingdom under these Rules must be made either by completing the relevant online application process in accordance with paragraph A34 (iii) or by using the specified application form in accordance with paragraphs 34A to 34D.

(i)   'The relevant online application process' means the application process accessible via the visas and immigration pages of the gov.uk website and identified there as relevant for applications for leave to remain for the immigration category under which the applicant wishes to apply.

(ii)   'Specified' in relation to the relevant online application process means specified in the online guidance accompanying that process.

(iii)   When the application is made via the relevant online application process:

    (a)   any specified fee in connection with the application must be paid in accordance with the method specified;

    (b)   if the online application process requires the applicant to provide biometric information that information must be provided as specified;

(c)   if the online application process requires supporting documents to be submitted by post then any such documents specified as mandatory must be submitted in the specified manner within 15 working days of submission of the online application;

(d)   if the online application process requires the applicant to make an appointment to attend a public enquiry office of the United Kingdom Border Agency the applicant must, within 45 working days of submission of the online application, make and attend that appointment; and comply with any specified requirements in relation to the provision of biometric information and documents specified as mandatory; and

(e)   the requirements of paragraph 34BB must be met.

Notice of invalidity will be given in writing and deemed to be received on the date it is given, except where it is sent by post, in which case it will be deemed to be received on the second day after it was posted excluding any day which is not a business day.

34.   An application form is specified when:

(i)   it is posted on the visas and immigration pages of the gov.uk website of the Home Office,

(ii)   it is marked on the form that it is a specified form for the purpose of the immigration rules,

(iii)   it comes into force on the date specified on the form and/or in any accompanying announcement.

34A.   Where an application form is specified, the application or claim must also comply with the following requirements:

(i)   Subject to paragraph A34 the application or claim must be made using the specified form,

(ii)   any specified fee in connection with the application or claim must be paid in accordance with the method specified in the application form, separate payment form and/or related guidance notes, as applicable,

(iii)   any section of the form which is designated as mandatory in the application form and/or related guidance notes must be completed as specified,

(iv)   if the application form and/or related guidance notes require the applicant to provide biometric information, such information must be provided as specified,

(v)   an appointment for the purposes stated in subparagraph (iv) must be made and must take place by the dates specified in any subsequent notification by the Secretary of State following receipt of the application, or as agreed by the Secretary of State,

(vi)   where the application or claim is made by post or courier, or submitted in person:

(a)   the application or claim must be accompanied by the photographs and documents specified as mandatory in the application form and/or related guidance notes,

(ab)   those photographs must be in the same format specified as mandatory in the application form and/or related guidance notes, and

(b)   the form must be signed by the applicant, and where applicable, the applicant's spouse, civil partner, same-sex partner or unmarried partner, save that where the applicant is under the age of eighteen, the form may be signed by the parent or legal guardian of the applicant on his behalf, and

(vii)   the requirements of paragraph 34BB must be met.

34B.   Where an application form is specified, it must be sent by prepaid post to the Home Office at the address specified on the application form for such purposes, or submitted in person at a Home Office premium service centre. Application types permitted in person at a Home Office premium service centre are listed on the visa and immigration pages of the gov.uk website.

(i)   an application may be sent by courier to the Home Office at the address specified on the application form for such purposes if it is an application for:

(a)   limited or indefinite leave to remain as a sole representative, retired person of independent means or as a Tier 1 Migrant or Tier 2 Migrant;

(b)   limited leave to remain for work permit employment, as a seasonal agricultural worker, for the purpose of employment under the Sectors-Based Scheme.

(c)   Indefinite leave to remain as a businessperson, investor or innovator, or

(d)   limited leave to remain as a Tier 5 (Temporary Worker) Migrant.

(ii)   an applicant may submit an application online where this option is available on the visa and immigration pages of the gov.uk website

(iii) an application may not be sent by pre-paid post, and must be made online, if it is an application for a Tier 2, Tier 4 or Tier 5 (Temporary Worker) sponsorship licence.

34BB. (1) Where an application for limited or indefinite leave to remain in the United Kingdom is made by completing the relevant online application process, the supporting documents submitted in accordance with paragraph A34(iii)(c) must be accompanied by an original, valid passport, travel document or (unless the applicant is a Points Based System Migrant) national identity card issued to the applicant and to any dependant included in the application, unless sub-paragraph (3) applies.

(2) Where an application for limited or indefinite leave to remain in the United Kingdom is made, for which an application form is specified, the application must be accompanied by an original, valid passport, travel document or (unless the applicant is a Points Based System Migrant) national identity card issued to the applicant and to any dependant included in the application, unless sub-paragraph (3) applies.

(3) This sub-paragraph applies where:

(i) the application is made:

(a) for limited leave to enable access to public funds pending an application under paragraph 289A of, or under Part 6 of Appendix Armed Forces or section DVILR of Appendix FM to, these Rules; or

(b) by a stateless person or the family member of a stateless person under Part 14 of these Rules; or

(c) by a person in the UK with refugee status or humanitarian protection; or

(ii) the passport, travel document or national identity card of the applicant or (as the case may be) the dependant is held by the Home Office at the date of application; or

(iii) the Secretary of State considers that there is a good reason beyond the control of the applicant or (as the case may be) the dependant, given in or with the application, why an original, valid passport, travel document or (unless the applicant is a Points Based System Migrant) national identity card cannot be provided, e.g. where it has been retained by an employer or other person in circumstances which have led to the applicant being the subject of a positive conclusive grounds decision made by a competent authority under the National Referral Mechanism, or where it has been permanently lost and there is no functioning national government to issue a replacement.

(4) Where sub-paragraph (3)(iii) applies, the Secretary of State may require the person to provide alternative satisfactory evidence of his or her identity and nationality.

(5) Where sub-paragraph (3)(ii) or (iii) applies to the applicant or (as the case may be) to a dependant included in the application, the requirement in sub- paragraph (1) or (as the case may be) (2) continues to apply to any other person included in the application.

34C. Where an application or claim in connection with immigration for which an application form is specified does not comply with the requirements in paragraph 34A, or where an application for leave to remain in the United Kingdom is made by completing the relevant online application process, and does not comply with the requirements of paragraph A34(iii), the following applies:

(a) Subject to sub-paragraph (b), the application will be invalid and will not be considered. Notice of invalidity will be given in writing and deemed to be received on the date it is given, except where it is sent by post, in which case it will be deemed to be received on the second day after it was posted excluding any day which is not a business day, unless the contrary is proved.

(b) The decision maker may contact the applicant or their representative in writing and give the applicant a single opportunity to correct any omission or error which renders the application invalid, save for failure to enrol their biometric information. The amended application and/or any requested documents must be received at the address specified in the request within 10 business days of the date on which the request was sent.

34D. Where the main applicant wishes to include applications or claims by any members of his family as his dependants on his own application form, the applications or claims of the dependants must meet the following requirements or they will be invalid and will not be considered:

(i) the application form must expressly permit the applications or claims of dependants to be included, and

(ii) such dependants must be:

(a) the spouse, civil partner, unmarried or same-sex partner of the main applicant; and/or

(b)   children of the main applicant aged under 18; and/or

(c)   where permitted by the Rules for the immigration category under which the applicant wishes to apply, any dependants of the main applicant aged 18 or over.

Variation of Applications or Claims for Leave to Remain

34E.   If a person wishes to vary the purpose of an application or claim for leave to remain in the United Kingdom and an application form is specified for such new purpose or paragraph A34 applies, the variation must comply with the requirements of paragraph 34A or paragraph A34 (as they apply at the date the variation is made) as if the variation were a new application or claim, or the variation will be invalid and will not be considered.

34F.   Any valid variation of a leave to remain application will be decided in accordance with the immigration rules in force at the date such variation is made.

Determination of the date of an application or claim (or variation of an application or claim) for leave to remain

34G.   For the purposes of these rules, the date on which an application or claim (or a variation in accordance with paragraph 34E) is made is as follows:

(i)   where the application form is sent by post by Royal Mail, the date of posting,

(ii)   where the application form is submitted in person, the date on which it is accepted by a Home Office premium service centre,

(iii)   where the application form is sent by courier, or other postal services provider, the date on which it is delivered to the Home Office, or

(iv)   where the application is made via the online application process, on the date on which the online application is submitted.

34H.   Applications or claims for leave to remain made before 29 February 2008 for which a form was prescribed prior to 29 February 2008 shall be subject to the forms and procedures as in force on the date on which the application or claim was made.

34I.   Where an application or claim is made no more than 21 days after the date on which a form is specified under the immigration rules and on a form that was permitted for such application or claim immediately prior to the date of such specification, the application or claim shall be deemed to have been made on the specified form.

Withdrawn applications or claims for leave to remain in the United Kingdom

34J.   Where a person whose application or claim for leave to remain is being considered requests the return of his passport for the purpose of travel outside the common travel area, the application for leave shall, provided it has not already been determined, be treated as withdrawn on the date that request is received by the Home Office.

34K.   Paragraph 34J does not apply to an applicant who is applying as a Tier 2 Migrant or a Tier 5 Migrant and whose application is supported by a Certificate of Sponsorship from a Premium Sponsor.

34L.–34Y.   OMITTED

Undertakings

35.   A sponsor of a person seeking leave to enter or remain in the United Kingdom may be asked to give an undertaking in writing to be responsible for that person's maintenance, accommodation and (as appropriate) personal care for the period of any leave granted, including any further variation or for a period of 5 years from date of grant where indefinite leave to enter or remain is granted. Under the Social Security Administration Act 1992 and the Social Security Administration (Northern Ireland) Act 1992, the Department of Social Security or, as the case may be, the Department of Health and Social Services in Northern Ireland, may seek to recover from the person giving such an undertaking any income support paid to meet the needs of the person in respect of whom the undertaking has been given. Under the Immigration and Asylum Act 1999 the Home Office may seek to recover from the person giving such an undertaking amounts attributable to any support provided under section 95 of the Immigration and Asylum Act 1999 (support for asylum seekers) to, or in respect of, the person in respect of whom the undertaking has been given. Failure by the sponsor to maintain that person in accordance with the undertaking, may also be an offence under section 105 of the Social Security Administration Act 1992 and/or under section 108 of the Immigration and Asylum Act 1999 if, as a consequence, asylum support and/or income support is provided to, or in respect of, that person.

Medical

36. A person who intends to remain in the United Kingdom for more than 6 months should normally be referred to the Medical Inspector for examination. If he produces a medical certificate he should be advised to hand it to the Medical Inspector. Any person seeking entry who mentions health or medical treatment as a reason for his visit, or who appears not to be in good mental or physical health, should also be referred to the Medical Inspector; and the Immigration Officer has discretion, which should be exercised sparingly, to refer for examination in any other case.

37. Where the Medical Inspector advises that a person seeking entry is suffering from a specified disease or condition which may interfere with his ability to support himself or his dependants, the Immigration Officer should take account of this, in conjunction with other factors, in deciding whether to admit that person. The Immigration Officer should also take account of the Medical Inspector's assessment of the likely course of treatment in deciding whether a person seeking entry for private medical treatment has sufficient means at his disposal.

38. A returning resident should not be refused leave to enter or have existing leave to enter or remain cancelled on medical grounds. But where a person would be refused leave to enter or have existing leave to enter or remain cancelled on medical grounds if he were not a returning resident or in any case where it is decided on compassionate grounds not to exercise the power to refuse leave to enter or to cancel existing leave to enter or remain, or in any other case where the Medical Inspector so recommends, the Immigration Officer should give the person concerned a notice requiring him to report to the Medical Officer of Environmental Health designated by the Medical Inspector with a view to further examination and any necessary treatment.

A39. Any person making an application for entry clearance to come to the UK for more than six months or as a fiancé(e) or proposed civil partner applying for leave to enter under Section EC-P:Entry clearance as a partner under Appendix FM, having been present in a country listed in Appendix T for more than six months immediately prior to their application, must present, at the time of application, a valid medical certificate issued by a medical practitioner approved by the Secretary of State for these purposes, as listed on the Gov.uk website, confirming that they have undergone screening for active pulmonary tuberculosis and that this tuberculosis is not present in the applicant.

B39. Applicants seeking leave to enter as a returning resident under paragraph 19 of these rules, having been absent from the United Kingdom for more than two years are also subject to the requirements in paragraph A39.

C39. Where a person has lawfully been present in a country not mentioned in Appendix T for more than six months and they are applying for entry clearance as in A39 in a country in Appendix T but have not been in that country or any other country mentioned in Appendix T for more than six months immediately before making their application, they will not be required to produce a medical certificate showing they are free from active pulmonary TB. This does not alter the discretionary powers as in paragraph 39 below.

39. The Entry Clearance Officer has the same discretion as an Immigration Officer to refer applicants for entry clearance for medical examination and the same principles will apply to the decision whether or not to issue an entry clearance.

Students

39A. An application for a variation of leave to enter or remain made by a student who is sponsored by a government or international sponsorship agency may be refused if the sponsor has not given written consent to the proposed variation.

Specified documents

39B. (a) Where these Rules state that specified documents must be provided, that means documents specified in these Rules as being specified documents for the route under which the applicant is applying. If the specified documents are not provided, the applicant will not meet the requirement for which the specified documents are required as evidence.

  (b) Where these Rules specify documents that are to be provided, those documents are considered to be specified documents, whether or not they are named as such, and as such are subject to the requirements in (c) to (f) below.

  (c) If the Entry Clearance Officer or Secretary of State has reasonable cause to doubt the genuineness of any document submitted by an applicant which is, or which purports to be, a specified document under these Rules, and having taken reasonable steps to verify the document is unable to verify that it is genuine, the document will be discounted for the purposes of this application.

(d)   Specified documents must be originals, not copies, except where stated otherwise.

(e)   Specified documents must contain, or the applicant must provide, full contact details to allow each document to be verified.

(f)   Where any specified documents provided are not in English or Welsh, the applicant must provide the original and a full translation that can be independently verified by the Entry Clearance Officer, Immigration Officer or the Secretary of State. The translation must be dated and include:

   (i)   confirmation that it is an accurate translation of the original document;

   (ii)   the full name and original signature of the translator or an authorised official of the translation company;

   (iii) the translator or translation company's contact details; and

   (iv)   if the applicant is applying for leave to remain or indefinite leave to remain, certification by a qualified translator and details of the translator or translation company's credentials.

Indefinite leave to enter or remain

39C.   (a)   An applicant for indefinite leave to enter or remain must, unless the applicant provides a reasonable explanation, comply with any request made by the Secretary of State to attend an interview.

   (b)   If the decision-maker has reasonable cause to doubt (on examination or interview or on any other basis) that any document submitted by an applicant for the purposes of satisfying the requirements of Appendix KoLL of these Rules was genuinely obtained, that document may be discounted for the purposes of the application.

   (c)   Where sub-paragraph (b) applies, the decision-maker may request the applicant to provide additional evidence of knowledge of the English language and/or knowledge about life in the UK (as set out in paragraphs 3.2(b)(ii) and 3.3 of Appendix KoLL) for the purposes of demonstrating sufficient knowledge of the English language requirement and sufficient knowledge about life in the United Kingdom in accordance with Appendix KoLL.

   (d)   A decision-maker will not request evidence under sub-paragraph (c) where the decision-maker does not anticipate that the supply of that evidence will lead to a grant of leave to enter or remain in the United Kingdom because the application may be refused for other reasons.

Power to interview a person with limited leave to enter or remain

39D.   For the purpose of assessing whether any of the grounds of curtailment under paragraphs 245DE(c), 245EE(c), 276BD1, 276BN1, 276BS1, 323 (other than 323(vii)), 323A, 323B, or 323C, apply the Secretary of State may request a person who holds limited leave to enter or remain in the UK to:

   (i)   provide additional information and evidence to the Home Office at the address specified in the request within 28 calendar days of the date the request is sent; and/or

   (ii)   attend an interview.

Part 2 – Transitional provisions Part 2 and Appendix V: Immigration Rules for Visitors

1   Appendix V: Immigration Rules for Visitors will apply to all visitor applications for entry clearance, leave to enter or remain decided on or after 24 April 2015. Any references in legislation or in a ministerial authorisation made under paragraph 17(4), Schedule 3 of the Equality Act 2010 to an application for entry clearance, leave to enter or remain under Part 2 of the Immigration Rules shall, in relation to any application made by a visitor on or after 24th April 2015 and unless the context otherwise requires, be read as a reference to an application for a visit visa under Appendix V: Immigration Rules for Visitors.

2   An application made under paragraphs 56K to 56M for a student visit before 24 April 2015 will be decided as if it were an application for short-term study under paragraphs A57A to A57H of these Rules.

3   An application made under paragraphs 56A to 56C for a parent of a child at school visitor before 24 April 2015 will be decided as if it were an application for a Tier 4 (child) student under paragraphs 276BT1 to 276BV1 of these Rules.

4   From 24 April 2015 the following provisions of these rules will not apply to visitors, except where specifically provided for in Appendix V: Immigration Rules for Visitors:

a.   Paragraph 6;

b.   Part 1;

c.   Part 9;

d.   Appendix 1;

e.   Appendix R.

Part 3 – Persons seeking to enter or remain in the United Kingdom for studies

Students

Persons seeking to enter the UK for short-term study

Introduction

A57A. These Rules apply to persons who wish to study in the UK as a short- term student for up to and including 6 months or, for persons aged 18 and over, for up to and including 11 months for English language study only.

A57B. In paragraphs A57A to A57H:

(a)   English language study means study on a course that is entirely English language, not one that includes study of other subjects;

(b)   State-maintained school or institution is one which provides a free education and is primarily funded from public funds.

(c)   An accredited institution must be:

(i)   the holder of a sponsor licence for Tier 4 of the Points Based System; or

(ii)   the holder of valid accreditation from Accreditation UK, the Accreditation Body for Language Services (ABLS), the British Accreditation Council (BAC) or the Accreditation Service for International Colleges (ASIC); or

(iii)   the holder of a valid and satisfactory full institutional inspection, review or audit by one of the following bodies: Bridge Schools Inspectorate; Estyn; Education Scotland; the Independent Schools Inspectorate; Office for Standards in Education; the Quality Assurance Agency for Higher Education; the Schools Inspection Service or the Education and Training Inspectorate Northern Ireland; or

(iv)   an overseas Higher Education Institution offering only part of their programmes in the United Kingdom, holding its own national accreditation and offering programmes that are an equivalent level to a United Kingdom degree.

Requirements for entry clearance or leave to enter – Short-Term Student

A57C. All applicants for entry clearance or leave to enter the UK as a short-term student must meet the following requirements:

(a)   the applicant does not fall for refusal under the general grounds for refusal; and,

(b)   meets all of the following requirements. The student:

(i)   is aged 18 or over.

(ii)   does not intend to study at a state-maintained school or institution.

(iii)   does not intend to study in the UK for extended periods through frequent or successive periods as a short-term student.

(iv)   does not intend to take employment, including paid or unpaid work, a work placement or work experience in the UK.

(v)   does not intend to undertake self-employment or engage in business activities or any professional activity in the UK.

(vi)   has enough funds to meet the cost of his return or onward journey from the UK.

(vii)   will be maintained and accommodated adequately out of funds available to him.

(viii) will not have recourse to public funds.

A57D. Applicants for entry clearance or leave to enter the UK as a short-term student for up to and including 6 months must meet the requirements in A57C and all of the following requirements:

(a)   Either;

(i)   has been accepted on a course of study of no more than 6 months, which is to be provided by an accredited institution; or

(ii)   is enrolled on a course of study abroad equivalent to at least degree level study in the UK and has been accepted by a UK recognised body or a body in receipt of public funding as a higher education institution from the Department for Employment and Learning in Northern Ireland, the Higher Education Funding Council for England, the Higher Education Funding Council for Wales or the Scottish Funding Council to undertake research or be taught about research (research tuition) at the UK institution, provided that the overseas course provider confirms that the research or research tuition is part of or relevant to the course of study that they are enrolled on overseas, and the student is not to be employed as a sponsored researcher under the relevant Tier 5 Government Authorised Exchange scheme, or under Tier 2 of the Points-Based System, at the UK institution;

and

(b)   intends to leave the UK at the end of the study or at the end of 6 months whichever is sooner.

(c)   holds a valid entry clearance as a short-term student for 6 months unless he is a non-visa national.

A57E.   Applicants for entry clearance or leave to enter the UK as a short-term student for up to and including 11 months must meet the requirements in A57C and all of the following requirements:

(a)   has been accepted on a course of study in English language of no more than 11 months which is to be provided by an accredited institution; and

(b)   intends to leave the UK at the end of the study or at the end of 11 months whichever is sooner; and

(c)   holds a valid entry clearance as a short-term student for a period not exceeding 11 months.

Period and conditions of grant of entry clearance or leave to enter for short- term students

A57F.   (a)   Entry clearance or leave to enter the UK as a short-term student will be granted for a period not exceeding 6 months where paragraph A57D applies;

(b)   Entry clearance to enter the UK as a short-term student will be granted for a period not exceeding 11 months where paragraph A57E applies.

Requirements for entry clearance or leave to enter – Short-term student (child)

A57G.   The requirements for entry clearance or leave to enter for short-term students (child) are that the applicant:

(a)   does not fall for refusal under the general grounds for refusal; and,

(b)   meets all of the following requirements. That the student:

(i)   is aged under 18;

(ii)   has been accepted on a course of study which is to be provided by an accredited institution which is not a state-maintained school or institution;

(iii)   does not intend to study at a state-maintained school or institution;

(iv)   intends to leave the UK at the end of 6 months;

(v)   does not intend to study in the UK for extended periods through frequent or successive periods as a short-term student;

(vi)   does not intend to take employment, including paid or unpaid work, work placements or work experience in the UK;

(vii)   does not intend to undertake self-employment or engage in business or any professional activities in the UK;

(viii) has enough funds to meet the cost of his return or onward journey from the UK;

(ix)   will be maintained and accommodated adequately out of funds available to him

(x)   will not have recourse to public funds;

(xi)   can demonstrate that suitable arrangements have been made for his travel to, and reception and care in the UK;

(xii)   has a parent or guardian in his home country or country of habitual residence who is responsible for his care and who confirms that they consent to the arrangements for the applicant's travel, reception and care in the UK; and

(xiii) if a visa national;

(a) the applicant holds a valid United Kingdom entry clearance for entry as an accompanied short-term student (child) and is travelling in the company of the adult identified on the entry clearance, who is on the same occasion being admitted to the United Kingdom; or

(b) the applicant holds a valid United Kingdom entry for entry as an unaccompanied short-term student (child).

Period and conditions of grant of entry clearance or leave to enter as a short-term student (child)

A57H. Entry clearance or leave to enter as a short-term student (child) will be granted for a period not exceeding 6 months.

59.–75. DELETED.

Spouses or civil partners or students granted leave under paragraphs 57-75 (but not A57A to A57H)

Requirements for leave to enter or remain as the spouse or civil partner of a student granted leave under paragraphs 57-75 (but not A57A to A57H)

76. The requirements to be met by a person seeking leave to enter or remain in the United Kingdom as the spouse or civil partner of a student granted leave under paragraphs 57-75 (but not A57A to A57H) are that:

(i) the applicant is married to or the civil partner of a person admitted to or allowed to remain in the United Kingdom under paragraphs 57–75; and

(ii) each of the parties intends to live with the other as his or her spouse or civil partner during the applicant's stay and the marriage or the civil partner of is subsisting; and

(iii) there will be adequate accommodation for the parties and any dependants without recourse to public funds; and

(iv) the parties will be able to maintain themselves and any dependants adequately without recourse to public funds; and

(v) the applicant does not intend to take employment except as permitted under paragraph 77 below; and

(vi) the applicant intends to leave the United Kingdom at the end of any period of leave granted to him; and

(vii) if seeking leave to remain must not be in the UK in breach of immigration laws except that any period of overstaying for a period of 28 days or less will be disregarded.

Leave to enter or remain as the spouse or civil partner of a student or leave to remain as the spouse or civil partner of a prospective student

77. A person seeking leave to enter or remain in the United Kingdom as the spouse or civil partner of a student granted leave under paragraphs 57-75 (but not A57A to A57H) may be admitted or allowed to remain for a period not in excess of that granted to the student provided the Immigration Officer or, in the case of an application for limited leave to remain, the Secretary of State is satisfied that each of the requirements of paragraph 76 is met. Employment may be permitted where the period of leave granted to the student is, or was, 12 months or more. Study subject to the condition set out in Part 15 of these Rules.

Refusal of leave to enter or remain as the spouse or civil partner of a student granted leave under paragraphs 57-75 (but not A57A to A57H)

78. Leave to enter or remain as the spouse or civil partner of a student granted leave under paragraphs 57-75 (but not A57A to A57H) is to be refused if the Immigration Officer or, in the case of an application for limited leave to remain, the Secretary of State is not satisfied that each of the requirements of paragraph 76 is met.

Children of students granted leave under paragraphs 57-75 (but not A57A to A57H)

Requirements for leave to enter or remain as the child of a student granted leave under paragraphs 57-75 (but not A57A to A57H)

79. The requirements to be met by a person seeking leave to enter or remain in the United Kingdom as the child of a student granted leave under paragraphs 57-75 (but not A57A to A57H) are that he:

(i) is the child of a parent admitted to or allowed to remain in the United Kingdom as a student under paragraphs 57–75; and

(ii) is under the age of 18 or has current leave to enter or remain in this capacity; and

      (iii)   is not married or in a civil partnership, has not formed an independent family unit and is not leading an independent life; and

      (iv)   can, and will, be maintained and accommodated adequately without recourse to public funds; and

      (v)   will not stay in the United Kingdom beyond any period of leave granted to his parent; and

      (vi)   meets the requirements of paragraph 79A; and

      (vii)   if seeking leave to remain must not be in the UK in breach of immigration laws except that any period of overstaying for a period of 28 days or less will be disregarded.

79A.   Both of the applicant's parents must either be lawfully present in the UK, or being granted entry clearance or leave to remain at the same time as the applicant or one parent must be lawfully present in the UK and the other being granted entry clearance or leave to remain at the same time as the applicant, unless:

      (i)   The student is the applicant's sole surviving parent, or

      (ii)   The student parent has and has had sole responsibility for the applicant's upbringing, or

      (iii)   there are serious or compelling family or other considerations which would make it desirable not to refuse the application and suitable arrangements have been made in the UK for the applicant's care.

Leave to enter or remain as the child of a student granted leave under paragraphs 57-75 (but not A57A to A57H)

80.   A person seeking leave to enter or remain in the United Kingdom as the child of a student granted leave under paragraphs 57-75 (but not A57A to A57H) may be admitted or allowed to remain for a period not in excess of that granted to the student provided the Immigration Officer or, in the case of an application for limited leave to remain, the Secretary of State is satisfied that each of the requirements of paragraph 79 is met. Employment may be permitted where the period of leave granted to the student is, or was, 12 months or more. Study subject to the condition set out in Part 15 of these Rules where the applicant is 18 years of age or over at the time their leave is granted, or will be aged 18 or over before their period of limited leave expires.

Refusal of leave to enter or remain as the child of a student granted leave under paragraphs 57-75 (but not A57A to A57H)

81.   Leave to enter or remain in the United Kingdom as the child of a student granted leave under paragraphs 57-75 (but not A57A to A57H) is to be refused if the Immigration Officer or, in the case of an application for limited leave to remain, the Secretary of State, is not satisfied that each of the requirements of paragraph 79 is met.

A82–87F.   DELETED.

Part 4 – OMITTED

Part 5 – Persons seeking to enter or remain in the United Kingdom for employment

128A.–143F.   OMITTED

Representatives of overseas businesses

Requirements for leave to enter as a representative of an overseas business

144.   The requirements to be met by a person seeking leave to enter the United Kingdom as a representative of an overseas business are that he:

      (i)   has been recruited and taken on as an employee outside the United Kingdom of a business which has its headquarters and principal place of business outside the United Kingdom; and

      (ii)   is seeking entry to the United Kingdom:

            (a)   as a senior employee of an overseas business which has no branch, subsidiary or other representative in the United Kingdom with full authority to take operational decisions on behalf of the overseas business for the purpose of representing it in the United Kingdom by establishing and operating a registered branch or wholly owned subsidiary of that overseas business, the branch or subsidiary of which will be concerned with same type of business activity as the overseas business; or

(b) as an employee of an overseas newspaper, news agency or broadcasting organisation being posted on a long-term assignment as a representative of their overseas employer.

(iii) where entry is sought under (ii)(a), the person:

 (a) will be the sole representative of the employer present in the United Kingdom under the terms of this paragraph;

 (b) intends to be employed full time as a representative of that overseas business; and

 (c) is not a majority shareholder in that overseas business.

(iv) where entry is sought under (ii)(b), the person intends to work full-time as a representative of their overseas employer.

(v) does not intend to take employment except within the terms of this paragraph; and

(vi) has competence in the English language to the required standard on the basis that

 (a) the applicant is a national of one of the following countries: Antigua and Barbuda; Australia; the Bahamas; Barbados; Belize; Canada; Dominica; Grenada; Guyana; Jamaica; New Zealand; St Kitts and Nevis; St Lucia; St Vincent and the Grenadines; Trinidad and Tobago; United States of America; and provides the specified documents in paragraph 144-SD(a) or

 (b) the applicant has a knowledge of English equivalent to level A1 or above of the Council of Europe's Common European Framework for Language Learning, and

  (1) provides the specified documents from an English language test provider approved by the Secretary of State for these purposes, as listed in Appendix O, which clearly show the applicant's name, the qualification obtained (which must meet or exceed the standard described above) and the date of the award, or

  (2) has obtained an academic qualification (not a professional or vocational qualification) which is deemed by UK NARIC to meet the recognised standard of a Bachelor's degree in the UK, and

   (i) provides the specified documents in paragraph 144-SD(b) to show he has the qualification, and

   (ii) UK NARIC has confirmed that the qualification was taught or researched in English to level C1 of the Council of Europe's Common European Framework for Language learning or above, or

  (3) has obtained an academic qualification (not a professional or vocational qualification) which is deemed by UK NARIC to meet or exceed the recognised standard of a Bachelor's or Master's degree in the UK, and provides the specified documents in paragraph 144-SD(c) to show that:

   (i) he has the qualification, and

   (ii) the qualification was taught or researched in English, or

  (4) has obtained an academic qualification (not a professional or vocational qualification), which is deemed by UK NARIC to meet the recognised standard of a Bachelor's or Master's degree or PhD in the UK, from an educational establishment in one of the following countries: Antigua and Barbuda; Australia; The Bahamas; Barbados; Belize; Dominica; Grenada; Guyana; Ireland; Jamaica; New Zealand; St Kitts and Nevis; St Lucia; St Vincent and The Grenadines; Trinidad and Tobago; the UK; the USA; and provides the specified documents in paragraph 144-SD(b).

(vii) can maintain and accommodate himself and any dependants adequately without recourse to public funds; and

(viii) holds a valid United Kingdom entry clearance for entry in this capacity.

Specified documents

144-SD. (a) The specified documents in paragraph 144(vi)(a) as evidence of nationality are the applicant's current valid original passport or travel document. If the applicant is unable to provide these, the UK Border Agency may exceptionally consider this requirement to have been met where the applicant provides full reasons in the passport section of the application form, and either:

  (1) a current national identity document, or

(2)   an original letter from his home government or embassy, on the letter-headed paper of the government or embassy, which has been issued by an authorised official of that institution and confirms the applicant's full name, date of birth and nationality.

(b)   The specified documents in paragraph 144(vi)(b)(2)(i) and paragraph 144(vi)(4) as evidence of qualifications taught in English are:

(1)   the original certificate of the award, or

(2)   if the applicant is awaiting graduation having successfully completed the qualification, or no longer has the certificate and the awarding institution is unable to provide a replacement, an academic transcript (or original letter in the case of a PhD qualification) from the awarding institution on its official headed paper, which clearly shows:

(a)   the applicant's name,

(b)   the name of the awarding institution,

(c)   the title of the award,

(d)   confirmation that the qualification has been or will be awarded, and

(e)   the date that the certificate will be issued (if the applicant has not yet graduated) or confirmation that the institution is unable to reissue the original certificate or award.

(c)   The specified documents in paragraph 144(vi)(b)(3)(i) as evidence of qualifications taught in English are:

(1)   the specified documents in (b) above, and

(2)   an original letter from the awarding institution on its official headed paper, which clearly shows:

(a)   the applicant's name,

(b)   the name of the awarding institution,

(c)   the title of the award,

(d)   the date of the award, and

(e)   confirmation that the qualification was taught in English.

Leave to enter as a representative of an overseas business

145.   A person seeking leave to enter the United Kingdom as a representative of an overseas business may be admitted for a period not exceeding 3 years provided he is able to produce to the Immigration Officer, on arrival, a valid United Kingdom entry clearance for entry in this capacity, and his leave may be subject to the following conditions:

(i)   no recourse to public funds,

(ii)   registration with the police, if this is required by paragraph 326 of these Rules,

(iii)   no employment other than working for the business which the applicant has been admitted to represent, and

(iv)   study subject to the condition set out in Part 15 of these Rules.

Refusal of leave to enter as a representative of an overseas business

146.   Leave to enter as a representative of an overseas business is to be refused if a valid United Kingdom entry clearance for entry in this capacity is not produced to the Immigration Officer on arrival.

Requirements for an extension of stay as a representative of an overseas business

147.   The requirements for an extension of stay as a representative of an overseas business are that the applicant:

(i)   entered the United Kingdom with a valid United Kingdom entry clearance as:

(a)   a sole representative of an overseas business, including entry under the rules providing for the admission of sole representatives in force prior to 1 October 2009; or

(b)   a representative of an overseas newspaper, news agency or broadcasting organisation;

(ii)   the person was admitted in accordance with paragraph 144(ii)(a) and can show that:

(a)   the overseas business still has its headquarters and principal place of business outside the United Kingdom; and

(b)   he is employed full time as a representative of that overseas business and has established and is in charge of its registered branch or wholly owned subsidiary; and

(c)   he is still required for the employment in question, as certified by his employer;

(iii)   the person was admitted in accordance with paragraph 144(ii)(b) and can show that:

(a)   he is still engaged in the employment for which the entry clearance was granted; and

(b)   he is still required for the employment in question, as certified by his employer.

(iv)   does not intend to take employment except within the terms of this paragraph; and

(v)   can maintain and accommodate himself and any dependants adequately without recourse to public funds; and

(vi)   must not be in the UK in breach of immigration laws except that any period of overstaying for a period of 28 days or less will be disregarded.

Extension of stay as a representative of an overseas business

148.   An extension of stay as a representative of an overseas business may be granted provided the Secretary of State is satisfied that each of the requirements of paragraph 147 is met. The extension of stay will be granted for:

(i)   a period not exceeding 2 years, unless paragraph (ii) applies.

(ii)   a period not exceeding 3 years, if the applicant was last granted leave prior to 1 October 2009, and will be subject to the following conditions:

(i)   no recourse to public funds,

(ii)   registration with the police, if this is required by paragraph 326 of these Rules, and

(iii)   no employment other than working for the business which the applicant has been admitted to represent.

Refusal of extension of stay as a representative of an overseas business

149.   An extension of stay as a representative of an overseas business is to be refused if the Secretary of State is not satisfied that each of the requirements of paragraph 147 is met.

Indefinite leave to remain for a representative of an overseas business

150.   Indefinite leave to remain may be granted, on application, to a representative of an overseas business provided the applicant:

(i)   has spent a continuous period of 5 years lawfully in the United Kingdom in this capacity; and

(ii)   has met the requirements of paragraph 147 throughout the 5 year period; and

(iii)   is still required for the employment in question, as certified by the employer; and

(iv)   has demonstrated sufficient knowledge of the English language and sufficient knowledge about life in the United Kingdom, in accordance with Appendix KoLL, and

(v)   does not fall for refusal under the general grounds for refusal; and

(vi)   is not in the UK in breach of immigration laws except that any period of overstaying for a period of 28 days or less will be disregarded; and

(vii) provides the specified documents in paragraph 150-SD to evidence the reason for the absences set out in paragraph 128A.

Specified documents

150-SD.   The specified documents referred to in paragraph 150(vii) are:

(a)   A letter from the employer detailing the purpose and period of absences in connection with the employment, including periods of annual leave.

(b)   Where the absence was due to a serious or compelling reason, a personal letter from the applicant which includes full details of the reason for the absences and all original supporting documents in relation to those reasons – e.g. medical certificates, birth/death certificates, information about the reasons which led to the absence from the UK.

Refusal of indefinite leave to remain for a sole representative of an overseas business

151.   Indefinite leave to remain in the United Kingdom for a representative of an overseas business is to be refused if the Secretary of State is not satisfied that each of the requirements of paragraph 150 is met.

152–185.   OMITTED

Persons with United Kingdom ancestry

Requirements for leave to enter on the grounds of United Kingdom ancestry

186.   The requirements to be met by a person seeking leave to enter the United Kingdom on the grounds of his United Kingdom ancestry are that he:

(i)   is a Commonwealth citizen; and

(ii)   is aged 17 or over; and

(iii)   is able to provide proof that one of his grandparents was born in the United Kingdom and Islands and that any such grandparent is the applicant's blood grandparent or grandparent by reason of an adoption recognised by the laws of the United Kingdom relating to adoption; and

(iv)   is able to work and intends to take or seek employment in the United Kingdom; and

(v)   will be able to maintain and accommodate himself and any dependants adequately without recourse to public funds; and

(vi)   holds a valid United Kingdom entry clearance for entry in this capacity.

Leave to enter the United Kingdom on the grounds of United Kingdom ancestry

187.   A person seeking leave to enter the United Kingdom on the grounds of his United Kingdom ancestry may be given leave to enter for a period not exceeding 5 years, subject to a condition on study as set out in Part 15 of these Rules, provided he is able to produce to the Immigration Officer, on arrival, a valid United Kingdom entry clearance for entry in this capacity.

Refusal of leave to enter on the grounds of United Kingdom ancestry

188.   Leave to enter the United Kingdom on the grounds of United Kingdom ancestry is to be refused if a valid United Kingdom entry clearance for entry in this capacity is not produced to the Immigration Officer on arrival.

Requirements for an extension of stay on the grounds of United Kingdom ancestry

189.   The requirements to be met by a person seeking an extension of stay on the grounds of United Kingdom ancestry are that:

(i)   he is able to meet each of the requirements of paragraph 186 (i)–(v); and

(ii)   he was admitted to the United Kingdom on the grounds of United Kingdom ancestry in accordance with paragraphs 186 to 188 or has been granted an extension of stay in this capacity; and

(iii)   he is not in the UK in breach of immigration laws except that any period of overstaying for a period of 28 days or less will be disregarded.

Extension of stay on the grounds of United Kingdom ancestry

190.   An extension of stay on the grounds of United Kingdom ancestry may be granted for a period not exceeding 5 years, subject to a condition on study as set out in Part 15 of these Rules, provided the Secretary of State is satisfied that each of the requirements of paragraph 189 is met.

Refusal of extension of stay on the grounds of United Kingdom ancestry

191.   An extension of stay on the grounds of United Kingdom ancestry is to be refused if the Secretary of State is not satisfied that each of the requirements of paragraph 189 is met.

Indefinite leave to remain on the grounds of United Kingdom ancestry

192.   Indefinite leave to remain may be granted, on application, to a Commonwealth citizen with a United Kingdom born grandparent provided the applicant:

(i)   meets the requirements of paragraph 186 (i)–(v); and

(ii)   has spent a continuous period of 5 years lawfully in the United Kingdom in this capacity; and

(iii)   has demonstrated sufficient knowledge of the English language and sufficient knowledge about life in the United Kingdom, in accordance with Appendix KoLL; and

(iv)   does not fall for refusal under the general grounds for refusal; and

(v)   is not in the UK in breach of immigration laws except that any period of overstaying for a period of 28 days or less will be disregarded; and

(vi)   provides the specified documents in paragraph 192-SD to evidence the reason for the absences set out in paragraph 128A, where the absence was due to a serious or compelling reason.

Specified documents

192-SD. The specified documents referred to in paragraph 192(vi) are:

A personal letter from the applicant which includes full details of the reason for the absences and all original supporting documents in relation to those reasonse.g. medical certificates, birth/death certificates, information about the reasons which led to the absence from the UK.

Refusal of indefinite leave to remain on the grounds of United Kingdom ancestry

193. Indefinite leave to remain in the United Kingdom on the grounds of a United Kingdom born grandparent is to be refused if the Secretary of State is not satisfied that each of the requirements of paragraph 192 is met.

Partners of persons who have or have had leave to enter or remain under paragraphs 128–193 (but not paragraphs 135I–135K)

193A. Nothing in paragraphs 194–196F is to be construed as allowing a person to be granted entry clearance, leave to enter, leave to remain or variation of leave as a partner of a person granted entry clearance or leave to enter under Paragraph 159A where that entry clearance or leave to enter was granted under 159A on or after 6 April 2012.

Requirements for leave to enter as the partner of a person with limited leave to enter or remain in the United Kingdom under paragraphs 128–193 (but not paragraphs 135I–135K)

194. The requirements to be met by a person seeking leave to enter the United Kingdom as the partner of a person with limited leave to enter or remain in the United Kingdom under paragraphs 128–193 (but not paragraphs 135I–135K) are that:

(i) the applicant is the spouse, civil partner, unmarried or same-sex partner of a person with limited leave to enter in the United Kingdom under paragraphs 128–193 (but not paragraphs 135I–135K); and

(ii) if an unmarried or same-sex partner:

(1) any previous marriage or civil partnership (or similar relationship) by either partner has permanently broken down; and

(2) the parties are not involved in a consanguineous relationship with one another; and

(3) the parties have been living together in a relationship akin to marriage or civil partnership which has subsisted for 2 years or more; and

(iii) each of the parties intends to live with the other as his or her partner during the applicant's stay and the relationship is subsisting; and

(iv) there will be adequate accommodation for the parties and any dependants without recourse to public funds in accommodation which they own or occupy exclusively; and

(v) the parties will be able to maintain themselves and any dependants adequately without recourse to public funds; and

(vi) the applicant does not intend to stay in the United Kingdom beyond any period of leave granted to his partner; and

(vii) the applicant does not fall for refusal under the general grounds for refusal; and

(viii) the applicant holds a valid United Kingdom entry clearance for entry in this capacity.

Leave to enter as the partner of a person with limited leave to enter or remain in the United Kingdom under paragraphs 128–193 (but not paragraphs 135I–135K)

195. A person seeking leave to enter the United Kingdom as the partner of a person with limited leave to enter or remain in the United Kingdom under paragraphs 128–193 (but not paragraphs 135I–135K) may be given leave to enter for a period not in excess of that granted to the person with limited leave to enter or remain under paragraphs 128–193 (but not paragraphs 135I–135K), subject to a condition on study as set out in Part 15 of these Rules, provided the Immigration Officer is satisfied that each of the requirements of paragraph 194 is met. If the person is seeking leave to enter as the partner of a Highly Skilled Migrant, leave which is granted will be subject to a condition prohibiting Employment as a Doctor or Dentist in Training, unless the applicant has obtained a degree in medicine or dentistry at bachelor's level or above from a UK institution that is a UK recognised or listed body, or which holds a sponsor licence under Tier 4 of the Points Based System and provides evidence of this degree.

Refusal of leave to enter as the partner of a person with limited leave to enter or remain in the United Kingdom under paragraphs 128–193 (but not paragraphs 135I–135K)

196. Leave to enter the United Kingdom as the partner of a person with limited leave to enter or remain in the United Kingdom under paragraphs 128–193 (but not paragraphs 135I–135K) is to be refused if the Immigration Officer is not satisfied that each of the requirements of paragraph 194 is met.

Requirements for extension of stay as the partner of a person who has or has had leave to enter or remain in the United Kingdom under paragraphs 128–193 (but not paragraphs 135I–135K)

196A. The requirements to be met by a person seeking an extension of stay in the United Kingdom as the partner of a person who has or has had leave to enter or remain in the United Kingdom under paragraphs 128–193 (but not paragraphs 135I–135K) are that the applicant:

   (i)   is the spouse, civil partner, unmarried or same sex partner of a person who:

      (1)   has limited leave to enter or remain in the United Kingdom under paragraphs 128–193 (but not paragraphs 135I–135K); or

      (2)   has indefinite leave to remain in the United Kingdom or has become a British citizen, and who had limited leave to enter or remain in the United Kingdom under paragraphs 128–193 (but not paragraphs 135I–135K) immediately before being granted indefinite leave to remain; and

   (ii)   meets the requirements of paragraph 194(ii)–(vii); and

   (iii)   was not last granted:

      (1)   entry clearance or leave as a visitor, short-term student or short-term student (child),

      (2)   temporary admission, or

      (3)   temporary release; and

   (iv)   must not be in the UK in breach of immigration laws except that any period of overstaying for a period of 28 days or less will be disregarded.

Extension of stay as the partner of a person who has or has had leave to enter or remain in the United Kingdom under paragraphs 128–193 (but not paragraphs 135I–135K)

196B. An extension of stay in the United Kingdom as:

   (i)   the partner of a person who has limited leave to enter or remain under paragraphs 128–193 (but not paragraphs 135I–135K) may be granted, subject to a condition on study as set out in Part 15 of these Rules, for a period not in excess of that granted to the person with limited leave to enter or remain; or

   (ii)   the partner of a person who is being admitted at the same time for settlement, or the partner of a person who has indefinite leave to remain or has become a British citizen, may be granted for a period not exceeding 2 years, subject to a condition on study as set out in Part 15 of these Rules, in both instances, provided the Secretary of State is satisfied that each of the requirements of paragraph 196A is met.

If the person is seeking an extension of stay as the partner, of a Highly Skilled Migrant, leave which is granted will be subject to a condition prohibiting Employment as a Doctor or Dentist in Training, unless the applicant:

   (1)   has obtained a primary degree in medicine or dentistry at bachelor's level or above from a UK institution that is a UK recognised or listed body, or which holds a sponsor licence under Tier 4 of the Points Based System; or

   (2)   has, or has last been granted, entry clearance, leave to enter or leave to remain that was not subject to any condition restricting him from taking employment as a Doctor in Training, and has been employed during that leave as a Doctor in Training; or

   (3)   has, or has last been granted, entry clearance, leave to enter or leave to remain that was not subject to any condition restricting him from taking employment as a Dentist in Training, and has been employed during that leave as a Dentist in Training.

Refusal of extension of stay as the partner of a person who has or has had leave to enter or remain in the United Kingdom under paragraphs 128–193 (but not paragraphs 135I–135K)

196C. An extension of stay in the United Kingdom as the partner of a person who has or has had leave to enter or remain in the United Kingdom under paragraphs 128–193 (but not paragraphs 135I–135K) is to be refused if the Secretary of State is not satisfied that each of the requirements of paragraph 196A is met.

Requirements for indefinite leave to remain for the partner of a person who has or has had leave to enter or remain in the United Kingdom under paragraphs 128–193 (but not paragraphs 135I–135K)

196D. The requirements to be met by a person seeking indefinite leave to remain in the United Kingdom as the partner of a person who has or has had leave to enter or remain in the United Kingdom under paragraphs 128–193 (but not paragraphs 135I–135K) are that the applicant:

(i) is the spouse, civil partner, unmarried or same-sex partner of a person who:

(1) has limited leave to enter or remain in the United Kingdom under paragraphs 128–193 (but not paragraphs 135I–135K) and who is being granted indefinite leave to remain at the same time; or

(2) is the spouse, civil partner, unmarried or same-sex partner of a person who has indefinite leave to remain in the United Kingdom or has become a British citizen, and who had limited leave to enter or remain in the United Kingdom under paragraphs 128–193 (but not paragraphs 135I–135K) immediately before being granted indefinite leave to remain; and

(ii) meets the requirements of paragraph 194(ii)–(vii); and

(iii) has demonstrated sufficient knowledge of the English language and sufficient knowledge about life in the United Kingdom, in accordance with Appendix KoLL; and

(iv) was not last granted:

(1) entry clearance or leave as a visitor, short-term student or short-term student (child),

(2) temporary admission, or

(3) temporary release; and

(v) must not be in the UK in breach of immigration laws except that any period of overstaying for a period of 28 days or less will be disregarded.

Indefinite leave to remain as the partner of a person who has or has had leave to enter or remain in the United Kingdom under paragraphs 128–193 (but not paragraphs 135I–135K)

196E. Indefinite leave to remain in the United Kingdom as the partner of a person who has or has had leave to enter or remain in the United Kingdom under paragraphs 128–193 (but not paragraphs 135I–135K) may be granted provided the Secretary of State is satisfied that each of the requirements of paragraph 196D is met.

Refusal of indefinite leave to remain as the partner of a person who has or has had leave to enter or remain in the United Kingdom under paragraphs 128–193 (but not paragraphs 135I–135K)

196F. Indefinite leave to remain in the United Kingdom as the partner of a person who has or has had limited leave to enter or remain in the United Kingdom under paragraphs 128–193 (but not paragraphs 135I–135K) is to be refused if the Secretary of State is not satisfied that each of the requirements of paragraph 196D is met.

Children of persons with limited leave to enter or remain in the United Kingdom under paragraphs 128–193 (but not paragraphs 135i–135k)

196G. Nothing in paragraphs 197–199 is to be construed as allowing a person to be granted entry clearance, leave to enter, leave to remain or variation of leave as the child of a person granted entry clearance or leave to enter under Paragraph 159A where that entry clearance or leave to enter was granted under 159A on or after 6 April 2012.

Requirements for leave to enter or remain as the child of a person with limited leave to enter or remain in the United Kingdom under paragraphs 128–193 (but not paragraphs 135I–135K)

197. The requirements to be met by a person seeking leave to enter or remain in the United Kingdom as a child of a person with limited leave to enter or remain in the United Kingdom under paragraphs 128–193 (but not paragraphs 135I–135K) are that:

(i) he is the child of a parent with limited leave to enter or remain in the United Kingdom under paragraphs 128–193 (but not paragraphs 135I–135K) or, in respect of applications for leave to remain only, of a parent who has indefinite leave to remain in the UK but who immediately before that grant had limited leave to enter or remain under those paragraphs; and

(ii) he is under the age of 18 or has current leave to enter or remain in this capacity; and

(iii)   he is unmarried and is not a civil partner, has not formed an independent family unit and is not leading an independent life; and

(iv)   he can and will be maintained and accommodated adequately without recourse to public funds in accommodation which his parent(s) own or occupy exclusively; and

(v)   he will not stay in the United Kingdom beyond any period of leave granted to his parent(s); and

(vi)   both parents are being or have been admitted to or allowed to remain in the United Kingdom save where:

   (a)   the parent he is accompanying or joining is his sole surviving parent; or

   (b)   the parent he is accompanying or joining has had sole responsibility for his upbringing; or

   (c)   there are serious and compelling family or other considerations which make exclusion from the United Kingdom undesirable and suitable arrangements have been made for his care; and

(vii) if seeking leave to enter, he holds a valid United Kingdom entry clearance for entry in this capacity or, if seeking leave to remain, he was not last granted:

   (1)   entry clearance or leave as a visitor, short-term student or short-term student (child),

   (2)   temporary admission, or

   (3)   temporary release; and

(viii) if seeking leave to remain, must not be in the UK in breach of immigration laws except that any period of overstaying for a period of 28 days or less will be disregarded.

Leave to enter or remain as the child of a person with limited leave to enter or remain in the United Kingdom under paragraphs 128–193 (but not paragraphs 135I–135K)

198.   (a)   A person seeking leave to enter or remain in the United Kingdom as the child of a person with limited leave to enter or remain in the United Kingdom under paragraphs 128–193 (but not paragraphs 135I–135K), subject to a condition on study as set out in Part 15 of these Rules where the applicant is 18 years of age or over at the time their leave is granted, or will be aged 18 before their period of limited leave expires, may be given leave to enter or remain in the United Kingdom for a period of leave not in excess of that granted to the person with limited leave to enter or remain under paragraphs 128–193 (but not paragraphs 135I–135K) provided that:

   (i)   in relation to an application for leave to enter, he is able to produce to the Immigration Officer, on arrival, a valid United Kingdom entry clearance for entry in this capacity; or

   (ii)   in the case of an application for limited leave to remain, he was not last granted:

      (1)   entry clearance or leave as a visitor, short-term student or short-term student (child),

      (2)   temporary admission, or

      (3)   temporary release,

   and is able to satisfy the Secretary of State that each of the requirements of paragraph 197(i)–(vi) and (viii) is met.

   (b)   A person seeking leave to remain as the child of a parent who has indefinite leave to remain in the UK and who had limited leave under paragraphs 128 – 193 (but not paragraphs 135I–135K) immediately before being granted indefinite leave may be given leave to remain in the UK for a period of 30 months, subject to a condition on study as set out in Part 15 of these Rules where the applicant is 18 years of age or over at the time their leave is granted, or will be aged 18 before their period of limited leave expires, provided he is in the UK with valid leave under paragraph 198 and is able to satisfy the Secretary of State that each of the requirements of paragraph 197(i) and 197 (ii)–(vi) and (viii) is met.

Refusal of leave to enter or remain as the child of a person with limited leave to enter or remain in the United Kingdom under paragraphs 128–193 (but not paragraphs 135I–135K)

198A.   Leave to enter or remain in the United Kingdom as the child of a person with limited leave to enter or remain in the United Kingdom under paragraphs 128–193 (but not paragraphs 135I–135K) is to be refused if:

   (i)   in relation to an application for leave to enter, a valid United Kingdom entry clearance for entry in this capacity is not produced to the Immigration Officer on arrival; or

   (ii)   in the case of an application for limited leave to remain, if the applicant was last granted:

      (1)   entry clearance or leave as a visitor, short-term student or short-term student (child),

      (2)   temporary admission, or

      (3)   temporary release,

or is unable to satisfy the Secretary of State that each of the requirements of paragraph 197(i)–(vi) and (viii) is met.

Requirements for indefinite leave to remain as the child of a person who has or has had leave to enter or remain in the United Kingdom under paragraphs 128–193 (but not paragraphs 135I–135K)

199. The requirements to be met by a person seeking indefinite leave to remain in the United Kingdom as the child of a person who has or has had leave to enter or remain in the United Kingdom under paragraphs 128–193 (but not paragraphs 135I–135K) are that the applicant:

(i) is the child of a person who:

    (1) has limited leave to enter or remain in the United Kingdom under paragraphs 128–193 (but not paragraphs 135I–135K) and who is being granted indefinite leave to remain at the same time; or

    (2) has indefinite leave to remain in the United Kingdom and who had limited leave to enter or remain in the United Kingdom under paragraphs 128–193 (but not paragraphs 135I–135K) immediately before being granted indefinite leave to remain; and

(ii) meets the requirements of paragraph 197(i)–(vi) and (viii); and

(iii) was not last granted:

    (1) entry clearance or leave as a visitor,

    (2) temporary admission, or

    (3) temporary release; and

(iv) does not fall for refusal under the general grounds for refusal; and

(v) must not be in the UK in breach of immigration laws except that any period of overstaying for a period of 28 days or less will be disregarded; and

(vi) has demonstrated sufficient knowledge of the English language and sufficient knowledge about life in the United Kingdom, in accordance with Appendix KoLL, unless he is under the age of 18 at the date on which the application is made.

Indefinite leave to remain as the child of a person who has or has had leave to enter or remain in the United Kingdom under paragraphs 128–193 (but not paragraphs 135I–135K)

199A. Indefinite leave to remain in the United Kingdom as the child of a person who has or has had leave to enter or remain in the United Kingdom under paragraphs 128–193 (but not paragraphs 135I–135K) may be granted provided the Secretary of State is satisfied that each of the requirements of paragraph 199 is met.

Refusal of indefinite leave to remain as the child of a person who has or has had leave to enter or remain in the United Kingdom under paragraphs 128–193 (but not paragraphs 135I–135K)

199B. Indefinite leave to remain in the United Kingdom as the child of a person who has or has had limited leave to enter or remain in the United Kingdom under paragraphs 128–193 (but not paragraphs 135I–135K) is to be refused if the Secretary of State is not satisfied that each of the requirements of paragraph 199 is met.

Part 6 – OMITTED

Part 6A – Points-based system

General requirements for indefinite leave to remain

245AAA. For the purposes of references in this Part to requirements for indefinite leave to remain, except for those in paragraphs 245BF, 245DF and 245EF:

(a) 'continuous period of 5 years lawfully in the UK' means, subject to paragraphs 245CD, 245GF and 245HF, residence in the United Kingdom for an unbroken period with valid leave, and for these purposes a period shall not be considered to have been broken where:

    (i) the applicant has been absent from the UK for a period of 180 days or less in any of the five consecutive 12 month periods preceding the date of the application for leave to remain, except that any absence from the UK for the purpose of assisting with the Ebola crisis which began in

West Africa in 2014 shall not count towards the 180 days, if the applicant provides evidence that this was the purpose of the absence(s) and that his Sponsor agreed to the absence(s);

    (ii)   the applicant has existing limited leave to enter or remain upon their departure and return except that where that leave expired no more than 28 days prior to a further application for entry clearance, that period and any period pending the determination of an application made within that 28 day period shall be disregarded; and

    (iii)   the applicant has any period of overstaying between periods of entry clearance, leave to enter or leave to remain of up to 28 days and any period of overstaying pending the determination of an application made within that 28 day period disregarded.

(b)   Except for periods when the applicant had leave as a Tier 1 (General) Migrant, a Tier 1 (Investor) Migrant, a Tier 1 (Entrepreneur) Migrant, a Tier 1 (Exceptional Talent) Migrant, a highly skilled migrant, a Businessperson, an Innovator, an Investor, a self-employed lawyer or a writer, composer or artist, the applicant must have been employed in the UK continuously throughout the five years, under the terms of their Certificate of Sponsorship, work permit or in the employment for which they were given leave to enter or remain, except that any breaks in employment in which they applied for leave as a Tier 2 Migrant, or, under Tier 5 Temporary Worker (International Agreement) Migrant as a private servant in a diplomatic household, where in the latter case they applied to enter the UK before 6 April 2012, to work for a new employer shall be disregarded, provided this is within 60 days of the end of their employment with their previous employer or Sponsor.

(c)   Except for periods where the applicant had leave as a Tier 1(Investor) Migrant, a Tier 1(Entrepreneur) Migrant, a Tier 1(Exceptional Talent) Migrant or a highly skilled migrant, any absences from the UK during the five years must have been for a purpose that is consistent with the applicant's basis of stay here, including paid annual leave, or for serious or compelling reasons.

Documents not submitted with applications

245AA.   (a)   Where Part 6A or any appendices referred to in Part 6A state that specified documents must be provided, the Entry Clearance Officer, Immigration Officer or the Secretary of State will only consider documents that have been submitted with the application, and will only consider documents submitted after the application where they are submitted in accordance with subparagraph (b).

(b)   If the applicant has submitted specified documents in which:

    (i)   Some of the documents in a sequence have been omitted (for example, if one bank statement from a series is missing);

    (ii)   A document is in the wrong format (for example, if a letter is not on letterhead paper as specified); or

    (iii)   A document is a copy and not an original document; or

    (iv)   A document does not contain all of the specified information;

the Entry Clearance Officer, Immigration Officer or the Secretary of State may contact the applicant or his representative in writing, and request the correct documents. The requested documents must be received at the address specified in the request within 7 working days of the date of the request.

(c)   Documents will not be requested where a specified document has not been submitted (for example an English language certificate is missing), or where the Entry Clearance Officer, Immigration Officer or the Secretary of State does not anticipate that addressing the omission or error referred to in subparagraph (b) will lead to a grant because the application will be refused for other reasons.

(d)   If the applicant has submitted a specified document:

    (i)   in the wrong format; or

    (ii)   which is a copy and not an original document; or

    (iii)   which does not contain all of the specified information, but the missing information is verifiable from:

        (1)   other documents submitted with the application,

        (2)   the website of the organisation which issued the document, or

        (3)   the website of the appropriate regulatory body;

the application may be granted exceptionally, providing the Entry Clearance Officer, Immigration Officer or the Secretary of State is satisfied that the specified documents are genuine and the applicant meets all the other requirements. The Entry Clearance Officer, Immigration Officer or the Secretary of

State reserves the right to request the specified original documents in the correct format in all cases where (b) applies, and to refuse applications if these documents are not provided as set out in (b).

Specified documents for students previously sponsored by an overseas government or international scholarship agency

245A.   Where Part 6A of these Rules state that specified documents must be provided to show that a sponsoring government or international scholarship agency has provided its unconditional written consent to the application, the specified documents are original letters, on the official letter-headed paper or stationery of the organisation(s), bearing the official stamp of that organisation and issued by an authorised official of that organisation. The documents must confirm that the organisation gives the applicant unconditional consent to remain in or re-enter the UK for an unlimited time.

Tier 1 (Exceptional Talent) Migrants

Purpose

245B.   This route is for exceptionally talented individuals in particular fields, who wish to work in the UK. These individuals are those who are already internationally recognised at the highest level as world leaders in their particular field, or who have already demonstrated exceptional promise and are likely to become world leaders in their particular area.

Entry to the UK

245BA.   All migrants arriving in the UK and wishing to enter as a Tier 1 (Exceptional Talent) Migrant must have a valid entry clearance for entry under this route. If they do not have a valid entry clearance, entry will be refused.

Requirements for entry clearance

245BB.   To qualify for entry clearance as a Tier 1 (Exceptional Talent) Migrant, an applicant must meet the requirements listed below. If the applicant meets these requirements, entry clearance will be granted. If the applicant does not meet these requirements, the application will be refused.

Requirements:

(a)   The applicant must not fall for refusal under the general grounds for refusal.

(c)   The applicant must have a minimum of 75 points under paragraphs 1 to 6 of Appendix A.

(d)   an applicant who has, or was last granted, leave as a student or a Postgraduate Doctor or Dentist, a Student Nurse, a Student Writing-Up a Thesis, a Student Re-Sitting an Examination or as a Tier 4 Migrant and:

    (i)   is currently being sponsored by a government or international scholarship agency, or

    (ii)   was being sponsored by a government or international scholarship agency, and that sponsorship came to an end 12 months ago or less,

must provide the unconditional written consent of the sponsoring Government or agency to the application and must provide the specified documents as set out in paragraph 245A above to show that this requirement has been met.

Period and conditions of grant

245BC.   (a)   Entry clearance will be granted for a period of:

    (i)   1 year,

    (ii)   2 years,

    (iii)   3 years,

    (iv)   4 years, or

    (v)   5 years and 4 months,

    as requested by the applicant.

(b)   Entry clearance will be granted subject to the following conditions:

    (i)   no recourse to public funds,

    (ii)   registration with the police, if this is required by paragraph 326, (iii) no employment as a Doctor or Dentist in Training, and

    (iv)   no employment as a professional sportsperson (including as a sports coach).

(v)   study subject to the condition set out in Part 15 of these Rules, where the applicant is 18 years of age or over at the time their leave is granted, or will be aged 18 before their period of limited leave expires

Requirements for leave to remain

245BD.   To qualify for leave to remain as a Tier 1 (Exceptional Talent) Migrant, an applicant must meet the requirements listed below. If the applicant meets these requirements, leave to remain will be granted. If the applicant does not meet these requirements, the application will be refused.

Requirements:

(a)   The applicant must not fall for refusal under the general grounds for refusal, and must not be an illegal entrant.

(b)   The applicant must have a minimum of 75 points under paragraphs 1 to 6 of Appendix A.

(c)   The applicant must have, or have last been granted, entry clearance, leave to enter or remain as:

(i)   a Tier 1 Migrant,

(ii)   a Tier 2 Migrant, or

(iii)   as a Tier 5 (Temporary Worker) Migrant, sponsored in the Government Authorised Exchange sub-category in an exchange scheme for sponsoredresearchers.

(d)   The applicant must not be in the UK in breach of immigration laws except that any period of overstaying for a period of 28 days or less will be disregarded.

Period and conditions of grant

245BE.   (a)   Leave to remain will be granted for a period of:

(i)   1 year,

(ii)   2 years,

(iii)   3 years,

(iv)   4 years, or

(v)   5 years,

as indicated by the applicant.

(b)   Leave to remain under this route will be subject to the following conditions:

(i)   no recourse to public funds,

(ii)   registration with the police, if this is required by paragraph 326,

(iii)   no employment as a Doctor or Dentist in Training, and

(iv)   no employment as a professional sportsperson (including as a sports coach), and

(v)   study subject to the condition set out in Part 15 of these Rules where the applicant is 18 years of age or over at the time their leave is granted, or will be aged 18 before their period of limited leave expires.

Requirements for indefinite leave to remain

245BF.   To qualify for indefinite leave to remain, a Tier 1 (Exceptional Talent) Migrant must meet the requirements listed below. If the applicant meets these requirements, indefinite leave to remain will be granted. If the applicant does not meet these requirements, the application will be refused.

Requirements:

(a)   DELETED

(b)   The applicant must not fall for refusal under the general grounds for refusal, and must not be an illegal entrant.

(c)   The applicant must have spent a continuous period of 5 years lawfully in the UK as follows:

(i)   The applicant must have, or have last been granted, leave as a Tier 1 (Exceptional Talent) Migrant;

(ii)   The 5 years must have been spent with leave as a Tier 1 Migrant (excluding as a Tier 1 (Graduate Entrepreneur) Migrant or Tier 1 (Post-Study Work) Migrant) or as a Tier 2 Migrant (excluding as a Tier 2 (Intra-Company Transfer) Migrant); and

(iii)   The applicant must have had absences from the UK of no more than 180 days in any 12 calendar months during the 5 years.

(d)   The applicant must have a minimum of 75 points under paragraphs 1 to 6 of Appendix A.

(e)   The applicant must have demonstrated sufficient knowledge of the English language and sufficient knowledge about life in the United Kingdom, in accordance with Appendix KoLL.

(f)   The applicant must not be in the UK in breach of immigration laws except that any period of overstaying for a period of 28 days or less will be disregarded.

Tier 1 (General) Migrants

Purpose

245C.   This route is now closed except for indefinite leave to remain applications.

Requirements for leave to remain

245CA, 245CB.   DELETED

Requirements for indefinite leave to remain

245CD.   To qualify for indefinite leave to remain, a Tier 1 (General) Migrant must meet the requirements listed below. If the applicant meets these requirements, indefinite leave to remain will be granted. If the applicant does not meet these requirements, the application will be refused.

Requirements:

(a)   DELETED

(b)   The applicant must not fall for refusal under the general grounds for refusal (except that paragraph 322(1C) shall not apply if the applicant meets the conditions in (f)(i)-(iii) below), and must not be an illegal entrant.

(c)   The applicant must have spent a continuous period as specified in (d) lawfully in the UK, of which the most recent period must have been spent with leave as a Tier 1 (General) Migrant, in any combination of the following categories:

    (i)   as a Tier 1 (General) Migrant,

    (ii)   as a Highly Skilled Migrant,

    (iii)   as a Work Permit Holder,

    (iv)   as an innovator,

    (v)   as a Self-Employed Lawyer,

    (vi)   as a Writer, Composer or Artist,

    (vii)   as a Tier 2 (General) Migrant, a Tier 2 (Minister of Religion) Migrant or a Tier 2 (Sportsperson) Migrant, or

    (viii)   as a Tier 2 (Intra-Company Transfer) Migrant, provided the continuous period of 5 years spent lawfully in the UK includes a period of leave as a Tier 2 (Intra-Company Transfer) Migrant granted under the Rules in place before 6 April 2010, or as a Work Permit Holder where the work permit was granted because the applicant was the subject of an Intra-Company Transfer.

(d)   The continuous period in (c) is:

    (i)   4 years, if the applicant:

        (1)   received a Highly Skilled Migrant Programme approval letter issued on the basis of an application made before 3 April 2006,

        (2)   was subsequently granted entry clearance or leave to remain on the basis of that letter, and

        (3)   has not since been granted entry clearance or leave to remain in any category other than as a Highly Skilled Migrant or Tier 1 (General) Migrant; or

    (ii)   5 years, in all other cases.

(e)   If the applicant has or has had leave as a Highly Skilled Migrant, a Writer, Composer or artist, a self-employed lawyer or as a Tier 1 (General) Migrant under the Rules in place before 19 July 2010, and has not been granted leave in any categories other than these under the Rules in place since 19 July 2010, the applicant must have 75 points under paragraphs 7 to 34 of Appendix A.

(f)   Where the applicant:

    (i)   received a Highly Skilled Migrant Programme approval letter issued on the basis of an application made before 7 November 2006,

(ii)   was subsequently granted entry clearance or leave to remain on the basis of that letter, and

(iii)   has not since been granted entry clearance or leave to remain in any category other than as a Highly Skilled Migrant or Tier 1 (General) Migrant,

the applicant must be economically active in the UK, in employment or self-employment or both.

(g)   in all cases other than those referred to in (e) or (f) above, the applicant must have 80 points under paragraphs 7 to 34 of Appendix A.

(h)   The applicant must have sufficient knowledge of the English language and sufficient knowledge about life in the United Kingdom, in accordance with Appendix KoLL of these Rules, unless the applicant meets the conditions in (f)(i)-(iii) above.

(i)   The applicant must not be in the UK in breach of immigration laws except that any period of overstaying for a period of 28 days or less will be disregarded, unless the applicant meets the conditions in (f)(i)-(iii) above.

(j)   The applicant must provide the specified documents in paragraph 245CD-SD to evidence the reason for the absences set out in paragraph 245AAA, unless the applicant meets the conditions in (f)(i)-(iii) above.

(k)   For the purposes of sub-paragraph (c), time spent with valid leave in the Bailiwick of Guernsey, the Bailiwick of Jersey or the Isle of Man in a category equivalent to those set out in (c)(i) to (viii) may be included in the continuous period of 5 years lawful residence in the UK, provided that:

(i)   the most recent period of leave was granted in the UK as a Tier 1 (General) Migrant; and

(ii)   any period of leave granted in the Bailiwick of Guernsey, the Bailiwick of Jersey or the Isle of Man as a work permit holder or a Tier 2 Migrant was for employment:

(a)   in a job which appears on the list of occupations skilled to National Qualifications Framework level 3 or above (or from 6 April 2011, National Qualifications Framework level 4 or above or from 14 June 2012, National Qualifications Framework level 6 or above), as stated in the Codes of Practice in Appendix J, or

(b)   in a job which appears in the Creative Sector Codes of Practice in Appendix J, or

(c)   as a professional sportsperson (including as a sports coach).

(iii)   In any such case, references to the 'UK' in paragraph 245AAA shall include a reference to the Bailiwick of Guernsey, Bailiwick of Jersey or the Isle of Man, as the case may be.

(l)   For the purposes of paragraph (e), time spent with valid leave in the Bailiwick of Guernsey, the Bailiwick of Jersey and the Isle of Man in a category equivalent to those set out in (e)(i) to (iv) may be included in the continuous period of 5 years (or 4 years as the case may be) lawful residence in the UK, provided that:

(i)   the most recent period of leave was granted in the UK as a Tier 1 (General) Migrant; and

(ii)   any period of leave granted in the Bailiwick of Guernsey, the Bailiwick of Jersey or the Isle of Man as a work permit holder or a Tier 2 Migrant was for employment:

(a)   in a job which appears on the list of occupations skilled to National Qualifications Framework level 3 or above (or from 6 April 2011, National Qualifications Framework level 4 or above or from 14 June 2012, National Qualifications Framework level 6 or above), as stated in the Codes of Practice in Appendix J, or

(b)   in a job which appears in the Creative Sector Codes of Practice in Appendix J, or

(c)   as a professional sportsperson (including as a sports coach).

(iii)   In any such case, references to the 'UK' in paragraph 245AAA shall include a reference to the Bailiwick of Guernsey, Bailiwick of Jersey or the Isle of Man, as the case may be.

(m)   The application for indefinite leave to remain must have been made before 6 April 2018.

Specified documents

245CD-SD.   The specified documents referred to in paragraph 245CD(j) are:

(a)   For periods where the applicant was in employment in the UK, a letter from the employer detailing the purpose and period of absences in connection with the employment, including periods of annual leave.

(b)   For periods where the applicant was self-employed or in business in the UK, or looking for work or setting up in business in the UK, a personal letter from the applicant detailing the purpose and period of absences in relation to those activities.

(c)   A personal letter from the applicant which includes full details of the reason for the absences and all original supporting documents in relation to those reasons – e.g. medical certificates, birth/death certificates, information about the reasons which led to the absence from the UK.

Tier 1 (Entrepreneur) Migrants

Purpose of this route and meaning of business

245D.   (a)   This route is for migrants who wish to establish, join or take over one or more businesses in the UK.

(b)   For the purpose of paragraphs 245D to 245DF and paragraphs 35 to 53 of Appendix A 'business' means an enterprise as:

(i)   a sole trader,

(ii)   a partnership, or

(iii)   a company registered in the UK.

(c)   Where paragraphs 245D to 245DF and paragraphs 35 to 53 of Appendix A refer to investing funds in a business or businesses, or to money remaining available to the applicant until such time as it is spent for the purposes of his business or businesses:

(i)   'Available' means that the funds are:

(1)   in the applicant's own possession,

(2)   in the financial accounts of a UK incorporated business of which he is the director, or

(3)   available from the third party or parties named in the application under the terms of the declaration(s) referred to in paragraph 41-SD(b) of Appendix A.

(ii)   'Invested' or 'spent' excludes spending on:

(1)   the applicant's own remuneration,

(2)   buying the business from a previous owner, where the money ultimately goes to that previous owner (irrespective of whether it is received or held directly or indirectly by that previous owner) rather than into the business being purchased (This applies regardless of whether the money is channelled through the business en route to the previous owner, for example by means of the applicant or business purchasing 'goodwill' or other assets which were previously part of the business.),

(3)   investing in other businesses, and

(4)   any spending which is not directly for the purpose of establishing or running the applicant's own business or businesses.

Entry to the UK

245DA. All migrants arriving in the UK and wishing to enter as a Tier 1 (Entrepreneur) Migrant must have a valid entry clearance for entry under this route. If they do not have a valid entry clearance, entry will be refused.

Requirements for entry clearance

245DB. To qualify for entry clearance as a Tier 1 (Entrepreneur) Migrant, an applicant must meet the requirements listed below. If the applicant meets those requirements, entry clearance will be granted. If the applicant does not meet these requirements, the application will be refused.

Requirements:

(a)   The applicant must not fall for refusal under the general grounds for refusal.

(b)   The applicant must have a minimum of 75 points under paragraphs 35 to 53 of Appendix A.

(c)   The applicant must have a minimum of 10 points under paragraph 1 to 15 of Appendix B.

(d)   The applicant must have a minimum of 10 points under paragraph 1 to 2 of Appendix C.

(e)   An applicant who has, or was last granted, leave as a Student or a Postgraduate Doctor or Dentist, a Student Nurse, a Student Writing-Up a Thesis, a Student Re-Sitting an Examination or as a Tier 4 Migrant and:

(i)   is currently being sponsored by a government or international scholarship agency, or

(ii)   was being sponsored by a government or international scholarship agency, and that sponsorship came to an end 12 months ago or less, must provide the unconditional written consent of the sponsoring Government or agency to the application and must provide the specified documents as set out in paragraph 245A above, to show that this requirement has been met.

(f)   Where the applicant is being assessed under Table 4 of Appendix A, the Entry Clearance Officer must be satisfied that:

    (i)   the applicant genuinely intends and is able to establish, take over or become a director of one or more businesses in the UK within the next six months;

    (ii)   the applicant genuinely intends to invest the money referred to in Table 4 of Appendix A in the business or businesses referred to in (i);

    (iii)   that the money referred to in Table 4 of Appendix A is genuinely available to the applicant, and will remain available to him until such time as it is spent for the purposes of his business or businesses.

    (iv)   that the applicant does not intend to take employment in the United Kingdom other than under the terms of paragraph 245DC;

(g)   The applicant must provide a business plan, setting out his proposed business activities in the UK and how he expects to make his business succeed.

(h)   In making the assessment in (f), the Entry Clearance Officer will assess the balance of probabilities. The Entry Clearance Officer may take into account the following factors:

    (i)   the evidence the applicant has submitted;

    (ii)   the viability and credibility of the source of the money referred to in Table 4 of Appendix A;

    (iii)   the viability and credibility of the applicant's business plan and market research into their chosen business sector;

    (iv)   the applicant's previous educational and business experience (or lack thereof);

    (v)   the applicant's immigration history and previous activity in the UK; and

    (vi)   any other relevant information.

(i)   Where the applicant has had entry clearance, leave to enter or leave to remain as a Tier 1 (Entrepreneur) Migrant, a Businessperson or an Innovator in the 12 months immediately before the date of application, and is being assessed under Table 5 of Appendix A, the Entry Clearance Officer must be satisfied that:

    (i)   the applicant has established, taken over or become a director of one or more genuine businesses in the UK, and has genuinely operated that business or businesses while he had leave as a Tier 1 (Entrepreneur) Migrant, a Businessperson or an Innovator; and

    (ii)   the applicant has genuinely invested the money referred to in Table 5 of Appendix A into one or more genuine businesses in the UK to be spent for the purpose of that business or businesses; and

    (iii)   the applicant genuinely intends to continue operating one or more businesses in the UK; and

    (iv)   the applicant does not intend to take employment in the United Kingdom other than under the terms of paragraph 245DE.

(j)   In making the assessment in (i), the Entry Clearance Officer will assess the balance of probabilities. The Entry Clearance Officer may take into account the following factors:

    (i)   the evidence the applicant has submitted;

    (ii)   the viability and credibility of the source of the money referred to in Table 5 of Appendix A;

    (iii)   the credibility of the financial accounts of the business or businesses;

    (iv)   the credibility of the applicant's business activity in the UK, including when he had leave as a Tier 1 (Entrepreneur) Migrant, Businessperson or an Innovator;

    (v)   the credibility of the job creation for which the applicant is claiming points in Table 5 of Appendix A;

    (vii)   if the nature of the business requires mandatory accreditation, registration and/or insurance, whether that accreditation, registration and/or insurance has been obtained; and

    (viii)   any other relevant information.

(k)   The Entry Clearance Officer reserves the right to request additional information and evidence to support the assessment in (f) or (i), and to refuse the application if the information or evidence is not provided. Any requested documents must be received by the Entry Clearance Officer at the address specified in the request within 28 calendar days of the date of the request.

(l)   If the Entry Clearance Officer is not satisfied with the genuineness of the application in relation to a points-scoring requirement in Appendix A, those points will not be awarded.

(m)   The Entry Clearance Officer may decide not to carry out the assessment in (f) or (i) if the application already falls for refusal on other grounds, but reserves the right to carry out this assessment in any reconsideration of the decision.

(n)   The applicant must, unless he provides a reasonable explanation, comply with any request made by the Entry Clearance Officer to attend for interview.

(o)   The applicant must be at least 16 years old.

(p)   Where the applicant is under 18 years of age, the application must be supported by the applicant's parents or legal guardian or by one parent if that parent has sole legal responsibility for the child.

(q)   Where the applicant is under 18 years of age, the applicant's parents or legal guardian, or one parent if that parent has sole legal responsibility for the child, must confirm that they consent to the arrangements for the applicant's care in the UK.

Period and conditions of grant

245DC.   (a)   Entry clearance will be granted for a period of 3 years and four months and will be subject to the following conditions:

    (i)   no recourse to public funds,

    (ii)   registration with the police, if this is required by paragraph 326 of these Rules, and

    (iii)   no employment other than working for the business(es) the applicant has established, joined or taken over, but working for such business(es) does not include anything undertaken by the applicant pursuant to a contract of service or apprenticeship, whether express or implied and whether oral or written, with another business,

    (iv)   no employment as a professional sportsperson (including as a sports coach), and

    (v)   study subject to the condition set out in Part 15 of these Rules where the applicant is 18 years of age or over at the time their leave is granted, or will be aged 18 before their period of limited leave expires.

Requirements for leave to remain

245DD.   To qualify for leave to remain as a Tier 1 (Entrepreneur) Migrant under this rule, an applicant must meet the requirements listed below. If the applicant meets these requirements, leave to remain will be granted. If the applicant does not meet these requirements, the application will be refused.

Requirements:

(a)   The applicant must not fall for refusal under the general grounds for refusal, except that paragraph 322(10) shall not apply, and must not be an illegal entrant.

(b)   The applicant must have a minimum of 75 points under paragraphs 35 to 53 of Appendix A.

(c)   The applicant must have a minimum of 10 points under paragraphs 1 to 15 of Appendix B.

(d)   The applicant must have a minimum of 10 points under paragraphs 1 to 2 of Appendix C.

(e)   The applicant who is applying for leave to remain must have, or have last been granted, entry clearance, leave to enter or remain:

    (i)   as a Highly Skilled Migrant,

    (ii)   as a Tier 1 (General) Migrant,

    (iii)   as a Tier 1 (Entrepreneur) Migrant,

    (iv)   as a Tier 1 (Investor) Migrant,

    (v)   as a Tier 1 (Graduate Entrepreneur) Migrant

    (vi)   as a Tier 1 (Post-Study Work) Migrant,

    (vii)   as a Businessperson,

    (viii)   as an Innovator,

    (ix)   as an Investor,

    (x)   as a Participant in the Fresh Talent: Working in Scotland Scheme,

    (xi)   as a Participant in the International Graduates Scheme (or its predecessor, the Science and Engineering Graduates Scheme),

    (xii)   as a Postgraduate Doctor or Dentist,

> (xiii) as a Self-employed Lawyer,
>
> (xiv) as a Student,
>
> (xv) as a Student Nurse,
>
> (xvi) as a Student Re-sitting an Examination,
>
> (xvii) as a Student Writing Up a Thesis,
>
> (xviii) as a Work Permit Holder,
>
> (xix) as a Writer, Composer or Artist,
>
> (xx) as a Tier 2 Migrant
>
> (xxi) as a Tier 4 (General) Student and, in respect of such leave, is or was last sponsored by:
>
>> (1) a UK recognised body or a body in receipt of public funding as a higher education institution from the Department of Employment and Learning in Northern Ireland, the Higher Education Funding Council for England, the Higher Education Funding Council for Wales or the Scottish Funding Council; or
>>
>> (2) an overseas higher education institution to undertake a short-term study abroad programme in the United Kingdom; or
>>
>> (3) an Embedded College offering Pathway Courses,
>
> (xxii) as a Tier 4 (Child) Student, or
>
> (xxiii) as a visitor who has been undertaking permitted activities as a prospective entrepreneur.

(f) An applicant who has, or was last granted, leave as a Student or a Postgraduate Doctor or Dentist, Student Nurse, Student Re-Sitting an Examination, a Student Writing-Up a Thesis or as a Tier 4 Migrant and:

> (i) is currently being sponsored by a government or international scholarship agency, or
>
> (ii) was being sponsored by a government or international scholarship agency, and that sponsorship came to an end 12 months ago or less,

must provide the unconditional written consent of the sponsoring Government or agency to the application and must provide the specified documents as set out in paragraph 245A above, to show that this requirement has been met.

(g) The applicant must not be in the UK in breach of immigration laws except that any period of overstaying for a period of 28 days or less will be disregarded.

(h) Where the applicant is being assessed under Table 4 of Appendix A, the Secretary of State must be satisfied that:

> (i) the applicant genuinely:
>
>> (1) intends and is able to establish, take over or become a director of one or more businesses in the UK within the next six months, or
>>
>> (2) has established, taken over or become a director of one or more businesses in the UK and continues to operate that business or businesses; and
>
> (ii) the applicant genuinely intends to invest the money referred to in Table 4 of Appendix A in the business or businesses referred to in (i);
>
> (iii) the money referred to in Table 4 of Appendix A is genuinely available to the applicant, and will remain available to him until such time as it is spent for the purposes of his business or businesses.
>
> (iv) that the applicant does not intend to take employment in the United Kingdom other than under the terms of paragraph 245DE.

(i) The applicant must provide a business plan, setting out his proposed business activities in the UK and how he expects to make his business succeed.

(j) In making the assessment in (h), the Secretary of State will assess the balance of probabilities. The Secretary of State may take into account the following factors:

> (i) the evidence the applicant has submitted;
>
> (ii) the viability and credibility of the source of the money referred to in Table 4 of Appendix A;
>
> (iii) the viability and credibility of the applicant's business plans and market research into their chosen business sector;
>
> (iv) the applicant's previous educational and business experience (or lack thereof);

(v)   the applicant's immigration history and previous activity in the UK;

(vi)   where the applicant has already registered in the UK as self-employed or as the director of a business, and the nature of the business requires mandatory accreditation, registration and/or insurance, whether that accreditation, registration and/or insurance has been obtained; and

(vii)   any other relevant information.

(k) Where the applicant has, or was last granted, leave as a Tier 1 (Entrepreneur) Migrant, a Businessperson or an Innovator, and is being assessed under Table 5 of Appendix A, the Secretary of State must be satisfied that:

(i)   the applicant has established, taken over or become a director of one or more genuine businesses in the UK, and has genuinely operated that business or businesses while he had leave as a Tier 1 (Entrepreneur) Migrant, a Businessperson or an Innovator; and

(ii)   the applicant has genuinely invested the money referred to in Table 5 of Appendix A into one or more genuine businesses in the UK to be spent for the purpose of that business or businesses; and

(iii)   the applicant genuinely intends to continue operating one or more businesses in the UK; and

(iv)   the applicant does not intend to take employment in the United Kingdom other than under the terms of paragraph 245DE.

(l)   In making the assessment in (k), the Secretary of State will assess the balance of probabilities. The Secretary of State may take into account the following factors:

(i)   the evidence the applicant has submitted;

(ii)   the viability and credibility of the source of the money referred to in Table 5 of Appendix A;

(iii)   the credibility of the financial accounts of the business or businesses;

(iv)   the credibility of the applicant's business activity in the UK, including when he had leave as a Tier 1 (Entrepreneur) Migrant, a Businessperson or an Innovator;

(v)   the credibility of the job creation for which the applicant is claiming points in Table 5 of Appendix A;

(vii)   if the nature of the business requires mandatory accreditation, registration and/or insurance, whether that accreditation, registration and/or insurance has been obtained; and

(viii) any other relevant information.

(m) The Secretary of State reserves the right to request additional information and evidence to support the assessment in (h) or (k), and to refuse the application if the information or evidence is not provided. Any requested documents must be received by the Secretary of State at the address specified in the request within 28 calendar days of the date of the request.

(n) If the Secretary of State is not satisfied with the genuineness of the application in relation to a points-scoring requirement in Appendix A, those points will not be awarded.

(o) The Secretary of State may decide not to carry out the assessment in (h) or (k) if the application already falls for refusal on other grounds, but reserves the right to carry out this assessment in any reconsideration of the decision.

(p) The applicant must, unless he provides a reasonable explanation, comply with any request made by the Secretary of State to attend for interview.

(q) The applicant must be at least 16 years old.

(r) Where the applicant is under 18 years of age, the application must be supported by the applicant's parents or legal guardian or by one parent if that parent has sole legal responsibility for the child.

(s) Where the applicant is under 18 years of age, the applicant's parents or legal guardian, or one parent if that parent has sole legal responsibility for the child, must confirm that they consent to the arrangements for the applicant's care in the UK.

Period, conditions and curtailment of grant

245DE. (a) Leave to remain will be granted:

(i)   for a period of 2 years, to an applicant who has, or was last granted, leave as a Tier 1 (Entrepreneur) Migrant,

(ii)   for a period of 3 years, to any other applicant.

(b) Leave to remain under this route will be subject to the following conditions:

(i) no recourse to public funds,

(ii) registration with the police, if this is required by paragraph 326 of these Rules, and

(iii) no employment, other than working for the business or businesses which he has established, joined or taken over, but working for such business(es) does not include anything undertaken by the applicant pursuant to a contract of service or apprenticeship, whether express or implied and whether oral or written, with another business, and

(iv) no employment as a professional sportsperson (including as a sports coach), and

(v) study subject to the condition set out in Part 15 of these Rules where the applicant is 18 years of age or over at the time their leave is granted, or will be aged 18 before their period of limited leave expires.

(c) Without prejudice to the grounds for curtailment in paragraph 323 of these Rules, leave to enter or remain granted to a Tier 1 (Entrepreneur) Migrant may be curtailed if:

(i) within 6 months of the date specified in paragraph (d), the applicant has not done one or more of the following things:

(1) registered with HM Revenue and Customs as self-employed,

(2) registered a new business in which he is a director, or

(3) registered as a director of an existing business, or

(ii) the funds referred to in the relevant sections of Appendix A cease to be available to him, except where they have been spent for the purposes of his business or businesses.

(d) The date referred to in paragraph (c) is:

(i) the date of the applicant's entry to the UK, in the case of an applicant granted entry clearance as a Tier 1 (Entrepreneur) Migrant where there is evidence to establish the applicant's date of entry to the UK,

(ii) the date of the grant of entry clearance to the applicant, in the case of an applicant granted entry clearance as a Tier 1 (Entrepreneur) Migrant where there is no evidence to establish the applicant's date of entry to the UK, or

(iii) the date of the grant of leave to remain to the applicant, in any other case.

(e) Paragraph 245DE(c) does not apply where the applicant's last grant of leave prior to the grant of the leave that he currently has was as a Tier 1 (Entrepreneur) Migrant, a Businessperson or an Innovator.

Requirements for indefinite leave to remain

245DF. To qualify for indefinite leave to remain as a Tier 1 (Entrepreneur) Migrant, an applicant must meet the requirements listed below. If the applicant meets these requirements, indefinite leave to remain will be granted. If the applicant does not meet these requirements, the application will be refused.

Requirements:

(a) DELETED

(b) The applicant must not fall for refusal under the general grounds for refusal, and must not be an illegal entrant.

(c) The applicant must have a minimum of 75 points under paragraphs 35 to 53 of Appendix A.

(d) The applicant must have demonstrated sufficient knowledge of the English language and sufficient knowledge about life in the United Kingdom, in accordance with Appendix KoLL.

(e) The applicant must not be in the UK in breach of immigration laws except that any period of overstaying for a period of 28 days or less will be disregarded.

(f) The Secretary of State must be satisfied that:

(i) the applicant has established, taken over or become a director of one or more genuine businesses in the UK, and has genuinely operated that business or businesses while he had leave as a Tier 1 (Entrepreneur) Migrant, a Businessperson or an Innovator; and

(ii) the applicant has genuinely invested the money referred to in Table 6 of Appendix A into one or more businesses in the UK to be spent for the purpose of that business or businesses; and

(iii) the applicant genuinely intends to continue operating one or more businesses in the UK.

(g) In making the assessment in (f), the Secretary of State will assess the balance of probabilities. The Secretary of State may take into account the following factors:

(i) the evidence the applicant has submitted;

    (ii)   the viability and credibility of the source of the money referred to in Table 6 of Appendix A;

    (iii)   the credibility of the financial accounts of the business or businesses;

    (iv)   the credibility of the applicant's business activity in the UK, including when he had leave as a Tier 1 (Entrepreneur) Migrant, a Businessperson or an Innovator;

    (v)   the credibility of the job creation for which the applicant is claiming points in Table 6 of Appendix A;

    (vii)   if the nature of the business requires mandatory accreditation, registration and/or insurance, whether that accreditation, registration and/or insurance has been obtained; and

    (viii)   any other relevant information.

(h)   The Secretary of State reserves the right to request additional information and evidence to support the assessment in (f), and to refuse the application if the information or evidence is not provided. Any requested documents must be received by the Secretary of State at the address specified in the request within 28 calendar days of the date of the request.

(i)   If the Secretary of State is not satisfied with the genuineness of the application in relation to a points-scoring requirement in Appendix A, those points will not be awarded.

(j)   The Secretary of State may decide not to carry out the assessment in (f) if the application already falls for refusal on other grounds, but reserves the right to carry out this assessment in any reconsideration of the decision.

(k)   The applicant must, unless he provides a reasonable explanation, comply with any request made by the Secretary of State to attend for interview.

Tier 1 (Investor) Migrants

Purpose

245E.   This route is for high net worth individuals making a substantial financial investment to the UK.

Entry to the UK

245EA.   All migrants arriving in the UK and wishing to enter as a Tier 1 (Investor) Migrant must have a valid entry clearance for entry under this route. If they do not have a valid entry clearance, entry will be refused.

Requirements for entry clearance

245EB.   To qualify for entry clearance or leave to remain as a Tier 1 (Investor) Migrant, an applicant must meet the requirements listed below. If the applicant meets these requirements, entry clearance will be granted. If the applicant does not meet these requirements, the application will be refused.

Requirements:

(a)   The applicant must not fall for refusal under the general grounds for refusal.

(b)   The applicant must have a minimum of 75 points under paragraphs 54 to 65-SD of Appendix A.

(c)   An applicant who has, or was last granted, leave as a Student or a Postgraduate Doctor or Dentist, a Student Nurse, a Student Re-Sitting an Examination, a Student Writing-Up a Thesis or as a Tier 4 Migrant and:

    (i)   is currently being sponsored by a government or international scholarship agency, or

    (ii)   was being sponsored by a government or international scholarship agency, and that sponsorship came to an end 12 months ago or less

must provide the unconditional written consent of the sponsoring Government or agency to the application and must provide the specified documents to as set out in paragraph 245A above, show that this requirement has been met.

(d)   The applicant must be at least 18 years old and the assets and investment he is claiming points for must be wholly under his control.

(e)   The Entry Clearance Officer must not have reasonable grounds to believe that:

    (i)   notwithstanding that the applicant has provided the relevant specified documents required under Appendix A, the applicant is not in control of and at liberty to freely invest the money specified in their application for the purposes of meeting the requirements of Table 7 of Appendix A to these Rules (where relevant); or

    (ii)   any of the money specified in the application for the purposes of meeting the requirements of Table 7 of Appendix A to these Rules held by:

(1)   the applicant; or

(2)   where any of the specified money has been made available to the applicant by another party, that party,

has been acquired by means of conduct which is unlawful in the UK, or would constitute unlawful conduct if it occurred in the UK; or

(iii)   where any of the money specified in the application for the purposes of meeting the requirements of Table 7 of Appendix A to these Rules has been made available by another party, the character, conduct or associations of that party are such that approval of the application would not be conducive to the public good,

and where the Entry Clearance Officer does have reasonable grounds to believe one or more of the above applies, no points from Table 7 (where relevant) will be awarded.

Period and conditions of grant

245EC.   (a)   Entry clearance will be granted for a period of 3 years and four months and will be subject to the following conditions:

(i)   no recourse to public funds,

(ii)   registration with the police, if this is required by paragraph 326 of these Rules,

(iii)   no Employment as a Doctor or Dentist in Training, unless the applicant has obtained a primary degree in medicine or dentistry at bachelor's level or above from a UK institution that is a UK recognised or listed body, or which holds a sponsor licence under Tier 4 of the Points Based System, and

(iv)   no employment as a professional sportsperson (including as a sports coach), and

(v)   study subject to the condition set out in Part 15 of these Rules.

Requirements for leave to remain

245ED.   To qualify for leave to remain as a Tier 1 (Investor) Migrant, an applicant must meet the requirements listed below. If the applicant meets these requirements, leave to remain will be granted. If the applicant does not meet these requirements, the application will be refused.

Requirements:

(a)   The applicant must not fall for refusal under the general grounds for refusal, and must not be an illegal entrant.

(b)   The applicant must have a minimum of 75 points under paragraphs 54 to 65-SD of Appendix A.

(c)   The applicant must have, or have last been granted, entry clearance, leave to enter or remain:

(i)   as a Highly Skilled Migrant,

(ii)   as a Tier 1 (General) Migrant,

(iii)   as a Tier 1 (Entrepreneur) Migrant,

(iv)   as a Tier 1 (Investor) Migrant,

(v)   as a Tier 1 (Post-Study Work) Migrant,

(vi)   as a Businessperson,

(vii)   as an Innovator,

(viii)   as an Investor,

(ix)   as a Student,

(x)   as a Student Nurse,

(xi)   as a Student Re-Sitting an Examination,

(xii)   as a Student Writing Up a Thesis,

(xiii)   as a Work Permit Holder,

(xiv)   as a Writer, Composer or Artist,

(xv)   as a Tier 2 Migrant,

(xvi)   as a Tier 4 (General) Student and, in respect of such leave, is or was last sponsored by:

(1)   a UK recognised body or a body in receipt of public funding as a higher education institution from the Department of Employment and Learning in Northern Ireland, the

Higher Education Funding Council for England, the Higher Education Funding Council for Wales or the Scottish Funding Council; or

(2)   an overseas higher education institution to undertake a short-term study abroad programme in the United Kingdom; or

(3)   an Embedded College offering Pathway Courses, or

(xvii) as a Tier 4 (Child) Student.

(d)   An applicant who has, or was last granted, leave as a Student Nurse, Student Re-Sitting an Examination, Student Writing-Up a Thesis or as a Tier 4 Migrant and:

(i)   is currently being sponsored by a government or international scholarship agency, or

(ii)   was being sponsored by a government or international scholarship agency, and that sponsorship came to an end 12 months ago or less,

must provide the unconditional written consent of the sponsoring Government or agency to the application and must provide the specified documents as set out in paragraph 245A above, to show that this requirement has been met.

(e)   The applicant must be at least 18 years old and the assets and investment he is claiming points for must be wholly under his control.

(f)   The applicant must not be in the UK in breach of immigration laws except that any period of overstaying for a period of 28 days or less will be disregarded.

(g)   The Secretary of State must not have reasonable grounds to believe that:

(i)   notwithstanding that the applicant has provided the relevant specified documents required under Appendix A, the applicant is not in control of and at liberty to freely invest the money specified in their application for the purposes of meeting the requirements of Table 7 of Appendix A to these Rules (where relevant); or

(ii)   any of the money specified in the application for the purposes of meeting the requirements of Table 7 of Appendix A to these Rules held by:

(1)   the applicant; or

(2)   where any of the specified money has been made available to the applicant by another party, that party,

has been acquired by means of conduct which is unlawful in the UK, or would constitute unlawful conduct if it occurred in the UK; or

(iii) where any of the money specified in the application for the purposes of meeting the requirements of Table 7 of Appendix A to these Rules has been made available by another party, the character, conduct or associations of that party are such that approval of the application would not be conducive to the public good,

and where the Secretary of State does have reasonable grounds to believe one or more of the above applies, no points from Table 7 (where relevant) will be awarded.

Period, conditions and curtailment of grant

245EE.   (a)   Leave to remain will be granted:

(i)   for a period of 2 years, to an applicant who has, or was last granted, leave as a Tier 1 (Investor) Migrant,

(ii)   for a period of 3 years, to any other applicant.

(b)   Leave to remain under this route will be subject to the following conditions:

(i)   no recourse to public funds,

(ii)   registration with the police, if this is required by paragraph 326 of these Rules,

(iii) no Employment as a Doctor or Dentist in Training, unless the applicant:

(1)   has obtained a primary degree in medicine or dentistry at bachelor's level or above from a UK institution that is a UK recognised or listed body, or which holds a sponsor licence under Tier 4 of the Points Based System, and provides evidence of this degree; or

(2)   has, or has last been granted, entry clearance, leave to enter or leave to remain that was not subject to any condition restricting him from taking employment as a Doctor in Training, has been employed during that leave as a Doctor in Training, and provides a letter from the Postgraduate Deanery or NHS Trust employing them which confirms that

they have been working in a post or programme that has been approved by the General Medical Council as a training programme or post; or

    (3)   has, or has last been granted, entry clearance, leave to enter or leave to remain that was not subject to any condition restricting him from taking employment as a Dentist in Training, has been employed during that leave as a Dentist in Training, and provides a letter from the Postgraduate Deanery or NHS Trust employing them which confirms that they have been working in a post or programme that has been approved by the Joint Committee for Postgraduate Training in Dentistry as a training programme or post, and

    (iv)   no employment as a professional sportsperson (including as a sports coach), and

    (v)   study subject to the condition set out in Part 15 of these Rules.

(c)   Without prejudice to the grounds for curtailment in paragraph 323 of these Rules, leave to enter or remain as a Tier 1 (Investor) Migrant may be curtailed if:

    (i)   within 3 months of the date specified in paragraph (d), the applicant has not invested, or had invested on his behalf, at least the amount of capital specified in paragraph (e) in the UK by way of UK Government bonds, share capital or loan capital in active and trading UK registered companies other than those principally engaged in property investment, or

    (ii)   the applicant does not maintain at least the level of investment in (i) throughout the remaining period of his leave.

(d)   The date referred to in paragraph (c) is:

    (i)   the date of the applicant's entry to the UK, in the case of an applicant granted entry clearance as a Tier 1 (Investor) Migrant where there is evidence to establish the applicant's date of entry to the UK,

    (ii)   the date of the grant of entry clearance to the applicant, in the case of an applicant granted entry clearance as a Tier 1 (Investor) Migrant where there is no evidence to establish the applicant's date of entry to the UK, or

    (iii)   the date of the grant of leave to remain to the applicant, in any other case.

(e)   The amount of capital referred to in paragraph (c) is:

    (i)   at least £2 million if the applicant was last granted leave under the Rules in place from 6 November 2014 and was awarded points as set out in Table 7 or Table 8A of Appendix A to these Rules in that last grant, or

    (ii)   at least £750,000 if the applicant was last granted leave under the Rules in place before 6 November 2014 or was awarded points as set out in Table 8B of Appendix A to these Rules in his last grant.

(f)   Paragraph 245EE(c) does not apply where the applicant's two most recent grants of leave were either as a Tier 1 (Investor) Migrant and / or as an Investor.

Requirements for indefinite leave to remain

245EF.   To qualify for indefinite leave to remain, a Tier 1 (Investor) Migrant must meet the requirements listed below. if the applicant meets these requirements, indefinite leave to remain will be granted. if the applicant does not meet these requirements, the application will be refused.

Requirements:

(a)   DELETED

(b)   The applicant must not fall for refusal under the general grounds for refusal, and must not be an illegal entrant.

(c)   The applicant must have a minimum of 75 points under paragraphs 54 to 65-SD of Appendix A

(d)   The applicant must have demonstrated sufficient knowledge of the English language and sufficient knowledge about life in the United Kingdom, in accordance with Appendix KoLL.

(e)   The applicant must not be in the UK in breach of immigration laws except that any period of overstaying for a period of 28 days or less will be disregarded.

Tier 1 (Graduate Entrepreneur) Migrants

Purpose of the route and meaning of business

245F.   (a)   This route is for:

(i)   UK graduates who have been identified by Higher Education Institutions as having developed genuine and credible business ideas and entrepreneurial skills to extend their stay in the UK after graduation to establish one or more businesses in the UK; and

(ii)   Graduates who have been identified by UK Trade and Investment as elite global graduate entrepreneurs to establish one or more businesses in the UK.

(b)   For the purpose of paragraphs 245F to 245FC and paragraphs 66 to 72 of Appendix A 'business' means an enterprise as:

(i)   a sole trader,

(ii)   a partnership, or

(iii) a company registered in the UK.

Entry to the UK

245FA.   All migrants arriving in the UK and wishing to enter as a Tier 1 (Graduate Entrepreneur) Migrant must have a valid entry clearance for entry under this route. If they do not have a valid entry clearance, entry will be refused.

Requirements for entry clearance or leave to remain

245FB.   To qualify for entry clearance or leave to remain as a Tier 1 (Graduate Entrepreneur) Migrant, an applicant must meet the requirements listed below. If the applicant meets these requirements, entry clearance or leave to remain will be granted. If the applicant does not meet these requirements, the application will be refused.

Requirements:

(a)   The applicant must not fall for refusal under the general grounds for refusal, and must not be an illegal entrant.

(b)   The applicant must have a minimum of 75 points under paragraphs 66 to 72 of Appendix A.

(c)   The applicant must have a minimum of 10 points under paragraphs 1 to 15 of Appendix B.

(d)   The applicant must have a minimum of 10 points under paragraphs 1 to 2 of Appendix C. 11

(e)   If applying for leave to remain, the applicant must have, or have last been granted, entry clearance, leave to enter or remain:

(i)   as a Tier 4 Migrant and, in respect of such leave, is or was last sponsored by:

(1)   a UK recognised body or a body in receipt of public funding as a higher education institution from the Department of Employment and Learning in Northern Ireland, the Higher Education Funding Council for England, the Higher Education Funding Council for Wales or the Scottish Funding Council; or

(2)   an overseas higher education institution to undertake a short-term study abroad programme in the United Kingdom.

(ii)   as a Student,

(iii) as a Student Nurse,

(iv) as a Student Re-sitting an Examination,

(v)   as a Student Writing Up a Thesis,

(vi) as a Postgraduate Doctor or Dentist,

(vii) as a Tier 1 (Graduate Entrepreneur) Migrant, or

(viii) as a Tier 2 (General) Migrant.

(f)   An applicant who is applying for leave to remain and has, or was last granted, entry clearance or leave to remain as a Tier 2 (General) Migrant must have been granted leave to work as a post-doctoral researcher for the same institution which is endorsing his application as a Tier 1 (Graduate Entrepreneur) Migrant.

(g)   The applicant must not have previously been granted entry clearance, leave to enter or remain as a Tier 1 (Post-Study Work) Migrant, a Participant in the Fresh Talent: Working in Scotland Scheme, or a Participant in the International Graduates Scheme (or its predecessor, the Science and Engineering Graduates Scheme).

(h)   The applicant must not previously have been granted leave as a Tier 1 (Graduate Entrepreneur) Migrant on more than 1 occasion.

(i)   An applicant who does not have, or was not last granted, leave to remain as a Tier 1 (Graduate Entrepreneur) Migrant and:

(i)   is currently being sponsored in his studies by a government or international scholarship agency, or

(ii)   was being sponsored in his studies by a government or international scholarship agency, and that sponsorship came to an end 12 months ago or less,

must provide the unconditional written consent of the sponsoring government or agency to the application and must provide the specified documents as set out in paragraph 245A above, to show that this requirement has been met.

(j)   The applicant must not be in the UK in breach of immigration laws except that any period of overstaying for a period of 28 days or less will be disregarded.

Period and conditions of grant

245FC.   Entry clearance or leave to remain will be granted for a period of 1 year and will be subject to the following conditions:

(i)   no recourse to public funds,

(ii)   registration with the police, if this is required by paragraph 326 of these Rules,

(iii) no employment as a Doctor or Dentist in Training

(iv)   no employment as a professional sportsperson (including as a sports coach), and

(v)   study subject to the condition set out in Part 15 of these Rules where the applicant is 18 years of age or over at the time their leave is granted, or will be aged 18 before their period of limited leave expires.

Tier 2 Migrants

Tier 2 (Intra-Company Transfer) Migrants

Purpose of this route and definitions

245G.   This route enables multinational employers to transfer their existing employees from outside the EEA to their UK branch for training purposes or to fill a specific vacancy that cannot be filled by a British or EEA worker. There are four sub-categories in this route:

(i)   Short Term staff: for established employees of multi-national companies who are being transferred to a skilled job in the UK for 12 months or less that could not be carried out by a new recruit from the resident workforce;

(ii)   Long Term staff: for established employees of multi-national companies who are being transferred to a skilled job in the UK which will, or may, last for more than 12 months and could not be carried out by a new recruit from the resident workforce;

(iii) Graduate Trainee: for recent graduate recruits of multi-national companies who are being transferred to the UK branch of the same organisation as part of a structured graduate training programme, which clearly defines progression towards a managerial or specialist role;

(iv)   Skills Transfer: for overseas employees of multi-national companies who are being transferred to the UK branch of the same organisation in a graduate occupation to learn the skills and knowledge they will need to perform their jobs overseas, or to impart their specialist skills to the UK workforce.

Entry clearance

245GA.   All migrants arriving in the UK and wishing to enter as a Tier 2 (Intra-Company Transfer) Migrant must have a valid entry clearance for entry under this route. If they do not have a valid entry clearance, entry will be refused.

Requirements for entry clearance

245GB.   To qualify for entry clearance as a Tier 2 (Intra-Company Transfer) Migrant, an applicant must meet the requirements listed below. If the applicant meets these requirements, entry clearance will be granted. if the applicant does not meet these requirements, the application will be refused.

Requirements:

(a)   The applicant must not fall for refusal under the general grounds for refusal.

(b)   The applicant must have a minimum of 50 points under paragraphs 73 to 75E of Appendix A.

(c)   The applicant must have a minimum of 10 points under paragraphs 4 to 5 of Appendix C.

(d)   Except where the period of engagement recorded by the Certificate of Sponsorship used in support of such entry clearance or leave to remain was granted for a period of three months or less, the applicant must not have had entry clearance or leave to remain as a Tier 2 Migrant at any time during the 12 months immediately before the date of the application, unless paragraph (e) below applies.

(e)   Paragraph (d) above does not apply to an applicant who:

    (i)   was not in the UK with leave as a Tier 2 migrant at any time during the above 12-month period, and provides evidence to show this,

    (ii)   is applying under the Long Term Staff sub-category and who has, or last had entry clearance or leave to remain as a Tier 2 (Intra-Company Transfer) Migrant in the Short Term staff, Graduate Trainee or Skills Transfer sub-categories, or under the Rules in place before 6 April 2011, or

    (iii)   will be paid a gross annual salary (as recorded by the Certificate of Sponsorship Checking Service entry, and including such allowances as are specified as acceptable for this purpose in paragraph 75 of Appendix A) of £155,300 or higher.

(f)   an applicant who has, or was last granted, leave as a Student, a Student Nurse, a Student Re-Sitting an Examination, a Student Writing-Up a Thesis, a Postgraduate Doctor or Dentist or a Tier 4 Migrant and:

    (i)   is currently being sponsored by a government or international scholarship agency, or

    (ii)   was being sponsored by a government or international scholarship agency, and that sponsorship came to an end 12 months ago or less,

must provide the unconditional written consent of the sponsoring Government or agency to the application and must provide the specified documents as set out in paragraph 245A above, to show that this requirement has been met.

(g)   The applicant must be at least 16 years old.

(h)   Where the applicant is under 18 years of age, the application must be supported by the applicant's parents or legal guardian, or by one parent if that parent has sole legal responsibility for the child.

(i)   Where the applicant is under 18 years of age, the applicant's parents or legal guardian, or just one parent if that parent has sole responsibility for the child, must confirm that they consent to the arrangements for the applicant's travel to, and reception and care in, the UK.

Period and conditions of grant

245GC.   (a)   Entry clearance will be granted for whichever is the shorter of:

    (i)   a period equal to the length of the period of engagement plus 1 month, or

    (ii)   the maximum time, as set out in (b).

(b)   The maximum time referred to in (a)(ii) is:

    (i)   6 months, if the applicant is applying in the Skills Transfer subcategory,

    (ii)   12 months, if the applicant is applying in either of the Graduate Trainee or Short Term Staff sub-categories, or

    (iii)   5 years and 1 month, if the applicant is applying in the Long Term Staff sub-category.

(c)   entry clearance will be granted with effect from 14 days before the date that the Certificate of Sponsorship Checking Service records as the start date for the applicant's employment in the UK, unless entry clearance is being granted less than 14 days before that date, in which case it will be granted with immediate effect.

(d)   Entry clearance will be subject to the following conditions:

    (i)   no recourse to public funds,

    (ii)   registration with the police, if this is required by paragraph 326,

    (iii)   no employment except:

        (1)   working for the sponsor in the employment that the Certificate of Sponsorship Checking Service records that the migrant is being sponsored to do, subject to any notification of a change to the details of that employment, other than prohibited changes as defined in paragraph 323AA,

        (2)   voluntary work, and

> (iv) study subject to the condition set out in Part 15 of these Rules where the applicant is 18 years of age or over at the time their leave is granted, or will be aged 18 before their period of limited leave expires.

Requirements for leave to remain

245GD.   To qualify for leave to remain as a Tier 2 (Intra-Company Transfer) Migrant under this rule, an applicant must meet the requirements listed below. If the applicant meets these requirements, leave to remain will be granted. If the applicant does not meet these requirements, the application will be refused.

Requirements:

(a)   The applicant must not fall for refusal under the general grounds for refusal, and must not be an illegal entrant.

(b)   if the applicant is applying for leave to remain as a Tier 2 (Intra-Company Transfer) Migrant in the Long Term Staff sub-category:

    (i)   the applicant must have, or have last been granted, entry clearance, leave to enter or leave to remain as either:

        (1)   a Tier 2 (Intra-Company Transfer) Migrant in the Long Term Staff sub-category, or

        (2)   a Tier 2 (Intra-Company Transfer) Migrant in the established Staff sub-category under the Rules in place before 6 April 2011, or

        (3)   a Tier 2 (Intra-Company Transfer) Migrant granted under the Rules in place before 6 April 2010, or

        (4)   a Qualifying Work Permit Holder, provided that the work permit was granted because the applicant was the subject of an Intra-Company Transfer, or

        (5)   as a representative of an overseas Business, and

    (ii)   the applicant must still be working for the same employer as he was at the time of that earlier grant of leave.

(c)   if the applicant is applying for leave to remain as a Tier 2 (Intra-Company Transfer) Migrant in the Short Term Staff sub-category:

    (i)   the applicant must have, or have last been granted, entry clearance, leave to enter or leave to remain as a Tier 2 (Intra-Company Transfer) Migrant in the Short Term Staff sub-category, and

    (ii)   the applicant must still be working for the same employer as he was at the time of that earlier grant of leave.

(d)   if the applicant is applying for leave to remain as a Tier 2 (Intra-Company Transfer) Migrant in the Graduate Trainee sub-category:

    (i)   the applicant must have, or have last been granted, entry clearance, leave to enter or leave to remain as a Tier 2 (Intra-Company Transfer) Migrant in the Graduate Trainee sub-category, and

    (ii)   the applicant must still be working for the same employer as he was at the time of that earlier grant of leave.

(e)   if the applicant is applying for leave to remain as a Tier 2 (Intra-Company Transfer) Migrant in the Skills Transfer sub-category:

    (i)   the applicant must have, or have last been granted, entry clearance, leave to enter or leave to remain as a Tier 2 (Intra-Company Transfer) Migrant in the skills Transfer sub-category, and

    (ii)   the applicant must still be working for the same employer as he was at the time of that earlier grant of leave.

(f)   in all cases the applicant must have a minimum of 50 points under paragraphs 73 to 75E of Appendix A.

(g)   DELETED.

(h)   The applicant must have a minimum of 10 points under paragraphs 4 to 5 of Appendix C.

(i)   The applicant must be at least 16 years old.

(j)   Where the applicant is under 18 years of age, the application must be supported by the applicant's parents or legal guardian or by one parent if that parent has sole legal responsibility for the child.

(k)   Where the applicant is under 18 years of age, the applicant's parents or legal guardian, or one parent if that parent has sole legal responsibility for the child, must confirm that they consent to the arrangements for the applicant's care in the UK.

(l)   The applicant must not be in the UK in breach of immigration laws except that any period of overstaying for a period of 28 days or less will be disregarded.

Period and conditions of grant

245GE.   (a)   Leave to remain will be granted for whichever of the following is the shortest:

    (i)   the length of the period of engagement plus 14 days,

    (ii)   5 years, or

    (iii)   the difference between the continuous period of leave that the applicant has already been granted (notwithstanding any breaks between periods of leave of up to 28 days) as a Tier 2 (Intra-Company Transfer) Migrant, and the maximum time, as set out in (b).

If the calculation of period of leave comes to zero or a negative number, leave to remain will be refused.

(b)   The maximum time referred to in (a)(iii) is:

    (i)   6 months, if the applicant is applying in the Skills Transfer subcategory,

    (ii)   12 months, if the applicant is applying in either of the Graduate Trainee or Short Term Staff sub-categories,

    (iii)   5 years, if:

        (1)   the applicant is applying in the Long Term Staff subcategory,

        (2)   the Certificate of Sponsorship Checking Service entry records that the applicant's gross annual salary (including such allowances as are specified as acceptable for this purpose in paragraph 75 of Appendix A) to be paid by the Sponsor is less than £155,300, (or £153,500 if the Certificate of Sponsorship used in support of the application was assigned to him before 6 April 2015) and

        (3)   Paragraph (v) below does not apply,

    (iv)   9 years, if:

        (1)   the applicant is applying in the Long Term Staff subcategory,

        (2)   the Certificate of Sponsorship Checking Service entry records that the applicant's gross annual salary (including such allowances as are specified as acceptable for this purpose in paragraph 75 of Appendix A) to be paid by the Sponsor is £155,300, (or £153,500 if the Certificate of Sponsorship used in support of the application was assigned to him before 6 April 2015) or higher, and

        (3)   Paragraph (v) below does not apply,

        or

    (v)   No limit, if the applicant:

        (1)   is applying in the Long Term Staff sub-category,

        (2)   previously had leave as a Tier 2 (Intra-Company Transfer) Migrant under the Rules in place before 6 April 2011 or as a Qualifying Work Permit Holder, and

        (3)   has not been granted entry clearance in this or any other route since the grant of leave referred to in (2) above.

(c)   In addition to the period in (a), leave to remain will be granted for the period between the date that the application is decided and the date that the Certificate of Sponsorship Checking Service records as the start date of employment in the UK, provided this is not a negative value.

(d)   Leave to remain will be granted subject to the following conditions:

    (i)   no recourse to public funds,

    (ii)   registration with the police, if this is required by paragraph 326, and

    (iii)   no employment except:

        (1)   working for the sponsor in the employment that the Certificate of Sponsorship Checking Service records that the migrant is being sponsored to do, subject to any notification of a change to the details of that employment, other than prohibited changes as defined in paragraph 323AA,

        (2)   supplementary employment, and

        (3)   voluntary work.

Requirements for indefinite leave to remain

245GF.   To qualify for indefinite leave to remain as a Tier 2 (Intra-Company Transfer) Migrant, an applicant must meet the requirements listed below. If the applicant meets these requirements, indefinite leave to remain will be granted. if the applicant does not meet these requirements, the application will be refused.

Requirements:

(a)   DELETED

(b)   The applicant must not fall for refusal under the general grounds for refusal, and must not be an illegal entrant.

(c)   The applicant must have spent a continuous period of 5 years lawfully in the UK, of which the most recent period must have been spent with leave as a Tier 2 (Intra-Company Transfer) Migrant, in any combination of the following categories:

   (i)   as a Tier 2 (Intra-Company Transfer) Migrant,

   (ii)   as a Qualifying Work Permit Holder, or

   (iii)   as a representative of an overseas Business.

(d)   The continuous period of 5 years referred to in paragraph (c) must include a period of leave as:

   (i)   a Tier 2 (Intra-Company Transfer) Migrant granted under the Rules in place before 6 April 2010, or

   (ii)   a Qualifying Work Permit Holder, provided that the work permit was granted because the applicant was the subject of an Intra-Company Transfer.

(e)   The Sponsor that issued the Certificate of Sponsorship that led to the applicant's last grant of leave must:

   (i)   still hold, or have applied for a renewal of, a Tier 2 (Intra-Company Transfer) Sponsor licence; and

   (ii)   certify in writing that:

      (1)   he still requires the applicant for the employment in question, and

      (2)   the applicant is paid at or above the appropriate rate for the job as stated in the Codes of Practice in Appendix J, or where the applicant is not paid at that rate only due to maternity, paternity or adoption leave, the date that leave started and that the applicant was paid at the appropriate rate immediately before the leave.

(f)   The applicant provides the specified documents in paragraph 245GF-SD to evidence the sponsor's certification in subsection (e) (ii) and to evidence the reason for the absences set out in paragraph 245AAA.

(g)   The applicant must have sufficient knowledge of the English language and sufficient knowledge about life in the United Kingdom, in accordance with Appendix KoLL.

(h)   The applicant must not be in the UK in breach of immigration laws except that any period of overstaying for a period of 28 days or less will be disregarded.

(i)   For the purposes of sub-paragraph (c), time spent with valid leave in the Bailiwick of Guernsey, the Bailiwick of Jersey or the Isle of Man in a category equivalent to the categories set out in (c)(i) to (iii) above, may be included in the continuous period of 5 years lawful residence, provided that:

   (i)   the continuous period of 5 years includes a period of leave as a Tier 2 (Intra-Company Transfer) Migrant granted before 6 April 2010, or a Qualifying Work Permit Holder (provided the work permit was granted because the applicant was the subject of an Intra-Company Transfer); and

   (ii)   any period of leave granted in the Bailiwick of Guernsey, the Bailiwick of Jersey or the Isle of Man as a work permit holder or as a Tier 2 Migrant was for employment:

      (a)   in a job which appears on the list of occupations skilled to National Qualifications Framework level 3 or above (or from 6 April 2011, National Qualifications Framework level 4 or above or from 14 June 2012, National Qualifications Framework level 6 or above), as stated in the Codes of Practice in Appendix J, or

      (b)   in a job which appears in the Creative Sector Codes of Practice in Appendix J, or

      (c)   as a professional sportsperson (including as a sports coach); and

   (iii)   the most recent period of leave was granted in the UK as a Tier 2 (Intra-Company Transfer) Migrant.

In such cases, references to the 'UK' in paragraph 245AAA shall include a reference to the Bailiwick of Guernsey, Bailiwick of Jersey or the Isle of Man, as the case may be.

Specified documents

245GF-SD.   The specified documents referred to in paragraph 245GF(f) are set out in A, B and C below:

A.   Either a payslip and a personal bank or building society statement, or a payslip and a building society pass book.

   (a)   Payslips must be:

      (i)   the applicant's most recent payslip,

      (ii)   dated no earlier than one calendar month before the date of the application, and

      (iii)   either:

          (1)   an original payslip,

          (2)   on company-headed paper, or

          (3)   accompanied by a letter from the applicant's Sponsor, on company headed paper and signed by a senior official, confirming the payslip is authentic.

   (b)   Personal bank or building society statements must:

      (i)   be the applicant's most recent statement,

      (ii)   be dated no earlier than one calendar month before the date of the application,

      (iii)   clearly show:

          (1)   the applicant's name,

          (2)   the applicant's account number,

          (3)   the date of the statement,

          (4)   the financial institution's name,

          (5)   the financial institution's logo, and

          (6)   transactions by the Sponsor covering the period no earlier than one calendar month before the date of the application, including the amount shown on the specified payslip as at 245GF-SD A.(a)

      (iv)   be either:

          (1)   printed on the bank's or building society's letterhead,

          (2)   electronic bank or building society statements, accompanied by a supporting letter from the bank or building society, on company headed paper, confirming the statement provided is authentic, or

          (3)   electronic bank or building society statements, bearing the official stamp of the bank or building society on every page,

     and

      (v)   not be mini-statements from automatic teller machines (ATMs).

   (c)   Building society pass books must

      (i)   clearly show:

          (1)   the applicant's name,

          (2)   the applicant's account number,

          (3)   the financial institution's name,

          (4)   the financial institution's logo, and

          (5)   transactions by the sponsor covering the period no earlier than one calendar month before the date of the application, including the amount shown on the specified payslip as at 245GF-SD A.(a)

     and

      (ii)   be either:

          (1)   the original pass book, or

          (2)   a photocopy of the pass book which has been certified by the issuing building society on company headed paper, confirming the statement provided is authentic.

B.　A letter from the employer detailing the purpose and period of absences in connection with the employment, including periods of annual leave. Where the absence was due to a serious or compelling reason, a personal letter from the applicant which includes full details of the reason for the absences and all original supporting documents in relation to those reasons – e.g. medical certificates, birth/death certificates, information about the reasons which led to the absence from the UK.

C.　Where the applicant is not being paid the appropriate rate in Appendix J due to maternity, paternity or adoption leave:

(a)　Payslips must be:

(i)　the applicant's payslip from the month immediately preceding the leave,

(ii)　the applicant's payslips for each month of the period of the leave,

(iii)　as set out in A(a)(iii) above.

(b)　Bank or building society statements must be:

(i)　the applicant's statement from the month immediately preceding the leave,

(ii)　the applicant's statement for each month of the period of the leave,

(iii)　as set out in A(b)(iii) above.

Tier 2 (General) Migrants, Tier 2 (Minister of Religion) Migrants and Tier 2 (Sportsperson) Migrants

Purpose of these routes and definitions

245H.　These routes enable UK employers to recruit workers from outside the EEA to fill a particular vacancy that cannot be filled by a British or EEA worker.

Entry clearance

245HA.　All Migrants arriving in the UK and wishing to enter as a Tier 2 (General) Migrant, Tier 2 (Minister of Religion) Migrant or Tier 2 (Sportsperson) Migrant must have a valid entry clearance for entry under the relevant one of these routes. If they do not have a valid entry clearance, entry will be refused.

Requirements for entry clearance

245HB.　To qualify for entry clearance as a Tier 2 (General) Migrant, Tier 2 (Minister of Religion) Migrant or Tier 2 (Sportsperson) Migrant, an applicant must meet the requirements listed below. If the applicant meets these requirements, entry clearance will be granted. if the applicant does not meet these requirements, the application will be refused.

Requirements:

(a)　The applicant must not fall for refusal under the general grounds for refusal.

(b)　If applying as a Tier 2 (General) Migrant, the applicant must have a minimum of 50 points under paragraphs 76 to 84A of Appendix A.

(c)　If applying as a Tier 2 (Minister of religion) Migrant, the applicant must have a minimum of 50 points under paragraphs 85 to 92A of Appendix A.

(d)　If applying as a Tier 2 (sportsperson) Migrant, the applicant must have a minimum of 50 points under paragraphs 93 to 100 of Appendix A.

(e)　The applicant must have a minimum of 10 points under paragraphs 1 to 18 of Appendix B.

(f)　The applicant must have a minimum of 10 points under paragraphs 4 to 5 of Appendix C.

(g)　Except where the period of engagement recorded by the Certificate of Sponsorship used in support of such entry clearance or leave to remain was three months or less, the applicant must not have had entry clearance or leave to remain as a Tier 2 Migrant at any time during the 12 months immediately before the date of the application, unless the applicant:

(i)　was not in the UK with leave as a Tier 2 Migrant during this period, and provides evidence to show this, or

(ii)　will be paid a gross annual salary (as recorded by the Certificate of Sponsorship Checking Service entry, and including such allowances as are specified as acceptable for this purpose in paragraph 79 of Appendix A) of £155,300 or higher.

(h)　An applicant who has, or was last granted, leave as a Student, a Student Nurse, a Student Re-Sitting an Examination, a Student Writing-Up a Thesis, a Postgraduate Doctor or Dentist or a Tier 4 Migrant and:

(i) is currently being sponsored by a government or international scholarship agency, or

(ii) was being sponsored by a government or international scholarship agency, and that sponsorship came to an end 12 months ago or less

must provide the unconditional written consent of the sponsoring Government or agency to the application and must provide the specified documents as set out in paragraph 245A above, to show that this requirement has been met.

(i) The applicant must be at least 16 years old.

(j) Where the applicant is under 18 years of age, the application must be supported by the applicant's parents or legal guardian, or by one parent if that parent has sole legal responsibility for the child.

(k) Where the applicant is under 18 years of age, the applicant's parents or legal guardian, or one parent if that parent has sole responsibility for the child, must confirm that they consent to the arrangements for the applicant's travel to, and reception and care in, the UK.

(l) If the Sponsor is a limited company, the applicant must not own more than 10% of its shares, unless the gross annual salary (as recorded by the Certificate of Sponsorship Checking Service entry, and including such allowances as are specified as acceptable for this purpose in paragraph 79 of Appendix A) is £155,300 or higher.

(m) If the applicant is applying as a Tier 2 (Minister of Religion) Migrant, the Entry Clearance Officer must be satisfied that the applicant:

(i) genuinely intends to undertake, and is capable of undertaking, the role recorded by the Certificate of Sponsorship Checking Service; and

(ii) will not undertake employment in the United Kingdom other than under the terms of paragraph 245HC(d)(iii).

(n) To support the assessment in paragraph 245HB(m), the Entry Clearance Officer may:

(i) request additional information and evidence, and refuse the application if the information or evidence is not provided. Any requested documents must be received by the Home Office at the address specified in the request within 28 calendar days of the date the request is sent, and

(ii) request the applicant attends an interview, and refuse the application if the applicant fails to comply with any such request without providing a reasonable explanation.

(o) If the Entry Clearance Officer is not satisfied following the assessment in paragraph 245HB(m), no points will be awarded under paragraphs 85 to 92A of Appendix A.

(p) The Entry Clearance Officer may decide not to carry out the assessment in paragraph 245HB(m) if the application already falls for refusal on other grounds, but reserves the right to carry out this assessment in any reconsideration of the decision.

Period and conditions of grant

245HC. (a) Entry clearance will be granted for whichever of the following is the shorter:

(i) a period equal to the length of the period of engagement plus 1 month, or

(ii) the maximum time, as set out in (b).

(b) The maximum time referred to in (a)(ii) is:

(i) 5 years and 1 month, if the applicant is applying as a Tier 2 (General) Migrant; or

(ii) 3 years and 1 month, if the applicant is applying as a Tier 2 (Minister of Religion) Migrant or a Tier 2 (Sportsperson) Migrant.

(c) Entry clearance will be granted with effect from 14 days before the date that the Certificate of Sponsorship Checking Service records as the start date for the applicant's employment in the UK, unless entry clearance is being granted less than 14 days before that date, in which case it will be granted with immediate effect.

(d) Entry clearance will be subject to the following conditions:

(i) no recourse to public funds,

(ii) registration with the police, if this is required by paragraph 326 of these Rules, and

(iii) no employment except:

(1) working for the sponsor in the employment that the Certificate of Sponsorship Checking Service records that the migrant is being sponsored to do, subject to any notification of a change to the details of that employment, other than prohibited changes as defined in paragraph 323AA,

(2)   supplementary employment,

(3)   voluntary work, and

(4)   if the applicant is applying as a Tier 2 (Sportsperson) Migrant, employment as a sportsperson for his national team while his national team is in the UK and Temporary Engagement as a Sports Broadcaster, and

(iv)   study subject to the condition set out in Part 15 of these Rules where the applicant is 18 years of age or over at the time their leave is granted, or will be aged 18 before their period of limited leave expires.

(e)   (i)   Applicants who meet the requirements for entry clearance and who obtain points under paragraphs 76 to 79D of Appendix A shall be granted entry clearance as a Tier 2 (General) Migrant.

(ii)   Applicants who meet the requirements for entry clearance and who obtain points under paragraphs 85 to 92 of Appendix A shall be granted entry clearance as a Tier 2 (Minister of Religion) Migrant.

(iii)   Applicants who meet the requirements for entry clearance and who obtain points under paragraphs 93 to 100 of Appendix A shall be granted entry clearance as a Tier 2 (Sportsperson) Migrant.

Requirements for leave to remain

245HD.   To qualify for leave to remain as a Tier 2 (General) Migrant, Tier 2 (Minister of Religion Migrant or Tier 2 (Sportsperson) Migrant under this rule, an applicant must meet the requirements listed below. if the applicant meets these requirements, leave to remain will be granted. if the applicant does not meet these requirements, the application will be refused.

Requirements:

(a)   The applicant must not fall for refusal under the general grounds for refusal, and must not be an illegal entrant.

(b)   the applicant must:

(i)   have, or have last been granted, entry clearance, leave to enter or leave to remain as:

(1)   a Tier 1 Migrant,

(2)   a Tier 2 Migrant,

(3)   a Highly Skilled Migrant,

(4)   an Innovator,

(5)   a Jewish Agency Employee,

(6)   a Member of the Operational Ground Staff of an Overseas-owned Airline,

(7)   a Minister of Religion, Missionary or Member of a Religious Order,

(8)   a Participant in the Fresh Talent: Working in Scotland Scheme,

(9)   a Participant in the International Graduates Scheme (or its predecessor, the Science and Engineering Graduates Scheme),

(10)   a Qualifying Work Permit Holder,

(11)   a Representative of an Overseas Business,

(12)   a Representative of an Overseas Newspaper, News Agency or Broadcasting Organisation,

(13)   a Tier 5 (Temporary Worker) Migrant, or

(14)   the partner of a Relevant Points Based System Migrant if the relevant Points Based System Migrant is a Tier 4 Migrant,

or

(ii)   have, or have last been granted, entry clearance, leave to enter or leave to remain as:

(1)   a Tier 4 Migrant and, in respect of such leave, is or was last sponsored by:

(1)   a UK recognised body or a body in receipt of public funding as a higher education institution from the Department of Employment and Learning in Northern Ireland, the Higher Education Funding Council for England, the Higher Education Funding Council for Wales or the Scottish Funding Council; or

(2)   an overseas higher education institution to undertake a short-term study abroad programme in the United Kingdom

      (2)   a Student,

      (3)   a Student Nurse,

      (4)   a Student Re-Sitting an Examination,

      (5)   a Person Writing Up a Thesis,

      (6)   an Overseas Qualified Nurse or Midwife,

      (7)   a Postgraduate Doctor or Dentist, or

      (8)   a Student Union Sabbatical Officer.

(c)   An applicant who has, or was last granted leave as a Tier 2 (Intra-Company Transfer) Migrant must:

    (i)   have previously had leave as a Tier 2 (Intra-Company Transfer) Migrant under the Rules in place before 6 April 2010, or in the Established Staff sub-category under the Rules in place before 6 April 2011,

    (ii)   not have been granted entry clearance in this or any other route since the grant of leave referred to in (i) above; and

    (iii)   not be applying to work for the same Sponsor as sponsored him when he was last granted leave.

(d)   An applicant under the provisions in (b)(ii) above must meet the following requirements:

    (i)   The applicant must have completed and passed:

      (1)   a UK recognised bachelor's or master's degree (not a qualification of equivalent level which is not a degree),

      (2)   a UK Postgraduate Certificate in Education or Professional Graduate Diploma of Education (not a qualification of equivalent level),

    or the applicant must have completed a minimum of 12 months study in the UK towards a UK PhD.

    (ii)   The applicant (other than an applicant under b(ii)(1) above) must have studied for the course in (d)(i) at a UK institution that is a UK recognised or listed body, or which holds a sponsor licence under Tier 4 of the Points Based System.

    (iii)   The applicant must have studied the course referred to in (d)(i) during:

      (1)   his last grant of leave, or

      (2)   a period of continuous leave which includes his last grant of leave, (for these purposes continuous leave will not be considered to have been broken if any of the circumstances set out in paragraphs 245AAA(a)(i) to (iii) of these Rules apply.).

    (iv)   The applicant's periods of UK study and/or research towards the course in (i) must have been undertaken whilst he had entry clearance, leave to enter or leave to remain in the UK that was not subject to a restriction preventing him from undertaking that course of study and/or research.

    (v)   If the institution studied at is removed from the Tier 4 Sponsor Register, the applicant's qualification must not have been obtained on or after the date of removal from the Sponsor Register.

    (vi)   If the applicant:

      (1)   is currently being sponsored by a government or international scholarship agency, or

      (2)   was being sponsored by a government or international scholarship agency, and that sponsorship came to an end 12 months ago or less,

    the applicant must provide the unconditional written consent of the sponsoring Government or agency to the application and must provide the specified documents as set out in paragraph 245A above, to show that this requirement has been met.

    (vii)   The applicant must provide an original degree certificate, academic transcript or an academic reference on official headed paper of the institution, which clearly shows:

      (1)   The applicant's name,

      (2)   the course title/award,

      (3)   the course duration (except in the case of a degree certificate), and

      (4)   unless the course is a PhD course, the date of course completion and pass (or the date of award in the case of a degree certificate).

(e)   an applicant who was last granted leave as a Tier 5 (Temporary Worker) Migrant must have been granted such leave in the Creative and Sporting sub-category of Tier 5 in order to allow the applicant to work as a professional footballer, and the applicant must be applying for leave to remain as a Tier 2 (Sportsperson) Migrant.

(f) If applying as a Tier 2 (General) Migrant, the applicant must have a minimum of 50 points under paragraphs 76 to 79D of Appendix A.

(g) If applying as a Tier 2 (Minister of Religion) Migrant, the applicant must have a minimum of 50 points under paragraphs 85 to 92A of Appendix A.

(h) If applying as a Tier 2 (Sportsperson) Migrant, the applicant must have a minimum of 50 points under paragraphs 93 to 100 of Appendix A.

(i) The applicant must have a minimum of 10 points under paragraphs 1 to 16 of Appendix B.

(j) The applicant must have a minimum of 10 points under paragraphs 4 to 5 of Appendix C.

(k) Except where the period of engagement recorded by the Certificate of Sponsorship used in support of such entry clearance or leave to remain was three months or less, the applicant must not have had entry clearance or leave to remain as a Tier 2 Migrant at any time during the 12 months immediately before the date of the application, unless:

    (i) the applicant's last grant of leave was as a Tier 2 Migrant,

    (ii) the applicant was not in the UK with leave as a Tier 2 Migrant during this period, and provides evidence to show this, or

    (iii) the applicant will be paid a gross annual salary (as recorded by the Certificate of Sponsorship Checking Service entry, and including such allowances as are specified as acceptable for this purpose in paragraph 79 of Appendix A) of £155,300 or higher.

(l) The applicant must be at least 16 years old.

(m) Where the applicant is under 18 years of age, the application must be supported by the applicant's parents or legal guardian, or by just one parent if that parent has sole legal responsibility for the child.

(n) Where the applicant is under 18 years of age, the applicant's parents or legal guardian, or just one parent if that parent has sole legal responsibility for the child, must confirm that they consent to the arrangements for the applicant's care in the UK.

(o) if the sponsor is a limited company, the applicant must not own more than 10% of its shares, unless the gross annual salary (as recorded by the Certificate of Sponsorship Checking Service entry, and including such allowances as are specified as acceptable for this purpose in paragraph 79 of Appendix A) is £155,300 or higher.

(p) The applicant must not be in the UK in breach of immigration laws except that any period of overstaying for a period of 28 days or less will be disregarded.

(q) If the applicant is applying as a Tier 2 (Minister of Religion) Migrant, the Secretary of State must be satisfied that the applicant:

    (i) genuinely intends to undertake, and is capable of undertaking, the role recorded by the Certificate of Sponsorship Checking Service; and

    (ii) will not undertake employment in the United Kingdom other than under the terms of paragraph 245HE(d)(iii).

(r) To support the assessment in paragraph 245HD(q), the Secretary of State may:

    (i) request additional information and evidence, and refuse the application if the information or evidence is not provided. Any requested documents must be received by the Home Office at the address specified in the request within 28 calendar days of the date the request is sent, and

    (ii) request the applicant attends an interview, and refuse the application if the applicant fails to comply with any such request without providing a reasonable explanation.

(s) If the Secretary of State is not satisfied following the assessment in paragraph 245HD(q), no points will be awarded under paragraphs 85 to 92A of Appendix A.

(t) The Secretary of State may decide not to carry out the assessment in paragraph 245HD(q) if the application already falls for refusal on other grounds, but reserves the right to carry out this assessment in any reconsideration of the decision.

Period and conditions of grant

245HE. (a) Leave to remain will be granted for whichever of the following is the shortest:

    (i) the length of the period of engagement plus 14 days,

    (ii) 5 years if the applicant is applying as a Tier 2 (General) Migrant, or

(iii)   3 years if the applicant is applying as a Tier 2 (Minister of Religion) Migrant or a Tier 2 (Sportsperson) Migrant, or

(iv)   except where (b) applies, the difference between the continuous period of leave that the applicant has already been granted (notwithstanding any breaks between periods of leave of up to 28 days) as a Tier 2 Migrant (other than as a Tier 2 (Intra-Company Transfer) Migrant), and 6 years.

If the calculation of period of leave comes to zero or a negative number, leave to remain will be refused.

(b)   The 6 year restriction set out in (a)(iv) will not apply if the applicant:

(i)   previously had leave under the Rules in place before 6 April 2011 as:

(1)   a Tier 2 (General) Migrant,

(2)   a Tier 2 (Minister of Religion) Migrant,

(3)   a Tier 2 (Sportsperson) Migrant,

(4)   a Jewish Agency Employee,

(5)   a Member of the Operational Ground Staff of an Overseas-owned Airline,

(6)   a Minister of Religion, Missionary or Member of a Religious Order,

(7)   a Qualifying Work Permit Holder, or

(8)   a Representative of an Overseas Newspaper, News Agency or Broadcasting Organisation,

and

(ii)   has not been granted entry clearance as a Tier 2 (General) Migrant, Tier 2 (Minister of Religion) Migrant or Tier 2 (Sportsperson) Migrant under the Rules in place from 6 April 2011, and

(iii)   has not been granted entry clearance, leave to enter or leave to remain in any other category since the grant of leave referred to in (i) above.

(c)   In addition to the period in (a), leave to remain will be granted for the period between the date that the application is decided and the date that the Certificate of Sponsorship Checking Service records as the start date of employment in the UK, provided this is not a negative value.

(d)   leave to remain will be granted subject to the following conditions:

(i)   no recourse to public funds,

(ii)   registration with the police, if this is required by paragraph 326 of these Rules,

(iii)   no employment except:

(1)   working for the sponsor in the employment that the Certificate of Sponsorship Checking Service records that the migrant is being sponsored to do, subject to any notification of a change to the details of that employment, other than prohibited changes as defined in paragraph 323AA,

(2)   supplementary employment,

(3)   voluntary work,

(4)   until the start date of the period of engagement, any employment which the applicant was lawfully engaged in on the date of his application, and

(5)   if the applicant is applying as a Tier 2 (Sportsperson) Migrant, employment as a sportsperson for his national team while his national team is in the UK and Temporary Engagement as a Sports Broadcaster.

(iv)   study subject to the condition set out in Part 15 of these Rules where the applicant is 18 years of age or over at the time their leave is granted, or will be aged 18 before their period of limited leave expires.

(e)   (i)   Applicants who meet the requirements for leave to remain and who obtain points under paragraphs 76 to 79D of Appendix A shall be granted leave to remain as a Tier 2 (General) Migrant.

(ii)   Applicants who meet the requirements for leave to remain and who obtain points under paragraphs 85 to 92 of Appendix A shall be granted leave to remain as a Tier 2 (Minister of Religion) Migrant.

(iii)   Applicants who meet the requirements for leave to remain and who obtain points under paragraphs 93 to 100 of Appendix A shall be granted leave to remain as a Tier 2 (Sportsperson) Migrant.

Requirements for indefinite leave to remain

245HF.   To qualify for indefinite leave to remain as a Tier 2 (General) Migrant, Tier 2 (Minister of Religion) Migrant or Tier 2 (Sportsperson) Migrant, an applicant must meet the requirements listed below. If the applicant meets these requirements, indefinite leave to remain will be granted. If the applicant does not meet these requirements, the application will be refused.

Requirements:

(a)   DELETED.

(b)   The applicant must not fall for refusal under the general grounds for refusal, and must not be an illegal entrant.

(c)   The applicant must have spent a continuous period of 5 years lawfully in the UK, of which the most recent period must have been spent with leave as a Tier 2 Migrant, in any combination of the following categories:

  (i)   as a Member of the Operational Ground Staff of an Overseas-owned Airline,

  (ii)   as a Minister of Religion, Missionary or Member of a Religious Order,

  (iii) as a Qualifying Work Permit Holder,

  (iv)   as a Representative of an Overseas Business,

  (v)   as a Representative of an Overseas Newspaper, News Agency or Broadcasting Organisation,

  (vi)   as a Tier 1 Migrant, other than a Tier 1 (Post Study Work) Migrant or a Tier 1 (Graduate Entrepreneur) Migrant,

  (vii) as a Highly Skilled Migrant,

  (viii) as an innovator,

  (ix)   as a Tier 2 (General) Migrant, a Tier 2 (Minister of Religion) Migrant or a Tier 2 (Sportsperson) Migrant, or

  (x)   as a Tier 2 (Intra-Company Transfer) Migrant, provided the continuous period of 5 years spent lawfully in the UK includes a period of leave as:

    (1)   a Tier 2 (Intra-Company Transfer) Migrant granted under the Rules in place before 6 April 2010, or

    (2)   a Qualifying Work Permit Holder, provided that the work permit was granted because the applicant was the subject of an Intra-Company Transfer.

(d)   The Sponsor that issued the Certificate of Sponsorship that led to the applicant's last grant of leave must:

  (i)   still hold, or have applied for a renewal of, a Tier 2 Sponsor licence in the relevant category; and

  (ii)   certify in writing that:

    (1)   he still requires the applicant for the employment in question, and

    (2)   in the case of a Tier 2 (General) Migrant applying for settlement, the applicant is paid at or above the appropriate rate for the job as stated in the Codes of Practice in Appendix J, or where the applicant is not paid at that rate only due to maternity, paternity or adoption leave, the date that leave started and that the applicant was paid at the appropriate rate immediately before the leave.

(e)   The applicant provides the specified documents in paragraph 245HF-SD to evidence the sponsor's certification in subsection (d)(ii) and to evidence the reason for the absences set out in paragraph 245AAA.

(f)   The applicant must have sufficient knowledge of the English language and sufficient knowledge about life in the United Kingdom, in accordance with Appendix KoLL.

(g)   The applicant must not be in the UK in breach of immigration laws except that any period of overstaying for a period of 28 days or less will be disregarded.

(h)   For the purposes of sub-paragraph (c), time spent with valid leave in the Bailiwick of Guernsey, the Bailiwick of Jersey or the Isle of Man in a category equivalent to any of the categories set out in (c)(i) to (x), may be included in the continuous period of 5 years lawful residence, provided that:

  (i)   where the leave is in category (x), the continuous period of 5 years includes a period of leave as a Tier 2 (Intra-Company Transfer) Migrant granted before 6 April 2010, or a Qualifying Work Permit Holder (provided the work permit was granted because the applicant was the subject of an Intra-Company Transfer); and

(ii)   any period of leave granted in the Bailiwick of Guernsey, the Bailiwick of Jersey or the Isle of Man as a work permit holder or as a Tier 2 Migrant was for employment:

    (a)   in a job which appears on the list of occupations skilled to National Qualifications Framework level 3 or above (or from 6 April 2011, National Qualifications Framework level 4 or above or from 14 June 2012, National Qualifications Framework level 6 or above), as stated in the Codes of Practice in Appendix J, or

    (b)   in a job which appears in the Creative Sector Codes of Practice in Appendix J, or

    (c)   as a professional sportsperson (including as a sports coach); and

(iii)   the most recent period of leave was granted in the UK as a Tier 2 Migrant.

In any such case, references to the 'UK' in paragraph 245AAA shall include a reference to the Bailiwick of Guernsey, Bailiwick of Jersey or the Isle of Man, as the case may be.

Specified documents

245HF-SD.

The specified documents referred to in paragraph 245HF(e) are set out in A, B and C below:

A.   Either a payslip and a personal bank or building society statement, or a payslip and a building society pass book.

    (a)   Payslips must be:

        (i)   the applicant's most recent payslip,

        (ii)   dated no earlier than one calendar month before the date of the application, and

        (iii)   either:

            (1)   an original payslip,

            (2)   on company-headed paper, or

            (3)   accompanied by a letter from the applicant's Sponsor, on company headed paper and signed by a senior official, confirming the payslip is authentic.

    (b)   Personal bank or building society statements must:

        (i)   be the applicant's most recent statement,

        (ii)   be dated no earlier than one calendar month before the date of the application,

        (iii)   clearly show:

            (1)   the applicant's name,

            (2)   the applicant's account number,

            (3)   the date of the statement,

            (4)   the financial institution's name,

            (5)   the financial institution's logo, and

            (6)   transactions by the Sponsor covering the period no earlier than one calendar month before the date of the application, including the amount shown on the specified payslip as at 245HF-SD A.(a)

        (iv)   be either:

            (1)   printed on the bank's or building society's letterhead,

            (2)   electronic bank or building society statements, accompanied by a supporting letter from the bank or building society, on company headed paper, confirming the statement provided is authentic, or

            (3)   electronic bank or building society statements, bearing the official stamp of the bank or building society on every page,

        and

        (v)   not be mini-statements from automatic teller machines (ATMs).

    (c)   Building society pass books must

        (i)   clearly show:

            (1)   the applicant's name,

            (2)   the applicant's account number,

            (3)   the financial institution's name,

            (4)   the financial institution's logo, and

(5) transactions by the sponsor covering the period no earlier than one calendar month before the date of the application, including the amount shown on the specified payslip as at 245HF-SD A.(a)

and

(ii) be either:

(1) the original pass book, or

(2) a photocopy of the pass book which has been certified by the issuing building society on company headed paper, confirming the statement provided is authentic.

B. A letter from the employer detailing the purpose and period of absences in connection with the employment, including periods of annual leave. Where the absence was due to a serious or compelling reason, a personal letter from the applicant which includes full details of the reason for the absences and all original supporting documents in relation to those reasons – e.g. medical certificates, birth/death certificates, information about the reasons which led to the absence from the UK.

C. Where the applicant is not being paid the appropriate rate in Appendix J due to maternity, paternity or adoption leave:

(a) Payslips must be:

(i) the applicant's payslip from the month immediately preceding the leave,

(ii) the applicant's payslips for each month of the period of the leave,

(iii) as set out in A(a)(iii) above.

(b) Bank or building society statements must be:

(i) the applicant's statement from the month immediately preceding the leave,

(ii) the applicant's statements for each month of the period of the leave,

(iii) as set out in A(b)(iii) above.

245ZI.–245ZS.   OMITTED

Tier 4 (General) Student

Purpose of this route

245ZT. This route is for migrants aged 16 or over who wish to study in the UK at an institution that is not an Academy or a school maintained by a local authority.

Entry clearance

245ZU. All migrants arriving in the UK and wishing to enter as a Tier 4 (General) Student must have a valid entry clearance for entry under this route. If they do not have a valid entry clearance, entry will be refused.

Requirements for entry clearance

245ZV. To qualify for entry clearance as a Tier 4 (General) Student, an applicant must meet the requirements listed below. If the applicant meets these requirements, entry clearance will be granted. If the applicant does not meet these requirements, the application will be refused.

Requirements:

(a) The applicant must not fall for refusal under the General Grounds for Refusal.

(b) The applicant must have a minimum of 30 points under paragraphs 113 to 120 of Appendix A.

(c) The applicant must have a minimum of 10 points under paragraphs 10 to 14 of Appendix C.

(ca) The applicant must, if required to do so on examination or interview, be able to demonstrate without the assistance of an interpreter English language proficiency of a standard to be expected from an individual who has reached the standard specified in a Confirmation of Acceptance for Studies assigned in accordance with Appendix A paragraph 118(b) (for the avoidance of doubt, the applicant will not be subject to a test at the standard set out in Appendix A, paragraph 118(b).

(da) if the applicant wishes to undertake a course:

(i) undergraduate or postgraduate studies leading to a Doctorate or Masters degree by research in one of the disciplines listed in paragraph 1 of Appendix 6 of these Rules, or

(ii) undergraduate or postgraduate studies leading to a taught Masters degree or other postgraduate qualification in one of the disciplines listed in paragraph 2 of Appendix 6 of these Rules, or

        (iii)   a period of study or research in excess of 6 months in one of the disciplines listed in paragraphs 1 or 2 of Appendix 6 of these Rules at an institution of higher education where this forms part of an overseas postgraduate qualification

the applicant must hold a valid Academic Technology Approval Scheme clearance certificate from the Counter-Proliferation Department of the Foreign and Commonwealth Office which relates to the course, or area of research, that the applicant will be taking and at the institution at which the applicant wishes to undertake it and must provide a print-out of his Academic Technology Approval Scheme clearance certificate to show that these requirements have been met.

(e)   If the applicant wishes to be a postgraduate doctor or dentist on a recognised Foundation Programme:

    (i)   the applicant must have successfully completed a recognised UK degree in medicine or dentistry from:

        (1)   an institution with a Tier 4 sponsor licence,

        (2)   a UK publicly funded institution of further or higher education or

        (3)   a UK bona fide private education institution which maintains satisfactory records of enrolment and attendance,

    (ii)   the applicant must have previously been granted leave:

        (1)   as a Tier 4 (General) Student, or as a Student, for the final academic year of the studies referred to in paragraph (i) above, and

        (2)   as a Tier 4 (General) Student, or as a Student, for at least one other academic year (aside from the final year) of the studies referred to in paragraph (i) above,

    (iii)   if the applicant has previously been granted leave as a Postgraduate Doctor or Dentist, the applicant must not be seeking entry clearance or leave to enter or remain to a date beyond 3 years from the date on which he was first granted leave to enter or remain in that category, and

    (iv)   if the applicant has previously been granted leave as a Tier 4 (General) Student to undertake a course as a postgraduate doctor or dentist, the applicant must not be seeking entry clearance or leave to enter or remain to a date beyond 3 years from the date on which the applicant was first granted leave to undertake such a course.

(f)   If the applicant is currently being sponsored by a Government or international scholarship agency, or within the last 12 months has come to the end of such a period of sponsorship, the applicant must provide the written consent of the sponsoring Government or agency to the application and must provide the specified documents as set out in paragraph 245A above, to show that this requirement has been met.

(g)   If the course is below degree level the grant of entry clearance the applicant is seeking must not lead to the applicant having spent more than 2 years in the UK as a Tier 4 Migrant since the age of 18 studying courses that did not consist of degree level study.

(ga)   If the course is at degree level or above, the grant of entry clearance the applicant is seeking must not lead to the applicant having spent more than 5 years in the UK as a Tier 4 (General) Migrant, or as a Student, studying courses at degree level or above unless:

    (i)   the applicant has successfully completed a course at degree level in the UK of a minimum duration of 4 academic years, and will follow a course of study at Master's degree level sponsored by a UK recognised body or a body in receipt of public funding as a higher education institution from the Department of Employment and Learning in Northern Ireland, the Higher Education Funding Council for England, the Higher Education Funding Council for Wales or the Scottish Funding Council, and the grant of entry clearance must not lead to the applicant having spent more than 6 years in the UK as a Tier 4 (General) Migrant, or as a Student, studying courses at degree level or above; or

    (ii)   the grant of entry clearance is to follow a course leading to the award of a PhD, and the applicant is sponsored by a UK recognised body or a body in receipt of public funding as a higher education institution from the Department of Employment and Learning in Northern Ireland, the Higher Education Funding Council for England, the Higher Education Funding Council for Wales or the Scottish Funding Council; or

    (iii)   the applicant is following a course of study in;

        (1)   Architecture;

        (2)   Medicine;

(3)   Dentistry;

(4)   Law, where the applicant has completed a course at degree level in the UK and is progressing to:

    a.   a law conversion course validated by the Joint Academic Stage Board in England and Wales, a Masters in Legal Science (MLegSc) in Northern Ireland, or an accelerated graduate LLB in Scotland; or

    b.   the Legal Practice Course in England and Wales, the Solicitors Course in Northern Ireland, or a Diploma in Professional Legal Practice in Scotland; or

    c.   the Bar Professional Training Course in England and Wales, or the Bar Course in Northern Ireland.

(5)   Veterinary Medicine & Science; or

(6)   Music at a music college that is a member of Conservatoires UK (CUK).

(gb)   If the applicant has completed a course leading to the award of a PhD in the UK, the grant of entry clearance the applicant is seeking must not lead to the applicant having spent more than 8 years in the UK as a Tier 4 (General) Migrant, or as a Student.

(h)   The applicant must be at least 16 years old.

(i)   Where the applicant is under 18 years of age, the application must be supported by the applicant's parents or legal guardian, or by just one parent if that parent has sole legal responsibility for the child.

(j)   Where the applicant is under 18 years of age, the applicant's parents or legal guardian, or just one parent if that parent has sole responsibility for the child, must confirm that they consent to the arrangements for the applicant's travel to, and reception and care in, the UK.

(k)   The Entry Clearance Officer must be satisfied that the applicant is a genuine student.

Period and conditions of grant

245ZW.   (a)   Subject to paragraph (b), entry clearance will be granted for the duration of the course.

    (b)   In addition to the period of entry clearance granted in accordance with paragraph (a), entry clearance will also be granted for the periods set out in the following table. Notes to accompany the table appear below the table.

Type of course	Period of entry clearance to be granted before the course starts	Period of entry clearance to be granted after the course ends
12 months or more	1 month before the course starts or 7 days before the intended date of travel, whichever is later	4 months
6 months or more but less than 12 months	1 month before the course starts or 7 days before the intended date of travel, whichever is later	2 months
Pre-sessional course of less than 6 months	1 month before the course starts or 7 days before the intended date of travel, whichever is later	1 month
Course of less than 6 months that is not a pre-sessional course	7 days before the course starts	7 days
Postgraduate doctor or dentist	1 month before the course starts or 7 days before the intended date of travel, whichever is later	1 month

Notes

(i)   If the grant of entry clearance is made less than 7 days before the intended date of travel, entry clearance will be granted with immediate effect.

(aii)   The intended date of travel is the date recorded by the applicant either through the relevant online application process or in the specified application form for Tier 4 (General) Students, as their intended date for travel to the UK.

(ii)   A pre-sessional course is a course which prepares a student for the student's main course of study in the UK.

(iii) The additional periods of entry clearance granted further to the table above will be included for the purposes of calculating whether a migrant has exceeded the limits specified at 245ZV(g) to 245ZV(gb).

(c) Entry clearance will be granted subject to the following conditions:

(i) no recourse to public funds,

(ii) registration with the police, if this is required by paragraph 326 of these Rules,

(iii) no employment except:

(1) employment during term time of no more than 20 hours per week and employment (of any duration) during vacations, where the student is following a course of degree level study and is either:

(a) sponsored by a UK recognised body or a body in receipt of public funding as a higher education institution from the Department of Employment and Learning in Northern Ireland, the Higher Education Funding Council for England, the Higher Education Funding Council for Wales or the Scottish Funding Council; or

(b) sponsored by an overseas higher education institution to undertake a short-term study abroad programme in the United Kingdom.

(2) employment during term time of no more than 10 hours per week and employment (of any duration) during vacations, where the student is following a course of below degree level study and is sponsored by a a Recognised Body or a body in receipt of public funding as a higher education institution from the Department of Employment and Learning in Northern Ireland, the Higher Education Funding Council for England, the Higher Education Funding Council for Wales or the Scottish Funding Council,

(3) DELETED

(4) employment as part of a course-related work placement which forms an assessed part of the applicant's course and provided that any period that the applicant spends on that placement does not exceed one third of the total length of the course undertaken in the UK except:

(i) where it is a United Kingdom statutory requirement that the placement should exceed one third of the total length of the course; or

(ii) where the placement does not exceed one half of the total length of the course undertaken in the UK and the student is following a course of degree level study and is either:

(a) sponsored by a UK recognised body or a body in receipt of public funding as a higher education institution from the Department of Employment and Learning in Northern Ireland, the Higher Education Funding Council for England, the Higher Education Funding Council for Wales or the Scottish Funding Council; or

(b) sponsored by an overseas higher education institution to undertake a short-term Study Abroad Programme in the United Kingdom.

(5) employment as a Student Union Sabbatical Officer, for up to 2 years, provided the post is elective and is at the institution which is the applicant's sponsor or they must be elected to a national National Union of Students (NUS) position.

(6) employment as a Postgraduate Doctor or Dentist on a recognised Foundation Programme

(7) until such time as a decision is received from the Home Office on an application which is supported by a Certificate of Sponsorship assigned by a licensed Tier 2 Sponsor and which is made following successful completion of course at degree level or above at a UK recognised body or a body in receipt of public funding as a higher education institution from the Department of Employment and Learning in Northern Ireland, the Higher Education Funding Council for England, the Higher Education Funding Council for Wales or the Scottish Funding Council and while the applicant has extant leave, and any appeal or administrative review against that decision has been determined, employment with the Tier 2 Sponsor, in the role for which they assigned the Certificate of Sponsorship to the Tier 4 migrant,

(8)   self-employment, providing the migrant has made an application for leave to remain as a Tier 1 (Graduate Entrepreneur) Migrant which:

(a)   is supported by an endorsement from a qualifying Higher Education Institution,

(b)   is made following successful completion of a UK recognised Bachelor degree, Masters degree or PhD (not a qualification of equivalent level which is not a degree) course at a UK recognised body or a body in receipt of public funding as a higher education institution from the Department of Employment and Learning in Northern Ireland, the Higher Education Funding Council for England, the Higher Education Funding Council for Wales or the Scottish Funding Council, and

(c)   is made while the applicant has extant leave,

until such time as a decision is received from the Home Office on that application and any appeal or administrative review against that decision has been determined,

provided that the migrant is not self-employed other than under the conditions of (8) above, or employed as a Doctor or Dentist in Training other than under the conditions of (v) below, professional sportsperson (including a sports coach) or an entertainer, and provided that the migrant's employment would not fill a permanent full time vacancy other than under the conditions of (7) above, or a vacancy on a recognised Foundation Programme or as a sabbatical officer; and

(iv)   no study except:

(1)   study at the institution that the Confirmation of Acceptance for Studies Checking Service records as the migrant's sponsor, unless:

(a)   the migrant is studying at an institution which is a partner institution of the migrant's sponsor; or

(b)   until such time as a decision is received from the Home Office on an application which is supported by a Confirmation of Acceptance for Studies assigned by a sponsor with Tier 4 Sponsor status and which is made while the applicant has extant leave, and any appeal or administrative review against that decision has been determined, the migrant is studying at the sponsor with Tier 4 Sponsor status that the Confirmation of Acceptance for Studies Checking Service records as having assigned such Confirmation of Acceptance for Studies to the migrant; or

(c)   the study is supplementary study, and

(2)   study on the course, or courses where a pre-sessional is included, for which the Confirmation of Acceptance for Studies was assigned, unless the student:

(a)   has yet to complete the course for which the Confirmation of Acceptance for Studies was assigned; and

(b)   begins studying a new course at their sponsor institution, instead of the course for which the Confirmation of Acceptance for Studies was assigned, that represents academic progress (as set out paragraph 120A (b) of Appendix A to these Rules) from the course(s) preceding the migrant's last grant of leave, and:

the new course is either:

1.   at a higher or the same level as the course for which the Confirmation of Acceptance for Studies was assigned; or

2.   at a lower level than the course for which the Confirmation of Acceptance for Studies was assigned, provided that the requirements and conditions of the migrant's grant of leave as at the date of commencement of the new course are the same requirements and conditions to which the migrant's leave would have been subject had he made an application to study at that lower level under the Rules in force at the time of commencement of the new course,

and

(3)   subject to (1) and (2) above, study on a course (or period of research) to which paragraph 245ZV(da) applies only if the migrant holds a valid Academic Technology Approval Scheme certificate issued prior to the commencement of the course (or period of

research) that specifically relates to the course (or area of research) and to the institution at which the migrant undertakes such course (or period of research). Where:

    (a)   the migrant's course (or research) completion date reported on the Confirmation of Acceptance for Studies is postponed or delayed for a period of more than three calendar months, or if there are any changes to the course contents (or the research proposal), the migrant must apply for a new Academic Technology Approval Scheme certificate within 28 calendar days; and

    (b)   the migrant begins studying a new course (or period of research) as permitted in (2) above and the new course (or area of research) is of a type specified in paragraph 245ZV(da), the migrant must obtain an Academic Technology Approval Scheme clearance certificate relating to the new course (or area of research) prior to commencing it.

    (v)   no employment as a Doctor or Dentist in Training unless:

        (1)   the course that the migrant is being sponsored to do (as recorded by the Confirmation of Acceptance for Studies Checking Service) is a recognised Foundation Programme, or

        (2)   the migrant has made an application as a Tier 4 (General) Student which is supported by a Confirmation of Acceptance for Studies assigned by a sponsor with Tier 4 Sponsor status to sponsor the applicant to do a recognised Foundation Programme, and this study satisfies the requirements of (iv)(2) above, or

        (3)   the migrant has made an application as a Tier 2 (General) Migrant which is supported by a Certificate of Sponsorship assigned by a licensed Tier 2 Sponsor to sponsor the applicant to work as a Doctor or Dentist in Training, and this employment satisfies the conditions of (iii)(7) above.

    (vi)   no study at Academies or schools maintained by a local authority.

Requirements for leave to remain

245ZX.   To qualify for leave to remain as a Tier 4 (General) Student under this rule, an applicant must meet the requirements listed below. If the applicant meets these requirements, leave to remain will be granted. If the applicant does not meet these requirements, the applicant will be refused.

Requirements:

    (a)   The applicant must not fall for refusal under the general grounds for refusal and must not be an illegal entrant.

    (b)   The applicant must have, or have last been granted, entry clearance, leave to enter or leave to remain:

        (i)   as a Tier 4 (General) Student, and, in respect of such leave, is or was last sponsored by:

            (1)   a UK recognised body or a body in receipt of public funding as a higher education institution from the Department of Employment and Learning in Northern Ireland, the Higher Education Funding Council for England, the Higher Education Funding Council for Wales or the Scottish Funding Council; or

            (2)   an overseas higher education institution to undertake a short-term study abroad programme in the United Kingdom; or

            (3)   an Embedded College offering Pathway Courses.

        (ii)   as a Tier 4 (Child) Student,

        (iii)   as a Tier 1 (Post-study Work) Migrant,

        (iv)   as a Tier 2 Migrant,

        (v)   as a Participant in the International Graduates Scheme (or its predecessor, the Science and Engineering Graduates Scheme),

        (vi)   as a Participant in the Fresh Talent: Working in Scotland Scheme,

        (vii)   as a Postgraduate Doctor or Dentist,

        (viii)   DELETED

        (ix)   as a Student,

        (x)   as a Student Nurse,

        (xi)   as a Student Re-sitting an Examination,

        (xii)   as a Student Writing-Up a Thesis,

(xiii)   as a Student Union Sabbatical Officer, or

(xiv)   as a Work Permit Holder.

(c)   The applicant must have a minimum of 30 points under paragraphs 113 to 120 of Appendix A.

(d)   The applicant must have a minimum of 10 points under paragraphs 10 to 14 of Appendix C.

(da)   The applicant must, if required to do so on examination or interview, be able to demonstrate without the assistance of an interpreter English language proficiency of a standard to be expected from an individual who has reached the standard specified in a Confirmation of Acceptance for Studies assigned in accordance with Appendix A paragraph 118(b) (for the avoidance of doubt, the applicant will not be subject to a test at the standard set out in Appendix A, paragraph 118(b)).

(ea)   if the applicant wishes to undertake a course:

(i)   undergraduate or postgraduate studies leading to a Doctorate or Masters degree by research in one of the disciplines listed in paragraph 1 of Appendix 6 of these Rules, or

(ii)   undergraduate or postgraduate studies leading to a taught Masters degree or other postgraduate qualification in one of the disciplines listed in paragraph 2 of Appendix 6 of these Rules, or

(iii)   a period of study or research in excess of 6 months in one of the disciplines listed in paragraphs 1 or 2 of Appendix 6 of these Rules at an institution of higher education where this forms part of an overseas postgraduate qualification

the applicant must hold a valid Academic Technology Approval Scheme clearance certificate from the Counter-Proliferation Department of the Foreign and Commonwealth Office which relates to the course, or area of research, that the applicant will be taking and at the institution at which the applicant wishes to undertake it and must provide a print-out of his Academic Technology Approval Scheme clearance certificate to show that these requirements have been met. Applicants applying for leave to remain under the doctorate extension scheme are not required to meet the conditions of paragraph 245ZX (ea) if they continue to study on a course (or period of research) for which they have a valid Academic Technology Approval Scheme certificate.

(f)   If the applicant wishes to be a postgraduate doctor or dentist on a recognised Foundation Programme:

(i)   the applicant must have successfully completed a recognised UK degree in medicine or dentistry from:

(1)   an institution with a Tier 4 sponsor licence,

(2)   a UK publicly funded institution of further or higher education or

(3)   a UK bona fide private education institution which maintains satisfactory records of enrolment and attendance,

(ii)   the applicant must have previously been granted leave:

(1)   as a Tier 4 (General) Student, or as a Student, for the final academic year of the studies referred to in paragraph (i) above, and

(2)   as a Tier 4 (General) Student, or as a Student, for at least one other academic year (aside from the final year) of the studies referred to in paragraph (i) above,

(iii)   if the applicant has previously been granted leave as a Postgraduate Doctor or Dentist the applicant must not be seeking entry clearance or leave to enter or remain to a date beyond 3 years from the date on which he was first granted leave to enter or remain in that category, and

(iv)   if the applicant has previously been granted leave as a Tier 4 (General) Student to undertake a course as a postgraduate doctor or dentist, the applicant must not be seeking entry clearance or leave to enter or remain to a date beyond 3 years from the date on which he was first granted leave to undertake such a course.

(g)   If the applicant is currently being sponsored by a Government or international scholarship agency, or within the last 12 months has come to the end of such a period of sponsorship, the applicant must provide the unconditional written consent of the sponsoring Government or agency to the application and must provide the specified documents as set out in paragraph 245A above, to show that this requirement has been met.

(h)   If the course is below degree level the grant of leave to remain the applicant is seeking must not lead to the applicant having spent more than 2 years in the UK as a Tier 4 Migrant since the age of 18 studying courses that did not consist of degree level study.

(ha) If the course is at degree level or above, the grant of leave to remain the applicant is seeking must not lead to the applicant having spent more than 5 years in the UK as a Tier 4 (General) Migrant, or as a Student, studying courses at degree level or above unless:

   (i) the applicant has successfully completed a course at degree level in the UK of a minimum duration of 4 academic years, and will follow a course of study at Master's degree level sponsored by a UK recognised body or a body in receipt of public funding as a higher education institution from the Department of Employment and Learning in Northern Ireland, the Higher Education Funding Council for England, the Higher Education Funding Council for Wales or the Scottish Funding Council, and the grant of leave to remain must not lead to the applicant having spent more than 6 years in the UK as a Tier 4 (General) Migrant, or as a Student, studying courses at degree level or above; or

   (ii) the grant of leave to remain is to follow a course leading to the award of a PhD and the applicant is sponsored by a recognised body or a body in receipt of public funding as a higher education institution from the Department of Employment and Learning in Northern Ireland, the Higher Education Funding Council for England, the Higher Education Funding Council for Wales or the Scottish Funding Council; or

   (iii) the applicant is following a course of study in;

      (1) Architecture;

      (2) Medicine;

      (3) Dentistry;

      (4) Law, where the applicant has completed a course at degree level in the UK and is progressing to:

         a. a law conversion course validated by the Joint Academic Stage Board in England and Wales, a Masters in Legal Science (MLegSc) in Northern Ireland, or an accelerated graduate LLB in Scotland; or

         b. the Legal Practice Course in England and Wales, the Solicitors Course in Northern Ireland, or a Diploma in Professional Legal Practice in Scotland; or

         c. the Bar Professional Training Course in England and Wales, or the Bar Course in Northern Ireland.

      (5) Veterinary Medicine & Science; or

      (6) Music at a music college that is a member of Conservatoires UK (CUK).

(hb) If the applicant has completed a course leading to the award of a PhD in the UK, the grant of leave to remain the applicant is seeking must not lead to the applicant having spent more than 8 years in the UK as a Tier 4 (General) Migrant, or as a Student.

(i) The applicant must be at least 16 years old.

(j) Where the applicant is under 18 years of age, the application must be supported by the applicant's parents or legal guardian, or by just one parent if that parent has sole legal responsibility for the child.

(k) Where the applicant is under 18 years of age, the applicant's parents or legal guardian, or just one parent if that parent has sole legal responsibility for the child, must confirm that they consent to the arrangements for the applicant's care in the UK.

(l) Unless applying for leave to remain as a Tier 4 (General) Student on the doctorate extension scheme, the applicant must be applying for leave to remain for the purpose of studies which commence within 28 days of the expiry of the applicant's current leave to enter or remain or, where the applicant has overstayed, within 28 days of when that period of overstaying began.

(m) The applicant must not be in the UK in breach of immigration laws except that any period of overstaying for a period of 28 days or less will be disregarded.

(n) Where the applicant is applying for leave to remain as a Tier 4 (General) Student on the doctorate extension scheme:

   (i) leave to remain as a Tier 4 (General) Student on the doctorate extension scheme must not have previously been granted;

   (ii) the applicant must have leave to remain as a Tier 4 (General) Student and must be following a course leading to the award of a PhD;

   (iii) the applicant must be sponsored by a UK recognised body or a body in receipt of public funding as a higher education institution from the Department of Employment and Learning in

Northern Ireland, the Higher Education Funding Council for England, the Higher Education Funding Council for Wales or the Scottish Funding Council and that sponsor will be the sponsor awarding the PhD; and

(iv)   the date of the application must be within 60 days of the expected end date of a course leading to the award of a PhD.

(o)   the Secretary of State must be satisfied that the applicant is a genuine student.

Period and conditions of grant

245ZY.   (a)   Subject to paragraphs (b), (ba) and (c) below, leave to remain will be granted for the duration of the course.

(b)   In addition to the period of leave to remain granted in accordance with paragraph (a), leave to remain will also be granted for the periods set out in the following table. Notes to accompany the table appear below the table.

Type of course	Period of leave to remain to be granted before the course starts	Period of leave to remain to be granted after the course ends
12 months or more	1 month	4 months
6 months or more but less than 12 months	1 month	2 months
Pre-sessional course of less than 6 months	1 month	1 month
Course of less than 6 months that is not a pre-sessional course	7 days	7 days
Postgraduate doctor or dentist	1 month	1 month

Notes

(i)   If the grant of leave to remain is being made less than 1 month or, in the case of a course of less than 6 months that is not a pre-sessional course, less than 7 days before the start of the course, leave to remain will be granted with immediate effect.

(ii)   A pre-sessional course is a course which prepares a student for the student's main course of study in the UK.

(iii)   The additional periods of leave to remain granted further to the table above will be included for the purposes of calculating whether a migrant has exceeded the limits specified at 245ZX(h) to 245ZX(hb).

(ba)   Leave to remain as a Tier 4 (General) Student on the doctorate extension scheme will be granted for 12 months, commencing on the expected end date of a course leading to the award of a PhD.

(bb)   Leave to remain as a Tier 4 (General) Student on the doctorate extension scheme will not be subject to the conditions on the limited time that can be spent as a Tier 4 (General) Student or as a student, specified at 245ZX (hb).

(c)   Leave to remain will be granted subject to the following conditions:

(i)   no recourse to public funds,

(ii)   registration with the police, if this is required by paragraph 326 of these Rules,

(iii)   no employment except:

(1)   employment during term time of no more than 20 hours per week and employment (of any duration) during vacations, where the student is following a course of degree level study and is either:

(a)   sponsored by a UK recognised body or a body in receipt of public funding as a higher education institution from the Department of Employment and Learning in Northern Ireland, the Higher Education Funding Council for England, the Higher Education Funding Council for Wales or the Scottish Funding Council; or

(b)   sponsored by an overseas higher education institution to undertake a short-term Study Abroad Programme in the United Kingdom.

(2)   employment during term time of no more than 10 hours per week and employment (of any duration) during vacations, where the student is following a course of below degree level study and is sponsored by a UK recognised body or a body in receipt of public funding as a higher education institution from the Department of Employment and

Learning in Northern Ireland, the Higher Education Funding Council for England, the Higher Education Funding Council for Wales or the Scottish Funding Council,

(3)   DELETED

(4)   employment as part of a course-related work placement which forms an assessed part of the applicant's course and provided that any period that the applicant spends on that placement does not exceed one third of the total length of the course undertaken in the UK except:

    (i)   where it is a United Kingdom statutory requirement that the placement should exceed one third of the total length of the course; or

    (ii)   where the placement does not exceed one half of the total length of the course undertaken in the UK and the student is following a course of degree level study and is either:

        (a)   sponsored by a Recognised Body or a body in receipt of public funding as a higher education institution from the Department of Employment and Learning in Northern Ireland, the Higher Education Funding Council for England, the Higher Education Funding Council for Wales or the Scottish Funding Council; or

        (b)   sponsored by an overseas higher education institution to undertake a short-term study abroad programme in the United Kingdom.

(5)   employment as a Student Union Sabbatical Officer for up to 2 years provided the post is elective and is at the institution which is the applicant's sponsor or they must be elected to a national National Union of Students (NUS) position,

(6)   employment as a Postgraduate Doctor or Dentist on a recognised Foundation Programme

(7)   until such time as a decision is received from the Home Office on an application which is supported by a Certificate of Sponsorship assigned by a licensed Tier 2 Sponsor and which is made following successful completion of course at degree level or above at a UK recognised body or a body in receipt of public funding as a higher education institution from the Department of Employment and Learning in Northern Ireland, the Higher Education Funding Council for England, the Higher Education Funding Council for Wales or the Scottish Funding Council and while the applicant has extant leave, and any appeal or administrative review against that decision has been determined, employment with the Tier 2 Sponsor institution, in the role for which they assigned the Certificate of Sponsorship to the Tier 4 migrant,

(8)   self-employment, providing the migrant has made an application for leave to remain as a Tier 1 (Graduate Entrepreneur) Migrant which is supported by an endorsement from a qualifying Higher Education Institution and which is made following successful completion of a course at degree level or above at a UK recognised body or a body in receipt of public funding as a higher education institution from the Department of Employment and Learning in Northern Ireland, the Higher Education Funding Council for England, the Higher Education Funding Council for Wales or the Scottish Funding Council and while the applicant has extant leave, until such time as a decision is received from the Home Office on an application and any appeal or administrative review against that decision has been determined,

provided that the migrant is not self-employed other than under the conditions of (8) above, or employed as a Doctor or Dentist in Training other than under the conditions of (v) below, a professional sportsperson (including a sports coach) or an entertainer, and provided that the migrant's employment would not fill a permanent full time vacancy other than under the conditions of (7) above, or a vacancy on a recognised Foundation Programme or as a sabbatical officer.

(9)   where, during the current period of leave, the migrant has successfully completed a PhD at a UK recognised body or a body in receipt of public funding as a higher education institution from the Department of Employment and Learning in Northern Ireland, the Higher Education Funding Council for England, the Higher Education Funding Council for Wales or the Scottish Funding Council, and has been granted leave to remain as a Tier 4 (General) Student on the doctorate extension scheme or has made a valid application

for leave to remain as a Tier 4 (General) Student on the doctorate extension scheme but has not yet received a decision from the Home Office on that application, there will be no limitation on the type of employment that may be taken, except for:

(a)   no employment as a Doctor or Dentist in Training other than under the conditions of (v) below;

(b)   no employment as a professional sportsperson (including a sports coach).

(iv)   no study except:

(1)   study at the institution that the Confirmation of Acceptance for Studies Checking Service records as the migrant's sponsor, unless:

(a)   the migrant is studying at an institution which is a partner institution of the migrant's sponsor; or

(b)   until such time as a decision is received from the Home Office on an application which is supported by a Confirmation of Acceptance for Studies assigned by a sponsor with Tier 4 Sponsor status and which is made while the applicant has extant leave, and any appeal or administrative review against that decision has been determined, the migrant is studying at the sponsor with Tier 4 Sponsor status that the Confirmation of Acceptance for Studies Checking Service records as having assigned such Confirmation of Acceptance for Studies to the migrant; or

(c)   the study is supplementary study, and

(2)   study on the course, or courses where a pre-sessional is included, for which the Confirmation of Acceptance for Studies was assigned, unless the student:

(a)   has yet to complete the course for which the Confirmation of Acceptance for Studies was assigned; and

(b)   begins studying a new course at their sponsor institution, instead of the course for which the Confirmation of Acceptance for Studies was assigned, that represents academic progress (as set out paragraph 120A (b) of Appendix A to these Rules) on the course(s) preceding the migrant's last grant of leave, and:

the new course is either:

1.   at a higher or the same level as the course for which the Confirmation of Acceptance for Studies was assigned; or

2.   at a lower level than the course for which the Confirmation of Acceptance for Studies was assigned, provided that the requirements and conditions of the migrant's grant of leave as at the date of commencement of the new course are the same requirements and conditions to which the migrant's leave would have been subject had he made an application to study at that lower level under the Rules in force at the time of commencement of the new course,

and

(3)   subject to (1) and (2), study on a course (or period of research) to which paragraph 245ZX(ea) applies only if the migrant holds a valid Academic Technology Approval Scheme certificate issued prior to the commencement of the course (or period of research) that specifically relates to the course (or area of research) and to the institution at which the migrant undertakes such course (or period of research). Where:

(a)   the migrant's course (or research) completion date reported on the Confirmation of Acceptance for Studies is postponed or delayed for a period of more than three calendar months, or if there are any changes to the course contents (or the research proposal), the migrant must apply for a new Academic Technology Approval Scheme certificate within 28 calendar days.

(b)   the migrant begins studying a new course (or period of research) as permitted in (2) above and the new course (or period of research) is of a type specified in paragraph 245ZX(ea), the migrant must obtain an Academic Technology Approval Scheme clearance certificate from the Counter- Proliferation Department of the Foreign and Commonwealth Office relating to the new course (or area of research) prior to commencing it.

(v) no employment as a Doctor or Dentist in Training unless:

    (1) the course that the migrant is being sponsored to do (as recorded by the Confirmation of Acceptance for Studies Checking Service) is a recognised Foundation Programme, or

    (2) the migrant has made an application as a Tier 4 (General) Student which is supported by a Confirmation of Acceptance for Studies assigned by a sponsor with Tier 4 Sponsor Status to sponsor the applicant to do a recognised Foundation Programme, and this study satisfies the requirements of (iv)(2) above, or

    (3) the migrant has made an application as a Tier 2 (General) Migrant which is supported by a Certificate of Sponsorship assigned by a licensed Tier 2 Sponsor to sponsor the applicant to work as a Doctor or Dentist in Training, and this employment satisfies the conditions of (iii)(7) above.

(vi) no study at Academies or schools maintained by a local authority.

245ZZ.–245ZZE.   OMITTED

Part 7 – Other Categories

Requirements for leave to enter the United Kingdom as a person exercising rights of access to a child resident in the United Kingdom

A246. Paragraphs 246 to 248F apply only to a person who has made an application before 9 July 2012 for leave to enter or remain or indefinite leave to remain as a person exercising rights of access to a child resident in the UK, or who before 9 July 2012 has been granted leave to enter or remain as a person exercising rights of access to a child resident in the UK.

AB246. Where an application for leave to enter or remain is made on or after 9 July 2012 as a person exercising rights of access to a child resident in the UK Appendix FM will apply.

246. The requirements to be met by a person seeking leave to enter the United Kingdom to exercise access rights to a child resident in the United Kingdom are that:

(i) the applicant is the parent of a child who is resident in the United Kingdom; and

(ii) the parent or carer with whom the child permanently resides is resident in the United Kingdom; and

(iii) the applicant produces evidence that he has access rights to the child in the form of:

    (a) a Residence Order or a Contact Order granted by a Court in the United Kingdom; or

    (b) a certificate issued by a district judge confirming the applicant's intention to maintain contact with the child; and

(iv) the applicant intends to take an active role in the child's upbringing; and

(v) the child is under the age of 18; and

(vi) there will be adequate accommodation for the applicant and any dependants without recourse to public funds in accommodation which the applicant owns or occupies exclusively; and

(vii) the applicant will be able to maintain himself and any dependants adequately without recourse to public funds; and

(viii) the applicant holds a valid United Kingdom entry clearance for entry in this capacity.

Leave to enter the United Kingdom as a person exercising rights of access to a child resident in the United Kingdom

247. Leave to enter as a person exercising access rights to a child resident in the United Kingdom may be granted for 12 months in the first instance, provided that a valid United Kingdom entry clearance for entry in this capacity is produced to the Immigration Officer on arrival.

Refusal of leave to enter the United Kingdom as a person exercising rights of access to a child resident in the United Kingdom

248. Leave to enter as a person exercising rights of access to a child resident in the United Kingdom is to be refused if a valid United Kingdom entry clearance for entry in this capacity is not produced to the Immigration Officer on arrival.

Requirements for leave to remain in the United Kingdom as a person exercising rights of access to a child resident in the United Kingdom

248A.   The requirements to be met by a person seeking leave to remain in the United Kingdom to exercise access rights to a child resident in the United Kingdom are that:

(i)   the applicant is the parent of a child who is resident in the United Kingdom; and

(ii)   the parent or carer with whom the child permanently resides is resident in the United Kingdom; and

(iii)   the applicant produces evidence that he has access rights to the child in the form of:

(a)   a Residence Order or a Contact Order granted by a Court in the United Kingdom; or

(b)   a certificate issued by a district judge confirming the applicant's intention to maintain contact with the child; or

(c)   a statement from the child's other parent (or, if contact is supervised, from the supervisor) that the applicant is maintaining contact with the child; and

(iv)   the applicant takes and intends to continue to take an active role in the child's upbringing; and

(v)   the child visits or stays with the applicant on a frequent and regular basis and the applicant intends this to continue; and

(vi)   the child is under the age of 18; and

(vii)   the applicant has limited leave to remain in the United Kingdom as the spouse, civil partner, unmarried partner or same-sex partner of a person present and settled in the United Kingdom who is the other parent of the child; and

(viii) the applicant has not remained in breach of the immigration laws; and

(ix)   there will be adequate accommodation for the applicant and any dependants without recourse to public funds in accommodation which the applicant owns or occupies exclusively; and

(x)   the applicant will be able to maintain himself and any dependants adequately without recourse to public funds.

Leave to remain in the United Kingdom as a person exercising rights of access to a child resident in the United Kingdom

248B.   Leave to remain as a person exercising access rights to a child resident in the United Kingdom may be granted for 12 months in the first instance, provided the Secretary of State is satisfied that each of the requirements of paragraph 248A is met.

Refusal of leave to remain in the United Kingdom as a person exercising rights of access to a child resident in the United Kingdom

248C.   Leave to remain as a person exercising rights of access to a child resident in the United Kingdom is to be refused if the Secretary of State is not satisfied that each of the requirements of paragraph 248A is met.

Indefinite leave to remain in the United Kingdom as a person exercising rights of access to a child resident in the United Kingdom

248D.   The requirements for indefinite leave to remain in the United Kingdom as a person exercising rights of access to a child resident in the United Kingdom are that:

(i)   the applicant was admitted to the United Kingdom or granted leave to remain in the United Kingdom for a period of 12 months as a person exercising rights of access to a child and has completed a period of 12 months as a person exercising rights of access to a child; and

(ii)   the applicant takes and intends to continue to take an active role in the child's upbringing; and

(iii)   the child visits or stays with the applicant on a frequent and regular basis and the applicant intends this to continue; and

(iv)   there will be adequate accommodation for the applicant and any dependants without recourse to public funds in accommodation which the applicant owns or occupies exclusively; and

(v)   the applicant will be able to maintain himself and any dependants adequately without recourse to public funds; and

(vi)   the child is under 18 years of age; and

(vii)   The applicant must have demonstrated sufficient knowledge of the English language and sufficient knowledge about life in the United Kingdom, in accordance with Appendix KoLL; and

(viii) the applicant does not fall for refusal under the general grounds for refusal.

Indefinite leave to remain as a person exercising rights of access to a child resident in the United Kingdom

248E. Indefinite leave to remain as a person exercising rights of access to a child may be granted provided the Secretary of State is satisfied that each of the requirements of paragraph 248D is met.

Refusal of indefinite leave to remain in the United Kingdom as a person exercising rights of access to a child resident in the United Kingdom

248F. Indefinite leave to remain as a person exercising rights of access to a child is to be refused if the Secretary of State is not satisfied that each of the requirements of paragraph 248D is met.

249.–265. DELETED

266–276. OMITTED

Long residence

Long residence in the United Kingdom

276A. For the purposes of paragraphs 276B to 276D and 276ADE(1).

(a) 'continuous residence' means residence in the United Kingdom for an unbroken period, and for these purposes a period shall not be considered to have been broken where an applicant is absent from the United Kingdom for a period of 6 months or less at any one time, provided that the applicant in question has existing limited leave to enter or remain upon their departure and return, but shall be considered to have been broken if the applicant:

    (i) has been removed under Schedule 2 of the 1971 Act, section 10 of the 1999 Act, has been deported or has left the United Kingdom having been refused leave to enter or remain here; or

    (ii) has left the United Kingdom and, on doing so, evidenced a clear intention not to return; or

    (iii) left the United Kingdom in circumstances in which he could have had no reasonable expectation at the time of leaving that he would lawfully be able to return; or

    (iv) has been convicted of an offence and was sentenced to a period of imprisonment or was directed to be detained in an institution other than a prison (including, in particular, a hospital or an institution for young offenders), provided that the sentence in question was not a suspended sentence; or

    (v) has spent a total of more than 18 months absent from the United Kingdom during the period in question.

(b) 'lawful residence' means residence which is continuous residence pursuant to:

    (i) existing leave to enter or remain; or

    (ii) temporary admission within section 11 of the 1971 Act where leave to enter or remain is subsequently granted; or

    (iii) an exemption from immigration control, including where an exemption ceases to apply if it is immediately followed by a grant of leave to enter or remain.

(c) 'lived continuously' and 'living continuously' mean 'continuous residence', except that paragraph 276A(a)(iv) shall not apply.

276A0. For the purposes of paragraph 276ADE(1) the requirement to make a valid application will not apply when the Article 8 claim is raised:

    (i) as part of an asylum claim, or as part of a further submission in person after an asylum claim has been refused;

    (ii) where a migrant is in immigration detention. A migrant in immigration detention or their representative must submit any application or claim raising Article 8 to a prison officer, a prisoner custody officer, a detainee custody officer or a member of Home Office staff at the migrant's place of detention; or

    (iii) in an appeal (subject to the consent of the Secretary of State where applicable).

276A00. Where leave to remain is granted under paragraphs 276ADE-276DH, or where an applicant does not meet the requirements in paragraph 276ADE(1) but the Secretary of State grants leave to remain outside the rules on Article 8 grounds, (and without prejudice to the specific provision that is made in paragraphs 276ADE-276DH in respect of a no recourse to public funds condition), that leave may be subject to such conditions as the Secretary of State considers appropriate in a particular case.

276A01. (1) Where an applicant for leave to enter the UK remains in the UK on temporary admission or temporary release and satisfies the requirements in paragraph 276ADE(1), as if those were requirements for leave to enter not leave to remain (and except that the reference to 'leave to remain' in sub-paragraph (ii) is to be read as if it said 'leave to enter'), or the Secretary of State decides to grant leave to enter outside the rules on Article 8 grounds:

(a) paragraph 276BE(1) shall apply, as if the first reference in paragraph 276BE(1) to limited leave to remain were to limited leave to enter and as if the wording from 'provided that' to 'under this sub-paragraph' were omitted; and

(b) paragraph 276BE(2) shall apply, as if the reference in paragraph 276BE(2) to limited leave to remain were to limited leave to enter.

(2) Where leave to enter is granted in accordance with paragraph 276A01(1), paragraph 276BE(1) shall apply to an application for leave to remain on the grounds of private life in the UK as if for 'leave to remain under this sub-paragraph' there were substituted 'leave to enter in accordance with paragraph 276A01(1)'.

276A02. In all cases where:

(a) limited leave on the grounds of private life in the UK is granted under paragraph 276BE(1) or 276DG; or

(b) limited leave is granted outside the rules on Article 8 grounds under paragraph 276BE(2),

leave will normally be granted subject to a condition of no recourse to public funds, unless the applicant has provided the decision-maker with (i) satisfactory evidence that the applicant is destitute as defined in section 95 of the Immigration and Asylum Act 1999, or (ii) satisfactory evidence that there are particularly compelling reasons relating to the welfare of a child of a parent in receipt of a very low income.

276A03. Where a person aged 18 or over is granted limited leave to remain under this Part on the basis of long residence or private life in the UK or limited leave to enter in accordance with paragraph 276A01(1) (or limited leave to enter or remain outside the rules on Article 8 grounds), or where a person granted such limited leave to enter or remain will be aged 18 before that period of limited leave expires, the leave will, in addition to any other conditions which may apply, be granted subject to the conditions in Part 15 of these rules.

276A04. Where a person who has made an application for indefinite leave to remain under this Part does not meet the requirements for indefinite leave to remain but falls to be granted limited leave to remain under this Part on the basis of long residence or private life in the UK, or outside the rules on Article 8 grounds:

(a) The Secretary of State will treat that application for indefinite leave to remain as an application for limited leave to remain;

(b) The Secretary of State will notify the applicant in writing of any requirement to pay an immigration health charge under the Immigration (Health Charge) Order 2015; and

(c) If there is such a requirement and that requirement is not met, the application for limited leave to remain will be invalid and the Secretary of State will not refund any application fee paid in respect of the application for indefinite leave to remain.

Requirements for an extension of stay on the ground of long residence in the United Kingdom

276A1. The requirement to be met by a person seeking an extension of stay on the ground of long residence in the United Kingdom is that the applicant meets each of the requirements in paragraph 276B(i)–(ii) and (v).

Extension of stay on the ground of long residence in the United Kingdom

276A2. An extension of stay on the ground of long residence in the United Kingdom may be granted for a period not exceeding 2 years provided that the Secretary of State is satisfied that the requirement in paragraph 276A1 is met (but see paragraph 276A04), and a person granted such an extension of stay following an application made before 9 July 2012 will remain subject to the rules in force on 8 July 2012.

Conditions to be attached to extension of stay on the ground of long residence in the United Kingdom

276A3. Where an extension of stay is granted under paragraph 276A2:

(i) if the applicant has spent less than 20 years in the UK , the grant of leave should be subject to the same conditions attached to his last period of lawful leave, or

(ii)   if the applicant has spent 20 years or more in the UK, the grant of leave should not contain any restriction on employment.

Refusal of extension of stay on the ground of long residence in the United Kingdom

276A4.   An extension of stay on the ground of long residence in the United Kingdom is to be refused if the Secretary of State is not satisfied that the requirement in paragraph 276A1 is met.

Requirements for indefinite leave to remain on the ground of long residence in the United Kingdom

276B.   The requirements to be met by an applicant for indefinite leave to remain on the ground of long residence in the United Kingdom are that:

(i)   (a)   he has had at least 10 years continuous lawful residence in the United Kingdom.

(ii)   having regard to the public interest there are no reasons why it would be undesirable for him to be given indefinite leave to remain on the ground of long residence, taking into account his:

    (a)   age; and

    (b)   strength of connections in the United Kingdom; and

    (c)   personal history, including character, conduct, associations and employment record; and

    (d)   domestic circumstances; and

    (e)   compassionate circumstances; and

    (f)   any representations received on the person's behalf; and

(iii)   the applicant does not fall for refusal under the general grounds for refusal.

(iv)   the applicant has demonstrated sufficient knowledge of the English language and sufficient knowledge about life in the United Kingdom, in accordance with Appendix KoLL.

(v)   the applicant must not be in the UK in breach of immigration laws except that any period of overstaying for a period of 28 days or less will be disregarded, as will any period of overstaying between periods of entry clearance, leave to enter or leave to remain of up to 28 days and any period of overstaying pending the determination of an application made within that 28 day period.

Indefinite leave to remain on the ground of long residence in the United Kingdom

276C.   Indefinite leave to remain on the ground of long residence in the United Kingdom may be granted provided that the Secretary of State is satisfied that each of the requirements of paragraph 276B is met.

Refusal of indefinite leave to remain on the ground of long residence in the United Kingdom

276D.   Indefinite leave to remain on the ground of long residence in the United Kingdom is to be refused if the Secretary of State is not satisfied that each of the requirements of paragraph 276B is met.

Private life

Requirements to be met by an applicant for leave to remain on the grounds of private life

276ADE(1).   The requirements to be met by an applicant for leave to remain on the grounds of private life in the UK are that at the date of application, the applicant:

(i)   does not fall for refusal under any of the grounds in Section S-LTR 1.2 to S-LTR 2.3. and S-LTR.3.1. in Appendix FM; and

(ii)   has made a valid application for leave to remain on the grounds of private life in the UK; and

(iii)   has lived continuously in the UK for at least 20 years (discounting any period of imprisonment); or

(iv)   is under the age of 18 years and has lived continuously in the UK for at least 7 years (discounting any period of imprisonment) and it would not be reasonable to expect the applicant to leave the UK; or

(v)   is aged 18 years or above and under 25 years and has spent at least half of his life living continuously in the UK (discounting any period of imprisonment); or

(vi)   subject to sub-paragraph (2), is aged 18 years or above, has lived continuously in the UK for less than 20 years (discounting any period of imprisonment) but there would be very significant obstacles to the applicant's integration into the country to which he would have to go if required to leave the UK.

276ADE(2).   Sub-paragraph (1)(vi) does not apply, and may not be relied upon, in circumstances in which it is proposed to return a person to a third country pursuant to Schedule 3 to the Asylum and Immigration (Treatment of Claimants, etc) Act 2004.

Leave to remain on the grounds of private life in the UK

276BE(1).   Limited leave to remain on the grounds of private life in the UK may be granted for a period not exceeding 30 months provided that the Secretary of State is satisfied that the requirements in paragraph 276ADE(1) are met or, in respect of the requirements in paragraph 276ADE(1)(iv) and (v), were met in a previous application which led to a grant of limited leave to remain under this sub-paragraph. Such leave shall be given subject to a condition of no recourse to public funds unless the Secretary of State considers that the person should not be subject to such a condition.

276BE(2).   Where an applicant does not meet the requirements in paragraph 276ADE(1) but the Secretary of State grants leave to remain outside the rules on Article 8 grounds, the applicant will normally be granted leave for a period not exceeding 30 months and subject to a condition of no recourse to public funds unless the Secretary of State considers that the person should not be subject to such a condition.

276BE(3).   Where an applicant has extant leave at the date of application, the remaining period of that extant leave up to a maximum of 28 days will be added to the period of limited leave to remain granted under paragraph 276BE(1) (which may therefore exceed 30 months).

Refusal of limited leave to remain on the grounds of private life in the UK

276CE.   Limited leave to remain on the grounds of private life in the UK is to be refused if the Secretary of State is not satisfied that the requirements in paragraph 276ADE(1) are met.

Requirements for indefinite leave to remain on the grounds of private life in the UK

276DE.   The requirements to be met for the grant of indefinite leave to remain on the grounds of private life in the UK are that:

(a)   the applicant has been in the UK with continuous leave on the grounds of private life for a period of at least 120 months. This continuous leave will disregard any period of overstaying between periods of leave on the grounds of private life where the application was made no later than 28 days after the expiry of the previous leave. Any period pending the determination of the application will also be disregarded;

(b)   the applicant meets the requirements of paragraph 276ADE(1) or, in respect of the requirements in paragraph 276ADE(1) (iv) and (v), the applicant met the requirements in a previous application which led to a grant of limited leave to enter or remain under paragraph 276BE(1);

(c)   the applicant does not fall for refusal under any of the grounds in Section S-ILR: Suitability-indefinite leave to remain in Appendix FM;

(d)   the applicant has demonstrated sufficient knowledge of the English language and sufficient knowledge about life in the United Kingdom, in accordance with Appendix KoLL; and

(e)   there are no reasons why it would be undesirable to grant the applicant indefinite leave to remain based on the applicant's conduct, character or associations or because the applicant represents a threat to national security.

Indefinite leave to remain on the grounds of private life in the UK

276DF.   Indefinite leave to remain on the grounds of private life in the UK may be granted provided that the Secretary of State is satisfied that each of the requirements of paragraph 276DE is met.

276DG.   If the applicant does not meet the requirements for indefinite leave to remain on the grounds of private life in the UK only for one or both of the following reasons–

(a)   paragraph S-ILR.1.5. or S-ILR.1.6. in Appendix FM applies;

(b)   the applicant has not demonstrated sufficient knowledge of the English language or about life in the UK in accordance with Appendix KoLL,

subject to compliance with any requirement notified under paragraph 276A04(b), the applicant may be granted further limited leave to remain on the grounds of private life in the UK for a period not exceeding 30 months, and subject to a condition of no recourse to public funds unless the Secretary of State considers that the person should not be subject to such a condition.

Refusal of indefinite leave to remain on the grounds of private life in the UK

276DH. Indefinite leave to remain on the grounds of private life in the UK is to be refused if the Secretary of State is not satisfied that each of the requirements of paragraph 276DE is met, subject to paragraph 276DG.

276E–276BV1. OMITTED

Part 8 – Family members

A277–295O. OMITTED

Children

296. Nothing in these Rules shall be construed as permitting a child to be granted entry clearance, leave to enter or remain, or variation of leave where his parent is party to a polygamous marriage or civil partnership and any application by that parent for admission or leave to remain for settlement or with a view to settlement would be refused pursuant to paragraphs 278 or 278A.

Leave to enter or remain in the United Kingdom as the child of a parent, parents or a relative present and settled or being admitted for settlement in the United Kingdom

Requirements for indefinite leave to enter the United Kingdom as the child of a parent, parents or a relative present and settled or being admitted for settlement in the United Kingdom

297. The requirements to be met by a person seeking indefinite leave to enter the United Kingdom as the child of a parent, parents or a relative present and settled or being admitted for settlement in the United Kingdom are that he:

(i) is seeking leave to enter to accompany or join a parent, parents or a relative in one of the following circumstances:

    (a) both parents are present and settled in the United Kingdom; or

    (b) both parents are being admitted on the same occasion for settlement; or

    (c) one parent is present and settled in the United Kingdom and the other is being admitted on the same occasion for settlement; or

    (d) one parent is present and settled in the United Kingdom or being admitted on the same occasion for settlement and the other parent is dead; or

    (e) one parent is present and settled in the United Kingdom or being admitted on the same occasion for settlement and has had sole responsibility for the child's upbringing; or

    (f) one parent or a relative is present and settled in the United Kingdom or being admitted on the same occasion for settlement and there are serious and compelling family or other considerations which make exclusion of the child undesirable and suitable arrangements have been made for the child's care; and

(ii) is under the age of 18; and

(iii) is not leading an independent life, is unmarried and is not a civil partner, and has not formed an independent family unit; and

(iv) can, and will, be accommodated adequately by the parent, parents or relative the child is seeking to join without recourse to public funds in accommodation which the parent, parents or relative the child is seeking to join, own or occupy exclusively; and

(v) can, and will, be maintained adequately by the parent, parents, or relative the child is seeking to join, without recourse to public funds; and

(vi) holds a valid United Kingdom entry clearance for entry in this capacity; and

(vii) does not fall for refusal under the general grounds for refusal.

Requirements for indefinite leave to remain in the United Kingdom as the child of a parent, parents or a relative present and settled or being admitted for settlement in the United Kingdom

298. The requirements to be met by a person seeking indefinite leave to remain in the United Kingdom as the child of a parent, parents or a relative present and settled in the United Kingdom are that he:

(i)   is seeking to remain with a parent, parents or a relative in one of the following circumstances:

     (a)   both parents are present and settled in the United Kingdom; or

     (b)   one parent is present and settled in the United Kingdom and the other parent is dead; or

     (c)   one parent is present and settled in the United Kingdom and has had sole responsibility for the child's upbringing or the child normally lives with this parent and not their other parent; or

     (d)   one parent or a relative is present and settled in the United Kingdom and there are serious and compelling family or other considerations which make exclusion of the child undesirable and suitable arrangements have been made for the child's care; and

(ii)   has or has had limited leave to enter or remain in the United Kingdom, and

     (a)   is under the age of 18; or

     (b)   was given leave to enter or remain with a view to settlement under paragraph 302 or Appendix FM; or

     (c)   was admitted into the UK in accordance with paragraph 319R and has completed a period of 2 years limited leave as the child of a refugee or beneficiary of humanitarian protection who is now present and settled in the UK or as the child of a former refugee or beneficiary of humanitarian protection who is now a British Citizen, or

     (d)   the applicant *has limited leave to enter or remain* in the United Kingdom in accordance with paragraph 319X, as the child of a relative with limited leave to remain as a refugee or beneficiary of humanitarian protection in the United Kingdom and who is now present and settled here; or

     (e)   was last given limited leave to remain under paragraph 298A; and

(iii)   is not leading an independent life, is unmarried, and has not formed an independent family unit; and

(iv)   can, and will, be accommodated adequately by the parent, parents or relative the child was admitted to join, without recourse to public funds in accommodation which the parent, parents or relative the child was admitted to join, own or occupy exclusively; and

(v)   can, and will, be maintained adequately by the parent, parents or relative the child was admitted to join, without recourse to public funds; and

(vi)   does not fall for refusal under the general grounds for refusal; and

(vii)   if aged 18 or over, was admitted to the United Kingdom under paragraph 302, or Appendix FM, or 319R or 319X and has demonstrated sufficient knowledge of the English language and sufficient knowledge about life in the United Kingdom in accordance with Appendix KoLL.

298A.   If an applicant does not meet the requirements of paragraph 298 only because:

     (a)   the applicant does not meet the requirement in paragraph 298(vi) by reason of a sentence or disposal of a type mentioned in paragraph 322(1C)(iii) or (iv); or

     (b)   an applicant aged 18 or over does not meet the requirement in paragraph 298(vii); or

     (c)   the applicant would otherwise be refused indefinite leave to remain under paragraph 322(1C)(iii) or (iv),

the applicant may be granted limited leave to remain for a period not exceeding 30 months and subject to a condition of no recourse to public funds.

Indefinite leave to enter or remain in the United Kingdom as the child of a parent, parents or a relative present and settled or being admitted for settlement in the United Kingdom

299.   Indefinite leave to enter the United Kingdom as the child of a parent, parents or a relative present and settled or being admitted for settlement in the United Kingdom may be granted provided a valid United Kingdom entry clearance for entry in this capacity is produced to the Immigration Officer on arrival. Indefinite leave to remain in the United Kingdom as the child of a parent, parents or a relative present and settled in the United Kingdom may be granted provided the Secretary of State is satisfied that each of the requirements of paragraph 298 is met.

Refusal of indefinite leave to enter or remain in the United Kingdom as the child of a parent, parents or a relative present and settled or being admitted for settlement in the United Kingdom

300.   Indefinite leave to enter the United Kingdom as the child of a parent, parents or a relative present and settled or being admitted for settlement in the United Kingdom is to be refused if a valid United Kingdom entry clearance for entry in this capacity is not produced to the Immigration Officer on arrival. Indefinite leave to

remain in the United Kingdom as the child of a parent, parents or a relative present and settled in the United Kingdom is to be refused if the Secretary of State is not satisfied that each of the requirements of paragraph 298 is met.

Requirements for limited leave to enter or remain in the United Kingdom with a view to settlement as the child of a parent or parents given limited leave to enter or remain in the United Kingdom with a view to settlement

301. The requirements to be met by a person seeking limited leave to enter or remain in the United Kingdom with a view to settlement as the child of a parent or parents given limited leave to enter or remain in the United Kingdom with a view to settlement are that he:

    (i)   is seeking leave to enter to accompany or join or remain with a parent or parents in one of the following circumstances:

        (a)   one parent is present and settled in the United Kingdom or being admitted on the same occasion for settlement and the other parent is being or has been given limited leave to enter or remain in the United Kingdom with a view to settlement; or

        (b)   one parent is being or has been given limited leave to enter or remain in the United Kingdom with a view to settlement and has had sole responsibility for the child's upbringing; or

        (c)   one parent is being or has been given limited leave to enter or remain in the United Kingdom with a view to settlement and there are serious and compelling family or other considerations which make exclusion of the child undesirable and suitable arrangements have been made for the child's care; and

    (ii)   is under the age of 18; and

    (iii)   is not leading an independent life, is unmarried and is not a civil partner, and has not formed an independent family unit; and

    (iv)   can, and will, be accommodated adequately without recourse to public funds, in accommodation which the parent or parents own or occupy exclusively; and

    (iva)   can, and will, be maintained adequately by the parent or parents without recourse to public funds; and

    (ivb)   does not qualify for limited leave to enter as a child of a parent or parents given limited leave to enter or remain as a refugee or beneficiary of humanitarian protection under paragraph 319R; and

    (v)   (where an application is made for limited leave to remain with a view to settlement) has limited leave to enter or remain in the United Kingdom; and

    (vi)   if seeking leave to enter, holds a valid United Kingdom entry clearance for entry in this capacity.

Limited leave to enter or remain in the United Kingdom with a view to settlement as the child of a parent or parents given limited leave to enter or remain in the United Kingdom with a view to settlement

302. A person seeking limited leave to enter the United Kingdom with a view to settlement as the child of a parent or parents given limited leave to enter or remain in the United Kingdom with a view to settlement may be admitted for a period not exceeding 27 months provided he is able, on arrival, to produce to the Immigration Officer a valid United Kingdom entry clearance for entry in this capacity. A person seeking limited leave to remain in the United Kingdom with a view to settlement as the child of a parent or parents given limited leave to enter or remain in the United Kingdom with a view to settlement may be given limited leave to remain for a period not exceeding 27 months provided the Secretary of State is satisfied that each of the requirements of paragraph 301 (i)–(v) is met.

Refusal of limited leave to enter or remain in the United Kingdom with a view to settlement as the child of a parent or parents given limited leave to enter or remain in the United Kingdom with a view to settlement

303. Limited leave to enter the United Kingdom with a view to settlement as the child of a parent or parents given limited leave to enter or remain in the United Kingdom with a view to settlement is to be refused if a valid United Kingdom entry clearance for entry in this capacity is not produced to the Immigration Officer on arrival. Limited leave to remain in the United Kingdom with a view to settlement as the child of a parent or parents given limited leave to enter or remain in the United Kingdom with a view to settlement is to be refused if the Secretary of State is not satisfied that each of the requirements of paragraph 301 (i)–(v) is met.

Leave to enter and extension of stay in the United Kingdom as the child of a parent who is being, or has been admitted to the united kingdom as a fiance(e) or proposed civil partner

Requirements for limited leave to enter the United Kingdom as the child of a fiance(e) or proposed civil partner

303A.   The requirements to be met by a person seeking limited leave to enter the United Kingdom as the child of a fiance(e) or proposed civil partner, are that:

(i)   he is seeking to accompany or join a parent who is, on the same occasion that the child seeks admission, being admitted as a fiance(e) or proposed civil partner , or who has been admitted as a fiance(e) or proposed civil partner; and

(ii)   he is under the age of 18; and

(iii)   he is not leading an independent life, is unmarried and is not a civil partner, and has not formed an independent family unit; and

(iv)   he can and will be maintained and accommodated adequately without recourse to public funds with the parent admitted or being admitted as a fiance(e) or proposed civil partner; and

(v)   there are serious and compelling family or other considerations which make the child's exclusion undesirable, that suitable arrangements have been made for his care in the United Kingdom, and there is no other person outside the United Kingdom who could reasonably be expected to care for him; and

(vi)   he holds a valid United Kingdom entry clearance for entry in this capacity.

Limited leave to enter the United Kingdom as the child of a parent who is being, or has been admitted to the United Kingdom as a fiance(e) or proposed civil partner

303B.   A person seeking limited leave to enter the United Kingdom as the child of a fiance(e) or proposed civil partner, may be granted limited leave to enter the United Kingdom for a period not in excess of that granted to the fiance(e) or proposed civil partner, provided that a valid United Kingdom entry clearance for entry in this capacity is produced to the Immigration Officer on arrival. Where the period of limited leave granted to a fiance(e) will expire in more than 6 months, a person seeking limited leave to enter as the child of the fiance(e) or proposed civil partner should be granted leave for a period not exceeding six months.

Refusal of limited leave to enter the United Kingdom as the child of a parent who is being, or has been admitted to the United Kingdom as a fiance(e) or proposed civil partner

303C.   Limited leave to enter the United Kingdom as the child of a fiance(e) or proposed civil partner, is to be refused if a valid United Kingdom entry clearance for entry in this capacity is not produced to the Immigration Officer on arrival.

Requirements for an extension of stay in the United Kingdom as the child of a fiance(e) or proposed civil partner

303D.   The requirements to be met by a person seeking an extension of stay in the United Kingdom as the child of a fiance(e) or proposed civil partner are that:

(i)   the applicant was admitted with a valid United Kingdom entry clearance as the child of a fiance(e) or proposed civil partner; and

(ii)   the applicant is the child of a parent who has been granted limited leave to enter, or an extension of stay, as a fiance(e) or proposed civil partner; and

(iii)   the requirements of paragraph 303A (ii)–(v) are met.

Extension of stay in the United Kingdom as the child of a fiance(e) or proposed civil partner

303E.   An extension of stay as the child of a fiance(e) or proposed civil partner may be granted provided that the Secretary of State is satisfied that each of the requirements of paragraph 303D is met.

Refusal of an extension of stay in the United Kingdom as the child of a fiance(e) or proposed civil partner

303F.   An extension of stay as the child of a fiance(e) or proposed civil partner is to be refused if the Secretary of State is not satisfied that each of the requirements of paragraph 303D is met.

Children born in the United Kingdom who are not British citizens

304. This paragraph and paragraphs 305–309 apply only to dependent children under 18 years of age who are unmarried and are not civil partners and who were born in the United Kingdom on or after 1 January 1983 (when the British Nationality Act 1981 came into force) but who, because neither of their parents was a British Citizen or settled in the United Kingdom at the time of their birth, are not British Citizens and are therefore subject to immigration control. Such a child requires leave to enter where admission to the United Kingdom is sought, and leave to remain where permission is sought for the child to be allowed to stay in the United Kingdom. If he qualifies for entry clearance, leave to enter or leave to remain under any other part of these Rules, a child who was born in the United Kingdom but is not a British Citizen may be granted entry clearance, leave to enter or leave to remain in accordance with the provisions of that other part.

Requirements for leave to enter or remain in the United Kingdom as the child of a parent or parents given leave to enter or remain in the United Kingdom

305. The requirements to be met by a child born in the United Kingdom who is not a British Citizen who seeks leave to enter or remain in the United Kingdom as the child of a parent or parents given leave to enter or remain in the United Kingdom are that he:

    (i)   (a)   is accompanying or seeking to join or remain with a parent or parents who have, or are given, leave to enter or remain in the United Kingdom; or

            (b)   is accompanying or seeking to join or remain with a parent or parents one of whom is a British Citizen or has the right of abode in the United Kingdom; or

            (c)   is a child in respect of whom the parental rights and duties are vested solely in a local authority; and

    (ii)   is under the age of 18; and

    (iii)   was born in the United Kingdom; and

    (iv)   is not leading an independent life, is unmarried and is not a civil partner, and has not formed an independent family unit; and

    (v)   (where an application is made for leave to enter) has not been away from the United Kingdom for more than 2 years.

Leave to enter or remain in the United Kingdom

306. A child born in the United Kingdom who is not a British Citizen and who requires leave to enter or remain in the circumstances set out in paragraph 304 may be given leave to enter for the same period as his parent or parents where paragraph 305 (i)(a) applies, provided the Immigration Officer is satisfied that each of the requirements of paragraph 305 (ii)–(v) is met. Where leave to remain is sought, the child may be granted leave to remain for the same period as his parent or parents where paragraph 305 (i)(a) applies, provided the Secretary of State is satisfied that each of the requirements of paragraph 305 (ii)–(iv) is met. Where the parent or parents have or are given periods of leave of different duration, the child may be given leave to whichever period is longer except that if the parents are living apart the child should be given leave for the same period as the parent who has day to day responsibility for him.

307. If a child does not qualify for leave to enter or remain because neither of his parents has a current leave, (and neither of them is a British Citizen or has the right of abode), he will normally be refused leave to enter or remain, even if each of the requirements of paragraph 305 (ii)–(v) has been satisfied. However, he may be granted leave to enter or remain for a period not exceeding 3 months if both of his parents are in the United Kingdom and it appears unlikely that they will be removed in the immediate future, and there is no other person outside the United Kingdom who could reasonably be expected to care for him.

308. A child born in the United Kingdom who is not a British Citizen and who requires leave to enter or remain in the United Kingdom in the circumstances set out in paragraph 304 may be given indefinite leave to enter where paragraph 305 (i)(b) or (i)(c) applies provided the Immigration Officer is satisfied that each of the requirements of paragraph 305 (ii)–(v) is met. Where an application is for leave to remain, such a child may be granted indefinite leave to remain where paragraph 305 (i)(b) or (i)(c) applies, provided the Secretary of State is satisfied that each of the requirements of paragraph 305 (ii)–(iv) is met.

Refusal of leave to enter or remain in the United Kingdom

309. Leave to enter the United Kingdom where the circumstances set out in paragraph 304 apply is to be refused if the Immigration Officer is not satisfied that each of the requirements of paragraph 305 is met. Leave to

remain for such a child is to be refused if the Secretary of State is not satisfied that each of the requirements of paragraph 305 (i)–(iv) is met.

309A.–319.   OMITTED

Family members of relevant points-based system migrants

Partners of relevant points-based system migrants

319AA.   In paragraphs 319A to 319K and Appendix E, 'Relevant Points Based System Migrant' means a migrant granted to leave as a Tier 1 Migrant, a Tier 2 Migrant, a Tier 4 (General) Student or a Tier 5 (Temporary Worker) Migrant.

Purpose

319A.   This route is for the spouse, civil partner, unmarried or same-sex partner of a Relevant Points Based System Migrant (Partner of a Relevant Points Based System Migrant). Paragraphs 277 to 280 of these Rules apply to spouses or civil partners of Relevant Points Based System Migrant; paragraph 277 of these Rules applies to civil partners of Relevant Points Based System Migrant; and paragraph 295AA of these Rules applies to unmarried and same-sex partners of Relevant Points Based System Migrant

Entry to the UK

319B.   (a)   Subject to paragraph (b), all migrants wishing to enter as the Partner of a relevant Points Based System Migrant must have a valid entry clearance for entry under this route. If they do not have a valid entry clearance, entry will be refused.

(b)   A Migrant arriving in the UK and wishing to enter as a partner of a Tier 5 (Temporary Worker) Migrant, who does not have a valid entry clearance will not be refused entry if the following conditions are met:

(i)   the migrant wishing to enter as partner is not a visa national,

(ii)   the migrant wishing to enter as a Partner is accompanying an applicant who at the same time is being granted leave to enter under paragraph 245ZN(b), and

(iii)   the migrant wishing to enter as a Partner meets the requirements of entry clearance in paragraph 319C.

Requirements for entry clearance or leave to remain

319C.   To qualify for entry clearance or leave to remain as the Partner of a Relevant Points Based System Migrant, an applicant must meet the requirements listed below. If the applicant meets these requirements, entry clearance or leave to remain will be granted. If the applicant does not meet these requirements, the application will be refused.

Requirements:

(a)   The applicant must not fall for refusal under the general grounds for refusal, and if applying for leave to remain, must not be an illegal entrant.

(b)   The applicant must be the spouse or civil partner, unmarried or same-sex partner of a person who:

(i)   has valid leave to enter or remain as a Relevant Points Based System Migrant, or

(ii)   is, at the same time, being granted entry clearance or leave to remain as a Relevant Points Based System Migrant, or

(iii)   has indefinite leave to remain as a Relevant Points Based System Migrant, or is at the same time being granted indefinite leave to remain as a Relevant Points Based System Migrant, where the applicant is applying for further leave to remain, or has been refused indefinite leave to remain solely because the applicant has not met the requirements of paragraph 319E(g), and was last granted leave:

(1)   as the partner of that same Relevant Points Based System Migrant: or

(2)   as the spouse or civil partner, unmarried or same-sex partner of that person at a time when that person had leave under another category of these Rules; or

(iv)   has become a British Citizen where prior to that they held indefinite leave to Remain as a Relevant Points Based System Migrant and where the applicant is applying for further leave to remain, or has been refused indefinite leave to remain solely because the applicant has not met the requirements of paragraph 319E(g), and was last granted leave:

(1)   as the partner of that same Relevant Points Based System Migrant, or

(2)   as the spouse or civil partner, unmarried or same-sex partner of that person at a time when that person had leave under another category of these Rules.

(c)   An applicant who is the unmarried or same-sex partner of a Relevant Points Based System Migrant must also meet the following requirements:

(i)   any previous marriage or civil partnership or similar relationship by the applicant or the Relevant Points Based System Migrant with another person must have permanently broken down,

(ii)   the applicant and the Relevant Points Based System Migrant must not be so closely related that they would be prohibited from marrying each other in the UK, and

(iii)   the applicant and the Relevant Points Based System Migrant must have been living together in a relationship similar to marriage or civil partnership for a period of at least 2 years.

(d)   The marriage or civil partnership, or relationship similar to marriage or civil partnership, must be subsisting at the time the application is made.

(e)   The applicant and the Relevant Points Based System Migrant must intend to live with the other as their spouse or civil partner, unmarried or same-sex partner throughout the applicants stay in the UK.

(f)   The applicant must not intend to stay in the UK beyond any period of leave granted to the Relevant Points Based System Migrant .

(g)   Unless the Relevant Points Based System Migrant is a Tier 1 (Investor) Migrant or a Tier 1 (Exceptional Talent) Migrant, there must be a sufficient level of funds available to the applicant, as set out in Appendix E.

(h)   An applicant who is applying for leave to remain must not have last been granted:

(i)   entry clearance or leave as a:

(a)   visitor, including where they entered the United Kingdom from the Republic of Ireland to stay under the terms of articles 3A and 4 of the Immigration (Control of Entry through the Republic of Ireland) Order 1972 (as amended by the Immigration (Control of Entry through Republic of Ireland) (Amendment) Order 2014) on the basis of a visa issued by the Republic of Ireland authorities endorsed with the letters 'BIVS' for the purpose of travelling and staying in the Republic for a period of 90 days or fewer; or

(b)   short-term student or short term student (child); or

(c)   parent of a Tier 4 (child) student

unless the Relevant Points Based System Migrant has, or is being granted, leave to remain as a Tier 5 (Temporary Worker) Migrant in the creative and sporting subcategory on the basis of having met the requirement at paragraph 245ZQ(b)(ii);

(ii)   temporary admission; or

(iii)   temporary release.

(i)   Where the relevant Points Based System Migrant is applying for, or has been granted, entry clearance, leave to enter, or leave to remain in the United Kingdom as a Tier 4 (General) Student either:

(i)   the relevant Points Based System Migrant must be a government sponsored student who is applying for, or who has been granted, entry clearance or leave to remain to undertake a course of study longer than six months;

(ii)   the relevant Points Based System Migrant must:

(1)   be applying for, or have been granted entry clearance or leave to remain in order to undertake a course of study at post-graduate level that is 12 months or longer in duration; and

(2)   be sponsored by a sponsor who is a UK recognised body or a body in receipt of funding as a higher education institution from either:

(a)   the Department for Employment and Learning in Northern Ireland;

(b)   the Higher Education Funding Council for England;

(c)   the Higher Education Funding Council for Wales; or

(d)   the Scottish Funding Council;

(iii)   the relevant Points Based System Migrant must be applying for, or have been granted leave to remain as a Tier 4 (General) Student on the doctorate extension scheme; or

(iv)   the following conditions must be met:

(1)   the relevant Points Based System Migrant must be applying for entry clearance, leave to enter, or leave to remain, to undertake a course of study that is longer than six months and either:

(a)   have entry clearance, leave to enter, or leave to remain as a Tier 4 (General) Student or as a student to undertake a course of study longer than six months; or

(b)   have last had entry clearance, leave to enter, or leave to remain within the three months preceding the application as a Tier 4 (General) Student or as a student to undertake a course of study longer than six months; and

(2)   the Partner must either:

(a)   have entry clearance, leave to enter, or leave to remain as the Partner of a Tier 4 (General) Student or a student with entry clearance, leave to enter, or leave to remain, to undertake a course of study longer than six months; or

(b)   have last had entry clearance, leave to enter, or leave to remain within the three months preceding the application as the Partner of a Tier 4 (General) Student or as a student to undertake a course of study longer than six months; and

(3)   the relevant Points Based System Migrant and the Partner must be applying at the same time.

(j)   The applicant must not be in the UK in breach of immigration laws except that any period of overstaying for a period of 28 days will be disregarded.

Period and conditions of grant

319D.   (a)   (i)   Entry clearance or limited leave to remain will be granted for a period which expires on the same day as the leave granted to the Relevant Points Based System Migrant, or

(ii)   If the Relevant Points-Based System Migrant has indefinite leave to remain as a Relevant Points Based System Migrant, or is, at the same time being granted indefinite leave to remain as a Relevant Points Based System Migrant, or where the Relevant Points-Based System Migrant has since become a British Citizen, leave to remain will be granted to the applicant for a period of 3 years.

(b)   Entry clearance and leave to remain under this route will be subject to the following conditions:

(i)   no recourse to public funds,

(ii)   registration with the police, if this is required under paragraph 326 of these Rules,

(iii)   no Employment as a Doctor or Dentist in Training, unless the applicant:

(1)   has obtained a primary degree in medicine or dentistry at bachelor's level or above from a UK institution that is a UK recognised or listed body, or which holds a sponsor licence under Tier 4 of the Points Based System, and provides evidence of this degree; or

(2)   is applying for leave to remain and has, or has last been granted, entry clearance, leave to enter or leave to remain that was not subject to any condition restricting him from taking employment as a Doctor in Training, has been employed during that leave as a Doctor in Training, and provides a letter from the Postgraduate Deanery or NHS Trust employing them which confirms that they have been working in a post or programme that has been approved by the General Medical Council as a training programme or post; or

(3)   is applying for leave to remain and has, or has last been granted, entry clearance, leave to enter or leave to remain that was not subject to any condition restricting him from taking employment as a Dentist in Training, has been employed during that leave as a Dentist in Training, and provides a letter from the Postgraduate Deanery or NHS Trust employing them which confirms that they have been working in a post or programme that has been approved by the Joint Committee for Postgraduate Training in Dentistry as a training programme or post.

(iv)   if the Relevant Points Based System Migrant is a Tier 4 (General) Student and the Partner meets the requirements of paragraphs 319C(i)(iv)(1),(2) and (3) and:

(1)   the Relevant Points Based System Migrant is a Tier 4 (General) Student applying for leave for less than 12 months, no employment, or

(2)   the Relevant Points Based System Migrant is a Tier 4 (General) Student who is following a course of below degree level study, no employment.

(v)   no employment as a professional sportsperson (including as a sports coach).

Requirements for indefinite leave to remain

319E. To qualify for indefinite leave to remain as the Partner of a Relevant Points Based System Migrant, an applicant must meet the requirements listed below. If the applicant meets these requirements, indefinite leave to remain will be granted. If the applicant does not meet these requirements, the application will be refused.

Requirements:

(a) The applicant must not fall for refusal under the general grounds for refusal, and must not be an illegal entrant.

(b) The applicant must be the spouse or civil partner, unmarried or same-sex partner of a person who:

    (i) has indefinite leave to remain as a Relevant Points Based System Migrant; or

    (ii) is, at the same time being granted indefinite leave to remain as a Relevant Points Based System Migrant, or

    (iii) has become a British Citizen where prior to that they held indefinite leave to remain as a Relevant Points Based System Migrant.

(c) The applicant must have, or have last been granted, leave as the partner of the Relevant Points Based System Migrant who:

    (i) has indefinite leave to remain as a Relevant Points Based System Migrant; or

    (ii) is, at the same time being granted indefinite leave to remain as a Relevant Points Based System Migrant, or

    (iii) has become a British Citizen where prior to that they held indefinite leave to remain as a Relevant Points Based System Migrant.

(d) The applicant and the Relevant Points Based System Migrant must have been living together in the UK in a marriage or civil partnership, or in a relationship similar to marriage or civil partnership, for at least the period specified in (i) or (ii):

    (i) If the applicant was granted leave as:

        (a) the Partner of that Relevant Points Based System Migrant, or

        (b) the spouse or civil partner, unmarried or same-sex partner of that person at a time when that person had leave under another category of these Rules under the Rules in place before 9 July 2012, and since then has had continuous leave as the Partner of that Relevant Points based System Migrant, the specified period is 2 years

    (ii) If (i) does not apply, the specified period is a continuous period of 5 years, during which the applicant must:

        (a) have been in a relationship with the same Relevant Points Based System Migrant for this entire period,

        (b) have spent the most recent part of the 5 year period with leave as the Partner of that Relevant Points Based System Migrant, and during that part of the period have met all of the requirements of paragraph 319C(a) to (e), and

        (c) have spent the remainder of the 5 year period, where applicable, with leave as the spouse or civil partner, unmarried or same-sex partner of that person at a time when that person had leave under another category of these Rules.

(e) The marriage or civil partnership, or relationship similar to marriage or civil partnership, must be subsisting at the time the application is made.

(f) The applicant and the Relevant Points Based System Migrant must intend to live permanently with the other as their spouse or civil partner, unmarried or same-sex partner.

(g) The applicant has demonstrated sufficient knowledge of the English language and sufficient knowledge about life in the United Kingdom, in accordance with Appendix KoLL.

(h) DELETED

(i) The applicant must not be in the UK in breach of immigration laws except that any period of overstaying for a period of 28 days will be disregarded.

Children of relevant points-based system migrants

Purpose

319F.   This route is for the children of a Relevant Points Based System Migrant who are under the age of 18 when they apply to enter under this route. Paragraph 296 of these Rules applies to children of a Relevant Points Based System Migrants.

Entry to the UK

319G.   (a)   Subject to paragraph (b), all migrants wishing to enter as the Child of a relevant Points Based System Migrant must have a valid entry clearance for entry under this route. If they do not have a valid entry clearance, entry will be refused.

(b)   A Migrant arriving in the UK and wishing to enter as a child of a Tier 5 (Temporary Worker) Migrant, who does not have a valid entry clearance will not be refused entry if the following conditions are met:

(i)   the migrant wishing to enter as a child is not a visa national,

(ii)   the migrant wishing to enter as a child is accompanying an applicant who at the same time is being granted leave to enter under paragraph 245ZN(b), and

(iii)   the migrant wishing to enter as a Child meets the requirements of entry clearance in paragraph 319H.

Requirements for entry clearance or leave to remain

319H.   To qualify for entry clearance or leave to remain under this route, an applicant must meet the requirements listed below. If the applicant meets these requirements, entry clearance or leave to remain will be granted. If the applicant does not meet these requirements, the application will be refused.

Requirements:

(a)   The applicant must not fall for refusal under the general grounds for refusal, and if applying for leave to remain, must not be an illegal entrant.

(b)   The applicant must be the child of a parent who has, or is at the same time being granted, valid entry clearance, leave to enter or remain, or indefinite leave to remain, as:

(i)   a Relevant Points Based System Migrant, or

(ii)   the partner of a Relevant Points Based System Migrant,

or who has obtained British citizenship having previously held indefinite leave to remain as above.

(c)   The applicant must be under the age of 18 on the date the application is made, or if over 18 and applying for leave to remain, must have, or have last been granted, leave as the child of a **Relevant Points Based System Migrant** or as the child of the parent who had leave under another category of these Rules and who has since been granted, or, is at the same time being granted, leave to remain as a Relevant Points Based System Migrant.

(d)   The applicant must not be married or in a civil partnership, must not have formed an independent family unit, and must not be leading an independent life and, if he is over the age of 16 on the date the application is made, he must provide the specified documents and information in paragraph 319H-SD to show that this requirement is met.

(e)   The applicant must not intend to stay in the UK beyond any period of leave granted to the Relevant Points Based System Migrant parent.

(f)   Both of the applicant's parents must either be lawfully present in the UK, or being granted entry clearance or leave to remain at the same time as the applicant or one parent must be lawfully present in the UK and the other is being granted entry clearance or leave to remain at the same time as the applicant, unless:

(i)   The Relevant Points Based System Migrant is the applicant's sole surviving parent, or

(ii)   The Relevant Points Based System Migrant parent has and has had sole responsibility for the applicant's upbringing, or

(iii)   there are serious or compelling family or other considerations which would make it desirable not to refuse the application and suitable arrangements have been made in the UK for the applicant's care.

(g)   Unless the Relevant Points Based System Migrant is a Tier 1 (Investor) Migrant or a Tier 1 (Exceptional Talent) Migrant, there must be a sufficient level of funds available to the applicant, as set out in Appendix E.

(h)   An applicant who is applying for leave to remain must not have last been granted:

   (i)   entry clearance or leave as a:

      (a)   visitor, including where they entered the United Kingdom from the Republic of Ireland to stay under the terms of articles 3A and 4 of the Immigration (Control of Entry through the Republic of Ireland) Order 1972 (as amended by the Immigration (Control of Entry through Republic of Ireland) (Amendment) Order 2014) on the basis of a visa issued by the Republic of Ireland authorities endorsed with the letters 'BIVS' for the purpose of travelling and staying in the Republic for a period of 90 days or fewer; or

      (b)   short-term student (child)

      unless the Relevant Points Based System Migrant has, or is being granted, leave to remain as a Tier 5 (Temporary Worker) Migrant in the creative and sporting subcategory on the basis of having met the requirement at paragraph 245ZQ(b)(ii);

   (ii)   temporary admission; or

   (iii)   temporary release.

(i)   Where the relevant Points Based System Migrant is applying for, or has been granted, entry clearance, leave to enter, or leave to remain in the United Kingdom as a Tier 4 (General) Student either:

   (i)   the relevant Points Based System Migrant must be a government sponsored student who is applying for, or who has been granted, entry clearance or leave to remain to undertake a course of study longer than six months;

   (ii)   the relevant Points Based System Migrant must:

      (1)   be applying for, or have been granted entry clearance or leave to remain in order to undertake a course of study at post-graduate level that is 12 months or longer in duration; and

      (2)   be sponsored by a sponsor who is a UK recognised body or a body in receipt of funding as a higher education institution from either:

         (a)   the Department for Employment and Learning in Northern Ireland;

         (b)   the Higher Education Funding Council for England;

         (c)   the Higher Education Funding Council for Wales; or

         (d)   the Scottish Funding Council;

   (iii)   the relevant Points Based System Migrant must be applying for, or have been granted leave to remain as a Tier 4 (General) Student on the doctorate extension scheme; or

   (iv)   the following conditions must be met:

      (1)   the relevant Points Based System Migrant must be applying for entry clearance, leave to enter, or leave to remain, to undertake a course of study that is longer than six months and either:

         (a)   have entry clearance, leave to enter, or leave to remain as a Tier 4 (General) Student or as a student to undertake a course of study longer than six months; or

         (b)   have last had entry clearance, leave to enter, or leave to remain within the three months preceding the application as a Tier 4 (General) Student or as a student to undertake a course of study longer than six months; and

      (2)   the Child must either:

         (a)   have entry clearance, leave to enter, or leave to remain as the Child of a Tier 4 (General) Student or a student with entry clearance, leave to enter, or leave to remain, to undertake a course of study longer than six months; or

         (b)   have last had entry clearance, leave to enter, or leave to remain within the three months preceding the application as the Child of a Tier 4 (General) Student or as a student to undertake a course of study longer than six months; and

      (3)   the relevant Points Based System Migrant and the Child must be applying at the same time.

(j)   A Child whose parent is a Relevant Points Based System Migrant, who is a Tier 4 (General) Student or Student, and who does not otherwise meet the requirements of paragraph 319H(i):

(1)   must have been born during the Relevant Points Based System Migrant's most recent grant of entry clearance, leave to enter or leave to remain as a Tier 4 (General) Student or Student with leave for a course of more than six months duration; or

(2)   where the Relevant Points Based System Migrant's most recent grant of entry clearance, leave to enter or leave to remain was to re-sit examinations or repeat a module of a course, must either have been born during a period of leave granted for the purposes of re-sitting examinations or repeating a module of a course or during the Relevant Points Based System Migrant's grant of leave for a course of more than six months, where that course is the same as the one for which the most recent grant of leave was to re-sit examinations or repeat a module; or

(3)   must have been born no more than three months after the expiry of that most recent grant of leave; and

(4)   must be applying for entry clearance.

(k)   If the applicant is a child born in the UK to a Relevant Points Based System migrant and their partner, the applicant must provide a full UK birth certificate showing the names of both parents.

(l)   All arrangements for the child's care and accommodation in the UK must comply with relevant UK legislation and regulations.

(m)   The applicant must not be in the UK in breach of immigration laws except that any period of overstaying for a period of 28 days will be disregarded.

Specified documents and information

319H-SD.   Applicants who are over the age of 16 on the date the application is made must provide the following specified documents and information:

(a)   The applicant must provide two items from the list below confirming his residential address:

(i)   bank statements,

(ii)   credit card bills,

(iii)   driving licence,

(iv)   NHS Registration document,

(v)   letter from his current school, college or university, on official headed paper and bearing the official stamp of that organisation, and issued by an authorised official of that organisation.

(b)   The documents submitted must be from two separate sources and dated no more than one calendar month before the date of the application.

(c)   If the applicant pays rent or board, he must provide details of how much this amounts to each calendar month.

(d)   If the applicant is residing separately from the Relevant Points Based System Migrant, he must provide:

(i)   reasons for residing away from the family home. Where this is due to academic endeavours he must provide confirmation from his university or college confirming his enrolment and attendance on the specific course, on official headed paper and bearing the official stamp of that organisation, and issued by an authorised official of that organisation,

(ii)   the following evidence that he has been supported financially by his parents whilst residing away from the family home:

(1)   bank statements for the applicant covering the three months before the date of the application clearly showing the origin of the deposits; and

(2)   bank statements for the applicant's parent covering the three months before the date of the application also showing corroborating payments out of their account.

Period and conditions of grant

319I.   (a)   Entry clearance and leave to remain will be granted for:

(i)   a period which expires on the same day as the leave granted to the parent whose leave expires first, or

(ii)   where both parents have, or are at the same time being granted, indefinite leave to remain, or have since become British citizens, leave to remain will be granted to the applicant for a period of 3 years.

(b)   Entry clearance and leave to remain under this route will be subject to the following conditions:

(i)   no recourse to public funds,

    (ii)   registration with the police, if this is required under paragraph 326 of these Rules, and

    (iii)   if the Relevant Points Based System Migrant is a Tier 4 (General) Student and the Child meets the requirements of paragraphs 319H(i)(iv)(1), (2) and (3) or 319H(j) and:

        (1)   the Relevant Points Based System Migrant is a Tier 4 (General) Student applying for leave for less than 12 months, no employment, or

        (2)   the Relevant Points Based System Migrant is a Tier 4 (General) Student who is following a course of below degree level study, no employment.

Requirements for indefinite leave to remain

319J.   To qualify for indefinite leave to remain under this route, an applicant must meet the requirements listed below. If the applicant meets these requirements, indefinite leave to remain will be granted. If the applicant does not meet these requirements, the application will be refused.

Requirements:

(a)   The applicant must not fall for refusal under the general grounds for refusal, and must not be an illegal entrant.

(b)   The applicant must be the child of a parent who has, or is at the same time being granted, indefinite leave to remain as:

    (i)   a Relevant Points Based System Migrant, or

    (ii)   the partner of a Relevant Points Based System Migrant.

(c)   The applicant must have, or have last been granted, leave as the child of or have been born in the United Kingdom to, the Points Based System Migrant, or the partner of a Points Based System migrant who is being granted indefinite leave to remain.

(d)   The applicant must not be married or in a civil partnership, must not have formed an independent family unit, and must not be leading an independent life, and if he is over the age of 16 on the date the application is made, he must provide the specified documents and information in paragraph 319H-SD to show that this requirement is met.

(e)   Both of an applicant's parents must either be lawfully settled in the UK, or being granted indefinite leave to remain at the same time as the applicant, unless:

    (i)   The Points Based System Migrant is the applicant's sole surviving parent, or

    (ii)   The Points Based System Migrant parent has and has had sole responsibility for the applicant's upbringing, or

    (iii) there are serious and compelling family or other considerations which would make it desirable not to refuse the application and suitable arrangements have been made for the applicant's care, or

    (iv) One parent is, at the same time, being granted indefinite leave to remain as a Relevant Points Based System Migrant, the other parent is lawfully present in the UK or being granted leave at the same time the applicant, and the applicant was granted leave as the child of a Relevant Points Based System Migrant under the Rules in place before 9 July 2012.

(f)   The applicant has demonstrated sufficient knowledge of the English language and sufficient knowledge about life in the United Kingdom, in accordance with Appendix KoLL, unless he is under the age of 18 at the date on which the application is made.

(g)   If the applicant is a child born in the UK to a Relevant Points Based System migrant and their partner, the applicant must provide a full UK birth certificate showing the names of both parents.

(h)   All arrangements for the child's care and accommodation in the UK must comply with relevant UK legislation and regulations.

(i)   The applicant must not be in the UK in breach of immigration laws except that any period of overstaying for a period of 28 days will be disregarded.

Please note in the printed version of CM5829 these points appear in error numbered as an alternative version of 316D (iii) and (iv).

319L.–319Y.   OMITTED

Part 9 – General grounds for the refusal of entry clearance, leave to enter or variation of leave to enter or remain in the United Kingdom

Refusal of entry clearance or leave to enter the United Kingdom

A320.   Paragraphs 320 (except subparagraph (3), (10) and (11)) and 322 do not apply to an application for entry clearance, leave to enter or leave to remain as a Family Member under Appendix FM, and Part 9 (except for paragraph 322(1)) does not apply to an application for leave to remain on the grounds of private life under paragraphs 276ADE–276DH.

320.   In addition to the grounds of refusal of entry clearance or leave to enter set out in Parts 2–8 of these Rules, and subject to paragraph 321 below, the following grounds for the refusal of entry clearance or leave to enter apply:

Grounds on which entry clearance or leave to enter the United Kingdom is to be refused

(1)   the fact that entry is being sought for a purpose not covered by these Rules;

(2)   the fact that the person seeking entry to the United Kingdom:

    (a)   is currently the subject of a deportation order; or

    (b)   has been convicted of an offence for which they have been sentenced to a period of imprisonment of at least 4 years; or

    (c)   has been convicted of an offence for which they have been sentenced to a period of imprisonment of at least 12 months but less than 4 years, unless a period of 10 years has passed since the end of the sentence; or

    (d)   has been convicted of an offence for which they have been sentenced to a period of imprisonment of less than 12 months, unless a period of 5 years has passed since the end of the sentence.

Where this paragraph applies, unless refusal would be contrary to the Human Rights Convention or the Convention and Protocol Relating to the Status of Refugees, it will only be in exceptional circumstances that the public interest in maintaining refusal will be outweighed by compelling factors.

(2A)   Failure, if required to do so, by a person seeking entry to the United Kingdom to provide a criminal record certificate from the relevant authority in any country in which they have been resident for 12 months or more, in the past 10 years. Such evidence will not normally be required where:

    i.   The applicant is aged 17 years old or under at the date the application is made; or

    ii.   It is not reasonably practicable for the applicant to obtain such evidence from the relevant authorities.

(3)   failure by the person seeking entry to the United Kingdom to produce to the Immigration Officer a valid national passport or other document satisfactorily establishing his identity and nationality;

(4)   failure to satisfy the Immigration Officer, in the case of a person arriving in the United Kingdom or seeking entry through the Channel Tunnel with the intention of entering any other part of the common travel area, that he is acceptable to the immigration authorities there;

(5)   failure, in the case of a visa national, to produce to the Immigration Officer a passport or other identity document endorsed with a valid and current United Kingdom entry clearance issued for the purpose for which entry is sought;

(6)   where the Secretary of State has personally directed that the exclusion of a person from the United Kingdom is conducive to the public good;

(7)   save in relation to a person settled in the United Kingdom or where the Immigration Officer is satisfied that there are strong compassionate reasons justifying admission, confirmation from the Medical Inspector that, for medical reasons, it is undesirable to admit a person seeking leave to enter the United Kingdom.

(7A)   where false representations have been made or false documents or information have been submitted (whether or not material to the application, and whether or not to the applicant's knowledge), or material facts have not been disclosed, in relation to the application or in order to obtain documents from the Secretary of State or a third party required in support of the application.

(7B)   where the applicant has previously breached the UK's immigration laws (and was 18 or over at the time of his most recent breach) by:

    (a)   Overstaying;

(b)   breaching a condition attached to his leave;

(c)   being an Illegal Entrant;

(d)   using Deception in an application for entry clearance, leave to enter or remain, or in order to obtain documents from the Secretary of State or a third party required in support of the application (whether successful or not);

unless the applicant:

(i)   Overstayed for 90 days or less and left the UK voluntarily, not at the expense (directly or indirectly) of the Secretary of State;

(ii)   used Deception in an application for entry clearance more than 10 years ago;

(iii)   left the UK voluntarily, not at the expense (directly or indirectly) of the Secretary of State, more than 12 months ago;

(iv)   left the UK voluntarily, at the expense (directly or indirectly) of the Secretary of State, more than 2 years ago; and the date the person left the UK was no more than 6 months after the date on which the person was given notice of liability for removal, or no more than 6 months after the date on which the person no longer had a pending appeal or administrative review; whichever is the later;

(v)   left the UK voluntarily, at the expense (directly or indirectly) of the Secretary of State, more than 5 years ago;

(vi)   was removed or deported from the UK more than 10 years ago or;

(vii)   left or was removed from the UK as a condition of a caution issued in accordance with section 22 of the Criminal Justice Act 2003 more than 5 years ago.

Where more than one breach of the UK's immigration laws has occurred, only the breach which leads to the longest period of absence from the UK will be relevant under this paragraph.

(7D)   failure, without providing a reasonable explanation, to comply with a request made on behalf of the Entry Clearance Officer to attend for interview.

Grounds on which entry clearance or leave to enter the United Kingdom should normally be refused

(8)   failure by a person arriving in the United Kingdom to furnish the Immigration Officer with such information as may be required for the purpose of deciding whether he requires leave to enter and, if so, whether and on what terms leave should be given;

(8A)   where the person seeking leave is outside the United Kingdom, failure by him to supply any information, documents, copy documents or medical report requested by an Immigration Officer;

(9)   failure by a person seeking leave to enter as a returning resident to satisfy the Immigration Officer that he meets the requirements of paragraph 18 of these Rules, or that he seeks leave to enter for the same purpose as that for which his earlier leave was granted;

(10)   production by the person seeking leave to enter the United Kingdom of a national passport or travel document issued by a territorial entity or authority which is not recognised by Her Majesty's Government as a state or is not dealt with as a government by them, or which does not accept valid United Kingdom passports for the purpose of its own immigration control; or a passport or travel document which does not comply with international passport practice;

(11)   where the applicant has previously contrived in a significant way to frustrate the intentions of the Rules by:

(i)   overstaying; or

(ii)   breaching a condition attached to his leave; or

(iii)   being an illegal entrant; or

(iv)   using deception in an application for entry clearance, leave to enter or remain or in order to obtain documents from the Secretary of State or a third party required in support of the application (whether successful or not);

and there are other aggravating circumstances, such as absconding, not meeting temporary admission/reporting restrictions or bail conditions, using an assumed identity or multiple identities, switching nationality, making frivolous applications or not complying with the re-documentation process.

(12)   DELETED

(13)   failure, except by a person eligible for admission to the United Kingdom for settlement, to satisfy the Immigration Officer that he will be admitted to another country after a stay in the United Kingdom;

(14)   refusal by a sponsor of a person seeking leave to enter the United Kingdom to give, if requested to do so, an undertaking in writing to be responsible for that person's maintenance and accommodation for the period of any leave granted;

(16)   failure, in the case of a child under the age of 18 years seeking leave to enter the United Kingdom otherwise than in conjunction with an application made by his parent(s) or legal guardian to provide the Immigration Officer, if required to do so, with written consent to the application from his parent(s) or legal guardian; save that the requirement as to written consent does not apply in the case of a child seeking admission to the United Kingdom as an asylum seeker;

(17)   save in relation to a person settled in the United Kingdom, refusal to undergo a medical examination when required to do so by the Immigration Officer;

(18)   DELETED

(18A)   within the 12 months prior to the date on which the application is decided, the person has been convicted of or admitted an offence for which they received a non-custodial sentence or other out of court disposal that is recorded on their criminal record;

(18B)   in the view of the Secretary of State:

(a)   the person's offending has caused serious harm; or

(b)   the person is a persistent offender who shows a particular disregard for the law.

(19)   The immigration officer deems the exclusion of the person from the United Kingdom to be conducive to the public good. For example, because the person's conduct (including convictions which do not fall within paragraph 320(2)), character, associations, or other reasons, make it undesirable to grant them leave to enter.

(20)   failure by a person seeking entry into the United Kingdom to comply with a requirement relating to the provision of physical data to which he is subject by regulations made under section 126 of the Nationality, Immigration and Asylum Act 2002.

(21)   DELETED

(22)   where one or more relevant NHS body has notified the Secretary of State that the person seeking entry or leave to enter has failed to pay a charge or charges with a total value of at least £1000 in accordance with the relevant NHS regulations on charges to overseas visitors.

Refusal of leave to enter in relation to a person in possession of an entry clearance

321.   A person seeking leave to enter the United Kingdom who holds an entry clearance which was duly issued to him and is still current may be refused leave to enter only where the Immigration Officer is satisfied that:

(i)   False representations were made or false documents or information were submitted (whether or not material to the application, and whether or not to the holder's knowledge), or material facts were not disclosed, in relation to the application for entry clearance; or in order to obtain documents from the Secretary of State or a third party required in support of the application.

(ii)   a change of circumstances since it was issued has removed the basis of the holder's claim to admission, except where the change of circumstances amounts solely to the person becoming over age for entry in one of the categories contained in paragraphs 296–316 of these Rules since the issue of the entry clearance; or

(iii)   on grounds which would have led to a refusal under paragraphs 320(2), 320(6), 320(18A), 320(18B) or 320(19) (except where this sub-paragraph applies in respect of an entry clearance issued under Appendix Armed Forces it is to be read as if for 'paragraphs 320(2), 320(6), 320(18A), 320(18B) or 320(19)' it said 'paragraph 8(a), (b), (c) or (g) and paragraph 9(d)').

Grounds on which leave to enter or remain which is in force is to be cancelled at port or while the holder is outside the United Kingdom

321A.   The following grounds for the cancellation of a person's leave to enter or remain which is in force on his arrival in, or whilst he is outside, the United Kingdom apply;

(1)   there has been such a change in the circumstances of that person's case since the leave was given, that it should be cancelled; or

(2)   false representations were made or false documents were submitted (whether or not material to the application, and whether or not to the holder's knowledge), or material facts were not disclosed, in

relation to the application for leave; or in order to obtain documents from the Secretary of State or a third party required in support of the application or,

(3)   save in relation to a person settled in the United Kingdom or where the Immigration Officer or the Secretary of State is satisfied that there are strong compassionate reasons justifying admission, where it is apparent that, for medical reasons, it is undesirable to admit that person to the United Kingdom; or

(4)   where the Secretary of State has personally directed that the exclusion of that person from the United Kingdom is conducive to the public good; or

(4A) Grounds which would have led to a refusal under paragraphs 320(2), 320(6), 320(18A), 320(18B) or 320(19) if the person concerned were making a new application for leave to enter or remain (except where this sub-paragraph applies in respect of leave to enter or remain granted under Appendix Armed Forces it is to be read as if for paragraphs 320(2), 320(6), 320(18A), 320(18B) or 320(19)' it said 'paragraph 8(a), (b), (c) or (g) and paragraph 9(d)'); or

(5)   The Immigration Officer or the Secretary of State deems the exclusion of the person from the United Kingdom to be conducive to the public good. For example, because the person's conduct (including convictions which do not fall within paragraph 320(2)), character, associations, or other reasons, make it undesirable to grant them leave to enter the United Kingdom; or

(6)   where that person is outside the United Kingdom, failure by that person to supply any information, documents, copy documents or medical report requested by an Immigration Officer or the Secretary of State.

Refusal of leave to remain, variation of leave to enter or remain or curtailment of leave

322. In addition to the grounds for refusal of extension of stay set out in Parts 2–8 of these Rules, the following provisions apply in relation to the refusal of an application for leave to remain, variation of leave to enter or remain or, where appropriate, the curtailment of leave, except that only paragraphs (1A), (1B), (5), (5A), (9) and (10) shall apply in the case of an application made under paragraph 159I of these Rules.

Grounds on which leave to remain and variation of leave to enter or remain in the United Kingdom are to be refused

(1)   the fact that variation of leave to enter or remain is being sought for a purpose not covered by these Rules.

(1A) where false representations have been made or false documents or information have been submitted (whether or not material to the application, and whether or not to the applicant's knowledge), or material facts have not been disclosed, in relation to the application or in order to obtain documents from the Secretary of State or a third party required in support of the application.

(1B) the applicant is, at the date of application, the subject of a deportation order or a decision to make a deportation order;

(1C) where the person is seeking indefinite leave to enter or remain:

(i)   they have been convicted of an offence for which they have been sentenced to imprisonment for at least 4 years; or

(ii)   they have been convicted of an offence for which they have been sentenced to imprisonment for at least 12 months but less than 4 years, unless a period of 15 years has passed since the end of the sentence; or

(iii) they have been convicted of an offence for which they have been sentenced to imprisonment for less than 12 months, unless a period of 7 years has passed since the end of the sentence; or

(iv)   they have, within the 24 months prior to the date on which of the application is decided, been convicted of or admitted an offence for which they have received a non-custodial sentence or other out of court disposal that is recorded on their criminal record.

(1D) DELETED.

Grounds on which leave to remain and variation of leave to enter or remain in the United Kingdom should normally be refused

(2)   the making of false representations or the failure to disclose any material fact for the purpose of obtaining leave to enter or a previous variation of leave or in order to obtain documents from the Secretary of State or a third party required in support of the application for leave to enter or a previous variation of leave.

(2A)   the making of false representations or the failure to disclose any material fact for the purpose of obtaining a document from the Secretary of State that indicates the person has a right to reside in the United Kingdom.

(3)   failure to comply with any conditions attached to the grant of leave to enter or remain;

(4)   failure by the person concerned to maintain or accommodate himself and any dependants without recourse to public funds;

(5)   the undesirability of permitting the person concerned to remain in the United Kingdom in the light of his conduct (including convictions which do not fall within paragraph 322(1C), character or associations or the fact that he represents a threat to national security;

(5A)   it is undesirable to permit the person concerned to enter or remain in the United Kingdom because, in the view of the Secretary of State:

(a)   their offending has caused serious harm; or

(b)   they are a persistent offender who shows a particular disregard for the law;

(6)   refusal by a sponsor of the person concerned to give, if requested to do so, an undertaking in writing to be responsible for his maintenance and accommodation in the United Kingdom or failure to honour such an undertaking once given;

(7)   failure by the person concerned to honour any declaration or undertaking given orally or in writing as to the intended duration and/or purpose of his stay;

(8)   failure, except by a person who qualifies for settlement in the United Kingdom or by the spouse or civil partner of a person settled in the United Kingdom, to satisfy the Secretary of State that he will be returnable to another country if allowed to remain in the United Kingdom for a further period;

(9)   failure by an applicant to produce within a reasonable time information, documents or other evidence required by the Secretary of State to establish his claim to remain under these Rules;

(10)   failure, without providing a reasonable explanation, to comply with a request made on behalf of the Secretary of State to attend for interview;

(11)   failure, in the case of a child under the age of 18 years seeking a variation of his leave to enter or remain in the United Kingdom otherwise than in conjunction with an application by his parent(s) or legal guardian, to provide the Secretary of State, if required to do so, with written consent to the application from his parent(s) or legal guardian; save that the requirement as to written consent does not apply in the case of a child who has been admitted to the United Kingdom as an asylum seeker.

(12)   where one or more relevant NHS body has notified the Secretary of State that the person seeking leave to remain or a variation of leave to enter or remain has failed to pay a charge or charges with a total value of at least £1000 in accordance with the relevant NHS regulations on charges to overseas visitors.

Grounds on which leave to enter or remain may be curtailed

323.   A person's leave to enter or remain may be curtailed:

(i)   on any of the grounds set out in paragraph 322(2)–(5A) above (except where this paragraph applies in respect of a person granted leave under Appendix Armed Forces 'paragraph 322(2)-(5A) above' is to read as if it said 'paragraph 322(2) and (3) above and paragraph 8(e) and (g) of Appendix Armed Forces'); or

(ia)   if he uses deception in seeking (whether successfully or not) leave to remain or a variation of leave to remain; or

(ii)   if he ceases to meet the requirements of the Rules under which his leave to enter or remain was granted; or

(iii)   if he is the dependant, or is seeking leave to remain as the dependant, of an asylum applicant whose claim has been refused and whose leave has been curtailed under section 7 of the1993 Act, and he does not qualify for leave to remain in his own right, or

(iv)   on any of the grounds set out in paragraph 339A (i)–(vi) and paragraph 339G (i)–(vi), or

(v)   where a person has, within the first 6 months of being granted leave to enter, committed an offence for which they are subsequently sentenced to a period of imprisonment, or

(vi)   if he was granted his current period of leave as the dependent of a person ('P') and P's leave to enter or remain is being, or has been, curtailed; or

(vii)   if, without a reasonable explanation, he fails to comply with a request made by or on behalf of the Secretary of State under paragraph 39D.

Curtailment of leave in relation to a Tier 2 Migrant, a Tier 5 Migrant or a Tier 4 Migrant

323A.   In addition to the grounds specified in paragraph 323, the leave to enter or remain of a Tier 2 Migrant, a Tier 4 Migrant or a Tier 5 Migrant:

    (a)   is to be curtailed if:

        (i)   in the case of a Tier 2 Migrant or a Tier 5 Migrant:

            (1)   the migrant fails to commence, or

            (2)   the migrant ceases, or will cease, before the end date recorded on the Certificate of Sponsorship Checking Service,

        the employment, volunteering, training or job shadowing (as the case may be) that the migrant has been sponsored to do.

        (ii)   in the case of a Tier 4 Migrant:

            (1)   the migrant fails to commence studying with the sponsor, or

            (2)   the sponsor has excluded or withdrawn the migrant, or the migrant has withdrawn, from the course of studies, or

            (2A)   the migrant's course of study has ceased, or will cease, before the end date recorded on the Certificate of Sponsorship Checking Service, or'

            (3)   the sponsor withdraws their sponsorship of a migrant on the doctorate extension scheme, or

            (4)   the sponsor withdraws their sponsorship of a migrant who, having completed a pre-sessional course as provided in paragraph 120(b) (i) of Appendix A, does not have a knowledge of English equivalent to level B2 of the Council of Europe's Common European Framework for Language Learning in all four components (reading, writing, speaking and listening) or above.

    (b)   may be curtailed if:

        (i)   the migrant's sponsor ceases to have a sponsor licence (for whatever reason); or

        (ii)   the migrant's sponsor transfers the business for which the migrant works, or at which the migrant is studying, to another person; and

            (1)   that person does not have a sponsor licence; and

            (2)   fails to apply for a sponsor licence within 28 days of the date of the transfer of the business; or

            (3)   applies for a sponsor licence but is refused; or

            (4)   makes a successful application for a sponsor licence, but the sponsor licence granted is not in a category that would allow the sponsor to issue a Certificate of Sponsorship or Confirmation of Acceptance for Studies to the migrant;

        (iii)   in the case of a Tier 2 Migrant or a Tier 5 Migrant, if the employment that the Certificate of Sponsorship Checking Service records that the migrant is being sponsored to do undergoes a prohibited change as specified in paragraph 323AA;

        (iv)   paragraph (a) above applies but:

            (1)   the migrant is under the age of 18;

            (2)   the migrant has a dependant child under the age of 18;

            (3)   leave is to be varied such that when the variation takes effect the migrant will have leave to enter or remain and the migrant has less than 60 days extant leave remaining;

            (4)   the migrant has been granted leave to enter or remain with another Sponsor or under another immigration category; or

            (5)   the migrant has a pending application for leave to remain, or variation of leave, with the UK Border Agency, or has a pending appeal under Section 82 of the Nationality, Immigration and Asylum Act 2002, or has a pending administrative review.

Prohibited changes to employment for Tier 2 Migrants and Tier 5 Migrants

323AA.   The following are prohibited changes, unless a further application for leave to remain is granted which expressly permits the changes:

(a)   The migrant is absent from work without pay for 30 days or more in total (whether over a single period or more than one period), during any calendar year (1 January to 31 December), unless the absence from work is due solely to:

    (i)   maternity leave,

    (ii)   paternity leave,

    (iii)   adoption leave, or

    (iv)   long term sick leave of one calendar month or more during any one period.

(b)   The employment changes such that the migrant is working for a different employer or Sponsor, unless:

    (i)   the migrant is a Tier 5 (Temporary Worker) Migrant in the Government Authorised Exchange sub-category and the change of employer is authorised by the Sponsor and under the terms of the work, volunteering or job shadowing that the Certificate of Sponsorship Checking Service records that the migrant is being sponsored to do,

    (ii)   the migrant is working for a different Sponsor under arrangements covered by the Transfer of Undertakings (Protection of Employment) Regulations 2006 or similar protection to continue in the same job, or

    (iii)   the migrant is a Tier 2 (Sportsperson) Migrant or a Tier 5 (Temporary Worker) Migrant in the creative and sporting sub-category and the following conditions are met:

        (1)   The migrant's sponsor is a sports club;

        (2)   The migrant is sponsored as a player only and is being temporarily loaned as a player to another sports club;

        (3)   Player loans are specifically permitted in rules set down by the relevant sports governing body listed in Appendix M;

        (4)   The migrant's sponsor has made arrangements with the loan club to enable the sponsor to continue to meet its sponsor duties; and

        (5)   The migrant will return to working for the sponsor at the end of the loan.

(c)   The employment changes to a job in a different Standard Occupational Classification (SOC) code to that recorded by the Certificate of Sponsorship Checking Service.

(d)   If the migrant is a Tier 2 (Intra-Company Transfer) Migrant or a Tier 2 (General) Migrant, the employment changes to a different job in the same Standard Occupational Classification code to that recorded by the Certificate of Sponsorship Checking Service, and the gross annual salary (including such allowances as are specified as acceptable for this purpose in Appendix A) is below the appropriate salary rate for that new job as specified in the Codes of Practice in Appendix J.

(e)   If the migrant was required to be Sponsored for a job at a minimum National Qualification Framework level in the application which led to his last grant of entry clearance or leave to remain, the employment changes to a job which the Codes of Practice in Appendix J record as being at a lower level.

(f)   If the migrant is a Tier 2 (General) Migrant and scored points from the shortage occupation provisions of Appendix A, the employment changes to a job which does not appear in the Shortage Occupation List in Appendix K.

(g)   Except where (h) applies, the gross annual salary (including such allowances as are specified as acceptable for this purpose in Appendix A) reduces below:

    (i)   any minimum salary threshold specified in Appendix A of these Rules, where the applicant was subject to or relied on that threshold in the application which led to his current grant of entry clearance or leave to remain, or

    (ii)   the appropriate salary rate for the job as specified in the Codes of Practice in Appendix J, or

    (iii)   in cases where there is no applicable threshold in Appendix A and no applicable salary rate in Appendix J, the salary recorded by the Certificate of Sponsorship Checking Service.

(h)   Other reductions in salary are permitted if the reduction coincides with a period of:

    (i)   maternity leave,

    (ii)   paternity leave,

    (iii)   adoption leave,

    (iv)   long term sick leave of one calendar month or more,

    (v)   working for the sponsor's organisation while the migrant is not physically present in the UK, if the migrant is a Tier 2 (Intra-Company Transfer) Migrant, or

(vi)   undertaking professional examinations before commencing work for the sponsor, where such examinations are a regulatory requirement of the job the migrant is being sponsored to do, and providing the migrant continues to be sponsored during that period.

Curtailment of leave in relation to a Tier 1 (Exceptional Talent) Migrant

323B.   In addition to the grounds specified in paragraph 323, the leave to enter or remain of a Tier 1 (Exceptional Talent) Migrant may be curtailed if the Designated Competent Body that endorsed the application which led to the migrant's current grant of leave withdraws its endorsement of the migrant.

Curtailment of leave in relation to a Tier 1 (Graduate Entrepreneur) Migrant

323C.   In addition to the grounds specified in paragraph 323, the leave to enter or remain of a Tier 1 (Graduate Entrepreneur) Migrant may be curtailed if the endorsing body that endorsed the application which led to the migrant's current grant of leave:

(a)   loses its status as an endorsing institution for Tier 1 (Graduate Entrepreneur) Migrants,

(b)   ceases to be a sponsor with Tier 4 Sponsor status,

(c)   ceases to be an A-rated Sponsor under Tier 2 or Tier 5 of the Points-Based System because its Tier 2 or Tier 5 Sponsor licence is downgraded or revoked by the UK Border Agency, or

(d)   withdraws its endorsement of the migrant.

Crew members

324.   A person who has been given leave to enter to join a ship, aircraft, hovercraft, hydrofoil or international train service as a member of its crew, or a crew member who has been given leave to enter for hospital treatment, repatriation or transfer to another ship, aircraft, hovercraft, hydrofoil or international train service in the United Kingdom, is to be refused leave to remain unless an extension of stay is necessary to fulfil the purpose for which he was given leave to enter or unless he meets the requirements for an extension of stay as a spouse or civil partner in paragraph 284.

Part 10 – Registration with the police

For the purposes of paragraph 326, a 'relevant foreign national' is a person aged 16 or over who is:

325.   (i)   a national or citizen of a country or territory listed in Appendix 2 to these Rules;

(ii)   a stateless person; or

(iii) a person holding a non-national travel document.

326.   (1)   Subject to sub-paragraph (2) below, a condition requiring registration with the police should normally be imposed on any relevant foreign national who is:

(i)   given limited leave to enter the United Kingdom for longer than six months; or

(ii)   given limited leave to remain which has the effect of allowing him to remain in the United Kingdom for longer than six months, reckoned from the date of his arrival (whether or not such a condition was imposed when he arrived).

(2)   Such a condition should not normally be imposed where the leave is given:

(i)   as a seasonal agricultural worker;

(ii)   as a Tier 5 (Temporary Worker) Migrant, provided the Certificate of Sponsership Checking System refrence for which points were awarded records that the applicant is being sponsored as an overseas goverment employee or a private servant is a diplomatic household;

(iii) as a Tier 2 (Minister of Religion) Migrant;

(iv)   on the basis of marriage to or civil partnership with a person settled in the United Kingdom or as the unmarried or same-sex partner of a person settled in the United Kingdom

(v)   as a person exercising access rights to a child resident in the United Kingdom;

(vi)   as the parent of a child at school; or

(vii) following the grant of asylum.

(3)   Such a condition should also be imposed on any foreign national given limited leave to enter the United Kingdom where, exceptionally, the Immigration Officer considers it necessary to ensure that he complies with the terms of the leave.

Part 11 – Asylum

Procedure

326A. The procedures set out in these Rules shall apply to the consideration of asylum and humanitarian protection.

326B. Where the Secretary of State is considering a claim for asylum or humanitarian protection under this Part, she will consider any Article 8 elements of that claim in line with the provisions of Appendix FM (family life) which are relevant to those elements and in line with paragraphs 276ADE to 276DH (private life) of these Rules unless the person is someone to whom Part 13 of these Rules applies.

Definition of asylum applicant

327. Under the Rules an asylum applicant is a person who either;

(a) makes a request to be recognised as a refugee under the Geneva Convention on the basis that it would be contrary to the United Kingdom's obligations under the Geneva Convention for him to be removed from or required to leave the United Kingdom, or

(b) otherwise makes a request for international protection. 'Application for asylum' shall be construed accordingly.

327A. Every person has the right to make an application for asylum on his own behalf.

Applications for asylum

328. All asylum applications will be determined by the Secretary of State in accordance with the Geneva Convention. Every asylum application made by a person at a port or airport in the United Kingdom will be referred by the Immigration Officer for determination by the Secretary of State in accordance with these Rules.

328A. The Secretary of State shall ensure that authorities which are likely to be addressed by someone who wishes to make an application for asylum are able to advise that person how and where such an application may be made.

329. Until an asylum application has been determined by the Secretary of State or the Secretary of State has issued a certificate under Part 2, 3, 4 or 5 of Schedule 3 to the Asylum and Immigration (Treatment of Claimants, etc.) Act 2004 no action will be taken to require the departure of the asylum applicant or his dependants from the United Kingdom.

330. If the Secretary of State decides to grant asylum and the person has not yet been given leave to enter, the Immigration Officer will grant limited leave to enter.

331. If a person seeking leave to enter is refused asylum or their application for asylum is withdrawn or treated as withdrawn under paragraph 333C of these Rules, the Immigration Officer will consider whether or not he is in a position to decide to give or refuse leave to enter without interviewing the person further. If the Immigration Officer decides that a further interview is not required he may serve the notice giving or refusing leave to enter by post. If the Immigration Officer decides that a further interview is required, he will then resume his examination to determine whether or not to grant the person leave to enter under any other provision of these Rules. If the person fails at any time to comply with a requirement to report to an Immigration Officer for examination, the Immigration Officer may direct that the person's examination shall be treated as concluded at that time. The Immigration Officer will then consider any outstanding applications for entry on the basis of any evidence before him.

332. If a person who has been refused leave to enter applies for asylum and that application is refused or withdrawn or treated as withdrawn under paragraph 333C of these Rules, leave to enter will again be refused unless the applicant qualifies for admission under any other provision of these Rules.

333. Written notice of decisions on applications for asylum shall be given in reasonable time. Where the applicant is legally represented, notice may instead be given to the representative. Where the applicant has no legal representative and free legal assistance is not available, he shall be informed of the decision on the application for asylum and, if the application is rejected, how to challenge the decision, in a language that he may reasonably be supposed to understand.

333A. The Secretary of State shall ensure that a decision is taken by him on each application for asylum as soon as possible, without prejudice to an adequate and complete examination.

Where a decision on an application for asylum cannot be taken within six months of the date it was recorded, the Secretary of State shall either:

(a) inform the applicant of the delay; or

(b)   if the applicant has made a specific written request for it, provide information on the timeframe within which the decision on his application is to be expected. The provision of such information shall not oblige the Secretary of State to take a decision within the stipulated time-frame.

333B.   Applicants for asylum shall be allowed an effective opportunity to consult, at their own expense or at public expense in accordance with provision made for this by the Legal Services Commission or otherwise, a person who is authorised under Part V of the Immigration and Asylum Act 1999 to give immigration advice. This paragraph shall also apply where the Secretary of State is considering revoking a person's refugee status in accordance with these Rules.

Withdrawal of applications

333C.   If an application for asylum is withdrawn either explicitly or implicitly, consideration of it may be discontinued. An application will be treated as explicitly withdrawn if the applicant signs the relevant form provided by the Secretary of State. An application may be treated as impliedly withdrawn if an applicant leaves the United Kingdom without authorisation at any time prior to the conclusion of his or her asylum claim, or fails to complete an asylum questionnaire as requested by the Secretary of State or fails to attend the personal interview as provided in paragraph 339NA of these Rules unless the applicant demonstrates within a reasonable time that that failure was due to circumstances beyond his or her control. The Secretary of State will indicate on the applicant's asylum file that the application for asylum has been withdrawn and consideration of it has been discontinued.

Grant of asylum

334.   An asylum applicant will be granted asylum in the United Kingdom if the Secretary of State is satisfied that:

(i)   he is in the United Kingdom or has arrived at a port of entry in the United Kingdom;

(ii)   he is a refugee, as defined in regulation 2 of The Refugee or Person in Need of International Protection (Qualification) Regulations 2006;

(iii)   there are no reasonable grounds for regarding him as a danger to the security of the United Kingdom;

(iv)   he does not, having been convicted by a final judgment of a particularly serious crime, he does not constitute danger to the community of the United Kingdom; and

(v)   refusing his application would result in him being required to go (whether immediately or after the time limited by any existing leave to enter or remain) in breach of the Geneva Convention, to a country in which his life or freedom would threatened on account of his race, religion, nationality, political opinion or membership of a particular social group.

335.   If the Secretary of State decides to grant asylum to a person who has been given leave to enter (whether or not the leave has expired) or to a person who has entered without leave, the Secretary of State will vary the existing leave or grant limited leave to remain.

Refusal of asylum

336.   An application which does not meet the criteria set out in paragraph 334 will be refused. Where an application for asylum is refused, the reasons in fact and law shall be stated in the decision and information provided in writing on how to challenge the decision.

337.   DELETED

338.   When a person in the United Kingdom is notified that asylum has been refused he may, if he is liable to removal as an illegal entrant , removal under section 10 of the Immigration and Asylum Act 1999 or to deportation, at the same time be notified of removal directions, served with a notice of intention to make a deportation order, or served with a deportation order, as appropriate.

339.   DELETED

Revocation or refusal to renew a grant of asylum

339A.   A person's grant of asylum under paragraph 334 will be revoked or not renewed if the Secretary of State is satisfied that:

(i)   he has voluntarily re-availed himself of the protection of the country of nationality;

(ii)   having lost his nationality, he has voluntarily re-acquired it; or

(iii)   he has acquired a new nationality, and enjoys the protection of the country of his new nationality;

(iv)   he has voluntarily re-established himself in the country which he left or outside which he remained owing to a fear of persecution;

(v)   he can no longer, because the circumstances in connection with which he has been recognised as a refugee have ceased to exist, continue to refuse to avail himself of the protection of the country of nationality;

(vi)   being a stateless person with no nationality, he is able, because the circumstances in connection with which he has been recognised a refugee have ceased to exist, to return to the country of former habitual residence;

(vii)   he should have been or is excluded from being a refugee in accordance with regulation 7 of The Refugee or Person in Need of International Protection (Qualification) Regulations 2006;

(viii)   his misrepresentation or omission or facts, including the use of false documents, were decisive for the grant of asylum;

(ix)   there are reasonable grounds for regarding him as a danger to the security of the United Kingdom; or

(x)   having been convicted by a final judgment of a particularly serious crime he constitutes danger to the community of the United Kingdom.

In considering (v) and (vi), the Secretary of State shall have regard to whether the change of circumstances is of such a significant and non-temporary nature that the refugee's fear of persecution can no longer be regarded as well-founded.

Where an application for asylum was made on or after the 21st October 2004, the Secretary of State will revoke or refuse to renew a person's grant of asylum where he is satisfied that at least one of the provisions in sub-paragraph (i)–(vi) apply.

339B.   When a person's grant of asylum is revoked or not renewed any limited leave which they have may be curtailed.

339BA.   Where the Secretary of State is considering revoking refugee status in accordance with these Rules, the person concerned shall be informed in writing that the Secretary of State is reconsidering his qualification for refugee status and the reasons for the reconsideration. That person shall be given the opportunity to submit, in a personal interview or in a written statement, reasons as to why his refugee status should not be revoked. If there is a personal interview, it shall be subject to the safeguards set out in these Rules. However, where a person acquires British citizenship status, his refugee status is automatically revoked in accordance with paragraph 339A (iii) upon acquisition of that status without the need to follow the procedure set out above.

Grant of humanitarian protection

339C.   A person will be granted humanitarian protection in the United Kingdom if the Secretary of State is satisfied that:

(i)   he is in the United Kingdom or has arrived at a port of entry in the United Kingdom;

(ii)   he does not qualify as a refugee as defined in regulation 2 of The Refugee or Person in Need of International Protection (Qualification) Regulations 2006;

(iii)   substantial grounds have been shown for believing that the person concerned, if he returned to the country of return, would face a real risk of suffering serious harm and is unable, or, owing to such risk, unwilling to avail himself of the protection of that country; and

(iv)   he is not excluded from a grant of humanitarian protection.

Serious harm consists of:

(i)   the death penalty or execution;

(ii)   unlawful killing;

(iii)   torture or inhuman or degrading treatment or punishment of a person in the country of return; or

(iv)   serious and individual threat to a civilian's life or person by reason of indiscriminate violence in situations of international or internal armed conflict.

Exclusion from humanitarian protection

339D.   A person is excluded from a grant of humanitarian protection under paragraph 339C (iv) where the Secretary of State is satisfied that:

(i)   there are serious reasons for considering that he has committed a crime against peace, a war crime, a crime against humanity, or any other serious crime or instigated or otherwise participated in such crimes;

(ii)   there are serious reasons for considering that he is guilty of acts contrary to the purposes and principles of the United Nations or has committed, prepared or instigated such acts or encouraged or induced others to commit, prepare or instigate instigated such acts;

(iii) there are serious reasons for considering that he constitutes a danger to the community or to the security of the United Kingdom; or

(iv) prior to his admission to the United Kingdom the person committed a crime outside the scope of (i) and (ii) that would be punishable by imprisonment were it committed in the United Kingdom and the person left his country of origin solely in order to avoid sanctions resulting from the crime.

339E. If the Secretary of State decides to grant humanitarian protection and the person has not yet been given leave to enter, the Secretary of State or an Immigration Officer will grant limited leave to enter. If the Secretary of State decides to grant humanitarian protection to a person who has been given limited leave to enter (whether or not that leave has expired) or a person who has entered without leave, the Secretary of State will vary the existing leave or grant limited leave to remain.

Refusal of humanitarian protection

339F. Where the criteria set out in paragraph 339C is not met humanitarian protection will be refused.

Revocation of humanitarian protection

339G. A person's humanitarian protection granted under paragraph 339C will be revoked or not renewed if the Secretary of State is satisfied that at least one of the following applies:

(i) the circumstances which led to the grant of humanitarian protection have ceased to exist or have changed to such a degree that such protection is no longer required;

(ii) the person granted humanitarian protection should have been or is excluded from humanitarian protection because there are serious reasons for considering that he has committed a crime against peace, a war crime, a crime against humanity, or any other serious crime or instigated or otherwise participated in such crimes;

(iii) the person granted humanitarian protection should have been or is excluded from humanitarian protection because there are serious reasons for considering that he is guilty of acts contrary to the purposes and principles of the United Nations or has committed, prepared or instigated such acts or encouraged or induced others to commit, prepare or instigate such acts;

(iv) the person granted humanitarian protection should have been or is excluded from humanitarian protection because there are serious reasons for considering that he constitutes a danger to the community or to the security of the United Kingdom;

(v) the person granted humanitarian protection misrepresented or omitted facts, including the use of false documents, which were decisive to the grant of humanitarian protection; or

(vi) the person granted humanitarian protection should have been or is excluded from humanitarian protection because prior to his admission to the United Kingdom the person committed a crime outside the scope of (ii) and (iii) that would be punishable by imprisonment had it been committed in the United Kingdom and the person left his country of origin solely in order to avoid sanctions resulting from the crime.

In applying (i) the Secretary of State shall have regard to whether the change of circumstances is of such a significant and non-temporary nature that the person no longer faces a real risk of serious harm;

339H. When a person's humanitarian protection is revoked or not renewed any limited leave which they have may be curtailed.

Consideration of applications

339HA. The Secretary of State shall ensure that the personnel examining applications for asylum and taking decisions on his behalf have the knowledge with respect to relevant standards applicable in the field of asylum and refugee law.

339I. When the Secretary of State considers a person's asylum claim, eligibility for a grant of humanitarian protection or human rights claim it is the duty of the person to submit to the Secretary of State as soon as possible all material factors needed to substantiate the asylum claim or establish that he is a person eligible for humanitarian protection or substantiate the human rights claim, which the Secretary of State shall assess in cooperation with the person.

The material factors include:

(i) the person's statement on the reasons for making an asylum claim or on eligibility for a grant of humanitarian protection or for making a human rights claim;

(ii)   all documentation at the person's disposal regarding the person's age, background (including background details of relevant relatives), identity, nationality(ies), country(ies) and place(s) of previous residence, previous asylum applications, travel routes; and

(iii)   identity and travel documents.

339IA. For the purposes of examining individual applications for asylum

(i)   information provided in support of an application and the fact that an application has been made shall not be disclosed to the alleged actor(s) of persecution of the applicant, and

(ii)   information shall not be obtained from the alleged actor(s) of persecution that would result in their being directly informed that an application for asylum has been made by the applicant in question and would jeopardise the physical integrity of the applicant and his dependants, or the liberty and security of his family members still living in the country of origin.

This paragraph shall also apply where the Secretary of State is considering revoking a person's refugee status in accordance with these Rules.

339J.   The assessment by the Secretary of State of an asylum claim, eligibility for a grant of humanitarian protection or a human rights claim will be carried out on an individual, objective and impartial basis. This will include taking into account in particular:

(i)   all relevant facts as they relate to the country of origin or country of return at the time of taking a decision on the grant; including laws and regulations of the country of origin or country of return and the manner in which they are applied;

(ii)   relevant statements and documentation presented by the person including information on whether the person has been or may be subject to persecution or serious harm;

(iii)   the individual position and personal circumstances of the person, including factors such as background, gender and age, so as to assess whether, on the basis of the person's personal circumstances, the acts to which the person has been or could be exposed would amount to persecution or serious harm;

(iv)   whether the person's activities since leaving the country of origin or country of return were engaged in for the sole or main purpose of creating the necessary conditions for making an asylum claim or establishing that he is a person eligible for humanitarian protection or a human rights claim, so as to assess whether these activities will expose the person to persecution or serious harm if he returned to that country; and

(v)   whether the person could reasonably be expected to avail himself of the protection of another country where he could assert citizenship.

339JA. Reliable and up-to-date information shall be obtained from various sources as to the general situation prevailing in the countries of origin of applicants for asylum and, where necessary, in countries through which they have transited. Such information shall be made available to the personnel responsible for examining applications and taking decisions and may be provided to them in the form of a consolidated country information report.

This paragraph shall also apply where the Secretary of State is considering revoking a person's refugee status in accordance with these Rules.

339K.   The fact that a person has already been subject to persecution or serious harm, or to direct threats of such persecution or such harm, will be regarded as a serious indication of the person's well-founded fear of persecution or real risk of suffering serious harm, unless there are good reasons to consider that such persecution or serious harm will not be repeated.

339L.   It is the duty of the person to substantiate the asylum claim or establish that he is a person eligible humanitarian protection or substantiate his human rights claim. Where aspects of the person's statements are not supported by documentary or other evidence, those aspects will not need confirmation when all of the following conditions are met:

(i)   the person has made a genuine effort to substantiate his asylum claim or establish that he is a person eligible humanitarian protection or substantiate his human rights claim;

(ii)   all material factors at the person's disposal have been submitted, and a satisfactory explanation regarding any lack of other relevant material has been given;

(iii)   the person's statements are found to be coherent and plausible and do not run counter to available specific and general information relevant to the person's case;

(iv)   the person has made an asylum claim or sought to establish that he is a person eligible for humanitarian protection or made a human rights claim at the earliest possible time, unless the person can demonstrate good reason for not having done so; and

(v)   the general credibility of the person has been established.

339M.   The Secretary of State may consider that a person has not substantiated his asylum claim or established that he is a person eligible for humanitarian protection or substantiated his human rights claim, and thereby reject his application for asylum, determine that he is not eligible for humanitarian protection or reject his human rights claim, if he fails, without reasonable explanation, to make a prompt and full disclosure of material facts, either orally or in writing, or otherwise to assist the Secretary of State in establishing the facts of the case; this includes, for example, failure to report to a designated place to be fingerprinted, failure to complete an asylum questionnaire or failure to comply with a requirement to report to an immigration officer for examination.

339MA.   Applications for asylum shall be neither rejected nor excluded from examination on the sole ground that they have not been made as soon as possible.

339N.   In determining whether the general credibility of the person has been established the Secretary of State will apply the provisions in s.8 of the Asylum and Immigration (Treatment of Claimants, etc.) Act 2004.

Personal interview

339NA.   Before a decision is taken on the application for asylum, the applicant shall be given the opportunity of a personal interview on his application for asylum with a representative of the Secretary of State who is legally competent to conduct such an interview.

The personal interview may be omitted where:

(i)   the Secretary of State is able to take a positive decision on the basis of evidence available;

(ii)   the Secretary of State has already had a meeting with the applicant for the purpose of assisting him with completing his application and submitting the essential information regarding the application;

(iii)   the applicant, in submitting his application and presenting the facts, has only raised issues that are not relevant or of minimal relevance to the examination of whether he is a refugee, as defined in regulation 2 of the Refugee or Person in Need of International Protection (Qualification) Regulations 2006;

(iv)   the applicant has made inconsistent, contradictory, improbable or insufficient representations which make his claim clearly unconvincing in relation to his having been the object of persecution;

(v)   the applicant has submitted a subsequent application which does not raise any relevant new elements with respect to his particular circumstances or to the situation in his country of origin;

(vi)   the applicant is making an application merely in order to delay or frustrate the enforcement of an earlier or imminent decision which would result in his removal; and

(vii)   it is not reasonably practicable, in particular where the Secretary of State is of the opinion that the applicant is unfit or unable to be interviewed owing to enduring circumstances beyond his control.

The omission of a personal interview shall not prevent the Secretary of State from taking a decision on the application.

Where the personal interview is omitted, the applicant and dependants shall be given a reasonable opportunity to submit further information.

339NB.   (i)   The personal interview mentioned in paragraph 339NA above shall normally take place without the presence of the applicant's family members unless the Secretary of State considers it necessary for an appropriate examination to have other family members present.

(ii)   The personal interview shall take place under conditions which ensure appropriate confidentiality.

339NC.   (i)   A written report shall be made of every personal interview containing at least the essential information regarding the asylum application as presented by the applicant in accordance with paragraph 339I of these Rules.

(ii)   The Secretary of State shall ensure that the applicant has timely access to the report of the personal interview and that access is possible as soon as necessary for allowing an appeal to be prepared and lodged in due time.

339ND.   The Secretary of State shall provide at public expense an interpreter for the purpose of allowing the applicant to submit his case, wherever necessary. The Secretary of State shall select an interpreter who can ensure appropriate communication between the applicant and the representative of the Secretary of State who conducts the interview.

Internal relocation

339O.   (i)   The Secretary of State will not make:

(a)   a grant of asylum if in part of the country of origin a person would not have a well founded fear of being persecuted, and the person can reasonably be expected to stay in that part of the country; or

(b)   a grant of humanitarian protection if in part of the country of return a person would not face a real risk of suffering serious harm, and the person can reasonably be expected to stay in that part of the country.

(ii)   In examining whether a part of the country of origin or country of return meets the requirements in (i) the Secretary of State, when making his decision on whether to grant asylum or humanitarian protection, will have regard to the general circumstances prevailing in that part of the country and to the personal circumstances of the person.

(iii)   (i) applies notwithstanding technical obstacles to return to the country of origin or country of return

Sur place claims

339P.   A person may have a well-founded fear of being persecuted or a real risk of suffering serious harm based on events which have taken place since the person left the country of origin or country of return and/or activates which have been engaged in by a person since he left he country of origin or country of return, in particular where it is established that the activities relied upon constitute the expression and continuation of convictions or orientations held in the country of origin or country of return.

Residence Permits

339Q.   (i)   The Secretary of State will issue to a person granted asylum in the United Kingdom a United Kingdom Residence Permit (UKRP) as soon as possible after the grant of asylum. The UKRP may be valid for five years and renewable, unless compelling reasons of national security or public order otherwise require or where there are reasonable grounds for considering that the applicant is a danger to the security of the UK or having been convicted by a final judgment of a particularly serious crime, the applicant constitutes a danger to the community of the UK or the person's character, conduct or associations otherwise require.

(ii)   The Secretary of State will issue to a person granted humanitarian protection in the United Kingdom a UKRP as soon as possible after the grant of humanitarian protection. The UKRP may be valid for five years and renewable, unless compelling reasons of national security or public order otherwise require or where there are reasonable grounds for considering that the person granted humanitarian protection is a danger to the security of the UK or having been convicted by a final judgment of a serious crime, this person constitutes a danger to the community of the UK or the person's character, conduct or associations otherwise require.

(iii)   The Secretary of State will issue a UKRP to a family member of a person granted asylum or humanitarian protection where the family member does not qualify for such status. A UKRP may be granted for a period of five years. The UKRP is renewable on the terms set out in (i) and (ii) respectively. 'Family member' for the purposes of this sub-paragraph refers only to those who are treated as dependants for the purposes of paragraph 349.

(iv)   The Secretary of State may revoke or refuse to renew a person's UKRP where their grant of asylum or humanitarian protection is revoked under the provisions in the immigration rules.

Requirements for indefinite leave to remain for persons granted asylum or humanitarian protection

339R.   The requirements for indefinite leave to remain for a person granted asylum or humanitarian protection, or their dependants granted asylum or humanitarian protection in line with the main applicant or any dependant granted in accordance with the requirements of paragraphs 352A to 352FJ of these Rules (Family Reunion), are that:

(i)   the applicant has held a UK Residence Permit (UKRP) issued under paragraph 339Q for a continuous period of five years in the UK; and

(ii)   the applicant's UKRP has not been revoked or not renewed under paragraphs 339A or 339G of the immigration rules; and

(iii)   the applicant has not:

(a)   been convicted of an offence for which they have been sentenced to imprisonment for at least 4 years; or

(b)   been convicted of an offence for which they have been sentenced to imprisonment for at least 12 months but less than 4 years, unless a period of 15 years has passed since the end of the sentence; or

(c)   been convicted of an offence for which they have been sentenced to imprisonment for less than 12 months, unless a period of 7 years has passed since the end of the sentence; or

(d)   within the 24 months prior to the date on which the application has been decided been convicted of or admitted an offence for which they have received a non-custodial sentence or other out of court disposal that is recorded on their criminal record; or

(e)   in the view of the Secretary of State caused serious harm by their offending or persistently offended and shown a particular disregard for the law; or

(f)   or in the view of the Secretary of State, at the date on which the application has been decided, demonstrated the undesirability of granting settlement in the United Kingdom in light of his or her conduct (including convictions which do not fall within paragraphs 339R(iii)(a-e)), character or associations; or the fact that he or she represents a threat to national security.

Indefinite leave to remain for a person granted asylum or humanitarian protection

339S.   Indefinite leave to remain for a person granted asylum or humanitarian protection will be granted where each of the requirements in paragraph 339R is met.

Refusal of indefinite leave to remain for a person granted asylum or humanitarian protection

339T.   (i)   Indefinite leave to remain for a person granted asylum or humanitarian protection is to be refused if any of the requirements of paragraph 339R is not met.

(ii)   An applicant refused indefinite leave to remain under paragraph 339T(i) may apply to have their UK Residence Permit extended in accordance with paragraph 339Q.

Consideration of asylum applications and human rights claims

340.   DELETED

341.   DELETED

342.   The actions of anyone acting as an agent of the asylum applicant or human rights claimant may also be taken into account in regard to the matters set out in paragraphs 340 and 341.

343.   DELETED

344.   DELETED

Travel documents

344A.   (i)   After having received a complete application for a travel document, the Secretary of State will issue to a person granted asylum in the United Kingdom and their family members travel documents, in the form set out in the Schedule to the Geneva Convention, for the purpose of travel outside the United Kingdom, unless compelling reasons of national security or public order otherwise require.

(ii)   After having received a complete application for a travel document, the Secretary of State will issue travel documents to a person granted humanitarian protection in the United Kingdom where that person is unable to obtain a national passport or other identity documents which enable him to travel, unless compelling reasons of national security or public order otherwise require.

(iii)   Where the person referred to in (ii) can obtain a national passport or identity documents but has not done so, the Secretary of State will issue that person with a travel document where he can show that he has made reasonable attempts to obtain a national passport or identity document and there are serious humanitarian reasons for travel.

Access to Employment

344B.   The Secretary of State will not impose conditions restricting the employment or occupation in the United Kingdom of a person granted asylum or humanitarian protection.

Information

344C.   A person who is granted asylum or humanitarian protection will be provided with access to information in a language that they may reasonably be supposed to understand which sets out the rights and obligations relating to that status. The Secretary of State will provide the information as soon as possible after the grant of asylum or humanitarian protection.

Third country cases

345. (1)   In a case where the Secretary of State is satisfied that the conditions set out in Paragraphs 4 and 5(1), 9 and 10(1), 14 and 15(1) or 17 of Schedule 3 to the Asylum and Immigration (Treatment of Claimants, etc.) Act 2004 are fulfilled, he will normally decline to examine the asylum application substantively and issue a certificate under Part 2, 3, 4 or 5 of Schedule 3 to the Asylum and Immigration (Treatment of Claimants, etc.) Act 2004 as appropriate.

(2)   The Secretary of State shall not issue a certificate under Part 2, 3, 4 or 5 of Schedule 3 to the Asylum and Immigration (Treatment of Claimants, etc.) Act 2004 unless:

   (i)   the asylum applicant has not arrived in the United Kingdom directly from the country in which he claims to fear persecution and has had an opportunity at the border or within the third country or territory to make contact with the authorities of that third country or territory in order to seek their protection; or

   (ii)   there is other clear evidence of his admissibility to a third country or territory.

Provided that he is satisfied that a case meets these criteria, the Secretary of State is under no obligation to consult the authorities of the third country or territory before the removal of an asylum applicant to that country or territory.

(2A)   Where a certificate is issued under Part 2, 3, 4 or 5 of Schedule 3 to the Asylum and Immigration (Treatment of Claimants, etc.) Act 2004 the asylum applicant shall:

   (i)   be informed in a language that he may reasonably be expected to understand regarding his removal to a safe third country;

   (ii)   be provided with a document informing the authorities of the safe third country, in the language of that country, that the asylum application has not been examined in substance by the authorities in the United Kingdom;

   (iii)   sub-paragraph 345(2A)(ii) shall not apply if removal takes place with reference to the arrangements set out in Regulation (EC) No. 343/2003 or Regulation (EC) No 604/2013 (the Dublin Regulation); and

   (iv)   if an asylum applicant removed under this paragraph is not admitted to the safe third country (not being a country to which the Dublin Regulation applies as specified in paragraph 345(2A)(iii)), subject to determining and resolving the reasons for his nonadmission, the asylum applicant shall be admitted to the asylum procedure in the United Kingdom.

(3)   Where a certificate is issued under Part 2, 3, 4 or 5 of Schedule 3 to the Asylum and Immigration (Treatment of Claimants, etc.) Act 2004 in relation to the asylum claim and the person is seeking leave to enter the Immigration Officer will consider whether or not he is in a position to decide to give or refuse leave to enter without interviewing the person further. If the Immigration Officer decides that a further interview is not required he may serve the notice giving or refusing leave to enter by post. If the Immigration Officer decides that a further interview is required, he will then resume his examination to determine whether or not to grant the person leave to enter under any other provision of these Rules. If the person fails at any time to comply with a requirement to report to an Immigration Officer for examination, the Immigration Officer may direct that the person's examination shall be treated as concluded at that time. The Immigration Officer will then consider any outstanding applications for entry on the basis of any evidence before him.

(4)   Where a certificate is issued under Part 2, 3, 4 or 5 of Schedule 3 to the Asylum and Immigration (Treatment of Claimants, etc.) Act 2004 the person may, if liable to removal as an illegal entrant, or removal under section 10 of the Immigration and Asylum Act 1999 or to deportation, at the same time be notified of removal directions, served with a notice of intention to make a deportation order, or served with a deportation order, as appropriate.

Previously rejected applications

346.   DELETED

347.   DELETED

Rights of appeal

348.   DELETED

Dependants

349. A spouse, civil partner, unmarried or same-sex partner, or minor child accompanying a principal applicant may be included in his application for asylum as his dependant, provided, in the case of an adult dependant with legal capacity, the dependant consents to being treated as such at the time the application is lodged. A spouse, civil partner, unmarried or same-sex partner or minor child may also claim asylum in his own right. If the principal applicant is granted asylum or humanitarian protection and leave to enter or remain any spouse, civil partner, unmarried or same-sex partner or minor child will be granted leave to enter or remain for the same duration. The case of any dependant who claims asylum in his own right will be also considered individually in accordance with paragraph 334 above. An applicant under this paragraph, including an accompanied child, may be interviewed where he makes a claim as a dependant or in his own right.

If the spouse, civil partner, unmarried or same-sex partner, or minor child in question has a claim in his own right, that claim should be made at the earliest opportunity. Any failure to do so will be taken into account and may damage credibility if no reasonable explanation for it is given. Where an asylum or humanitarian protection application is unsuccessful, at the same time that asylum or humanitarian protection is refused the applicant may be notified of removal directions or served with a notice of the Secretary of State's intention to deport him, as appropriate. In this paragraph and paragraphs 350–352 a child means a person who is under 18 years of age or who, in the absence of documentary evidence establishing age, appears to be under that age. An unmarried or same sex partner for the purposes of this paragraph, is a person who has been living together with the principal applicant in a subsisting relationship akin to marriage or a civil partnership for two years or more.

Unaccompanied children

350. Unaccompanied children may also apply for asylum and, in view of their potential vulnerability, particular priority and care is to be given to the handling of their cases.

351. A person of any age may qualify for refugee status under the Convention and the criteria in paragraph 334 apply to all cases. However, account should be taken of the applicant's maturity and in assessing the claim of a child more weight should be given to objective indications of risk than to the child's state of mind and understanding of his situation. An asylum application made on behalf of a child should not be refused solely because the child is too young to understand his situation or to have formed a well founded fear of persecution. Close attention should be given to the welfare of the child at all times.

352. Any child over the age of 12 who has claimed asylum in his own right shall be interviewed about the substance of his claim unless the child is unfit or unable to be interviewed. When an interview takes place it shall be conducted in the presence of a parent, guardian, representative or another adult independent of the Secretary of State who has responsibility for the child. The interviewer shall have specialist training in the interviewing of children and have particular regard to the possibility that a child will feel inhibited or alarmed. The child shall be allowed to express himself in his own way and at his own speed. If he appears tired or distressed, the interview will be suspended. The interviewer should then consider whether it would be appropriate for the interview to be resumed the same day or on another day.

352ZA. The Secretary of State shall as soon as possible after an unaccompanied child makes an application for asylum take measures to ensure that a representative represents and/or assists the unaccompanied child with respect to the examination of the application and ensure that the representative is given the opportunity to inform the unaccompanied child about the meaning and possible consequences of the interview and, where appropriate, how to prepare himself for the interview. The representative shall have the right to be present at the interview and ask questions and make comments in the interview, within the framework set by the interviewer.

352ZB. The decision on the application for asylum shall be taken by a person who is trained to deal with asylum claims from children.

Requirements for limited leave to remain as an unaccompanied asylum seeking child.

352ZC. The requirements to be met in order for a grant of limited leave to remain to be made in relation to an unaccompanied asylum seeking child under paragraph 352ZE are:

(a) the applicant is an unaccompanied asylum seeking child under the age of 17 ½ years throughout the duration of leave to be granted in this capacity;

(b) the applicant must have applied for asylum and been refused Refugee Leave and Humanitarian Protection;

(c) there are no adequate reception arrangements in the country to which they would be returned if leave to remain was not granted;

    (d)   the applicant must not be excluded from a grant of asylum under Regulation 7 of the Refugee or Person in Need of International Protection (Qualification) Regulations 2006 or excluded from a grant of Humanitarian Protection under paragraph 339D or both;

    (e)   there are no reasonable grounds for regarding the applicant as a danger to the security of the United Kingdom;

    (f)   the applicant has not been convicted by a final judgment of a particularly serious crime, and the applicant does not constitute a danger to the community of the United Kingdom; and

    (g)   the applicant is not, at the date of their application, the subject of a deportation order or a decision to make a deportation order.

352ZD.   An unaccompanied asylum seeking child is a person who:

    (a)   is under 18 years of age when the asylum application is submitted.

    (b)   is applying for asylum in their own right; and

    (c)   is separated from both parents and is not being cared for by an adult who in law or by custom has responsibility to do so.

352ZE.   Limited leave to remain should be granted for a period of 30 months or until the child is 17 ½ years of age whichever is shorter, provided that the Secretary of State is satisfied that the requirements in paragraph 352ZC are met.

352ZF.   Limited leave granted under this provision will cease if

    (a)   any one or more of the requirements listed in paragraph 352ZC cease to be met, or

    (b)   a misrepresentation or omission of facts, including the use of false documents, were decisive for the grant of leave under 352ZE.

352A.   The requirements to be met by a person seeking leave to enter or remain in the United Kingdom as the spouse civil partner of a refugee are that:

    (i)   the applicant is married to or the civil partner of a person who is currently a refugee granted status as such under the immigration rules in the United Kingdom ; and

    (ii)   the marriage or civil partnership did not take place after the person granted asylum left the country of his former habitual residence in order to seek asylum; an

    (iii)   the applicant would not be excluded from protection by virtue of article 1F of the United Nations Convention and Protocol relating to the Status of Refugees if he were to seek asylum in his own right; and

    (iv)   each of the parties intends to live permanently with the other as his or her spouse civil partner and the marriage is subsisting; and

    (v)   if seeking leave to enter, the applicant holds a valid United Kingdom entry clearance for entry in this capacity.

352AA.   The requirements to be met by a person seeking leave to enter or remain in the United Kingdom as the unmarried or the same-sex partner of a refugee are that:

    (i)   the applicant is the unmarried or same-sex partner of a person who is currently a refugee granted status as such under the immigration rules in the United Kingdom and was granted that status in the UK on or after 9th October 2006; and

    (ii)   the parties have been living together in a relationship akin to either a marriage or a civil partnership which has subsisted for two years or more; and

    (iii)   the relationship existed before the person granted asylum left the country of his former habitual residence in order to seek asylum; and

    (iv)   the applicant would not be excluded from protection by virtue of paragraph 334(iii) or

    (v)   of these Rules or article 1F of the Geneva Convention if he were to seek asylum in his own right; and

    (vi)   each of the parties intends to live permanently with the other as his or her unmarried or same-sex partner and the relationship is subsisting; and

    (vii)   if seeking leave to enter, the applicant holds a valid United Kingdom entry clearance for entry in this capacity.

    (viii)   the parties are not involved in a consanguineous relationship with one another; and

352B.   Limited leave to enter the United Kingdom as the spouse civil partner of a refugee may be granted provided a valid United Kingdom entry clearance for entry in this capacity is produced to the Immigration Officer on arrival. Limited leave to remain in the United Kingdom as the spouse of a refugee may be granted provided the Secretary of State is satisfied that each of the requirements of paragraph 352A (i)–(v) are met.

352BA.   Limited leave to enter the United Kingdom as the unmarried or same-sex partner of a refugee may be granted provided a valid United Kingdom entry clearance for entry in this capacity is produced to the Immigration Officer on arrival. Limited leave to remain in the United Kingdom as the unmarried or same sex partner of a refugee may be granted provided the Secretary of State is satisfied that each of the requirements of paragraph 352AA (i)–(vii) are met.

352C.   Limited leave to enter the United Kingdom as the spouse civil partner of a refugee is to be refused if a valid United Kingdom entry clearance for entry in this capacity is not produced to the Immigration Officer on arrival. Limited leave to remain as the spouse civil partner of a refugee is to be refused if the Secretary of State is not satisfied that each of the requirements of paragraph 352A (i)–(v) are met.

352CA.   Limited leave to enter the United Kingdom as the unmarried or same-sex partner of a refugee is to be refused if a valid United Kingdom entry clearance for entry in this capacity is not produced to the Immigration Officer on arrival. Limited leave to remain as the unmarried or same sex partner of a refugee is to be refused if the Secretary of State is not satisfied that each of the requirements of paragraph 352AA (i)–(vi) are met.

352D.   The requirements to be met by a person seeking leave to enter or remain in the United Kingdom in order to join or remain with the parent who is currently a refugee granted status as such under the immigration rules in the United Kingdom are that the applicant:

(i)   is the child of a parent who is currently a refugee granted status as such under the immigration rules in the United Kingdom; and

(ii)   is under the age of 18, and

(iii)   is not leading an independent life, is unmarried and is not a civil partner, and has not formed an independent family unit; and

(iv)   was part of the family unit of the person granted asylum at the time that the person granted asylum left the country of his habitual residence in order to seek asylum; and

(v)   would not be excluded from protection by virtue of article 1F of the United Nations Convention and Protocol relating to the Status of Refugees if he were to seek asylum in his own right; and

(vi)   if seeking leave to enter, holds a valid United Kingdom entry clearance for entry in this capacity.

352E.   Limited leave to enter the United Kingdom as the child of a refugee may be granted provided a valid United Kingdom entry clearance for entry in this capacity is produced to the Immigration Officer on arrival. Limited leave to remain in the United Kingdom as the child of a refugee may be granted provided the Secretary of State is satisfied that each of the requirements of paragraph 352D (i)–(v) are met.

352F.   Limited leave to enter the United Kingdom as the child of a refugee is to be refused if a valid United Kingdom entry clearance for entry in this capacity is not produced to the Immigration Officer on arrival. Limited leave to remain as the child of a refugee is to be refused if the Secretary of State is not satisfied that each of the requirements of paragraph 352D (i)–(v) are met.

352FA.   The requirements to be met by a person seeking leave to enter or remain in the United Kingdom as the spouse or civil partner of a person who is currently a beneficiary of humanitarian protection granted under the immigration rules in the United Kingdom and was granted that status on or after 30 August 2005 are that:

(i)   the applicant is married to or the civil partner of a person who is currently a beneficiary of humanitarian protection granted under the immigration rules and was granted that status on or after 30 August 2005; and

(ii)   the marriage or civil partnership did not take place after the person granted humanitarian protection left the country of his former habitual residence in order to seek asylum in the UK; and

(iii)   the applicant would not be excluded from a grant of humanitarian protection for any of the reasons in paragraph 339D; and

(iv)   each of the parties intend to live permanently with the other as his or her spouse or civil partner and the marriage or civil partnership is subsisting; and

(v)   if seeking leave to enter, the applicant holds a valid United Kingdom entry clearance for entry in this capacity.

352FB.   Limited leave to enter the United Kingdom as the spouse or civil partner of a person granted humanitarian protection may be granted provided a valid United Kingdom entry clearance for entry in this capacity is produced to the Immigration Officer on arrival. Limited leave to remain in the United Kingdom as the spouse or civil partner of a person granted humanitarian protection may be granted provided the Secretary of State is satisfied that each of the requirements in sub paragraphs 352FA(i)–(iv) are met.

352FC.   Limited leave to enter the United Kingdom as the spouse or civil partner of a person granted humanitarian protection is to be refused if a valid United Kingdom entry clearance for entry in this capacity is not produced to the Immigration Officer on arrival. Limited leave to remain as the spouse or civil partner of a person granted humanitarian protection is to be refused if the Secretary of State is not satisfied that each of the requirements in sub paragraphs 352FA (i)–(iv) are met.

352FD.   The requirements to be met by a person seeking leave to enter or remain in the United Kingdom as the unmarried or same-sex partner of a person who is currently a beneficiary of humanitarian protection granted under the immigration rules in the United Kingdom are that:

   (i)   the applicant is the unmarried or same-sex partner of a person who is currently a beneficiary of humanitarian protection granted under the immigration rules and was granted that status on or after 9th October 2006; and

   (ii)   the parties have been living together in a relationship akin to either a marriage or a civil partnership which has subsisted for two years or more; and

   (iii)   the relationship existed before the person granted humanitarian protection left the country of his former habitual residence in order to seek asylum; and

   (iv)   the applicant would not be excluded from a grant of humanitarian protection for any of the reasons in paragraph 339D; and

   (v)   each of the parties intends to live permanently with the other as his or her unmarried or same-sex partner and the relationship is subsisting; and

   (vi)   the parties are not involved in a consanguineous relationship with one another; and

   (vii)   if seeking leave to enter, the applicant holds a valid United Kingdom entry clearance for entry in this capacity.

352FE.   Limited leave to enter the United Kingdom as the unmarried or same-sex partner of a person granted humanitarian protection may be granted provided a valid United Kingdom entry clearance for entry in this capacity is produced to the Immigration Officer on arrival. Limited leave to remain in the United Kingdom as the unmarried or same sex partner of a person granted humanitarian protection may be granted provided the Secretary of State is satisfied that each of the requirements in subparagraphs 352FD (i)–(vi) are met.

352FF.   Limited leave to enter the United Kingdom as the unmarried or same-sex partner of a person granted humanitarian protection is to be refused if a valid United Kingdom entry clearance for entry in this capacity is not produced to the Immigration Officer on arrival. Limited leave to remain as the unmarried or same sex partner of a person granted humanitarian protection is to be refused if the Secretary of State is not satisfied that each of the requirements in sub paragraphs 352FD(i)–(vi) are met.

352FG.   The requirements to be met by a person seeking leave to enter or remain in the United Kingdom in order to join or remain with their parent who is currently a beneficiary of humanitarian protection granted under the immigration rules in the United Kingdom and was granted that status on or after 30 August 2005 are that the applicant:

   (i)   is the child of a parent who is currently a beneficiary of humanitarian protection granted under the immigration rules in the United Kingdom and was granted that status on or after 30 August 2005; and

   (ii)   is under the age of 18, and

   (iii)   is not leading an independent life, is unmarried or is not in a civil partnership, and has not formed an independent family unit; and

   (iv)   was part of the family unit of the person granted humanitarian protection at the time that the person granted humanitarian protection left the country of his habitual residence in order to seek asylum in the UK; and

   (v)   would not be excluded from a grant of humanitarian protection for any of the reasons in paragraph 339D; and

   (vi)   if seeking leave to enter, holds a valid United Kingdom entry clearance for entry in this capacity.

352FH.   Limited leave to enter the United Kingdom as the child of a person granted humanitarian protection may be granted provided a valid United Kingdom entry clearance for entry in this capacity is produced to the Immigration Officer on arrival. Limited leave to remain in the United Kingdom as the child of a person granted humanitarian protection may be granted provided the Secretary of State is satisfied that each of the requirements in sub paragraphs 352FG (i)–(v) are met.

352FI.   Limited leave to enter the United Kingdom as the child of a person granted humanitarian protection is to be refused if a valid United Kingdom entry clearance for entry in this capacity is not produced to the Immigration Officer on arrival. Limited leave to remain as the child of a person granted humanitarian protection is to be refused if the Secretary of State is not satisfied that each of the requirements in sub paragraphs 352FG (i)–(v) are met.

352FJ. Nothing in paragraphs 352A–352FI shall allow a person to be granted leave to enter or remain in the United Kingdom as the spouse or civil partner, unmarried or same sex partner or child of a refugee, or of a person granted humanitarian protection under the immigration rules in the United Kingdom on or after 30 August 2005, if the refugee or, as the case may be, person granted humanitarian protection, is a British Citizen.

Interpretation

352G. For the purposes of this Part:

(a) 'Geneva Convention' means the United Nations Convention and Protocol relating to the Status of Refugees;

(b) 'Country of return' means a country or territory listed in paragraph 8(c) of Schedule 2 of the Immigration Act 1971;

(c) 'Country of origin' means the country or countries of nationality or, for a stateless person, or former habitual residence.

Restriction on study

352H here a person is granted leave in accordance with the provisions set out in Part 11 of the Immigration Rules that leave will, in addition to any other conditions which may apply, be granted subject to the condition in Part 15 of these Rules.

Part 11A – Temporary Protection

Definition of Temporary Protection Directive

354. For the purposes of paragraphs 355 to 356B, 'Temporary Protection Directive' means Council Directive 2001/55/EC of 20 July 2001 regarding the giving of temporary protection by Member States in the event of a mass influx of displaced persons.

Grant of temporary protection

355. An applicant for temporary protection will be granted temporary protection if the Secretary of State is satisfied that:

(i) the applicant is in the United Kingdom or has arrived at a port of entry in the United Kingdom; and

(ii) the applicant is a person entitled to temporary protection as defined by, and in accordance with, the Temporary Protection Directive; and

(iii) the applicant does not hold an extant grant of temporary protection entitling him to reside in another Member State of the European Union. This requirement is subject to the provisions relating to dependants set out in paragraphs 356 to 356B and to any agreement to the contrary with the Member State in question; and

(iv) the applicant is not excluded from temporary protection under the provisions in paragraph 355A.

355A. An applicant or a dependant may be excluded from temporary protection if:

(i) there are serious reasons for considering that:

(a) he has committed a crime against peace, a war crime, or a crime against humanity, as defined in the international instruments drawn up to make provision in respect of such crimes; or

(b) he has committed a serious non-political crime outside the United Kingdom prior to his application for temporary protection; or

(c) he has committed acts contrary to the purposes and principles of the United Nations, or

(ii) there are reasonable grounds for regarding the applicant as a danger to the security of the United Kingdom or, having been convicted by a final judgment of a particularly serious crime, to be a danger to the community of the United Kingdom.

Consideration under this paragraph shall be based solely on the personal conduct of the applicant concerned. Exclusion decisions or measures shall be based on the principle of proportionality.

355B. If temporary protection is granted to a person who has been given leave to enter or remain (whether or not the leave has expired) or to a person who has entered without leave, the Secretary of State will vary the existing leave or grant limited leave to remain.

355C.   A person to whom temporary protection is granted will be granted limited leave to enter or remain, which is not to be subject to a condition prohibiting employment, for a period not exceeding 12 months. On the expiry of this period, he will be entitled to apply for an extension of this limited leave for successive periods of 6 months thereafter.

355D.   A person to whom temporary protection is granted will be permitted to return to the United Kingdom from another Member State of the European Union during the period of a mass influx of displaced persons as established by the Council of the European Union pursuant to Article 5 of the Temporary Protection Directive.

355E.   A person to whom temporary protection is granted will be provided with a document in a language likely to be understood by him in which the provisions relating to temporary protection and which are relevant to him are set out. A person with temporary protection will also be provided with a document setting out his temporary protection status.

355F.   The Secretary of State will establish and maintain a register of those granted temporary protection. The register will record the name, nationality, date and place of birth and marital status of those granted temporary protection and their family relationship to any other person who has been granted temporary protection.

355G.   If a person who makes an asylum application is also eligible for temporary protection, the Secretary of State may decide not to consider the asylum application until the applicant ceases to be entitled to temporary protection.

Dependants

356.   In this part:

'dependant' means a family member or a close relative.

'family member' means:

(i)   the spouse or civil partner of an applicant for, or a person who has been granted, temporary protection; or

(ii)   the unmarried or same-sex partner of an applicant for, or a person who has been granted, temporary protection where the parties have been living together in a relationship akin to marriage which has subsisted for 2 years or more; or

(iii)   the minor child (who is unmarried and not a civil partner); of an applicant for, or a person who has been granted, temporary protection or his spouse,

who lived with the principal applicant as part of the family unit in the country of origin immediately prior to the mass influx.

'close relative' means:

(i)   the adult child (who is unmarried and not a civil partner), parent or grandparent of an applicant for, or person who has been granted, temporary protection; or

(ii)   sibling (who is unmarried and not a civil partner or the uncle or aunt of an applicant for, or person who has been granted, temporary protection, who lived with the principal applicant as part of the family unit in the country of origin immediately prior to the mass influx and was wholly or mainly dependent upon the principal applicant at that time, and would face extreme hardship if reunification with the principal applicant did not take place.

356A.   A dependant may apply for temporary protection. Where the dependant falls within paragraph 356 and does not fall to be excluded under paragraph 355A, he will be granted temporary protection for the same duration and under the same conditions as the principal applicant.

356B.   When considering any application by a dependant child, the Secretary of State shall take into consideration the best interests of that child.

Part 11B – Asylum

Reception Conditions for non-EU asylum applicants

357.   Part 11B only applies to asylum applicants (within the meaning of these Rules) who are not nationals of a member State.

Information to be provided to asylum applicants

357A.   The Secretary of State shall inform asylum applicants in a language they may reasonably be supposed to understand and within a reasonable time after their claim for asylum has been recorded of the procedure to be followed, their rights and obligations during the procedure, and the possible consequences of non-compliance and non-co-operation. They shall be informed of the likely timeframe for consideration of the application and the means at their disposal for submitting all relevant information.

358.	The Secretary of State shall inform asylum applicants within a reasonable time not exceeding fifteen days after their claim for asylum has been recorded of the benefits and services that they may be eligible to receive and of the rules and procedures with which they must comply relating to them. The Secretary of State shall also provide information on non-governmental organisations and persons that provide legal assistance to asylum applicants and which may be able to help asylum applicants or provide information on available benefits and services.

358A.	The Secretary of State shall ensure that the information referred to in paragraph 358 is available in writing and, to the extent possible, will provide the information in a language that asylum applicants may reasonably be supposed to understand. Where appropriate, the Secretary of State may also arrange for this information to be supplied orally.

Information to be provided by asylum applicants

358B.	An asylum applicant must notify the Secretary of State of his current address and of any change to his address or residential status. If not notified beforehand, any change must be notified to the Secretary of State without delay after it occurs.

The United Nations High Commissioner for Refugees

358C.	A representative of the United Nations High Commissioner for Refugees (UNHCR) or an organisation working in the United Kingdom on behalf of the UNHCR pursuant to an agreement with the government shall:

(a)	have access to applicants for asylum, including those in detention;

(b)	have access to information on individual applications for asylum, on the course of the procedure and on the decisions taken on applications for asylum, provided that the applicant for asylum agrees thereto;

(c)	be entitled to present his views, in the exercise of his supervisory responsibilities under Article 35 of the Geneva Convention, to the Secretary of State regarding individual applications for asylum at any stage of the procedure.

This paragraph shall also apply where the Secretary of State is considering revoking a person's refugee status in accordance with these Rules.

Documentation

359.	The Secretary of State shall ensure that, within three working days of recording an asylum application, a document is made available to that asylum applicant, issued in his own name, certifying his status as an asylum applicant or testifying that he is allowed to remain in the United Kingdom while his asylum application is pending. For the avoidance of doubt, in cases where the Secretary of State declines to examine an application it will no longer be pending for the purposes of this rule.

359A.	The obligation in paragraph 359 above shall not apply where the asylum applicant is detained under the Immigration Acts, the Immigration and Asylum Act 1999 or the Nationality, Immigration and Asylum Act 2002.

359B.	A document issued to an asylum applicant under paragraph 359 does not constitute evidence of the asylum applicant's identity.

359C.	In specific cases the Secretary of State or an Immigration Officer may provide an asylum applicant with evidence equivalent to that provided under rule 359. This might be, for example, in circumstances in which it is only possible or desirable to issue a time-limited document.

Right to request permission to take up employment

360.	An asylum applicant may apply to the Secretary of State for permission to take up employment if a decision at first instance has not been taken on the applicant's asylum application within one year of the date on which it was recorded. The Secretary of State shall only consider such an application if, in the Secretary of State's opinion, any delay in reaching a decision at first instance cannot be attributed to the applicant.

360A.	If permission to take up employment is granted under paragraph 360, that permission will be subject to the following restrictions:

        (i)   employment may only be taken up in a post which is, at the time an offer of employment is accepted, included on the list of shortage occupations published by the United Kingdom Border Agency (as that list is amended from time to time);

        (ii)   no work in a self-employed capacity; and

        (iii)   no engagement in setting up a business.

360B.   If an asylum applicant is granted permission to take up employment under paragraph 360 this shall only be until such time as his asylum application has been finally determined.

360C.   Where an individual makes further submissions which raise asylum grounds and which fall to be considered under paragraph 353 of these Rules, that individual may apply to the Secretary of State for permission to take up employment if a decision pursuant to paragaph 353 of these Rules has not been taken on the further submissions within one year of the date on which they were recorded. The Secretary of State shall only consider such an application if, in the Secretary of State's opinion, any delay in reaching a decision pursuant to paragraph 353 of these Rules cannot be attributed to the individual.

360D.   If permission to take up employment is granted under paragraph 360C, that permission will be subject to the following restrictions:

        (i)   employment may only be taken up in a post which is, at the time an offer of employment is accepted, included on the list of shortage occupations published by the United Kingdom Border Agency (as that list is amended from time to time);

        (ii)   no work in a self-employed capacity; and

        (iii)   no engagement in setting up a business.

360E.   Where permission to take up employment is granted pursuant to paragraph 360C, this shall only be until such time as:

        (i)   a decision has been taken pursuant to paragraph 353 that the further submissions do not amount to a fresh claim; or

        (ii)   where the further submissions are considered to amount to a fresh claim for asylum pursuant to paragraph 353, all rights of appeal from the immigration decision made in consequence of the rejection of the further submissions have been exhausted.

Interpretation

361.   For the purposes of this Part–

        (a)   'working day' means any day other than a Saturday or Sunday, a bank holiday, Christmas day or Good Friday;

        (b)   'member State' has the same meaning as in Schedule 1 to the European Communities Act 1972.

Part 12 – Procedure and rights of appeal

Fresh Claims

353.   When a human rights or asylum claim has been refused or withdrawn or treated as withdrawn under paragraph 333C of these Rules and any appeal relating to that claim is no longer pending, the decision maker will consider any further submissions and, if rejected, will then determine whether they amount to a fresh claim. The submissions will amount to a fresh claim if they are significantly different from the material that has previously been considered. The submissions will only be significantly different if the content:

        (i)   had not already been considered; and

        (ii)   taken together with the previously considered material, created a realistic prospect of success, notwithstanding its rejection.

This paragraph does not apply to claims made overseas.

353A.   Consideration of further submissions shall be subject to the procedures set out in these Rules. An applicant who has made further submissions shall not be removed before the Secretary of State has considered the submissions under paragraph 353 or otherwise.

Exceptional Circumstances

353B.   Where further submissions have been made and the decision maker has established whether or not they amount to a fresh claim under paragraph 353 of these Rules, or in cases with no outstanding further submissions whose appeal rights have been exhausted and which are subject to a review, the decision maker will also have regard to the migrant's:

(i)   character, conduct and associations including any criminal record and the nature of any offence of which the migrant concerned has been convicted;

(ii) compliance with any conditions attached to any previous grant of leave to enter or remain and compliance with any conditions of temporary admission or immigration bail where applicable;

(iii) length of time spent in the United Kingdom spent for reasons beyond the migrant's control after the human rights or asylum claim has been submitted or refused; in deciding whether there are exceptional circumstances which mean that removal from the United Kingdom is no longer appropriate.

This paragraph does not apply to submissions made overseas.

This paragraph does not apply where the person is liable to deportation.

Part 13 – Deportation

A deportation order

A362.   Where Article 8 is raised in the context of deportation under Part 13 of these Rules, the claim under Article 8 will only succeed where the requirements of these rules as at 24 July 2014 are met, regardless of when the notice of intention to deport or the deportation order, as appropriate, was served.

362.   A deportation order requires the subject to leave the United Kingdom and authorises his detention until he is removed. It also prohibits him from re-entering the country for as long as it is in force and invalidates any leave to enter or remain in the United Kingdom given him before the Order is made or while it is in force.

363.   The circumstances in which a person is liable to deportation include:

(i)   where the Secretary of State deems the person's deportation to be conducive to the public good;

(ii) where the person is the spouse or civil partner or child under 18 of a person ordered to be deported; and

(iii) where a court recommends deportation in the case of a person over the age of 17 who has been convicted of an offence punishable with imprisonment.

363A.   Prior to 2 October 2000, a person would have been liable to deportation in certain circumstances in which he is now liable to administrative removal. However, such a person remains liable to deportation, rather than administrative removal where:

(i)   a decision to make a deportation order against him was taken before 2 October 2000; or

(ii) the person has made a valid application under the Immigration (Regularisation Period for Overstayers) Regulations 2000.

Deportation of family members

364.   DELETED

364A.   DELETED

365.   The Secretary of State will not normally decide to deport the spouse or civil partner of a deportee under section 5 of the Immigration Act 1971 where:

(i)   he has qualified for settlement in his own right; or

(ii) he has been living apart from the deportee.

366.   The Secretary of State will not normally decide to deport the child of a deportee under section 5 of the Immigration Act 1971 where:

(i)   he and his mother or father are living apart from the deportee; or

(ii) he has left home and established himself on an independent basis; or

(iii) he married or formed a civil partnership before deportation came into prospect.

367.   DELETED

368.   DELETED

369.–375.   DELETED

Hearing of appeals

376.–380.   DELETED

Procedure

381.   When a decision to make a deportation order has been taken (otherwise than on the recommendation of a court) a notice will be given to the person concerned informing him of the decision.

382.   Following the issue of such a notice the Secretary of State may authorise detention or make an order restricting a person as to residence, employment or occupation and requiring him to report to the police, pending the making of a deportation order.

383., 384.   DELETED

Arrangements for removal

385.   A person against whom a deportation order has been made will normally be removed from the United Kingdom. The power is to be exercised so as to secure the person's return to the country of which he is a national, or which has most recently provided him with a travel document, unless he can show that another country will receive him. In considering any departure from the normal arrangements, regard will be had to the public interest generally, and to any additional expense that may fall on public funds.

386.   DELETED

Supervised departure

387.   DELETED

Returned deportees

388.   Where a person returns to the UK when a deportation order is in force against him, he may be deported under the original order. The Secretary of State will consider every such case in the light of all the relevant circumstances before deciding whether to enforce the order.

Returned family members

389.   Persons deported in the circumstances set out in paragraphs 365–368 above (deportation of family members) may be able to seek re-admission to the United Kingdom under the Immigration Rules where:

(i)   a child reaches 18 (when he ceases to be subject to the deportation order); or

(ii)   in the case of a spouse or civil partner, the marriage or civil partnership comes to an end.

Revocation of deportation order

390.   An application for revocation of a deportation order will be considered in the light of all the circumstances including the following:

(i)   the grounds on which the order was made;

(ii)   any representations made in support of revocation;

(iii)   the interests of the community, including the maintenance of an effective immigration control;

(iv)   the interests of the applicant, including any compassionate circumstances.

390A.   Where paragraph 398 applies the Secretary of State will consider whether paragraph 399 or 399A applies and, if it does not, it will only be in exceptional circumstances that the public interest in maintaining the deportation order will be outweighed by other factors.

391.   In the case of a person who has been deported following conviction for a criminal offence, the continuation of a deportation order against that person will be the proper course:

(a)   in the case of a conviction for an offence for which the person was sentenced to a period of imprisonment of less than 4 years, unless 10 years have elapsed since the making of the deportation order, when, if an application for revocation is received, consideration will be given on a case by case basis to whether the deportation order should be maintained, or

(b)   in the case of a conviction for an offence for which the person was sentenced to a period of imprisonment of at least 4 years, at any time,

Unless, in either case, the continuation would be contrary to the Human Rights Convention or the Convention and Protocol Relating to the Status of Refugees, or there are other exceptional circumstances that mean the continuation is outweighed by compelling factors.

391A.   In other cases, revocation of the order will not normally be authorised unless the situation has been materially altered, either by a change of circumstances since the order was made, or by fresh information coming to light which was not before the appellate authorities or the Secretary of State. The passage of time since the person was deported may also in itself amount to such a change of circumstances as to warrant revocation of the order.

392. Revocation of a deportation order does not entitle the person concerned to re-enter the United Kingdom; it renders him eligible to apply for admission under the Immigration Rules. Application for revocation of the order may be made to the Entry Clearance Officer or direct to the Home Office.

Rights of appeal in relation to a decision not to revoke a deportation order

393.–395. DELETED

396. Where a person is liable to deportation the presumption shall be that the public interest requires deportation. It is in the public interest to deport where the Secretary of State must make a deportation order in accordance with section 32 of the UK Borders Act 2007.

397. A deportation order will not be made if the person's removal pursuant to the order would be contrary to the UK's obligations under the Refugee Convention or the Human Rights Convention. Where deportation would not be contrary to these obligations, it will only be in exceptional circumstances that the public interest in deportation is outweighed.

Deportation and Article 8

A398. These rules apply where:

(a) a foreign criminal liable to deportation claims that his deportation would be contrary to the United Kingdom's obligations under Article 8 of the Human Rights Convention;

(b) a foreign criminal applies for a deportation order made against him to be revoked.

398. Where a person claims that their deportation would be contrary to the UK's obligations under Article 8 of the Human Rights Convention, and

(a) the deportation of the person from the UK is conducive to the public good and in the public interest because they have been convicted of an offence for which they have been sentenced to a period of imprisonment of at least 4 years;

(b) the deportation of the person from the UK is conducive to the public good and in the public interest because they have been convicted of an offence for which they have been sentenced to a period of imprisonment of less than 4 years but at least 12 months; or

(c) the deportation of the person from the UK is conducive to the public good and in the public interest because, in the view of the Secretary of State, their offending has caused serious harm or they are a persistent offender who shows a particular disregard for the law,

the Secretary of State in assessing that claim will consider whether paragraph 399 or 399A applies and, if it does not, the public interest in deportation will only be outweighed by other factors where there are very compelling circumstances over and above those described in paragraphs 399 and 399A.

399. This paragraph applies where paragraph 398 (b) or (c) applies if –

(a) the person has a genuine and subsisting parental relationship with a child under the age of 18 years who is in the UK, and

  (i) the child is a British Citizen; or

  (ii) the child has lived in the UK continuously for at least the 7 years immediately preceding the date of the immigration decision; and in either case

   (a) it would be unduly harsh for the child to live in the country to which the person is to be deported; and

   (b) it would be unduly harsh for the child to remain in the UK without the person who is to be deported; or

(b) the person has a genuine and subsisting relationship with a partner who is in the UK and is a British Citizen or settled in the UK, and

  (i) the relationship was formed at a time when the person (deportee) was in the UK lawfully and their immigration status was not precarious; and

  (ii) it would be unduly harsh for that partner to live in the country to which the person is to be deported, because of compelling circumstances over and above those described in paragraph EX.2. of Appendix FM; and

  (iii) it would be unduly harsh for that partner to remain in the UK without the person who is to be deported.

399A.   This paragraph applies where paragraph 398(b) or (c) applies if –

(a)   the person has been lawfully resident in the UK for most of his life; and

(b)   he is socially and culturally integrated in the UK; and

(c)   there would be very significant obstacles to his integration into the country to which it is proposed he is deported.

399B.   Where an Article 8 claim from a foreign criminal is successful:

(a)   in the case of a person who is in the UK unlawfully or whose leave to enter or remain has been cancelled by a deportation order, limited leave may be granted for periods not exceeding 30 months and subject to such conditions as the Secretary of State considers appropriate;

(b)   in the case of a person who has not been served with a deportation order, any limited leave to enter or remain may be curtailed to a period not exceeding 30 months and conditions may be varied to such conditions as the Secretary of State considers appropriate;

(c)   indefinite leave to enter or remain may be revoked under section 76 of the 2002 Act and limited leave to enter or remain granted for a period not exceeding 30 months subject to such conditions as the Secretary of State considers appropriate;

(d)   revocation of a deportation order does not confer entry clearance or leave to enter or remain or re-instate any previous leave.

399C.   Where a foreign criminal who has previously been granted a period of limited leave under this Part applies for further limited leave or indefinite leave to remain his deportation remains conducive to the public good and in the public interest notwithstanding the previous grant of leave.

399D.   Where a foreign criminal has been deported and enters the United Kingdom in breach of a deportation order enforcement of the deportation order is in the public interest and will be implemented unless there are very exceptional circumstances.

400.   Where a person claims that their removal under paragraphs 8 to 10 of Schedule 2 to the Immigration Act 1971, section 10 of the Immigration and Asylum Act 1999 or section 47 of the Immigration, Asylum and Nationality Act 2006 would be contrary to the UK's obligations under Article 8 of the Human Rights Convention, the Secretary of State may require an application under paragraph 276ADE(1) (private life) or under paragraphs RLTRP.1.1.(a), (b) and (d), R-LTRPT.1.1.(a), (b) and (d) and EX.1. of Appendix FM (family life as a partner or parent) of these rules. Where an application is not required, in assessing that claim the Secretary of State or an immigration officer will, subject to paragraph 353, consider that claim against the requirements to be met (except the requirement to make a valid application) under paragraph 276ADE(1) (private life) or paragraphs RLTRP.1.1.(a), (b) and (d), R-LTRPT.1.1.(a), (b) and (d) and EX.1. of Appendix FM (family life as a partner or parent) of these rules as appropriate and if appropriate the removal decision will be cancelled.

Parts 14, 15 – OMITTED

Appendix 1 – DELETED

Appendix 2 – Countries or territories whose nationals or citizens are relevant foreign nationals for the purposes of Part 10 of these Rules

Registration with the police

Afghanistan
Algeria
Argentina
Armenia
Azerbaijan
Bahrain
Belarus
Bolivia
Brazil
China
Colombia

Cuba
Egypt
Georgia
Iran
Iraq
Israel
Jordan
Kazakhstan
Kuwait
Kyrgyzstan
Lebanon
Libya
Moldova
Morocco
North Korea
Oman
Palestine
Peru
Qatar
Russia
Saudi Arabia
Sudan
Syria
Tajikistan
Tunisia
Turkey
Turkmenistan
United Arab Emirates
Ukraine
Uzbekistan
Yemen

Appendix 3–5 – DELETED

Appendix 6, 7 – OMITTED

Appendix A – Attributes

Attributes for Tier 1 (Exceptional Talent) Migrants

1. An applicant applying for entry clearance, leave to remain or indefinite leave to remain as a Tier 1 (Exceptional Talent) Migrant must score 75 points for attributes.

2. Available points are shown in Table 1.

3. Notes to accompany the table are shown below the table.

Table 1

Applications for entry clearance and leave to remain where the applicant does not have, or has not last had, leave as a Tier 1 (Exceptional Talent) Migrant

Criterion	Points
Endorsed by Designated Competent Body according to that Body's criteria as set out in Appendix L.	75

All other applications for entry clearance and leave to remain and applications for indefinite leave to remain

Criterion		Points
(i)	During his most recent period of leave as a Tier 1 (Exceptional Talent) Migrant, the applicant has earned money in the UK as a result of employment or self- employment in his expert field as previously endorsed by a Designated Competent Body; and	75
(ii)	That Designated Competent Body has not withdrawn its endorsement of the applicant.	

Notes

Tier 1 (Exceptional Talent) Limit

4. (a) The Secretary of State shall be entitled to limit the total number of Tier 1 (Exceptional Talent) endorsements Designated Competent Bodies may make in support of successful applications, for entry clearance and leave to remain in a particular period, to be referred to as the Tier 1 (Exceptional Talent) Limit.

    (b) The Tier 1 (Exceptional Talent) Limit is 1,000 endorsements in total per year (beginning on 6 April and ending on 5 April) which will be allocated to the Designated Competent Bodies as follows:

        (i) 250 endorsements to The Arts Council for the purpose of endorsing applicants with exceptional talent in the fields of arts and culture;

        (ii) 250 endorsements to The Royal Society for the purpose of endorsing applicants with exceptional talent in the fields of natural sciences and medical science research;

        (iii) 150 endorsements to The Royal Academy of Engineering for the purpose of en- dorsing applicants with exceptional talent in the field of engineering

        (iv) endorsements to The British Academy for the purpose of endorsing applicants with exceptional talent in the fields of humanities and social sciences; and

        (v) 200 endorsements to Tech City UK for the purpose of endorsing applicants with exceptional talent in the field of digital technology.

    (c) The Tier 1 (Exceptional Talent) Limit will be operated according to the practice set out in paragraph 5 below.

    (d) If a Designated Competent Body chooses to transfer part of its unused allocation of endorsements to another Designated Competent Body by mutual agreement of both bodies and the Secretary of State, the allocations of both bodies will be adjusted accordingly and the adjusted allocations will be published on the visas and immigration pages of the gov.uk website.

5. (a) Before an applicant applies for entry clearance or leave to remain (unless he has, or last had, leave as a Tier 1 (Exceptional Talent) Migrant), he must make an application for a Designated Competent Body endorsement, and this application must:

        (i) be made to the UK Border Agency using the specified form,

        (ii) state which Designated Competent Body he wishes to endorse his application, and

        (iii) provide the specified evidence set out in Appendix L.

    (b) A number of endorsements will be made available for each Designated Competent Body, as follows:

        (i) From 6 April to 30 September each year, half that body's allocated endorsements under paragraph 4 above.

        (ii) From 1 October to 5 April each year, that body's remaining unused allocated endorsements under paragraph 4 above.

    (c) Unused endorsements will not be carried over from one year to the next.

    (d) If a Designated Competent Body endorses an application for an endorsement, the applicant subsequently uses that endorsement to make an application for entry clearance or leave to remain which is refused, and that refusal is not subsequently overturned, the used endorsement will be returned to the number of endorsements available for the relevant Designated Competent Body, providing the end of the period (6 April to 5 April) to which it relates has not yet passed.

    (e) An application for a Designated Competent Body endorsement will be refused if the Designated Competent Body has reached or exceeded the number of endorsements available to it.

    (f) The number of endorsements available for each Designated Competent Body to endorse Tier 1 (Exceptional Talent) applicants in a particular period, will be reduced by one for each Croatian national that body endorses in that period for the purposes of applying to be deemed a highly skilled person under the Accession of Croatia (Immigration and Worker Authorisation) Regulations 2013.

Endorsement by the relevant Designated Competent Body

6. Points will only be awarded in an application for entry clearance or leave to remain (except where the applicant has, or last had, leave as a Tier 1 (Exceptional Talent) Migrant) for an endorsement from the relevant Designated Competent Body if:

   (a) the applicant provides a valid approval letter from the UK Border Agency for a Designated Competent Body endorsement, which was granted to him no more than three months before the date of the application for entry clearance or leave to remain, and

   (b) the endorsement has not been withdrawn by the relevant Designated Competent Body at the time the application is considered by the UK Border Agency.

Money earned in the UK

6A. Points will only be awarded for money earned in the UK if the applicant provides the following specified documents:

   (a) If the applicant is a salaried employee, the specified documents are at least one of the following:

      (i) payslips confirming his earnings, which must be either:

         (1) original formal payslips issued by the employer and showing the employer's name, or

         (2) accompanied by a letter from the applicant's employer, on company headed paper and signed by a senior official, confirming the payslips are authentic;

      or

      (ii) personal bank statements on official bank stationery, showing the payments made to the applicant; or

      (iii) electronic bank statements, which either:

         (1) are accompanied by a supporting letter from the bank on company headed paper confirming that the documents are authentic, or

         (2) bear the official stamp of the issuing bank on every page of the document;

      or

      (iv) official tax document produced by HM Revenue & Customs or the applicant's employer, which shows earnings on which tax has been paid or will be paid in a tax year, and is either:

         (1) a document produced by HM Revenue & Customs that shows details of declarable taxable income on which tax has been paid or will be paid in a tax year, such as a tax refund letter or tax demand,

         (2) a P60 document produced by an employer as an official return to HM Revenue & Customs, showing details of earnings on which tax has been paid in a tax year, or

         (3) a document produced by a person, business, or company as an official return to HM Revenue & Customs, showing details of earnings on which tax has been paid or will be paid in a tax year, and which has been approved, registered, or stamped by HM Revenue & Customs;

      or

      (v) Dividend vouchers, confirming the gross and net dividend paid by a company to the applicant, normally from its profits. The applicant must provide a separate dividend voucher or payment advice slip for each dividend payment.

   (b) If the applicant has worked in a self-employed capacity, the specified documents are at least one of the following:

      (i) A letter from the applicant's accountant (who must be either a fully qualified chartered accountant or a certified accountant who is a member of a registered body in the UK), on headed paper, which shows a breakdown of the gross and net earnings. The letter should give a breakdown of salary, dividends, profits, tax credits and dates of net payments earned. If the applicant's earnings are a share of the net profit of the company, the letter should also explain this; or

      (ii) Company or business accounts that meet statutory requirements and clearly show:

         (1) the net profit of the company or business made over the earnings period to be assessed,

        (2)   both a profit and loss account (or income and expenditure account if the organisation is not trading for profit), and

        (3)   a balance sheet signed by a director;

or

   (iii)   the applicant has worked as a sponsored researcher, a letter on official headed paper to the applicant from the institution providing the funding, which confirms:

        (1)   the applicant's name,

        (2)   the name of the sponsoring institution providing the funding,

        (3)   the name of the host institution where the applicant's sponsored research is based,

        (4)   the title of the post, and

        (5)   details of the funding provided.

(c)   All applicants must also provide at least one of the following specified documents:

    (i)   A contract of service or work between the applicant and a UK employer or UK institution which indicates the field of work he has undertaken; or

   (ii)   A letter from a UK employer or UK institution on its official headed paper, confirming that the applicant has earned money in his expert field.

7–34-SD.   OMITTED

Attributes for Tier 1 (Entrepreneur) Migrants

35.   An applicant applying for entry clearance, leave to remain or indefinite leave to remain as a Tier 1 (Entrepreneur) Migrant must score 75 points for attributes.

36.   Subject to paragraph 37, available points for applications for entry clearance or leave to remain are shown in Table 4.

36A.   An applicant who is applying for leave to remain and has, or was last granted, entry clearance, leave to enter or leave to remain as:

(i)   a Tier 4 Migrant,

(ii)   a Student,

(iii)   a Student Nurse,

(iv)   a Student Re-sitting an Examination, or

(v)   a Student Writing Up a Thesis,

will only be awarded points under the provisions in (b)(ii) or (b)(iii) in Table 4.

36B.   An applicant who is applying for leave to remain and has, or was last granted, entry clearance, leave to enter or leave to remain as a Tier 1 (Post-Study Work) Migrant will only be awarded points under the provisions in (b)(ii), (b)(iii) or (d) in Table 4.

37.   Available points are shown in Table 5 for an applicant who:

(a)   has had entry clearance, leave to enter or leave to remain as a Tier 1 (Entrepreneur) Migrant, a Businessperson or an Innovator in the 12 months immediately before the date of application, or

(b)   is applying for leave to remain and has, or was last granted, entry clearance, leave to enter or leave to remain as a Tier 1 (Entrepreneur) Migrant, a Businessperson or an Innovator.

38.   Available points for applications for indefinite leave to remain are shown in Table 6.

39.   (a)   Notes to accompany Table 4 appear below Table 4.

    (b)   Notes to accompany Tables 4, 5 and 6 appear below Table 6.

40.   In all cases, an applicant cannot use the same funds to score points for attributes under this Appendix and to score points for maintenance funds for himself or his dependants under Appendices C or E.

Table 4: Applications for entry clearance or leave to remain referred to in paragraph 36

Investment and business activity	Points
(a) The applicant has access to not less than £200,000, or	25
(b) The applicant has access to not less than £50,000 from:	
(i) one or more registered venture capitalist firms regulated by the Financial Conduct Authority (FCA),	

Investment and business activity	Points
(ii) one or more UK Entrepreneurial seed funding competitions which is listed as endorsed on the UK Trade & Investment website, or	
(iii) one or more UK Government Departments, or Devolved Government Departments in Scotland, Wales or Northern Ireland, and made available by the Department(s) for the specific purpose of establishing or expanding a UK business, or	
(c) The applicant:	
(i) is applying for leave to remain,	
(ii) has, or was last granted, leave as a Tier 1 (Graduate Entrepreneur) Migrant, and	
(iii) has access to not less than £50,000, or	
(d) The applicant:	
(i) is applying for leave to remain,	
(ii) has, or was lasted granted, leave as a Tier 1 (Post-Study Work) Migrant, and	
(iii) has access to not less than £50,000.	
An applicant who is applying for leave to remain and has, or was last granted leave as a Tier 1 (General) Migrant will be awarded no points under (a) or (b)(i) above, unless he meets the additional requirements in (1) and (2) below.	
An applicant who is applying for leave to remain and has, or was last granted leave as a Tier 1 (Post-Study Work) Migrant will be awarded no points under (d) above, unless he meets the additional requirements in (1) and (2) below.	
(1) Since before the specified date below and up to the date of his application, the applicant must have been continuously engaged in business activity which was not, or did not amount to, activity pursuant to a contract of service with a business other than his own and, during such period, has been continuously: • registered with HM Revenue & Customs as self-employed, or • registered with Companies House as a director of a new or an existing business. Directors who are on the list of disqualified directors provided by Companies House will not be awarded points.	
(2) Since before the specified date below and up to the date of his application, has continuously been working in an occupation which appears on the list of occupations skilled to National Qualifications Framework level 4 or above, as stated in the Codes of Practice in Appendix J, and provides the specified evidence in paragraph 41-SD. 'Working' in this context means that the core service his business provides to its customers or clients involves the business delivering a service in an occupation at this level. It excludes any work involved in administration, marketing or website functions for the business, and. The specified date in (1) and (2) above is: • 11 July 2014 if the applicant has, or was lasted granted, leave as a Tier 1 (Post-Study Work) Migrant, or • 6 April 2015 if the applicant has, or was last granted, leave as a Tier 1 (General) Migrant.	
The money is held in one or more regulated financial institutions	25
The money is disposable in the UK If the applicant is applying for leave to remain, the money must be held in the UK.	25

Investment: notes

41.   An applicant will only be considered to have access to funds if:

     (a)   The specified documents in paragraph 41-SD are provided to show cash money to the amount required (this must not be in the form of assets and, where multiple documents are provided, they must show the total amount required is available on the same date);

(b)   The specified documents in paragraph 41-SD are provided to show that the applicant has permission to use the money to invest in a business in the UK;

(c)   Where the applicant has held the money for less than a consecutive 90-day period of time, ending no earlier than 31 days before the date of application, the applicant must provide the specified documents for third party funding in paragraph 41-SD, as evidence of the source of the money;

(d)   The money is either held in a UK regulated financial institution or is transferable to the UK; and

(e)   The money will remain available to the applicant until such time as it is spent for the purposes of the applicant's business or businesses. The Secretary of State reserves the right to request further evidence or otherwise verify that the money will remain available, and to refuse the application if this evidence is not provided or it is unable to satisfactorily verify.

41-SD.   The specified documents in Table 4 and paragraph 41, and associated definitions, are as follows:

(a)   Where this paragraph refers to funding being available, unless stated otherwise, this means funding available to:

(i)   the applicant;

(ii)   the entrepreneurial team, if the applicant is applying under the provisions in paragraph 52 of this Appendix; or

(iii)   the applicant's business.

(b)   Where sub-paragraph (a)(iii) above applies and this paragraph refers to the applicant's business, the business must be a company and the applicant must be registered as a director of that business in the UK, and provide a Companies House document showing the address of the registered office in the UK, or head office in the UK if it has no registered office, and the applicant's name, as it appears on the application form, as a director.

(c)   The specified documents to show evidence of the funding available to invest, whether from the applicant's own funds or from one or more third parties, are one or more of the following specified documents:

(i)   A letter from each financial institution holding the funds, to confirm the amount of money available. Each letter must:

(1)   be an original document and not a copy,

(2)   be on the institution's headed paper,

(3)   have been issued by an authorised official of that institution,

(4)   have been produced within the 31 days immediately before the date of application,

(5)   confirm that the institution is regulated by the appropriate body,

(6)   state the applicant's name, and his team partner's name where relevant,

(7)   show the account number and,

(8)   state the date of the document,

(9)   confirm the minimum balance available from the applicant's own funds (if applicable) that has been held in that institution during a consecutive 90-day period of time, ending on the date of the letter,

(10)   for money available from any third party (if applicable) that is held in that institution, confirm that the third party has informed the institution of the amount of money it intends to make available, and that the institution is not aware of the third party having promised to make that money available to any other person,

(11)   confirm the name of each third party and their contact details, including their full address including postal code, and where available landline phone number and any email address, and

(12)   confirm that if the money is not in an institution regulated by the Financial Conduct Authority (FCA) and the Prudential Regulation Authority (PRA), the money can be transferred into the UK; or

(ii)   For money held in the UK only, recent personal bank or building society statements covering a consecutive 90-day period of time, with the most recent statement being dated no earlier than 31 days before the date of application, from each UK financial institution holding the funds, which confirms the amount of money available. Each statement must satisfy the following requirements:

(1)   the statements must be original documents and not copies;

(2)   the bank or building society holding the money must be based in the UK and regulated by the Financial Conduct Authority (FCA) and the Prudential Regulation Authority (PRA);

(3)   the money must be in cash in the account, not Individual Savings Accounts or assets such as stocks and shares;

(4)   the account must be in the applicant's own name only (or both names for an entrepreneurial team or where it is a joint account with the applicant's spouse, civil partner or partner as set out in paragraph 53 below), not in the name of a business or third party;

(5)   each statement must be on the institution's official stationery showing the institution's name and logo, and confirm the applicant's name (and, where relevant, the applicant's entrepreneurial team partner's name), the account number and the date of the statement;

(6)   each statement must have been issued by an authorised official of that institution; and

(7)   if the statements are printouts of electronic statements, they must either be accompanied by a supporting letter from the bank, on the bank's headed paper, confirming the authenticity of the statements, or bear the official stamp of the bank in question on each page of the statement; or

(iii)   For £50,000 from a Venture Capital firm, Seed Funding Competition or UK or Devolved Government Department, a letter from:

(1)   an accountant, who is a member of the Institute of Chartered Accountants in England and Wales, the Institute of Chartered Accountants in Scotland, the Institute of Chartered Accountants in Ireland, the Association of Chartered Certified Accountants, the Association of Authorised Public Accountants, the Chartered Institute of Public Finance and Accountancy, the Institute of Financial Accountants, the Chartered Institute of Management Accountants, or the Association of International Accountants, or

(2)   in the case of money made available from a UK or Devolved Government Department only, an authorised official of either:

a.   the UK or Devolved Government Department, or

b.   an intermediary public body which has been authorised by the UK or Devolved Government Department to award funds from that Department for the specific purpose of establishing or expanding UK businesses.

(iv)   Each letter referred to in (iii) above must:

(1)   be an original document and not a copy,

(2)   be on the organisation's official headed paper,

(3)   be dated within the three months immediately before the date of the application,

(4)   state the applicant's name, and his team partner's name where relevant, or the name of the applicant's business,

(5)   state the date of the document,

(6)   confirm the amount of money available to the applicant, the entrepreneurial team or the applicant's business from the Venture Capital firm, Seed Funding Competition or UK or Devolved Government Department,

(7)   confirm the name of the Venture Capital firm, Seed funding competition or UK or Devolved Government Department providing the funding, and

(8)   include the contact details of an official of the organisation, including their full address, postal code and, where available, landline phone number and any email address,

(d)   If the applicant is applying using money from a third party, which is either held by the third party or has been transferred to the applicant less than 90 days before the date of the application, he must provide all of the following specified documents, in addition to the specified documents in (c) above:

(i)   An original written declaration from every third party that they have made the money available to invest in a business in the United Kingdom, containing:

(1)   the names of the third party and the applicant (and his team partner's name where relevant), or the name of the applicant's business,

(2)   the date of the declaration,

(3)   the applicant's signature and the signature of the third party (and the signature of the applicant's team partner where relevant),

(4)   the amount of money available in pounds sterling,

(5)   the relationship(s) of the third party to the applicant,

(6)   if the third party is a Venture Capital firm, confirmation of whether this body is registered with the Financial Conduct Authority (FCA) and its entry in the register includes a permission to arrange, deal in or manage investments, or to manage alternative investment funds,

(7)   if the third party is a UK Seed Funding Competition, confirmation that the applicant, the entrepreneurial team or the applicant's business has been awarded money and that the competition is listed as endorsed on the UK Trade & Investment website, together with the amount of the award and naming the applicant, the entrepreneurial team or the applicant's business as a winner,

(8)   if the third party is a UK or Devolved Government Department (or intermediary public body authorised to award funds from that Department), confirmation that the UK or Devolved Government Department has made money available for the specific purpose of establishing or expanding a UK business, and the amount,

(9)   if the third party is another business in which the applicant is self- employed or a director, evidence of the applicant's status within that business and that the applicant is the sole controller of that business's finances, or, where the applicant is not the sole controller, the letter must be signed by another authorised official of that business who is not the applicant, and

(10)   confirmation that the money will remain available until such time as it is transferred to the applicant, the entrepreneurial team or the applicant's business.

and

(ii)   A letter from a legal representative who is independent from the third party or third parties, confirming the validity of signatures on each third-party declaration provided, which confirms that the declaration(s) from the third party or parties contains the signatures of the people stated. It can be a single letter covering all third-party permissions, or several letters from several legal representatives. It must be an original letter and not a copy, and it must be from a legal representative permitted to practise in the country where the third party or the money is. The letter must clearly show the following:

(1)   the name of the legal representative confirming the details,

(2)   the registration or authority of the legal representative to practise legally in the country in which the permission or permissions was or were given,

(3)   the date of the confirmation letter,

(4)   the applicant's name (and the name of the applicant's team partner's name where relevant) and, where (b) applies, that the applicant is a director of the business named in each third-party declaration,

(5)   the third party's name (which cannot be the legal representative themselves or their client),

(6)   that the declaration from the third party is signed and valid, and

(7)   if the third party is not a Venture Capital firm, Seed Funding Competition or UK or Devolved Government Department (or intermediary public body authorised to award funds from that Department), the number of the third party or their authorised representative's identity document (such as a passport or national identity card), the place of issue and dates of issue and expiry.

(e)   If the applicant is applying for leave to remain, and has, or was lasted granted, leave as a Tier 1 (General) Migrant or a Tier 1 (Post-Study Work) Migrant, he must also provide the following evidence that he meets the additional requirements set out in Table 4:

(i)   his job title,

(ii)   the Standard Occupational Classification (SOC) code of the occupation that the applicant has been working in since before 11 July 2014 or 6 April 2015 (as applicable) up to the date of his application, which must appear on the list of occupations skilled to National Qualifications Framework level 4 or above, as stated in the Codes of Practice in Appendix J,

(iii)   one or more of the following specified documents covering (either together or individually) a continuous period commencing before 11 July 2014 up to no earlier than three months before the date of his application:

    (1)   advertising or marketing material, including printouts of online advertising, that has been published locally or nationally

       (_a)   showing the applicant's name (and the name of the business if applicable) together with the business activity; or

       (_b)   where his business is trading online, confirmation of his ownership of the domain name of the business's website.

    (2)   article(s) or online links to article(s) in a newspaper or other publication showing the applicant's name (and the name of the business if applicable) together with the business activity,

    (3)   information from a trade fair, at which the applicant has had a stand or given a presentation to market his business, showing the applicant's name (and the name of the business if applicable) together with the business activity, or

    (4)   personal registration with a UK trade body linked to the applicant's occupation; and

(iv)   one or more of the following documents showing trading, which must cover (either together or individually) a continuous period commencing before 11 July 2014 or 6 April 2015 (as applicable) up to no earlier than three months before the date of his application:

    (1)   one or more contracts for service. If a contract is not an original the applicant must sign each page. Each contract must show:

       (_a)   the applicant's name and the name of the business,

       (_b)   the service provided by the applicant's business;

       (_c)   the name of the other party or parties involved in the contract and their contact details, including their full address, postal code and, where available, landline phone number and any email address; and

       (_d)   the duration of the contract; or

    (2)   one or more original letters from UK-regulated financial institutions with which the applicant has a business bank account, on the institution's headed paper, confirming the dates the business was trading during the period referred to at (iv) above; and

(v)   (1)   if claiming points for being self-employed, the following specified documents to show the applicant's compliance with National Insurance requirements:

       (_a)   the original bills covering the continuous billing period during which the applicant claims to have been self-employed, if his Class 2 National Insurance is paid by bill;

       (_b)   bank statements covering the continuous period during which the applicant claims to have been self-employed, showing the direct debit payment of Class 2 National Insurance to HM Revenue & Customs;

       (_c)   all original small earnings exception certificates issued to the applicant by HM Revenue & Customs covering the continuous tax period during which the applicant claims to have been self-employed, if he has low earnings; or

       (_d)   if the applicant has, or was last granted leave as a Tier 1 (General) Migrant and is applying before 31 October 2015, the original, dated welcome letter from HM Revenue & Customs containing the applicant's unique taxpayer reference number, if he has not yet become liable for paying National Insurance, or has not yet received the documents in (_c); or

    (2)   (_a)   if claiming points for being a director of a UK company at the time of his application, a printout from Companies House of the company's filing history page and of a Current Appointment Report, listing the applicant as a director of a company that is actively trading (and not dormant, or struck-off, or dissolved or in liquidation), and showing the date of his appointment as a director of that company; and

       (_b)   if claiming points for being a director of a UK company other than the company referred to in (_a) above, at any time before the date of his application, a printout from Companies House of the applicant's personal appointments history, showing that the applicant has held directorships continuously during the period in which he claims to have been a director, as well as a printout of the company's filing history page.

The evidence at (1) and (2) above must cover (either together or individually) a continuous period commencing before 11 July 2014 or 6 April 2015 (as applicable), and ending on a date no earlier than three months before the date of his application. The only exception is if the applicant is claiming points for being self-employed at the time of his application, and the evidence consists of documents issued by HM Revenue & Customs referred to at (v)(1)(_a) or (_c) above. If this is the case, the applicant must submit the most recent document issued before the date of his application; and

(vi)   if the applicant is currently a director, the following evidence that his business has business premises in the UK and is subject to UK taxation:

(1)   a printout of a Companies House document showing the address of the registered office in the UK, or head office in the UK if it has no registered office, and the applicant's name, as it appears on the application form, as a director; and

(2)   documentation from HM Revenue & Customs which confirms that the business is registered for corporation tax;

and

(vii)   the following evidence that the business has a UK bank account of which the applicant is a signatory:

(1)   if the applicant is currently self-employed, a personal or business bank statement, showing transactions for his business (which must be currently active), or a letter from the UK bank in question, on its headed paper, confirming that he has a business and acts through that bank for the purposes of that business, or

(2)   if the applicant is currently a director, a company bank statement showing that the company has a UK account and transactions for that company, or a letter from the UK bank in question, on its headed paper, confirming that the company has a bank account and the applicant is a signatory of that account,

and the evidence at (vi) and (vii)(2) above must relate to a company that is actively trading and not dormant, or struck-off, or dissolved or in liquidation.

42.   Subject to paragraphs 36A and 36B above, points will only be awarded to an applicant to whom Table 4, paragraph (b) applies if the total sum of those funds derives from one or more of the sources listed in (b)(i) to (iii) in Table 4.

43.   A regulated financial institution is one, which is regulated by the appropriate regulatory body for the country in which the financial institution operates.

44.   Money is disposable in the UK if all of the money is held in a UK based financial institution or if the money is freely transferable to the UK and convertible to sterling. Funds in a foreign currency will be converted to pounds sterling (£) using the spot exchange rate which appeared on www.oanda.com* on the date on which the application was made.

45.   If the applicant has invested the money referred to in Table 4 in the UK before the date of the application, points will be awarded for funds available as if the applicant had not yet invested the funds, providing:

(a)   the investment was made no more than 12 months (or 24 months if the applicant was last granted leave as a Tier 1 (Graduate Entrepreneur) Migrant) before the date of the application; and

(b)   all of the specified documents required in paragraphs 46-SD (a) to (g) are provided to show:

(i)   the amount of money invested; and

(ii)   that the applicant has established a business in the UK, in which the money was invested.

45A.   No points will be awarded where the specified documents show that the funds are held in a financial institution listed in Appendix P as being an institution with which the UK Border Agency is unable to make satisfactory verification checks.

Table 5: Applications for entry clearance or leave to remain referred to in paragraph 37

Investment and business activity	Points
The applicant has invested, or had invested on his behalf, not less than £200,000 (or £50,000 if, in his last grant of leave, he was awarded points for funds of £50,000) in cash directly into one or more businesses in the UK.	25
The applicant has: (a) registered with HM revenue and Customs as self-employed, or (b) registered with Companies House as a director of a new or an existing business. Directors who are on the list of disqualified directors provided by Companies House will not be awarded points. Where the applicant's last grant of entry clearance, leave to enter or leave to remain was as a Tier 1 (Entrepreneur) Migrant, the above condition must have been met within 6 months of his entry to the UK (if he was granted entry clearance as a Tier 1 (Entrepreneur) Migrant and there is evidence to establish his date of arrival to the UK), or, in any other case, the date of the grant of leave to remain.	20
On a date no earlier than three months prior to the date of application, the applicant was: (a) registered with HM revenue and Customs as self-employed, or (b) registered with Companies House as a director of a new or an existing business. Directors who are on the list of disqualified directors provided by Companies House will not be awarded points.	15
The applicant has: (a) established a new business or businesses that has or have created the equivalent of at least two new full time jobs for persons settled in the UK, or (b) taken over or invested in an existing business or businesses and his services or investment have resulted in a net increase in the employment provided by the business or businesses for persons settled in the UK by creating the equivalent of at least two new full time jobs. Where the applicant's last grant of entry clearance or leave to enter or remain was as a Tier 1 (Entrepreneur) Migrant, the jobs must have existed for at least 12 months of the period for which the previous leave was granted.	20

Table 6: Applications for indefinite leave to remain as referred to in paragraph 38

Row	Investment and business activity	Points
1	The applicant has invested, or had invested on his behalf, not less than £200,000 (or £50,000 if, in his last grant of leave, he was awarded points for funds of £50,000) in cash directly into one or more businesses in the UK. The applicant will not need to provide evidence of this investment if he was awarded points for it, as set out in Table 5, in his previous grant of entry clearance or leave to remain as a Tier 1 (Entrepreneur) Migrant.	20
2	On a date no earlier than three months prior to the date of application, the applicant was: (a) registered with HM Revenue and Customs as self-employed, or (b) registered with Companies House as a director of a new or an existing business. Directors who are on the list of disqualified directors provided by Companies House will not be awarded points.	20
3	The applicant has: (a) established a new UK business or businesses that has or have created the equivalent of X new full time jobs for persons settled in the UK, or	20

Row	Investment and business activity	Points
	(b) taken over or invested in an existing UK business or businesses and his services or investment have resulted in a net increase in the employment provided by the business or businesses for persons settled in the UK by creating the equivalent of X new full time jobs where X is at least 2. Where the applicant's last grant of entry clearance or leave to enter or remain was as a Tier 1 (Entrepreneur) Migrant, the jobs must have existed for at least 12 months during that last grant of leave.	

4	The applicant has spent the specified continuous period lawfully in the UK, with absences from the UK of no more than 180 days in any 12 calendar months during that period.
	
	The specified period must have been spent with leave as a Tier 1 (Entrepreneur) Migrant, as a Businessperson and/or as an Innovator, of which the most recent period must have been spent with leave as a Tier (1) (Entrepreneur) Migrant.
	
	The specified continuous period is:
	
	(a) 3 years if the number of new full time jobs, X, referred to in row 3 above is at least 10, or
	
	(b) 3 years if the applicant has:
	
	    (i) established a new UK business that has had an income from business activity of at least £5 million during a 3 year period in which the applicant has had leave as a Tier 1 (Entrepreneur) Migrant, or
	
	    (ii) taken over or invested in an existing UK business and his services or investment have resulted in a net increase in income from business activity to that business of £5 million during a 3 year period in which the applicant has had leave as a Tier 1 (Entrepreneur) Migrant, when compared to the immediately preceding 3 year period,
	
	or
	
	(c) 5 years in all other cases.
	
	Time spent with valid leave in the Bailiwick of Guernsey, the Bailiwick of Jersey or the Isle of Man in a category equivalent to the categories set out above may be included in the continuous period of lawful residence, provided the most recent period of leave was as a Tier 1 (Entrepreneur) Migrant in the UK. In any such case, the applicant must have absences from the Bailiwick of Guernsey, the Bailiwick of Jersey or the Isle of Man (as the case may be) of no more than 180 days in any 12 calendar months during the specified continuous period.
		15

Investment and business activity: notes

46.   Documentary evidence must be provided in all cases. The specified documents in paragraph 46-SD must be provided as evidence of any investment and business activity that took place when the applicant had leave as a Tier 1 (Entrepreneur) Migrant or a Tier 1 (Post- Study Work) Migrant, and any investment made no more than 12 months (or 24 months if the applicant was last granted leave as a Tier 1 (Graduate Entrepreneur) Migrant) before the date of the application for which the applicant is claiming points.

46-SD.   The specified documents in paragraphs 45 and 46 are as follows:

(a)   The applicant must provide all the appropriate specified documents needed to establish the amount of money he has invested from the following list:

    (i)   If the applicant's business is a registered company that is required to produce audited accounts, the audited accounts must be provided;

    (ii)   If the applicant's business is not required to produce audited accounts, unaudited accounts and an accounts compilation report must be provided from an accountant who is a member of a UK Recognised Supervisory Body (as defined in the Companies Act 2006);

    (iii)   the applicant has made the investment in the form of a director's loan, it must be shown in the relevant set of accounts provided, and the applicant must also provide a legal agreement, between the applicant (in the name that appears on his application) and the company, showing:

- (1) the terms of the loan,
- (2) any interest that is payable,
- (3) the period of the loan, and
- (4) that the loan is unsecured and subordinated in favour of third-party creditors.

- (iv) the applicant is claiming points for investing £50,000 from a Venture Capital firm, Seed Funding Competition or UK Government Department, and has not been awarded points in a previous application for having those funds available, he must provide a letter as specified in paragraph 41-SD(c)(iii) (except that the letter does not need to have been produced within the three months immediately before the date of the application) as evidence of the source of those funds.

(b) Audited or unaudited accounts must show the investment in money made directly by the applicant, in his own name or on his behalf (and showing his name). If he has invested by way of share capital the business accounts must show the shareholders, the amount and value of the shares (on the date of purchase) in the applicant's name as it appears on his application. If the value of the applicant's share capital is not shown in the accounts, then share certificates must be submitted as documentary evidence. The accounts must clearly show the name of the accountant, the date the accounts were produced, and how much the applicant has invested in the business. The accounts must be prepared and signed off in accordance with statutory requirements,

(c) The applicant must provide the following specified documents to show that he has established a UK business:

- (i) Evidence that the business has business premises in the United Kingdom:
    - (1) If the applicant is self employed, his registration with HM Revenue and Customs to show that the business is based in the UK, or
    - (2) If the applicant is a director, printout of a Companies House document showing the address of the registered office in the UK, or head office in the UK if it has no registered office, and the applicant's name, as it appears on the application form, as a director,

    and

- (ii) Evidence that the business has a UK bank account of which the applicant is a signatory:
    - (1) If the applicant is self employed, a personal bank statement showing transactions for his business, or a business bank statement, or a letter from a UK-regulated financial institution, on the institution's headed paper, confirming that he has a business and acts through that bank for the purposes of that business, or
    - (2) If the applicant is a director, a company bank statement showing that the company has a UK account, or a letter from a UK-regulated financial institution, on the institution's headed paper, confirming that the company has a bank account and the applicant is a signatory of that account,

    and

- (iii) Evidence that the business is subject to UK taxation:
    - (1) If the applicant is self-employed, he must be registered as self- employed for National Insurance assessment and provide either the welcome letter from HM Revenue & Customs, the Small Earnings Exception certificate, a copy of the National Insurance bill from HM Revenue & Customs, or the applicant's bank statement showing that National Insurance is taken by HM Revenue & Customs by direct debit, or
    - (2) If the applicant is a director of a business, the business must be registered for corporation tax and the applicant must provide documentation from HM Revenue & Customs which confirms this.

(d) If the applicant has bought property that includes residential accommodation the value of this part of the property will not be counted towards the amount of the business investment. The applicant must provide an estimate of the value of the living accommodation if it is part of the premises also used for the business, from a surveyor who is a member of the Royal Institution of Chartered Surveyors. This valuation must be produced in the three months prior to the date of application.

(e) If the applicant scores points from paragraph 45 above and only some of the money has been invested into a business in the UK, the balance of funds must be held in a regulated financial institution and disposable in the UK, and the applicant must provide the specified documents required in paragraph

41-SD for the previous investment of money together with the specified documents required in paragraph 41-SD required for his access to the balance of sufficient funds.

(f)   Where Table 5 applies and the applicant's last grant of entry clearance, leave to enter or leave to remain was as a Tier 1 (Entrepreneur) Migrant, he must provide the following specified documents as evidence of his registration as self-employed or as a director within the 6 months after the specified date in the relevant table:

(i)   If the applicant was self-employed, he must provide one of the following:

(1)   an original, dated welcome letter from HM Revenue & Customs containing the applicant's unique taxpayer reference number, dated no more than 8 months from the specified date in the relevant table,

(2)   an original Exception Certificate from HM Revenue & Customs, dated no more than 8 months from the specified date in the relevant table,

(3)   an original National Insurance bill from the HM Revenue & Customs dated during the 6 months after the specified date in the relevant table, or

(4)   a bank statement dated in the 6 months after the specified date in the relevant table, showing the direct debit payment of National Insurance to HM Revenue & Customs.

(ii)   If the applicant was a director of a new or existing company, he must provide a printout from Companies House of the company's filing history page and of the applicant's personal appointments history, showing the date of his appointment as a director of that company, which must be no more than 8 months after the specified date in the relevant table.

(g)   The applicant must provide the following specified documents as evidence of his current registration as self-employed or as a director:

(i)   If the applicant is claiming points for being currently self-employed, he must provide the following specified documents to show that he is paying Class 2 National Insurance contributions:

(1)   the original bill from the billing period immediately before the application, if his Class 2 National Insurance is paid by bill,

(2)   the most recent bank statement issued before the application, showing the direct debit payment of National Insurance to HM Revenue & Customs, if his National Insurance is paid by direct debit,

(3)   an original small earnings exception certificate issued by HM Revenue & Customs for the most recent return date, if he has low earnings, or

(4)   the original, dated welcome letter from HM Revenue & Customs containing the applicant's unique taxpayer reference number, if he has not yet received the documents in (1) to (3).

(ii)   If the applicant is claiming points for currently being a director of a UK company, he must provide a printout of a Current Appointment Report from Companies House, dated no earlier than three months before the date of the application, listing the applicant as a director of the company, and confirming the date of his appointment. The company must be actively trading and not struck-off, or dissolved or in liquidation on the date that the printout was produced.

(h)   If the applicant is required to score points for creating the net increase in employment in Table 5 or Table 6, he must provide the following information and specified documents:

(i)   A HM Revenue & Customs Employee Payment Record, showing details of the earnings for the settled worker for each week that he worked for the applicant, and signed and dated by the applicant;

(ii)   If the date of the start of the employment is not shown in the Employee Payment Record, an original HM Revenue & Customs form P45 or form P46 (also called a Full Payment Submission) for the settled worker, showing the starting date of the employment;

(iii)   If any of the period of employment for which points are claimed is covered by Real Time Information for PAYE, printouts of all Full Payment Submissions sent to HM Revenue & Customers, including the first one (which includes the start date of the settled worker), which are initialled by the applicant;

(iv)   Duplicate payslips or wage slips for each settled worker for whom points are being claimed, covering the full period of the employment for which points are being claimed;

(v)   Confirmation of the hourly rate for each settled worker used to claim points, including any changes in the hourly rate and the dates of the changes, enabling calculation of the hours of work created for each settled worker;

(vi)   Documents which show that the employment was created for settled workers, such as the passport pages from a UK passport that contain the employee's personal details, and the page containing the UK Government stamp or endorsement, if appropriate, or the worker's full birth certificate, showing the name of at least one parent;

(vii) If the applicant was a director of a company, a printout from Companies House of the company's filing history page and of the applicant's personal appointments history, and showing the date of his appointment as a director of that company, to confirm that he was a director of the company that employed the settled worker at the time that the settled worker was employed;

(viii) If the applicant was self-employed, the specified documents in (c) above showing the dates that the applicant became self-employed, the names on the Employee Payment Record and bank account, and the address of the business;

(ix)   If the applicant took over or joined a business that employed workers before he joined it, he must also provide one of the following types of payroll documentation:

(1)   a duplicate HM Revenue & Customs Full Payment Submission for the year before the jobs were created and the year that the jobs were created, showing the net increase in employment, and signed and dated by the applicant (If the posts were created too recently for a Full Payment Submission to have been produced, the applicant must provide a draft copy), or

(2)   a printout of the information sent to HM Revenue & Customs, initialled by the applicant, if the employer is taking part in the Real Time Initiative pilot;

(x)   If the applicant took over or joined a business that employed workers before he joined it, he must also provide an original accountant's letter verifying the net increase in employment and confirming the number of posts. The accountant must be a member of the Institute of Chartered Accountants in England and Wales, the Institute of Chartered Accountants in Scotland, the Institute of Chartered Accountants in Ireland, the Association of Chartered Certified Accountants, the Association of Authorised Public Accountants, the Chartered Institute of Public Finance and Accountancy, the Institute of Financial Accountants, the Chartered Institute of Management Accountants, or the Association of International Accountants. The letter must contain:

(1)   the name and contact details of the business,

(2)   the applicant's status in the business,

(3)   the number of posts created in the business and the hours worked,

(4)   the dates of the employment created,

(5)   the registration or permission of the accountant to operate in the United Kingdom,

(6)   the date that the accountant created the letter on the applicant's behalf, and

(7)   that the accountant will confirm the content of the letter to the UK Border Agency on request.

47. For the purposes of tables 4, 5 and 6, 'investment and business activity' does not include investment in any residential accommodation, property development or property management, and must not be in the form of a director's loan unless it is unsecured and subordinated in favour of the business. 'Property development or property management' in this context means any development of property owned by the applicant or his business to increase the value of the property with a view to earning a return either through rent or a future sale or both, or management of property (whether or not it is owned by the applicant or his business) for the purposes of renting it out or resale. The principle is that the business income must be generated from the supply of goods and/or services, and not derived from the increased value of property or any income generated from property, such as rent.

48. Points will only be awarded in respect of a UK business or businesses.

(a)   A business will be considered to be a UK business if:

(i)   it is trading within the UK economy, and

(ii)   it has a registered office in the UK, except where the applicant is registered with HM revenue & Customs as self-employed and does not have a business office, and

      (iii)   it has a UK bank account, and

      (iv)   it is subject to UK taxation.

(b)   Multinational companies that are registered as UK companies with either a registered office or head office in the UK are considered to be UK businesses for the purposes of Tables 4, 5 and 6.

(c)   Subject to (d) below, a business will only be considered to be a "new" business for the purposes of Tables 5 and 6 if it was established no earlier than 12 months before the start of a period throughout which the applicant has had continuous leave as a Tier 1 (Entrepreneur) Migrant, and which includes the applicant's last grant of leave. (For these purposes continuous leave will not be considered to have been broken if any of the circumstances set out in paragraphs 245AAA(a)(i) to (iii) of these Rules apply.)

(d)   If the applicant held entry clearance or leave to remain as a Tier 1 (Graduate Entrepreneur) Migrant no more than 28 days before the application which led to the start of the period of continuous leave as a Tier 1 (Entrepreneur) Migrant referred to in (c) above, a business will only be considered to be a 'new' business for the purposes of Tables 5 and 6 if it was established no earlier than 24 months before the start of the period in (c).

49.   A full time job is one involving at least 30 hours of work a week. Two or more part time jobs that add up to 30 hours a week will count as one full time job but one full time job of more than 30 hours work a week will not count as more than one full time job.

50.   Where the applicant's last grant of entry clearance or leave was as a Tier (Entrepreneur) Migrant, the jobs must have existed for a total of at least 12 months during the period in which the migrant had leave in that category. This need not consist of 12 consecutive months and the jobs need not exist at the date of application, provided they existed for at least 12 months during the period in which the migrant had leave as a Tier 1 (Entrepreneur) Migrant.

51.   The jobs must comply with all relevant UK legislation including, but not limited to, the national Minimum Wage and the Working Time Directive.

Entrepreneurial teams: Notes

52.   Two applicants, and no more than two applicants, may claim points for the same investment and business activity in Tables 4, 5 or 6 providing the following requirements are met.

Requirements:

(a)   The applicants have equal level of control over the funds and/or the business or businesses in question;

(b)   The applicants are both shown by name in each other's applications and in the specified evidence required in the relevant table; and

(c)   Neither applicant has previously been granted leave as a Tier 1 (Entrepreneur) Migrant on the basis of investment and/or business activity linked in this way with any applicant other than each other if the same funds are being relied on as in a previous application.

53.   (a)   No points will be awarded for funds that are made available to any individual other than the applicant, except:

      (i)   under the terms of paragraph 52 above; or

      (ii)   where the money is held in a joint account with the applicant's spouse, civil partner or partner (defined as a person who has been living together with the applicant in a relationship akin to a marriage or civil partnership for at least two years prior to the date of application), and that spouse or partner is not (or is not applying to be) another Tier 1 (Entrepreneur) Migrant.

(b)   No points will be awarded for investment and business activity shared with another Tier 1 (Entrepreneur) applicant, except under the terms of paragraph 52 above.

(c)   If the applicant is not the sole partner or director in the business, he must state:

      (i)   the names of the other partners or directors,

      (ii)   whether any of the other partners or directors are also Tier 1 (Entrepreneur) Migrants, and

      (iii)   If so:

          (1)   the dates they became partners or directors,

          (2)   whether they are applying under the provisions in paragraph 52 above, and

          (3)   if they have made (or are making at the same time) an application in which they claimed points for creating jobs, the names of the jobholders in question.

Attributes for Tier 1 (Investor) Migrants

54. An applicant applying for entry clearance, leave to remain or indefinite leave to remain as a Tier 1 (Investor) Migrant must score 75 points for attributes.

55. Except where paragraph 56 applies, available points for applications for entry clearance or leave to remain are shown in Table 7.

56. (a) Available points for entry clearance or leave to remain are shown in Table 8A for an applicant who:

        (i) has had entry clearance, leave to enter or leave to remain as a Tier 1 (Investor) Migrant, which was granted under the Rules in place from 6 November 2014, in the 12 months immediately before the date of application, or

        (ii) is applying for leave to remain and has, or was last granted, entry clearance, leave to enter or leave to remain as a Tier 1 (Investor) Migrant, which was granted under the Rules in place from 6 November 2014.

    (b) Available points for entry clearance or leave to remain are shown in Table 8B for an applicant who:

        (i) has had entry clearance, leave to enter or leave to remain as a Tier 1 (Investor) Migrant, under the Rules in place before 6 November 2014, or as an Investor, in the 12 months immediately before the date of application;, or

        (ii) is applying for leave to remain and has, or was last granted, entry clearance, leave to enter or leave to remain as a Tier 1 (Investor) Migrant, under the Rules in place before 6 November 2014, or as an Investor.

57. (a) Available points for applications for indefinite leave to remain are shown in Table 9A for an applicant who was last granted as a Tier 1 (Investor) Migrant under the Rules in place from 6 November 2014, and was awarded points as set out in Table 7 or Table 8A of Appendix A to these Rules in that last grant.

    (b) Available points for applications for indefinite leave to remain are shown in Table 9B for an applicant who was last granted as a Tier 1 (Investor) Migrant under the Rules in place before 6 November 2014, or was awarded points as set out in Table 8B of Appendix A in his last grant.58. Notes to accompany Tables 7 to Table 9B appear below Table 9B.

Table 7: applications for entry clearance or leave to remain referred to in paragraph 55

Money to invest in the UK	Points
The applicant: (a) has money of his own under his control held in a regulated financial institution and disposable in the UK amounting to not less than £2 million; and (b) has opened an account with a UK regulated bank for the purposes of investing not less than £2 million in the UK.	75

Table 8A: Applications for entry clearance or leave to remain from applicants who initially applied to enter the category from 6 November 2014 as referred to in paragraph 56(a)

Money and investment	Points
The applicant has invested not less than £2 million in the UK by way of UK Government bonds, share capital or loan capital in active and trading UK registered companies, subject to the restrictions set out in paragraph 65 below. The investment referred to above was made: (1) within 3 months of the applicant's entry to the UK, if he was granted entry clearance as a Tier 1 (Investor) Migrant and there is evidence to establish his date of entry to the UK, unless there are exceptionally compelling reasons for the delay in investing, or (2) where there is no evidence to establish his date of entry in the UK or where the applicant was granted entry clearance in a category other than Tier 1 (Investor) Migrant, within 3 months of the date of the grant of entry clearance or leave to remain as a Tier 1 (Investor) Migrant, unless there are exceptionally compelling reasons for the delay in investing, or (3) where the investment was made prior to the application which led to the first grant of leave as a Tier 1 (Investor) Migrant, no earlier than 12 months before the date of such application,	75

Money and investment	Points
and in each case the level of investment has been at least maintained for the whole of the remaining period of that leave.	
'Compelling reasons for the delay in investing' must be unforeseeable and outside of the applicant's control. Delays caused by the applicant failing to take timely action will not be accepted. Where possible, the applicant must have taken reasonable steps to mitigate such delay.	

Table 8B: Applications for entry clearance or leave to remain from applicants who initially applied to enter the category before 6 November 2014 as referred to in paragraph 56(b)

Money and investment	Points
The applicant: (a) has money of his own under his control in the UK amounting to not less than £1 million, or (b) (i) owns personal assets which, taking into account any liabilities to which they are subject, have a value of not less than £2 million, and (ii) has money under his control and disposable in the UK amounting to not less than £1 million which has been loaned to him by a UK regulated financial institution.	30
The applicant has invested not less than £750,000 of his capital in the UK by way of UK Government bonds, share capital or loan capital in active and trading UK registered companies, subject to the restrictions set out in paragraph 65 below and has invested the remaining balance of £1,000,000 in the UK by the purchase of assets or by maintaining the money on deposit in a UK regulated financial institution.	30

(i) The investment referred to above was made:
 	
   (1) within 3 months of the applicant's entry to the UK, if he was granted entry clearance as a Tier 1 (Investor) Migrant and there is evidence to establish his date of entry to the UK, unless there are exceptionally compelling reasons for the delay in investing, or
 	
   (2) where there is no evidence to establish the date of his entry in the UK or where the applicant was granted entry clearance in a category other than Tier 1 (Investor) Migrant, within 3 months of the date of the grant of entry clearance or leave to remain as a Tier 1 (Investor) Migrant, unless there are exceptionally compelling reasons for the delay in investing, or
 	
   (3) where the investment was made prior to the application which led to the first grant of leave as a Tier 1 (Investor) Migrant, no earlier than 12 months before the date of such application,
 	
   and in each case the investment has been at least maintained for the whole of the remaining period of that leave;
 	
   or
 	
(ii) The migrant has, or was last granted, entry clearance, leave to enter or leave to remain as an Investor.
 	
'Compelling reasons for the delay in investing' must be unforeseeable and outside of the applicant's control. Delays caused by the applicant failing to take timely action will not be accepted. Where possible, the applicant must have taken reasonable steps to mitigate such delay.
	15

Table 9A: Applications for indefinite leave to remain from applicants who initially applied to enter the category from 6 November 2014 as referred to in paragraph 57(a)

Row	Money and investment	Points
1	The applicant has invested money of his own under his control amounting to at least: (a) £10 million; or (b) £5 million; or	40

Row	Money and investment	Points
	(c) £2 million in the UK by way of UK Government bonds, share capital or loan capital in active and trading UK registered companies, subject to the restrictions set out in paragraph 65 below.	
2	The applicant has spent the specified continuous period lawfully in the UK, with absences from the UK of no more than 180 days in any 12 calendar months during that period. The specified continuous period must have been spent with leave as a Tier 1 (Investor) Migrant. The specified continuous period is: (a) 2 years if the applicant scores points from row 1(a) above; (b) 3 years if the applicant scores points from row 1(b) above; or (c) 5 years if the applicant scores points from row 1(c) above.	20
3	Time spent with valid leave in the Bailiwick of Guernsey, the Bailiwick of Jersey or the Isle of Man in a category equivalent to the categories set out above may be included in the continuous period of lawful residence, provided the most recent period of leave was as a Tier 1 (Investor) Migrant in the UK. In any such case, the applicant must have absences from the Bailiwick of Guernsey, the Bailiwick of Jersey or the Isle of Man (as the case may be) of no more than 180 days in any 12 calendar months during the specified continuous period. The investment referred to above was made no earlier than 12 months before the date of the application which led to the first grant of leave as a Tier 1 (Investor) Migrant. The level of investment has been at least maintained throughout the relevant specified continuous period referred to in row 2, other than in the first 3 months of that period, and the applicant has provided the specified documents to show that this requirement has been met. When calculating the specified continuous period, the first day of that period will be taken to be the later of: (a) the date the applicant first entered the UK as a Tier 1 (Investor) Migrant (or the date entry clearance was granted as a Tier 1 (Investor) Migrant), or the date the applicant first entered the Bailiwick of Guernsey, the Bailiwick of Jersey or the Isle of Man with leave in a category equivalent to Tier 1 (Investor) if this is earlier, or (b) the date 3 months before the full specified amount was invested in the UK, or before the full required amount in an equivalent category was invested in the Bailiwick of Guernsey, the Bailiwick of Jersey or the Isle of Man.	15

Table 9B: Applications for indefinite leave to remain from applicants who initially applied to enter the category before 6 November 2014 as referred to in paragraph 57(b)

Row	Assets and investment	Points

1	The applicant:
	
	(a) (i) has money of his own under his control in the UK amounting to not less than £10 million; or
	
	        (ii) (1) owns personal assets which, taking into account any liabilities to which they are subject, have a value of not less than £20 million; and
	
	                (2) has money under his control and disposable in the UK amounting to not less than £10 million which has been loaned to him by a UK regulated financial institution, or
		20

Row	Assets and investment	Points
	(b) (i) has money of his own under his control in the UK amounting to not less than £5 million; or (ii) (1) owns personal assets which, taking into account any liabilities to which they are subject, have a value of not less than £10 million; and (2) has money under his control and disposable in the UK amounting to not less than £5 million which has been loaned to him by a UK regulated financial institution; or (c) (i) has money of his own under his control in the UK amounting to not less than £1 million; or (ii) (1) owns personal assets which, taking into account any liabilities to which they are subject, have a value of not less than £2 million; and (2) has money under his control and disposable in the UK amounting to not less than £1 million which has been loaned to him by a UK regulated financial institution.	
2	The applicant has invested not less than 75% of the specified invested amount of his capital in the UK by way of UK Government bonds, share capital or loan capital in active and trading UK registered companies, subject to the restrictions set out in paragraph 65 below, and has invested the remaining balance of the specified invested amount in the UK by the purchase of assets or by maintaining the money on deposit in a UK regulated financial institution. The specified invested amount is: (a) £10,000,000 if the applicant scores points from row 1(a) above, (b) £5,000,000 if the applicant scores points from row 1(b) above, or (c) £1,000,000 if the applicant scores points from row 1(c) above.	20
3	The applicant has spent the specified continuous period lawfully in the UK, with absences from the UK of no more than 180 days in any 12 calendar months during that period. The specified continuous period must have been spent with leave as a Tier 1 (Investor) Migrant and/or as an Investor, of which the most recent period must have been spent with leave as a Tier 1 (Investor) Migrant. The specified continuous period is: (a) 2 years if the applicant scores points from row 1(a) above, (b) 3 years if the applicant scores points from row 1(b) above, or (c) 5 years if the applicant scores points from row 1(c) above. Time spent with valid leave in the Bailiwick of Guernsey, the Bailiwick of Jersey or the Isle of Man in a category equivalent to the categories set out above may be included in the continuous period of lawful residence, provided the most recent period of leave was as a Tier 1 (Investor) Migrant in the UK. In any such case, the applicant must have absences from the Bailiwick of Guernsey, the Bailiwick of Jersey or the Isle of Man (as the case may be) of no more than 180 days in any 12 calendar months during the specified continuous period.	20
4	The investment referred to above was made no earlier than 12 months before the date of the application which led to the first grant of leave as a Tier 1 (Investor) Migrant. The level of investment has been at least maintained throughout the time spent with leave as a Tier 1 (Investor) Migrant in the UK in the relevant specified continuous period referred to in row 3, other than in the first 3 months of that period.	15

Row	Assets and investment	Points
	In relation to time spent with leave as a Tier 1 (Investor) Migrant in the UK, the applicant has provided specified documents to show that this requirement has been met. When calculating the specified continuous period, the first day of that period will be taken to be the later of: (a) the date the applicant first entered the UK as a Tier 1 (Investor) Migrant (or the date entry clearance was granted as a Tier 1 (Investor) Migrant), or the date the applicant first entered the Bailiwick of Guernsey, the Bailiwick of Jersey or the Isle of Man with leave in a category equivalent to Tier 1 (Investor) if this is earlier, or (b) the date 3 months before the full specified amount was invested in the UK, or before the full required amount in an equivalent category was invested in the Bailiwick of Guernsey, the Bailiwick of Jersey or the Isle of Man.	

UK bank account: notes

59. In the case of an application where Table 7 applies, in addition to the evidence relating to money to invest, the applicant must provide an original letter issued by an authorised official of a UK regulated bank, on the official letter-headed paper of the institution, which:

(a) is dated within the three months immediately before the date of the application;

(b) states the applicant's name and account number; and

(c) confirms that:

    (i) the applicant has opened an account with that bank for the purposes of investing not less than £2 million in the UK; and

    (ii) the bank is regulated by the Financial Conduct Authority for the purposes of accepting deposits.

60. Money is disposable in the UK if all of the money is held in a UK based financial institution or if the money is freely transferable to the UK and convertible to sterling. funds in a foreign currency will be converted to pounds sterling (£) using the spot exchange rate which appeared on www.oanda.com* on the date on which the application was made.

61. 'Money of his own', 'personal assets' and 'his capital' include money or assets belonging to the applicant's spouse, civil partner or unmarried or same-sex partner, provided that:

(a) the applicant's spouse, civil partner or unmarried or same-sex partner meets the requirements of paragraphs 319C(c) and (d) of these rules, and the specified documents in paragraph 61-SD are provided, and

(b) specified documents in paragraph 61-SD are provided to show that the money or assets are under the applicant's control and that he is free to invest them.

61A. In Tables 7 to 9B, 'money of his own under his control' and 'money under his control' exclude money that a loan has been secured against, where another party would have a claim on the money if loan repayments were not met, except where:

(i) the applicant made an application before 13 December 2012 which is undecided or which led to a grant of entry clearance or leave to remain as an Investor or a Tier 1 (Investor) migrant,

(ii) the applicant has not been granted entry clearance, leave to enter or leave to remain in any other category since the grant referred to in (i), and

(iii) money is under the applicant's control, except for the fact that the loan referred to in paragraph (b) in Table 8B or row 1 of Table 9B has been secured against it.

61-SD. The specified documents in paragraph 61, as evidence of the relationship and to show that the money or assets are under the applicant's control and that he is free to invest them, are as follows:

(a) The applicant must provide:

    (i) The original certificate of marriage or civil partnership, to confirm the relationship, which includes the name of the applicant and the husband, wife or civil partner, or

    (ii) At least three of the following types of specified documents to demonstrate a relationship similar in nature to marriage or civil partnership, including unmarried and same-sex relationships, covering a full two-year period immediately before the date of the application:

(1)   a bank statement or letter from a bank confirming a joint bank account held in both names,

(2)   an official document such as a mortgage agreement showing a joint mortgage,

(3)   official documents such as deeds of ownership or a mortgage agreement showing a joint investment, such as in property or business,

(4)   a joint rent (tenancy) agreement,

(5)   any other official correspondence linking both partners to the same address, such as example bills for council tax or utilities,

(6)   a life insurance policy naming the other partner as beneficiary,

(7)   birth certificates of any children of the relationship, showing both partners as parents, or

(8)   any other evidence that adequately demonstrates the couple's long-term commitment to one another.

(b)   The applicant must provide an original declaration from the applicant's husband, wife, civil partner, or unmarried or same-sex partner that he will permit all joint or personal money used to claim points for the application to be under the control of the applicant in the UK, known as a gift of beneficial ownership of the money while retaining the legal title, which clearly shows:

(1)   the names of husband, wife, civil partner, or unmarried or same-sex partner and the applicant,

(2)   the date of the declaration,

(3)   the signatures of the husband, wife, civil partner, or unmarried or same-sex partner and applicant,

(4)   the amount of money available, and

(5)   a statement that the husband, wife, civil partner, or unmarried or same-sex partner agrees that the applicant has sole control over the money.

(c)   The applicant must provide a letter, from a legal adviser who is permitted to practise in the country where the declaration was made, confirming that the declaration is valid and which clearly shows:

(1)   the name of the legal adviser confirming that the declaration is valid,

(2)   the registration or authority of the legal adviser to practise legally in the country in which the document was drawn up,

(3)   the date of the confirmation of the declaration,

(4)   the names of the applicant and husband, wife, civil partner, or unmarried or same-sex partner, and

(5)   that the declaration is signed and valid according to the laws of the country in which it was made.

62.   'Regulated financial institution' is defined in paragraph 43, Appendix A.

63.   In the case of an application where Table 7 applies, where the money referred to in Table 7 has already been invested in the UK before the date of application, points will only be awarded if it was invested in the UK no more than 12 months before the date of application.

Source of money: notes

64.   In the case of an application where Table 7 applies, points will only be awarded if the applicant:

(a)   has had the money referred to in Table 7 for a consecutive 90-day period of time, ending no earlier than one calendar month before the date of application, and provides the specified documents in paragraph 64-SD; or

(b)   provides the additional specified documents in paragraph 64A-SD of the source of the money.

64-SD.   The specified document requirements in paragraph 64(a), as evidence of having held the money for the specified 90-day period, are as follows:

(a)   The applicant must provide:

(i)   A portfolio report produced by a UK regulated financial institution, or a breakdown of investments in an original letter produced by a UK regulated financial institution, on the official letter-headed paper of the institution, issued by an authorised official of that institution. The portfolio report or letter must cover a consecutive 90-day period of time, ending no earlier than one calendar month before the date of application. The portfolio report or letter must confirm all the following:

(1)   the amount of the money held in the investments,

(2)   the beneficial owner of the funds,

(3)   the date of the investment period covered,

(4)   that the institution is a UK regulated financial institution, with the details of the registration shown on the documentation, and

(5)   that the money can be transferred into the UK should the application be successful, if it is held abroad, or that the money has already been invested in the UK in the form of UK Government bonds, share capital or loan capital in active and trading UK registered companies, and the dates of these investments;

(ii)   If the applicant manages his own investments, or has a portfolio manager who does not operate in the UK and is not therefore regulated by the Financial Conduct Authority (FCA) (and the Prudential Regulation Authority (PRA) where applicable), he must provide one or more of the documents from the list below, as relevant to their type of investments, covering a consecutive 90-day period of time, ending no earlier than one calendar month before the date of application:

(1)   certified copies of bond documents showing the value of the bonds, the date of purchase and the owner;

(2)   share documents showing the value of the shares, the date of purchase and the owner,

(3)   the latest audited annual accounts of the organisation in which the investment has been made, clearly showing the amount of money held in the investments, the name of the applicant (or applicant and/or husband, wife, civil partner, or unmarried or same-sex partner), and the date of investment, or, if no accounts have been produced, a certificate from an accountant showing the amount of money held in the investments, and

(4)   original trust fund documents from a legal adviser showing the amount of money in the fund, the date that the money is available and the beneficial owner, and including the name and contact details of the legal adviser and at least one of the trustees;

(iii)   Original personal bank statements on the official bank stationery from a bank that is regulated by the official regulatory body for the country in which the institution operates and the funds are located, showing the account number and the amount of money available in the name of the applicant (or applicant and/or husband, wife, civil partner, or unmarried or same-sex partner), covering a consecutive 90-day period of time, ending no earlier than one calendar month before the date of application. The most recent statement must be no more than one calendar month old at the date of application. Electronic bank statements must be accompanied by a supporting letter from the bank on the institution's official headed paper, issued by an authorising official of that institution, confirming the content and that the document is genuine;

(iv)   If the applicant cannot provide bank statements, an original letter from a bank that is regulated by the official regulatory body for the country in which the institution operates and the funds are located. The letter must be on the institution's official headed paper, issued by an authorised official of that institution, and dated no more than one calendar month before the date of application. The letter must confirm:

(1)   the name of the applicant (or applicant and/or husband, wife, civil partner, or unmarried or same-sex partner), and that the money is available in their name(s),

(2)   the account number,

(3)   that the bank is regulated by the official regulatory body for the country in which the institution operates and the funds are located,

(4)   the dates of the period covered, including both the day the letter was produced and three full consecutive months immediately before the date of the letter, and

(5)   the balance of the account to cover the required amount of money as a minimum credit balance on the date of the letter and throughout the three full consecutive months before the date of the letter;

(b)   If the funds are not held in the UK, the applicant must also provide an original letter from a bank or financial institution that is regulated by the official regulatory body for the country in which the institution operates and the funds are located, on the institution's official headed paper, issued by an authorised official of that institution, which confirms:

(1)   the name of the beneficial owner, which should be the applicant (or applicant and/or husband, wife, civil partner, or unmarried or same-sex partner),

(2)   the account number,

(3)   the date of the letter,

(4)   the amount of money to be transferred,

(5)   that the money can be transferred to the UK if the application is successful, and

(6)   that the institution will confirm the content of the letter to the Home Office on request.

If the applicant is providing the letter in (a)(iv) above, this information may be contained in the same letter.

(c)   If specified documents are provided from accountants, the accountant must:

   (i)   if based in the UK, be a member of the Institute of Chartered Accountants in England and Wales, the Institute of Chartered Accountants in Scotland, the Institute of Chartered Accountants in Ireland, the Association of Chartered Certified Accountants, the Association of Authorised Public Accountants, the Chartered Institute of Public Finance and Accountancy, the Institute of Financial Accountants, the Chartered Institute of Management Accountants, or the Association of International Accountants, or

   (ii)   if not based in the UK, be a member of an equivalent, appropriate supervisory or regulatory body in the country in which they operate.

64A-SD.   Where paragraph 64(b) states that specified documents are required as evidence that the money is under the applicant's control and that he is free to invest it, the applicant must provide all the specified documents from the following list, with contact details that enable verification:

(a)   Original documents in the form of:

   (i)   Money given to the applicant (or applicant and/or husband, wife, civil partner, or unmarried or same-sex partner) within the three months immediately before the application must be shown in an irrevocable memorandum of gift, which clearly shows:

      (1)   the name and signature of the person receiving the gift,

      (2)   the name and signature of the person giving the gift,

      (3)   the date of the memorandum,

      (4)   the relationship between the person giving the gift and the person receiving it,

      (5)   the amount of money being given,

      (6)   a statement that the legal ownership of the gift is transferred and that the document is the memorandum of transfer,

      (7)   a clear description of the gift, and

      (8)   a statement that the gift is irrevocable;

   (ii)   If a memorandum of gift in (i) is provided, it must be accompanied by an original confirmation letter from a legal adviser permitted to practise in the country where the gift was made, which clearly shows:

      (1)   the name of the legal adviser who is confirming the details,

      (2)   the registration or authority of the legal adviser to practise legally in the country in which the gift was made,

      (3)   the date of the confirmation of the memorandum,

      (4)   the names of the person giving the gift and the person receiving it,

      (5)   the relationship between the person giving the gift and the person receiving it,

      (6)   the amount of money given,

      (7)   the date that the money was transferred to the applicant, or to the husband, wife, civil partner, or unmarried partner or same-sex partner of the applicant,

      (8)   that the memorandum is signed and valid,

      (9)   that the gift is irrevocable, and

      (10)   that the memorandum is binding according to the laws of the country in which it was made;

   (iii)   of sale of assets such as business or property, if the applicant has generated these funds within the three months immediately before the date of application, which meet the relevant legal requirements of the country of sale and clearly show:

(1) the name of the applicant (or applicant and/or husband, wife, civil partner, or unmarried or same-sex partner),

(2) the amount of money raised, and

(3) the date of the sale;

(iv) If a deed of sale in (iii) is provided, it must be accompanied by an original confirmation letter from a legal adviser permitted to practise in the country where the sale was made, which clearly shows:

(1) the name of the legal adviser confirming the details,

(2) the registration or authority of the legal adviser to practise legally in the country in which the sale was made,

(3) the date of the sale,

(4) the date of production of the letter confirming the sale,

(5) the details of what was sold and the amount of money received from the sale,

(6) the relationship between the person making the will and the beneficiary,

(7) the name of the person receiving the money from the sale,

(8) the date that the money was transferred, and

(9) that the sale was valid according to the laws of the country in which it was made;

(v) If the funds are currently held in the applicant's business (or the business of the applicant and/or the applicant's husband, wife, civil partner, or unmarried or same- sex partner), the applicant must provide business accounts, which:

(1) are profit and loss accounts (or income and expenditure accounts if the organisation is not trading for profit),

(2) are prepared and signed off in accordance with statutory requirements, and

(3) clearly show the amount of money available for investment;

(vi) business accounts in (v) are provided, they must be accompanied by an original letter from a legal adviser who is permitted to practise in the country where business was operating, confirming that the applicant (or applicant and/or husband, wife, civil partner, or unmarried or same-sex partner) can lawfully extract the money from the business, which clearly shows:

(1) the name of the legal adviser who is confirming the details,

(2) the registration or authority of the legal adviser to practise legally in the country in which the business is operating,

(3) the date on which the details are confirmed, and

(4) that the applicant (or applicant and/or husband, wife, civil partner, or unmarried or same-sex partner) can lawfully extract the money from the business in question;

(vii) If the applicant (or applicant and/or husband, wife, civil partner, or unmarried or same sex partner) has been the beneficiary of a will within the three months before making the application, and has received money as a result, the applicant must provide a notarised copy of the will. If the applicant (or applicant and/or husband, wife, civil partner, or unmarried or same-sex partner) has received possessions or assets, rather than money, then the applicant (or applicant and/or husband, wife, civil partner, or unmarried or same-sex partner) may not use estimates of the value of the items as evidence of funds for investment. The notarised copy of the will must clearly show:

(1) the date of the will,

(2) the beneficiary of the will (this should be the applicant or applicant and/or husband, wife, civil partner, or unmarried or same-sex partner),

(3) the amount of money that the applicant (or applicant and/or husband, wife, civil partner, or unmarried or same-sex partner) has inherited, and

(4) the names of any executors, plus any codicils (additions) to the will that affect the amount of money that was received;

(viii) If a notarised copy of a will in (vii) is provided, it must be accompanied by an original confirmation letter from a legal adviser who is permitted to practise in the country where will was made, confirming the validity of the will, which clearly shows:

(1) the name of the legal adviser confirming the details,

(2) the registration or authority of the legal adviser to practise legally in the country in which the will was made,

(3) the date of the document produced by the legal adviser confirming the will,

(4) the date that the applicant received the money as a result of the settlement of the will,

(5) the names of the person making the will and the beneficiary,

(6) the relationship between the person making the will and the beneficiary,

(7) confirmation of the amount of money received by the applicant (or applicant and/or husband, wife, civil partner, or unmarried or same-sex partner),

(8) that the will is signed and valid, and

(9) that the will is valid according to the laws of the country in which it was made;

(ix) the applicant (or applicant and/or husband, wife, civil partner, or unmarried or same-sex partner) has obtained money as a result of a divorce settlement within the three months immediately before the date of application, the applicant must provide a notarised copy of a financial agreement following a divorce. If the applicant (or applicant and/or husband, wife, civil partner, or unmarried or same- sex partner) has received possessions or assets, rather than money, estimates of the value of the items will not be accepted as evidence of money for investment.

(x) If a divorce settlement in (ix) is provided, it must be accompanied by an original confirmation letter from a legal adviser who is permitted to practise in the country where the divorce took place, which clearly shows:

(1) the name of the legal adviser confirming the details,

(2) the registration or authority of the legal adviser to practise legally in the country in which the divorce took place,

(3) the date of the document produced by the legal adviser confirming the divorce settlement,

(4) the date that the applicant received the money as a result of the settlement,

(5) the names of the persons who are divorced,

(6) confirmation of the amount of money received by the applicant (or applicant and/or husband, wife, civil partner, or unmarried or same-sex partner,

(7) that the divorce settlement is complete and valid, and

(8) that the divorce settlement is valid according to the laws of the country in which it was made;

(xi) If the applicant is relying on a financial award or winnings as a source of funds, he must provide an original letter from the organisation issuing the financial award or winnings, which clearly shows:

(1) the name of the applicant (or applicant and/or husband, wife, civil partner, or unmarried or same-sex partner),

(2) the date of the award,

(3) the amount of money won,

(4) the winnings are genuine, and

(5) the contact details for the organisation issuing the award or winnings;

(xii) If a letter showing a financial award or winnings in (xi) is provided, it must be accompanied by an original confirmation letter from a legal adviser who is permitted to practise in the country where the award was made, which clearly shows:

(1) the name of the legal adviser confirming the details,

(2) the registration or authority of the legal adviser to practise legally in the country in which the award was made,

(3) the date of the letter of confirmation,

(4) the date of the award,

(5) the name of the recipient of the award,

(6) the amount of the winnings,

(7) the source of the winnings, and

      (8)   the date that the money was transferred to the applicant, or husband, wife, civil partner, or unmarried or same-sex partner;

   (xiii)   If the applicant (or applicant and/or husband, wife, civil partner, or unmarried or same-sex partner) has received money from a source not listed above, the applicant must provide relevant original documentation as evidence of the source of the money, together with independent supporting evidence, which both clearly confirm:

      (1)   the amount of money received,

      (2)   the date that the money was received,

      (3)   the source of the money, and

      (4)   that the applicant (or applicant and/or husband, wife, civil partner, or unmarried or same-sex partner) was the legal recipient of the money.

Source of additional money (Table 9A and Table 9B): notes

64B-SD. In the case of an application where Table 9A, row 1 (a) or (b), or Table 9B, row 1 (a)(i) or (b)(i) applies, points will only be awarded if the applicant:

(a)   (i)   has had the additional money (or the additional assets in respect of an application to which either row 1 (a)(i) or (b)(i) of Table 9B applies) that he was not awarded points for in his previous grant of leave for a consecutive 90-day period of time, ending on the date(s) this additional capital was invested (as set out in row 1 of Table 9A or row 2 of Table 9B), and

      (ii)   provides the specified documents in paragraph 64-SD (or the additional assets in respect of an application to which either row 1 (a)(i) or (b)(i) of Table 9B applies), with the difference that references to 'date of application' in that paragraph are taken to read 'date of investment'; or

(b)   provides the additional specified documents in paragraph 64A-SD of the source of the additional money (with the difference that references to 'date of application' in that paragraph are taken to read 'date of investment').

64C-SD. In the case of an application where Table 9B, row 1 (a)(ii) or (b)(ii) applies, points will only be awarded if the applicant provides an original letter of confirmation from each UK regulated financial institution the applicant has taken out a loan with to obtain the additional funds that he was not awarded points for in his previous grant of leave. The letter must have been issued by an authorised official, on the official letter-headed paper of the institution(s), and confirm:

(i)   the amount of money that the institution(s) has loaned to the applicant,

(ii)   the date(s) the loan(s) was taken out by the applicant, which must be no later than the date(s) this additional capital was invested (as set out in Table 9B, row 2),

(iii)   that the institution is a UK regulated financial institution for the purpose of granting loans,

(iv)   that the applicant has personal assets with a net value of at least £2 million, £10 million or £20 million (as appropriate), and

(v)   that the institution(s) will confirm the content of the letter to the Home Office on request.

Qualifying investments (Table 8A to Table 9B): notes

65. Investment excludes investment by the applicant by way of:

(a)   an offshore company or trust, or investments that are held in offshore custody except that investments held in offshore custody shall not be excluded where the applicant made an application before 13 December 2012 which is undecided or which led to a grant of entry clearance or leave to remain as an Investor or a Tier 1 (Investor) migrant and has not since been granted entry clearance, leave to enter or leave to remain in any other category,

(b)   Open-ended investment companies, investment trust companies or pooled investment vehicles,

(c)   Companies mainly engaged in property investment, property management or property development (meaning in this context any investment or development of property to increase the value of the property with a view to earning a return either through rent or a future sale or both, or management of property for the purposes of renting it out or resale. The principle is that business income must be generated from the supply of goods and/or services and not derived from the increased value of property or any income generated through property, such as rent.),

(d)   Deposits with a bank, building society or other enterprise whose normal course of business includes the acceptance of deposits,

(e)   ISAs, premium bonds and saving certificates issued by the National Savings and Investment Agency (NS&I), for an applicant who has, or last had leave as a Tier 1 (Investor) Migrant, or

(f)   Leveraged investment funds, except where the leverage in question is the security against the loan referred to in paragraph (b) in Table 8B or row 1 of Table 9B (as appropriate), and paragraph 61A(i)-(iii) apply.

65A.   'Active and trading UK registered companies' means companies which:

(a)   have a registered office or head office in the UK;

(b)   have a UK bank account showing current business transactions; and

(c)   are subject to UK taxation.

65B.   No points will be awarded where the specified documents show that the funds are held in a financial institution listed in Appendix P as being an institution with which the UK Border Agency is unable to make satisfactory verification checks.

65C.   (a)   In the case of an application where Table 8A or Table 9A applies, points for maintaining the level of investment for the specified continuous period of leave will only be awarded:

(i)   if the applicant has purchased a portfolio of qualifying investments for a price of at least £2 million (or £5 million or £10 million, as appropriate); and

(ii)   where any part of the qualifying investments in the portfolio is sold (whether at a gain or at a loss) during the specified continuous period of leave, their gross proceeds are re-invested in qualifying investments before the end of the next reporting period, or within six months of the date of completion of the sale, whichever is sooner.

(b)   In the case of an application where Table 8B or Table 9B applies, points for maintaining the level of investment for the relevant period of leave will only be awarded if:

(i)   the applicant has maintained a portfolio of qualifying investments with a market value of at least £750,000 (or £3,750,000 or £7,500,000 as appropriate);

(ii)   any fall in the market value of the portfolio below the amount in (i) is corrected before the end of the next reporting period, or within six months of the date of completion of the sale, whichever is sooner, by the purchase of further qualifying investments with a market value equal to the amount of any such fall; and

(iii)   the applicant has maintained a total level of investment (including the qualifying investments at (i) and (ii) above) of £1,000,000.

(c)   In the case of an application where one of Tables 8A, 8B, 9A or 9B applies:

(i)   The applicant may withdraw interest and dividend payments generated by the qualifying investments from the portfolio;

(ii)   Fees, for example those charged by institutions for managing the portfolio, and transaction costs and tax incurred through buying and selling investments cannot be paid for from the investment funds for which the applicant scores points; and

(iii)   If the applicant has invested more than the required level in qualifying investments, the fees, transaction costs and tax referred to in (ii) above may be paid from the surplus investment, providing the surplus investment was made at the same time or before the fees, transaction costs and tax were incurred (for example, if the applicant scores points for investing £2 million in qualifying investments, but has actually invested £2.1 million in qualifying investments, up to £100,000 in fees, transaction costs and tax may be paid for from the investment funds. The applicant must have invested £2.1 million at or by the time he pays these costs; he cannot pay out of a £2 million investment and invest a further £100,000 at a later date to compensate).

65-SD.   The following specified documents must be provided as evidence of investment:

(a)   The applicant must provide a series of investment portfolio reports, certified as correct by a UK regulated financial institution, which must:

(i)   cover the required period, beginning no later than the end of the 3 month timescale specified in the relevant table;

(ii)   continue to the last reporting date of the most recent reporting period directly before the date of the application;

(iii)   include the price of the investments;

(iv)   certify that the total investment was maintained as required by paragraph 65C as applicable;

(v)   show the dates that the investments were made;

(vi)   show the destination of the investments;

(vii)   for investments made as loan funds to companies, be accompanied by audited accounts or unaudited accounts with an accounts compilation report for the investments made, giving the full details of the applicant's investment. The accountant must be a member of the Institute of Chartered Accountants in England and Wales, the Institute of Chartered Accountants in Scotland, the Institute of Chartered Accountants in Ireland, the Association of Chartered Certified Accountants, the Association of Authorised Public Accountants, the Chartered Institute of Public Finance and Accountancy, the Institute of Financial Accountants, the Chartered Institute of Management Accountants, or the Association of International Accountants;

(viii)   include the name and contact details of the financial institution that has certified the portfolio as correct, and confirmation that this institution is regulated by the Financial Conduct Authority (FCA) (and the Prudential Regulation Authority (PRA) where applicable);

(ix)   confirm that the investments were made in the applicant's name and/or that of his spouse, civil partner, unmarried or same-sex partner and not in the name of an offshore company or trust even if this is wholly owned by the applicant;

(x)   include the date that each portfolio report was certified by the financial institution; and

(xi)   state that the institution will confirm the content of the reports to the Home Office on request.

(b)   Where the applicant is applying under Table 8B or Table 9B, previously had leave as an Investor and is unable to provide the evidence listed above because he manages his own investments, or because he has a portfolio manager who does not operate in the UK and is therefore not regulated by the Financial Conduct Authority (FCA) (and the Prudential Regulation Authority (PRA) where applicable), the applicant must provide the following specified documents showing his holdings used to claim points, as relevant to the type of investment:

(i)   Certified copies of bond documents showing the value of the bonds, the date of purchase and the owner;

(ii)   Share documents showing the value of the shares, the date of purchase and the owner;

(iii)   The latest audited annual accounts of the organisation in which the investment has been made, which have been prepared and signed off in accordance with statutory requirements, and clearly show:

(1)   the amount of money held in the investments,

(2)   the name of the applicant (or applicant and/or husband, wife, civil partner, or unmarried or same-sex partner), and

(3)   the date of investment.

(iv)   the organisation in (iii) is not required to produce accounts, the applicant must provide a certificate showing the amount of money held in the investments, from an accountant who is a member of the Institute of Chartered Accountants in England and Wales, the Institute of Chartered Accountants in Scotland, the Institute of Chartered Accountants in Ireland, the Association of Chartered Certified Accountants, the Association of Authorised Public Accountants, the Chartered Institute of Public Finance and Accountancy, the Institute of Financial Accountants, the Chartered Institute of Management Accountants, or the Association of International Accountants.

(c)   Where the applicant is applying under Table 8B or Table 9B and has invested at least 75% of the specified investment amount but less than 100%, he must provide one or more of the following specified documents as evidence of the balance of the funds required to bring his total investment in the UK up to the specified investment amount:

(i)   Documents confirming the purchase of assets in the UK, showing the assets purchased, the value of these assets and the dates of purchase. When using property only the unmortgaged portion of the applicant's own home can be considered and the valuation must be provided on a report issued by a surveyor (who is a member of the Royal Institution of Chartered Surveyors) in the six months prior to the date of application;

(ii)   If the applicant maintained money on deposit in the UK, a statement or statements of account on the official stationery of the institution that holds the funds. These statements must be in the name of the applicant (or applicant and/or the husband, wife, civil partner, or unmarried or same-sex partner of the applicant) and confirm the dates and amount of money held. The applicant must ensure that the institution will confirm the content of the statement to the Home Office on request;

(iii)   An original letter from the financial institution that holds the cash on deposit, on the institution's official headed paper, issued by an authorised official of that institution, which confirms the dates and amount of money held and that the institution will confirm the content of the letter to the UK Border Agency on request.

(d)   If the applicant wishes the start of the 3 month timescale specified in Table 8A, Table 8B, Table 9A or Table 9B to be taken as the date he entered the UK, he must provide evidence which proves this date, such as a stamp in the applicant's passport, or an aircraft boarding card.

(e)   Evidence of the investment having been maintained, from the date that the funds were invested for the full period of remaining leave, will be determined using the portfolio reports provided in (a).

Attributes for Tier 1 (Graduate Entrepreneur) Migrants

66.   An applicant applying for entry clearance or leave to remain as a Tier 1 (Graduate Entrepreneur) Migrant must score 75 points for attributes.

67.   Available points are shown in Table 10.

68.   Notes to accompany the table appear below the table.

Table 10

Criterion	Points
(a) The applicant has been endorsed by a UK Higher Education Institution which: (i) is a sponsor with Tier 4 Sponsor status, (ii) is an A-rated Sponsor under Tier 2 of the Points-Based System if a Tier 2 licence is held, (iii) is an A-rated Sponsor under Tier 5 of the Points-Based System if a Tier 5 licence is held, (iv) has degree-awarding powers, and (v) has established processes and competence for identifying, nurturing and developing entrepreneurs among its undergraduate and postgraduate population; or (b) The applicant has been endorsed by UK Trade and Investment.	25
The applicant has been awarded a degree qualification (not a qualification of equivalent level which is not a degree) which meets or exceeds the recognised standard of a Bachelor's degree in the UK. For overseas qualifications, the standard must be confirmed by UK NARIC.	25
The endorsement must confirm that the endorsing body has assessed the applicant and considers that: (a) the applicant has a genuine and credible business idea, and (b) the applicant will spend the majority of his working time on developing business ventures, and (c) if the applicant is applying for leave to remain and his last grant of leave was as a Tier 1 (Graduate Entrepreneur), he has made satisfactory progress in developing his business since that leave was granted. The endorsement must also confirm the applicant's intended business sector or business intention. Points will not be awarded if this business will be mainly engaged in property development or property management. 'Property development or property management' in this context means any development of property owned by the applicant or his business to increase the value of the property with a view to earning a return either through rent or a future sale or both, or management of property (whether or not it is owned by the applicant or his business) for the purposes of renting it out or resale. The principle is that business income must be generated from the supply of goods and/or services and not derived from the increased value of property or any income generated through property, such as rent.	25

Notes Tier 1 (Graduate Entrepreneur) Limit

69. (a) The Secretary of State shall be entitled to limit the total number of Tier 1 (Graduate Entrepreneur) endorsements qualifying endorsing bodies may make in support of successful applications in a particular period, to be referred to as the Tier 1 (Graduate Entrepreneur) Limit.

    (b) The Tier 1 (Graduate Entrepreneur) Limit is 2,000 places per year (beginning on 6 April and ending on 5 April), which will be allocated as follows:

      (i) 1, 900 places will be allocated to qualifying Higher Education Institutions as set out in (c) below; and

      (ii) 100 places will be allocated to UK Trade and Investment.

    (c) Places for qualifying Higher Education Institutions will be allocated as follows:

      (i) The UK Border Agency will, on an annual basis, invite all UK Higher Education Institutions which meet the requirements in (a)(i) to (iv) in the first row of Table 10 to take part as endorsing institutions, with responses required by 5 April for the year beginning the next day.

      (ii) The endorsements will be allocated between all invited Higher Education Institutions who confirm that:

        (1) They wish to take part, and

        (2) They meet the requirement in (a)(v) in the first row of Table 10 above.

      (iii) Each qualifying body in (ii) will be allocated the smallest of:

        (1) The number of endorsements it has requested,

        (2) Its equal share of the number of endorsements available (If the result is not an integer it will be rounded down to the next lowest integer), or

        (3) 20 endorsements.

      (iv) If the result of (i) to (iii) is that there are fewer than 1,850 endorsements allocated to qualifying Higher Education Institutions for the year, the Home Office will invite all UK Higher Education Institutions which meet the requirements in (a)(i) to (iv) in the first row of Table 10 to request the remaining endorsements for the year ending 5 April, with responses required by 30 September.

      (v) The remaining endorsements will be allocated between all invited Higher Education Institutions who meet the criteria in (ii), regardless of whether they were previously allocated endorsements for the year.

      (vi) If all requests can be met without exceeding the number of remaining places available, each Higher Education Institution in (v) will be allocated the number of endorsements it has requested.

      (vii) If all requests cannot be met without exceeding the number of remaining places available, each Higher Education Institution in (v) will be allocated the smaller of:

        (1) The number of endorsements it has requested, or

        (2) Its equal share of the remaining number of endorsements available (If the result is not an integer it will be rounded down to the next lowest integer).

      (viii) the result of (iv) to (vii) is that there are still remaining places in the Tier 1 (Graduate Entrepreneur) Limit for the year, those places will not be allocated.

    (d) If:

      (i) an applicant does not make a valid application within 3 months of the date of his endorsement, or

      (ii) an application is refused, and that refusal is not subsequently overturned,

      the endorsement used in that application will be cancelled and the relevant endorsing body's unused allocation of endorsements will be increased by one, providing the end of the period (6 April to 5 April) to which it relates has not yet passed.

    (e) The Tier 1 (Graduate Entrepreneur) limit will not apply to applications for leave to remain where the applicant has, or last had, leave to remain as a Tier 1 (Graduate Entrepreneur).

    (f) Endorsements which have not been used by endorsing bodies cannot be carried over from one year (beginning on 6 April and ending on 5 April) to the next.

Endorsement

70. Points will only be awarded for an endorsement if:

    (a)   the endorsement was issued to the applicant no more than 3 months before the date of application,

    (b)   the endorsement has not been withdrawn by the relevant endorsing body at the time the application is considered by the entry clearance officer or the Secretary of State, and

    (c)   the applicant provides an original endorsement from the relevant endorsing body, which shows:

        (i)   the endorsement reference number,

        (ii)   the date of issue (including a statement on how long the letter is valid for),

        (iii)   the applicant's name,

        (iv)   the applicant's date of birth,

        (v)   the applicant's nationality,

        (vi)   the applicant's current passport number,

        (vii)   details of any dependants of the applicant who are already in the UK or who the applicant intends to bring to the UK,

        (viii) the name of the endorsing body,

        (ix)   the name and contact details of the authorising official of the endorsing body,

        (x)   the name, level and date of award of the applicant's qualification, this was shown in a previous successful Tier 1 (Graduate Entrepreneur) application,

        (xi)   the applicant's intended business sector or business intention,

        (xii)   what has led the endorsing body to endorse the application, and

        (xiii) if the applicant is applying for leave to remain and was last granted leave as a Tier 1 (Graduate Entrepreneur) Migrant, confirmation that the endorsing body is satisfied that he has made satisfactory progress.

Qualifications

71. Points will be awarded for a degree qualification if the endorsement:

    (a)   is by the UK Higher Education Institution which awarded the qualification; and

    (b)   contains the specified details of the qualification, as set out in paragraph 70(c).

72. (a)   In cases other than those in paragraph 71, points will only be awarded for a degree qualification if the applicant provides the following specified documents:

        (i)   The original certificate of award of the qualification, which clearly shows the:

            (1)   applicant's name,

            (2)   title of the award,

            (3)   date of the award, and

            (4)   name of the awarding institution, or

        (ii)   if:

            (1)   the applicant is awaiting graduation having successfully completed his degree, or

            (2)   the applicant no longer has the certificate and the institution who issued the certificate is unable to produce a replacement, an original academic reference from the institution that is awarding, or has awarded, the degree together with an original academic transcript, unless (d) applies.

    (b)   The academic reference referred to in (a)(ii) must be on the official headed paper of the institution and clearly show the:

        (1)   applicant's name,

        (2)   title of award,

        (3)   date of award, confirming that it has been or will be awarded, and

        (4)   either the date that the certificate will be issued (if the applicant has not yet graduated) or confirmation that the institution is unable to re-issue the original certificate or award.

    (c)   The academic transcript referred to in (a)(ii) must be on the institution's official paper and must show the:

        (1)   applicant's name,

        (2)   name of the academic institution,

        (3)   course title, and

        (4)   confirmation of the award.

(d)   If the applicant cannot provide his original certificate for one of the reasons given in (a)(ii) and is claiming points for a qualification with a significant research bias, such as a doctorate, an academic transcript is not required, providing the applicant provides an academic reference which includes all the information detailed in (b) above.

(e)   Where the degree is an overseas qualification and an applicant cannot find details of it on the points based calculator on the visas and immigration pages of the gov.uk website, he must, in addition to the document or documents in (a), provide an original letter or certificate from UK NARIC confirming the equivalency of the level of his qualification.

Attributes for Tier 2 (Intra-Company Transfer) Migrants

73.   An applicant applying for entry or leave to remain as a Tier 2 (Intra-Company Transfer) Migrant must score 50 points for attributes.

73A.   Available points for entry clearance or leave to remain are shown in Table 11.

73B.   Notes to accompany Table 11 appear below the table.

Table 11

Criterion	Points
Certificate of Sponsorship	30
Appropriate salary	20

Notes

Certificate of Sponsorship

74.   In order to obtain points for a Certificate of Sponsorship, the applicant must provide a valid Certificate of Sponsorship reference number.

74A.   A Certificate of Sponsorship reference number will only be considered to be valid if:

(a)   the number supplied links to a Certificate of Sponsorship Checking Service entry that names the applicant as the migrant and confirms that the Sponsor is Sponsoring him as a Tier 2 (Intra- Company Transfer) Migrant and specifies the sub-category of Tier 2 (Intra-Company Transfer) under which he is applying,

(b)   the Sponsor assigned the Certificate of Sponsorship reference number to the migrant no more than 3 months before the application for entry clearance or leave to remain is made,

(c)   the application for entry clearance or leave to remain is made no more than 3 months before the start of the employment as stated on the Certificate of Sponsorship,

(d)   the migrant must not previously have applied for entry clearance, leave to enter or leave to remain using the same Certificate of Sponsorship reference number, if that application was either approved or refused (not rejected as an invalid application declared void or withdrawn),

(e)   that reference number must not have been withdrawn or cancelled by the Sponsor or by the UK Border Agency since it was assigned, including where it has been cancelled by the UK Border Agency due to having been used in a previous application, and

(f)   the Sponsor is an A-rated Sponsor, unless the application is for leave to remain and the applicant has, or was last granted, leave as a Tier 2 (Intra-Company) Migrant or a Qualifying Work Permit Holder.

74B.   No points will be awarded for a Certificate of Sponsorship unless:

(a)   the job that the Certificate of Sponsorship Checking Service entry records that the person is being sponsored to do appears on:

    (i)   the list of occupations skilled to National Qualifications Framework level 6 or above, as stated in the codes of practice in Appendix J, or

    (ii)   one of the following creative sector occupations skilled to National Qualifications Framework level 4 or above:

        (1)   3411 Artists,

        (2)   3412 Authors, writers and translators,

        (3)   3413 Actors, entertainers and presenters,

(4)   3414 Dancers and choreographers, or

(5)   3422 Product, clothing and related designers, or

(b)   (i)   the applicant is applying for leave to remain,

(ii)   the applicant previously had leave as a Tier 2 (Intra-Company Transfer) Migrant under the Rules in place between 6 April 2011 and 13 June 2012, and has not since been granted leave to remain in any other route, or entry clearance or leave to enter in any route, and

(iii)   the job that the Certificate of Sponsorship Checking Service entry records that the person is being sponsored to do appears on the list of occupations skilled to National Qualifications Framework level 4 or above, as stated in the codes of practice in Appendix J

(c)   (i)   the applicant is applying for leave to remain as a Tier 2 (Intra-Company Transfer) Migrant in the Long Term Staff sub-category,

(ii)   the applicant previously had leave as:

(1)   a Tier 2 (Intra-Company Transfer) Migrant under the rules in place before 6 April 2011, or

(2)   a Qualifying Work Permit Holder,

and has not since been granted leave to remain in any other route, or entry clearance or leave to enter in any route, and

(iii)   the job that the Certificate of Sponsorship Checking Service entry records that the person is being sponsored to do appears on the list of occupations skilled to National Qualifications Framework level 3 or above, as stated in the codes of practice in Appendix J, or the applicant is a Senior Care Worker or an Established Entertainer as defined in paragraph 6 of these Rules, or

(d)   (i)   the applicant was last granted entry clearance or leave as a Tier 2 (Intra-Company Transfer) Migrant,

(ii)   the applicant is applying for leave to remain to work in the same occupation for the same Sponsor as in the application which led to his previous grant of leave,

(iii)   the Certificate of Sponsorship used in support of the applicant's previous application was assigned by the Sponsor before 6 April 2013, and

(iv)   the occupation fails to meet the required skill level in (a) to (c) above solely due to reclassification from the SOC 2000 system to the SOC 2010 system.

74C.   (a)   if the applicant is applying as a Tier 2 (Intra-Company Transfer) Migrant in either the Short Term Staff or Long Term Staff sub-categories, no points will be awarded for a Certificate of Sponsorship unless:

(i)   the Certificate of Sponsorship Checking Service entry confirms that the applicant has been working for the Sponsor for at least 12 months as specified in paragraphs (b) and (c) below, and

(ii)   the applicant provides, if requested to do so, the specified documents as set out in paragraph 74C-SD(a) below, unless he was last granted leave to work for the same Sponsor in the same sub-category as he is currently applying under. The application may be granted without these specified documents, but the Home Office reserves the right to request the specified documents, and to refuse applications if these documents are not received at the address specified in the request within 7 working days of the date of the request.

(b)   Throughout the 12 months referred to in paragraph (a)(i) above, the applicant must have been working for the Sponsor:

(i)   outside the UK, or

(ii)   in the UK, provided he had leave to work for the Sponsor as:

(1)   a Tier 2 (Intra-Company Transfer) Migrant in either of the Short Term Staff or Long Term Staff sub-categories,

(2)   a Tier 2 (Intra-Company Transfer) Migrant in the established staff sub-category under the rules in place before 6 April 2011,

(3)   a Tier 2 (Intra-Company Transfer) Migrant under the rules in place before 6 April 2010,

(4)   a Qualifying Work Permit Holder (provided that the work permit was granted because the holder was the subject of an Intra-Company Transfer), and/or

(5)   a representative of an Overseas Business, and

(c)   The specified period referred to in paragraph (a)(i) above is:

(i)   a continuous period of 12 months immediately prior to the date of application, or

    (ii)   an aggregated period of at least 12 months within the 24 month period immediately before the date of application, if at some point within the 12 months preceding the date of application, the applicant has been:

        (1)   on maternity, paternity or adoption leave, or

        (2)   on long-term sick leave lasting one month or longer,

        and if requested to provide the specified documents set out in paragraph 74C-SD(a) below, also provides, at the same time, the specified documents as set out in paragraph 74C-SD(c) below, or

    (iii)   an aggregated period of at least 12 months overseas within any timeframe, providing the applicant has been working continuously and lawfully for the sponsor (either overseas or in the UK) since the start of that aggregated 12-month period.

74C-SD.   (a)   The specified documents in paragraph 74C(a) are:

    (i)   Original formal payslips issued by the employer and showing the employer's name covering the full specified period (The most recent payslip must be dated no earlier than 31 days before the date of the application);

    (ii)   Other payslips covering the full specified period (The most recent payslip must be dated no earlier than 31 days before the date of the application), accompanied by a letter from the Sponsor, on company headed paper and signed by a senior official, confirming the authenticity of the payslips;

    (iii)   Personal bank or building society statements covering the full specified period, which clearly show:

        (1)   the applicant's name,

        (2)   the account number,

        (3)   the date of the statement (The most recent statement must be dated no earlier than 31 days before the date of the application),

        (4)   the financial institution's name and logo, and

        (5)   transactions by the Sponsor covering the full specified period; or

    (iv)   A building society pass book, which clearly shows:

        (1)   the applicant's name,

        (2)   the account number,

        (3)   the financial institution's name and logo, and

        (4)   transactions by the Sponsor covering the full specified period.

    (b)   If the applicant provides the bank or building society statements in (a)(iii):

    (i)   The statements must:

        (1)   be printed on paper bearing the bank or building society's letterhead,

        (2)   bear the official stamp of the bank on every page, or

        (3)   be accompanied by a supporting letter from the issuing bank or building society, on company headed paper, confirming the authenticity of the statements provided;

    (ii)   The statements must not be mini-statements obtained from an Automated Teller Machine.

    (c)   The specified documents as evidence of periods of maternity, paternity or adoption leave, as required in paragraph 74C(b), are:

    (i)   The original full birth certificate or original full certificate of adoption (as appropriate) containing the names of the parents or adoptive parents of the child for whom the leave was taken, if this is available; and

    (ii)   At least one (or both, if the document in (i) is unavailable) of the following, if they are available:

        (1)   An original letter from the applicant and his sponsor, on company headed paper, confirming the start and end dates of the applicant's leave,

        (2)   One of the types of documents set out in (a) above, covering the entire period of leave, and showing the maternity, paternity or adoption payments.

        and

    (iii)   If the applicant cannot provide two of the types of specified document in (i) and (ii), at least one of the types of specified documents in either (i) or (ii), a full explanation of why the other documents cannot be provided, and at least one of the following specified documents, from an official source and which is independently verifiable:

    (1)   official adoption papers issued by the relevant authority,

    (2)   any relevant medical documents, or

    (3)   a relevant extract from a register of birth which is accompanied by an original letter from the issuing authority.

(d)   The specified documents as evidence of periods of long term sick leave, as required in paragraph 74C(b), are:

    (i)   An original letter from the applicant's Sponsor, on company headed paper, confirming the start and end dates of the applicant's leave, if this is available;

    (ii)   One of the types of documents set out in (a) above, covering the entire period of leave, and showing the statutory sick pay and/or sick pay from health insurance, if these documents are available; and

    (iii)   If the applicant cannot provide the specified documents in both (i) and (ii), the specified documents in either (i) or (ii), a full explanation of why the other documents cannot be provided, and any relevant medical documents, from an official source and which are independently verifiable.

74D.   If the applicant is applying as a Tier 2 (Intra-Company Transfer) Migrant in the Graduate Trainee sub-category, no points will be awarded for a Certificate of Sponsorship unless:

(a)   the job that the Certificate of Sponsorship Checking Service entry records that the person is being Sponsored to do is part of a structured graduate training programme, with clearly defined progression towards a managerial or specialist role within the organisation,

(b)   the Sponsor has assigned Certificates of Sponsorship to 5 applicants or fewer, including the applicant in question, under the Graduate Trainee sub-category in the current year, beginning 6 April and ending 5 April each year, and

(c)   the Certificate of Sponsorship Checking Service entry confirms that the applicant has been working for the Sponsor outside the UK for a continuous period of 3 months immediately prior to the date of application and, if requested to do so, the applicant provides the specified documents in paragraph 74C-SD(a) above to prove this. The application may be granted without these specified documents, but the UK Border Agency reserves the right to request the specified documents, and to refuse applications if these documents are not received at the address specified in the request within 7 working days of the date of the request.

74E.   If the applicant is applying as a Tier 2 (Intra-Company Transfer) Migrant in the Skills Transfer subcategory, no points will be awarded for a Certificate of Sponsorship unless the job that the Certificate of Sponsorship Checking Service entry records that the person is being Sponsored to do is for the sole purpose of transferring skills to or from the Sponsor's UK work environment. The appointment must be additional to staffing requirements that is the role in the UK would not exist but for the need for skills transfer.

74F.   An applicant cannot score points for a Certificate of Sponsorship from Table 11 if the job that the Certificate of Sponsorship Checking Service entry records that he is being Sponsored to do is as a sports person or a Minister of Religion.

74G.   No points will be awarded for a Certificate of Sponsorship if the job that the Certificate of Sponsorship Checking Service entry records that the applicant is being sponsored to do amounts to:

(a)   the hire of the applicant to a third party who is not the sponsor to fill a position with that party, whether temporary or permanent, or

(b)   contract work to undertake an ongoing routine role or to provide an ongoing routine service for a third party who is not the sponsor,

regardless of the nature or length of any arrangement between the sponsor and the third party.

74H.   No points will be awarded for a Certificate of Sponsorship if the Entry Clearance Officer or the Secretary of State has reasonable grounds to believe, notwithstanding that the applicant has provided the evidence required under the relevant provisions of Appendix A, that:

(a)   the job as recorded by the Certificate of Sponsorship Checking Service is not a genuine vacancy, if the applicant is applying as a Tier 2 (Intra-Company Transfer) Migrant in either of the Short Term Staff or Long Term Staff subcategories, or

(b)   the applicant is not appropriately qualified to do the job in question.

74I.   To support the assessment in paragraph 74H, the Entry Clearance Officer or the Secretary of State may request additional information and evidence from the applicant or the Sponsor, and refuse the application if the information or evidence is not provided. Any requested documents must be received by the Entry Clearance Officer or the Secretary of State at the address specified in the request within 28 calendar days of the date the request is sent.

Appropriate salary

75.   The points awarded for appropriate salary will be based on the applicant's gross annual salary to be paid by the Sponsor, subject to the following conditions:

   (i)   Points will be awarded based on basic pay (excluding overtime);

   (ii)   Allowances will be included in the salary for the awarding of points where they are part of the guaranteed salary package and:

      (1)   would be paid to a local settled worker in similar circumstances, or

      (2)   are paid to cover the additional cost of living in the UK;

   (iii)   Where allowances are made available solely for the purpose of accommodation, they will only be included up to a value of:

      (1)   40% of the total salary package for which points are being awarded, if the applicant is applying in either the Short Term Staff, Graduate Trainee or Skills Transfer sub-categories, or

      (2)   30% of the total salary package for which points are being awarded, if the applicant is applying in the Long Term Staff sub-category;

   (iv)   Other allowances and benefits, such as bonus or incentive pay, employer pension contributions, and allowances to cover business expenses, including (but not limited to) travel to and from the sending country, will not be included;

   (v)   If the applicant has exchanged some of his UK employment rights for shares as an employee-owner, the value of those shares will not be included.

75A.   No points will be awarded if the salary referred to in paragraph 75 above is less than £41,500 per year where the applicant is applying in the Long Term Staff sub-category, unless the applicant is applying for leave to remain and previously had leave as:

   (i)   a Qualifying Work Permit Holder, or

   (ii)   a Tier 2 (Intra-Company Transfer) Migrant under the rules in place before 6 April 2011,

   and has not been granted entry clearance in this or any other route since that grant of leave.

75B.   No points will be awarded if the salary referred to in paragraph 75 above is less than £24,800 per year where the applicant is applying in the Short Term Staff, Graduate Trainee or Skills Transfer sub-categories, unless the applicant is applying for leave to remain and has, or last had entry clearance, leave to enter or leave to remain as a Tier 2 (Intra-Company Transfer) Migrant under the rules in place before 6 April 2011.

75C.   No points will be awarded if the salary referred to in paragraph 75 above is less than the appropriate rate for the job as stated in the codes of practice in Appendix J, unless the applicant is an established entertainer as defined in paragraph 6 of these Rules.

75D.   Where the applicant is paid hourly, the appropriate salary consideration will be based on earnings up to a maximum of 48 hours a week, even if the applicant works for longer than this. For example, an applicant who works 60 hours a week for £8 per hour be considered to have a salary of £19,968 (8x48x52) and not £25,960 (8x60x52), and will therefore not be awarded points for appropriate salary.

75E.   No points will be awarded for appropriate salary if the applicant does not provide a valid Certificate of Sponsorship reference number with his application.

Attributes for Tier 2 (General) Migrants

76.   An applicant applying for entry or leave to remain as a Tier 2 (General) Migrant must score 50 points for attributes.

76A.   Available points for entry clearance or leave to remain are shown in Table 11A.

76B.   Notes to accompany Table 11A appear below the table.

Table 11A

Certificate of Sponsorship	Points	Appropriate salary	Points
Job offer passes Resident Labour Market Test	30	Appropriate salary	20
Resident Labour Market Test exemption applies	30		
Continuing to work in the same occupation for the same Sponsor			

Notes

Certificate of Sponsorship

77. Points may only be scored for one entry in the Certificate of Sponsorship column.

77A. In order to obtain points for a Certificate of Sponsorship, the applicant must provide a valid Certificate of Sponsorship reference number.

77B. The only Certificates of Sponsorship to be allocated to Sponsors for applicants to be Sponsored as Tier 2 (General) Migrants are:

(a) Certificates of Sponsorship to be assigned to applicants as a Tier 2 (General) Migrant, as allocated to Sponsors under the Tier 2 (General) limit, which is set out in paragraphs 80 to 84A below.

(b) Certificates of Sponsorship to be assigned to specified applicants for leave to remain as a Tier 2 (General) Migrant, as set out in paragraph 77D of Appendix A,

(c) Certificates of Sponsorship to be assigned to an applicant to do a job for which the gross annual salary (including such allowances as are specified as acceptable for this purpose in paragraph 79 of this Appendix) is £155,300 (or £153,500, if the recruitment took place before 6 April 2015) or higher, and

77C. A Certificate of Sponsorship reference number will only be considered to be valid if:

(a) the number supplied links to a Certificate of Sponsorship Checking Service entry that names the applicant as the migrant and confirms that the Sponsor is Sponsoring him as a Tier 2 (General) Migrant,

(b) the Sponsor assigned that reference number to the migrant no more than 3 months after the Sponsor was allocated the Certificate of Sponsorship, if the Certificate of Sponsorship was allocated to the Sponsor under the Tier 2 (General) limit,

(c) the Sponsor assigned that reference number to the migrant no more than 3 months before the application for entry clearance or leave to remain is made,

(d) the application for entry clearance or leave to remain is made no more than 3 months before the start of the employment as stated on the Certificate of Sponsorship,

(e) the migrant must not previously have applied for entry clearance, leave to enter or leave to remain using the same Certificate of Sponsorship reference number, if that application was either approved or refused (not rejected as an invalid application, declared void or withdrawn),

(f) that reference number must not have been withdrawn or cancelled by the Sponsor or by the UK Border Agency since it was assigned, including where it has been cancelled by the UK Border Agency due to having been used in a previous application, and

(g) the Sponsor is an A-rated Sponsor, unless:

(1) the application is for leave to remain, and

(2) the applicant has, or was last granted, leave as a Tier 2 (General) Migrant, a Jewish Agency Employee, a Member of the Operational Ground Staff of an Overseas-owned Airline, a Representative of an Overseas Newspaper, News Agency or Broadcasting Organisation, or a Qualifying Work Permit Holder, and

(3) the applicant is applying to work for the same employer named on the Certificate of Sponsorship or Work Permit document which led to his last grant of leave or, in the case of an applicant whose last grant of leave was as a Jewish Agency Employee, a Member of the Operational Ground Staff of an Overseas-owned Airline, a Representative of an Overseas Newspaper, News Agency or Broadcasting Organisation, the same employer for whom the applicant was working or stated he was intending to work when last granted leave.

77D. No points will be awarded for a Certificate of Sponsorship unless:

(a) in the case of a Certificate of Sponsorship which was allocated to the Sponsor under the Tier 2 (General) limit, the number supplied links to a Certificate of Sponsorship Checking Service entry which contains the same job and at least the same salary details as stated in the Sponsor's application for that Certificate of Sponsorship,

(b) in the case of a Certificate of Sponsorship which was not allocated to the Sponsor under the Tier 2 (General) limit:

    (i) the applicant:

        (1) is applying for leave to remain, and

        (2) does not have, or was not last granted entry clearance, leave to enter or leave to remain as the partner of a Relevant Points Based System Migrant,

    or

    (ii) the number supplied links to a Certificate of Sponsorship Checking Service entry which shows that the applicant's gross annual salary (including such allowances as are specified as acceptable for this purpose in paragraph 79 of this appendix) to be paid by the Sponsor is £155,300 (or £153,500 if the recruitment took place before 6 April 2015) or higher.

77E. No points will be awarded for a Certificate of Sponsorship unless:

(a) the job that the Certificate of Sponsorship Checking Service entry records that the person is being sponsored to do appears on:

    (i) the list of occupations skilled to National Qualifications Framework level 6 or above, as stated in the codes of practice in Appendix J, or

    (ii) one of the following creative sector occupations skilled to National Qualifications Framework level 4 or above:

        (1) 3411 Artists,

        (2) 3412 Authors, writers and translators,

        (3) 3413 Actors, entertainers and presenters,

        (4) 3414 Dancers and choreographers, or

        (5) 3422 Product, clothing and related designers,

    or

(b) the job that the Certificate of Sponsorship Checking Service entry records that the person is being sponsored to do is skilled to National Qualifications Framework level 4 or above, and appears on the shortage occupation list in Appendix K,

    or

(c) (i) the applicant is applying for leave to remain,

    (ii) the applicant previously had leave as a Tier 2 (General) Migrant or a Qualifying Work Permit Holder, and has not since been granted leave to remain in any other route, or entry clearance or leave to enter in any route,

    (iii) at the time a Certificate of Sponsorship or Work Permit which led to a grant of leave in (ii) was issued, the job referred to in that Certificate of Sponsorship or Work Permit appeared on the shortage occupation list in Appendix K, and

    (iv) the job that the Certificate of Sponsorship Checking service entry records that the person is being sponsored to do in his current application is the same as the job referred to in (iii), for either the same or a different employer,

    or

(d) (i) the applicant is applying for leave to remain,

    (ii) the applicant previously had leave as a Tier 2 (General) Migrant under the Rules in place between 6 April 2011 and 13 June 2012, and has not since been granted leave to remain in any other route, or entry clearance or leave to enter in any route, and

    (iii) the job that the Certificate of Sponsorship Checking Service entry records that the person is being sponsored to do appears on the list of occupations skilled to National Qualifications Framework level 4 or above, as stated in the codes of practice in Appendix J,

    or

(e) (i) the applicant is applying for leave to remain,

    (ii) the applicant previously had leave as:

(1)   a Tier 2 (General) Migrant under the rules in place before 6 April 2011,

(2)   a Qualifying Work Permit Holder,

(3)   a Representative of an Overseas Newspaper, News Agency or Broadcasting Organisation,

(4)   a Member of the Operational Ground Staff of an Overseas-owned Airline

(5)   a Jewish Agency Employee,

and has not since been granted leave to remain in any other route, or entry clearance or leave to enter in any route, and

(iii)   the job that the Certificate of Sponsorship Checking Service entry records that the person is being sponsored to do appears on the list of occupations skilled to National Qualifications Framework level 3 or above, as stated in the codes of practice in Appendix J, or the applicant is a Senior Care Worker or an Established Entertainer as defined in paragraph 6 of these Rules.

(f)   (i)   the applicant was last granted as a Tier 2 (General) Migrant,

(ii)   the applicant is applying for leave to remain to work in the same occupation for the same Sponsor as in the application which led to his previous grant of leave,

(iii)   the Certificate of Sponsorship used in support of the applicant's previous application was assigned by the Sponsor before 6 April 2013, and

(iv)   the occupation fails to meet the required skill level in (a) to (e) above solely due to reclassification from the SOC 2000 system to the SOC 2010 system.

77F.   An applicant cannot score points for a Certificate of Sponsorship from Table 11A if the job that the Certificate of Sponsorship Checking Service entry records that he is being sponsored to do is as a sports person or a Minister of Religion.

77G.   No points will be awarded for a Certificate of Sponsorship if the job that the Certificate of Sponsorship Checking Service entry records that the applicant is being sponsored to do amounts to:

(a)   the hire of the applicant to a third party who is not the sponsor to fill a position with that party, whether temporary or permanent, or

(b)   contract work to undertake an ongoing routine role or to provide an ongoing routine service for a third party who is not the sponsor,

regardless of the nature or length of any arrangement between the sponsor and the third party.

77H.   No points will be awarded for a Certificate of Sponsorship if the Entry Clearance Officer or the Secretary of State has reasonable grounds to believe, notwithstanding that the applicant has provided the evidence required under the relevant provisions of Appendix A, that:

(a)   the job as recorded by the Certificate of Sponsorship Checking Service is not a genuine vacancy,

(b)   the applicant is not appropriately qualified or registered to do the job in question (or will not be, by the time they begin the job), or

(c)   the stated requirements of the job as recorded by the Certificate of Sponsorship Checking Service and in any advertisements for the job are inappropriate for the job on offer and / or have been tailored to exclude resident workers from being recruited.

77I.   To support the assessment in paragraph 77H(b), if the applicant is not yet appropriately qualified or registered to do the job in question, he must provide evidence with his application showing that he can reasonably be expected to obtain the appropriate qualifications or registrations by the time he begins the job, for example, a letter from the relevant body providing written confirmation that the applicant has registered to sit the relevant examinations.

77J.   To support the assessment in paragraph 77H(a)-(c), the Entry Clearance Officer or the Secretary of State may request additional information and evidence from the applicant or the Sponsor, and refuse the application if the information or evidence is not provided. Any requested documents must be received by the Entry Clearance Officer or the Secretary of State at the address specified in the request within 28 calendar days of the date the request is sent.

Job offer passes Resident Labour Market Test

78.   Points will only be awarded for a job offer that passes the Resident Labour Market Test if:

(a)   the Sponsor has advertised (or had advertised on its behalf) the job as set out in Tables 11B and 11C below; and

(b)   The advertisements have stated:

(i)   the job title,

    (ii)   the main duties and responsibilities of the job (job description),

    (iii)   the location of the job,

    (iv)   an indication of the salary package or salary range or terms on offer,

    (v)   the skills, qualifications and experience required for the job, and

    (vi)   the closing date for applications, unless it is part of the Sponsor's rolling recruitment programme, in which case the advertisement should show the period of the recruitment programme;

    and

(c)   The advertisements were published in English (or Welsh if the job is based in Wales); and

(d)   The Sponsor can show that no suitable settled worker is available to fill the job unless the job is in a PhD-level occupation listed in Appendix J. Settled workers will not be considered unsuitable on the basis that they lack qualifications, experience or skills (including language skills) that were not specifically requested in the job advertisement; and

(e)   The Certificate of Sponsorship Checking Service entry contains full details of when and where the job was advertised, and any advertisement reference numbers, including the Universal Jobmatch (or other Jobcentre Plus online service) or JobCentre Online vacancy reference number where relevant.

Table 11B: Advertising methods and duration which satisfy the Resident Labour Market Test

Type of job	Methods of advertising/ recruitment	Duration/timing of advertising
New graduate jobs or internships	• University milkround visits to at least 3 UK universities (or all UK universities which provide the relevant course, whichever is the lower number), • At least one of the following websites: – www.jobs.ac.uk, – www.milkround.com, – www.prospects.ac.uk, or – www.targetjobs.co.uk and • At least one other medium listed in Table 11C	At least 28 days within the **4 years** immediately before the Sponsor assigned the Certificate of Sponsorship to the applicant
Pupillages for trainee barristers	• At least two media (or one medium if the job was advertised before 6 April 2013) listed in Table 11C	At least 28 days within the **2 years** immediately before the Sponsor assigned the Certificate of Sponsorship to the applicant
Jobs in PhD-level occupations as listed in Appendix J	• At least two media (or one medium if the job was advertised before 6 April 2013) listed in Table 11C	At least 28 days within the **1 year** immediately before the Sponsor assigned the Certificate of Sponsorship to the applicant
Jobs where the appropriate salary, as determined by paragraphs 79 to 79D of Appendix A, is at least £72,500 per year (or £71,600 per year if the job was advertised before 6 April 2015) or there is a stock exchange disclosure requirement	• At least two media (or one medium if the job was advertised before 6 April 2013) listed in Table 11C	At least 28 days within the **6 months** immediately before the Sponsor assigned the Certificate of Sponsorship to the applicant
Creative sector jobs covered by Table 9 of Appendix J	• As set out in Table 9 of Appendix J	As set out in Table 9 of Appendix J

Type of job	Methods of advertising/recruitment	Duration/timing of advertising
Orchestral musicians	• Universal Jobmatch (or other Jobcentre Plus online service) for jobs based in England, Scotland or Wales, or JobCentre Online for jobs based in Northern Ireland, and • At least one other medium listed in Table 11C	At least 28 days within the **2 years** immediately before the Sponsor assigned the Certificate of Sponsorship to the applicant
Positions in the NHS where the Resident Labour Market Test includes advertising on NHS Jobs between 19 November 2012 and 6 April 2015	• NHS Jobs	At least 28 days within the **6 months** immediately before the Sponsor assigned the Certificate of Sponsorship to the applicant
All other jobs	• Universal Jobmatch (or other Jobcentre Plus online service) for jobs based in England, Scotland or Wales, or JobCentre Online for jobs based in Northern Ireland, and • At least one other medium listed in Table 11C	At least 28 days within the **6 months** immediately before the Sponsor assigned the Certificate of Sponsorship to the applicant

Table 11C: Advertising media which satisfy the Resident Labour Market Test

Type of medium	Criteria for suitable media
Newspaper	Must be: • marketed throughout the UK or throughout the whole of the devolved nation in which the job is located, and • published at least once a week
Professional journal	Must be: • available nationally through retail outlets or through subscription, • published at least once a month, and • related to the nature of the job i.e. a relevant trade journal, official journal of a professional occupational body, or subject-specific publication
Website	Must be one of the following: • Universal Jobmatch (or other Jobcentre Plus online service), for jobs based in England, Scotland or Wales, • JobCentre Online, for jobs based in Northern Ireland, • an online version of a newspaper or professional journal which would satisfy the criteria above, • the website of a prominent professional or recruitment organisation, which does not charge a fee to jobseekers to view job advertisements or to apply for jobs via those advertisements, or • if the Sponsor is a multinational organisation or has over 250 permanent employees in the UK, the Sponsor's own website

Resident Labour Market Test exemption applies

Shortage occupation

78A.   In order for a Resident Labour Market Test exemption to apply for a job offer in a shortage occupation:

(a)   the job must, at the time the Certificate of Sponsorship was assigned to the applicant, have appeared on the shortage occupation list in Appendix K,

(b)   in all cases, contracted working hours must be for at least 30 hours a week, and

(c)   in all cases, if the UK Border Agency list of shortage occupations indicates that the job appears on the 'Scotland only' shortage occupation list, the job offer must be for employment in which the applicant will be working at a location in Scotland.

Post-Study Work

78B.   In order for a Resident Labour Market Test exemption to apply for post-study work:

(a)   the applicant must be applying for leave to remain,

(b)   the applicant must have, or have last been granted, entry clearance, leave to enter or leave to remain as:

(1)   a Tier 1 (Graduate Entrepreneur) Migrant,

(2)   a Tier 1 (Post-Study Work) Migrant,

(3)   a Participant in the International Graduates Scheme (or its predecessor, the Science and Engineering Graduates Scheme),

(4)   a Participant in the Fresh Talent: Working in Scotland Scheme,

(5)   a Tier 4 Migrant,

(6)   a Student,

(7)   a Student Nurse,

(8)   a Student Re-Sitting an Examination,

(9)   a Person Writing Up a Thesis,

(10)   an Overseas Qualified Nurse or Midwife,

(11)   a Postgraduate Doctor or Dentist, or

(12)   a Student Union Sabbatical Officer,

and

(c)   Where (b)(5) to (12) apply, the applicant must meet the requirements of paragraph 245HD(d) of these Rules.

Other exemptions

78C.   In order for another Resident Labour Market Test exemption to apply, either:

(a)   the Certificate of Sponsorship Checking Service entry must show that the applicant's gross annual salary (including such allowances as are specified as acceptable for this purpose in paragraph 79 of this appendix) to be paid by the Sponsor is £155,300 (or £153,500, if the recruitment took place before 6 April 2015) or higher; or

(b)   the job offer must be in a supernumerary research position where the applicant has been issued a non-transferable scientific research Award or Fellowship by an external organisation which is not the Sponsor, meaning that the role is over and above the Sponsor's normal requirements and if the applicant was not there, the role would not be filled by anyone else; or

(c)   the job offer must be to continue working as a Doctor or Dentist in training, under the same NHS Training Number which was assigned to the applicant for previous lawful employment as a Doctor or Dentist in Training in the UK; or

(d)   the job offer must be as a Doctor in Speciality Training where the applicant's salary and the costs of his training are being met by the government of another country under an agreement with that country and the United Kingdom Government; or

(e)   the job offer must be to resume a post in a Higher Education Institution, working for the same Sponsor as in a previous grant of entry clearance or leave to remain as a Tier 2 (General) Migrant, where the break in employment is due solely to a period of academic leave;

and the Certificate of Sponsorship Checking Service entry must provide full details of why an exemption applies.

Continuing to work in the same occupation for the same Sponsor

78D.　In order for the applicant to be awarded points for continuing to work in the same occupation for the same Sponsor:

    (a)　the applicant must be applying for leave to remain,

    (b)　the applicant must have, or have last been granted, entry clearance or leave to remain as:

        (i)　a Tier 2 (General) Migrant,

        (ii)　a Qualifying Work Permit Holder,

        (iii)　a Representative of an Overseas Newspaper, News Agency or Broadcasting Organisation,

        (iv)　a Member of the Operational Ground Staff of an Overseas-owned Airline or

        (v)　a Jewish Agency Employee,

    (b)　the Sponsor must be the same employer:

        (i)　as the Sponsor on the previous application that was granted, in the case of an applicant whose last grant of leave was as a Tier 2 (General) Migrant,

        (ii)　that the work permit was issued to, in the case of an applicant whose last grant of leave was as a Qualifying Work Permit Holder,

        (iii)　for whom the applicant was working or stated he was intending to work when last granted leave, in the case of an applicant whose last grant of leave was a Representative of an Overseas Newspaper, News Agency or Broadcasting Organisation, a Member of the Operational Ground Staff of an Overseas-owned Airline, or a Jewish Agency Employee.

    (c)　the job that the Certificate of Sponsorship Checking Service entry records the applicant as having been engaged to do must be the same occupation:

        (i)　in respect of which the Certificate of Sponsorship that led to the previous grant was issued, in the case of an applicant whose last grant of leave was as a Tier 2 (General) Migrant,

        (ii)　in respect of which the previous work permit was issued, in the case of an applicant whose last grant of leave was as a Qualifying Permit Holder, or

        (iii)　that the applicant was doing, or intended to do, when he received his last grant of leave, in the case of an applicant whose last grant of leave was a Representative of an Overseas Newspaper, News Agency or Broadcasting Organisation, a Member of the Operational Ground Staff of an Overseas-owned Airline, or a Jewish Agency Employee,

Appropriate salary

79.　The points awarded for appropriate salary will be based on the applicant's gross annual salary to be paid by the Sponsor, subject to the following conditions:

    (i)　Points will be awarded based on basic pay (excluding overtime);

    (ii)　Allowances, such as London weighting, will be included in the salary for the awarding of points where they are part of the guaranteed salary package and would be paid to a local settled worker in similar circumstances;

    (iii)　Other allowances and benefits, such as bonus or incentive pay, employer pension contributions, travel and subsistence (including travel to and from the applicant's home country), will not be included.

    (iv)　the applicant has exchanged some of his UK employment rights for shares as an employee-owner, the value of those shares will not be included.

79A.　No points will be awarded if the salary referred to in paragraph 79 above is less than £20,800 per year, unless:

    (a)　the applicant:

        (i)　is applying for leave to remain and

        (ii)　previously had leave as:

            (1)　a Qualifying Work Permit Holder,

            (2)　a Representative of an Overseas Newspaper, News Agency or Broadcasting Organisation,

            (3)　a Member of the operational Ground Staff of an Overseas-owned Airline

            (4)　a Jewish Agency Employee, or

            (5)　a Tier 2 (General) Migrant under the Rules in place before 6 April 2011;

      and

        (iii)　has not been granted entry clearance in this or any other route since that grant of leave; or

(b)   the Certificate of Sponsorship checking service entry records the applicant:

    (i)   is being sponsored as a pre-registration candidate nurse or candidate midwife on the basis that:

        (1)   the applicant obtained a Nursing and Midwifery Council permission before 30 March 2015 to undertake the Overseas Nursing Programme or the Adaptation to Midwifery Programme, and is being sponsored to undertake a supervised practice placement as part of the programme, which has been approved by the Nursing and Midwifery Council, or

        (2)   the applicant will sit an Observed Structured Clinical Examination (OSCE) to obtain Nursing and Midwifery Council registration no later than 3 months after the stated employment start date, and familiarisation training will be permitted until the application for registration with the Nursing and Midwifery Council Registration is either successfully completed, otherwise closed, or 8 months, whichever is earlier;

    and

    (ii)   will continue to be sponsored as a nurse or midwife by the Sponsor after achieving Nursing and Midwifery Council registration; and

    (iii)   will be paid at least £20,800 per year once that registration is achieved;

    and the applicant or his Sponsor provides evidence of the above, if requested to do so.

79B.   No points will be awarded for appropriate salary if the salary referred to in paragraph 79 above is less than the appropriate rate for the job as stated in the codes of practice in Appendix J, unless the applicant is an established entertainer as defined in paragraph 6 of these Rules.

79C.   Where the applicant is paid hourly, the appropriate salary consideration will be based on earnings up to a maximum of 48 hours a week, even if the applicant works for longer than this. for example, an applicant who works 60 hours a week for £8 per hour be considered to have a salary of £19,968 (8x48x52) and not £25,960 (8x60x52), and will therefore not be awarded points for appropriate salary.

79D.   No points will be awarded for appropriate salary if the applicant does not provide a valid Certificate of Sponsorship reference number with his application.

Tier 2 (General) limit

Overview

80.   The Secretary of State shall be entitled to limit the number of Certificates of Sponsorship available to be allocated to Sponsors in any specific period under the Tier 2 (General) limit referred to in paragraph 77B(a) above;

80A.   The Tier 2 (General) limit is 20,700 Certificates of Sponsorship in each year (beginning on 6 April and ending on 5 April).

80B.   The process by which Certificates of Sponsorship shall be allocated to Sponsors under the Tier 2 (General) limit is set out in paragraphs 80C to 84a and Tables 11D below.

80C.   A Sponsor must apply to the Secretary of State for a Certificate of Sponsorship.

80D.   Available points for an application for a Certificate of Sponsorship are shown in Table 11D. No application will be granted unless it scores a minimum of 20 points under the heading 'Type of Job' and a minimum of 1 point under the heading 'Salary'.

80E.   Notes to accompany Table 11D appear below the table.

"**Table 11D** Applications for Certificates of Sponsorship under the Tier 2 (General) limit

Type of job	Points	Salary	Points
Shortage occupation	130	£100,000 - £155,299.99	60
		£75,000 - £99,999.99	55
PhD-level occupation code and job passes Resident Labour Market Test or an exception applies	75	£70,000 - £74,999.99	50
		£65,000 - £69,999.99	45
		£60,000 - £64,999.99	40
		£55,000 - £59,999.99	35
		£50,000 - £54,999.99	30
Job passes Resident Labour Market	20	£45,000 - £49,999.99	25

Type of job	Points	Salary	Points
Test or an exception applies		£44,000 - £44,999.99	24
		£43,000 - £43,999.99	23
		£42,000 - £42,999.99	22
		£41,000 - £41,999.99	21
		£40,000 - £40,999.99	20
		£39,000 - £39,999.99	19
		£38,000 - £38,999.99	18
		£37,000 - £37,999.99	17
		£36,000 - £36,999.99	16
		£35,000 - £35,999.99	15
		£34,000 - £34,999.99	14
		£33,000 - £33,999.99	13
		£32,000 - £32,999.99	12
		£31,000 - £31,999.99	11
		£30,000 - £30,999.99	10
		£29,000 - £29,999.99	9
		£28,000 - £28,999.99	8
		£27,000 - £27,999.99	7
		£26,000 - £26,999.99	6
		£25,000 - £25,999.99	5
		£24,000 - £24,999.99	4
		£23,000 - £23,999.99	3
		£22,000 - £22,999.99	2
		£20,800 - £21,999.99	1

Notes

81.   Points may only be scored for one entry in each column.

81A.   No points will be awarded under the heading 'Type of Job' unless the job described in the Sponsor's application for a Certificate of Sponsorship:

(a)   appears on:

(i)   the list of occupations skilled to National Qualifications Framework level 6 or above, as stated in the codes of practice in Appendix J, or

(ii)   one of the following creative sector occupations skilled to National Qualifications Framework level 4 or above:

(1)   3411 Artists,

(2)   3412 Authors, writers and translators,

(3)   3413 Actors, entertainers and presenters,

(4)   3414 Dancers and choreographers, or

(5)   3422 Product, clothing and related designers,

or

(b)   is skilled to National Qualifications Framework level 4 or above, and appears on the shortage occupation list in Appendix K.

81B.   In order for the Sponsor's application to be awarded points for a job in a shortage occupation, the job must, at the time the application for a Certificate of Sponsorship is decided, appear on the the shortage occupation list in Appendix K, and contracted working hours must be for at least 30 hours a week. Furthermore, if the shortage occupation list in Appendix K, indicates that the job appears on the 'Scotland only' shortage occupation list, the job must be for employment in Scotland.

81C. In order for the Sponsor's application to be awarded points for a job in a PhD-level occupation code, the job must be in an occupation code which appears on the list of PhD-level occupation codes as stated in the codes of practice in Appendix J. The Sponsor's application must also meet the requirements of paragraph 81D.

81D. In order for the Sponsor's application to be awarded points for a job that passes the resident labour market test or an exemption applies, the Sponsor must certify that it has met the requirements of that test, as defined in guidance published by the UK Border Agency, in respect of the job, or that one of the exemptions set out in paragraphs 78B or 78C of this Appendix applies.

81E. The points awarded under the heading 'Salary on Offer' will be based on the gross annual salary on offer to be paid by the Sponsor, as stated in the Sponsor's application, subject to the following conditions:

    (i) Points will be awarded based on basic pay (excluding overtime);

    (ii) Allowances, such as London weighting, will be included in the salary for the awarding of points where they are part of the guaranteed salary package and would be paid to a local settled worker in similar circumstances;

    (iii) Other allowances and benefits, such as bonus or incentive pay, travel and subsistence (including travel to and from the applicant's home country), will not be included.

    (iv) If the applicant has exchanged some of his UK employment rights for shares as an employee-owner, the value of those shares will not be included.

81F. No points will be awarded for the salary on offer if the salary referred to in paragraph 81e above is less than the appropriate rate for the job as stated in the codes of practice in Appendix J.

81G. Where the salary on offer will be paid hourly, the salary on offer will be calculated on the basis of earnings up to a maximum of 48 hours a week, even if the jobholder works for longer than this.

81H. No points will be awarded for a Certificate of Sponsorship if the Secretary of State has reasonable grounds to believe that:

    (a) the job described in the application is not a genuine vacancy, or

    (b) the stated requirements of the job described in the application and in any advertisements for the job are inappropriate for the job on offer and / or have been tailored to exclude resident workers from being recruited.

81I. To support the assessment in paragraph 81H, the Secretary of State may request additional information and evidence from the Sponsor. This request will follow the procedure for verification checks as set out in paragraph 82C.

82–84A. OMITTED

Attributes for Tier 2 (Ministers of Religion) Migrants

85. An applicant applying for entry clearance or leave to remain as a Tier 2 (Ministers of Religion) Migrant must score 50 points for attributes.

86. Available points are shown in Table 12 below.

87. Notes to accompany Table 12 appear below that table.

Table 12

Criterion	Points
Certificate of Sponsorship	50

88.–92A. OMITTED

Attributes for Tier 2 (Sportsperson) Migrants

93. An applicant applying for entry clearance or leave to remain as a Tier 2 (Sportsperson) Migrant must score 50 points for attributes.

94. Available points are shown in Table 13 below

95. Notes to accompany Table 13 appear below that table.

Criterion	Points
Certificate of Sponsorship	50

96.–100. OMITTED

Attributes for Tier 5 (Youth Mobility Scheme) Temporary Migrants

101. An applicant applying for entry clearance as a Tier 5 (Youth Mobility Scheme) Temporary Migrant must score 40 points for attributes

102. Available points are shown in Table 14 below.

103. Notes to accompany Table 14 below.

Table 14

Criterion	Points
Citizen of a country or rightful holder of a passport issued by a territory listed in Appendix G or Is a British Overseas Citizen, British Territories Overseas Citizen or British National (Overseas.)	30
Will be 18 or over when his entry clearance becomes valid for use and was under the age of 31 on the date his application was made.	10

Notes

104. The applicant must provide a valid passport as evidence of all of the above.

Attributes for Tier 5 (Temporary Worker) Migrants

105. An applicant applying for entry clearance or leave enter or remain as a Tier 5 (Temporary Worker) Migrant must score 30 points for attributes.

106. Available points are shown in Table 15 below.

107. Notes to accompany Table 15 appear below in that table.

Table 15

Criterion	Points awarded
Holds a Tier 5 (Temporary Worker) Certificate of Sponsorship	30

108.–112   OMITTED

Attributes for Tier 4 (General) Students

113. An applicant applying for entry clearance or leave to remain as a Tier 4 (General) Student must score 30 points for attributes.

114. Available points are shown in Table 16 below.

115. Notes to accompany Table 16 appear below that table.

Table 16

Criterion	Points awarded
Confirmation of Acceptance for Studies	30

Notes

115A. In order to obtain points for a Confirmation of Acceptance for Studies, the applicant must provide a valid Confirmation of Acceptance for Studies reference number.

115B.–115I   DELETED

116. A Confirmation of Acceptance for Studies will only be considered to be valid if:

   (a)   it was issued no more than 6 months before the application is made,

   (b)   the application for entry clearance or leave to remain is made no more than 3 months before the start date of the course of study as stated on the Confirmation of Acceptance for Studies,

   (c)   the sponsor has not withdrawn the offer since the Confirmation of Acceptance for Studies was issued,

   (d)   it was issued by an institution with a Tier 4 sponsor licence,

   (da)   where the application for entry clearance or leave to remain is for the applicant to commence a new course of study, not for completion of a course already commenced by way of re-sitting examinations or repeating a module of a course, the sponsor must not be a Legacy Sponsor,

   (db)   where the Confirmation of Acceptance for Studies is issued by a Legacy Sponsor, the Confirmation of Acceptance for Studies will only be valid if it is issued for completion of a course already commenced by way of re-sitting examinations or repeating a module of a course and the Confirmation of Acceptance for Studies must be for the same course as the course for which the last period of leave was granted to study with that same sponsor,

(e) the institution must still hold such a licence at the time the application for entry clearance or leave to remain is determined

(ea) the migrant must not previously have applied for entry clearance, leave to enter or leave to remain using the same Confirmation of Acceptance for Studies reference number where that application was either approved or refused (not rejected as an invalid application declared void or withdrawn),

(f) it contains the following mandatory information:

    (i) the applicant's:

        (1) name,

        (2) date of birth,

        (3) gender,

        (4) nationality, and

        (5) passport number;

    (ii) the course:

        (1) title,

        (2) level,

        (3) start and end dates, and

        (4) hours per week, including confirmation that the course is full-time;

    (iii) confirmation if the course is one in which the applicant must hold a valid Academic Technology Approval Scheme clearance certificate from the Counter- Proliferation Department of the Foreign and Commonwealth Office;

    (iv) confirmation if the course is a recognised Foundation Programme for postgraduate doctors or dentists, and requires a certificate from the Postgraduate Dean;

    (v) the main study address;

    (vi) details of how the Tier 4 sponsor has assessed the applicant's English language ability including, where relevant, the applicant's English language test scores in all four components (reading, writing, speaking and listening);

    (vii) details of any work placements relating to the course;

    (viii) accommodation, fees and boarding costs;

    (ix) details of any partner institution, if the course will be provided by an education provider that is not the Tier 4 sponsor; and

    (x) the name and address of the overseas higher education institution, if the course is part of a study abroad programme.

(g) it was not issued for a course of studies, it was issued for a full-time, salaried, elected executive position as a student union sabbatical officer to an applicant who is part-way through their studies or who is being sponsored to fill the position in the academic year immediately after their graduation,

(h) it was not issued for a course of studies, it was issued within 60 days of the expected end date of a course leading to the award of a PhD and the migrant is sponsored by a UK recognised body or a body in receipt of public funding as a higher education institution from the Department of Employment and Learning in Northern Ireland, the Higher Education Funding Council for England, the Higher Education Funding Council for Wales or the Scottish Funding Council, to enable the migrant to remain in the UK as a Tier 4 (General) Student on the doctorate extension scheme.

117. A Confirmation of Acceptance for Studies reference number will only be considered to be valid if:

(a) the number supplied links to a Confirmation of Acceptance for Studies Checking Service entry that names the applicant as the migrant and confirms that the sponsor is sponsoring him in the Tier 4 category indicated by the migrant in his application for leave to remain (that is, as a Tier 4 (General) Student or a Tier 4 (Child) Student), and

(b) that reference number must not have been withdrawn or cancelled by the sponsor or the Home Office since it was assigned.

118. No points will be awarded for a Confirmation of Acceptance for Studies unless:

(a)   the applicant supplies, as evidence of previous qualifications, the specified documents, as set out in paragraph 120-SD(a), that the applicant used to obtain the offer of a place on a course from the sponsor unless the applicant is sponsored by a sponsor with Tier 4 Sponsor status, is a national of one of the countries or the rightful holder of a qualifying passport issued by one of the relevant competent authorities, as appropriate, listed in Appendix H, and is applying for entry clearance in his country of nationality or in the territory related to the passport he holds, as appropriate, or leave to remain in the UK. The UK Border Agency reserves the right to request the specified documents from these applicants. The application will be refused if the specified documents are not provided in accordance with the request made; and

(b)   One of the requirements in (i) to (iii) below is met:

(i)   the course is degree level study and the Confirmation of Acceptance for Studies has been assigned by a Sponsor which is a UK recognised body or a body in receipt of funding as a higher education institution from the Department for Employment and Learning in Northern Ireland, the Higher Education Funding Council for England, the Higher Education Funding Council for Wales, or the Scottish Funding Council, and:

(1)   the applicant is a national of one of the following countries: Antigua and Barbuda; Australia; The Bahamas; Barbados; Belize; Canada; Dominica; Grenada; Guyana; Jamaica; New Zealand; St Kitts and Nevis; St Lucia; St Vincent and the Grenadines; Trinidad and Tobago; United States of America, and provides the specified documents set out in paragraph 120-SD(b); or

(2)   has obtained an academic qualification (not a professional or vocational qualification), which is deemed by UK NARIC to meet or exceed the recognised standard of a Bachelor's or Master's degree or a PhD in the UK, from an educational establishment in one of the following countries: Antigua and Barbuda; Australia; The Bahamas; Barbados; Belize; Dominica; Grenada; Guyana; Ireland; Jamaica; New Zealand; St Kitts and Nevis; St Lucia; St Vincent and The Grenadines; Trinidad and Tobago; the UK; the USA, and provides the specified documents set out in paragraph 120-SD(a); or

(3)   the applicant has successfully completed a course as a Tier 4 (Child) Student (or under the student rules that were in force before 31 March 2009, where the student was granted permission to stay whilst he was under 18 years old) which:

i.   was at least six months in length, and

ii.   ended within two years of the date the sponsor assigned the Confirmation of Acceptance for Studies; or

(4)   the Confirmation of Acceptance for Studies Checking Service entry confirms that the applicant has a knowledge of English equivalent to level B2 of the Council of Europe's Common European Framework for Language Learning in all four components (reading, writing, speaking and listening), or above, or that the sponsor is satisfied that on completion of a pre-sessional course as provided for in paragraph 120(b)(i) of this Appendix, the applicant will have a knowledge of English as set out in this paragraph; or

(ii)   the course is degree level study and the Confirmation of Acceptance for Studies has been assigned by a Sponsor which is not a UK recognised body or is not a body in receipt of funding as a higher education institution from the Department for Employment and Learning in Northern Ireland, the Higher Education Funding Council for England, the Higher Education Funding Council for Wales, or the Scottish Funding Council, and:

(1)   the applicant is a national of one of the following countries: Antigua and Barbuda; Australia; The Bahamas; Barbados; Belize; Canada; Dominica; Grenada; Guyana; Jamaica; New Zealand; St Kitts and Nevis; St Lucia; St Vincent and the Grenadines; Trinidad and Tobago; United States of America, and provides the specified documents set out in paragraph 120-SD(b); or

(2)   has obtained an academic qualification (not a professional or vocational qualification), which is deemed by UK NARIC to meet or exceed the recognised standard of a Bachelor's or Master's degree or a PhD in the UK, from an educational establishment in one of the following countries: Antigua and Barbuda; Australia; The Bahamas; Barbados; Belize; Dominica; Grenada; Guyana; Ireland; Jamaica; New Zealand; St Kitts and Nevis; St Lucia; St Vincent and The Grenadines; Trinidad and Tobago; the UK; the USA, and provides the specified documents set out in paragraph 120-SD(a); or

(3)   the applicant has successfully completed a course as a Tier 4 (Child) Student (or under the student rules that were in force before 31 March 2009, where the student was granted permission to stay whilst he was under 18 years old) which:

    i.   was at least six months in length, and

    ii.   ended within two years of the date the sponsor assigned the Confirmation of Acceptance for Studies; or

(4)   the applicant provides the specified documents from an English language test provider approved by the Secretary of State for these purposes as listed in Appendix O, which clearly show:

    i.   the applicant's name,

    ii.   that the applicant has achieved or exceeded level B2 of the Council of Europe's Common European Framework for Language learning in all four components (reading, writing, speaking and listening), unless exempted from sitting a component on the basis of the applicant's disability,

    iii.   the date of the award, and

    iv.   that the test is within its validity date (where applicable), and

    v.   the test centre at which the test was taken is approved by the Secretary of State as a Secure English Language Test Centre.

Or

(iii)   the course is for below degree level study and:

(1)   the applicant is a national of one of the following countries: Antigua and Barbuda; Australia; The Bahamas; Barbados; Belize; Canada; Dominica; Grenada; Guyana; Jamaica; New Zealand; St Kitts and Nevis; St Lucia; St Vincent and the Grenadines; Trinidad and Tobago; United States of America, and provides the specified documents set out in paragraph 120-SD(b); or

(2)   has obtained an academic qualification (not a professional or vocational qualification), which is deemed by UK NARIC to meet or exceed the recognised standard of a Bachelor's or Master's degree or a PhD in the UK, from an educational establishment in one of the following countries: Antigua and Barbuda; Australia; The Bahamas; Barbados; Belize; Dominica; Grenada; Guyana; Ireland; Jamaica; New Zealand; St Kitts and Nevis; St Lucia; St Vincent and The Grenadines; Trinidad and Tobago; the UK; the USA, and provides the specified documents set out in paragraph 120-SD(a); or

(3)   the applicant has successfully completed a course as a Tier 4 (Child) student (or under the student rules that were in force before 31 March 2009, where the student was granted permission to stay whilst he was under 18 years old) which:

    i.   was at least six months in length, and

    ii.   ended within two years of the date the sponsor assigned the Confirmation of Acceptance for Studies; or

(4)   the applicant provides the specified documents from an English language test provider approved by the Secretary of State for these purposes as listed in Appendix O, which clearly show:

    i.   the applicant's name,

    ii.   that the applicant has achieved or exceeded level B1 of the Council of Europe's Common European Framework for Language learning in all four components (reading, writing, speaking and listening), unless exempted from sitting a component on the basis of the applicant's disability,

    iii.   the date of the award, and

    iv.   that the test is within its validity date (where applicable), and

    v.   the test centre at which the test was taken is approved by the Secretary of State as a Secure English Language Test Centre.

119.   If the applicant is re-sitting examinations or repeating a module of a course, the applicant must not previously have re-sat the same examination or repeated the same module more than once, unless the sponsor has Tier 4 Sponsor status. If this requirement is not met then no points will be awarded for the Confirmation of Acceptance for Studies, unless the sponsor has Tier 4 Sponsor status.

120. Points will only be awarded for a Confirmation of Acceptance for Studies (even if all the requirements in paragraphs 116 to 119 above are met) if the course in respect of which it is issued meets each of the following requirements:

    (a)   The course must meet the following minimum academic requirements:

        i.   for applicants applying to study in England, Wales or Northern Ireland, the course must be at National Qualifications Framework (NQF) / Qualifications and Credit Framework (QCF) Level 3 or above if the sponsor has Tier 4 Sponsor status; or

        ii.   for applicants applying to study in England, Wales or Northern Ireland, the course must be at National Qualifications Framework (NQF) / Qualifications and Credit Framework (QCF) Level 4 or above if the sponsor has Probationary Sponsor status; or

        iii.   for applicants applying to study in Scotland, the course must be accredited at Level 6 or above in the Scottish Credit and Qualifications Framework (SCQF) by the Scottish Qualifications Authority and the Sponsor must be a Highly Trusted Sponsor; or

        iv.   for applicants applying to study in Scotland, the course must be accredited at Level 7 or above in the Scottish Credit and Qualifications Framework (SCQF) by the Scottish Qualifications Authority if the Sponsor is an A-Rated Sponsor or B-Rated Sponsor; or

        v.   the course must be a short-term Study Abroad Programme in the United Kingdom as part of the applicant's qualification at an overseas higher education institution, and that qualification must be confirmed as the same as a United Kingdom degree level by the National Recognition Information Centre for the United Kingdom (UK NARIC); or

        vi   the course must be an English language course at level B2 or above of the Common European Framework of Reference for Languages; or

        vii.   the course must be a recognised Foundation Programme for postgraduate doctors or dentists.

    (b)   The Confirmation of Acceptance for Studies must be for a single course of study except where the Confirmation of Acceptance for Studies is:

        (i)   issued by a UK recognised body or a body in receipt of funding as a higher education institution from the Department for Employment and Learning in Northern Ireland, the Higher Education Funding Council for England, the Higher Education Funding Council for Wales, or the Scottish Funding Council to cover both a pre-sessional course of no longer than three months' duration and a course of degree level study at that sponsor; and

        (ii)   the applicant has an unconditional offer of a place on a course of degree level study at that sponsor or that where the offer is made in respect of an applicant whose knowledge of English is not at B2 level of the Council of Europe's Common European Framework for Language Learning in all four components (reading, writing, speaking and listening) or above, the sponsor is satisfied that on completion of a pre-sessional course as provided for in (i) above, the applicant will have a knowledge of English at as set out in this paragraph; and

        (iii)   the course of degree level study commences no later than one month after the end date of the pre-sessional course.

    (c)   The course must, except in the case of a pre-sessional course, lead to an approved qualification as defined in (cb) below.

    (ca)   If a student is specifically studying towards an Association of Certified Chartered Accountants (ACCA) qualification or an ACCA Foundations in Accountancy qualification, the sponsor must be an ACCA approved learning partner - student tuition (ALP-st) at either Gold or Platinum level.

    (cb)   An approved qualification is one that is:

        (1)   validated by Royal Charter,

        (2)   awarded by a body that is on the list of recognised bodies produced by the Department for Business, Innovation and Skills,

        (3)   recognised by one or more recognised bodies through a formal articulation agreement with the awarding body,

        (4)   in England, Wales and Northern Ireland, on the Register of Regulated Qualifications (http://register.ofqual.gov.uk/) at National Qualifications Framework (NQF) / Qualifications and Credit Framework (QCF) level 3 or above,

        (5)   in Scotland, accredited at Level 6 or above in the Scottish Credit and Qualifications Framework (SCQF) by the Scottish Qualifications Authority,

(6)   an overseas qualification that UK NARIC assesses as valid and equivalent to National Qualifications Framework (NQF) / Qualifications and Credit Framework (QCF) level 3 or above, or

(7)   covered by a formal legal agreement between a UK recognised body and another education provider or awarding body. An authorised signatory for institutional agreements within the UK recognised body must sign this. The agreement must confirm the UK recognised body's own independent assessment of the level of the Tier 4 sponsor's or the awarding body's programme compared to the National Qualifications Framework (NQF) / Qualifications and Credit Framework (QCF) or its equivalents. It must also state that the UK recognised body would admit any student who successfully completes the Tier 4 sponsor's or the awarding body's named course onto a specific or a range of degree-level courses it offers.

(d)   Other than when the applicant is on a course-related work placement or a pre-sessional course, all study that forms part of the course must take place on the premises of the sponsoring educational institution or an institution which is a partner institution of the migrant's sponsor.

(e)   The course must meet one of the following requirements:

i.   be a full time course of degree level study that leads to an approved qualification as defined in (cb) above;

ii.   be an overseas course of degree level study that is recognised as being equivalent to a UK Higher Education course and is being provided by an overseas Higher Education Institution; or

iii.   be a full time course of study involving a minimum of 15 hours per week organised daytime study and, except in the case of a pre-sessional course, lead to an approved qualification, below bachelor degree level as defined in (cb) above.

(f)   Where the student is following a course of below degree level study including course –related work placement, the course can only be offered by a sponsor with Tier 4 Sponsor status. If the course contains a course-related work placement, any period that the applicant will be spending on that placement must not exceed one third of the total length of the course spent in the United Kingdom except :

(i)   where it is a United Kingdom statutory requirement that the placement should exceed one third of the total length of the course; or

(ii)   where the placement does not exceed one half of the total length of the course undertaken in the UK and the student is following a course of degree level study and is either:

(a)   sponsored by a UK recognised body or a body in receipt of public funding as a higher education institution from the Department of Employment and Learning in Northern Ireland, the Higher Education Funding Council for England, the Higher Education Funding Council for Wales or the Scottish Funding Council; or

(b)   sponsored by an overseas higher education institution to undertake a short-term Study Abroad Programme in the United Kingdom.

Specified documents

120-SD.   Where paragraphs 118 to 120 of this Appendix refer to specified documents, those specified documents are as follows:

(a)   In the case of evidence relating to previous qualifications, the applicant must provide, for each qualification, either:

(i)   The original certificate(s) of qualification, which clearly shows:

(1)   the applicant's name,

(2)   the title of the award,

(3)   the date of the award, and

(4)   the name of the awarding institution;

(ii)   The transcript of results, which clearly shows:

(1)   the applicant's name,

(2)   the name of the academic institution,

(3)   their course title, and

(4)   confirmation of the award;

This transcript must be original unless the applicant has applied for their course through UCAS (Universities and Colleges Admissions Service), and:

(a)   the applicant is applying in the UK to study at a Higher Education Institution which has Tier 4 Sponsor status, and

(b)   the qualification is issued by a UK awarding body for a course that the applicant has studied in the UK;

or

(iii)   the applicant's Tier 4 sponsor has assessed the applicant by using one or more references, and the Confirmation of Acceptance for Studies Checking Service entry includes details of the references assessed, the original reference(s) (or a copy, together with an original letter from the Tier 4 sponsor confirming it is a true copy of the reference they assessed), which must contain:

(1)   the applicant's name,

(2)   confirmation of the type and level of course or previous experience; and dates of study or previous experience,

(3)   date of the letter, and

(4)   contact details of the referee.

(b)   In the case of evidence of the applicant's nationality, the specified documents are the applicant's current valid original passport or travel document. If the applicant is unable to provide this, the Home Office may exceptionally consider this requirement to have been met where the applicant provides full reasons in the passport section of the application form, and either:

(1)   a current national identity document, or

(2)   an original letter from his home government or embassy, on the letter-headed paper of the government or embassy, which has been issued by an authorised official of that institution and confirms the applicant's full name, date of birth and nationality.

120A.   (a)   Points will only be awarded for a valid Confirmation of Acceptance for Studies (even if all the requirements in paragraphs 116 to 120-SD above are met) if the sponsor has confirmed that the course for which the Confirmation of Acceptance for Studies has been assigned represents academic progress, as defined in (b) below, from previous study undertaken during the last period of leave as a Tier 4 (General) Student or as a Student where the applicant has had such leave, except where:

(i)   the applicant is re-sitting examinations or repeating modules in accordance with paragraph 119 above,

(ii)   the applicant is applying for leave to remain to complete the PhD or other doctoral qualification for which the Confirmation of Acceptance for Studies relating to the study undertaken during the last period of leave as a Tier 4 (General) Student or as a Student was assigned, or

(iii)   the applicant is making a first application to move to a new institution to complete a course commenced at a Tier 4 sponsor that has had its licence revoked.

(b)   For a course to represent academic progress from previous study the course must be above the level of the previous course for which the applicant was granted leave as a Tier 4 (General) Student or as a Student, unless:

(i)   the course is taught by a UK recognised body or a body in receipt of public funding as a higher education institution from the Department of Employment and Learning in Northern Ireland, the Higher Education Funding Council for England, the Higher Education Funding Council for Wales or the Scottish Funding Council which is also the sponsor;

(ii)   the sponsor has Tier 4 Sponsor status; and

(iii)   the sponsor confirms that:

(1)   the course is related to the previous course for which the applicant was granted leave as a Tier 4 (General) Student, meaning that it is either connected to the previous course, part of the same subject group, or involves deeper specialisation; or

(2)   the previous course and the new course in combination support the applicant's genuine career aspirations.

Attributes for Tier 4 (Child) Students

121.   An applicant applying for entry clearance or leave to remain as a Tier 4 (Child) Student must score 30 points for attributes.

122.   Available points are show in Table 17 below.

123.   Notes to accompany Table 17 appear below that table.

123A.   In order to obtain points for a Confirmation of Acceptance for Studies, the applicant must provide a valid Confirmation of Acceptance for Studies reference number.

Table 17

Criterion	Points awarded
Confirmation of Acceptance for Studies	30

Notes

124.   Confirmation of Acceptance for Studies will be considered to be valid only if:

(a)   it was issued by an Independent School,

(b)   it was issued no more than 6 months before the application is made,

(c)   the application for entry clearance or leave to remain is made no more than 3 months before the start date of the course of study as stated on the Confirmation of Acceptance for Studies,

(d)   the sponsor has not withdrawn the offer since the Confirmation of Acceptance for Studies was issued,

(e)   it was issued by an Independent School with a Tier 4 (Child) Student sponsor licence,

(f)   the Independent School must still hold such a licence at the time the application for entry clearance or leave to remain is determined,

(fa)   the migrant must not previously have applied for entry clearance, leave to enter or leave to remain using the same Confirmation of Acceptance for Studies reference number, if that application was either approved or refused (not rejected as an invalid application declared void or withdrawn), and

(g)   it contains such information as is specified as mandatory in these immigration rules.

125.   A Confirmation of Acceptance for Studies reference number will only be considered to be valid if:

(a)   the number supplied links to a Confirmation of Acceptance for Studies Checking Service entry that names the applicant as the migrant and confirms that the sponsor is sponsoring him in the Tier 4 category indicated by the migrant in his application for leave to remain (that is, as a Tier 4 (General) Student or a Tier 4 (Child) Student), and

(b)   that reference number must not have been withdrawn or cancelled by the sponsor or the Home Office since it was assigned.

125A.   Points will only be awarded for a Confirmation of Acceptance for Studies if the applicant:

(a)   supplies, as evidence of previous qualifications, the specified documents set out in paragraph 125-SD that the applicant used to obtain the offer of a place on a course from the sponsor,

(b)   is sponsored by a sponsor with Tier 4 Sponsor status, is a national of one of the countries or the rightful holder of a qualifying passport issued by one of the relevant competent authorities, as appropriate, listed in Appendix H and is applying for entry clearance in his country of nationality or in the territory related to the passport he holds, as appropriate, or leave to remain in the UK. The Home Office reserves the right to request the specified documents set out in paragraph 125-SD from these applicants. The application will be refused if the specified documents are not provided in accordance with the request made; or

(c)   where the application for entry clearance or leave to remain is for the applicant to commence a new course of study, not for completion of a course already commenced by way of re-sitting examinations or repeating a module of a course, the Sponsor must not be a Legacy Sponsor, or

(d)   where the Confirmation of Acceptance for Studies is issued by a Legacy Sponsor, the Confirmation of Acceptance for Studies will only be valid if it is issued for completion of a course already commenced by way of re-sitting examinations or repeating a module of a course and the Confirmation of Acceptance for Studies must be for the same course as the course for which the last period of leave was granted to study with that same sponsor.

Specified documents

125-SD.   Where paragraph 125 of this Appendix refers to specified documents evidence relating to previous qualifications, those specified documents are:

(i)   The original certificate(s) of qualification, which clearly shows:

(1)   the applicant's name,

(2)   the title of the award,

(3)   the date of the award, and

(4)   the name of the awarding institution;

(ii)   The original transcript of results, which clearly shows:

(1)   the applicant's name,

(2)   the name of the academic institution,

(3)   their course title, and

(4)   confirmation of the award;

126.   Points will not be awarded under Table 17 unless the course that the student will be pursuing meets one of the following requirements:

(a)   be taught in accordance with the National Curriculum,

(b)   be taught in accordance with the National Qualification Framework (NQF) and must not be a foundation course intended to prepare the student for entry to a higher education institution,

(c)   be accepted as being of equivalent academic status to (a) or (b) above by Ofsted (England), the Education and Training Inspectorate (Northern Ireland), Education Scotland (Scotland) or Estyn (Wales),

(d)   be provided as required by prevailing Independent School education inspection standards.

(e)   be a single course of study, except where the Confirmation of Acceptance for Studies is:

(i)   issued by an Independent School to cover both a pre-sessional course and a course at an Independent School; and

(ii)   the applicant has an unconditional offer of a place at the Independent School; and

(iii)   duration of the pre-sessional course and period of study at the Independent School does not exceed the maximum period of entry clearance or leave to remain that can be granted under paragraphs 245ZZB and 245ZZD of the Immigration Rules.

Appendix AR – OMITTED

Appendix Armed Forces – OMITTED

Appendix B – English language

1.   An applicant applying as a Tier 1 Migrant or Tier 2 Migrant must have 10 points for English language, unless applying for entry clearance or leave to remain:

(i)   as a Tier 1 (Exceptional Talent) Migrant,

(ii)   as a Tier 1 (Investor) Migrant, or

(iii)   as a Tier 2 (Intra-Company Transfer) Migrant.

2.   The levels of English language required are shown in Table 1.

3.   Available points for English language are shown in Table 2.

4.   Notes to accompany the tables are shown below each table.

Table 1 Level of English language required to score points

Tier 1

Row	Category	Applications	Level of English language required
B	Tier 1 (Entrepreneur)	Entry clearance and leave to remain	A knowledge of English equivalent to level B1 or above of the Council of Europe's Common European Framework for Language Learning
C	Tier 1 (Graduate Entrepreneur)	Entry clearance and leave to remain	A knowledge of English equivalent to level B1 or above of the Council of Europe's Common European Framework for Language Learning

Tier 2

Row	Category	Applications	Level of English language required
E	Tier 2 (Minister of Religion)	Entry clearance and leave to remain	A knowledge of English equivalent to level B2 or above of the Council of Europe's Common European Framework for Language Learning
F	Tier 2 (General)	Entry clearance and leave to remain, other than the cases in paragraph 5 below	A knowledge of English equivalent to level B1 or above of the Council of Europe's Common European Framework for Language Learning
G	Tier 2 (General)	Leave to remain cases in paragraph 5 below	A knowledge of English equivalent to level A1 or above of the Council of Europe's Common European Framework for Language Learning
H	Tier 2 (Sportsperson)	Entry clearance and leave to remain	A knowledge of English equivalent to level A1 or above of the Council of Europe's Common European Framework for Language Learning

Notes

5. An applicant applying for leave to remain as a Tier 2 (General) Migrant must have competence of English to a level A1 or above as set out in Table 1 above if:

(i) he previously had leave as:

    (1) a Tier 2 (General) Migrant under the rules in place before 6 April 2011,

    (2) a Qualifying Work Permit Holder,

    (3) a representative of an overseas newspaper, news agency or Broadcasting organisation,

    (4) a Member of the Operational Ground Staff of an Overseas-owned Airline, or

    (5) a Jewish Agency Employee,

    and

(ii) he has not been granted leave to remain in any other routes, or entry clearance or leave to enter in any route, since the grant of leave referred to in (i) above.

Table 2 Points available for English language

Factor	Points
National of a majority English speaking country	10
Degree taught in English	10
Passed an English language test	10
Met requirement in a previous grant of leave	10
Transitional arrangements	10

Notes

National of a majority English speaking country

6. 10 points will only be awarded for being a national of a majority English speaking country if the applicant has the relevant level of English language shown in Table 1 and:

(i) is a national of one of the following countries:
Antigua and Barbuda
Australia
The Bahamas
Barbados
Belize
Canada
Dominica

Grenada
Guyana
Jamaica
New Zealand
St Kitts and Nevis
St Lucia
St Vincent and the Grenadines
Trinidad and Tobago
USA
and

(ii)   provides his current valid original passport or travel document to show that this requirement is met. If the applicant is unable to do so, the UK Border Agency may exceptionally consider this requirement to have been met where the applicant provides full reasons in the passport section of the application form, and either:

(1)   a current national identity document, or

(2)   an original letter from his home government or embassy, on the letter-headed paper of the government or embassy, which has been issued by an authorised official of that institution and confirms the applicant's full name, date of birth and nationality.

Degree taught in English

7.   10 points will be awarded for a degree taught in English if the applicant has the relevant level of English language shown in Table 1 and:

(i)   has obtained an academic qualification (not a professional or vocational qualification) which either:

(1)   is deemed by UK NARIC to meet the recognised standard of a Bachelor's or Master's degree or a PhD in the UK, and UK NARIC has confirmed that the degree was taught or researched in English to level C1 of the Council of Europe's Common European Framework for Language learning or above

or:

(2)   is deemed by UK NARIC to meet or exceed the recognised standard of a Bachelor's or Master's degree or a PhD in the UK, and is from an educational establishment in one of the following countries:

Antigua and Barbuda
Australia
The Bahamas
Barbados
Belize
Dominica
Grenada
Guyana
Ireland
Jamaica
New Zealand
St Kitts and Nevis
St Lucia
St Vincent and The Grenadines
Trinidad and Tobago
the UK
the USA,
and

(ii)   provides the following specified documents to show he has the qualification:

(1)   the original certificate of the award, or

(2)   if the applicant is awaiting graduation having successfully completed the qualification, or no longer has the certificate and the awarding institution is unable to provide a replacement, an academic transcript (or original letter in the case of a PhD qualification) from the awarding institution on its official headed paper, which clearly shows:

(a)   the applicant's name,

(b)   the name of the awarding institution,

(c)   the title of the award,

(d)   confirmation that the qualification has been or will be awarded, and

(e)   the date that the certificate will be issued (if the applicant has not yet graduated) or confirmation that the institution is unable to reissue the original certificate or award.

8.   If the applicant is required to have competence of English to level A1 as set out in Table 1 above (rows G and H), 10 points will be awarded for a degree taught in English if the applicant has the relevant level of English language shown in Table 1 and:

(i)   has obtained an academic qualification (not a professional or vocational qualification) which is deemed by UK NARIC to meet or exceed the recognised standard of a Bachelor's or Master's degree or a PhD in the UK,

(ii)   provides the specified documents in paragraph 7(ii) evidence to show that he has the qualification, and

(iii)   provides provide an original letter from the awarding institution on its official headed paper, which clearly shows:

(1)   the applicant's name,

(2)   the name of the awarding institution,

(3)   the title of the award,

(4)   the date of the award, and

(5)   confirmation that the qualification was taught in English.

9.   An applicant for entry clearance or leave to remain as a Tier 1 (Graduate Entrepreneur) Migrant does not need to provide evidence of a qualification taught in English if:

(a)   the applicant scores points from Appendix A for an endorsement by the UK Higher Education Institution which awarded the qualification; and

(b)   the endorsement letter contains the specified details of the qualification, as set out in paragraph 70(c) of Appendix A.

Passed an English language test

10.   10 points will only be awarded for passing an English language test if the applicant has the relevant level of English language shown in Table 1 and provides the specified documents from an English language test provider approved by the Secretary of State for these purposes, as listed in Appendix O, for a test taken at a test centre approved by the Secretary of State as a Secure English Language Test centre, which clearly show:

(1)   the applicant's name,

(2)   the qualification obtained, which must meet or exceed the relevant level shown in Table 1 in all four components (reading, writing, speaking and listening), unless the applicant was exempted from sitting a component on the basis of his disability,

(3)   the date of the award,

(4)   the test centre at which the test was taken, and

(5)   that the test is within its validity date (where applicable).

Met requirement in a previous grant of leave

11.   Subject to paragraph 15 below, 10 points will be awarded for meeting the requirement in a previous grant of leave if the applicant:

(i)   has ever been granted leave as a Tier 1 (General) Migrant, a Tier 1 (Entrepreneur) Migrant or Business person, or a Tier 1 (Post-Study Work) Migrant, or

(ii)   has ever been granted leave as a Highly Skilled Migrant under the Rules in place on or after 5 December 2006.

12.   Subject to paragraph 15 below, where the application falls under rows B to H of Table 1 above, 10 points will be awarded for meeting the requirement in a previous grant of leave if the applicant has ever been granted leave:

(a)   as a Minister of Religion (not as a Tier 2 (Minister of Religion) Migrant) under the Rules in place on or after 19 April 2007,

(b) as a Tier 2 (Minister of Religion) Migrant, provided that when he was granted that leave he obtained points for English language for being a national of a majority English speaking country, a degree taught in English, or passing an English language test, or

(c) as a Tier 4 (General) student, and the Confirmation of Acceptance for Studies used to support that application was assigned on or after 21 April 2011 for a course of at least degree level study.

13. Subject to paragraph 15 below, where the application falls under rows B to C or rows F to H of Table 1 above, 10 points will be awarded for meeting the requirement in a previous grant of leave if the applicant has ever been granted leave:

(a) as a Tier 1 (Graduate Entrepreneur) Migrant,

(b) as a Tier 2 (General) Migrant under the Rules in place on or after 6 April 2011, or

(c) as a Tier 4 (General) student, and the Confirmation of Acceptance for Studies used to support that application was assigned on or after 21 April 2011,

provided that when he was granted that leave he obtained points for having knowledge of English equivalent to level B1 of the Council of Europe's Common European Framework for Language Learning or above.

14. Subject to paragraph 15 below, where the application falls under rows G and H of table 1 above, 10 points will be awarded for meeting the requirement in a previous grant of leave if the applicant has ever been granted:

(i) leave as a Minister of Religion (not as a Tier 2 (Minister of Religion) Migrant) under the Rules in place on or after 23 August 2004,

(ii) leave as a Tier 2 Migrant, provided that when he was granted that leave he obtained points for English language for being a national of a majority English speaking country, a degree taught in English, or passing an English language test.

15. No points will be awarded for meeting the requirement in a previous grant of leave if false representations were made or false documents or information were submitted (whether or not to the applicant's knowledge) in relation to the requirement in the application for that previous grant of leave.

Transitional arrangements

16. 10 points will be awarded for English language if the applicant:

(a) is applying for leave to remain as a Tier 2 (General) Migrant, and

(b) has previously been granted entry clearance, leave to enter or leave to remain as:

(i) a Jewish Agency Employee,

(ii) a Member of the Operational Ground Staff of an Overseas-owned Airline,

(iii) a Minister of Religion, Missionary or Member of a Religious Order,

(iv) a Qualifying Work Permit Holder,

(v) a Representative of an Overseas Newspaper, News Agency or Broadcasting Organisation

and

(c) has not been granted leave in any categories other than Tier 2 (General), Tier 2 (Intra-Company Transfer) and those listed in (b) above under the Rules in place since 28 November 2008.

17. 10 points will be awarded for English language if the applicant:

(a) is applying for leave to remain as a Tier 2 (Minister of Religion) Migrant,

(b) has previously been granted entry clearance, leave to enter and/or leave to remain as a Minister of Religion, Missionary or Member of a Religious Order, and

(c) has not been granted leave in any categories other than Tier 2 (Minister of Religion) and those listed in (b) above under the Rules in place since 28 November 2008.

18. 10 points will be awarded for English language if the applicant:

(a) is applying for leave to remain as a Tier 2 (Sportsperson) Migrant,

(b) has previously been granted entry clearance, leave to enter and/or leave to remain as a Qualifying Work Permit Holder, and

(c) has not been granted leave in any categories other than Tier 2 (Sportsperson) and as a Qualifying Work Permit Holder under the Rules in place since 28 November 2008.

Appendix C – Maintenance (funds)

1A.   In all cases where an applicant is required to obtain points under Appendix C, the applicant must meet the requirements listed below:

    (a)   The applicant must have the funds specified in the relevant part of Appendix C at the date of the application;

    (b)   If the applicant is applying as a Tier 1 Migrant, a Tier 2 Migrant or a Tier 5 (Temporary Worker) Migrant, the applicant must have had the funds referred to in (a) above for a consecutive 90-day period of time, unless applying as a Tier 1 (Exceptional Talent) Migrant or a Tier 1 (Investor) Migrant;

    (c)   If the applicant is applying as a Tier 4 Migrant, the applicant must have had the funds referred to in (a) above for a consecutive 28-day period of time;

    (ca) If the applicant is applying for entry clearance or leave to remain as a Tier 4 Migrant, he must confirm that the funds referred to in (a) above are:

        (i)   available in the manner specified in paragraph 13 below for his use in studying and living in the UK; and

        (ii) that the funds will remain available in the manner specified in paragraph 13 below unless used to pay for course fees and living costs;

    (d)   If the funds were obtained when the applicant was in the UK, the funds must have been obtained while the applicant had valid leave and was not acting in breach of any conditions attached to that leave;

    (e)   Where the funds are in one or more foreign currencies, the applicant must have the specified level of funds when converted to pound sterling (£) using the spot exchange rate which appears on www.oanda.com* for the date of the application;

    (f)   Where the applicant is applying as a Tier 1 Migrant, a Tier 2 Migrant or a Tier 5 Migrant, the funds must have been under his own control on the date of the application and for the period specified in (b) above; and

    (g)   Where the application is made at the same time as applications by the partner or child of the applicant (such that the applicant is a Relevant Points Based System Migrant for the purposes of paragraph 319AA), each applicant must have the total requisite funds specified in the relevant parts of appendices C and E. If each applicant does not individually meet the requirements of appendices C and / or E, as appropriate, all the applications (the application by the Relevant Points Based System Migrant and applications as the partner or child of that relevant Points Based system Migrant) will be refused.

    (h)   the end date of the 90-day and 28-day periods referred to in (b) and (c) above will be taken as the date of the closing balance on the most recent of the specified documents (where specified documents from two or more accounts are submitted, this will be the end date for the account that most favours the applicant), and must be no earlier than 31 days before the date of application.

    (i)   No points will be awarded where the specified documents show that the funds are held in a financial institution listed in Appendix P as being an institution with which the UK Border Agency is unable to make satisfactory verification checks.

    (j)   Maintenance must be in the form of cash funds. Other accounts or financial instruments such as shares, bonds, credit cards, pension funds etc, regardless of notice period are not acceptable.

    (k)   If the applicant wishes to rely on a joint account as evidence of available funds, the applicant (or for children under 18 years of age, the applicant's parent or legal guardian who is legally present in the United Kingdom) must be named on the account as one of the account holders.

    (l)   Overdraft facilities will not be considered towards funds that are available or under an applicant's own control.

1B.   In all cases where Appendix C or Appendix E states that an applicant is required to provide specified documents, the specified documents are:

    (a)   Personal bank or building society statements which satisfy the following requirements:

        (i)   The statements must cover:

            (1)   a consecutive 90-day period of time, if the applicant is applying as a Tier 1 Migrant, a Tier 2 Migrant a Tier 5 (Temporary Worker) Migrant, or the Partner or Child of a Relevant Points Based System Migrant in any of these categories,

            (2)   a single date within 31 days of the date of the application, if the applicant is applying as a Tier 5 (Youth Mobility Scheme) Migrant, or

(3)   a consecutive 28-day period of time, if the applicant is applying as a Tier 4 Migrant or the Partner or Child of a Relevant Points Based System Migrant who is a Tier 4 Migrant

(ii)   The most recent statement must be dated no earlier than 31 days before the date of the application;

(iii)   The statements must clearly show:

(1)   the name of:

(i)   the applicant,

(ii)   the applicant's parent(s) or legal guardian's name, if the applicant is applying as Tier 4 Migrant,

(iii)   the name of the Relevant Points-Based System Migrant, if the applicant is applying as a Partner or Child of a Relevant Points-Based System Migrant, or

(iv)   the name of the applicant's other parent who is legally present in the UK, if the applicant is applying as a Child of a Relevant Points-Based System Migrant,

(2)   the account number,

(3)   the date of each statement,

(4)   the financial institution's name,

(5)   the financial institution's logo,

(6)   any transactions during the specified period, and

(7)   that the funds in the account have been at the required level throughout the specified period;

(iv)   The statements must be be either:

(1)   printed on the bank's or building society's letterhead,

(2)   electronic bank or building society statements, accompanied by a supporting letter from the bank or building society, on company headed paper, confirming the statement provided is authentic, or

(3)   electronic bank or building society statements, bearing the official stamp of the bank or building society on every page,

(v)   The statements must not be mini-statements from automatic teller machines (ATMs);

or

(b)   A building society pass book which satisfies the following requirements:

(i)   The building society pass book must cover:

(1)   a consecutive 90-day period of time, if the applicant is applying as a Tier 1 Migrant, a Tier 2 Migrant a Tier 5 (Temporary Worker) Migrant, or the Partner or Child of a Relevant Points Based System Migrant in any of these categories,

(2)   a single date within 31 days of the date of the application, if the applicant is applying as a Tier 5 (Youth Mobility Scheme) Migrant, or

(3)   a consecutive 28-day period of time, if the applicant is applying as a Tier 4 Migrant or the Partner or Child of a Relevant Points Based System Migrant who is a Tier 4 Migrant

(ii)   The period covered by the building society pass book must end no earlier than 31 days before the date of the application;

(iii)   The building society pass book must clearly show:

(1)   the name of:

(i)   the applicant,

(ii)   he applicant's parent(s) or legal guardian's name, if the applicant is applying as Tier 4 Migrant,

(iii)   the name of the Relevant Points-Based System Migrant, if the applicant is applying as a Partner or Child of a Relevant Points-Based System Migrant, or

(iv)   the name of the applicant's other parent who is legally present in the UK, if the applicant is applying as a Child of a Relevant Points-Based System Migrant,

(2)   the account number,

(3)   the building society's name and logo,

(4)   any transactions during the specified period, and

    (5)   that there have been enough funds in the applicant's account throughout the specified period;

or

(c)   A letter from the applicant's bank or building society, or a letter from a financial institution regulated for the purpose of personal savings accounts by the Financial Conduct Authority (FCA) and the Prudential Regulation Authority (PRA) or, for overseas accounts, the official regulatory body for the country in which the institution operates and the funds are located, which satisfies the following requirements:

    (i)   The letter must confirm the level of funds and that they have been held for:

        (1)   a consecutive 90-day period of time, if the applicant is applying as a Tier 1 Migrant, a Tier 2 Migrant a Tier 5 (Temporary Worker) Migrant, or the Partner or Child of a Relevant Points Based System Migrant in any of these categories,

        (2)   a single date within 31 days of the date of the application, if the applicant is applying as a Tier 5 (Youth Mobility Scheme) Migrant, or

        (3)   a consecutive 28-day period of time, if the applicant is applying as a Tier 4 Migrant or the Partner or Child of a Relevant Points Based System Migrant who is a Tier 4 Migrant;

    (ii)   The period covered by the letter must end no earlier than 31 days before the date of the application;

    (iii)   The letter must be dated no earlier than 31 days before the date of the application;

    (iv)   The letter must be on the financial institution's letterhead or official stationery;

    (v)   The letter must clearly show:

        (1)   the name of:

            (i)   the applicant,

            (ii)   the applicant's parent(s) or legal guardian's name, if the applicant is applying as Tier 4 Migrant,

            (iii)   the name of the Relevant Points-Based System Migrant, if the applicant is applying as a Partner or Child of a Relevant Points-Based System Migrant, or

            (iv)   the name of the applicant's other parent who is legally present in the UK, if the applicant is applying as a Child of a Relevant Points-Based System Migrant,

        (2)   the account number,

        (3)   the date of the letter,

        (4)   the financial institution's name and logo,

        (5)   the funds held in the applicant's account, and

        (5)   confirmation that there have been enough funds in the applicant's account throughout the specified period;

or

(d)   If the applicant is applying as a Tier 4 Migrant, an original loan letter from a financial institution regulated for the purpose of student loans by either the Financial Conduct Authority (FCA) and the Prudential Regulation Authority (PRA) or, in the case of overseas accounts, the official regulatory body for the country the institution is in and where the money is held, which is dated no more than 6 months before the date of the application and clearly shows:

    (1)   the applicant's name,

    (2)   the date of the letter,

    (3)   the financial institution's name and logo,

    (4)   the money available as a loan,

    (5)   for applications for entry clearance, that the loan funds are or will be available to the applicant before he travels to the UK, unless the loan is an academic or student loan from the applicant's country's national government and will be released to the applicant on arrival in the UK,

    (6)   there are no conditions placed upon the release of the loan funds to the applicant, other than him making a successful application as a Tier 4 Migrant, and

    (7)   the loan is provided by the national government, the state or regional government or a government sponsored student loan company or is part of an academic or educational loans scheme.

Tier 1 Migrants

1. An applicant applying for entry clearance or leave to remain as a Tier 1 Migrant must score 10 points for funds, unless applying as a Tier 1 (Exceptional Talent) Migrant or a Tier 1 (Investor) Migrant.

2. 10 points will only be awarded if an applicant:

    (a) applying for entry clearance, has the level of funds shown in the table below and provides the specified documents in paragraph 1B above, or

Category	Level of funds	Points
Tier 1 (Entrepreneur)	£3,310	10
Tier 1 (Graduate Entrepreneur)	£1,890	10

    (b) applying for leave to remain, has the level of funds shown in the table below and provides the specified documents in paragraph 1B above, or

Level of funds	Points
£945	10

    (c) applying as a Tier 1 (Graduate Entrepreneur) Migrant scores points from Appendix A for an endorsement from UK Trade and Investment, and UK Trade and Investment has confirmed in the endorsement letter that it has awarded funding of at least £1,890 (for entry clearance applications) or £945 (for leave to remain applications) to the applicant.

3. Where the applicant is applying as a Tier 1 (Entrepreneur) Migrant, he cannot use the same funds to score points for attributes under Appendix A and to score points for maintenance funds for himself or his dependants under this Appendix or Appendix E.

Tier 2 Migrants

4. An applicant applying for entry clearance or leave to remain as a Tier 2 Migrant must score 10 points for Funds.

5. 10 points will only be awarded if:

    (a) the applicant has the level of funds shown in the table below and provides the specified documents in paragraph 1B above, or

Level of funds	Points awarded
£945	10

    (b) the applicant has entry clearance, leave to enter or leave to remain as:

    (i)   a Tier 2 Migrant
    (ii)   a Jewish Agency Employee
    (iii) A member of the Operational Ground Staff of an Overseas-owned Airline,
    (iv)   a Minister of Religion, Missionary or Member of a Religious Order,
    (v)   a Representative of an Overseas Newspaper, News Agency or Broadcasting Organisation, or
    (vi)   a Work Permit Holder, or

    (c) the Sponsor is an a rated Sponsor and has certified on the Certificate of Sponsorship that, should it become necessary, it will maintain and accommodate the migrant up to the end of the first month of his employment. The Sponsor may limit the amount of the undertaking but any limit must be at least £945. Points will only be awarded if the applicant provides a valid Certificate of Sponsorship reference number with his application.

Tier 5 (Youth Mobility) Temporary Migrants

6. An applicant applying for entry clearance as a Tier 5 (Youth Mobility) Temporary Migrant must score 10 points for funds.

7. 10 points will only be awarded if an applicant has the level of funds shown in the table below and provides the specified documents in paragraph 1B above:

Level of funds	Points awarded
£1890	10

Tier 5 (Temporary Worker) Migrants

8. A migrant applying for entry clearance or leave to remian as a Tier 5 (Temporary Worker) Migrant must score 10 points for funds.

9. 10 points will only be awarded if an applicant has the level of funds shown in the table below and provides the specified documents in paragraph 1B above:

Criterion	Points awarded
Meets one of the following criteria: Has £945; or The Sponsor is an A rated Sponsor and the Certificate of Sponsorship Checking Service confirms that the Sponsor has certified that the applicant will not claim public funds during his period of leave as a Tier 5 (Temporary Worker) Migrant. Points will only be awarded if the applicant provides a valid Certificate of Sponsorship reference number with his application.	10

Tier 4 (General) Students

10. A Tier 4 (General) Student must score 10 points for funds.

11. 10 points will only be awarded if the funds shown in the table below are available in the manner specified in paragraph 13 and 13A below to the applicant. The applicant must either:

    (a)   provide the specified documents in paragraph 1B above to show that the funds are available to him, or

    (b)   where the applicant is sponsored by a sponsor with Tier 4 Sponsor status, is a national of one of the countries or the rightful holder of a qualifying passport issued by one of the relevant competent authorities, as appropriate, listed in Appendix H, and is applying for entry clearance in his country of nationality or in the territory related to the passport he holds, as appropriate, or leave to remain in the UK, confirm that the funds are available to him in the specified manner. The Home Office reserves the right to request the specified documents in paragraph 1B above from these applicants to support this confirmation. The application will be refused if the specified documents are not provided in accordance with the request made.

Criterion	Points
If studying in London: (i) Where the applicant is applying for leave to remain on the doctorate extension scheme, the applicant must have £1,265 for each month remaining of the course up to a maximum of two months. (ii) In all other circumstances, the applicant must have funds amounting to the full course fees for the first academic year of the course, or for the entire course if it is less than a year long, plus £1,265 for each month of the course up to a maximum of nine months.	10
If studying outside London and elsewhere in the United Kingdom: (iii) Where the applicant is applying for leave to remain on the doctorate extension scheme, the applicant must have £1,015 for each month remaining of the course up to a maximum of two months. (iv) In all other circumstances, the applicant must have funds amounting to the full course fees for the first academic year of the course, or for the entire course if it is less than a year long, plus £1,015 for each month of the course up to a maximum of nine months.	10

Notes

12. An applicant will be considered to be studying in London studying at the University of London, or institutions wholly or partly within the area comprising the City of London and the Former Metropolitan Police District (as defined in paragraph 12AA below). If the applicant will be studying at more than one site, one or more of which is in London and one or more outside, then the applicant will be considered to be studying in London if the applicant's Confirmation of Acceptance for Studies states that the applicant will be spending the majority of time studying at a site or sites situated within the area comprising the City of London and the Former Metropolitan Police District (as defined in paragraph 12AA below).

12AA. 'Former Metropolitan Police District' means:

    (i)   London, excluding the City of London, the Inner Temple and the Middle Temple;

(ii)   in the county of Essex, in the district of Epping Forest— the area of the former urban district of Chigwell, the parish of Waltham Abbey;

(iii)   in the county of Hertfordshire— in the borough of Broxbourne, the area of the former urban district of Cheshunt, the district of Hertsmere, in the district of Welwyn Hatfield, the parish of Northaw; and

(iv)   in the county of Surrey— in the borough of Elmbridge, the area of the former urban district of Esher, the boroughs of Epsom and Ewell and Spelthorne, in the district of Reigate and Banstead, the area of the former urban district of Banstead.

12A.   If the length of the applicant's course includes a part of a month, the time will be rounded up to the next full month.

13.   Funds will be available to the applicant only where the specified documents show or, where permitted by these Rules, the applicant confirms that the funds are held or provided by:

(i)   the applicant (whether as a sole or joint account holder); and/or

(ii)   the applicant's parent(s) or legal guardian(s), and the parent(s) or legal guardian(s) have provided written consent that their funds may be used by the applicant in order to study in the UK; and/or

(iii)   an official financial sponsor which must be Her Majesty's Government, the applicant's home government, the British Council or any international organisation, international company, University or Independent School.

13A.   In assessing whether the requirements of Appendix C, paragraph 11 are met, where an applicant pays a deposit on account to the sponsor for accommodation costs this amount, up to a maximum of £1,265, can be offset against the total maintenance requirement if he will be staying in accommodation arranged by the Tier 4 sponsor and he has paid this money to that Tier 4 sponsor.

13B.   If the applicant is relying on the provisions in paragraph 13(ii) above, he must provide:

(a)   one of the following original (or notarised copy) documents:

(i)   his birth certificate showing names of his parent(s),

(ii)   his certificate of adoption showing the names of both parent(s) or legal guardian, or

(iii)   a Court document naming his legal guardian;

and

(b)   a letter from his parent(s) or legal guardian, confirming:

(1)   the relationship between the applicant and his parent(s) or legal guardian, and

(2)   that the parent(s) or legal guardian give their consent to the applicant using their funds to study in the UK.

13C.   If the applicant has already paid all or part of the course fees to his Tier 4 sponsor:

(a)   the Confirmation of Acceptance for Studies Checking Service entry must confirm details of the fees already paid; or

(b)   the applicant must provide an original paper receipt issued by the Tier 4 sponsor, confirming details of the fees already paid.

13D.   If the applicant has an official financial sponsor as set out in paragraph 13(iii) above:

(a)   the Confirmation of Acceptance for Studies Checking Service entry must confirm details of the official financial sponsorship, if it is the Tier 4 sponsor who is the official financial sponsor; or

(b)   the applicant must provide a letter of confirmation from his official financial sponsor, on official letter-headed paper or stationery of that organisation and bearing the official stamp of that organisation, which clearly shows:

(1)   the applicant's name,

(2)   the name and contact details of the official financial sponsor,

(3)   the date of the letter,

(4)   the length of the official financial sponsorship, and

(5)   the amount of money the official financial sponsor is giving to the applicant, or a statement that the official financial sponsor will cover all of the applicant's fees and living costs.

14.   DELETED

Tier 4 (Child) Students

15.   A Tier 4 (Child) Student must score 10 points for funds.

16.   10 points will only be awarded if the funds shown in the table below are available in the manner specified in paragraph 21 *and* 21A below to the applicant. The applicant must either:

(a)   provide the specified documents in paragraph 1B above to show that the funds are available to him, or

(b)   where the applicant is sponsored by a sponsor with Tier 4 Sponsor status, is a national of one of the countries or the rightful holder of a qualifying passport issued by one of the relevant competent authorities, as appropriate, listed in Appendix H, and is applying for entry clearance in his country of nationality or in the territory related to the passport he holds, as appropriate, or leave to remain in the UK, confirm that the funds are available to him in the specified manner. The Home Office reserves the right to request the specified documents in paragraph 1B above from these applicants to support this confirmation. The application will be refused if the specified documents are not provided in accordance with the request made.

Criterion	Points
Where the child is (or will be) studying at a residential Independent School: sufficient funds are available to the applicant to pay boarding fees (being course fees plus board/lodging fees) for an academic year.	10
Where the child is (or will be) studying at a non-residential Independent School and is in a private foster care arrangement (see notes below) or staying with and cared for by a close relative (see notes below): sufficient funds are available to the applicant to pay school fees for an academic year, the foster carer or relative (who must meet the requirements specified in paragraph 19 of this Appendix) has undertaken to maintain and accommodate the child for the duration of the course, and that foster carer or relative has funds equivalent to at least £570 per month, for up to a maximum of nine months, to support the child while he is in the United Kingdom.	10
Where the child is (or will be) studying at a non-residential Independent School, is under the age of 12 and is (or will be) accompanied by a parent, sufficient funds are available to the applicant to pay school fees for an academic year, plus: • if no other children are accompanying the applicant and the parent, £1,560 per month of stay up to a maximum of nine months; or • if other children are accompanying the applicant and the parent, £1,560 per month, plus £625 per month for each additional child, up to a maximum of nine months.	10
Where the child is aged 16 or 17 years old and is living independently and studying at a non-residential Independent School in London: Where the applicant does not have an established presence studying in the United Kingdom, the applicant must have funds amounting to the full course fees for the first academic year of the course, or for the entire course if it is less than a year long, plus £1,265 for each month of the course up to a maximum of nine months.	10
Where the child is aged 16 or 17 years old, is living independently and studying at a non-residential Independent School outside London or elsewhere in the United Kingdom: Where the applicant does not have an established presence studying in the United Kingdom, the applicant must have funds amounting to the full course fees for the first academic year of the course, or for the entire course if it is less than a year long, plus £1,015 for each month of the course up to a maximum of nine months.	10

17.–22.   OMITTED

Appendix D – OMITTED

Appendix E – Maintenance (funds) for the family of Relevant Points Based Systems Migrants

A sufficient level of funds must be available to an applicant applying as the Partner or Child of a Relevant Points Based System Migrant. A sufficient level of funds will only be available if the requirements below are met.

(aa)   Paragraphs 1A and 1B of Appendix C also apply to this Appendix.

(ab)   Where the application is connected to a Tier 1 (Entrepreneur) Migrant, the applicant cannot use the same funds to score points for maintenance funds from this Appendix as the Tier 1 (Entrepreneur) Migrant used to score points for attributes under Appendix A.

(a)   Where the application is connected to a Tier 1 Migrant (other than a Tier 1 (Investor) Migrant or a Tier 1 (Exceptional Talent) Migrant) who is outside the UK or who has been in the UK for a period of less than 12 months, there must be:

  (i)   £1,260 in funds, where the application is connected to a Tier 1 (Graduate Entrepreneur) Migrant;

  (ii)   £1,890 in funds in other cases.

(b)   Where:

  (i)   paragraph (a) does not apply, and

  (ii)   the application is connected to a Relevant Points Based System Migrant who is not a Tier 1 (Investor) Migrant a Tier 1 (Exceptional Talent) Migrant or a Tier 4 (General) Student there must be £630 in funds.

(ba)   (i)   Where the application is connected to a Tier 4 (General) Student:

    (1)   if the Tier 4 (General) Student is studying in London (as defined in paragraph 12 of Appendix C), there must be £845 in funds for each month for which the applicant would, if successful, be granted leave under paragraph 319D(a), up to a maximum of nine months, or

    (2)   if the Tier 4 (General) Student is not studying in London (as defined in paragraph 12 of Appendix C), there must be £680 in funds for each month for which the applicant would, if successful, be granted leave under paragraph 319D(a), up to a maximum of nine months,

    and in each case

    (3)   the applicant must confirm that the funds referred to in (1) or (2) above are:

      (i)   available in the manner specified in paragraph (f) below for use in living costs in the UK; and

      (ii)   that the funds will remain available in the manner specified in paragraph (f) below unless used to pay for living costs.

(c)   Where the applicant is applying as the Partner of a Relevant Points Based System Migrant the relevant amount of funds must be available to either the applicant or the Relevant Points Based System Migrant.

(d)   Where the applicant is applying as the Child of a Relevant Points Based System Migrant, the relevant amount of funds must be available to the applicant, the Relevant Points Based System Migrant, or the applicant's other parent who is Lawfully present in the UK or being granted entry clearance, or leave to enter or remain, at the same time.

(e)   Where the Relevant Points Based System Migrant is applying for entry clearance or leave to remain at the same time as the applicant, the amount of funds available to the applicant must be in addition to the level of funds required separately of the Relevant Points Based System Migrant.

(f)   In all cases, the funds in question must be available to:

  (i)   the applicant, or

  (ii)   where he is applying as the partner of a Relevant Points Based System Migrant, either to him or to that Relevant Points Based System Migrant, or

  (iii)   where he is applying as the child of a Relevant Points Based System Migrant, either to him, to the Relevant Points Based System Migrant or to the child's other parent who is lawfully present in the UK or being granted entry clearance, or leave to enter or remain, at the same time;

(g)   The funds in question must have been available to the person referred to in (f) above on the date of the application and for:

  (i)   a consecutive 90-day period of time, if the applicant is applying as the Partner or Child of a Tier 1 Migrant (other than a Tier 1 (Investor) Migrant) or a Tier 1 (Exceptional Talent) Migrant, a Tier 2 Migrant or a Tier 5 (Temporary Worker) Migrant;

  (ii)   a consecutive 28-day period of time, if the applicant is applying as the Partner or Child of a Tier 4 (General) Student;

(h)   If the funds in question were obtained when the person referred to in (f) above was in the UK, the funds must have been obtained while that person had valid leave and was not acting in breach of any conditions attached to that leave; and

(i)   In the following cases, sufficient funds will be deemed to be available where all of the following conditions are met:

    (1)   the Relevant Points Based System Migrant to whom the application is connected has, or is being granted, leave as a Tier 2 Migrant,

    (2)   the Sponsor of that Relevant Points Based System Migrant is A-rated, and

    (3)   that Sponsor has certified on the Certificate of Sponsorship that, should it become necessary, it will maintain and accommodate the dependants of the relevant Points Based System Migrant up to the end of the first month of the dependant's leave, if granted. The undertaking may be limited provided the limit is at least £630 per dependant. If the relevant Points Based System Migrant is applying at the same time as the applicant, points will only be awarded if the Relevant Points Based System Migrant provides a valid Certificate of Sponsorship reference number with his application.

(ia)   Sufficient funds will not be deemed to be available to the Partner or Child if the specified documents, as set out in paragraph 1B of Appendix C, show that the funds are held in a financial institution listed in Appendix P as being an institution with which the Home Office is unable to make satisfactory verification checks.

(ib)   Sufficient funds will be deemed to be available where the application is connected to a Tier 1 (Graduate Entrepreneur) Migrant who scores, or scored, points from Appendix A for an endorsement from UK Trade and Investment, and UK Trade and Investment has confirmed in the endorsement letter that it has awarded funding that is at least sufficient to cover the required maintenance funds for the Tier 1 (Graduate Entrepreneur) Migrant, the applicant and any other dependants.

(j)   In all cases the applicant must provide the specified documents as set out in paragraph 1B of Appendix C, unless the applicant is applying at the same time as the Relevant Points Based System Migrant who is a Tier 4 (General) Student sponsored by a sponsor with Tier 4 Sponsor status, is a national of one of the countries or the rightful holder of a qualifying passport issued by one of the relevant competent authorities, as appropriate, listed in Appendix H, and is applying for entry clearance in his country of nationality or in the territory related to the passport he holds, as appropriate, or leave to remain in the UK and the applicant is also a national of the same country, and confirms these requirements are met, in which case the specified documents shall not be required. The Home Office reserves the right to request the specified documents from these applicants. The application will be refused if the specified documents are not provided in accordance with the request made.

(k)   Where the funds are in one or more foreign currencies, the applicant must have the specified level of funds when converted to pound sterling (£) using the spot exchange rate which appears on www.oanda.com* for the date of the application.

(l)   Where the application is one of a number of applications made at the same time as a partner or child of a Relevant Points Based System Migrant (as set out in paragraphs 319A and 319F) each applicant, including the Relevant Points Based System Migrant if applying at the same time, must have the total requisite funds specified in the relevant parts of appendices C and E. if each applicant does not individually meet the requirements of appendices C and / or E, as appropriate, all the applications (the application by the Relevant Points Based System Migrant and applications as the partner or child of that Relevant Points Based System Migrant) will be refused.

(m)   The end date of the 90-day and 28-day periods referred to in (g) above will be taken as the date of the closing balance on the most recent of the specified documents (where specified documents from two or more accounts are submitted, this will be the end date for the account that most favours the applicant), as set out in paragraph 1B of Appendix C, and must be no earlier than 31 days before the date of application.

(n)   If:

    (i)   the Relevant Points-Based System Migrant is a Tier 4 (General) Student who has official financial sponsorship as set out in paragraph 13(iii) of Appendix C, and

    (ii)   this sponsorship is intended to cover costs of the Relevant Points-Based System Migrant's family member(s), the applicant must provide a letter of confirmation from the Tier 4 (General) Student's official financial sponsor which satisfies the requirements in paragraph 13D of Appendix C, and confirms that the sponsorship will cover costs of the applicant in addition to costs of the Relevant Points-Based System Migrant.

(o)   Where the Relevant Points Based System Migrant is applying for entry clearance or leave to remain at the same time as the applicant, and is not required to provide evidence of maintenance funds because of the provisions in paragraph 5(b) of Appendix C, the applicant is also not required to provide evidence of maintenance funds.

(p)   Overdraft facilities will not be considered towards funds that are available or under an applicant's own control.

Appendix F – OMITTED

Appendix FM family members

Section GEN: General

Purpose

GEN.1.1.   This route is for those seeking to enter or remain in the UK on the basis of their family life with a person who is a British Citizen, is settled in the UK, or is in the UK with limited leave as a refugee or person granted humanitarian protection (and the applicant cannot seek leave to enter or remain in the UK as their family member under Part 11 of these rules). It sets out the requirements to be met and, in considering applications under this route, it reflects how, under Article 8 of the Human Rights Convention, the balance will be struck between the right to respect for private and family life and the legitimate aims of protecting national security, public safety and the economic well-being of the UK; the prevention of disorder and crime; the protection of health or morals; and the protection of the rights and freedoms of others (and in doing so also reflects the relevant public interest considerations as set out in Part 5A of the Nationality, Immigration and Asylum Act 2002). It also takes into account the need to safeguard and promote the welfare of children in the UK, in line with the Secretary of State's duty under section 55 of the Borders, Citizenship and Immigration Act 2009.

GEN.1.11A.   In all cases where:

(a)   limited leave is granted under paragraph D-LTRP.1.2., D-ILRP.1.3., D- LTRPT.1.2. or D-ILRPT.1.3.; or

(b)   limited leave is granted outside the rules on Article 8 grounds under paragraph GEN.1.10. or GEN.1.11.,

leave will normally be granted subject to a condition of no recourse to public funds, unless the applicant has provided the decision-maker with (i) satisfactory evidence that the applicant is destitute as defined in section 95 of the Immigration and Asylum Act 1999, or (ii) satisfactory evidence that there are particularly compelling reasons relating to the welfare of a child of a parent in receipt of a very low income.

Definitions

GEN.1.2.   For the purposes of this Appendix 'partner' means–

(i)   the applicant's spouse;

(ii)   the applicant's civil partner;

(iii)   the applicant's fiancé(e) or proposed civil partner; or

(iv)   a person who has been living together with the applicant in a relationship akin to a marriage or civil partnership for at least two years prior to the date of application,

unless a different meaning of partner applies elsewhere in this Appendix.

GEN.1.3.   For the purposes of this Appendix

(a)   'application for leave to remain' also includes an application for variation of leave to enter or remain by a person in the UK;

(b)   references to a person being present and settled in the UK also include a person who is being admitted for settlement on the same occasion as the applicant; and

(c)   references to a British Citizen in the UK also include a British Citizen who is coming to the UK with the applicant as their partner or parent.

GEN.1.4.   In this Appendix 'specified' means specified in Appendix FM-SE, unless otherwise stated.

GEN.1.5.   If the Entry Clearance Officer, or Secretary of State, has reasonable cause to doubt the genuineness of any document submitted in support of an application, and having taken reasonable steps to verify the document, is unable to verify that it is genuine, the document will be discounted for the purposes of the application.

GEN.1.6.   For the purposes of paragraph E-ECP.4.1.(a); E-LTRP.4.1.(a); EECPT. 4.1(a) and E-LTRPT.5.1.(a) the applicant must be a national of Antigua and Barbuda; Australia; the Bahamas; Barbados; Belize; Canada; Dominica; Grenada; Guyana; Jamaica; New Zealand; St Kitts and Nevis; St Lucia; St Vincent and the Grenadines; Trinidad and Tobago; or the United States of America.

GEN.1.7.   In this Appendix references to paragraphs are to paragraphs of this Appendix unless the context otherwise requires.

GEN.1.8.   Paragraphs 277–280, 289AA, 295AA and 296 of Part 8 of these Rules shall apply to this Appendix.

GEN.1.9.   In this Appendix:

   (a)   the requirement to make a valid application will not apply when the Article 8 claim is raised:

      (i)   as part of an asylum claim, or as part of a further submission in person after an asylum claim has been refused;

      (ii)   where a migrant is in immigration detention. A migrant in immigration detention or their representative must submit any application or claim raising Article 8 to a prison officer, a prisoner custody officer, a detainee custody officer or a member of Home Office staff at the migrant's place of detention; or

      (iii)   in an appeal (subject to the consent of the Secretary of State where applicable); and

   (b)   where an application or claim raising Article 8 is made in any of the circumstances specified in paragraph GEN.1.9.(a), or is considered by the Secretary of State under paragraph A277C of these rules, the requirements of paragraphs R-LTRP.1.1.(c) and R-LTRPT.1.1.(c) are not met.

GEN.1.10.   Where an applicant does not meet the requirements of this Appendix as a partner or parent but the decision-maker grants entry clearance or leave to enter or remain outside the rules on Article 8 grounds, the applicant will normally be granted entry clearance for a period not exceeding 33 months, or leave to enter or remain for a period not exceeding 30 months, and subject to a condition of no recourse to public funds unless the decision-maker considers that the person should not be subject to such a condition.

GEN.1.11.   Where entry clearance or leave to enter or remain is granted under this Appendix, or where an applicant does not meet the requirements of this Appendix as a partner or parent but the decision-maker grants entry clearance or leave to enter or remain outside the rules on Article 8 grounds, (and without prejudice to the specific provision that is made in this Appendix in respect of a no recourse to public funds condition), that leave may be subject to such conditions as the decision-maker considers appropriate in a particular case.

GEN.1.12.   In paragraphs GEN.1.10. and GEN.1.11. 'decision-maker' refers to the Secretary of State or an Entry Clearance Officer.

GEN.1.13.   For the purposes of paragraphs D-LTRP.1.1., D-LTRP.1.2., DILRP.1.2., D-LTRPT.1.1., D-LTRPT.1.2., and D-ILRPT.1.2. (excluding a grant of limited leave to remain as a fiancé(e) or proposed civil partner), where the applicant has extant leave at the date of application, the remaining period of that extant leave up to a maximum of 28 days will be added to the period of limited leave to remain granted under that paragraph (which may therefore exceed 30 months).

GEN.1.14.   Where a person aged 18 or over is granted entry clearance or limited leave to enter or remain under this Appendix (or outside the rules on Article 8 grounds), or where a person granted such entry clearance or limited leave to enter or remain will be aged 18 before that period of entry clearance or limited leave expires, the entry clearance or leave will, in addition to any other conditions which may apply, be granted subject to the conditions in Part 15 of these rules.

GEN.1.15.   Where, pursuant to paragraph D-ILRP.1.2., D-ILRP.1.3., D-ILRPT.1.2. or D-ILRPT.1.3., a person who has made an application for indefinite leave to remain under this Appendix does not meet the requirements for indefinite leave to remain but falls to be granted limited leave to remain under those provisions or paragraphs 276ADE(1) to 276DH, or outside the rules on Article 8 grounds:

   (a)   The Secretary of State will treat that application for indefinite leave to remain as an application for limited leave to remain;

   (b)   The Secretary of State will notify the applicant in writing of any requirement to pay an immigration health charge under the Immigration (Health Charge) Order 2015; and

   (c)   If there is such a requirement and that requirement is not met, the application for limited leave to remain will be invalid and the Secretary of State will not refund any application fee paid in respect of the application for indefinite leave to remain.

Leave to enter

GEN.2.1.   Subject to paragraph GEN.2.3., the requirements to be met by a person seeking leave to enter the UK under this route are that the person–

(a)   must have a valid entry clearance for entry under this route; and

(b)   must produce to the Immigration Officer on arrival a valid national passport or other document satisfactorily establishing their identity and nationality.

GEN.2.2.   If a person does not meet the requirements of paragraph GEN.2.1. entry will be refused.

GEN.2.3.   (1)   Where an applicant for leave to enter the UK remains in the UK on temporary admission or temporary release and the requirements of sub-paragraph (2) are met, paragraph GEN.1.10., D-LTRP.1.2., D-LTRC.1.1. or D-LTRPT.1.2. (as appropriate) will apply, as if paragraph D-LTRP.1.2., D-LTRC.1.1. or D- LTRPT.1.2. (where relevant) provided for the granting of leave to enter not leave to remain (and except that the references to leave to remain and limited leave to remain are to be read as leave to enter).

(2)   The requirements of this sub-paragraph are met where:

(a)   the applicant satisfies the requirements in paragraph R-LTRP.1.1.(a), (b) and (d), paragraph R-LTRC.1.1.(a), (b) and (d) or paragraph R-LTRPT.1.1.(a), (b) and (d), as if those were requirements for leave to enter not leave to remain (and except that the references to leave to remain and indefinite leave to remain are to be read as leave to enter);

(b)   a parent of the applicant has been granted leave to enter in accordance with this paragraph and the applicant satisfies the requirements in paragraph R- LTRC.1.1.(a), (b) and (d), as if those were requirements for leave to enter not leave to remain and as if paragraph R-LTRC.1.1.(d)(iii) referred to a parent of the applicant being or having been granted leave to enter in accordance with this paragraph (and except that the references to leave to remain are to be read as leave to enter); or

(c)   the Secretary of State decides to grant leave outside the rules on Article 8 grounds.

Family life with a Partner

Section EC-P: Entry clearance as a partner

EC-P.1.1.   The requirements to be met for entry clearance as a partner are that–

(a)   the applicant must be outside the UK;

(b)   the applicant must have made a valid application for entry clearance as a partner;

(c)   the applicant must not fall for refusal under any of the grounds in Section S-EC: Suitability–entry clearance; and

(d)   the applicant must meet all of the requirements of Section E-ECP:

Eligibility for entry clearance as a partner.

Section S-EC: Suitability-entry clearance

S-EC.1.1.   The applicant will be refused entry clearance on grounds of suitability if any of paragraphs S-EC.1.2. to 1.8. apply.

S-EC.1.2.   The Secretary of State has personally directed that the exclusion of the applicant from the UK is conducive to the public good.

S-EC.1.3.   The applicant is currently the subject of a deportation order.

S-EC.1.4.   The exclusion of the applicant from the UK is conducive to the public good because they have:

(a)   been convicted of an offence for which they have been sentenced to a period of imprisonment of at least 4 years; or

(b)   been convicted of an offence for which they have been sentenced to a period of imprisonment of at least 12 months but less than 4 years, unless a period of 10 years has passed since the end of the sentence; or

(c)   been convicted of an offence for which they have been sentenced to a period of imprisonment of less than 12 months, unless a period of 5 years has passed since the end of the sentence.

Where this paragraph applies, unless refusal would be contrary to the Human Rights Convention or the Convention and Protocol Relating to the Status of Refugees, it will only be in exceptional circumstances that the public interest in maintaining refusal will be outweighed by compelling factors.

S-EC.1.5. The exclusion of the applicant from the UK is conducive to the public good because, for example, the applicant's conduct (including convictions which do not fall within paragraph S-EC.1.4.), character, associations, or other reasons, make it undesirable to grant them entry clearance.

S-EC.1.6. The applicant has failed without reasonable excuse to comply with a requirement to–

(a) attend an interview;

(b) provide information;

(c) provide physical data; or

(d) undergo a medical examination or provide a medical report.

S-EC.1.7. It is undesirable to grant entry clearance to the applicant for medical reasons.

S-EC.1.8. The applicant left or was removed from the UK as a condition of a caution issued in accordance with section 22 of the Criminal Justice Act 2003 less than 5 years prior to the date on which the application is decided.

S-EC.2.1. The applicant will normally be refused on grounds of suitability if any of paragraphs S-EC.2.2. to 2.5. apply.

S-EC.2.2. Whether or not to the applicant's knowledge–

(a) false information, representations or documents have been submitted in relation to the application (including false information submitted to any person to obtain a document used in support of the application); or

(b) there has been a failure to disclose material facts in relation to the application.

S-EC.2.3. One or more relevant NHS body has notified the Secretary of State that the applicant has failed to pay charges in accordance with the relevant NHS regulations on charges to overseas visitors and the outstanding charges have a total value of at least £1000.

S-EC.2.4. A maintenance and accommodation undertaking has been requested or required under paragraph 35 of these Rules or otherwise and has not been provided.

S-EC.2.5. The exclusion of the applicant from the UK is conducive to the public good because:

(a) within the 12 months prior to the date on which the application is decided, the person has been convicted of or admitted an offence for which they received a non-custodial sentence or other out of court disposal that is recorded on their criminal record; or

(b) in the view of the Secretary of State:

(i) the person's offending has caused serious harm; or

(ii) the person is a persistent offender who shows a particular disregard for the law.

Section E-ECP: Eligibility for entry clearance as a partner

E-ECP.1.1. To meet the eligibility requirements for entry clearance as a partner all of the requirements in paragraphs E-ECP.2.1. to 4.2. must be met.

Relationship requirements

E-ECP.2.1. The applicant's partner must be–

(a) a British Citizen in the UK, subject to paragraph GEN.1.3.(c); or

(b) present and settled in the UK, subject to paragraph GEN.1.3.(b); or

(c) in the UK with refugee leave or with humanitarian protection.

E-ECP.2.2. The applicant must be aged 18 or over at the date of application.

E-ECP.2.3. The partner must be aged 18 or over at the date of application.

E-ECP.2.4. The applicant and their partner must not be within the prohibited degree of relationship.

E-ECP.2.5. The applicant and their partner must have met in person.

E-ECP.2.6. The relationship between the applicant and their partner must be genuine and subsisting.

E-ECP.2.7. If the applicant and partner are married or in a civil partnership it must be a valid marriage or civil partnership, as specified.

E-ECP.2.8. If the applicant is a fiancé(e) or proposed civil partner they must be seeking entry to the UK to enable their marriage or civil partnership to take place.

E-ECP.2.9. Any previous relationship of the applicant or their partner must have broken down permanently, unless it is a relationship which falls within paragraph 278(i) of these Rules.

E-ECP.2.10. The applicant and partner must intend to live together permanently in the UK.

Financial requirements

E-ECP.3.1. The applicant must provide specified evidence, from the sources listed in paragraph E-ECP.3.2., of–

    (a) a specified gross annual income of at least–

        (i) £18,600;

        (ii) an additional £3,800 for the first child; and

        (iii) an additional £2,400 for each additional child; alone or in combination with

    (b) specified savings of–

        (i) £16,000; and

        (ii) additional savings of an amount equivalent to 2.5 times the amount which is the difference between the gross annual income from the sources listed in paragraph E-ECP.3.2.(a)–(d) and the total amount required under paragraph E-ECP.3.1.(a); or

    (c) the requirements in paragraph E-ECP.3.3.being met.

In this paragraph 'child' means a dependent child of the applicant who is–

    (a) under the age of 18 years, or who was under the age of 18 years when they were first granted entry under this route;

    (b) applying for entry clearance as a dependant of the applicant, or has limited leave to enter or remain in the UK;

    (c) not a British Citizen or settled in the UK; and

    (d) not an EEA national with a right to be admitted under the Immigration (EEA) Regulations 2006.

E-ECP.3.2. When determining whether the financial requirement in paragraph EECP.3.1. is met only the following sources will be taken into account–

    (a) income of the partner from specified employment or self-employment, which, in respect of a partner returning to the UK with the applicant, can include specified employment or self-employment overseas and in the UK;

    (b) specified pension income of the applicant and partner;

    (c) any specified maternity allowance or bereavement benefit received by the partner in the UK or any specified payment relating to service in HM Forces received by the applicant or partner;

    (d) other specified income of the applicant and partner; and

    (e) specified savings of the applicant and partner.

E-ECP.3.3. The requirements to be met under this paragraph are–

    (a) the applicant's partner must be receiving one or more of the following –

        (i) disability living allowance;

        (ii) severe disablement allowance;

        (iii) industrial injury disablement benefit;

        (iv) attendance allowance;

        (v) carer's allowance;

        (vi) personal independence payment;

        (vii) Armed Forces Independence Payment or Guaranteed Income Payment under the Armed Forces Compensation Scheme; or

        (viii) Constant Attendance Allowance, Mobility Supplement or War Disablement Pension under the War Pensions Scheme; and

    (b) the applicant must provide evidence that their partner is able to maintain and accommodate themselves, the applicant and any dependants adequately in the UK without recourse to public funds.

E-ECP.3.4. The applicant must provide evidence that there will be adequate accommodation, without recourse to public funds, for the family, including other family members who are not included in the application but who live in the same household, which the family own or occupy exclusively: accommodation will not be regarded as adequate if–

    (a) it is, or will be, overcrowded; or

    (b) it contravenes public health regulations.

English language requirement

E-ECP.4.1. The applicant must provide specified evidence that they–

(a)   are a national of a majority English speaking country listed in paragraph GEN.1.6.;

(b)   have passed an English language test in speaking and listening at a minimum of level A1 of the Common European Framework of Reference for Languages with a provider approved by the Secretary of State;

(c)   have an academic qualification recognised by UK NARIC to be equivalent to the standard of a Bachelor's or Master's degree or PhD in the UK, which was taught in English; or

(d)   are exempt from the English language requirement under paragraph E-ECP.4.2.

E-ECP.4.2.   The applicant is exempt from the English language requirement if at the date of application–

(a)   the applicant is aged 65 or over;

(b)   the applicant has a disability (physical or mental condition) which prevents the applicant from meeting the requirement; or

(c)   there are exceptional circumstances which prevent the applicant from being able to meet the requirement prior to entry to the UK.

Section D-ECP: Decision on application for entry clearance as a partner

D-ECP.1.1.   If the applicant meets the requirements for entry clearance as a partner the applicant will be granted entry clearance for an initial period not exceeding 33 months, and subject to a condition of no recourse to public funds; or, where the applicant is a fiancé(e) or proposed civil partner, the applicant will be granted entry clearance for a period not exceeding 6 months, and subject to a condition of no recourse to public funds and a prohibition on employment.

D-ECP.1.2.   Where the applicant does not meet the requirements for entry clearance as a partner the application will be refused.

Section R-LTRP: Requirements for limited leave to remain as a partner

R-LTRP.1.1.   The requirements to be met for limited leave to remain as a partner are–

(a)   the applicant and their partner must be in the UK;

(b)   the applicant must have made a valid application for limited or indefinite leave to remain as a partner; and either

(c)   (i)   the applicant must not fall for refusal under Section S-LTR: Suitability leave to remain; and

  (ii)   the applicant meets all of the requirements of Section E-LTRP: Eligibility for leave to remain as a partner; or

(d)   (i)   the applicant must not fall for refusal under Section S-LTR: Suitability leave to remain; and

  (ii)   the applicant meets the requirements of paragraphs E-LTRP.1.2-1.12. and E-LTRP.2.1.–2.2.; and

  (iii)   paragraph EX.1. applies.

Section S-LTR: Suitability-leave to remain

S-LTR.1.1.   The applicant will be refused limited leave to remain on grounds of suitability if any of paragraphs S-LTR.1.2. to 1.7. apply.

S-LTR.1.2.   The applicant is currently the subject of a deportation order.

S-LTR.1.3.   The presence of the applicant in the UK is not conducive to the public good because they have been convicted of an offence for which they have been sentenced to imprisonment for at least 4 years.

S-LTR.1.4.   The presence of the applicant in the UK is not conducive to the public good because they have been convicted of an offence for which they have been sentenced to imprisonment for less than 4 years but at least 12 months.

S-LTR.1.5.   The presence of the applicant in the UK is not conducive to the public good because, in the view of the Secretary of State, their offending has caused serious harm or they are a persistent offender who shows a particular disregard for the law.

S-LTR.1.6.   The presence of the applicant in the UK is not conducive to the public good because their conduct (including convictions which do not fall within paragraphs S-LTR.1.3. to 1.5.), character, associations, or other reasons, make it undesirable to allow them to remain in the UK.

S-LTR.1.7.   The applicant has failed without reasonable excuse to comply with a requirement to–

(a)   attend an interview;

(b)   provide information;

(c)   provide physical data; or

(d)   undergo a medical examination or provide a medical report.

S-LTR.2.1.   The applicant will normally be refused on grounds of suitability if any of paragraphs S-LTR.2.2. to 2.4. apply.

S-LTR.2.2.   Whether or not to the applicant's knowledge –

(a)   false information, representations or documents have been submitted in relation to the application (including false information submitted to any person to obtain a document used in support of the application); or

(b)   there has been a failure to disclose material facts in relation to the application.

S-LTR.2.3.   One or more relevant NHS body has notified the Secretary of State that the applicant has failed to pay charges in accordance with the relevant NHS regulations on charges to overseas visitors and the outstanding charges have a total value of at least £1000.

S-LTR.2.4.   A maintenance and accommodation undertaking has been requested under paragraph 35 of these Rules and has not been provided.

S-LTR.3.1.   When considering whether the presence of the applicant in the UK is not conducive to the public good any legal or practical reasons why the applicant cannot presently be removed from the UK must be ignored.

Section E-LTRP: Eligibility for limited leave to remain as a partner

E-LTRP.1.1.   To qualify for limited leave to remain as a partner all of the requirements of paragraphs E-LTRP.1.2. to 4.2. must be met.

Relationship requirements

E-LTRP.1.2.   The applicant's partner must be–

(a)   a British Citizen in the UK;

(b)   present and settled in the UK; or

(c)   in the UK with refugee leave or as a person with humanitarian protection.

E-LTRP.1.3.   The applicant must be aged 18 or over at the date of application.

E-LTRP.1.4.   The partner must be aged 18 or over at the date of application.

E-LTRP.1.5.   The applicant and their partner must not be within the prohibited degree of relationship.

E-LTRP.1.6.   The applicant and their partner must have met in person.

E-LTRP.1.7.   The relationship between the applicant and their partner must be genuine and subsisting.

E-LTRP.1.8.   If the applicant and partner are married or in a civil partnership it must be a valid marriage or civil partnership, as specified.

E-LTRP.1.9.   Any previous relationship of the applicant or their partner must have broken down permanently, unless it is a relationship which falls within paragraph 278(i) of these Rules.

E-LTRP.1.10.   The applicant and their partner must intend to live together permanently in the UK and, in any application for further leave to remain as a partner (except where the applicant is in the UK as a fiancé(e) or proposed civil partner) and in any application for indefinite leave to remain as a partner, the applicant must provide evidence that, since entry clearance as a partner was granted under paragraph D-ECP1.1. or since the last grant of limited leave to remain as a partner, the applicant and their partner have lived together in the UK or there is good reason, consistent with a continuing intention to live together permanently in the UK, for any period in which they have not done so.

E-LTRP.1.11.   If the applicant is in the UK with leave as a fiancé(e) or proposed civil partner and the marriage or civil partnership did not take place during that period of leave, there must be good reason why and evidence that it will take place within the next 6 months.

E-LTRP.1.12.   The applicant's partner cannot be the applicant's fiancé(e) or proposed civil partner, unless the applicant was granted entry clearance as that person's fiancé(e) or proposed civil partner.

Immigration status requirements

E-LTRP.2.1.   The applicant must not be in the UK–

(a)   as a visitor; or

(b)   with valid leave granted for a period of 6 months or less, unless that leave is as a fiancé(e) or proposed civil partner, or was granted pending the outcome of family court or divorce proceedings.

E-LTRP.2.2.   The applicant must not be in the UK–

(a)   on temporary admission or temporary release, unless the applicant has been so for a continuous period of more than 6 months at the date of application and paragraph EX.1. applies; or

(b)   in breach of immigration laws (disregarding any period of overstaying for a period of 28 days or less), unless paragraph EX.1. applies.

Financial requirements

E-LTRP.3.1.   The applicant must provide specified evidence, from the sources listed in paragraph E-LTRP.3.2., of–

    (a)   a specified gross annual income of at least–

        (i)   £18,600;

        (ii)   an additional £3,800 for the first child; and

        (iii)   an additional £2,400 for each additional child; alone or in combination with

    (b)   specified savings of–

        (i)   £16,000; and

        (ii)   additional savings of an amount equivalent to 2.5 times the amount which is the difference between the gross annual income from the sources listed in paragraph E-LTRP.3.2.(a)–(f) and the total amount required under paragraph E-LTRP.3.1.(a); or

    (c)   the requirements in paragraph E-LTRP.3.3.being met, unless paragraph EX.1. applies.

In this paragraph 'child' means a dependent child of the applicant who is–

    (a)   under the age of 18 years, or who was under the age of 18 years when they were first granted entry under this route;

    (b)   applying for entry clearance or is in the UK as a dependant of the applicant;

    (c)   not a British Citizen or settled in the UK; and

    (d)   not an EEA national with a right to remain in the UK under the Immigration (EEA) Regulations 2006.

E-LTRP.3.2.   When determining whether the financial requirement in paragraph ELTRP.3.1. is met only the following sources may be taken into account–

    (a)   income of the partner from specified employment or self-employment;

    (b)   income of the applicant from specified employment or self-employment unless they are working illegally;

    (c)   specified pension income of the applicant and partner;

    (d)   any specified maternity allowance or bereavement benefit received by the applicant and partner in the UK or any specified payment relating to service in HM Forces received by the applicant or partner;

    (e)   other specified income of the applicant and partner;

    (f)   income from the sources at (b), (d) or (e) of a dependent child of the applicant under paragraph E-LTRP.3.1. who is aged 18 years or over; and

    (g)   specified savings of the applicant, partner and a dependent child of the applicant under paragraph E-LTRP.3.1. who is aged 18 years or over.

E-LTRP.3.3.   The requirements to meet this paragraph are–

    (a)   the applicant's partner must be receiving one or more of the following –

        (i)   disability living allowance;

        (ii)   severe disablement allowance;

        (iii)   industrial injury disablement benefit;

        (iv)   attendance allowance;

        (v)   carer's allowance;

        (vi)   personal independence payment;

        (vii)   Armed Forces Independence Payment or Guaranteed Income Payment under the Armed Forces Compensation Scheme; or

        (viii) Constant Attendance Allowance, Mobility Supplement or War Disablement Pension under the War Pensions Scheme; and

    (b)   the applicant must provide evidence that their partner is able to maintain and accommodate themselves, the applicant and any dependants adequately in the UK without recourse to public funds.

E-LTRP.3.4.   The applicant must provide evidence that there will be adequate accommodation, without recourse to public funds, for the family, including other family members who are not included in the application but who live in the same household, which the family own or occupy exclusively, unless paragraph EX.1. applies: accommodation will not be regarded as adequate if–

(a)   it is, or will be, overcrowded; or

(b)   it contravenes public health regulations.

English language requirement

E-LTRP.4.1.   If the applicant has not met the requirement in a previous application for leave as a partner or parent, the applicant must provide specified evidence that they–

(a)   are a national of a majority English speaking country listed in paragraph GEN.1.6.;

(b)   have passed an English language test in speaking and listening at a minimum of level A1 of the Common European Framework of Reference for Languages with a provider approved by the Secretary of State;

(c)   have an academic qualification recognised by UK NARIC to be equivalent to the standard of a Bachelor's or Master's degree or PhD in the UK, which was taught in English; or

(d)   are exempt from the English language requirement under paragraph E-LTRP.4.2;

unless paragraph EX.1. applies.

E-LTRP.4.2.   The applicant is exempt from the English language requirement if at the date of application–

(a)   the applicant is aged 65 or over;

(b)   the applicant has a disability (physical or mental condition) which prevents the applicant from meeting the requirement; or

(c)   there are exceptional circumstances which prevent the applicant from being able to meet the requirement.

Section D-LTRP: Decision on application for limited leave to remain as a partner

D-LTRP.1.1.   If the applicant meets the requirements in paragraph R-LTRP.1.1.(a) to (c) for limited leave to remain as a partner the applicant will be granted limited leave to remain for a period not exceeding 30 months, and subject to a condition of no recourse to public funds, and they will be eligible to apply for settlement after a continuous period of at least 60 months with such leave or in the UK with entry clearance as a partner under paragraph D-ECP1.1. (excluding in all cases any period of entry clearance or limited leave as a fiance(e) or proposed civil partner); or, if paragraph E-LTRP.1.11. applies, the applicant will be granted limited leave for a period not exceeding 6 months and subject to a condition of no recourse to public funds and a prohibition on employment.

D-LTRP.1.2.   If the applicant meets the requirements in paragraph R-LTRP.1.1.(a), (b) and (d) for limited leave to remain as a partner they will be granted leave to remain for a period not exceeding 30 months and subject to a condition of no recourse to public funds unless the Secretary of State considers that the person should not be subject to such a condition, and they will be eligible to apply for settlement after a continuous period of at least 120 months with such leave, with limited leave as a partner under paragraph D-LTRP.1.1., or in the UK with entry clearance as a partner under paragraph D-ECP1.1. (excluding in all cases any period of entry clearance or limited leave as a fiancé(e) or proposed civil partner), or, if paragraph E-LTRP.1.11. applies, the applicant will be granted limited leave for a period not exceeding 6 months and subject to a condition of no recourse to public funds and a prohibition on employment.

D-LTRP.1.3.   If the applicant does not meet the requirements for limited leave to remain as a partner the application will be refused.

Section R-ILRP: Requirements for indefinite leave to remain (settlement) as a partner

R-ILRP.1.1.   The requirements to be met for indefinite leave to remain as a partner are that-

(a)   the applicant and their partner must be in the UK;

(b)   the applicant must have made a valid application for indefinite leave to remain as a partner;

(c)   the applicant must not fall for refusal under any of the grounds in Section S-ILR: Suitability for indefinite leave to remain;

(d)   the applicant:

(i)   must meet all of the requirements of Section E-LTRP: Eligibility for leave to remain as a partner (but in applying paragraph ELTRP.3.1.(b)(ii) delete the words '2.5 times'); or

(ii)   must meet the requirements of paragraphs E-LTRP.1.2.-1.12. and E-LTRP.2.1. and paragraph EX.1. applies; and

(e)   the applicant must meet all of the requirements of Section E-ILRP: Eligibility for indefinite leave to remain as a partner.

Section S-ILR: Suitability for indefinite leave to remain

S-ILR.1.1.   The applicant will be refused indefinite leave to remain on grounds of suitability if any of paragraphs S-ILR.1.2. to 1.9. apply.

S-ILR.1.2.   The applicant is currently the subject of a deportation order.

S-ILR.1.3.   The presence of the applicant in the UK is not conducive to the public good because they have been convicted of an offence for which they have been sentenced to imprisonment for at least 4 years.

S-ILR.1.4.   The presence of the applicant in the UK is not conducive to the public good because they have been convicted of an offence for which they have been sentenced to imprisonment for less than 4 years but at least 12 months, unless a period of 15 years has passed since the end of the sentence.

S-ILR.1.5.   The presence of the applicant in the UK is not conducive to the public good because they have been convicted of an offence for which they have been sentenced to imprisonment for less than 12 months, unless a period of 7 years has passed since the end of the sentence.

S-ILR.1.6.   The applicant has, within the 24 months prior to the date on which the application is decided, been convicted of or admitted an offence for which they received a non-custodial sentence or other out of court disposal that is recorded on their criminal record.

S-ILR.1.7.   The presence of the applicant in the UK is not conducive to the public good because, in the view of the Secretary of State, their offending has caused serious harm or they are a persistent offender who shows a particular disregard for the law.

S-ILR.1.8.   The presence of the applicant in the UK is not conducive to the public good because their conduct (including convictions which do not fall within paragraphs S-ILR.1.3. to 1.6.), character, associations, or other reasons, make it undesirable to allow them to remain in the UK.

S-ILR.1.9.   The applicant has failed without reasonable excuse to comply with a requirement to–

(a)   attend an interview;

(b)   provide information;

(c)   provide physical data; or

(d)   undergo a medical examination or provide a medical report.

S-ILR.2.1.   The applicant will normally be refused on grounds of suitability if any of paragraphs S-ILR.2.2. to 2.4. apply.

S-ILR.2.2.   Whether or not to the applicant's knowledge–

(a)   false information, representations or documents have been submitted in relation to the application (including false information submitted to any person to obtain a document used in support of the application); or

(b)   there has been a failure to disclose material facts in relation to the application.

S-ILR.2.3.   One or more relevant NHS body has notified the Secretary of State that the applicant has failed to pay charges in accordance with the relevant NHS regulations on charges to overseas visitors and the outstanding charges have a total value of at least £1000.

S-ILR.2.4.   A maintenance and accommodation undertaking has been requested under paragraph 35 of these Rules and has not been provided.

S-ILR.3.1.   When considering whether the presence of the applicant in the UK is not conducive to the public good, any legal or practical reasons why the applicant cannot presently be removed from the UK must be ignored.

Section E-ILRP: Eligibility for indefinite leave to remain as a partner

E-ILRP.1.1.   To meet the eligibility requirements for indefinite leave to remain as a partner all of the requirements of paragraphs E-ILRP.1.2. to 1.6. must be met.

E-ILRP.1.2.   The applicant must be in the UK with valid leave to remain as a partner (disregarding any period of overstaying for a period of 28 days or less).

E-ILRP.1.3.   The applicant must have completed a continuous period of at least 60 months with limited leave as a partner under paragraph R-LTRP.1.1.(a) to (c) or in the UK with entry clearance as a partner under paragraph D-ECP.1.1.; or a continuous period of at least 120 months with limited leave as a partner under paragraph R-LTR.P.1.1(a), (b) and (d) or in the UK with entry clearance as a partner under paragraph D-ECP.1.1.; or a continuous period of at least 120 months with limited leave as a partner under a combination of these paragraphs, excluding in all cases any period of entry clearance or limited leave as a fiancé(e) or proposed civil partner.

E-ILRP.1.4.   In calculating the periods under paragraph E-ILRP.1.3. only the periods when the applicant's partner is the same person as the applicant's partner for the previous period of limited leave shall be taken into account.

E-ILRP.1.5.   In calculating the periods under paragraph E-ILRP.1.3. the words 'in the UK' in that paragraph shall not apply to any period(s) to which the evidence in paragraph 26A of Appendix FM-SE applies.

E-ILRP.1.6.   The applicant must have demonstrated sufficient knowledge of the English language and sufficient knowledge about life in the United Kingdom in accordance with the requirements of Appendix KoLL of these Rules.

Section D-ILRP: Decision on application for indefinite leave to remain as a partner

D-ILRP.1.1.   If the applicant meets all of the requirements for indefinite leave to remain as a partner the applicant will be granted indefinite leave to remain.

D-ILRP.1.2.   If the applicant does not meet the requirements for indefinite leave to remain as a partner only for one or both of the following reasons–

(a)   paragraph S-ILR.1.5. or S-ILR.1.6. applies;

(b)   The applicant has not demonstrated sufficient knowledge of the English language or about life in the United Kingdom in accordance with Appendix KoLL,

subject to compliance with any requirement notified under paragraph GEN.1.15.(b), the applicant will be granted further limited leave to remain as a partner for a period not exceeding 30 months, and subject to a condition of no recourse to public funds.

D-ILRP.1.3.   If the applicant does not meet all the eligibility requirements for indefinite leave to remain as a partner, and does not qualify for further limited leave to remain as a partner under paragraph DILRP. 1.2., the application will be refused, unless the applicant meets the requirements in paragraph R-LTRP.1.1.(a), (b) and (d) for limited leave to remain as a partner. Where they do, and subject to compliance with any requirement notified under paragraph GEN.1.15.(b), the applicant will be granted further limited leave to remain as a partner for a period not exceeding 30 months under paragraph D-LTRP.1.2. and subject to a condition of no recourse to public funds unless the Secretary of State considers that the person should not be subject to such a condition.

Family members

Section EX: Exceptions to certain eligibility requirements for leave to remain as a partner or parent

EX.1.   This paragraph applies if

(a)   (i)   the applicant has a genuine and subsisting parental relationship with a child who–

(aa)   is under the age of 18 years, or was under the age of 18 years when the applicant was first granted leave on the basis that this paragraph applied;

(bb)   is in the UK;

(cc)   is a British Citizen or has lived in the UK continuously for at least the 7 years immediately preceding the date of application; and

(ii)   it would not be reasonable to expect the child to leave the UK; or

(b)   the applicant has a genuine and subsisting relationship with a partner who is in the UK and is a British Citizen, settled in the UK or in the UK with refugee leave or humanitarian protection, and there are insurmountable obstacles to family life with that partner continuing outside the UK.

EX.2.   For the purposes of paragraph EX.1.(b) 'insurmountable obstacles' means the very significant difficulties which would be faced by the applicant or their partner in continuing their family life together outside the UK and which could not be overcome or would entail very serious hardship for the applicant or their partner.

Bereaved partner

Section BPILR: Indefinite leave to remain (settlement) as a bereaved partner

BPILR.1.1.   The requirements to be met for indefinite leave to remain in the UK as a bereaved partner are that–

(a)   the applicant must be in the UK;

(b)   the applicant must have made a valid application for indefinite leave to remain as a bereaved partner;

(c)   the applicant must not fall for refusal under any of the grounds in Section S-ILR: Suitability-indefinite leave to remain; and

(d)   the applicant must meet all of the requirements of Section E-BPILR: Eligibility for indefinite leave to remain as a bereaved partner.

Section E-BPILR: Eligibility for indefinite leave to remain as a bereaved partner

E-BPILR.1.1.   To meet the eligibility requirements for indefinite leave to remain as a bereaved partner all of the requirements of paragraphs E-BPILR1.2. to 1.4. must be met.

E-BPILR.1.2.   The applicant's last grant of limited leave must have been as–

     (a)   a partner (other than a fiancé(e) or proposed civil partner) of a British Citizen or a person settled in the UK; or

     (b)   a bereaved partner.

E-BPILR.1.3.   The person who was the applicant's partner at the time of the last grant of limited leave as a partner must have died.

E-BPILR.1.4.   At the time of the partner's death the relationship between the applicant and the partner must have been genuine and subsisting and each of the parties must have intended to live permanently with the other in the UK.

Section D-BPILR: Decision on application for indefinite leave to remain as a bereaved partner

D-BPILR.1.1.   If the applicant meets all of the requirements for indefinite leave to remain as a bereaved partner the applicant will be granted indefinite leave to remain.

D-BPILR.1.2.   If the applicant does not meet the requirements for indefinite leave to remain as a bereaved partner only because paragraph S-ILR.1.5. or S-ILR.1.6. applies, the applicant will be granted further limited leave to remain for a period not exceeding 30 months, and subject to a condition of no recourse to public funds.

D-BPILR.1.3.   If the applicant does not meet the requirements for indefinite leave to remain as a bereaved partner, or limited leave to remain as a bereaved partner under paragraph D-BPILR.1.2., the application will be refused.

Victim of domestic violence

Section DVILR: Indefinite leave to remain (settlement) as a victim of domestic violence

DVILR.1.1.   The requirements to be met for indefinite leave to remain in the UK as a victim of domestic violence are that–

     (a)   the applicant must be in the UK;

     (b)   the applicant must have made a valid application for indefinite leave to remain as a victim of domestic violence;

     (c)   the applicant must not fall for refusal under any of the grounds in Section S-ILR: Suitability-indefinite leave to remain; and

     (d)   the applicant must meet all of the requirements of Section E-DVILR:

Eligibility for indefinite leave to remain as a victim of domestic violence.

Section E-DVILR: Eligibility for indefinite leave to remain as a victim of domestic violence

E-DVILR.1.1.   To meet the eligibility requirements for indefinite leave to remain as a victim of domestic violence all of the requirements of paragraphs E-DVILR.1.2. and 1.3. must be met.

E-DVILR.1.2.   The applicant's first grant of limited leave under this Appendix must have been as a partner (other than a fiancé(e) or proposed civil partner) of a British Citizen or a person settled in the UK under paragraph D-ECP.1.1., DLTRP.1.1. or D-LTRP.1.2. of this Appendix and any subsequent grant of limited leave must have been:

     (a)   granted as a partner (other than a fiancé(e) or proposed civil partner) of a British Citizen or a person settled in the UK under paragraph D-ECP.1.1., DLTRP.1.1. or D-LTRP.1.2. of this Appendix; or

     (b)   granted to enable access to public funds pending an application under DVILR and the preceding grant of leave was granted as a partner (other than a fiancé(e) or proposed civil partner) of a British Citizen or a person settled in the UK under paragraph D-ECP.1.1., D-LTRP.1.1. or D-LTRP.1.2. of this Appendix; or

     (c)   granted under paragraph D-DVILR.1.2.

E-DVILR.1.3.   The applicant must provide evidence that during the last period of limited leave as a partner of a British Citizen or a person settled in the UK under paragraph D-ECP.1.1., D-LTRP.1.1. or D-LTRP.1.2. of this Appendix the applicant's relationship with their partner broke down permanently as a result of domestic violence.

Section D-DVILR: Decision on application for indefinite leave to remain as a victim of domestic violence

D-DVILR.1.1.   If the applicant meets all of the requirements for indefinite leave to remain as a victim of domestic violence the applicant will be granted indefinite leave to remain.

D-DVILR.1.2.   If the applicant does not meet the requirements for indefinite leave to remain as a victim of domestic violence only because paragraph S-ILR.1.5. or S-ILR.1.6. applies, the applicant will be granted further limited leave to remain for a period not exceeding 30 months.

D-DVILR.1.3.   If the applicant does not meet the requirements for indefinite leave to remain as a victim of domestic violence, or further limited leave to remain under paragraph D-DVILR.1.2. the application will be refused.

Family life as a child of a person with limited leave as a partner or parent

This route is for a child whose parent is applying for entry clearance or leave, or who has limited leave, as a partner or parent. For further provision on a child seeking to enter or remain in the UK for the purpose of their family life see Part 8 of these Rules.

Section EC-C: Entry clearance as a child

EC-C.1.1.   The requirements to be met for entry clearance as a child are that–

(a)   the applicant must be outside the UK;

(b)   the applicant must have made a valid application for entry clearance as a child;

(c)   the applicant must not fall for refusal under any of the grounds in Section S-EC: Suitability for entry clearance; and

(d)   the applicant must meet all of the requirements of Section E-ECC: Eligibility for entry clearance as a child.

Section E-ECC: Eligibility for entry clearance as a child

E-ECC.1.1.   To meet the eligibility requirements for entry clearance as a child all of the requirements of paragraphs E-ECC.1.2. to 2.4. must be met.

Relationship requirements

E-ECC.1.2.   The applicant must be under the age of 18 at the date of application.

E-ECC.1.3.   The applicant must not be married or in a civil partnership.

E-ECC.1.4.   The applicant must not have formed an independent family unit.

E-ECC.1.5.   The applicant must not be leading an independent life.

E-ECC.1.6.   One of the applicant's parents must be in the UK with limited leave to enter or remain, or be applying, or have applied, for entry clearance, as a partner or a parent under this Appendix (referred to in this section as the 'applicant's parent'), and

(a)   the applicant's parent's partner under Appendix FM is also a parent of the applicant; or

(b)   the applicant's parent has had and continues to have sole responsibility for the child's upbringing; or

(c)   there are serious and compelling family or other considerations which make exclusion of the child undesirable and suitable arrangements have been made for the child's care.

Financial requirement

E-ECC.2.1.   Where a parent of the applicant has, or is applying or has applied for, entry clearance or limited leave to enter or remain as a partner under this Appendix, the applicant must provide specified evidence, from the sources listed in paragraph E-ECC.2.2., of–

(a)   a specified gross annual income of at least–

(i)   £18,600;

(ii)   an additional £3,800 for the first child; and

(iii)   an additional £2,400 for each additional child; alone or in combination with

(b)   specified savings of

(i)   £16,000; and

(ii)   additional savings of an amount equivalent to 2.5 times the amount which is the difference between the gross annual income from the sources listed in paragraph E-ECC.2.2.(a)–(f) and the total amount required under paragraph E-ECC.2.1.(a); or

(c)   the requirements in paragraph E-ECC.2.3. being met.

In this paragraph 'child' means the applicant and any other dependent child of the applicant's parent who is–

(a)   under the age of 18 years, or who was under the age of 18 years when they were first granted entry under this route;

(b)   in the UK;

(c)   not a British Citizen or settled in the UK; and

(d)   not an EEA national with a right to remain in the UK under the Immigration (EEA) Regulations 2006.

E-ECC.2.2.   When determining whether the financial requirement in paragraph EECC. 2.1. is met only the following sources may be taken into account–

(a)   income of the applicant's parent's partner from specified employment or self-employment, which, in respect of an applicant's parent's partner returning to the UK with the applicant, can include specified employment or self-employment overseas and in the UK;

(b)   income of the applicant's parent from specified employment or self employment if they are in the UK unless they are working illegally;

(c)   specified pension income of the applicant's parent and that parent's partner;

(d)   any specified maternity allowance or bereavement benefit received by the applicant's parent and that parent's partner in the UK or any specified payment relating to service in HM Forces received by the applicant's parent and that parent's partner;

(e)   other specified income of the applicant's parent and that parent's partner;

(f)   income from the sources at (b), (d) or (e) of a dependent child of the applicant's parent under paragraph E-ECC.2.1. who is aged 18 years or over; and

(g)   specified savings of the applicant's parent, that parent's partner and a dependent child of the applicant's parent under paragraph E-ECC.2.1. who is aged 18 years or over.

E-ECC.2.3.   The requirements to be met under this paragraph are–

(a)   the applicant's parent's partner must be receiving one or more of the following–

(i)   disability living allowance;

(ii)   severe disablement allowance;

(iii)   industrial injury disablement benefit;

(iv)   attendance allowance;

(v)   carer's allowance;

(vi)   personal independence payment;

(vii)   Armed Forces Independence Payment or Guaranteed Income Payment under the Armed Forces Compensation Scheme; or

(viii)   Constant Attendance Allowance, Mobility Supplement or War Disablement Pension under the War Pensions Scheme; and

(b)   the applicant must provide evidence that their parent's partner is able to maintain and accommodate themselves, the applicant's parent, the applicant and any dependants adequately in the UK without recourse to public funds.

E-ECC.2.3A.   Where a parent of the applicant has, or is applying or has applied for, entry clearance or limited leave to enter or remain as a parent under this Appendix, the applicant must provide evidence that that parent is able to maintain and accommodate themselves, the applicant and any other dependants adequately in the UK without recourse to public funds.

E-EEC.2.4.   The applicant must provide evidence that there will be adequate accommodation, without recourse to public funds, for the family, including other family members who are not included in the application but who live in the same household, which the family own or occupy exclusively: accommodation will not be regarded as adequate if–

(a)   it is, or will be, overcrowded; or

(b)   it contravenes public health regulations.

Section D-ECC: Decision on application for entry clearance as a child

D-ECC.1.1.   If the applicant meets the requirements for entry clearance as a child they will be granted entry clearance of a duration which will expire at the same time as the leave granted to the applicant's parent, and subject to a condition of no recourse to public funds.

D-ECC.1.2.   If the applicant does not meet the requirements for entry clearance as a child the application will be refused.

Section R-LTRC: Requirements for leave to remain as a child

R-LTRC.1.1.   The requirements to be met for leave to remain as a child are that–

(a)   the applicant must be in the UK;

(b)   the applicant must have made a valid application for leave to remain as a child;

and either

(c)   (i)   the applicant must not fall for refusal under any of the grounds in Section S-LTR: Suitability-leave to remain; and

(ii)   the applicant meets all of the requirements of Section E-LTRC: Eligibility for leave to remain as a child; or

(d)   (i)   the applicant must not fall for refusal under any of the grounds in Section S-LTR: Suitability-leave to remain; and

(ii)   the applicant meets the requirements of paragraphs E-LTRC.1.2.–1.6.; and

(iii)   a parent of the applicant has been or is at the same time being granted leave to remain under paragraph D-LTRP.1.2. or D-LTRPT.1.2. or indefinite leave to remain under this Appendix (except as an adult dependent relative).

Section E-LTRC: Eligibility for leave to remain as a child

E-LTRC.1.1.   To qualify for limited leave to remain as a child all of the requirements of paragraphs E-LTRC.1.2. to 2.4. must be met (except where paragraph R-LTRC.1.1.(d)(ii) applies).

Relationship requirements

E-LTRC.1.2.   The applicant must be under the age of 18 at the date of application or when first granted leave as a child under this route.

E-LTRC.1.3.   The applicant must not be married or in a civil partnership.

E-LTRC.1.4.   The applicant must not have formed an independent family unit.

E-LTRC.1.5.   The applicant must not be leading an independent life.

E-LTRC.1.6.   One of the applicant's parents (referred to in this section as the 'applicant's parent') must be in the UK and have leave to enter or remain or indefinite leave to remain, or is at the same time being granted leave to remain or indefinite leave to remain, under this Appendix (except as an adult dependent relative), and

(a)   the applicant's p and compelling family or other considerations which make exclusion of the child undesirable and suitable arrangements have been made for the child's care.

Financial requirements

E-LTRC.2.1.   Where a parent of the applicant has, or is applying or has applied for, limited leave to remain as a partner under this Appendix, the applicant must provide specified evidence, from the sources listed in paragraph E-LTRC.2.2., of –

(a)   a specified gross annual income of at least–

(i)   £18,600;

(ii)   an additional £3,800 for the first child; and

(iii)   an additional £2,400 for each additional child; alone or in combination with

(b)   specified savings of–

(i)   £16,000; and

(ii)   additional savings of an amount equivalent to 2.5 times (or if the parent is applying for indefinite leave to remain 1 times) the amount which is the difference between the gross annual income from the sources listed in paragraph E-LTRC.2.2.(a)–(f) and the total amount required under paragraph E-LTRC.2.1.(a); or

(c)   the requirements in paragraph E-LTRC.2.3. being met.

In this paragraph 'child' means the applicant and any other dependent child of the applicant's parent who is–

(i)   under the age of 18 years, or who was under the age of 18 years when they were first granted entry under this route;

(ii)   in the UK;

(iii)   not a British Citizen or settled in the UK; and

(iv)   not an EEA national with a right to remain in the UK under the Immigration (EEA) Regulations 2006.

E-LTRC.2.2.   When determining whether the financial requirement in paragraph ELTRC. 2.1. is met only the following sources may be taken into account–

(a)   income of the applicant's parent's partner from specified employment or self-employment;

(b)   income of the applicant's parent from specified employment or selfemployment;

(c)   specified pension income of the applicant's parent and that parent's partner;

(d)   any specified maternity allowance or bereavement benefit received by the applicant's parent and that parent's partner in the UK or any specified payment relating to service in HM Forces received by the applicant's parent and that parent's partner;

(e)   other specified income of the applicant's parent and that parent's partner;

(f)   income from the sources at (b), (d) or (e) of a dependent child of the applicant's parent under paragraph E-LTRC.2.1. who is aged 18 years or over; and

(g)   specified savings of the applicant's parent, that parent's partner and a dependent child of the applicant's parent under paragraph E-ECC.2.1. who is aged 18 years or over.

E-LTRC.2.3.   The requirements to be met under this paragraph are–

(a)   the applicant's parent's partner must be receiving one or more of the following–

(i)   disability living allowance;

(ii)   severe disablement allowance;

(iii)   industrial injury disablement benefit;

(iv)   attendance allowance;

(v)   carer's allowance;

(vi)   personal independence payment;

(vii)   Armed Forces Independence Payment or Guaranteed Income Payment under the Armed Forces Compensation Scheme; or

(viii)   Constant Attendance Allowance, Mobility Supplement or War Disablement Pension under the War Pensions Scheme; and

(b)   the applicant must provide evidence that their parent's partner is able to maintain and accommodate themselves, the applicant's parent, the applicant and any dependants adequately in the UK without recourse to public funds.

E-LTRC.2.3A.   Where a parent of the applicant has, or is applying or has applied for, limited leave to remain as a parent under this Appendix, the applicant must provide evidence that that parent is able to maintain and accommodate themselves, the applicant and any other dependants adequately in the UK without recourse to public funds.

E-LTRC.2.4.   The applicant must provide evidence that there will be adequate accommodation in the UK, without recourse to public funds, for the family, including other family members who are not included in the application but who live in the same household, which the family own or occupy exclusively: accommodation will not be regarded as adequate if–

(a)   it is, or will be, overcrowded; or

(b)   it contravenes public health regulations.

Section D-LTRC: Decision on application for leave to remain as a child

D-LTRC.1.1.   If the applicant meets the requirements for leave to remain as a child the applicant will be granted leave to remain of a duration which will expire at the same time as the leave granted to the applicant's parent, and subject to a condition of no recourse to public funds. To qualify for indefinite leave to remain as a child of a person with indefinite leave to remain as a partner or parent, the applicant must meet the requirements of paragraph 298 of these rules.

D-LTRC.1.2.   If the applicant does not meet the requirements for leave to remain as a child the application will be refused.

Family life as a parent

Family life as a parent of a child in the UK

Section EC-PT: Entry clearance as a parent of a child in the UK

EC-PT.1.1.   The requirements to be met for entry clearance as a parent are that–

(a)   the applicant must be outside the UK;

(b)   the applicant must have made a valid application for entry clearance as a parent;

(c)   the applicant must not fall for refusal under any of the grounds in Section S-EC: Suitability–entry clearance; and

(d)   the applicant must meet all of the requirements of Section E-ECPT: Eligibility for entry clearance as a parent.

Section E-ECPT: Eligibility for entry clearance as a parent

E-ECPT.1.1.   To meet the eligibility requirements for entry clearance as a parent all of the requirements in paragraphs E-ECPT.2.1. to 4.2. must be met.

Relationship requirements

E-ECPT.2.1.   The applicant must be aged 18 years or over.

E-ECPT.2.2.   The child of the applicant must be–

(a)   under the age of 18 years at the date of application;

(b)   living in the UK; and

(c)   a British Citizen or settled in the UK.

E-ECPT.2.3.   Either–

(a)   the applicant must have sole parental responsibility for the child; or

(b)   the parent or carer with whom the child normally lives must be–

    (i)   a British Citizen in the UK or settled in the UK;

    (ii)   not the partner of the applicant; and

    (iii)   the applicant must not be eligible to apply for entry clearance as a partner under this Appendix.

E-ECPT.2.4.   (a)   The applicant must provide evidence that they have either–

    (i)   sole parental responsibility for the child; or

    (ii)   direct access (in person) to the child, as agreed with the parent or carer with whom the child normally lives or as ordered by a court in the UK; and

(b)   The applicant must provide evidence that they are taking, and intend to continue to take, an active role in the child's upbringing.

Financial requirements

E-ECPT.3.1.   The applicant must provide evidence that they will be able to adequately maintain and accommodate themselves and any dependants in the UK without recourse to public funds

E-ECPT.3.2.   The applicant must provide evidence that there will be adequate accommodation in the UK, without recourse to public funds, for the family, including other family members who are not included in the application but who live in the same household, which the family own or occupy exclusively: accommodation will not be regarded as adequate if–

(a)   it is, or will be, overcrowded; or

(b)   it contravenes public health regulations.

English language requirement

E-ECPT.4.1.   The applicant must provide specified evidence that they–

(a)   are a national of a majority English speaking country listed in paragraph GEN.1.6.;

(b)   have passed an English language test in speaking and listening at a minimum of level A1 of the Common European Framework of Reference for Languages with a provider approved by the Secretary of State;

(c)   have an academic qualification recognised by UK NARIC to be equivalent to the standard of a Bachelor's or Master's degree or PhD in the UK, which was taught in English; or

(d)   are exempt from the English language requirement under paragraph E-ECPT.4.2.

E-ECPT.4.2.   The applicant is exempt from the English language requirement if at the date of application–

(a)   the applicant is aged 65 or over;

(b)   the applicant has a disability (physical or mental condition) which prevents the applicant from meeting the requirement; or

(c)   there are exceptional circumstances which prevent the applicant from being able to meet the requirement prior to entry to the UK.

Section D-ECPT: Decision on application for entry clearance as a parent

D-ECPT.1.1.   If the applicant meets the requirements for entry clearance as a parent they will be granted entry clearance for an initial period not exceeding 33 months, and subject to a condition of no recourse to public funds.

D-ECPT.1.2.   If the applicant does not meet the requirements for entry clearance as a parent the application will be refused.

Section R-LTRPT: Requirements for limited leave to remain as a parent

R-LTRPT.1.1.   The requirements to be met for limited leave to remain as a parent are–

(a)   the applicant and the child must be in the UK;

(b)   the applicant must have made a valid application for limited or indefinite leave to remain as a parent or partner; and either

(c)   (i)   the applicant must not fall for refusal under Section S-LTR: Suitability leave to remain; and

(ii)   the applicant meets all of the requirements of Section ELTRPT: Eligibility for leave to remain as a parent, or

(d)   (i)   the applicant must not fall for refusal under S-LTR:

Suitability leave to remain; and

(ii)   the applicant meets the requirements of paragraphs E-LTRPT.2.2-2.4. and E-LTRPT.3.1.–3.2.; and

(iii)   paragraph EX.1. applies.

Section E-LTRPT: Eligibility for limited leave to remain as a parent

E-LTRPT.1.1.   To qualify for limited leave to remain as a parent all of the requirements of paragraphs E-LTRPT.2.2. to 5.2. must be met.

Relationship requirements

E-LTRPT.2.2.   The child of the applicant must be–

(a)   under the age of 18 years at the date of application, or where the child has turned 18 years of age since the applicant was first granted entry clearance or leave to remain as a parent under this Appendix, must not have formed an independent family unit or be leading an independent life;

(b)   living in the UK; and

(c)   a British Citizen or settled in the UK; or

(d)   has lived in the UK continuously for at least the 7 years immediately preceding the date of application and paragraph EX.1. applies.

E-LTRPT.2.3.   Either–

(a)   the applicant must have sole parental responsibility for the child or the child normally lives with the applicant and not their other parent (who is a British Citizen or settled in the UK); or

(b)   the parent or carer with whom the child normally lives must be–

(i)   a British Citizen in the UK or settled in the UK;

(ii)   not the partner of the applicant (which here includes a person who has been in a relationship with the applicant for less than two years prior to the date of application); and

(iii)   the applicant must not be eligible to apply for leave to remain as a partner under this Appendix.

E-LTRPT.2.4.   (a)   The applicant must provide evidence that they have either–

(i)   sole parental responsibility for the child, or that the child normally lives with them; or

(ii)   direct access (in person) to the child, as agreed with the parent or carer with whom the child normally lives or as ordered by a court in the UK; and

(b)   The applicant must provide evidence that they are taking, and intend to continue to take, an active role in the child's upbringing.

Immigration status requirement

E-LTRPT.3.1.   The applicant must not be in the UK–

(a)   as a visitor; or

       (b)   with valid leave granted for a period of 6 months or less, unless that leave was granted pending the outcome of family court or divorce proceedings.

E-LTRPT.3.2.   The applicant must not be in the UK–

       (a)   on temporary admission or temporary release, unless the applicant has been so for a continuous period of more than 6 months at the date of application and paragraph EX.1. applies; or

       (b)   in breach of immigration laws (disregarding any period of overstaying for a period of 28 days or less), unless paragraph EX.1. applies.

Financial requirements

E-LTRPT.4.1.   The applicant must provide evidence that they will be able to adequately maintain and accommodate themselves and any dependants in the UK without recourse to public funds, unless paragraph EX.1. applies.

E-LTRPT.4.2.   The applicant must provide evidence that there will be adequate accommodation in the UK, without recourse to public funds, for the family, including other family members who are not included in the application but who live in the same household, which the family own or occupy exclusively, unless paragraph EX.1. applies: accommodation will not be regarded as adequate if–

       (a)   it is, or will be, overcrowded; or

       (b)   it contravenes public health regulations.

English language requirement

E-LTRPT.5.1.   If the applicant has not met the requirement in a previous application for leave as a parent or partner, the applicant must provide specified evidence that they–

       (a)   are a national of a majority English speaking country listed in paragraph GEN.1.6.;

       (b)   have passed an English language test in speaking and listening at a minimum of level A1 of the Common European Framework of Reference for Languages with a provider approved by the Secretary of State;

       (c)   have an academic qualification recognised by UK NARIC to be equivalent to the standard of a Bachelor's or Master's degree or PhD in the UK, which was taught in English; or

       (d)   are exempt from the English language requirement under paragraph E-LTRPT.5.2, unless paragraph EX.1. applies.

E-LTRPT.5.2.   The applicant is exempt from the English language requirement if at the date of application–

       (a)   the applicant is aged 65 or over;

       (b)   the applicant has a disability (physical or mental condition) which prevents the applicant from meeting the requirement; or

       (c)   there are exceptional circumstances which prevent the applicant from being able to meet the requirement.

Section D-LTRPT: Decision on application for limited leave to remain as a parent

D-LTRPT.1.1.   If the applicant meets the requirements in paragraph R-LTRPT.1.1. (a) to (c) for limited leave to remain as a parent the applicant will be granted limited leave to remain for a period not exceeding 30 months, and subject to a condition of no recourse to public funds, and they will be eligible to apply for settlement after a continuous period of at least 60 months with such leave or in the UK with entry clearance as a parent under paragraph D-ECPT.1.1.

D-LTRPT.1.2.   If the applicant meets the requirements in paragraph LTRPT.1.1. (a), (b) and (d) for limited leave to remain as a parent they will be granted leave to remain for a period not exceeding 30 months and subject to a condition of no recourse to public funds unless the Secretary of State considers that the person should not be subject to such a condition, and they will be eligible to apply for settlement after a continuous period of at least 120 months with such leave, with limited leave as a parent under paragraph D-LTRPT.1.1., or in the UK with entry clearance as a parent under paragraph D-ECPT.1.1.

D-LTRPT.1.3.   If the applicant does not meet the requirements for limited leave to remain as a parent the application will be refused.

Section R-ILRPT: Requirements for indefinite leave to remain (settlement) as a parent

R-ILRPT.1.1.   The requirements to be met for indefinite leave to remain as a parent are that–

       (a)   the applicant must be in the UK;

       (b)   the applicant must have made a valid application for indefinite leave to remain as a parent;

(c)   the applicant must not fall for refusal under any of the grounds in Section S-ILR: Suitability-indefinite leave to remain;

(d)   the applicant must meet all of the requirements of Section E-LTRPT: Eligibility for leave to remain as a parent; and

(e)   the applicant must meet all of the requirements of Section E-ILRPT: Eligibility for indefinite leave to remain as a parent.

Section E-ILRPT: Eligibility for indefinite leave to remain as a parent

E-ILRPT.1.1.   To meet the eligibility requirements for indefinite leave to remain as a parent all of the requirements of paragraphs E-ILRPT.1.2. to 1.5. must be met.

E-ILRPT.1.2.   The applicant must be in the UK with valid leave to remain as a parent (disregarding any period of overstaying for 28 days or less).

E-ILRPT.1.3.   The applicant must have completed a continuous period of at least 60 months with limited leave as a parent under paragraph R-LTRPT.1.1.(a) to (c) or in the UK with entry clearance as a parent under paragraph D-ECPT.1.1.; or a continuous period of at least 120 months with limited leave as a parent, under paragraphs R-LTRPT.1.1(a), (b) and (d) or in the UK with entry clearance as a parent under paragraph D-ECPT.1.1.; or a continuous period of at least 120 months with limited leave as a parent under a combination of these paragraphs.

E-ILRPT.1.4.   DELETED.

E-ILRPT.1.5.   The applicant must have demonstrated sufficient knowledge of the English language and sufficient knowledge about life in the United Kingdom in accordance with the requirements of Appendix KoLL of these Rules.

Section D-ILRPT: Decision on application for indefinite leave to remain as a parent

D-ILRPT.1.1.   If the applicant meets all of the requirements for indefinite leave to remain as a parent the applicant will be granted indefinite leave to remain.

D-ILRPT.1.2.   If the applicant does not meet the requirements for indefinite leave to remain as a parent only for one or both of the following reasons–

(a)   paragraph S-ILR.1.5. or S-ILR.1.6. applies; or

(b)   The applicant has not demonstrated sufficient knowledge of the English language or about life in the United Kingdom in accordance with Appendix KoLL,

subject to compliance with any requirement notified under paragraph GEN.1.15.(b), the applicant will be granted further limited leave to remain as a parent for a period not exceeding 30 months, and subject to a condition of no recourse to public funds.

D-ILRPT.1.3.   If the applicant does not meet all the eligibility requirements for indefinite leave to remain as a parent, and does not qualify for further limited leave to remain under paragraph D-ILRPT.1.2., the application will be refused, unless the applicant meets the requirements in paragraph R-LTRPT.1.1.(a), (b) and (d) for limited leave to remain as a parent. Where they do, and subject to compliance with any requirement notified under paragraph GEN.1.15.(b), the applicant will be granted further limited leave to remain as a parent for a period not exceeding 30 months under paragraph D-LTRPT.1.2. and subject to a condition of no recourse to public funds unless the Secretary of State considers that the person should not be subject to such a condition.

Adult dependent relatives

Section EC-DR: Entry clearance as an adult dependent relative

EC-DR.1.1.   The requirements to be met for entry clearance as an adult dependent relative are that–

(a)   the applicant must be outside the UK;

(b)   the applicant must have made a valid application for entry clearance as an adult dependent relative;

(c)   the applicant must not fall for refusal under any of the grounds in Section S-EC: Suitability for entry clearance; and

(d)   the applicant must meet all of the requirements of Section E-ECDR: Eligibility for entry clearance as an adult dependent relative.

Section E-ECDR: Eligibility for entry clearance as an adult dependent relative

E-ECDR.1.1.   To meet the eligibility requirements for entry clearance as an adult dependent relative all of the requirements in paragraphs E-ECDR.2.1. to 3.2. must be met.

Relationship requirements

E-ECDR.2.1.   The applicant must be the–

(a)   parent aged 18 years or over;

(b)   grandparent;

(c)   brother or sister aged 18 years or over; or

(d)   son or daughter aged 18 years or over

of a person ('the sponsor') who is in the UK.

E-ECDR.2.2.   If the applicant is the sponsor's parent or grandparent they must not be in a subsisting relationship with a partner unless that partner is also the sponsor's parent or grandparent and is applying for entry clearance at the same time as the applicant.

E-ECDR.2.3.   The sponsor must at the date of application be–

(a)   aged 18 years or over; and

(b)   (i)   a British Citizen in the UK; or

   (ii)   present and settled in the UK; or

   (iii)   in the UK with refugee leave or humanitarian protection.

E-ECDR.2.4.   The applicant or, if the applicant and their partner are the sponsor's parents or grandparents, the applicant's partner, must as a result of age, illness or disability require long-term personal care to perform everyday tasks.

E-ECDR.2.5.   The applicant or, if the applicant and their partner are the sponsor's parents or grandparents, the applicant's partner, must be unable, even with the practical and financial help of the sponsor, to obtain the required level of care in the country where they are living, because–

(a)   it is not available and there is no person in that country who can reasonably provide it; or

(b)   it is not affordable.

Financial requirements

E-ECDR.3.1.   The applicant must provide evidence that they can be adequately maintained, accommodated and cared for in the UK by the sponsor without recourse to public funds.

E-ECDR.3.2.   If the applicant's sponsor is a British Citizen or settled in the UK, the applicant must provide an undertaking signed by the sponsor confirming that the applicant will have no recourse to public funds, and that the sponsor will be responsible for their maintenance, accommodation and care, for a period of 5 years from the date the applicant enters the UK if they are granted indefinite leave to enter.

Section D-ECDR: Decision on application for entry clearance as an adult dependent relative

D-ECDR.1.1.   If the applicant meets the requirements for entry clearance as an adult dependent relative of a British Citizen or person settled in the UK they will be granted indefinite leave to enter.

D-ECDR.1.2.   If the applicant meets the requirements for entry clearance as an adult dependent relative and the sponsor has limited leave the applicant will be granted limited leave of a duration which will expire at the same time as the sponsor's limited leave, and subject to a condition of no recourse to public funds. If the sponsor applies for further limited leave, the applicant may apply for further limited leave of the same duration, if the requirements in EC-DR.1.1. (c) and (d) continue to be met, and subject to no recourse to public funds.

D-ECDR.1.3.   If the applicant does not meet the requirements for entry clearance as an adult dependent relative the application will be refused.

Section R-ILRDR: Requirements for indefinite leave to remain as an adult dependent relative

R-ILRDR.1.1.   The requirements to be met for indefinite leave to remain as an adult dependent relative are that–

(a)   the applicant is in the UK;

(b)   the applicant must have made a valid application for indefinite leave to remain as an adult dependent relative;

(c)   the applicant must not fall for refusal under any of the grounds in Section S-ILR: Suitability-indefinite leave to remain; and

(d)   the applicant must meet all of the requirements of Section E-ILRDR: Eligibility for indefinite leave to remain as an adult dependent relative.

Section E-ILRDR: Eligibility for indefinite leave to remain as an adult dependent relative

E-ILRDR.1.1.   To qualify for indefinite leave to remain as an adult dependent relative all of the requirements of paragraphs E-ILRDR.1.2. to 1.5. must be met.

E-ILRDR.1.2.   The applicant must be in the UK with valid leave to remain as an adult dependent relative (disregarding any period of overstaying for a period of 28 days or less).

E-ILRDR.1.3.   The applicant's sponsor must at the date of application be

    (a)   present and settled in the UK; or

    (b)   in the UK with refugee leave or as a person with humanitarian protection and have made an application for indefinite leave to remain.

E-ILRDR.1.4.   The applicant must provide evidence that they can be adequately maintained, accommodated and cared for in the UK by the sponsor without recourse to public funds.

E-ILRDR.1.5.   The applicant must provide an undertaking signed by the sponsor confirming that the applicant will have no recourse to public funds, and that the sponsor will be responsible for their maintenance, accommodation and care, for a period ending 5 years from the date the applicant entered the UK with limited leave as an adult dependent relative.

Section D-ILRDR: Decision on application for indefinite leave to remain as an adult dependent relative

D-ILRDR.1.1.   If the applicant meets the requirements for indefinite leave to remain as an adult dependent relative and the applicant's sponsor is settled in the UK, the applicant will be granted indefinite leave to remain as an adult dependent relative.

D-ILRDR.1.2.   If the applicant does not meet the requirements for indefinite leave to remain as an adult dependent relative because paragraph S-ILR.1.5. or S-ILR.1.6. applies, the applicant will be granted further limited leave to remain as an adult dependent relative for a period not exceeding 30 months, and subject to a condition of no recourse to public funds.

D-ILRDR.1.3.   If the applicant's sponsor has made an application for indefinite leave to remain and that application is refused, the applicant's application for indefinite leave to remain will be refused. If the sponsor is granted limited leave, the applicant will be granted further limited leave as an adult dependent relative of a duration which will expire at the same time as the sponsor's further limited leave, and subject to a condition of no recourse to public funds.

D-ILRDR.1.4.   Where an applicant does not meet the requirements for indefinite leave to remain, or further limited leave to remain under paragraphs D-ILRDR.1.2. or 1.3., the application will be refused.

Deportation and removal

Where the Secretary of State or an immigration officer is considering deportation or removal of a person who claims that their deportation or removal from the UK would be a breach of the right to respect for private and family life under Article 8 of the Human Rights Convention that person may be required to make an application under this Appendix or paragraph 276ADE(1), but if they are not required to make an application Part 13 of these Rules will apply.

Appendix FM-SE

Family Members – Specified Evidence

A.   This Appendix sets out the specified evidence applicants need to provide to meet the requirements of rules contained in Appendix FM and, where those requirements are also contained in other rules, including armed forces, and unless otherwise stated, the specified evidence applicants need to provide to meet the requirements of those rules.

B.   Where evidence is not specified by Appendix FM, but is of a type covered by this Appendix, the requirements of this Appendix shall apply.

C.   In this Appendix references to paragraphs are to paragraphs of this Appendix unless the context otherwise requires.

D.   (a)   In deciding an application in relation to which this Appendix states that specified documents must be provided, the Entry Clearance Officer or Secretary of State ('the decision-maker') will consider documents that have been submitted with the application, and will only consider documents submitted after the application where sub-paragraph (b) or (e) applies.

(b)   If the applicant:

    (i)   Has submitted:

        (aa)   A sequence of documents and some of the documents in the sequence have been omitted (e.g. if one bank statement from a series is missing);

        (bb)   A document in the wrong format (for example, if a letter is not on letterhead paper as specified); or

        (cc)   A document that is a copy and not an original document; or

        (dd)   A document which does not contain all of the specified information; or

    (ii)   Has not submitted a specified document,

the decision-maker may contact the applicant or his representative in writing or otherwise, and request the document(s) or the correct version(s). The material requested must be received at the address specified in the request within a reasonable timescale specified in the request.

(c)   The decision-maker will not request documents where he or she does not anticipate that addressing the error or omission referred to in sub-paragraph (b) will lead to a grant because the application will be refused for other reasons.

(d)   If the applicant has submitted:

    (i)   A document in the wrong format; or

    (ii)   A document that is a copy and not an original document, or

    (iii)   A document that does not contain all of the specified information, but the missing information is verifiable from:

        (1)   other documents submitted with the application,

        (2)   the website of the organisation which issued the document, or

        (3)   the website of the appropriate regulatory body,

the application may be granted exceptionally, providing the decision-maker is satisfied that the document(s) is genuine and that the applicant meets the requirement to which the document relates. The decision-maker reserves the right to request the specified original document(s) in the correct format in all cases where sub-paragraph (b) applies, and to refuse applications if this material is not provided as set out in sub-paragraph (b).

(e)   Where the decision-maker is satisfied that there is a valid reason why a specified document(s) cannot be supplied, e.g. because it is not issued in a particular country or has been permanently lost, he or she may exercise discretion not to apply the requirement for the document(s) or to request alternative or additional information or document(s) be submitted by the applicant.

(f)   Before making a decision under Appendix FM or this Appendix, the decision-maker may contact the applicant or their representative in writing or otherwise to request further information or documents. The material requested must be received at the address specified in the request within a reasonable timescale specified in the request.

Evidence of Financial Requirements under Appendix FM

A1.   To meet the financial requirement under paragraphs E-ECP.3.1., E-LTRP.3.1., E-ECC.2.1. and E-LTRC.2.1. of Appendix FM, the applicant must meet:

(a)   The level of financial requirement applicable to the application under Appendix FM; and

(b)   The requirements specified in Appendix FM and this Appendix as to:

    (i)   The permitted sources of income and savings;

    (ii)   The time periods and permitted combinations of sources applicable to each permitted source relied upon; and

    (iii)   The evidence required for each permitted source relied upon.

1.   In relation to evidencing the financial requirements in Appendix FM the following general provisions shall apply:

(a)   Bank statements must:

    (i)   be from a financial institution regulated by the appropriate regulatory body for the country in which that institution is operating.

   (ii) not be from a financial institution on the list of excluded institutions in Appendix P of these rules.

   (iii) in relation to personal bank statements be only in the name of:

    (1) the applicant's partner, the applicant or both as appropriate; or

    (2) if the applicant is a child the applicant parent's partner, the applicant's parent or both as appropriate; or

    (3) if the applicant is an adult dependent relative, the applicant's sponsor or the applicant, unless otherwise stated.

   (iv) cover the period(s) specified.

   (v) be:

    (1) on official bank stationery; or

    (2) electronic bank statements which are either accompanied by a letter from the bank on its headed stationery confirming that the documents are authentic or which bear the official stamp of the issuing bank on every page.

 (aa) Where a bank statement is specified in this Appendix, a building society statement, a building society pass book, a letter from the applicant's bank or building society, or a letter from a financial institution regulated by the Financial Conduct Authority and the Prudential Regulation Authority or, for overseas accounts, the appropriate regulatory body for the country in which the institution operates and the funds are located, may be submitted as an alternative to a bank statement(s) provided that:

  (1) the requirements in paragraph 1(a)(i)–(iv) are met as if the document were a bank statement; and

  (2) a building society pass book must clearly show:

   (i) the account number;

   (ii) the building society's name and logo; and

   (iii) the information required on transactions, funds held and time period(s) or as otherwise specified in this Appendix in relation to bank statements; and/or

  (3) a letter must be on the headed stationery of the bank, building society or other financial institution and must clearly show:

   (i) the account number,

   (ii) the date of the letter;

   (iii) the financial institution's name and logo; and

   (iv) the information required on transactions, funds held and time period(s) or as otherwise specified in this Appendix in relation to bank statements.

 (b) Promises of third party support will not be accepted. Third party support will only be accepted in the form of:

  (i) payments from a former partner of the applicant for the maintenance of the applicant or any children of the applicant and the former partner, and payments from a former partner of the applicant's partner for the maintenance of that partner.

  (ii) income from a dependent child who has turned 18, remains in the same UK household as the applicant and continues to be counted towards the financial requirement under Appendix FM;

  (iii) gift of cash savings (whose souce must be declared) evidenced at paragraph 1(a)(iii), provided that the cash savings have been held by the person or persons at paragraph 1(a)(iii) for at least 6 months prior to the date of application and are under their control; and

  (iv) a maintenance grant or stipend associated with undergraduate study or postgraduate study or research.

 (bb) Payslips must be:

  (i) original formal payslips issued by the employer and showing the employer's name; or

  (ii) accompanied by a letter from the employer, on the employer's headed paper and signed by a senior official, confirming the payslips are authentic;

 (c) The employment or self employment income of an applicant will only be taken into account if they are in the UK, aged 18 years or over and working legally, and prospective employment income will not be taken into account (except that of an applicant's partner or parent's partner who is returning to employment or self-employment in the UK at paragraphs E-ECP.3.2.(a) and E-ECC.2.2.(a) of Appendix FM).

(cc)   The income of an applicant or sponsor working in the UK in salaried or non-salaried employment or in self-employment can include income from work undertaken overseas, provided paragraph E-LTRP.1.10 of Appendix FM and the other requirements of this Appendix are met.

(d)   All income and savings must be lawfully derived.

(e)   Savings must be held in cash.

(f)   Income or cash savings in a foreign currency will be converted to pounds sterling using the closing spot exchange rate which appears on www.oanda.com* on the date of application.

(g)   Where there is income or cash savings in different foreign currencies, each will be converted into pounds sterling before being added together, and then added to any UK income or savings to give a total amount.

(h)   All documentary evidence must be original, unless otherwise stated.

(i)   Evidence of profit from the sale of a business, property, investment, bond, stocks, shares or other asset will:

(i)   not be accepted as evidence of income, but

(ii)   the associated funds will be accepted as cash savings subject to the requirements of this Appendix and Appendix FM.

(j)   Where any specified documents provided are not in English or Welsh, the applicant must provide the original and a full translation that can be independently verified by the Entry Clearance Officer, Immigration Officer or the Secretary of State. The translation must be dated and include:

(i)   confirmation that it is an accurate translation of the original document;

(ii)   the full name and original signature of the translator or an authorised official of the translation company;

(iii)   the translator or translation company's contact details; and

(iv)   if the applicant is applying for leave to remain or indefinite leave to remain, certification by a qualified translator and details of the translator or translation company's credentials.

(k)   Where the gross (pre-tax) amount of any income cannot be properly evidenced, the net (post-tax) amount will be counted, including towards a gross income requirement.

(l)   Where this Appendix requires the applicant to provide specified evidence relating to a period which ends with the date of application, that evidence, or the most recently dated part of it, must be dated no earlier than 28 days before the date of application.

(m)   Cash income on which the correct tax has been paid may be counted as income under this Appendix, subject to the relevant evidential requirements of this Appendix.

(n)   The gross amount of any cash income may be counted where the person's specified bank statements show the net amount which relates to the gross amount shown on their payslips (or in the relevant specified evidence provided in addition to the specified bank statements in relation to non-employment income). Otherwise, only the net amount shown on the specified bank statements may be counted.

(o)   In this Appendix, a reference to the 'average' is a reference to the mean average.

2.   In respect of salaried employment in the UK (except where paragraph 9 applies), all of the following evidence must be provided:

(a)   Payslips covering:

(i)   a period of 6 months prior to the date of application if the person has been employed by their current employer for at least 6 months (and where paragraph 13(b) of this Appendix does not apply); or

(ii)   any period of salaried employment in the period of 12 months prior to the date of application if the person has been employed by their current employer for less than 6 months (or at least 6 months but the person does not rely on paragraph 13(a) of this Appendix), or in the financial year(s) relied upon by a self-employed person.

(b)   A letter from the employer(s) who issued the payslips at paragraph 2(a) confirming:

(i)   the person's employment and gross annual salary;

(ii)   the length of their employment;

        (iii)   the period over which they have been or were paid the level of salary relied upon in the application; and

        (iv)   the type of employment (permanent, fixed-term contract or agency).

(c)   Personal bank statements corresponding to the same period(s) as the payslips at paragraph 2(a), showing that the salary has been paid into an account in the name of the person or in the name of the person and their partner jointly.

(d)   Where the person is a director of a limited company based in the UK, evidence that the company is not of a type specified in paragraph 9(a). This can include the latest Annual Return filed at Companies House.

(e)   Where a person appointed as a non-executive director of a limited company based in the UK, which is not a company of the type specified in paragraph 9(a), is paid a fee instead of a salary, this income may be treated and evidenced as though it were income received for employment in that capacity.

2A.   (i)   In respect of salaried employment in the UK (paragraph 2 of this Appendix), statutory or contractual maternity, paternity, adoption or sick pay in the UK (paragraph 5 or 6 of this Appendix), or a director's salary paid to a self-employed person (paragraph 9 of this Appendix), the applicant may, in addition to the payslips and personal bank statements required under that paragraph, submit the P60 for the relevant period(s) of employment relied upon (if issued). If they do not, the Entry Clearance Officer or Secretary of State may grant the application if otherwise satisfied that the requirements of this Appendix relating to that employment are met. The Entry Clearance Officer or Secretary of State may request that the applicant submit the document(s) in accordance with paragraph D of this Appendix.

        (ii)   In respect of salaried employment in the UK (paragraph 2 of this Appendix), or statutory or contractual maternity, paternity, adoption or sick pay in the UK (paragraph 5 or 6 of this Appendix), the applicant may, in addition to the letter from the employer(s) required under that paragraph, submit a signed contract of employment. If they do not, the Entry Clearance Officer or Secretary of State may grant the application if otherwise satisfied that the requirements of this Appendix relating to that employment are met. The Entry Clearance Officer or Secretary of State may request that the applicant submit the document(s) in accordance with paragraph D of this Appendix.

3.   In respect of salaried employment outside of the UK, evidence should be a reasonable equivalent to that set out in paragraph 2 and (where relevant) paragraph 2A. In respect of an equity partner whose income from the partnership is treated as salaried employment under paragraph 17, the payslips and employer's letter referred to in paragraph 2 may be replaced by other evidence providing the relevant information in paragraph 2 (which may include, but is not confined to, a letter on official stationery from an accountant, solicitor or business manager acting for the partnership).

4.   In respect of a job offer in the UK (for an applicant's partner or parent's partner returning to salaried employment in the UK at paragraphs E-ECP.3.2.(a) and E-ECC.2.2.(a) of Appendix FM) a letter from the employer must be provided:

(a)   confirming the job offer, the gross annual salary and the starting date of the employment which must be within 3 months of the applicant's partner's return to the UK; or

(b)   enclosing a signed contract of employment, which must have a starting date within 3 months of the applicant's partner's return to the UK.

5.   In respect of statutory or contractual maternity, paternity or adoption pay all of the following, and in respect of parental leave in the UK only the evidence at paragraph 5(c), must be provided:

(a)   Personal bank statements corresponding to the same period(s) as the payslips at paragraph 5(b), showing that the salary has been paid into an account in the name of the person or in the name of the person and their partner jointly.

(b)   Payslips covering:

        (i)   a period of 6 months prior to the date of application or to the commencement of the maternity, paternity or adoption leave, if the applicant has been employed by their current employer for at least 6 months (and where paragraph 13(b) does not apply); or

        (ii)   any period of salaried employment in the period of 12 months prior to the date of application or to the commencement of the maternity, paternity or adoption leave, if the applicant has been employed by their current employer for less than 6 months (or at least 6 months but the person does not rely on paragraph 13(a)).

(c)   A letter from the employer confirming:

        (i)   the length of the person's employment;

      (ii)   the gross annual salary and the period over which it has been paid at this level;

      (iii)   the entitlement to maternity, paternity, parental or adoption leave; and

      (iv)   the date of commencement and the end-date of the maternity, paternity, parental or adoption leave.

6.   In respect of statutory or contractual sick pay in the UK all of the following must be provided:

    (a)   Personal bank statements corresponding to the same period(s) as the payslips at paragraph 6(b), showing that the salary has been paid into an account in the name of the person or in the name of the person and their partner jointly.

    (b)   Payslips covering:

      (i)   a period of 6 months prior to the date of application or to the commencement of the sick leave, if the applicant has been employed by their current employer for at least 6 months (and where paragraph 13(b) does not apply); or,

      (ii)   any period of salaried employment in the period of 12 months prior to the date of application or to the commencement of the sick leave, if the applicant has been employed by their current employer for less than 6 months (or at least 6 months but the person does not rely on paragraph 13(a)).

    (c)   A letter from employer confirming:

      (i)   the length of the person's employment;

      (ii)   the gross annual salary and the period over which it has been paid at this level;

      (iii)   that the person is in receipt of statutory or contractual sick pay; and

      (iv)   the date of commencement of the sick leave.

7.   In respect of self-employment in the UK as a partner, as a sole trader or in a franchise all of the following must be provided:

    (a)   Evidence of the amount of tax payable, paid and unpaid for the last full financial year.

    (b)   The following documents for the last full financial year, or for the last two such years (where those documents show the necessary level of gross income as an average of those two years):

      (i)   annual self-assessment tax return to HMRC (a copy or print-out); and

      (ii)   Statement of Account (SA300 or SA302).

    (c)   Proof of registration with HMRC as self-employed if available.

    (d)   Each partner's Unique Tax Reference Number (UTR) and/or the UTR of the partnership or business.

    (e)   Where the person holds or held a separate business bank account(s), bank statements for the same 12-month period as the tax return(s).

    (f)   personal bank statements for the same 12-month period as the tax return(s) showing that the income from self-employment has been paid into an account in the name of the person or in the name of the person and their partner jointly.

    (g)   Evidence of ongoing self-employment through evidence of payment of Class 2 National Insurance contributions, or (where the person has reached state pension age) through alternative evidence (which may include, but is not confined to, evidence of ongoing payment of business rates, business-related insurance premiums, employer National Insurance contributions or franchise payments to the parent company).

    (h)   One of the following documents must also be submitted:

      (i)   (aa)   If the business is required to produce annual audited accounts, such accounts for the last full financial year; or

            (bb)   If the business is not required to produce annual audited accounts, unaudited accounts for the last full financial year and an accountant's certificate of confirmation, from an accountant who is a member of a UK Recognised Supervisory Body (as defined in the Companies Act 2006);

      (ii)   A certificate of VAT registration and the latest VAT return (a copy or print-out) confirming the VAT registration number, if turnover is in excess of £79,000 or was in excess of the threshold which applied during the last full financial year;

      (iii)   Evidence to show appropriate planning permission or local planning authority consent is held to operate the type/class of business at the trading address (where this is a local authority requirement); or

        (iv)   A franchise agreement signed by both parties.

    (i)   The document referred to in paragraph 7(h)(iv) must be provided if the organisation is a franchise.

8.   In respect of self-employment outside of the UK, evidence should be a reasonable equivalent to that set out in paragraph 7.

9.   In respect of income from employment and/or shares in a limited company based in the UK of a type specified in paragraph 9(a), the requirements of paragraph 9(b)–(e) shall apply in place of the requirements of paragraphs 2 and 10(b).

    (a)   The specified type of limited company is one in which:

        (i)   the person is a director of the company (or another company within the same group); and

        (ii)   shares are held (directly or indirectly) by the person, their partner or the following family members of the person or their partner: parent, grandparent, child, stepchild, grandchild, brother, sister, uncle, aunt, nephew, niece or first cousin; and

        (iii)   any remaining shares are held (directly or indirectly) by fewer than five other persons.

    (b)   All of the following must be provided:

        (i)   Company Tax Return CT600 (a copy or print-out) for the last full financial year and evidence this has been filed with HMRC, such as electronic or written acknowledgment from HMRC.

        (ii)   Evidence of registration with the Registrar of Companies at Companies House.

        (iii)   If the company is required to produce annual audited accounts, such accounts for the last full financial year.

        (iv)   If the company is not required to produce annual audited accounts, unaudited accounts for the last full financial year and an accountant's certificate of confirmation, from an accountant who is a member of a UK Recognized Supervisory Body (as defined in the Companies Act 2006).

        (v)   Corporate/business bank statements covering the same 12-month period as the Company Tax Return CT600.

        (vi)   A current Appointment Report from Companies House.

        (vii)   One of the following documents must also be provided:

            (1)   A certificate of VAT registration and the VAT return for the last full financial year (a copy or print-out) confirming the VAT registration number, if turnover is in excess of £79,000 or was in excess of the threshold which applied during the last full financial year.

            (2)   Proof of ownership or lease of business premises.

            (3)   Original proof of registration with HMRC as an employer for the purposes of PAYE and National Insurance, proof of PAYE reference number and Accounts Office reference number. This evidence may be in the form of a certified copy of the documentation issued by HMRC.

    (c)   Where the person is listed as a director of the company and receives a salary from the company, all of the following documents must also be provided:

        (i)   Payslips and P60 (if issued) covering the same period as the Company Tax Return CT600.

        (ii)   Personal bank statements covering the same 12-month period as the Company Tax Return CT600 showing that the salary as a director was paid into an account in the name of the person or in the name of the person and their partner jointly.

    (d)   Where the person receives dividends from the company, all of the following documents must also be provided:

        (i)   Dividend vouchers for all dividends declared in favour of the person during or in respect of the period covered by the Company Tax Return CT600 showing the company's and the person's details with the person's net dividend amount and tax credit.

        (ii)   Personal bank statement(s) showing that those dividends were paid into an account in the name of the person or in the name of the person and their partner jointly.

    (e)   For the purposes of paragraph 19(a), evidence of ongoing employment as a director of the company or of ongoing receipt of dividend income from the company must be provided. This evidence may include payslips (or dividend vouchers) and personal bank statements showing that, in the period since the latest 12-month period covered by the Company Tax Return CT600, the person's salary as a director of the company (or dividend income from the company) was paid into an account in the name of the person or in the name of the person and their partner jointly. Alternative evidence may include evidence of ongoing payment of business rates, business-related insurance premiums or employer National Insurance contributions in relation to the company.

10. In respect of non-employment income all the following evidence, in relation to the form of income relied upon, must be provided:

(a) To evidence property rental income:

(i) Confirmation that the person or the person and their partner jointly own the property for which the rental income is received, through:

(1) A copy of the title deeds of the property or of the title register from the Land Registry (or overseas equivalent); or

(2) A mortgage statement.

(ii) personal bank statements for or from the 12-month period prior to the date of application showing the income relied upon was paid into an account in the name of the person or of the person and their partner jointly.

(iii) A rental agreement or contract.

(b) To evidence dividends (except where paragraph 9 applies) or other income from investments, stocks, shares, bonds or trust funds:

(i) A certificate showing proof of ownership and the amount(s) of any investment(s).

(ii) A portfolio report (for a financial institution regulated by the Financial Conduct Authority (and the Prudential Regulation Authority where applicable) in the UK) or a dividend voucher showing the company and person's details with the person's net dividend amount and tax credit.

(iii) personal bank statements for or from the 12-month period prior to the date of application showing that the income relied upon was paid into an account in the name of the person or of the person and their partner jointly.

(iv) Where the person is a director of a limited company based in the UK, evidence that the company is not of a type specified in paragraph 9(a). This can include the latest Annual Return filed at Companies House.

(c) To evidence interest from savings:

(i) personal bank statements for or from the 12-month period prior to the date of application showing the amount of the savings held and that the interest was paid into an account in the name of the person or of the person and their partner jointly.

(d) To evidence maintenance payments (from a former partner of the applicant to maintain their and the applicant's child or children or the applicant, or from a former partner of the applicant's partner to maintain the applicant's partner):

(i) Evidence of a maintenance agreement through any of the following:

(1) A court order;

(2) Written voluntary agreement; or

(3) Child Support Agency documentation.

(ii) personal bank statements for or from the 12-month period prior to the date of application showing the income relied upon was paid into an account in the name of the person or the person and their partner jointly.

(e) To evidence a pension:

(i) Official documentation from:

(1) The Department for Work and Pensions (in respect of the Basic State Pension and the Additional or Second State Pension) or other government department or agency, including the Veterans Agency;

(2) An overseas pension authority; or

(3) A pension company,

confirming pension entitlement and amount (and, where applicable, reflecting any funds withdrawn from the pension account or fund).

(ii) At least one personal bank statement in the 12-month period prior to the date of application showing payment of the pension into the person's account.

        (iii)   For the purposes of sub-paragraph (i), War Disablement Pension, War Widow's/Widower's Pension and any other pension or equivalent payment for life made under the War Pensions Scheme, the Armed Forces Compensation Scheme or the Armed Forces Attributable Benefits Scheme may be treated as a pension, unless excluded under paragraph 21 of this Appendix.

    (f)   To evidence UK Maternity Allowance, Bereavement Allowance, Bereavement Payment and Widowed Parent's Allowance:

        (i)   Department for Work and Pensions documentation confirming the person or their partner is or was in receipt of the benefit in the 12-month period prior to the date of application.

        (ii)   personal bank statements for or from the 12-month period prior to the date of application showing the income was paid into the person's account.

    (ff)   Subject to paragraph 12, to evidence payments under the War Pensions Scheme, the Armed Forces Compensation Scheme or the Armed Forces Attributable Benefits Scheme which are not treated as a pension for the purposes of paragraph 10(e)(i):

        (i)   Veterans Agency or Department for Work and Pensions documentation in the form of an award notification letter confirming the person or their partner is or was in receipt of the payment at the date of application.

        (ii)   personal bank statements for or from the 12-month period prior to the date of application showing the income was paid into the person's account.

    (g)   To evidence a maintenance grant or stipend (not a loan) associated with undergraduate study or postgraduate study or research:

        (i)   Documentation from the body or company awarding the grant or stipend confirming that the person is currently in receipt of the grant or stipend or will be within 3 months of the date of application, confirming that the grant or stipend will be paid for a period of at least 12 months or for at least one full academic year from the date of application or from the date on which payment of the grant or stipend will commence, and confirming the annual amount of the grant or stipend. Where the grant or stipend is or will be paid on a tax-free basis, the amount of the gross equivalent may be counted as income under this Appendix.

        (ii)   personal bank statements for or from any part of the 12-month period prior to the date of the application during which the person has been in receipt of the grant or stipend showing the income was paid into the person's account.

    (h)   To evidence ongoing insurance payments (such as, but not exclusively, payments received under an income protection policy):

        (i)   documentation from the insurance company confirming:

            (a)   that in the 12 months prior to the date of application the person has been in receipt of insurance payments and the amount and frequency of the payments.

            (b)   the reason for the payments and their expected duration.

            (c)   that, provided any relevant terms and conditions continue to be met, the payment(s) will continue for at least the 12 months following the date of application.

        (ii)   personal bank statements for or from the 12-month period prior to the date of application showing the insurance payments were paid into the person's account.

    (i)   To evidence ongoing payments (other than maintenance payments under paragraph 10(d)) arising from a structured legal settlement (such as, but not exclusively, one arising from settlement of a personal injury claim):

        (i)   documentation from a court or the person's legal representative confirming:

            (a)   that in the 12 months prior to the date of application the person has been in receipt of structured legal settlement payments and the amount and frequency of those payments.

            (b)   the reason for the payments and their expected duration.

            (c)   that the payment(s) will continue for at least the 12 months following the date of application.

        (ii)   personal bank statements for or from the 12-month period prior to the date of application showing the payments were paid into the person's account, either directly or via the person's legal representative.

11.   In respect of cash savings the following must be provided:

(a)   personal bank statements showing that at least the level of cash savings relied upon in the application has been held in an account(s) in the name of the person or of the person and their partner jointly throughout the period of 6 months prior to the date of application.

(b)   A declaration by the account holder(s) of the source(s) of the cash savings.

11A.   In respect of cash savings:

(a)   The savings may be held in any form of bank/savings account (whether a deposit or investment account), provided that the account allows the savings to be accessed immediately (with or without a penalty for withdrawing funds without notice). This can include savings held in a pension savings account which can be immediately withdrawn.

(b)   Paid out competition winnings or a legacy which has been paid can contribute to cash savings.

(c)   Funds held as cash savings by the applicant, their partner or both jointly at the date of application can have been transferred from investments,stocks, shares, bonds or trust funds within the period of 6 months prior to the date of application, provided that:

   (i)   The funds have been in the ownership and under the control of the applicant, their partner or both jointly for at least the period of 6 months prior to the date of application.

   (ii)   The ownership of the funds in the form of investments, stocks, shares, bonds or trust funds; the cash value of the funds in that form at or before the beginning of the period of 6 months prior to the date of application; and the transfer of the funds into cash, are evidenced by a portfolio report or other relevant documentation from a financial institution regulated by the appropriate regulatory body for the country in which that institution is operating.

   (iii)   The requirements of this Appendix in respect of the cash savings held at the date of application are met, except that the period of 6 months prior to the date of application in paragraph 11(a) will be reduced by the amount of that period in which the relevant funds were held in the form of investments, stocks, shares, bonds or trust funds.

   (iv)   For the purposes of sub-paragraph 11A(c), 'investments' includes funds held in an investment account or pension account or fund which does not meet the requirements of paragraphs 11 and 11A(a).

(d)   Funds held as cash savings by the applicant, their partner or both jointly at the date of application can be from the proceeds of the sale of property, in the form only of a dwelling, other building or land, which took place within the period of 6 months prior to the date of application, provided that:

   (i)   The property (or relevant share of the property) was owned at the beginning of the period of 6 months prior to the date of application and at the date of sale by the applicant, their partner or both jointly.

   (ii)   Where ownership of the property was shared with a third party, only the proceeds of the sale of the share of the property owned by the applicant, their partner or both jointly may be counted.

   (iii)   The funds deposited as cash savings are the net proceeds of the sale, once any mortgage or loan secured on the property (or relevant share of the property) has been repaid and once any taxes and professional fees associated with the sale have been paid.

   (iv)   The decision-maker is satisfied that the requirements in sub-paragraphs (i)–(iii) are met on the basis of information and documents submitted in support of the application. These may include for example:

      (1)   Registration information or documentation (or a copy of this) from the Land Registry (or overseas equivalent).

      (2)   A letter from a solicitor (or other relevant professional, if the sale takes place overseas) instructed in the sale of the property confirming the sale price and other relevant information.

      (3)   A letter from a lender (a bank or building society) on its headed stationery regarding the repayment of a mortgage or loan secured on the property.

      (4)   Confirmation of payment of taxes or professional fees associated with the sale.

      (5)   Any other relevant evidence that the requirements in subparagraphs (i)–(iii) are met.

   (v)   The requirements of this Appendix in respect of the cash savings held at the date of application are met, except that the period of 6 months mentioned in paragraph 11(a) will be reduced by the amount of time which passed between the start of that 6-month period and the deposit of the proceeds of the sale in an account mentioned in paragraph 11(a).

12. Where a person is in receipt of Carer's Allowance, Disability Living Allowance, Severe Disablement Allowance, Industrial Injuries Disablement Benefit, Attendance Allowance or Personal Independence Payment, or Armed Forces Independence Payment or Guaranteed Income Payment under the Armed Forces Compensation Scheme or Constant Attendance Allowance, Mobility Supplement or War Disablement Pension under the War Pensions Scheme, all the following must be provided:

(a) Official documentation from the Department for Work and Pensions or Veterans Agency confirming the current entitlement and the amount currently received.

(b) At least one personal bank statement in the 12-month period prior to the date of application.showing payment of the amount of the benefit or allowance to which the person is currently entitled into their account.

12A. Where the financial requirement the applicant must meet under Appendix FM relates to adequate maintenance, paragraphs 2 to 12 apply only to the extent and in the manner specified by this paragraph. Where such a financial requirement applies, the applicant must provide the following evidence:

(a) Where the current salaried employment in the UK of the applicant or their partner, parent, parent's partner or sponsor is relied upon:

(i) A letter from the employer confirming the employment, the gross annual salary and the annual salary after income tax and National Insurance contributions have been paid, how long the employment has been held, and the type of employment (permanent, fixed-term contract or agency).

(ii) Payslips covering the period of 6 months prior to the date of application or such shorter period as the current employment has been held.

(iii) personal bank statement covering the same period as the payslips, showing that the salary has been paid into an account in the name of the person or in the name of the person and their partner jointly.

(b) Where statutory or contractual maternity, paternity, adoption or sick pay in the UK of the applicant or their partner, parent, parent's partner or sponsor are relied upon, paragraph 5(b)(i) and (c) or paragraph 6(b)(i) and (c) apply as appropriate.

(c) Where self-employment in the UK of the applicant or their partner, parent, parent's partner or sponsor, or income from employment and/or shares in a limited company based in the UK of a type to which paragraph 9 applies, is relied upon, paragraph 7 or 9 applies as appropriate.

(d) Where the non-employment income of the applicant or their partner, parent, parent's partner or sponsor is relied upon, paragraph 10 applies and paragraph 10(f) shall apply as if it referred to any UK welfare benefit or tax credit relied upon and to HMRC as well as Department for Work and Pensions or other official documentation.

(e) Where the cash savings of the applicant or their partner, parent, parent's partner or sponsor are relied upon, paragraphs 11 and 11A apply.

(f) The monthly housing and Council Tax costs for the accommodation in the UK in which the applicant (and any other family members who are or will be part of the same household) lives or will live if the application is granted.

(g) Where the applicant is an adult dependent relative applying for entry clearance, the applicant must in addition provide details of the care arrangements in the UK planned for them by their sponsor (which can involve other family members in the UK), of the cost of these arrangements and of how that cost will be met by the sponsor.

12B. Where the financial requirement an applicant must meet under Part 8 (excluding an applicant who is a family member of a Relevant Points Based System Migrant) or under Appendix FM relates to adequate maintenance and where cash savings are relied upon to meet the requirement in full or in part, the decision-maker will:

(a) Establish the total cash savings which meet the requirements of paragraphs 11 and 11A;

(b) Divide this figure by the number of weeks of limited leave which would be issued if the application were granted, or by 52 if the application is for indefinite leave to enter or remain;

(c) Add the figure in sub-paragraph 12B(b) to the weekly net income (before the deduction of housing costs) available to meet the requirement.

Calculating Gross Annual Income under Appendix FM

13.   Based on evidence that meets the requirements of this Appendix, and can be taken into account with reference to the applicable provisions of Appendix FM, gross annual income under paragraphs E-ECP.3.1., E-LTRP.3.1., E-ECC.2.1. and E-LTRC.2.1. will be calculated in the following ways:

(a)   Where the person is in salaried employment in the UK at the date of application, has been employed by their current employer for at least 6 months and has been paid throughout the period of 6 months prior to the date of application at a level of gross annual salary which equals or exceeds the level relied upon in paragraph 13(a)(i), their gross annual income will be (where paragraph 13(b) does not apply) the total of:

(i)   The level of gross annual salary relied upon in the application;

(ii)   The gross amount of any specified non-employment income (other than pension income) received by them or their partner in the 12 months prior to the date of application; and

(iii) The gross annual income from a UK or foreign State pension or a private pension received by them or their partner.

(b)   Where the person is in salaried employment in the UK at the date of application and has been employed by their current employer for less than 6 months (or at least 6 months but the person does not rely on paragraph 13(a)), their gross annual income will be the total of:

(i)   The gross annual salary from employment as it was at the date of application;

(ii)   The gross amount of any specified non-employment income (other than pension income) received by them or their partner in the 12 months prior to the date of application; and

(iii) The gross annual income from a UK or foreign State pension or a private pension received by them or their partner.

In addition, the requirements of paragraph 15 must be met.

(c)   Where the person is the applicant's partner, is in salaried employment outside of the UK at the date of application, has been employed by their current employer for at least 6 months, and is returning to the UK to take up salaried employment in the UK starting within 3 months of their return, the person's gross annual income will be calculated:

(i)   On the basis set out in paragraph 13(a); and also

(ii)   On that basis but substituting for the gross annual salary at paragraph 13(a)(i) the gross annual salary in the salaried employment in the UK to which they are returning.

(d)   Where the person is the applicant's partner, has been in salaried employment outside of the UK within 12 months of the date of application, and is returning to the UK to take up salaried employment in the UK starting within 3 months of their return, the person's gross annual income will be calculated:

(i)   On the basis set out in paragraph 13(a) but substituting for the gross annual salary at paragraph 13(a)(i) the gross annual salary in the salaried employment in the UK to which they are returning; and also

(ii)   On the basis set out in paragraph 15(b).

(e)   Where the person is self-employed, their gross annual income will be the total of their gross income from their self-employment, from any salaried or non-salaried employment they have had or their partner has had (if their partner is in the UK with permission to work), from specified non-employment income received by them or their partner, and from income from a UK or foreign State pension or a private pension received by them or their partner, in the last full financial year or as an average of the last two full financial years. The requirements of this Appendix for specified evidence relating to these forms of income shall apply as if references to the date of application were references to the end of the relevant financial year(s). The relevant financial year(s) cannot be combined with any financial year(s) to which paragraph 9 applies and vice versa.

(f)   Where the person is self-employed, they cannot combine their gross annual income at paragraph 13(e) with specified savings in order to meet the level of income required under Appendix FM.

(g)   Where the person is not relying on income from salaried employment or self-employment, their gross annual income will be the total of:

(i)   The gross amount of any specified non-employment income (other than pension income) received by them or their partner in the 12 months prior to the date of application; and

(ii)   The gross annual income from a UK or foreign State pension or a private pension received by them or their partner.

(h)   Where the person is the applicant's partner and is in self-employment outside the UK at the date of application and is returning to the UK to take up salaried employment in the UK starting within 3 months of their return, the person's gross annual income will be calculated:

  (i)   On the basis set out in paragraph 13(a) but substituting for the gross annual salary at paragraph 13(a)(i) the gross annual salary in the salaried employment in the UK to which they are returning; and also

  (ii)   On the basis set out in paragraph 13(e).

(i)   Any period of unpaid maternity, paternity, adoption, parental or sick leave in the 12 months prior to the date of application will not be counted towards any period relating to employment, or any period relating to income from employment, for which this Appendix provides.

(j)   The provisions of paragraph 13 which apply to self-employment and to a person who is self-employed also apply to income from employment and/or shares in a limited company based in the UK of a type to which paragraph 9 applies and to a person in receipt of such income.

(k)   Where the application relies on the employment income of the applicant and the sponsor, all of that income must be calculated either under subparagraph 13(a) or under sub-paragraph 13(b) and paragraph 15, and not under a combination of these methods.

14.   Where the requirements of this Appendix and Appendix FM are met by the combined income or cash savings of more than one person, the income or the cash savings must only be counted once unless stated otherwise.

15.   In respect of paragraph 13(b) and paragraph 13(d), the provisions in this paragraph also apply:

(a)   In order to evidence the level of gross annual income required by Appendix FM, the person must meet the requirements in paragraph 13(b) or paragraph 13(d)(i); and

(b)   The person must also meet the level of gross annual income required by Appendix FM on the basis that their income is the total of:

  (i)   The gross income from salaried employment in the UK or overseas earned by the person in the 12 months prior to the date of application;

  (ii)   The gross amount of any specified non-employment income (other than pension income) received by the person or their partner in the 12 months prior to the date of application;

  (iii)   The gross amount received from a UK or foreign State pension or a private pension by the person or their partner in the 12 months prior to the date of application; and

  (iv)   The person cannot combine the gross annual income at paragraph 15(b)(i)–(iii) with specified savings in order to meet the level of income required.

16.   Where a person is in receipt of maternity, paternity, adoption or sick pay or has been so in the 6 months prior to the date of application, this paragraph applies:

(a)   the relevant date for considering the length of employment with their current employer will be the date that the maternity, paternity, adoption or sick leave commenced or the date of application; and

(b)   the relevant period for calculating income from their salaried employment will be the period prior to the commencement of the maternity, paternity, adoption or sick pay or to the date of application.

17.   If a person is an equity partner, for example in a law firm, the income they draw from the partnership (including where this is in the form of a profit share) will be treated as salaried employment for the purposes of this Appendix and Appendix FM.

17A.   Where a person is a subcontractor under the Construction Industry Scheme administered by HMRC and does not rely on paragraph 13(e), the income they receive as a subcontractor under the Construction Industry Scheme may be treated as income from salaried employment for the purposes of this Appendix and Appendix FM. In that case, the requirements for specified evidence in paragraph 2 must be met, subject to applying those requirements so as to reflect the person's status as a subcontractor under the Construction Industry Scheme.

18.   When calculating income from salaried employment under paragraphs 12A and 13 to 16, this paragraph applies:

(a)   Basic pay, skills-based allowances, and UK location-based allowances will be counted as income provided that:

  (i)   They are contractual; and

  (ii)   Where these allowances make up more than 30% of the total salary, only the amount up to 30% is counted.

(b)   Overtime, commission-based pay and bonuses (which can include tips and gratuities paid via a tronc scheme registered with HMRC) will be counted as income, where they have been received in the relevant period(s) of employment or self-employment relied upon in the application.

(bb)   In respect of a person in salaried employment at the date of application, the amount of income in sub-paragraph (b) which may be added to their gross annual salary, and counted as part of that figure for the purposes of paragraph 13(a)(i) or 13(b)(i), is the annual equivalent of the person's average gross monthly income from that income in their current employment in the 6 months prior to the date of application.

(c)   UK and overseas travel, subsistence and accommodation allowances, and allowances relating to the cost of living overseas will not be counted as income.

(d)   Gross income from non-salaried employment will be calculated on the same basis as income from salaried employment, except as provided in paragraph 18(e) and 18(f), and the requirements of this Appendix for specified evidence relating to salaried employment shall apply as if references to salary were references to income from non-salaried employment. Non-salaried employment includes that paid at an hourly or other rate (and the number and/or pattern of hours required to be worked may vary), or paid an amount which varies according to the work undertaken, whereas salaried employment includes that paid at a minimum fixed rate (usually annual) and is subject usually to a contractual minimum number of hours to be worked.

(e)   For the purpose of paragraph 13(a)(i), in respect of a person in non-salaried employment at the date of application 'the level of gross annual salary relied upon in the application' shall be no greater than the annual equivalent of the person's average gross monthly income from non-salaried employment in the 6 months prior to the date of application, where that employment was held throughout that period.

(f)   For the purpose of paragraph 13(b)(i), 'the gross annual salary from employment as it was at the date of application' of a person in non-salaried employment at the date of application shall be considered to be the annual equivalent of the person's average gross monthly income from non-salaried employment in the 6 months prior to the date of application, regardless of whether that employment was held throughout that period.

(g)   For the purpose of paragraphs 13(c)(ii) and 13(d)(i), 'the gross annual salary in the salaried employment in the UK to which they are returning' of a person who is returning to the UK to take up non-salaried employment in the UK starting within 3 months of their return is the gross annual income from that employment, based on the rate or amount of pay, and the standard or core hours of work, set out in the document(s) from the employer provided under paragraph 4. Notwithstanding paragraph 18(b), this may include the gross 'on-target' earnings which may be expected from satisfactory performance in the standard or core hours of work.

19.   When calculating income from self-employment under paragraphs 12A and 13(e), and in relation to income from employment and/or shares in a limited company based in the UK of a type to which paragraph 9 applies, this paragraph applies:

(a)   There must be evidence of ongoing self-employment, and (where income from salaried employment is also relied upon or where paragraph 9(c) applies) ongoing employment, at the date of application.

(b)   Where the self-employed person is a sole trader or is in a partnership or franchise agreement, the income will be:

(i)   the gross taxable profits from their share of the business; and

(ii)   allowances or deductible expenses which are not taxed will not be counted towards income.

(c)   Where income to which paragraph 19 applies is being used to meet the financial requirement for an initial application for leave to remain as a partner under Appendix FM by an applicant who used such income to meet that requirement in an application for entry clearance as a fiancé(e) or proposed civil partner under that Appendix in the last 12 months, the Secretary of State may continue to accept the same level and evidence of income to which paragraph 19 applies that was accepted in granting the application for entry clearance, provided that there is evidence of ongoing self-employment, and (where income from salaried employment is also relied upon or where paragraph 9(c) applies) ongoing employment, at the date of the application for leave to remain.

(d)   The financial year(s) to which paragraph 7 refers is the period of the last full financial year(s) to which the required Statement(s) of Account (SA300 or SA302) relates.

(e)   The financial year(s) to which paragraph 9 refers is the period of the last full financial year(s) to which the required Company Tax Return(s) CT600 relates.

20. When calculating income from specified non-employment sources under paragraphs 12A and 13 to 15, this paragraph applies:

    (a) Assets or savings must be in the name of the person, or jointly with their partner.

    (b) Any asset or savings on which income is based must be held or owned by the person at the date of application.

    (c) Any rental income from property, in the UK or overseas, must be from a property that is:

        (i) owned by the person;

        (ii) not their main residence and will not be so if the application is granted, except in the circumstances specified in paragraph 20(e); and

        (iii) if ownership of the property is shared with a third party, only income received from their share of the property can be counted.

    (cc) The amount of rental income from property received before any management fee was deducted may be counted.

    (d) Equity in a property cannot be used to meet the financial requirement.

    (e) Where the applicant and their partner are resident outside the UK at the date of application, rental income from a property in the UK that will become their main residence if the application is granted may only be counted under paragraph 13(c)(i) and paragraph 13(d)(ii).

    (f) Any future entitlement to a maintenance grant or stipend of the type specified in paragraph 10(g) may be counted as though the person had received the annual amount of that grant or stipend in the 12 months prior to the date of application.

20A. When calculating the gross annual income from pension under paragraph 13, the gross annual amount of any pension received may be counted where the pension has become a source of income at least 28 days prior to the date of application.

21. When calculating income under paragraphs 13 to 16, the following sources will not be counted:

    (a) Loans and credit facilities.

    (b) Income-related benefits: Income Support, income-related Employment and Support Allowance, Pension Credit, Housing Benefit, Council Tax Benefit or Support (or any equivalent) and income-based Jobseeker's Allowance.

    (c) The following contributory benefits: contribution-based Jobseeker's Allowance, contribution-based Employment and Support Allowance and Incapacity Benefit.

    (cc) Unemployability Allowance, Allowance for a Lowered Standard of Occupation and Invalidity Allowance under the War Pension Scheme.

    (d) Child Benefit.

    (e) Working Tax Credit.

    (f) Child Tax Credit.

    (ff) Universal Credit.

    (g) Any other source of income not specified in this appendix.

Evidence of Marriage or Civil Partnerships

22. A claim to have been married in the United Kingdom must be evidenced by a marriage certificate.

23. A claim to be divorced in the United Kingdom must be evidenced by a decree absolute from a civil court.

24. A civil partnership in the United Kingdom must be evidenced by a civil partnership certificate.

25. The dissolution of a civil partnership in the UK must be evidenced by a final order of civil partnership dissolution from a civil court.

26. Marriages, civil partnerships or evidence of divorce or dissolution from outside the UK must be evidenced by a reasonable equivalent to the evidence detailed in paragraphs 22 to 25, valid under the law in force in the relevant country.

Evidence of the Applicant Living Overseas with a Crown Servant

26A. Where

    (a) An applicant for entry clearance, limited leave to enter or remain or indefinite leave to remain as a partner under Appendix FM (except as a fiancé(e) or proposed civil partner) intends to enter or remain in the UK to begin their probationary period (or has done so) and then to live outside the UK for the time being with their sponsor (or is doing so or has done so) before the couple live together permanently in the UK; and

(b)   The sponsor, who is a British Citizen or settled in the UK, is a permanent member of HM Diplomatic Service or a comparable UK-based staff member of the British Council, the Department for International Development or the Home Office on a tour of duty outside the UK,

the applicant must provide a letter on official stationery from the sponsor's head of mission confirming the information at (a) and (b) and confirming the start date and expected end date of the sponsor's tour of duty outside the UK.

Evidence of English Language Requirements

27.   Evidence of passing an English language test in speaking and listening must take the form of a certificate and/ or other document(s) for the relevant test (which may include a print out of the online score from a PTE (Pearson) test or the Home Office must be able to verify the evidence online) as specified in Appendix O that:

(i)   is from an English language test provider approved by the Secretary of State for these purposes as specified in Appendix O of these rules;

(ii)   is for a test approved by the Secretary of State for these purposes as specified in Appendix O of these rules;

(iii)   shows the applicant's name;

(iv)   shows the qualification obtained (which must meet or exceed level A1 of the Common European Framework of Reference);

(v)   shows the date of award;

(vi)   shows that the test is within its validity date (where applicable); and

(vii)   is for a test taken at a test centre approved by the Secretary of State as a Secure English Language Test centre.

28.   The evidence required to show that a person is a citizen or national of a majority English speaking country is a valid passport or travel document, unless paragraphs 29 and 30 apply. A dual national may invoke either of their nationalities.

29.   If the applicant has not provided their passport or travel document other evidence of nationality can be supplied in the following circumstances only (as indicated by the applicant on their application form):

(a)   where the passport or travel document has been lost or stolen;

(b)   where the passport or travel document has expired and been returned to the relevant authorities; or

(c)   where the passport or travel document is with another part of the Home Office.

30.   Alternative evidence as proof of nationality, if acceptable, must be either:

(a)   A current national identity document; or

(b)   An original letter from the applicant's national government, Embassy or High Commission confirming the applicant's full name, date of birth and nationality.

31.   Evidence of an academic qualification (recognised by UK NARIC to be equivalent to the standard of a Bachelor's or Master's degree or PhD in the UK) and was taught in English must be either:

(a)   A certificate issued by the relevant institution confirming the award of the academic qualification showing:

(i)   the applicant's name;

(ii)   the title of award;

(iii)   the date of award;

(iv)   the name of the awarding institution; and,

(v)   that the qualification was taught in English

Or,

(b)   If the applicant is awaiting graduation or no longer has the certificate and cannot get a new one, the evidence must be:

(i)   an original academic reference from the institution awarding the academic qualification that;

(1)   is on official letter headed paper;

(2)   shows the applicant's name;

(3)   shows the title of award;

(4)   confirms that the qualification was taught in English;

(5)   explains when the academic qualification has been, or will be awarded; and

(6)   states either the date that the certificate will be issued (if the applicant has not yet graduated) or confirms that the institution is unable to re-issue the original certificate of award.

or

(ii)   an original academic transcript that

(1)   is on official letter headed paper

(2)   shows the applicant's name;

(3)   the name of the academic institution;

(4)   the course title;

(5)   confirms that the qualification was taught in English; and,

(6)   provides confirmation of the award.

32.   If the qualification was taken in one of the following countries, it will be assumed for the purpose of paragraph 31 that it was taught in English: Antigua and Barbuda, Australia, the Bahamas, Barbados, Belize, Dominica, Grenada, Guyana, Ireland, Jamaica, New Zealand, St Kitts and Nevis, St Lucia, St Vincent and the Grenadines, Trinidad and Tobago, the UK, the USA.

32A.   For the avoidance of doubt paragraphs 27 to 32D of this Appendix apply to fiancé(e), proposed civil partner, spouse, civil partner, unmarried partner and same sex partner applications for limited leave to enter or remain made under Part 8 of these Rules where English language requirements apply, regardless of the date of application. Paragraphs 27 to 32D of this Appendix also apply to spouse, civil partner, unmarried partner and same sex partner applications which do not meet the requirements of Part 8 of these Rules for indefinite leave to remain (where the application is for indefinite leave to remain) and are being considered for a grant of limited leave to remain where paragraph A277A(b) of these Rules applies. Any references in paragraphs 27 to 32D of this Appendix to 'limited leave to enter or remain' shall therefore be read as referring to all applicants referred to in this paragraph.

32B.   Where the decision-maker has:

(a)   reasonable cause to doubt that an English language test in speaking and listening at a minimum of level A1 of the Common Framework of Reference for Languages relied on at any time to meet a requirement for limited leave to enter or remain in Part 8 or Appendix FM was genuinely obtained; or

(b)   information that the test certificate or result awarded to the applicant has been withdrawn by the test provider for any reason,

the decision-maker may discount the test certificate or result and require the applicant to provide a new test certificate or result from an approved provider which shows that they meet the requirement, if they are not exempt from it.

32C.   If an applicant applying for limited leave to enter or remain under Part 8 or Appendix FM submits an English language test certificate or result which has ceased by the date of application to be:

(a)   from an approved test provider, or

(b)   in respect of an approved test, or

(c)   from an approved test centre,

the decision-maker will not accept that certificate or result as valid, unless the decision-maker does so in accordance with paragraph 32D of this Appendix and subject to any transitional arrangements made in respect of the test provider, test or test centre in question.

32D.   If an applicant applying for limited leave to enter or remain under Part 8 or Appendix FM submits an English language test certificate or result and the Home Office has already accepted it as part of a successful previous partner or parent application (but not where the application was refused, even if on grounds other than the English language requirement), the decision-maker may accept that certificate or result as valid if it is:

(a)   from a provider which is no longer approved, or

(b)   from a provider who remains approved but the test the applicant has taken with that provider is no longer approved, or

(c)   from a test centre which is no longer approved, or

(d)   past its validity date (if a validity date is required under Appendix O),

provided that when the subsequent application is made:

(i)   the applicant has had continuous leave (disregarding any period of overstaying of no more than 28 days) as a partner or parent since the Home Office accepted the test certificate as valid; and

(ii)   the award to the applicant does not fall within the circumstances set out in paragraph 32B of this Appendix.

Adult dependent relatives

33. Evidence of the family relationship between the applicant(s) and the sponsor should take the form of birth or adoption certificates, or other documentary evidence.

34. Evidence that, as a result of age, illness or disability, the applicant requires long-term personal care should take the form of:

(a)   Independent medical evidence that the applicant's physical or mental condition means that they cannot perform everyday tasks; and

(b)   This must be from a doctor or other health professional.

35. Independent evidence that the applicant is unable, even with the practical and financial help of the sponsor in the UK, to obtain the required level of care in the country where they are living should be from:

(a)   a central or local health authority;

(b)   a local authority; or

(c)   a doctor or other health professional.

36. If the applicant's required care has previously been provided through a private arrangement, the applicant must provide details of that arrangement and why it is no longer available.

37. If the applicant's required level of care is not, or is no longer, affordable because payment previously made for arranging this care is no longer being made, the applicant must provide records of that payment and an explanation of why that payment cannot continue. If financial support has been provided by the sponsor or other close family in the UK, the applicant must provide an explanation of why this cannot continue or is no longer sufficient to enable the required level of care to be provided.

Appendix G – Countries and Territories participating in the Tier 5 Youth Mobility Scheme and annual allocations of places for 2015

Places available for use by Countries and Territories with Deemed Sponsorship Status:

Australia – 38,000 places
Canada – 5,000 places
Japan – 1,000 places
New Zealand – 11,000 places
Monaco – 1,000 places

Places available for use by Countries and Territories without Deemed Sponsorship Status:

Taiwan – 1,000 places
South Korea – 1,000 places
Hong Kong – 1,000 places

Appendix H – Applicants who are subject to different documentary requirements under Tier 4 of the Points Based System

An applicant will be subject to different documentary requirements under Tier 4 of the Points Based System where he is a national of one of the following countries and he is applying for entry clearance in his country of nationality or leave to remain in the UK:

Argentina
Australia
Barbados
Botswana
Brunei
Canada
Chile

Japan
Malaysia
New Zealand
Oman
Qatar
Singapore
South Korea
Trinidad and Tobago
United Arab Emirates
United States of America

Where an applicant is a dual national, and only one of their nationalities is listed above, he will be able to apply using the different documentary requirements that apply to these nationals, provided he is applying either for entry clearance in his country of nationality listed above or for leave to remain in the UK.

An applicant will be subject to different documentary requirements under Tier 4 of the Points Based System where he is the rightful holder of one of the following passports, which has been issued by the relevant competent authority, and where he is applying for leave to remain in the UK or for entry clearance in the territory related to the passport he holds:

British National (Overseas)

Hong Kong

Taiwan (those who hold a passport issued by Taiwan that includes the number of the identification card issued by the competent authority in Taiwan)

Where an applicant is the rightful holder of a passport issued by a relevant competent authority listed above and also holds another passport or is the national of a country not listed above, he will be able to apply using the different documentary requirements that apply to rightful holders of those passports listed in this Appendix provided he is applying either for entry clearance in the territory related to the passport he holds or for leave to remain in the UK.

Appendix I, J – OMITTED

Appendix K: Shortage Occupation List

1. Where these Rules refer to jobs which appear on the Shortage Occupation List, this means only those specific jobs within each Standard Occupational Classification code stated in Tables 1 and 2 below and, where stated, where the further specified criteria are met.

2. Jobs which appear on the United Kingdom Shortage Occupation List are set out in Table 1.

3. Jobs which appear on the Scotland Only Shortage Occupation List are set out in Table 2.

Table 1: United Kingdom Shortage Occupation List

Standard Occupational Classification (SOC) code and description	Job titles included on the United Kingdom Shortage Occupation List and further criteria
Production managers and directors in mining and energy (1123)	**Only** the following jobs in this occupation code: The following jobs in the decommissioning and waste management areas of the nuclear industry: – managing director – programme director – site director The following jobs in the electricity transmission and distribution industry: – project manager – site manager

Standard Occupational Classification (SOC) code and description	Job titles included on the United Kingdom Shortage Occupation List and further criteria
2113 Physical Scientists	**Only** the following jobs in this occupation code: the following jobs in the construction-related ground engineering industry: – engineering geologist – hydrogeologist – geophysicist The following jobs in the oil and gas industry: – geophysicist – geoscientist – geologist – geochemist technical services manager in the decommissioning and waste areas of the nuclear industry senior resource geologist and staff geologist in the mining sector
2121 Civil engineers	**Only** the following jobs in this occupation code: the following jobs in the construction-related ground engineering industry: – geotechnical engineer – tunnelling engineer the following jobs in the oil and gas industry: – petroleum engineer – drilling engineer – completions engineer – fluids engineer – reservoir engineer – offshore and subsea engineer – control and instrument engineer – process safety engineer – wells engineer senior mining engineer in the mining sector
2122 Mechanical engineers	**Only** the following job in this occupation code: mechanical engineer in the oil and gas industry
2123 Electrical engineers	**Only** the following jobs in this occupation code: electrical engineer in the oil and gas industry the following jobs in the electricity transmission and distribution industry: – power system engineer – control engineer – protection engineer the following jobs in the aerospace industry: – electrical machine design engineer – power electronics engineer

Standard Occupational Classification (SOC) code and description	Job titles included on the United Kingdom Shortage Occupation List and further criteria
2124 Electronics Engineers	**Only** the following jobs in this occupation code: the following jobs in the railway industry: – signalling design manager – signalling design engineer – signalling principles designer – senior signalling design checker – signalling design checker – signalling systems engineer specialist electronics engineer in the automotive manufacturing and design industry
2126 Design and development engineers	**Only** the following jobs in this occupation code: design engineer in the electricity transmission and distribution industry the following jobs in the automotive design and manufacturing industry: – product development engineer – product design engineer the following jobs in the electronics system industry: – integrated circuit design engineer – integrated circuit test engineer
2127 Production and process engineers	**Only** the following jobs in this occupation code: chemical engineer manufacturing engineer (process planning) in the aerospace industry technical services representative in the decommissioning and waste areas of the nuclear industry

Standard Occupational Classification (SOC) code and description	Job titles included on the United Kingdom Shortage Occupation List and further criteria
2129 Engineering professionals not elsewhere classified	**Only** the following jobs in this occupation code: the following jobs in the electricity transmission and distribution industry: – project engineer – proposals engineer the following jobs in the aerospace industry: – aerothermal engineer – stress engineer – chief of engineering – advance tool and fixturing engineer the following jobs in the decommissioning and waste management areas of the civil nuclear industry: – operations manager – decommissioning specialist manager – project/planning engineer – radioactive waste manager – radiological protection advisor The following jobs in the civil nuclear industry: – nuclear safety case engineer – mechanical design engineer (pressure vehicles) – piping design engineer – mechanical design engineer (stress) – thermofluids/process engineer
2135 IT Business analysts, architects and systems designers	**Only** the following jobs in this occupation code: systems engineer in visual effects and 2D/3D computer animation for the film, television or video games sectors
2136 Programmers and software development professionals	**Only** the following jobs in this occupation code: the following jobs in visual effects and 2D/3D computer animation for the film, television or video games sectors: – software developer – shader writer – games designer the following jobs in the electronics system industry: – driver developer – embedded communications engineer
2142 Environmental Professionals	**Only** the following jobs in this occupation code: the following jobs in the construction-related ground engineering industry: – contaminated land specialist – geoenvironmental specialist – landfill engineer

Standard Occupational Classification (SOC) code and description	Job titles included on the United Kingdom Shortage Occupation List and further criteria
2211 Medical practitioners	**Only** the following jobs in this occupation code: Consultants in the following specialities: – clinical radiology – emergency medicine – old age psychiatry CT3 trainee and ST4 to ST7 trainee in emergency medicine Core trainee in psychiatry Non-consultant, non-training, medical staff post in the following specialities: – emergency medicine (including specialist doctors working in accident and emergency) – old age psychiatry – paediatrics
2217 Medical radiographers	**Only** the following jobs in this occupation code: – HPC registered diagnostic radiographer – nuclear medicine practitioner – radiotherapy physics practitioner – radiotherapy physics scientist – sonographer Sponsors must retain evidence of the individual's HPC registration and provide this to the Home Office on request. (Registration may need to be done after the individual has entered the United Kingdom but must be done before starting work).
2219 Health professionals not elsewhere classified	**Only** the following jobs in this occupation code: – neurophysiology healthcare scientist – neurophysiology practitioner – nuclear medicine scientist
2229 Therapy professionals not elsewhere classified	**Only** the following jobs in this occupation code: – orthotist – prosthetist
2314 Secondary education teaching professionals	**Only** the following jobs in this occupation code: secondary education teachers in the subjects of maths and science (chemistry and physics only)
2425 Actuaries, economists and statisticians	**Only** the following jobs in this occupation code: – bio-informatician – informatician
2442 Social workers	**Only** the following jobs in this occupation code: social worker working in children's and family services
2461 Quality control and planning engineers	**Only** the following jobs in this occupation code: the following jobs in the electricity transmission and distribution industry: – planning / development engineer – quality, health, safety and environment (QHSE) engineer

Standard Occupational Classification (SOC) code and description	Job titles included on the United Kingdom Shortage Occupation List and further criteria

3113 Engineering technicians	**Only** the following jobs in this occupation code:
	
	the following jobs in the electricity transmission and distribution industry:
	
	   – commissioning engineer
	   – substation electrical engineer

3213 Paramedics	**All** jobs in this occupation code
3411 Artist	**Only** the following jobs in this occupation code: Animator in visual effects and 2D/3D computer animation for the film, television or video games sectors

3414 Dancers and choreographers	**Only** the following jobs in this occupation code:
	
	skilled classical ballet dancers who meet the standard required by internationally recognised United Kingdom ballet companies (e.g. Birmingham Royal Ballet, English National Ballet, Northern Ballet Theatre, The Royal Ballet and Scottish Ballet). The company must either:
	
	   – have performed at or been invited to perform at venues of the calibre of the Royal Opera House, Sadler's Wells or Barbican, either in the United Kingdom or overseas; or
	
	   – attract dancers and/or choreographers and other artists from other countries; or
	
	   – be endorsed as being internationally recognised by a United Kingdom industry body such as the Arts Councils (of England, Scotland and/or Wales)
	
	skilled contemporary dancers who meet the standard required by internationally recognised United Kingdom contemporary dance companies (e.g. Shobana Jeyasingh Dance Company, Scottish Dance Theatre and Rambert Dance Company). The company must either:
	
	   – have performed at or been invited to perform at venues of the calibre of Sadler's Wells, the Southbank Centre or The Place, either in the United Kingdom or overseas; or
	
	   – attract dancers and/or choreographers and other artists from all over the world; or
	
	   – be endorsed as being internationally recognised by a United Kingdom industry body such as the Arts Councils (of England, Scotland and/or Wales)

3415 Musicians	**Only** the following jobs in this occupation code: skilled orchestral musicians who are leaders, principals, sub-principals or numbered string positions, and who meet the standard required by internationally recognised UK orchestras (including London Symphony Orchestra, London Philharmonic Orchestra, Philharmonia Orchestra and Royal Philharmonic Orchestra)

Standard Occupational Classification (SOC) code and description	Job titles included on the United Kingdom Shortage Occupation List and further criteria
3416 Arts officers, producers and directors	**Only** the following jobs in this occupation code: the following jobs in visual effects and 2D/3D computer animation for the film, television or video games sectors: – 2D supervisor – 3D supervisor – computer graphics supervisor – producer – production manager – technical director – visual effects supervisor
3421 Graphic designers	**Only** the following jobs in this occupation code: the following jobs in visual effects and 2D/3D computer animation for the film, television or video games sectors: – compositing artist – matte painter – modeller – rigger – stereo artist – texture artist
3541 Buyers and purchasing officers	**Only** the following job in this occupation code: manufacturing engineer (purchasing) in the aerospace industry
5215 Welding trades	**Only** the following job in this occupation code: high integrity pipe welder where the job requires three or more years' related on-the-job experience Sponsors must retain references from the individual's past employer(s) detailing three or more years' related on-the-job experience and provide these to the Home Office on request. Sponsors must also retain relevant evidence to enable them to justify the following: 1) – Why does the job require someone with three or more years' related on-the-job experience? What elements of the job require this experience and why? 2) – Why could the job not be carried out to the required standard by someone with less experience? 3) – How would you expect a settled worker to gain this experience before being appointed to the post?
5235 Aircraft maintenance and related trades	**Only** the following jobs in this occupation code: licensed and military certifying engineer/inspector technician
5249 Line repairers and cable jointers	**Only** the following job in this occupation code: overhead linesworker at Linesman Erector 2 (LE2) level and above, where the pay is at least £32,000 per year

Standard Occupational Classification (SOC) code and description	Job titles included on the United Kingdom Shortage Occupation List and further criteria
5434 Chefs	**Only** the following job in this occupation code: skilled chef where: – the pay is at least £29,570 per year after deductions for accommodation, meals etc; **and** – the job requires five or more years relevant experience in a role of at least equivalent status to the one they are entering; **and** – the job is not in either a fast food outlet, a standard fare outlet, or an establishment which provides a take-away service; **and** – the job is in one of the following roles: – executive chef – limited to one per establishment – head chef – limited to one per establishment – sous chef – limited to one for every four kitchen staff per establishment – specialist chef – limited to one per speciality per establishment A fast food outlet is one where food is prepared in bulk for speed of service, rather than to individual order. A standard fare outlet is one where the menu is designed centrally for outlets in a chain / franchise, rather than by a chef or chefs in the individual restaurant. Standard fare outlets also include those where dishes and / or cooking sauces are bought in ready-made, rather than prepared from fresh / raw ingredients. Sponsors must retain references from the individual's past employer(s) detailing five or more years' relevant experience in a role of at least equivalent status and provide these to the Home Office on request. Sponsors must also retain relevant evidence to enable them to justify the following: 1) – Why does the job require someone with at least five years' previous experience in a role of at least equivalent status? What elements of the job require this experience and why? 2) – Why could the job not be carried out to the required standard by someone with less experience? 3) – How would you expect a settled worker to gain this experience before being appointed to the post?

Table 2: Scotland Only Shortage Occupation List

Standard Occupational Classification (SOC) code and description	Job titles included on the Scotland Only Shortage Occupation List and further specified criteria
All	**All** job titles and occupations on the United Kingdom Shortage Occupation List

Standard Occupational Classification (SOC) code and description	Job titles included on the Scotland Only Shortage Occupation List and further specified criteria

2211 Medical practitioners	**Only** the following jobs in this occupation code:
	jobs on the United Kingdom Shortage Occupation List
	   – jobs on the United Kingdom Shortage Occupation List
	   – consultant in clinical oncology
	   – non-consultant, non-training, medical staff post in clinical radiology
	   – CT3 trainee and ST4 to ST7 trainee in clinical radiology
	   – all grades except CPT1 in psychiatry
	   – all grades in anaesthetics, paediatrics, obstetrics and gynaecology

2217 Medical radiographers	**Only** the following jobs in this occupation code:
	   – jobs on the United Kingdom Shortage Occupation List
	   – medical physicist
	   – staff working in diagnostics radiology (including magnetic resonance imaging)

2231 Nurses	**Only** the following jobs in this occupation code: – specialist nurse working in neonatal intensive care units Sponsors must retain evidence of the individual's provisional / full NMC registration and provide this to the Home Office on request.

APPENDIX KOLL

PART 1. GENERAL

Purpose

1.1 This Appendix sets out how an applicant for indefinite leave to enter or remain must demonstrate sufficient knowledge of the English language and about life in the United Kingdom where it is a requirement of the Rules to demonstrate this for the purposes of an application for indefinite leave to enter or remain. It also sets out general exemptions to the requirement on grounds of age and enables the decision maker to waive the requirement in light of special circumstances in any particular case.

'Specified' in this Appendix means 'specified in Part 4 of this appendix'

PART 2 – KNOWLEDGE OF LANGUAGE AND LIFE

2.1 An applicant for leave to enter or remain has sufficient knowledge of the English language and about life in the United Kingdom for the purpose of an application for indefinite leave to enter or remain made under these Rules if the requirements set out in paragraphs 2.2 and 2.3 are met unless the exceptions set out in Part 3 apply.

2.2 For the purposes of paragraph 2. 1, an applicant demonstrates sufficient knowledge of the English language if:

(a) the applicant has provided specified documentary evidence that:

    (i) the applicant is a national or citizen of one of the following countries:

        Antigua and Barbuda
        Australia
        The Bahamas Barbados
        Belize
        Canada
        Dominica
        Grenada
        Guyana
        Jamaica

New Zealand
St Kitts and Nevis
St Lucia
St Vincent and the Grenadines
Trinidad and Tobago
USA.

or

(ii)   the applicant has passed an English language test in speaking and listening at a minimum level B 1 of the Common European Framework of Reference for Languages with a provider approved by the Secretary of State as specified in Appendix O to these Rules and taken at a test centre approved by the Secretary of State as a Secure English Language Test centre; or

(iii)   the applicant has obtained an academic qualification (not a professional or vocational qualification), which is deemed by UK NARIC to meet the recognised standard of a Bachelor's or Master's degree or PhD in the UK, from an educational establishment in one of the following countries: Antigua and Barbuda; Australia; The Bahamas; Barbados; Belize; Dominica; Grenada; Guyana; Ireland; Jamaica; New Zealand; St Kitts and Nevis; St Lucia; St Vincent and The Grenadines; Trinidad and Tobago; the UK; the USA; and provides the specified documents; or

(iv)   the applicant has obtained an academic qualification (not a professional or vocational qualification) which is deemed by UK NARIC to meet the recognised standard of a Bachelor's or Master's degree or PhD in the UK, and

(1)   provides the specified documentary evidence to show he has the qualification, and

(2)   UK NARIC has confirmed that the qualification was taught or researched in English; or

(v)   the applicant has obtained an academic qualification (not a professional or vocational qualification) which is deemed by UK NARIC to meet the recognised standard of a Bachelor's or Master's degree or PhD in the UK, and provides the specified evidence to show:

(1)   he has the qualification, and

(2)   that the qualification was taught or researched in English; or.

(vi)   the applicant has taken and passed in England, Wales or Northern Ireland a qualification in English for Speakers of Other Languages (ESOL) which:

(aa)   includes speaking and listening;

(bb)   is at ESOL Entry level 3, level 1, level 2 or level 3,

(cc)   is regulated by the Office of Qualifications and Examinations Regulation (OFQUAL), the Welsh Government or the Council for Curriculum, Examinations and Assessment (CCEA), and

(dd)   is listed as an ESOL qualification on the Register of Regulated Qualifications,

or

(vii)   the applicant has passed in Scotland a National Qualification in English for Speakers of Other Languages at Scottish Credit and Qualifications Framework (SCQF) level 4, 5 or 6 awarded by the Scottish Qualifications Authority;

or

(b)   the applicant–

(i)   has limited leave to enter or remain in the UK, and

(ii)   that leave (or a grant of leave which preceded it provided any periods of leave since have been unbroken) was given on the basis that the applicant had an English language qualification at a minimum level of B 1 on the Common European Framework of Reference for Languages, and

(iii) at the date of application, the provider of that qualification continues to be approved by the Secretary of State as specified in Appendix O to these Rules.

2.3   For the purposes of sub-paragraph (1), an applicant demonstrates sufficient knowledge about life in the United Kingdom if:

(a)   the applicant has passed the test known as the 'Life in the UK test administered by learndirect limited;

or

(b)   in respect of an applicant who was resident in the Isle of Man, the applicant took and passed the test in the Isle of Man known as the 'Life in the UK test' and which was administered by an educational institution or other person approved for that purpose by the Lieutenant Governor; or

(c)   in respect of an applicant who was resident in the Bailiwick of Guernsey or in the Bailiwick of Jersey, the applicant took and passed the test known as the 'Citizenship Test' and which was administered by an educational institution or other person approved for that purpose by the Lieutenant Governor of Guernsey or Jersey (as the case may be).

PART 3 EXCEPTIONS

3.1   Notwithstanding any requirement to the contrary in these Rules, for the purposes of this appendix, an applicant will not be required to demonstrate sufficient knowledge of the English language and about life in the UK where:

(a)   the applicant is under 18 years of age at the date of his or her application, or

(b)   the applicant is at least 65 years of age at the date of his or her application, or

(c)   in all the circumstances of the case, the decision maker considers that, because of the applicant's mental or physical condition, it would be unreasonable to expect the applicant to fulfil that requirement.

3.2   In the following circumstances an applicant will be deemed to have demonstrated sufficient knowledge of the English language and about life in the UK:

(a)   Where the application for indefinite leave to enter or remain in the United Kingdom is made under:

    (i)   paragraph 196D and the applicant has had, as at the day on which the application is made, continuous leave to enter or remain in the United Kingdom for at least 15 years as the spouse or civil partner of a person who has or has had leave to enter or remain under paragraphs 128–193 (but not paragraphs 135I–135K), or

    (ii)   paragraph 199 and the applicant has had, as at the day on which the application was made, continuous leave to enter or remain in the United Kingdom for at least 15 years as the child of a person who has or has had leave to enter or remain in the United Kingdom under paragraphs 128–193 (but not paragraphs 135l–135K), or

    (iii)   paragraph 248D and the applicant has had, as at the day on which the application was made, continuous leave to enter or remain in the United Kingdom for at least 15 years as a person exercising rights of access to a child resident in the United Kingdom and that child is under the age of 18 at the day on which the applicant's application for indefinite leave is made under paragraph 248D, or

    (iv)   paragraph 273D and the applicant has had, as at the day on which the application is made, continuous leave to enter or remain in the United Kingdom for at least 15 years as a spouse or civil partner of a person who has or has had leave to enter or remain in the United Kingdom as a retired person of independent means, or

    (v)   paragraph 275A and the applicant has had, as at the day on which the application was made, continuous leave to enter or remain in the United Kingdom for at least 15 years as the child of a person who has or has had leave to enter or remain in the United Kingdom as a retired person of independent means, or

    (vi)   paragraph 287 and the applicant has had, as at the day on which the application is made, continuous leave to enter or remain in the United Kingdom for at least 15 years under paragraph 281 or paragraph 284, or

    (vii)   paragraph 295G and the applicant has had, as at the day on which the application is made, continuous leave to enter or remain in the United Kingdom for at least 15 years under paragraph 295B or paragraph 295D, or

    (viii)   paragraph 298 and the applicant has had, as at the day on which the application is made, continuous leave to enter or remain in the United Kingdom for at least 15 years under paragraph 302 or Appendix FM or paragraph 319R or paragraph 319X, or

    (ix)   paragraph 319E and the applicant has had, as at the day on which the application is made, continuous leave to enter or remain in the United Kingdom for at least 15 years as the partner of a relevant points based system migrant

(x)   paragraph 319J and the applicant has had, as at the day on which the application is made, continuous leave to enter or remain in the United Kingdom for at least 15 years as the child of a relevant points based system migrant

(xi)   section E-ILRP of Appendix FM and the applicant has had, as at the day on which the application is made, continuous leave to enter or remain in the United Kingdom for at least 15 years on the day on which the application is made as a partner (except where leave is as a fiancé or proposed civil partner) under section D-LTRP of Appendix FM; or

(xii)   section E-ILRPT of Appendix FM and the applicant has had, as at the day on which the application is made, continuous leave to enter or remain in the United Kingdom for at least 15 years on the day on which the application is made as a parent under section D-ILRPT of Appendix FM,

or,

(xiii)   paragraph 25 or 31 of Appendix Armed Forces and the applicant has completed, on the date on which the application is made, a continuous period of leave to enter or remain in the United Kingdom of at least 15 years as the partner of a member of HM Forces under that Appendix, or

(xiv)   paragraph 45 or 49 of Appendix Armed Forces and the applicant has completed on the date on which the application is made, a continuous period of leave to enter or remain in the United Kingdom of at least 15 years as the child of a member of HM Forces under that Appendix,

and

(b)   (i)   the applicant has provided specified documentary evidence of an English language speaking and listening qualification at A2 CEFR or ESOL entry level 2 or Scottish Credit and Qualification Framework level 3; or

(ii)   where paragraph 39C(c) of these Rules applies, the applicant has provided specified documentary evidence of an English language speaking and listening qualification at A2 CEFR with a provider approved by the Secretary of State as specified in Appendix O to these Rules.

and

(c)   the applicant has provided specified documentary evidence from a qualified English language teacher that the applicant has made efforts to learn English but does not yet have sufficient knowledge of the English language to pass a qualification at B1 CEFR, or ESOL entry level 3 or Scottish Credit and Qualification Framework level 4.

and

(d)   the applicant is not a national or a citizen of one of the following countries:
Antigua and Barbuda
Australia
The Bahamas
Barbados Belize
Canada
Dominica
Grenada
Guyana
Jamaica
New Zealand
St Kitts and Nevis
St Lucia
St Vincent and the Grenadines
Trinidad and Tobago
USA.

3.3   Where paragraph 39C(c) of these Rules applies, an applicant demonstrates sufficient knowledge of the English language and about life in the UK where:

(i)   upon a request by the decision-maker to provide additional evidence of knowledge of the English language, he or she has provided specified documentary evidence that he or she has passed an English language test in speaking and listening at a minimum B1 of the Common European Framework of Reference for Languages with a provider approved by the Secretary of State as specified in Appendix O to these Rules, unless paragraph 3.2 of this Appendix applies; or

(ii) upon a request by the decision-maker to provide additional evidence of knowledge about life in the UK, he or she has provided specified evidence that he or she has passed the test known as the 'Life in the UK test' administered by learndirect limited under arrangements approved by the decision-maker; or

(iii) upon a request by the decision-maker to provide additional evidence of knowledge of the English language and about life in the UK, he or she has provided the evidence set out in sub-paragraphs (i) and (ii).

PART 4 SPECIFIED DOCUMENTS

4.1 Where these Rules require an applicant to demonstrate sufficient knowledge of the English language and of life in the United Kingdom, the applicant must supply the documents specified in paragraphs 4.6 to 4.14 below.

4.2 The decision maker will only consider evidence submitted after the date on which an application is made where the circumstances in paragraph 39(C)(c) of these Rules or paragraphs 4.3 or 4.6 of this Appendix apply.

4.3 Where an applicant has submitted:

(i) a document in the wrong format (for example, if a letter is not on letterhead paper as specified); or

(ii) a document that is a copy and not an original document, or

(iii) a document which does not contain all of the specified information,

or

(iv) fails to submit a specified document,

the decision-maker may contact the applicant or his or her representative (in writing or otherwise), and request the document or the correct version of the document. The document must be received by the Home Office at the address specified in the request within such timescale (which will not be unreasonable) as is specified.

4.4 A decision-maker may decide not to request a document under paragraph 4.3 where he or she does not anticipate that the supply of that document will lead to a grant of leave to enter or remain in the United Kingdom because the application may be refused for other reasons.

4.5 Without prejudice to the decision maker's discretion under paragraph 4.2 and also his or her right in all cases to request the original or specified document and refuse an application in circumstances in which they are not provided, where an applicant submits a specified document:

(i) in the wrong format, or

(ii) which is a copy and not an original document, or

(iii) which does not contain all of the specified information but the missing information is verifiable from,

    (aa) other documents submitted with the application,

    (bb) the website of the organisation which issued the document,

        or

    (cc) the website of the appropriate regulatory body;

the application for leave to enter or remain in the United Kingdom may be granted exceptionally providing the decision-maker is satisfied that the specified documents are genuine and that the applicant meets all the other requirements.

4.6 Where the decision-maker is satisfied that there is a valid reason why a document has not been and cannot be supplied, (for example, because the document has been permanently lost or destroyed), he or she may waive the requirement for the document to be provided or may instead request alternative or additional evidence (which may include confirmation of evidence from the organisation which issued the original document).

4.7 The evidence specified for the purposes of paragraph 2.2 of this Appendix is:

(a) a cerificate that:

    (i) is from an English language test provider approved by the Secretary of State for the purposes of limited leave to enter or remain as specified in Appendix O of these Rules, and is in respect of a test approved by the Secretary of State as specified in that Appendix, and

    (ii) shows the applicant's name; and

    (iii) shows the qualification obtained, and

    (iv) shows that the level of speaking and listening skills attained by the applicant met or exceeded level B 1 of the Common European Framework of Reference, and

    (v) shows the date of award of the qualification;

or,

(b)   a print out of the online score from a PTE Academic (Pearson) test which:

    (i)   is from an English language test provider approved by the Secretary of State for the purposes of limited (ii)leave to enter or remain as specified in Appendix O of these rules, and

    (ii)   is in respect of a test approved by the Secretary of State as specified in that Appendix , and

    (iii)   can be used to show the qualification obtained; and,

    (iv)   shows that the level of speaking and listening skills attained by the applicant met or exceeded level B 1 of the Common European Framework of Reference;

or

(c)   a certificate or other document issued by an awarding organisation that is recognised either by Ofqual, the Welsh Government, or CCEA that

    (i)   is issued in England, Wales or Northern Ireland in respect of a qualification listed as an ESOL qualification in the OFQUAL Register of Regulated Qualifications, and

    (ii)   shows that the level of speaking and listening skills attained by the applicant met or exceeded ESOL entry level 3;

or

(d)   a certificate that

    (i)   is issued in Scotland in respect of a National Qualification in English for Speakers of Other Languages awarded by the Scottish Qualifications Authority, and

    (ii)   shows that the level of speaking and listening skills attained by the applicant met or exceeded Scottish Credit and Qualifications Framework level 4

4.8   Subject to paragraphs 4.9 and 4.10 the documentary evidence specified for the purposes of paragraph 2.2 of this Appendix as showing that a person is a national or a citizen of one of the countries listed in paragraph 2.2 is a valid passport or travel document which satisfactorily establishes the applicant's nationality.

4.9   If the applicant cannot provide their passport or travel document other evidence of nationality of the type described in paragraph 4.10 may exceptionally be supplied in the following circumstances (the reason for which must be indicated by the applicant on their application form), where:

(a)   the applicant's passport has been lost or stolen, or

(b)   the applicant's passport has expired and has been returned to the relevant authorities, or

(c)   the applicant's passport is with another part of the Home Office.

4.10   Where paragraph 4.9 applies, the alternative evidence specified for the purposes of establishing the applicant's nationality is:

(a)   a valid national identity document; or

(b)   an original letter from the applicant's Home Government or Embassy confirming the applicant's full name, date of birth and nationality.

4.11   The evidence specified for the purposes of paragraph 2.2(a)(iii) to 2.2(a)(v) (academic qualification recognised by UK NARIC) is:

(a)   a certificate issued by the relevant institution confirming the award of the academic qualification and showing:

    (i)   the applicant's name,

    (ii)   the title of the award,

    (iii)   the date of the award,

    (iv)   the name of the awarding institution, and,

    (v)   for paragraph 2.2(a) (iii) that the qualification was taught in English or,

(b)   where an applicant has not, at the date of application, formally graduated or no longer has his or her certificate and is unable to obtain a duplicate certificate:

    (i)   an original academic reference from the institution awarding the academic qualification that:

        (aa)   is on official letter headed paper,

        (bb)   shows the applicant's name,

        (cc)   shows the title of the award,

        (dd)   confirms that the qualification was taught in English,

        (ee)   states when the academic qualification was (or as the case may be, will be) awarded, and (ff)   confirms that the institution is unable to issue a duplicate certificate of award or (as the case may be in respect of an applicant who has not yet graduated) the date on which the certificate will be issued.

or

(ii)   an original academic transcript that;

(aa)   is on official letter headed paper,

(bb)   shows the applicant's name,

(cc)   shows the name of the academic institution,

(dd)   shows the course title,

(ee)   confirms that the qualification was taught in English, and, (ff) confirms the award given.

4.12   In the absence of any evidence to the contrary, a qualification obtained in one of the following countries will be assumed for the purposes of this Appendix to have been taught in English: Antigua and Barbuda, Australia, the Bahamas, Barbados, Belize, Dominica, Grenada, Guyana, Ireland, Jamaica, New Zealand, St Kitts and Nevis, St Lucia, St Vincent and the Grenadines, Trinidad and Tobago, the UK or the USA.

4.13   The evidence specified for the purposes of paragraph 3.2(b)(i) (evidence of English language speaking and listening) is the same as that specified for the purposes of paragraphs 2.2(a)(vi) and 2.2(a)(vii) except that:

(a)   references to B 1 are to be read as references to A2,

(b)   references to ESOL levels Entry 3, level 1, level 2 and level 3 are to be read as references to ESOL Entry level 2, and

(c)   references to Scottish Credit and Qualification Framework Level 4, 5 and 6 are to be read as references to Scottish Qualification Framework Level 3.

4.13A.   The evidence specified for the purposes of paragraph 3.2(b)(ii) (evidence of English language speaking and listening) is the same as that specified for the purposes of paragraph 2.2(a)(ii) except that references to B1 are to be read as references to A2.

4.14   (a)   The evidence specified for the purposes of paragraph 3.2(c) (evidence from qualified English teacher) is a letter from the teacher which is signed by him or her and dated no more than 3 months before the date on which the application for indefinite leave to remain is made and which includes the following information:

(i)   the applicant's name,

(ii)   confirmation that the applicant has attended an English language class taught by that teacher for at least 75 guided learning hours and which was taught during the period of 12 months immediately preceding the date on which the application for indefinite leave to remain was made,

(iii)   confirmation that the teacher has assessed that the speaking and listening level attained by the applicant is not at B 1 level or above,

(iv)   confirmation that the applicant is considered unlikely to attain B 1 level through further study

(v)   confirmation of the teacher's qualifications as an English language teacher within the meaning of this Appendix.

(b)   For the purposes of paragraph (a)(ii) 'guided learning hours' means the time during which a person is taught or given instruction and does not include any time spent on unsupervised preparation or study.

4.15   The documentary evidence specified for the purposes of paragraph 2.3 of this Appendix is:

(a)   a pass notification letter issued by learndirect limited in respect of the test known as the 'Life in the UK test', or

(b)   where the 'Life in the UK test' was taken and passed in the Isle of Man, a pass certificate in respect of the test issued by the relevant educational institution or other person approved for that purpose by the Lieutenant Governor, or

(c)   where the 'Citizenship test' was taken in the Bailiwick of Guernsey or, as the case may be, in the Bailiwick of Jersey, a pass certificate issued by the relevant educational institution or other person approved for that purpose by the Lieutenant Governor of Guernsey or Jersey (as the case may be).

4.16.   The evidence specified for the purposes of paragraph 3.3(i) of this Appendix (evidence of English language speaking and listening) is the same as that specified for the purpose of paragraph 2.2(a)(ii) of this Appendix.

4.17.   The evidence specified for the purposes of paragraph 3.3(ii) of this Appendix (evidence of knowledge about life in the UK) is the same as that specified at paragraph 4.15(a) of this Appendix.

PART 5 INTERPRETATION

5.1   For the purposes of this Appendix 'decision maker' means an Entry Clearance Officer or the Secretary of State.

5.2   For the purposes of this Appendix, 'qualified English language teacher' means a person who holds a qualification in teaching English as a foreign language or in teaching English to speakers of other languages which was awarded by an awarding organisation regulated by OFQUAL or the Welsh Government or the CCEA or the Scottish Qualification Authority.

Appendix L–P – OMITTED

Appendix Q–R – OMITTED

Appendix T – OMITTED

APPENDIX V: Immigration Rules for visitors

Introduction

A visitor is a person who is coming to the UK, usually for up to six months, for a temporary purpose, for example as a tourist, to visit friends or family or to carry out a business activity.

Visitors cannot work or study in the UK unless this is allowed by the permitted activities that are set out in these Visitor Rules.

Each visitor must meet the requirements of these Visitor Rules, even if they are travelling as, for example, a family group, a tour group or a school party.

Applications are decided based on the information provided by the applicant and any other relevant circumstances at the date of decision.

Definitions of terms and phrases used in these Visitor Rules are in Appendix 1.

PART V1. Entry to the UK

Types of permission to enter the UK

V 1.1   A person who wishes to enter the UK as a visitor must have permission to do so. That permission may be granted as a visit visa or as leave to enter.

Who needs a visit visa

V 1.2   A visa national must obtain a visit visa before they arrive in the UK. Appendix 2 sets out who is a visa national. A visa national who arrives in the UK without a visit visa will be refused leave to enter.

V 1.3   A non-visa national may apply for a visit visa, but is not required to unless they are:

(a)   visiting the UK to marry or to form a civil partnership, or to give notice of this; or

(b)   seeking to visit the UK for more than 6 months.

Who can apply for leave to enter on arrival

V 1.4   A non-visa national may apply for leave to enter as a visitor on arrival at the UK border, unless V 1.3 (a) or (b) applies.

Types and lengths of visit visa and leave to enter or remain

V 1.5   There are four types of visitor routes which depend on the purpose of the visit:

	Types of visit visa/Leave to enter or remain	Visitors of this type can:	The maximum length of stay that can be granted for each type of visitor:
(a)	Visit (standard)	Do the permitted activities in Appendix 3 except visitors entering under the Approved Destination Status agreement who may only do the activities in paragraph 3 of Appendix 3 to these Rules;	up to 6 months, except: (i) a visitor who is coming to the UK for private medical treatment may be granted a visit visa of up to 11 months; or (ii) an academic, who is employed by an overseas institution and is carrying out the specific permitted activities paragraph 12 of Appendix 3,of these Rules, along with their spouse or partner and children, may be granted a visit visa of up to 12 months; or (iii) a visitor under the Approved Destination Status Agreement (ADS Agreement) may be granted a visit visa for a period of up to 30 days.
(b)	Marriage / civil partnership visit	Visit to marry or to form a civil partnership, or to give notice of this, in the UK, and do the permitted activities in Appendix 3;	up to 6 months.
(c)	Permitted Paid Engagements (PPE) visit	Do the paid engagements in Appendix 4 and do the permitted activities in Appendix 3;	up to 1 month.
(d)	Transit visit	Transit the UK.	up to 48 hours, except for leave to enter as a transit visitor under the Transit Without Visa Scheme which may be granted until 23:59 hours on the next day after the day the applicant arrived.

V 1.6   Within the period for which the visit visa is valid, a visitor may enter and leave the UK multiple times, unless the visit visa is endorsed as a single- or dual-entry visa.

PART V2. Making an application for a visit visa

How to apply for a visit visa

V 2.1   An application for a visit visa must be made while the applicant is outside the UK.

V 2.2   To apply for a visit visa the applicant must:

(a)   complete the online application process on the visas and immigration pages of the gov.uk website; and

(b)   pay any fee that applies; and

(c)   provide their biometrics if required; and

(d)   provide a valid travel document.

Where the online application process is not available, the applicant must follow the instructions provided by the local visa post or application centre on how to make an application.

Date of application

V 2.3   An application for a visit visa is made on the date on which the fee is paid.

V 2.4   Where a fee is not required, the date of application is the date on which the application is submitted online.

V 2.5   Where a fee is not required and an online application is not available, the date of application is the date on which the paper application form is received by the relevant visa post or application centre.

Withdrawing an application and return of a travel document

V 2.6   An applicant may withdraw their application at any time before a decision is made on it. The request must be made in writing or email to the visa post or application centre where the application was submitted. When notice of withdrawal is received no decision will be made on the application and the applicant's travel document and any other documents will be returned. The fee will not be refunded.

V 2.7   A request from an applicant for return of their travel document after an application has been submitted must be made in writing or email to the visa post or application centre where the application was submitted. It will be treated as a notice of withdrawal of the application, unless the visa post states otherwise.

PART V3. SUITABILITY REQUIREMENTS FOR ALL VISITORS

V 3.1   This Part applies to all applications for visit visas, leave to enter, and an extension of stay as a visitor except where explicitly stated otherwise.

Not conducive to the public good: exclusion and deportation

V 3.2   An application will be refused if:

(a)   the Secretary of State has personally directed that the applicant's exclusion from the UK is conducive to the public good; or

(b)   the applicant is currently the subject of a deportation order or a decision to make a deportation order.

V 3.3   An application will be refused if the decision maker believes that exclusion of the applicant from the UK is conducive to the public good because, for example, the applicant's conduct (including convictions which do not fall within paragraph V 3.4), character, associations, or other reasons, make it undesirable to grant their application.

Not conducive to the public good: criminal convictions, etc.

V 3.4   An application (except for an application for an extension of stay as a visitor) will be refused if the applicant has been convicted of a criminal offence for which they have been sentenced to a period of imprisonment of:

(a)   at least 4 years; or

(b)   between 12 months and 4 years, unless at least 10 years have passed since the end of the sentence; or

(c)   less than 12 months, unless at least 5 years has passed since the end of the sentence.

Where this paragraph applies, it will only be in exceptional circumstances that the public interest in maintaining refusal will be outweighed by compelling factors.

V 3.5   An application will normally be refused if:

(a)   within the period of 12 months before the application is decided, the applicant has been convicted of or admitted an offence for which they received a non-custodial sentence or out of court disposal that is recorded on their criminal record (except for an application for an extension of stay as a visitor); or

(b)   in the view of the Secretary of State the applicant's offending has caused serious harm; or

(c)   in the view of the Secretary of State the applicant is a persistent offender who shows a particular disregard for the law.

False information in relation to an application

V 3.6   An applicant will be refused where:

(a)   false representations have been made or false documents or information have been submitted (whether or not material to the application, and whether or not to the applicant's knowledge); or

(b)   material facts have not been disclosed,

in relation to their application or in order to obtain documents from the Secretary of State or a third party provided in support of their application.

Breaches of UK immigration laws

V 3.7   An applicant will be refused:

(a)   if the applicant previously breached UK immigration laws as described at V 3.9; and

(b)   if the applicant is outside the UK, the application is made within the relevant re-entry ban time period in V 3.10 (which time period is relevant will depend on the manner in which the applicant left the UK).

V 3.8   If the applicant has previously breached UK immigration laws but is outside the relevant re-entry ban time period the application will normally be refused if there are other aggravating circumstances, such as a failure to cooperate with immigration control or enforcement processes. This applies even where the applicant has overstayed for 90 days or less and left voluntarily and not at public expense.

V 3.9   An applicant, when aged 18 years or over, breached the UK's immigration laws:

(a)   by overstaying (except where this was for 90 days or less and they left the UK voluntarily and not at public expense); or

(b)   by breaching a condition attached to their leave; or

(c)   by being an illegal entrant; or

(d)   if deception was used in relation to an application or documents used in support of an application (whether successful or not).

V 3.10   The duration of a re-entry ban is as follows:

Duration of re entry ban from date they left the UK (or date of refusal of entry clearance under paragraph f)	This applies where the applicant	and	and
(a) 12 months	left voluntarily	at their own expense.	–
(b) 2 years	left voluntarily	at public expense	Within 6 months of being given notice of liability for removal or when they no longer had a pending appeal or administrative review, whichever is later.
(c) 5 years	left voluntarily	at public expense,	more than 6 months after being given notice of liability for removal or when they no longer had a pending appeal or administrative review, whichever is later.
(d) 5 years	left or was removed from the UK	as a condition of a caution issued in accordance with section 22 of the Criminal Justice Act 2003 (and providing that any condition prohibiting their return to the UK has itself expired)	–
(e) 10 years	was deported from the UK or was removed from the UK	at public expense	–
(f) 10 years	used deception in an application for entry clearance (including a visit visa).	–	–

V 3.11   Where more than one breach of the UK's immigration laws has occurred, only the breach which leads to the longest period of absence from the UK will be relevant.

Failure to produce satisfactory identity documents or provide other information

V 3.12   An applicant will be refused where the applicant:

(a)   fails to produce a valid travel document that satisfies the decision maker as to their identity and nationality.

(b)   fails without reasonable excuse to comply with a requirement to:

(i)   attend an interview; or

(ii)   provide information; or

(iii)   provide biometrics; or

(iv)   undergo a medical examination or provide a medical report.

Medical

V 3.13   An applicant will normally be refused where, on the advice of the medical inspector, it is undesirable to grant the application for medical reasons.

Debt to the NHS

V 3.14   An applicant will normally be refused where a relevant NHS body has notified the Secretary of State that the applicant has failed to pay charges under relevant NHS regulations on charges to overseas visitors and the outstanding charges have a total value of at least £1000.

Admission to the Common Travel Area or other countries

V 3.15   An applicant will be refused where they are seeking entry to the UK with the intention of entering another part of the Common Travel Area, and fails to satisfy the decision maker that they are acceptable to the immigration authorities there.

V 3.16   An applicant will normally be refused where they fail to satisfy the decision maker that they will be admitted to another country after a stay in the UK.

PART V4. ELIGIBILITY REQUIREMENTS FOR VISITORS (STANDARD)

V 4.1   The decision maker must be satisfied that the applicant meets all of the eligibility requirements in paragraphs V 4.2 – V 4.10. The decision maker must be satisfied that the applicant meets any additional eligibility requirements, where the applicant:

(a)   is a child at the date of application, they must also meet the additional requirements at V 4.11 – V 4.13; or

(b)   is coming to the UK to receive private medical treatment, they must also meet the additional requirements at V 4.14 – V 4.16; or

(c)   is coming to the UK as an organ donor, they must also meet the additional requirements at V 4.17 – V 4.20; or

(d)   is coming to the UK under the ADS agreement, they must also meet the additional requirements at V 4.21; or

(e)   is an academic seeking a 12 month visit visa, they must also meet the additional requirements at V 4.22.

Genuine intention to visit

V 4.2   The applicant must satisfy the decision maker that they are a genuine visitor. This means that the applicant:

(a)   will leave the UK at the end of their visit; and

(b)   will not live in the UK for extended periods through frequent or successive visits, or make the UK their main home; and

(c)   is genuinely seeking entry for a purpose that is permitted by the visitor routes (these are listed in Appendices 3, 4 and 5); and

(d)   will not undertake any prohibited activities set out in V 4.5 – V 4.10; and

(e)   must have sufficient funds to cover all reasonable costs in relation to their visit without working or accessing public funds. This includes the cost of the return or onward journey, any costs relating to dependants, and the cost of planned activities such as private medical treatment.

Funds, maintenance and accommodation provided by a third party

V 4.3 A visitor's travel, maintenance and accommodation may be provided by a third party where the decision maker is satisfied that they:

(a) have a genuine professional or personal relationship with the visitor; and

(b) are not, or will not be, in breach of UK immigration laws at the time of decision or the visitor's entry to the UK; and

(c) can and will provide support to the visitor for the intended duration of their stay.

V 4.4 The third party may be asked to give an undertaking in writing to be responsible for the applicant's maintenance and accommodation. In this case paragraph 35 of Part 1 of these Rules applies also to Visitors. An applicant will normally be refused where, having been requested to do so, the applicant fails to provide a valid written undertaking from a third party to be responsible for their maintenance and accommodation for the period of any visit.

Prohibited activities

Work

V 4.5 The applicant must not intend to work in the UK, which includes the following:

(a) taking employment in the UK;

(b) doing work for an organisation or business in the UK;

(c) establishing or running a business as a self-employed person;

(d) doing a work placement or internship;

(e) direct selling to the public;

(f) providing goods and services;

unless expressly allowed by the permitted activities in Appendices 3, 4 or 5.

V 4.6 Permitted activities must not amount to the applicant taking employment, or doing work which amounts to them filling a role or providing short-term cover for a role within a UK based organisation. In addition, where the applicant is already paid and employed outside of the UK, they must remain so. Payment may only be allowed in specific circumstances set out in V 4.7.

Payment

V 4.7 The applicant must not receive payment from a UK source for any activities undertaken in the UK, except for the following:

(a) reasonable expenses to cover the cost of their travel and subsistence, including fees for directors attending board-level meetings; or

(b) prize money; or

(c) billing a UK client for their time in the UK, where the applicant's overseas employer is contracted to provide services to a UK company, and the majority of the contract work is carried out overseas. Payment must be lower than the amount of the applicant's salary; or

(d) multi-national companies who, for administrative reasons, handle payment of their employees' salaries from the UK; or

(e) where the applicant is engaged in Permitted Paid Engagements (PPE) as listed at Appendix 4, provided the applicant holds a visa or leave to enter as a PPE visitor; or

(f) paid performances at a permit free festival as listed in Appendix 5.

Study

V 4.8 The applicant must not intend to study in the UK, except where they are undertaking a maximum of 30 days incidental study as permitted by Appendix 3.

Medical

V 4.9 The applicant must not intend to access medical treatment other than private medical treatment or to donate an organ (for either of these activities they must meet the relevant additional requirements).

Marriage or civil partnership

V 4.10 The applicant must not intend to marry or form a civil partnership, or to give notice of this, in the UK, except where they have a visit visa endorsed for marriage or civil partnership.

Additional eligibility requirements for children

V 4.11   Adequate arrangements must have been made for their travel to, reception and care in the UK.

V 4.12   If the applicant is not applying or travelling with a parent or guardian based in their home country or country of ordinary residence who is responsible for their care; that parent or guardian must confirm that they consent to the arrangements for the child's travel to, and reception and care in the UK. Where requested, this consent must be given in writing.

V 4.13   A child who holds a visit visa must either:

(a)   hold a valid visit visa that states they are accompanied and will be travelling with an adult identified on that visit visa; or

(b)   hold a visit visa which states they are unaccompanied;

if neither applies, the child may be refused entry unless they meet the requirements of V 4.12.

Additional eligibility requirements for visitors coming to the UK to receive private medical treatment

V 4.14   If the applicant is suffering from a communicable disease, they must have satisfied the medical inspector that they are not a danger to public health.

V 4.15   The applicant must have arranged their private medical treatment before they travel to the UK, and must provide a letter from their doctor or consultant detailing:

(a)   the medical condition requiring consultation or treatment; and

(b)   the estimated costs and likely duration of any treatment which must be of a finite duration; and

(c)   where the consultation or treatment will take place.

V 4.16   If the applicant is applying for an 11 month visit visa for the purposes of private medical treatment they must also:

(a)   provide evidence from their medical practitioner in the UK that the proposed treatment is likely to exceed 6 months but not more than 11 months; and

(b)   if required under paragraph A39 and Appendix T Part 1 of these Rules, provide a valid medical certificate issued by a medical practitioner listed in Appendix T Part 2 of these Rules confirming that they have undergone screening for active pulmonary tuberculosis and that this tuberculosis is not present in the applicant.

Additional eligibility requirements for visitors coming to the UK to donate an organ

V 4.17   An applicant must satisfy the decision maker that they genuinely intend to donate an organ, or be assessed as a potential organ donor, to an identified recipient in the UK with whom they have a genetic or close personal relationship.

V 4.18   The applicant must provide written confirmation of medical tests to show that they are a donor match to the identified recipient, or that they are undergoing further tests to be assessed as a potential donor to the identified recipient.

V 4.19   The applicant must provide a letter, dated no more than three months prior to the applicant's intended date of arrival in the UK from either:

(a)   the lead nurse or coordinator of the UK's NHS Trust's Living Donor kidney Transplant team; or

(b)   a UK registered medical practitioner who holds an NHS consultant post or who appears in the Specialist Register of the General Medical Council; which confirms that the visitor meets the requirements in V 4.17 and V 4.18 and confirms when and where the planned organ transplant or medical tests will take place.

V 4.20   The applicant must be able to demonstrate, if required to do so, that the identified recipient is legally present in the United Kingdom or will be at the time of the planned organ transplant.

Additional eligibility requirements for visitors coming under the ADS agreement

V 4.21   An applicant under the Approved Destination Status (ADS) Agreement with China must:

(a)   be a national of the People's Republic of China; and

(b)   intend to enter, leave and travel within the UK as a member of a tourist group under the ADS agreement.

Additional eligibility requirements for academics

V 4.22 An academic applying for a 12 month visit visa (standard) must intend to do one (or more) of the permitted activities set out in paragraph 12 of Appendix 3; and:

    (a) be highly qualified within their own field of expertise; and

    (b) currently working in that field at an academic institution or institution of higher education overseas; and

    (c) if required under paragraph A39 and Appendix T Part 1 of these Rules, provide a valid medical certificate issued by a medical practitioner listed in Appendix T Part 2 of these Rules confirming that they have undergone screening for active pulmonary tuberculosis and that this tuberculosis is not present in the applicant

Conditions

V 4.23 Visit visas, leave to enter or an extension of stay as a visitor will be subject to the following conditions:

    (a) no recourse to public funds; and

    (b) no study (which does not prohibit the incidental study allowed by the permitted activities at Appendix 3); and

    (c) no work (which does not prohibit the permitted activities in Appendix 3, 4 or 5 as set out in V1.5).

PART V5. ELIGIBILITY REQUIREMENTS FOR A PPE VISITOR

V 5.1 An applicant for permitted paid engagements must satisfy the decision maker that they meet the requirements at V 4.2 - V 4.10.

Additional eligibility requirements for a permitted paid engagements visit visa or leave to enter

V 5.2 An applicant must intend to do one (or more) of the permitted paid engagements set out in Appendix 4 to these Rules, which must:

    (a) be arranged before the applicant travels to the UK; and

    (b) be declared as part of the application for a visit visa or leave to enter; and

    (c) be evidenced by a formal invitation, as required by Appendix 4; and

    (d) relate to the applicant's area of expertise and occupation overseas.

V 5.3 An applicant must not be a child.

PART V6. ELIGIBILITY REQUIREMENTS FOR A MARRIAGE OR CIVIL PARTNERSHIP VISIT VISA

V 6.1 An applicant for a marriage or civil partnership visit visa must satisfy the decision maker that they meet the requirements at V 4.2 - V 4.10 and must be aged 18 or over.

V 6.2 On arrival in the UK a visitor coming to marry or form a civil partnership, or give notice of this, in the UK must have a valid visit visa endorsed with this purpose and the name of the holder's fiancé(e) or proposed civil partner.

Additional eligibility requirements for a marriage or civil partnership visit visa

V 6.3 An applicant seeking to come to the UK as a visitor who wishes to give notice of marriage or civil partnership, or marry or form a civil partnership, in the UK during that visit must satisfy the decision maker that they:

    (a) intend to give notice of marriage or civil partnership; or

    (b) intend to marry or form a civil partnership; and

    (c) do not intend to give notice of or enter into a sham marriage or sham civil partnership,

within the validity period covered by their visit visa.

PART V7. TRANSIT VISITOR

Transit visitor

V 7.1   A transit visitor is a person who seeks to travel via the UK en route to another destination country outside the common travel area.

V 7.2   Individuals seeking to transit the UK without passing through the UK border may need a Direct Airside Transit Visa. These are provided for by the Immigration (Passenger Transit Visa) Order 2014 (as amended).

V 7.3   This Part does not apply to crew members who are employed in the working or service of their ship, aircraft, hovercraft, hydrofoil or train who fall under section 8(1) of the Immigration Act 1971.

V 7.4   A visa national must either hold a transit visit visa or, if they meet the requirements for admission under the transit without visa scheme in V 7.6 – V 7.8, they may seek leave to enter at the UK border.

Eligibility requirements for a transit visa or leave to enter for transit

V 7.5   An applicant must satisfy the decision maker that they:

(a)   are genuinely in transit to another country outside the common travel area, meaning the main purpose of their visit is to transit the UK and that the applicant is taking a reasonable transit route; and

(b)   will not access public funds or medical treatment, work or study in the UK; and

(c)   genuinely intend and are able to leave the UK within 48 hours after their arrival; and

(d)   are assured entry to their country of destination and any other countries they are transiting on their way there.

Transit Without Visa Scheme

V 7.6   To be granted leave to enter under the transit without visa scheme a visa national must meet all the requirements at V 7.7 and one of the requirements at V 7.8.

V 7.7   The applicant must:

(a)   have arrived by air and will be departing by air; and

(b)   be genuinely in transit to another country, meaning the purpose of their visit is to transit the UK and that the applicant is taking a reasonable transit route; and

(c)   will not access public funds or medical treatment, work or study in the UK; and

(d)   genuinely intend and be able to leave the UK before 23:59 hours on the day after the day when they arrived; and

(e)   have a confirmed booking on a flight departing the UK before 23:59 hours on the day after the day when they arrived; and

(f)   be assured entry to their country of destination and any other countries they are transiting through on their way there.

V 7.8   The applicant must also:

(a)   be travelling to or from (or on part of a reasonable journey to or from) Australia, Canada, New Zealand or the USA and have a valid visa for that country; or

(b)   be travelling from (or on part of a reasonable journey from) Australia, Canada, New Zealand or the USA and it is less than 6 months since he last entered that country with a valid entry visa; or

(c)   hold a valid permanent residence permit issued by either:

(i)   Australia;

(ii)   Canada, issued after 28 June 2002;

(iii)   New Zealand; or

(d)   hold a valid USA, I-551 permanent resident card issued on or after 21 April 1998; or

(e)   hold a valid USA I-551 temporary immigrant visa (a wet-ink stamp version will not be accepted); or

(f)   hold an expired USA I-551 permanent resident card issued on or after 21 April 1998, provided it is accompanied by a valid I-797 letter authorising extension of the period of permanent residency; or

(g)   hold a valid standalone US immigration form 155A/155B attached to a sealed brown envelope; or

(h)   hold a valid common format residence permit issued by an EEA state (pursuant to Council Regulation (EC) No. 1030/2002) or Switzerland; or

(i)   hold a valid uniform format category D visa for entry to a state in the European Economic Area (EEA) or Switzerland; or

(j)   be travelling on to the Republic of Ireland and have a valid Irish biometric visa; or

(k)   be travelling from the Republic of Ireland and it is less than three months since the applicant was last given permission to land or be in the Republic by the Irish authorities with a valid Irish biometric visa.

V 7.8.1   Paragraph V 7.8 (a) and (b) shall not apply where the transit passenger is a citizen or national of Syria holding a B1 or B2 category visa for entry to the United States of America.

V7.9   Electronic versions of any documents listed in paragraph V7.8, such as electronic visas (including printed versions), will not be accepted.

PART V8. EXTENSION OF STAY AS A VISITOR

Who can apply for an extension of stay as a visitor

V 8.1   It is not possible to switch to become a visitor while in the UK where a person is in the UK in breach of immigration laws or has entry clearance or leave to enter or remain for another purpose.

Making an application for an extension of stay as a visitor in the UK

V 8.2   An application for an extension of stay as a visitor must comply with the requirements in paragraphs A34 – 34D of Part 1 of these Rules.

Eligibility requirements for an extension of stay in the UK as a visitor

V 8.3   The applicant must be in the UK as a visitor. Visitors for permitted paid engagements and transit visitors may not apply for an extension of stay as a visitor.

V 8.4   An application for an extension of stay as a visitor must satisfy the decision maker that they continue to meet all the suitability and eligibility requirements for a visit visa.

V 8.5   The applicant must not be in the UK in breach of immigration laws, except for any period of overstaying of 28 days or less which will be discounted.

V 8.6   If the applicant is applying for an extension of stay as a visitor for the purpose of receiving private medical treatment they must also satisfy the decision maker they:

(a)   have met the costs of any medical treatment received so far; and

(b)   provide a letter from a registered medical practitioner, at a private practice or NHS hospital, who holds an NHS consultant post or who appears in the Specialist Register of the General Medical Council, detailing the medical condition requiring further treatment.

How long can a visitor extend their stay in the UK

V 8.7   A visitor (standard) and a visitor for marriage or civil partnership, who was granted a visit visa or leave to enter for less than 6 months may be granted an extension of stay as a visitor so that the total period they can remain the UK (including both the original grant and the extension of stay) does not exceed 6 months.

V 8.8   A visitor (standard) who is in the UK for private medical treatment may be granted an extension of stay as a visitor for a further 6 months, provided this is for private medical treatment.

V 8.9   A visitor (standard) who is an academic on sabbatical leave and is in the UK undertaking their own research, or the spouse, partner or child accompanying such an academic, can be granted an extension of stay as a visitor so that the total period they can remain in the UK (including both the original grant and the extension of stay) does not exceed 12 months.

V 8.10   A visitor (standard) may be granted an extension of stay as a visitor for up to 6 months in order to resit the Professional and Linguistic Assessment Board (PLAB) Test, provided they meet the requirements at Appendix 3, paragraph 22(b)(i).

V 8.11   A visitor (standard) who is successful in the Professional and Linguistic Assessment Board Test may be granted an extension of stay as a visitor to undertake an unpaid clinical attachment, provided they meet the requirements of Appendix 3, paragraph 22(a) so that the total period they can remain in the UK (including both the original grant and the extension of stay) does not exceed 18 months.

PART V9. GROUNDS FOR CANCELLATION OF A VISIT VISA OR LEAVE BEFORE OR ON ARRIVAL AT THE UK BORDER AND CURTAILMENT OF LEAVE

Cancellation of a visit visa or leave to enter or remain as a visitor on or before arrival at the UK border

V 9.1   A current visit visa or leave to enter or remain as a visitor may be cancelled whilst the person is outside the UK or on arrival in the UK, if any of paragraphs V 9.2 – V 9.7 apply.

Change of circumstances

V 9.2   Where there has been such a change in the circumstances of the case since the visit visa or leave to enter or remain was granted that the basis of the visitor's claim to admission or stay has been removed and the visa or leave should be cancelled.

Change of purpose

V 9.3   Where the visitor holds a visit visa and their purpose in arriving in the United Kingdom is different from the purpose specified in the visit visa.

False information or failure to disclose a material fact

V 9.4   Where:

(a)   false representations were made or false documents or information submitted (whether or not material to the application, and whether or not to the applicant's knowledge); or

(b)   material facts were not disclosed,

in relation to the application for a visit visa or leave to enter or remain as a visitor, or in order to obtain documents from the Secretary of State or a third party provided in support of their application.

Medical

V 9.5   Where it is undesirable to admit the visitor to the UK for medical reasons, unless there are strong compassionate reasons justifying admission.

Not conducive to the public good

V 9.6   Where the criteria in V 3.2 - V 3.5. apply.

Failure to supply information

V 9.7   Where the person is outside the UK and there is a failure to supply any information, documents, or medical reports requested by a decision maker.

Curtailment

V 9.8   A visit visa or leave to enter or remain as a visitor may be curtailed while the person is in the UK if any of paragraphs V 9.9 – V 9.13 apply.

False information or failure to disclose a material fact

V 9.9   Where:

(a)   false representations were made or false documents or information were submitted (whether or not material to the application, and whether or not to the applicant's knowledge); or

(b)   material facts were not disclosed,

in relation to any application for an entry clearance or leave to enter or remain, or for the purpose of obtaining either a document from the Secretary of State or third party required in support of the application, or a document from the Secretary of State that indicates the person has a right to reside in the UK.

Requirements of the Rules

V 9.10   If the visitor ceases to meet the requirements of the Visitor Rules.

Failure to comply with conditions

V 9.11   If the visitor fails to comply with any conditions of their leave to enter or remain.

Not conducive to the public good

V 9.12   Where either:

(a)   the visitor has, within the first 6 months of being granted a visit visa or leave to enter, committed an offence for which they are subsequently sentenced to a period of imprisonment; or

(b)   in the view of the Secretary of State the applicant's offending has caused serious harm; or

(c)   in the view of the Secretary of State the applicant is a persistent offender who shows a particular disregard for the law; or

(d)   it would be undesirable to permit the visitor to remain in the UK in light of their conduct, character, associations, or the fact that they represent a threat to national security.

APPENDIX 2

The European Union and Associated States

Member States of the European Union (see Chapter 4)

Austria

Belgium

Bulgaria

Croatia (but see the Accession of Croatia (Immigration and Worker Authorisation) Regulations 2013
(SI 2013/1460)

Cyprus

Czech Republic

Denmark

Estonia

Finland

France

Germany

Greece

Hungary

Republic of Ireland

Italy

Latvia

Lithuania

Luxembourg

Malta

The Netherlands

Poland

Portugal

Romania

Slovakia

Slovenia

Spain

Sweden

United Kingdom

Other Members of the European Economic Area (see Chapter 4)

Iceland

Norway

Liechtenstein

(As to Switzerland, see **4.1**)

Directive 2004/38/EC

CHAPTER I – GENERAL PROVISIONS

Article 1 – Subject

This Directive lays down:

(a) the conditions governing the exercise of the right of free movement and residence within the territory of the Member States by Union citizens and their family members;

(b) the right of permanent residence in the territory of the Member States for Union citizens and their family members;

(c) the limits placed on the rights set out in (a) and (b) on grounds of public policy, public security or public health.

Article 2 – Definitions

For the purposes of this Directive:

1. 'Union citizen' means any person having the nationality of a Member State;

2. 'family member' means:

    (a) the spouse;

    (b) the partner with whom the Union citizen has contracted a registered partnership, on the basis of the legislation of a Member State, if the legislation of the host Member State treats registered partnerships as equivalent to marriage and in accordance with the conditions laid down in the relevant legislation of the host Member State;

    (c) the direct descendants who are under the age of 21 or are dependants and those of the spouse or partner as defined in point (b);

    (d) the dependent direct relatives in the ascending line and those of the spouse or partner as defined in point (b);

3. 'host Member State' means the Member State to which a Union citizen moves in order to exercise his/her right of free movement and residence.

Article 3 – Beneficiaries

1. This Directive shall apply to all Union citizens who move to or reside in a Member State other than that of which they are a national, and to their family members as defined in point 2 of Article 2 who accompany or join them.

2. Without prejudice to any right to free movement and residence the persons concerned may have in their own right, the host Member State shall, in accordance with its national legislation, facilitate entry and residence for the following persons:

    (a) any other family members, irrespective of their nationality, not falling under the definition in point 2 of Article 2 who, in the country from which they have come, are dependants or members of the household of the Union citizen having the primary right of residence, or where serious health grounds strictly require the personal care of the family member by the Union citizen;

    (b) the partner with whom the Union citizen has a durable relationship, duly attested.

    The host Member State shall undertake an extensive examination of the personal circumstances and shall justify any denial of entry or residence to these people.

CHAPTER II – RIGHT OF EXIT AND ENTRY

Article 4 – Right of exit

1. Without prejudice to the provisions on travel documents applicable to national border controls, all Union citizens with a valid identity card or passport and their family members who are not nationals of a Member State and who hold a valid passport shall have the right to leave the territory of a Member State to travel to another Member State.

2. No exit visa or equivalent formality may be imposed on the persons to whom paragraph 1 applies.

3. Member States shall, acting in accordance with their laws, issue to their own nationals, and renew, an identity card or passport stating their nationality.

4. The passport shall be valid at least for all Member States and for countries through which the holder must pass when travelling between Member States. Where the law of a Member State does not provide for identity cards to be issued, the period of validity of any passport on being issued or renewed shall be not less than five years.

Article 5 – Right of entry

1. Without prejudice to the provisions on travel documents applicable to national border controls, Member States shall grant Union citizens leave to enter their territory with a valid identity card or passport and shall grant family members who are not nationals of a Member State leave to enter their territory with a valid passport.

    No entry visa or equivalent formality may be imposed on Union citizens.

2. Family members who are not nationals of a Member State shall only be required to have an entry visa in accordance with Regulation (EC) No 539/2001 or, where appropriate, with national law. For the purposes of this Directive, possession of the valid residence card referred to in Article 10 shall exempt such family members from the visa requirement.

    Member States shall grant such persons every facility to obtain the necessary visas. Such visas shall be issued free of charge as soon as possible and on the basis of an accelerated procedure.

3. The host Member State shall not place an entry or exit stamp in the passport of family members who are not nationals of a Member State provided that they present the residence card provided for in Article 10.

4. Where a Union citizen, or a family member who is not a national of a Member State, does not have the necessary travel documents or, if required, the necessary visas, the Member State concerned shall, before turning them back, give such persons every reasonable opportunity to obtain the necessary documents or have them brought to them within a reasonable period of time or to corroborate or prove by other means that they are covered by the right of free movement and residence.

5. The Member State may require the person concerned to report his/her presence within its territory within a reasonable and non-discriminatory period of time. Failure to comply with this requirement may make the person concerned liable to proportionate and non-discriminatory sanctions.

CHAPTER III – RIGHT OF RESIDENCE

Article 6 – Right of residence for up to three months

1. Union citizens shall have the right of residence on the territory of another Member State for a period of up to three months without any conditions or any formalities other than the requirement to hold a valid identity card or passport.

2. The provisions of paragraph 1 shall also apply to family members in possession of a valid passport who are not nationals of a Member State, accompanying or joining the Union citizen.

Article 7 – Right of residence for more than three months

1. All Union citizens shall have the right of residence on the territory of another Member State for a period of longer than three months if they:

(a)   are workers or self-employed persons in the host Member State; or

(b)   have sufficient resources for themselves and their family members not to become a burden on the social assistance system of the host Member State during their period of residence and have comprehensive sickness insurance cover in the host Member State; or

(c)   —   are enrolled at a private or public establishment, accredited or financed by the host Member State on the basis of its legislation or administrative practice, for the principal purpose of following a course of study, including vocational training; and

            —   have comprehensive sickness insurance cover in the host Member State and assure the relevant national authority, by means of a declaration or by such equivalent means as they may choose, that they have sufficient resources for themselves and their family members not to become a burden on the social assistance system of the host Member State during their period of residence; or

(d)   are family members accompanying or joining a Union citizen who satisfies the conditions referred to in points (a), (b) or (c).

2.   The right of residence provided for in paragraph 1 shall extend to family members who are not nationals of a Member State, accompanying or joining the Union citizen in the host Member State, provided that such Union citizen satisfies the conditions referred to in paragraph 1(a), (b) or (c).

3.   For the purposes of paragraph 1(a), a Union citizen who is no longer a worker or self-employed person shall retain the status of worker or self-employed person in the following circumstances:

(a)   he/she is temporarily unable to work as the result of an illness or accident;

(b)   he/she is in duly recorded involuntary unemployment after having been employed for more than one year and has registered as a job-seeker with the relevant employment office;

(c)   he/she is in duly recorded involuntary unemployment after completing a fixed-term employment contract of less than a year or after having become involuntarily unemployed during the first twelve months and has registered as a job-seeker with the relevant employment office. In this case, the status of worker shall be retained for no less than six months;

(d)   he/she embarks on vocational training. Unless he/she is involuntarily unemployed, the retention of the status of worker shall require the training to be related to the previous employment.

4.   By way of derogation from paragraphs 1(d) and 2 above, only the spouse, the registered partner provided for in Article 2(2)(b) and dependent children shall have the right of residence as family members of a Union citizen meeting the conditions under 1(c) above. Article 3(2) shall apply to his/her dependent direct relatives in the ascending lines and those of his/her spouse or registered partner.

Article 8 – Administrative formalities for Union citizens

1.   Without prejudice to Article 5(5), for periods of residence longer than three months, the host Member State may require Union citizens to register with the relevant authorities.

2.   The deadline for registration may not be less than three months from the date of arrival. A registration certificate shall be issued immediately, stating the name and address of the person registering and the date of the registration. Failure to comply with the registration requirement may render the person concerned liable to proportionate and non-discriminatory sanctions.

3.   For the registration certificate to be issued, Member States may only require that

     —   Union citizens to whom point (a) of Article 7(1) applies present a valid identity card or passport, a confirmation of engagement from the employer or a certificate of employment, or proof that they are self-employed persons,

     —   Union citizens to whom point (b) of Article 7(1) applies present a valid identity card or passport and provide proof that they satisfy the conditions laid down therein,

     —   Union citizens to whom point (c) of Article 7(1) applies present a valid identity card or passport, provide proof of enrolment at an accredited establishment and of comprehensive sickness insurance cover and the declaration or equivalent means referred to in point (c) of Article 7(1). Member States may not require this declaration to refer to any specific amount of resources.

4.   Member States may not lay down a fixed amount which they regard as 'sufficient resources', but they must take into account the personal situation of the person concerned. In all cases this amount shall not be higher than the threshold below which nationals of the host Member State become eligible for

social assistance, or, where this criterion is not applicable, higher than the minimum social security pension paid by the host Member State.

5. For the registration certificate to be issued to family members of Union citizens, who are themselves Union citizens, Member States may require the following documents to be presented:

    (a)   a valid identity card or passport;

    (b)   a document attesting to the existence of a family relationship or of a registered partnership;

    (c)   where appropriate, the registration certificate of the Union citizen whom they are accompanying or joining;

    (d)   in cases falling under points (c) and (d) of Article 2(2), documentary evidence that the conditions laid down therein are met;

    (e)   in cases falling under Article 3(2)(a), a document issued by the relevant authority in the country of origin or country from which they are arriving certifying that they are dependants or members of the household of the Union citizen, or proof of the existence of serious health grounds which strictly require the personal care of the family member by the Union citizen;

    (f)   in cases falling under Article 3(2)(b), proof of the existence of a durable relationship with the Union citizen.

Article 9 – Administrative formalities for family members who are not nationals of a Member State

1. Member States shall issue a residence card to family members of a Union citizen who are not nationals of a Member State, where the planned period of residence is for more than three months.

2. The deadline for submitting the residence card application may not be less than three months from the date of arrival.

3. Failure to comply with the requirement to apply for a residence card may make the person concerned liable to proportionate and non-discriminatory sanctions.

Article 10 – Issue of residence cards

1. The right of residence of family members of a Union citizen who are not nationals of a Member State shall be evidenced by the issuing of a document called 'Residence card of a family member of a Union citizen' no later than six months from the date on which they submit the application. A certificate of application for the residence card shall be issued immediately.

2. For the residence card to be issued, Member States shall require presentation of the following documents:

    (a)   a valid passport;

    (b)   a document attesting to the existence of a family relationship or of a registered partnership;

    (c)   the registration certificate or, in the absence of a registration system, any other proof of residence in the host MemberState of the Union citizen whom they are accompanying or joining;

    (d)   in cases falling under points (c) and (d) of Article 2(2), documentary evidence that the conditions laid down therein are met;

    (e)   in cases falling under Article 3(2)(a), a document issued by the relevant authority in the country of origin or country from which they are arriving certifying that they are dependants or members of the household of the Union citizen, or proof of the existence of serious health grounds which strictly require the personal care of the family member by the Union citizen;

    (f)   in cases falling under Article 3(2)(b), proof of the existence of a durable relationship with the Union citizen.

Article 11 – Validity of the residence card

1. The residence card provided for by Article 10(1) shall be valid for five years from the date of issue or for the envisaged period of residence of the Union citizen, if this period is less than five years.

2. The validity of the residence card shall not be affected by temporary absences not exceeding six months a year, or by absences of a longer duration for compulsory military service or by one absence of

a maximum of 12 consecutive months for important reasons such as pregnancy and childbirth, serious illness, study or vocational training, or a posting in another Member State or a third country.

Article 12 – Retention of the right of residence by family members in the event of death or departure of the Union citizen

1. Without prejudice to the second subparagraph, the Union citizen's death or departure from the host Member State shall not affect the right of residence of his/her family members who are nationals of a Member State.

    Before acquiring the right of permanent residence, the persons concerned must meet the conditions laid down in points (a), (b), (c) or (d) of Article 7(1).

2. Without prejudice to the second subparagraph, the Union citizen's death shall not entail loss of the right of residence of his/her family members who are not nationals of a Member State and who have been residing in the host Member State as family members for at least one year before the Union citizen's death.

    Before acquiring the right of permanent residence, the right of residence of the persons concerned shall remain subject to the requirement that they are able to show that they are workers or self-employed persons or that they have sufficient resources for themselves and their family members not to become a burden on the social assistance system of the host Member State during their period of residence and have comprehensive sickness insurance cover in the host Member State, or that they are members of the family, already constituted in the host Member State, of a person satisfying these requirements. 'Sufficient resources' shall be as defined in Article 8(4).

    Such family members shall retain their right of residence exclusively on a personal basis.

3. The Union citizen's departure from the host Member State or his/her death shall not entail loss of the right of residence of his/her children or of the parent who has actual custody of the children, irrespective of nationality, if the children reside in the host Member State and are enrolled at an educational establishment, for the purpose of studying there, until the completion of their studies.

Article 13 – Retention of the right of residence by family members in the event of divorce, annulment of marriage or termination of registered partnership

1. Without prejudice to the second subparagraph, divorce, annulment of the Union citizen's marriage or termination of his/her registered partnership, as referred to in point 2(b) of Article 2 shall not affect the right of residence of his/her family members who are nationals of a Member State.

    Before acquiring the right of permanent residence, the persons concerned must meet the conditions laid down in points (a), (b), (c) or (d) of Article 7(1).

2. Without prejudice to the second subparagraph, divorce, annulment of marriage or termination of the registered partnership referred to in point 2(b) of Article 2 shall not entail loss of the right of residence of a Union citizen's family members who are not nationals of a Member State where:

    (a) prior to initiation of the divorce or annulment proceedings or termination of the registered partnership referred to in point 2(b) of Article 2, the marriage or registered partnership has lasted at least three years, including one year in the host Member State; or

    (b) by agreement between the spouses or the partners referred to in point 2(b) of Article 2 or by court order, the spouse or partner who is not a national of a Member State has custody of the Union citizen's children; or

    (c) this is warranted by particularly difficult circumstances, such as having been a victim of domestic violence while the marriage or registered partnership was subsisting; or

    (d) by agreement between the spouses or partners referred to in point 2(b) of Article 2 or by court order, the spouse or partner who is not a national of a Member State has the right of access to a minor child, provided that the court has ruled that such access must be in the host Member State, and for as long as is required.

    Before acquiring the right of permanent residence, the right of residence of the persons concerned shall remain subject to the requirement that they are able to show that they are workers or self-employed persons or that they have sufficient resources for themselves and their family members not to become a burden on the social assistance system of the host Member State during their period of residence and have comprehensive sickness insurance cover in the host Member State, or that they are members of the family, already constituted in the host Member State, of a person satisfying these requirements. 'Sufficient resources' shall be as defined in Article 8(4).

Such family members shall retain their right of residence exclusively on personal basis.

Article 14 – Retention of the right of residence

1. Union citizens and their family members shall have the right of residence provided for in Article 6, as long as they do not become an unreasonable burden on the social assistance system of the host Member State.

2. Union citizens and their family members shall have the right of residence provided for in Articles 7, 12 and 13 as long as they meet the conditions set out therein.

    In specific cases where there is a reasonable doubt as to whether a Union citizen or his/her family members satisfies the conditions set out in Articles 7, 12 and 13, Member States may verify if these conditions are fulfilled. This verification shall not be carried out systematically.

3. An expulsion measure shall not be the automatic consequence of a Union citizen's or his or her family member's recourse to the social assistance system of the host Member State.

4. By way of derogation from paragraphs 1 and 2 and without prejudice to the provisions of Chapter VI, an expulsion measure may in no case be adopted against Union citizens or their family members if:

    (a) the Union citizens are workers or self-employed persons, or

    (b) the Union citizens entered the territory of the host Member State in order to seek employment. In this case, the Union citizens and their family members may not be expelled for as long as the Union citizens can provide evidence that they are continuing to seek employment and that they have a genuine chance of being engaged.

Article 15 – Procedural safeguards

1. The procedures provided for by Articles 30 and 31 shall apply by analogy to all decisions restricting free movement of Union citizens and their family members on grounds other than public policy, public security or public health.

2. Expiry of the identity card or passport on the basis of which the person concerned entered the host Member State and was issued with a registration certificate or residence card shall not constitute a ground for expulsion from the host Member State.

3. The host Member State may not impose a ban on entry in the context of an expulsion decision to which paragraph 1 applies.

CHAPTER IV – RIGHT OF PERMANENT RESIDENCE

Section I – Eligibility

Article 16 – General rule for Union citizens and their family members

1. Union citizens who have resided legally for a continuous period of five years in the host Member State shall have the right of permanent residence there. This right shall not be subject to the conditions provided for in Chapter III.

2. Paragraph 1 shall apply also to family members who are not nationals of a Member State and have legally resided with the Union citizen in the host Member State for a continuous period of five years.

3. Continuity of residence shall not be affected by temporary absences not exceeding a total of six months a year, or by absences of a longer duration for compulsory military service, or by one absence of a maximum of 12 consecutive months for important reasons such as pregnancy and childbirth, serious illness, study or vocational training, or a posting in another Member State or a third country.

4. Once acquired, the right of permanent residence shall be lost only through absence from the host Member State for a period exceeding two consecutive years.

Article 17 – Exemptions for persons no longer working in the host Member State and their family members

1. By way of derogation from Article 16, the right of permanent residence in the host Member State shall be enjoyed before completion of a continuous period of five years of residence by:

    (a) workers or self-employed persons who, at the time they stop working, have reached the age laid down by the law of that Member State for entitlement to an old age pension or workers who cease paid employment to take early retirement, provided that they have been working in that Member State for at least the preceding twelve months and have resided there continuously for more than three years.

    If the law of the host Member State does not grant the right to an old age pension to certain categories of self-employed persons, the age condition shall be deemed to have been met once the person concerned has reached the age of 60;

    (b) workers or self-employed persons who have resided continuously in the host Member State for more than two years and stop working there as a result of permanent incapacity to work.

    If such incapacity is the result of an accident at work or an occupational disease entitling the person concerned to a benefit payable in full or in part by an institution in the host Member State, no condition shall be imposed as to length of residence;

    (c) workers or self-employed persons who, after three years of continuous employment and residence in the host Member State, work in an employed or self-employed capacity in another Member State, while retaining their place of residence in the host Member State, to which they return, as a rule, each day or at least once a week.

    For the purposes of entitlement to the rights referred to in points (a) and (b), periods of employment spent in the Member State in which the person concerned is working shall be regarded as having been spent in the host Member State.

    Periods of involuntary unemployment duly recorded by the relevant employment office, periods not worked for reasons not of the person's own making and absences from work or cessation of work due to illness or accident shall be regarded as periods of employment.

2. The conditions as to length of residence and employment laid down in point (a) of paragraph 1 and the condition as to length of residence laid down in point (b) of paragraph 1 shall not apply if the worker's or the self-employed person's spouse or partner as referred to in point 2(b) of Article 2 is a national of the host Member State or has lost the nationality of that Member State by marriage to that worker or self-employed person.

3. Irrespective of nationality, the family members of a worker or a self-employed person who are residing with him in the territory of the host Member State shall have the right of permanent residence in that Member State, if the worker or self-employed person has acquired himself the right of permanent residence in that Member State on the basis of paragraph 1.

4. If, however, the worker or self-employed person dies while still working but before acquiring permanent residence status in the host Member State on the basis of paragraph 1, his family members who are residing with him in the host Member State shall acquire the right of permanent residence there, on condition that:

    (a) the worker or self-employed person had, at the time of death, resided continuously on the territory of that Member State for two years; or

    (b) the death resulted from an accident at work or an occupational disease; or

    (c) the surviving spouse lost the nationality of that Member State following marriage to the worker or self-employed person.

Article 18 – Acquisition of the right of permanent residence by certain family members who are not nationals of a Member State

Without prejudice to Article 17, the family members of a Union citizen to whom Articles 12(2) and 13(2) apply, who satisfy the conditions laid down therein, shall acquire the right of permanent residence after residing legally for a period of five consecutive years in the host Member State.

Section II – Administrative formalities

Article 19 – Document certifying permanent residence for Union citizens

1. Upon application Member States shall issue Union citizens entitled to permanent residence, after having verified duration of residence, with a document certifying permanent residence.
2. The document certifying permanent residence shall be issued as soon as possible.

Article 20 – Permanent residence card for family members who are not nationals of a Member State

1. Member States shall issue family members who are not nationals of a Member State entitled to permanent residence with a permanent residence card within six months of the submission of the application. The permanent residence card shall be renewable automatically every 10 years.
2. The application for a permanent residence card shall be submitted before the residence card expires. Failure to comply with the requirement to apply for a permanent residence card may render the person concerned liable to proportionate and non-discriminatory sanctions.
3. Interruption in residence not exceeding two consecutive years shall not affect the validity of the permanent residence card.

Article 21 – Continuity of residence

For the purposes of this Directive, continuity of residence may be attested by any means of proof in use in the host Member State. Continuity of residence is broken by any expulsion decision duly enforced against the person concerned.

CHAPTER V – PROVISIONS COMMON TO THE RIGHT OF RESIDENCE AND THE RIGHT OF PERMANENT RESIDENCE

Article 22 – Territorial scope

The right of residence and the right of permanent residence shall cover the whole territory of the host Member State. Member States may impose territorial restrictions on the right of residence and the right of permanent residence only where the same restrictions apply to their own nationals.

Article 23 – Related rights

Irrespective of nationality, the family members of a Union citizen who have the right of residence or the right of permanent residence in a Member State shall be entitled to take up employment or self-employment there.

Article 24 – Equal treatment

1. Subject to such specific provisions as are expressly provided for in the Treaty and secondary law, all Union citizens residing on the basis of this Directive in the territory of the host Member State shall enjoy equal treatment with the nationals of that Member State within the scope of the Treaty. The benefit of this right shall be extended to family members who are not nationals of a Member State and who have the right of residence or permanent residence.
2. By way of derogation from paragraph 1, the host Member State shall not be obliged to confer entitlement to social assistance during the first three months of residence or, where appropriate, the longer period provided for in Article 14(4)(b), nor shall it be obliged, prior to acquisition of the right of permanent residence, to grant maintenance aid for studies, including vocational training, consisting in student grants or student loans to persons other than workers, self-employed persons, persons who retain such status and members of their families.

Article 25 – General provisions concerning residence documents

1. Possession of a registration certificate as referred to in Article 8, of a document certifying permanent residence, of a certificate attesting submission of an application for a family member residence card, of a residence card or of a permanent residence card, may under no circumstances be made a precondition for the exercise of a right or the completion of an administrative formality, as entitlement to rights may be attested by any other means of proof.

2. All documents mentioned in paragraph 1 shall be issued free of charge or for a charge not exceeding that imposed on nationals for the issuing of similar documents.

Article 26 – Checks

Member States may carry out checks on compliance with any requirement deriving from their national legislation for non-nationals always to carry their registration certificate or residence card, provided that the same requirement applies to their own nationals as regards their identity card. In the event of failure to comply with this requirement, Member States may impose the same sanctions as those imposed on their own nationals for failure to carry their identity card.

CHAPTER VI – RESTRICTIONS ON THE RIGHT OF ENTRY AND THE RIGHT OF RESIDENCE ON GROUNDS OF PUBLIC POLICY, PUBLIC SECURITY OR PUBLIC HEALTH

Article 27 – General principles

1. Subject to the provisions of this Chapter, Member States may restrict the freedom of movement and residence of Union citizens and their family members, irrespective of nationality, on grounds of public policy, public security or public health. These grounds shall not be invoked to serve economic ends.

2. Measures taken on grounds of public policy or public security shall comply with the principle of proportionality and shall be based exclusively on the personal conduct of the individual concerned. Previous criminal convictions shall not in themselves constitute grounds for taking such measures.

   The personal conduct of the individual concerned must represent a genuine, present and sufficiently serious threat affecting one of the fundamental interests of society. Justifications that are isolated from the particulars of the case or that rely on considerations of general prevention shall not be accepted.

3. In order to ascertain whether the person concerned represents a danger for public policy or public security, when issuing the registration certificate or, in the absence of a registration system, not later than three months from the date of arrival of the person concerned on its territory or from the date of reporting his/her presence within the territory, as provided for in Article 5(5), or when issuing the residence card, the host Member State may, should it consider this essential, request the Member State of origin and, if need be, other Member States to provide information concerning any previous police record the person concerned may have. Such enquiries shall not be made as a matter of routine. The Member State consulted shall give its reply within two months.

4. The Member State which issued the passport or identity card shall allow the holder of the document who has been expelled on grounds of public policy, public security, or public health from another Member State to re-enter its territory without any formality even if the document is no longer valid or the nationality of the holder is in dispute.

Article 28 – Protection against expulsion

1. Before taking an expulsion decision on grounds of public policy or public security, the host Member State shall take account of considerations such as how long the individual concerned has resided on its territory, his/her age, state of health, family and economic situation, social and cultural integration into the host Member State and the extent of his/her links with the country of origin.

2. The host Member State may not take an expulsion decision against Union citizens or their family members, irrespective of nationality, who have the right of permanent residence on its territory, except on serious grounds of public policy or public security.

3. An expulsion decision may not be taken against Union citizens, except if the decision is based on imperative grounds of public security, as defined by Member States, if they:

    (a) have resided in the host Member State for the previous 10 years; or

    (b) are a minor, except if the expulsion is necessary for the best interests of the child, as provided for in the United Nations Convention on the Rights of the Child of 20 November 1989.

Article 29 – Public health

1. The only diseases justifying measures restricting freedom of movement shall be the diseases with epidemic potential as defined by the relevant instruments of the World Health Organisation and other infectious diseases or contagious parasitic diseases if they are the subject of protection provisions applying to nationals of the host Member State.

2. Diseases occurring after a three-month period from the date of arrival shall not constitute grounds for expulsion from the territory.

3. Where there are serious indications that it is necessary, Member States may, within three months of the date of arrival, require persons entitled to the right of residence to undergo, free of charge, a medical examination to certify that they are not suffering from any of the conditions referred to in paragraph 1. Such medical examinations may not be required as a matter of routine.

Article 30 – Notification of decisions

1. The persons concerned shall be notified in writing of any decision taken under Article 27(1), in such a way that they are able to comprehend its content and the implications for them.

2. The persons concerned shall be informed, precisely and in full, of the public policy, public security or public health grounds on which the decision taken in their case is based, unless this is contrary to the interests of State security.

3. The notification shall specify the court or administrative authority with which the person concerned may lodge an appeal, the time limit for the appeal and, where applicable, the time allowed for the person to leave the territory of the Member State. Save in duly substantiated cases of urgency, the time allowed to leave the territory shall be not less than one month from the date of notification.

Article 31 – Procedural safeguards

1. The persons concerned shall have access to judicial and, where appropriate, administrative redress procedures in the host Member State to appeal against or seek review of any decision taken against them on the grounds of public policy, public security or public health.

2. Where the application for appeal against or judicial review of the expulsion decision is accompanied by an application for an interim order to suspend enforcement of that decision, actual removal from the territory may not take place until such time as the decision on the interim order has been taken, except:

    — where the expulsion decision is based on a previous judicial decision; or

    — where the persons concerned have had previous access to judicial review; or

    — where the expulsion decision is based on imperative grounds of public security under Article 28(3).

3. The redress procedures shall allow for an examination of the legality of the decision, as well as of the facts and circumstances on which the proposed measure is based. They shall ensure that the decision is not disproportionate, particularly in view of the requirements laid down in Article 28.

4. Member States may exclude the individual concerned from their territory pending the redress procedure, but they may not prevent the individual from submitting his/her defence in person, except when his/her appearance may cause serious troubles to public policy or public security or when the appeal or judicial review concerns a denial of entry to the territory.

Article 32 – Duration of exclusion orders

1. Persons excluded on grounds of public policy or public security may submit an application for lifting of the exclusion order after a reasonable period, depending on the circumstances, and in any event after

three years from enforcement of the final exclusion order which has been validly adopted in accordance with Community law, by putting forward arguments to establish that there has been a material change in the circumstances which justified the decision ordering their exclusion.

The Member State concerned shall reach a decision on this application within six months of its submission.

2. The persons referred to in paragraph 1 shall have no right of entry to the territory of the Member State concerned while their application is being considered.

Article 33 – Expulsion as a penalty or legal consequence

1. Expulsion orders may not be issued by the host Member State as a penalty or legal consequence of a custodial penalty, unless they conform to the requirements of Articles 27, 28 and 29.

2. If an expulsion order, as provided for in paragraph 1, is enforced more than two years after it was issued, the Member State shall check that the individual concerned is currently and genuinely a threat to public policy or public security and shall assess whether there has been any material change in the circumstances since the expulsion order was issued.

CHAPTER VII – FINAL PROVISIONS

Article 34 – Publicity

Member States shall disseminate information concerning the rights and obligations of Union citizens and their family members on the subjects covered by this Directive, particularly by means of awareness-raising campaigns conducted through national and local media and other means of communication.

Article 35 – Abuse of rights

Member States may adopt the necessary measures to refuse, terminate or withdraw any right conferred by this Directive in the case of abuse of rights or fraud, such as marriages of convenience. Any such measure shall be proportionate and subject to the procedural safeguards provided for in Articles 30 and 31.

Article 36 – Sanctions

Member States shall lay down provisions on the sanctions applicable to breaches of national rules adopted for the implementation of this Directive and shall take the measures required for their application. The sanctions laid down shall be effective and proportionate. Member States shall notify the Commission of these provisions not later than 30 April 2006 and as promptly as possible in the case of any subsequent changes.

Article 37 – More favourable national provisions

The provisions of this Directive shall not affect any laws, regulations or administrative provisions laid down by a Member State which would be more favourable to the persons covered by this Directive.

Article 38 – Repeals

1. Articles 10 and 11 of Regulation (EEC) No 1612/68 shall be repealed with effect from 30 April 2006.

2. Directives 64/221/EEC, 68/360/EEC, 72/194/EEC, 73/148/EEC, 75/34/EEC, 75/35/EEC, 90/364/EEC, 90/365/EEC and 93/96/EEC shall be repealed with effect from 30 April 2006.

3. References made to the repealed provisions and Directives shall be construed as being made to this Directive.

Article 39 – Report

No later than 30 April 2006 the Commission shall submit a report on the application of this Directive to the European Parliament and the Council, together with any necessary proposals, notably on the opportunity to extend the period of time during which Union citizens and their family members may reside in the territory of the host Member State without any conditions. The Member States shall provide the Commission with the information needed to produce the report.

Article 40 – Transposition

1.   Member States shall bring into force the laws, regulations and administrative provisions necessary to comply with this Directive by 30 April 2006.

When Member States adopt those measures, they shall contain a reference to this Directive or shall be accompanied by such a reference on the occasion of their official publication. The methods of making such reference shall be laid down by the Member States.

2.   Member States shall communicate to the Commission the text of the provisions of national law which they adopt in the field covered by this Directive together with a table showing how the provisions of this Directive correspond to the national provisions adopted.

Article 41 – Entry into force

This Directive shall enter into force on the day of its publication in the *Official Journal of the European Union*.

Article 42 – Addressees

This Directive is addressed to the Member States.

Done at Strasbourg, 29 April 2004.

Immigration (European Economic Area) Regulations 2006 (SI 2006/1003, as amended)

PART I

INTERPRETATION ETC

1. Citation and commencement

These Regulations may be cited as the Immigration (European Economic Area) Regulations 2006 and shall come into force on 30th April 2006.

2. General interpretation

(1) In these Regulations—

'the 1971 Act' means the Immigration Act 1971;

'the 1999 Act' means the Immigration and Asylum Act 1999;

'the 2002 Act' means the Nationality, Immigration and Asylum Act 2002;

'the 2014 Act" means the Immigration Act 2014;

'the Accession Regulations' means the Accession (Immigration and Worker Registration) Regulations 2004;

'civil partner' does not include—

(a) a party to a civil partnership of convenience; or

(b) the civil partner ('C') of a person ('P') where a spouse, civil partner or durable partner of C or P is already present in the United Kingdom;

'decision maker' means the Secretary of State, an immigration officer or an entry clearance officer (as the case may be);

'deportation order' means an order made pursuant to regulation 24(3);

'derivative residence card' means a card issued to a person, in accordance with regulation 18A, as proof of the holder's derivative right to reside in the United Kingdom as at the date of issue;

'document certifying permanent residence' means a document issued to an EEA national, in accordance with regulation 18, as proof of the holder's permanent right of residence under regulation 15 as at the date of issue;

'durable partner' does not include the durable partner ('D') of a person ('P') where a spouse, civil partner or durable partner of D or P is already present in the United Kingdom and where that marriage, civil partnership or durable partnership is subsisting;

'EEA decision' means a decision under these Regulations that concerns—

(a) a person's entitlement to be admitted to the United Kingdom;

(b) a person's entitlement to be issued with or have renewed, or not to have revoked, a registration certificate, residence card, derivative residence card, document certifying permanent residence or permanent residence card;

(c) a person's removal from the United Kingdom; or

(d) the cancellation, pursuant to regulation 20A, of a person's right to reside in the United Kingdom;

but does not include decisions under regulations 24AA (human rights considerations and interim orders to suspend removal) or 29AA (temporary admission in order to submit case in person).

'EEA family permit' means a document issued to a person, in accordance with regulation 12, in connection with his admission to the United Kingdom;

'EEA national' means a national of an EEA State who is not also a British citizen;

'EEA State' means—

(a) a member State, other than the United Kingdom;

(b) Norway, Iceland or Liechtenstein; or

(c) Switzerland;

'entry clearance' has the meaning given in section 33(1) of the 1971 Act;

'entry clearance officer' means a person responsible for the grant or refusal of entry clearance;

'exclusion order' means an order made under regulation 19(1B);

'immigration rules' has the meaning given in section 33(1) of the 1971 Act;

'military service' means service in the armed forces of an EEA State;

'permanent residence card' means a card issued to a person who is not an EEA national, in accordance with regulation 18, as proof of the holder's permanent right of residence under regulation 15 as at the date of issue;

'qualifying EEA State residence card' means—

(a)   a document called a 'Residence card of a family member of a Union Citizen' issued under Article 10 of Council Directive 2004/38/EC (as applied, where relevant, by the EEA Agreement) by an EEA State listed in sub-paragraph (b) to a non-EEA family member of an EEA national as proof of the holder's right of residence in that State;

(b)   Germany and Estonia;

'registration certificate' means a certificate issued to an EEA national, in accordance with regulation 16, as proof of the holder's right of residence in the United Kingdom as at the date of issue;

'relevant EEA national' in relation to an extended family member has the meaning given in regulation 8(6);

'residence card' means a card issued to a person who is not an EEA national, in accordance with regulation 17, as proof of the holder's right of residence in the United Kingdom as at the date of issue;

'spouse' does not include—

(a)   a party to a marriage of convenience; or

(b)   the spouse ('S') of a person ('P') where a spouse, civil partner or durable partner of S or P is already present in the United Kingdom;

(2)   Paragraph (1) is subject to paragraph 1(a) of Schedule 4 (transitional provisions).

(3)   Section 11 of the 1971 Act (construction of references to entry) shall apply for the purpose of determining whether a person has entered the United Kingdom for the purpose of these Regulations as it applies for the purpose of determining whether a person has entered the United Kingdom for the purpose of that Act.

3. Continuity of residence

(1)   This regulation applies for the purpose of calculating periods of continuous residence in the United Kingdom under regulation 5(1) and regulation 15.

(2)   Continuity of residence is not affected by—

(a)   periods of absence from the United Kingdom which do not exceed six months in total in any year;

(b)   periods of absence from the United Kingdom on military service; or

(c)   any one absence from the United Kingdom not exceeding twelve months for an important reason such as pregnancy and childbirth, serious illness, study or vocational training or an overseas posting.

(3)   But continuity of residence is broken if a person is removed from the United Kingdom under these Regulations.

4. 'Worker', 'self-employed person', 'self-sufficient person' and 'student'

(1)   In these Regulations —

(a)   'worker' means a worker within the meaning of Article 39 of the Treaty establishing the European Community;

(b)   'self-employed person' means a person who establishes himself in order to pursue activity as a self-employed person in accordance with Article 43 of the Treaty establishing the European Community;

(c)   'self-sufficient person' means a person who has—

(i)   sufficient resources not to become a burden on the social assistance system of the United Kingdom during his period of residence; and

(ii)   comprehensive sickness insurance cover in the United Kingdom;

(d)   'student' means a person who—

       (i)   is enrolled, for the principal purpose of following a course of study (including vocational training), at a public or private establishment which is—

          (aa)   financed from public funds; or

          (bb)   otherwise recognised by the Secretary of State as an establishment which has been accredited for the purpose of providing such courses or training within the law or administrative practice of the part of the United Kingdom in which the establishment is located;

       (ii)   has comprehensive sickness insurance cover in the United Kingdom; and

       (iii)   assures the Secretary of State, by means of a declaration, or by such equivalent means as the person may choose, that he has sufficient resources not to become a burden on the social assistance system of the United Kingdom during his period of residence.

(2)   For the purposes of paragraph (1)(c) or (d), where family members of the person concerned reside in the United Kingdom and their right to reside is dependent upon their being family members of that person—

    (a)   the requirement for that person to have sufficient resources not to become a burden on the social assistance system of the United Kingdom during his period of residence shall only be satisfied if his resources and those of the family members are sufficient to avoid him and the family members becoming such a burden;

    (b)   the requirement for that person to have comprehensive sickness insurance cover in the United Kingdom shall only be satisfied if he and his family members have such cover.

(3)   ...

(4)   For the purposes of paragraphs (1)(c) and (d) and paragraph (2), the resources of the person concerned and, where applicable, any family members, are to be regarded as sufficient if—

    (a)   they exceed the maximum level of resources which a British citizen and his family members may possess if he is to become eligible for social assistance under the United Kingdom benefit system; or

    (b)   paragraph (a) does not apply but, taking into account the personal situation of the person concerned and, where applicable, any family members, it appears to the decision maker that the resources of the person or persons concerned should be regarded as sufficient.

(5)   For the purpose of regulation 15A(2) references in this regulation to 'family members' includes a 'primary carer' as defined in regulation 15A(7).

5. 'Worker or self-employed person who has ceased activity'

(1)   In these Regulations, 'worker or self-employed person who has ceased activity' means an EEA national who satisfies the conditions in paragraph (2), (3), (4) or (5).

(2)   A person satisfies the conditions in this paragraph if he—

    (a)   terminates his activity as a worker or self-employed person and—

       (i)   has reached the age at which he is entitled to a state pension on the date on which he terminates his activity; or

       (ii)   in the case of a worker, ceases working to take early retirement;

    (b)   pursued his activity as a worker or self-employed person in the United Kingdom for at least twelve months prior to the termination; and

    (c)   resided in the United Kingdom continuously for more than three years prior to the termination.

(3)   A person satisfies the conditions in this paragraph if—

    (a)   he terminates his activity in the United Kingdom as a worker or self-employed person as a result of a permanent incapacity to work; and

    (b)   either—

       (i)   he resided in the United Kingdom continuously for more than two years prior to the termination; or

       (ii)   the incapacity is the result of an accident at work or an occupational disease that entitles him to a pension payable in full or in part by an institution in the United Kingdom.

(4)   A person satisfies the conditions in this paragraph if—

    (a)   he is active as a worker or self-employed person in an EEA State but retains his place of residence in the United Kingdom, to which he returns as a rule at least once a week; and

    (b)   prior to becoming so active in that EEA State, he had been continuously resident and continuously active as a worker or self-employed person in the United Kingdom for at least three years.

(5)   A person who satisfies the condition in paragraph (4)(a) but not the condition in paragraph (4)(b) shall, for the purposes of paragraphs (2) and (3), be treated as being active and resident in the United Kingdom during any period in which he is working or self-employed in the EEA State.

(6)   The conditions in paragraphs (2) and (3) as to length of residence and activity as a worker or self-employed person shall not apply in relation to a person whose spouse or civil partner is a British citizen.

(7)   Subject to regulations 6(2), 7A(3) or 7B(3), for the purposes of this regulation—

    (a)   periods of inactivity for reasons not of the person's own making;

    (b)   periods of inactivity due to illness or accident; and

    (c)   in the case of a worker, periods of involuntary unemployment duly recorded by the relevant employment office,

shall be treated as periods of activity as a worker or self-employed person, as the case may be.

6. 'Qualified person'

(1)   In these Regulations, 'qualified person' means a person who is an EEA national and in the United Kingdom as—

    (a)   a jobseeker;

    (b)   a worker;

    (c)   a self-employed person;

    (d)   a self-sufficient person; or

    (e)   a student.

(2)   Subject to regulations 7A(4) and 7B(4), a person who is no longer working shall not cease to be treated as a worker for the purpose of paragraph (1)(b) if—

    (a)   he is temporarily unable to work as the result of an illness or accident;

    (b)   he is in duly recorded involuntary unemployment after having been employed in the United Kingdom for at least one year, provided that he—

        (i)   has registered as a jobseeker with the relevant employment office; and

        (ii)   satisfies conditions A and B;

    (ba)   he is in duly recorded involuntary unemployment after having been employed in the United Kingdom for less than one year, provided that he—

        (i)   has registered as a jobseeker with the relevant employment office; and

        (ii)   satisfies conditions A and B;

    (c)   he is involuntarily unemployed and has embarked on vocational training; or

    (d)   he has voluntarily ceased working and embarked on vocational training that is related to his previous employment.

(2A)   A person to whom paragraph (2)(ba) applies may only retain worker status for a maximum of six months.

(3)   A person who is no longer in self-employment shall not cease to be treated as a self-employed person for the purpose of paragraph (1)(c) if he is temporarily unable to pursue his activity as a self-employed person as the result of an illness or accident.

(4)   For the purpose of paragraph (1)(a), a 'jobseeker' is a person who satisfies conditions A, B and, where relevant, C.

(5)   Condition A is that the person—

    (a)   entered the United Kingdom in order to seek employment; or

    (b)   is present in the United Kingdom seeking employment, immediately after enjoying a right to reside pursuant to paragraph (1)(b) to (e) (disregarding any period during which worker status was retained pursuant to paragraph (2)(b) or (ba)).

(6)   Condition B is that the person can provide evidence that he is seeking employment and has a genuine chance of being engaged.

(7) A person may not retain the status of a worker pursuant to paragraph (2)(b), or jobseeker pursuant to paragraph (1)(a), for longer than the relevant period unless he can provide compelling evidence that he is continuing to seek employment and has a genuine chance of being engaged.

(8) In paragraph (7), 'the relevant period' means—

    (a) in the case of a person retaining worker status pursuant to paragraph (2)(b), a continuous period of six months;

    (b) in the case of a jobseeker, 91 days, minus the cumulative total of any days during which the person concerned previously enjoyed a right to reside as a jobseeker, not including any days prior to a continuous absence from the United Kingdom of at least 12 months.

(9) Condition C applies where the person concerned has, previously, enjoyed a right to reside under this regulation as a result of satisfying conditions A and B—

    (a) in the case of a person to whom paragraph (2)(b) or (ba) applied, for at least six months; or

    (b) in the case of a jobseeker, for at least 91 days in total,

unless the person concerned has, since enjoying the above right to reside, been continuously absent from the United Kingdom for at least 12 months.

(10) Condition C is that the person has had a period of absence from the United Kingdom.

(11) Where condition C applies—

    (a) paragraph (7) does not apply; and

    (b) condition B has effect as if 'compelling' were inserted before 'evidence'.

7. Family member

(1) Subject to paragraph (2), for the purposes of these Regulations the following persons shall be treated as the family members of another person—

    (a) his spouse or his civil partner;

    (b) direct descendants of his, his spouse or his civil partner who are—

        (i) under 21; or

        (ii) dependants of his, his spouse or his civil partner;

    (c) dependent direct relatives in his ascending line or that of his spouse or his civil partner;

    (d) a person who is to be treated as the family member of that other person under paragraph (3).

(2) A person shall not be treated under paragraph (1)(b) or (c) as the family member of a student residing in the United Kingdom after the period of three months beginning on the date on which the student is admitted to the United Kingdom unless—

    (a) in the case of paragraph (b), the person is the dependent child of the student or of his spouse or civil partner; or

    (b) the student also falls within one of the other categories of qualified persons mentioned in regulation 6(1).

(3) Subject to paragraph (4), a person who is an extended family member and has been issued with an EEA family permit, a registration certificate or a residence card shall be treated as the family member of the relevant EEA national for as long as he continues to satisfy the conditions in regulation 8(2), (3), (4) or (5) in relation to that EEA national and the permit, certificate or card has not ceased to be valid or been revoked.

(4) Where the relevant EEA national is a student, the extended family member shall only be treated as the family member of that national under paragraph (3) if either the EEA family permit was issued under regulation 12(2), the registration certificate was issued under regulation 16(5) or the residence card was issued under regulation 17(4).

7A. Application of the Accession Regulations

(1) This regulation applies to an EEA national who was an accession State worker requiring registration on 30th April 2011 ('an accession worker').

(2) In this regulation—

'accession State worker requiring registration' has the same meaning as in regulation 1(2)(d) of the Accession Regulations;

'legally working' has the same meaning as in regulation 2(7) of the Accession Regulations.

(3)   In regulation 5(7)(c), where the worker is an accession worker, periods of involuntary unemployment duly recorded by the relevant employment office shall be treated only as periods of activity as a worker—

    (a)   during any period in which regulation 5(4) of the Accession Regulations applied to that person; or

    (b)   when the unemployment began on or after 1st May 2011.

(4)   Regulation 6(2) applies to an accession worker where he—

    (a)   was a person to whom regulation 5(4) of the Accession Regulations applied on 30th April 2011; or

    (b)   became unable to work, became unemployed or ceased to work, as the case maybe, on or after 1st May 2011.

(5)   For the purposes of regulation 15, an accession worker shall be treated as having resided in accordance with these Regulations during any period before 1st May 2011 in which the accession worker—

    (a)   was legally working in the United Kingdom; or

    (b)   was a person to whom regulation 5(4) of the Accession Regulations applied.

(6)   Subject to paragraph (7), a registration certificate issued to an accession worker under regulation 8 of the Accession Regulations shall, from 1st May 2011, be treated as if it was a registration certificate issued under these Regulations where the accession worker was legally working in the United Kingdom for the employer specified in that certificate on—

    (a)   30th April 2011; or

    (b)   the date on which the certificate is issued where it is issued after 30th April 2011.

(7)   Paragraph (6) does not apply—

    (a)   if the Secretary of State issues a registration certificate in accordance with regulation 16 to an accession worker on or after 1st May 2011; and

    (b)   from the date of registration stated on that certificate.

7B. Application of the EU2 Regulations

(1)   This regulation applies to an EEA national who was an accession State national subject to worker authorisation before 1st January 2014.

(2)   In this regulation—

'accession State national subject to worker authorisation' has the same meaning as in regulation 2 of the EU2 Regulations;

'the EU2 Regulations' means the Accession (Immigration and Worker Authorisation) Regulations 2006.

(3)   Regulation 2(12) of the EU2 Regulations (accession State national subject to worker authorisation: legally working) has effect for the purposes of this regulation as it does for regulation 2(3) and (4) of the EU2 Regulations.

(4)   In regulation 5(7)(c), where the worker is an accession State national subject to worker authorisation, periods of involuntary unemployment duly recorded by the relevant employment office must only be treated as periods of activity as a worker when the unemployment began on or after 1st January 2014.

(5)   Regulation 6(2) applies to an accession State national subject to worker authorisation where the accession State national subject to worker authorisation became unable to work, became unemployed or ceased to work, as the case may be, on or after 1st January 2014.

(6)   For the purposes of regulation 15, an accession State national subject to worker authorisation must be treated as having resided in accordance with these Regulations during any period before 1st January 2014 in which the accession State national subject to worker authorisation was legally working in the United Kingdom.

(7)   An accession worker card issued to an accession State national subject to worker authorisation under regulation 11 of the EU2 Regulations before 1st January 2014 must be treated as if it were a registration certificate issued under these Regulations so long as it has not expired.

8. 'Extended family member'

(1)   In these Regulations 'extended family member' means a person who is not a family member of an EEA national under regulation 7(1)(a), (b) or (c) and who satisfies the conditions in paragraph (2), (3), (4) or (5).

(2)   A person satisfies the condition in this paragraph if the person is a relative of an EEA national, his spouse or his civil partner and—

   (a)   the person is residing in a country other than the United Kingdom and is dependent upon the EEA national or is a member of his household;

      (b)   the person satisfied the condition in paragraph (a) and is accompanying the EEA national to the United Kingdom or wishes to join him there; or

      (c)   the person satisfied the condition in paragraph (a), has joined the EEA national in the United Kingdom and continues to be dependent upon him or to be a member of his household.

(3)   A person satisfies the condition in this paragraph if the person is a relative of an EEA national or his spouse or his civil partner and, on serious health grounds, strictly requires the personal care of the EEA national his spouse or his civil partner.

(4)   A person satisfies the condition in this paragraph if the person is a relative of an EEA national and would meet the requirements in the immigration rules (other than those relating to entry clearance) for indefinite leave to enter or remain in the United Kingdom as a dependent relative of the EEA national were the EEA national a person present and settled in the United Kingdom.

(5)   A person satisfies the condition in this paragraph if the person is the partner of an EEA national (other than a civil partner) and can prove to the decision maker that he is in a durable relationship with the EEA national.

(6)   In these Regulations 'relevant EEA national' means, in relation to an extended family member, the EEA national who is or whose spouse or civil partner is the relative of the extended family member for the purpose of paragraph (2), (3) or (4) or the EEA national who is the partner of the extended family member for the purpose of paragraph (5).

9.   Family members of British citizens

(1)   If the conditions in paragraph (2) are satisfied, these Regulations apply to a person who is the family member of a British citizen as if the British citizen ('P') were an EEA national.

(2)   The conditions are that—

   (a)   P is residing in an EEA State as a worker or self-employed person or was so residing before returning to the United Kingdom;

   (b)   if the family member of P is P's spouse or civil partner, the parties are living together in the EEA State or had entered into the marriage or civil partnership and were living together in the EEA State before the British citizen returned to the United Kingdom; and

   (c)   the centre of P's life has transferred to the EEA State where P resided as a worker or self-employed person.

(3)   Factors relevant to whether the centre of P's life has transferred to another EEA State include—

   (a)   the period of residence in the EEA State as a worker or self-employed person;

   (b)   the location of P's principal residence;

   (c)   the degree of integration of P in the EEA State.

(4)   Where these Regulations apply to the family member of P, P is to be treated as holding a valid passport issued by an EEA State for the purpose of the application of regulation 13 to that family member.

10.   'Family member who has retained the right of residence'

(1)   In these Regulations, 'family member who has retained the right of residence' means, subject to paragraph (8), a person who satisfies the conditions in paragraph (2), (3), (4) or (5).

(2)   A person satisfies the conditions in this paragraph if—

   (a)   he was a family member of a qualified person or of an EEA national with a permanent right residence when that person died;

   (b)   he resided in the United Kingdom in accordance with these Regulations for at least the year immediately before the death of the qualified person or the EEA national with a permanent right of residence; and

   (c)   he satisfies the condition in paragraph (6).

(3)   A person satisfies the conditions in this paragraph if—

   (a)   he is the direct descendant of—

      (i)   qualified person or an EEA national with a permanent right of residence who has died;

> (ii) a person who ceased to be a qualified person on ceasing to reside in the United Kingdom; or
>
> (iii) the person who was the spouse or civil partner of the qualified person or an EEA national with a permanent right of residence mentioned in sub-paragraph (i) when he died or is the spouse or civil partner of the person mentioned in sub-paragraph (ii); and

(b) he was attending an educational course in the United Kingdom immediately before the qualified person or an EEA national with a permanent right of residence died or ceased to be a qualified person and continues to attend such a course.

(4) A person satisfies the conditions in this paragraph if the person is the parent with actual custody of a child who satisfies the condition in paragraph (3).

(5) A person satisfies the conditions in this paragraph if—

(a) he ceased to be a family member of a qualified person or of an EEA national with a permanent right of residence on the termination of the marriage or civil partnership of that person;

(b) he was residing in the United Kingdom in accordance with these Regulations at the date of the termination;

(c) he satisfies the condition in paragraph (6); and

(d) either—

> (i) prior to the initiation of the proceedings for the termination of the marriage or the civil partnership the marriage or civil partnership had lasted for at least three years and the parties to the marriage or civil partnership had resided in the United Kingdom for at least one year during its duration;
>
> (ii) the former spouse or civil partner of the qualified person or the EEA national with a permanent right of residence has custody of a child of the qualified person;
>
> (iii) the former spouse or civil partner of the qualified person or the EEA national with a permanent right of residence has the right of access to a child of the qualified person or the EEA national with a permanent right of residence, where the child is under the age of 18 and where a court has ordered that such access must take place in the United Kingdom; or
>
> (iv) the continued right of residence in the United Kingdom of the person is warranted by particularly difficult circumstances, such as he or another family member having been a victim of domestic violence while the marriage or civil partnership was subsisting.

(6) The condition in this paragraph is that the person—

(a) is not an EEA national but would, if he were an EEA national, be a worker, a self-employed person or a self-sufficient person under regulation 6; or

(b) is the family member of a person who falls within paragraph (a).

(7) In this regulation, 'educational course' means a course within the scope of Article 12 of Council Regulation (EEC) No. 1612/68 on freedom of movement for workers.

(8) A person with a permanent right of residence under regulation 15 shall not become a family member who has retained the right of residence on the death or departure from the United Kingdom of the qualified person or the EEA national with a permanent right of residence or the termination of the marriage or civil partnership, as the case may be, and a family member who has retained the right of residence shall cease to have that status on acquiring a permanent right of residence under regulation 15.

PART 2

EEA RIGHTS

11. Right of admission to the United Kingdom

(1) An EEA national must be admitted to the United Kingdom if he produces on arrival a valid national identity card or passport issued by an EEA State.

(2) A person who is not an EEA national must be admitted to the United Kingdom if he is—

(a) a family member of an EEA national and produces on arrival a valid passport and a qualifying EEA State residence card, provided the conditions in regulation 19(2)(a) (non-EEA family member to be accompanying or joining EEA national in the United Kingdom) and (b) (EEA national must have a right to reside in the United Kingdom under these Regulations) are met; or

(b)   a family member of an EEA national, a family member who has retained the right of residence, a person who meets the criteria in paragraph (5) or a person with a permanent right of residence under regulation 15 and produces on arrival—

    (i)   a valid passport; and

    (ii)   an EEA family permit, a residence card, a derivative residence card or a permanent residence card.

(3)   An immigration officer must not place a stamp in the passport of a person admitted to the United Kingdom under this regulation who is not an EEA national if the person produces a residence card, a derivative residence card, a permanent residence card or a qualifying EEA State residence card.

(4)   Before an immigration officer refuses admission to the United Kingdom to a person under this regulation because the person does not produce on arrival a document mentioned in paragraph (1) or (2), the immigration officer must give the person every reasonable opportunity to obtain the document or have it brought to him within a reasonable period of time or to prove by other means that he is—

(a)   an EEA national;

(b)   a family member of an EEA national with a right to accompany that national or join him in the United Kingdom;

(ba)   a person who meets the criteria in paragraph (5); or

(c)   a family member who has retained the right of residence or a person with a permanent right of residence under regulation 15.

(5)   A person ('P') meets the criteria in this paragraph where—

(a)   P previously resided in the United Kingdom pursuant to regulation 15A(3) and would be entitled to reside in the United Kingdom pursuant to that regulation were P in the country;

(b)   P is accompanying an EEA national to, or joining an EEA national in, the United Kingdom and P would be entitled to reside in the United Kingdom pursuant to regulation 15A(2) were P and the EEA national both in the United Kingdom;

(c)   P is accompanying a person ('the relevant person') to, or joining the relevant person in, the United Kingdom and—

    (i)   the relevant person is residing, or has resided, in the United Kingdom pursuant to regulation 15A(3); and

    (ii)   P would be entitled to reside in the United Kingdom pursuant to regulation 15A(4) were P and the relevant person both in the United Kingdom;

(d)   P is accompanying a person who meets the criteria in (b) or (c) ('the relevant person') to the United Kingdom and—

    (i)   P and the relevant person are both—

        (aa)   seeking admission to the United Kingdom in reliance on this paragraph for the first time; or

        (bb)   returning to the United Kingdom having previously resided there pursuant to the same provisions of regulation 15A in reliance on which they now base their claim to admission; and

    (ii)   P would be entitled to reside in the United Kingdom pursuant to regulation 15A(5) were P and the relevant person there; or

(e)   P is accompanying a British citizen to, or joining a British citizen in, the United Kingdom and P would be entitled to reside in the United Kingdom pursuant to regulation 15A(4A) were P and the British citizen both in the United Kingdom.

(6)   Paragraph (7) applies where—

(a)   a person ('P') seeks admission to the United Kingdom in reliance on paragraph (5)(b), (c) or (e); and

(b)   if P were in the United Kingdom, P would have a derived right of residence by virtue of regulation 15A(7)(b)(ii).

(7)   Where this paragraph applies a person ('P') will only be regarded as meeting the criteria in paragraph (5)(b), (c) or (e) where P—

(a)   is accompanying the person with whom P would on admission to the United Kingdom jointly share care responsibility for the purpose of regulation 15A(7)(b)(ii); or

(b)   has previously resided in the United Kingdom pursuant to regulation 15A(2), (4) or (4A) as a joint primary carer and seeks admission to the United Kingdom in order to reside there again on the same basis.

(8)   But this regulation is subject to regulations 19(1), (1A), (1AB) and (2) and 23A.

12.   Issue of EEA family permit

(1)   An entry clearance officer must issue an EEA family permit to a person who applies for one if the person is a family member of an EEA national and—

    (a)   the EEA national—

        (i)   is residing in the UK in accordance with these Regulations; or

        (ii)   will be travelling to the United Kingdom within six months of the date of the application and will be an EEA national residing in the United Kingdom in accordance with these Regulations on arrival in the United Kingdom; and

    (b)   the family member will be accompanying the EEA national to the United Kingdom or joining the EEA national there.

(1A)   An entry clearance officer must issue an EEA family permit to a person who applies and provides proof that, at the time at which he first intends to use the EEA family permit, he—

    (a)   would be entitled to be admitted to the United Kingdom by virtue of regulation 11(5); and

    (b)   will (save in the case of a person who would be entitled to be admitted to the United Kingdom by virtue of regulation 11(5)(a)) be accompanying to, or joining in, the United Kingdom any person from whom his right to be admitted to the United Kingdom under regulation 11(5) will be derived.

(1B)   An entry clearance officer must issue an EEA family permit to a family member who has retained the right of residence.

(2)   An entry clearance officer may issue an EEA family permit to an extended family member of an EEA national who applies for one if—

    (a)   the relevant EEA national satisfies the condition in paragraph (1)(a);

    (b)   the extended family member wishes to accompany the relevant EEA national to the United Kingdom or to join him there; and

    (c)   in all the circumstances, it appears to the entry clearance officer appropriate to issue the EEA family permit.

(3)   Where an entry clearance officer receives an application under paragraph (2) he shall undertake an extensive examination of the personal circumstances of the applicant and if he refuses the application shall give reasons justifying the refusal unless this is contrary to the interests of national security.

(4)   An EEA family permit issued under this regulation shall be issued free of charge and as soon as possible.

(5)   But an EEA family permit shall not be issued under this regulation if the applicant or the EEA national concerned is is not entitled to be admitted to the United Kingdom as a result of regulation 19(1A) or (1AB) or falls to be excluded in accordance with regulation 19(1B).

(6)   An EEA family permit will not be issued under this regulation to a person ('A') who is the spouse, civil partner or durable partner of a person ('B') where a spouse, civil partner or durable partner of A or B holds a valid EEA family permit.

13.   Initial right of residence

(1)   An EEA national is entitled to reside in the United Kingdom for a period not exceeding three months beginning on the date on which he is admitted to the United Kingdom provided that he holds a valid national identity card or passport issued by an EEA State.

(2)   A family member of an EEA national or a family member who has retained the right of residence who is residing in the United Kingdom under paragraph (1) who is not himself an EEA national is entitled to reside in the United Kingdom provided that he holds a valid passport.

(3)   An EEA national or his family member who becomes an unreasonable burden on the social assistance system of the United Kingdom will cease to have a right to reside under this regulation.

(4)   A person who otherwise satisfies the criteria in this regulation will not be entitled to reside in the United Kingdom under this regulation where the Secretary of State or an immigration officer has made a decision under—

    (a)   regulation 19(3)(b), 20(1), 20A(1) or 23A; or

(b)   regulation 21B(2), where that decision was taken in the preceding twelve months.

(5)   But—

    (a)   this regulation is subject to regulation 19(3)(b); and

    (b)   an EEA national or his family member who becomes an unreasonable burden on the social assistance system of the United Kingdom shall cease to have the right to reside under this regulation.

14. Extended right of residence

(1)   A qualified person is entitled to reside in the United Kingdom for so long as he remains a qualified person.

(2)   A family member of a qualified person residing in the United Kingdom under paragraph (1) or of an EEA national with a permanent right of residence under regulation 15 is entitled to reside in the United Kingdom for so long as he remains the family member of the qualified person or EEA national.

(3)   A family member who has retained the right of residence is entitled to reside in the United Kingdom for so long as he remains a family member who has retained the right of residence.

(4)   A right to reside under this regulation is in addition to any right a person may have to reside in the United Kingdom under regulation 13 or 15.

(5)   A person who otherwise satisfies the criteria in this regulation will not be entitled to a right to reside in the United Kingdom under this regulation where the Secretary of State or an immigration officer has made a decision under—

    (a)   regulation 19(3)(b), 20(1), 20A(1) or 23A; or

    (b)   regulation 21B(2) (not including such a decision taken on the basis of regulation 21B(1)(a) or (b)), where that decision was taken in the preceding twelve months.

15. Permanent right of residence

(1)   The following persons shall acquire the right to reside in the United Kingdom permanently—

    (a)   an EEA national who has resided in the United Kingdom in accordance with these Regulations for a continuous period of five years;

    (b)   a family member of an EEA national who is not himself an EEA national but who has resided in the United Kingdom with the EEA national in accordance with these Regulations for a continuous period of five years;

    (c)   a worker or self-employed person who has ceased activity;

    (d)   the family member of a worker or self-employed person who has ceased activity;

    (e)   a person who was the family member of a worker or self-employed person where—

        (i)   the worker or self-employed person has died;

        (ii)   the family member resided with him immediately before his death; and

        (iii)   the worker or self-employed person had resided continuously in the United Kingdom for at least the two years immediately before his death or the death was the result of an accident at work or an occupational disease;

    (f)   a person who—

        (i)   has resided in the United Kingdom in accordance with these Regulations for a continuous period of five years; and

        (ii)   was, at the end of that period, a family member who has retained the right of residence.

(1A)   Residence in the United Kingdom as a result of a derivative right of residence does not constitute residence for the purpose of this regulation.

(2)   The right of permanent residence under this regulation shall be lost only through absence from the United Kingdom for a period exceeding two consecutive years.

(3)   A person who satisfies the criteria in this regulation will not be entitled to a permanent right to reside in the United Kingdom where the Secretary of State or an immigration officer has made a decision under—

    (a)   regulation 19(3)(b), 20(1), 20A(1) or 23A; or

    (b)   regulation 21B(2) (not including such a decision taken on the basis of regulation 21B(1)(a) or (b)), where that decision was taken in the preceding twelve months.

15A.   Derivative right of residence

(1)   A person ('P') who is not an exempt person and who satisfies the criteria in paragraph (2), (3), (4), (4A) or (5) of this regulation is entitled to a derivative right to reside in the United Kingdom for as long as P satisfies the relevant criteria.

(2)   P satisfies the criteria in this paragraph if—

    (a)   P is the primary carer of an EEA national ('the relevant EEA national'); and

    (b)   the relevant EEA national—

        (i)   is under the age of 18;

        (ii)   is residing in the United Kingdom as a self-sufficient person; and

        (iii)   would be unable to remain in the United Kingdom if P were required to leave.

(3)   P satisfies the criteria in this paragraph if—

    (a)   P is the child of an EEA national ('the EEA national parent');

    (b)   P resided in the United Kingdom at a time when the EEA national parent was residing in the United Kingdom as a worker; and

    (c)   P is in education in the United Kingdom and was in education there at a time when the EEA national parent was in the United Kingdom.

(4)   P satisfies the criteria in this paragraph if—

    (a)   P is the primary carer of a person meeting the criteria in paragraph (3) ('the relevant person'); and

    (b)   the relevant person would be unable to continue to be educated in the United Kingdom if P were required to leave.

(4A)   P satisfies the criteria in this paragraph if—

    (a)   P is the primary carer of a British citizen ('the relevant British citizen');

    (b)   the relevant British citizen is residing in the United Kingdom; and

    (c)   the relevant British citizen would be unable to reside in the UK or in another EEA State if P were required to leave.

(5)   P satisfies the criteria in this paragraph if—

    (a)   P is under the age of 18;

    (b)   P's primary carer is entitled to a derivative right to reside in the United Kingdom by virtue of paragraph (2) or (4);

    (c)   P does not have leave to enter, or remain in, the United Kingdom; and

    (d)   requiring P to leave the United Kingdom would prevent P's primary carer from residing in the United Kingdom.

(6)   For the purpose of this regulation—

    (a)   'education' excludes nursery education;

    (b)   'worker' does not include a jobseeker or a person who falls to be regarded as a worker by virtue of regulation 6(2); and

    (c)   'an exempt person' is a person—

        (i)   who has a right to reside in the United Kingdom as a result of any other provision of these Regulations;

        (ii)   who has a right of abode in the United Kingdom by virtue of section 2 of the 1971 Act;

        (iii)   to whom section 8 of the 1971 Act, or any order made under subsection (2) of that provision, applies; or

        (iv)   who has indefinite leave to enter or remain in the United Kingdom.

(7)   P is to be regarded as a 'primary carer' of another person if

    (a)   P is a direct relative or a legal guardian of that person; and

    (b)   P—

        (i)   is the person who has primary responsibility for that person's care; or

        (ii)   shares equally the responsibility for that person's care with one other person who is not an exempt person.

(7A)   Where P is to be regarded as a primary carer of another person by virtue of paragraph (7)(b)(ii) the criteria in paragraphs (2)(b)(iii), (4)(b) and (4A)(c) shall be considered on the basis that both P and the person with whom care responsibility is shared would be required to leave the United Kingdom.

(7B)   Paragraph (7A) does not apply if the person with whom care responsibility is shared acquired a derivative right to reside in the United Kingdom as a result of this regulation prior to P assuming equal care responsibility.

(8)   P will not be regarded as having responsibility for a person's care for the purpose of paragraph (7) on the sole basis of a financial contribution towards that person's care.

(9)   A person who otherwise satisfies the criteria in paragraph (2), (3), (4), (4A) or (5) will not be entitled to a derivative right to reside in the United Kingdom where the Secretary of State or an immigration officer has made a decision under regulation—

   (a)   regulation 19(3)(b), 20(1), 20A(1) or 23A; or

   (b)   regulation 21B(2), where that decision was taken in the preceding twelve months.

15B.   Continuation of a right of residence

(1)   This regulation applies during any period in which, but for the effect of regulation 13(4), 14(5), 15(3) or 15A(9), a person ('P') who is in the United Kingdom would be entitled to reside here pursuant to these Regulations.

(2)   Where this regulation applies, any right of residence will (notwithstanding the effect of regulation 13(4), 14(5), 15(3) or 15A(9)) be deemed to continue during any period in which—

   (a)   an appeal under regulation 26 could be brought, while P is in the United Kingdom, against a relevant decision (ignoring any possibility of an appeal out of time with permission); or

   (b)   an appeal under regulation 26 against a relevant decision, brought while P is in the United Kingdom, is pending.

(3)   Periods during which residence pursuant to regulation 14 is deemed to continue as a result of paragraph (2) will not constitute residence for the purpose of regulation 15 unless and until—

   (a)   a relevant decision is withdrawn by the Secretary of State; or

   (b)   an appeal against a relevant decision is allowed and that appeal is finally determined.

(4)   Periods during which residence is deemed to continue as a result of paragraph (2) will not constitute residence for the purpose of regulation 21(4)(a) unless and until—

   (a)   a relevant decision is withdrawn by the Secretary of State; or

   (b)   an appeal against a relevant decision is allowed and that appeal is finally determined.

(5)   A 'relevant decision' for the purpose of this regulation means a decision pursuant to regulation 19(3)(b) or (c), 20(1) or 20A(1) which would, but for the effect of paragraph (2), prevent P from residing in the United Kingdom pursuant to these Regulations.

(6)   This regulation does not affect the ability of the Secretary of State to give directions for P's removal while an appeal is pending or before it is finally determined.

(7)   In this regulation, 'pending' and 'finally determined' have the meanings given in section 104 of the 2002 Act.

PART 3
RESIDENCE DOCUMENTATION

16.   Issue of registration certificate

(1)   The Secretary of State must issue a registration certificate to a qualified person immediately on application and production of—

   (a)   a valid identity card or passport issued by an EEA State;

   (b)   proof that he is a qualified person.

(2)   In the case of a worker, confirmation of the worker's engagement from his employer or a certificate of employment is sufficient proof for the purposes of paragraph (1)(b).

(3)   The Secretary of State must issue a registration certificate to an EEA national who is the family member of a qualified person or of an EEA national with a permanent right of residence under regulation 15 immediately on application and production of—

   (a)   a valid identity card or passport issued by an EEA State; and

   (b)   proof that the applicant is such a family member.

(4)   The Secretary of State must issue a registration certificate to an EEA national who is a family member who has retained the right of residence on application and production of—

    (a)   a valid identity card or passport; and

    (b)   proof that the applicant is a family member who has retained the right of residence.

(5)   The Secretary of State may issue a registration certificate to an extended family member not falling within regulation 7(3) who is an EEA national on application if—

    (a)   the relevant EEA national in relation to the extended family member is a qualified person or an EEA national with a permanent right of residence under regulation 15; and

    (b)   in all the circumstances it appears to the Secretary of State appropriate to issue the registration certificate.

(6)   Where the Secretary of State receives an application under paragraph (5) he shall undertake an extensive examination of the personal circumstances of the applicant and if he refuses the application shall give reasons justifying the refusal unless this is contrary to the interests of national security.

(7)   A registration certificate issued under this regulation shall state the name and address of the person registering and the date of registration.

(8)   But this regulation is subject to regulation 7A(6) and 20(1).

17.   Issue of residence card

(1)   The Secretary of State must issue a residence card to a person who is not an EEA national and is the family member of a qualified person or of an EEA national with a permanent right of residence under regulation 15 on application and production of—

    (a)   a valid passport; and

    (b)   proof that the applicant is such a family member.

(2)   The Secretary of State must issue a residence card to a person who is not an EEA national but who is a family member who has retained the right of residence on application and production of—

    (a)   a valid passport; and

    (b)   proof that the applicant is a family member who has retained the right of residence.

(3)   On receipt of an application under paragraph (1) or (2) and the documents that are required to accompany the application the Secretary of State shall immediately issue the applicant with a certificate of application for the residence card and the residence card shall be issued no later than six months after the date on which the application and documents are received.

(4)   The Secretary of State may issue a residence card to an extended family member not falling within regulation 7(3) who is not an EEA national on application if—

    (a)   the relevant EEA national in relation to the extended family member is a qualified person or an EEA national with a permanent right of residence under regulation 15; and

    (b)   in all the circumstances it appears to the Secretary of State appropriate to issue the residence card.

(5)   Where the Secretary of State receives an application under paragraph (4) he shall undertake an extensive examination of the personal circumstances of the applicant and if he refuses the application shall give reasons justifying the refusal unless this is contrary to the interests of national security.

(6)   A residence card issued under this regulation may take the form of a stamp in the applicant's passport and shall be valid for—

    (a)   five years from the date of issue; or

    (b)   in the case of a residence card issued to the family member or extended family member of a qualified person, the envisaged period of residence in the United Kingdom of the qualified person,

whichever is the shorter.

(6A)   A residence card issued under this regulation shall be entitled 'Residence card of a family member of an EEA national' or 'Residence card of a family member who has retained the right of residence', as the case may be.

(7)   ...

(8)   But this regulation is subject to regulations 20(1) and (1A).

18.   Issue of a document certifying permanent residence and a permanent residence card

(1)   The Secretary of State must issue an EEA national with a permanent right of residence under regulation 15 with a document certifying permanent residence as soon as possible after an application for such a document and proof that the EEA national has such a right is submitted to the Secretary of State.

(2)   The Secretary of State must issue a person who is not an EEA national who has a permanent right of residence under regulation 15 with a permanent residence card no later than six months after the date on which an application for a permanent residence card and proof that the person has such a right is submitted to the Secretary of State.

(3)   Subject to paragraph (5), a permanent residence card shall be valid for ten years from the date of issue and must be renewed on application.

(4)   ...

(5)   A document certifying permanent residence and a permanent residence card shall cease to be valid if the holder ceases to have a right of permanent residence under regulation 15.

(6)   But this regulation is subject to regulation 20.

18A.   Issue of a derivative residence card

(1)   The Secretary of State must issue a person with a derivative residence card on application and on production of—

(a)   a valid identity card issued by an EEA State or a valid passport; and

(b)   proof that the applicant has a derivative right of residence under regulation 15A.

(2)   On receipt of an application under paragraph (1) the Secretary of State must issue the applicant with a certificate of application as soon as possible.

(3)   A derivative residence card issued under paragraph (1) may take the form of a stamp in the applicant's passport and will be valid until—

(a)   a date five years from the date of issue; or

(b)   any other date specified by the Secretary of State when issuing the derivative residence card.

(4)   A derivative residence card issued under paragraph (1) must be issued as soon as practicable.

(5)   But this regulation is subject to regulations 20(1) and 20(1A).

PART 4

REFUSAL OF ADMISSION AND REMOVAL ETC

19.   Exclusion and removal from the United Kingdom

(1)   A person is not entitled to be admitted to the United Kingdom by virtue of regulation 11 if his exclusion is justified on grounds of public policy, public security or public health in accordance with regulation 21.

(1A)   A person is not entitled to be admitted to the United Kingdom by virtue of regulation 11 if that person is subject to a deportation or exclusion order, except where the person is temporarily admitted pursuant to regulation 29AA.

(1AB)   A person is not entitled to be admitted to the United Kingdom by virtue of regulation 11 if the Secretary of State considers there to be reasonable grounds to suspect that his admission would lead to the abuse of a right to reside in accordance with regulation 21B(1).

(1B)   If the Secretary of State considers that the exclusion of an EEA national or the family member of an EEA national is justified on the grounds of public policy, public security or public health in accordance with regulation 21 the Secretary of State may make an order for the purpose of these Regulations prohibiting that person from entering the United Kingdom.

(2)   A person is not entitled to be admitted to the United Kingdom as the family member of an EEA national under regulation 11(2) unless, at the time of his arrival—

(a)   he is accompanying the EEA national or joining him in the United Kingdom; and

(b)   the EEA national has a right to reside in the United Kingdom under these Regulations.

(3)   Subject to paragraphs (4) and (5), an EEA national who has entered the United Kingdom or the family member of such a national who has entered the United Kingdom may be removed if—

(a)   that person does not have or ceases to have a right to reside under these Regulations;

(b)   the Secretary of State has decided that the person's removal is justified on grounds of public policy, public security or public health in accordance with regulation 21; or

> (c)   the Secretary of State has decided that the person's removal is justified on grounds of abuse of rights in accordance with regulation 21B(2).

(4)   A person must not be removed under paragraph (3) as the automatic consequence of having recourse to the social assistance system of the United Kingdom.

(5)   A person must not be removed under paragraph (3) if he has a right to remain in the United Kingdom by virtue of leave granted under the 1971 Act unless his removal is justified on the grounds of public policy, public security or public health in accordance with regulation 21.

20.   Refusal to issue or renew and revocation of residence documentation

(1)   The Secretary of State may refuse to issue, revoke or refuse to renew a registration certificate, a residence card, a document certifying permanent residence or a permanent residence card if the refusal or revocation is justified on grounds of public policy, public security or public health or on grounds of abuse of rights in accordance with regulation 21B(2).

(1A)   A decision under regulation 19(3) or 24(4) to remove a person from the United Kingdom, or a decision under regulation 23A to revoke a person's admission to the United Kingdom will (save during any period in which a right of residence is deemed to continue as a result of regulation 15B(2)) invalidate a registration certificate, residence card, document certifying permanent residence or permanent residence card held by that person or an application made by that person for such a certificate, card or document.

(2)   The Secretary of State may revoke a registration certificate or a residence card or refuse to renew a residence card if the holder of the certificate or card has ceased to have, or never had, a right to reside under these Regulations.

(3)   The Secretary of State may revoke a document certifying permanent residence or a permanent residence card or refuse to renew a permanent residence card if the holder of the certificate or card has ceased to have, or never had, a right of permanent residence under regulation 15.

(4)   An immigration officer may, at the time of a person's arrival in the United Kingdom—

> (a)   revoke that person's residence card if he is not at that time the family member of a qualified person or of an EEA national who has a right of permanent residence under regulation 15, a family member who has retained the right of residence or a person with a right of permanent residence under regulation 15;

> (b)   revoke that person's permanent residence card if he is not at that time a person with a right of permanent residence under regulation 15.

(5)   An entry clearance officer or immigration officer may at any time revoke a person's s EEA family permit if—

> (a)   the revocation is justified on grounds of public policy, public security or public health; or

> (b)   the person is not at that time the family member of an EEA national with the right to reside in the United Kingdom under these Regulations or is not accompanying that national or joining him in the United Kingdom.

(6)   Any action taken under this regulation on grounds of public policy, public security or public health shall be in accordance with regulation 21.

20A.   Cancellation of a right of residence

(1)   Where the conditions in paragraph (2) are met the Secretary of State may cancel a person's right to reside in the United Kingdom pursuant to these Regulations.

(2)   The conditions in this paragraph are met where—

> (a)   a person has a right to reside in the United Kingdom as a result of these Regulations;

> (b)   the Secretary of State has decided that the cancellation of that person's right to reside in the United Kingdom is justified on grounds of public policy, public security or public health in accordance with regulation 21 or on grounds of abuse of rights in accordance with regulation 21B(2);

> (c)   the circumstances are such that the Secretary of State cannot make a decision under regulation 20(1); and

> (d)   it is not possible for the Secretary of State to remove the person from the United Kingdom pursuant to regulation 19(3)(b) or (c).

20B.   Verification of a right of residence

(1)   This regulation applies when the Secretary of State—

    (a)   has reasonable doubt as to whether a person ('A') has a right to reside under regulation 14(1) or (2); or

    (b)   wants to verify the eligibility of a person ('A') to apply for documentation issued under Part 3.

(2)   The Secretary of State may invite A to—

    (a)   provide evidence to support the existence of a right to reside, or to support an application for documentation under Part 3; or

    (b)   attend an interview with the Secretary of State.

(3)   If A purports to be entitled to a right to reside on the basis of a relationship with another person ('B'), the Secretary of State may invite B to—

    (a)   provide information about their relationship with A; or

    (b)   attend an interview with the Secretary of State.

(4)   If, without good reason, A or B fail to provide the additional information requested or, on at least two occasions, fail to attend an interview if so invited, the Secretary of State may draw any factual inferences about A's entitlement to a right to reside as appear appropriate in the circumstances.

(5)   The Secretary of State may decide following an inference under paragraph (4) that A does not have or ceases to have a right to reside.

(6)   But the Secretary of State must not decide that A does not have or ceases to have a right to reside on the sole basis that A failed to comply with this regulation.

(7)   This regulation may not be invoked systematically.

(8)   In this regulation, 'a right to reside' means a right to reside under these Regulations.

21.   Decisions taken on public policy, public security and public health grounds

(1)   In this regulation a 'relevant decision' means an EEA decision taken on the grounds of public policy, public security or public health.

(2)   A relevant decision may not be taken to serve economic ends.

(3)   A relevant decision may not be taken in respect of a person with a permanent right of residence under regulation 15 except on serious grounds of public policy or public security.

(4)   A relevant decision may not be taken except on imperative grounds of public security in respect of an EEA national who—

    (a)   has resided in the United Kingdom for a continuous period of at least ten years prior to the relevant decision; or

    (b)   is under the age of 18, unless the relevant decision is necessary in his best interests, as provided for in the Convention on the Rights of the Child adopted by the General Assembly of the United Nations on 20th November 1989.

(5)   Where a relevant decision is taken on grounds of public policy or public security it shall, in addition to complying with the preceding paragraphs of this regulation, be taken in accordance with the following principles—

    (a)   the decision must comply with the principle of proportionality;

    (b)   the decision must be based exclusively on the personal conduct of the person concerned;

    (c)   the personal conduct of the person concerned must represent a genuine, present and sufficiently serious threat affecting one of the fundamental interests of society;

    (d)   matters isolated from the particulars of the case or which relate to considerations of general prevention do not justify the decision;

    (e)   a person's previous criminal convictions do not in themselves justify the decision.

(6)   Before taking a relevant decision on the grounds of public policy or public security in relation to a person who is resident in the United Kingdom the decision maker must take account of considerations such as the age, state of health, family and economic situation of the person, the person's length of residence in the United Kingdom, the person's social and cultural integration into the United Kingdom and the extent of the person's links with his country of origin.

(7)   In the case of a relevant decision taken on grounds of public health—

    (a)   a disease that does not have epidemic potential as defined by the relevant instruments of the World Health Organisation or is not a disease listed in Schedule 1 to the Health Protection (Notification) Regulations 2010 shall not constitute grounds for the decision; and

(b)   if the person concerned is in the United Kingdom, diseases occurring after the three month period beginning on the date on which he arrived in the United Kingdom shall not constitute grounds for the decision.

21A.   Application of Part 4 to persons with a derivative right of residence

(1)   Where this regulation applies Part 4 of these Regulations applies subject to the modifications listed in paragraph (3).

(2)   This regulation applies where a person—

(a)   would, notwithstanding Part 4 of these Regulations, have a right to be admitted to, or reside in, the United Kingdom by virtue of a derivative right of residence arising under regulation 15A(2), (4), (4A) or (5);

(b)   holds a derivative residence card; or

(c)   has applied for a derivative residence card.

(3)   Where this regulation applies Part 4 applies in relation to the matters listed in paragraph (2) as if—

(a)   references to a matter being justified on grounds of public policy, public security or public health in accordance with regulation 21 referred instead to a matter being 'conducive to the public good';

(b)   the reference in regulation 20(5)(a) to a matter being 'justified on grounds of public policy, public security or public health' referred instead to a matter being 'conducive to the public good';

(c)   references to 'the family member of an EEA national' referred instead to 'a person with a derivative right of residence';

(d)   references to 'a registration certificate, a residence card, a document certifying permanent residence or a permanent residence card' referred instead to 'a derivative residence card';

(e)   the reference in regulation 19(1A) to a deportation or exclusion order referred also to a deportation or exclusion order made under any provision of the immigration Acts.

(f)   regulation 20(4) instead conferred on an immigration officer the power to revoke a derivative residence card where the holder is not at that time a person with a derivative right of residence; and

(g)   regulations 20(3), 20(6) and 21 were omitted.

21B.   Abuse of rights or fraud

(1)   The abuse of a right to reside includes—

(a)   engaging in conduct which appears to be intended to circumvent the requirement to be a qualified person;

(b)   attempting to enter the United Kingdom within 12 months of being removed pursuant to regulation 19(3)(a), where the person attempting to do so is unable to provide evidence that, upon re-entry to the United Kingdom, the conditions for any right to reside, other than the initial right of residence under regulation 13, will be met;

(c)   entering, attempting to enter or assisting another person to enter or attempt to enter, a marriage or civil partnership of convenience; or

(d)   fraudulently obtaining or attempting to obtain, or assisting another to obtain or attempt to obtain, a right to reside.

(2)   The Secretary of State may take an EEA decision on the grounds of abuse of rights where there are reasonable grounds to suspect the abuse of a right to reside and it is proportionate to do so.

(3)   Where these Regulations provide that an EEA decision taken on the grounds of abuse in the preceding twelve months affects a person's right to reside, the person who is the subject of that decision may apply to the Secretary of State to have the effect of that decision set aside on grounds that there has been a material change in the circumstances which justified that decision.

(4)   An application under paragraph (3) may only be made whilst the applicant is outside the United Kingdom.

(5)   This regulation may not be invoked systematically.

(6)   In this regulation, 'a right to reside' means a right to reside under these Regulations.

PART 5

PROCEDURE IN RELATION TO EEA DECISIONS

22. Person claiming right of admission

(1) This regulation applies to a person who claims a right of admission to the United Kingdom under regulation 11 as—

    (a) a person, not being an EEA national, who—

        (i) is a family member of an EEA national;

        (ii) is a family member who has retained the right of residence;

        (iii) has a derivative right of residence;

        (iv) has a permanent right of residence under regulation 15; or

        (v) is in possession of a qualifying EEA State residence card;

    (b) an EEA national, where there is reason to believe that he may fall to be excluded under regulation 19(1), (1A) or (1AB); or

    (c) a person to whom regulation 29AA applies.

(2) A person to whom this regulation applies is to be treated as if he were a person seeking leave to enter the United Kingdom under the 1971 Act for the purposes of paragraphs 2, 3, 4, 7, 16 to 18 and 21 to 24 of Schedule 2 to the 1971 Act (administrative provisions as to control on entry etc), except that—

    (a) the reference in paragraph 2(1) to the purpose for which the immigration officer may examine any persons who have arrived in the United Kingdom is to be read as a reference to the purpose of determining whether he is a person who is to be granted admission under these Regulations;

    (b) the references in paragraphs 4(2A), 7 and 16(1) to a person who is, or may be, given leave to enter are to be read as references to a person who is, or may be, granted admission under these Regulations; and

    (c) a medical examination is not be carried out under paragraph 2 or paragraph 7 as a matter of routine and may only be carried out within three months of a person's arrival in the United Kingdom.

(3) For so long as a person to whom this regulation applies is detained, or temporarily admitted or released while liable to detention, under the powers conferred by Schedule 2 to the 1971 Act, he is deemed not to have been admitted to the United Kingdom.

23. Person refused admission

(1) This regulation applies to a person who is in the United Kingdom and has been refused admission to the United Kingdom—

    (a) because he does not meet the requirement of regulation 11 (including where he does not meet those requirements because his EEA family permit, residence card, derivative residence card or permanent residence card has been revoked by an immigration officer in accordance with regulation 20); or

    (b) in accordance with regulation 19(1), (1A), (1AB) or (2).

(2) A person to whom this regulation applies, is to be treated as if he were a person refused leave to enter under the 1971 Act for the purpose of paragraphs 8, 10, 10A, 11, 16 to 19 and 21 to 24 of Schedule 2 to the 1971 Act, except that the reference in paragraph 19 to a certificate of entitlement, entry clearance or work permit is to be read as a reference to an EEA family permit, residence card, derivative residence card, a qualifying EEA State residence card, or a permanent residence card.

23A. Revocation of admission

(1) This regulation applies to a person admitted to the United Kingdom under regulation 11 in circumstances where, pursuant to regulation 19(1) (exclusion justified on grounds of public policy, public security or public health), (1A) (person subject to deportation order or exclusion order) or (1AB) (reasonable grounds to suspect that admission would lead to the abuse of a right to reside), that person was not entitled to be admitted.

(2) Paragraph 6(2) of Schedule 2 to the 1971 Act (administrative provisions as to control on entry: refusal of leave to enter) applies to a person to whom this regulation applies, as though the references—

    (a) to that person's examination under paragraph 2 of Schedule 2 to the 1971 Act were to that paragraph as applied by regulation 22(2)(a) and (c) of these Regulations;

    (b) to notices of leave to enter the United Kingdom were to a decision to admit that person to the United Kingdom under these Regulations;

(c)   to the cancellation of such a notice and the refusal of leave to enter were to revocation of the decision to admit that person to the United Kingdom under this regulation.

(3)   Where a person's admission to the United Kingdom is revoked, that person is to be treated as a person to whom admission to the United Kingdom has been refused and regulation 23 applies accordingly.

24.   Person subject to removal

(1)   If there are reasonable grounds for suspecting that a person is someone who may be removed from the United Kingdom under regulation 19(3)(b), that person may be detained under the authority of the Secretary of State pending a decision whether or not to remove the person under that regulation, and paragraphs 17 and 18 of Schedule 2 to the 1971 Act shall apply in relation to the detention of such a person as those paragraphs apply in relation to a person who may be detained under paragraph 16 of that Schedule.

(2)   Where a decision is taken to remove a person under regulation 19(3)(a) or (c), the person is to be treated as if he were a person to whom section 10(1)(a) of the 1999 Act applied, and section 10 of that Act (removal of certain persons unlawfully in the United Kingdom) is to apply accordingly.

(3)   Where a decision is taken to remove a person under regulation l9(3)(b), the person is to be treated as if he were a person to whom section 3(5)(a) of the 1971 Act (liability to deportation) applied, and section 5 of that Act (procedure for deportation) and Schedule 3 to that Act (supplementary provision as to deportation) are to apply accordingly.

(4)   A person who enters the United Kingdom in breach of a deportation or exclusion order, or in circumstances where that person was not entitled to be admitted pursuant to regulation 19(1) or (1AB), shall be removable as an illegal entrant under Schedule 2 to the 1971 Act and the provisions of that Schedule shall apply accordingly.

(5)   Where such a deportation order is made against a person but he is not removed under the order during the two year period beginning on the date on which the order is made, the Secretary of State shall only take action to remove the person under the order after the end of that period if, having assessed whether there has been any material change in circumstances since the deportation order was made, he considers that the removal continues to be justified on the grounds of public policy, public security or public health.

(6)   A person to whom this regulation applies shall be allowed one month to leave the United Kingdom, beginning on the date on which he is notified of the decision to remove him, before being removed pursuant to that decision except—

(a)   in duly substantiated cases of urgency;

(b)   where the person is detained pursuant to the sentence or order of any court;

(c)   where a person is a person to whom regulation 24(4) applies.

(7)   Paragraph (6) of this regulation does not apply where a decision has been taken under regulation 19(3) on the basis that the relevant person—

(a)   has ceased to have a derivative right of residence; or

(b)   is a person who would have had a derivative right of residence but for the effect of a decision to remove under regulation 19(3)(b).

24AA.   Human rights considerations and interim orders to suspend removal

(1)   This regulation applies where the Secretary of State intends to give directions for the removal of a person ('P') to whom regulation 24(3) applies, in circumstances where—

(a)   P has not appealed against the EEA decision to which regulation 24(3) applies, but would be entitled, and remains within time, to do so from within the United Kingdom (ignoring any possibility of an appeal out of time with permission); or

(b)   P has so appealed but the appeal has not been finally determined.

(2)   The Secretary of State may only give directions for P's removal if the Secretary of State certifies that, despite the appeals process not having been begun or not having been finally determined, removal of P to the country or territory to which P is proposed to be removed, pending the outcome of P's appeal, would not be unlawful under section 6 of the Human Rights Act 1998 (public authority not to act contrary to Human Rights Convention).

(3)   The grounds upon which the Secretary of State may certify a removal under paragraph (2) include (in particular) that P would not, before the appeal is finally determined, face a real risk of serious irreversible harm if removed to the country or territory to which P is proposed to be removed.

(4)   If P applies to the appropriate court or tribunal (whether by means of judicial review or otherwise) for an interim order to suspend enforcement of the removal decision, P may not be removed from the United Kingdom until such time as the decision on the interim order has been taken, except—

(a)   where the expulsion decision is based on a previous judicial decision;

(b)   where P has had previous access to judicial review; or

(c)   where the removal decision is based on imperative grounds of public security.

(5)   In this regulation, 'finally determined' has the same meaning as in Part 6.

24A. Revocation of deportation and exclusion orders

(1)   A deportation or exclusion order shall remain in force unless it is revoked by the Secretary of State under this regulation.

(2)   A person who is subject to a deportation or exclusion order may apply to the Secretary of State to have it revoked if the person considers that there has been a material change in the circumstances that justified the making of the order.

(3)   An application under paragraph (2) shall set out the material change in circumstances relied upon by the applicant and may only be made whilst the applicant is outside the United Kingdom.

(4)   On receipt of an application under paragraph (2), the Secretary of State shall revoke the order if the Secretary of State considers that the criteria for making such an order are no longer satisfied.

(5)   The Secretary of State shall take a decision on an application under paragraph (2) no later than six months after the date on which the application is received.

PART 6

APPEALS UNDER THESE REGULATIONS

25. Interpretation of Part 6

(1)   In this Part—

'Commission' has the same meaning as in the Special Immigration Appeals Commission Act 1997;

(2)   For the purposes of this Part, and subject to paragraphs (3) and (4), an appeal is to be treated as pending during the period when notice of appeal is given and ending when the appeal is finally determined, withdrawn or abandoned.

(3)   An appeal is not to be treated as finally determined while a further appeal may be brought; and, if such a further appeal is brought, the original appeal is not to be treated as finally determined until the further appeal is determined, withdrawn or abandoned.

(4)   A pending appeal is not to be treated as abandoned solely because the appellant leaves the United Kingdom.

26. Appeal rights

(1)   Subject to the following paragraphs of this regulation, a person may appeal under these Regulations against an EEA decision.

(2)   If a person claims to be an EEA national, he may not appeal under these Regulations unless he produces a valid national identity card or passport issued by an EEA State.

(2A)   If a person claims to be in a durable relationship with an EEA national he may not appeal under these Regulations unless he produces—

(a)   a passport; and

(b)   either—

(i)   an EEA family permit; or

(ii)   sufficient evidence to satisfy the Secretary of State that he is in a relationship with that EEA national.

(3)   If a person to whom paragraph (2) does not apply claims to be a family member who has retained the right of residence or the family member or relative of an EEA national he may not appeal under these Regulations unless he produces—

(a)   a passport; and

(b)   either—

(i)   an EEA family permit;

(ia)   a qualifying EEA State residence card;

(ii)   proof that he is the family member or relative of an EEA national; or

       (iii)   in the case of a person claiming to be a family member who has retained the right of residence, proof that he was a family member of the relevant person.

(3A)   If a person claims to be a person with a derivative right of entry or residence he may not appeal under these Regulations unless he produces a valid national identity card issued by an EEA State or a passport, and either—

    (a)   an EEA family permit; or

    (b)   proof that—

        (i)   where the person claims to have a derivative right of entry or residence as a result of regulation 15A(2), he is a direct relative or guardian of an EEA national who is under the age of 18;

        (ii)   where the person claims to have a derivative right of entry or residence as a result of regulation 15A(3), he is the child of an EEA national;

        (iii)   where the person claims to have a derivative right of entry or residence as a result of regulation 15A(4), he is a direct relative or guardian of the child of an EEA national;

        (iv)   where the person claims to have a derivative right of entry or residence as a result of regulation 15A(5), he is under the age of 18 and is a dependant of a person satisfying the criteria in (i) or (iii);

        (v)   where the person claims to have a derivative right of entry or residence as a result of regulation 15A(4A), he is a direct relative or guardian of a British citizen.

(4)   A person may not bring an appeal under these Regulations on a ground certified under paragraph (5) or rely on such a ground in an appeal brought under these Regulations.

(5)   The Secretary of State or an immigration officer may certify a ground for the purposes of paragraph (4) if it has been considered in a previous appeal brought under these Regulations or under section 82(1) of the 2002 Act.

(6)   Except where an appeal lies to the Commission, an appeal under these Regulations lies to the First-tier Tribunal or Upper Tribunal.

(7)   The provisions of or made under the 2002 Act referred to in Schedule 1 shall have effect for the purposes of an appeal under these Regulations to the First-tier Tribunal or Upper Tribunal in accordance with that Schedule.

(8)   For the avoidance of doubt, nothing in this Part prevents a person who enjoys a right of appeal under this regulation from appealing to the First-tier Tribunal under section 82(1) of the 2002 Act (right of appeal to the Tribunal), or, where relevant, to the Commission pursuant to section 2 of the Special Immigration Appeals Act 1997 (jurisdiction of the Commission: appeals), provided the criteria for bringing such an appeal under those Acts are met.

27.   Out of country appeals

(1)   Subject to paragraphs (2) and (3), a person may not appeal under regulation 26 whilst he is in the United Kingdom against an EEA decision—

    (a)   to refuse to admit him to the United Kingdom;

    (zaa)   to revoke his admission to the United Kingdom;

    (aa)   to make an exclusion order against him;

    (b)   to refuse to revoke a deportation or exclusion order made against him;

    (c)   to refuse to issue him with an EEA family permit;

    (ca)   to revoke, or to refuse to issue or renew any document under these Regulations where that decision is taken at a time when the relevant person is outside the United Kingdom; or

    (d)   to remove him from the United Kingdom after he has entered the United Kingdom in breach of a deportation or exclusion order, or in circumstances where that person was not entitled to be admitted pursuant to regulation 19(1) or (1AB).

(2)   Paragraphs (1)(a) to (aa) do not apply where the person is in the United Kingdom and—

    (a)   the person held a valid EEA family permit, registration certificate, residence card, derivative residence card, document certifying permanent residence, permanent residence card or qualifying EEA State residence card on his arrival in the United Kingdom or can otherwise prove that he is resident in the United Kingdom; or

(b)   the person is deemed not to have been admitted to the United Kingdom under regulation 22(3) but at the date on which notice of the decision to refuse to admit him is given he has been in the United Kingdom for at least 3 months.

28.   Appeals to the Commission

(1)   An appeal against an EEA decision lies to the Commission where paragraph (2) or (4) applies.

(2)   This paragraph applies if the Secretary of State certifies that the EEA decision was taken—

    (a)   by the Secretary of State wholly or partly on a ground listed in paragraph (3); or

    (b)   in accordance with a direction of the Secretary of State which identifies the person to whom the decision relates and which is given wholly or partly on a ground listed in paragraph (3).

(3)   The grounds mentioned in paragraph (2) are that the person's exclusion or removal from the United Kingdom is—

    (a)   in the interests of national security; or

    (b)   in the interests of the relationship between the United Kingdom and another country.

(4)   This paragraph applies if the Secretary of State certifies that the EEA decision was taken wholly or partly in reliance on information which in his opinion should not be made public—

    (a)   in the interests of national security;

    (b)   in the interests of the relationship between the United Kingdom and another country; or

    (c)   otherwise in the public interest.

(5)   In paragraphs (2) and (4) a reference to the Secretary of State is to the Secretary of State acting in person.

(6)   Where a certificate is issued under paragraph (2) or (4) in respect of a pending appeal to the First-tier Tribunal or Upper Tribunal the appeal shall lapse.

(7)   An appeal against an EEA decision lies to the Commission where an appeal lapses by virtue of paragraph (6).

(8)   The Special Immigration Appeals Commission Act 1997 shall apply to an appeal to the Commission under these Regulations as it applies to an appeal under section 2 of that Act to which subsection (2) of that section applies (appeals against an immigration decision) but paragraph (i) of that subsection shall not apply in relation to such an appeal.

28A.   National security: EEA Decisions

(1)   Section 97A(3) of the 2002 Act applies to an appeal against an EEA decision where the Secretary of State has certified under regulation 28(2) or (4) that the EEA decision was taken in the interests of national security.

(2)   Where section 97A so applies, it has effect as if—

    (a)   the references in that section to a deportation order were to an EEA decision;

    (b)   subsections (1), (1A), (2)(b) and (4) were omitted;

    (c)   the reference in subsection (2)(a) to section 79 were a reference to regulations 27(2) and (3) and 29 of these Regulations; and

    (d)   in subsection (2A), for sub-paragraphs (a) and (b), 'against an EEA decision' were substituted.

29.   Effect of appeals to the Asylum and Immigration Tribunal

(1)   This Regulation applies to appeals under these Regulations made to the First-tier Tribunal or Upper Tribunal.

(2)   If a person in the United Kingdom appeals against an EEA decision to refuse to admit him to the United Kingdom (other than a decision under regulation 19(1), (1A) or (1B)), any directions for his removal from the United Kingdom previously given by virtue of the refusal cease to have effect, except in so far as they have already been carried out, and no directions may be so given while the appeal is pending.

(3)   If a person in the United Kingdom appeals against an EEA decision to remove him from the United Kingdom (other than a decision under regulation 19(3)(b)), any directions given under section 10 of the 1999 Act or Schedule 3 to the 1971 Act for his removal from the United Kingdom are to have no effect, except in so far as they have already been carried out, while the appeal is pending.

(4)   But the provisions of Part I of Schedule 2, or as the case may be, Schedule 3 to the 1971 Act with respect to detention and persons liable to detention apply to a person appealing against a refusal to admit him, or a decision to revoke his admission, or a decision to remove him as if there were in force directions

for his removal from the United Kingdom, except that he may not be detained on board a ship or aircraft so as to compel him to leave the United Kingdom while the appeal is pending.

(4A) In paragraph (4), the words 'except that he' to the end do not apply to an EEA decision to which regulation 24AA applies.

(5) In calculating the period of two months limited by paragraph 8(2) of Schedule 2 to the 1971 Act for—

(a) the giving of directions under that paragraph for the removal of a person from the United Kingdom; and

(b) the giving of a notice of intention to give such directions,

any period during which there is pending an appeal by him under is to be disregarded (except in cases where the EEA decision was taken pursuant to regulation 19(1), (1A), (1B) or (3)(b)).

(6) If a person in the United Kingdom appeals against an EEA decision to remove him from the United Kingdom, a deportation order is not to be made against him under section 5 of the 1971 Act while the appeal is pending.

(7) Paragraph 29 of Schedule 2 to the 1971 Act (grant of bail pending appeal) applies to a person who has an appeal pending under these Regulations as it applies to a person who has an appeal pending under section 82(1) of the 2002 Act.

29AA.   Temporary admission in order to submit case in person

(1) This regulation applies where—

(a) a person ('P') was removed from the United Kingdom pursuant to regulation 19(3)(b);

(b) P has appealed against the decision referred to in sub-paragraph (a);

(c) a date for P's appeal has been set by the First Tier Tribunal or Upper Tribunal; and

(d) P wants to make submissions before the First Tier Tribunal or Upper Tribunal in person.

(2) P may apply to the Secretary of State for permission to be temporarily admitted (within the meaning of paragraphs 21 to 24 of Schedule 2 to the 1971 Act, as applied by this regulation) to the United Kingdom in order to make submissions in person.

(3) The Secretary of State must grant P permission, except when P's appearance may cause serious troubles to public policy or public security.

(4) When determining when P is entitled to be given permission, and the duration of P's temporary admission should permission be granted, the Secretary of State must have regard to the dates upon which P will be required to make submissions in person.

(5) Where—

(a) P is temporarily admitted to the United Kingdom pursuant to this regulation;

(b) a hearing of P's appeal has taken place; and

(c) the appeal is not finally determined,

P may be removed from the United Kingdom pending the remaining stages of the redress procedure (but P may apply to return to the United Kingdom to make submissions in person during the remaining stages of the redress procedure in accordance with this regulation).

(6) Where the Secretary of State grants P permission to be temporarily admitted to the United Kingdom under this regulation, upon such admission P is to be treated as if P were a person refused leave to enter under the 1971 Act for the purposes of paragraphs 8, 10, 10A, 11, 16 to 18 and 21 to 24 of Schedule 2(4) to the 1971 Act.

(7) Where Schedule 2 to the 1971 Act so applies, it has effect as if—

(a) the reference in paragraph 8(1) to leave to enter were a reference to admission to the United Kingdom under these Regulations; and

(b) the reference in paragraph 16(1) to detention pending a decision regarding leave to enter or remain in the United Kingdom were to detention pending submission of P's case in person in accordance with this regulation.

(8) P will be deemed not to have been admitted to the United Kingdom during any time during which P is temporarily admitted pursuant to this regulation.

29A.   Alternative evidence of identity and nationality

(1) Subject to paragraph (2), where a provision of these Regulations requires a person to hold or produce a valid identity card issued by an EEA State or a valid passport the Secretary of State may accept

alternative evidence of identity and nationality where the person is unable to obtain or produce the required document due to circumstances beyond his or her control.

(2)   This regulation does not apply to regulation 11.

SCHEDULE 1
APPEALS TO THE FIRST-TIER TRIBUNAL

1.   The following provisions of, or made under, the 2002 Act have effect in relation to an appeal under these Regulations to the First-tier Tribunal as if it were an appeal against a decision of the Secretary of State under section 82(1) of the 2002 Act (right of appeal to the Tribunal)—

section 84 (grounds of appeal), as though the sole permitted ground of appeal were that the decision breaches the appellant's rights under the EU Treaties in respect of entry to or residence in the United Kingdom ('an EU ground of appeal');

section 85 (matters to be considered), as though—

(i)   the references to a statement under section 120 of the 2002 Act include, but are not limited to, a statement under that section as applied by paragraph 4 of Schedule 2 to these Regulations; and

(ii)   a 'matter' in subsection (2) and a 'new matter' in subsection (6) include a ground of appeal of a kind listed in section 84 of the 2002 Act and an EU ground of appeal;

section 86 (determination of appeal);

section 105 and any regulations made under that section; and

section 106 and any rules made under that section.

2.   Tribunal Procedure Rules have effect in relation to appeals under these Regulations.

SCHEDULE 2
EFFECT ON OTHER LEGISLATION

1.   Leave under the 1971 Act

(1)   In accordance with section 7 of the Immigration Act 1988, a person who is admitted to or acquires a right to reside in the United Kingdom under these Regulations shall not require leave to remain in the United Kingdom under the 1971 Act during any period in which he has a right to reside under these Regulations but such a person shall require leave to remain under the 1971 Act during any period in which he does not have such a right.

(2)   Subject to sub-paragraph (3), where a person has leave to enter or remain under the 1971 Act which is subject to conditions and that person also has a right to reside under these Regulations, those conditions shall not have effect for as long as the person has that right to reside.

(3)   Where the person mentioned in sub-paragraph (2) is an accession State national subject to worker authorisation working in the United Kingdom during the accession period and the document endorsed to show that the person has leave is an accession worker authorisation document, any conditions to which that leave is subject restricting his employment shall continue to apply.

(4)   In sub-paragraph (3)—

(a)   'accession period' has the meaning given in regulation 1(2)(c) of the Accession (Immigration and Worker Authorisation) Regulations 2006;

(b)   'accession State national subject to worker authorisation' has the meaning given in regulation 2 of those Regulations; and

(c)   'accession worker authorisation document' has the meaning given in regulation 9(2) of those Regulations.

2.   Persons not subject to restriction on the period for which they may remain

(1)   For the purposes of the 1971 Act and the British Nationality Act 1981, a person who has a permanent right of residence under regulation 15 shall be regarded as a person who is in the United Kingdom without being subject under the immigration laws to any restriction on the period for which he may remain.

(2)   But a qualified person, the family member of a qualified person, a person with a derivative right of residence and a family member who has retained the right of residence shall not, by virtue of that status, be so regarded for those purposes.

3.   Carriers' liability under the 1999 Act

For the purposes of satisfying a requirement to produce a visa under section 40(1)(b) of the 1999 Act (charges in respect of passenger without proper documents), 'a visa of the required kind' includes an EEA family permit, a residence card, a derivative residence card , a qualifying EEA State residence card, permission to be temporarily admitted under regulation 29AA, or a permanent residence card required for admission under regulation 11(2).

4. **Appeals under the 2002 Act and previous immigration Acts**

(1)–(7) ...

(8)   Section 120 of the 2002 Act applies to a person ('P') if an EEA decision has been taken or may be taken in respect of P and, accordingly, the Secretary of State or an immigration officer may by notice require a statement from P under subsection (2) of that section, and that notice has effect for the purpose of section 96(2) of the 2002 Act.

(9)   Where section 120 of the 2002 Act so applies, it has effect as though—

(a)   subsection (3) also provides that a statement under subsection (2) need not repeat reasons or grounds relating to the EEA decision under challenge previously advanced by P; and

(b)   subsection (5) also applies where P does not have a right to reside in the United Kingdom under these Regulations, or only has such a right to reside by virtue of regulation 15B of these Regulations (continuation of a right of residence).

(10)   For the purposes of an appeal brought pursuant to section 82(1) of the 2002 Act, subsections (2) and (6)(a) of section 85 (matters to be considered) have effect as though section 84 included a ground of appeal that the decision appealed against breaches the appellant's rights under the EU Treaties in respect of entry to or residence in the United Kingdom.

Extracts from the European Convention on Human Rights

Article 2 – right to life

1. Everyone's right to life shall be protected by law. No one shall be deprived of his life intentionally save in the execution of a sentence of a court following his conviction of a crime for which this penalty is provided by law.

2. Deprivation of life shall not be regarded as inflicted in contravention of this Article when it results from the use of force which is no more than absolutely necessary:

Article 3 – prohibition of torture

No one shall be subjected to torture or to inhuman or degrading treatment or punishment.

Article 5 – right to liberty and security

1. Everyone has the right to liberty and security of person. No one shall be deprived of his liberty save in the following cases and in accordance with a procedure prescribed by law:

    (a) the lawful detention of a person after conviction by a competent court;

    (b) the lawful arrest or detention of a person for non-compliance with the lawful order of a court or in order to secure the fulfilment of any obligation prescribed by law;

    (c) the lawful arrest or detention of a person effected for the purpose of bringing him before the competent legal authority on reasonable suspicion of having committed an offence or when it is reasonably considered necessary to prevent his committing an offence or fleeing after having done so;

    (d) the detention of a minor by lawful order for the purpose of educational supervision or his lawful detention for the purpose of bringing him before the competent legal authority;

    (e) the lawful detention of persons for the prevention of the spreading of infectious diseases, of persons of unsound mind, alcoholics or drug addicts or vagrants;

    (f) the lawful arrest or detention of a person to prevent his effecting an unauthorised entry into the country or of a person against whom action is being taken with a view to deportation or extradition.

2. Everyone who is arrested shall be informed promptly, in a language which he understands, of the reasons for his arrest and of any charge against him.

3. Everyone arrested or detained in accordance with the provisions of paragraph 1(c) of this Article shall be brought promptly before a judge or other officer authorised by law to exercise judicial power and shall be entitled to trial within a reasonable time or to release pending trial. Release may be conditioned by guarantees to appear for trial.

4. Everyone who is deprived of his liberty by arrest or detention shall be entitled to take proceedings by which the lawfulness of his detention shall be decided speedily by a court and his release ordered if the detention is not lawful.

5. Everyone who has been the victim of arrest or detention in contravention of the provisions of this Article shall have an enforceable right to compensation.

Article 6 – right to a fair trial

1. In the determination of his civil rights and obligations or of any criminal charge against him, everyone is entitled to a fair and public hearing within a reasonable time by an independent and impartial tribunal established by law. Judgment shall be pronounced publicly but the press and public may be excluded from all or part of the trial in the interest of morals, public order or national security in a democratic society, where the interests of juveniles or the protection of the private life of the parties so

require, or to the extent strictly necessary in the opinion of the court in special circumstances where publicity would prejudice the interests of justice.

2. Everyone charged with a criminal offence shall be presumed innocent until proved guilty according to law.

3. Everyone charged with a criminal offence has the following minimum rights:

   (a) to be informed promptly, in a language which he understands and in detail, of the nature and cause of the accusation against him;

   (b) to have adequate time and facilities for the preparation of his defence;

   (c) to defend himself in person or through legal assistance of his own choosing or, if he has not sufficient means to pay for legal assistance, to be given it free when the interests of justice so require;

   (d) to examine or have examined witnesses against him and to obtain the attendance and examination of witnesses on his behalf under the same conditions as witnesses against him;

   (e) to have the free assistance of an interpreter if he cannot understand or speak the language used in court.

Article 8 – right to respect for private and family life

1. Everyone has the right to respect for his private and family life, his home and his correspondence.

2. There shall be no interference by a public authority with the exercise of this right except such as is in accordance with the law and is necessary in a democratic society in the interests of national security, public safety or the economic well-being of the country, for the prevention of disorder or crime, for the protection of health or morals, or for the protection of the rights and freedoms of others.

Article 9 – freedom of thought, conscience and religion

1. Everyone has the right to freedom of thought, conscience and religion; this right includes freedom to change his religion or belief and freedom, either alone or in community with others and in public or private, to manifest his religion or belief, in worship, teaching, practice and observance.

2. Freedom to manifest one's religion or beliefs shall be subject only to such limitations as are prescribed by law and are necessary in a democratic society in the interests of public safety, for the protection of public order, health or morals, or for the protection of the rights and freedoms of others.

Article 10 – freedom of expression

1. Everyone has the right to freedom of expression. This right shall include freedom to hold opinions and to receive and impart information and ideas without interference by public authority and regardless of frontiers. This Article shall not prevent States from requiring the licensing of broadcasting, television or cinema enterprises.

2. The exercise of these freedoms, since it carries with it duties and responsibilities, may be subject to such formalities, conditions, restrictions or penalties as are prescribed by law and are necessary in a democratic society, in the interests of national security, territorial integrity or public safety, for the prevention of disorder or crime, for the protection of health or morals, for the protection of the reputation or rights of others, for preventing the disclosure of information received in confidence, or for maintaining the authority and impartiality of the judiciary.

Article 11 – freedom of assembly and association

1. Everyone has the right to freedom of peaceful assembly and to freedom of association with others, including the right to form and to join trade unions for the protection of his interests.

2. No restrictions shall be placed on the exercise of these rights other than such as are prescribed by law and are necessary in a democratic society in the interests of national security or public safety, for the prevention of disorder or crime, for the protection of health or morals or for the protection of the rights and freedoms of others. This Article shall not prevent the imposition of lawful restrictions on the exercise of these rights by members of the armed forces, of the police or of the administration of the State.

Article 12 – right to marry

Men and women of marriageable age have the right to marry and to found a family, according to the national laws governing the exercise of this right.

Article 14 – prohibition of discrimination

The enjoyment of the rights and freedoms set forth in this Convention shall be secured without discrimination on any ground such as sex, race, colour, language, religion, political or other opinion, national or social origin, association with a national minority, property, birth or other status.

The First Protocol, Article 1 – protection of property

Every natural or legal person is entitled to the peaceful enjoyment of his possessions. No one shall be deprived of his possessions except in the public interest and subject to the conditions provided for by law and by the general principles of international law.

The preceding provisions shall not, however, in any way impair the right of a State to enforce such laws as it deems necessary to control the use of property in accordance with the general interest or to secure the payment of taxes or other contributions or penalties.

British Citizenship: A Summary

The BNA 1981 sets out some basic rules for determining who is a British citizen. The following series of questions can be used to work out if a person may be a British citizen. However, remember that nationality law can be complex, and you will not always be able to work out if a person is a British citizen or not without detailed research of the law and facts.

Q1. When was the person born?

    (a)   Before [1st January] 1983: go to Q2.

    (b)   After [31st December] 1982: go to Q9.

Q2. Where was the person born?

    (a)   In the UK: he is a British citizen otherwise than by descent (see **2.2.1**).

    (b)   Outside the UK: go to Q3.

Q3. Was the person's father born [or registered/naturalised before he was born] in the UK?

    (a)   Yes: go to Q4.

    (b)   No: go to Q5.

Q4. Was the person's father married to their mother? [If after the child's birth, did that marriage legitimise the child?]

    (a)   Yes: he is a British citizen by descent (see **2.2.2**).

    (b)   No: go to Q5.

Q5. Was the person's mother born [or registered/naturalised before he was born] in the UK?

    (a)   Yes: go to Q6.

    (b)   No: go to Q7.

Q6. Did the person's mother register him as a British citizen?

    (a)   Yes: he is a British citizen by descent (see **2.2.6.2**).

    (b)   No: go to Q7.

Q7. Has the person registered as a British citizen?

    (a)   Yes: he is a British citizen by descent (see **2.2.6.2**).

    (b)   No: go to Q8.

Q8. Has the person naturalised in the UK as a British citizen?

    (a)   Yes: he is a British citizen otherwise than by descent (see **2.2.7**).

    (b)   No: he is not a British citizen under these rules but a detailed analysis of law and facts is required.

Q9. Was the person born in the UK?

    (a)   Yes: go to Q10.

    (b)   No: go to Q13.

Q10. Was either of the person's parents a British citizen or settled in the UK when he was born?

    (a)   Yes: he is a British citizen otherwise than by descent (see **2.2.3**).

    (b)   No: go to Q11.

Q11. Did either of the person's parents subsequently become a British citizen or settled in the UK?

    (a)   Yes: he can apply to register as a British citizen otherwise than by descent (see **2.2.6.1**).

    (b)   No: go to Q12.

Q12. Has the person remained in the UK for the first 10 years of his life and not been absent for more than 90 days?

(a)   Yes: he is a British citizen otherwise than by descent (see **2.2.6.1**).

(b)   No: he is not a British citizen under these rules but a detailed analysis of law and facts is required.

Q13. Was one of the person's parents a British citizen otherwise than by birth, registration or naturalisation in the UK before he was born?

(a)   Yes: he is a British citizen by descent (see **2.2.4**).

(b)   No: he is not a British citizen under these rules but a detailed analysis of the law and facts is required.

Note 1: a parent in this context includes the father of an illegitimate child born before or after 1 July 2006 if certain conditions are met (see **2.2.3** and **2.2.4**).

Note 2: as to second generation children born outside UK, see **2.2.5**.

Naturalisation: A Summary

The following series of questions can be used to work out if a person may be eligible to apply for naturalisation as a British citizen.

Q1.   Is the person settled in the UK (this includes an EEA national who has permanent residence in the UK)?

  (a)   Yes: go to Q2.

  (b)   No: ineligible.

Q2.   Is the person married to a British citizen or in a civil partnership with a British citizen?

  (a)   Yes: go to Q3.

  (b)   No: go to Q7.

Q3.   Has the person been living in the UK legally for three years continuously before making the application?

  (a)   Yes: go to Q4.

  (b)   No: ineligible.

Q4.   Has the person been absent for less than 270 days in total and not more than 90 days in the year immediately before the application?

  (a)   Yes: go to Q5.

  (b)   No: ineligible but check Home Office policy.

Q5.   Can the person produce written evidence to show sufficient knowledge of English (Welsh or Scottish Gaelic) and Life in the UK?

  (a)   Yes: go to Q6.

  (b)   No: ineligible but check to see if Home Office might waive this requirement.

Q6.   Can the person show good character?

  (a)   Yes: may be granted naturalisation as a British citizen at discretion of Home Secretary.

  (b)   No: application will be refused.

Q7.   Has the person been settled in the UK (this includes an EEA national who has permanent residence in the UK) for at least one year before making the application?

  (a)   Yes: go to Q8.

  (b)   No: ineligible.

Q8.   Has the person been living in the UK legally for five years continuously before making the application?

  (a)   Yes: go to Q9.

  (b)   No: ineligible.

Q9.   Has the person been absent for less than 450 days in total and not more than 90 days in the year immediately before the application?

  (a)   Yes: go to Q10.

  (b)   No: ineligible but check Home Office policy.

Q10. Can the person produce written evidence to show sufficient knowledge of English (Welsh or Scottish Gaelic) and Life in the UK?

  (a)   Yes: go to Q11.

  (b)   No: ineligible but check to see if Home Office might waive this requirement.

Q11. Can the person show good character?

  (a)   Yes: go to Q12.

  (b)   No: application will be refused.

Q12. Can the person show an intention to live in the UK?

    (a)   Yes: may be granted naturalisation as a British citizen at discretion of Home Secretary.

    (b)   No: application will be refused.

Criminality under the Immigration Rules

Criminality grounds on which entry clearance or leave to enter the UK will be refused under the Immigration Rules

A. By paragraph 320(2) a person seeking entry to the UK will be refused if he:

   (a) is currently the subject of a deportation order; or

   (b) has been convicted of an offence for which he has been sentenced to a period of imprisonment of at least 4 years; or

   (c) has been convicted of an offence for which he has been sentenced to a period of imprisonment of at least 12 months but less than 4 years, unless a period of 10 years has passed since the end of the sentence; or

   (d) has been convicted of an offence for which he has been sentenced to a period of imprisonment of less than 12 months, unless a period of 5 years has passed since the end of the sentence.

   Where this paragraph applies, unless refusal would be contrary to the Human Rights Convention or the Convention and Protocol Relating to the Status of Refugees, it will only be in exceptional circumstances that the public interest in maintaining refusal will be outweighed by compelling factors.

B. By paragraph 320(7B)(vii) a person who left or was removed from the UK as a condition of a caution issued in accordance with s134 Legal Aid, Sentencing and Punishment of Offenders Act 2012 will be refused entry clearance or leave to enter unless a period of 5 years has passed since he left or was removed.

Criminality grounds on which entry clearance or leave to enter the UK is normally refused

A. By paragraph 320(18A) a person seeking entry to the UK will normally be refused if within the 12 months preceding the date of the application he has been convicted of or admitted an offence for which he received a non-custodial sentence or other out of court disposal that is recorded on his criminal record.

B. By paragraph 320(18B) a person seeking entry to the UK will normally be refused if in the view of the Secretary of State: (a) his offending has caused serious harm; or (b) he is a persistent offender who shows a particular disregard for the law.

C. By paragraph 320(19) a person seeking entry to the UK will normally be refused if the immigration officer deems their exclusion from the UK to be conducive to the public good. For example, because the person's conduct (including convictions which do not fall within paragraph 320(2)), character, associations, or other reasons, make it undesirable to grant them leave to enter.

Criminality grounds on which leave to remain and variation of leave to enter or remain in the UK will be refused

A. By paragraph 322(1B) an applicant will be refused if, at the date of application, he is the subject of a deportation order or a decision to make a deportation order;

B. By paragraph 322(1C) where the person is seeking indefinite leave to enter or remain the application will be refused if:

   (i) he has been convicted of an offence for which he has been sentenced to imprisonment for at least 4 years; or

   (ii) he has been convicted of an offence for which he has been sentenced to imprisonment for at least 12 months but less than 4 years, unless a period of 15 years has passed since the end of the sentence; or

   (iii) he has been convicted of an offence for which he has been sentenced to imprisonment for less than 12 months, unless a period of 7 years has passed since the end of the sentence; or

   (iv) he has, within the 24 months preceding the date of the application, been convicted of or admitted an offence for which he has received a non-custodial sentence or other out of court disposal that is recorded on their criminal record.

Criminality grounds on which leave to remain and variation of leave to enter or remain in the UK is normally refused

By paragraph 322(5A) that it is undesirable to permit the person concerned to enter or remain in the UK because, in the view of the Secretary of State (a) his offending has caused serious harm; or (b) he is a persistent offender who shows a particular disregard for the law.

APPENDIX 9

Commonwealth Citizens

Citizens of the following countries are currently Commonwealth citizens according to Sch 3 to the British Nationality Act 1981 (as amended).

Antigua and Barbuda	Mozambique
Australia	Namibia
The Bahamas	Nauru
Bangladesh	New Zealand
Barbados	Nigeria
Belize	Pakistan
Botswana	Papua New Guinea
Brunei	Saint Christopher and Nevis
Cameroon	Saint Lucia
Canada	Saint Vincent and the Grenadines
Republic of Cyprus	Seychelles
Dominica	Sierra Leone
Fiji	Singapore
The Gambia	Solomon Islands
Ghana	South Africa
Grenada	Sri Lanka
Guyana	Swaziland
India	Tanzania
Jamaica	Tonga
Kenya	Trinidad and Tobago
Kiribati	Tuvalu
Lesotho	Uganda
Malawi	Vanuatu
Malaysia	Western Samoa
Maldives	Zambia
Malta	Zimbabwe
Mauritius	

Note that British citizens, and some other categories of British Nationals (including British dependent territories citizens and British overseas citizens) are Commonwealth citizens by virtue of s 37 of the 1981 Act.

It is important to note that as Cameroon, Mozambique, Namibia, Pakistan and South Africa were not members of the Commonwealth on 31 December 1982, then nationals of those countries cannot take advantage of the provisions dealt with at **2.3**.

Commonwealth Citizen with Right of Abode: A Summary

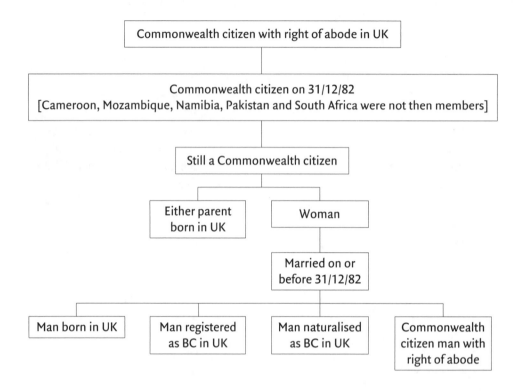

APPENDIX 11

British Overseas Territories

The following are currently British Overseas Territories according to Sch 6 to the British Nationality Act 1981 (as amended).

Anguilla

Bermuda

British Antarctic Territory

British Indian Ocean Territory

Cayman Islands

Gibraltar

Montserrat

Pitcairn, Henderson, Ducie and Oeno Islands

St Helena and Dependencies

South Georgia

South Sandwich Islands

The Sovereign Base Areas of Akrotiri and Dhekelia

Turks and Caicos Islands

Virgin Islands

Note that people from the Falkland Islands were made into full British citizens under the British Nationality (Falkland Islands) Act 1983.

Tier 1 Entrepreneur: Overview

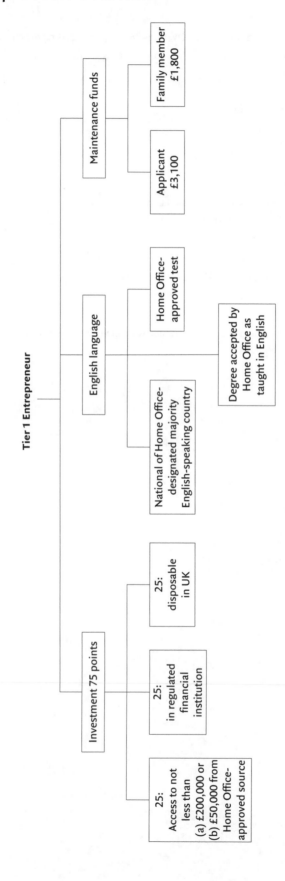

Home Office Definition of Common Ownership or Control

The Home Office states that common ownership or control may be defined as follows:

- one entity controls the composition of the other entity's board; or
- one entity is in a position to cast, or control the casting of, more than half the maximum number of votes that might be cast at a general meeting of the other entity; or
- one entity holds more than half the issued share capital of the other entity (excluding any part of that issued share capital that carries no right to participate beyond a specified amount in a distribution of either profits or capital); or
- both entities have a common parent entity that itself or through other entities meets one of the requirements of the first three bullet points above in relation to both entities that are the subject of the intra-company transfer; or
- one entity is related to the other entity as both entities are party to a joint venture agreement; or
- one entity is related to the other entity in that one entity is party to a joint venture agreement and the other entity is the entity formed by that joint venture agreement; or
- one entity is related to the other entity by agreement that would constitute a joint venture agreement other than for the fact that joint venture agreements are not permitted in the country of operation or one of the entities is not permitted to enter into joint ventures in the country of operation; or
- one entity is related to the other entity in that one entity is party to an agreement that would constitute a joint venture agreement other than for the fact that joint venture agreements are not permitted in the country of operation or that entity is not permitted to enter into joint ventures in the country of operation and the other entity is the entity formed by that agreement; or
- where both entities are either accountancy or law firms, one entity is related to the other entity by agreement which allows both entities to use a trademark which is registered or established under the laws of the United Kingdom and the jurisdiction of the other entity's country of operation; or
- where both entities are either accountancy or law firms, one entity is related to the other entity by agreement which allows both entities to operate under the same name in the United Kingdom and in the jurisdiction of the other entity's country of operation; or
- in the case of unincorporated associations, the receiving entity is a linked company if it is a registered company and its Articles of Association with the sending entity indicate a relationship of control (for example, one Member has the power to appoint the other's trustees).

Refugee or Person in Need of International Protection (Qualification) Regulations 2006

SI 2006/2525

1.　　Citation and commencement

　　(1)　　These Regulations may be cited as The Refugee or Person in Need of International Protection (Qualification) Regulations 2006 and shall come into force on 9th October 2006.

　　(2)　　These Regulations apply to any application for asylum which has not been decided and any immigration appeal brought under the Immigration Acts (as defined in section 64(2) of the Immigration, Asylum and Nationality Act 2006) which has not been finally determined.

2.　　Interpretation

In these Regulations—

'application for asylum' means the request of a person to be recognised as a refugee under the Geneva Convention;

'Geneva Convention' means the Convention Relating to the Status of Refugees done at Geneva on 28 July 1951 and the New York Protocol of 31 January 1967;

'immigration rules' means rules made under section 3(2) of the Immigration Act 1971;

'persecution' means an act of persecution within the meaning of Article 1(A) of the Geneva Convention;

'person eligible for humanitarian protection' means a person who is eligible for a grant of humanitarian protection under the immigration rules;

'refugee' means a person who falls within Article 1(A) of the Geneva Convention and to whom regulation 7 does not apply;

'residence permit' means a document confirming that a person has leave to enter or remain in the United Kingdom whether limited or indefinite;

'serious harm' means serious harm as defined in the immigration rules;

'person' means any person who is not a British citizen.

3.　　Actors of persecution or serious harm

In deciding whether a person is a refugee or a person eligible for humanitarian protection, persecution or serious harm can be committed by:

　　(a)　　the State;

　　(b)　　any party or organisation controlling the State or a substantial part of the territory of the State;

　　(c)　　any non-State actor if it can be demonstrated that the actors mentioned in paragraphs (a) and (b), including any international organisation, are unable or unwilling to provide protection against persecution or serious harm.

4.　　Actors of protection

　　(1)　　In deciding whether a person is a refugee or a person eligible for humanitarian protection, protection from persecution or serious harm can be provided by:

　　　　(a)　　the State; or

　　　　(b)　　any party or organisation, including any international organisation, controlling the State or a substantial part of the territory of the State.

　　(2)　　Protection shall be regarded as generally provided when the actors mentioned in paragraph (1)(a) and (b) take reasonable steps to prevent the persecution or suffering of serious harm by operating an effective legal system for the detection, prosecution and punishment of acts constituting persecution or serious harm, and the person mentioned in paragraph (1) has access to such protection.

(3)   In deciding whether a person is a refugee or a person eligible for humanitarian protection the Secretary of State may assess whether an international organisation controls a State or a substantial part of its territory and provides protection as described in paragraph (2).

5.   Act of persecution

(1)   In deciding whether a person is a refugee an act of persecution must be:

(a)   sufficiently serious by its nature or repetition as to constitute a severe violation of a basic human right, in particular a right from which derogation cannot be made under Article 15 of the Convention for the Protection of Human Rights and Fundamental Freedoms; or

(b)   an accumulation of various measures, including a violation of a human right which is sufficiently severe as to affect an individual in a similar manner as specified in (a).

(2)   An act of persecution may, for example, take the form of:

(a)   an act of physical or mental violence, including an act of sexual violence;

(b)   a legal, administrative, police, or judicial measure which in itself is discriminatory or which is implemented in a discriminatory manner;

(c)   prosecution or punishment, which is disproportionate or discriminatory;

(d)   denial of judicial redress resulting in a disproportionate or discriminatory punishment;

(e)   prosecution or punishment for refusal to perform military service in a conflict, where performing military service would include crimes or acts falling under regulation 7.

(3)   An act of persecution must be committed for at least one of the reasons in Article 1(A) of the Geneva Convention.

6.   Reasons for persecution

(1)   In deciding whether a person is a refugee:

(a)   the concept of race shall include consideration of, for example, colour, descent, or membership of a particular ethnic group;

(b)   the concept of religion shall include, for example, the holding of theistic, non-theistic and atheistic beliefs, the participation in, or abstention from, formal worship in private or in public, either alone or in community with others, other religious acts or expressions of view, or forms of personal or communal conduct based on or mandated by any religious belief;

(c)   the concept of nationality shall not be confined to citizenship or lack thereof but shall include, for example, membership of a group determined by its cultural, ethnic, or linguistic identity, common geographical or political origins or its relationship with the population of another State;

(d)   a group shall be considered to form a particular social group where, for example:

(i)   members of that group share an innate characteristic, or a common background that cannot be changed, or share a characteristic or belief that is so fundamental to identity or conscience that a person should not be forced to renounce it, and

(ii)   that group has a distinct identity in the relevant country, because it is perceived as being different by the surrounding society;

(e)   a particular social group might include a group based on a common characteristic of sexual orientation but sexual orientation cannot be understood to include acts considered to be criminal in accordance with national law of the United Kingdom;

(f)   the concept of political opinion shall include the holding of an opinion, thought or belief on a matter related to the potential actors of persecution mentioned in regulation 3 and to their policies or methods, whether or not that opinion, thought or belief has been acted upon by the person.

(2)   In deciding whether a person has a well-founded fear of being persecuted, it is immaterial whether he actually possesses the racial, religious, national, social or political characteristic which attracts the persecution, provided that such a characteristic is attributed to him by the actor of persecution.

7.   Exclusion

(1)   A person is not a refugee, if he falls within the scope of Article 1D, 1E or 1F of the Geneva Convention.

(2)   In the construction and application of Article 1F(b) of the Geneva Convention:

(a)   the reference to serious non-political crime includes a particularly cruel action, even if it is committed with an allegedly political objective;

(b)   the reference to the crime being committed outside the country of refuge prior to his admission as a refugee shall be taken to mean the time up to and including the day on which a residence permit is issued.

(3)   Article 1F(a) and (b) of the Geneva Convention shall apply to a person who instigates or otherwise participates in the commission of the crimes or acts specified in those provisions.

___

Pre-Action Protocol for Judicial Review

INTRODUCTION

1. This Protocol applies to proceedings within England and Wales only. It does not affect the time limit specified by Rule 54.5(1) of the Civil Procedure Rules (CPR), which requires that any claim form in an application for judicial review must be filed promptly and in any event not later than 3 months after the grounds to make the claim first arose. Nor does it affect the shorter time limits specified by Rules 54.5(5) and (6), which set out that a claim form for certain planning judicial reviews must be filed within 6 weeks and the claim form for certain procurement judicial reviews must be filed within 30 days.[1]

2. This Protocol sets out a code of good practice and contains the steps which parties should generally follow before making a claim for judicial review.

3. The aims of the protocol are to enable parties to prospective claims to—

    (a) understand and properly identify the issues in dispute in the proposed claim and share information and relevant documents;

    (b) make informed decisions as to whether and how to proceed;

    (c) try to settle the dispute without proceedings or reduce the issues in dispute;

    (d) avoid unnecessary expense and keep down the costs of resolving the dispute; and

    (e) support the efficient management of proceedings where litigation cannot be avoided.

4. Judicial review allows people with a sufficient interest in a decision or action by a public body to ask a judge to review the lawfulness of—

    • an enactment; or

    • a decision, action or failure to act in relation to the exercise of a public function.[2]

5. Judicial review should only be used where no adequate alternative remedy, such as a right of appeal, is available. Even then, judicial review may not be appropriate in every instance. Claimants are strongly advised to seek appropriate legal advice as soon as possible when considering proceedings. Although the Legal Aid Agency will not normally grant full representation before a letter before claim has been sent and the proposed defendant given a reasonable time to respond, initial funding may be available, for eligible claimants, to cover the work necessary to write this. (See Annex C for more information.)

6. This protocol will not be appropriate in very urgent cases. In this sort of case, a claim should be made immediately. Examples are where directions have been set for the claimant's removal from the UK or where there is an urgent need for an interim order to compel a public body to act where it has unlawfully refused to do so, such as where a local housing authority fails to secure interim accommodation for a homeless claimant. A letter before claim, and a claim itself, will not stop the implementation of a disputed decision, though a proposed defendant may agree to take no action until its response letter has been provided. In other cases, the claimant may need to apply to the court for an urgent interim order. Even in very urgent cases, it is good practice to alert the defendant by telephone and to send by email (or fax) to the defendant the draft Claim Form which the claimant intends to issue. A claimant is also normally required to notify a defendant when an interim order is being sought.

7. All claimants will need to satisfy themselves whether they should follow the protocol, depending upon the circumstances of the case. Where the use of the protocol is appropriate, the court will normally expect all parties to have complied with it in good time before proceedings are issued and will take into account compliance or non-compliance when giving directions for case management of proceedings or when making orders for costs.[3]

8. The Upper Tribunal Immigration and Asylum Chamber (UTIAC) has jurisdiction in respect of judicial review proceedings in relation to most immigration decisions.[4] The President of UTIAC has issued a Practice Statement to the effect that, in judicial review proceedings in UTIAC, the parties will be expected to follow this protocol, where appropriate, as they would for proceedings in the High Court.

Alternative Dispute Resolution

9. The courts take the view that litigation should be a last resort. The parties should consider whether some form of alternative dispute resolution ('ADR') or complaints procedure would be more suitable than litigation, and if so, endeavour to agree which to adopt. Both the claimant and defendant may be required by the court to provide evidence that alternative means of resolving their dispute were considered. Parties are warned that if the protocol is not followed (including this paragraph) then the court must have regard to such conduct when determining costs. However, parties should also note that a claim for judicial review should comply with the time limits set out in the Introduction above. Exploring ADR may not excuse failure to comply with the time limits. If it is appropriate to issue a claim to ensure compliance with a time limit, but the parties agree there should be a stay of proceedings to explore settlement or narrowing the issues in dispute, a joint application for appropriate directions can be made to the court.

10. It is not practicable in this protocol to address in detail how the parties might decide which method to adopt to resolve their particular dispute. However, summarised below are some of the options for resolving disputes without litigation which may be appropriate, depending on the circumstances—

    • Discussion and negotiation.

    • Using relevant public authority complaints or review procedures.

    • Ombudsmen – the Parliamentary and Health Service and the Local Government Ombudsmen have discretion to deal with complaints relating to maladministration. The British and Irish Ombudsman Association provide information about Ombudsman schemes and other complaint handling bodies and this is available from their website at www.bioa.org.uk. Parties may wish to note that the Ombudsmen are not able to look into a complaint once court action has been commenced.

    • Mediation – a form of facilitated negotiation assisted by an independent neutral party.

11. The Civil Justice Council and Judicial College have endorsed The Jackson ADR Handbook by Susan Blake, Julie Browne and Stuart Sime (2013, Oxford University Press). The Citizens Advice Bureaux website also provides information about ADR: http://www.ad viceguide.org.uk/england/law_e/law_legal_system_e/law_taking_legal_action_e/alternatives_to_court.htm.

    Information is also available at: http://www.civilmediation.justice.gov.uk/

12. If proceedings are issued, the parties may be required by the court to provide evidence that ADR has been considered. A party's silence in response to an invitation to participate in ADR or refusal to participate in ADR might be considered unreasonable by the court and could lead to the court ordering that party to pay additional court costs.

Requests for information and documents at the pre-action stage

13. Requests for information and documents made at the pre-action stage should be proportionate and should be limited to what is properly necessary for the claimant to understand why the challenged decision has been taken and/or to present the claim in a manner that will properly identify the issues. The defendant should comply with any request which meets these requirements unless there is good reason for it not to do so. Where the court considers that a public body should have provided relevant documents and/or information, particularly where this failure is a breach of a statutory or common law requirement, it may impose costs sanctions.

The letter before claim

14. In good time before making a claim, the claimant should send a letter to the defendant. The purpose of this letter is to identify the issues in dispute and establish whether they can be narrowed or litigation can be avoided.

15. Claimants should normally use the suggested standard format for the letter outlined at Annex A. For Immigration, Nationality and Asylum cases, the Home Office has a standardised form which can be used. It can be found online at: https://www.gov.uk/government/publications/chapter-27-judicial-review-guidance-part-1

16. The letter should contain the date and details of the decision, act or omission being challenged, a clear summary of the facts and the legal basis for the claim. It should also contain the details of any information that the claimant is seeking and an explanation of why this is considered relevant. If the claim is considered to be an Aarhus Convention claim (see Rules 45.41 to 45.44 and Practice Direction 45), the letter should state this clearly and explain the reasons, since specific rules as to costs apply to such claims. If the claim is

considered appropriate for allocation to the Planning Court and/or for classification as "significant" within that court, the letter should state this clearly and explain the reasons.

17. The letter should normally contain the details of any person known to the claimant who is an Interested Party. An Interested Party is any person directly affected by the claim.[5] They should be sent a copy of the letter before claim for information. Claimants are strongly advised to seek appropriate legal advice when considering proceedings which involve an Interested Party and, in particular, before sending the letter before claim to an Interested Party or making a claim.

18. A claim should not normally be made until the proposed reply date given in the letter before the claim has passed, unless the circumstances of the case require more immediate action to be taken. The claimant should send the letter before claim in good time so as to enable a response which can then be taken into account before the time limit for issuing the claim expires, unless there are good reasons why this is not possible.

19. Any claimant intending to ask for a protective costs order (an order that the claimant will not be liable for the costs of the defendant or any other party or to limit such liability) should explain the reasons for making the request, including an explanation of the limit of the financial resources available to the claimant in making the claim.

The letter of response

20. Defendants should normally respond within 14 days using the standard format at Annex B. Failure to do so will be taken into account by the court and sanctions may be imposed unless there are good reasons.[6] Where the claimant is a litigant in person, the defendant should enclose a copy of this Protocol with its letter.

21. Where it is not possible to reply within the proposed time limit, the defendant should send an interim reply and propose a reasonable extension, giving a date by which the defendant expects to respond substantively. Where an extension is sought, reasons should be given and, where required, additional information requested. This will not affect the time limit for making a claim for judicial review[7] nor will it bind the claimant where he or she considers this to be unreasonable. However, where the court considers that a subsequent claim is made prematurely it may impose sanctions.

22. If the claim is being conceded in full, the reply should say so in clear and unambiguous terms.

23. If the claim is being conceded in part or not being conceded at all, the reply should say so in clear and unambiguous terms, and—

   (a) where appropriate, contain a new decision, clearly identifying what aspects of the claim are being conceded and what are not, or, give a clear timescale within which the new decision will be issued;

   (b) provide a fuller explanation for the decision, if considered appropriate to do so;

   (c) address any points of dispute, or explain why they cannot be addressed;

   (d) enclose any relevant documentation requested by the claimant, or explain why the documents are not being enclosed;

   (e) where documents cannot be provided within the time scales required, then give a clear timescale for provision. The claimant should avoid making any formal application for the provision of documentation/information during this period unless there are good grounds to show that the timescale proposed is unreasonable;

   (f) where appropriate, confirm whether or not they will oppose any application for an interim remedy; and

   (g) if the claimant has stated an intention to ask for a protective costs order, the defendant's response to this should be explained.

   If the letter before claim has stated that the claim is an Aarhus Convention claim but the defendant does not accept this, the reply should state this clearly and explain the reasons. If the letter before claim has stated that the claim is suitable for the Planning Court and/or categorisation as "significant" within that court but the defendant does not accept this, the reply should state this clearly and explain the reasons.

24. The response should be sent to all Interested Parties 8 identified by the claimant and contain details of any other persons who the defendant considers are Interested Parties.

ANNEX A

Letter before claim

Section 1. Information required in a letter before claim

1 Proposed claim for judicial review

To

(Insert the name and address of the proposed defendant – see details in section 2.)

2 The claimant

(Insert the title, first and last name and the address of the claimant.)

3 The defendant's reference details

(When dealing with large organisations it is important to understand that the information relating to any particular individual's previous dealings with it may not be immediately available, therefore it is important to set out the relevant reference numbers for the matter in dispute and/or the identity of those within the public body who have been handling the particular matter in dispute – see details in section 3.)

4 The details of the claimants' legal advisers, if any, dealing with this claim

(Set out the name, address and reference details of any legal advisers dealing with the claim.)

5 The details of the matter being challenged

(Set out clearly the matter being challenged, particularly if there has been more than one decision.)

6 The details of any Interested Parties

(Set out the details of any Interested Parties and confirm that they have been sent a copy of this letter.)

7 The issue

(Set out a brief summary of the facts and relevant legal principles, the date and details of the decision, or act or omission being challenged, and why it is contended to be wrong.)

8 The details of the action that the defendant is expected to take

(Set out the details of the remedy sought, including whether a review or any interim remedy are being requested.)

9 ADR proposals

(Set out any proposals the claimant is making to resolve or narrow the dispute by ADR.)

10 The details of any information sought

(Set out the details of any information that is sought which is related to identifiable issues in dispute so as to enable the parties to resolve or reduce those issues. This may include a request for a fuller explanation of the reasons for the decision that is being challenged.)

11 The details of any documents that are considered relevant and necessary

(Set out the details of any documentation or policy in respect of which the disclosure is sought and explain why these are relevant.)

12 The address for reply and service of court documents

(Insert the address for the reply.)

13 Proposed reply date

(The precise time will depend upon the circumstances of the individual case. However, although a shorter or longer time may be appropriate in a particular case, 14 days is a reasonable time to allow in most circumstances.)

Section 2. Address for sending the letter before claim

Public bodies have requested that, for certain types of cases, in order to ensure a prompt response, letters before claim should be sent to specific addresses.

- Where the claim concerns a decision in an Immigration, Asylum or Nationality case (including in relation to an immigration decision taken abroad by an Entry Clearance Officer)— The claim should be sent electronically to the following Home Office email address: UKVIPAP@homeoffice.gsi.gov.uk

Alternatively the claim may be sent by post to the following Home Office postal address:

Litigation Operations Allocation Hub

Status Park 2

4 Nobel Drive
Harlington
Hayes
Middlesex UB3 5EY

The Home Office has a standardised form which claimants may find helpful to use for communications with the Home Office in Immigration, Asylum or Nationality cases pursuant to this Protocol, to assist claimants to include all relevant information and to promote speedier review and response by the Home Office. The Home Office form may be filled out in electronic or hard copy format. It can be found online at: https://www.gov.uk/government/publications/chapter-27-judicial-review-guidance-part-1

- Where the claim concerns a decision by the Legal Aid Agency—

  The address on the decision letter/notification;
  Legal Director
  Corporate Legal Team
  Legal Aid Agency
  102 Petty France
  London SW1H 9AJ

- Where the claim concerns a decision by a local authority—

  The address on the decision letter/notification; and
  their legal department[9]

- Where the claim concerns a decision by a department or body for whom Treasury Solicitor acts and Treasury Solicitor has already been involved in the case a copy should also be sent, quoting the Treasury Solicitor's reference, to—

  The Treasury Solicitor,
  One Kemble Street,
  London WC2B 4TS

In all other circumstances, the letter should be sent to the address on the letter notifying the decision.

Section 3. Specific reference details required

Public bodies have requested that the following information should be provided, if at all possible, in order to ensure prompt response. Where the claim concerns an Immigration, Asylum or Nationality case, dependent upon the nature of the case—

- The Home Office reference number;
- The Port reference number;
- The Asylum and Immigration Tribunal reference number;
- The National Asylum Support Service reference number; or, if these are unavailable:
- The full name, nationality and date of birth of the claimant.

Where the claim concerns a decision by the Legal Aid Agency—

- The certificate reference number.

ANNEX B

Response to a letter before claim

Information required in a response to a letter before claim

1 The claimant

(Insert the title, first and last names and the address to which any reply should be sent.)

2 From

(Insert the name and address of the defendant.)

3 Reference details

(Set out the relevant reference numbers for the matter in dispute and the identity of those within the public body who have been handling the issue.)

4 The details of the matter being challenged

(Set out details of the matter being challenged, providing a fuller explanation of the decision, where this is considered appropriate.)

5 Response to the proposed claim

(Set out whether the issue in question is conceded in part, or in full, or will be contested. Where an interim reply is being sent and there is a realistic prospect of settlement, details should be included. If the claimant is a litigant in person, a copy of the Pre-Action Protocol should be enclosed with the letter.)

6 Details of any other Interested Parties

(Identify any other parties who you consider have an interest who have not already been sent a letter by the claimant.)

7 ADR proposals

(Set out the defendant's position on any ADR proposals made in the letter before claim and any ADR proposals by the defendant.)

8 Response to requests for information and documents

(Set out the defendant's answer to the requests made in the letter before claim including reasons why any requested information or documents are not being disclosed.)

9 Address for further correspondence and service of court documents

(Set out the address for any future correspondence on this matter)

ANNEX C

Notes on public funding for legal costs in judicial review

Public funding for legal costs in judicial review is available from legal professionals and advice agencies which have contracts with the Legal Aid Agency. Funding may be provided for—

- Legal Help to provide initial advice and assistance with any legal problem; or
- Legal Representation to allow you to be represented in court if you are taking or defending court proceedings. This is available in two forms—

Investigative Help is limited to funding to investigate the strength of the proposed claim. It includes the issue and conduct of proceedings only so far as is necessary to obtain disclosure of relevant information or to protect the client's position in relation to any urgent hearing or time limit for the issue of proceedings. This includes the work necessary to write a letter before claim to the body potentially under challenge, setting out the grounds of challenge, and giving that body a reasonable opportunity, typically 14 days, in which to respond.

Full Representation is provided to represent you in legal proceedings and includes litigation services, advocacy services, and all such help as is usually given by a person providing representation in proceedings, including steps preliminary or incidental to proceedings, and/or arriving at or giving effect to a compromise to avoid or bring to an end any proceedings. Except in emergency cases, a proper letter before claim must be sent and the other side must be given an opportunity to respond before Full Representation is granted.

Further information on the type(s) of help available and the criteria for receiving that help may be found in the Legal Aid Agency's pages on the Ministry of Justice website at: https://www.justice.gov.uk/legal-aid

A list of contracted firms and Advice Agencies may be found at: http://find-legal-advice.justice.gov.uk"

Footnotes

1. The court has a discretion to extend time. It cannot be taken that compliance with the protocol will of itself be sufficient to excuse delay or justify an extension of time, but it may be a relevant factor. Under rule 54.5(2), judicial review time limits cannot be extended by agreement between the parties. However, a court will take account of a party's agreement 'not to take a time point' so far as concerns delay while they were responding to a letter before claim.

2. Civil Procedure Rules, Rule 54.1(2).

3. Civil Procedure Rules, Practice Directions 44-48.

4. See the Direction made by the Lord Chief Justice dated 21 August 2013 (as amended on 17 October 2014), available in the UTIAC section of the www. justice.gov.uk website. Also, the High Court can order the transfer of judicial review proceedings to the UTIAC.

5. See Civil Procedure Rules, Rule 54.1(2).

6. See Civil Procedure Rules, Practice Direction – Pre-Action Conduct and Protocols, paragraphs 2-3.

7. See Civil Procedure Rules, Rule 54.5(1).

8. See Civil Procedure Rules, Rule 54.1(2)(f).

9. The relevant address should be available from a range of sources such as the Phone Book; Business and Services Directory, Thomson's Local Directory, CAB, etc.

Index

C000008838

A

WISDEN

COLLECTION
volume two

A
WISDEN
COLLECTION
volume two

EDITED BY JONATHAN RICE

A & C Black · London

DEDICATION

For all who aspire to feature in *Wisden*, but don't.

First published in 2005 by
A & C Black Ltd
38 Soho Square
London W1D 3HB

www.acblack.com

This title is published by A & C Black Ltd under licence from
John Wisden & Co. Ltd

A copy of the CIP entry for this book is available from the British Library

ISBN-10: 0–7136–7506–3
ISBN-13: 9–780–7136–7506–1

10 9 8 7 6 5 4 3 2 1

A & C Black uses paper produced with elemental chlorine-free pulp, harvested from managed sustainable forests.

Typeset by RefineCatch Ltd, Bungay, Suffolk
Printed and bound in Great Britain by Clays Ltd, St Ives plc

CONTENTS

Advertisement from *Wisden* 1898

INTRODUCTION

C. L. R. James, in his endlessly (but deservedly) quoted work *Beyond A Boundary*, asks "What do they know of cricket who only cricket know?" He goes on to note that "English people, for example, have a conception of themselves bred from birth. Drake and mighty Nelson, Shakespeare, Waterloo, the Charge of the Light Brigade, the few who did so much for so many, the success of parliamentary democracy, those and such as those, constitute a national tradition." He then argues, quite validly, that the West Indian national tradition is based on heroes such as Worrell, Weekes and Walcott, Sobers, Headley and the rest. The heroes of these traditions may be quite different in many ways – where Britain's heroes are warriors or giants of our language, West Indian heroes are those who achieved greatness for their country by their exploits on playing fields – but to learn of these national traditions, we have to be told about them, from the cradle. If there were no books recording the exploits of Drake, Nelson or the Few, they would not be part of an English person's national tradition. The West Indian tradition may be younger, and there are many still alive who saw the Three Ws play (myself included) but unless there is somewhere to record their brilliance for future generations, a cultural heritage is lost.

That's where *Wisden* comes in. The cultural tradition of the game is built up from writings and recollections, and *Wisden* is at the very centre of that tradition. Although the Almanack claims, with every justification, merely to be a record of matches played in the previous twelve months, in fact it acts not just as a recorder of events but also as a shaper of the culture of cricket and in many ways as a guardian of the spirit of cricket. Without *Wisden* over the past 140-plus years, cricket would be a different game. The medium is the message, as Marshall McLuhan was wont to go on about in the 1960s.

In many ways, a *Wisden* "collection" is a bit of a cheat. The joy of reading *Wisden* is in the way that one thing inevitably leads to another, and what started out as a quick two-minute check on whether Kent beat Sussex last season, or whether Frank Tyson ever played a Test at Lord's, turns into a rummage through the obscurer corners of a year's cricket, at practically all levels and in all parts of the globe. As Rowland Ryder observed in 1965, "There is one thing you can be quite certain of in 'looking it up in *Wisden*' and that is that you will pick up a whole miscellany of information before you find the thing you have been looking for."

However, the *Wisden Collection* is by definition a miscellany. As Graeme Wright noted when he set the tone with the first *Wisden Collection* in 2004, "Like cricket itself, *Wisden* is an English institution." Unlike the Almanack, which tries – and usually succeeds – to be a complete record of all cricket played in the previous year, this little volume has no pretensions of completeness: I would like to think of it more as an *aide-mémoire* for any cricket follower with the kind of devious yet devoted mind that stores nuggets of cricket lore as shrewdly and as thoroughly as a squirrel storing nuts for winter. It is my belief that all readers of *Wisden* fall into that category to some extent, at least.

It is an impossible task to make a selection that will satisfy everyone – or quite possibly anyone – as I have taken the eclectic route wherever possible. On reassessing the pieces that have been chosen I see that the one-day game has come off rather badly (apart from the chapter on matches begun and finished in one day) but you can't have everything. What we have tried to do is bring back to life some of the cricketers of the distant past and the recent past, using the words of *Wisden* rather than the statistics. There are a number of match scorecards included in this collection and a few statistical tables, but what we wanted was to show how *Wisden* described the way Alfred Shaw or Tom Goddard bowled, for example, rather than the raw statistics of the number of batsmen who fell victim to their skills.

The term "collection" is also a slight misnomer: in fact I am beginning to think that this volume is rather like the Holy Roman Empire, which was described as being very correctly named, apart from the fact that it was not Holy, Roman, nor an Empire.

This collection is at least a *Wisden* book, and it is Volume Two, but whether such a random shuffling of clippings can be described as a "collection" is a moot point. Collections are well-ordered, cross-referenced and consisting of items that sit together logically and well. This collection is only a collection in the sense that pebbles, rocks and shells may be brought home from the seaside to make a collection – anything and everything might find its way in here. But that's the way *Wisden* is, and that's part of its appeal. You never know what you are likely to stumble across next.

Over the years the Almanack itself has become thicker and thicker, as it strives to be fully comprehensive, with details of every match played around the world each year. The recent revelation in *Wisden* that Graham Gooch scored more top-level runs (including one-day runs) than even Jack Hobbs confirms just how much cricket is being played in the twenty-first century. The golden days of counties playing a mere 32 three-day games a year are long gone, and the sheer idleness of bowlers like Alec Bedser who sent down no more than 2,000 overs each summer must be a source of envy for the overworked professionals of today. As the public appetite for live cricket – or at least televised live cricket – seems insatiable all over the world, we must assume that the main problem for the publishers of *Wisden* in years to come will be how to keep the pages bound together as the width of the spine heads for the 25-centimetre mark.

In compiling this second *Wisden Collection* we have had no such problems. I am aware that names like Alec Bedser, Ian Botham and Allan Border, to name but three great men of cricket, have just a few passing mentions in these pages, but their turn will come. I have enjoyed retracing the steps of such men as the Reverend Walter Fellows, William Ewart Astill, Roger Harman and Rodney Redmond, who have their own little niches in cricket history, and I make no apology for the fact that even Sir Donald Bradman keeps a comparatively low profile in this collection. You've read all there is to read about him, so now wallow in some of the more recondite parts of cricket's glorious heritage, as recorded by *Wisden Cricketers' Almanack*.

ACKNOWLEDGEMENTS

In putting together the book, I have been helped by many people, most notably Nicky Thompson and Robert Foss at Bloomsbury, Christopher Lane, Martin Williamson and Steven Lynch at *Wisden*, and of course Graeme Wright, who gave me several useful hints for researching the full archive with a minimum of fuss. My son Alex Rice helped with the research, turning up stories about Lionel Tennyson and strange stumpings, among others, and my wife Jan supplied coffee and support in equal quantities. I am grateful to them all.

They have all contributed, but if there are any mistakes, the fault is mine.

Jonathan Rice
July 2005

NOTE: The edition of *Wisden Cricketers' Almanack* from which an extract has been taken is indicated by the year that appears either above the extract, or alongside its heading or the name of its author.

Some notes and footnotes, marked *, have been specially added for this edition and do not appear in the original *Wisden*.

NOTES BY THE EDITOR

Almost from the very beginning of *Wisden*, the few pages in each Almanack headed "Notes by the Editor" has been a keen focus of interest. It was not always thus: for the first few years, the editors were careful not to comment on the play or players, but merely to be "a readier reference and a more convenient companion than larger volumes with greater pretensions". But that philosophy changed, pretensions became greater and once the Almanack got into its stride, the editor's chair at *Wisden* became one of the great cricketing pulpits of every age.

It was not until 1901 that a section entitled "Some Notes by the Editor" actually appeared in the Almanack, but even before then, the editors had taken it upon themselves to rage against the grave cricketing sins of their time. Needless to say, most of those great issues of their time are still great issues of our time. What the editor of *Wisden* has to say about them – and about some of the not so great issues – is what makes good copy for the sports pages the day after publication of each year's Almanack, and is what stirs or concludes some of the major cricketing debates of the past century and a bit.

Some editors have taken the "Thunderer" approach, choosing their words carefully and brooking no dissent. Others have tossed pebbles into the stream of cricket thinking, and waited to see what kind of ripples, if any, they may create. All of them have been united in their love for the game, and for the people who play the game (with a few exceptions). Sometimes they have been years ahead of their time in the issues they discuss, sometimes they have been the last hurrah for the old guard before some new-fangled idea sweeps past them. But whichever line they took on whatever subject bestirred them during the long winter of compilation, they have always been stimulating and worth reading.

Or almost always.

TO THE READER 1864

In offering our first edition of the CRICKETERS' ALMANACK to the patrons of the "Noble Game", we have taken great pains to collect a certain amount of information, which we trust will prove interesting to all those that take pleasure in this glorious pastime. Should the present work meet with but moderate success, it is intended next year to present our readers with a variety of other matches, which the confined nature of an Almanack precludes us from doing this year.

TO THE READER 1865

John Wisden and Co. return their most sincere thanks to the Cricketing Public for the support given by them to this little work. Induced by the flattering patronage of many of the most distinguished Cricketers of the day, they have ventured upon the publication of a second number, trusting that its contents will win for it the same generous support as its predecessor. J. W. and Co. hope that the selection of matches they have made will give satisfaction to their Readers, and that they will find the Almanack, from its size, a readier reference and a more convenient companion than larger volumes with greater pretensions.

It was our wish to have published in this year's Almanack a list of Secretaries of Clubs with their addresses, as we think it would be a useful reference in making matches with each other, and have advertised our intention of doing so in three different Sporting papers; but not having received so many answers as we hoped, we shall postpone the idea for another year, trusting in the meantime we may receive the desirable information from those of our readers whom it may concern.

TO THE READER 1866

John Wisden and Co. have again to thank the Cricketing Public for the encouragement given to the Almanack, and they beg respectfully to offer the third number for the perusal of their friends, trusting that it will be received with as much favour as its predecessors.

J. W. and Co. have this year published the matches of the three All-England Elevens, feeling certain, from the great favour with which these celebrated Elevens are received in all parts of the country, their doings will be read with interest.

J. W. and Co. have carefully avoided making any remarks upon the play or players, as the purport of this little work is to record the scores of the matches published as a book of reference.

THROWING

by Sydney H. Pardon, 1901 [The first set of notes]

I had intended to write at considerable length on the subject of unfair bowling and the no-balling of Mold and Tyler by James Phillips, but before I had started on my task the announcement appeared that at the meeting of county captains at Lord's, on December 10, an agreement had been made to take united action in the season of 1901, for the purpose of ridding English cricket of all throwing and dubious bowling. Up to the time of these lines being written – December 14 – full details of the method to be employed have not yet officially been made public, but I am assured on the highest authority that very strong measures have been determined on. Some bowlers will not be put on at all in county matches and others will receive a significant warning. "Better late than never," but I cannot help thinking what a number of scandals and what an immense amount of grumbling would have been avoided if, in the middle of the Eighties, the county captains had taken concerted action. At that time, however, Lord Harris alone had the courage of his convictions, and really tried to grapple with an admitted evil. It will not be forgotten that in 1885, Kent, at Lord Harris's instigation, dropped their return match with Lancashire on the grounds that the northern county employed unfair bowlers. Things have never since been so bad as they were about that time, when on one occasion three unmistakeable throwers took part in a Gentlemen v Players match at Lord's, but within the last few years there has unquestionably been great laxity. I think that the necessity of doing something was first brought home to the MCC committee and the county authorities when Jones and McKibbin so flagrantly disregarded Law 10 during the Australian tour of 1896. Even the least observant of cricketers must have been struck by the change that had come over Australian bowling since Spofforth, Boyle, Garrett, Palmer, Turner and Ferris earned their laurels on English cricket grounds. The mortifying fact was that the deplorable change was due entirely to our own weakness in not having the laws of the game carried out. The Australians only did against us what we had over and over again done against them. Now that at last English cricketers are taking steps to put their house in order, I think I may, without undue egotism, take some small credit to myself for having tried, year after year, to get rid of unfair bowling.

1906
by Sydney H. Pardon

It would ill become me to allow the retirement of James Phillips from the post of umpire in first-class cricket to pass without comment. Now that we are almost entirely free from the curse of throwing the value of what Phillips did for the cause of fair bowling is beginning to be realised. He had the courage to act when other umpires were content to express their opinions in private, and for the great improvement that has resulted from the concerted action of the county captains and the present happy condition of things, thanks are chiefly due to him. The concerted action of the captains only came when the question had been brought within the range of cricket politics. It is a little humiliating to think that an Australian umpire undertook a duty that our own men had shirked, but the fact must be borne in mind that Phillips stood in a rather more independent position than most of his colleagues. The courage lay in the initial steps as, the plunge once taken, Phillips soon found that he had authority behind him. As one who in a modest way laboured for many years to rid English cricket of throwing, I have special reason to rejoice at the change that has been brought about, and as I gave Phillips all the support I possibly could at a time when he was subjected to a good deal of criticism and even abuse, I may now congratulate him on his good work. No one could watch first-class cricket last season without being conscious of the great change that had come over the game. There was plenty of very fast bowling, but Cotter, Brearley, Knox, Warren and others were all so unimpeachably fair in delivery that not the slightest question could be raised with regard to any one of them. I do not think for a moment that there would have been this general fairness of action if Phillips had not stood up for the enforcement of Law 10.

1914
by Sydney H. Pardon

There is one rather delicate point of which I would like to write a few words. Alletson, the big hitter of the Notts eleven, won the Kent match at Trent Bridge by his bowling, but during the rest of the season he practically bowled no more. I am told that the reason for this was that exception was taken to his delivery. Assuming this to be the correct explanation, we may congratulate ourselves on the welcome change that has come about in the last ten years. The county captains did a truly wise thing when they took the question of unfair bowling into their own hands. As the result of their united action throwing in first-class cricket has practically disappeared.

SOUTH AFRICA'S DECISION
by Norman Preston, 1960

Early this year Mr A. H. Coy, President of the South African Cricket Association, was reported to have said that the number of bowlers with suspect actions had reached such proportions that the law would have to be more clearly defined. He considered that each country should ensure that such bowlers were corrected or kept out of first-class cricket and he added, "South Africa must make certain that touring teams do not include any bowler whose action is likely to cause controversy or embarrassment." There were a few suspicious cases in England last summer. Umpires are not likely to invoke the wrath of spectators or deprive a man of his living by making open examples during the course of a match. Nevertheless, umpires could report cases to Lord's and if a panel were appointed to deal with these matters, suspect actions could be watched. Then if the panel were satisfied with the umpires' opinions, the offenders and the counties concerned could be informed that unless such a bowler mended his ways immediately his presence in the game would no longer be tolerated.

1964
by Norman Preston

Another umpire, C. Egar, of Australia, has no-balled I. Meckiff in the opening over of the First Test between Australia and South Africa at Brisbane. Controversy has centred on Meckiff's bent-arm action ever since he helped to put out Peter May's England team for 87 in the Second Test at Melbourne five years ago by snatching six wickets for 38. The ruling bodies in England and Australia are determined to stamp out throwing, but it needs courage on the part of an umpire to take action in the excitement of a big match when perhaps 30,000 or so partisans are present. In Australia the gallant Egar needed police protection whereas the offending bowler reaped a harvest by selling his story and generally being hailed as something of a hero.

TWO DIVISION COUNTY CHAMPIONSHIP
by Sydney H. Pardon, 1907

No season goes by without producing some discussion as to the County Championship, and 1906 did not prove an exception to the rule. It was rather surprising, however, to find a proposal to arrange the Championship in two divisions, after the style of the Football League, emanating from W. G. Grace. I am, as everyone must be, quite conscious of the anomalies inevitable in a competition in which 16 counties play an unequal number of matches, but for the two divisions suggestion I have no liking whatsoever. I cannot bring myself to look with any favour on a scheme which might, as the result of one unlucky season, involve the most famous counties being put down into the second rank. The traditions of cricket are all against such a system. One has only to think of Surrey, Notts, or Kent, with the splendid records of half a century or more behind them, being suddenly degraded to feel that the scheme would never work.

1910
by Sydney H. Pardon

Since the season ended, there has once more been a good deal of talk of dividing the counties into two divisions, a strong hint in this direction coming from Yorkshire. Personally I hope nothing of the sort will come about. My own idea is that county cricket needs to be a little more elastic than it is at present, and that anything in the shape of increased rigidity should be avoided. For this reason, I can never get up the least interest in the discussion so often raised about the defects of the MCC's method of deciding the Championship. It is enough for me that under the existing system no county has won the Championship without fairly deserving the honour.

1991
by Graeme Wright

The intended elevation of Durham from Minor County to first-class status in 1992 brings with it an opportunity to reshape the County Championship more radically than merely by an increase in the number of counties for the first time since 1921. One possible change is the introduction of a Championship consisting of 17 four-day games per county; this, basically, is the recommendation of the TCCB's England Cricket and Marketing committees, which was rejected by a majority of the counties last spring. Whether this is sufficient to bring about a more competitive Championship is another matter.

What about dividing the counties into two leagues of nine, with the teams in each league playing the others home and away?

Worthwhile prize money, plus the prospect of promotion and relegation, might provide the keen competition which to me seems to be missing from much County Championship cricket.

2001
by Graeme Wright

After advocating a two-division County Championship in these Notes in 1991, I could hardly turn on it now it has come to pass. Not that I would want to. Three-up three-down may be one too many in a nine-team division, but the third place certainly concentrated some minds last summer. Not all the cricket was noticeably better ... However, if there are fewer meaningless matches, there should be more meaningful cricketers. Not Test cricketers, perhaps, but players people will want to watch, and who will stiffen the sinews of those destined for the England team. Even if the county game's role is playing second fiddle to international cricket, it's still a lovely way to spend a day.

OVERSEAS PLAYERS IN ENGLISH COUNTY CRICKET 1907
by Sydney H. Pardon

One subject has come up for discussion since the end of the season. At the meeting of the Advisory Committee at Lord's on December 19, a proposal was brought forward by Kent that in the case of a cricketer coming to this country to make a livelihood out of the game the period of qualification should be extended, this being substituted for a far more drastic proposition of which Essex had given notice. The proposal was lost but only by a majority of one, there being seven votes in its favour and eight against. Indeed, but for the fact of Mr Jessop losing his train and being late for the meeting the decision, as a recommendation to the MCC, would, it is understood, have been decided one way or the other by the casting vote of the chairman. The question is a very delicate one and there is much to be said on both sides. No one I think wishes Australian or other Colonial players to be excluded absolutely from our county elevens but at the same time there is a very strong feeling that the free importation of ready-made players does not make for the good of county cricket. Counties like Yorkshire and Kent that do all they can to encourage and develop home-grown talent feel that they are exposed to unfair competition. Moreover, there is a conviction in many quarters that a healthy state of things can only be brought about by limiting the choice of players to those who have some real connection with the counties they represent. It was certainly not a good thing for county cricket that Gloucestershire should years ago have made their unfortunate arrangement with poor Ferris or that in more recent days Lancashire should have brought Kermode all the way from New South Wales.

1927
by C. Stewart Caine

There is to most of us something objectionable in the idea of a man battling for Australia in Test matches one season, and a year later figuring as a paid player for an English local club. Of course, an Australian cricketer has a perfect right to turn professional if he thinks fit and, in that event, to sell his abilities in the best market. If the matter ended with the fact of a man accepting a situation, there would – much as one might regret the occurrence – be nothing more to be said on the subject. Unfortunately there is the precedent in the case of McDonald who, after playing a great part in Australia's triumph over England in 1921, accepted an engagement with a League club and, as soon as he had completed two years' residence, became a member of the Lancashire County eleven. In the ordinary nature of things, a similar course might be followed by Arthur Richardson, if that player takes up employment in this country. Against such a development there would, I feel confident, be a very general and very proper outcry. In qualifying Australians, Lancashire and Middlesex – and still further back, Gloucestershire – were big sinners, but the practice happily died out, and I am not aware that Lancashire County, even if prompted to avail themselves of McDonald's services, had anything to do with bringing that fine bowler back to this country. Obviously, however, if Richardson does join a League club, there must exist, as things are, something more than a possibility of that player also in two years' time finding his way into the ranks of the Lancashire eleven. How the situation should be tackled it is difficult to say. In what has happened – and still more in what may happen – there is a danger that the fine spirit which now exists in County cricket will be lost.

SOBERS SIGNS FOR NOTTINGHAMSHIRE 1968
by Norman Preston

County cricket has taken its biggest step forward in recent years by opening the door to overseas players through the process of immediate registration. This bold move could be the salvation of the three-day County Championship and I am only surprised that the plunge was not taken sooner. The numerous provisos safeguard the welfare of English-born players and the very fact that a heavy responsibility will now rest upon the star cricketer should help the promising youngster to take his place in first-class company without the worry that any temporary failure will weigh heavily against his side.

Heading for a Transfer System?

No county will be allowed to engage a second star within three years of taking on the first and at no time will more than two overseas players be specially registered for the same county, though after five years, under a previous arrangement, a player from another country enters the same category as a home-born man. Hence, the fears that cricket may be heading for a transfer system similar to professional football can be regarded as groundless. Yet when one takes into account all the publicity and the interest that League football gains from the exchange of players, is the time so very far distant when cricket will be conducted in similar fashion?

While Yorkshire with their broad acres and vast resources must be admired for their adherence to local talent, the imported player from outside the county border and from overseas is no stranger among the other 16 counties. Did not Warwickshire win the Championship in 1951 with only C. W. Grove and F. C. Gardner of the regular side born within the county? When Nottinghamshire met Leicestershire at Newark last season half the players who took part in the match were former players of other counties.

One of the reasons why the Advisory Committee retained the two-year qualification rule for so long was because our Test opponents, and Australia in particular, feared the draining of their resources if there was a steady flow of leading stars to the United Kingdom. That state of affairs no longer exists because now a man who is qualifying by residence may at any time play for the country of his birth. Hence, Lance Gibbs, who will assist Warwickshire this summer, was able to play for West Indies in the recent Test series against England.

DOMINANCE OF OVERSEAS PLAYERS 1983
by John Woodcock

In English county cricket overseas players were again pre-eminent, occupying seven of the first ten places in the batting averages and nine of the first eleven in the bowling figures.

PROFESSIONAL CAPTAINS 1928
by C. Stewart Caine

In the course of the autumn, Yorkshire cricket circles were greatly perturbed by the announcement that, in succession to Major Lupton, Herbert Sutcliffe had been appointed captain of the county team. Objection was taken to this action by two different parties. Some people urged the undesirability of having a professional captain; others argued that, if the committee thought fit to choose a professional, the post should be given to Wilfred Rhodes rather than to Sutcliffe. Happily the trouble was eventually settled to the satisfaction of all concerned. Sutcliffe declined the honour and, an invitation being extended to Captain Worsley, that gentleman stepped into the breach.

The matter naturally raised the question whether the practice which so generally obtains of giving the captaincy of a county eleven to an amateur, even of moderate attainments, carries with it greater advantages than the appointment of an experienced professional. Personally I think it does. Professionals, it is true, have in the past often captained leading counties – notably Yorkshire and Notts – but the system possesses more or less certain drawbacks. The professional may have difficulty in enforcing discipline. He would naturally hesitate to suggest to his committee that this player or that should be dropped, and so be instrumental in depriving the man in question of some part of his livelihood. Further, feeling that an error of judgement would prejudice his standing with the committee, he might well hesitate to take risks. The amateur is altogether differently placed. If a man is possessed of the qualities of leadership, he can insist upon strict obedience, and silent acquiescence in his orders. His views as to whether a player should be left out are not likely to be determined by any question of that player's earnings, and he can run risks with the knowledge that the worst that can befall him is the possibility he may not be given charge of the side another year.

WARWICKSHIRE CHAMPIONS 1952
by Norman Preston

And here let me congratulate Warwickshire on winning the County Championship. Their triumph emphasised the importance of skilled leadership, for in Tom Dollery they possessed a man able to get the best out of his team both on and off the field. Dollery, a professional, led an all-professional eleven, and while twentieth-century conditions rob the game of the real amateur, Dollery showed that the paid player can become a captain in the real sense of the word. By his astute work, Dollery has raised the status of the professional just as Hobbs did in the days when every county club had one dressing-room for the paid and another for the unpaid.

1953
by Norman Preston

Here was evidence of the sound work accomplished by the selectors, N. W. D. Yardley, R. E. S. Wyatt, F. R. Brown and L. E. G. Ames, and the new captain, L. Hutton. In breaking with tradition and choosing a professional as captain the Selection Committee made a vital decision in the interests of England, because it should mean in future no man will be picked as leader unless he is worth a place in the side.

On the other hand, the time may not be far distant when we have an amateur in charge again if P. B. H. May and D. S. Sheppard continue to improve. The task of captain is seldom a sinecure, and for a professional it could be onerous if disciplinary action was necessary against a fellow professional.

1960

by Norman Preston

For the first time for many years, Yorkshire now have a professional captain in J. V. Wilson, who has been appointed to succeed J. R. Burnet. Thirty-five years ago the late Lord Hawke said some strong things about professional captains and during the course of time the leadership of Yorkshire has been linked with them, whereas he was expressing his opinion about England.

In the summer of 1924, C. Parkin, then at his zenith, criticised A. E. R. Gilligan, the England captain, for not calling upon him to bowl on the third morning of the Edgbaston Test when South Africa, dismissed by Gilligan and Tate for 30, followed on. Parkin wrote disparagingly about Gilligan's captaincy in general and said he would never play for England again. At the Yorkshire annual meeting in the following January, Lord Hawke touched on this matter and said, "Pray God no professional will ever captain the England side. I love professionals, every one of them, but we have always had an amateur skipper. If the time comes when we are to have no more amateurs captaining England, well, I don't say England will become exactly like League football, but it will be a thousand pities, and it will not be for the good of the game."

Lord Hawke did not live to see Leonard Hutton, a Yorkshire professional, restore England's post-war cricket fortunes, nor to learn of the knighthood Hutton received for his services to cricket.

In the early years of his long reign as captain of Yorkshire (1883–1909) Lord Hawke was often helped by Louis Hall, a professional who at one time was termed assistant-captain and led Yorkshire throughout the summer of 1885 when Lord Hawke was away.

I also wonder what Lord Hawke's reaction would have been to recent suggestions that the present time may be the twilight of the amateur. It is seriously suggested that all players should be termed "cricketers" and that there should be no distinction between amateur and professional. In the past I may have thought along these lines, but when one remembers the great work done by B. H. Lyon for Gloucestershire, R. W. V. Robins for Middlesex, A. B. Sellers and J. R. Burnet for Yorkshire, and W. S. Surridge and P. B. H. May for Surrey, surely, no matter what the financial set-up, English cricket, and particularly county cricket, cannot afford to lose the amateur.

DISAPPEARANCE OF THE AMATEUR 1963

To many people the abolition of the amateur status in first-class cricket provided yet another big surprise. Four years earlier the MCC had conducted a full inquiry into this matter and arrived at certain conclusions which were accepted by the Advisory County Cricket Committee. Among them were the following:

> The wish to preserve in first-class cricket the leadership and general approach to the game traditionally associated with the Amateur player.

> The Committee rejected any solution to the problem on the lines of abolishing the distinction between Amateur and Professional and regarding them all alike as "cricketers".

> They considered that the distinctive status of the amateur cricketer was not obsolete, was of great value to the game and should be preserved.

The members of this Committee were: The Duke of Norfolk (chairman), H. S. Altham, G. O. Allen, M. J. C. Allom, Col. R. J. de C. Barber, F. R. Brown, E. D. R. Eagar, C. A. F. Hastilow,

C. G. Howard, D. J. Insole, P. B. H. May, C. H. Palmer, Col. R. S. Rait Kerr, A. B. Sellers, Rev. D. S. Sheppard, R. Aird (secretary).

It seems strange that within four years the opinions of some people appear to have been completely reversed. We live in a changing world. Conditions are vastly different from the days of our grandparents; but is it wise to throw everything overboard?

We have inherited the game of cricket. The story of its development during the last hundred years is appropriately given full treatment in this edition of *Wisden*. Right through these hundred years the amateur has played a very important part.

In the time of Dr W. G. Grace there was talk that the amateur received liberal expenses. Whether this was true or not, I do not believe cricket, as we know it today, would be such a popular attraction, or so remunerative to the professional, without the contribution which Dr Grace and his contemporaries made as amateurs.

By doing away with the amateur, cricket is in danger of losing the spirit of freedom and gaiety which the best amateur players brought to the game.

OTHER MATTERS 1926
by Sydney H. Pardon

Just as the Almanack is going to press comes a letter from Hobart, stating that in a match there between New Town and North West Hobart "A" Grade on November 21 last, A. O. Burrows of New Town bowled one of his opponents with a ball which sent the bail 83 yards 1 foot 9 inches. The statement is vouched for by no fewer than half a dozen different men associated with one club or the other, among these being Joe Darling, the famous left-handed batsman who captained Australia in this country in 1899, 1902 and 1905, and who is now President of the New Town club. Previously the record was 70½ yards by A. F. Morcom for Bedfordshire against Suffolk at Luton in 1908.

1933
by C. Stewart Caine

For the moment even the shakiest of counties must feel encouraged to battle on, seeing that they may expect a substantial sum of money as the result of the profits made by the MCC tour in Australia.

At the moment of writing these notes the Third Test Match has just ended in a handsome victory for England but while followers of cricket in this country rejoice exceedingly over that success, the public in Australia appear to be getting very excited about the fast bowling of some of the Englishmen and what is variously known as the "leg theory", "shock tactics" and "body-line methods".

. . . The ball to which such strong exception is being taken in Australia is not slow or slow-medium but fast. It is dropped short and is alleged in certain quarters to be aimed at the batsman rather than at the wicket. It may at once be said that, if the intention is to hit the batsman and so demoralise him, the practice is altogether wrong – calculated, as it must be, to introduce an element of pronounced danger and altogether against the spirit of the game of cricket. Upon this point practically everybody will agree. No one wants such an element introduced. That English bowlers, to dispose of their opponents, would of themselves pursue such methods or that Jardine would acquiesce in such a course is inconceivable.

ERRATA IN *WISDEN* 1987

Page 1140. In the match at Jodhpur on November 17, 18, 19, Vidarbha batted first and third, Rajasthan second and fourth. Because of the playing conditions in Indian domestic cricket, which provide for the addition of penalty points for slow over-rates, Rajasthan won by 9 runs, despite batting last.

1966
by Norman Preston

Three of the best opening batsmen in England could not score a century in first-class cricket last season. The two England openers, R. W. Barber and G. Boycott, who did so well on the true pitches of Australia and made that memorable first-wicket stand of 234 in under four hours before tea at Sydney, reached top scores of 94 and 95 respectively. Barber steadfastly pursued his enterprising policy and finished the season in 61st place in the batting list, average 26.93. Boycott came 15th, average 35.29. A third example was D. M. Green of Lancashire. Another free stroke-maker, Green managed an aggregate of 2,037 runs from 63 knocks with a top score of 85, which shows his wonderful consistency, and he averaged 32.85.

Surely it is time that groundsmen returned to the old method of using marl, cow-manure and the heaviest possible roller. The way back to better first-class cricket is to remember that the state of the pitch governs the play. Fine weather is essential and, when the sun shines, batsmen should be able to know that the ball will behave reasonably as it comes off a fast, true surface. Bowlers will then learn that accurate length and direction, allied to speed or spin, are the main ingredients of success. The worst pitches were considered to be Bath, Old Trafford, Bradford, Chesterfield, Edgbaston, Headingley (county matches), Hove, Loughborough, Middlesbrough, Northampton, Romford, Sheffield, Southampton, Trent Bridge and Worcester.

LESS WIELDY BATS 1985
by John Woodcock

Helmets, especially those with visors attached, are cumbersome to wear. They can weigh as much as 3½lb and inevitably slow down a batsman's reactions. The weight of the modern bat has also led to a change in batting styles, the cut and the hook being the strokes to have suffered most. In 1956, when Gunn and Moore supplied the Australian touring team with bats, the order was for 16 between 2lb 2oz and 2lb 4oz and one of 2lb 6oz. This last one was for Mackay, who had a method all his own, involving no detectable pick-up of the bat. Today's average weight is nearer 2lb 10oz, not a few being of 3lb or more. Is it surprising, therefore, that is has become fashionable to stand with the bat already raised above the shoulder? No less an authority than Bradman sees this as a "negative and regressive idea" and one which "detracts greatly from the style and flow of batsmanship". Bradman's own bats weighed 2lb 2oz. So did Compton's. Using a modern mallet they could never have played with such marvellous dexterity.

BEFORE I NOD OFF . . . 2000
by Matthew Engel

In his autobiography, *Tiger by the Tail*, Lord MacLaurin, the chairman of the ECB, has the following passage: "It is no longer possible to capture the somnolence of John Arlott's poem 'Cricket at Worcester, 1938', when 'Drowsing in a deck-chair's gentle curve, through half-closed eyes, I watched the cricket'. Those times are long gone."

I am not entirely sure what Lord MacLaurin is on about. He is right in the sense that there are no deck-chairs at Worcester these days, rather those plastic tip-up thingies, which are less conducive to drowsing. I still don't find it impossible. I half-dozed very happily on a sunny September afternoon last year; there was even someone called Hutton batting. Does he think county cricket isn't somnolent any more? Has he *been* to Worcester lately?

Heaven knows, I am not against reforming cricket where it is desirable and essential. I have been banging on about it in this space for the past eight years, and Lord MacLaurin can go on tinkering with the game in his way if he insists. But he really ought to leave us snoozers alone. They have done away with the deck-chairs. There are those whose future plans for cricket would include doing away with Worcester. Do away with somnolence, and you will do away with cricket once and for all. And England with it, probably.

A FIRST TEST VICTORY

There are now ten countries who compete internationally at Test level. With the exception of Australia, who won the first ever Test match in 1877, all these national sides have had to wait for their first Test victory, making it all the sweeter when it actually came. *Wisden* failed to mention the scores of the first Test match series at the time, listing only the names of the players who went on the tour, but subsequently reported all the other Test matches – even those that were not recognised as Tests at the time – some more in passing than in detail. Many of them were not particularly great matches, but for the winning teams and the countries they represented, these first Test victories will always be a significant part of their cricket history.

Only two countries – England and Pakistan – recorded their first Test victories away from home, but in all other cases, the players who achieved the breakthrough first victory have been on home soil (which in some instances was an important element in the win). England have been the losers in four of the ten first victories, India have been on the receiving end twice, and Australia, Pakistan, West Indies and Zimbabwe once each. Only South Africa, New Zealand and Bangladesh have never suffered the ignominy of conceding a debut Test win – an impossibility for Bangladesh who were only granted Test status after all the other nine had already notched up their first wins. Bangladesh did, however, go on to match South Africa and Sri Lanka as the only teams to translate a first Test victory promptly into a first series win: South Africa's first win was part of a 4–1 drubbing of

England under P. F. Warner in 1905/06, Sri Lanka won the only victory in a three Test series against India in 1985/86 and Bangladesh won one and drew one against an enfeebled Zimbabwe team in 2004/05. New Zealand, having waited 26 years for their first Test victory, made it in the fourth and final Test against West Indies in 1955/56, having lost each of the first three.

These Tests seem to have produced not just the history-making result, but also a plethora of individual and team performances to remember. George Headley became the first man to score centuries in both innings of a Test (or Representative Match, as *Wisden* coyly reported it) as West Indies gained their first win. In Zimbabwe's victory, Andy and Grant Flower broke the Test record for a batting partnership by brothers, and their winning margin – an innings and 64 runs – was the largest ever by a team winning a Test match for the first time. In Sri Lanka's first win, their wicketkeeper S. A. R. Silva opened the batting, scored 111, and also took eight catches and made one stumping (Gavaskar stumped for 52 – whatever was he thinking?), the best all-round performance by a wicketkeeper in a Test to that time. India's first Test win was delayed by the death of King George VI, but helped by their wicketkeeper, Sen, who stumped four men in England's first innings, at the time a Test record. S. C. Guillen, the New Zealand wicketkeeper, had already played Test cricket for the team New Zealand beat, West Indies, who in losing made their lowest Test score to date. Amir Elahi, on Pakistan's winning side, had also previously represented their opponents, India, before partition. Vinoo Mankad of India, Enamul Haque jnr. of Bangladesh and Heath Streak of Zimbabwe achieved the best bowling figures yet for their country in the debut win, while Henry Olonga, on debut, was no-balled for throwing. Every quirk of cricket is in these games.

AUSTRALIA AND ENGLAND

There are no accounts in *Wisden* of the first ever Test series, in Australia in 1876/77. The only mentions, apart from statistics in the Test records section of *Wisden* each year, are these:

1878

James Lillywhite's team – time of visit 1876/77.

Jas. Lillywhite (captain); T. Armitage; Henry Charlwood; Thomas Emmett; Andrew Greenwood; Allen Hill; Henry Jupp; Edward Pooley; J. Selby; Alfred Shaw; James Southerton; George Ulyett.

This team played 23 matches; won 11; lost 4; and 8 were drawn.

1951

Cricket Books, 1950, by John Arlott

The First Test Match, by E. C. Brogden, is a very skilfully contrived and detailed account of the first Test match played – England v Australia at Melbourne in 1877. This story has been compiled under the ideal circumstances of access to Australian press files and local tradition to produce one of the few studies which, perhaps, no English cricket library could have bettered in its profusion of basic material. As a novelty, as a highly detailed vignette and a piece of basic history, it will find an easy place in any collection of cricket books.

BANGLADESH

2005

BANGLADESH v ZIMBABWE

First Test Match

At Chittagong, January 6, 7, 8, 9, 10, 2005. Bangladesh won by 226 runs. Toss: Bangladesh. Against a weakened Zimbabwe, Bangladesh won their first Test victory at the 35th attempt, after 31 defeats and three draws. Their total of 488 was their highest yet, despite containing no hundreds; eighteen-year-old slow left-armer Enamul Haque's six for 45 was their best innings return, until he beat it the following week.

He took seven for 95 in Zimbabwe's first innings in the next Test.

Bangladesh 488 (Javed Omar 33, Nafis Iqbal 56, Habibul Bashar 94, Rajin
Saleh 89, Khaled Mashud 49, Mohammed Rafique 69, Mashrafe bin
Mortaza 48; C. B. Mpofu four for 109) **and 204** for nine declared.
(Habibul Bashar 55; D. T. Hondo three for 61, E. Chigumbura five for 54).

Zimbabwe 312 (B. R. M. Taylor 39, T. Taibu 92, E. Chigumbura 71;
Mashrafe bin Mortaza three for 59, Mohammed Rafique five for 65)
and 154 (H. Masakadza 56, B. R. M. Taylor 42; Enamul Haque, jnr. six
for 45).

INDIA
1953
INDIA v ENGLAND
Fifth Test Match

At Madras, February 6, 8, 9, 10, 1952. India won by an innings
and eight runs. India made history by recording their first Test
victory, and they did it in emphatic style. Undoubtedly India were
the superior all-round side and they went all out for success from
the first ball. Their hero was Mankad, who bowled superbly in
each innings, taking 12 wickets in the match for 108. His performance of eight for 55 in the first innings has seldom been bettered in
Test cricket when it is considered that the pitch gave him little
assistance. Mankad's bowling inspired the whole side, the fielding
being far better than in previous matches and the batting possessed a more adventurous spirit, necessary for the occasion.
England disappointed badly. There was no real reason for the
batting collapse in the first innings which virtually decided the
match. Hopes that they could stage one of their renowned recover-
ies were dashed when the pitch turned difficult after the third day.

Yet again India made five changes from their previous side.
Manjrekar, Nayudu, Shinde, Joshi and Adhikari stood down for
Mushtaq Ali, Amarnath, Gopinath, Divecha and Sen. As originally chosen the side included Adhikari and omitted Umrigar, but
a wrist injury due to a fall gave Umrigar another opportunity
which he seized splendidly. Carr led England for the first time,
Howard standing down with pleurisy, this being the one change
from the Kanpur side.

Carr won the toss, giving England a 3–2 advantage in tosses

won in the series, but they were soon in difficulties, Lowson being bowled by a splendid breakback with three runs on the board. Spooner and Graveney looked like bringing about a recovery, but the advent of Mankad at 65 changed the course of the match. Two or three times Mankad almost lured Graveney out of his ground before the batsman could resist no longer and moved forward to a ball well on the off and was stumped.

Spooner and Robertson added 60 for the next stand, but again, just when England looked to be getting themselves out of trouble, a wicket fell, Spooner, who stayed two hours 50 minutes, being caught at cover off Hazare's second ball. For a change, Watkins failed and Poole was never comfortable. With half the side out for 197 only two recognised batsmen, Robertson and Carr, remained. They made a good effort with a partnership of 47 before Robertson was brilliantly caught and bowled after a stay of four and a half hours. Mankad followed this by taking the last four wickets which fell for 22, three of them stumped when lured forward by the flight.

During the afternoon the death of King George VI was announced and arrangements were changed, the second day being made the rest day. Subsequently India batted consistently, with Roy again in fine form. Fourth out at 191, he scored his second century of the series and hit 15 fours in 111, made in three hours 50 minutes. India really took control after the fall of the fifth wicket, Phadkar and Umrigar adding 104 and Umrigar and Gopinath 93 in 80 minutes. Umrigar carried his bat for 130 after four hours 35 minutes, a splendid effort following a run of disappointing scores in the Tests.

England, 191 behind, survived the last quarter of an hour on the third day, but with the pitch wearing they were soon struggling next day. Robertson again batted well and top scored for the second time, Watkins showed he was still full of fight, but they were almost alone in their resistance and the match ended before tea on the fourth day. The scenes at the finish were surprisingly subdued, but the Indian officials and players were delighted at the first victory by their country at the 25th attempt to win a Test match.

England

F. A. Lowson b Phadkar	1	– c Mankad b Phadkar	7
R. T. Spooner c Phadkar b Hazare	66	– lbw b Divecha	6
T. W. Graveney st Sen b Mankad	39	– c Divecha b Ghulam Ahmed	25
J. D. Robertson c and b Mankad	77	– lbw b Ghulam Ahmed	56
A. J. Watkins c Gopinath b Mankad	9	– c and b Mankad	48
C. J. Poole b Mankad	15	– c Divecha b Ghulam Ahmed	3
D. B. Carr st Sen b Mankad	40	– c Mankad b Ghulam Ahmed	5
M. J. Hilton st Sen b Mankad	0	– st Sen b Mankad	15
J. B. Statham st Sen b Mankad	6	– c Gopinath b Mankad	9
F. Ridgway lbw b Mankad	0	– b Mankad	0
R. Tattersall not out	2	– not out	0
B 4, l-b 4, n-b 3	11	B 7, l-b 2	9
	266		**183**

1/3 2/71 3/131 4/174 5/197 6/244 7/252 8/261 9/261

1/13 2/15 3/68 4/117 5/135 6/159 7/159 8/178 9/178

Bowling: *First Innings* – Phadkar 16–2–49–1; Divecha 12–2–27–0; Amarnath 27–6–56–0; Ghulam Ahmed 18–5–53–0; Mankad 38.5–15–55–8; Hazare 10–5–15–1. *Second Innings* – Phadkar 9–2–17–1; Divecha 7–1–21–1; Amarnath 3–0–6–0; Ghulam Ahmed 26–5–77–4; Mankad 30.4–9–53–4.

India

Mushtaq Ali st Spooner b Carr	22
P. Roy c Watkins b Tattersall	111
V. S. Hazare b Hilton	20
V. Mankad c Watkins b Carr	22
L. Amarnath c Spooner b Statham	31
D. G. Phadkar b Hilton	61
P. Umrigar not out	130
C. D. Gopinath b Tattersall	35
R. V. Divecha c Spooner b Ridgway	12
P. Sen b Watkins	2
Ghulam Ahmed not out	1
B 8, l-b 2	10
(9 wkts dec.)	**457**

1/53 2/97 3/157 4/191 5/216 6/320 7/413 8/430 9/448

Bowling: Statham 19–3–54–1; Ridgway 17–2–47–1; Tattersall 40–9–100–2; Hilton 39–13–94–2; Carr 19–2–84–2; Watkins 14–1–50–1; Robertson 5–1–18–0.

Umpires: B. J. Mohoni and M. G. Vijayasarathy.

SCOTTISH ENTHUSIASM 1953

With the Australians due to finish their tour at Paisley and Edinburgh in the third week of September, interest in cricket in Scotland should last throughout the summer. They have many excellent and picturesque grounds over the border as well as plenty of cricket enthusiasts. One of the keenest is James Fleming, Scotland's former opening batsman and wicketkeeper. During the winter he founded a Cricket Society of Scotland, and in six weeks it became a flourishing body with over 160 members, including the Lord Provost of Edinburgh and many well-known and influential people. For the New Year festivities a cricket match was organised and it proved a great success. It was a lovely sunny morning and as there were five degrees of frost the pitch was nice and "firm". J. Aitchison lived up to his reputation by scoring 55. Each side bowled 15 overs in the morning and then gathered in the pavilion for lunch. This comprised Scotch broth, haggis with neeps (turnips) and mash, and whisky, and was played in by a piper in full regalia. Then they talked cricket until 5 p.m.

NEW ZEALAND
1957
NEW ZEALAND v WEST INDIES
Fourth Test Match

At Auckland, March 9, 10, 12, 13, 1956. New Zealand won by 190 runs. Local offices closed and excited crowds streamed to the Eden Park ground on the last afternoon as Cave and Beard bowled New Zealand to their first victory in 26 years of Test cricket. New Zealand owed much to the example of Reid, their captain. Until his arrival at the crease on the opening day nothing about New Zealand's cricket suggested their eventual triumph. Miller and MacGibbon struggled unconvincingly against a keen attack, following the early dismissal of McGregor, and Reid brought the first touch of mastery to the batting. Free, attacking strokes enabled him to hit 11 fours in his 84, and he dominated a partnership of 104 with the dour Beck.

Bad light ended the first day 40 minutes early with New Zealand 203 for six, and as the players left the field a tropical cyclone broke over the ground. Quicker bowlers were in their element next day. Dewdney swiftly accounted for the remaining New Zealand batsmen but MacGibbon and Cave proved equally menacing when West Indies batted. Weekes was, for once, among the early batting casualties and, despite a painstaking display by Furlonge, West Indies finished 110 behind.

Atkinson made a valiant attempt to retrieve the touring side's position with another whole-hearted bowling performance, but sensibly brisk batting by Guillen helped Reid to set them the formidable task of scoring 268 in four hours. Against the hostile bowling of Cave and Beard, West Indies collapsed so completely on a good batting wicket that the board soon showed 22 for six. Weekes and Binns rallied their team briefly but, after Alabaster dismissed both in an economical spell of leg-breaks, Cave and Beard completed West Indies' rout for their lowest score in Test cricket.

New Zealand

S. N. McGregor c Smith b Dewdney	2 –	c Binns b Atkinson 5
L. S. M. Miller c Weekes b Valentine	47 –	c Weekes b Atkinson 25
A. R. MacGibbon b Smith	9 –	c Weekes b Atkinson 35
D. D. Taylor lbw b Valentine . .	11 –	c Valentine b Atkinson 16
J. R. Reid hit wkt b Dewdney . .	84 –	c Binns b Atkinson 12
J. E. F. Beck c Sobers b Ramadhin	38 –	lbw b Atkinson 2
S. C. Guillen run out	6 –	st Binns b Valentine 41
M. E. Chapple c Atkinson b Dewdney	3 –	lbw b Ramadhin 1
D. D. Beard c Binns b Dewdney	3 –	not out 6
H. B. Cave c Smith b Dewdney .	11 –	not out 0
J. C. Alabaster not out	1 –	b Atkinson 5
B 7, l-b 5 12		B 4, l-b 5 9

1/9 2/45 3/66 4/87 5/191 6/203   255   1/14 2/61 3/66   (9 wkts. dec.) 157
7/205 8/210 9/250   4/91 5/100 6/101 7/109
                                       8/146 9/155

Bowling: *First Innings* – Dewdney 19.5–11–21–5; Atkinson 32–14–45–0; Valentine 41–20–46–2; Ramadhin 23–8–41–1; Smith 31–19–55–1; Sobers 20–7–35–0. *Second Innings* – Dewdney 12–5–22–0; Atkinson 40–21–53–7; Valentine 6–0–29–1; Ramadhin 18–6–26–1; Smith 4–0–18–0.

West Indies

H. Furlonge c Guillen b Cave..	64	– c MacGibbon b Beard	3
B. Pairaudeau c MacGibbon b Cave.................	9	– b Cave..................	3
G. Sobers c Guillen b MacGibbon...........	1	– run out............	1
E. D. Weekes c Guillen b MacGibbon...........	5	– c MacGregor b Alabaster.....	31
O. G. Smith b Beard.........	2	– b Cave..................	0
D. Atkinson b Reid	28	– c Chapple b Cave...........	10
A. Roberts b MacGibbon.....	28	– b Beard.................	0
A. P. Binns lbw b MacGibbon .	0	– b Alabaster................	20
S. Ramadhin b Cave........	3	– c Miller b Beard...........	0
A. L. Valentine c Taylor b Cave	0	– st Guillen b Cave...........	5
T. Dewdney not out	0	– not out..................	4
B 1, l-b 3, n-b 1...........	5		

1/25 2/32 3/46 4/59 5/94   145   1/4 2/16 3/16 4/16 5/18 6/22   77
6/139 7/140 8/145 9/145   7/68 8/68 9/68

Bowling: *First Innings* – MacGibbon 21–5–44–4; Cave 27.3–17–22–4; Reid 18–8–48–1; Beard 9–4–20–1; Alabaster 3–1–6–0. *Second Innings* – MacGibbon 6–1–16–0; Cave 13.1–9–21–4; Reid 6–2–14–0; Beard 15–7–22–3; Alabaster 5–4–4–2.

Umpires: J. C. Harris and T. M. Pearce.

PAKISTAN
1953
Pakistan in India, 1952

Pakistan's performance on their entry into official Test cricket was not without encouragement for the future. They gained only one victory in twelve first-class fixtures, but individual achievements suggested that they possessed the youthful talent on which to build for subsequent engagements. Their one success came in the Second Test, and with India winning two and two drawn, the series remained open until the end.

INDIA v PAKISTAN
Second Test Match

At Lucknow, October 23, 24, 25, 26, 1952. Pakistan won by an innings and 43 runs. With Hazare, Adhikari and Mankad unable to appear, India were as unconvincing as Pakistan had been in the previous Test. They were dismissed in their second innings in three hours 25 minutes, and Pakistan required only 15 minutes of the fourth day to complete their success, which was mainly due to the bowling of Fazal Mahmood and Mahmood Hussain. On a jute-matting pitch the two medium pacers perplexed all except Amarnath, the Indian captain. He gave an admirable performance in the second innings after being dropped by Zulfiqar Ahmed at square leg when six. Fazal Mahmood's splendid bowling earned him a match analysis of 12 for 92. Nazar Mohammed took the batting honours for Pakistan. He carried his bat after a painstaking display that lasted eight hours 35 minutes.

India

P. Roy lbw b Fazal Mahmood .	30 –	c Imtiaz Ahmed b Mahmood Hussain	2
D. K. Gaekwad b Maqsood Ahmed	6 –	c Nazar Mohammed b Fazal Mahmood	32
Gul Mohammed lbw b Maqsood Ahmed	0 –	b Fazal Mahmood	2
V. L. Manjrekar b Fazal Mahmood	3 –	lbw b Fazal Mahmood	3
G. Kishenchand lbw b Fazal Mahmood	0 –	c Nazar Mohammed b Fazal Mahmood	20
P. R. Umrigar b Mahmood Hussain	15 –	lbw b Fazal Mahmood	32
L. Amarnath c Zulfiqar Ahmed b Mahmood Hussain	10 –	not out	61
P. G. Joshi b Mahmood Hussain	9 –	b Amir Elahi	15
H. G. Gaekwad b Fazal Mahmood	14 –	b Fazal Mahmood	8
S. Nyalchand not out	6 –	lbw b Fazal Mahmood	1
Ghulam Ahmed c Hanif Mohammad b Fazal Mahmood	8 –	c sub b Amir Elahi	0
Extras	5	Extras	6
	106		182

1/17 2/17 3/20 4/24 5/55 6/65   106   1/4 2/27 3/43 4/73 5/77 6/103   182
7/68 8/85 9/93   7/115 8/170 9/170

Bowling: *First Innings* – Mahmood Hussain 23–7–35–3; Kardar 3–2–2–0; Fazal Mahmood 24.1–8–52–5; Maqsood Ahmed 5–1–12–2. *Second Innings* – Mahmood Hussain 19–5–57–1; Kardar 13–5–15–0; Fazal Mahmood 27.3–11–42–7; Maqsood Ahmed 5–0–25–0; Amir Elahi 7–1–20–2; Zulfiqar Ahmed 5–1–17–0.

Pakistan

Nazar Mohammed not out	124
Hanif Mohammad c Umrigar b Ghulam Ahmed	34
Waqar Hassan lbw b Amarnath	23
Imtiaz Ahmed lbw b Amarnath	0
Maqsood Ahmed lbw b Nyalchand	41
A. H. Kardar c Ghulam Ahmed b Nyalchand	16
Anwar Hussain b Nyalchand	5
Fazal Mahmood c Joshi b Gul Mohammed	29
Mahmood Hussain b Ghulam Ahmed	13
Zulfiqar Ahmed lbw b Ghulam Ahmed	34
Amir Elahi b Gul Mohammed	4
Extras	8
	331

1/63 2/118 3/120 4/167 5/194 6/201 7/239 8/302 9/318

Bowling: Amarnath 40–18–74–2; H. G. Gaekwad 37–21–47–0; Umrigar 1–0–1–0; Ghulam Ahmed 45–19–83–3; Nyalchand 64–33–97–3; Gul Mohammed 7.3–2–21–2. Umpires: B. J. Mohoni and J. R. Patel.

SOUTH AFRICA
1907
The MCC's Team in South Africa

The tour in South Africa during December 1905 and January, February and March 1906 was, as regards first-class cricket, a sad failure. The general result – 17 wins, 5 defeats and 4 drawn games – looks exceedingly well on paper, but unfortunately most of the victories were gained in matches against odds to which no interest attached. Everything else in the tour was naturally subordinate to the five Test matches with South Africa, and of these the Englishmen won the Fourth and lost the other four – three at Johannesburg and one, in a single innings in the last fixture of the tour, at Capetown. Of course, nothing that was done could compensate for these defeats and the team left the Cape somewhat crestfallen.

SOUTH AFRICA v ENGLISH TEAM

Played at Johannesburg, Tuesday, Wednesday, Thursday January 2, 3, 4, 1906. The first of the five Test matches was the most remarkable of the series, the Englishmen being beaten by one wicket after they had seemed to have the game in their hands. South Africa had 284 to get in the last innings, and when their sixth wicket fell before lunch the score was only 134. White played wonderfully well, resisting the bowling for four hours and ten minutes, but despite all his efforts he was eighth out at 226 – 45 runs were still required when Sherwell, the last man, joined Nourse. Amid ever-increasing excitement the runs came, South Africa thus winning by one wicket. Nourse was batting three hours and 40 minutes for his 93 not out – in every way a splendid innings. There was nothing exceptional in the cricket of the English team, but Crawford played two good innings and Lees bowled finely.

English Team

Mr P. F. Warner c Snooke b Schwarz	6 –	b Vogler ... 51
Mr F. L. Fane c Schwarz b Faulkner	1 –	b Snooke ... 3
D. Denton c Faulkner b Schwarz	0 –	b Faulkner ... 34
Capt. E. G. Wynyard st Sherwell b Schwarz	29 –	b Vogler ... 0
E. G. Hayes c and b Vogler	20 –	c Schwarz b Snooke ... 3
Mr J. N. Crawford c Nourse b Sinclair	44 –	b Nourse ... 43
A. E. Relf b White	8 –	c Sherwell b Faulkner ... 17
S. Haigh b Faulkner	23 –	lbw b Nourse ... 0
J. H. Board not out	9 –	lbw b Faulkner ... 7
W. Lees st Sherwell b White	11 –	not out ... 1
C. Blythe b Sinclair	17 –	b Faulkner ... 0
B 6, l-b 9, n-b 1	16	B 23, l-b 8 ... 31
	184	**190**

Bowling: *First Innings* – Schwarz 21–5–72–3; Faulkner 22–7–35–2; Sinclair 11–1–36–2; Vogler 3–0–10–1; White 5–1–13–2; Nourse 1–0–2–0. *Second Innings* – Schwarz 8–1–24–0; Faulkner 12.5–5–26–4; Sinclair 5–1–25–0; Vogler 11–3–24–2; White 4–0–15–0; Nourse 6–4–7–2; Snooke 12–4–38–2.

South Africa

L. J. Tancred c Board b Lees ..	3 – c Warner b Blythe...........	10
W. A. Shalders c Haigh		
b Blythe	4 – run out....................	38
M. Hathorn b Lees..........	5 – c Crawford b Lees	4
G. C. White c Blythe b Lees ...	8 – b Relf	81
S. J. Snooke c Board b Blythe..	19 – lbw b Lees	9
J. H. Sinclair c and b Lees.....	0 – c Fane b Lees	5
G. A. Faulkner b Blythe......	4 – run out	6
A. D. Nourse not out	18 – not out	93
A. E. E. Vogler b Crawford....	14 – b Hayes	2
R. O. Schwarz c Relf		
b Crawford	5 – c and b Relf	2
P. W. Sherwell lbw b Lees	1 – not out	22
B 9, l-b 1	10 B 6, l-b 2, n-b 7	15
	91 (for 9 wkts)	287

Bowling: *First Innings* – Lees 23.1–10–34–5; Blythe 16–5–33–3; Crawford 7–1–14–2. *Second Innings* – Lees 33–10–74–3; Blythe 28–12–50–1; Crawford 17–4–49–0; Haigh 1–0–9–0; Relf 21.5–7–47–2; Wynyard 3–0–15–0; Hayes 9–1–28–1.

SRI LANKA
1987
SRI LANKA v INDIA
Second Test Match

At P. Saravanamuttu Stadium, Colombo, September 6, 7, 8, 10, 11, 1985. Sri Lanka won by 149 runs. Sri Lanka's epochal Test win, in only their 14th Test match, came despite their own slow batting at the start, but their well-directed seam attack, bowling on and outside off stump, put them well in the hunt by establishing a convincing first-innings lead. India's woeful catching on the first day enabled Silva and Madugalle to build a steady foundation of 168 by the close, and Dias's polished 95 increased the advantage on the second day. Although the last six wickets fell for 17, the Sri Lankan bowlers maintained the pressure by capturing three Indian wickets for 6 runs by the end of the day's play.

Despite half-centuries from Srikkanth, Gavaskar and Amarnath on the third day, India frittered away their margin of safety by losing four quick wickets for 34 runs on the fourth morning.

This left Sri Lanka 141 runs ahead with time to set up a declaration on the fourth afternoon, and Dias and Aravinda de Silva obliged with quick-fire knocks that left their bowlers a whole day to bring about the country's first Test win.

Notwithstanding two dubious decisions on the final morning, India, set a target of 348 in 333 minutes plus 20 overs, could have batted out for a draw. However, Ratnayake swung the match for Sri Lanka by running through the middle order. His five for 49 included the wicket of the Indian captain Kapil Dev, who scored a defiant 78, and sealed a victory which led to a nationwide celebration and a public holiday the following day. Silva's century and nine dismissals in the match were an unprecedented feat by a wicketkeeper in a Test match.

Sri Lanka

S. Wettimuny run out	19	– c Rajput b Chetan	32
S. A. R. Silva c Viswanath b Shastri	111	– c Vengsarkar b Kapil Dev	11
R. S. Madugalle lbw b Chetan	54		
R. L. Dias c Viswanath b Chetan	95	– not out	60
L. R. D. Mendis c Shastri b Amarnath	51	– not out	13
A. Ranatunga lbw b Chetan	21		
P. A. de Silva c Azharuddin b Chetan	2	– (3) b Shastri	75
A. L. F. de Mel lbw b Shastri	0		
R. J. Ratnayake c Sivaramakrishnan b Shastri	7		
C. D. U. S. Weerasinghe b Chetan	3		
F. S. Ahangama not out	0		
L-b 3, w 4, n-b 15	22	B 4, l-b 6, n-b 5	15
	385	**(3 wkts dec.)**	**206**

1/74 2/169 3/229 4/328 5/368 6/372 7/375 8/375 9/379

1/46 2/48 3/180

Bowling: *First Innings* – Kapil Dev 32–10–69–0; Chetan 33–3–118–5; Shastri 45.3–11–74–3; Sivaramakrishnan 31–4–90–0; Amarnath 15–2–31–1. *Second Innings* – Kapil Dev 20–4–73–1; Chetan 13–1–55–1; Shastri 13–4–41–1; Sivaramakrishnan 7–1–27–0.

India

L. S. Rajput c Silva b de Mel ..	0	– lbw b de Mel	12
K. Srikkanth c Mendis b Ahangama	64	– lbw b Ratnayake	25
M. Azharuddin c Silva b Ratnayake	0	– c Silva b de Mel	25
D. B. Vengsarkar c Ranatunga b Ratnayake	1	– c Silva b Ratnayake	0
L. Sivaramakrishnan c Wettimuny b Ratnayake	18	– (9) c Silva b de Mel	21
S. M. Gavaskar st Silva b Ranatunga	52	– (5) c Silva b Ratnayake	19
M. Amarnath c Ahangama b de Mel	60	– (6) c de Silva b Ratnayake	10
R. J. Shastri c Silva b Ahangama	17	– (7) c Silva b Ahangama	4
*Kapil Dev c Ratnayake b Ahangama	6	– (8) c and b Ratnayake	78
†S. Viswanath c Wettimuny b Ratnayake	7	– lbw b Ahangama	0
Chetan Sharma not out	4	– not out	0
B 4, l-b 6, w 1, n-b 4	15	L-b 2, n-b 2	4
1/0 2/1 3/3 4/79 5/88	244	1/39 2/39 3/41 4/84 5/84	198
6/178 7/218 8/229 9/238		6/98 7/98 8/168 9/169	

Bowling: *First Innings* – de Mel 31–8–63–2; Ratnayake 25.1–5–76–4; Ahangama 18–3–59–3; Weerasinghe 16–7–28–0; Ranatunga 5–1–8–1. *Second Innings* – de Mel 22–4–64–3; Ratnayake 23.2–6–49–5; Ahangama 14–3–56–2; Weerasinghe 3–1–8–0; Ranatunga 4–0–19–0.

Umpires: S. Ponnadurai and P. W. Vidanagamage.

WEST INDIES
1931

WEST INDIES v MCC TEAM

Third Representative Match

Played at Georgetown, February 21, 22, 24, 25, 26, 1930. The third meeting with the full strength of the West Indies ended in defeat for MCC by 289 runs. In achieving a noteworthy victory, West Indies owed a great deal to the batting of Headley who created a record by scoring a hundred in each innings of a representative engagement and to that of Roach, and also some effective fast bowling by Constantine and Francis. MCC's fielding was badly at fault when West Indies opened their first innings with a stand of 144, Hunte being missed four times. Roach, however, played brilliantly for rather less than five hours, hitting three sixes and 22 fours, and in partnership with Headley he added 196. The total stood on 425 at the fall of the fifth wicket but the remaining batsmen were dismissed for 46. The only real resistance in the MCC's first innings came from Hendren and Ames and the West Indies went in again leading by 326. Their casual approach in the field almost deprived the home team of success for MCC, when facing the task of getting 617 runs, set themselves to save the game and held out until within a quarter of an hour from time. Hendren, carefully waiting for the right ball to hit, had 21 fours in his sixth century of the tour.

West Indies

C. A. Roach c Haig b Townsend	209	– st Ames b Astil	22
E. Hunte c Wyatt b Townsend	53	– b Townsend	14
G. A. Headley run out	114	– c Townsend b Haig	112
M. P. Fernandes c Ames b Rhodes	22	– c Calthorpe b Rhodes	19
J. E. D. Sealy c and b Rhodes	0	– c Hendren b Rhodes	10
C. V. Wight b Wyatt	10	– b Haig	22
L. N. Constantine st Ames b Wyatt	13	– b Astill	0
C. R. Browne b Voce	22	– not out	70
C. Jones c Ames b Voce	6	– b Townsend	2
E. St Hill st Ames b Haig	3	– b Astill	3
G. N. Francis not out	5	– lbw b Astill	2
Extras	14	Extras	14
	471		**290**

Bowling: *First Innings* – Voce 26–4–81–2; Haig 23–7–61–1; Townsend 16–6–48–2; Rhodes 40–8–96–2; Astill 28–3–92–0; Calthorpe 6–0–23–0; Wyatt 9–0–56–2. *Second Innings* – Voce 16–4–44–0; Haig 10–1–44–2; Townsend 7.3–2–25–2; Rhodes 51–23–93–2; Astill 43–17–70–4.

MCC Team

G. Gunn hit wkt b Francis	11	– c Hunte b Francis	45
A. Sandham c Hunte			
b Browne	9	– c and b Constantine	0
Mr R. E. S. Wyatt c Francis			
b Constantine	0	– c Jones b Constantine	28
E. Hendren b Constantine	56	– lbw b St Hill	123
L. E. G. Ames c Hunte			
b Francis	31	– c Francis b Constantine	3
W. E. Astill run out	0	– hit wkt b Constantine	5
Mr N. Haig b Constantine	4	– b Browne	0
Hon. F. S. G. Calthorpe			
c Headley b Constantine	15	– c Jones b Roach	49
W. Rhodes b Francis	0	– not out	10
W. Voce not out	1	– lbw b Francis	2
Extras	15	Extras	41
	145		327

Bowling: *First Innings* – Francis 21–5–40–4; Constantine 16.3–6–35–4; Browne 10–2–29–1; St Hill 14–4–26–0. *Second Innings* – Francis 26.5–11–69–2; Constantine 40–17–87–5; Browne 33–15–32–1; St Hill 33–15–61–1; Roach 9–2–18–1; Headley 2–0–8–0; Jones 10–7–5–0; Wight 5–1–6–0.

ZIMBABWE

by Qamar Ahmed, 1996

ZIMBABWE v PAKISTAN

First Test Match

At Harare, January 31, February 1, 2, 4, 1995. Zimbabwe won by an innings and 64 runs. Toss: Zimbabwe. Test debuts: S. V. Carlisle, H. K. Olonga

Zimbabwe not only created history with their first victory in their 11th Test match, but they did it with style, by an innings inside four days. The Flowers took control on the first afternoon in a record-breaking fourth-wicket partnership, and Pakistan never got back into the game. Streak forced them to follow on and they folded in 62 overs on their second attempt.

The match had a farcical start when the referee, Jackie Hendriks, demanded a second toss. Salim Malik had called "Bird", the national symbol on one side of the Zimbabwean coin, instead of "Heads"; Andy Flower congratulated him on winning but Hendriks said he had not heard the call. Flower won at the second attempt and chose to bat. Until lunch, Pakistan seemed to shrug off their frustration. Aqib Javed and Wasim Akram dismissed Dekker, Campbell and Houghton as Zimbabwe reached 42. After the interval, Wasim bowled seven maiden overs in succession. But from then on, the Flowers flourished.

Andy, the elder brother, was the dominant partner, reaching his second Test century in three and a half hours. The brothers' stand passed 194, Zimbabwe's all-wicket record set by Campbell and Houghton against Sri Lanka three months earlier, and was 247 at the close, with Andy on 142 and Grant on 88. Next day they took it to 269, overtaking the fraternal Test record of 264 shared by Greg and Ian Chappell for Australia's third wicket against New Zealand in 1973/74, before Andy was out. But there was no relief for the bowlers. Whittall joined Grant in another double-hundred partnership. Both completed maiden Test centuries; Grant, who had been dropped on 24 and 98, took 343 balls to reach his hundred but then speeded up to convert it to a double in another 177. He had batted for 11 hours and hit only ten fours in a marathon display of discipline and concentration. His brother declared at 544 for four, Zimbabwe's highest Test total, beating their 462 for nine against Sri Lanka in October.

Pakistan lost one wicket on the second evening, to Henry Olonga, the first non-white player to appear for Zimbabwe. His first delivery went for four wides, his second was a bouncer, and Andy Flower caught Saeed Anwar down the leg-side off the third. But Olonga's debut ended in disaster the next day. As in the previous tour match, he was no-balled for throwing, by umpire Robinson – the first recognised bowler to be called in a Test since Ian Meckiff for Australia against South Africa in Brisbane in 1963/64 – and later retired with a side strain. But accurate medium-pace bowling by Streak, with six for 90, brilliant fielding and some careless shots by batsmen finished off Pakistan 222 in arrears. Aamir Sohail, Salim Malik and Ijaz Ahmed all made a start before getting themselves out; Inzamam-ul-Haq, batting at No. 8 after damaging his shoulder in the slips, showed more authority in making 71. Inzamam was also the principal source of resistance when Pakistan followed on and collapsed to 35 for five. He and Rashid Latif added 96 but, apart from them and Wasim, no one else reached double figures. There were three wickets each for seamers Streak, who returned the best Test analysis yet for Zimbabwe, Brain and Whittall, as Pakistan were all out for an ignominious 158.

Men of the Match: A. Flower and G. W. Flower.

Zimbabwe

M. H. Dekker c Rashid Latif b Aqib Javed		2
G. W. Flower not out		201
A. D. R. Campbell lbw b Wasim Akram		1
D. L. Houghton c Aamir Sohail b Aqib Javed		23
A. Flower c Wasim Akram b Kabir Khan		156
G. J. Whittall not out		113
B 4, l-b 19, w 3, n-b 22		48
1/4 2/9 3/42 4/311	(4 wkts. dec.)	544

S. V. Carlisle, P. A. Strang, H. H. Streak, D. H. Brain and H. K. Olonga did not bat.

Bowling: Wasim Akram 39.5–12–95–1; Aqib Javed 34.1–8–73–2; Kabir Khan 35–5–142–1; Salim Malik 9–0–42–0; Akram Raza 34–6–112–0; Asif Mujtaba 7–0–30–0; Aamir Sohail 6–1–27–0.

Pakistan

Aamir Sohail c Houghton b Brain	61	– c Campbell b Brain		5
Saeed Anwar c A. Flower b Olonga	8	– lbw b Whittall		7
Akram Raza c Whittall b Streak	19	– (9) not out		2
Asif Mujtaba c Carlisle b Streak	2	– (3) b Brain		4
Salim Malik c Carlisle b Whittall	32	– (4) c A. Flower b Brain		6
Ijaz Ahmed c G. W. Flower b Streak	65	– (5) c Brain b Streak		2
Rashid Latif c Campbell b Whittall	6	– c Houghton b Whittall		38
Inzamam-ul-Haq c G. W. Flower b Streak	71	– (6) c A. Flower b Whittall		65

Wasim Akram c Carlisle

b Streak	27	– (8) c Dekker b Strang	19
Kabir Khan not out	2	– b Streak	0
Aqib Javed lbw b Streak	0	– b Streak	2
B 3, l-b 4, w 9, n-b 13	29	W 2, n-b 6	8
1/36 2/82 3/88 4/131	322	1/13 2/16 3/26	158
5/135 6/151 7/271 8/317 9/322		4/29 5/35 6/131 7/142 8/156 9/156	

Bowling: *First Innings* – Streak 39–11–90–6; Brain 27–4–94–1; Olonga 10–0–27–1; Whittall 29–10–49–2; Strang 15–5–45–0; Dekker 4–1–10–0. *Second Innings* – Brain 16–4–50–3; Streak 11–5–15–3; Strang 19–3–35–1; Whittall 16–3–58–3.

Umpires: M. J. Kitchen (England) and I. D. Robinson (Zimbabwe).

Referee: J. L. Hendriks (West Indies).

MR CHARLES ABSOLON – THE VETERAN 1874

"Age does not wither, nor custom stale the infinite success of his bowling."

Mr C. Absolon's bowling had all ten wickets (4 bowled) in the second innings of Shoreham v St Mary's Cray, at Shoreham, last June. Mr C. Absolon's bowling had seven wickets (4 bowled) in Shoreham's first innings; so in that match the old boy's bowling had 17 wickets.

Mr C. Absolon's bowling also had 17 wickets in another match played in 1873; this match was Wood Green v Junior Southgate, played at Southgate, last August. In this match *Bell's Life* reports Mr Absolon to have bowled nine wickets (the other was run out) in the Juniors' first innings, and to have bowled seven, and had another lbw, in their second innings. Bowling 16 wickets in an 11-a-side match is an unusually successful bit of bowling.

It was stated that Mr Absolon's bowling in 60 innings in 1873 averaged over six wickets per innings. What makes all this so surprising is the advanced age and great weight of Mr Absolon.

Mr Absolon was 56 years old in 1873.

W. G. GRACE

I make no apology for devoting a chapter of this collection to W. G. Grace. There is a strong case for considering him the greatest cricketer who ever lived, or who ever will live, based not only on his astonishing statistics (practically all of which have now been surpassed by somebody or other) but more on the changes he wrought in the game. When he first played at Lord's, in July 1864 (just a month or two after the publication of the first *Wisden*), the game had not yet refound the popularity that it had held in the great days of Hambledon and the early days of MCC three-quarters of a century before, but thanks almost entirely to his achievements on the cricket field, and to the extent by which he surpassed all of his team-mates and opponents, the public imagination was captured by cricket in a way that it had never been before, nor, many would argue, has been since. What is more, he stayed at the top for 30 years or so. He had to cope with the development of round-arm and overarm bowling, the decline of the great All-England elevens and the rise of the County Championship, the beginnings of Test cricket and touring overseas to places where there was often little Western civilisation let alone a decent wicket. Yet he coped with them all, and remained "The Champion".

Modern aficionados will argue, with justification, that the standard of wickets, bowling and – especially – fielding was much lower in W. G.'s day, and that some of the greats of more recent times, Bradman, Sobers, Viv Richards and Botham, for instance, were better cricketers than W. G. Given the improvement in quality that has come with the application of sports science to every athletic endeavour, these people could even have a case, but that does not alter the fact that under conditions which applied to all his contemporaries, he outdid them all by such a distance that he brought cricket to the forefront of national life. It was said that his face was, after Queen Victoria's, the best known in England. The one with the beard was W. G. *Wisden* always supported W. G. In many ways he was the making of the Almanack, whose job it was to record the amazing things the Champion (or "the doctor" or "the crack" or the "grand old man") did on the cricket field. In this collection, I have not tried to record too many of his cricketing achievements, but rather to seek out those writers who have tried to get to the essence of the man.

1874

Of the 2,239 runs scored from the bat for Gloucestershire in 1873 the three Graces made 1,140, or more than half.

1877
The Canterbury Week, 1876

Saturday was the last day of the Week, and Mr Grace's Day; for on that day he completed the largest innings ever played for MCC, made three-fifths of the runs in the largest innings ever scored on the Canterbury ground, and had – according to the *Kent Herald* – completely settled the Kentish Twelve.

The day was intensely hot, and so was the hitting of the MCC two – Mr W. Grace and Mr Crutchley – who resumed their innings at noon, and were not parted until late in the afternoon when they had increased the score by 227 runs! as Mr Crutchley went to wickets with the score at 203, and was out for 84 with it at 430. There were then five wickets down at an average of 86 runs per wicket, and Mr Grace as full of fine hitting as he had been at any phase of this great display, and he kept on hitting, scoring, and fagging the field until near the end, for he was not out until 546 runs had been scored, and play finally ceased when the score was at 557, nine wickets having then fallen. Then time was up for the Canterbury Week of 1876; and this stupendous run-getting match was drawn; 19 different bowlers having bowled therein; 1,999 balls bowled; 1,099 runs from the bat, and 75 extra scored, and 31 wickets having fallen.

Mr W. Grace commenced MCC's second innings; he was 6 hours and 20 minutes at wickets, and had scored 344 runs out of the 540 booked, when he was caught out at mid-off, *Bell's Life* stating, "He scored those 344 runs without positively giving a chance. His hits consisted of 76 singles, twenty twos, eight threes, and 51 fours (204 runs by fourers in one innings!)".

Kent 473 (Lord Harris 154; W. G. Grace four for 116).

MCC 144 (Fellowes five for 50) **and 557** (W. G. Grace 344, Crutchley 84; Lord Harris four for 59).

1916
Deaths in 1915 – W. G. Grace

In no branch of sport has anyone ever enjoyed such unquestioned supremacy as that of W. G. Grace in the cricket field. In his great days he stood alone, without a rival. Not even George Fordham and Fred Archer, as jockeys, or John Roberts as a billiard player, had such a marked superiority over the men who were nearest to them in point of ability. Whatever may be in store for the game of cricket in future it seems safe to say that such a player will never be seen again. A rare combination of qualities went to the making of W. G. Grace. Blessed with great physical advantages, he united to a strength of constitution that defied fatigue a devotion to the game which time was powerless to affect. When he was in his prime no sun was too hot and no day too long for him. It is on record that when, for a cricketer, he was no longer young, he spent the whole night by the bedside of a patient, and on the following day stepped on to the Clifton College ground and scored over 200 runs . . .

With Mr Grace's characteristics as a batsman I must deal rather briefly. He was, in the main, quite orthodox in style, his bat being as perfectly straight as Fuller Pilch's, but he greatly enlarged the domain of orthodoxy, playing a far more aggressive and punishing game than any of the classic batsmen who came before him. It should be explained here that E. M. Grace, who first made the family name famous, played a game of his own and was a little outside comparisons. W. G. developed the art of batting to an extraordinary degree, but he was not, like E. M., a revolutionist. There is his own authority for stating that he did not indulge in the pull till he was forty. A splendid all-round hitter, he excelled all his predecessors in his power of placing the ball on the on-side. A story is told of a cricketer who had regarded Fuller Pilch as the last word in batting, being taken in his old age to see Mr Grace bat for the first time. He watched the great man for a quarter of an hour or so and then broke out into expressions of boundless delight. "Why," he said, "this man scores continually from balls that old Fuller would have been thankful to stop." The words conveyed everything. Mr Grace when he went out at the ball did so for the purpose of getting runs. Pilch and his imitators, on the other hand, constantly used forward play for defence alone.

When the wicket was difficult and the ball turning, Mr Grace trusted for defence to that strong back play which, even in his boyhood, convinced his people at home that he would be a greater batsman than his brother E. M. Mr Grace's batting from 1868 onwards quite overshadowed his bowling, and yet during his career he took many hundreds of wickets. Indeed, old Bob Thoms, the umpire, always contended that if he had not been such a wonderful batsman he would have been the best slow bowler in England. Even as it was he held his own very well with such masters as Alfred Shaw and Southerton. He bowled medium pace with a purely round-arm action in his young days, but slackened his speed about 1872.

His superb strength and health enabled him to stand any amount of cricket, but in his two best years as a bowler – 1875 and 1877 – his batting fell off 50 per cent. He did not rely much on break, only turning in a little from leg, but he had a great command over length and very seldom indeed pitched short. His chief strength lay in head work. No one was quicker to find out the weak points of a batsman or more certain to lure an impetuous hitter to his doom. In Gloucestershire's great days he was much helped by brilliant fielding, Fred Grace in particular, at deep square leg, being invaluable to him. When he first appeared for the Gentlemen, Mr Grace was a splendid outfield, capable of throwing the ball a hundred yards, but as time went on he took to fielding near the wicket and for many years he had no superior at point except his brother E. M.

Personally, W. G. struck me as the most natural and unspoiled of men. Whenever and wherever one met him he was always the same. There was not the smallest trace of affectation about him. If anything annoyed him he was quick to show anger, but his little outbursts were soon over. One word I will add. No man who won such world-wide fame could have been more modest in speaking of his own doings.

PERSONAL RECOLLECTIONS OF W. G. GRACE 1896
by Lord Harris

From about '76 to '86 I saw a good deal of the old man's play and I shall never see such all-round play again. There may arise a bat as good, and at point and to his own bowling a field as good and, of course, there have been, and will be, bowlers as good, but I doubt one generation producing two such all-round cricketers. And remember, my young friends, that this super-excellence was not the result of eminent physical fitness only, it depended a good deal also on the careful life the old man led. He did not play brilliantly despite how he lived as some, whose all too brief careers I can remember, did, but he regulated his habits of life with such care and moderation that his physical capacity was always at its best, and has lasted in the most marvellous manner . . .

I always thought the old man depended rather too much on the umpire for leg before, particularly when I was on the opposite side. He crossed the wicket so far to the off himself that he could not in many instances judge with any accuracy whether the ball pitched straight or not, and I don't think a bowler ought to ask for leg before unless he is pretty sure as to the pitch. I remember one day at Canterbury, the wind was blowing pretty strongly across the ground, and W. G. was lobbing them up in the air to get all advantage of the wind. I kept on fetching them round to sharp long leg – I never hit him square – or trying to, and every time the ball hit my leg, he asked, and every time he asked Willsher shook his head, and the old man was getting almost savage, when, at last, I got my left leg too much to the off, and the ball went through my legs and bowled me. Of course, W. G. held that was proof positive that all the others would have hit the wicket too, whilst I held that that was possible, but that none of them had pitched straight.

1896

by A. G. Steel

W. G. has, so it goes without saying, a thorough knowledge of the game, and I recollect well in the summer of 1878 an incident which well illustrates the fact. North v South was being played at Lord's. Barlow, the Lancashire professional, was batting, and W. G. was fielding point. Now Barlow had a trick of tapping the ball away after he had played it, and occasionally, in order to excite a laugh from the onlookers, would scamper down the pitch for a yard or two and then back again. On this occasion he just stopped the ball and it lay by his crease; he then tapped it towards point, and perhaps thinking he would hustle that fielder, he went through his performance of dashing down the pitch and back again. He must have been thoroughly upset by the action of point, who, ignoring the ball, quietly asked the umpire, "How's that for hitting the ball twice?" and out Barlow had to go – a lesson which he never forgot.

1879

NORTH v SOUTH

Played at Lord's, June 10, 11 and 12, 1878, for the benefit of the MCC Professional Cricketers' Fund. Whit Monday broke bright, breezy, and hopeful for the enjoyment of the holiday folks, and up to the early afternoon of that day the people streamed up St John's Wood Road to Lord's so continuously that – notwithstanding a showery stormy afternoon, that undoubtedly lessened the attendance – the official return stated: 10,538 paid their 6d for admission.

Lord's Ground on that day was indeed a sight, the equal of which had never been seen on a Whit Monday. The people thronged the Grand Stand – they crowded to inconvenience the players' seats at the north end of the Pavilion – they filled to an inch the embankment seats at the NE and SW corners – they completely blocked up the Tavern steps – they sat as closely together as they could sit on the garden wall tops – every window looking on the ground was filled with lookers on, and not only did the visitors stand five or six deep behind the ring, but at top and bottom of the ground, they swarmed in hundreds before the ring, thereby materially contracting the fielding space, and rendering "hits to the people" not worth more than half the runs they were booked for. But for all that, the 10,000 present were, as a rule, a jolly and good-tempered crowd; and when Mr W. G. Grace went to and entreated them, in his well-known bland and courteous manner, to get back a bit and give a little more fielding space, they laughed at, chaffed, and shook hands with the crack in the most enjoyable, merry, and free and easy form; and by this and other ways practically proved that "the enlightened foreigner" who wrote that "the English took their pleasures churlishly" knew nothing of the matter, and wrote a famous fib.

The South 202 (Ridley 49, W. G. Grace 45; Shaw six for 60) **and 203**
(W. G. Grace b Barlow 77).

The North 180 (Greenwood 36 not out, Shaw 35, Barlow 20 "given out for infringing Rule XX"; W. G. Grace five for 60, Hadow 4–88) **and 226** for six (Lockwood 38, W. G. Grace four for 89). The North won by 4 wickets.

SPECTACLES 1916

Inevitably even W. G. failed sometimes – in four minor games, he was out for a duck in both innings, but he never suffered this fate in a first-class match.

XXII of Lansdown v The England Eleven, on the Sydenham

Field, Bath, May 28, 29, 30, 1863: c Clarke (A.) b Tinley 0; c Anderson b Tinley 0

Clifton v Lansdown, on the Sydenham Field, Bath, August 7, 8, 1863: lbw b E. M. Grace 0; b E. M. Grace 0

USEE v XXII of the Cadoxton CC (with Howitt) in Knoll Park, Neath, May 21, 22, 23, 1868: c Struve b Howitt 0; c and b Howitt 0

Bedminster v Great Western Railway (Swindon), at Bedminster, May 7, 1870: c and b Laverick 0; c Dormand b Laverick 0

SIR DONALD BRADMAN
BY R. C. ROBERTSON-GLASGOW, 1949

There are humorously affectionate stories about most great cricketers; intimate if somewhat apocryphal tales about them; of what Dr Grace said when Ernest Jones bowled a ball through his beard; of Patsy Hendren's reply to a criticism from the Sydney "Hill"; of what Johnny Douglas uttered when second slip floored a catch. But there are no funny stories about the Don. No one ever laughed about Bradman. He was no laughing matter.

W. G. GRACE CENTENARY 1949
by Hubert Preston

My personal knowledge of his greatness by means of eyesight commenced in 1884 at The Oval Test match in which Australia scored 551. How W. G. kept wicket and caught Midwinter off the Hon. Alfred Lyttelton, who, with his pads on, bowled lobs from the Vauxhall End and finished Australia's innings by taking the last four wickets for eight runs, remains a clear picture to me . . . And so by various pictures on to 1895 at Gravesend, where he came to the Press tent during lunch time and wrote a telegram. To my delight, Edgar Pardon, my chief, introduced me to the Doctor, so making the occasion even more memorable to me – though unforgettable for anyone present. That was the match in which W. G. scored 257 out of 443 before being last out on the Saturday. Then after lunch Kent were dismissed for 76. Of the 106 runs which gave Gloucestershire victory by nine wickets

W. G. scored 73, while to complete the remarkable three days, during which he was on the field while every ball was bowled, he trotted from the dressing tent in his tweed tail suit and hard felt hat, carrying his heavy cricket bag to a four-wheeled cab which took him to the station.

THE GREAT MEN OF GLOUCESTERSHIRE 1957
by H. F. Hutt

The date of the formation of Gloucestershire as a county club is given as 1871, but the side, which was purely amateur and remained so until 1876, made a start in the world of fairly important cricket in the early 1860s. A team under the name of Gloucestershire played a fixture against Devon in 1862, and there is a note of a Gloucestershire v. Somerset game in 1863. In 1868, Gloucestershire beat MCC in two days at Lord's, but it was not until 1870 that the enthusiasm of the Grace family – well known as a cricketing family long before W. G. was born at Downend in 1848 – put the club on a sound basis and enabled Gloucestershire to play other counties in a more or less settled programme.

The West Country team, soon to be dubbed the County of the Graces, engaged in first-class county matches for the first time in 1870. In 1873, Gloucestershire were admitted to the newly-formed County Championship as one of the nine sides considered first-class. Their amateur talent, under the captaincy of W. G., immediately showed their worth in a competition of largely professional strength by sharing the Championship with Nottinghamshire who usually had ten or eleven paid players.

The black-bearded W. G. strode through these early years of Gloucestershire successes like a colossus. He and his brothers – E. M. and G. F. – dominated match after match and in 1876 and 1877 Gloucestershire carried off the Championship on their own. Until beaten by the first Australian eleven in 1878 the team never lost a match at home. The glory faded after the death of G. F. Grace in 1880, and apart from brief revivals the team over a whole season have not recaptured it.

Second place in 1930, 1931 and 1947 was the nearest the county came to finishing top since the great days of the 1870s.

Still, Gloucestershire's valuable contribution to the game cannot be measured by match results.

The feats of W. G., who died in 1915, aged 67, are legendary. He led Gloucestershire from 1870 to 1899 and did more to popularise cricket than anyone else. As a batsman he achieved almost everything of distinction – two centuries in a match, three hundreds in succession, 2,000 runs in a season and three scores of over 300. A bowler of medium pace, with round-arm action and a little break from leg, he took all ten wickets in an innings, and he did the Double on eight occasions. W. G. hit 126 centuries, 51 of them for Gloucestershire, with a highest score for the county of 318 not out, and the remarkable average of 40.80 spread over 30 years with the club. In 1895, when 47 years old, he scored 1,000 runs in May – an amazing performance.

1944
by Sir Stanley Jackson (in an interview)

Of all the fast bowlers the Australians have sent to this country, I think Jones was the best in my time. I have very good reasons for remembering him, as I took part in the first match he played in this country against Lord Sheffield's XI at Sheffield Park, Sussex, in 1896. He was one of the most powerful men I ever met. I believe he was a miner, and in his early days of the tour was very wild in his delivery. This was probably because the Australians came practically straight off the ship to the match and were short of practice. Jones gave me the impression that his main effort was to show his immense pace. The wicket was dry and he bowled short, bumpy stuff.

I went in first with W. G. Grace and we had to dance about a bit. One ball from Jones hit W. G. under the arm, and later in the innings another one went head-high past him and over Kelly's head to the boundary. This was the ball about which the Beard Story originated. I can see W. G. now. He threw his head back, which caused his beard to stick out. Down the pitch went W. G., stroking his beard, to Harry Trott and said: "Here, what is all this?" And Trott said: "Steady, Jonah." To which Jones made that famous remark: "Sorry, Doctor, she slipped." I do not think the

ball actually touched W. G.'s beard. That story was told afterwards, and I believe I was responsible. When I was out and
returned to the Pavilion, I said: "Did you see that one go through
W. G.'s beard?"

A HISTORY OF DERBYSHIRE CRICKET 1953
BY W. T. TAYLOR

Derbyshire's inability to secure any additional county opponents
caused a good deal of despondency among officials and supporters,
but the turning point came in 1873 when a match was arranged at
Wirksworth between sixteen of the county and the Nottinghamshire
eleven. Considering that at the time Nottinghamshire were a cricket
power, the result was staggering. Derbyshire won by an innings and
eight runs. In their first innings Nottinghamshire scored a beggarly 14
runs; Joe Flint took six wickets for seven runs and William Mycroft
four for six.

Through the years a tale has been handed down about that batting
debacle. The story is that a local Derbyshire celebrity, a keen and
generous supporter of the club – and the proprietor of an important
wine and spirit business, where he blended an attractive and potent
brand of whisky – entertained the visitors lavishly at his establishment on the morning when they were to begin their innings.

Who can say that his fanatical enthusiasm for Derbyshire was
responsible for the heaviness of his hand when he poured out
refreshment for his guests? Might it not have been just the warmth of
his hospitality?

1957

There have been many memorials to W. G. and the cradle in
which he was rocked in his home at Downend more than one
hundred years ago is now in Bristol Museum.

THE DR W. G. GRACE 1967
by Norman Preston

The first Public House to bear the name of the Grand Old Man
of Cricket was opened last July at Elmers End. It stands within
200 yards of his grave and between the two sites is Birkbeck

railway station. In the saloon bar is an attractive mirror tinged with copper with the head of Dr Grace superimposed. The architect, a lover of cricket, attended the previous year's ceremony commemorating the 50th anniversary of the death of W. G. and so the new hostelry got its name. Cricket could not wish for a better advertisement, thousands of commuters to the City pass its doors, and some enter, day by day. The Rev. A. N. B. Sugden, a chaplain at the cemetery, who has since returned to his native Yorkshire as the Vicar of St Peter's Harrogate, blessed the house and pulled the first pint. The next day he was present when Mr C. Stuart Chiesman, Chairman of Kent CCC, unveiled a commemorative plaque to W. G. on his final home, Fairmont, Mottingham, where he died in 1915. Downend House, Gloucestershire, the birthplace of W. G., was also in the news at the same time for it was sold by auction for £12,600 to a Bristol engineering design firm. In 1942, it fetched only £1,200.

SHILLINGS FOR W. G. 1973
by Sir Compton Mackenzie

The year 1895 was to become a remarkable one in the history of cricket. The prodigious performance of W. G. Grace in scoring over 1,000 runs in 22 days in the month of May inspired the whole country with a tremendous interest in cricket and cricketers. There had been nothing like it and, moreover, more than 30 years passed before it was repeated by another Gloucestershire stalwart, W. R. Hammond, in 25 days.

There must have been three or four periodicals produced in 1895 devoted to cricket records and the personalities of the various cricketers. It may have been due to this interest at this time that, as I remember, five were promoted to first-class counties that year. These were Hampshire, Derbyshire, Warwickshire, Leicestershire and Essex.

It was a batsman's year. W. G. Grace was in his forty-eighth year and he had taken considerable pains to get himself into the best physical condition possible. He was by far the heaviest player taking part in the great matches and he was in his 31st season in first-class cricket. Moreover, he played many long innings without a mistake: 288 against Somerset at Bristol in five hours 20 minutes; it was his hundredth century; 257 against Kent at Gravesend and the Champion was on the field during every ball of the match.

Enthusiastic crowds flocked to see him wherever he appeared and he finished that memorable summer in making 2,346 runs, the largest aggregate of the year. He was entertained at banquets in London and Bristol; a National Testimonial was organised and the *Daily Telegraph*, the paper with which I was later to have some connection, collected £5,000, by means of a shilling subscription. Schoolboys all over the country were invited to contribute. I can still recall from 80 years ago our determination not to let our pocket-money of sixpence per week be given to cigarettes until we had the necessary shilling for W. G.

THE CAREER FIGURES OF W. G. GRACE 1982
by John Woodcock

There follows an article by Michael Fordham, *Wisden*'s chief statistician since 1979, in which he gives his reasons, and those of the Association of Cricket Statisticians, for wanting to change, quite significantly, the career record of W. G. Grace. While acknowledging the amount of work done by Mr Fordham and his fellow scrutineers, and though grateful for the pleasure they give us, I prefer to leave the great man's figures as they have been for as long as anyone cares to remember.

That they appeared in *Wisden* 1981, my first year as editor, in their revised form was because Mr Fordham thought, mistakenly, that he had cleared them with me. In future, various books of reference, though not *Wisden*, will show W. G. as having scored not 126 but 124 hundreds. To avoid confusion, the figures now claimed by the Association of Cricket Statisticians are to be found in footnotes on pages 180 and 200.

No amount of research could, to my mind, justify changing a record so honoured by time and custom. If wrong decisions are thought to have been made, they should be altered reasonably soon or left to stand. That one-day games played more than a century ago should have been termed first-class need not surprise

us: there were no regulations in those days stipulating the minimum time for a first-class match. Then, as now, contemporary
opinion was the best criterion.

So, in *Wisden* at any rate, W. G.'s 152 at Lord's for the England
team that had toured North America in 1872 against Fourteen
Gentlemen of MCC (with Rylott) survives, as does his 113 for
Gloucestershire against Somerset at Clifton in 1879. To remove
them, as the Association of Cricket Statisticians would have us
do, would, I think, be presumptuous and sadly unromantic. The
first of them, anyway, is referred to in *Wisden* 1874 as having been
one of the Doctor's superb lot of *first-class* triple figure scores.

Who, too, would wish to invalidate such historic occasions as
W. G.'s hundredth 100, the origin, as *Wisden* put it at the time, of
a national testimonial taken up with enthusiasm in many places
far beyond the limits of the United Kingdom, or the great match
at Taunton when Jack Hobbs first equalled Grace's total of hundreds and then passed it? In recognition of Hobbs's feat, *Wisden*
wrote how the match was rendered forever memorable by the
triumph of Hobbs, who, playing innings of 101 and 101 not out,
beat the "Grand Old Man's" record. Circumstances generally
combined to invest the occasion with exceptional excitement.
Tremendous cheering greeted the accomplishment of the feat:
indeed so pronounced was the enthusiasm that the progress of
the game was delayed while at the end of the over all players in
the field shook hands with Hobbs and the Surrey captain brought
out a drink for the hero, who raised his glass high and bowed to
the crowd before partaking of the refreshment! Far be it from me
to say that that might as well never have happened.

TWO THOUSAND WICKETS

In all of cricket history, only 33 men have taken as many as 2,000 wickets in their first-class careers. This compares with the 24 men who have scored one hundred first-class hundreds (two men feature in both lists: W. G. Grace and Kent's peerless Frank Woolley) and 38 who have scored as many as 35,000 first-class runs. But cricket is a batsman's game and bowlers never seem to get the credit they deserve.

R. C. Robertson-Glasgow, writing in *Wisden* in 1963, was one of the few who believed that cricket is a bowler's game. "It is the bowler in cricket who knows the deepest joy; because he can hit his victim and pretend to be sorry about it; because he is artist and workman in one; because he can make mistakes and yet suddenly enter the paradise of triumph.

"Myself, I go back once more to Taunton in 1926. Clarence Grimmett, who could bowl deadly spinners from somewhere near his right kidney, was at the wicket. Not a great batsman, Clarrie; not even a fairly good one. Never mind. He had raised his bat to cut me square. The ball chose to come in from the off, and it knocked out his middle stump. Leonardo da Vinci should have been there, to paint the incredulity of the batsman, and the unconfined joy of the bowler.

"Rejoice, then, cricketers; but, most of all, ye bowlers. For, whatever the books may say, yours is the best part in the best play yet invented."

I'm not sure that many of the editors of *Wisden* have been so enthusiastic about bowling. It was not until 1939 that *Wisden* listed all those bowlers who had taken more than 1,500 wickets in their careers, a list that was shortened in the first post-war edition, in 1946, to those who had taken 2,000 wickets. The achievement of taking 2,000 wickets is a career milestone which often has no particular bearing on the match being played at the time, and the inaccuracy of early records means that in most cases the feat has gone entirely unnoticed by *Wisden*, and probably by the bowlers themselves.

The top two men on the list of wicket-takers, Wilfred Rhodes and "Tich" Freeman, probably had little idea how many wickets they had taken in their careers, and when Rhodes retired, his official tally was set by *Wisden* at 4,184 wickets. This was upped to 4,188 a few seasons later, and then reduced finally to 4,187 in 1957. In that same 1957 edition, Freeman's career total, which had stood at 3,775 since his retirement two decades earlier, suddenly went up to 3,776. W. G. Grace and Alex Kennedy of Hampshire have also swapped places on the list, years after both men had died. Alfred Shaw of Nottinghamshire had 45 wickets deducted from his total half a century after his death. If *Wisden*'s statisticians at the time had little idea when the 2,000-wicket milestones were passed, it is not surprising that the rest of the cricket world had little idea either. When the most recent member of the club, Norman Gifford, took his 2,000th wicket, against Kent at Folkestone, I remember that there was just a ripple of polite applause that would accompany the fall of any Kent wicket within the county, although *Wisden* did deign to mention the fact.

Now that the opportunities to take first-class wickets have been reduced, it is difficult to imagine anybody adding their names to the list of these 33 immortals. At the start of the 2005 English season, the leading active wicket-taker was thirty-nine-year-old Phil DeFreitas with 1,236 wickets. So we ought to celebrate those giants of the past who have achieved a haul of wickets that current players can only dream of.

BOWLERS WHO HAVE TAKEN 2,000 WICKETS, 2005

W. Rhodes	1898–1930	4,187
A. P. Freeman	1914–1936	3,776
C. W. L. Parker	1903–1935	3,278
J. T. Hearne	1888–1923	3,061
T. W. J. Goddard	1922–1952	2,979
W. G. Grace	1865–1908	2,876
A. S. Kennedy	1907–1936	2,874
D. Shackleton	1948–1969	2,857
G. A. R. Lock	1946–1970	2,844
F. J. Titmus	1949–1982	2,830
M. W. Tate	1912–1937	2,784
G. H. Hirst	1891–1929	2,739
C. Blythe	1899–1914	2,506
D. L. Underwood	1963–1987	2,465
W. E. Astill	1906–1939	2,431
J. C. White	1909–1937	2,356
W. E. Hollies	1932–1957	2,323
F. S. Trueman	1949–1969	2,304
J. B. Statham	1950–1968	2,260
R. T. D. Perks	1930–1955	2,233
J. Briggs	1879–1900	2,221
D. J. Shepherd	1950–1972	2,218
E. G. Dennett	1903–1926	2,147
T. Richardson	1892–1905	2,104
T. E. Bailey	1945–1967	2,082
R. Illingworth	1951–1983	2,072
N. Gifford	1960–1988	2,068
F. E. Woolley	1906–1938	2,068
G. Geary	1912–1938	2,063
D. V. P. Wright	1932–1957	2,056
J. A. Newman	1906–1930	2,032
A. Shaw	1864–1897	2.027
S. Haigh	1895–1913	2,012

W. RHODES

Wilfred Rhodes took his 2,000th wicket in 1908, his 3,000th in 1920 and his 4,000th in 1929. *Wisden* missed the lot.

1931

Wilfred Rhodes, now 53 years of age, has announced that, although he obtained more than 70 wickets for less than 20 runs apiece last summer and had a batting average of nearly 23, he will take no further part in first-class cricket. So comes to an end a splendid career which, including the years of war, extended over 33 seasons.

The distinction peculiar to Rhodes consists in his achievement – after gaining great fame as the leading bowler in the country for a dozen years or more – of developing his batting to such an extent that for a time in Test matches he regularly opened England's innings in company with Hobbs.

That attainment would of itself have invested Rhodes' career with special quality but, as it happened, his prowess did not end with his advance to such high rank as a batsman. After the war, with Yorkshire's attack enormously weakened owing to the deaths of Booth and Drake, Rhodes was once again called upon for a huge amount of work with the ball and, as happily his skill had not deserted him, he found himself able to respond so handsomely to the demands of his county that, when over forty, he took in the course of six seasons 828 wickets for 13 runs each.

A. P. FREEMAN

Freeman's 2,000th wicket was taken in 1929, and his 3,000th in 1933.

A. P. Freeman in the Cricket Field, 1937

After the close of the 1936 season, the engagement of A. P. Freeman with the Kent County Club was not renewed. The acceptance of an offer from Walsall, a Birmingham and District League club, suggests that Freeman will not play any more county cricket; so an epitome of his career is opportune. One of the smallest first-class players, he became a great slow bowler by the diverse way he found to spin and flight the ball with his strong right hand.

Born on May 17, 1889, at Lewisham, Freeman played first for Kent in 1914 when twenty-five years of age, and the break in county cricket until 1919 delayed the development of his full powers until the completion of his thirtieth year.

This prolonged hindrance makes his aggregate of 3,775 wickets taken in first-class cricket all the more remarkable. Wilfred Rhodes, with 4,184 wickets, alone has surpassed this figure, and the Yorkshire slow left-hander, starting when twenty, accomplished this from 1898 to 1930–29 seasons, compared with Freeman's 19.

Nearly all his best work has been accomplished for Kent, and his bowling in the six seasons 1928–1933, when 1,673 wickets fell to him, was little short of astounding.

C. W. L. PARKER
Five Cricketers of the Year, 1923

I have seen Parker so seldom that I can say little about his bowling from personal observation. His main strength lies, I think, in the fact that with the left-handed slow bowler's usual spin and break he combines a little extra speed. He is not strictly speaking a slow bowler, but rather a bowler on the slow side of medium pace. This is, I admit, a nice distinction, but it makes him more difficult to hit. The batsman thinks twice before jumping out to drive him.

J. T. HEARNE 1892

To a player who has done so much in a short time, a brilliant career should be merely a question of health. He has everything in his favour, and certainly, since the days of George Howitt, Middlesex have had no bowler who could for a moment be compared to him. He is a pupil of the school of which Spofforth was the master – a high delivery, an off-break, and good variety of pace being the characteristics of his method. He has proved his excellence on all sorts of wickets, and nearly all the leading batsmen to whom he was opposed last season were loud in his praise.

He is a very good field, and though he has not yet done much in batting, it is likely enough that in that department of the game he will improve with experience. For the present, however, it is a sufficient distinction for him that he has supplied the need of a first-class bowler from which the Middlesex eleven had been suffering for nearly 20 years.

T. W. J. GODDARD
1940
SURREY v GLOUCESTERSHIRE

At Kennington Oval, July 12, 13, 14, 1939. Surrey won by seven wickets. Gloucestershire sorely felt the absence of W. R. Hammond, suffering from lumbago, but Goddard bowled so well that only a last wicket stand of 88 between Mobey and Gover enabled Surrey to snatch the lead.

Goddard's 2,000th wicket was: A. R. Gover b Goddard 31

1967

The early days of Goddard's career gave no hint of the success he was later to achieve. Born on October 1, 1900, he first played for Gloucestershire in 1922 as a fast bowler. Despite his strong physique he made little progress and in six years took only 153 wickets at a cost of 34 runs each.

At the end of the 1927 season he left the county and joined the MCC ground staff at Lord's. There he decided to experiment with off-breaks and his long, strong fingers were ideally suited to this type of bowling. Beverley Lyon, the Gloucestershire captain, saw him in the nets at Lord's and, immediately struck by Goddard's new-found ability, persuaded Gloucestershire to re-engage him. The effect was immediate and dramatic. In 1929 Goddard took 184 wickets at 16 runs apiece and he never looked back.

W. G. GRACE 1896
by A. G. Steel

The first occasion I ever played against W. G. was at Cambridge in the summer of 1878, and this was also the first time I ever saw him play. I remember being desperately anxious to get him out, but I was disappointed, and on my telling him what pleasure it would give me to get him out, he laughingly replied, "It's only a question of time; if you go on long enough you are bound to get me out". I was not, however, successful on that occasion, but I shall never forget the kindly encouragement I, a young cricketer, received from W. G. the first time I met him. It was not, however, his batting, oddly enough, which struck me as so wonderful, it was his bowling. Never, as far as I know, did any bowler give the same peculiar flight to the ball as W. G. does, and well justified is the remark I have often heard him make of a newly-arrived batsman, "Oh, he's a young one, is he? I think I ought to do for him," and he generally does.

A. S. KENNEDY
Five Cricketers of the Year, 1933

Kennedy has, over a long period of years, been one of the best county bowlers in the country and, as in the case of Astill, it is a little difficult to understand why such a fine bowler and more than useful bat has never appeared for England against Australia.

Perhaps some explanation for this may be found in the fact that some years ago when he was at the height of his powers there were rumours that his action was not above suspicion.

Bowling with his hand very high, almost indeed directly above his head, Kennedy relied for his success on accuracy of length combined with an in-swing which, fortified by spin off the pitch, made him, on his day, a very difficult bowler against whom to prevail. It was this high delivery with a real or apparent flick which gave rise to the idea his action was open to question.

Very naturally he resented in most strenuous fashion the accusation but, unfortunately for him, there remained in the minds of the successive selection committees the germ of the suspicion. This probably has stood in the way of his being picked for a representative match in this country or for an England team going out to Australia.

D. SHACKLETON 1963

Shackleton performed magnificently. In his 15th season with Hampshire and at thirty-eight years of age, he bowled more overs and took more wickets than ever before. His figures in all matches were 1,717 overs for 172 wickets – the 14th successive time he had taken one hundred wickets in a summer.

HAMPSHIRE v DERBYSHIRE

At Portsmouth, July 7, 9, 10, 1962. Drawn, Hampshire taking four points. On a perfect pitch and a fast outfield, batsmen maintained the upper hand throughout the game.

Shackleton's 2,000th wicket: G. W. Richardson b Shackleton 1
Bowling analysis: Shackleton 41.5–13–112–5

1964
ENGLAND v WEST INDIES
Second Test Match

At Lord's, June 20, 21, 22, 24, 25. Drawn. Shackleton joined Allen with 19 minutes left and 15 runs required. They fell further behind the clock and when Hall began his last dramatic over eight runs were needed. Singles came off the second and third balls, but Shackleton was run out off the fourth when Worrell raced from short-leg with the ball and beat the batsman to the bowler's end.

That meant Cowdrey had to come in with two balls left and six wanted.

G. A. R. LOCK 1963
INDIA v ENGLAND
First Test Match

At Bombay, November 11, 12, 14, 15, 16, 1961. Drawn. Excellent slow bowling by Allen and Lock kept India fighting and, despite a fifth-wicket stand of 142 by Borde and Durani and sound innings by Manjrekar and Jaisimha, England led by 110.

Lock's 2,000th wicket: B. K. Kunderan lbw b Lock 5

F. J. TITMUS 1969
MCC in West Indies, 1967/68

From the English viewpoint the 1967/68 MCC tour of West Indies was a conspicuous success. The team, under the captaincy of Cowdrey and the management of Ames, went unbeaten through a programme containing 12 first-class matches, and the Test series was won. A team in the full sense of the word played good cricket in most testing circumstances. Neither on nor off the field did they obviously put a foot wrong . . .

Titmus lost four toes when his left foot was caught in the screw of a small boat, placed in the middle of the craft and, contrary to regulations, without a guard. Titmus could take no further part in the tour, and when he went home Lock, who had been leading Western Australia to top place in the Sheffield Shield, was recalled to Test cricket.

Titmus' 2,000th wicket, a catch by Tom Graveney to dismiss Seymour Nurse for 41 in the First Test at Trinidad, was taken a few days before his accident.

M. W. TATE
Bowler of the Year, 1924

He has all the good qualities of bowlers of his type – accuracy of length and power to make the ball break back or go away a little with his arm – but his prime merit is extra pace off the pitch. Though much slower than Arthur Gilligan through the air he often, I am assured, comes off the ground quite as fast. Whether in him will be found the Test bowler of whom we are so badly in need remains to be seen, but many of the best judges are very hopeful about him. It is a great point in his favour that, thanks to his beautiful delivery, he can get through a lot of work without undue fatigue. He had so much to do last summer that he might well have been tired out, but except for one day at The Oval in September he was effective to the end, and finished up quite fresh. Tate is a good, free-hitting batsman, capable at any time of getting his 50 runs, but one hopes that for the next few years, at least, the lure of long scores will not attract him. With heavy tasks ahead for English cricket his business is to take wickets.

G. H. HIRST
My Favourite Summer
by A. A. Thomson, 1967

The 1902 rubber began at Edgbaston with a rain-wrecked game, which England must have won if a full third day's play had been possible. This match had everything except a positive ending. It had what was reckoned the best integrated side that England ever put into the field: MacLaren, Fry, Tyldesley, Ranjitsinhji, Jackson, Braund, Jessop, Hirst, Lilley, Lockwood and Rhodes.

It saw a swordsman's century by Tyldesley which dragged England's batting back from the abyss; it staged Australia's dismissal for 36 (Hirst, three for 15 and Rhodes seven for 17) of which total Trumper magnificently scored half; it then alas, suffered an almost empty last day. (C. B. Fry told me long afterwards that, though Rhodes took seven wickets, it was Hirst who broke the batting's back.)

For full measure the scorecard carried a classic misprint which sets down the extras as three wides. There were, of course, really three byes, probably due to Hirst's terrific swerve. I doubt if Hirst ever bowled three wides in a season or Rhodes three wides in his whole career.

C. BLYTHE
by Frank Woolley, 1939

My heart and soul were in cricket. I was fortunate enough to bowl to Colin Blythe and he mentioned my name to the Kent manager, Mr Tom Pawley. That was in 1902, but as I had rather outgrown my strength at that age, being very tall and thin, they allowed me to attend the ground on mornings only. In 1903 I became a regular member of the staff. Colin Blythe was without doubt one of the greatest left-hand bowlers I have ever seen. He had a perfect action and run-up. I do not think I copied him. His style was so different from mine.

1918

Test matches, owing to his tendency to epileptic fits, were very trying to him, and after having had a big share in England's victory over Australia at Birmingham in 1909 he was practically forbidden to play at Lord's. Still he was, out by himself, England's best bowler in the three matches with the famous South African team of 1907, taking 26 wickets for less than 10½ runs apiece. Only one of the three matches was finished, England winning at Leeds by 53 runs. Blythe on that occasion bowled himself to a standstill, but he had his reward, clearly winning the game for his country.

D. L. UNDERWOOD
1982

HAMPSHIRE v KENT

At Bournemouth, August 29, 31, September 1, 1981. Kent won by eight wickets. Kent 23 pts, Hampshire 3 pts. Hampshire took three quick wickets before Aslett, making his debut for Kent, began to stamp his authority on the game. He put on 81 for the fourth wicket with Cowdrey, before finding an excellent partner in Johnson with whom he added 123 for the fifth wicket. Aslett went on to reach 146 not out, the highest score by a Kent batsman on his debut. Hampshire lost half their wickets for 29, and despite some late resistance from Southern and Stevenson, who put on 51 for the ninth wicket, were forced to follow on 170 behind. Greenidge and Tremlett gave Hampshire a better start to their second innings, but at the close on the second day were still five behind with six wickets remaining. Underwood became only the 32nd bowler to take 2,000 wickets in first-class cricket when he removed Turner at the start of the third day and, although Pocock and Parks gave Hampshire some hope, Kent were left to score only 109 to win.

Bowling analysis: Underwood 31–12–72–3

Five Cricketers of the Year, 1969

Few young cricketers have made such a direct impact on their entry to first-class cricket as Derek Leslie Underwood, hero of England's victory over Australia in the final Test at The Oval last season. At the age of twenty-three this left-arm slow-medium paced bowler of Kent may be said to be on the threshold of a great career in world cricket.

In six years he has taken 744 wickets, no doubt a record for one so young, and he bids fair to follow in the wake of such renowned England left-arm slow bowlers as Bobby Peel, John Briggs, Wilfred Rhodes, Hedley Verity and Tony Lock. His England and county captain, Colin Cowdrey, believes he will beat them all.

1871
SURREY v SUSSEX

Played at The Oval, June 23, 24, 25, 1870. Southerton started the bowling in this match with extraordinary success for Sussex; from the first ball he delivered Jupp was smartly stumped; from the second ball Stephenson made 2; from the third ball "H. H. S." was had at point, and from the fourth ball Griffith was caught out at long field; and inasmuch as Sussex won by two wickets only, there can be no doubt but that this three-wicket *mitrailleuse* kind of over of Southerton's really won the match.

W. E. ASTILL
Five Cricketers of the Year, 1933

Having appeared in the county eleven in the one game in 1906, he took part in every match for Leicestershire for the next four years – a very remarkable performance. During that period – in 1907 and 1908 – he headed the bowling averages; he was second in 1909 and fifth in 1910.

Already then he had justified his early inclusion and it was quite obvious that in him Leicestershire had discovered a medium-pace spin bowler of more than usual skill. In the course of time he has not altered his style very much and still bowls with a nice, easy action with the ability to turn the ball either way, though at the present time his arm is not so high as formerly.

J. C. WHITE
Five Cricketers of the Year, 1929

In addition to possessing much power of spinning the ball and great command of length, White uses his brains as much as any bowler of the present time. Given a wicket at all tricky, he spins the ball and, pitching on the leg stump to go across, never gives the batsman any peace. His faster ball on the bad wicket is well disguised, for he makes no difference in the pace of his run up to the wicket. On the hard wicket which gives the bowler no help, White depends mostly on flight, a slight swerve in the air, and a slow ball well outside the off-stump to which is imparted real finger-spin. With a certain wind to help him, White swerves late and makes the ball dip. With any wind against him, he will make the ball swerve and he is one of the few bowlers who can control the swerve so that the ball does not do too much.

W. E. HOLLIES
1956

WARWICKSHIRE v WORCESTERSHIRE

At Birmingham, May 11, 12, 13, 1955. Drawn. Rain again ruined the match, no play being possible on the final day. When Gardner and Horner began with a stand of 92 Warwickshire looked set for a big score, but the nine remaining wickets fell for 50. Perks, making the occasional ball lift, and Berry, genuine left-arm spin, caused the breakdown. Kenyon and Outschoorn were even more successful in their opening partnership but, like their opponents, most of the other Worcestershire batsmen were dismissed cheaply. Hollies, whose leg breaks and googlies accounted for seven wickets, became the first Warwickshire bowler to pass 2,000 wickets in his career.

Warwickshire 142 and 171 for 4.
Worcestershire 223 (Hollies 49–20–69–7).

1949
ENGLAND v AUSTRALIA
Fifth Test Match

At Kennington Oval, August 14, 16, 17, 18, 1948. Australia won by an innings and 149 runs. Shortly before six o'clock Bradman walked to the wicket amidst continued applause from the standing crowd. Yardley shook hands with Bradman and called on the England team for three cheers, in which the crowd joined. Evidently deeply touched by the enthusiastic reception, Bradman survived one ball, but, playing forward to the next, was clean bowled by a sharply turning break-back – possibly a googly. As if to avenge the fall of these two wickets in an over, Morris twice hooked Hollies to the boundary and the score rose to 153.

England 52 (Hutton 30; Lindwall six for 20) **and 188** (Hutton 64; Johnston four for 40).

Australia 389 (Morris 196, D. G. Bradman, b Hollies 0; Hollies 56–14–131–5).

F. S. TRUEMAN
1966
YORKSHIRE v ESSEX

At Bradford, July 24, 26, 27, 1965. Drawn. Yorkshire narrowly escaped defeat, being outplayed for most of the game. They were dismissed by Bailey and Knight in two and a half hours in the first innings. Smith, although barracked for slow scoring, and Fletcher, were mainly responsible for Essex gaining a lead of 199. During the innings, Trueman took the 2,000th wicket of his career. Knight again upset Yorkshire in the second innings, but Illingworth played a defiant innings lasting two hours, 40 minutes and the last pair, Chadwick and Waring, held out for the final 25 minutes. Yorkshire were still one run behind at the finish.

Yorkshire 75 (Trueman 14; Knight five for 41, Bailey five for 27) **and 198** for nine.

Essex 274 (Fletcher 81; Trueman four for 60).

1965
ENGLAND v AUSTRALIA
Fifth Test Match

At Kennington Oval, August 13, 14, 15, 17, 18, 1964. Drawn. Trueman, previously ineffective, suddenly bowled Redpath middle stump and had McKenzie caught at slip off successive balls.

There was no time for another delivery before the interval and the crowd hurried back to their places to see whether Trueman could complete his hat-trick. He also needed one more wicket to become the only bowler to take 300 wickets in Test matches. Hawke survived the first ball, but eventually provided Trueman with his 300th victim. Trueman followed by dismissing Corling and finished with four for 87.

J. B. STATHAM

Statham's 2,000th wicket was taken in 1966, for Lancashire v Nottinghamshire. *Wisden* does not record the feat.

J. B. Statham – Gentleman George
by Sir Neville Cardus, 1969

He was a fairly certain selection for Sir Leonard Hutton's conquering contingent which won the rubber in Australia, 1954/55. This was the rubber in which Frank Tyson achieved a hair-raising speed, so fast that Arthur Morris told me that Tyson was "through you almost before you had picked up your bat". Tyson stole all the limelight, but he was indebted for much of his blinding efficiency to Statham. And most generously has he acknowledged this indebtedness, in print, for he has written, "The glamour of success was undoubtedly mine. When in the second innings of the Sydney Test I captured six for 85, few spared a thought for Statham, who on that day bowled unremittingly for two hours into a stiff breeze and took three for 45."

Tyson adds that he "owed much to desperation injected into the batsmen's methods by Statham's relentless pursuit. To me it felt like having Menuhin playing second fiddle to my lead."

This is the most generous tribute paid by one cricketer to another since MacLaren maintained in a conversation with me,

"Talk about class and style? Well, I was supposed to be a batsman of some majesty but, believe me, compared to Victor Trumper I was like a cab-horse side by side with a thoroughbred Derby winner."

The Statham-Trueman collaboration of speed is recent history. Trueman in Test matches took 307 wickets, average 21.57. Statham in Tests took 252, average 24.84. It is useless to measure one against the other. As well we might try to assess Wagner and Mozart on the same level. Trueman, on occasion, nearly lost a big match by loss of technical (and temperamental) control; Statham never.

I particularly like Frank Tyson's story of the West Indies bowler who hit Laker over the eye. When subsequently the West Indies bouncer came in to bat and reluctantly took guard, somebody asked Statham to retaliate in kind and explosive kick. "No," said Statham, "I think I'll just bowl him out."

Here, in a phrase, is the essence of Statham's character. Gentleman "George". Sometimes he bowled too superbly to tail-end batsmen, they were not good enough to get into touch. It is rare for a fast bowler to play all round the world for nearly 20 years and not suffer animosity or verbal abuse from the opposition.

In his first-class seasons of the game, Statham overthrew no fewer than 2,259 batsmen, and each of them were glad to call him a friend.

R. T. D. PERKS
1953
ESSEX v WORCESTERSHIRE

At Chelmsford, August 1, 3, 4, 1952. Essex won by seven wickets. Bailey showed his value as an all-rounder by splendid fast bowling which broke the back of the early Worcestershire batting and then with an exhibition of enterprising stroke-play quite different from the dour tactics he adopted in the Test matches. Worcestershire, captained by Perks in the absence of Bird, never found their best batting form, but Perks took the eye with well-controlled swing bowling. When he dismissed Preston, Perks took his

2,000th wicket in first-class cricket. Worcestershire were without Ashman, who returned home because of his wife's illness, for the last two days. The ground was flooded the day preceding the match and wet portions of the square off the pitch had to be returfed before the match started at 3.30 p.m. D. W. Richardson, younger brother of the Worcestershire opening batsman, also a left-hander, made his first Championship appearance.

Worcestershire 133 (Bailey five for 43) **and 111** (Smith five for 51, Preston four for 32).

Essex 169 (Bailey 75, K. C. Preston c Broadbent b Perks. 2; Perks 25.3–11–40–6) **and 76** for three (Perks 10.5–4–33–2).

1978

In 1939 he had played twice for England, in the notorious time-less Test at Durban and against the West Indies at The Oval, and had performed respectably without meeting with spectacular success. He was then twenty-eight. When cricket was resumed he was thirty-five and had missed the years when a bowler of his type would naturally be in his prime. Now he was perhaps just past it and had moreover Bedser to compete with.

A tall man who made full use of his height, he bowled fast-medium right-hand, swinging the ball both ways, and was very steady, a great trier, endlessly cheerful and quite tireless. A left-handed bat, he started as a poor player but made himself into a useful tail-end hitter. Born at Hereford, he first appeared for Worcestershire in 1930 and his first victim was Jack Hobbs.

J. BRIGGS

1900
ENGLAND v AUSTRALIA
Third Test Match

Played at Leeds, Thursday, Friday, Saturday, June 29, 30, July 1, 1899. Drawn. The selection of Briggs had, as everyone knows, a disastrous result, the popular player being seized on the Thursday evening with illness of so serious a character as to prevent him playing any more during the season and rendering necessary his detention in the Cheadle Asylum. It was a sad end to a very brilliant career. On the form in which he had been bowling there was some reason for picking Briggs, but the committee made a bad mistake in not retaining Rhodes.

1903

Johnny Briggs died on January 11. The last reports as to the condition of Briggs's health had been so discouraging that the news of his death did not cause much surprise. Though he rallied so wonderfully from his seizure at Leeds, during the Test match in 1899, as to bowl with nearly all his old skill and success throughout the season of 1900, it was known that his ailment – a form of epilepsy – admitted of no permanent cure, and was liable to recur at any time. He had another attack sooner than had been expected; was compelled to go back to Cheadle Asylum; and took no part in the cricket of 1901. Five or six weeks before his death it was announced that he had again rallied after a serious relapse, but this time the improvement was of very brief duration. Briggs had a long career, but at the time of his death he was only a little over thirty-nine.

D. J. SHEPHERD 1970

GLAMORGAN v WORCESTERSHIRE

At Cardiff, September 3, 4, 5, 1969. Glamorgan won by 147 runs. Glamorgan 17 pts, Worcestershire 4 pts. A week's stirring cricket had its great climax at Cardiff where Glamorgan entered their last game happy in the knowledge that if they won they were virtual champions with an unassailable lead. And win they did. Sophia Gardens broke out in pandemonium and the celebrations ran well into the evening. Yet this match did not have the mounting tension of the Middlesex and Essex thrillers because Glamorgan were always in comfortable command. They were never in danger after Majid's century. He scored 156 out of 214 in three hours 20 minutes, his highest for Glamorgan. Good bowling by Nash and Shepherd resulted in Glamorgan gaining a lead of 82. Worcestershire had to get 256 to win in as many minutes on a wicket of unpredictable bounce. This time Cordle (five for 42) supported

Shepherd's spin and Worcestershire were all out for 108. It was not only a great day for Glamorgan but also for Don Shepherd, who in the match took his 2,000th wicket in first-class cricket.

Glamorgan 265 (Majid Jahangir 156; Gifford seven for 99) **and 173** for five declared (Walker 63 not out).

Worcestershire 183 (Headley 71; Shepherd three for 69) **and 108** (Cordle five for 42, Shepherd four for 20).

E. G. DENNETT
The Great Men of Gloucestershire
by H. F. Hutt, 1957

Dennett, master of flight and spin, was the first of Gloucestershire's famous left-arm bowlers, and had he not been contemporary with Rhodes and Blythe he must have gained Test honours. In 11 consecutive seasons to 1914, Dennett averaged nearly 150 wickets for under 20 runs each. In 1906 he took all ten Essex wickets in the first innings at Bristol for 40 runs, and in 1907 at Gloucester he shared with Jessop the distinction of dismissing Northamptonshire for 12 runs – the lowest total recorded in any county match. Dennett took eight wickets for nine runs and Jessop the other two for three runs. Dennett, who played for Gloucestershire from 1903 to 1926, captured 2,082 wickets for the county at 19.88 runs apiece.

T. RICHARDSON
A Hundred Years of Surrey Cricket
by H. D. G. Leveson Gower, 1946

In dealing with Surrey cricket from 1900 up to World War I it is somewhat difficult to decide whether the county sides were stronger than from 1887 to 1900. Although the decline of Richardson and Lockwood – surely there were never a finer pair of fast bowlers – had begun, there was distinct compensation in the rise of Hayward to his zenith, the arrival of Hobbs and J. N. Crawford.

It has been claimed that Lockwood at his best was the finest bowler of all time and Richardson the most consistent. This is probably the best summing-up of their respective merits. Day in and day out, Richardson has had no superior; Lockwood, on his day, with that slow ball of his, was the most difficult.

T. E. BAILEY
1955
WEST INDIES v ENGLAND
Fifth Test Match

Played at Sabina Park, Kingston, Jamaica, March 30, 31 April 1, 2, 3, 1954. England won by nine wickets. The architect of England's bowling triumph was the vice-captain, Bailey, who, had Statham been fit to play, might well have been confined to a few overs. Instead Bailey, inspired by constant successes, beginning with a fine short-leg catch by Lock from his fifth ball, swung a little either way to a spot length and occasionally cut sharply off the seam. One such ball whipped back from the off and bowled Weekes. When Worrell, stabbing apprehensively at a fast short ball immediately following a bumper, gave a catch to short-leg, four men were out for 13 runs in 40 minutes. Three fell to Bailey for five runs.

Walcott led a partial recovery, but Bailey could not be denied for long and he achieved easily his best analysis in Test cricket. As Bailey himself was first to say, he would have been pleased with figures only half as good in a county match played in similar conditions.

West Indies 139 (Walcott 50; Bailey 16–7–34–7) **and 346** (Walcott 116, Stollmeyer 64; Laker four for 71).

England 414 (Hutton 205, Wardle 66; Sobers four for 75) **and 72** for one.

R. ILLINGWORTH
1978
NOTTINGHAMSHIRE v LEICESTERSHIRE

At Nottingham, September 7, 8, 9, 1977. Leicestershire won by an innings and five runs. Leicestershire 20 pts, Nottinghamshire 1 pt. Although Leicestershire lost Steele, run out with only a single on the board, they proceeded to take heavy toll of the Nottinghamshire attack. Balderstone, with 22 fours compiled his highest score, 178 not out, and shared stands of 219 with

Dudleston and 106 with Davison. In the face of accurate bowling Nottinghamshire crumbled to 162 all out. Following on 164 behind, they fared no better against the spin of Balderstone and Illingworth, who had the satisfaction of leading his side to a resounding victory and in the process collected his 2,000th wicket in first-class cricket.

Bowling analysis: Illingworth 9.5–3–23–3

1996
by Matthew Engel

The South African tour, with Illingworth in charge, was mostly harmonious and the arrival of the diplomatic John Barclay as assistant manager was extremely helpful. The handling of gifted but problematic individuals remained woeful. It was hard to fathom what Illingworth thought he was achieving in his dealings with Mark Ramprakash and Devon Malcolm. Other teams are deeply into sports psychology; Illingworth expresses his contempt for the very idea.

Theoretically, Illingworth had more power than anyone has ever had over the national team. And he would regularly flex his muscles, laying down iron principles for the untrammelled exercise of his power and for selecting the team. Then, suddenly, those principles would prove unexpectedly changeable. Ultimately, it became clear that teams were being chosen much as they had been before, by a coalition in which the captain's voice was extremely important. And Mike Atherton's reputation, as a cricketer and captain, had recovered after his difficult 1994; indeed, it was sky-high – both because of the way he held the batting together (saving the Johannesburg Test was merely the most dramatic example) and because of the sensible manner in which he appeared to deal with his master. There was something rather endearing about Illy's claims to total power, which became a great deal less insistent when things were going wrong. It is clear, though, that if the counties are ever to agree to let the England selectors have a say in the way they handle their players, it will come only when Illingworth gives way to a more emollient figure.

N. GIFFORD
1987
KENT v WARWICKSHIRE

At Folkestone, September 3, 4, 5, 1986. Kent won by an innings and 30 runs. Kent 22 pts, Warwickshire 4 pts. Bad light and rain brought five interruptions on the first day of a match in which bowlers generally had the better of conditions. On a more pleasant second day Kent fared better as their captain, Cowdrey, moved towards his only hundred of the season. Marsh, who had equalled Kent's wicketkeeping record of six dismissals in Warwickshire's innings, hit a career-best 70. Gifford's marathon spell – on the second day he had taken his 2,000th first-class wicket – forecast trouble for Warwickshire in their second innings and so it proved when Underwood returned one of his most remarkable analyses. He was backed by some fine close catching, Christopher Cowdrey holding five catches in an innings for the second time in his career, and was well supported by another left-arm spinner, Davis, who was making his county debut.

Bowling analyses: Gifford 49.5–15–96–5; Underwood 35.5–29–11–7

Five Cricketers of the Year, 1975

A serene type of player, he celebrated his appointment as Worcestershire's captain by being recalled by England. He derived a great deal of pleasure from being a member of the side which defeated Pakistan by 25 runs at Leeds after England had left their opponents a seemingly easy target of 231 runs to win.

Even after this success, his appearances for England have been infrequent because of the strong competition from Derek Underwood. To date he has played in 15 Tests and captured 33 wickets. He now feels that his Test career may be over, but Gifford is a player who cannot be written off, as he had proved on countless occasions.

Over the years he has emerged as a formidable opponent with Worcestershire one of the most competitive teams. Gifford emphasises that it is very much a team effort at New Road with regular tactical discussions on the opposition.

Gifford, who outside the game works for a West Bromwich firm of industrial and domestic decorators on the costing and estimating side of the business, is, however, disturbed by the present attitude, engendered by the public, of winning at all costs. He feels the fear of losing has been detrimental to the game. Gifford says there is no disgrace in losing – if the game has been played in the right sort of spirit. It was, after all, this approach which enabled Worcestershire to win the County Championship last summer for the third time in a decade when all hope was seemingly lost.

F. E. WOOLLEY
1937
KENT v INDIA

Played at Canterbury, Wednesday, Thursday, Friday, August 26, 27, 28, 1936. Kent won by an innings and 202 runs. Outplaying their visitors almost from the start, they passed the opposition total without loss. Except for a stand of 68 between Dilawar Hussain and Sir Vijaya, the India batsmen, when going in 350 behind, shaped poorly. Woolley showed some of his old skill in bowling.

Woolley's 2,000th wicket was [most probably]: Maharaj Sir Vijaya Vizianagram c Chalk b Woolley . . . 39
Bowling analysis: Woolley 13–7–22–4

1957

Woolley on C. B. Fry: "He was one of the most solid batsmen I ever bowled against. He had a tremendous amount of determination, especially on difficult pitches, and the patience to play the type of game required. I remember once bowling to him on a 'sticky' when the ball was turning a lot. I beat him several times in one over without getting his wicket. Next over, to my surprise, he demonstrated that I was not pitching the ball on the right spot and it was going over the stumps. That was typical of him. He was a great theorist."

G. GEARY
1938
LEICESTERSHIRE v NORTHAMPTONSHIRE

At Leicester July 31, August 2, 3, 1937. Drawn. Although behind on the first innings, Leicestershire went very close to winning the game for, having set their opponents to get 299, they dismissed six batsmen for 112. Partridge foiled their bid for victory.

There is no mention of Geary's feat in the match report. His 2,000th wicket was his second of the innings, probably: Mr G. B. Cuthbertson lbw b Geary . . . 7
Bowling analysis: Geary 37–14–63–4

1982

His last season for Leicestershire was 1938 and then he became the professional at Charterhouse. He showed himself a great coach and in particular was one of the few who could really teach bowling. Feeling that at 65 he would be rash to undertake another three-year contract, he left Charterhouse in 1959 with great reluctance on both sides, but Rugby were desperate for help and persuaded him to come and stand behind their nets. Before the end of the first net he could bear it no longer, had his coat off and continued to bowl for another 11 years.

Few professionals have been more popular and more respected, and deservedly. No one ever saw him out of temper: he was always cheerful and smiling and had a wonderful sense of humour which made him a splendid raconteur. E. W. Dawson said that, when he took over the Leicestershire captaincy immediately after coming down from Cambridge and utterly inexperienced, he owed everything to Geary, who, though not yet the senior professional, looked after him like a father.

In all first-class matches he made 13,500 runs (including eight centuries) with an average of 19.80 and took 2,063 wickets at 20.03.

Peter May, who was coached by Geary at Charterhouse, writes: "George really fired me with the enthusiasm and ambition to play first-class cricket and to get to the top. When he told me of his

great experiences in Australia and India and the wonderful
friends he had made, I knew that this was something which I
really wanted to follow. You will be judged by your scores. Never
give your wicket away. I shall always have the happiest memories
of this great man."

1930

TASMANIA v MCC

Played at Launceston, Saturday, Monday, Tuesday, January 12, 14,
15, 1929. Journeying over to Tasmania, the MCC team gained an
easy victory in the first match against a Tasmanian XI by an innings
and 116 runs. Freeman, in each innings, and Tate, in the second,
bowled very well. G. F. Martin, a tall resolute batsman, stayed in
for over two hours and hit 10 fours, showing excellent form. When
Larwood bowled him, one of the bails was sent a distance of 66
yards.

D. V. P. WRIGHT

Wright's 2,000th wicket came on August 4, 1956, at Canterbury, when
Derek Shackleton of Hampshire was caught by Stuart Leary for 0.

Googly Bowlers and Captains Retire
by E. M. Wellings, 1958

Wright was the most controversial bowler of his period, regarded
by some as an expensive luxury. There were times when he was
costly, and his Test record was not remarkable. Others, and I
number myself among them, regard Wright as a magnificent
bowler. He bowled leg-breaks and googlies at a pace not
attempted by his rivals, and there were occasions when he was
quite unplayable. At such times, unfortunately, he was liable to
beat bat, wicket, stumper and everything and thus often missed
his due reward.

Wright's Test record is a faulty guide. He began on the too-
perfect pitches of the 1930s against an Australian batting side
containing Bradman, McCabe, Brown, Fingleton and Hassett.
Even then he was unlucky. When at last he found a favourable

pitch at Leeds in 1938, he took three wickets so quickly that a remarkable win for England was in prospect, but a missed catch in the slips allowed Hassett to play the match-winning innings. Again at Sydney in 1947 Wright had his chance. Once more a vital catch was dropped off his bowling, for Bradman escaped when only two and stayed to make sure that Australia would win.

J. A. NEWMAN 1952

For years bowling had been Hampshire's weakness. Llewellyn – the first bowler of the Chinaman and that most dangerous of all balls, the left-hander's googly – carried the attack almost unaided from 1899. Now he received some much-needed help. Three successive seasons, 1906, 1907, and 1908, brought a trio of world-famous characters and cricketers to the game in Jack Newman, Alex Kennedy and George Brown.

Kennedy and Newman – what names to conjure with! No pair of bowlers can have performed so often and so well, with so little rest as did these two throughout their long careers. Between them they took just short of 5,000 wickets, and if this was not enough, the pair found time and strength to score 30,000 runs.

A. SHAW 1908

As a bowler Alfred Shaw placed his chief reliance on accuracy of pitch. In this respect he has never been surpassed. When in his prime he could keep up his end for hours, without ever becoming short or getting in any way loose. In being able to get through so much work he was greatly helped by his delivery, which, from the beginning of his career to its close, was beautifully easy and natural. When the ground helped him, he broke back a good deal, but he never set much store on a big break, always arguing that the most dangerous ball was the one that did just enough to beat the bat. Unlike most of the present-day bowlers, he regarded the off theory as more or less a waste of time, preferring to keep on the wicket and trust to variations of pace and elevation to deceive the batsmen.

S. HAIGH

Haigh is the only one of the 33 men to have taken 2,000 wickets to have taken four of those wickets in successive balls. He did this for MCC against an Army XI in Pretoria in 1905/06. *Wisden* does not mention this feat, either!

1897
AUSTRALIANS v YORKSHIRE

At Bradford Monday, Tuesday, Wednesday June 29, 30 July 1, 1896. There were two great personal successes in the match, Iredale following up his performance at Nottingham with a splendid innings of 114, and Schofield Haigh on the second afternoon gaining the first of his triumphs as a bowler for Yorkshire.

Australians 224 (Graham 67; Hirst five for 79) **and 251** (Iredale 114; Haigh 39.1–13–78–8).

Yorkshire 145 (McKibbin seven for 23) **and 190** (Tunnicliffe 59; Jones four for 40).

1951
Essex v Warwickshire

At Ilford, June 3, 5, 6, 1950. Drawn. Essex needed 316 in three and a half hours, and when Dodds and Avery began with 50 in half an hour a definite finish seemed probable. Cray helped himself to one six and ten fours, but he concentrated so much on defence that his side fell behind the clock. Kardar, at slip, smartly "stumped" Vigar off Hollies, but as the wicketkeeper did not remove the bails the bowler under Laws 41 and 42 was not credited with the wicket.

F. H. Vigar, run out. . . . 20

ALL-ROUND GOOD GUYS

The all-rounder, the player who can do two things equally well, is the pivot of a successful side. In the classic tradition of W. G. Grace, Trevor Bailey and Jacques Kallis, they are men who are worth their place in the team for both their batting and their bowling. If their batting fails, they are worth their place in the side for their bowling, and vice versa. This distinguishes them from the bits and pieces men so revered by limited-overs selectors, who can almost do two things well, but anyway have only got to be on song for a few overs.

The term all-rounder also applies to men like Alec Stewart and, supremely, Adam Gilchrist, who follow in the tradition of Les Ames as wicketkeepers who bat in the top six. We could also almost add men like Jonty Rhodes and Stuart Surridge, whose fielding was a part of their value to the side at least on a par with their basic skills of batting or bowling. These days everybody has to aspire to being an all-rounder, even if the levels attained by Gary Sobers or Keith Miller will be forever out of reach.

Finally, there are the all-rounders like Rupert Brooke, Samuel Beckett and Sam Mendes: *Wisden* has always been tolerant of cricketers with reputations in other corners of foreign fields. The tribute to C. B. Fry from the 1957 Almanack typifies this attitude. Fry was perversely most certainly not a cricketing all-rounder – his bowling action was very doubtful, and even his team-mates were known to express the opinion that he was a chucker – but as a man he was the beau ideal of Corinthian masculinity.

W. E. ROLLER 1886
SURREY v SUSSEX
A Record

Played at Kennington Oval, Monday, Tuesday, Wednesday, June 29, 30, July 1, 1885. The innings of 631 played by Surrey in this match was the highest ever made in a contest between county teams of first-class rank, and in absolutely first-class matches in England had been beaten on only one occasion, viz., by the Australians at Brighton in 1882, when the colonial team scored 643 against Sussex. Surrey had first innings, and when play came to an end on the opening day the home team had scored 462, and had still three wickets to fall, the batting throughout the greater part of the afternoon being of the most brilliant description. Mr Shuter made 27 out of 31 scored for the first wicket; 22 were added before Mr Diver was bowled; and then Mr W. W. Read and Abel put on 36 for the third. So far the batting had been good, but not remarkable. When, however, Maurice Read joined Mr W. W. Read a complete mastery was obtained over the Sussex bowling, and 78 runs were scored before the batsmen were parted, while the succeeding partnership, that of Messrs Read and Roller, added no fewer than 144. Messrs Roller and Bowden increased that total by 94, and finally Mr Roller and Wood put together 57 before the latter was caught a minute or two before time. Mr Read scored 163 out of 258 put on while he was in, and Mr Roller was seen to almost equal advantage in making 131 not out, out of 295. Mr Read's hitting was of a much more dashing character throughout than Mr Roller's, although the latter batted very freely towards the close. The former occupied but three hours and ten minutes, while Mr Roller was batting for 40 minutes longer. Mr Read's score was made up of 21 fours, 5 threes, 17 twos, and 30 singles. At the commencement of the game the weather was very gloomy, but after luncheon it became bright and fine.

The last Surrey wicket was not obtained until three-quarters of an hour after luncheon on the Tuesday, occupying in all eight hours and three-quarters in compiling. Mr Roller, who had made 131 on the Monday, was the ninth man out with the total at 585, having been in while 418 runs were put on. Like Mr Read, he made his long and splendid score apparently without a mistake, and the figures of his 204 – the highest innings scored by him during the season – were 17 fours, 17 threes, 27 twos and 31 singles . . .

Sussex, whose bowling and fielding had been thoroughly worn out, started their batting at 3.55 p.m. and were dismissed in just over three hours for 168, their last wicket falling within a few minutes of time. The first two or three batsmen did fairly well, and indeed 130 went up with only four out, but then came a series of disasters. Mr Roller was put on to bowl, and after being hit for several overs he performed the "hat trick" by getting J. Hide caught at point from the last ball of one over and bowling Humphreys and Mr Brann with the first two balls of his following over . . . This match of 1,041 runs resulted in victory for Surrey by an innings and 221 runs.

Surrey 631 (Roller 204, W. W. Read 163).

Sussex 168 (Roller four for 28) **and 242** (Newham 62, J. Phillips 56, H. Phillips 55 not out; Roller two for 16).

1894

In this year, *Wisden*'s portraits were of "Five Great All-Rounders". In the case of four of them (the lucky escapee being F. S. Jackson), the pen portraits ended with some waspish comments.

Edward Wainwright

He had the honour of playing for England against Australia at Lord's, and would also have played at The Oval if the Yorkshire Committee had been willing to let him off from a county match. Wainwright is emphatically an all-round cricketer, his fielding being quite as good as his batting and bowling. As a bowler he only misses greatness by reason of the fact that his accuracy of pitch is not commensurate with his break and spin.

George Giffen

Apart from a couple of long innings against Gloucestershire and Yorkshire his batting fell far below his Australian standard.

Indeed, in the matches generally regarded as representative in character, his average was only 12. It cannot be said, therefore, that his fourth visit to England added to his reputation. Of course he did a lot of good work, but he did not prove the tower of strength on the side that his friends in South Australia had expected. Still, whatever his shortcomings in England in 1893, his record during the last ten years in Australia is sufficient to stamp him one of the world's greatest all-round players.

Albert Trott

As a bowler he is very effective against moderate batsmen, but there is always a sense of exhilaration amongst the spectators when he is tried against first-rates. Experience has proved that though he may now and then get a wicket, runs are sure to come at the rate of six or eight an over. Judged by the best English standards we should not consider Trott a great field at point, but he is very good.

Alec Hearne

He is now probably at the height of his powers, and is good enough for any eleven. The weak point in his cricket is that he is rather apt to drop catches.

W. STORER 1899
Five Great Players of the Season

William Storer, certainly the greatest cricketer who has ever appeared for Derbyshire, was born on January 26, 1868. Though he had been assisting Derbyshire for several seasons it was not perhaps until 1893 that his remarkable qualities as a wicketkeeper were recognised by the general body of the cricket public. He was chosen to keep wicket at Lord's that season for the MCC in their return match with the Australians and so brilliantly did he acquit himself that his position in the front rank was thenceforward assured. In the course of the match he caught four batsmen and stumped another and what is more he did not, in the Australians' second innings, with Mr Kortright bowling his fastest, give away a single bye . . . At his best as a wicketkeeper to fast bowling he was not unworthy of comparison with Pinder and Pilling. As a batsman he does not boast any special beauty of style, but he has immense resources. He is very strong in defence and when in a hitting mood can "pull" with astonishing certainty. Over and above his batting and wicketkeeping, Storer can bowl slow leg-breaks with no small amount of skill, and taking him altogether he may without exaggeration be described as a great player – good enough for any eleven in the world.

G. H. HIRST 1907

In finishing up second on the list, Yorkshire had chiefly to thank George Hirst. Alike as batsman and bowler, that great cricketer was the mainstay of the side. Having regard to the responsibilities that rested upon him, it is safe to say that he was a better all-round man than ever. His batting and bowling figures, remarkable as they are, do not give anything like an adequate idea of what his presence meant to the eleven. When runs had to be made under trying conditions, he made them; when the opposing side had to be got rid of for a moderate score, he was, as a rule, the most successful bowler. As instances of his wonderful resources as a batsman, we may mention particularly his hitting on a more or less ruined wicket against Lancashire at Old Trafford, and his great though unsuccessful effort to draw the game with Surrey at The Oval. He played many other fine innings, but these two were among his very best. In bowling he was perhaps never better than when he helped to win the return match with Surrey – a triumph that afforded more satisfaction than even the victories against Lancashire. Coming to figures, Hirst set up a record that may possibly never be equalled. In Yorkshire matches alone, he scored over 2,000 runs and took over 200 wickets, a double feat without precedent in first-class cricket. Only a very strong man in perfect health would have been equal to the mere physical labour involved, but Hirst thrives on hard work and at the end of the season he was so fresh and well that nobody seeing him bat or bowl could have guessed that any extra demands had been made upon him. Indeed, he bowled in quite his finest form when the Rest of England beat Kent at The Oval in September – the last fixture of the year. In his general form he was much the same as he has been since his bowling developed its special qualities. As a batsman, his only fault was an occasional tendency to attempt daring pulls before he had got the pace of the ground, and in bowling he was deadly just in proportion as he could get his peculiar swerve on the ball. As an all-round man in county cricket, there has been no one to surpass him since W. G. Grace in the 1870s lifted Gloucestershire to the top of the tree.

G. H. Hirst in 1906:

Batting:

	M	Inns	N.O.	Runs	H. S.	Avge	100s
For Yorkshire	32	53	6	2164	169	46.04	6
All Matches	35	58	6	2385	169	45.86	6

Bowling:

	Overs	Mdns	Runs	Wkts	Avge
For Yorkshire	1211.1	262	3089	201	15.36
All Matches	1306.1	271	3434	208	16.50

1908

Edward Pooley, the once famous Surrey wicketkeeper, died in Lambeth Infirmary on July 18. He had for a long time been in very poor circumstances and was often compelled to seek the shelter of the workhouse ... Of the faults of private character that marred Pooley's career and were the cause of the poverty in which he spent the later years of his life there is no need now to speak. He was in many ways his own enemy, but even to the last he had a geniality and sense of humour that to a certain extent condoned his weaknesses.

J. H. PARKS 1938
Five Cricketers of the Year

JAMES HORACE PARKS, whose all-round form for Sussex attracted so much attention last season, was born at Haywards Heath on May 12, 1903. Actually, he never played cricket at school and did not take up the game seriously until reaching the age of sixteen. When, after the War, sport again came into its own, Parks, at the instance of his father, joined the Haywards Heath Club, who had advertised for second-team players, and on the strength of his first-rate slip fielding he was picked for the first eleven almost immediately. Parks was given two trials by Sussex, but achieved nothing of much note until the Sussex Club and Ground side, strongly represented towards the end of the season, paid a visit to Haywards Heath. So well did Parks perform with bat and ball that he made 50 runs – the next highest score was 9 – and took six wickets for 44.

That performance impressed many of those who saw it and in 1923 Parks joined the Sussex Nursery. His first outstanding success was as a bowler, and this came in 1924 as the indirect result of the choice of Arthur Gilligan and Maurice Tate to play for England. It was the third appearance of Parks in the county eleven and given, for the first time, the opportunity of bowling with the new ball, he took seven wickets for 17 runs in Leicestershire's second innings at Horsham and paved the way to a victory for Sussex by ten wickets. At the time, the regular Sussex opening bowlers were engaged in dismissing South Africa at Edgbaston for 30 runs.

In developing his batting, Parks owed a lot to Albert Relf, but bowling came naturally to him and he found himself able early in his career to swing the ball with little apparent effort. During his early days in the Sussex team, his safe fielding proved a big asset to him. In 1929, Parks and Bowley set up a new Sussex first-wicket record by scoring 368 in three hours against Gloucestershire at Hove, Parks' share of the runs being 110. Not until 1934, however, did he take a place among the leading all-rounders. In the following summer, he scored 1,633 runs and took 103 wickets, and in 1937, when completing the Cricketers' Double for the second time, he obtained 3,003 runs, averaging nearly 51, and 101 wickets, at an average of 25.83. No other cricketer has scored more than 3,000 runs and taken over 100 wickets in a season.

1946

GANDAR-DOWER, MR KENNETH CECIL, was lost at sea through Japanese action in February 1944 at the age of 36 . . . One of the most versatile players of games of any period, he was amateur squash champion of 1938, won amateur championships at fives, and played lawn tennis for Great Britain. In all, he represented Cambridge at six forms of sport: tennis, lawn tennis, Rugby fives, Eton fives, squash rackets and billiards. In fact, time hardly sufficed for their rival calls. He probably created a record when he played simultaneously in the Freshmen's Match and the Freshmen's Tournament, with the connivance of the tennis but not the cricket authorities; he disappeared to play-off a round during the early part of his side's innings, with relays of cyclist friends to keep him informed as to the fall of wickets! He flew a private aeroplane to India. In spite of other demands he continued to allow time for cricket, making some ten appearances for the Frogs each season almost to the outbreak of war, and got many runs and wickets.

Famous as a big game shot, and extensive traveller, he introduced a team of cheetahs from the Kenya jungle to London and on greyhound tracks they set up speed records. A writer of articles and books, he acted as War Correspondent in various theatres of operations up to the time of his death.

A. K. DAVIDSON 1951
Australian Tour of New Zealand, 1950

The Australian bowling, although perhaps flattered by the rather low level of batsmanship in New Zealand, gave a very good account of itself. L. Johnson, with right-arm fast-medium deliveries, headed the averages by capturing 18 wickets for 11.27 runs apiece, and with A. Davidson and C. Puckett formed a hostile pace attack. Davidson (fast left-arm) met with phenomenal success against Wairarapa, taking all ten wickets for 29 runs and also scoring 157 not out.

C. B. FRY 1957
by Hubert Preston

CAPTAIN CHARLES BURGESS FRY, who died at his home at Hampstead, London, on September 7, 1956, aged 84, was probably the greatest all-rounder of his or any generation. He was a brilliant scholar and an accomplished performer in almost every branch of outdoor sport. Fry was the perfect amateur; he played games because he loved them and never for personal gain. He captained England in Test Matches, and the Mother Country never lost under his captaincy. He played Association Football for England against Ireland in 1901; he was at full-back for Southampton in the FA Cup Final of 1902; and he put up a world's long jump record of 23ft 5in in 1892 which stood for 21 years. But it was at cricket that his outstanding personality found its fullest expression.

Charles Fry secured a place in the Repton XI in 1888 and retained it for the next three years, being captain in 1890 and 1891. In his last season at school his average reached nearly 50. When he went up to Oxford, Fry was captain of the cricket and Association football XIs and president of the athletic club, acting as first string in the 100 yards and the long-jump. He also played a good deal of Rugby football, and his friends insisted that but for an unfortunate injury he would have added a Rugger Blue to his other honours. Charles Fry was also a fine boxer, a passable golfer, swimmer, sculler, tennis player and javelin thrower. But it was on the cricket field that he achieved his greatest triumphs. He represented three counties – Sussex, Hampshire and Surrey – scoring altogether 30,886 runs in first-class matches, average 50.22. His total of centuries reached 94 and five times he scored two separate hundreds in a match.

Fry's best season was 1901 when his aggregate reached 3,147, average 78.67. In that summer he scored 13 hundreds and made six in successive innings – a feat equalled only by Sir Donald Bradman . . .

Considering the very high rank he attained among batsmen, Fry, at the outset, was a stiff ungainly performer and was still somewhat laboured in stroke-production when he went up to Oxford. But from the time he began playing for Sussex with "Ranji" his game improved. He was a natural on-side batsman with a powerful straight drive and many useful leg-side strokes.

The records contain very few details of Fry's achievements as a bowler. Yet he figured in a somewhat heated controversy in the 1890s about "unfair deliveries". Cricket writers generally regarded him as a thrower. Fry was equally insistent that all his deliveries were scrupulously fair. In his writings, Fry recalled how Jim Phillips, an Australian heavyweight slow bowler turned umpire, was sent to Hove specially to "no-ball" him.

"A bright move," commented Fry, "because, of course, I rolled up my sleeve above my elbow and bowled with my arm as rigidly straight as a poker. The great Jim, sighting himself as a strong umpire, was not deterred. Large as an elephant, he bluffly no-balled me nine times running. It was a farce and the Sussex authorities and players were angry. However, I bowled often afterwards unscathed, even in Gentlemen v Players at Lord's and in a Test Match."

LIONEL TENNYSON 1962
BY H. L. V. DAY

One of his pleasant little habits was to send telegrams to his batsmen on the field. One day at Trent Bridge I was trying to cope with the Notts fast bowlers. I failed completely to connect with a very short long hop and duly received it around the heart. It flattened me.

As I sat on the ground recovering my composure, I got a telegram which read, "What do you think your — bat is for" signed Lionel. Another young amateur, striving to find his touch, received this encouraging message, "For God's sake get out and let someone else take a hundred off this jam."

SIR GARFIELD SOBERS, CRICKET'S MOST VERSATILE PERFORMER
by John Arlott, 1975

Sir Garfield Sobers, the finest all-round player in the history of cricket, has announced his retirement from full-time county cricket at the age of thirty-eight ... In a historically sapping career, Sobers has played for Barbados for 21 seasons; in English league cricket for eight, for South Australia in the Sheffield Shield for three, and Nottinghamshire for seven; he turned out regularly for the Cavaliers on Sundays for several years before there was a Sunday League in England; made nine tours for West Indies, two with Rest of the World sides and several in lesser teams; 89 of his

93 Tests for the West Indies were consecutive and he averaged more than four a year for 20 years. There is no doubt, also, that his car accident in which Collie Smith was killed affected him more profoundly and for longer than most people realised.

The wonder was not that the spark grew dim but that it endured so bright for so long. Though it happened so frequently and for so many years, it was always thrilling even to see Sobers come to the wicket. As lately as 1968 he hit six sixes from a six-ball over. In 1974, on his "farewell" circuit of England he still, from time to time, recaptured his former glory, playing a lordly stroke or making the ball leave the pitch faster than the batsman believed possible. As he walked away afterwards, though, his step dragged. He was a weary man – as his unparalleled results do not merely justify, but demand. Anyone who ever matches Garfield Sobers' performances will have to be an extremely strong man – and he, too, will be weary.

MIKE PROCTER – A GREAT ALL-ROUNDER
by Alan Gibson, 1982

Before the 1968 season began, I had my first news of Procter as a player, from David Green who had also just joined Gloucestershire from Lancashire, and had batted against him in nets and trials. "This man is extraordinary," David said. "He bowls at a hundred miles an hour from extra cover off the wrong foot." The two men were to become fast friends, though this did not prevent Procter giving him a fearful bouncer when they were playing against each other in Rhodesia. David went for the hook, missed, caught it with his head, and was laid out. Procter unperturbedly began his long walk back, throwing scarcely a glance over his shoulder, until about halfway through it came the casual query, "You all right, Greeny?"

. . . Of all the overseas cricketers who have decorated our domestic game, I know of none who has identified himself with his adopted county more whole-heartedly than Procter. He is "Our Mike" as Goddard used to be "Our Tom" and Hammond "Our Walter". In 1980 he became qualified for England, as the rules stood. I thought he should have been picked. The rules may be silly, but so long as they are there you should play within them. There was no doubt that he was still good enough. Indeed, with Botham in trouble, and Brearley's return unforeseen, he looked by far the best choice for captain. Not that it was ever likely to happen. I suppose he took up his English "citizenship" only because it gave Gloucestershire a chance to sign another overseas player. But if Roland Butcher could play for England, as he did, and as Allan Lamb presumably will, there was no logic in not choosing Procter. He would have liked to play. He had more of an affinity with English cricket than Tony Greig ever had.

Where does he stand among the all-rounders of cricket? I suppose Sobers must come before him, because Sobers was three different sorts of bowler, Procter only two. Sobers also had far more opportunities of demonstrating his skills at the highest level. Rhodes had a mighty pile of figures, in a very long career, but his best years as a batsman did not coincide with his best as a bowler. Sobers and Procter had to do both at the same time. Their careers were more concentrated. George Hirst, in 1906, scored 2,385 runs and took 208 wickets, something nobody had done before; and never will again while anything like the present system lasts. There can scarcely have been, ever, a better simultaneous all-rounder than Hirst was in 1906. I doubt if Sobers could have done it, even if he had grown up to that sort of grind. He would have become bored. But Procter might have done. He had the strength and the spirit for it.

R. J. HADLEE 1985

Few people remember who comes second: that was the tragedy of Nottinghamshire's 1984 season, which must still go down as one of the most successful in the club's history ... As in previous seasons, much emanated from the talents of the New Zealand all-rounder Richard Hadlee. His remarkable displays, which brought him the coveted double of 1,000 runs and 100 wickets, were a constant source of inspiration to his colleagues. Not since Fred Titmus in 1967 had anyone achieved the "Double", and there was a lot more first-class cricket in those days. Hadlee's displays overshadowed the contribution of anyone else at Trent Bridge.

NOTTINGHAMSHIRE v WARWICKSHIRE

At Nottingham, August 25, 27, 28, 1984. Nottinghamshire won by seven wickets.

Nottinghamshire 24 pts. Warwickshire 5 pts. Despite some splendid batting by Amiss, Nottinghamshire eased to a seven-wicket win. Amiss and Humpage held together the Warwickshire first innings after they had been put in, and not even Hadlee's six for 55 could prevent them from reaching a respectable 261. Randall's 113, scored in 212 minutes and including nine fours, made sure that Nottinghamshire replied positively. He shared a second-wicket stand of 178 with Robinson, whose 97 took 220 minutes, and then Hadlee became the first player to complete the "Double" since F. J. Titmus in 1967. Nottinghamshire declared 89 runs ahead, and with Hemmings taking six for 49 against his former county, Warwickshire would have been in serious trouble but for Amiss's 62. He was last out, leaving Nottinghamshire to get 117.

Warwickshire 261 (Humpage 89, Amiss 70: Hadlee six for 55) **and 205** (Amiss 62; Hemmings six for 49, Hadlee three for 48).

Nottinghamshire 350 for six declared (Randall 113, Robinson 97, Hadlee 39; Ferreira three for 65) **and 117** for three (Rice 41 not out).

I. V. A. RICHARDS 1988

NEW ZEALAND v WEST INDIES

First One-Day International

At Dunedin, March 18, 1987. West Indies won by 95 runs. A magnificent all-round performance by Richards, who became the first player to score a hundred and take five wickets in a one-day international, overshadowed all else. His 119, made from 113 balls with four sixes and ten fours, was his ninth at this level and his partnership of 120 with Hooper lifted West Indies from a shaky start after they had been put in. Hooper batted impressively on his international debut. New Zealand never looked like getting close to their target as Richards captured his five wickets, mainly with slow-medium swing.

Man of the Match: I. V. A. Richards.

West Indies 237 for nine (50 overs) (Richards 119, Hooper 48).
New Zealand 142 (42.1 overs) (Wright 34; Richards 10–0–41–5).

This all-round feat was not equalled until this volume was almost complete, when Paul Collingwood of England scored 112 not out and took 6 for 31 against Bangladesh at Trent Bridge on June 21, 2005.

F. D. STEPHENSON 1989
Nottinghamshire

By the end of a summer that was not without its traumas, Nottinghamshire had achieved levels of success that even the most optimistic Trent Bridge regular would have doubted at the outset. In finishing fifth in the Britannic Assurance Championship, and so claiming a share of the prize money, they won only one game fewer than they did in winning the title 12 months earlier. And in the West Indian all-rounder Franklyn Stephenson, they had the Championship Player of the Year.

. . . Nottinghamshire's health blossomed thanks largely to the marvellous bowling of the new-ball pair, Stephenson and Kevin Cooper. Both topped 100 wickets, and not since the days before the Championship was reduced in 1969 has any county boasted such an achievement. For Stephenson, heading the list of first-class wicket-takers in the country with 125 was just part of a remarkable performance in his first season on the staff. He had been signed as a replacement for Hadlee, indeed had been recommended by Hadlee himself, but no one expected him to emulate his predecessor's great successes. How wrong everyone was. Stephenson, as self-motivated as Hadlee, proved his all-round ability by repeating the New Zealander's previously unique Double of 1984 and so became the second player to score 1,000 runs and take 100 wickets in a season since 1969. Moreover, Stephenson completed the feat in two fewer games, and he did so in style, taking two hundreds off Yorkshire in the last game of the season. Only once before had he reached three figures.

NOTTINGHAMSHIRE v YORKSHIRE

At Nottingham, September 14, 15, 16, 17, 1988. Yorkshire won by 127 runs. Yorkshire 24 pts, Nottinghamshire 5 pts. Toss: Yorkshire. The game will go down in history as "Stephenson's Match". It was perhaps appropriate that in the year celebrating the 150th anniversary of Trent Bridge, the final match of the season should produce a feat never before seen on the ground. Only twice in first-class cricket had a player scored, as Stephenson did against Yorkshire, two hundreds and taken ten wickets in a match: B. J. T. Bosanquet, Middlesex v Surrey at Lord's in 1905, and G. H. Hirst, Yorkshire v Somerset at Bath in 1906. At the start of the match, Stephenson required 210 runs to complete the "Double" for the season. Bearing in mind that he had never scored a hundred for Nottinghamshire, the feat appeared beyond him. In the first innings, however, when only Johnson among his colleagues mastered the bowling, he hit 111 in 157 minutes, including a six and 18 fours. In the second innings his 117 came in 137 minutes with 20 fours and two sixes, and while he chanced his arm, he gave no actual chances. Nine minutes after he was lbw to the persevering Fletcher, the match was over. Stephenson's all-round brilliance swamped the rest of the match details, but Bairstow, returning to the Yorkshire side after six matches, reached 1,000 dismissals for his county when he caught Johnson in the first innings. He then came close to celebrating his achievement with a century, hitting 15 fours and a six as he raced to 94 from 99 balls before the close. Instead, Carrick declared at the overnight score to leave his bowlers all day to dismiss Nottinghamshire.

Yorkshire 380 (Robinson 98, Moxon 68; Stephenson four for 105) **and 340** for seven declared (Bairstow 94 not out, Robinson 80; Stephenson seven for 117).

Nottinghamshire 296 (Stephenson 111, Johnson 59; Sidebottom seven for 89) **and 297** (Stephenson 117, Randall 59; Fletcher six for 74).

K. D. JAMES 1991
HAMPSHIRE v INDIANS

At Southampton, June 29, 30, July 1, 1990. Drawn. Toss: Hampshire. This will go down in history as Kevan James's match. The 35-year-old left-arm seamer, who had begun the season in the second eleven, became the first man ever to take four wickets with successive balls and score a century in the same game. For the rest, it was largely forgettable, and rain ended proceedings shortly before lunch on the final day. James's four-in-four came on Saturday afternoon; the Indians had advanced smoothly to 207 for one when he struck in his 16th over. Rathore was stumped down the leg side; Tendulkar's inside-edge gave a simple catch to short leg; Dravid played down the wrong line and Manjrekar nicked to slip. After that, normality returned, as the immaculate Ganguly completed a wristy century and put on 155 with Kumble. Laney then hit a mature hundred, but James took centre stage again as he scored 103, with three sixes off Hirwani and ten fours. Hampshire closed the second day 21 runs ahead, with one wicket remaining. But, with the Indians spurning a contrived finish, Stephenson instructed his last pair to bat as long as possible. They survived to lunch, with No. 11 Milburn completing a maiden 50 in 54 balls. Then the weather took over.

Indians 362 for five declared (Ganguly 100 not out, Rathore 95, Jadeja 91; James five for 74).

Hampshire 458 for nine (James 103, Laney 100).

1939

Before the 1938 season began, the highest innings played by an Englishman in a home Test Match against Australia was 182 not out by C. P. Mead at The Oval in 1921. Last summer no fewer than four different batsmen beat that record. Paynter made 216 not out at Nottingham, W. R. Hammond scored 240 in the Lord's Test and in the memorable Fifth Test at The Oval both Leyland (187) and Hutton (364) surpassed the figure reached by Mead 17 years previously.

Then there are the wicketkeepers who have other skills as well.

HON. A. LYTTELTON 1885
AUSTRALIA v ENGLAND [the 25th match]

Played at Kennington Oval, Monday, Tuesday, Wednesday, August 11, 12, 13, 1884.

The third and last of the three great matches arranged to be played against the full strength of England resulted in a draw, England wanting 120 runs to avert a single innings defeat, with eight wickets to go down. The fact that three individual scores of over 100 runs each were scored on the first day rendered the match unique in the annals of the game. When stumps were drawn on the first day, the score stood as under:

Australia

A. C. Bannerman, c Read b Peate	4
P. S. M'Donnell, c Ulyett b Peate	103
W. L. Murdoch, not out	145
H. J. H. Scott, not out	101
B4, lb 6	10
For two wickets	363

Bannerman was out with the score at 15, and M'Donnell at 158, but 205 more runs were added that day without further loss. On the Tuesday Scott was caught at the wicket after adding a single to his overnight score, but Murdoch was not dismissed until he had compiled 211, being the sixth batsman out with the total at 494. The remainder of the innings was alone remarkable for the success which attended Lyttelton's lobs. He went on for the second time when six wickets were down for 532, and took the last four wickets in eight overs for only 8 runs.

Australia 551 (Murdoch 211, M'Donnell 103, Scott 102; Lyttelton four for 19).

England 346 (Read 117, Scotton 90; Palmer four for 90) **and 85** for two.

D. G. BRADMAN 1939
NEW SOUTH WALES v SOUTH AUSTRALIA

At Sydney, January 15, 17, 18, 19, 1938. New South Wales won by four wickets. The moderately cheap dismissal of Bradman at the start influenced the course of the game, but with his first run the crack batsman set up a record aggregate for an Australian in first-class matches. McCabe and Jackson batted splendidly for New South Wales who gained a lead of 108. Bradman did quite well when he kept wicket in place of Walker who injured a finger. Bradman at his second attempt put together a fine century, during which he reached 1,000 runs for the season. Badcock also drove very hard in making a hundred, but New South Wales were not left a very serious task. They wanted 227 and, despite some first-rate wicketkeeping by Bradman, who caught three men, they won comfortably.

South Australia 187 and 334 (Badcock 132, Bradman 104; O'Reilly four for 65).

New South Wales 295 (McCabe 83, Jackson 63, O'Reilly st Bradman b Ward 20; Ward 4–51) **and 227 for six** (Fingleton 74).

1994

by Matthew Engel

In such a year, it is easy to overlook a lengthy list of other very, very good cricketers who have retired. Richards, Botham and Gower played for seven counties between them. Derek Randall was perhaps the last of the true local heroes – it was impossible to imagine him playing for anyone except Nottinghamshire. Yet his fame spread from Retford round the globe. On the 1982/83 Ashes tour, I met a man in a bar in a South Australian bush town. "That Randall," he said, "he bats like an octopus with piles."

A. C. SMITH 1966
ESSEX v WARWICKSHIRE

At Clacton, August 4, 5, 6, 1965. Drawn, the last pair of Essex batsmen surviving the closing quarter of an hour. Restrained batting by Stewart saved Warwickshire from first-innings failure against Knight and Bailey. Essex lost seven wickets for 77, mostly to the pace of Bannister, but the left-handed Wrightson, after two "lives", held out for over four hours. Amiss took the honours when Warwickshire batted again and in the end Essex needed 203 in three hours 55 minutes.

With Webster unable to bowl, A. C. Smith, the wicketkeeper, joined the attack and he performed the hat-trick at the expense of Barker, G. Smith and Fletcher. When disposing of Bailey, Smith had taken four wickets in 34 deliveries without cost, but grim defence saved Essex.

Warwickshire 160 (Stewart 54; Knight five for 38) **and 205** (Amiss 54).

Essex 163 (Wrightson 84; Bannister five for 47) **and 141** for nine (Knight 44; A.C. Smith 21–10–36–4).

W. R. JAMES 1997
FINAL: MATABELELAND v MASHONALAND
COUNTRY DISTRICTS

At Bulawayo Athletic Club, Bulawayo, April 19, 20, 21, 1996. Matabeleland won by six wickets. Toss: Mashonaland Country Districts. First-class debuts: G. D. Ferreira, J. M. Oates, K. R. Scott.

Home captain Wayne James dominated the match in a manner unprecedented in world cricket. He made nine dismissals in the Districts' first innings, to equal the world record of Tahir Rashid, who caught eight and stumped one for Habib Bank v PACO in 1992/93. In the second innings, he added four more to set a new record of 13 dismissals in a match, beating 12 by Edward Pooley for Surrey v Sussex in 1868, Don Tallon for Queensland v New South Wales in 1938/39 and Brian Taber for New South Wales v South Australia in 1968/69. He also scored 99 in both Matabele innings, though he might have reached his century in the second if the wicketkeeper had not conceded four byes to give the home side victory. Only one player is known to have scored two 99s in a first-class match, Amay Khurasia of Madhya Pradesh, against Vidarbha in 1991/92. He was also left stranded in the second innings – but did not break the world wicketkeeping record.

Matabeleland had home advantage, although the Districts headed the table and would have won the cup on their first-innings lead in the event of a draw. But that was never likely in a match of sudden collapses. Chasing 174, the Matabeles were 15 for four early on the final morning, before James and Dekker began their match-winning stand of 161. Both sides had difficulty raising a full team. Jason Oates – who managed to elude James' gloves – became the third player to score a century for a Zimbabwean or Rhodesian team on first-class debut, while 46-year-old Denis Streak joined his son Heath in the Matabele line-up for his first first-class match since he toured England in 1985.

Mashonaland Country Districts 265 (Oates 115, B.C. Strang 66) **and 128**
(Rennie six for 42).

Matabeleland 220 (James 99; Strang four for 69) **and 176** for four
(James 99 not out, Dekker 57 not out).

T. TAIBU 2005
ZIMBABWE v SRI LANKA
First Test Match

At Harare, May 6, 7, 8, 2004. Sri Lanka won by an innings and 240 runs. The bowlers exhibited enthusiasm and reasonable accuracy, but had little more to offer as Atapattu and Jayasuriya put on 281, a first-wicket record against Zimbabwe. Jayasuriya scored 157 off 147 balls without ever looking to be forcing the pace. The breakthrough finally came on the second afternoon when Taibu took off his pads to bowl his skiddy medium-pacers, only to get his third delivery to bounce unexpectedly from the pitch, off Jayasuriya's gloves and into the gully.

Sri Lanka 541 (Atapattu 170, Jayasuriya 157; Taibu 8–1–27–1).
Zimbabwe 199 and 102.

A DAY IN THE LIFE

Before one-day cricket became the dominant form of the game, in the halcyon days when three-day county games were attended by tens of thousands of men wrapped up against the worst the English summer could throw at them, in dark overcoats and trilby hats, there were those matches which were meant to run for three days, but still managed to end in one day. *Wisden* has listed them all, but they are largely features of the middle ages of cricket, in the Victorian era and (once) even earlier than that. First-class matches do not last just three sessions any more; this is perhaps because county committees need the gate money and the chip van receipts, so they discourage their managers and captains from anything so rash and as economically unviable as a quick and crushing victory.

This is what *Wisden* wrote about some of them, including one of the three benefit matches on the list, from the Somerset section of the 1954 Almanack. In all, four Lancashire v Somerset County Championship matches have ended in one day, with Lancashire winning all of them. Somerset have also lost to Yorkshire, Middlesex and Derbyshire within one day, so there must be a feeling of elation in the Somerset dressing-room whenever they reach close of play on the first day with a match still in progress.

It is amusing to note that in the early days, *Wisden* used words like "remarkable" and "curious" to describe these matches, with a strong undertone of approval at the come-uppance dished out to the batsmen. Several of the teams involved in the early matches listed here were sorely mismatched, as the report of the North v South match from the 1876 Almanack shows. That report also shows the florid style of writing that sometimes was allowed to flow unchecked across the pages of early *Wisdens*, but which now has to be kept under a tight rein, lest the Almanack stretch to 2,000 pages or more. By the 1950s and 1960s, when cricket had once and for all become a batsman's game, the pitches were condemned as "disgraceful" and "treacherous", and since 1960, this remarkable and curious circumstance of disgraceful treachery has never recurred.

1873

MCC AND GROUND v THE COUNTY OF SURREY

Played at Lord's, Tuesday May 14, 1872. This was the most remarkable match of the MC [*sic*] season. Seven MCC wickets, including the crack's, being got rid of before a run was scored. Eight noughts were booked in that innings of MCC's, whose eleven were out in three-quarters of an hour for a total of 16 runs. Nineteen was the highest score made in the match, which was commenced at 10 past 12 and concluded at 20 minutes to 7; the whole number of runs made in the match being 175, and that, too, notwithstanding such batsmen as Mr W. Grace, Jupp, John Smith, Richard Humphrey, Pooley, T. Hearne, T. Humphrey and Mr L. S. Howell had played their innings.

Incessant rain from dawn to dusk on the 13th (the day set to commence the match) necessitated a postponement until the following day, when on dead, deceitful playing wickets, and in a queer light for batting, Mr W. Grace and John Smith commenced (!) MCC's marvellous little innings of 16 runs, wherein seven of the wickets (including the crack's) went down before a run was scored, in this form: To the fourth ball delivered, Mr Grace was lbw; from the sixth ball Smith was caught out by long-stop; the 15th ball shot down Mr Coote's wicket, and the 22nd bowled Shaw. From the 23rd ball Mr Onslow was smartly had at mid-off; the 35th thoroughly beat and bowled Mr Brune, and the very next ball slick bowled Hearne; seven wickets – and good ones too – in this way falling in 25 minutes before a run was scored; the bowling at that phase of the match standing in the score books in the following unique form:

Southerton: ... w .... w w
Marten: . w ..... w .. w w. ....

Captain Beecher then made a 2 from the first ball of Marten's fifth over, but in Southerton's sixth over (another maiden) a clever catch by Pooley got rid of Biddulph; then Captain Beecher made his score 8 when a truly splendid left-hand catch – low down – by Marten settled him; Captain Beecher (ninth man out) *having made all the runs (8) then scored for the Club.* When Rylott and Howitt had doubled the score Marten bowled Howitt, and so, in exactly 45 minutes, were the MCC eleven out for an innings of 16 runs, their wickets having fallen in the following curious form:

1/0, 2/0, 3/0, 4/0, 5/0, 6/0, 7/0, 8/2, 9/8 and 10/16.

At ten minutes past one the Surrey innings was commenced; at 2.30 it was concluded for 49 runs, made from 46 overs (less one ball). At five minutes past three, the second innings of MCC was commenced by Mr Grace and Mr Onslow; with the score at 21, Mr Onslow was bowled and at 22, Mr Grace was bowled. John Smith made 19 – the top score in the match; but at 5.30, the innings was over for 71 runs, made from 77 overs (less one ball).

At a quarter to six, Jupp and R. Humphrey commenced Surrey's second innings, and at 20 minutes to 7, the County had won by five wickets; but if Captain Beecher had not missed R. Humphrey when he had scored only three runs, and Mr Howell when he had scored but two, the probability was the match would have been a very close affair.

MCC and Ground 16 (Southerton four for 5, Marten six for 11) **and 71**
　　(Southerton seven for 38, Strachan two for 7).
Surrey 49 (Howitt four for 6) **and 39** for five (Howitt four for 15).

1875

MIDDLESEX v OXFORD UNIVERSITY

Played at Prince's, June 18, 1874. Some of the most accomplished amateur batsmen in England played in this match, and yet when 173 overs had been bowled, 29 wickets had fallen, six hours' cricket had been played and 231 runs scored, the match was a page of the past, and Oxford had won by an innings and 15 runs. The reason why of all this was stated to have been wet heavy wickets "which had been watered too much". Although the Oxonians won so easily, they lost three wickets before they scored a run; then Mr Ridley and Lord Harris made 61 (the exact number of Middlesex's innings) for the fourth wicket; Mr Wallroth and Mr Jones increased the score from 76 to 116, and the end was a one-innings victory for Oxford. (Only ten men batted in Middlesex's second, Mr V. E. Walker having left late under the general impression that his side could not possibly be got out for another innings that evening).

Middlesex 61 (Buller 29; Lang six for 27, Jones four for 33) **and 47** (Jones six for 26, Ridley two for 5).

Oxford University 123 (Lord Harris 39, Wallroth 36; Rutter four for 34).

1876

NORTH v SOUTH

Played at Lord's, May 17, 1875 (for the benefit of the MCC Professional Fund). The Whit Monday of 1875 was most enjoyably fine, the bright hot sun that beamed down upon the millions of holiday folks out that day pleasure taking, being agreeably tempered by a cool and brisk breeze from the east. Lord's was thronged, as many as 8,342 having paid for admission to the old ground, which, as evening drew near, presented all the familiarly free and easy appearance of a great match on a great holiday. The pavilion seats and roof had a much larger number of occupants than had ever been seen thereon at preceding Whit Monday matches. The grand stand was largely patronised. The tavern balcony was as full as the many bottles of champagne that were uncorked there on that day. The top of Mr Frank Dark's garden wall was covered by those "who would climb and did not fear to fall". The "reporters' stall" was filled by an unusually large number of "the gentlemen of the press"; and around the ground the people sat, or stood, five or six deep, crowding in front of the score box throughout the afternoon and evening as they were never before allowed to crowd, and, it is to be hoped, they will never again be allowed to crowd; for the angry disputations, the noisy chaff, the frequent question-asking to the scorers, and the (at times) interception of all sight of the wickets by that upstanding throng of men – some of them six-footers – rendered the perfect fulfilment of the scorers' duties next door to an impossibility.

The match – as a fair trial of the cricketing strength of North and South – was a thorough failure, owing to the absence of many of the best cricketers of the North. Mr A. N. Hornby did not play; Richard Daft, William Oscroft, Martin McIntyre, J. C. Shaw, Mycroft, Flint and Frost were playing at Nottingham in the Notts v Derbyshire match; Ephraim Lockwood, Andrew Greenwood, Pinder, Allen Hill, Emmett and Ullyett were playing against a Twenty-Two at Hallam (or thereabouts); Watson – the Southerton of the North – was playing at Old Trafford; Rylott was absent; and F. Randon was playing at Leicester. So the North team had to be made up from men engaged on the ground, colts, veterans etc.: consequently the surprise was not that the Northerners were so emphatically licked, but that they were enabled to get that very strong batting eleven of the South out for an innings of 123 runs.

The North won choice, and were the first to bat; they lost a wicket when six runs only had been scored, another when eight were booked, a third at 16, their fourth at 17, their fifth at 22, and their sixth at 29; then the Yorkshire colt – A. Marshall (a free hitter) – and Alfred Shaw made a bit of a stand, brought on Mr F. Grace to bowl v Mr W. Grace, and had hit the score to 48 when the colt collapsed for 13. Clayton then got hold of one or two, but left at 64; and at 75 Biddulph was stumped, all the nine wickets down having fallen to Southerton, who had a wicket to perform on that suited him to a nicety, and who bowled with such skill and success, that a moiety of his overs were maidens, and his nine wickets were obtained at a trifle over three runs per wicket. All hoped the "Mitcham Figaro", as his pen-and-ink friends term Southerton, would complete the innings by obtaining the tenth wicket, but fate foiled him for that wicket (Morley's) was splendidly run out by Mr W. Grace, and thereby the innings was finished at five minutes to two for 90 runs, Alfred Shaw taking out his bat for 26, a bit of batting that brought out a lot of lusty cheering from the holiday lads, some hundreds of whom triumphantly escorted Alfred from the wickets to the players' room.

At ten minutes past two, Mr W. Grace and Jupp commenced the South's innings to the bowling of Alfred Shaw and Morley. When three byes only had been scored, Shaw clean bowled Jupp for 0. Mr W. Grace and Mr Gilbert then made the score 20 when "dinner" (at 2.30) was called. After dinner, Mr Gilbert was had at mid-off, the score still at 20; and at 33 Mr W. Grace hit out at one from Morley, the bat swinging out of his hands from the wicket to mid-on, and the ball going to cover-slip, where it was caught by Rawlinson, the crack being thus curiously out for a hard-earned 9. Before another run was made, Mr Renny-Tailyour was bowled; Mr F. Grace and, at 70, both Mr Hadow and Richard Humphrey were bowled by Morley; and when, at 76, Biddulph settled Charlwood for 24, and eight wickets had gone down, the visitors began to fancy the Northmen would after all make a match of it, in so far as the first innings went. But on Pooley and Pearce (from Herts) getting together, a stand was made and the score increased to 103, when Shaw bowled Pooley for 22, an innings that testified to the old Pooley form being still in full vigour. Southerton then stayed until Pearce had, in really good style, increased the score to 123, when Biddulph caught out the young man from Herts for 21; and so the innings ended at five minutes to five, the match being then half played out with an advantage of 33 runs to the South.

The North's second innings was indeed a brief affair; commenced at 5.12, it was done with at 6.40. Mr C. Booth and Hicks began the batting to the bowling of Southerton and Mr W. Grace; they had made 17 runs before the first wicket (Mr Booth's) fell, but at 25, the second and third both went; at 37, the fourth wicket fell, and at 42, half the wickets had gone. Bold, resolute, hard – aye, and good – hitting by Clayton was the main reason why the sixth wicket stood up until the score reached 64, but before another run had been made, the seventh went; the eighth collapsed at 65, and the ninth at 66, Clayton being then very cleverly caught out by Mr W. Grace for 27, a hard driving innings, and the largest score hit for the North in the match. Morley then had a go at one or two, but was stumped for 5, and so the innings ended for 72, leaving the Southerners only 40 to make to win. It was then 20 minutes to seven, and under the impression there would be no more play that day, hundreds of visitors left the ground, and thereby lost a brief but busy bit of batting. A consultation was held, and a decision to play out the match that evening promptly come to; the clear-the-ground bell rang out forthwith, the people settled down in their places, and at 6.50 out came Mr W. Grace and Jupp to get the 40 runs. They got them in dashing form. The bowlers were Alfred Shaw and Morley. Jupp commenced with a three, a single was then over-thrown into a five, a four followed that, and in this way the first 20 runs were made from six overs; then Mr Grace made a four, a four and a two (all on-drives) from one over of Alfred Shaw's; and when nine overs had been bowled, 31 runs had been made; five more runs were made from the next over, and five more from the following four balls, and so the match was won, the 41 runs having been made from 11 overs in exactly 15 minutes, and thus was this uninteresting "North v South" match played out in one day, the South the winners by ten wickets.

The North 90 (Shaw 26 not out; Southerton nine for 30) **and** 72 (Clayton 27; Southerton seven for 22, W. G. Grace three for 47).

The South 123 (Charlwood 24; Morley five for 55, Shaw four for 52) **and 41** for none (W. G. Grace 28 not out, Jupp 13 not out).

1885

THE AUSTRALIANS v AN ELEVEN OF ENGLAND

Played at Birmingham, Monday May 26, 1884. This contest was one of the most remarkable played during the year, and though the Australians won it by four wickets, it was not a victory of which they could feel proud considering the composition of their opponents' team. The match was played out in four hours of actual cricket, 36 wickets falling for 197 runs from the bat, of which 80 were made by three batsmen. It was to Spofforth's phenomenal bowling in the second essay of the Englishmen, and M'Donnell's dashing play in both innings that the Australians owed their victory. Spofforth's extraordinary success is chronicled in the score book as under:

. w 2. . . . . w . . . . w . w 1 . w w . . . . . . w

The wicket on which this match was played was almost bare of grass, and was said to have been freely watered on the previous evening. Whether that was so or not it is certain that the extremely low scoring was alone due to the badness of it.

Eleven of England 82 (Docker 19; Spofforth seven for 34) **and 26**
  (Spofforth seven for 3).
Australians 76 (M'Donnell 21; Barlow seven for 31) **and 33** for six
  (M'Donnell 17; Christopherson four for 10).

1892

MCC AND GROUND v NOTTINGHAMSHIRE

Played at Lord's, Monday, June 1, 1891. After nearly a fortnight of bad weather there was a hot sun shining on the soft ground at Lord's when this match commenced, and the spectators present were fully prepared to see some curious cricket, though few could have anticipated that the game would begin and end in the single day. Such, however, proved to be the case. Mr Grace on winning the toss put Notts in, and the county, weakened by the absence of Arthur Shrewsbury and Mr Dixon, failed so completely that they were all dismissed by Mr Ferris and Rawlin in the course of 25 overs for the paltry score of 21. Seven members of the team failed to get a run between them, and Mr C. W. Wright, though he only obtained 5, alone showed any ability against the bowling. Poor as was the total, it will be noticed that there were six extras. When the Club went in, some far superior batting was witnessed, though certainly the ground had slightly improved. Mr Grace and Mr Ferris made 37 for the first partnership, and Mr Pope and Mr Murdoch 33 for the third, while a useful contribution later on by Davidson helped the total to 127 before all the side were got rid of. The county had a balance of 106 against them, and though they did better than before they only made 69, and in the end were beaten in an innings with 37 runs to spare. Mr Wright, as at the first attempt, batted capitally, and he and William Attewell actually put together 37 for the first wicket, but no one else reached double figures and there were four more "duck's eggs". The victory was a memorable one for the MCC, and the honours were fairly borne off by the four Australians playing. Messrs Ferris, Pope and Murdoch made 68 runs between them, while James Phillips obtained five wickets in the second innings for 30 runs.

Nottinghamshire 21 (Ferris six for 7, Rawlin four for 8) **and 69** (Wright 39; Ferris five for 25, Phillips five for 30).

MCC and Ground 127 (Pope 31; Redgate three for 8, Attewell three for 28).

1893

LANCASHIRE v SOMERSET

Played at Manchester, Monday, Tuesday, August 8, 9, 1892. This return match furnished another instance of a first-class fixture being commenced and finished in a single day, a similar occurrence having been recorded in connection with the same ground when Surrey beat Lancashire in 1888. Rain prevented any cricket at all on the Monday, and Somerset, going in to bat on the following morning, put on 60 for the loss of two men, but then the other eight wickets went down for 28 runs, and Lancashire were dismissed for 116, the home side getting a very useful lead of 28. Palairet played very skilfully when Somerset went in a second time, but the innings being all over for 58, Lancashire had no great difficulty in gaining a victory – some time after the usual hour for drawing stumps – with eight wickets to spare. Briggs took 12 wickets for 83 runs and Mold eight for 40.

Somerset 88 (Hewett 35; Briggs six for 62, Mold three for 13) **and 58** (Palairet 22 not out; Briggs five for 21, Mold five for 27).

Lancashire 116 (Hedley four for 18, Woods four for 50) **and 32** for two.

1895
LANCASHIRE v SOMERSET

Played at Manchester, Monday, Tuesday, July 16, 17, 1894. Some extraordinary cricket was witnessed in this game, in which no start could be made on the Monday. The second day's cricket, however, made full amends, for on a difficult wicket the play proved so sensational that the game was commenced and finished between 20 minutes to twelve and a quarter past six. Curiously enough, only two years before Lancashire had similarly beaten Somerset in the course of one day's cricket. The triumph for the northern county in the match under notice was mainly the work of Frank Sugg and Mold. The fast bowler did the "hat-trick" in the first innings of the western team, who were all out in 50 minutes for 31. Three wickets fell at 19, and four others at 21, Mold narrowly missing the "hat-trick" for the second time in the innings, and actually obtaining seven wickets for 10 runs. Up to this point Sugg had done scarcely anything worthy of his reputation, but he came out on the slow wicket in his finest form, and hit up an innings of 105 by one five, nineteen fours, a three, five twos and 11 singles. Smith helped him put on 133 runs in 65 minutes for the second wicket. In the second innings of the visitors Lionel Palairet played a great game for his side, and scored a splendid innings of 69 in 80 minutes, but no one except Fowler gave him much assistance, and before time Somerset were beaten by an innings and 68 runs.

Somerset 31 (Mold seven for 10, Briggs three for 16) **and 132** (Palairet 69, Mold six for 50, Briggs three for 50).

Lancashire 231 (Sugg 105, Smith 50; Woods four for 100).

1899
HAMPSHIRE v YORKSHIRE
(For Mr H. Baldwin's Benefit)

Played at Southampton, Thursday, Friday, May 26, 27, 1898. After rain had prevented a ball being bowled on the opening day, the wicket proved so treacherous that between twelve o'clock and five minutes past six on Friday the game was finished off, Yorkshire doing a noteworthy performance in winning in one afternoon by an innings and 79 runs. With all their Army officers away the Hampshire batting proved lamentably weak on the soft ground which had caked on the top. In the two innings, which in the aggregate realised but 78 runs, only one man reached double figures and he was let off. Haigh carried off the bowling honours and no one could have turned such an opportunity to better account. Varying his pace skilfully, he got a wonderful break on the ball and had the batsmen completely at his mercy. His record for the match was extraordinary – 14 wickets for 43 runs – and he hit the stumps no fewer than ten times. Between the two collapses of the home side Yorkshire put together the capital score of 157, in making which they were largely assisted by the weakness of the bowling opposed to them. Certainly the Hampshire men failed where Haigh succeeded so brilliantly, but still great credit belongs to Tunnicliffe for an admirable 58. He was in the whole of the time the innings lasted. Much disappointment was occasioned through the match being brought to such a summary conclusion, as it had been set aside as the benefit for the Hampshire bowler H. Baldwin.

Hampshire 42 (Haigh eight for 21) **and 36** (Haigh six for 22, Jackson two for 2).

Yorkshire 157 (Tunnicliffe 58; Baldwin four for 37).

1900
MIDDLESEX v SOMERSET
(For W. Flowers's Benefit)

Played at Lord's, Monday, Tuesday, May 22, 23, 1899. By arrangement between Middlesex and the Marylebone Club the

Whit Monday match was allotted to Wilfrid Flowers for his benefit, the Notts cricketer having been a member of the ground staff at Lord's since 1878. Unfortunately, as a benefit, the match was ruined by the weather. Not a ball could be bowled on the Bank Holiday, and so difficult was the wicket on the following day that in the course of little more than three hours' actual play, the game was begun and finished, Middlesex winning by an innings and seven runs. With the ground as it was Albert Trott and J. T. Hearne proved quite irresistible, and in neither innings of Somerset was a change found necessary. In the first innings eight wickets fell in four overs for eight runs, and it seemed quite possible that Somerset would be out for the smallest score on record in first-class matches. This, however, was averted by Woods and Newton. Middlesex could not do very much on the difficult wicket, but, inasmuch as the first two batsmen scored 24 before they were separated, the home team were always sure of being well ahead on the first innings. When Somerset went in for the second time with a balance of 51 runs against them, five wickets were lost for five runs and eight were down with the score at 18. After that Nichols and Newton played up with great pluck, but they did not succeed in averting the single innings defeat.

Somerset 35 (Woods 20; Hearne five for 14, Trott four for 18) **and 44** (Nichols 18; Trott seven for 13, Hearne three for 30).

Middlesex 86 (Foley 20; Tyler eight for 42).

1909

MIDDLESEX v GENTLEMEN OF PHILADELPHIA

Played at Lord's, Monday July 20, 1908. So complete a mastery did the ball obtain over the bat, that on a treacherous pitch this match was played out in one day, Middlesex winning by seven wickets. For their success the county were indebted almost entirely to Tarrant, Trott and Bruce, the last of whom appeared for Middlesex for the first time. Tarrant, in addition to playing an invaluable innings, took ten wickets for 46 runs, and Trott obtained nine wickets for 59, the two men bowling unchanged through the two innings of the Philadelphians. Bruce hit with

refreshing confidence under conditions which rendered most of
the batsmen powerless. The Philadelphians' bowling proved far
better than their batting, Lester in the latter department alone
showing real skill on the sticky wicket. Middlesex, it will be
noted, placed a moderate side in the field.

Gentlemen of Philadelphia 58 (Tarrant five for 19, Trott five for 31) **and 55**
(Tarrant five for 27, Trott four for 28).

Middlesex 92 (Bruce 39; King four for 19, Lester three for 12) **and 24** for
three (King two for 11).

1910
GLOUCESTERSHIRE v MIDDLESEX

Played at Bristol, Thursday August 26, 1909. For the first time in
the history of the county, Gloucestershire were beaten in one day,
Middlesex winning by an innings and 31 runs. In gaining their
startling victory, Middlesex owed nearly everything to Tarrant,
who enjoyed a remarkable all-round triumph. He began by taking seven wickets for 18 runs, followed that feat by playing a not
out innings of 55 – the highest individual score in the match –
and then obtained six more wickets for 49 runs. In making his 55
Tarrant was batting for about an hour and a half, and only gave
one difficult chance. Brown showed that the Middlesex bowling
could be hit, but his effort came too late to affect the situation.

Gloucestershire 33 (Tarrant seven for 18, Hearne three for 10) **and 81**
(Brown 32; Tarrant six for 49).

Middlesex 145 (Tarrant 55 not out; Huggins four for 13).

1920
KENT v SUSSEX

Played at Tonbridge, Friday and Saturday, June 20, 21, 1919. In
the first two months of the season, Sussex had such an excessively
weak team at command that success was almost out of the question. Their outlook at Tonbridge was hopeless from the start, but
naturally it came as a surprise to find the game finished off in one
day – after rain had made Friday a blank – Kent declaring with
six wickets down and winning by an innings and 123 runs. Not

since 1909 had a county match been so rapidly completed. The
game began in startling fashion, Sussex, on going in first, losing
five wickets for five runs. Up to that point Fairservice had sent
down five overs, three maidens, for three runs and three wickets.
In the circumstances it was surprising that the total reached the
modest total of 60. Kent's batting was consistently good.
Woolley hit up 59 out of 86 in 50 minutes, and Troughton 54 out
of 91 in 40 minutes. Woolley's innings included three sixes.
Hubble, though less vigorous than his two partners, played
admirably for an hour and three-quarters and was still not out
when the closure was put in force. Sussex started their second
innings shortly before half past four and were all out at half past
six, Wilson alone making any stand against the capital bowling.
Woolley finished off the match by taking five wickets in four
overs and a ball for eight runs. As he scored 59 and took in all
12 wickets the chief honours of the game were clearly with him.

Sussex 60 (Woolley six for 33, Fairservice four for 21) **and 78** (Wilson 34;
Woolley six for 28, Fairservice three for 25).

Kent 261 for six declared (Hubble 71 not out, Woolley 59, Troughton 54;
Tate four for 97).

1926

LANCASHIRE v SOMERSET

Played at Manchester, Wednesday, Thursday, May 20, 21, 1925.
Somerset had not played Lancashire for 14 years and the renewal
of the fixture was noteworthy, the game beginning and ending on
the Thursday, Lancashire winning by nine wickets. After the loss
of a day through rain, the captains agreed to play until quarter
past seven to permit an early finish on the Friday, and the winning hit was made at seven o'clock. Owing to the soaked state of
the pitch intended for the match a new wicket was prepared, and,
drying under sunshine, it gave bowlers such help that most of the
batsmen were helpless. Bligh stayed an hour and Earle hit up 43
out of 56 in 35 minutes, two drives for six and five fours being
included in the highest score of the day. Although Barnes batted
well for an hour before being run out, Lancashire held little

advantage until Richard Tyldesley and McDonald forced the game so effectively as to add 55. Batting a second time after tea Somerset fared worse than before until Daniell drove Parkin three times for six. The whole side were out in 80 minutes, and Lancashire quickly got the 18 runs wanted for victory. Parkin, McDonald and Richard Tyldesley used their opportunity skilfully, the slow bowler taking six wickets for 26 runs, his figures being identical in each innings. Hunt and White bowled admirably for Somerset.

Somerset 74 (Earle 43; McDonald five for 24, R. Tyldesley three for 13) **and 73** (Daniell 20; Parkin six for 44, R. Tyldesley three for 13).

Lancashire 130 (McDonald 35 not out; White five for 67, Hunt four for 63) **and 20** for one.

1937

In 1836, two professional cricketers, Wenman and Mills, defeated an Isle of Oxney XI, at Wittersham, Kent. At the end of that game it was agreed that another of the kind should take place in one hundred years' time.

The agreement was fulfilled on September 5, 1936, when Ashdown (Kent) and Wensley (Sussex) comprised the professional "team". Oxney batted first, scoring 153; then Wensley (96) and Ashdown (83 not out) made 186 and won by 33 runs.

1938

IRELAND v NEW ZEALANDERS

At Dublin, September 11, 1937. New Zealanders won by eight wickets. For the first time since 1925, a first-class match was begun and finished in a single day. Bowlers held the mastery to an astonishing degree, 32 wickets falling at an average cost of less than seven runs each. As may be gathered, the pitch was all against batsmen, and in the second innings of Ireland, which produced the smallest total on record by an Irish representative side, Cowie, as his analysis of 6 wickets for 3 runs indicates, proved well-nigh unplayable.

Ireland 79 (Lambert 25 not out; Gallichan three for 27, Moloney three for 26) **and 30** (Ingram 15; Cowie six for 3, Moloney two for 10).

New Zealanders 64 (Wallace 20; Boucher seven for 13) **and 46** for two (Lowry 30 not out).

1948
DERBYSHIRE v SOMERSET

At Chesterfield, June 11, 1947. Derbyshire won by an innings and 125 runs. This was the first County Championship match completed in one day since Lancashire beat Somerset in 1925. The game provided a personal triumph for Pope, who took 13 wickets for 50 runs. On a lively pitch, he bowled in-swingers with deadly accuracy against irresolute batsmen. He was unchanged in both innings and his figures were the more remarkable because he conceded 24 runs before taking a wicket. Vaulkhard, the most successful batsman for Derbyshire, hit three sixes.

Somerset 68 (Buse 23; Pope six for 34, Rhodes three for 20) **and 38** (Pope seven for 16, Gladwin two for 14).

Derbyshire 231 (Vaulkhard 84; Hazell five for 64).

1951
LANCASHIRE v SUSSEX

At Manchester, July 12, 1950. Lancashire won by an innings and 87 runs. For the third time since 1925, when Somerset were the victims, a match at Old Trafford ended in one day. Afterwards, James Langridge, Sussex professional captain, asserted that the pitch was not fit for three-day games, but he admitted that Lancashire were better equipped to exploit the conditions. During the day 30 wickets fell for 391 runs, and with Sussex in a hopeless plight at the end of the normal period, the captains agreed on extra time to complete the match. Hilton, Lancashire's slow left-arm bowler, did his best work for the county, returning match figures of 11 wickets for 50 runs. Greenwood, with off-breaks, took nine for 67. Although John Langridge carried his bat, and J. Oakes hit two sixes and five fours, six players failed to score and Sussex were dismissed in 105 minutes before lunch. J. Oakes also bowled well, but Edrich and Barlow batted forcefully for

Lancashire, who gained a lead of 138. Sussex again fell to pieces in their second innings, being put out in 70 minutes.

Sussex 101 (John Langridge 48 not out, J. Oakes 35; Hilton six for 32, Greenwood four for 43) **and 51** (Hilton five for 18, Greenwood five for 24).
Lancashire 239 (G. A. Edrich 89; J. Oakes five for 107).

1954
SURREY v WARWICKSHIRE

At The Oval, May 16, 1953. Surrey won by an innings and 49 runs. Members rose as one when the triumphant Surrey team walked from the field having begun their Championship programme with victory in a day. The last and only time that a first-class match had been completed in a day at the Oval was in 1857. Special applause was accorded to A. Bedser, who took 12 wickets for 35 runs, and Laker, who performed the hat-trick. Bedser bowled magnificently when play commenced at noon. Unable to obtain a proper foothold on the wet turf, he attacked the leg stump at below normal pace, and, helped by fine catches, he equalled his previous best analysis of eight for 18. Surrey also found the pitch treacherous, but, chiefly through a sound innings by Constable, they took the lead with only two wickets down. The score then went from 50 for 2 to 81 for 7 and only the aggressiveness of Surridge, who hit three sixes in four balls from Hollies, Laker and Lock enabled them to gain a substantial lead. Lock became the second highest scorer before a blow above the right eye led to a visit to hospital and his retirement from the game. Laker was called into the attack for the first time when Warwickshire batted again and he began the final rout by achieving the first hat-trick of the season. Warwickshire, batting for ten minutes of the extra half hour, were all out in 70 minutes, five minutes less than in their first innings. No Warwickshire batsman was bowled during a day in which 29 wickets fell for 243 runs – a fact that emphasised Surrey's excellent fielding.

Warwickshire 45 (A. Bedser 13.5–4–18–8) **and 52** (A. Bedser 13.4–7–17–4; Laker 13–6–29–5).
Surrey 146 (Constable 37; K. Dollery 11–4–40–4).

1954
SOMERSET v LANCASHIRE
(For H. T. F. Buse's Benefit)

At Bath, June 6, 1953. Lancashire won by an innings and 24 runs. A newly-laid pitch brought financial disaster for Buse, the match ending before six o'clock on the first day when 30 wickets fell for 292 runs. Tattersall, the England and Lancashire off-spin bowler, carried everything before him, taking 13 for 69. His seven victims in the first innings, when not one Somerset player reached double figures, were all caught. The best stand of the match for the losers came in their second innings, Redman and Langford adding 35 in a plucky final partnership. Ironical as it seemed, Buse proved Somerset's central figure with the ball. Although hit for 18 in one over, he dismissed six batsmen for 41 runs. Lancashire, who lost half their side for 46, were put in a winning position by Marner and Wharton, whose fierce hitting brought 70 for the sixth stand in 25 minutes. Four times Marner cleared the boundary with huge hits for six.

Somerset 55 (Tattersall seven for 25, Hilton two for 12) **and 79** (Tattersall six for 44, Statham four for 13).
Lancashire 158 (Marner 44, Buse six for 41).

1961
KENT v WORCESTERSHIRE

At Tunbridge Wells, June 15, 1960. Kent won by an innings and 101 runs, taking 14 points from the first match to be completed in a day since 1953. The pitch, grassless and soft at first, dried under a hot sun, leaving crusty edges on the indentations made when the ball dug in earlier. No two deliveries behaved alike; many rising sharply, some keeping low and nearly all deviating to an unaccustomed degree. Worcestershire, not the strongest of batting sides, floundered against Brown and Halfyard, both of whom needed to do little more than turn over their arms. The pitch did the rest.

An enterprising innings by Jones, who hit two sixes and nine fours in scoring 73 in one hour 35 minutes, helped Kent to a reasonable total while the pitch was drying out. Worcestershire commenced their first innings at ten minutes to four and, with tea intervening, were all out at 5.25 after batting 75 minutes. Six wickets were down for nine runs and there never seemed a chance of them hitting the 38 needed to avoid the follow-on. Slade, with two fours off successive balls from Brown, became top scorer with nine, and six extras bolstered the total to 25, the lowest since Hampshire were dismissed by Derbyshire for 23 in August 1958, and only one run better than the lowest in Worcestershire's history.

Brown, six for 12, and Halfyard, four for 7, bowled throughout and continued to demolish Worcestershire when they went in again 162 behind. The second innings stretched ten minutes into the extra half-hour – mainly because of the determination of Broadbent who stayed for one hour ten minutes, and a bold front by Slade and Booth, whose dismissal was indicative of the pitch, described afterwards by Cowdrey as "disgraceful". The ball flew off one of the many patches on to the top of the bat, struck Booth on the cheekbone and produced a catch.

Kent 187 (P. H. Jones 73; Gifford six for 63).

Worcestershire 25 (Halfyard four for 7, Brown six for 12) **and 61** (Broadbent 22; Halfyard five for 20, Brown three for 22, Shenton two for 12).

WHAT HAVE I DONE TO DESERVE THIS?

There are plenty of players who have earned just one Test cap in their lives. These are men who were probably on the edge of selection for a couple of seasons, and got their chance when a first-choice player was unavailable, usually through injury. After one performance of average success, these players ceded their place to the original occupant and went back to county or inter-state cricket, secure in the knowledge that they did at least have their one moment of international glory, and perhaps knowing in their hearts that Test cricket was indeed one step too far for them. Still, for those of us whose sporting skills have never taken us within sniffing distance of county cricket, let alone Test cricket, a Test cap is the ultimate, and only a curmudgeon would point out that a hundred Test caps is rather more impressive than just the one.

There are some strange stories hidden behind *Wisden*'s words: J. J. Ferris only played once for England, but he had already played eight Tests for Australia. In that same Test, Billy Murdoch, the former Australian captain, also won a first and only cap for England after 18 Tests for Australia. On the South African side, Frank Hearne was playing his first Test for South Africa, having three years earlier played twice for England against South Africa. His brothers, Alec and George, were playing their only Test (for England), along with their cousin J. T. Hearne. This is still the only instance of brothers playing on opposing sides in a Test match. G. G. Hearne had a Test career even less statistically distinguished than poor Fred Grace – out for nought in his only innings, he also neither bowled nor took a catch.

Among the one-Test wonders, there are a few who must have felt aggrieved when their place was reclaimed by another. These are the men who did so well on debut that they should have had a long Test career. Runs, wickets, catches, stumpings – they racked them up and looked back on their first Test as a job well done and a great start to their time in the national side. But they, to a man, had reckoned without the cruel fates that conspire, in the shape of injuries, selectors and international Test schedules, to name but three reasons why even the brightest start can sometimes also be a bright finish. These are the men whose one Test was certainly not enough – but that was all they had.

C. A. SMITH 1890

It was never intended, or considered necessary, to take out a representative English team for a first trip to the Cape, and certain laments which were indulged in at home when the news of the early defeats came to hand were found to be quite uncalled for. The heroes of the trip were undoubtedly Abel and Briggs, the former with the bat and Briggs with the ball literally doing marvels. Three times Abel exceeded the hundred, and his play all through was some of the best ever shown for a travelling side. Mr J. H. Roberts, who went out with the team, was recalled to England by a domestic bereavement, and George Ulyett journeyed to the Cape to take his place. Mr C. A. Smith, the captain of the side, and Mr M. P. Bowden remained behind in South Africa when the tour ended.

SOUTH AFRICA v ENGLAND
First Test Match

Played at Port Elizabeth, 12, 13 March, 1889. The first of the two eleven-a-side matches that were played, and a victory for the Englishmen by eight wickets. Good all-round cricket, rather than any specially noteworthy individual achievement, brought around this gratifying result. Mr Smith, however, had a capital bowling average in the first innings of South Africa. Abel, as on many other occasions, made the best score for his side.

South Africa 84 (Tancred 29, Dunell 26; Smith five for 19, Briggs four for 39) **and 129** (Tancred 29; Fothergill four for 19, Smith two for 42).
England 148 (Abel 46, Fothergill 32; Innes five for 43) **and 67** for two (Abel 23 not out).

THE MARYLEBONE CLUB IN 1877
THE DINNER

After the usual loyal toasts, the President proposed "Cricket, and success to the MCC". After stating the pleasure he had experienced during his year of office, and expressing his thanks for the assistance he had received from the Committee in the performance of his duties, the noble lord (Londesbrough) said that he had great satisfaction in proposing the Duke of Beaufort as his successor in office, and that he felt sure that no one would fill the post more worthily than his Grace. He said that he owed an apology to the Duke, who was absent from the dinner through having been misinformed by him as to the day.

J. J. FERRIS AND W. L. MURDOCH 1893

During the winter of 1891/92 a band of English cricketers, under the captaincy of Mr Walter Read, visited South Africa, and had, from a cricket point of view, a most successful tour. Though, with one exception, opposing odds, the Englishmen did not meet with a single reverse, and of the 20 matches played 13 were won. The remaining seven games were left unfinished, and except, perhaps, in one instance, the draws were all in favour of the visitors. With some few exceptions, the form shown by the South African cricketers was very moderate; but their batsmen were subjected to a very severe test in being opposed to the bowling of Ferris, J. T. Hearne, Martin, Pougher and Alec Hearne. Against such variety of attack it is no matter for surprise that the colonial batsmen gave but a poor account of themselves, and the extent of their failure may well be gathered from the fact that the averages of these five bowlers ranged from less than six to under nine runs a wicket. The wear and tear of the tour apparently had an effect upon the bowlers, as in the English summer of 1892 Mr Ferris, J. T. Hearne, and Martin, who in South Africa took between them 507 wickets, were less effective than in former seasons.

Financially the trip was a failure, but ... the cricketers were cordially received.

SOUTH AFRICA v ENGLAND

Played at Newlands, Cape Town, March 19, 20, 21, 1892. Owing to the absence of A. B. Tancred, the best all-round cricketer in South Africa, and two of three other prominent players, the home team was not fully representative. The South African eleven went in first, but with the exception of F. Hearne (24), G. Cuffs (18) and W. H. Milton, an old Marlborough boy (21), fared badly. The Englishmen treated the home bowling with scant courtesy, and Wood, by some vigorous cricket, hit up 134 not out, in the home team's second innings F. Hearne made 23 and C. Mills 21, but the general resistance offered to the English bowling was poor, the visitors finished their tour with a brilliant victory by an innings and 189 runs.

South Africa 97 (F. Hearne 24; Ferris six for 54) **and 83** (F. Hearne 23; Ferris seven for 37).

England 369 (Wood 134 not out, Ferris 16, Murdoch 12).

T. F. JOHNSON, N. OLDFIELD AND V. H. STOLLMEYER 1940
ENGLAND v WEST INDIES
Third Test Match

Played at Kennington Oval, 19, 21, 22 August, 1939. The final Test was notable for the enterprising batting of both teams. In the course of three days 1,216 runs were scored while only 23 wickets fell. The West Indies had special cause for satisfaction as, after facing a total of 352, they so severely thrashed the England bowling that they gained a first innings lead of 146 runs. The two Stollmeyers, Weekes and Constantine, were in brilliant form and

R. S. Grant's men proved that, given real cricketing weather, West Indies could hold their own in the best company. For various reasons England called on only six of the men, Hammond, Hutton, Compton, Wood, Hardstaff and Wright, who took part in the defeat of Australia on the same ground 12 months previously. For once, since Hammond took over the captaincy, England fielded poorly and the absence of Bowes, Copson and Verity left the bowling somewhat wanting in hostility and guile.

Though Hammond's luck in the toss deserted him in the first two Tests, it returned and England gained first innings on a perfect pitch. They soon suffered a setback as with only two runs on the board, Keeton played the ball on to his leg stump. In this way Johnson, the West Indies tall, left-arm fast bowler, claimed a wicket with his first delivery in Test cricket, repeating his achievement in the match at Worcester where he took a wicket with his first ball in first-class cricket in England.

West Indies, encouraged by this early success, bowled and fielded splendidly but a second wicket stand of 131 between Hutton and Oldfield enabled England to recover. Oldfield, like Johnson, was new to Test cricket and he seized the opportunity to prove his worth. He scored freely with a delightful late cut, timed his leg glances with masterly skill and also drove fluently. Hutton played a very different innings compared with his marathon 364 at The Oval in 1938. The young Yorkshireman never neglected a scoring chance and his off-driving off the back foot was superb. In contrast Hammond spent an hour and three-quarters over 43 before falling to a grand catch at short-leg. Nor was Compton at his best, but Hardstaff treated the crowd to a magnificent display. He drove cleanly and vigorously and with Nichols put on 89 in 65 minutes. This stand was proving very troublesome to West Indies when Constantine, the bowler, fielded the ball at cover and threw down the wicket in amazing style. This incident led the way for the West Indies to dismiss the tail cheaply, for the last four wickets went down for 19. Hardstaff made a great effort to reach a hundred but, with his colleagues falling so quickly, he abandoned all caution and was last out, bowled middle stump,

Throughout the innings not a single full toss was bowled and Grant managed his attack shrewdly. Johnson bowled better than at any time during the tour and Constantine, mixing his pace, cunningly, was never mastered. Clarke, too, bowled his leg-breaks better than the analysis would suggest.

Before stumps were drawn on Saturday, West Indies lost Grant, caught in the gully, and they resumed on Monday with their total 27 for one wicket. Not for a long time had England spent such an unsatisfactory day in the field. In brilliant sunshine the West Indies batsmen gave an exhibition of the cricket they play in their own islands. First thing J. B. Stollmeyer and Headley set out on a policy of wearing down the bowling which Hammond changed with bewildering frequency. For two hours England laboured unsuccessfully and then Hutton, in his second over, broke the stand, which yielded 113, by getting J. B. Stollmeyer caught at mid-on. In this way the younger Stollmeyer made way for his brother Victor, who, owing to tonsillitis, had to defer his Test debut until this match.

Early in his innings V. H. Stollmeyer was unfortunate to cause Headley to be run out. Apparently he did not see Hardstaff behind the square-leg umpire and attempted a single which Headley at first declined, but afterwards attempted with fatal results. During a stay of two hours 20 minutes, Headley made some delightful square-cuts, strong forcing shots off his legs and a few excellent drives. His dismissal was, at the time, a severe mishap for West Indies and, as Gomez failed to settle down, four men were out for 164.

Any hopes England entertained of bringing about a collapse were frustrated by the promotion in the batting order of Weekes. The left-hander and V. Stollmeyer quickly took complete control and the bowling received drastic punishment. Whereas the first 200 runs occupied three hours and 50 minutes, the next hour yielded 110, 43 coming in four overs when Nichols and Perks took the new ball. England's fielding became very slack and Wright made a particularly costly blunder when he dropped a simple catch offered by Weekes when 52, off Nichols. The partnership had put on 163 in 100 minutes when Stollmeyer, playing a defensive stroke, was stumped. He made his 96, which included eleven fours, in two and a quarter hours and, besides revealing perfect style, produced plenty of strokes. Weekes raced to his first century in Test cricket in 110 minutes and when he fell to a superb right-hand catch by Hammond high at first slip, he had scored 137 out of 225 in two and a quarter hours. Besides lifting Hutton for six, he hit 18 fours. Weekes always hit fearlessly though his stance and footwork were somewhat unorthodox. After tea when Weekes and Sealy were hammering the bowling to all parts of the field, a thunderstorm held up the game for over an hour and though little rain fell it certainly saved England finishing the day a long way in arrears. As it was, Grant's men had to be content with a lead of 43 with four wickets in hand.

It was a real joy to watch the carefree cricket of the West Indies on the last day. Constantine, in the mood suggesting his work in Saturday afternoon League cricket, brought a welcome air of gaiety to the Test arena. He revolutionised all the recognised features of cricket and, surpassing Bradman in his amazing stroke play, he was absolutely impudent in his aggressive treatment of bowling shared by Nichols and Perks. While the four remaining wickets fell those two bowlers delivered 92 balls from which Constantine made 78 runs out of 103. Seldom can there have been such a spreadeagled field with no slips, and Hammond did not dare risk further trouble by changing his attack. With an astonishing stroke off the back foot Constantine thumped Perks for six to the Vauxhall end – a very long carry – and helped himself to 11 fours before he was last out to a very fine catch by Wood; running towards the pavilion the wicketkeeper held the ball that had gone high over his head.

England lost Keeton and Oldfield for 77 and then Hutton and Hammond, with a definite result already impossible, set up a new Test world record third-wicket partnership by adding 264 in three hours. Hutton enjoyed another personal triumph at the Oval for, following his 364 against Australia a year before, he hit 283 for once out in this match. Hutton never looked in trouble and, defying the bowling for five hours and ten minutes, he claimed 17 fours. Towards the end of his innings Hammond hit at everything and, although it was not one of his best efforts, there were 21 fours in his 138.

Altogether, 42,252 people paid at the turnstiles to watch the match and it was estimated that the attendances were 20,000 on Saturday; 23,500 on Monday, and 9,000 on Tuesday.

England 352 (Hardstaff 94, Oldfield 80, Hutton 73; Constantine five for 75) **and 366** for three declared (Hutton 165 not out, Hammond 138).

West Indies 498 (K. Weekes 137, V. Stollmeyer 96, Constantine 79; Perks five for 156).

None of the three debutants ever played Test cricket again, largely because this was the final Test before six years of World War.

A. G. GANTEAUME 1949
WEST INDIES v ENGLAND
Second Test Match

At Queen's Park Oval, Port of Spain, February 11, 12, 13, 14, 16, 1948. Drawn. For holding West Indies to a draw England were indebted mainly to Griffith. In the absence through illness or injury of Brookes, Place and Hardstaff, the batting was sadly weakened, and in his dilemma Allen pressed Griffith into service as opening batsman. Like a true cricketer, the Sussex amateur never allowed the responsibility to worry him. Instead, he curbed his natural impulse, did not attempt anything reckless, and pursued this course so rigidly that he gained the distinction of scoring his maiden century in first-class cricket on his first Test appearance. One cannot praise Griffith too highly for this stupendous effort. At the same time, credit must be given also to Ganteaume, a twenty-seven-year-old clerk in the Trinidad Civil Service, who, in the absence through injury of J. B. Stollmeyer, stepped into the breach and, like Griffith, claimed a century in his first Test. In the course of the match all four opening batsmen reached three figures. England were soon in trouble; brilliant fielding by Gaskin at cover when Griffith called for a sharp single led to Robertson being narrowly run out with only five runs on the board. Ikin, Allen and Evans all began in promising style; in fact Evans hit five grand fours; but the end of the first day found six England wickets down for 230 with Griffith 110. Seventh to leave at 288, Griffith defied the West Indies bowling for six minutes short of six hours. His only serious error occurred when 75 with the total 157; he lifted Ferguson to long leg, where Christiani, blinded by the sun, lost sight of the ball. Griffith hit 15 fours with a variety of strokes, of which the cover drive was especially attractive. Smithson helped him add 87 for the seventh wicket, and then came a fine display by Laker, who, last out, hit seven fours in a stay of 70 minutes. Butler gave valuable support while the last stand realised 56.

Daring strokeplay by Carew quickly established a complete mastery over the English bowling. Wearing a chocolate-coloured felt hat and chewing gum the whole time, Carew, in an unorthodox display, used the hook and pull freely in a dazzling exhibition. Butler alone looked at all difficult, and when eight and again at 41 Carew offered hard chances off the Nottinghamshire bowler to the slips; but at the drawing of stumps on the second day the West Indies score reached 160 without loss, with Carew 101 and Ganteaume 52. Early next day the big stand ended at 173, when Carew, whose fours numbered 16, was lbw. Weekes enjoyed an early escape, being dropped at first slip off Robertson* when only one, but otherwise he hit convincingly, getting six fours before Butler bowled him with a very fine ball. Meanwhile Ganteaume maintained his defiant attitude, but by this time everyone was admiring the cultured batting of Worrell. Ganteaume duly reached 100 out of 279 in four and a half hours, but only 46 runs came in an hour, and Gomez, the West Indies captain, realised that his men were falling behind the clock. A note was sent out to Ganteaume, who promptly replied by lifting the ball to extra cover, where Ikin accepted the catch. Mainly by off-drives, Ganteaume hit 13 fours. Walcott did his utmost to obey his captain and force the pace, but it was Gomez himself who really pushed the score along. His fifth-wicket stand with Worrell, who claimed one six and nine fours, produced 99. Whereas

* This must be an error as Robertson did not bowl in the Test. Presumably Weekes was dropped by Robertson.

Worrell spent three and a quarter hours over his 97, Gomez made 62 in 86 minutes, West Indies raising their total to 447 for six wickets on the third day. On Saturday Williams attempted to repeat his Barbados performance, and in 16 minutes helped himself to seven fours and three singles before Butler finished the innings, which gave West Indies a well-deserved lead of 135.

England's only hope was to play for a draw. Rain cut short the cricket on Saturday by two hours, leaving the outfield slow, and the bowlers used towels to dry the ball when Robertson and Griffith began the grim task. Robertson defended splendidly and Ikin kept up his end for over an hour, but three wickets fell for 70 before stumps were drawn.

At one time on the final day West Indies looked likely to force a win, the seventh wicket going at 196, but Robertson received valuable assistance from Smithson, who stayed 75 minutes. Then Robertson duly completed his first Test hundred; he altogether stayed five and three-quarter hours before being ninth out, having hit 15 fours. West Indies, wanting 141 for victory in 57 minutes, sent in Weekes and Walcott, with Williams No. 3. Weekes fell to a wonderful right-hand catch by Evans, and at no time did the batsmen look like achieving their objective. Best bowling for England was by Butler, Laker, Ikin and Howorth, but no one looked as good as Ferguson, the stocky leg-break expert, who at times tossed his deliveries skilfully into the wind. His was a very fine performance in taking eleven wickets on the easy-paced matting wicket. Near the end Allen pulled up lame after sending down two balls in his fifth over.

England 362 (Griffith 140, Laker 55; Ferguson five for 137) **and 275** (Robertson 133; Ferguson six for 92).

West Indies 497 (Ganteaume 112, Carew 107, Worrell 97) **and 72** for three.

Both Ganteaume and Griffith were dropped for the rest of the series. Griffith played two Tests against South Africa the following winter, and Ganteaume was picked nine years later for the 1957 tour of England. However, he played no more Tests. *Wisden* reported in 1958 that "none of the four recognised opening batsmen, Pairaudeau, Ganteaume, Asgarali and Rohan Kanhai, came up to expectations."

R. E. REDMOND 1974
NEW ZEALAND v PAKISTAN
Third Test Match

Played at Eden Park, Auckland, February 16, 17, 18, 19, 1973. Match drawn. With a prudent approach to the match, Pakistan held New Zealand at arm's length and thus recorded their first Test rubber success away from home. It was a remarkable match, full of interest almost until the end. Intikhab again won the toss, but this was of little moment for the pitch played quite easily after it had given a little bounce and movement before lunch on the first day. Once more Majid Khan led the Pakistan batting, but this was a very subdued innings, compared with his earlier brilliance. He was in almost four and a half hours for 110. Taylor and Howarth commanded considerable respect as Pakistan went to 300 for seven at the close. Once more the New Zealand catching was below standard. Khan and Mushtaq scored 104 for the third wicket, then Asif Iqbal was with Khan while 86 were added. During the day Wadsworth broke the New Zealand Test wicket-keeping record of 50 (set by A. E. Dick) and in the last over he took a magnificent diving catch to give Taylor his 100th wicket in Tests, only the second New Zealander to reach that mark. In Pakistan's second innings he took two more wickets to leave R. C. Motz's record behind.

The second day, a Saturday, was a study in contrasts. Pakistan, determined to take no chance, batted on for three hours to add 102. Saleem was undefeated for 53, made in three hours and Pervez, sharing a last-wicket stand of 48, had a personal Test best, much to his and everyone's delight. Wasim Bari stayed nearly two hours for 30 as Pakistan made the game safe. In his Test debut the tall, fair-haired left-hander, Redmond, contributed a spectacular century. Diffident and unsound at first, he began to attack vigorously after the first half-hour. Strangely, the only other New Zealanders – J. E. Mills and Taylor – to make centuries on their Test debuts were also left-handers. Redmond, driving, cutting and pulling with tremendous confidence, reached his century in two hours 12 minutes from 110 balls. He hit 20 fours and one five in a scintillating display. When Khan bowled, Redmond hit all of the first five balls to the fence. At 97, he thumped a ball away to mid-wicket and it seemed a certain four. A crowd of about 300 boys and youths streamed on to the field to congratulate Redmond, but on the boundary Asif Iqbal had made a magnificent save and Redmond was only 99. This demonstration, which lasted several minutes, was without parallel in New Zealand domestic cricket. Redmond was hoisted shoulder high, a bail was souvenired, an umpire slightly injured in the jostling throng. But Redmond went to his century with another four. With Redmond was Turner, playing a flawless innings as New Zealand scored 159 for the first wicket. Once the stand was broken, Intikhab took command with another splendid display of spin bowling. On the third morning he took five for 42 as New Zealand wickets tumbled and at lunch nine were down with Hastings fighting grimly for survival and two runs still needed to avoid the follow-on.

In this crisis, Collinge batted with extraordinary solidity and aggression. Using his considerable reach, he played the spinners safely and from time to time let go with powerful attacking strokes. As soon as the batsmen had forced the removal of Sarfraz from a close leg-side catching position, their progress became easier and faster. Hastings, although not batting without blemish, won admiration for his concentration and his cutting and driving. Soon they left the New Zealand tenth-wicket record behind, and went on to beat the world record of 130 set by Rhodes and Foster almost 70 years earlier. They went past that mark when Collinge crashed Pervez through the covers, and they were not separated until they had added 151 and the totals were level. They made the runs in two hours, 35 minutes. Hastings batted over four and a half hours.

New Zealand made further progress by capturing three wickets for 73 before the close, but could not get wickets quickly enough on the last day to have a chance of victory. Asif was missed very early and batted another 70 minutes: New Zealand were always a little behind the striking rate needed.

It was a determined defensive action by Pakistan. The normally ebullient Mushtaq batted two hours 50 minutes for 52,

Saleem an hour and three-quarters for 11 but Raja shaped well. In New Zealand's second innings Redmond was even more convincing than in the first and scored a fine 56.

Pakistan 402 (Majid Khan 110, Mushtaq Mohammad 61; Taylor four for 86) **and 271** (Mushtaq Mohammad 52).

New Zealand 402 (Hastings 110, Redmond 107; Intikhab Alam six for 127) **and 92** for three (Redmond 56; Wasim Raja three for 32).

S. G. LAW 1997
AUSTRALIA v SRI LANKA
First Test Match

At Perth, December 8, 9, 10, 11, 1995. Australia won by an innings and 36 runs. Toss: Sri Lanka. Test debuts: S. G. Law, R. T. Ponting. Australia won inside four days for the fifth time in eight Tests. But the controversy that dogged the series began on the second morning, when the umpires decided someone in Sri Lanka's attack had doctored the seam of the ball. The tourists protested vehemently. The umpires failed to impound the ball, so that any evidence was lost, while referee Graham Dowling seemed assured of their guilt before hearing the Sri Lankans' story. They became the first team convicted of ball-tampering in Test cricket, but the ICC reversed the finding a fortnight later.

On a flat opening day, eight Sri Lankan batsmen reached double figures, but only Kaluwitharana managed 50. Warne's reputation, rather than his spin, spurred de Silva into suicide-by-bravado right on lunch. When Australia replied, the Sri Lankan attack looked below par; strike bowler Vaas was toying with his run and his confidence after back problems. Muralitharan's action attracted plenty of attention; Khizar Hayat spent an over or two watching closely from square leg, but appeared more satisfied than some television commentators, who nearly burned out their slow-motion replay. Taylor and Slater ran up 228, their second-highest opening stand in Tests, before Taylor became the first of two Australians lbw on 96. But Slater slept on a career-best 189 and completed his maiden double-hundred in the morning. Mark Waugh's tenth Test century, an imperious 111 off 223 balls, was so smooth it almost slipped by without notice. One section of the crowd even ragged him for not having a go. Debutant Ricky Ponting, nine days short of his 21st birthday, was cruelly denied a hundred. Hayat ruled him leg-before when replays showed the ball heading over the stumps. Ponting soon lent a sober perspective. He'd been lucky to survive an outside edge first ball, he said, and besides, he would "gladly cop 96 each hit".

Taylor declared as soon as Ponting was out, with the other newcomer, Stuart Law, unbeaten on 54. Australia led by 366 and, after 12 hours' hunting leather, Sri Lanka slumped to 105 for four in the next two. A century from Tillekeratne could not stave off defeat but suggested that the remaining Tests might be less one-sided. His 119 from 206 balls outpaced Waugh's and, though he became Warne's 201st Test wicket when he was last out, Warne found him as elusive as any along the way in his 42 Tests. Indeed, he conceded more than four an over while Tillekeratne and his fellow left-hander Ranatunga were together. Tillekeratne used his long reach and soft hands to good effect; his captain was more ungainly but equally threatening – and turned to the umpires after colliding with McDermott, one of a string of incidents that came to irritate the Australians. Ranatunga finally fell, for 46 in 64 balls, to a yorker from round the wicket – a calculated piece of bowling by McGrath. Taylor claimed the extra half-hour to complete the game on the fourth evening.

Man of the Match: M. J. Slater. Attendance: 28,883.

Sri Lanka 251 (Kaluwitharana 50; McGrath four for 81) **and 330** (Tillekeratne 119).

Australia 617 for five declared (Slater 219, M. E. Waugh 111, Ponting 96, Law 54 not out).

Five Cricketers of the Year 1998

Law cherishes his one Test appearance, against Sri Lanka in Perth in December 1995, in which he made an unbeaten and effortless half-century in Australia's only innings (and so, of course, he does not have a Test average). "To actually don the baggy green cap . . . I can take that to the grave with me," he said. By the next Test, Steve Waugh was fit again, Australia were not quite ready to drop David Boon, and Law was jettisoned.

1998

PAKISTAN V NEW ZEALAND

Second Test Match

At Rawalpindi, November 28, 29, 30, December 1, 1996. Pakistan won by an innings and 13 runs. Toss: Pakistan. Test debut: Mohammad Zahid. Pakistan struck back to draw the series an hour after lunch on the fourth day. The Test occupied only 258.4 overs, though the opening day saw several hold-ups. One was caused by sunlight dazzling the batsmen after tea, another, more conventionally, by bad light, but the oddest occurred at the start, when play was delayed 20 minutes because the Pakistan Cricket Board had forgotten to supply balls. The match eventually got under way using a ball bought from a local sports shop.

C. S. MARRIOTT 1934

ENGLAND v WEST INDIES

Third Test Match

Played at Kennington Oval, Saturday, Monday, Tuesday, August 12, 14, 15, 1933. After their capital work at Manchester, the cricket of the West Indies in the concluding Test match proved disappointing, and early on the third morning England were successful in an innings with 17 runs to spare. Once again no great fault could be found with the bowling and fielding of the tourists, but the batting proved unworthy of a Test match and they did not display any marked ability in dealing with some really splendid bowling by C. S. Marriott. Taking part in his first Test match, the Kent amateur made the most of his opportunity and by clever flighting of the ball, perfect length and spin, he obtained in the two innings 11 wickets for 96 runs – one of the best performances accomplished by a bowler when playing for England for the first time. England won the toss and, staying in for practically the whole of the first day, put together in the course of five hours and three-quarters actual cricket, a total of 312. On Monday the West Indies were dismissed in two hours for 100 runs and following on 212 behind, lost eight wickets for 190 before stumps were drawn, so that, with only two men to be dismissed, they still wanted 22 runs to save the innings defeat when they went in on Tuesday. As it happened, ten minutes' cricket on the last morning proved sufficient to bring the match to an end, but it was a very near thing, for rain, which for some time had threatened, began to fall heavily five minutes after the players had left the field.

It is only fair to the West Indies to observe that the conditions when they went in on Monday were not favourable to them. There had been a little rain in the early morning, but although this did not affect the pitch to any alarming extent, the atmosphere remained gloomy, so that against bowlers of the pace of Clark and Nichols, the visiting batsmen laboured under a considerable handicap. All the same, they never recovered from a bad start, nobody being able to stay long enough and show that the bowling could be dealt with . . .

In the first innings of the West Indies Sealy stayed for about half an hour but nobody dealt with the bowling of Marriott, Clark and Nichols either confidently or successfully. Marriott disguised his spin very well and never made the ball break too much while taking his five wickets for just over seven runs apiece. There might have been a different story if Headley had escaped damage, but two painful blows – one on the thigh from Clark and one on the body from Nichols – affected his play. Ames kept wicket admirably, giving away only one bye and having a hand in the dismissal of four men. When the West Indies followed on Roach batted in a most bright and attractive style. He hooked the ball with great power and certainty and the first wicket produced 77 runs in 40 minutes. Two later Roach was out, having obtained his runs in 45 minutes with a six and five fours as his chief hits. The rest of the cricket was rather dull, nearly everyone playing a sedate game. At tea the score was 137, but Headley and Da Costa were both out at 138, Da Costa having been in for about 80 minutes. Later on Grant received a blow on the arm and had to retire, but on resuming his innings he and Achong stayed together until nearly 25 minutes past six, Grant being eighth out at 183. Martindale was missed first ball, but, as already observed, the match soon ended on the third morning. It is interesting to note that for the first time in the history of Test matches at the Oval, Surrey had no representative in the England team.

England 312 (Bakewell 107, Barnett 52; Martindale five for 93).

West Indies 100 (Marriott five for 37) **and 195** (Roach 56; Marriott six for 59).

1967

MARRIOTT, CHARLES STOWELL, who died on October 13, aged 71, was one of the best leg-break and googly bowlers of his era. In all first-class cricket he took 724 wickets at an average cost of 20.04 runs and his bowling skill so far exceeded his ability as a batsman that his victims exceeded his aggregate of runs by 169. Cunning flighting, allied to the ability to turn the ball sharply, made him a menace to batsmen even on good pitches and when the turf gave him help, he could be well-nigh unplayable. His action was high with a free, loose arm which he swung behind his back before delivery in a manner reminiscent of Colin Blythe. From 1919 to 1921 he appeared for Lancashire and when beginning a long association with Dulwich College as master-in-charge of cricket, he threw in his lot with Kent, whom he assisted during the school holidays from 1924 to 1937 . . .

He met with great success on the occasion of his one appearance in a Test match for England. That was at The Oval in 1933, when he so bewildered the batsmen that he took five wickets for 37 runs in the first innings and, with second innings figures of six for 59, hurried the West Indies to defeat by an innings and 17 runs – a feat described by *Wisden* of the time as one of the best accomplished by a bowler when playing for England for the first time.

"Father" Marriott, as he was popularly known, engaged in two tours abroad. In 1924/25 he was a member of Lord – then the Hon. Lionel – Tennyson's side in South Africa and in 1933/34 he went with D. R. Jardine's MCC team to India, where, against Madras, he did the "hat-trick" for the only time in his first-class career. During World War II he served as an anti-aircraft gunner in the Home Guard.

M. F. MALONE 1978
ENGLAND v AUSTRALIA
Fifth Test Match
by Geoffrey Wheeler

At Kennington Oval, August 25, 26, 27, 29, 30, 1977. Match drawn. Toss: Australia. Test debuts: K. J. Hughes, M. F. Malone.

The Australians ended a rain-ruined game with a clear advantage, but there was little hope of a result once the first day had been lost because sections of the square and outfield were waterlogged.

Chappell's team did their best to make up for lost time by dismissing nine England batsmen for 181 on the Friday before the surrender of another four and three-quarter hours to the weather on Saturday ended their hopes of salvaging a win from a disastrous summer. An atmosphere of anti-climax hung over the match because the series was already decided and there was also an air of sadness that this might be the last meeting between full strength sides of the two countries for a number of years.

The key player for Australia proved to be Malone, the swing bowler who with limited opportunities had previously achieved little on the tour. He entered his first Test because of a doubt about Pascoe's fitness. Two more players from Western Australia were also brought in, Hughes being preferred to Robinson for his Test debut and Serjeant recalled to partner McCosker.

England played Lever for the unfit Botham as their only change, although there had been a strong lobby to omit the Packer signatories in the cause of experiment. Brearley's arguments for the strongest available side won the day. However, there was no denying that the fine edge had gone from England's form. The close catching, all but faultless in the first four matches, was of a poor standard and the batting lacked concentration.

Yet this was not a charge that could be levelled against Boycott and Brearley who, after England had been put in, launched the innings with a partnership of 86 in two hours 50 minutes before

Walker broke through. The breach was well exploited by the tall and powerful Malone, who after an innocuous first few overs caused everyone trouble by his movement away from the bat.

At the close of the first day, when England were 181 for nine, Malone had bowled 43 overs and taken five for 53, showing a splendid appetite for work. His only break was for two overs just before lunch. Other than the opening batsmen only Roope of the specialists looked comfortable before he was nonplussed by Thomson's speed with the new ball.

In Saturday's brief spell of play Willis and Hendrick added 33, taking England to a more respectable total of 214. Hendrick had the distinction of striking the only boundary off Malone in his 47 overs. The tenth wicket pair hit seven of the 16 boundaries in the innings.

Australia, who began their innings in indifferent light, were 11 for one when a mid-afternoon storm washed out further play for the day. While the pitch still showed traces of damp on Monday, Australia struggled and might have been put out cheaply yet again had McCosker been caught at slip by Hendrick when he was two. He stayed for three and a quarter hours until the pitch became a typically slow Oval surface. Hookes then entertained a large Bank Holiday crowd in an innings of 85 which compensated for Underwood's dismissal of Chappell when the Australian captain seemed set to play a major farewell innings. Hookes needed some luck on and around the off-stump but so sweetly timed were his off-side strokes that he was always good to watch.

Using the same weathered bat with which he scored five centuries in six Sheffield Shield innings Hookes, in company with Marsh, rescued the side from 104 for five. When Hookes was sixth out at 184, having hit 12 fours, Australia were in sight of a first-innings lead for only the second time in the series.

Yet with an advantage of only 12 runs on the final morning with four wickets in hand they had little chance of forcing a win. Marsh and Bright soon perished but Malone, surviving a slip chance to Greig before he had scored, and Walker, badly missed by Brearley at 19, put on exactly 100 mainly by reputable stroke-making. Malone did not fall until the last ball before lunch while

Walker finished unbeaten with his highest score, 78 (ten fours), made in two hours 20 minutes. Willis's five wickets for 102 brought his tally for the five Tests to 27, easily a record for an England fast bowler in a home series with Australia.

There were fewer than three hours remaining when England went in for their second innings. In a final burst of speed, before he limped off with a damaged ankle, Thomson removed Brearley. Malone rounded off an auspicious debut by dismissing Woolmer, but Boycott, who when on two completed 5,000 runs in Tests – the eighth Englishman to do so – was still batting solidly when the game was given up soon after a stoppage for bad light at 4.50 p.m. Attendance: 54,000. Receipts £125,000.

England 214 (Malone five for 63, Thomson four for 87) **and 57** for two (Malone one for 14).

Australia 385 (Hookes 85, Walker 78 not out, Marsh 57, Malone 46).

THE JOHNSONS AND
THE TAYLORS

From 1877 to 2005, there have been over 2,000 people who have been able to call themselves Test cricketers. *Wisden*'s full list takes up over 40 pages of tightly packed names. There have been fathers, sons, brothers, grandsons, cousins, half-brothers, great-grandsons and even, with the advent of the Marshalls, James and Hamish, of New Zealand in 2005, a pair of identical twin brothers. However, it is the unrelated players sharing the same surname that seem to leap out from the list.

If we begin with that most common of Anglo-Saxon surnames, Smith, we quickly see that it has spread round the cricketing world. Not only are there the brothers Chris and Robin, South African-born but England Test players, but there are also A. C., Mike, C. I. J., Sir Aubrey, two Davids, a Denis and a Don, Ed, Ernest, Harry, M. J. K. and a Peter to add to the list, a total of 15 Smiths who have played cricket for England. Cammie, Collie, Devon and Dwayne Smith have all played for West Indies, and another four, C. J. E., Fred, Ian and the 2005 captain Graeme, have all worn Springbok colours. Brunton, Dennis and Ian have played for New Zealand, and David and Steve for Australia, a total of 28 Test cricketers Smith.

The five countries the Smiths have played for is not, however, a record. The Richardson clan has also represented five countries (England, Australia, South Africa, West Indies and New Zealand), but pride of place must go to the Johnsons and the Taylors, who have each represented six different Test-playing nations. There have been Browns playing for four different nations, and two more at One-Day International level, but Johnson and Taylor are the only names to have appeared on the Test scorecards of six different nations.

Some have had very long and distinguished Test careers, with three of them captaining their country (Mark and Herbie Taylor, and Ian Johnson). Some have been in and out of their national side before anybody, except probably their mothers, seemed to notice. Les Taylor of England, for example, played two Tests, both against Australia and both of which England won by an innings, but then was never called on again. This was despite the fact that his final act as a Test cricketer was to take the wicket that regained the Ashes. Paul Taylor of England batted four times in his two Tests, making a symmetrical 17 and 17 not out in his first Test, and an even more symmetrical 0 and 0 not out in his last. Len Johnson played just one – victorious – Test for Australia, but was never seen again. The West Indian Johnsons, Hines and Tyrell, have four caps between them, which at least is more than the three that C. L. Johnson of South Africa and David Johnson of India amassed between them. Mark Taylor, with 104 Test appearances, has more caps than all eight Johnsons combined, and, perhaps not surprisingly, the combined Test caps of the three Test captains, 191, is more than half the 360 caps the massed ranks of 23 Johnsons and Taylors have been awarded, by a total of seven different nations.

This is the full list (apart from Claire Taylor, one of England's leading female batsmen and Clare Taylor, the England opening bowler, who retired at the end of the 2005 season).

THE JOHNSONS
AUSTRALIA
Ian William Geddes Johnson 1957

The gradual decline in Australia's cricketing strength since the retirement of Sir Donald Bradman at the end of his triumphant tour in 1948 was not halted by the team of 17 players led by Ian Johnson in 1956. Although they lost the rubber by the bare margin of two wins by England (at Leeds and Manchester) against one by themselves (at Lord's) they were more or less outplayed in four of the five Tests and gave a disappointing display against the majority of the counties . . .

Whenever they faced Laker, they feared his off-spin. In seven matches, including two for Surrey, Laker claimed 63 wickets against them. Yet his whole tally for the season came to no more than 132.

The Test which Australia won was played under dry conditions when, happily for them, Johnson won the toss. Otherwise Australia had the worst of the weather, the pitches and the toss, which May won four times. Unlike England, who possessed plenty of bowlers for any type of pitch, Australia were sadly deficient in spin . . . The team possessed three slow bowlers of repute, Johnson, Benaud and Wilson. Between them they claimed only 14 wickets in the five Tests compared with 61 obtained by Laker and Lock. Johnson, who came to England in 1948 but was omitted from the 1953 team, carried a big responsibility. He could not approach Laker's skill on English wickets, but he was a shrewd and skilful captain who led his men conscientiously both on and off the field.

Test Career Statistics

Matches: 45 (Captain 17 times)

Runs	HS	Avge	100s	Ct/St	Wkts	Runs	Avge	5 w/i	10 w/m	BB
1,000	77	18.51	–	30/-	109	3,182	29.19	3	–	7–44

Leonard Joseph Johnson 1949
AUSTRALIA v INDIA
Fifth Test Match

At Melbourne, February 6, 7, 9, 10, 1948. Australia won by an innings and 177 runs . . . Chief honours fell to Neil Harvey, a nineteen-year-old left-hander playing in his second Test match. He hit the first hundred of his career, showing the confidence of an experienced cricketer. He scored 153 in just over four hours and his only mistake occurred shortly before his dismissal. He hit a five and 11 fours. Loxton, driving powerfully, helped Harvey in a stand of 159, and with useful contributions coming from

Lindwall, Tallon, L. Johnson and W. Johnston, Bradman declared at tea-time on the second day.

Test Career Statistics

Matches: 1

Runs	HS	Avge	100s	Ct/St	Wkts	Runs	Avge	5 w/i	10 w/m	BB
25	25*	–	–	2/-	6	74	12.33	–	–	3–8

ENGLAND
Richard Leonard Johnson 1995
DERBYSHIRE v MIDDLESEX

At Derby, June 30, July 1, 2, 1994. Middlesex won by an innings and 96 runs. Middlesex 23 pts, Derbyshire 5 pts. Toss: Derbyshire. Nineteen-year-old seamer Richard Johnson of Middlesex became the first bowler to take all ten wickets in the Championship for 30 years, since Ian Thomson, for Sussex against Warwickshire at Worthing in 1964. In Derbyshire's second innings, Johnson captured seven for 17 in his first nine overs, rested after 12 and completed his task after tea when Taylor was caught at third slip. The opening batsman Haynes bowled the last two overs from the other end, in an attempt to ensure that Johnson took the final wicket, and had a fright when Malcolm almost played on. Although Johnson was helped by reckless batting, it was an outstanding feat by a young man in his first full season. Only one player younger than Johnson had taken ten in a first-class innings: eighteen-year-old Imran Adil of Bahawalpur in 1989/90. Johnson's previous best was four for 64 against Durham a week earlier – though he had attracted attention by dismissing Lara in both the Benson and Hedges Cup and the Championship. "It hasn't quite sunk in," he said afterwards. "The ball did a little bit off the seam, but it didn't really swing."

2004
ENGLAND v ZIMBABWE
Second npower Test Match

At Chester-le-Street, June 5, 6, 7, 2003. England won by an innings and 69 runs. Test debut: R. L. Johnson. For England,

Richard Johnson made his debut in place of the injured Hoggard, nine years after first entering the national consciousness by taking ten wickets in an innings for Middlesex. His analysis here was eye-catching too, if not quite as spectacular, and he instantly found a good length and some accurate in-swing. Helped by two wickets in his first over, he followed Anderson at Lord's in claiming a five-wicket haul in his first Test. His eventual figures of six for 33 were the sixth-best by an Englishman on Test debut.

Test Career Statistics

Matches: 3

Runs	HS	Avge	100s	Ct/St	Wkts	Runs	Avge	5 w/i	10 w/m	BB
59	26	14.25	–	–/–	16	275	17.18	2	–	6–33

INDIA
David Jude Johnson 1998
SOUTH AFRICA v INDIA
First Test Match

At Durban, December 26, 27, 28, 1996. South Africa won by 328 runs. Bacher was lbw to Srinath's first ball after lunch, Prasad induced edges from Cullinan and Cronje, and Johnson, who had been expensive in the morning, dismissed Gibbs.

Test Career Statistics

Matches: 2

Runs	HS	Avge	100s	Ct/St	Wkts	Runs	Avge	5 w/i	10 w/m	BB
12	8	4.00	–	–/–	3	143	47.66	–	–	2–52

SOUTH AFRICA
Clement Lecky Johnson 1909

In 1893, owing to ill-health, he left his native country (Ireland) and in the following year came to England as a member of the first South African team. During the tour he scored 508 runs with an average of 14.32 and took 50 wickets at a cost of 17.27 runs each. He afterwards represented the Transvaal and in 1896 was included in a South African eleven which met Lord Hawke's team at Johannesburg. He was a fast right-handed bowler and a good bat.

Test Career Statistics
Matches: 1

Runs	HS	Avge	100s	Ct/St	Wkts	Runs	Avge	5 w/i	10 w/m	BB
10	7	5.00	–	1/–	0	57	–	–	–	0–57

WEST INDIES
Hophnie Hobah Hines Johnson 1949
WEST INDIES v ENGLAND
Fourth Test Match

At Sabina Park, Kingston, March 27, 29, 30, 31, April 1, 1948. West Indies won by ten wickets. The superior team, they thoroughly deserved to repeat their success of the previous Test. For this match West Indies were able to include for the first time the two Jamaica fast bowlers, Johnson and Kentish, but were without Headley, so the captaincy devolved on Goddard. Weekes, filling the vacancy, scored his first Test century. At the age of 36, Johnson, standing 6 feet 3 inches, looked a truly great fast bowler. At no time did he attempt to intimidate the England batsmen by pitching short, but maintained a splendid pace, and by consistently keeping the ball well up the pitch compelled his opponents to make strokes. His reward was five wickets in each innings – ten for 96 – and these were easily the best bowling figures in the whole series.

Test Career Statistics
Matches: 3

Runs	HS	Avge	100s	Ct/St	Wkts	Runs	Avge	5 w/i	10 w/m	BB
38	22	9.5	–	–/–	13	238	18.30	2	1	5–41

Tyrell Fabian Johnson 1940
ENGLAND v WEST INDIES
Third Test Match

At Kennington Oval, August 19, 21, 22, 1939. Drawn. The final Test was notable for the enterprising batting of both teams. In the course of three days 1,216 runs were scored while only 23 wickets fell . . .

Though Hammond's luck in the toss deserted him in the first two Tests, it returned and England gained first innings on a perfect pitch. They soon suffered a setback as with only two runs on the board, Keeton played the ball on to his leg stump. In this way Johnson, the West Indies tall, left-arm fast bowler, claimed a wicket with his first delivery in Test cricket, repeating his achievement in the match at Worcester where he took a wicket with his first ball in first-class cricket in England . . . Johnson bowled better than at any time during the tour, and Constantine, mixing his pace cunningly, was never mastered.

Test Career Statistics

Matches: 1

Runs	HS	Avge	100s	Ct/St	Wkts	Runs	Avge	5 w/i	10 w/m	BB
9	9*	–	–	1/–	3	129	43.00	–	–	2–53

ZIMBABWE
Neil Clarkson Johnson 2000
PAKISTAN v ZIMBABWE
First Test Match

At Peshawar, November 27, 28, 29, 30, 1999. Zimbabwe won by seven wickets. Toss: Zimbabwe. Zimbabwe completed their first overseas Test win on the fourth morning, after a run-chase led by Goodwin, who hit an unbeaten 73. Like Johnson, who scored a vital first-innings century, Goodwin had returned to his native Zimbabwe after sharpening his skills overseas; he had played in Australia, Johnson in South Africa and England. But the bowlers who set up the victory by skittling Pakistan for just 103 in their second innings were the black pace men, Olonga and Mbangwa, and their white compatriot Streak, who had all come up through Zimbabwe's ranks . . .

Grant Flower was dropped twice in scoring 15, which carried him past 2,000 Test runs (his brother Andy was the only other Zimbabwean to have reached the landmark), but was caught in the slips off Waqar shortly afterwards. Waqar added Goodwin and Andy Flower, with successive balls. Johnson avoided the hat-trick, stood firm as his side stumbled to a precarious 115 for six, and then turned the innings round in a 103-run partnership with Streak. He was dropped on 99, by second slip Mahmood off Wasim, but survived to complete a maiden century in his second Test. Mahmood had another chance the next morning and caught Johnson at his overnight score of 107, which took only 117 balls and included sixteen fours. It was Wasim's 350th Test wicket, in his 82nd game. But shoddy fielding had let Zimbabwe off the hook; their tail reduced the first-innings deficit to 58. Then came the ignominious collapse, and the final target was 162, which Zimbabwe's top order briskly achieved.

Man of the Match: N. C. Johnson.

Test Career Statistics

Matches: 13

Runs	HS	Avge	100s	Ct/St	Wkts	Runs	Avge	5 w/i	10 w/m	BB
532	107	24.18	1	12/–	15	594	39.60	–	–	4–77

1869

BY W. H. KNIGHT

Mr Tylecote's 404 was made in a Clifton College practice match, and was hit in six hours, or at the rate of about 67 runs per hour, thus Mr Tylecote was first man in of his side, played about half an hour and scored 34 runs on the first day (it was an afternoon's match); on the second afternoon he resumed his innings at 2.45, played up to 5.30, and increased his score to 199; and on the third day he was also at the wickets from 2.45 to 5.30, when he carried his bat out for 404 (out of 630). Mr Tylecote's hits were one seven, five fives, 21 fours, 39 threes, 42 twos, and 77 singles, and barring one four (a hit of Mr T.'s out of the field) he ran all the runs made by his side.

THE TAYLORS
AUSTRALIA
John Morris Taylor
1972

TAYLOR, JOHN MORRIS, who died in a Sydney hospital following a heart attack on May 12, aged 75, was a polished batsman and a brilliant fieldsman at cover point, who played in 20 matches for Australia between 1920 and 1926 – 18 against England and two against South Africa in 1921/22.

1922

Taylor, who did not have the best of health, scarcely lived up to the reputation he enjoys at Sydney, but he often played well, and was at his best against England at The Oval.

1926

AUSTRALIA v ENGLAND
First Test Match

Played at Sydney, Friday, Saturday, Monday, Tuesday, Wednesday, Friday, Saturday December 19, 20, 22, 23, 24, 26, 27, 1924. After a prolonged struggle which established a record by lasting into the seventh day, Australia won the First Test match by 195 runs.

... Arthur Richardson and Taylor were the great batsmen in Australia's second innings. Richardson this time went in first with Bardsley while Taylor was No. 8 on the list. Mailey helped put on 127 for the last wicket and, though England had got eight men out for 286, they were set the overwhelming task of making 605 in the last innings ... Hobbs scored his seventh Test match hundred, beating MacLaren's record, and Taylor enjoyed this success for the first time in a match of this kind.

Test Career Statistics

Matches: 20

Runs	HS	Avge	100s	Ct/St	Wkts	Runs	Avge	5 w/i	10 w/m	BB
997	108	35.60	1	11/–	1	45	45.00	–	–	1–25

Peter Laurence Taylor 1988
AUSTRALIA v ENGLAND
Fifth Test Match

At Sydney, January 10, 11, 12, 14, 15, 1987. Australia won by 55 runs. When, with one over left, Sleep bowled Emburey to complete Australia's first Test win in more than a year, it was an unexpected as well as welcome victory . . .

If their leg-spinner delivered Australia's *coup de grâce*, however, there was no question that their hero was the thirty-year-old Taylor, a sandy-haired off-spinner from Sydney's Northern District Club, who had played only six first-class matches in his life, and only one that season, restricted to few appearances for New South Wales by their three Test spinners. So little was known about him that when Australia announced a twelve containing only one opening batsman, Marsh, there was speculation in some quarters that he owed selection to an error in transmission, confusing him with M. A. Taylor, a dour left-handed opener who had been making runs for New South Wales.

There was no substance to the allegations, and in a saga that developed along the lines of a story in *Boy's Own*, the unassuming Taylor gloriously vindicated the selectors' judgement, not to say courage, with a performance of such merit that he was named player of the match. Figures of six for 78 in England's first innings and two for 76 in the second revealed him as a thoughtful bowler with more than average powers of spin. But well as he did in his specialist department, it was his batting – angular, left-handed and blessed with common sense – that made possible Australia's win. Going in at No. 9, he batted for 244 minutes in both innings while 142 runs were scored, enabling Jones to add 111 with his last three partners in the first innings and sharing a stand of 98 with Waugh in the second when Australia's needs were even greater.

Test Career Statistics

Matches: 13

Runs	HS	Avge	100s	Ct/St	Wkts	Runs	Avge	5 w/i	10 w/m	BB
431	87	26.93	–	10/–	27	1,068	39.55	1	–	6–78

Mark Anthony Taylor
PAKISTAN v AUSTRALIA
Second Test Match
by Mark Ray, 2000

At Peshawar, October 15, 16, 17, 18, 19, 1999. Drawn. Toss: Australia. If ever a sound typified a Test then it was the mellow thwack of the ball meeting the middle of Mark Taylor's bat during his undefeated 334 in this game. On a flat, evenly grassed yellow pitch, which had hardly changed appearance over five days, Taylor played as well as he ever had in his ten-year Test career. After a less than perfect start against some very fast bowling from Shoaib Akhtar, Taylor made barely an error, hitting the ball with the sweet spot of his bat for hour after hour. His pulling was brutal, his cutting precise . . .

On the second day, Australia added 375 for the loss of three wickets. At stumps they were 599 for four, with Taylor unbeaten on 334 and level with Bradman's Australian record at Headingley in 1930. He clipped the final ball of the day, from Aamir Sohail, towards square leg, but Ijaz, who had hardly excelled in the field before then, threw down a hand and managed to stop what would have been a record-breaking single.

Taylor had batted for exactly 12 hours and 564 balls, hitting 32 fours and a six. His innings was the seventh highest score in Test history, the 15th triple-century and the fifth by an Australian. He also became the fourth Australian to pass 7,000 Test runs. Yet more drama followed next morning as the news spread around the ground – and the world – that Taylor had sacrificed the chance of breaking both Bradman's mark and Lara's world record by declaring. Immediately the theorising and myth-making began. The local experts could not believe that Taylor would deny himself a shot at the record. One explanation that quickly gained currency, though it was later denied by Taylor, was that he had refused to pass the record of Bradman, the greatest batsman the game has produced and a living legend of Australian society. The simplest explanation was the correct one: Taylor thought 599 in two days was more than enough runs, and he wanted to try to win by giving his bowlers a chance at

Pakistan's batsmen from the start of the third day. There were a number of team meetings that evening, and several players urged Taylor to bat on and beat Lara. But it was typical of his approach to the game that he should be aware of the record without being obsessed by it.

Taylor: His Place in the Pantheon
by Scyld Berry, 2000

When Mark Taylor came off the field for the final time in Test cricket, on January 5, 1999, he was wearing his baggy green cap, not his normal hat, to signal that retirement was at hand. It was the end of an era not just for Australian cricket, but for the game worldwide, because he had no challenger as the finest captain of modern times.

It would be fruitless to compare "Tubby" with the leaders of other ages. Warwick Armstrong, who was tubbier still, never had to address TV viewers ten minutes after the breathless finish of a day/night international, as Taylor did with unfailing articulacy. Sir Donald Bradman did not have to calculate net run-rate and work to keep the media onside: newspapers then were deferential. When Richie Benaud was captain, he knew the workings of the media all right, but he did not have to speak to them about players taking money from an Indian bookmaker, as Taylor did, with the diplomacy of an elder statesman.

Taylor can only be compared with other captains of the post-Packer era. And – bearing in mind that Mike Brearley led in just eight Tests in this period – among them he was unquestionably supreme.

Test Career Statistics

Matches: 104   (Captain 50 times)

Runs	HS	Avge	100s	Ct/St	Wkts	Runs	Avge	5 w/i	10 w/m	BB
7,525	334*	43.49	19	157/– 1	26	26.00	–	–		1–11

ENGLAND
Kenneth Taylor 1965
by Norman Preston
ENGLAND v AUSTRALIA
Third Test Match

At Leeds, July 2, 3, 4, 6, 1964. Australia won by seven wickets with more than a day to spare ... Just before the match began, Cowdrey (England) and O'Neill (Australia) had to stand down through being unfit, and during the contest England suffered three more casualties. Taylor, who replaced Cowdrey, received two blows on the right hand while batting on the first day, which chipped a bone; Parfitt cracked a bone in his left hand while fending off a bouncer in the England second innings and Flavell went lame with a sore Achilles tendon and could not bowl in Australia's second innings.

Test Career Statistics
Matches: 3

Runs	HS	Avge	100s	Ct/St	Wkts	Runs	Avge	5 w/i	10 w/m	BB
57	24	11.40	–	1/–	0	6	–	–	–	0–6

Robert William Taylor 1977
Five Cricketers of the Year
by Michael Carey

Wicketkeepers the world over will rejoice in the news that the editor of *Wisden* has stepped in where England's selectors have so often feared to tread and recognised the skill of Bob Taylor, whose artistry – there is no other word for it – behind the stumps has long illumined even the darkest hours of Derbyshire cricket. Appropriately, the honour comes after the season in which he joined the small band of wicketkeepers who have captured 1,000 victims, but one likes to think that it is as much an acknowledgement of Taylor's self-imposed high standards, discipline and courteous attitude down the years. Indeed, it is a measure of his consistency that Taylor could be regarded as a cricketer of any year, not merely the last one.

Like many a true craftsman, he has plied his trade quietly and honestly, rarely showing extreme flashes of temperament or histrionics, making some catches or stumpings look deceptively easy, earning the admiration of team-mate and opponent alike with the sheer brilliance of others and shunning acrobatics and showmanship for the sake of it. For day in, day out diligence and efficiency, he has been without peer in the world for some years and would clearly have graced the England team but for Alan Knott, whose ability with the bat has often swayed the selectors, not least when his performances behind the stumps have fallen short of his own high standards.

ROBERT WILLIAM TAYLOR was born in Stoke-on-Trent on July 17, 1941 and first appeared for Derbyshire 20 years later. Having followed George Dawkes and Harry Elliott, who also had 1,000 victims in first-class cricket, he is only the county's third post-war wicketkeeper. As a schoolboy he kept wicket on the cinder car park adjoining Stoke City FC's ground near his home. He was in the school under-15 XI at the age of twelve; at fifteen he was playing for Bignall End in the North Staffs and South Cheshire League and he played for Staffordshire in the Minor Counties before he was sixteen.

In fact, when he arrived at Norton for his debut, against Shropshire, an over-zealous gateman would not allow the young Taylor into the ground, although he was carrying a cricket bag, until another player vouched for him. In an early League game, walking to the wicket in black plimsolls, grey trousers and pads which came up to his chest, he was asked by the groundsman, "Have you got a box on, lad?" Taylor had to admit he had not – he did not even know what a "box" was!

His first Championship victim was Sussex's Ken Suttle in a game which Taylor helped to save for Derbyshire, playing out time with Harold Rhodes, who was batting in suede shoes because of an injured foot. He broke Derbyshire's wicketkeeping record with 77 catches in 1962, his first full season, and since then only injury and occasional representative honours have kept him out of the side. His attention to fitness and ultra-professional approach probably stem from his experience in 1964 when he damaged an ankle playing football (he was with Port Vale for a time) and, having told Derbyshire he had slipped on the escalator at Lewis's in Hanley, missed the first seven matches of the season . . .

Laurie Johnson, his replacement, did so well that Derbyshire were tempted to leave Taylor out indefinitely and play an extra batsman. Ruefully telling the story against himself, Taylor now recalls that he might have quit there and then if they had gone ahead. Fortunately, after this writer and others had taken up their pens, the club realised their folly. Taylor was reinstated and his only other lengthy absence came in 1967 when he edged a ball from Jack Birkenshaw into his eye, suffered a detached retina and had to lie on his back for three weeks, wondering if his career was over . . .

When he joined Derbyshire (on the recommendation of Cliff Gladwin) Taylor was regarded as a "natural" but he knew he had much to learn, especially standing up. He persisted in standing up to medium pacers like Derek Morgan and Ian Buxton, even though the odd nick would go astray and they, like many bowlers, regularly badgered him to stand back and catch them. He became increasingly proficient in keeping to spin, too, even though in those days it was a luxury for Derbyshire.

He will discuss wicketkeeping only in terms of standing up. "Any decent slip catcher could do it standing back", he says, while conceding that widespread one-day fields have complicated the job. Indeed, for a long time Derbyshire's bowlers could not recall Taylor dropping other than a diving half chance while standing back. One day, he did drop a comfortable one off Alan Ward and the bowler refused to believe it until he checked with both batsman and wicketkeeper later!

Standing up, Taylor gets as close to the stumps as possible, even though this gives him less margin for error. Like all cricketers, he has bad patches but is quick to analyse why. "If I am keeping badly, it is usually because of one of three things – lack of concentration, standing up too soon or snatching at the ball," he says. "You must stay down that thousandth of a second longer because it means the difference between the ball hitting the middle of your glove or your fingertips".

He does not find concentration easy in front of small crowds, "But I am a professional and others rely on me and it is a crime to let them down. I once dropped Roy Fredericks three times in one innings, standing up. Possibly not many spectators realised it but I knew I was at fault and I knew my concentration was not right because it was a Sunday game in the middle of a match I was playing for MCC, and I had allowed myself to become too casual about it."

Such is Taylor's honest approach to the game, on and off the field. He believes too many players today want the glamour without the hard work. By the same token, he tries to be philosophical about the fact that his skill and dedication have brought him but one Test appearance, and that on an uneven pitch in New Zealand.

"There are about 300 county cricketers and we can't all play for England. Cricket has taken me to many places I would not otherwise have seen and I'm grateful for that. I am a pro and try to behave like one, but I will admit that I don't enjoy people coming up to me on tour and asking who I am. That's when it really hurts."

1987

ENGLAND v NEW ZEALAND
First Cornhill Test Match
by Terry Cooper

At Lord's, July 24, 25, 26, 28, 29, 1986. Drawn. England may have been spared another Lord's defeat in the 1980s when the sort of weather that spoiled so many Test matches there in the 1970s robbed this match of almost half the fourth day. None the less, England needed a long and commanding innings from Gooch, his second Test hundred at Lord's in 1986, to save the game.

It would hardly be a drawn Lord's Test without rain and bad light plus a much-discussed, if short-lived, controversy. This came on the second day when French, England's injured wicket-keeper, was replaced by the former England wicketkeeper, R. W. Taylor. French had been struck on the back of the helmet when he turned away from a Hadlee bouncer, the resulting cut

requiring three stitches and the blow leaving him groggy until
after the weekend. Athey deputised for two overs at the start of
New Zealand's innings until Taylor could hurry round the
ground – from his duties as host for Cornhill, the match's sponsor – and equip himself with an assortment of borrowed kit,
although he did, far-sightedly, have his own gloves in his car.
Despite having retired from first-class cricket two years earlier,
Taylor, at the age of 45, kept almost without blemish. He did his
old job until the 76th over, near the lunch interval on Saturday,
after which R. J. Parks of Hampshire, following his grandfather
and father, appeared in a Test match. However, Parks, a more
authentic substitute, should have been on stand-by at the start of
play because recovery from such a head wound is seldom
immediate. French finally assumed his appointed role for one ball
on Monday morning. All these switches were made with the generous permission of New Zealand's captain, Coney. With substitutes also needed for Willey and Foster and for Coney and Jeff
Crowe, 29 players took the field at various times.

Test Career Statistics
Matches: 57

Runs	HS	Avge	100s	Ct/St	Wkts	Runs	Avge	5 w/i	10 w/m	BB
1,156	97	16.28	–	167/7	0	6	–	–	–	0–6

Leslie Brian Taylor 1986

Leicestershire's pleasure at winning the Benson and Hedges Cup,
their first major trophy since the John Player League title in 1977,
was tempered by their lowest Championship placing since 1964
and a spate of late-season departures from their discontented
players.

They were, in fairness, one of the hardest hit of all the counties
by the weather, creating a John Player Sunday League record of
five "no-result" washouts, and losing no fewer than 116 playing
hours in first-class matches, most of them at home. In the Britannic
Championship alone, the time lost added up to one quarter of
their fixtures. The absence of key players for lengthy periods also
had a significant effect. Les Taylor and Jonathan Agnew did not

appear together until June because of injury, and Test calls
further restricted their Championship appearances. Taylor
missed three games, Agnew four, with the captain, David Gower,
absent in twelve, and the vice-captain, Peter Willey, in four.

1986

ENGLAND v AUSTRALIA
Sixth Cornhill Test

At The Oval, August 29, 30, 31, September 2, 1985. England won
by an innings and 94 runs . . . As on the previous three, every seat
had been sold in advance for the fourth day's play, a crowd of
15,000 assembling to see if Australia's captain had one more
heroic saving innings in him. And as at Old Trafford in the
Fourth Test, the day began ominously for England when in over-
cast conditions Downton missed Border in the first over before he
had added to his score, diving for a mistimed leg-glance off
Ellison. However, the captain's resolution struck no chord with
his team-mates. Ritchie, driving at a wide one, and Phillips, making room to cut, were swept aside in 50 minutes, and at eight
minutes past noon Australia's last vestige of resistance disappeared when Border edged Ellison to second slip. There was time
for Botham, leaping to his left to drag down a fast edge by
McDermott, to add another to his galaxy of slip catches before
Taylor caught and bowled Bennett to end the match and the series.
In 96 minutes Australia had lost six for 67, Ellison finishing with
five for 46.

As in 1926 and 1953, when the Ashes were also regained at The
Oval, several thousand spectators massed in front of the pavilion
when the match was over, to hail the England captain and his
team and to give Allan Border a heartfelt cheer. Gooch was
named Man of the Match and Gower Player of the Series. The
attendance was 60,000 and the match receipts £485,000.

Test Career Statistics
Matches: 2

Runs	HS	Avge	100s	Ct/St	Wkts	Runs	Avge	5 w/i	10 w/m	BB
1	1*	–	–	1/–	4	178	44.50	–	–	2–34

Jonathan Paul Taylor 1993
HAMPSHIRE v NORTHAMPTONSHIRE

At Bournemouth, August 14, 15, 17, 1992. Northamptonshire
won by ten wickets. Northamptonshire 22 pts, Hampshire 5 pts.
Toss: Hampshire. The penultimate first-class match at Dean Park
before the ground was mothballed did nothing to make Hampshire's players regret the county's decision to sacrifice the ground
to financial necessity; they produced another numbing demonstration of their batting fragility. Left-armer Taylor, bowling
well-controlled in-swing, took four wickets in an over, as six fell
in 18 balls, to reduce the home side from 79 for three to 80 for
nine in their second innings. Taylor claimed a career-best seven
for 23.

1995
ENGLAND v NEW ZEALAND
Second Cornhill Test

At Lord's, June 16, 17, 18, 19, 20, 1994. Drawn. Toss: New
Zealand. England made just one change, the Northamptonshire
left-armer Taylor coming in for his home Test debut in place of
Malcolm, who made a disgruntled return to his county 24 hours
before the Test began, after being told he would not be in the
team. For the second time, left-arm spinner Stemp was also omitted from the final eleven. Atherton, having lost his sixth successive Test toss, switched around seven bowlers with little joy. Only
when DeFreitas had the ball in his hand did the English attack
look anything but bland.

ENGLAND v NEW ZEALAND
Third Cornhill Test

At Manchester, June 30, July 1, 2, 4, 5, 1994. Drawn. Toss
England. Test debut: D. Gough.
England included the off-spinner, Such, ahead of leg-spinner
Salisbury on a hard surface expected to produce more bounce
than turn. England also gave a Test debut to the twenty-three-
year-old Yorkshireman, Gough, dispensing with Taylor's services
after just one Test.

Test Career statistics

Matches: 2

Runs	HS	Avge	100s	Ct/St	Wkts	Runs	Avge	5 w/i	10 w/m	BB
34	17*	17.00	–	–/–	3	156	52.00	–	–	1–18

NEW ZEALAND
Donald Dougal Taylor 1957
NEW ZEALAND v WEST INDIES
Third Test Match

At Wellington, March 3, 5, 6, 7, 1956. West Indies won by nine wickets. Due mainly to the recall of Taylor, whose only previous Test experience was against England nine years earlier, New Zealand gave a more spirited batting performance. Taylor's enterprising strokeplay in both innings was in refreshing contrast to the timidity of most of his colleagues. The chief batting honours, however, again went to Weekes who gave a sparkling display of clean hitting on the opening day, when the New Zealanders wasted a great chance of taking a grip on the game. Cave and MacGibbon sent back Pairaudeau, Goddard and Smith while the West Indies score rose from 117 to 119 and then Weekes, who had scored only two, was dropped at slip. Weekes gave New Zealand abundant reason to regret this lapse, which was the most important of several. He reached his third successive Test century in two and a quarter hours and shared in three-figure stands with Atkinson and Binns.

New Zealand were soon in deeper trouble, their score slumping from 23 for none to 28 for four, before Beck joined Taylor in a promising stand. A mix-up between the two caused Taylor to be run out by the length of the pitch but Beck, who spent nearly five hours over 55, found another valuable partner in Guillen. Following on 196 behind, New Zealand were indebted again to Taylor for narrowly avoiding their third consecutive innings defeat. Atkinson bowled his medium-paced deliveries with commendable accuracy.

1982

He is best remembered for his opening partnerships of 220 and 286 with Bert Sutcliffe for Auckland against Canterbury in 1948/

49, the only instance of two players putting up 200 in each innings of a first-class match. Taylor's own share was 99 and 143. After this he was perhaps unlucky not to be picked for the tour of England in 1949. Instead he came over and qualified for Warwickshire, but though he played some useful innings for them, notably 90 not out in as many minutes against Nottinghamshire at Trent Bridge in 1951, he could never command a regular place. He returned to New Zealand in 1953. A neat, attractive strokeplaying batsman, in all first-class cricket he scored 3,734 runs with an average of 23.63.

Test Career Statistics

Matches: 3

Runs	HS	Avge	100s	Ct/St	Wkts	Runs	Avge	5 w/i	10 w/m	BB
159	77	31.80	–	2/–	–	–	–	–	–	–

Bruce Richard Taylor 1966
INDIA v NEW ZEALAND
Second Test Match

At Calcutta, March 5, 6, 7, 8, 1965. Drawn. Everything else in this match was overshadowed by the remarkable Test debut of Taylor for New Zealand. Making the most of his height, Taylor, a forceful left-hander, attacked the Indian bowling freely while scoring his maiden century in first-class cricket and later he went on to take five wickets for 86 at right-arm fast-medium pace.

INDIA v NEW ZEALAND
Third Test Match

At Bombay, March 12, 13, 14, 15, 1965. Drawn. New Zealand missed a great opportunity of gaining the first victory in the series. Thanks mainly to a steady century by Dowling and 71 by Morgan they put together a total of 297 against some admirable fast bowling by Desai who took six of the first eight wickets.

India began their innings shortly before lunch on the second day and they were all out for 88 in under two and three-quarter hours. It was their lowest Test total in their own country and was due to the hard brick pitch allowing Taylor and Motz to bounce the ball disconcertingly. Taylor finished with five for 26 and as usual India's batting in such circumstances was irresolute. So India followed on 209 behind, but in the terrific heat Taylor and Motz could not repeat their earlier triumphs.

Test Career Statistics
Matches: 30

Runs	HS	Avge	100s	Ct/St	Wkts	Runs	Avge	5 w/i	10 w/m	BB
898	124	20.40	2	10/–	111	2,953	26.60	4	–	7–74

SOUTH AFRICA
Daniel Taylor

Test Career Statistics
Matches: 2

Runs	HS	Avge	100s	Ct/St	Wkts	Runs	Avge	5 w/i	10 w/m	BB
85	36	21.25	–	–/–	–	–	–	–	–	–

Apart from the scorecards of his two Test matches and of one game for Natal against MCC, Daniel Taylor rates no mention whatsoever in *Wisden*. His father, who died in 1927 without ever having played first-class cricket, rates an obituary, but Daniel, who died 30 years later, does not. The reports of the two Tests he played mention his brother's great achievements, but do not even refer to him as a family adjunct.

Herbert Wilfred Taylor 1925

Expert opinion was unanimous in placing Taylor among the best of living batsmen and yet, though he scored 1,925 runs, he disappointed both himself and his friends. He could not find his best form on the big occasions, his highest score in the five Test matches being 59 not out. There can be no doubt that the anxiety of captaining a beaten team told upon him and that he would have done far better if he had had nothing to think about but his own batting. In some of the smaller fixtures he was quite himself, hitting up hundreds against Essex, the Combined Services, Warwickshire and Northamptonshire. On his good days, there could be no question as to his class. In point of style, he was a model and the strength of his back play made his defence look almost impregnable.

Five Cricketers of the Year 1925

Herbert Wilfred Taylor, by far the most prominent figure in South African cricket today, was born at Durban on the 5th of May, 1879 [*sic, actually 1889*]. He first played cricket at Michael House School, where he was coached by George Cox, the Sussex bowler. After leaving school he had his first experience of public cricket, taking part in 1909 in a match against Leveson-Gower's eleven. Up to that time he had not played in the Currie Cup. He did not go to Australia with the South African team in 1910/11, but he came to England in 1912 for the Triangular Tournament, his career really beginning with that tour. His powers as a batsman were not fully matured, but he showed great promise, playing a fine, though lucky, innings of 93 against the Australians at Lord's, and coming out second to Nourse for the whole trip with an aggregate of 1,340 runs and an average of 25. His future was felt to be assured, and when the England team, with J. W. H. T. Douglas as captain, went to South Africa in the winter of 1913/14 he jumped to the top of the tree. Indeed, the Englishmen could not say too much in praise of his wonderful form against Barnes's bowling. South Africa lost four of the Test matches, the other being drawn in their favour, but Taylor himself had a series of triumphs, scoring 508 runs with an average of 50. During the War, Taylor had 18 months in the Royal Field Artillery and two years in the Flying Corps, and was awarded the MC. When international cricket resumed he played better than ever, hitting up three hundreds, with an average of 64, in the Test matches against the England team in South Africa in 1922/23. It is no injustice to him to say that in this country last summer he fell far below the expectations of his friends. He made plenty of runs and played many a fine innings, but the responsibility of captaining a losing side proved rather too much for him, and in the Test matches he did not do himself justice. He had not in any way lost his form, but circumstances were against him. Taylor's style is so good and his back play so exceptionally strong that one never while watching him has the least doubt as to his class as a batsman. Few players at the present day have so many scoring strokes in front of the wicket.

1930
ENGLAND v SOUTH AFRICA
Fifth Test Match

Played at Kennington Oval, Saturday, Monday, Tuesday, August 17, 19, 20, 1929. Contested all through on a splendid wicket the last Test match produced a lot of heavy scoring and ended in a draw ... The start of the South African innings proved truly deplorable, for in 35 minutes before lunch they lost three wickets for 25 runs. Thenceforward, however, everything went well for them. Their recovery was entirely due to a great partnership by Taylor and Deane who added 214 in three hours and ten minutes. The batting of both men reached a very high standard and, coming as it did in such circumstances, was easily the best in point of class and skill shown by the South Africans in the whole series of Tests. Deane was out at 234 and Taylor at 246 soon afterwards. The former hit only four fours in his 93, while Taylor had 12 fours. These figures clearly suggest they had a lot of good bowling to play. While exercising a pronounced mastery over the attack, the batsmen were not favoured by very many really bad balls. Deane, as far as was seen, did not give a chance, but Taylor was missed at the wicket off Woolley when 17 – a small blemish in a remarkable exhibition.

Test Career Statistics

Matches: 42   (Captain 18 times)

Runs	HS	Avge	100s	Ct/St	Wkts	Runs	Avge	5 w/i	10 w/m	BB
2,936	176	40.77	7	19/–	5	156	31.20	–	–	3–15

Alastair Innes Taylor 1958
SOUTH AFRICA v ENGLAND
First Test Match

At Johannesburg, December 24, 26, 27, 28, 29, 1956. England won by 131 runs in a slow scoring match ... This was the first Test match to be played on the new Wanderers ground, and although the pitch showed no sign of wear it always helped the faster bowlers because of the lift and movement in the air and off the turf they were able to obtain. South Africa were unfortunate to lose their captain and most dependable batsman, McGlew, who dropped out the day before the match with a slightly dislocated left shoulder.

Test Career Statistics
Matches: 1

Runs	HS	Avge	100s	Ct/St	Wkts	Runs	Avge	5 w/i	10 w/m	BB
18	12	9.00	–	–	–	–	–	–	–	–

Taylor's run total was such that he did not merit a mention in *Wisden*.

WEST INDIES
Jaswick Ossie Taylor 1959
WEST INDIES v PAKISTAN
Fifth Test Match

At Port of Spain, March 26, 27, 28, 29, 31, 1958. Pakistan won by an innings and one run . . . Saeed Ahmed and Wazir Mohammad mastered the West Indies attack, which suffered an early blow when Gilchrist sprained an ankle. Wazir, batting six hours and three-quarters and hitting 22 fours, shared stands of 169 with Saeed and 154 with his brother, Hanif. Making his first Test appearance, the West Indies fast bowler, Taylor, showing pace and persistency, performed admirably in taking five wickets in 37 overs.

Test Career Statistics
Matches: 3

Runs	HS	Avge	100s	Ct/St	Wkts	Runs	Avge	5 w/i	10 w/m	BB
4	4*	2.00	–	–/–	10	273	27.30	1	–	5–109

Jerome Everton Taylor 2004
WEST INDIES v SRI LANKA
First Test Match

At Gros Islet, St Lucia, June 20, 21, 22, 23, 24, 2003. Drawn. Toss: Sri Lanka. Test debut: J. E. Taylor. The wisdom of scheduling international cricket at the start of the Caribbean rainy season was again brought into question by the loss of more than half the third day and all of the fourth to the weather. The rain further dampened the spectators' already lukewarm response to St Lucia's first Test match. The president of the West Indies Cricket Board, Reverend Wes Hall, compared it with trying to play cricket in the English winter.

Despite being located in what is considered the driest part of the island, the new Beausejour Stadium – never more than half full – did not escape the showers for long, and a torrential downpour on the third afternoon left the ground waterlogged. Though the clouds lifted early on the fourth morning, it remained too soft underfoot for any play to be possible, which was a major blow to celebrations scheduled to mark the 75th anniversary of West Indies' first Test. Only a handful of fans watched the modest ceremony, at which relatives of the pioneering 1928 touring team to England were presented with a mounted photograph of the side.

Test Career Statistics

Matches: 3

Runs	HS	Avge	100s	Ct/St	Wkts	Runs	Avge	5 w/i	10 w/m	BB
22	9*	7.33	–	–/–	3	226	75.33	–	–	2–38

ZIMBABWE
Brendan Ross Murray Taylor 2005
ZIMBABWE v SRI LANKA
First Test Match

At Harare, May 6, 7, 8, 2004. Sri Lanka won by an innings and 240 runs. Toss: Sri Lanka. Test debuts: E. Chigumbura, A. Maregwede, T. Panyangara, B. R. M. Taylor, P. Utseya; M. F. Maharoof. The one-day embarrassments turned into a three-day humiliation once the Test series began. With the dispute between the Zimbabwe Cricket Union and the 15 dissidents unresolved, the home team was selected from the pool of players who had taken part in the one-day series, plus Mahwire and Vermeulen. In the first and last one-day games, the team had proved moderately competitive, but in Test cricket there is no hiding place. The eleven that took the field had 53 previous Test caps between them, and included five debutants. Taibu – the only man apart from Ebrahim whose Test career ran into double figures – became the youngest ever Test captain at 20 years 358 days. The result was Zimbabwe's heaviest Test defeat, a record that held for nine days.

ZIMBABWE v SRI LANKA
Second Test Match

At Bulawayo, May 14, 15, 16, 17, 2004. Sri Lanka won by an innings and 254 runs. Toss: Sri Lanka. Test debut: T. Mupariwa. The First Test showed up the inability of Zimbabwe's reserves to compete at international level; this was even worse. For the second match running, the Zimbabweans suffered the heaviest defeat in their Test history, and this time they managed just three Sri Lankan wickets.

Atapattu again put Zimbabwe in on a pitch even better for batting than the one in Harare. Vermeulen, the only contracted white player not to join the dissidents, was included, having finally been declared fit after a head injury in the one-day series in Australia, but he contributed little. Local seamer Tawanda Mupariwa made his debut, a remarkable turnaround after he had been omitted from the Under-19 World Cup team three months earlier. They replaced Mahwire, whose bowling action had been reported to the ICC after the First Test, and Utseya, who had injured his shoulder. So bare was the cupboard that the only slow bowler at a ground reputed to favour them was part-time spinner Matsikinyeri.

Matsikinyeri batted like a millionaire on the first morning, hitting 45 off 64 balls, while Ebrahim put his head down and grafted for 70 in his role as sheet anchor. But Taibu and Maregwede were cut off in their prime, and Zimbabwe just failed to last the day.

The second day was one for records, none favourable to Zimbabwe. Sri Lanka amassed 425 runs for the loss of a single wicket. The bowlers did at least carry out their plan against Jayasuriya, keeping him quiet so that his 48 took 95 balls, but they had no answer to Atapattu or Sangakkara, who piled up

438, the sixth-highest stand for any Test wicket. Shortly before the close, Atapattu reached his sixth Test double-century, his third against Zimbabwe and his second in two Tests on this ground. Sangakkara followed him past 200 next day, and both must have had their eyes on 300 or more. Against such weak opposition, it was perhaps a mercy that neither achieved the coveted landmark. Several hard chances were missed in the field before Atapattu, trying to push a single for his 250, edged to the keeper. He had batted eight hours 36 minutes, and struck 36 fours and a six in 324 balls.

After such a stand, Mahela Jayawardene must have felt like a bear aroused from hibernation as he emerged to bat, but he settled down for a century of his own, with Atapattu delaying his declaration until it was completed. And Brian Lara, who had made 400 not out a month earlier, could breathe again when Sangakkara, who had just beaten the ground record, Dave Houghton's 266 against Sri Lanka in the first Test at Queen's Sports Club almost ten years earlier, was well held by the diving Taibu. Sangakkara's 270 occupied seven hours 48 minutes and 365 balls; like Atapattu, he had 36 fours, but he hit a second six. There was one more unwelcome record: it was the first time six bowlers had conceded a century apiece in a Test innings. Taibu did not bowl in this match, but caught all three batsmen who were out.

This time Sri Lanka's lead was 485, and only the pursuit of personal milestones had prevented another three-day victory. A promising 61 by Taylor, studded with handsome off-side strokes, was the fourth day's main feature, Ebrahim again batted well and Panyangara hit merrily at the end. Zimbabwe might have done worse had Muralitharan not been handicapped by a bruised finger – he bowled spells of genuine leg-breaks at times – but another total mismatch finally persuaded ICC that something had to be done to preserve the integrity of Test cricket.

Test Career Statistics

Matches: 6

Runs	HS	Avge	100s	Ct/St	Wkts	Runs	Avge	5 w/i	10 w/m	BB
273	78	22.75	–	3/–	0	24	–	–	–	–

THE ALMANACK, 1878

September, 1878

Moon's Changes – First Quarter 3rd day, 8.25 p.m. Full Moon 11th day 3.49 p.m. Last Quarter 19th day 6.30 p.m. New Moon 26th day 2.10 p.m.

Su	1	Eleventh Sunday after Trinity	M	16	Germans evacuated France, 1873 . . . .
M	2	Capitulation of Sudan, 1870	Tu	17	First trial 81-ton gun, 1875 . . . .
Tu	3	M. Thiers died, 1877 . . .	W	18	Dr Johnson born, 1709
W	4	Mr A. Ridding died, 1876	Th	19	Cow sold for 2,200 guineas, 1877 . . . .
Th	5	Mr H. Fielden MP died, 1875	F	20	Indian Famine Fd £202,000, 1877 . . . .
F	6	HMS *Captain* lost, 1870	Sa .	21	Lillywhite's 12 left for Aus, 1876 . . . .
Sa	7	A calf sold for 2,000 Guineas, 1875	Su	22	Fourteenth Sunday after Trinity. . . . .
Su	8	Twelfth Sunday after Trinity	M	23	Battle of Assaye, 1803 . .
M	9	Sebastopol taken, 1855 .	Tu	24	Hell Gate blown up, 1876 . . . .
Tu	10	Indian Famine Fd £125,000, 1877	W	25	Mr Blenkiron died, 1871
W	11	Coll, in Channel, 108 lives lost, 1877	Th	26	Live whale at Aqm. died 29th, 1877 . . . .
Th	12	Silvio won Leger, 1877. .	F	27	} A second Summer, 1877 . . . .
F	13	Yearling horse sld for £3,000, 1877.	Sa	28	}
Sa	14	Yearling horse sld for 2,200 gs., 1877	Su	29	Fifteenth Sunday after Trinity . . Fierce gale in
Su	15	Thirteenth Sunday after Trinity	M	30	Ireland, 1876 . . . .

FESTIVALS AND BENEFITS

Festival cricket is a dying art. In the very early days of organised cricket, most cricket was of a festival type – matches purely for the enjoyment of players and spectators, with no extra significance riding on the result. Festival teams were created for the event – North v South, Over Thirty-Two v Under Thirty-Two (where that left those who were exactly thirty-two years old is not explained), Smokers v Non-Smokers and so on. It may not have been what third-millennium man would call serious cricket, but it was a great spectacle, and the holiday crowds loved it. The county players hoped to be included in the festival sides in order to complete their 1,000 runs or 100 wickets for the season, as well as for the carnival atmosphere and the bracing sea air. They almost always got them all. These days, Festival cricket has been killed off by a combination of commercialism, overseas holidays and the need to win at all costs. Easy runs and wickets are only available to professional cricketers when they play against the university sides, or in Tests against Bangladesh and Zimbabwe.

Or in their benefit match, in the days when one match a season was put aside for the benefit of a seasoned professional, and the taxman was persuaded not to consider the proceeds taxable. In those games, the beneficiary was usually allowed one off the mark, and few opponents took too many liberties with his bowling, however innocuous it might be. Nowadays the sums raised are enormous, because the fund raising goes on all the year round, with golf days, dinners, raffles, and even Concorde flights to Egypt, in the case of Allan Lamb. The main recipients of the megabenefits are those whose earnings from the game are large anyway: the Test players who today have little time for county cricket are often the ones who receive the largest benefits, money prised from the wallets and purses of people who rarely see them play.

Someday soon the taxman will change his mind and benefits will be no more.

THE CANTERBURY WEEK 1874

The clerical, staid, quiet, quaint old "City of the Men of Kent" was, from Monday morn until Saturday eve, dressed up in an unwonted gay form, the whole length of the *antiente* High Street being ablaze with flags: scarce a house in that long narrow and historically interesting thoroughfare but what had its bits of bunting blowing in the breeze, and at about every two score yards or so a string of flags of all colours streamed across the street. The Union Jack; the rampant White Horse of Kent; the famous old buff and blue of politics; the gorgeous red, black, and gold of "I Zingari"; the sombre black and blue of Kent's "Band Of Brothers"; the scarlet and black of "The Knickerbockers"; the ever popular red and gold of MCC; the dark blue of Oxford; the light blue of Cambridge; the blue and yellow of the RA; and lots of other banners crowdedly covered the house fronts in the High Street, and as the strong wind fluttered them they seemed cheerily to wave welcome to all comers to The Canterbury Week of 1873.

The attendance up at breezy old St Lawrence was unprecedentedly large on the Monday; very good on the Tuesday; middling ditto on the Wednesday; numerically large beyond any preceding "Ladies' Day" on the Thursday; but slack on the Friday and on the Saturday.

1937

In a rain-ruined match at Nottingham, G. O. Allen (Middlesex) batted on each of three days for 6 not out. Actually his innings occupied half an hour.

TOM HEARNE'S MATCH 1877
NORTH v SOUTH

Played at Lord's, Whit Monday, Tuesday, and Wednesday, June 5, 6, 7, 1876.

THE MARYLEBONE CLUB'S generously given permission for a three day's match to be played at Lord's for TOM HEARNE'S benefit, was a valuable and just acknowledgement of the old un's many season's zealous labours and excellent behaviour in the Club's service. The match arranged was North v South, to be played on Whit Monday, Tuesday, and Wednesday, a valuable concession, the compliment being greatly enhanced by the Club leaving the selection of the sides, and other arrangements solely to Hearne, with the single (and wise) stipulation that the daily admission charge to the ground during the match should not be more than the ordinary 6d. On this satisfactory ground-work Hearne's many friends worked heartily to ensure his match being a success, but none worked more willingly, so unremittingly, or more successfully, than Pearce, the ground superintendent at Lord's whose long and persevering labours resulted in the very best wickets that were played on at the old ground during 1876, or in any other year; wickets that, despite the wet weather, wore so well, and played so truthfully to the last, that they were the main reason why the match went into a third day, and thereby increased the value of the benefit by some £70. The score will tell how ably the sides were represented, the willing participation in the match by most of the front rank Gentlemen Cricketers of the period affording pleasant proof of Hearne's popularity among the best supporters of the game. The weather (told about elsewhere) was not favourable, nevertheless the gate transactions resulted in the following satisfactory form:

WHIT MONDAY	TUESDAY	WEDNESDAY
6,369 paid	4,602 paid	2,807 paid
Cash received £159 9s 6d	Cash received £115 17s 0d	Cash received £70 8s 6d

In *Bell's Life* of July 15, a Dr and Cr account up to date was published, wherein a balance of £308 5s. was credited to Hearne; this was, of course, exclusive of his subscription lists, which were to remain open throughout the season. The same opportunity was taken by Hearne to publicly express his thanks to the Gentlemen of the Marylebone Cricket Club for their kindness, and to the cricketing public for the handsome support they accorded him.

1878
MCC AND G. v YORKSHIRE
Played at Scarborough, August 30, 31 and September 1, 1877.

"Lord Londesborough and cricket" are now household words with all who participate in, or wish success to, England's national game. Yorkshire, and Yorkshire cricketers, largely enjoy his Lordship's patriotic devotion to the people's pastime; never more so than at the back end of the season, when, through Lord Londesborough's liberality, the Yorkshire eleven play the prominent part in The Scarborough Cricket Week at that fashionable seaside resort. To wing up the 1877 season a rare week's cricket had been arranged, the Yorkshire eleven having to play I Zingari the first three days, and MCC and G. the last three days of the week. Many of the most accomplished cricketers in the country had arranged to play, and nothing was wanting to ensure success but fair weather, but the weather was not fair: nay, it was so foul that the wickets were swamped, true cricket could not possibly be played, the commencement of either match was of necessity deferred and when commenced, play was frequently interrupted by rain.

SCARBOROUGH FESTIVAL 1951
NORTH v SOUTH
At Scarborough, September 6, 7, 8, 1950. South won by three wickets. Set to get 250 in two hours and a half, South succeeded in an exciting struggle within four minutes of time. Fishlock made the pace with 57 out of 119 in an hour; he and Graveney

made 73 in 30 minutes and no delay occurred before Jones finished the match with two fours. Hutton gave two splendid displays. A single in the first over completed his 2,000 runs for the season, and he scored freely in each innings with his customary delightful strokes all round the wicket. Rain stopped play on Wednesday afternoon, but the pitch, completely covered by tarpaulin, was not affected and Insole made 84 in two hours by his own methods, which are apt to look reckless. He, in turn, declared first thing on Friday, though South were four behind, and in true festive spirit Hutton, five fours, and Simpson put on 93 in 53 minutes. Lester, hitting two sixes and six fours, scored 78 out of 132 in 70 minutes before Yardley's second declaration gave a challenge which South accepted, and the lively cricket produced plenty of excitement for some 12,000 spectators – the average attendance throughout the nine days of Festival cricket.

1973

by Sir Compton Mackenzie

I recall the Scarborough Cricket Week of 1893 when I was taken by Frank Goodricke, the eldest son of the manager of the Spa, to see the South of England eleven playing Yorkshire. Well do I remember the venerated figure of W. W. Read, the Surrey batsman, in his chocolate-coloured cap; we were too much in awe of cricketers 80 years ago to pester them for autographs. I recall dark handsome Tom Richardson, the Surrey fast bowler, and fair handsome Lockwood; I recall the burly figure of Sir Timothy O'Brien making terrific swipes of the redoubtable Yorkshire bowler Peel, I recall F. R. Spofforth, the demon bowler, with his heavy drooping moustache; finally, I recall J. J. Ferris of Gloucestershire, a small left-handed bowler from Australia who only played a couple of seasons for Gloucestershire and went back to Australia in 1895. I have an impression that he took the wicket of the famous J. T. Brown; I certainly saw him take one Yorkshire wicket.

I fell into disgrace with Frank Goodricke because from where I was sitting in the pavilion I could see a football match going on. I can hear him now turning to me and saying, "This is the last time

I'll bring you to the Scarborough cricket week if you want to look at football". Frank Goodricke did not know that the ten-year-old boy looking at football, when the paragons of cricket were performing, was anticipating what the whole of the British public would be doing 20 years later.

PHILATELIC CRICKET 1984

Of the game's players to have featured on stamps, there are almost enough to form an eleven, immensely strong in batting. The first to be honoured was Sir Garfield Sobers, on a Barbados independence issue of 1966, and he subsequently appeared on two stamps of 1977 which showed the ceremony at Bridgetown Racecourse where he was knighted by the Queen. To join him he has W. G. Grace (GB 1973), K. S. Ranjitsinhji (India 1973), Vivian Richards (Antigua 1975 and 1976, Barbuda 1975), Sir Donald Bradman (anonymously on a South African stamp of 1976), Sir Frank Worrell (Turks and Caicos Islands 1980, but misspelt "Worrel") and Victor Trumper (Australia 1981), with middle-order support Sir William Milton (Rhodesia 1969), captain of South Africa in two of her early Test matches and subsequently administrator of Southern Rhodesia.

Andy Roberts, featured at the same times as Richards, would spearhead the attack, supported by Sobers, Grace, Worrell and Richards. To make up the side, with a wicketkeeper a priority, they might call on the unnamed Indian Test players on a 1971 stamp or some likely-looking performers from Grenada (1969). As umpire they could summon Sir Edmund Barton (Australia 1951 and 1969), the country's first prime minister and the only one to have stood in first-class matches.

THE CRICKETERS' FUND FRIENDLY SOCIETY 1889

We are glad to hear that the efforts which have been made in various ways to improve the position of this society have not been without effect. We still think that, considering the wealth and position of thousands who take a pleasure in cricket, the subscription-list is deplorably small, and that if the county clubs whose professionals, if debarred by accident from their profession, benefit by it, would organise a systematic application for pecuniary support, the subscription-list would be rapidly increased, with but little trouble. However something has been done. Subscriptions and donations from honorary subscribers amount this year to £170, as against, in last year, £152 8s. The MCC has, with its invariable liberality, given to the society 20 per cent of the gate at the Australian matches at Lord's Ground, and though the wet season curtailed the sum that might have been expected, the cheque was for £283 9s. 3d. But, in addition to this kindly help, the society has this year to thank the Surrey County for a most handsome donation in the shape of £71 18s. 5d., the net proceeds of the Surrey and Sussex match. The Incogniti have also been extremely generous, sending a donation of £15 15s., and we find that Gloucestershire, Cheshire, and Hampshire, in addition to Kent, are this year amongst the counties subscribing.

Altogether the society is to be congratulated on a more healthy financial condition. We find on the other side of the balance-sheet that 14 professional cricketers have benefited by their membership, and we are glad to see that amongst these is poor Bates, whose sad accident in Australia prevented his playing for Yorkshire during the past season. Surely such an instance of sudden disability as this may well appeal to lovers of cricket to come forward and help the society. They should remember that, but for the necessity forced on the society two years ago of reducing the benefits, these poor fellows would have been drawing larger sums, and been so much the better off.

We shall be unfeignedly glad if these words catch the eyes of some lovers of the game, and remind them of the many pleasant hours they spend in admiring, condemning, criticising the play of professional cricketers. If they do, we hope they will not be oblivious of the dangers and chances of a cricketer's life, of the temptations and hardships of the winter months if he can get no work to do, and will add their names to the list of honorary subscribers to the Cricketers' Fund Friendly Society.

Any application for information to Mr H. Luff, 21, Cranbourn-street, Leicester-square, will receive prompt attention.

1896
by Lord Harris

I have referred to poor Fred Grace's fine fielding, and I recall an incident at The Oval in a match we played late in the year for the benefit of the sufferers by the sinking of the *Princess Alice* an excursion boat. Fred was bowling, W. G. was at point, and I was mid-off. The batsman skied one so high on the off-side that we three had quite a conversation which of us should have it. It was a horribly cold day, and I had no particular fancy for it, and when Fred said he would have it I was quite ready to resign, knowing he was certain to hold it, which he did.

SUTCLIFFE'S BENEFIT 1930
YORKSHIRE v SURREY

Played at Leeds, Saturday, Monday, Tuesday, July 6, 8, 9, 1929. Singularly unfortunate was Sutcliffe, in a season favoured by so much fine weather, in having his benefit spoilt by rain. Not a ball could be bowled on Saturday. Better conditions prevailed on the other two days, but Saturday's "gate" having been lost, the receipts from the match amounted to no more than £506.

RECORD BENEFITS 1949

Nothing gave clearer proof of the increased popularity of cricket as an entertainment for all and sundry than record attendances at most grounds and the remarkable value of benefits for professionals. The record £8,083 made in 1947 for W. E. Bowes, the Yorkshire fast bowler, in his retiring year, was left far behind, over £14,000 being raised for the equally popular Lancashire and England opening batsman, Cyril Washbrook. The gate at the match with the Australians at Old Trafford in August Bank Holiday week was swollen by subscriptions, collections at local functions, and games played in various parts of the county. Leslie Ames, in a second benefit, received £4,336 as a well-merited reward notwithstanding unfavourable weather at Canterbury; T. H. Wade, of Essex, received £3,878; T. F. Smailes, of Yorkshire, and H. S. Squires, of Surrey, were rewarded by valuable tributes. Unfortunately the testimonial fund for Frank Chester, the best of umpires, fell below expectations and has been left open for another year. I sincerely hope that MCC will push this testimonial to the utmost; the cricketing public need only the right directive from Lord's to respond liberally. Chester deserves the fullest reward for all the great service he has done for cricket.

C. WASHBROOK'S BENEFIT 1949
LANCASHIRE v AUSTRALIANS

At Manchester, August 7, 9, 10, 1948. Drawn. Instead of enforcing the follow-on when leading by 191, the Australians batted again and Bradman delayed his declaration until lunch time on the last day when only two hours and three-quarters remained for play. Bradman for his highest score at Old Trafford batted three hours 35 minutes and hit 17 fours. Lancashire seemed certain to play out time, but with the new ball Lindwall bowled Ikin, who was dismissed for 99 in the second successive match, and Pollard with following deliveries. Thus, Washbrook being unfit, only two wickets were left when Lindwall began his last and very fast over, but Roberts held out. Although financially a great success, the game brought misfortune to Washbrook, for he injured his right thumb when batting against Lindwall and withdrew from the England team for the Fifth Test. Roberts, the left-arm slow bowler, did good work on a drying pitch on the first day, when he bowled 41 consecutive overs and took the first five wickets for 29 runs. The pace and life of Lindwall, Miller and Loxton sorely troubled Lancashire in their first innings, but Howard made some attractive strokes. Barnes gave two fine batting displays.

Australians 321 (Barnes 67; Roberts six for 73) **and 265** for three declared (Bradman 133 not out, Barnes 90).

Lancashire 130 (Washbrook 38; Johnson three for 5) **and 199** for seven (Ikin 99; Lindwall four for 27)

L. B. FISHLOCK'S BENEFIT 1951
SURREY v MIDDLESEX

At The Oval, July 29, 31, August 1, 1950. Surrey won by ten wickets. The reappearance of Denis Compton after being kept out of cricket for two months by his injured knee increased the interest in the always attractive visit of Middlesex, and on the three days 48,350 people paid £4,326 gate money, ensuring Fishlock a worthy reward for his splendid services. He marked the occasion by scoring 133 runs for once out, so helping materially in the victory which came to Surrey at three o'clock on Tuesday. Fishlock made 111 out of 205 in four hours ten minutes, hitting 13 fours, and he was out to a grand catch, Warr holding a hard low drive with his right hand at mid-on. Constable was out unluckily, his leg touching the stumps when he hit a boundary. McIntyre, 12 fours, and Laker followed by adding 102, the best stand of the innings. Denis Compton surpassed Fishlock's performance by scoring 140 for once out. The 85th century of his first-class career came in three hours 20 minutes, and altogether he batted three hours and three-quarters while the total was increased by 168; he hit 12 fours by perfect timing and avoided unnecessary risks. On the last day chief honours fell to Laker with eight wickets for 57, the batting breaking down after an opening stand of 78. On Saturday a collection for Fishlock realised £354.

Surrey 401 (Fishlock 111, McIntyre 85; Warr four for 79) **and 28** for none.

Middlesex 229 (D. Compton 115) **and 199** (Dewes 56; Laker eight for 57).

THEN AS NOW 1951

In the matter of benefit matches the professional today is far better placed than once he was. Such matches now receive more competent advance publicity and are organised more shrewdly. There is improvement in the timing and frequency of ground collections. There can seldom be occasion for a repetition of a famous West County professional's remark when asked if he would like to receive a second benefit, "No, thanks; I don't want to be ruined twice". All this is to the good in days when every million pounds count. But it could go too far. First-class cricket could be spoilt by money as well as by poverty.

THE ONES THAT GOT AWAY

Wisden has over the years been among the first to highlight the talents of many young players who have gone on to achieve great things in the sport, from Grace to Tendulkar and beyond. But there have also been some young players who flattered to deceive, who came onto the first-class scene with a bang, but failed to consolidate their place and disappeared with a corresponding whimper a year or two later. Second-season syndrome, rather like that difficult second album for some rock stars, has struck too often for it to be entirely in the mind: once a player has achieved some success, all opposing sides try to work out how to counter his success, and those who get found out get left out. Some young prodigies died young, and some went off to do other things, failing to become great for other reasons than lack of the necessary luck and talent. Some were geniuses in the nets but proved fallible at the wicket. So who are these brief shooting stars, whose hope of a season's fame proved only too close to the truth? Who are the Terence Trent D'Arbys and the Alanis Morissettes, not to mention the Richie Valens, of cricket?

These men are, by the nature of their failures, less well known than the Bothams, the Gowers and the Underwoods who graduated from youthful prodigies to great cricketers in their maturer years. All the same, it is fun to see what *Wisden* got slightly wrong, to see which players brought out the premature superlatives. Some of the players did go on to play for their country, if only briefly, but none fulfilled the early promise that *Wisden* had thought it had spotted.

Oh, and there are one or two written off by *Wisden*, who also went on to prove the editor and his teams of writers wrong.

A. E. J. COLLINS 1900
The Highest Individual Score on Record
CLIFTON COLLEGE – CLARKE'S v NORTH TOWN

A Junior House Match at Clifton College, begun on Thursday 22 June and completed on the following Wednesday, is noteworthy for having produced the greatest score known to have been made by a single player in a game of any description. The hero of the occasion, A. E. J. Collins, was batting for six hours and 50 minutes, his innings being continued in unequal instalments during five days. His hits included a six, four fives, 31 fours and 146 twos. The previous best score was that of A. E. Stoddart, who made 485 for the Hampstead Club against the Stoics in 1886. It is remarkable that it was in a Clifton College game that E. F. S. Tylecote made his score of 404 in 1868.

Clarke's 836 (Collins 628 not out).
North Town 87 (Collins 7 wickets) **and 61** (Collins 4 wickets).

1915

LIEUT ARTHUR EDWARD JEUNE COLLINS, of the Royal Engineers, who was killed in action on November 11, came suddenly into note by scoring 628 not out for Clarke's House v North Town, in a junior house match at Clifton College in June 1899, when only thirteen years old. Clarke's, who scored 836, won by an innings and 688 runs. Collins also obtained eleven wickets in the match, and in partnership with Redfern (13) put on as many as 183 for the last wicket. In 1901 and 1902 he was in the College XI, in the former year scoring 342 runs with an average of 38.00, his highest innings being 112 against Old Cliftonians. He was a free-hitting batsman, but his military duties prevented him from taking his cricket seriously: still he made many good scores in Army matches, and for Old Cliftonians v Trojans at Southampton in August 1913, he and F. G. Robinson made 141 without being parted for the first wicket in 38 minutes, Collins scoring 63 and his partner 77. His best performance at Lord's was to make 58 and 36 for RE v RA in 1913. He was born in India in 1885, gazetted second Lieutenant in 1904 and promoted Lieutenant in 1907.

R. HUMPHREY 1907

RICHARD HUMPHREY was found drowned in the Thames and was buried in St Pancras Cemetery, East Finchley, on February 28. He had for a long time been in poor circumstances and no doubt his mind became unhinged. He was a batsman who did not accomplish half of what was expected from him. Gaining a high reputation very early in his career, he had no sooner reached the top of the tree than he began to decline in power.

A. P. DAY 1910
Five Cricketers of the Year

Arthur Percival Day was born at Newton House, Blackheath on August 10, 1885, and thus plays for Kent by right of the qualification that can never be open to question. Fresh from school cricket, Mr Day was given a thorough trial by Kent in 1905, and splendidly he played, scoring 1,050 runs in county matches alone and averaging 35. Many public school batsmen have done great things in their first season in county cricket, but considering Mr Day took part in 19 matches it would be difficult to recall a better record. He made a hundred in each match against Gloucestershire, but his finest cricket was shown in winning Kent's match against Yorkshire at Hull. With Rhodes, Haigh and Hirst bowling at him on a slow wicket he scored 54 and not out 58. This performance settled all doubts as to his class and proved he was far more than a fast wicket batsman. Great things were expected of him in 1906 – the year in which Kent first carried off the Championship – but strangely enough that season brought with it a pronounced check in his career. He did not find his form in the early part of the summer and, Kent being tremendously strong in batting, he failed to keep his place in the eleven, only playing in nine county matches. In 1907 he appeared in eight county fixtures, his best score being 68. Then in 1908 he to a large extent recovered his ground. He played in 15 of Kent's 25 matches and was fifth in the averages. Still, it would be idle to say that up to the end of 1908 he had fulfilled the hopes of his first season for Kent. Last summer, however, he was quite at his best again, and might well have been given a place in the Gentlemen's eleven at The Oval and Lord's. He was in form all through the season and finished up with a particularly fine innings at The Oval against England. As it is understood that circumstances will admit of his keeping up the game he is one of the chief hopes of England's batting in the near future. He has a fine commanding style with plenty of hitting, but his sovereign merit is the watchful defence which enables him to do well on all sorts of wickets. In view of what may be in store for him one could wish that he had specialised a little more in fielding.

1970

DAY, ARTHUR PERCIVAL, who died on January 22, aged 83, played as an amateur for Kent from 1905 to 1923. His first summer at Kent was his most successful as a batsman, for he hit a century in each of the two matches with Gloucestershire and reached an aggregate of 1,050 runs, average 35. In 1908, when he scored 118 against Somerset at Taunton, he and E. Humphreys added 248, which remains a record for the Kent seventh wicket.

In all first-class cricket, Day scored 7,175 runs, including 13 centuries, average 32.31. Though for some years rarely employed as a bowler by Kent, he took 137 wickets for 26.56 runs each and he held 21 catches.

OUR YOUNG CRICKETERS 1911
by P. F. Warner

I have been asked by the editor of *Wisden*'s Almanack to write something about the young cricketers who came to the front during last summer, and after consultation with him, the following players were chosen: Mr M. C. Bird, Mr I. P. F. Campbell, Ducat and Hitch, of Surrey; Mr F. H. Knott of Kent; Newman, Mead and Brown of Hampshire; J. W. Hearne and Hendren of Middlesex; Mr F. R. Foster of Warwickshire; Booth of

Yorkshire: Shipman, the Leicestershire fast bowler; and Whysall of Notts.

This was a pretty good selection – between them they went on to earn over 130 Test caps for England, and in Hendren and Mead, Warner identified two of the only four men who have scored more runs than W. G. Grace in their careers. However, he and his editor, Sydney Pardon, got a couple wrong.

I. P. F. CAMPBELL

The only time I saw Mr I. P. F. Campbell play he batted extremely well against J. T. Hearne and Tarrant on a slow wicket at Lord's and I formed the opinion of him then that he was an England player in embryo. Strongly built, Mr Campbell drove splendidly, and his bat appeared to be very straight. Such good judges as J. T. Hearne and Hayward were enthusiastic about him.

from Surrey Notes, 1911

The discovery of the season was I. P. F. Campbell of Repton. His play at school was not such as to foreshadow the success that rewarded him directly he was given a place in the Surrey eleven. He seemed perfectly at home in county cricket, batting with the utmost confidence. Judged by figures, he did nothing extraordinary, but against Middlesex at Lord's he hit with such extreme brilliancy that critics at once began to speak of him as possibly an England batsman in the near future.

1964

CAMPBELL, IAN PERCY FITZGERALD, who died on December 25, aged 73, got his Blue as a Freshman at Oxford, playing in the University matches of 1911 and 1912 and playing Association Football against Cambridge in the same two years. At Repton he was in the cricket and football elevens from 1906 to 1910, and also represented the school at fives. He assisted Surrey Second XI as a batsman in 1908 and made occasional appearances for the county side until 1913. Twice in 1911 he appeared against the Players, being a member of the team at The Oval deemed by Sir Pelham Warner to be the best ever to represent the Gentlemen.

W. SHIPMAN

I have never had the good fortune to see Shipman bowl, but I have heard very flattering things said about him especially with regard to his form against Surrey at The Oval in August, when his quick off-break astonished everybody.

SURREY v LEICESTERSHIRE

Played at Kennington Oval, Thursday, Friday, Saturday September 1, 2, 3, 1910. Originally arranged to commence on May 9, but postponed owing to the death of King Edward, this match saw Surrey defeated by 63 runs, the reversal being only the second sustained by the county at Kennington Oval during the summer. In disposing of Leicestershire for 144, Surrey looked to have laid the foundation of a victory, but some splendid work by Shipman, upset calculations, the Leicestershire professional, with the ground in excellent order, bowling his fast break-backs so finely that in taking nine wickets he hit the stumps six times.

Leicestershire 144 (Hitch five for 80) **and 306** (Wood 95, Whitehead 81; Smith four for 90).

Surrey 166 (Hayes 51; Shipman nine for 83) **and 221** (Hobbs 61; Jayes five for 108).

1944

In 1911, his most successful season, he took 100 wickets in Championship matches at 25.61 apiece and averaged 16.27 with the bat, his best display, 69 out of 93 in 70 minutes, being an uphill struggle against Warwickshire at Hinckley. He bowled fast right-hand with off-break and showed to most advantage on hard turf.

In 1909 he did the hat-trick against Derbyshire. Twice he excelled against Yorkshire; in 1910 at Leeds he took their first five wickets for 12 runs, and Jayes dismissed seven men for 87 in the second innings, the two fast bowlers being mainly responsible for a victory by 259 runs – Leicestershire's first triumph over Yorkshire in a Championship match. Next year, at Leicester, Shipman got rid of seven opponents for 73, and with King, the slow right-hander – eight wickets for 17 – brought about the defeat of Yorkshire by an innings and 20 runs, the only win for Leicestershire that season. The war brought his county cricket career to an end, though he played once in 1921. Altogether he took 367 wickets, average 27.26, and scored 2,479 runs, average 14.18. Shipman joined Todmorden, the Lancashire League Club, in 1914, and afterwards played for Smethwick in the Birmingham League.

RECOLLECTIONS OF MR F. R. SPOFFORTH 1927
BY MR C. I. THORNTON

To get Spofforth and E. M. Grace on a side was to ensure a pleasant day's cricket if not necessarily a successful one. Spofforth was at his happiest at country matches where his stories – always told with an air of sincerity – used to amuse people immensely. One special one that never failed to please used to be given in the following circumstances. I would say to him at lunch, "How did you learn to be such a fine short-slip, Spoff?" And he would reply, "When I was quite young I made a boy, when out for a walk, throw stones into a hedge and, as the sparrows flew out, I caught 'em."

R. B. LAGDEN 1914

I have no wish to take up the role of prophet, but looking back on what happened last season, it will be disappointing indeed if, to mention only a few names, Lee of Notts, Kilner of Yorkshire, Jeeves of Warwickshire, Chester of Worcestershire, R. B. Lagden and D. J. Knight, do not do a great deal in the next few years. It was quite in accordance with recent precedent that Lagden, after playing splendidly for Cambridge, should have failed for the Gentlemen. The days seem to have gone by when University bats, such as Yardley, and Ottaway, could step as Freshmen into the Gentlemen's Eleven, and at once prove themselves good enough for the best company.

1945

LAGDEN, MR REGINALD BOUSFIELD, OBE, MC, was killed in an aeroplane accident while returning to India from England late in October. After representing Marlborough at cricket, rugby football, rackets and hockey, he went up to Pembroke College and gained his cricket Blue, besides playing hockey for Cambridge. Three times he played against Oxford, twice helping in victory at Lord's after hard fights and being on the losing side in 1914. He began by scoring 61 and 6 and taking four wickets, so having a large share in beating by three wickets an Oxford eleven which included his elder brother, R. O. Lagden, by whom he was bowled in the second innings. Cambridge won in 1913 by four wickets, R. B. Lagden again being conspicuous with 71 and 45; and he finished his cricket career at Cambridge with 20 and 19 and taking one wicket, Oxford being successful by 194 runs. So his six innings in these matches realised 222 runs at an average of 37.

A very good half-back, R. B. Lagden played hockey for Cambridge, finishing captain in 1914, and he became an international. After serving with distinction in the last war, he went on business to Bengal, where he played cricket and hockey for many years, giving valuable help in increasing the popularity of both games. Aged 51, R. B. Lagden left a widow and six children living at Guildford.

W. FLAMSON
from Leicestershire Notes, 1938

Except for Astill, who after many years of great service could not be regarded as in the top flight, the county did not possess a good slow bowler, and only when the pitch appeared at all fiery and helpful to fast bowlers did the attack look dangerous. At Basingstoke, Flamson and Smith found the wicket to their liking and bowled with such life that the Hampshire batsmen were powerless. Probably the only satisfactory feature of the bowling was the advance of Flamson, who in his first full season of county cricket, accomplished some splendid performances. He developed as the season progressed and towards the close often carried the attack on his shoulders. Powerfully built and with a run-up similar to that of George Geary, he put plenty of "shoulder" into his medium-fast deliveries and had the knack of making the ball keep unexpectedly low.

Season's average:
Overs 655.5, Maidens 106, Runs 2027, Wickets 60, Average 33.78.

1939

Flamson, of whom a lot was expected, suffered a lot through an injury which kept him out of the side for a month.

1940

In the first five county matches of the 1939 season, Flamson's first innings bowling analyses were:

v Sussex: 35–5–122–4; v Somerset 25–1–114–3; v Lancashire 23–1–104–0; v Northamptonshire 27–2–125–4; v Nottinghamshire 21.1–0–105–5

1946

Flamson, William Henry, who died in January in his fortieth year was a useful bowler for Leicestershire during the three seasons immediately preceding the outbreak of war. In 1936 he took 59 wickets but never played regularly owing to injury. Of powerful build, he bowled fast-medium with plenty of life, but want of a good length often made him expensive. He showed little skill in batting.

H. GIMBLETT 1979

His second summer dispelled any notion that his early successes had been a fluke, as he scored 1,608 runs with an average of 32.81. People sometimes talk as if after this he was a disappointment. In fact his one set-back, apart from being overlooked by the selectors, was when in 1938, probably listening to the advice of grave critics, he attempted more cautious methods and his average dropped to 27. But can one call disappointing a man who between 1936 and his retirement in 1953 never failed to get his 1,000 runs, who in his career scored over 23,000, more than any other Somerset player, and 50 centuries, the highest 310 against Sussex at Eastbourne in 1948, and whose average for his career was over 36? Moreover after his first season he habitually went in first and yet he hit 265 sixes, surely a record.

1983
Cricket Books, 1982

David Foot has sub-titled *Harold Gimblett* (Heinemann: £7.95) "Tormented Genius of Cricket" and his biography justifies it. This is no cosy recital of runs or wickets, of comfortable success, but of the mental agony of one man who, despite his outstanding cricket gifts, never gained the satisfaction they seemed to offer.

HON. L. R. WHITE 1945

No one revealed greater promise at headquarters than did the Hon. L. R. White, the most consistent Eton batsman. After doing well in a losing game for Lord's Schools, he scored 102 against a Lord's XI, and with 77 he made more than twice as many runs as came from anyone else on the strong Middlesex and Essex side in a keen fight with Kent and Surrey. He might develop into a county and England captain.

1946
SIR PELHAM WARNER'S XI v SECOND ARMY

June 29, 1945. Drawn. The extra leave arranged by General Dempsey for his players was put to good use, a hard-fought game with an exciting finish resulting. Had the Second Army batsmen been in full practice they would most likely have scored fast enough to win after G. O. Allen's declaration. The former England captain played one of his best innings. His off-side strokes were well timed and attractive; only a damp outfield restricted his biggest hits to seven fours, besides a five, all run. White, Allen's partner in a stand of 158 occupying an hour and three-quarters, obviously found inspiration from his captain. The on-drive, kept well down, showed the young Cantab to best advantage, and he took out his bat, with 11 fours to his credit, after two and a half hours at the wicket.

Sir Pelham Warner's XI 270 for three declared (Cadet Hon. L. R. White 132 not out, Lieut. Col. G. O. Allen 93).

Second Army 247 for eight (Capt. P. G. T. Kingsley 100 not out).

ENGLAND v AUSTRALIA
Third Victory Match

At Lord's, July 14, 16, 17, 1945. Australia won by four wickets. For this game England tried the experiment of playing three of the best schoolboy cricketers of 1944 – Dewes, White and Carr – but they scored only 47 runs and Carr, the bowler, sent down only nine overs ... After an eclipse of the sun earlier in the week, storms of wind and rain made cricket conditions problematical on Saturday, but, following a sharp shower that delayed the start until ten minutes past twelve, rain held off during the playing hours ...

By good defence White countered the menace of "silly" point and mid-on – both stood very close – for three-quarters of an hour, but Carr, the third tyro, soon fell to a fine ball that shook off the leg bail.

1991

Along with John Dewes and Donald Carr, White was subjected to the gaze of the whole nation when he was chosen to represent England in the third of the hastily arranged "Victory Tests" at Lord's against the Australian Services. He made 11 and 4, and in England's first innings he helped Hutton put on 55 for the fourth wicket, defending well when Hassett crowded him with close fielders. This was his first-class debut. He played in five more matches, three for Middlesex and one each for the RAF and MCC, his highest score being 46 for the RAF against Worcestershire at Worcester in June 1946. He had no ambitions to pursue a first-class career, preferring to enjoy his cricket for such clubs as MCC, the Ramblers and I Zingari.

R. HARMAN
1965

In a general all-round improvement in Surrey's cricket, perhaps the most important factor was the way Harman stepped so readily into the vacancy left by Lock. In all matches the persevering left-arm slow bowler with an easy action and genuine spin took 136 wickets, including eight for 12 against

Nottinghamshire at Trent Bridge and eight for 32 against Kent at The Oval.

1967

Pocock also made progress as an off-spinner, perhaps as much as could be expected in the current restricting conditions for slow bowlers, which have grievously set back Harman in the past two years.

1969

Harman had one outstanding performance but did little else.

At the end of 1968, Harman was released by Surrey, and his first-class career ended.

J. WHITEHOUSE
1973

The most encouraging feature of the batting was the immense promise and instant form of Whitehouse. Born in Nuneaton, Whitehouse concentrated on academic qualifications before turning his talents to cricket. After one match against Scotland in 1970, he burst upon the first-class scene with 173 against Oxford University – the fourth-highest score recorded by an English batsman on his first-class debut. Despite an unorthodox stance, Whitehouse, an excellent slip fielder, soon claimed a place at number five before replacing Abberley as Jameson's opening partner.

1978

One who did do his job commendably was Whitehouse, a model of consistency until he ran out of runs in the closing weeks. A fine off-side player despite his square stance, he was the obvious candidate for the captaincy, having filled this role in a winter tour of Zambia for which Brown was not available. A safe fielder anywhere, his best cricket may be yet to come.

Although he went on to captain Warwickshire, Whitehouse never quite fulfilled his early potential.

LIKELY ENGLAND TALENT 1975
by Norman Preston

Players have to be found this summer to take part in the Prudential (World) Cup and the four Test Matches that will follow against Australia. The time would seem to be ripe not only to look at the constitution of the team but also the make-up of the Selection Committee, which might include Charlie Elliott, a man of vast experience who is no longer on the Umpires' panel. Personally, I was disappointed that England relied on so many of the old brigade for the tour of the Antipodes. The side was rich in experience, but the three youngest, Willis, Old and Hendrick, were twenty-five. Kent have three men, besides Denness, Knott and Underwood, looking for a chance – Johnson, opening bat and off-spinner, Woolmer, batsman and medium pacer, and Ealham, a stocky hard-hitting bat and possibly the best outfielder in the country with a deadly return to the stumps.

Trevor Jesty, of Hampshire, is another all-rounder, and others who come to mind are two tall Somerset youngsters, Ian Botham, a nineteen-year-old opening bowler and splendid batsman, and Peter Denning, a left-handed bat. Another left-handed bat who looked very good last summer is Kennedy of Lancashire, and at Northampton there is Willey of upright cultured strokes. Challenging Underwood, is Edmonds, a former Cambridge University captain, who has shone for Middlesex with left arm slows of impeccable length and flight. . . . England found only one new Test batsman in 1974, David Lloyd, the twenty-seven-year-old Lancashire captain and left hander.

A. KENNEDY
1976

[Lancashire] attracted big crowds wherever they played and blooded several young players who promise to carry on the good work first revived by Bond and still carried on by David Lloyd and, in his absence through injury, by Clive Lloyd. Kennedy was awarded his county cap towards the end of the season and this stylish young left-handed batsman from Colne, in the Lancashire League, must rank as one of the most promising of England's new brigade of batsmen. A punishing as well as a stylish stroke player, Kennedy matched his flair with the bat with sound fielding in the gully or in the deep. His consistency indicated the right temperament and his fitness was never in doubt.

1983

Opening batsman Andrew Kennedy, a former winner of the Cricket Writers' award as Young Cricketer of the Year (1975), who at one time looked destined to be a future captain of Lancashire, all-rounder Bernard Reidy and wicket-keeper Chris Scott were not re-engaged.

1989

NEWSON, Edward Surrurier (Bob) OBE, who died in Durban on April 24, 1988, aged 77, opened the bowling in his three Test matches for South Africa, against England at Johannesburg in 1930/31 and eight years later in the last two Tests against Hammond's side. Yet he might easily have missed his debut, for he had not received notification of his selection and arrived at work as usual on the morning of the match. His father brought his kit to the Old Wanderers ground by tram as his son, recently turned twenty, lined up for the team photograph in borrowed clothes.

G. A. HICK 1989
We Always Knew He Could Bat
by Peter Roebuck

Test cricket awaits Hick. At Worcester Viv Richards saw a star on the rise. I wonder what he thought. Imran Khan has said that Hick might not be so effective at Test level because, like Zaheer Abbas, he is fundamentally a front-foot player. Hick is a tough, strong character, a man with the courage to meet every challenge. He will, I believe, be a major force in Test cricket. After his final innings of the 1988 season, one Glamorgan player said he was, "Unbelievable. I'd never seen anything like it. He played and missed only three or four times. He didn't seem to get the balls others were getting."

I don't think he ever will.

M. N. LATHWELL
1993

Lathwell, a twenty-year-old opening bat, educated in Devon and under Somerset eyes for a long time, delighted watchers all over the country with his busy, forceful batting. Besides 1,176 Championship runs at 36.75, he often excelled in one-day games. (It is interesting to recall that in his first year, Viv Richards had very similar figures: 1,223 at 33.05.) It was a major achievement to replace an opening pair of the calibre of Jimmy Cook and Peter Roebuck. Lathwell and the steady, cricket-wise Hayhurst, with nearly 1,200 runs, did it splendidly.

Why We Beat the Poms, 1994
by Ian Chappell

Until the advent of Atherton, England's selections had often lacked rhyme or reason. A classic case was the predicament of twenty-one-year-old Mark Lathwell in the one-day international series. At Lord's, Australia had an unbeatable 2–0 lead, so the selectors took the opportunity to play their talented twenty-one-year-old, Damien Martyn. As he made mincemeat of the bowling on his way to a glorious half-century, an MCC member said to me, "How come you Australians always produce good young batsmen?" With Lathwell needlessly sitting in the pavilion watching his third match in a row, the answer wasn't difficult. "We play them," I replied.

D. L. AMISS
1965

Jameson, when he made 165, shared with Amiss in the highest stand of the summer; 255 against Oxford University. Unfortunately Amiss, and also Richardson, failed to bridge the gap between minor cricket and the county game.

1975
WEST INDIES v ENGLAND
Second Test Match

At Kingston, Jamaica, February 16, 17, 19, 20, 21, 1974. Drawn. In the end this became the great escape story – a match apparently lost by England but finally saved by Amiss who batted for the last nine and a half hours and scored 262 not out ... In the end England made 432 for nine, at which point Amiss, who had never before in his first-class career scored a double century, led them off the field for the last time. His was the hero's role in a classic escape.

D. W. RANDALL
by Norman Preston, 1975

Two years ago, high opinions were held of Randall, of Nottinghamshire, a tall stylish bat, but he fell away. Perhaps his confidence will return in 1975.

CENTENARY TEST MATCH
Australia Victorious Again By 45 Runs
by Reg Hayter, 1978

Well as Amiss, Greig, Knott and Brearley batted, however, the innings to remember was played by Randall, a jaunty, restless, bubbling character, whose 174 took England to the doorstep of victory. The Australian crowds enjoyed his approach as much as Indian crowds had done on the tour just finished.

Once, when Lillee tested him with a bouncer, he tennis-batted it to the mid-wicket fence with a speed and power that made many a rheumy eye turn to the master of the stroke, the watching Sir Donald Bradman. Words cannot recapture the joy of that moment.

Australians 138 (Underwood three for 16; Old three for 39) **and 419** for 9 declared (Marsh 110 not out, Davis 68; Old four for 104).

England 95 (Lillee six for 26) **and 417** (Randall 174, Amiss 64; Lillee five for 139)

WOMEN IN *WISDEN*

As Norman Preston noted in his introduction to Netta Rheinberg's article on Enid Bakewell in the 1970 *Wisden*, "Women have played a far more important part in the development of cricket than many people realise. W. G. Grace and his brothers learnt the technicalities of the game from their mother, the only woman who has appeared in *Wisden*'s list of Births and Deaths. Mrs Foster inspired her seven sons at a very early age and long before most of them played with such distinction for Worcestershire." Nor should we forget Christina Willes, whose brother John began to experiment with round-arm bowling after seeing his sister solving the problem of how to bowl underarm while wearing a crinoline dress. His being no-balled in 1822 led to the legalisation of round-arm bowling, and the heralding of the modern era of cricket, half a dozen years later. When round-arm became overarm in 1864 – the first year of *Wisden's Cricketers' Almanack* – perhaps the gender of the true originator of the revolution had been forgotten, and it was not until the 75th edition in 1938 that the editor, Wilfrid Brookes, established something approaching a regular section devoted to women's cricket. Nowadays, women's cricket is becoming a more visible part of the public game, with some of the great names of recent generations becoming, if not as well known as their male counterparts, at least recognisable names among cricket aficionados.

1885

LANCASHIRE v GLOUCESTERSHIRE

Played at Manchester, Thursday, Friday July 24, 25, 1884. Owing to rain only three-quarters of an hour's play took place before luncheon, and during that time Gloucestershire, who went in first, lost three wickets for 25 runs. On resuming two more went down by the time the total reached 34. Dr W. G. Grace, who went in late in consequence of an injury to one of his fingers, then came to the rescue of his side, and by seven fours, one three, four twos and singles scored 53 out of 80 runs made while he was in. The Gloucestershire captain narrowly escaped being caught when he had scored 20, but that was the only fault in his innings. On Lancashire going in, Barlow was bowled without scoring, but Mr Hornby and Mr Taylor made a capital stand for the second wicket. By dashing, if not faultless, cricket, Mr Hornby made 46 out of the first 57 runs, and when he was dismissed Mr Taylor and Briggs carried the score to 79. At this total three wickets fell, and when time was called six wickets were down for 104 runs.

Three-quarters of a hour's play sufficed to finish off the Lancashire innings on the Friday, and Gloucestershire went in for the second time 22 runs to the bad. They had twelve minutes' batting before luncheon, and upon resuming Dr E. M. Grace was splendidly caught at mid-off, and his brother had just succeeded him when a telegram was received announcing the death of Mrs Grace, the mother of Drs E. M. and W. G. Grace. A short consultation was held, and it was decided to at once abandon the match.

1938

ENGLAND v AUSTRALIA TEST MATCHES

If, ten years ago, anyone had suggested that Test matches between women cricketers would take place in England, and that one day's play in such a game would attract five thousand spectators, the idea would have been laughed to scorn. Yet this ideal of women cricketers was realised in 1937 when people of the Midlands and elsewhere flocked to Northampton to witness the opening of the first Test Match in England between women's teams representing England and Australia.

Important occasion as was June 12 last summer, the historian must state a date shortly after Christmas in 1934 as the commencement of women's international cricket. On December 28 in that year England met Australia in a women's Test match, the game taking place at Brisbane, Australia, and ending in victory for England by nine wickets. Thus last year's visit of the Australian side completed a chapter in the development of women's cricket.

For the success of this phase of the game, the Women's Cricket Association has been largely responsible. Founded in 1926, the WCA, besides organising the tours, has helped to form clubs and county associations and has set up a complete organisation for the furtherance of women's cricket.

Women play under the MCC Laws of Cricket with the exception of that relating to the ball. For women's cricket in England the weight of the ball varies between $4\frac{15}{16}$ ounces and $5\frac{1}{16}$ ounces compared with the MCC specification of not less than $5\frac{1}{2}$ ounces and not more than $5\frac{3}{4}$ ounces. In no other respect does the material used for women's cricket differ from that for men. Of course, women employ bats, pads and gloves of suitable weight. There is a regulation mode of dress in white.

. . . Those who have seen women exponents of the highest class – and fully 10,000 people watched one game at Mitcham in 1937 – agree that they play cricket with skill, perseverance, a proper regard for the spirit of the game and with natural grace and charm. When prominent members of MCC attend women's Test matches, as happened last summer, it is obvious that the welcomed sanction of the male authority has been obtained. With the possession of outstanding players and capable legislators the women's game in England and Australia has an assured future.

WOMEN'S CRICKET – THE AUSTRALIAN TOUR OF ENGLAND, 1963

No one name stands out from the rest, though if there were to be another tour in say three years' time, it is safe to say that

Elizabeth Amos and Helen Lee would gain places of honour. Both showed undoubted signs of greatness. One major character stood out in England's cricket, that of Mary Duggan, with a long and solid reputation as an all-rounder behind her, and the first Test century by a woman at The Oval in the third Test suitably crowned her notable past achievements. Rachael Heyhoe, a reliable all-rounder, also certainly made a name for herself by noticeably enjoying her cricket. What a sign of the times it is that a player who shows her undoubted enjoyment of the game should become a subject for special comment!

1994

In 1966 Myrtle Maclagan was appointed MBE. At various times in her life she won prizes for squash, tennis, badminton and knitting. It was reported that so many people turned up for her eightieth birthday she had to make a speech from the top of a step-ladder and got attention by a blast on her whistle.

ENID BAKEWELL – CHAMPION WOMAN CRICKETER
by Netta Rheinberg, 1970

Mrs Enid Bakewell (née Turton) cannot remember when she first took up a bat, but the game of cricket attracted her at an early age and in 1950, when she was nine years old, she joined the local boys playing on a small field close to her home as, in her own words, "there were too few girls available". The only child of a non-cricketing family, her parents encouraged her enthusiasm, purchasing and supplying her with all her gear. At her Primary School at Newstead, Enid was soon better at cricket than the boys and when at Brincliffe County Grammar School, Nottingham, the boys used to borrow her gear.

At fourteen Enid had already graduated from her club, Notts Casuals WCC, to her county team. In those days she was a quiet, steady, right-hand opening bat, concentrating on staying at the wicket. The lessons of concentration and watchfulness learnt in those early years provided a solid basis for the future, as she found later, when the opportunity arose, that she was not only able to stay at the wicket, but also to score easily.

Mention of Enid Turton's batting ability first came in June 1957 when, at sixteen years of age, she scored 43 not out against Leicester out of a total of 101. A month later she followed this with 56 not out in the return match, an encouraging start for a youngster. Two years later Enid entered Dartford College of Physical Education, graduating in 1959, the same year in which she was chosen to tour Holland with the WCA team of young and promising players. At this stage Enid did not take her bowling seriously and it was only later, when she was coached at her club by Edna Valentine, now its President, and Eileen White, then Hon. Secretary of the County Association, that she began to think about her left-arm slow bowling, modelling it on that of Tony Lock, even to the extent of taking the same number of paces in the same run-up round the umpire. Later still, in 1967, having reached top-class cricket, Enid started seriously to concentrate on her bowling. "As a Nottingham girl," she says, "I was torn two ways. When I went to watch Nottinghamshire v Surrey I admired Tony Lock's bowling and delighted in Peter May's batting, so I sometimes hoped Surrey might win."

In 1963 Enid's name was among the possibles for Test selection against Australia then touring England. She says, "My first feelings were of excitement and surprise tempered somewhat on seeing the full list of names." She failed, however, to gain a place, and in 1966, when the New Zealanders toured England she had married and was having a baby. The recent tour, therefore, provided Mrs Bakewell with her first Test appearance and her first opportunity to do battle with Australian and New Zealand cricketers; the rest of the story is one of consistent and amazing success. On receiving the invitation to tour, Mrs Bakewell, mother of a two-year-old daughter and part-time schoolteacher (to help with funds) found the decision to accept a difficult one, not only on the score of separation from her family but also on financial grounds. However, her husband, Colin, a Rolls Royce electrical engineer, was most understanding and her parents at once offered to look after her small daughter while she was away.

Slight of build and small in stature, Enid has been described as "diminutive" and a "tiny blonde". Although she is small, she is athletically built and gives an impression of freshness, alertness and quickwittedness, following many previous cricketers of less than average build in nimbleness of footwork and quick reflex action. Enid's record on the tour of 1,031 runs and 118 wickets is now history. She finished with a batting average of 39.6 in 29 innings and a bowling average of 564.1 overs – 1,153 runs – 118 wickets – at an average of 9.7. On three occasions, once in Australia and twice in New Zealand, she took eight wickets in an innings, and on nine other occasions five or more wickets. On her first Test appearance against Australia she opened the innings with a maiden century (113) and also as opening batsman scored two consecutive Test centuries against New Zealand in the first innings of the First and Second Tests (124 and 114). She scored six half-centuries on the whole tour, and took ten catches, though ironically enough she dropped an easy chance at a vital stage in the Second Test against Australia. This proved to be the only time the pendulum swung the other way for her.

The consistency of her performances caused her opponents to respect her from the start, and the opposing bowlers and batsmen both suffered from the reputation which she built up. Headlines in the Australian and New Zealand press reflected her prowess. "English girl does a Sobers" stated an Adelaide newspaper reporting her top score of 59 against Victoria, followed by her skittling of seven batsmen for 28. Another reported the same performance with "Bakewell routs Vic". The second Test match in New Zealand, won by England by seven wickets, was called "Bakewell's Match". Her achievements were outstanding. She scored 114 and took four for 68 in the first innings followed by 66 not out and five for 56 in the second innings. Fittingly amid much excitement, she also scored the single a bare four minutes before the end, to give England their victory, their first win against New Zealand since 1954.

After this performance Enid began to be rated as the world's best woman all-rounder. The comments varied; they outdid each other in praise. The somewhat condescending comment, "Mainstay of an aggressive English knock was Enid Bakewell who played as correctly as any male Test player might have as she moved relentlessly towards her century" contrasted with, "an audacious batsman, fast between wickets, who uses her feet better than many Plunket Shield cricketers". As for her bowling, "her orthodox left-arm spinners were bowled with skill and consistency. She was able to drift the ball across the batsmen in the slight breeze and straighten it off the pitch with alarming sharpness."

. . . An engraved silver cup was presented to her at Heathrow on her arrival home by one of the men's teams against whom she played in aid of tour funds last season, and when Kirkby Council made her a gift of a dressing-table set, her three-year-old daughter Lorna commented loudly and brightly, "And what have we got this time?"

Enid's 1968 tour performances remain a challenge to women cricketers wherever they may play. They will remain unforgotten, not only by her fellow tourists but also by her opponents in Australia and New Zealand for a long time to come.

2003

Dr Roy Park played his only Test for Australia at Melbourne in 1920/21, as a replacement for the injured Charles Macartney. Legend has it that Park's wife dropped her knitting as he faced his first ball, bent down to pick it up, and missed his entire Test career – he was bowled by Harry Howell, and never played again.

THE YEAR THE CITADEL FELL
by Peter Hayter, 1999

What was a woman to think? Or a chap? The messages being thrown at women in cricket during 1998 were so confused and confusing that they made the head spin. In the early months of the year came three items of news that suggested that all the old attitudes were alive and well and living at Lord's.

In March, an industrial tribunal upheld a claim for sex discrimination by Theresa Harrild, a receptionist formerly employed by the England and Wales Cricket Board, who said she had been pressured and paid by the Board to have an abortion after becoming pregnant by a colleague.

Harrild's evidence – regarding the attitude of certain high-ranking Board officials towards women in their offices and in cricket at large – was damning. The ECB got into even more trouble when it denied her allegations after the hearing, having declined to contest them. This came only weeks after a case in which Geoffrey Boycott, one of the game's most public figures, was convicted by a French court of assaulting a girlfriend in a Riviera hotel room.

To the public, the conclusion that there was no smoke without fire was all but irresistible. Why would the man, or woman, in the street think otherwise? To them, all the available evidence, outside as well as inside the courtrooms, pointed to the same conclusion: the majority of men in cricket regarded women as simply fodder for jokes about maidens, tickles to fine legs and bouncers – or worse.

It was made all the more relevant because of events in the Marylebone Cricket Club barely a fortnight before the Harrild case. A blocking minority of the all-male MCC membership had voted against the proposal of their committee – pushed by the President, Colin Ingleby-Mackenzie – to admit persons of the opposite gender. They thus reaffirmed the club's 211-year-old position: not in here, madam.

By the end of the year, so much had changed that those of a cynical disposition might have been tempted to believe Rachael Heyhoe-Flint had been busy putting something in the gin-and-tonics at NW8. Ingleby-Mackenzie, having refused to take no for an answer, urged the members to think and vote again and, on September 28, they did, momentously. Just how influential in their final decision was the President's warning that no women meant no lottery money, who can tell? In the meantime, the Women's Cricket Association had voted to become an integral part of the ECB, thus establishing a single governing body for all cricket in the country. Women in MCC, and the ECB, as equals? Whatever next?

2001

ARCHDALE, HELEN ELIZABETH, MBE, who died on January 11, 2000, aged 92, was captain of the pioneering England women's team that toured Australia and New Zealand in 1934/35. The tour did much both to raise the status of women's cricket and to heal some of the damage done to Anglo-Australian cricket relations by Bodyline two years earlier. Betty Archdale herself earned much of the credit, "... her forthright yet engaging personality made her a popular figure to whom the sizable Australian crowds responded warmly", according to *Wisden Australia*. She was also a capable batsman, who twice made important 32s in a low-scoring series that England won. Instead of leading England again on the planned 1939/40 tour, she was commissioned in the WRNS and, after the war, emigrated to Australia. There she switched from a career in law to education, becoming principal of Sydney University Women's College and then head of Abbotsleigh Girls School, where she introduced sex education – and cricket. Betty Archdale also became a TV and radio personality, well-known for her witty and sensible approach to problems. In 1997 she was voted one of Australia's 100 Living Treasures and, in 1999, one of the first ten female honorary members of MCC. Her mother was a leading suffragette, imprisoned in 1912, and Betty was said to have collected stones for her to throw.

2001

All 11 players in the Cuddalore women's team failed to score against Chennai B in India. However, the side scraped to six all out – in reply to 158 for one declared – because of wides. One batswoman, Balasoundari, almost hit a four but the ball just failed to reach the boundary and she was unable to run because of cramp.

2003

Leslie Hylton, a Jamaican fast bowler who played six Tests for
West Indies in the 1930s, shot his wife Lurline dead in 1954 after
she admitted to adultery. Hylton was sentenced to death and
hanged in Jamaica in May 1955. Australia were touring the West
Indies, and when the Jamaican opener J. K. Holt followed a run
of low scores by dropping two catches in the Test at Bridgetown,
a placard urged "Save Hylton, hang Holt".

2003

In 2002, Australia's one-day captain Ricky Ponting, twenty-
seven, married Rianna Cantor, a twenty-three-year-old law student, in Sydney. His father, Graeme, said Rianna was "a very
special woman" who had helped give Ricky the maturity to lead
the national team. A hundred guests dined on oysters and
Tasmanian champagne at a reception paid for by a women's
magazine in exchange for exclusive access. The couple had met at
a Melbourne restaurant on Boxing Day 2000. "I had no idea who
he was," Rianna said. "I hate cricket with a passion."

2003

The record for the Test cricketer with the most marriages is believed
to be shared by two players: Bill Edrich, the England batsman of the
1940s, and Hugh Tayfield, the South African off-spinner of the 1950s,
with five each.

2003

Growing up in the New South Wales country town of Mudgee,
Lisa Keightley was barred from the primary school cricket team
because she was a girl. How those teachers would have been
shamed nearly two decades later, in 1998, when Keightley became
the first woman to make a century at Lord's, as Australia completed a 5–0 rout of England in a one-day series. Ushered into the
national team at the age of twenty-three following Australia's
disastrous World Cup loss in 1993, Keightley held down a place
for the next eight years, helped win the World Cup back in 1997

and formed a fine opening partnership with Belinda Clark. An elegant batsman, she loved socialising, surfing and sleeping. In December 2002, aged thirty-one, she retired, feeling her form was waning and that touring had lost its allure. She had scored 1,827 runs in 54 one-day internationals, making her Australia's third-highest scorer behind Clark and Karen Rolton. Keightley averaged 36.2 in her seven Tests, with three fifties, and 44.56 in one-dayers with two other hundreds apart from the famous one.

2004
Under-11 Cricket

Christ Church Primary School from Ealing in London won the National Under-11 BBC Kwik Cricket tournament. While plenty of the other 5,500 schools were coached by women, Christ Church were probably the only side trained by a female Sorbonne graduate with a French passport. Marie Holt was born in Paris, arrived in England in 1972 and developed an interest in cricket when her son David showed promise.

MY LIFE REPORTING CRICKET
BY ALEX BANNISTER, 1980

When they arrived in England, the combined experience of those little pals of mine, Ramadhin and Valentine, as the calypso went, was two first-class matches. It was Jack Mercer, the former Glamorgan bowler, then coaching in Jamaica, who urged the selectors to send Valentine. Mercer used to tell Valentine to spin until the blood showed from his fingers. Nobody could pick Ramadhin, and Valentine spun like a top. All John Goddard needed to do was put his slow bowlers on and they would do the rest. Valentine was charmingly vague. "When is the England captain coming in?" he asked when he was bowling out England in the Trent Bridge Test. "You dismissed him an hour ago", he was told.

Another story I associate with Jack Mercer involved Freddie Trueman on the 1953/54 tour of the West Indies. MCC were playing at Spanish Town, not far from Kingston, at a sugar plantation. Across the entrance was strung a banner exhorting the employees on the virtues of WORK, OBEDIENCE, DISCIPLINE. Trueman, who was sharing a car with Mercer and myself, looked with disgust at the banner and exploded: bloody well wouldn't work here!

CRICKETERS IN
HOLY ORDERS

Cricket and the Church of England have worked and played happily together since the beginning of cricket history. The Hambledon side of the late eighteenth century was held together by the Reverend Charles Powlett, bastard son of the third Duke of Bolton, although his motives were probably more based around the opportunities to bet on matches than for any intrinsic love of the game. Powlett's great-nephew, Fred Powlett, who emigrated to Australia and played first-class cricket for Victoria in pre-*Wisden* days, remains the only first-class cricketer who was also first cousin to an Archbishop of Canterbury. Lord Frederick Beauclerk was not only a priest and a nobleman, but also an early President of MCC, and an outstanding cricketer of his age. Throughout the Victorian era, cricketing priests kept the game going in rural communities and in the cities, and in the twentieth century, men such as David Sheppard, Ernest Killick and Frank Gillingham have left their mark on both church and cricket field. *Wisden* notes all of these players, and several others, whose achievements may have been less, but who added to the eccentricities of sport and religion in equal measure.

HENRY, CARDINAL MANNING 1893
CARDINAL MANNING died on January 14, 1892, aged eighty-three. It may seem a little strange to include Cardinal Manning's name in a cricket obituary, but inasmuch as he played

for Harrow against Winchester at Lord's in 1825, in the first match that ever took place between the two schools, his claim cannot be disputed.

REV. CANON A. CAZENOVE 1894

CANON CAZENOVE, who died in August while playing lawn tennis, performed an extraordinary bowling feat at Oxford on May 5, and 6, 1853. Playing for the Undergraduates of Oxford against Oxfordshire, he obtained no fewer than 16 wickets, securing all the ten in the first innings of the county, and six in the second. Five of the ten wickets were taken in one over, the umpire inadvertently allowing an extra ball. Canon Cazenove was born at Clapton in Middlesex on February 12, 1833, and played for Oxford against Cambridge at Lord's in 1851 and 1852. He was a round-arm bowler of medium pace.

REV. W. FELLOWS 1903

THE REVEREND WALTER FELLOWS, who was born at Rickmansworth, in Hertfordshire, on February 23, 1834, died at Toorak Parsonage, near Melbourne, July 23. He was educated at Westminster and Oxford, and is described in *Scores And Biographies* as "a hard slashing hitter, and a tremendous fast round-armed bowler". He was younger brother of Mr Harvey Fellows who still, happily, survives. For Westminster against Rugby, at Westminster, in 1852, he obtained nine wickets in the first innings and six in the second, but was on the losing side, Westminster making only 19 and 11 against Rugby's scores of 114 and 129. Although Mr Fellows' bowling was effective, it was certainly expensive, as there were 15 byes in the first innings, and 27 in the second. Moreover, he bowled 30 wides, thereby giving away as many runs as Westminster made in their two innings combined. For four years he assisted Oxford against Cambridge, namely from 1854 to 1857, and made scores of 33, 0 and 5, 35 and 30 (the highest in each innings), 24 and 3. In the 1855 match, he bowled 12 overs for 6 runs and 2 wickets. In 1855 and the two following years he appeared for the Gentlemen against the Players at Lord's, participating in the match in which Reginald

Hankey played his historical innings of 70. Whilst at practice on the Christ Church Ground, at Oxford, in 1856, Mr Fellows hit a ball, bowled by Rogers, a distance of 175 yards from hit to pitch, the length of the drive being carefully measured by E. Martin, the ground-keeper. In 1863 he emigrated to Australia and joined the Melbourne Club the following year. He was interested in the game to the last. Height 5ft. 11ins., and playing weight as much as 17st. 4lbs.

REV. J. DE SOYRES 1906

THE REV. JOHN DE SOYRES, Rector of St John The Evangelist, St John's, New Brunswick, who died suddenly on February 3 while undergoing an operation, was a great lover of cricket. He was born in Somerset in 1849 and educated at Brighton College and Gonville and Caius College, Cambridge, where he had a most distinguished career. He went out to New Brunswick in 1888 and had made for himself s reputation as the most distinguished preacher in Eastern Canada. He was a nephew of Edward Fitzgerald, the translator of Omar Khayyam.

REV. W. B. WEIGHELL 1907

THE REV. WILLIAM BARTHOLOMEW WEIGHELL, who was born at Cheddington, Bucks, on June 21, 1846, died on October 24, 1905. He was a very good fast round-armed bowler, and in the first over he ever delivered at Lord's – for Cambridge University against MCC Club and Ground, in 1866 – he bowled down the wickets of Mr W. Nicholson, Grundy and Mr C. F. Buller with consecutive balls. He was educated at Bedford Grammar School and Cambridge, and in 1866, 1868 and 1869 played against Oxford. His fielding was very good indeed, and his batting often effective; his highest score was 197 for Brighton v Horsham in 1876. He assisted Sussex 13 times between 1868 and 1878, and appeared for Norfolk in 1882 and 1883.

REV. A. J. LOWTH 1908

THE REV. ALFRED JAMES LOWTH, who was born at Grove House, Chiswick, on July 20, 1817, died at Winchester on

February 5, being at the time senior Wykehamist. He was left-handed both as a batsman as a bowler, but did not continue the game long after taking Holy Orders ... It is testimony to his greatness that in 1836 a deputation from the MCC went down to Winchester to see him bowl and, as a result, asked him to assist the Gentlemen against the Players at Lord's. He accepted the invitation and took nine wickets.

REV. CANON F. R. EVANS 1928

EVANS, CANON The REV. FREDERIC EVANS (a nephew of George Eliot), born at Griff House, near Nuneaton, on June 1, 1842, died at Bedworth Rectory, Warwickshire on March 4, aged 84. *Scores And Biographies* said of him, "Is a good bat, having patient defence, combined with great power of hitting; and is also a sure field, often (when not bowling) at long leg. Is most noted, however, as a high and fast round-armed bowler, occasionally difficult to play" ... In 1863 and two following seasons he was in the Oxford eleven under R. A. H. Mitchell, and in his three matches against Cambridge, all of which were won by Oxford, he scored exactly a hundred runs with an average of 20. Very little bowling indeed fell to his share in those games, the reason being that Mr Mitchell was not quite sure whether his action would satisfy the umpires. Umpires' decisions were then apt to vary; in the 1863 match Mr Collins was no-balled for getting his hand above his shoulder.

REV. CANON F. H. GILLINGHAM 1954

GILLINGHAM, CANON FRANK HAY, who died on April 1, aged seventy-seven, was a great personality in the Church and on the cricket field. Born in Tokyo on September 6, 1875, he came to England when eight, gained a place in the Dulwich XIs of 1891 and 1892, and appeared with much distinction for Durham University. When ordained in 1899, he became a curate at Leyton and so qualified for Essex. During this period he showed his love of the game when making his rounds of the parish by joining in street cricket with local boys.

After a few appearances for the second eleven, he first played for the Essex Championship side in 1903, and he appeared whenever his clerical duties permitted until 1928. Altogether he scored 9,942 runs, average 30.49, and brought off 102 catches. Tall and powerfully built, he was a strong believer in hitting the ball hard in front of the wicket, and, though the first to admit that he was not at ease against spin, he dealt firmly with bowlers of pace.

1905

MIDDLESEX v ESSEX

Played at Lord's Monday, Tuesday, Wednesday July 11, 12, 13, 1904. There was a splendid partnership between Gillingham and Perrin, who put on 227 runs. Perrin played a delightful innings, quite free from real blemish. Gillingham and Sewell afterwards punished the bowling severely, stumps being drawn with the total at 443 for seven wickets. Gillingham, in his 201, drove with great power and hit well in front of square leg. His innings was a very fine one.

Mr P. Perrin lbw b Trott 134
Rev. F. H. Gillingham c Bosanquet b Hearne 201

1954

A fine preacher who filled his churches to overflowing, he was appointed Chaplain to the King in 1939. He was also an after-dinner speaker with a wonderful sense of humour; his supremely funny anecdotes, told without the vestige of a smile, frequently convulsed listeners. As Sir Pelham Warner wrote of him in *The Cricketer*, "Gillingham was a man with a charming individuality who exerted a powerful and beneficial influence over people of various types and characteristics. He was a very human being, kind, gentle and understanding, who was the last to condemn. No one ever came to him in trouble without going away comforted. His friends and admirers were numerous indeed."

AND GILLIGAN LED THEM OUT

by Rowland Ryder, 1970

Sussex and England captain E. R. Dexter, discussed the subject of cricket and Christianity with Colin Cowdrey in a wireless broadcast (*Subject for Sunday*, April 1968). Dexter's own view is that Christianity comes into the actual playing of cricket – literally into batting and bowling, "I feel that Christ has an opinion about the use of bouncers and how much you appeal to the umpire, and whether you walk when you've hit it, and whether you are a selfish or an unselfish player." He quoted John Arlott's statement, "If you are to understand Colin Cowdrey you have to understand Colin Cowdrey's Christian faith and the way it affects his life."

Cowdrey himself goes deeply into the subject, "I was in some state of confusion on leaving Oxford as to whether one was justified in giving one's life to cricket. One of the tenets of the whole Christian faith is that life is a service, and could one honestly justify standing at first slip for two days of a Test match and touching the ball three times and then making nought and one and taking a week over it, and then in the evenings having the good fortune to meet with gifted people in other walks of life – perhaps a gifted surgeon who had just saved three lives and worked nine hours a day sweating flesh and blood in a tremendous life of service." Cowdrey recounted that he went to see Cuthbert Bardsley, the present Bishop of Coventry, who was then Bishop of Croydon, for advice. "One of the things he did say was that this [cricketing ability] surely must be one of the gifts that I'd been given, and that if I were to play cricket for a certain number of years then I must give myself a hundred per cent to it."

Cowdrey also made this vividly evocative statement, "Batting in a Test match, the build-up, the waiting for two or three hours at Melbourne, I think that's a picture which comes to mind with 70,000 Australians clamouring for an English wicket, or perhaps two or three wickets fall quickly and you are not the next one in, but the next after that, and the tension is built up, the radio's on in the home and you know that 20 million at home are listening in . . . One is terribly alone. And I think these are the moments when one desperately needs this abiding Christian faith which brings, I think, a mastery of oneself . . . without that feeling I think you are desperately on your own. I think you are in the jungle."

REV. R. H. MOSS 1972
Over Fifty in the County Championship
by E. L. Peake

Unique is the case of the Rev. R. H. Moss. Born on February 24, 1868, his first and only Championship appearance was for Worcestershire v Gloucestershire on May 23–26, 1925. He was thus over fifty-seven years old at the time; the greatest age at which any cricketer has played in a Championship match.

Moss is condemned to anonymity by *Wisden*. He does not merit a mention in the match report, despite making 2 and 0 (dismissed by Parker and Hammond no less), and taking a wicket (Capt. M. A. Green c Root b Moss 54). The scorecard describes him, correctly as Rev. R. H. Moss, but the season's averages show, Also batted: Rev. H. E. Moss 2 and 0. Also bowled Rev. F. H. Moss 3–0–5–1. When he died in 1956, he received no obituary in *Wisden*.

REV. G. W. GILLINGHAM 1954

GILLINGHAM, REV. GEORGE WILLIAM, who died on June 11 after a ministry of 52 years, played cricket for Gentlemen of Worcestershire before World War I. Though never attaining to first-class standards, he was a great cricket enthusiast who did much good work for Worcestershire. When becoming Rector of St Martin's Worcester, he revived and managed the Worcestershire Club and Ground matches, and in 1923 he organised a bazaar which realised £2,300 for the County Club. From 1929 he acted for some seasons as honorary secretary to Worcestershire in order that the secretary, C. F. Walters, could play for the county. During this period when, during the winter the River Severn flooded the county ground at Worcester, Gillingham swam across the ground to gain access to the Pavilion and returned with the account books. He was author of *The Cardinal's Treasure*, a romance of the Elizabethan age, part of the proceeds from which he devoted to the Worcestershire CCC and the RSPCA. When Vicar of St Mark's Coventry, he was for four years tenant of a condemned public house, The Barley Mow, which he transformed into a "Hooligans' Club" where boxing and Bible classes went hand-in-hand.

REV. E. T. KILLICK 1954

KILLICK, THE REVEREND EDGAR THOMAS, who died while taking part in a cricket match between the diocesan clergy of St Albans and Coventry at Northampton on May 18, aged 46, played for Cambridge University, Middlesex and England.

1930
ENGLAND v SOUTH AFRICA
First Test Match

Played at Birmingham, Saturday, Monday, Tuesday, June 15, 17, 18, 1929. On a pitch of very easy pace and devoid of life, a definite result in the First Test match always appeared unlikely and at ten minutes past six on the third day, the game was drawn.

Killick and Duleepsinhji were making their first appearance in a Test match, while splendid all round form in County cricket brought Fender back into the England side. But, if Killick did not actually fail, not one of the three accomplished anything of note.

ENGLAND v SOUTH AFRICA
Second Test Match

Played at Lord's Saturday, Monday, Tuesday, June 29, July 1, 2, 1929. Like that at Birmingham, the Second Test match was drawn, but the cricket proved vastly more interesting. Nothing could have been more sensational than the first half hour's play. Morkel, bowling from the Pavilion end, obtained such pace off the ground that the first three England wickets fell for 18 runs. Killick was bowled middle stump at eight, Hammond caught at second slip and O'Connor bowled first ball.

ENGLAND v SOUTH AFRICA
Third Test Match

Played at Leeds, Saturday, Monday, Tuesday July 13, 15, 16, 1929. The previous England teams not having given entire satisfaction, the younger element failing to rise to the occasion, the Selection Committee brought in Woolley, Bowley and Freeman for O'Connor, Killick and Robins. These changes were all to the good.

1932

MIDDLESEX v WARWICKSHIRE

Played at Lord's, Wednesday, Thursday, Friday August 12, 13, 14, 1931. To a single day's play was this game restricted, the weather turning so unkind that on Thursday the state of the ground precluded any possibility of cricket, while on Friday a heavy and continuous downpour compelled an early abandonment of the contest. The one day, however, resulted in a great triumph for two Middlesex batsmen – Stevens and Killick – who, withstanding the Warwickshire attack for four hours and ten minutes, shared in a first-wicket partnership of 277. Killick went on to beat the highest score he had previously put together – 201 for Cambridge University against Essex in 1929 – and, having accomplished that performance, gave a simple catch to mid-on. Fifth out at 380, he batted in splendid form for nearly five hours and a half, made no mistake, apart from a chance when 106, cut, hit to leg and pulled particularly well and had 18 fours and ten threes as his chief strokes. The drawing of stumps found Middlesex with seven men out and 408 on the board.

Mr G. T. S. Stevens c Smart b Wyatt 117
Rev. E. T. Killick c Kemp-Welch b Foster 206

1954

Curiously, this was the only time he played for the county that season. E. Hendren once described Killick as, "the prettiest forward player since Lionel Palairet". Certainly, there was a grace in his strokeplay and few batsmen executed the off-drive and square-cut with such ease of movement. As a fieldsman he delighted onlookers by his anticipation, swift running and clean picking up of the ball in the deep.

REV. J. M. MARSHALL 1905

REV. J. M. MARSHALL was found drowned in a river in New Zealand in September 1903. In an exhibition match against Lord Hawke's team at Wanganui in the previous season he scored over a hundred.

1904
ENGLISH TEAM v FIFTEEN OF WANGANUI

Played at Wanganui, Saturday, Monday, Tuesday January 3, 5, 6, 1903. The Wanganui fifteen ran Lord Hawke's team to 20 runs on the first innings, but failed badly at their second attempt before Hargreave and Bosanquet. The Englishmen, of whom twelve took part in the match, won by eight wickets.

English Team 140 and 59 for three.
Fifteen of Wanganui 120 and 77.

It seems unlikely that Marshall (who was definitely playing in this match because he is recorded as taking a catch) could have scored over 100 of Wanganui's 120, but is *Wisden* ever wrong?

REV. D. S. SHEPPARD
Five Cricketers of the Year, 1953

Few cricketers at the age of twenty-three have accomplished as much as DAVID STUART SHEPPARD, the Sussex and England opening batsman. Sheppard made his first-class debut in 1947, but not until 1949 did he appear with any regularity. In the next three years he represented Cambridge in three University matches, captaining the side in 1952, appeared in six Tests for England, toured Australia and New Zealand with MCC, scored a Test century against India, played for Gentlemen against the Players at Lord's, obtained over 2,000 runs in two successive seasons, shared in two opening partnerships of over 300, and, finally, headed the first-class batting averages.

Quiet and unassuming, Sheppard for a long time considered giving up regular cricket to concentrate on the Church. He has been a lay preacher in many parts of England. His loss to the game would be unfortunate, but in September it was announced that he had accepted an invitation to captain Sussex for 1953. Thus, for the moment Sheppard remains in cricket.

1957

ENGLAND v AUSTRALIA
Fourth Test Match

At Manchester, July 26, 27, 28, 30, 31, 1956. England won by an innings and 170 runs, with just over an hour to spare and so retained the "Ashes".

The England selectors sprang a surprise when they named Rev. D. S. Sheppard among the twelve from whom the team would be chosen. Sheppard, who had given up regular cricket to take up Holy Orders had played only four innings for Sussex during the season, when selected. One of these was 97 against the Australians at Hove. His previous Test appearance was two years earlier when he captained England against Pakistan. Like nearly every move the Selection Committee made during the season, this one proved fully justified.

A curiosity was that the first five England batsmen were all amateurs, something that had last happened against Australia in 1899 when C. B. Fry, A. C. MacLaren, K. S. Ranjitsinhji, C. L. Townsend and F. S. Jackson were the men concerned. Mutterings about the pitch could be heard that evening, but they rose to full fury the next day. The Australians could still not get the ball to bite as much as they ought to have done and England went gaily on, adding 152 in two hours 11 minutes before being all out for the highest total against Australia since 1948. Sheppard, 59 overnight, completed a chanceless century and batted for five minutes under five hours for 113, which included one six and 15 fours. He drove delightfully and gave not the slightest suggestion of lack of match practice.

1964

MCC Team in Australia and New Zealand, 1962/63

Sheppard helped to win the Second Test with 113 in the second innings, his only century, and he played a number of useful innings which enabled him to become one of four batsmen to complete 1,000 runs on the tour in first-class games. In the early weeks he missed many catches, probably because his reactions were not quick enough following his absence from regular cricket for some years. As he lost his tenseness later in the tour, he improved considerably in the field.

REV. T. H. BELCHER 1920

BELCHER, The REV. THOMAS HAYES, died on November 26 (1919). Born at Faringdon, Berkshire, on September 12, 1847, he was in his seventy-third year. Mr Belcher will always have a place in cricket history. He was the second of the victims to F. C. Cobden's memorable "hat trick" at the finish of the Oxford and Cambridge match in 1870. Of the three players he was the last survivor, S. E. Butler dying in 1903 and W. A. Stewart in 1883. As to his own share in the catastrophe, Mr Belcher, writing in *The Globe* in August 1901 – one of the endless discussions as to the details of the sensational was then being carried on – declared that he was bowled off his leg. To quote his exact words, he said, "Mr Cobden is right in saying that the ball that bowled me was of a good length. It entirely beat me, but it touched my right leg a little below the knee on the inside. Of this I am quite certain, but whether this slight touch turned it on to the wicket I cannot possibly say." Belcher played in the University match only in 1870. He was picked for his bowling and fully justified his selection, taking four wickets for 52 runs and two for 38. He was vicar of Bramley, Basingstoke, Hampshire, from 1893.

REV. R. H. FOWLER 1972

FOWLER, REV. RICHARD HAROLD, who died on October 27, 1970, played in a few matches for Worcestershire in 1921. After taking five Gloucestershire wickets for 33 runs at Stourbridge, he was told that only his cloth had saved him from being no-balled. This doubtless accounted for the brevity of his first-class career.

YORKSHIRE

Yorkshire, the strongest Championship team since the competition began, excites strong emotions among cricket lovers – you either love, like and admire those northern Tykes, or else you think they are too big for their boots and you relish their years of comparative failure since the 1970s. For *Wisden* it has been a great ongoing saga: articles and comment about Yorkshire abound. It would be easy to compile a complete book – or several complete books – of what *Wisden* says about Yorkshire. In the weak years there are articles wondering if the white rose will ever bloom again, and in the strong years people are wondering how Yorkshire can ever be beaten. In the end it is perhaps Yorkshire's never-ending ability to self-destruct that makes them so interesting. Just when everything seems to be fine, something bizarre happens which causes all sorts of unexpected (at least by the Yorkshire committee) difficulties. From Bobby Peel to Geoff Boycott, Yorkshire have had players who have been highly individualistic in their approach to cricket and life, but then so has every other county. Only Yorkshire have made a habit of turning their molehills into a range of mountains. And yet they have produced many of the greatest cricketers of the past 140 years of *Wisden*'s history. How do they do it?

COUNTY OF THE CENTURY
by Philip Bailey, 2000

To prove that the methods of the hare occasionally prevail, Yorkshire have clearly emerged as the county side of the twentieth century. They dominated the first seven decades, winning 26 Championships out of 60, and shared one of the others. Then they went to sleep, but still clearly emerged as the most successful county throughout.

Yorkshire achieved their 1,000th victory since 1900 at Trent Bridge in August 1999. No one else came close to reaching that target. They also lost almost 100 fewer matches than any of their rivals (excluding Durham). In many seasons, especially before the war, there were considerable disparities between the number of fixtures played by different counties. And since the points system has changed frequently, the percentage of wins was the fairest method to determine the century's champion county. But whichever criterion is used, the answer is the same.

Surrey had the second-highest number of wins overall and, on percentages, were just ahead of Kent and Middlesex. Further to the table of post-war success, published in *Wisden* 1996, Surrey

COUNTY CHAMPIONSHIP 1900–1999

		P	W	L	D	T	%W	%L	%D	Titles*
1	Yorkshire	2,331	1,001	351	977	2	42.94	15.05	41.91	26
2	Surrey	2,263	833	450	979	1	36.80	19.88	43.26	10
3	Kent	2,235	819	603	808	5	36.64	26.97	36.15	6
4	Middlesex	2,091	765	491	832	3	36.58	23.48	39.78	10
5	Lancashire	2,315	789	451	1,073	2	34.08	19.48	46.34	6
6	Gloucs	2,179	635	783	759	2	29.14	35.93	34.83	0
7	Essex	2,169	613	631	920	5	28.26	29.09	42.41	6
8	Sussex	2,303	646	715	936	6	28.05	31.04	40.64	0
9	Notts	2,151	593	585	972	1	27.56	27.19	45.18	4
10	Warwickshire	2,141	589	618	933	1	27.51	28.86	43.57	5
11	Hampshire	2,211	576	722	909	4	26.05	32.65	41.11	2
12	Derbyshire	2,105	528	726	850	1	25.08	34.48	40.38	1
13	Worcs	2,157	539	742	874	2	24.98	34.39	40.51	5
14	Northants	1,983	484	688	808	3	24.40	34.69	40.74	0
15	Somerset	2,091	492	812	784	3	23.52	38.83	37.49	0
16	Leics	2,143	493	755	894	1	23.00	35.23	41.71	3
17	Glamorgan	1,781	388	604	789	0	21.78	33.91	44.30	3
18	Durham	141	23	79	39	0	16.31	56.02	27.65	0

* Denotes "outright" titles as Lancashire, Surrey, Middlesex (twice), Yorkshire and Kent have all shared the title. The list totals 87 outright titles, omitting ten cancelled because of wars, and three shared.

have now climbed ahead of Middlesex as the most successful post-war team. Kent's record before then was exceptional. They and Yorkshire were the top two teams in each of the first four decades, even though Kent were not champions at all between the wars.

Over the course of the century, Somerset lost by far the most matches both numerically and (again excluding Durham) by percentage. On draws, the facts support the weather lore: Lancashire were the only county to draw more than 1,000 games. Their nearest rivals in percentage terms were Nottinghamshire (Trent Bridge pitches were once famously flat) and Glamorgan. Five of the top nine in the table will be in the Second Division in 2000.

FIELDING IN 1900
by D. L. A. Jephson, 1901

The success of Yorkshire is due, in a very large degree, to their fielding. There are many fine fields in their side, and an article of this description would be void of all interest if mention were not made of Hirst and Denton, perhaps the finest mid-off and the finest outfield of the year. The one is in front of you, and you may as well attempt to drive through a brick wall as pass those hands of iron; and the other, hovering on the edge of the green circle, has made you run many a three when you were crediting yourself with a four. They are cat-like in their activity; before the bat has struck the ball, by some strange intuition, they divine the direction it will take, and move, whilst the so-called fieldsman – the little mound of earth – stands open-mouthed, watching the ball go by. All through the season their catching has been good and their ground work perhaps better; their fielding has been full of life, full of vigour.

FIFTY YEARS OF YORKSHIRE COUNTY
by Lord Hawke, 1932

There would seem to be little doubt that the origin of the Yorkshire County Cricket Club is to be found in the series of matches between Sheffield and Nottingham which began in 1771. Though there were only 26 of such games, the last one being played in 1860, the fact that leading players of both counties took part in them gave to Sheffield the sort of right that is due to custom of being regarded as the home of the game in Yorkshire.

They were, by the way, evidently keen enough on the game in my county in those days, as the first match, in 1771, began at 9 a.m.! And, in 1784, in the York rules, I see that a fine of 3d was levied on any member who was not within sight of the wickets each morning before the Minster strikes five o'clock. Report has it that one of the Notts players was in the habit of rising before daybreak and riding on horseback all the way to Sheffield to play!

Nearly all these matches, however, were played for money – that of 1800, for example, for 200 guineas. In that year the second match took place on November 3, 4 and 5! These early games were played at Sheffield on Darnall Ground, the Hyde Park Ground, and at the present ground at Bramall Lane, where the first county match was Yorkshire v Sussex in 1855.

In the first Sheffield–Notts match at Bramall Lane there played for Sheffield (totals: Nottingham 130 and 93 against Sheffield 146 and 78 for six, Sheffield winning by four wickets) M. J. Ellison whom I succeeded in 1902 as President. Ellison held a record which must be very bad to beat, viz., that he shot grouse on the first day of the grouse-shooting season for 70 successive years. He was the second President of our County Club, a post he occupied from 1863 to 1898. Mr T. R. Barker was the first President in 1863, though I understand he never attended a meeting.

1911
by Sydney H. Pardon

Writing at the end of the year I am quite in the dark as to what the Advisory Committee will do with regard to Yorkshire's proposal to give points in county matches to sides leading on the first innings. Personally I hope the idea will not be entertained. No doubt it answers very well in the Minor Counties' "two days" matches, but I think that, especially in a dry season, it would encourage slow and laborious batting. I do not for a moment think that the salvation of County cricket will be found in a more complicated system of reckoning points. The end to aim at is to play every match on its own merits, let the final result be what it may.

1925
by Sydney H. Pardon

I have no wish to dwell at any length on the disagreement between Middlesex and Yorkshire that last season so disturbed the usually cheerful atmosphere of our cricket. For one reason I have only a dim idea of what led Middlesex to say they would not play Yorkshire in 1925. I heard no end of gossip, but scarcely any exact details. Still, one knows that the match that mainly caused the trouble was a thoroughly unpleasant one. The Sheffield public – false to all their old traditions of good sportsmanship – barracked for three days in most unseemly fashion and Butt, the umpire, felt it his duty to report Waddington to Lord's. Waddington duly apologised for his loss of temper and self-control, and there, so far as he was concerned, the matter ended. The quarrel was healed up, and in the coming season the two counties will meet as before. The trouble in Yorkshire cricket seems to have been confined to a minority of the players – from what I have been told not more than four. In this connection some remarks made by Lord Hawke at the Yorkshire annual meeting were very significant indeed. Speaking of individual doings for the county last summer he said Macaulay ought to have been in the MCC's team to Australia, and that it was entirely his own fault he was not chosen. To that stern condemnation not a word need be added.

YORKSHIRE v MIDDLESEX

Played at Sheffield, Saturday, Monday, Tuesday July 5, 7, 8, 1924. This will always be a match of unhappy memories. It led to no end of ill-feeling and was one of the chief causes of Middlesex coming to the decision – afterwards revoked – that they would not play Yorkshire in 1925. For some reason the Sheffield crowd, forgetting their old reputation for good sportsmanship, barracked more or less persistently all through the game, making the atmosphere almost unbearable. Under such conditions cricket could not be played in a proper spirit. Some fine work was done by both sides, but no one enjoyed the match.

1955

by J. M. Kilburn

There can be no doubt that much of the spirit inculcated into the Yorkshire side during the 1890s came directly from the leadership of Lord Hawke. It was his declared ambition to win for Yorkshire cricket not only admiration but respect, and he took some drastic steps to ensure that his teams became acceptable everywhere for their conduct both on the field and off. Lord Hawke could never be classed as an outstanding player. Experience gave him useful-ness as a batsmen in the lower half of the order and in his younger days he was certainly not a handicap to his team in the field, but other qualities than playing ability were needed to raise him to the eminence he attained on the fields and in the councils of cricket.

Those qualities were an abiding affection for his cause, which was Yorkshire cricket, and a happy understanding of the men who played under his captaincy. As a captain Lord Hawke was a martinet; in course of time firmness could have been seen as obstinacy, depending upon the viewpoint, and his major interest tended to become paramount. Yet there can be no denying that in developing Yorkshire cricket Lord Hawke did rare service to cricket in its widest sphere. He set standards that have survived him and he took cricket to Australia, India, Canada, United States, South Africa, West Indies and the Argentine. He was cap-tain of Yorkshire from 1883 to 1910 and President of the club from 1898 until his death in 1938.

The Sellers Era

It was not, of course, in the mere possession of individuals beyond the ordinary that Yorkshire found their strength. Great players do not necessarily establish great teams. Yorkshire had great players in the 1930s and they established a great team primarily because they were prepared to devote their special talents to a common cause. The character of the side became something more than the agglomerated characters of the members. Yorkshire cricket given to be the over-riding concern of every player and the personal achievement was the common satisfaction. The origin of this outlook lay far back in history but its development, or its renaissance, at least, was the contribution of A. B. Sellers who took over the captaincy in 1933 and held office for 15 seasons. Perhaps Lord Hawke did more than Sellers in that there was more to do, but neither Lord Hawke nor any other Yorkshire leader brought greater devotion or persistent efficiency to the task in hand.

Sellers drew loyalty because he gave loyalty. He maintained unswervingly the principle that team interests were paramount, and his principles were so clearly illustrated that they could not escape the notice of established player or newcomer. The Yorkshire of Brian Sellers' time would have been unmistakable in multi-coloured caps and disguised by beards. They carried their character on to every field they visited.

REBUILDING YORKSHIRE CRICKET
by A. B. Sellers, 1948

What's happened to Yorkshire? I heard on many occasions during last season. They aren't the cricketing machine that we knew before the war. I think everyone was inclined to agree, but when one stops to think for one moment and looks back two years, the answer is very clear.

In two playing seasons the county that won the Championship seven times out of nine between 1931–39, and once again in the first season after the war, has lost seven of its regular members, and of those seven members six were international players: H. Sutcliffe, H. Verity, M. Leyland, A. Mitchell, A. Wood and W. Barber. No team can stand a blow such as that in so short a time and be expected to be able to rebuild and continue to win the Championship.

Now another blow has befallen the team this year. That great match-winning bowler, Bill Bowes, has announced his retirement. It leaves a very big gap which will require a great deal of filling.

Are Yorkshire going down never to rise again? I should say NOT by a very long way. A trip behind the scenes and a talk with a very alive secretary, J. H. Nash, is well worth anyone's time. You will soon find out for yourself how Yorkshire discover and train her reserves, and as a rule the selected reserves are good enough for any county. Proof of that can be seen by the number of Yorkshire-born and trained players who have played and are playing in many other county teams today. The sole reason for this is that they couldn't find a regular place in the county team. Only eleven men can do this, and rather than restrict such men the County Committee allow them to qualify for other counties who require their services.

To gain a White Rose – the ambition of everyone who plays cricket in the county – is a very hard and long struggle. It begins at an early age, round about fourteen, when perhaps the boy catches the eye of an old player or a Committee member. Don't laugh at the mention of a Committee member, because the members of the Yorkshire County Cricket Club Committee are very enthusiastic members. They represent various districts throughout the county and are elected by the county members in their own districts, who expect them to help find the young players who will eventually step into the first team.

The young boy who has been noticed is watched very carefully and during the early winter he will be asked to attend special practices, under the county coach, Arthur Mitchell. These practices begin in January and are held twice a week up to the middle of April.

Everyone who attends them is paid return railway fares plus ten shillings out-of-pocket expenses. As these practices progress the youngsters gain much knowledge and experience. The better ones continue to be asked to attend right up to mid-April. At this period the regular members are called up for ten days' intensive practice. During these ten days the youngsters practise with the regular players and gain further knowledge. After these practices are over the young players go back to their clubs to begin their season. It is from these players that the second team is formed which makes the background and nursery for the first eleven.

We do not chop and change our first team about more than we can help. When we think we have the right man, in he goes to the first team and he stays there to make his name. Of course there have been misfits and mistakes, but not many. When he has settled down and made his place secure the great day arrives – the day he receives his county cap. When that day does come it is almost the end of the hard road, but not quite, because he knows that he must maintain his form to keep in the side, always remembering that other men are trying to do just what he did.

It is interesting to note that during the years 1932–39 the average number of men who represented the county during any one season was 19. Since the war the average has risen to 24–25. This requires very little explanation. We are rebuilding and looking ahead five or more years.

1956

Young Hutton was feeling in form, so after he had played himself in he decided to cut a rising ball outside the off-stump. Remember that he was fresh to the Yorkshire scene and policies. He actually lay back and cut hard and swiftly, with cavalier flourish. He cut under the ball by an inch, and it sped bang into the wicketkeeper's gloves. And Mitchell, from the other end of the pitch, looked hard at Hutton and said, "That's no **** use!" This was probably Hutton's true baptism, cleansing him of all vanity and lusts for insubstantial pageantry and temporal glory.

1968

WARWICKSHIRE v YORKSHIRE

At Birmingham, August 16, 17, 18, 1967. Drawn. This was the match with tremendous repercussions. The last hour and 40 minutes, in which Warwickshire had to score 142 to win and failed by nine runs, led to allegations of delaying tactics against Yorkshire and to the eventual censuring of their captain, Close. The last phase was in violent contrast to the urgency of the second day when Warwickshire just wrested the lead by four runs. Yorkshire bowled only 24 overs, and, in the last 15 minutes, during which they left the field to the umpires and the batsmen during a shower, sent down two overs, one from Trueman containing two no-balls and three bouncers. Before the acrimonious end, big hitting by Jameson – who hit a six over the bowler's head – and Amiss had kept Warwickshire up with the clock.

Yorkshire 238 (Hampshire 102, Boycott 57; Cartwright three for 46) **and 145** (Cartwright four for 26, Cook four for 66).

Warwickshire 242 (Amiss 53, Ibadulla 52; Nicholson six for 50) **and 133** for five (Amiss 46).

by J. M. Kilburn

To prevent Warwickshire from scoring 142 runs in one hundred minutes in the fourth innings Yorkshire indulged in blatant time-wasting tactics which brought down the wrath of spectators and disapproval of the critics. Report of this conduct raised an enquiry by the County Advisory executive committee which resulted in a public censure for the team with full responsibility laid on the Yorkshire captain.

[Close subsequently also lost the England captaincy.]

In the meantime a batting collapse brought a defeat by Essex at Scarborough and though Sussex were beaten at Eastbourne at the time of The Oval Test, Yorkshire reached their last two fixtures needing 14 points to be sure of finishing at the top of the table. With outright victories at Middlesbrough and Harrogate they achieved their purpose and confirmed their own belief that they were the strongest county side of the year.

1974

by Sir Neville Cardus

On the whole and naturally enough, Rhodes distrusted the romantic gesture. One day in conversation with him, I deplored the absence in modern cricket of the cut. "But it were never a business stroke," he maintained.

While he was actively engaged in the game he was not a man given to affability. He was known as a natterer on the field; and to natter in the North of England means to talk naggingly, most to oneself, with the intention of being overheard. At Old Trafford in the 1930s Lancashire reached a total of 500 against Yorkshire. The Lancashire captain, Leonard Green, was about to take the bowling of Rhodes when the score was 499. Green was sure in his mind that a total of 500 would never again, or not for decades, be achieved by Lancashire against Yorkshire. He therefore determined that come what may he would himself score the five hundredth run. So he blocked a ball from Rhodes, then ran like the wind. The ball was picked up by Emmott Robinson at silly-point, and hurled to the bowler's end, where it struck Rhodes on the wrist even as Green got home by the skin of his teeth. And in all the scurry and excitement Wilfred was heard to mutter, while he retrieved Robinson's violent throw, "There's somebody runnin' up and down this wicket. Ah don't know who it is, but there's somebody runnin' up and down this wicket."

TO BE DISLIKED AGAIN
by Roy Hattersley, 2002

On a warm afternoon in the late summer of 1946, my father – normally the most reticent of men – danced a little jig on the promenade in Morecambe. He had, as was his invariable summer habit, bought an evening paper to find out the cricket scores. To his delight he discovered that Yorkshire, already the county champions, had lost to Hampshire. He addressed my mother and me in a voice of triumph. "At least they haven't gone all season without being beaten." It was then that I realised that the Yorkshire County Cricket Club attracted the animosity that goes with near invincibility. With any luck, we will soon begin to attract it again.

. . . In the years that followed the war, we Yorkshire members grew used to success. Indeed, in the 1950s, when the team began to fail, we felt that the natural order of things had been disrupted. In 1958, when we came 11th in the Championship, Johnny Wardle, an ingenious spin bowler, prehensile close fielder and irresponsibly entertaining batsman, was sacked for defending himself from committee criticism in a newspaper. I attended the annual meeting with the intention of causing trouble about his treatment. The chairman welcomed members to the "AGM of the champion county" and added, "We know which the champion county is, whichever team happens to be at the top of the table at the end of any one year." After that, no criticism was possible.

After the 1950s the county recovered but continued in its profligate ways. Ray Illingworth left for Leicestershire – and became a highly successful England captain – following an argument about his contract. The accusation was that he was disloyal because he did not regard a year with Yorkshire as better than three with any other county. Brian Close, who led the last Championship-winning team, moved on to Somerset. Bill Athey went to Gloucestershire, and dozen of other players, less talented but highly able, drifted away. For a time it seemed that nothing could go right for Yorkshire. After the pride of a century was forgotten and an overseas player recruited, two of the world's greatest batsmen wore the white rose for a single season. Neither Sachin Tendulkar nor Richie Richardson was a success. Yorkshire remained in the wilderness.

Perhaps, even in the early 1990s, Yorkshire were still suffering from the repercussions of "the Boycott affair". Whatever the merits of the argument – Boycott versus the committee – the damage that the conflict did to the county was immense. In 1978, members were asked to vote on what some thought were rival propositions: endorse sacking Boycott as captain or ask the committee to resign. I voted "yes" to both, hoping that a clearout would put the damaging disputes behind us. It dragged on for year after year, making life impossible for some of the best Yorkshire cricketers of the age, John Hampshire, captain in impossible circumstances, amongst them.

It was all desperately different from 1938 when, as well as winning the Championship, Yorkshire provided five players for the final Test at The Oval. More than half of England's highest-ever total of 903 for seven was made by Len Hutton, with his record-beating 364, and Maurice Leyland, whose century he over-shadowed. Hutton, the greatest English batsman of his time, remains the example of what Yorkshire cricketers should be.

Genius is not enough. Determination and dedication are equally essential. When I read of Yorkshire fast bowlers who worry about the strains of playing two Championship matches in a week, I wonder if they recall that Hutton lost two inches of bone from his arm in a wartime accident, came back to first-class cricket and almost immediately faced Ray Lindwall and Keith Miller.

Not all the Yorkshire fast bowlers whine about being over-worked. Much to his credit, Matthew Hoggard, asked if he had fears about touring India, replied that he wanted to play for England and therefore had never considered refusing to go. Suddenly – partly owing to their academy and the new coaching regime – Yorkshire have a surfeit of fast bowlers and enough batting strength to make a second successive Championship a strong prospect. I still regret that Darren Lehmann, the star batsman of 2001's success, is Australian, and I wish that Michael Vaughan had been born in Yorkshire as well as being a clear candidate to succeed Nasser Hussain as England's captain. But the clock cannot be turned back – except in one particular. There is a real hope that Yorkshire will become so successful that we are really disliked again.

FIVE CRICKETERS OF THE YEAR 2003
by David Hopps

Yorkshiremen were quick to hail Vaughan as one of their own, although had the ancient tradition of fielding only players born within the county boundary been maintained a few years longer, he might easily have been representing the old foe, Lancashire. MICHAEL PAUL VAUGHAN was born at Salford's Hope Hospital on October 29, 1974, and lived in Manchester to the age of nine, when the family moved to Sheffield. Encouraged by his elder brother, he began netting at the Yorkshire League club Sheffield Collegiate, under the guidance of their junior coach, Jack Bethel, and Yorkshire age-group cricket quickly followed. It was while he was hitting a ball on the outfield at Abbeydale Park, during the interval of a county match, that Yorkshire's coach, the taciturn, gentle Doug Padgett, was stirred to put down his cup of tea on the pavilion balcony and wander on to the field to jot down his name. When Padgett heard that Vaughan had been born in Lancashire, he could barely conceal his dismay, but Yorkshire's junior ranks were relatively enlightened and Vaughan was repeatedly assured that the home-grown-only policy would soon be relaxed to encompass players raised within the county. So it did, although not before he had been invited to nets at both Lancashire and Northamptonshire (a perpetual scavenger of unwanted Yorkshire talent).

Vaughan's presence in the Yorkshire side was never likely to bring protests. Polite and eager to learn, he won over even the crabbiest defenders of a faith that seemed even more outdated once Headingley's doors had been flung open to overseas players. He proved adept, as he remains to this day, at filtering advice from many sources. From Martyn Moxon he understood something of the opening batsman's art. From David Byas came the value of discipline. He watched Michael Bevan, who had two seasons with Yorkshire, and wondered at his ability to pace an innings with such calm.

An upbringing on Headingley's inconsistent pitches is not easy even for a batsman of high pedigree. Vaughan does not cavil at suggestions that it slowed his entry into the England side. But equally he credits life at Headingley with toughening him mentally, teaching him with every rogue ball and waspish comment from the crowd that cricket did not bestow its favours easily.

2005

With David Byas back at Headingley as director of cricket and Craig White installed as captain, Yorkshire began 2004 confident that they had the know-how and the playing staff to make a big impression. They were wrong, and the club endured their worst season in 12 years.

The goal of promotion in both Championship and one-day league was missed, and in the Championship it was not even close . . .

POLITICS, ECONOMICS
AND CRICKET

In 1864, cricket and politics only mixed inasmuch as the President of MCC was likely to be a Privy Councillor, and on first-name terms with most of the House of Lords. If the Church of England was the Tory party at prayer, then MCC was the Tory party at play. Even cricket and economics merged only when professional cricketers began wrestling with the shackles of a paternalistic cricketing economy founded on the feudal traditions of the rural communities where the game was born. The Nottinghamshire strike of 1881 was an early example of professional cricketers trying to flex their muscles, but *Wisden*, even though founded by a professional cricketer, tended to take the establishment view on everything, and the establishment view was to brush as much as possible under the carpet.

But times change, and with it editorial policy. The difference in attitude between 1882 ("No good purpose would be served by entering into the details of a dispute which caused Nottinghamshire to take a back seat among the cricketing counties in 1881") and 2002, when Mihir Bose's thorough account of the match-fixing scandals pulled no punches, is complete. Even in 1937, in *Wisden*'s obituarist's brief reference to the death of King George V, there is a sense of hierarchy and obeisance which is alien to us today. Now even *Wisden* takes the common man's viewpoint from time to time, and is all the better for it.

The change came in the Sixties, when two events served to take the power away from the authorities and into the hands of players, spectators and press. The first was the abolition of the distinction between amateur and professional cricketers, when both Gentlemen and Players became "cricketers", and the second was the D'Oliveira affair, which once and for all showed that sport and politics have to mix, however uneasily they may come together.

NOTTINGHAMSHIRE 1882

No good purpose would be served by entering into the details of a dispute which caused Nottinghamshire to take a back seat among the cricketing counties in 1881. The subject has been worn threadbare, and however individual opinions may differ, one feeling is common and paramount with all lovers of the noble game – a feeling of deep regret that by any possibility a dispute could have arisen to bring about such deplorable results.

LANCASHIRE v NOTTINGHAMSHIRE

Played at Old Trafford, June 2, 3, 1881. With substitutes for seven of the best players of Notts, no other ending to this match could have been expected than the one attained – an easy victory for the home team.

Lancashire 239 and 5 for none.
Nottinghamshire 67 and 175.

MIDDLESEX v NOTTINGHAMSHIRE

Played at Lord's, June 9, 10, 1881. There was but a meagre attendance at this match. The cold, showery and unseasonable weather had much to do with it, but the composition of the sides was the principal reason of its unattractiveness. Owing to the unfortunate dispute between the Notts Committee and seven of the principal Notts players, the visiting eleven were not in the least representative, and Middlesex were not nearly up to their full strength. At 3.30 on the second day Middlesex had won the match by 51 runs.

Middlesex 107 and 128.
Nottinghamshire 68 and 116.

NOTTINGHAMSHIRE v SURREY

Played at Trent Bridge Ground, June 13, 14, 15, 1881. Owing to a disagreement between the Players and the Nottingham executive, neither Morley, Shaw, Barnes, Selby, Flowers, Shrewsbury, nor Scotton, took part in this match.

Nor did they for the rest of the season.

1936

H.M. KING GEORGE V died at Sandringham on January 20. As Duke of Cornwall, when Prince of Wales, His Majesty was ground landlord of Kennington Oval, and remained Patron of the Surrey club until his death. King George was also Patron of MCC, and the book *Lord's And MCC* by Lord Harris and F. S. Ashley-Cooper, published in 1914, was dedicated by gracious permission to His Majesty.

He habitually visited Lord's when Colonial teams were playing against England, and on such occasions the match was invariably interrupted in order that all the players and umpires could be presented to His Majesty in front of the pavilion, an informal ceremony which the spectators watched with keen interest marked by expressions of loyalty.

1946

by Hubert Preston

While we have Australia emphasising the value of cricket in cementing the brotherhood of all countries in the British Empire and the imperative desire to maintain the happy gestures always apparent when England and Australia take the field in the keenest of Test matches, the Government cannot see that entertainment tax charged on gate receipts, not on profits, of a match is a heavy drag on county cricket, besides handicapping the organisations responsible for the international fixtures which mean so much for the general welfare of Great Britain and our various Commonwealth visitors – Australia, South Africa, New Zealand, West Indies and India. This continuous drain on revenue becomes all the more serious now when all the countries face the heavy cost of renovating their grounds, rebuilding blitzed pavilions and stands, with improved accommodation necessary to meet the requirements of the large crowds which are certain to assemble. True, the Chancellor of the Exchequer has reduced the tax on some outdoor sports, a concession partly turned by cricket clubs to the benefit of the paying public. We may hope that more may be done in this direction, so helping the clubs which foster cricket as a game for recreative amusement and not for financial gain.

CENTURIES BY LICENCE 1951
by Hubert Preston

Cricket functions are renowned for the high quality of the speeches they usually produce. After spending a lifetime in the game I naturally expect something brilliant and witty, and it was therefore most appropriate from my point of view that the speakers at the John Wisden & Co. Ltd. Centenary luncheon in May lived up to the high tradition. This was a memorable occasion. Mr Oliver Lyttelton, in his happiest vein, when referring to the West Indies team, said, "I have it on the authority of no less a person than Mr Harold Wilson (President of the Board of Trade) that, if they won too many matches in this country, he would have seriously to consider setting up a working party to examine the low productivity of British batsmen and bowlers. And that might be followed by the setting up of a development council, and even the nationalisation of cricket itself. I warn West Indies that if they come again in a few years' time they may find that centuries will only be scored with a licence, and that maidens will only be obtained with a coupon."

Of this almanack Mr Lyttelton said, "Within *Wisden*'s well-known covers lie the records of our national game; and those who, like myself, turn its pages in a spirit of escapism can see in their mind's eye many of the beautiful grounds, some of them lying below the gleaming spires of our cathedrals or the smoking chimneys of our industrial life. We know that as long as we have the spirit and tradition of this game and allow them to endure, change and decay which we may discern in other nations will touch us only lightly with their dread fingers."

To Mr Harold Wilson fell the task of proposing the toast of "This Wonderful Century". He confessed that he was no cricketer himself, but he remarked, "I am a Yorkshireman, and cricket is never far from a Yorkshireman's thoughts." Then he amused us with an account of the last time he played cricket. He said it was in Moscow when he was there for trade talks with the Russians. "There was one Sunday afternoon, during a lull in the negotiations, when my delegation repaired to some woods not far from Moscow. A few weeks afterwards, following the breakdown of the discussions, the Moscow Press, who seem to have observed our innocent pastime, came out with an account of the 'orgies and strange pirouettes by the lakeside of the English delegation'." Continuing his reminiscence, Mr Wilson told this story, "My second over was interrupted by a gentleman from NKVD or Ogpu, who was appointed to follow us around and see that we came to no harm. He stood in the middle of the pitch and remonstrated with us in a very long Russian speech which we understood came to this – that we could not do that there there! He was supported by two men who came up on horseback with rifles. I persuaded him, after some negotiation, to take up his position at square leg, out of the way of even my bowling. The episode closed with the NKVD man's failure to make any attempt to catch a ball – and after that my opinion of the Russian secret police fell even lower." Mr Wilson suggested that the incident should be recorded in *Wisden* as the "only case of a catch missed at square leg by a member of the NKVD off an off-spinner by a visiting British minister".

CRICKET IN ETHIOPIA 1965

Perhaps the day may not be far distant when Ethiopia will be challenging England and Australia to Test matches. Until a few months ago cricket was unknown in that vast country. An Australian doctor resident there, Dr R. H. J. Hamlin, put forward the idea that it would be a good thing for morale if someone from Australia could go there and introduce the game. So W. A. Oldfield, who holds the wicketkeeping record for Tests between England and Australia with 90 victims in 38 matches, spent a month converting the natives to cricket. In that time he taught the game at four schools. He brought with him several complete sets of cricket gear, including bats, balls, pads, gloves and coir matting. The matting was laid over couch grass and the native boys took so readily to a game completely strange to them that before Oldfield left they played a charity match in which at the age of 66 he took part. The highlight of Bert Oldfield's visit was a 20-minute audience with the Emperor Haile Selassie, who accepted a bat for competition between the schools, two of which have English headmasters, presented by Sir Robert Menzies as a gesture of goodwill from Australia to Ethiopia.

PRIME MINISTERS AT CRICKET 1965
by Norman Preston

Sir Robert Menzies, Prime Minister of Australia, is a familiar figure at Test matches in his own country and he generally makes a special effort to be present at Lord's when Australia meet England. Last year, with the Prime Ministers' Conference taking place in London in mid-July, Sir Robert watched the Third Test at Headingley and had the good fortune to see Australia gain a splendid victory in the only match in the series brought to a definite conclusion. Sir Alec Douglas-Home, who made his name as a cricketer at Eton and for Middlesex when he was Lord Dunglass, paid a brief visit to the Old Trafford Test, as did his successor, Mr Harold Wilson. Another Prime Minister, Mr Ian Smith, of Rhodesia, went to Lord's in September when the Mashonaland County Districts played Cross Arrows.

SIR ALEC DOUGLAS-HOME 1967
by Norman Preston

Cricket is certainly fortunate in this vital year with the structure of the first-class game in England in the balance to have such a compelling personality as Sir Alec Douglas-Home in its most important office of all, that of President of MCC. He alone of all of the Prime Ministers of England has played first-class cricket. At Eton, as Lord Dunglass, he played in the XI for two years, making top score, 66, against Harrow in 1922 when he also played for the Lord's Schools against The Rest. A medium-paced bowler and capable batsman, he played for Oxford University and is a Harlequin, but did not gain a Blue. He also played for Middlesex and in 1926/27 went on MCC's tour to South America under the captaincy of Sir Pelham Warner. The only other Prime Minister who became President of MCC was Lord Baldwin, in 1938. In those days the Committee met at four and took tea at half-past, a very different state of affairs compared with the many arduous all-day meetings of the present time.

THEN AND NOW 1951
BY R. C. ROBERTSON-GLASGOW

Were we happier then than now? Philosophers since the world began have asked and been asked that question in vain. So how can mere cricketers answer it? All I can say is that we were happy in our cricket, happy as only those can be who laughed and sweated, loved and strove, quarrelled and were reconciled, got the softest bed and the best breakfast for 10s. 6d., and, at the advice of immortal Mrs Beeton, ate "Christmas Pudding (Rich), sufficient for eight to nine persons, at 1s 10d."

THE D'OLIVEIRA CASE 1969
by Michael Melford

The bitterness engendered by the sequence of events leading up to the cancellation of MCC's proposed tour of South Africa only six weeks before the scheduled starting date made a sad end to the 1968 English season.

Almost from the moment that England walked off the field at The Oval with a rare victory over Australia to their credit, English cricket was caught up in a whirlpool of acrimony and political argument such as it can seldom have known before. The culmination, on September 17, was the refusal by the South African Prime Minister, Mr John Vorster, to accept Basil D'Oliveira, a Cape Coloured, as a member of the MCC team, and the MCC committee's consequent cancellation of the tour.

Since D'Oliveira came successfully into English cricket, and even before he first played for England in 1966, it had been evident that a delicate situation might arise if he were selected for this tour of his native country. However, what appeared to be a relatively simple problem of whether he was acceptable or not had been greatly complicated when the time came, especially by his original omission from the team and the outcry which greeted it.

When the New Zealand Rugby Board were refused permission to bring their Maoris to South Africa in 1967 by Mr Vorster's predecessor, Dr Verwoerd, they cancelled the tour with so little rancour that it was soon being replanned for 1970 with the ban removed. Cricket, however, ever more exposed to publicity, had to endure charges and recrimination of a passion which resounded far outside the sporting world.

Not until December, when, at a special general meeting of MCC the Committee defeated three resolutions put forward by dissident members, was relief in sight from a period of unpleasantness which must have been a nightmare to the ordinary sensitive lover of cricket.

THE SOUTH AFRICAN DILEMMA 1983
by John Woodcock

It was ironic, some thought, that Lamb should be acceptable for England but not the 15 Englishmen, captained by Graham Gooch, who toured South Africa, Lamb's home country, in the spring of 1982 and were disqualified from Test cricket for three years for having done so. Having had their submission for re-entry into the Test fold persistently rejected, despite meeting in every detail the original conditions for this to happen, South Africa have run out of patience and decided that only with the aid of a cheque book can they give the game there the stimulus of international competition which it needs. They are, accordingly, offering cricketers the chance to become mercenaries. By the end of 1982 a team of Sri Lankans (the equivalent, perhaps of Sri Lanka's second eleven) had been slipped into South Africa, there, at the expense of their cricket careers at home, to earn more money in a few weeks than they could normally do in a lifetime.

There are, inevitably, unattractive aspects to this . . . Although the Englishmen who went to South Africa (12 of them had won Test caps, all except Amiss within the previous 18 months) were not in breach of the Gleneagles Agreement as it is interpreted by the British government (they would have been, of course, had they been an "official" team) they must have known that there would be repercussions. Five of the party had only recently returned from the England tour of India, which Mrs Gandhi had threatened to prohibit because of the connections of two of them (Boycott and Cook) with cricket in South Africa. It was hardly surprising, when Gooch, Boycott, Emburey, Lever and Underwood turned up in Johannesburg in March, that the Indians felt let down. In the autumn of 1981 the Test and County Cricket Board had warned, by letter, all county cricketers that if they went as members of a team to South Africa (the distinction between going collectively and to coach was clearly drawn) they might have to pay for it.

The Prime Minister's View

In the event, the reaction to their unheralded arrival in South Africa was little short of hysterical. Although they had widespread public support, the English players became, overnight, pawns in a fiercely political game. Predictably, the cricket boards of both India and Pakistan, guided by their governments, threatened to call off their forthcoming visits to England should they be expected to play against the English "rebels". One English county, Northamptonshire, so feared the financial consequences of such a cancellation that they called for a life ban, no less, on the offending players. The Prime Minister, on the other hand, refused to condemn them. Speaking in Parliament, Mrs Thatcher said, "We do not have the power to prevent any sportsmen or women from visiting South Africa or anywhere else. If we did, we would no longer be a free country." Trapped in the maelstrom, the TCCB, by imposing a three-year ban, "to preserve international multi-racial cricket", bowed to political pressures to the consternation not only of the players but also of the average cricket follower.

In politics, which this was, even a week is a long time. Three years is an eternity, as it is in a cricketer's career. In time the players appealed for some remission of their sentence. But again politics took over. When the West Indians were asked how they would view it if the players' suspensions were to be reduced from three years to two, they withheld their approval. This although, less than a month before, the ICC had agreed "unanimously" that on no account should one country be allowed to influence the team selection of another.

If that was not hypocritical, what is?

1997

The former Government minister John Redwood, who challenged John Major for the Conservative Party leadership in 1995, led a team of "Eurosceptics" to a five-wicket win over a team of "Europhiles", captained by Lord Archer, at Burton's Court, London.

A GAME IN SHAME 2001
by Mihir Bose

Companies such as Singer and Pepsi, American but with extensive interests in south Asia, saw the marketing advantages of being associated with subcontinental cricket, and sponsored many of these mini-series. Television companies, in particular Rupert Murdoch's Star, were also keen to reach this new economic group. It is estimated that every second person watching cricket in the world is an Indian, and their insatiable appetite for the one-day game since 1983 has created a market worth cultivating. As Justice Malik Mohammad Qayyum pointed out in his inquiry into match-fixing, submitted to the Pakistan government in 1999, "With the massive influx of money and sheer increase in the number of matches played, cricket has become a business." It was a business, however, that was run like a private members' club.

Not surprisingly, the game's new economic power stimulated the ambitions of Asia's cricket administrators. Our second incident, in the spring of 1996, provided the spur. It happened in the foyer of Taj Bengal, the luxurious Calcutta hotel just opposite the city's zoo, and gathered there were the subcontinent's leading administrators. The World Cup, which was just about to start in the subcontinent, had been thrown into chaos by the refusal of the Australians, for security reasons, to play their group matches in Sri Lanka. The television and sponsorship deals that the Asians had made for the World Cup, which would eventually bring them a profit in excess of $US75 million, were in jeopardy, and the game's governing body, the International Cricket Council, seemed powerless to act. It was against this background that Ana Punchihewa, President of the Sri Lankan board, turned to Jagmohan Dalmiya, the Indian convenor of the World Cup organising committee, and said, "We should have an Asian as the next chairman of the International Cricket Council."

Dalmiya picked up the baton and ran his election campaign as if it was an American presidential race, energetically wooing the ICC Associate Members. But despite winning a simple majority in two ballots, he found the old, established members reluctant to accept him. A bitter power struggle, essentially brown versus white (and black), saw England, Australia, New Zealand and West Indies ranged against the subcontinent. It was so vicious that the scars have never healed. The Asian countries resented the grudging acceptance of them by England and Australia; the old powers felt that the new kids on the block were not following the game's gentlemanly ways.

"There was, is, a power struggle in international cricket," one highly placed ICC source admitted, "and the Asian countries are resentful of England, the old colonial power, but then the sub-continent has not helped matters by being very defensive about match-fixing. We have known for years that match-fixing goes on, helped by the fact that betting is illegal and in the hands of criminals there. But in the past, whenever the matter has been raised, they have said we are cricket administrators, not cops. Then a clean-cut white South African, Hansie Cronje, was caught in the net, the game changed and everyone has had to come clean."

2005

Yorkshire gave a trial to Ismail Dawood, a twenty-seven-year-old keeper who had done the rounds elsewhere but, at Scarborough on July 21, made history by becoming the first British-born (Dewsbury, indeed) Asian to play Championship cricket for Yorkshire. That built on an earlier breakthrough, when Ajmal Shahzad, a nippy eighteen-year-old seam bowler from Bradford, played in the totesport League game against Worcestershire. Shahzad would have been given further opportunities if he had not been laid low with a bad back.

It therefore came as a surprise when in October Terry Rooney, the Labour MP for Bradford North, accused Yorkshire of "deep-rooted, embedded racism" during a parliamentary debate on social cohesion. The comments caused outrage at the club: if Rooney's view had ever been accurate, it certainly looked out of date in 2004.

1963

BY L. E. S. GUTTERIDGE

I have a catalogue issued by A. J. Gaston in 1899 of the library of T. Padwick. A set (1864–1898) of the Almanack was advertised for £10. One of the best cricket book catalogues ever produced was that of A. Maurice & Co., of Covent Garden. It was issued in 1909 and is itself a rare item.

It has no set for sale, but lists the rarer *Wisdens* at 5s. each. Gaston issued a further general catalogue of cricket books in 1925 and has a bound set (1864–1924) available, at fifty guineas. Sotheby's auction in 1937 of the library of J. A. H. Catton had a set (1864–1936) and a further 11 duplicate volumes unspecified. This fetched £33. Messrs Hodgson & Co., of Chancery Lane, auctioned a set (1864–1953) in 1954 and the price was £145. The present accepted price for a set in good condition and collated as completed is £250.

UMPIRES

The role of umpires has changed over the years, and *Wisden*'s attention to them has changed accordingly. Where once they were men in white coats who, as unobtrusively as possible, kept the game going by means of decisions, signals and occasional words to the players, now they are showmen with signals more suitable to the flight deck of an aircraft carrier than Lord's or the MCG. As Matthew Engel pointed out in his Notes in 2004, "In hot weather, the umpires now officiate at county games wearing polo shirts. Since, in the nature of things, not all of them are as svelte as they used to be, and the shirt is sometimes worn over a sub-stantial paunch, it makes them look less like figures of authority and more as if they've wandered in from a game of crazy golf with the grandchildren."

The natural authority of umpires is under pressure, not only from their sartorial preferences but also from the players. Yet we must be grateful for the fact that however much more money there is riding on umpires' decisions than there used to be, and however much a mistaken lbw decision might affect a player's livelihood, cricket umpires remain far less challenged or abused than referees in football, rugby or tennis, for example. This is despite their having an almost impossible job, especially when every decision is double-checked by Hawk-Eye and super-slow motion cameras for millions of viewers at home and, what's worse, inside the Test match and ODI grounds. Let's hear it for the umpires!

UMPIRES AND WHERE TO FIND THEM 1872

"Their decision should in every case be strictly obeyed, or there will be no pleasure in the game." Selkirk's *Guide to the Cricket Ground.*

G. BROCKWELL, Lower Clapton, E.

T. BURLINSON, Bradford, Yorks

G. BUTLER, Trent Bridge Ground Nottingham

JULIUS CAESAR, Godalming, Surrey

G. CHATTERTON, Sheffield, Yorks

S. DAKIN, Cambridge

W. H. FRYER, Coxheath, Linton, Staplehurst, Kent

DANIEL HAYWARD, Cambridge

H. HOLMES, Totton, near Southampton, Hants.

W. INWOOD, 39, Mansfield Place, Kentish Town, N.

GEORGE LEE, Lord's Cricket Ground, St John's Wood Road, N.W.

W. H. LUCK, Tunbridge Wells, Kent

G. MARTIN, Leigh, Tunbridge, Kent

W. MORTLOCK, Harleyford Street Kennington Oval, S.

H. ROYSTON, Lord's Cricket Ground St John's Wood Road, N.W.

THOS. SHERMAN, Mitcham, Surrey

JOHN THEWLIS, Lascelles Hall, near Huddersfield, Yorks

R. THOMS, 31, Princess Terrace, Regent's Park Road, N.W.

HENRY WRIGHT, Sheffield, Yorks

1892

There was a large and representative gathering at the annual meeting of county secretaries held on Tuesday, December 8, in the Members' Dining Room at Lord's Cricket Ground, for the purpose of arranging the fixtures for next season . . .

The meeting commenced at twelve o'clock, and the first hour and a half was devoted to the arrangement of fixtures. After lunch the Chairman placed before the meeting a memorial from a number of umpires which had been handed to him. In the memorial, which was signed by the umpires of Derbyshire, Essex, Gloucestershire, Hampshire, Kent, Lancashire, Leicestershire, Middlesex, Notts, Surrey, Sussex, Warwickshire and Yorkshire, application was made for an increase of payment to umpires for county matches from £5 to £6. The memorialists based their claim for an increase on the ground of the constant strain and long and arduous work which their duties involved, and pointed to the difference which existed between players and umpires. Most of the counties paid their professional players £6 for each match, but whereas the cricketers had the advantage of playing in home engagements, all matches at which umpires officiated were played away from home. It constantly happened that umpires had to make long journeys to reach the various towns which they had to visit. This very often entailed considerable extra expense, and at the present rate of remuneration they, the umpires, were but little gainers by their engagements. The memorialists concluded by asking the county secretaries to pass the following resolution: That county umpires for the future be paid £6 per match in all county matches played henceforth.

Mr E. M. GRACE said he had been asked by the umpires named to bring their memorial before the meeting of county secretaries, and he was entirely in favour of the increase asked for. It must not be forgotten that the work of umpires was very arduous, and as a matter of fact they worked much harder than the players. The umpires had to stand out in the field all through the day, while the cricketers were able at intervals to take a rest. He (Mr Grace) did not know whether any of the gentlemen present had officiated as umpires, but if they did so they would probably find it was extremely hard and tiring work. Speaking on behalf of Gloucestershire, he was entirely in favour of granting this extra £1 per match. If umpires were properly paid for their duties there was much less chance of having inferior men, and there would be no inducement for an umpire to give a man out leg-before-wicket when he was not out. Mr Grace concluded by moving that in future umpires be paid £6.

. . . After a little further conversation Mr OATES proposed, and Dr BENCRAFT seconded, "That all counties which nominate umpires for three-day matches send their answer to the memorial to the secretary of the MCC, the majority to decide," and this motion was carried.

1923

OXFORD UNIVERSITY v SOMERSET

Played at Oxford, Wednesday, Thursday, Friday, May 31, June 1, 2, 1922. It was in this match that G. T. S. Stevens was asked to continue his innings after having been given out leg-before-wicket, a course of action that led to reproof from Lord's.

CAMBRIDGE UNIVERSITY v FREE FORESTERS

Played at Cambridge, Saturday, Monday, Tuesday, June 10, 12, 13, 1922. It was in this match, the last of the Cambridge season, that the incident occurred that brought down such a sharp reproof from Lord's. J. N. Buchanan was not well enough to play on the second day, and G. B. Cuthbertson was allowed to bat in his place.

Lord Harris and Umpires' Decisions

Sharp reproof from Lord's in June with regard to certain irregularities in connection with matches at Oxford and Cambridge led to much discussion and quite a lively controversy in *The Times*, the action taken by MCC being vigorously attacked and defended. One writer even went to the length of suggesting that the University match should not be played unless the MCC sent an apology to the Cambridge captain. However, the storm soon blew over. The first letter from the MCC, a copy of which was sent to the county clubs as well as the Universities, was as under. It was, at the wish of the MCC, given the widest publicity through the newspapers.

The attention of MCC was recently called to a press report which alleged that in a match between Oxford University and Somerset, a batsman had, on the invitation of the fielding side, been allowed to continue his innings notwithstanding that the umpire had on appeal given him out lbw.

The respective captains and the umpires were asked to report what actually happened, and their replies are in agreement that the incident was as above stated.

MCC cannot too strongly remonstrate against such a disregard of the laws of cricket. Provision is made in the

"Instructions to Umpires" for an umpire to alter his decision if he feels satisfied that his first decision was wrong. In the above case the umpire did not alter his decision.

Umpires should feel confident that MCC will – to the full extent of their powers – support them in insisting that their decisions must be accepted, and in the event of refusal to do so they should report the case to MCC.

Yours faithfully,

F. E. Lacey (sec. MCC)

A few days later the second letter was made public in the following announcement:

"The MCC, through the Secretary, Mr F. E. Lacey, have sent the following letter to the Captain of Cricket, Cambridge University.

The MCC much regret again to have to comment upon a disregard of the Laws of cricket, this time at Cambridge.

In the match Cambridge University v Free Foresters it was agreed to allow a substitute on each side to bat in the second innings in the place of batsmen who had already batted in the first innings.

This is not provided for in the laws, and is quite contrary to the practice observed in first class cricket.

The MCC feel confident that they can rely on the Universities to support them in maintaining the Laws of cricket."

Dealing with this matter in his speech at the annual meeting of the Cricketers' Fund at Lord's on July 19, Lord Harris said:

". . . I know what I think is the true 'spirit' of the game – that it should be played boldly, uprightly without any chicanery – but that is merely an individual opinion, and there may be many other opinions and when the occasion comes for a decision to be made, who is the person who is to be responsible for deciding according to the 'spirit' of the game? The two sides? Is the game to be adjourned to take their opinion? Or the captains?

Supposing one captain is not on the field at the time, is the other captain to have the privilege of deciding according to his opinion provided it agrees with some other member of the other side? Don't you think if there is any merit in the suggestion at all that you would be landed in a maelstrom of complexity? Do you think that our ancestors were not actuated by great admiration for the game, and were just as anxious to preserve the 'spirit of the game' from defilement as we are?

But they evidently found that the 'spirit' of the game did not suffice, and that laws were necessary, and they handed us down a code which has been amended from time to time, and the most important factor upon which that code depends is that the decision of the umpire should be unquestioned. Whether right or wrong, every cricketer knows that in almost every match there are decisions of questionable accuracy, but the 'spirit' of the game has been for many decades to accept the umpire's decision. In one of the cases in question, the batsman was asked to continue his innings, and I understand it was even argued that it was justifiable to ask him to continue his innings, although he had been given out.

Then, of course, if that is justifiable, why not the converse, namely, that a batsman should be asked to go out although he had been given 'not out'. I can see no difference; one is as serious a breach of the law as the other. Might I not safely conclude, as Euclid frequently did, 'which is absurd'? . . . The most satisfactory way of playing the game is to adhere to the laws as laid down, and, above all, to honour the important factor of accepting the umpire's decision."

1988

History was made during the season when Pat Carrick of Christchurch became the first woman to umpire a men's first-class match in New Zealand. Mrs Carrick, a regular member of New Zealand women's teams between 1969 and 1978, joined the panel of first-class umpires and officiated in five Shell Cup and Trophy matches.

THE UMPIRE'S POINT OF VIEW 1933
Some Experiences and Suggestions
by Frank Chester

While it may not be considered within the province of an umpire to suggest tampering with the rules, there is one matter which I think merits very close consideration. Where a batsman, not out overnight, is not present on the ground to resume his innings next morning and the two minutes' grace has elapsed, he can, according to the existing laws, bat with the consent of the opposing captain. Surely, unless an unanswerable explanation or excuse is given, the batsman should be ruled out without the captain of the opposition being approached on the point. An incident touching on this rule occurred last season.

Another curious occurrence at a match in which I was standing umpire took place some years ago. A batsman deliberately ran after a ball and kicked it; then he started to run. I informed the batsman he could not run and no runs were allowed, but afterwards I was "called over the coals" and told there was no law whereby a man should not kick the ball. My defence of the action was that this was unfair play and that, had it occurred again, I should, had I been appealed to, have given the batsman out for impeding the wicketkeeper.

UMPIRING VAGARIES 1951
by Hubert Preston

From Frank Chester standing in the Test match at Trent Bridge to an official acting in a club game in Australia is a far cry, but each gave a decision beyond the knowledge of regular players and followers of cricket down the ages. Chester called "out" to an appeal for leg-before against D. J. Insole and insisted that his ruling should go on to the score sheet although the ball went off the batsman's pads on to the stumps; surely this meant bowled. How Chester contrived to signal "out" before the ball reached the stumps is difficult to realise, but, however that may be, his refusal to withdraw his verdict in favour of the more definite and satisfactory form of dismissal cannot be understood. Both for bowler and batsman "bowled" looks far better than "lbw" in the score, and the obstinacy of such an expert as Frank Chester, regarded as the most sagacious, quickest and reliable umpire for many years, in declining to alter his attitude is more than surprising. Can it be that having given his decision he regarded the ball as "dead" before it reached the stumps?

Umpires in Australia often come under criticism. An incident in a district game at Melbourne last October shows that clear understanding of the laws of the game is just as necessary as practical knowledge of the game. In the case under notice Neil Harvey, the left-hander, had scored 17 when a fast bowler hit the middle stump. Both bails flew into the air, but dropped back into the grooves of the stumps. Harvey was on his way back to the pavilion when the umpire recalled him, saying that he was not out, his reason being that the bails must fall to the ground. Nothing in the laws makes this essential to dismissal. The bails might lodge in the wicketkeeper's pads or be caught by fieldsmen. If these suggestions seem to be stretching the point, they are mentioned to emphasise Law 31, which reads, "The wicket shall be held to be 'down' if either ball or striker's bat or person completely removes either bail from the top of the stumps," etc.

Note to this law, "A wicket is not 'down' merely on account of disturbance of a bail, but it is 'down' if a bail in falling from the wicket lodges between two of the stumps." Surely this applied to the case in question when the "bails flew into the air".

1952
NEW ZEALAND v ENGLAND
First Test Match

At Lancaster Park, Christchurch, March 17, 19, 20, 21, 1951. Early in the England innings occurred an incident believed to be unique in Test cricket. Washbrook, when 13 and the total 27, was given out leg-before, but after Hadlee, the New Zealand captain, held a short consultation with the umpire he was recalled when on his way to the pavilion. Apparently Hadlee, who had stopped Washbrook on his way out, told the umpire that he felt certain Washbrook had hit the ball on to his pad. The ethics of this action caused considerable discussion.

UMPIRING 1960
by Tom Smith

In places where "gamesmanship" is accepted it is considered smart to try to deceive the umpire. Fieldsmen appeal at every opportunity, even if they know perfectly well that they have little or no justification. It stands to reason that the only man in a position to judge lbw is the umpire, but even he has difficulties. Yet we have players at mid-off and mid-on, and frequently in other positions, talking about a man being "plumb out". It is ridiculous and absurd, but it can become fashionable and infectious. The bowler who is standing at an angle of 20–30 degrees to the pitch after delivery, and is constantly throwing his hands up to the heavens with disappointment or anguished appeals is a menace to the game.

Not Cricket

This posturing may be amusing to some but it is not so to umpires and it is not cricket. Youngsters will always imitate their seniors and this behaviour is detrimental to the game as a whole.

There are matches, too, where batsmen who know full well they are out apply all their acting powers and "gimmicks" to try to confuse the umpire. Again, this can become fashionable and considered "clever" and it will be imitated and carried into junior cricket. Fair-minded people know that the umpire has a very small chance against the odds of bowler and batsman. In some cases his life becomes miserable. He grows bitter and unhappy, and thinks seriously about giving up. It is impossible to recruit the right type of man if he has to face hours of worry and anxiety in the field. He does not stick it for very long if he meets the wrong type of players.

My appeal to players in all grades of cricket is to recognise the umpire as a vital part of the game. Treat him with respect. Forget silly play-acting and gallery-appealing antics; control bad temper and incidents. Not only will this be doing something for umpires and umpiring but it will make cricket a happy game. It was always intended to be so.

1965

FILLISTON, JOSEPH W., who died in hospital on October 25, aged 102, three days after being knocked down by a motor scooter, acted as umpire to the BCC Cricket Club for many years. "Old Joe" stood in the Old England v Lord's Taverners match when over a hundred. In his younger days he played cricket with Dr W. G. Grace and he helped the Gentlemen of Kent defeat the Philadelphians by six wickets at Town Malling in 1889. He also played as a professional in the Staffordshire League. He liked to tell of the occasion when he gave "W. G." out leg-before in a London County game at Crystal Palace. The Doctor, he said, refused to leave his crease and, as nobody has the courage to contradict him, he continued his innings.

1965

ENGLAND v AUSTRALIA
First Test Match

At Trent Bridge, Nottingham, June 4, 5, 6, 8, 9, 1964. Titmus stayed with Boycott for an hour, surviving the occasional short lifting ball from Corling. Just before the Duke of Edinburgh piloted his helicopter round the ground, the Australians raised the biggest cheer of this brief day's cricket for a genuine act of sportsmanship.

Grout could have run out Titmus when Boycott placed Hawke towards mid-on and both batsmen dashed for a quick single. Hawke dived for the ball and in the process knocked Titmus over from behind. Titmus was far from home when the ball landed in the wicketkeeper's gloves, but Grout let him reach the crease and England were credited with a single.

This recalled a similar incident in the Test at Trent Bridge in 1960, when D. J. McGlew was impeded and Statham threw down the wicket, leaving no room for latitude. Cowdrey, the England captain that day, wished McGlew to be allowed to continue, but the umpires insisted that their decision in response to an appeal could not be changed.

1961
ENGLAND v SOUTH AFRICA
Third Test Match

At Trent Bridge, Nottingham, July 7, 8, 9, 11, 1960. For the first time on the tour, McGlew gave of his best. He looked a class batsman again and was receiving all the help he needed when, with the stand having put on 91 in two hours, the South African captain was run out. The left-handed O'Linn played a ball from Moss to extra cover and went for a reasonably quick single. Moss dashed across the pitch to chase it and McGlew ran into his back. He stumbled and darted for the crease, but Statham had picked up and with unerring aim hit the stumps.

Cowdrey and the other England players near the broken wicket promptly appealed and Elliott, the square-leg umpire, signalled out. Elliott's decision was correct because Moss had not deliberately baulked McGlew. McGlew never hesitates when given out, but as he hastened towards the pavilion the crowd voiced their disapproval of the circumstances of his dismissal. Three times Cowdrey called to him to come back, and when he did the England captain asked the umpires if it was possible to change the verdict, but they were adamant.

1966
SOUTH AFRICA v ENGLAND
Fourth Test Match

At Johannesburg, January 22, 23, 25, 26, 27, 1965. Drawn. On the third day there was another incident involving an umpire. After a ball had rested in the hands of Waite and tossed by him to leg slip, Smith went "gardening", whereupon van der Merwe threw down the wicket. Umpire Kidson gave Smith out, but was prevailed upon by Goddard to call him back.

1971
WARWICKSHIRE v NOTTINGHAMSHIRE

At Birmingham, August 5, 6, 7, 1970. Warwickshire won by five wickets. Warwickshire 12 pts, Nottinghamshire 7 pts. The match was marred by the untimely death of the Test umpire, J. S. Buller.

The former Yorkshire and Worcestershire wicketkeeper collapsed in the pavilion and died during a stoppage for rain on the third day.

Syd Buller – a Great Umpire
by his colleague, Frank Lee

Syd, as he became known the world over, made his first-class cricket debut in 1930, when he played one match for Yorkshire. He left his native county in 1934 and, having qualified by residence, he appeared for Worcestershire in 1936. Despite being involved in a car crash in 1939 while his new county were playing Essex at Chelmsford, when Syd was badly injured and his teammate Charlie Bull, was killed, he continued his playing career till 1947. Thereafter he acted as county coach and captain of the team in the Minor Counties competition till 1951, when he gained a place on the list of first-class umpires.

. . . He was a worthy successor to the late Frank Chester, who was to my mind the greatest umpire of my time. Those of us who played and umpired with Chester are fully aware that he blazed a trail for other umpires to follow. His fearlessness, not only on the field, but in his dealings with the authorities, resulted in the raising of the standard of umpiring to a very considerable degree.

Syd was one of the central figures in what developed into a big controversy at Lord's in 1960, when I was his partner as umpire. This became known as the "Griffin Affair". In the Second Test match between England and South Africa, it became my distinctly unpleasant duty to have to "no-ball" Geoff Griffin, the South African fast bowler, no fewer than 11 times for throwing during the England innings. I should point out that Griffin had been penalised in earlier fixtures with MCC at Lord's, Nottinghamshire at Trent Bridge and Hampshire at Southampton for the same offence.

As the Test match ended a quarter of an hour after lunch on the fourth day, the agreement to play an exhibition one-innings-each contest came into force. In this game, Griffin bowled only one over, but what an eventful over it was, for it consisted of 11 deliveries. Syd Buller "called" him for throwing four times in his first five balls. Syd did not take such strong measures without careful study of the bowler's action; he looked at him first from square leg and then from point before he raised a hand. Upon the advice of his captain, D. J. McGlew, Griffin decided to complete the over with underarm deliveries – only to be no-balled immediately by me because he omitted to notify the batsman of his intention to change his action!

A vast amount of discussion and bother followed from all this, both among people directly concerned with the running of cricket and in the Press, but the inexplicable thing to me was that, despite the part that I played during the actual Test, in which Buller, being at the bowler's end on each occasion Griffin bowled, had no opportunity to penalise him from throwing, most of the unpleasant publicity fell upon him. I felt at that time, and still do: why should a man be pilloried for conscientiously fulfilling his duty? Furthermore, the South Africans declined to agree to Syd umpiring in any of the remaining Tests, though I should say that the English authorities paid him the fees he would have received and restored him to his rightful place the following season.

1989
PAKISTAN v ENGLAND
Second Test Match
by Martin Johnson

Played at Iqbal Stadium, Faisalabad, on December 7, 8, 9, 11, 12, 1987. Match drawn. One of the most acrimonious Test matches in history almost brought about the cancellation of the tour, while the bitter rows that led to the loss of a whole day's play, and half an hour from another, might have cost England their chance of levelling the series.

Gatting won another good toss on a pitch which had again been prepared for the spinners, and this time England also included three slow bowlers. Broad's 421-minute hundred, his first of any kind since his 112 in Melbourne almost a year earlier, was the cornerstone of an England total well above par for the conditions. He shared half-century partnerships with Gooch and Athey, and put on 117 with his captain before reaching his century in the penultimate over of the day. Attacking the spinners, Gatting himself made 79 off only 81 deliveries, including 14 fours, a masterly innings apparently sparked by anger at what he considered to be another display of abject umpiring.

The official who most upset him during England's innings was Shakoor Rana, and three deliveries from the end of what had been an absorbing second day, with Pakistan struggling at 106 for five, the two of them became embroiled in an exchange which produced a situation provoking headlines in countries with only the vaguest interest in cricket. The incident occurred when Gatting moved Capel up from deep square leg to prevent a single. He had, he said later, told the batsman, Salim Malik, what he was doing. However, as Hemmings came in to bowl, Gatting signalled to Capel that he had come close enough, whereupon Shakoor Rana, standing at square leg, stopped play to inform Malik of Capel's position. Shakoor claimed that Gatting had been unfairly moving the fielder behind the batsman's back. Gatting informed the umpire that he was, in his opinion, overstepping his bounds. The language employed throughout the discourse was basic.

Shakoor's refusal to play on until he received an apology from Gatting was suspected by some of having more than a little to do with Pakistan's parlous position, and by the time Gatting's enforced apology had restored an uneasy truce, six hours of playing time had been lost. Ironically, a further three and a half hours were then lost to rain and bad light on the fourth day.

Having bowled Pakistan out for 191 by the close, England began the final day with a lead of 101. By lunch (106 for two), they had increased this to 207, Gooch giving them a good start with 65 from 74 balls. But Pakistan bowled just 24 overs in the morning session, and when four wickets fell in half an hour in the afternoon, England had little hope of victory. Realistically, their chance had evaporated once Pakistan refused to make up for the lost third day, Gatting's declaration left his bowlers 100 minutes in which to bowl out Pakistan, and they did not even get this long. In keeping with the conduct of everything to do with the match, Miandad called his batsmen in when the last 20 overs were due to start. That the Laws make no provision for such an early closure did not prevent the umpires from drawing stumps immediately.

Man of the Match: B. C. Broad.

England 292 (Broad 116; Iqbal Qasim five for 83) **and 137** for six declared
(Gooch 65; Abdul Qadir three for 45).
Pakistan 191 (Salim Malik 60; Foster four for 42) and 51 for one.

1950

OXFORD v CAMBRIDGE

At Lord's. This was the first time that Chester had acted as umpire in the University match. Another interesting item was the presentation on the opening day to the MCC by Mr F. T. Wynyard-Wright of the score-book kept by Magdalen Cricket Club from 1827. His grandfather, F. B. Wright, played for Oxford in 1829, and his father, F. W. Wright, in 1863, 1864 and 1865. This score-book is the earliest known to MCC and is therefore a valuable addition to their history of the game.

THE MAN WHO STOLE THE SHOW 1997
by Tony Lewis

Harold Dennis Bird, known to the cricket world as Dickie, retired from Test match umpiring in 1996, aged 63. He had completed 23 years at the top and his 66 Tests are a record; he stood in three World Cup Finals and 71 one-day internationals. His career coincided with the advent of television coverage of cricket by satellite to many parts of the world; consequently his fame was global. Frank Chester, who umpired in England between 1924 and 1955, was once described as "the most famous of all umpires". There is no doubt that this accolade now belongs to Dickie Bird.

. . . Chester virtually created the modern profession of umpiring by his serious approach to the smallest detail. After him, Syd Buller was outstanding: massively unobtrusive, entirely dependable. His decisions were quick and clean. Players were happy with his judgments; even if they had not been, no one would have dared leave the field with a shaking head. Charlie Elliott, another protector of the spirit of cricket, was often Buller's companion in Tests, and also operated without fuss or palaver. And so it must have been a fascinating umpires' room at Headingley in England's Third Test against New Zealand in 1973 when Elliott, of the old school, welcomed Dickie Bird to Test cricket.

"I have never seen anyone so nervous in my life," Elliott recalled. "I thought he would never make it to the middle let alone give good decisions. Then I saw something which was a clue to his future reputation. He gave Ray Illingworth out lbw. The bowler was the New Zealand seamer Bruce Taylor and he was bowling round the wicket. I thought from square leg, 'How can that be out? A seamer bowling right-arm round the wicket?' But I saw it later on television and I liked what I saw. Dickie was absolutely correct: the ball had moved back into Illingworth from the line of off-stump. It was a top-class instant decision."

. . . His final exit at Lord's, 1996, was incredible. He was given a Hollywood-style reception which has never been afforded to any player, let alone an umpire. Don Bradman and Viv Richards were applauded to the crease when they played their last innings in England, and the Don was given three cheers. Umpire Bird walked out of the Long Room and the whole of Lord's stood and applauded. Even more, the players of England and India sides were out on the grass to form a corridor of appreciation. Frank Chester would not have recognised the scene, nor, I guess, would he and his contemporaries have approved the elevation of an umpire so far above the real craftsmen who bat, bowl and field.

But if you wanted the essence of Dickie Bird encapsulated in a few minutes, you could have seen it that day. One moment he was dabbing at his tears with a handkerchief; then at the fifth ball of the match he gave a rock-solid decision for lbw against Mike Atherton, the England captain. It is probably true that Dickie was a natural character who became a conscious character. But he never allowed anything to stand in the way of the fair conduct of the game. That is why he retained the trust of the players and stayed at the top for so long.

FINISHING IN STYLE

The end of a sportsman's career is a traumatic period, and to finish in style is the hardest thing of all. Few players ever feel they are no longer good enough: even at the lowest level of sporting activity, we still feel that with a following wind and a bit of luck we could repeat the chanceless hundred or the seven for 11 we achieved 20 years earlier. Self-belief is a vital ingredient in any successful cricketer, but identifying the moment when self-belief becomes self-delusion is something very few can notice in themselves, however easy it may be to spot in a team-mate. Most professional sportsmen, therefore, find they have little opportunity to stage manage the finish they would like. Just as they are expecting a curtain call and tumultuous applause, the stage is being dismantled and the world is moving on, with a new leading man.

Some cricketers have managed the triumphant exit, and it is these men we salute in this chapter. These are the lucky few who managed to go out at the top, cricket's equivalent of Rocky Marciano, the only man to retire as the undefeated heavyweight boxing champion of the world.

P. F. WARNER 1921
by Sydney H. Pardon

There have been many greater cricketers than Pelham Warner but none more devoted to the game. Nothing has ever damped his enthusiasm. Whether winning or losing he has always been the same. When, having made up his mind to finish with county cricket last season, he had the extreme satisfaction of leading Middlesex to victory in the Championship it was suggested that though he had already found a place in the *Wisden* portrait gallery there could be no more appropriate picture for this year's issue of the Almanack than a special photograph of him at the end of his career. The previous portrait appeared in 1904, Middlesex then, as now, having gained first place among the counties. Mr Warner has had a long and varied experience of the cricket field. He has played in Australia, South Africa and the West Indies. From his earliest days in the Rugby eleven he was marked out for distinction, but it was not till he played regularly for Middlesex that he became famous as a batsman. He was only in the Oxford eleven in the last two of his four years, and though he scored fairly well he did nothing out of the common. A wonderful innings of 150 at Lord's for Middlesex against Yorkshire in 1899 gave him an assured position, and from that year right on to the time of his dangerous illness in Australia in 1911 he met with little but success. It is no secret that when during the War his illness recurred he almost despaired of playing cricket any more, but happily he made a good recovery and did much to keep the game going in the two dreary summers that preceded the Armistice. When cricket came to its own again he was not the batsman he had been, but even in 1919, when the long hours of two-day matches did not suit him at all, he managed to add one to his splendid list of hundreds at Lord's, and last summer he was something like his old self. Still it was not his batting but his skill as a captain that made his final season memorable. But for his leadership Middlesex would never have gained in August the wonderful series of victories that culminated with the triumph over Surrey. His great asset as a captain in that month of strenuous matches, counting for even more than his judgment in changing the bowling and placing the field, was his sanguine spirit. He was full of encouragement and got the very best out of his men by making them believe in themselves.

MIDDLESEX v SURREY

Played at Lord's, Saturday, Monday, Tuesday, August 28, 30, 31, 1920. This was the match of the season. Middlesex and Lancashire were running neck and neck for the Championship, and as Lancashire on the same days had the simplest of tasks against Worcestershire, Middlesex knew that nothing less than an actual victory would be of real value to them. Never before has a county match proved such an attraction at Lord's. On the Saturday there must have been nearly 25,000 people on the ground, 20,706 paying for admission at the gates. A great fight was looked forward to, and as it happened all expectations were exceeded. It was a game never to be forgotten, Middlesex in the end winning by 55 runs and so securing the Championship. Winning the toss, Middlesex had the advantage of batting first on a hard wicket, but nothing could have been less promising than their start. For once Lee and Hearne failed them, and in less than an hour three wickets were down for 35 runs. After these disasters nothing was risked and at the end of the afternoon the Middlesex score with eight men out had only reached 253. Warner was blamed in some quarters for over-caution, but he saved his side. In getting 79, he was batting for nearly four hours and a half. On the Monday there was again an enormous attendance, the number paying at the gates this time being 20,021. Owing nearly everything to Sandham, Surrey had the best of the day's cricket. Sandham had some luck – a chance of stumping at 40 and a chance at slip at 77 – but for the most part he played superbly, combining an ever-watchful defence with his clean hitting. For his 167 not out he was batting four hours and 20 minutes, his figures including 17 fours. With the object of getting Middlesex in before the end of the afternoon, Fender declared with nine wickets down, but his policy met with no reward, Skeet and Lee batting for 40 minutes and taking the score to 27. Lee was splendid and Skeet, though not so certain in timing the ball, played better than he had ever played before in a first-class match. Warner declared at 20 minutes to four, leaving Surrey to get 244 in a trifle over three hours. The downfall of Hobbs – caught in the slips at 22 – was discouraging, but Surrey went for the runs, and with Sandham playing even more finely than on the previous day, the hundred was up in an hour and a quarter for two wickets. However, Hendren got rid of Shepherd by means of a wonderful catch in the deep field – just in front of the screen with his hands above his head – this being really the turning point of the game. Surrey's great hope departed when Sandham – the sixth man out – was caught and bowled from a full pitch. In the end Middlesex won with ten minutes to spare. Warner was carried off the field shoulder high, and before the crowd dispersed he and Fender had to make speeches.

Middlesex 268 (Warner 79, Stevens 53; Fender four for 76) **and 316** for
    seven declared (Lee 108, Skeet 106; Rushby three for 73).
Surrey 341 for nine declared (Sandham 167 not out; Durston four for 97)
    and 188 (Sandham 68; Stevens five for 61).

ANDREW SANDHAM 1983

Sandham's career began as long ago as 1911 when in his first match he made 53 against Cambridge and in his second 60 against Lancashire, creating a great impression. None the less in 1912 he had only one match for the county. In 1913 he scored 196 against Sussex, adding 298 with Harrison for the sixth wicket, and one might have supposed that this would have made his place secure, but a month later he was dropped for D. J. Knight, who had just left Malvern, and in 1914 he appeared in only five matches. Even in 1919 he was dropped for some matches, but an innings of 175 not out against Middlesex at the beginning of August at last ensured him a regular place, which he retained until 1937 when, having made a century against Sussex at Hove in the last match of the season, he left it to the Surrey Committee to announce his retirement. By then he had made in all first-class matches 41,284 runs with an average of 44.83, including 107 centuries. Twenty times he had exceeded 1,000 runs, two of these occasions being on tours abroad, and his 219 for Surrey in 1934 is still the highest score made for a county against the Australians.

His first Test match was against Australia at The Oval in 1921, when he made a useful 21 at No. 5. In 1922/23 he went to South

Africa, where he played in all five Tests as an opener, but did little, although taking the tour as a whole he was the most consistent bat on the side, and in 1924 he played twice against South Africa, scoring 46 in his only innings. That winter he was a member of Arthur Gilligan's side in Australia. Hobbs and Sutcliffe were now in their prime as an opening pair and Sandham in his two Tests, going in lower down, met with no success. Finally in 1929/30 he went to West Indies and played innings of 152 at Bridgetown and 325 at Kingston. These matches were classified as Tests only at a later date: at the time they were called Representative Matches and in fact only one of the English team played in the Tests in England in the following summer.

1931
MCC Team in the West Indies 1929/30

Favoured by beautiful weather throughout their visit to the West Indies, the MCC team had a most enjoyable tour. Engaging in 13 matches they won four, lost two and drew seven . . . As for the outcome of the four Representative games, honours were even, each side winning one and the remaining two being left drawn. The Englishmen might have won the last match had Calthorpe, after establishing a lead of 563, enforced the follow-on but MCC batted a second time and, rain preventing any play on the last two days, the chance of victory vanished.

WEST INDIES V ENGLAND
Fourth Test Match

Played at Sabina Park, Kingston, Jamaica on April 3, 4, 5, 7, 8, 9, 10, 11, 12, 1930. Each side having won once and one game having been drawn, it was decided to play to a finish the Fourth Representative Match, but rain prevented cricket on the eighth and ninth days. By that time the MCC team were due to return home so no result could be reached. Had MCC, after gaining a first-innings lead of 563, enforced the follow-on, they might have won, but Calthorpe decided to bat again and the weather destroyed the possibility of victory. MCC placed themselves in a practically impregnable position during the first three days when they put together the tremendous total of 849. While the run-getting was very consistent and Ames registered a capital hundred, Sandham carried off the honours with an innings of 325 which, occupying ten hours, included a seven, a five and 27 fours. Nunes gave the West Indies a fair start but nobody stayed long afterwards. Although when batting again MCC failed to repeat their huge success of the first innings, they set their opponents the appalling task of getting 836 runs. Headley made a great effort for his side, staying six hours and a half and hitting 28 fours. He and Nunes put on 228, the West Indies at the end being 427 behind with half their wickets in hand.

England 849 (Sandham 325, Ames 149, Gunn 85; Scott five for 266) **and 272** for nine declared (Hendren 55, Sandham 50; Scott four for 108).

West Indies 286 (Nunes 66; Astill three for 73, Haig three for 73) **and 408** for five (Headley 223, Nunes 92).

by Norman Preston, 1938

Sandham remained a valuable member of the side and on one sunny Saturday at The Oval he delighted his admirers with a glorious 239 against Glamorgan in perfect style. He finished the season by hitting a hundred at Hove and then without any fuss or bother he allowed the county to announce his retirement. For 18 successive seasons he made over 1,000 runs and eight times he exceeded the 2,000 mark. Always placing first the interests of his side, Sandham has been the model professional.

1957

BURN, MR KENNETH EDWARD, who died in Hobart, Tasmania, on July 20, aged 92, was the oldest living Test cricketer. He took part in two Test matches for Australia during the 1890 tour of England, scoring 41 runs in four innings. *Wisden* of the time termed his selection as wicketkeeper "the one serious mistake in making up the side", and described how "only when he had accepted the terms offered him and joined the ship at Adelaide was the discovery made that he had never kept wicket in his life".

STUART SURRIDGE 1957
Surrey's Inspiration
by Douglas Jardine

Inspiration is the operative word.

Exactly what inspiration may mean varies too much for exact definition or analysis. Leave it, therefore, that most people would claim to recognise it when they see it, and what is quite as important, everyone appreciates the difference between being at the sending or at the receiving end of inspiration.

Having got his inspiration, Mr Stuart Surridge was able not only to digest it, but to pass it on to each and every Surrey side from 1952 to 1956. In this, rather than in changing personnel, can be summed up the difference between the sides of 1948 to 1951.

To some extent Surridge's advent as leader may, from his own point of view, be considered to have been fortunately timed. It is no secret that during the years from 1948 to 1951 there was a very general conviction among players and members alike that there was present in the team, in good measure, all the ability and talent needed to win the County Cricket Championship. But the title continued to elude the County's grasp. The ability was never quite harnessed, or the talent fully and firmly exploited.

It is improbable that many recognised Surridge's inspiration for what it was. Few, however, could fail to appreciate his enthusiasm and the tautened determination springing naturally from it. The fielding had never been bad; no Oval crowd would tolerate that. But there was, nevertheless, a world of difference between the good workmanlike stuff served up before Surridge and the dynamic current with which he has charged it for the last five years. Don't drop a catch and you won't lose the match is an old and tried adage. It would be no great exaggeration to say that the majority of catches missed by Surrey were chances only because they were made into possibles by the fieldsmen. Surridge supplied the electricity close in on the off-side, while Lock did as much on the leg-side. To the unfortunate who had made nought in the first innings and was looking for a chance to get off the mark in the second innings, the Surrey in-field must have offered anything but an alluring prospect.

Not long ago a county captain stated, in effect, that he regarded his team as first and foremost public entertainers, and impressed that fact upon them. To an elder generation such a statement strikes an altogether false note. A first invitation to play for a county couched in such terms would hardly appeal to the individual recipient, or be calculated to enhance the best interests of the game. By the same criterion a Master of Foxhounds would be a public entertainer, though both imagination and language might prove quite inadequate to record his reactions to the role suggested. Yet, to borrow a metaphor from the hunting field, Surridge would have been as popular a Master as he proved himself a successful captain. He showed great sport; he went for and achieved definite results, and the number of his kills was satisfactory to a degree.

In the course of doing this he undoubtedly entertained the public – but only incidentally. One knew that, had the fortunes of Surrey required it, entertainment would have been relegated to limbo.

. . . The temptation to go on for just one more year must have been well-nigh irresistible; yet he has resisted it, and we can only applaud his voluntary breaking of his wand as he takes his bow with a peerless record as a county captain.

One may regret that he never had the honour of captaining the Gentlemen against the Players at Lord's; still more that he was never entrusted with the task of taking, and bringing on, an England A Team overseas. But Surridge was ever a county man, first and last, and as such can have few if any regrets.

CHAMPION COUNTY (SURREY) v THE REST OF ENGLAND
At The Oval, September 8, 10, 11, 1956. The Rest won by 128 runs. The Champion County gave a sadly inept performance in the final match of the first-class season. Indeed, much of their batting bore unmistakeable signs of weariness after the stresses and strains involved in winning the title. The pitch, however, always favoured the bowlers and the Lancashire spinners, Hilton and Tattersall, who between them bowled out the champions in the rain-ruined county game a fortnight previously, were in their

element. They accounted for 16 of the 19 Surrey wickets, Stewart not batting in the second innings because of a sore eye. On the first day Milton defended admirably while the pitch was probably at its trickiest, and Smith and Taylor gave a flourish to the middle of the Rest's innings with a gay stand of 71. Rain prevented cricket on the second day and only a small crowd saw the final day's play in cold, gloomy conditions. Surrey lost 15 wickets for 134 runs and the only real moments of enthusiasm occurred when Surridge, the Surrey captain, appeared for his final innings. He was applauded all the way to the crease and again after Milton caught him superbly in the leg trap where Surridge himself was such a fearless fielder during five successful years as leader.

Rest of England 192 (D. V. Smith 63; A. Bedser four for 71) **and 79** for three declared.

Surrey 71 (Hilton six for 10) **and 72** (Tattersall six for 29).

RAMAN SUBBA ROW 1962
by Norman Preston
ENGLAND v AUSTRALIA
Fifth Test Match

At The Oval, August 17, 18, 19, 21, 22, 1961. Drawn. Although the destination of the Ashes had already been decided in Australia's favour, victory in this match would have enabled England to draw the rubber. Instead, England made such a poor start that they always seemed to be fighting against adversity.

England went into the match without a Yorkshireman in the side, the selectors preferring Flavell to Trueman while Australia played Gaunt for McKenzie. It was Gaunt's first Test against England. Cowdrey had an unfortunate match. Dismissed for a duck on the first day, he spent the next three days in bed with a high temperature caused by a return of the throat infection which had kept him out of the Fourth Test and though he batted on the fourth day he was not really fit.

Three Australian batsmen, O'Neill, Burge and Booth, carried off the main honours, the first two making their first centuries against England. Barrington played two sound innings for

England, and Subba Row, who had announced his retirement, stayed six hours and 40 minutes for 137 in ensuring England immunity from defeat.

. . . Rain reduced play on Monday to three hours. The loss of Pullar and Dexter first thing for only a single seemed to have destroyed England's chance of survival, but Subba Row, although handicapped with a groin injury which he received in the first innings, saw them through the crisis.

By adopting a more venturesome policy and giving the loose ball the punishment it deserved, both Subba Row and May set a good example. Despite a severe drenching the pitch never became treacherous – the delay lasted from twelve o'clock until four – and May drove superbly, treating Mackay with distain. He had hit seven fours in 33 when a lofted drive was well taken by O'Neill at deep mid-off despite colliding with Benaud who also went for the ball.

Mackay bowled craftily for two hours. He soon disposed of Cowdrey and then Subba Row (39) had Dexter as runner for the remainder of his innings.

With Barrington using the hook and cut to good purpose England were 155 for four wickets on Monday evening; Subba Row 69, Barrington 35.

With a difference of 83 still in Australia's favour, England faced another hard struggle on the last day and that they avoided defeat was due mainly to Subba Row and Barrington who played through the two and a half hours session before lunch on the final day to take the score at the interval to 245 for four, representing a lead of seven.

Their vigilant partnership lasted four hours and 20 minutes and yielded 172 before Subba Row presented a return catch to Benaud who had missed him off Davidson at silly mid-on when he was 100. Subba Row hooked Mackay for 6 and also hit 15 fours.

England 256 (May 71, Barrington 53; Davidson four for 83) **and 370** for eight (Subba Row 137, Barrington 83; Mackay five for 121).

Australia 494 (Burge 181, O'Neill 117, Booth 71; Allen four for 133).

ANTHONY STUART 1998
AUSTRALIA v PAKISTAN
Carlton & United Series 1996/97

At Melbourne, January 16 (day/night), 1997. Australia won by three wickets. Toss: Pakistan. With Australia already out of the finals, this was a meaningless match. But it came to life when lively pace bowler Anthony Stuart became only the second Australian to take a hat-trick at this level, following Bruce Reid, against New Zealand in 1985/86. Stuart was playing his third international, aged 27. As a teenager, he was a wicketkeeper, but found his niche in bowling history when Moin Khan edged a perfectly pitched leg-cutter to slip, and he finished with five for 26. Even then, his team struggled. Opener Inzamam-ul-Haq rallied Pakistan from 29 for five to reach 181, and Australia looked no certainties at 110 for four. But Bevan's cool 79 saw them home.

Man of the Match: A. M. Stuart. Attendance: 48,218.

Pakistan 181 for nine (50 overs) (Inzamam-ul-Haq 64; Stuart 10–1–26–5).
Australia 182 for seven (49.3 overs) (Bevan 79 not out; Wasim Akram 10–1–25–4).

New South Welshman Stuart was never selected for Australia again.

NASSER HUSSAIN 2005
by Mike Walters
ENGLAND v NEW ZEALAND
First npower Test Match

At Lord's, May 20, 21, 22, 23, 24, 2004. England won by seven wickets. Toss: New Zealand. Test debut: A.J. Strauss. Rarely has Lord's witnessed such a surge of affection for one of English cricket's grandees to match the final flourish of Nasser Hussain's career, which concluded an extraordinary sequence of events. The theory that a butterfly flapping its wings in Casablanca can lead to a hurricane in Cuba found powerful supporting evidence in this compelling match. It was a wonderful setting for anyone's farewell.

The first twist of a spellbinding plot came three days before a ball had been bowled in anger. Vaughan, the England captain, attempted an innocuous sweep at a nineteen-year-old net bowler, left-arm spinner Zac Taylor, collapsed in a heap and was carried from the Nursery practice ground with a twisted right knee. The repercussions were momentous: Trescothick stood in as captain for the first time in Tests and the Middlesex captain Andrew Strauss, not named in the original 13-man squad, became only the fourth player – after Australian Harry Graham (in 1893), England's John Hampshire (1969) and India's Sourav Ganguly (1996) – to launch his Test career with a century at Headquarters.

But Strauss was not the only adhesive left-hand opener to make an impact. For more than six hours on a stodgy first day, New Zealand's Richardson was a model of obduracy. Prompted by fears of a terrorist attack, Lord's stewards had been ordered to seal hampers and cool boxes left by spectators in the Coronation Garden for their picnic lunches, but for 266 balls of torpor it was Richardson who might have been removed from the premises as a suspect package. With delightful self-deprecation, he described his 93 as "dour, pokey and proddy", but it was undeniably valuable. He was robbed of a century by a poor lbw decision which disregarded an inside edge.

But that helped the innings perk up. There was Astle, with 11 fours in a 77-ball 64, and Oram, with a similarly breezy 67 from 82 balls, and finally there was a performance of awesome power and violence from Cairns. Four times in the space of ten deliveries, Simon Jones, Harmison and Flintoff (twice) disappeared into the back of beyond. In the process, Cairns surpassed Sir Vivian Richards' record of 84 sixes in Tests, and England's relief was palpable when he was last out, trying to hit Flintoff for a third straight six. He had ransacked 82 from 47 balls.

Without their fastest bowler, Bond, New Zealand's attack could hardly raise a gallop, and it was England's openers who made all the running with a fluent stand of 190 in 54 overs. Trescothick, punching 13 fours with the assurance of an immigration officer stamping passports, was finally beaten down the slope by Oram, 14 short of becoming only the third man to score a hundred in his first Test as England captain, after Archie MacLaren (1897/98) and Allan Lamb (1989/90). But Strauss, batting on his home ground and serenaded by the crowd warbling the "Blue Danube" in his honour, was not to be denied.

On 91, he enjoyed a miraculous sliver of good fortune when his inside edge off Martin brushed off stump firmly enough to make the timber wobble but somehow failed to dislodge the bails. Another trail of scorched earth through the covers soon confirmed England's first centurion on debut since Graham Thorpe in 1993, and their superiority. But the applause was accompanied by a sense of wonder: Vaughan would have to come back, and Strauss could hardly be dropped. So who would make way? No one was considering the implications more clearly than a thirty-six-year-old ex-captain already known to be close to retirement. Afterwards, the initiative slipped during a passage of hesitant batting and tighter bowling on the third morning, but Flintoff and Geraint Jones reclaimed it by hitting three sixes and 11 fours in a sparkling seventh-wicket stand of 105 in 19 overs, which led to a useful 55-run advantage.

With Richardson, a man whose batting fills the bars, in occupation again, the pendulum swung back towards New Zealand on the fourth morning. They clawed their way up to a 125-run lead with nine wickets in hand. McCullum, promoted to No. 3 because Astle had flu, responded with 14 fours and was within a heartbeat of a maiden Test hundred when he was becalmed and then broken by Simon Jones' reverse swing. After his near miss in the first innings, Richardson was rewarded with a century second time around; it occupied 309 balls and brought his time at the crease to more than 13 and a half hours.

Inexplicably, Trescothick ignored the second new ball and settled for the attrition of Giles, dutifully bowling over the wicket for 35 overs unchanged in a spell of three for 64, to suppress the scoring rate. He could argue that negativity served its purpose, but it took three wickets in 19 balls from Harmison to end the charade. England eventually needed 282 from 95 overs to win – 64 more than they had ever managed in the fourth innings to win in 105 previous Lord's Tests. At 35 for two, the chase began to look forlorn until Hussain – who had already decided, unknown to his team-mates, that this would be his final Test innings – marched out to join Strauss for his last hurrah. Strauss was the dominant partner in a 108-run stand and was on course for a century in each innings, a feat achieved on debut only by West Indian Lawrence Rowe and Pakistan's Yasir Hameed. Then he sacrificed himself in a Keystone Kops mix-up with Hussain. While the crestfallen Strauss would soon be mollified by the match award, Hussain was distraught after "doing a Boycott on the local lad" – a reference to Geoff Boycott running out Derek Randall against Australia at Trent Bridge 27 years earlier.

Only leading England to victory from the wreckage of Strauss's heartbreak would atone for Hussain's part in the catastrophe, and they were still 139 away. But few men are blessed with such willpower. Fortified by a succinct pep-talk from fellow warhorse Thorpe – "Stop whingeing and get on with it" – Hussain scrambled to his fifty in 158 deliveries before he was carried to glorious redemption, and the final curtain, on one last rush of adrenalin. His next fifty took only 45 balls; he reached his 14th Test hundred with a lofted on-drive and signature extra-cover drive off successive deliveries to level the scores, and the ovation had not subsided before he collared Martin through the covers again and swayed triumphantly into the sunset. Forgiveness rained down and, less than three days later, he confirmed what everyone had suspected from his nostalgic body language: after 96 Tests spanning 14 years, he was giving up the game in a blaze of glory.

Man of the Match: A.J. Strauss. Attendance 125,890; receipts £2,086,368.

New Zealand 386 (Richardson 93, Cairns 82, Oram 67, Astle 64; Harmison four for 126) **and 336** (Richardson 101, McCullum 96; Harmison four for 76).

England 441 (Strauss 112, Trescothick 86, Flintoff 63; Martin three for 94) **and 282** for three (Hussain 103 not out, Strauss 83, Thorpe 51 not out).

INDEX OF KEY PLAYERS, TEAMS AND TOPICS

Page numbers in *italic* refer to authors of articles